State of the Union

State of the Union

Presidential Rhetoric
from Woodrow Wilson
to George W. Bush

Edited by Deborah Kalb, Gerhard Peters,
and John T. Woolley

Introductory essay by Gerhard Peters
and John T. Woolley

State of the Union addresses provided
by the American Presidency Project
(http://www.presidency.ucsb.edu)

CQ PRESS

A Division of Congressional Quarterly Inc.
Washington, D.C.

CQ Press
1255 22nd Street, NW, Suite 400
Washington, DC 20037

Phone: 202-729-1900; toll-free, 1-866-4CQ-PRESS (1-866-427-7737)

Web: www.cqpress.com

Photo/illustration credits and acknowledgments can be found on page 1147, which constitutes a continuation of the copyright page.

Development editor: Timothy Arnquist
Production and copy editor: Kerry Kern
Compositor: Marcie Pottern
Indexer: Vicky Agee
Cover design: Tony Olivis
Interior design: Wayne Vincent

♾ The paper used in this publication exceeds the requirements of the American National Standard for Information Sciences—Permanence of Paper for Printed Library Materials, ANSI Z39.48-1992

Printed and bound in the United States of America

10   09   08   07   06   1   2   3   4   5

Library of Congress Cataloging-in-Publication Data
State of the union : presidential rhetoric from Woodrow Wilson to George W. Bush.
   p. cm.
   Includes bibliographical references and index.
   ISBN-13: 978-0-87289-433-4 (alk. paper)
   ISBN-10: 0-87289-433-9 (alk. paper)
   1. Presidents—United States—Messages.   2. Presidents—United States—Inaugural addresses.   3. Rhetoric—Political aspects—History—20th century—Sources.   4. Rhetoric—Political aspects—History—21st century—Sources.   5. United States—Politics and government—20th century—Sources.   6. United States—Politics and government—2001—Sources.   7. Speeches, addresses, etc., American.
   J81.4.S73 2007
   352.23'80973—dc22

                                                                2006035973

Contents

Herbert Hoover, 1929–1933

Franklin D. Roosevelt, 1933–1945

Harry S. Truman, 1945–1953

Dwight D. Eisenhower, 1953–1961

John F. Kennedy, 1961–1963

Lyndon B. Johnson, 1963–1969

Richard Nixon, 1969–1974

Gerald R. Ford, 1974–1977

Jimmy Carter, 1977–1981

Ronald Reagan, 1981–1989

George W. Bush, 2001–2006

Preface

Along with quadrennial presidential elections and their attendant inaugurals, the annual State of the Union speech is one of the most familiar, and unifying, rituals on the U.S. political calendar. One night each winter, under the Capitol dome, the president's oratory resounds through the chamber and is broadcast into millions of homes. With the nation watching, the chief executive fulfills an obligation as spelled out in Article II, Section 3, of the Constitution that the president "shall from time to time give to the Congress Information of the State of the Union, and recommend to their Consideration such Measures as he shall judge necessary and expedient."

Although the image of the president's annual pilgrimage to Congress has become deeply embedded in the political consciousness, it is a recent phenomenon. Every president from Thomas Jefferson to William Howard Taft only submitted a written annual message to Congress. In December 1913, President Woodrow Wilson decided to deliver his message in person. As the editors of this volume see it, Wilson's public State of the Union address forever changed the nature of this constitutional obligation. They therefore have compiled that message and every subsequent address, from Wilson's eight messages through George W. Bush's January 2006 speech, tracing the modern era of the presidency through each leader's words and vision. These addresses are distinctive not only for the personal style and rhetorical leadership of each president, but also for the policy prescriptions and political exhortations that flow from them.

This volume presents one hundred State of the Union messages in their entirety. The American Presidency Project provided them as a courtesy. Every attempt has been made to preserve the original spelling and punctuation of these documents, but to enhance clarity, the editors have included explanatory material in brackets within the texts. Introductory notes, written by Deborah Kalb, precede each document, providing historical context and a sense of how presidents have tailored their messages to engage the public and appeal to Congress. The introductory essay by Gerhard Peters and John T. Woolley presents a general history of these annual messages, noting their evolution over time as a distinctly American political and cultural phenomenon.

Presidents George H. W. Bush, William J. Clinton, and George W. Bush chose to give speeches before a joint session of Congress close on the heels of their first inaugurals. Although these speeches are not State of the Union addresses—they are officially titled an "Address before a Joint Session of Congress on Administration Goals"—they functioned in much the same way and are therefore included here.

An appendix contains three additional speeches because of their importance to the development of modern presidential rhetoric: Woodrow Wilson's 1913 speech on tariff reform, Franklin D. Roosevelt's 1933 inaugural address, and Ronald Reagan's 1981 inaugural address. The appendix also includes a list of all congressional members who have given opposition responses via network television to State of the Union speeches, a roster of the visitors recent presidents have invited to sit in the House gallery during the annual speeches, and an inventory of every written State of the Union message from George Washington in 1790 through William Howard Taft in 1912.

State of the Union: Presidential Rhetoric from Woodrow Wilson to George W. Bush is the brainchild of the development and acquisitions editors at CQ Press, who share a fascination with presidential rhetoric. We found the perfect team of outside editors to fulfill our vision in Deborah Kalb, who also contributes to the mega-book *Guide to the Presidency,* and Gerhard Peters and John T. Woolley, the creators and administrators of the American Presidency Project. Tim Arnquist, our editorial assistant, was the book's development editor. Anne Stewart and Diana Park provided photographic research. Kerry Kern edited the manuscript and handled production.

We hope this volume provides handy reference to these historic messages and enriches our understanding of the presidents who gave them and the evolution of rhetorical leadership in the modern era.

Kathryn C. Suárez
Director, Reference Publishing
CQ Press
Washington, D.C.

The State of the Union Address and the Rise of Rhetorical Leadership

On April 8, 1913, President Woodrow Wilson arrived at his cabinet meeting clad in his finest Prince Albert attire, prepared to visit the Capitol to deliver an address in person. Upon seeing the president, Secretary of the Navy Josephus Daniels teasingly suggested that perhaps Wilson thought more of Congress than his own cabinet.[1] The president knew that his speech later that day would be groundbreaking. Having served less than a month as president, Wilson was about to do what no president had done since John Adams in 1800; he was going to address Congress in person.

Today we would not call Wilson's April 1913 speech a "State of the Union" address, but it must be included in any discussion of the genesis of the modern annual message because of the historical significance of its break with political norms (it is included in this volume in the appendix). Officially, the speech was an "Address to a Joint Session of Congress on Tariff Reform" and was a relatively short discussion of the nation's fiscal priorities.[2] Nevertheless, our understanding of the genesis of this annual rhetorical ritual must begin with Wilson's precedent-setting act. With exceptions to be noted, what we today call the "State of the Union" message is a presidential speech delivered orally to a joint session of Congress, fulfilling the requirements of Article II, Section 3, of the Constitution.[3] Presidents have largely used this form since Wilson's fourth address to Congress, made December 2, 1913, entitled "Annual Message."[4]

The president's State of the Union message to Congress provides valuable data for students of a variety of disciplines. Unlike most forms of presidential communication, the distinctive scholarly value of the State of the Union address arises from its regularity. Although the specific date has varied, State of the Union messages have been submitted to Congress almost every year since 1790, at the start of each session of Congress. Frequently used by political scientists and historians, the State of the Union message allows academics in these disciplines to analyze the words of American presidents for their policy prescriptions, evidence of bargaining between the executive and legislative branches, and insights into the pressing issues of the time. In addition, State of the Union messages serve a scholarly function for students in fields as varied as communication, rhetoric, literature, geography, and economics. Language used in presidential communications reveals the chief executive's persuasive method and literary

---

[1] Josephus Daniels, "From the Diary of Josephus Daniels, April 8, 1913," in Arthur S. Link, ed., *The Papers of Woodrow Wilson,* vol. 27 (Princeton, N.J.: Princeton University Press, 1978), p. 267.

[2] But in covering the speech, the *New York Times* quoted the constitutional requirement that the president shall "from time to time give to the Congress Information of the State of the Union." "Congress Cheers Greet Wilson," *New York Times,* April 9, 1913, A1.

[3] "He shall from time to time give to the Congress Information of the State of the Union, and recommend to their Consideration such Measures as he shall judge necessary and expedient. . . ."

[4] In addition to Wilson's April 8, 1913, address on tariff reform, Wilson addressed Congress on June 23, 1913, on bank reform and on August 27, 1913, on Mexican affairs.

style, while the words may be analyzed in research models to explain demographic trends or economic changes throughout American history.

The Annual Message: Linking Branches in a Separated System

The Framers of the Constitution gave Congress the power to pass legislation and granted presidents the power to veto such measures. Continuing the British royal tradition, the Founders allowed the president to "recommend to their Consideration such Measures as he shall judge necessary and expedient." The language of Article II of the Constitution is somewhat vague in defining this executive role, as precedent was needed to establish the timing, frequency, and format of these recommendations. On the one hand, the drafters of the Constitution sought to limit the president's power over the legislature, lest they simply replace King George III with another tyrant. On the other hand, the Framers feared that tyranny could arise out of legislative majorities. Thus the delegates at the Constitutional Convention in 1787 sought a role for the executive in the law-making process, but it should be a limited role to be consistent with republican principles.

Article II, Section 3, of the Constitution provides the seed from which the annual message was born. It reads, "He shall from time to time give to the Congress Information of the State of the Union, and recommend to their Consideration such Measures as he shall judge necessary and expedient." This clause is filled with ambiguity. Exactly how often is "from time to time?" In what form should the president give this information to Congress? What is the implicit responsibility of Congress? Is Congress free simply to ignore the president's measures? Must Congress respond formally to what the president suggests? Knowing that George Washington would almost certainly become the first president of the United States, it was the hope and expectation of the convention delegates that the procedure of reporting to Congress on the state of the union would be further institutionalized by precedents set by the first president. After all, according to AlexanderHamilton in *Federalist* No. 77, this role of the president generated little concern among the convention delegates.[5]

With George Washington's first and second annual messages to Congress, some ambiguities were resolved. The definition of "from time to time" was clarified by Washington's precedent to mean "annually," although there is no legal obstacle to more frequent "messages." Washington also sought and received nonbinding replies to his various measures from the House and Senate. Washington delivered his annual messages around the beginning of each session of Congress, a practice that has continued to this day and has given the State of the Union a distinctive characteristic. This practice was regarded by many early observers to be alarmingly similar to the British monarch's convention of opening each session of Parliament with "requests" for legislation—the Speech from the Throne. But an even more disturbing resemblance to the monarchy came with Washington's decision to deliver the message in person.

Thomas Jefferson's reaction against this royalist tone led him to reverse Washington's precedent in 1801. An ardent advocate of limited executive power, Jefferson thought the spectacle of the president addressing Congress in person to be too similar to the practice of the British monarchs. Jefferson fulfilled his constitutional duty

---

[5.] Alexander Hamilton, *Federalist* No. 77.

by sending his message to Congress in written form, establishing a new tradition that lived for 112 years, along with the notion that presidential messages of all forms shall be institutionalized and impersonal.

Although Wilson reversed Jefferson's precedent of sending a written message to Congress when he asked to appear in person, the December timing for the message persisted until Franklin Delano Roosevelt's first term. In the eighteenth century it took a long time for the president-elect to prepare for office and travel potentially long distances. The president took office on March 4 and Congress assembled on the first Monday in December (Article I, Section 4). The Twentieth Amendment, passed by Congress in 1932 and ratified by the states in 1933, reordered the political calendar by specifying that a newly elected Congress would be sworn in on January 3 and the new president on January 20. As a result, in 1933 Roosevelt never submitted a December message, as was customary. To coincide with the opening of the second session of the seventy-third Congress in 1934, Franklin Roosevelt delivered his first annual message on January 3, 1934, and, with the exception of his 1945 message, set a modern precedent of addressing Congress in either January or early February each year. In 1942 Roosevelt also began the enduring practice of referring to the event as the "State of the Union" address.

Since then, these presidential appearances have been referred to by this name among the press and in public discourse, but it must be noted that there are a few exceptions. Beginning with the administration of George H. W. Bush in 1989, the address presidents have delivered to a joint session of Congress in the weeks immediately following their inaugurations are *not* considered to be State of the Union addresses. They are, however, important to include in the universe of "State of the Union" addresses because the timing of the speech and range of content are similar to the officially titled State of the Union addresses. They are delivered at the beginning of a new session of Congress and contain a variety of policy issues and recommendations, but they were never billed as State of the Union addresses when the White House formally requested an opportunity to speak. In February 1989 President Bush delivered an address entitled, "Address on Administration Goals before a Joint Session of Congress"; in February 1993 Bill Clinton's address was similarly titled, "Address before a Joint Session of Congress on Administration Goals"; and in February 2001 George W. Bush delivered his "Address before a Joint Session of the Congress on Administration Goals," which was considered a budget message address. The differences between these addresses are subtle and related more to the fact that these newly inaugurated presidents chose to place the focus of their speech on meeting election expectations rather than reporting on the past year of government. Nonetheless, they are often falsely considered to be State of the Union addresses. For that reason, aside from the gap in 1933 caused by the Twentieth Amendment, 1989, 1993, and 2001 are the only years in which a State of the Union message, whether oral or written, was never submitted to Congress.

From a contemporary perspective, the 113-year gap between the Adams and Wilson speeches might be more surprising to today's casual observer than the fact that Wilson sought to address Congress in person. In the age of television, Americans expect the president to pre-empt their prime-time shows one evening each winter. After all, it has become common practice to refer to these earlier *messages* as *addresses*. For example, in his 1982 State of the Union address, Ronald Reagan observed:

A hundred and twenty years ago, the greatest of all our Presidents delivered his second State of the Union message in this Chamber. "We cannot escape history," Abraham Lincoln warned. "We of this Congress and this administration will be remembered in spite of ourselves." The "trial through which we pass will light us down, in honor or dishonor, to the latest [last] generation."

But of course, Lincoln's message was delivered in writing and was not spoken by Lincoln "in this Chamber."

The Annual Address: Rise of Rhetorical Leadership

Shortly after Wilson's precedent-shattering speech, one of the era's most famous political cartoonists, Clifford Berryman, sketched a cartoon that nicely reflected the tectonic changes in presidential leadership occurring during that time. In Berryman's cartoon, reproduced here, an obviously annoyed Theodore Roosevelt sits clutching a newspaper featuring a picture of Wilson standing and orating to the seated members of Congress. In reaction to the headline, "President Wilson Delivers His Message to Congress in Person," a frustrated Roosevelt exclaims to himself, "Now why didn't I think of that!"

Theodore Roosevelt did not think to break Jefferson's tradition of sending written messages and, as a result, this collection of State of the Union messages begins with Wilson, not Roosevelt. But Roosevelt nonetheless had a profound influence on the creation of the "modern" presidency. One of the most important features of the modern presidency is the expectation that presidents will speak directly to the people using the latest communications technology. Presidents are commonly viewed by the electorate as the ones that set the political agenda, and in so doing they seek to address the pressing needs of the times. In Roosevelt's terms, he used his "bully pulpit" to rally the public. In this manner, rhetorical leadership enhanced the president's position of bargaining with Congress by allowing him a more proactive role in the legislative process. Thus Theodore Roosevelt began to show how charismatic public leadership could elevate the executive above the legislative as the most prominent political institution in the eyes of the public. He did so with direct appeals to the people for support of his progressive agenda, whether to preserve public lands for the good of the nation or to regulate big business. Wilson built on Theodore Roosevelt's practice to develop more fully this new relationship between the people and their president. Wilson believed that the people must know that their president is a person, not merely an institution. As he explained in his April 1913 address on tariff reform:

> I am very glad indeed to have this opportunity to address the two Houses directly and to verify for myself the impression that the President of the United States is a person, not a mere department of the Government hailing Congress from some isolated island of jealous power, sending messages, not speaking naturally and with his own voice—that he is a human being trying to cooperate with other human beings in a common service. After this pleasant experience I shall feel quite normal in all our dealings with one another.

Following Wilson, the annual message evolved slowly to its modern form. If not for Franklin Roosevelt, the ritual might have permanently reverted back to written form. After suffering a stroke in October 1919, Wilson was forced to write his last two annual messages. He was simply too incapacitated to appear before Congress in person. The next president, Warren Harding, addressed Congress in person, adopting a structure that resembled contemporary addresses in both length and content. In terms of length, Harding's 1921 and 1922 addresses were 5,606 and 5,748 words respectively, while the median word count for State of the Union addresses delivered orally from 1913 to 2006 was 4,914 words. Harding also spoke thematically and descriptively about the nation's priorities. While Harding is not remembered for having the persuasive style of Franklin Roosevelt or Ronald Reagan, it is nonetheless apparent that he understood the usefulness of speaking directly to a room of legislators.

Upon the death of Harding in August 1923, Calvin Coolidge became the country's fifth accidental president. Only four months later, in December, Coolidge delivered his first annual message. Coolidge's address is noteworthy for being the first to be broadcast across America via radio. Coolidge showed that a president could not only speak directly to Congress, but he could speak directly to the people as well. Although the speech was well received by the press and many public officials,[6] its organization around a laundry list of policy areas echoed the nineteenth-century *messages* more than Wilson's new form of *address.* Ironically, while Coolidge was known for using radio to connect with the American people, he would never again deliver such an address despite the dramatic growth of radio during the 1920s. His remaining annual messages were written, and they closely mirrored the list of administrative topics he read to the nation in 1923. Coolidge's successor, Herbert Hoover, also chose not to address Congress in person on the occasion of his annual messages.

Coolidge was not averse to speaking directly to the people and is considered to have been an effective orator, but both his and Hoover's attitude of avoiding overt rhetorical leadership became outmoded. With changes in public expectations of presidential leadership, the rhetorical model fashioned by Theodore Roosevelt and Woodrow Wilson rose to dominate the twentieth century. Shortly following the defeat of Herbert Hoover by Franklin Delano Roosevelt in the 1932 election, Coolidge, near death, explained to a friend that he felt he "no longer fit in with these

---

[6.] As evidenced by coverage of the event by the *New York Times.*

times."[7] What Coolidge saw approaching was the modern presidential era in which a skillful use of rhetorical leadership became a political necessity as mass communication began to transform politics.

The State of the Union Address: A Modern Presidency

The era ushered in by Franklin Roosevelt was characterized by the vigorous use of executive authority. To fundamentally alter the nature of the federal government in American society required a mastery of the art of persuasion. Roosevelt used his annual messages, as well as his "fireside chats," to speak directly and frankly to the American people. In the opening paragraph of Roosevelt's first annual message, he declared to the members of Congress:

> I come before you . . . not to make requests for special or detailed items of legislation; I come, rather, to counsel with you, who, like myself, have been selected to carry out a mandate of the whole people, in order that without partisanship you and I may cooperate to continue the restoration of our national wellbeing and, equally important, to build on the ruins of the past a new structure designed better to meet the present problems of modern civilization.

With these words the annual message effectively evolved into the modern State of the Union speech. Speaking to the nation over radio airwaves, Roosevelt transformed the address beyond its function as an executive communication to Congress and made it an instance of consultation between the president, Congress, and the people.

In many respects, Franklin Roosevelt's State of the Union addresses were unique in both length and style. Averaging just over 3,500 words, they were among the shortest speeches delivered on the state of the union, much shorter than the prime-time television age speeches of Bill Clinton and almost one-third shorter than the average of all State of the Union addresses since Wilson. More important, Roosevelt delivered his addresses by articulating broad themes, with the intention of persuading listeners of the merits of his causes. Throughout the 1930s Roosevelt used his addresses to stress the importance of shared sacrifice and to appeal to the people for support of the domestic regulatory regime constructed during the New Deal. In doing this, he sought to calm the American people in the face of economic hardship, and in 1936 he reiterated the plea from his inaugural addresses that, "The only thing we have to fear is fear itself."

War is a circumstance, especially in a democracy, that requires a leader to possess a special ability to persuade the people that the cause is just and the sacrifices necessary. While the general sentiment during the late 1930s in the United States supported neutrality, Roosevelt felt the need to prepare the American people for the coming conflict. Although the United States was not at war in January 1939, Roosevelt was keenly aware of the trouble brewing around the globe. Japan was well on its way to conquering more of East Asia, and Nazi forces had built a modern war machine that threatened the peace in Europe. To prepare the American people for the commitment needed to withstand what he saw as a looming national struggle, Roosevelt, as presi-

---

[7.] George H. Nash, "The 'Great Enigma' and the 'Great Engineer,'" in John Earl Haynes, ed., *Calvin Coolidge and the Coolidge Era* (Washington, D.C.: Library of Congress, 1998), p. 181.

dents throughout America's history have done, used appeals to faith to secure public support for mobilization. He stated in his sixth annual message:

> Storms from abroad directly challenge three institutions indispensable to Americans, now as always. The first is religion. It is the source of the other two —democracy and international good faith. . . . In a modern civilization, all three—religion, democracy and international good faith—complement and support each other. . . . An ordering of society which relegates religion, democracy and good faith among nations to the background can find no place within it for the ideals of the Prince of Peace. The United States rejects such an ordering, and retains its ancient faith.

In 1940, shortly after World War II began in Europe, Roosevelt sought to reassure the country that America would not meddle in the affairs of other nations. Identifying himself with George Washington's philosophy, he stated in his seventh annual message, "The first President of the United States warned us against entangling foreign alliances. The present President of the United States subscribes to and follows that precept." In the course of just one year, however, Europe was reeling from the Nazi onslaught: Great Britain was on the verge of military collapse; Poland and Czechoslovakia had been all but eliminated from the world map; and France, Norway, Belgium, Holland, and Denmark were occupied by fascist forces. In response, Roosevelt delivered what would arguably become the most famous and influential of all the State of the Union addresses. On January 6, 1941, he declared:

> As long as the aggressor. nations maintain the offensive, they—not we—will choose the time and the place and the method of their attack. That is why the future of all the American Republics is today in serious danger. That is why this annual message to Congress is unique in our history.

Despite Roosevelt's words of caution, the 1941 address is enshrined in American cultural history for its words of hope and dedication to the ideals that separated Americans from the forces of aggression waging war in the world. In communicating his vision for hope in the future, Roosevelt described a world in which four essential freedoms would prevail: freedom of speech and expression; freedom for every person to worship in his or her own way; freedom from want, meaning an economic understanding that promotes a healthy life for the people of all nations; and freedom from fear, specifically fear of aggression. So resonant were these words that when Norman Rockwell's depictions of the four freedoms appeared on the cover of the *Saturday Evening Post* on February 20, 1943, 25,000 readers sought reproductions suitable for framing.[8] Roosevelt's last State of the Union was a written message, but he still seized the leadership opportunity afforded by his duty to report to Congress by addressing the nation via radio, repeating key points of his message.

As the war and Franklin Roosevelt's era drew to an end, his impact on what was now commonly referred to as the State of the Union address would prove to be long lasting. Besides reestablishing Wilson's format of oral delivery, Roosevelt believed that,

---

[8.] "Rockwell's Four Freedoms," http://www.loc.gov/exhibits/treasures/trm142.html.

after the passage of the Twentieth Amendment, it would be proper for outgoing presidents to present a message with policy recommendations as they prepared to leave office. He reasoned:

> For the first time in our national history a President delivers his Annual Message to a new Congress within a fortnight of the expiration of his term of office. While there is no change in the Presidency this year, change will occur in future years. It is my belief that under this new constitutional practice, the President should in every fourth year, in so far as seems reasonable, review the existing state of our national affairs and outline broad future problems, leaving specific recommendations for future legislation to be made by the President about to be inaugurated.

Presidents from Harry S. Truman through Jimmy Carter accepted Roosevelt's recommendation, and, with the exceptions of incoming presidents Richard Nixon in 1969 and Reagan in 1981, Congress received two State of the Union messages in years in which there was a change in administrations. The format of these "lame duck" messages varied between written and oral. Presidents Truman in 1953, Dwight Eisenhower in 1961, and Carter in 1981 sent written messages to Congress (Carter's message was the longest of any annual message—a hefty 33,667 words), while Lyndon Johnson in 1969 and Gerald Ford in 1977 chose to speak to a joint session of Congress just days before leaving office. This tradition ended with Jimmy Carter's 1981 State of the Union message. Presidents Reagan, George H. W. Bush, and Clinton all decided against writing or speaking to Congress in their last months in office, choosing instead to allow the incoming president to set the policy agenda.

After Roosevelt's passing in April 1945, Truman declined the opportunity to address Congress for his first State of the Union in 1946. After that, however, no permanent reversion back to the nineteenth-century written style of Coolidge and Hoover would occur among non-outgoing presidents, and even the two exceptions since 1946 were at least accompanied by radio remarks to the people on the themes of the message. Quite the opposite trend was developing as the State of the Union entered the television age.

The State of the Union Address: Ready for Prime Time

In the late 1940s and throughout the 1950s television flourished and became a fixture in American homes, much the way the radio had throughout the 1920s and the Internet would in the 1990s. Just as American culture was affected by this development, so too was American politics, as Truman's 1947 State of the Union address was the first to be broadcast by television. The age of electronic media, combined with the presidency's position at center stage in American politics and a public expectation of rhetorical leadership, meant that—other than the three "lame duck" messages already noted—only two State of the Union messages from 1947 to the present were written. In 1956, while recovering in Key West, Florida, from a heart attack, President Eisenhower sent a written message to Congress. Like Franklin Roosevelt in 1945, he addressed the nation by summarizing his message on film and radio. In 1973, believing that his second inaugural address would suffice in communicating to the people his second-term agenda, Richard Nixon opted instead to submit six themed State of the Union messages in writing over the course of about six weeks. In February he submitted an overview message, followed by components on natural resources and the environment, the economy, human resources, and community development; finally, in March, he released a message on law enforcement and drug abuse prevention. A few days prior to sending each component, Nixon addressed the people via radio. Thus he summarized his messages and effectively fulfilled the dual responsibilities of the modern presidency: his constitutional obligation to report to Congress and his public obligation to speak to the people.

In the early 1960s John F. Kennedy furthered the State of the Union's importance as a vehicle for rhetorical leadership by using his addresses not only to advance his economic policies and strengthen American resolve during the depths of the Cold War, but also to persuade the nation about the importance of space exploration. Speaking on this subject in 1962 he said, "This Nation belongs among the first to explore it." Notable about the importance of the State of the Union message in helping Kennedy persuade the country to land on the moon was Kennedy's ambiguous and mistaken claim that a second address to a joint session of Congress in 1961 was also a State of the Union address. In his May 25, 1961, "Special Message to the Congress on Urgent National Needs," Kennedy opened his remarks with the statement,

> The Constitution imposes upon me the obligation to "from time to time give to the Congress Information of the State of the Union." While this has traditionally been interpreted as an annual affair, this tradition has been broken in extraordinary times. These are extraordinary times. And we face an extraordinary challenge. Our strength as well as our convictions have imposed upon this nation the role of leader in freedom's cause.

Kennedy's "special message" speech was technically not a State of the Union address. This was not because he had already delivered one four months earlier, but rather because the composition of the address was limited to a set of specific policies and not an overall assessment of the nation and its wide range of issues. Such structure is one of the hallmarks of what must be considered when determining which addresses before Congress are "State of the Unions." But, in retrospect, perhaps the greatest significance of Kennedy's words in this 1961 address is how well it illustrates that when presidents need the national stage for urgent appeals, they ask Congress for an audience and enter the House chamber with the same reception and applause they can expect from an official State of the Union address.

The last major development in State of the Union addresses came during the administration of Lyndon B. Johnson. Johnson's second State of the Union address, delivered shortly before his inauguration in 1965, was the first to be delivered on prime-time television. Addressing the nation as a president recently elected in his own right, Johnson spoke at 9:04 P.M.—early enough for East Coast viewers to watch and still get a good night's sleep, and late enough for West Coast commuters to get home from work in time to watch. In 1966—four years before the Federal Communications Commission's "equal time" doctrine, which required networks that provide free airtime to candidates of one party to also provide an equal amount of time to the opposition, took effect—the networks began offering time to the opposition party to respond to the president's address. While not mandated by law, this new tradition afforded a degree of fairness to the party outside the White House by giving them access to prime-time audiences. For this first occasion, Senator Everett Dirksen of Illinois and Representative Gerald Ford of Michigan represented the Republican Party.

The Reaganization of Presidential Rhetoric

Somewhere in 1917, on the western front of World War I, a typical man from a typical American town was gunned down in a hail of machine gun fire while attempting to carry a message to another platoon during battle. What distinguished Private Martin Treptow, in the eyes of a future American president, from the thousands of other brave and ordinary Americans who fought in the bloodiest war the world had ever seen, was the revelation of his personal commitment to his role in defending democracy, and thus America. As Ronald Reagan explained in his January 20, 1981, inaugural address:

> We're told that on his body was found a diary. On the flyleaf under the heading, "My Pledge," he had written these words: "America must win this war. Therefore I will work, I will save, I will sacrifice, I will endure, I will fight cheerfully and do my utmost, as if the issue of the whole struggle depended on me alone."

Reagan cited Treptow's personification of the American spirit of heroism and endurance in order to rally the American people behind the difficult choices Reagan expected them to make in the face of some of the worst economic conditions since the Great Depression. In doing so, Reagan also created a new, powerful precedent of personalizing the American political experience that would affect the State of the Union beginning with his first such address on January 26, 1982.

On an icy January 13, 1982, Air Florida Flight 90 took off from Washington's National Airport, ascending over the frozen Potomac River. Improperly de-iced wings combined with pilot error resulted in a crash into the 14th Street Bridge, causing the deaths of all aboard except four passengers and one crew member.[9] A commuter on the bridge, Lenny Skutnik, witnessed the desperate attempts by the few survivors to grasp lines dangling from rescue helicopters and, in an act of selflessness, dove into the frigid water to save a drowning woman. In his 1982 State of the Union address President Reagan used this heroism as an illustration of American courage. Skutnik would become enshrined in the history of the State of the Union address as the first of many invited guests referred to in the speech. President Reagan urged the American people to muster courage in order to endure the economic adjustments required by the Reagan revolution. Sitting next to First Lady Nancy Reagan, Lenny Skutnik was acknowledged by the president with these words:

> Just two weeks ago, in the midst of a terrible tragedy on the Potomac, we saw again the spirit of American heroism at its finest—the heroism of dedicated rescue workers saving crash victims from icy waters. And we saw the heroism of one of our young government employees, Lenny Skutnik, who, when he saw a

[9]. Ernest Holsendolph, "Jet's Icing Device Was Turned Off," *New York Times*, January 29, 1982, A14.

woman lose her grip on the helicopter line, dived into the water and dragged her to safety.

Since then, presidents have frequently referred to guests seated in the House gallery, often adjacent to the First Lady, in the State of the Union address. These moments have become known by presidential speechwriters as "Lenny Skutniks" and have been used in almost every State of the Union message since Reagan. President Clinton invited and recognized baseball slugger Sammy Sosa in 1998, following his exciting challenge of Roger Maris's home run record, and civil rights icon Rosa Parks in 1999. One of the most powerful uses of these gallery guests came in a seemingly impromptu moment during the 2005 State of the Union address. Iraqi human rights activist Safia Taleb al-Suhail and Janet and Bill Norwood, parents of slain Marine Corps Sergeant Byron Norwood, were sitting in the First Lady's gallery and were referred to by President George W. Bush. In a seemingly unscripted moment of emotion, Ms. al-Suhail turned to Mrs. Norwood and embraced her as a gesture of thanks for the ultimate sacrifice made by her son in the liberation of Iraq from Saddam Hussein. This interaction overshadowed any rhetorical attempt by the president to persuade the American people of the righteousness of the American cause in Iraq.

A Seemingly Entrenched Tradition

The United States was founded on a number of liberal principles, one of which is the rejection of monarchy in any form. For this reason, the president serves not just as the head of government, but also as its head of state, and the State of the Union address provides an annual ritual for displays of pomp and circumstance. During war and peace, recession and boom, and times of administration scandal, the State of the Union as a modern rhetorical tradition continues to take place, although there have been instances of controversy surrounding some presidents when they speak. In 1974, during the height of the Watergate scandal, President Nixon visited the House chamber to deliver his fourth address (fifth message), visibly uncomfortable and pausing frequently to wipe his brow. Bill Clinton, in 1999, became the only president to address a joint session of Congress while at the same time having been formally impeached by the House of Representatives. In each case, the president chose to focus on the policy issues relevant at the time, although Nixon also offered a personal appeal to Congress at the end of his address to "bring that investigation and the other investigations of this matter to an end."

Sometimes presidents create controversy with the words they use in the address. One such occurrence came in the years following George W. Bush's 2003 State of the Union. Seizing the opportunity to attempt to rally the American people to support the war in Iraq, the president claimed in his address that Iraqi dictator Saddam Hussein had attempted to purchase enriched uranium from sources in Niger. Two months later the United States invaded Iraq and toppled the Hussein regime, but no evidence of such nuclear aspiration was found, leading many to question the foundation of the president's foreign intelligence.

Today, the State of the Union remains entrenched in American political tradition. In an era in which presidents cannot rely on having the center stage afforded by monolithic television networks, they must now compete with the proliferation of alternate forms of entertainment for the public's attention. Cable television and the Internet give people opportunities to divert themselves from the annual ritual, but there is no evidence that the State of the Union will disappear as a cultural event any time soon. Just as politically disinterested citizens may turn to a variety of alternate programs or surf the Internet, these same developments in American cultural life reinforce the importance of the president's State of the Union address. Additional avenues for analysis of the president's message exist with the proliferation of multiple cable news networks, while the recent phenomenon of political blogs has extended public deliberation of public policy beyond the town square and onto the home computer of anyone with an Internet connection.

As long as the American presidency exists within the foundations of a republic with a system of separated powers and checks and balances, it will remain necessary for presidents to "go public" in an effort to win political support. Considering that no effort exists to amend the president's constitutional requirement to communicate to Congress "Information of the State of the Union," it is reasonable to suggest that the story of this established tradition of political communication will continue to evolve. What remains for the future are the additional precedents and modifications to this ritual as new leaders enter the Oval Office and leave their mark on this address.

Gerhard Peters and John T. Woolley
The American Presidency Project
University of California, Santa Barbara

Woodrow Wilson

1913–1921

*". . . the President of the United States
is a person, not a mere department
of the Government. . . ."*

ADDRESS TO A JOINT SESSION OF CONGRESS ON TARIFF REFORM, APRIL 8, 1913

Annual Message to Congress

December 2, 1913

Woodrow Wilson, who arrived in the White House espousing a reformist platform, shook up the practice of the president's annual State of the Union message by becoming the first chief executive since John Adams to deliver the message to Congress in person rather than in writing. In another move toward presidential openness, the new president also held weekly press conferences.

On April 8, 1913, Wilson had made his first in-person speech to Congress, urging tariff reform(see Appendix); he thus became the first president to appear before Congress since Adams.

The president's first State of the Union address took place nine months after his March 4, 1913, inauguration. It had been a productive first year in office for Wilson, with Congress passing two major pieces of legislation relating to issues that were high on his "New Freedom" agenda. The Underwood Tariff Act, which lowered tariffs to pre-Civil War levels, was approved, and the Federal Reserve Act, which created the regional federal banking system, was signed into law December 23, a few weeks after the State of the Union address.

In his speech, Wilson put in a plug for the banking reform legislation, urging Congress to complete its work on the bill. He also discussed his desire to fight harder against monopolies in business and said that agricultural reform was needed to create a more efficient farming system.

Wilson, a Democrat, had been elected in the unusual campaign of 1912, which pitted incumbent Republican president William Howard Taft against Wilson—but also against former GOP president Theodore Roosevelt, who disapproved of Taft, his successor, and thought he could do a better job himself. Roosevelt's entrance into the race—eventually at the head of his own new Progressive, or "Bull Moose," Party—split the Republican vote and gave Wilson the White House. He was the first Democrat to win the presidency since Grover Cleveland in 1892.

Wilson—a former Princeton University president who had been elected governor of New Jersey in 1910—had the good fortune of working with a Congress controlled by his own party. The House had gone Democratic in 1910 and the Senate in 1912.

Wilson's State of the Union speech focused primarily on domestic concerns, with the "one [international] cloud upon our horizon" being political instability in neighboring Mexico. Although Wilson foresaw "an age of settled peace and good will" among the nations, less than a year later World War I began in Europe—a conflict that would come to define Wilson's presidency; the United States would enter the war in 1917.

Gentlemen of the Congress:

In pursuance of my constitutional duty to "give to the Congress information of the state of the Union," I take the liberty of addressing you on several matters which ought, as it seems to me, particularly to engage the attention of your honorable bodies, as of all who study the welfare and progress of the Nation.

I shall ask your indulgence if I venture to depart in some degree from the usual custom of setting before you in formal review the many matters which have engaged the attention and called for the action of the several departments of the Government or which look to them for early treatment in the future, because the list is long, very long, and would suffer in the abbreviation to which I should have to subject it. I shall submit to you the reports of the heads of the several departments, in which these subjects are set forth in careful detail, and beg that they may receive the thoughtful attention of your committees and of all Members of the Congress who may have the leisure to study them. Their obvious importance, as constituting the very substance of the business of the Government, makes comment and emphasis on my part unnecessary.

The country, I am thankful to say, is at peace with all the world, and many happy manifestations multiply about us of a growing cordiality and sense of community of interest among the nations, foreshadowing an age of settled peace and good will. More and more readily each decade do the nations manifest their willingness to bind themselves by solemn treaty to the processes of peace, the processes of frankness and fair concession. So far the United States has stood at the front of such negotiations. She will, I earnestly hope and confidently believe, give fresh proof of her sincere adherence to the cause of international friendship by ratifying the several treaties of arbitration awaiting renewal by the Senate. In addition to these, it has been the privilege of the Department of State to gain the assent, in principle, of no less than 31 nations, representing four-fifths of the population of the world, to the negotiation of treaties by which it shall be agreed that whenever differences of interest or of policy arise which can not be resolved by the ordinary processes of diplomacy they shall be publicly analyzed, discussed, and reported upon by a tribunal chosen by the parties before either nation determines its course of action.

There is only one possible standard by which to determine controversies between the United States and other nations, and that is compounded of these two elements: Our own honor and our obligations to the peace of the world. A test so compounded ought easily to be made to govern both the establishment of new treaty obligations and the interpretation of those already assumed.

There is but one cloud upon our horizon. That has shown itself to the south of us, and hangs over Mexico. There can be no certain prospect of peace in America until Gen. Huerta has surrendered his usurped authority in Mexico; until it is understood on all hands, indeed, that such pretended governments will not be countenanced or dealt with by the Government of the United States. We are the friends of constitutional government in America; we are more than its friends, we are its champions; because in no other way can our neighbors, to whom we would wish in every way to make proof of our friendship, work out their own development in peace and liberty. Mexico has no Government. The attempt to maintain one at the City of Mexico has broken down, and a mere military despotism has been set up which has hardly more than the semblance of national authority. It originated in the usurpation of Victoriano Huerta, who, after a brief attempt to play the part of constitutional President, has at last cast aside even the pretense of legal right and declared himself dictator. As a consequence, a condition of affairs now exists in Mexico which has made it doubtful whether even the most elementary and fundamental rights either of her own people or of the citizens of other countries resident within her territory can long be successfully safeguarded, and which threatens, if long continued, to imperil the interests of peace, order, and tolerable life in the lands immediately to the south of us. Even if the usurper had succeeded in his purposes, in despite of the constitution of the Republic and the rights of its people, he would have set up nothing but a precarious and hateful power, which could have lasted but a little while, and whose eventual downfall would have left the country in a more deplorable condition than ever. But he has not succeeded. He has forfeited the respect and the moral support even of those who were at one time willing to see him succeed. Little by little he has been completely isolated. By a little every day his power and prestige are crumbling and the collapse is not far away. We shall not, 1 believe, be obliged to alter our policy of watchful waiting. And then, when the end comes, we shall hope to see constitutional order restored in distressed Mexico by the concert and energy of such of her leaders as prefer the liberty of their people to their own ambitions.

I turn to matters of domestic concern. You already have under consideration a bill for the reform of our system of banking and currency, for which the country waits with impatience, as for something fundamental to its whole business life and necessary to set credit free from arbitrary and artificial restraints. I need not say how earnestly I hope for its early enactment into law. I take leave to beg that the whole energy and attention of the Senate be concentrated upon it till the matter is successfully disposed of. And yet I feel that the request is not needed—that the Members of that great House need no urging in this service to the country.

I present to you, in addition, the urgent necessity that special provision be made also for facilitating the credits needed by the farmers of the country. The pending currency bill does the farmers a great service. It puts them upon an equal footing with other business men and masters of enterprise, as it should; and upon its passage they will find themselves quit of many of the difficulties which now hamper them in the field of credit. The farmers, of course, ask and should be given no special privilege, such as extending to them the credit of the Government itself. What they need and should obtain is legislation which will make their own abundant and substantial credit resources available as a foundation for joint, concerted local action in their own behalf in getting the capital they must use. It is to this we should now address ourselves.

It has, singularly enough, come to pass that we have allowed the industry of our farms to lag behind the other activities of the country in its development. I need not stop to tell you how fundamental to the life of the Nation is the production of its food. Our thoughts may ordinarily be concentrated upon the cities and the hives of industry, upon the cries of the crowded market place and the clangor of the factory, but it is from the quiet interspaces of the open valleys and the free hillsides that we draw the sources of life and of prosperity, from the farm and the ranch, from the forest and the mine. Without these every street would be silent, every office deserted, every factory fallen into disrepair. And yet the farmer does not stand upon the same footing with the forester and the miner in the market of credit. He is the servant of the seasons. Nature determines how long he must wait for his crops, and will not be hurried in her processes. He may give his note, but the season of its maturity depends upon the season when his crop matures, lies at the gates of the market where his products are sold. And the security he gives is of a character not known in the broker's office or as familiarly as it might be on the counter of the banker.

The Agricultural Department of the Government is seeking to assist as never before to make farming an efficient business, of wide co-operative effort, in quick touch with the markets for foodstuffs. The farmers and the Government will henceforth work together as real partners in this field, where we now begin to see our way very clearly and where many intelligent plans are already being put into execution. The Treasury of the United States has, by a timely and well-considered distribution of its deposits, facilitated the moving of the crops in the present season and prevented the scarcity of available funds too often experienced at such times. But we must not allow ourselves to depend upon extraordinary expedients. We must add the means by which the, farmer may make his credit constantly and easily available and command when he will the capital by which to support and expand his business. We lag behind many other great countries of the modern world in attempting to do this. Systems of rural credit have been studied and developed on the other side of the water while we left our farmers to shift for themselves in the ordinary money market. You have but to look about you in any rural district to see the result, the handicap and embarrassment which nave been put upon those who produce our food.

Conscious of this backwardness and neglect on our part, the Congress recently authorized the creation of a special commission to study the various systems of rural credit which have been put into operation in Europe, and this commission is already prepared to report. Its report ought to make it easier for us to determine what methods will be best suited to our own farmers. I hope and believe that the committees of the Senate and House will address themselves to this matter with the most fruitful results, and I believe that the studies and recently formed plans of the Department of Agriculture may be made to serve them very greatly in their work of framing appropriate and adequate legislation. It would be indiscreet and presumptuous in anyone to dogmatize upon so great and many-sided a question, but I feel confident that common counsel will produce the results we must all desire.

Turn from the farm to the world of business which centers in the city and in the factory, and I think that all thoughtful observers will agree that the immediate service we owe the business communities of the country is to prevent private monopoly more effectually than it has yet been prevented. I think it will be easily agreed that we should let the Sherman anti-trust law stand, unaltered, as it is, with its debatable ground about it, but that we should as much as possible reduce the area of that debatable ground by further and more explicit legislation; and should also supplement that great act by legislation which will not only clarify it but also facilitate its administration and make it fairer to all concerned. No doubt we shall all wish, and the country will expect, this to be the central subject of our deliberations during the present session; but it is a subject so many-sided and so deserving of careful and discriminating discussion that 1 shall take the liberty of addressing you upon it in a special message at a later date than this. It is of capital importance that the business men of this country should be relieved of all uncertainties of law with regard to their enterprises and investments and a clear path indicated which they can travel without anxiety. It is as important that they should be relieved of embarrassment and set free to prosper as that private monopoly should be destroyed. The ways of action should be thrown wide open.

I turn to a subject which I hope can be handled promptly and without serious controversy of any kind. I mean the method of selecting nominees for the Presidency of the United States. I feel confident that I do not misinterpret the wishes or the expectations of the country when I urge the prompt enactment of legislation which will provide for primary elections throughout the country at which the voters of the several parties may choose their nominees for the Presidency without the intervention of nominating conventions. I venture the suggestion that this legislation should provide for the retention of party conventions, but only for the purpose of declaring and accepting the verdict of the primaries and formulating the platforms of the parties; and I suggest that these conventions should consist not of delegates chosen for this single purpose, but of the nominees for Congress, the nominees for vacant seats in the Senate of the United States, the Senators whose terms have not yet closed, the national committees, and the candidates for the Presidency themselves, in order that platforms may be framed by those responsible to the people for carrying them into effect.

These are all matters of vital domestic concern, and besides them, outside the charmed circle of our own national life in which our affections command us, as well as our consciences, there stand out our obligations toward our territories over sea. Here we are trustees. Porto Rico, Hawaii, the Philippines, are ours, indeed, but not ours to do what we please with. Such territories, once regarded as mere possessions, are no longer to be selfishly exploited; they are part of the domain of public conscience and of serviceable and enlightened statesmanship. We must administer them for the people who live in them and with the same sense of responsibility to them as toward our own people in our domestic affairs. No doubt we shall successfully enough bind Porto Rico and the Hawaiian Islands to ourselves by ties of justice and interest and affection, but the performance of our duty toward the Philippines is a more difficult and debatable matter. We can satisfy the obligations of generous justice toward the people of Porto Rico by giving them the ample and familiar rights and privileges accorded our own citizens in our own territories and our obligations toward the people of Hawaii by perfecting the provisions for self-government already granted them, but in the Philippines we must go further. We must hold steadily in view their ultimate independence, and we must move toward the time of that independence as steadily as the way can be cleared and the foundations thoughtfully and permanently laid.

Acting under the authority conferred upon the President by Congress, I have already accorded the people of the islands a majority in both houses of their legislative body by appointing five instead of four native citizens to the membership of the commission. I believe that in this way we shall make proof of their capacity in counsel and their sense of responsibility in the exercise of political power, and that the success of this step will be sure to clear our view for the steps which are to follow. Step by step we should extend and perfect the system of self-government in the islands, making test of them and modifying them as experience discloses their successes and their failures; that we should more and more put under the control of the native citizens of the archipelago the essential instruments of their life, their local instrumentalities of government, their schools, all the common interests of their communities, and so by counsel and experience set tip a government which all the world will see to be suitable to a people whose affairs are under their own control. At last, I hope and believe, we are beginning to gain the confidence of the Filipino peoples. By their counsel and experience, rather than by our own, we shall learn how best to serve them and how soon it will be possible and wise to withdraw our supervision. Let us once find the path and set out with firm and confident tread upon it and we shall not wander from it or linger upon it.

A duty faces us with regard to Alaska which seems to me very pressing and very imperative; perhaps I should say a double duty, for it concerns both the political and the material development of the Territory. The people of Alaska should be given the full Territorial form of government, and Alaska, as a storehouse, should be unlocked. One key to it is a system of railways. These the Government should itself build and administer, and the ports and terminals it should itself control in the interest of all who wish to use them for the service and development of the country and its people.

But the construction of railways is only the first step; is only thrusting in the key to the storehouse and throwing back the lock and opening the door. How the tempting resources of the country are to be exploited is another matter, to which I shall take the liberty of from time to time calling your attention, for it is a policy which must be worked out by well-considered stages, not upon theory, but upon lines of practical expediency. It is part of our general problem of conservation. We have a freer hand in working out the problem in Alaska than in the States of the Union; and yet the principle and object are the same, wherever we touch it. We must use the resources of the country, not lock them up. There need be no conflict or jealousy as between State and Federal authorities, for there can be no essential difference of purpose between them. The resources in question must be used, but not destroyed or wasted; used, but not monopolized upon any narrow idea of individual rights as against the abiding interests of communities. That a policy can be worked out by conference and concession which will release these resources and yet not jeopard or dissipate them, I for one have no doubt; and it can be done on lines of regulation which need be no less acceptable to the people and governments of the States concerned than to the people and Government of the Nation at large, whose heritage these resources are. We must bend our counsels to this end. A common purpose ought to make agreement easy.

Three or four matters of special importance and significance I beg, that you will permit me to mention in closing.

Our Bureau of Mines ought to be equipped and empowered to render even more effectual service than it renders now in improving the conditions of mine labor and making the mines more economically productive as well as more safe. This is an all-important part of the work of conservation; and the conservation of human life and energy lies even nearer to our interests than the preservation from waste of our material resources.

We owe it, in mere justice to the railway employees of the country, to provide for them a fair and effective employers' liability act; and a law that we can stand by in this matter will be no less to the advantage of those who administer the railroads of the country than to the advantage of those whom they employ. The experience of a large number of the States abundantly proves that.

We ought to devote ourselves to meeting pressing demands of plain justice like this as earnestly as to the accomplishment of political and economic reforms. Social justice comes first. Law is the machinery for its realization and is vital only as it expresses and embodies it.

An international congress for the discussion of all questions that affect safety at sea is now sitting in London at the suggestion of our own Government. So soon as the conclusions of that congress can be learned and considered we ought to address ourselves, among other things, to the prompt alleviation of the very unsafe, unjust, and burdensome conditions which now surround the employment of sailors and render it extremely difficult to obtain the services of spirited and competent men such as every ship needs if it is to be safely handled and brought to port.

May I not express the very real pleasure I have experienced in co-operating with this Congress and sharing with it the labors of common service to which it has devoted itself so unreservedly during the past seven months of uncomplaining concentration upon the business of legislation? Surely it is a proper and pertinent part of my report on "the state of the Union" to express my admiration for the diligence, the good temper, and the full comprehension of public duty which has already been manifested by both the Houses; and I hope that it may not be deemed an impertinent intrusion of myself into the picture if I say with how much and how constant satisfaction I have availed myself of the privilege of putting my time and energy at their disposal alike in counsel and in action.

Woodrow Wilson, 1913–1917

Annual Message to Congress
December 8, 1914

Woodrow Wilson's second State of the Union message represented a departure from his first message a year earlier. While that first speech focused primarily on domestic concerns, the second was delivered against the backdrop of war in Europe.

World War I had begun in the summer of 1914, and while the United States would not officially enter the conflict until 1917, events across the Atlantic were clearly on Wilson's mind. "While we have worked at our tasks of peace the circumstances of the whole age have been altered by war," he said.

Wilson discussed national defense, stating his opposition to what he termed "compulsory military service in times of peace." He said that the United States was "at peace with all the world," referring to Americans as "the champions of peace and of concord." While he spoke against the idea of a large standing army, he did propose that volunteers be trained in weaponry and suggested strengthening the national guard.

While some had urged the president to move more directly toward creating a larger army, he was adamant, defending his own policies and stating that any more changes would cause the country to lose its sense of self.

Wilson also discussed the impact of the war on trade and suggested that the United States needed to be better prepared to play a greater role in international commerce. He criticized the readiness of the country's merchant marine system and pushed for passage of pending shipping legislation.

In his speech, Wilson touched only briefly on the domestic issues that had preoccupied much of his time as president. He spoke of having completed his program of business regulatory reform. Indeed, his successes with Congress in 1913 had continued into the following year, with the passage of the anti-monopolistic Clayton Anti-Trust Act. The Federal Trade Commission, which sought to ensure fair business practices, was also created in 1914.

In addition to the international changes that Wilson had seen in 1914, he also experienced a great personal loss: the death in August of his wife, Ellen, who suffered from kidney disease.

Wilson's speech came a month after the midterm congressional elections of November 1914, in which the president's Democratic Party held control of both the House and Senate, picking up additional Senate seats while losing seats in the House.

Gentlemen of the Congress:

The session upon which you are now entering will be the closing session of the Sixty-third Congress, a Congress, I venture to say, which will long be remembered for the great body of thoughtful and constructive work which it has done, in loyal response to the thought and needs of the country. I should like in this address to review the notable record and try to make adequate assessment of it; but no doubt we stand too near the work that has been done and are ourselves too much part of it to play the part of historians toward it.

Our program of legislation with regard to the regulation of business is now virtually complete. It has been put forth, as we intended, as a whole, and leaves no conjecture as to what is to follow. The road at last lies clear and firm before business. It is a road which it can travel without fear or embarrassment. It is the road to ungrudged, unclouded success. In it every honest man, every man who believes that the public interest is part of his own interest, may walk with perfect confidence.

Moreover, our thoughts are now more of the future than of the past. While we have worked at our tasks of peace the circumstances of the whole age have been altered by war. What we have done for our own land and our own people we did with the best that was in us, whether of character or of intelligence, with sober enthusiasm and a confidence in the principles upon which we were acting which sustained us at every step of the difficult undertaking; but it is done. It has passed from our hands. It is now an established part of the legislation of the country. Its usefulness, its effects will disclose themselves in experience. What chiefly strikes us now, as we look about us during these closing days of a year which will be forever memorable in the history of the world, is that we face new tasks, have been facing them these six months, must face them in the months to come,—face them without partisan feeling, like men who have forgotten everything but a common duty and the fact that we are representatives of a great people whose thought is not of us but of what America owes to herself and to all mankind in such circumstances as these upon which we look amazed and anxious.

War has interrupted the means of trade not only but also the processes of production. In Europe it is destroying men and resources wholesale and upon a scale unprecedented and appalling. There is reason to fear that the time is near, if it be not already at hand, when several of the countries of Europe will find it difficult to do for their people what they have hitherto been always easily able to do,—many essential and fundamental things. At any rate, they will need our help and our manifold services as they have never needed them before; and we should be ready, more fit and ready than we have ever been.

It is of equal consequence that the nations whom Europe has usually supplied with innumerable articles of manufacture and commerce of which they are in constant need and without which their economic development halts and stands still can now get only a small part of what they formerly imported and eagerly look to us to supply their all but empty markets. This is particularly true of our own neighbors, the States, great and small, of Central and South America. Their lines of trade have hitherto run chiefly athwart the seas, not to our ports but to the ports of Great Britain and of the older continent of Europe. I do not stop to inquire why, or to make any comment on probable causes. What interests us just now is not the explanation but the fact, and our duty and opportunity in the presence of it. Here are markets which we must supply, and we must find the means of action. The United States, this great people for whom we speak and act, should be ready, as never before, to serve itself and to serve mankind; ready with its resources, its energies, its forces of production, and its means of distribution.

It is a very practical matter, a matter of ways and means. We have the resources, but are we fully ready to use them? And, if we can make ready what we have, have we the means at hand to distribute it? We are not fully ready; neither have we the means of distribution. We are willing, but we are not fully able. We have the wish to serve and to serve greatly, generously; but we are not prepared as we should be. We are not ready to mobilize our resources at once. We are not prepared to use them immediately and at their best, without delay and without waste.

To speak plainly, we have grossly erred in the way in which we have stunted and hindered the development of our merchant marine. And now, when we need ships, we have not got them. We have year after year debated, without end or conclusion, the best policy to pursue with regard to the use of the ores and forests and water powers of our national domain in the rich States of the West, when we should have acted; and they are still locked up. The key is still turned upon them, the door shut fast at which thousands of vigorous men, full of initiative, knock clamorously for admittance. The water power of our navigable streams outside the national domain also, even in the eastern States, where we have worked and planned for generations, is still not used as it might be, because we will and we won't; because the laws we have made do not intelligently balance encouragement against restraint. We withhold by regulation.

I have come to ask you to remedy and correct these mistakes and omissions, even at this short session of a Congress which would certainly seem to have done all the work that could reasonably be expected of it. The time and the circumstances are extraordinary, and so must our efforts be also.

Fortunately, two great measures, finely conceived, the one to unlock, with proper safeguards, the resources of the national domain, the other to encourage the use of the navigable waters outside that domain for the generation of power, have already passed the House of Representatives and are ready for immediate consideration and action by the Senate. With the deepest earnestness I urge their prompt passage. In them both we turn our backs upon hesitation and makeshift and formulate a genuine policy of use and conservation, in the best sense of those words. We owe the one measure not only to the people of that great western country for whose free and systematic development, as it seems to me, our legislation has done so little, but also to the people of the Nation as a whole; and we as clearly owe the other fulfillment of our repeated promises that the water power of the country should in fact as well as in name be put at the disposal of great industries which can make economical and profitable use of it, the rights of the public being adequately guarded the while, and monopoly in the use prevented. To have begun such measures and not completed them would indeed mar the record of this great Congress very seriously. I hope and confidently believe that they will be completed.

And there is another great piece of legislation which awaits and should receive the sanction of the Senate: I mean the bill which gives a larger measure of self-government to the people of the Philippines. How better, in this time of anxious questioning and perplexed policy, could we show our confidence in the principles of liberty, as the source as well as the expression of life, how better could we demonstrate our own self-possession and steadfastness in the courses of justice and disinterestedness than by thus going calmly forward to fulfill our promises to a dependent people, who will now look more anxiously than ever to see whether we have indeed the liberality, the unselfishness, the courage, the faith we have boasted and professed. I can not believe that the Senate will let this great measure of constructive justice await the action of another Congress. Its passage would nobly crown the record of these two years of memorable labor.

But I think that you will agree with me that this does not complete the toll of our duty. How are we to carry our goods to the empty markets of which I have spoken if we have not the ships? How are we to build up a great trade if we have not the certain and constant means of transportation upon which all profitable and useful commerce depends? And how are we to get the ships if we wait for the trade to develop without them? To correct the many mistakes by which we have discouraged and all but destroyed the merchant marine of the country, to retrace the steps by which we have, it seems almost deliberately, withdrawn our flag from the seas, except where, here and there, a ship of war is bidden carry it or some wandering yacht displays it, would take a long time and involve many detailed items of legislation, and the trade which we ought immediately to handle would disappear or find other channels while we debated the items.

The case is not unlike that which confronted us when our own continent was to be opened up to settlement and industry, and we needed long lines of railway, extended means of transportation prepared beforehand, if development was not to lag intolerably and wait interminably. We lavishly subsidized the building of transcontinental railroads. We look back upon that with regret now, because the subsidies led to many scandals of which we are ashamed; but we know that the railroads had to be built, and if we had it to do over again we should of course build them, but in another way. Therefore I propose another way of providing the means of transportation, which must precede, not tardily follow, the development of our trade with our neighbor states of America. It may seem a reversal of the natural order of things, but it is true, that the routes of trade must be actually opened—by many ships and regular sailings and moderate charges—before streams of merchandise will flow freely and profitably through them.

Hence the pending shipping bill, discussed at the last session but as yet passed by neither House. In my judgment such legislation is imperatively needed and can not wisely be postponed. The Government must open these gates of trade, and open them wide; open them before it is altogether profitable to open them, or altogether reasonable to ask private capital to open them at a venture. It is not a question of the Government monopolizing the field. It should take action to make it certain that transportation at reasonable rates will be promptly provided, even where the carriage is not at first profitable; and then, when the carriage has become sufficiently profitable to attract and engage private capital, and engage it in abundance, the Government ought to withdraw. I very earnestly hope that the Congress will be of this opinion, and that both Houses will adopt this exceedingly important bill.

The great subject of rural credits still remains to be dealt with, and it is a matter of deep regret that the difficulties of the subject have seemed to render it impossible to complete a bill for passage at this session. But it can not be perfected yet, and therefore there are no other constructive measures the necessity for which I will at this time call your attention to; but I would be negligent of a very manifest duty were I not to call the attention of the Senate to the fact that the proposed convention for safety at sea awaits its confirmation and that the limit fixed in the convention itself for its acceptance is the last day of the present month. The conference in which this convention originated was called by the United States; the representatives of the United States played a very influential part indeed in framing the provisions of the proposed convention; and those provisions are in themselves for the most part admirable. It would hardly be consistent with the part we have played in the whole matter to let it drop and go by the board as if forgotten and neglected. It was ratified in May by the German Government and in August by the Parliament of Great Britain. It marks a most hopeful and decided advance in international civilization. We should show our earnest good faith in a great matter by adding our own acceptance of it.

There is another matter of which I must make special mention, if I am to discharge my conscience, lest it should escape your attention. It may seem a very small thing. It affects only a single item of appropriation. But many human lives and many great enterprises hang upon it. It is the matter of making adequate provision for the survey and charting of our coasts. It is immediately pressing and exigent in connection with the immense coast line of Alaska, a coast line greater than that of the United States themselves, though it is also very important indeed with regard to the older coasts of the continent. We can not use our great Alaskan domain, ships will not ply thither, if those coasts and their many hidden dangers are not thoroughly surveyed and charted. The work is incomplete at almost every point. Ships and lives have been lost in threading what were supposed to be well-known main channels. We have not provided adequate vessels or adequate machinery for the survey and charting. We have used old vessels that were not big enough or strong enough and which were so nearly unseaworthy that our inspectors would not have allowed private owners to send them to sea. This is a matter which, as I have said, seems small, but is in reality very great. Its importance has only to be looked into to be appreciated.

Before I close may I say a few words upon two topics, much discussed out of doors, upon which it is highly important that our judgment should be clear, definite, and steadfast?

One of these is economy in government expenditures. The duty of economy is not debatable. It is manifest and imperative. In the appropriations we pass we are spending the money of the great people whose servants we are,—not our own. We are trustees and responsible stewards in the spending. The only thing debatable and upon which we should be careful to make our thought and purpose clear is the kind of economy demanded of us. I assert with the greatest confidence that the people of the United States are not jealous of the amount their Government costs if they are sure that they get what they need and desire for the outlay, that the money is being spent for objects of which they approve, and that it is being applied with good business sense and management.

Governments grow, piecemeal, both in their tasks and in the means by which those tasks are to be performed, and very few Governments are organized, I venture to say, as wise and experienced business men would organize them if they had a clean sheet of paper to write upon. Certainly the Government of the United States is not. I think that it is generally agreed that there should be a systematic reorganization and reassembling of its parts so as to secure greater efficiency and effect considerable savings in expense. But the amount of money saved in that way would, I believe, though no doubt considerable in itself, running, it may be, into the millions, be relatively small,— small, I mean, in proportion to the total necessary outlays of the Government. It would be thoroughly worth effecting, as every saving would, great or small. Our duty is not altered by the scale of the saving. But my point is that the people of the United States do not wish to curtail the activities of this Government; they wish, rather, to enlarge them; and with every enlargement, with the mere growth, indeed, of the country itself, there must come, of course, the inevitable increase of expense. The sort of economy we ought to practice may be effected, and ought to be effected, by a careful study and assessment of the tasks to be performed; and the money spent ought to be made to yield the best possible returns in efficiency and achievement. And, like good stewards, we should so account for every dollar of our appropriations as to make it perfectly evident what it was spent for and in what way it was spent.

It is not expenditure but extravagance that we should fear being criticized for; not paying for the legitimate enterprise and undertakings of a great Government whose people command what it should do, but adding what will benefit only a few or pouring money out for what need not have been undertaken at all or might have been postponed or better and more economically conceived and carried out. The Nation is not niggardly; it is very generous. It will chide us only if we forget for whom we pay money out and whose money it is we pay. These are large and general standards, but they are not very difficult of application to particular cases.

The other topic I shall take leave to mention goes deeper into the principles of our national life and policy. It is the subject of national defense.

It can not be discussed without first answering some very searching questions. It is said in some quarters that we are not prepared for war. What is meant by being prepared? Is it meant that we are not ready upon brief notice to put a nation in the field, a nation of men trained to arms? Of course we are not ready to do that; and we shall never be in time of peace so long as we retain our present political principles and institutions. And what is it that it is suggested we should be prepared to do? To defend ourselves against attack? We have always found means to do that, and shall find them whenever it is necessary without calling our people away from their necessary tasks to render compulsory military service in times of peace.

Allow me to speak with great plainness and directness upon this great matter and to avow my convictions with deep earnestness. I have tried to know what America is, what her people think, what they are, what they most cherish and hold dear. I hope that some of their finer passions are in my own heart,—some of the great conceptions and desires which gave birth to this Government and which have made the voice of this people a voice of peace and hope and liberty among the peoples of the world, and that, speaking my own thoughts, I shall, at least in part, speak theirs also, however faintly and inadequately, upon this vital matter.

We are at peace with all the world. No one who speaks counsel based on fact or drawn from a just and candid interpretation of realities can say that there is reason to fear that from any quarter our independence or the integrity of our territory is threatened. Dread of the power of any other nation we are incapable of. We are not jealous of rivalry in the fields of commerce or of any other peaceful achievement. We mean to live our own lives as we will; but we mean also to let live. We are, indeed, a true friend to all the nations of the world, because we threaten none, covet the possessions of none, desire the overthrow of none. Our friendship can be accepted and is accepted without reservation, because it is offered in a spirit and for a purpose which no one need ever question or suspect. Therein lies our greatness. We are the champions of peace and of concord. And we should be very jealous of this distinction which we have sought to earn. Just now we should be particularly jealous of it because it is our dearest present hope that this character and reputation may presently, in God's providence, bring us an opportunity such as has seldom been vouchsafed any nation, the opportunity to counsel and obtain peace in the world and reconciliation and a healing settlement of many a matter that has cooled and interrupted the friendship of nations. This is the time above all others when we should wish and resolve to keep our strength by self-possession, our influence by preserving our ancient principles of action.

From the first we have had a clear and settled policy with regard to military establishments. We never have had, and while we retain our present principles and ideals we never shall have, a large standing army. If asked, Are you ready to defend yourselves? we reply, Most assuredly, to the utmost; and yet we shall not turn America into a military camp. We will not ask our young men to spend the best years of their lives making soldiers of themselves. There is another sort of energy in us. It will know how to declare itself and make itself effective should occasion arise. And especially when half the world is on fire we shall be careful to make our moral insurance against the spread of the conflagration very definite and certain and adequate indeed.

Let us remind ourselves, therefore, of the only thing we can do or will do. We must depend in every time of national peril, in the future as in the past, not upon a standing army, nor yet upon a reserve army, but upon a citizenry trained and accustomed to arms. It will be right enough, right American policy, based upon our accustomed principles and practices, to provide a system by which every citizen who will volunteer for the training may be made familiar with the use of modern arms, the rudiments of drill and maneuver, and the maintenance and sanitation of camps. We should encourage such training and make it a means of discipline which our young men will learn to value. It is right that we should provide it not only, but that we should make it as attractive as possible, and so induce our young men to undergo it at such times as they can command a little freedom and can seek the physical development they need, for mere health's sake, if for nothing more. Every means by which such things can be stimulated is legitimate, and such a method smacks of true American ideas. It is right, too, that the National Guard of the States should be developed and strengthened by every means which is not inconsistent with our obligations to our own people or with the established policy of our Government. And this, also, not because the time or occasion specially calls for such measures, but because it should be our constant policy to make these provisions for our national peace and safety.

More than this carries with it a reversal of the whole history and character of our polity. More than this, proposed at this time, permit me to say, would mean merely that we had lost our self-possession, that we had been thrown off our balance by a war with which we have nothing to do, whose causes can not touch us, whose very existence affords us opportunities of friendship and disinterested service which should make us ashamed of any thought of hostility or fearful preparation for trouble. This is assuredly the opportunity for which a people and a government like ours were raised up, the opportunity not only to speak but actually to embody and exemplify the counsels of peace and amity and the lasting concord which is based on justice and fair and generous dealing.

A powerful navy we have always regarded as our proper and natural means of defense, and it has always been of defense that we have thought, never of aggression or of conquest. But who shall tell us now what sort of navy to build? We shall take leave to be strong upon the seas, in the future as in the past; and there will be no thought of offense or of provocation in that. Our ships are our natural bulwarks. When will the experts tell us just what kind we should construct—and when will they be right for ten years together, if the relative efficiency of craft of different kinds and uses continues to change as we have seen it change under our very eyes in these last few months?

But I turn away from the subject. It is not new. There is no new need to discuss it. We shall not alter our attitude toward it because some amongst us are nervous and excited. We shall easily and sensibly agree upon a policy of defense. The question has not changed its aspects because the times are not normal. Our policy will not be for an occasion. It will be conceived as a permanent and settled thing, which we will pursue at all seasons, without haste and after a fashion perfectly consistent with the peace of the world, the abiding friendship of states, and the unhampered freedom of all with whom we deal. Let there be no misconception. The country has been misinformed. We have not been negligent of national defense. We are not unmindful of the great responsibility resting upon us. We shall learn and profit by the lesson of every experience and every new circumstance; and what is needed will be adequately done.

I close, as I began, by reminding you of the great tasks and duties of peace which challenge our best powers and invite us to build what will last, the tasks to which we can address ourselves now and at all times with free-hearted zest and with all the finest gifts of constructive wisdom we possess. To develop our life and our resources; to supply our own people, and the people of the world as their need arises, from the abundant plenty of our fields and our marts of trade to enrich the commerce of our own States and of the world with the products of our mines, our farms, and our factories, with the creations of our thought and the fruits of our character,—this is what will hold our attention and our enthusiasm steadily, now and in the years to come, as we strive to show in our life as a nation what liberty and the inspirations of an emancipated spirit may do for men and for societies, for individuals, for states, and for mankind.

Annual Message to Congress

December 7, 1915

World War I had been under way for more than a year when Woodrow Wilson gave his third State of the Union message. It was a lengthy speech, centered on one theme: how the United States should respond to the hostilities. While the country would not enter the conflict until 1917, it was becoming clearer that a protracted war would have a large impact on the United States and its people.

Wilson had tried to stay neutral in the conflict between the Allies, which included Great Britain and France, and their opponents, which included Germany and the Austro-Hungarian Empire. But neutrality was becoming harder to sustain, and the American public took note in May 1915 when the British liner *Lusitania,* with more than one hundred Americans on board, was sunk by a German submarine.

In his previous State of the Union speech, in December 1914, Wilson had spoken against an increase in the size of the country's standing army, arguing that he did not want to alter the character of the United States. But one year later, the president had changed his mind and endorsed a War Department plan that boosted the size of the army from 5,023 officers and 102,985 enlisted men to 7,136 officers and 134,707 enlisted men. The plan also called for a supplementary force of 400,000 men that would be available if needed. Wilson spoke of "making the country ready" to use its power if called upon to do so. In addition, the navy was seeking additions of 7,500 sailors, 2,500 apprentice seamen, and 1,500 marines. The following year, Congress approved legislation that strengthened the armed forces.

The president preached fiscal responsibility in his speech, calling for the country to use a "pay as we go" system to cover the increased expenditures for the military expansion; he also suggested increasing tax revenues.

While Wilson backed increasing the size of the military, he still stated that he did not see war as inevitable, maintaining his position of neutrality. Wilson, a Democrat, clearly had one eye on the political calendar; he gave this speech less than a year before the presidential election of 1916, in which he successfully sought reelection.

An issue that had concerned some of his political advisers was Wilson's quick second marriage to Edith Bolling Galt, a Washington widow, on December 18, 1915. His first wife, Ellen, had died in August 1914, and he had met Edith in March 1915. But in the end, the remarriage did not harm his reelection bid.

Gentlemen of the Congress:

Since I last had the privilege of addressing you on the state of the Union the war of nations on the other side of the sea, which had then only begun to disclose its portentous proportions, has extended its threatening and sinister scope until it has swept within its flame some portion of every quarter of the globe, not excepting our own hemisphere, has altered the whole face of international affairs, and now presents a prospect of reorganization and reconstruction such as statesmen and peoples have never been called upon to attempt before.

We have stood apart, studiously neutral. It was our manifest duty to do so. Not only did we have no part or interest in the policies which seem to have brought the conflict on; it was necessary, if a universal catastrophe was to be avoided, that a limit should be set to the sweep of destructive war and that some part of the great family of nations should keep the processes of peace alive, if only to prevent collective economic ruin and the breakdown throughout the world of the industries by which its populations are fed and sustained. It was manifestly the duty of the self-governed nations of this hemisphere to redress, if possible, the balance of economic loss and confusion in the other, if they could do nothing more. In the day of readjustment and recuperation we earnestly hope and believe that they can be of infinite service.

In this neutrality, to which they were bidden not only by their separate life and their habitual detachment from the politics of Europe but also by a clear perception of international duty, the states of America have become conscious of a new and more vital community of interest and moral partnership in affairs, more clearly conscious of the many common sympathies and interests and duties which bid them stand together.

There was a time in the early days of our own great nation and of the republics fighting their way to independence in Central and South America when the government of the United States looked upon itself as in some sort the guardian of the republics to the South of her as against any encroachments or efforts at political control from the other side of the water; felt it its duty to play the part even without invitation from them; and I think that we can claim that the task was undertaken with a true and disinterested enthusiasm for the freedom of the Americas and the unmolested self-government of her independent peoples. But it was always difficult to maintain such a role without offense to the pride of the peoples whose freedom of action we sought to protect, and without provoking serious misconceptions of our motives, and every thoughtful man of affairs must welcome the altered circumstances of the new day in whose light we now stand, when there is no claim of guardianship or thought of wards but, instead, a full and honorable association as of partners between ourselves and our neighbors, in the interest of all America, north and south. Our concern for the independence and prosperity of the states of Central and South America is not altered. We retain unabated the spirit that has inspired us throughout the whole life of our government and which was so frankly put into words by President Monroe. We still mean always to make a common cause of national independence and of political liberty in America. But that purpose is now better understood so far as it concerns ourselves. It is known not to be a selfish purpose. It is known to have in it no thought of taking advantage of any government in this hemisphere or playing its political fortunes for our own benefit. All the governments of America stand, so far as we are concerned, upon a footing of genuine equality and unquestioned independence.

We have been put to the test in the case of Mexico, and we have stood the test. Whether we have benefited Mexico by the course we have pursued remains to be seen. Her fortunes are in her own hands. But we have at least proved that we will not take advantage of her in her distress and undertake to impose upon her an order and government of our own choosing. Liberty is often a fierce and intractable thing, to which no bounds can be set, and to which no bounds of a few men's choosing ought ever to be set. Every American who has drunk at the true fountains of principle and tradition must subscribe without reservation to the high doctrine of the Virginia Bill of Rights, which in the great days in which our government was set up was everywhere amongst us accepted as the creed of free men. That doctrine is, "That government is, or ought to be, instituted for the common benefit, protection, and security of the people, nation, or community"; that "of all the various modes and forms of government, that is the best which is capable of producing the greatest degree of happiness and safety, and is most effectually secured against the danger of maladministration; and that, when any government shall be found inadequate or contrary to these purposes, a majority of the community hath an indubitable, inalienable, and indefeasible right to reform, alter, or abolish it, in such manner as shall be judged most conducive to the public weal." We have unhesitatingly applied that heroic principle to the case of Mexico, and now hopefully await the rebirth of the troubled Republic, which had so much of which to purge itself and so little sympathy from any outside quarter in the radical but necessary process. We will aid and befriend Mexico, but we will not coerce her; and our course with regard to her ought to be sufficient proof to all America that we seek no political suzerainty or selfish control.

The moral is, that the states of America are not hostile rivals but cooperating friends, and that their growing sense of community or interest, alike in matters political and in matters economic, is likely to give them a new significance as factors in international affairs and in the political history of the world. It presents them as in a very deep and true sense a unit in world affairs, spiritual partners, standing together because thinking together, quick with common sympathies and common ideals. Separated they are subject to all the cross currents of the confused politics of a world of hostile rivalries; united in spirit and purpose they cannot be disappointed of their peaceful destiny.

This is Pan-Americanism. It has none of the spirit of empire in it. It is the embodiment, the effectual embodiment, of the spirit of law and independence and liberty and mutual service.

A very notable body of men recently met in the City of Washington, at the invitation and as the guests of this Government, whose deliberations are likely to be looked back to as marking a memorable turning point in the history of America. They were representative spokesmen of the several independent states of this hemisphere and were assembled to discuss the financial and commercial relations of the republics of the two continents which nature and political fortune have so intimately linked together. I earnestly recommend to your perusal the reports of their proceedings and of the actions of their committees. You will get from them, I think, a fresh conception of the ease and intelligence and advantage with which Americans of both continents may draw together in practical cooperation and of what the material foundations of this hopeful partnership of interest must consist,—of how we should build them and of how necessary it is that we should hasten their building.

There is, I venture to point out, an especial significance just now attaching to this whole matter of drawing the Americans together in bonds of honorable partnership and mutual advantage because of the economic readjustments which the world must inevitably witness within the next generation, when peace shall have at last resumed its healthful tasks. In the performance of these tasks I believe the Americas to be destined to play their parts together. I am interested to fix your attention on this prospect now because unless you take it within your view and permit the full significance of it to command your thought I cannot find the right light in which to set forth the particular matter that lies at the very font of my whole thought as I address you to-day. I mean national defense.

No one who really comprehends the spirit of the great people for whom we are appointed to speak can fail to perceive that their passion is for peace, their genius best displayed in the practice of the arts of peace. Great democracies are not belligerent. They do not seek or desire war. Their thought is of individual liberty and of the free labor that supports life and the uncensored thought that quickens it. Conquest and dominion are not in our reckoning, or agreeable to our principles. But just because we demand unmolested development and the undisturbed government of our own lives upon our own principles of right and liberty, we resent, from whatever quarter it may come, the aggression we ourselves will not practice. We insist upon security in prosecuting our self-chosen lines of national development. We do more than that. We demand it also for others. We do not confine our enthusiasm for individual liberty and free national development to the incidents and movements of affairs which affect only ourselves. We feel it wherever there is a people that tries to walk in these difficult paths of independence and right. From the first we have made common cause with all partisans of liberty on this side the sea, and have deemed it as important that our neighbors should be free from all outside domination as that we ourselves should be,—have set America aside as a whole for the uses of independent nations and political freemen.

Out of such thoughts grow all our policies. We regard war merely as a means of asserting the rights of a people against aggression. And we are as fiercely jealous of coercive or dictatorial power within our own nation as of aggression from without. We will not maintain a standing army except for uses which are as necessary in times of peace as in times of war; and we shall always see to it that our military peace establishment is no larger than is actually and continuously needed for the uses of days in which no enemies move against us. But we do believe in a body of free citizens ready and sufficient to take care of themselves and of the governments which they have set up to serve them. In our constitutions themselves we have commanded that "the right of the people to keep and bear arms shall not be infringed," and our confidence has been that our safety in times of danger would lie in the rising of the nation to take care of itself, as the farmers rose at Lexington.

But war has never been a mere matter of men and guns. It is a thing of disciplined might. If our citizens are ever to fight effectively upon a sudden summons, they must know how modern fighting is done, and what to do when the summons comes to render themselves immediately available and immediately effective. And the government must be their servant in this matter, must supply them with the training they need to take care of themselves and of it. The military arm of their government, which they will not allow to direct them, they may properly use to serve them and make their independence secure,—and not their own independence merely but the rights also of those with whom they have made common cause, should they also be put in jeopardy. They must be fitted to play the great role in the world, and particularly in this hemisphere, for which they are qualified by principle and by chastened ambition to play.

It is with these ideals in mind that the plans of the Department of War for more adequate national defense were conceived which will be laid before you, and which I urge you to sanction and put into effect as soon as they can be properly scrutinized and discussed. They seem to me the essential first steps, and they seem to me for the present sufficient.

They contemplate an increase of the standing force of the regular army from its present strength of five thousand and twenty-three officers and one hundred and two thousand nine hundred and eighty-five enlisted men of all services to a strength of seven thousand one hundred and thirty-six officers and one hundred and thirty-four thousand seven hundred and seven enlisted men, or 141,843, all told, all services, rank and file, by the addition of fifty-two companies of coast artillery, fifteen companies of engineers, ten regiments of infantry, four regiments of field artillery, and four aero squadrons, besides seven hundred and fifty officers required for a great variety of extra service, especially the all important duty of training the citizen force of which I shall presently speak, seven hundred and ninety-two noncommissioned officers for service in drill, recruiting and the like, and the necessary quota of enlisted men for the Quartermaster Corps, the Hospital Corps, the Ordnance Department, and other similar auxiliary services. These are the additions necessary to render the army adequate for its present duties, duties which it has to perform not only upon our own continental coasts and borders and at our interior army posts, but also in the Philippines, in the Hawaiian Islands, at the Isthmus, and in Porto Rico.

By way of making the country ready to assert some part of its real power promptly and upon a larger scale, should occasion arise, the plan also contemplates supplementing the army by a force of four hundred thousand disciplined citizens, raised in increments of one hundred and thirty-three thousand a year throughout a period of three years. This it is proposed to do by a process of enlistment under which the serviceable men of the country would be asked to bind themselves to serve with the colors for purposes of training for short periods throughout three years, and to come to the colors at call at any time throughout an additional "furlough" period of three years. This force of four hundred thousand men would be provided with personal accoutrements as fast as enlisted and their equipment for the field made ready to be supplied at any time. They would be assembled for training at stated intervals at convenient places in association with suitable units of the regular army. Their period of annual training would not necessarily exceed two months in the year.

It would depend upon the patriotic feeling of the younger men of the country whether they responded to such a call to service or not. It would depend upon the patriotic spirit of the employers of the country whether they made it possible for the younger men in their employ to respond under favorable conditions or not. I, for one, do not doubt the patriotic devotion either of our young men or of those who give them employment,—those for whose benefit and protection they would in fact enlist. I would look forward to the success of such an experiment with entire confidence.

At least so much by way of preparation for defense seems to me to be absolutely imperative now. We cannot do less.

The programme which will be laid before you by the Secretary of the Navy is similarly conceived. It involves only a shortening of the time within which plans long matured shall be carried out; but it does make definite and explicit a programme which has heretofore been only implicit, held in the minds of the Committees on Naval Affairs and disclosed in the debates of the two Houses but nowhere formulated or formally adopted. It seems to me very clear that it will be to the advantage of the country for the Congress to adopt a comprehensive plan for putting the navy upon a final footing of strength and efficiency and to press that plan to completion within the next five years. We have always looked to the navy of the country as our first and chief line of defense; we have always seen it to be our manifest course of prudence to be strong on the seas. Year by year we have been creating a navy which now ranks very high indeed among the navies of the maritime nations. We should now definitely determine how we shall complete what we have begun, and how soon.

The programme to be laid before you contemplates the construction within five years of ten battleships, six battle cruisers, ten scout cruisers, fifty destroyers, fifteen fleet submarines, eighty-five coast submarines, four gunboats, one hospital ship, two ammunition ships, two fuel oil ships, and one repair ship. It is proposed that of this number we shall the first year provide for the construction of two battleships, two battle cruisers, three scout cruisers, fifteen destroyers, five fleet submarines, twenty-five coast submarines, two gunboats, and one hospital ship; the second year, two battleships, one scout cruiser, ten destroyers, four fleet submarines, fifteen coast submarines, one gunboat, and one fuel oil ship; the third year, two battleships, one battle cruiser, two scout cruisers, five destroyers, two fleet submarines, and fifteen coast submarines; the fourth year, two battleships, two battle cruisers, two scout cruisers, ten destroyers, two fleet submarines, fifteen coast submarines, one ammunition ship, and one fuel oil ship; and the fifth year, two battleships, one battle cruiser, two scout cruisers, ten destroyers, two fleet submarines, fifteen coast submarines, one gunboat, one ammunition ship, and one repair ship.

The Secretary of the Navy is asking also for the immediate addition to the personnel of the navy of seven thousand five hundred sailors, twenty-five hundred apprentice seamen, and fifteen hundred marines. This increase would be sufficient to care for the ships which are to be completed within the fiscal year 1917 and also for the number of men which must be put in training to man the ships which will be completed early in 1918. It is also necessary that the number of midshipmen at the Naval academy at Annapolis should be increased by at least three hundred in order that the force of officers should be more rapidly added to; and authority is asked to appoint, for engineering duties only, approved graduates of engineering colleges, and for service in the aviation corps a certain number of men taken from civil life.

If this full programme should be carried out we should have built or building in 1921, according to the estimates of survival and standards of classification followed by the General Board of the Department, an effective navy consisting of twenty-seven battleships of the first line, six battle cruisers, twenty-five battleships of the second line, ten armored cruisers, thirteen scout cruisers, five first class cruisers, three second class cruisers, ten third class cruisers, one hundred and eight destroyers, eighteen fleet submarines, one hundred and fifty-seven coast submarines, six monitors, twenty gunboats, four supply ships, fifteen fuel ships, four transports, three tenders to torpedo vessels, eight vessels of special types, and two ammunition ships. This would be a navy fitted to our needs and worthy of our traditions.

But armies and instruments of war are only part of what has to be considered if we are to provide for the supreme matter of national self-sufficiency and security in all its aspects. There are other great matters which will be thrust upon our attention whether we will or not. There is, for example, a very pressing question of trade and shipping involved in this great problem of national adequacy. It is necessary for many weighty reasons of national efficiency and development that we should have a great merchant marine. The great merchant fleet we once used to make us rich, that great body of sturdy sailors who used to carry our flag into every sea, and who were the pride and often the bulwark of the nation, we have almost driven out of existence by inexcusable neglect and indifference and by a hope lessly blind and provincial policy of so-called economic protection. It is high time we repaired our mistake and resumed our commercial independence on the seas.

For it is a question of independence. If other nations go to war or seek to hamper each other's commerce, our merchants, it seems, are at their mercy, to do with as they please. We must use their ships, and use them as they determine. We have not ships enough of our own. We cannot handle our own commerce on the seas. Our independence is provincial, and is only on land and within our own borders. We are not likely to be permitted to use even the ships of other nations in rivalry of their own trade, and are without means to extend our commerce even where the doors are wide open and our goods desired. Such a situation is not to be endured. It is of capital importance not only that the United States should be its own carrier on the seas and enjoy the economic independence which only an adequate merchant marine would give it, but also that the American hemisphere as a whole should enjoy a like independence and self-sufficiency, if it is not to be drawn into the tangle of European affairs. Without such independence the whole question of our political unity and self-determination is very seriously clouded and complicated indeed.

Moreover, we can develop no true or effective American policy without ships of our own,—not ships of war, but ships of peace, carrying goods and carrying much more: creating friendships and rendering indispensable services to all interests on this side the water. They must move constantly back and forth between the Americas. They are the only shuttles that can weave the delicate fabric of sympathy,—comprehension, confidence, and mutual dependence in which we wish to clothe our policy of America for Americans.

The task of building up an adequate merchant marine for America private capital must ultimately undertake and achieve, as it has undertaken and achieved every other like task amongst us in the past, with admirable enterprise, intelligence, and vigor; and it seems to me a manifest dictate of wisdom that we should promptly remove every legal obstacle that may stand in the way of this much to be desired revival of our old independence and should facilitate in every possible way the building, purchase, and American registration of ships. But capital cannot accomplish this great task of a sudden. It must embark upon it by degrees, as the opportunities of trade develop. Something must be done at once; done to open routes and develop opportunities where they are as yet undeveloped; done to open the arteries of trade where the currents have not yet learned to run,—especially between the two American continents, where they are, singularly enough, yet to be created and quickened; and it is evident that only the government can undertake such beginnings and assume the initial financial risks. When the risk has passed and private capital begins to find its way in sufficient abundance into these new channels, the government may withdraw. But it cannot omit to begin. It should take the first steps, and should take them at once. Our goods must not lie piled up at our ports and stored upon side tracks in freight cars which are daily needed on the roads; must not be left without means of transport to any foreign quarter. We must not await the permission of foreign ship-owners and foreign governments to send them where we will.

With a view to meeting these pressing necessities of our commerce and availing our-selves at the earliest possible moment of the present unparalleled opportunity of link-ing the two Americas together in bonds of mutual interest and service, an opportu-nity which may never return again if we miss it now, proposals will be made to the present Congress for the purchase or construction of ships to be owned and directed by the government similar to those made to the last Congress, but modified in some essential particulars. I recommend these proposals to you for your prompt acceptance with the more confidence because every month that has elapsed since the former pro-posals were made has made the necessity for such action more and more manifestly imperative. That need was then foreseen; it is now acutely felt and everywhere real-ized by those for whom trade is waiting but who can find no conveyance for their goods. I am not so much interested in the particulars of the programme as I am in taking immediate advantage of the great opportunity which awaits us if we will but act in this emergency. In this matter, as in all others, a spirit of common counsel should prevail, and out of it should come an early solution of this pressing problem.

There is another matter which seems to me to be very intimately associated with the question of national safety and preparation for defense. That is our policy towards the Philippines and the people of Porto Rico. Our treatment of them and their atti-tude towards us are manifestly of the first consequence in the development of our duties in the world and in getting a free hand to perform those duties. We must be free from every unnecessary burden or embarrassment; and there is no better way to be clear of embarrassment than to fulfil our promises and promote the interests of those dependent on us to the utmost. Bills for the alteration and reform of the gov-ernment of the Philippines and for rendering fuller political justice to the people of Porto Rico were submitted to the sixty-third Congress. They will be submitted also to you. I need not particularize their details. You are most of you already familiar with them. But I do recommend them to your early adoption with the sincere conviction that there are few measures you could adopt which would more serviceably clear the way for the great policies by which we wish to make good, now and always, our right to lead in enterprises of peace and good will and economic and political freedom.

The plans for the armed forces of the nation which I have outlined, and for the general policy of adequate preparation for mobilization and defense, involve of course very large additional expenditures of money,—expenditures which will considerably exceed the estimated revenues of the government. It is made my duty by law, when-ever the estimates of expenditure exceed the estimates of revenue, to call the attention of the Congress to the fact and suggest any means of meeting the deficiency that it may be wise or possible for me to suggest. I am ready to believe that it would be my duty to do so in any case; and I feel particularly bound to speak of the matter when it appears that the deficiency will arise directly out of the adoption by the Congress of measures which I myself urge it to adopt. Allow me, therefore, to speak briefly of the present state of the Treasury and of the fiscal problems which the next year will probably disclose.

On the thirtieth of June last there was an available balance in the general fund of the Treasury of $104,170,105.78. The total estimated receipts for the year 1916, on the assumption that the emergency revenue measure passed by the last Congress will not be extended beyond its present limit, the thirty-first of December, 1915, and that the present duty of one cent per pound on sugar will be discontinued after the first of May, 1916, will be $670,365,500. The balance of June last and these estimated revenues come, therefore, to a grand total of $774,535,605.78. The total estimated disbursements for the present fiscal year, including twenty-five millions for the Panama Canal, twelve millions for probable deficiency appropriations, and fifty thousand dollars for miscellaneous debt redemptions, will be $753,891,000; and the balance in the general fund of the Treasury will be reduced to $20,644,605.78. The emergency revenue act, if continued beyond its present time limitation, would produce, during the half year then remaining, about forty-one millions. The duty of one cent per pound on sugar, if continued, would produce during the two months of the fiscal year remaining after the first of May, about fifteen millions. These two sums, amounting together to fifty-six millions, if added to the revenues of the second half of the fiscal year, would yield the Treasury at the end of the year an available balance of $76,644,605.78.

The additional revenues required to carry out the programme of military and naval preparation of which I have spoken, would, as at present estimated, be for the fiscal year, 1917, $93,800,000. Those figures, taken with the figures for the present fiscal year which I have already given, disclose our financial problem for the year 1917. Assuming that the taxes imposed by the emergency revenue act and the present duty on sugar are to be discontinued, and that the balance at the close of the present fiscal year will be only $20,644,605.78, that the disbursements for the Panama Canal will again be about twenty-five millions, and that the additional expenditures for the army and navy are authorized by the Congress, the deficit in the general fund of the Treasury on the thirtieth of June, 1917, will be nearly two hundred and thirty-five millions. To this sum at least fifty millions should be added to represent a safe working balance for the Treasury, and twelve millions to include the usual deficiency estimates in 1917; and these additions would make a total deficit of some two hundred and ninety-seven millions. If the present taxes should be continued throughout this year and the next, however, there would be a balance in the Treasury of some seventy-six and a half millions at the end of the present fiscal year, and a deficit at the end of the next year of only some fifty millions, or, reckoning in sixty-two millions for deficiency appropriations and a safe Treasury balance at the end of the year, a total deficit of some one hundred and twelve millions. The obvious moral of the figures is that it is a plain counsel of prudence to continue all of the present taxes or their equivalents, and confine ourselves to the problem of providing one hundred and twelve millions of new revenue rather than two hundred and ninety-seven millions.

How shall we obtain the new revenue? We are frequently reminded that there are many millions of bonds which the Treasury is authorized under existing law to sell to reimburse the sums paid out of current revenues for the construction of the Panama Canal; and it is true that bonds to the amount of approximately $222,000,000 are now available for that purpose. Prior to 1913, $134,631,980 of these bonds had actually been sold to recoup the expenditures at the Isthmus; and now constitute a considerable item of the public debt. But I, for one, do not believe that the people of this country approve of postponing the payment of their bills. Borrowing money is short-sighted finance. It can be justified only when permanent things are to be accomplished which many generations will certainly benefit by and which it seems hardly fair that a single generation should pay for. The objects we are now proposing to spend money for cannot be so classified, except in the sense that everything wisely done may be said to be done in the interest of posterity as well as in our own. It seems to me a clear dictate of prudent statesmanship and frank finance that in what we are now, I hope, about to undertake we should pay as we go. The people of the country are entitled to know just what burdens of taxation they are to carry, and to know from the outset, now. The new bills should be paid by internal taxation.

To what sources, then, shall we turn? This is so peculiarly a question which the gentlemen of the House of Representatives are expected under the Constitution to propose an answer to that you will hardly expect me to do more than discuss it in very general terms. We should be following an almost universal example of modern governments if we were to draw the greater part or even the whole of the revenues we need from the income taxes. By somewhat lowering the present limits of exemption and the figure at which the surtax shall begin to be imposed, and by increasing, step by step throughout the present graduation, the surtax itself, the income taxes as at present apportioned would yield sums sufficient to balance the books of the Treasury at the end of the fiscal year 1917 without anywhere making the burden unreasonably or oppressively heavy. The precise reckonings are fully and accurately set out in the report of the Secretary of the Treasury which will be immediately laid before you.

And there are many additional sources of revenue which can justly be resorted to without hampering the industries of the country or putting any too great charge upon individual expenditure. A tax of one cent per gallon on gasoline and naphtha would yield, at the present estimated production, $10,000,000; a tax of fifty cents per horse power on automobiles and internal explosion engines, $15,000,000; a stamp tax on bank cheques, probably $18,000,000; a tax of twenty-five cents per ton on pig iron, $10,000,000; a tax of twenty-five cents per ton on fabricated iron and steel, probably $10,000,000. In a country of great industries like this it ought to be easy to distribute the burdens of taxation without making them anywhere bear too heavily or too exclusively upon any one set of persons or undertakings. What is clear is, that the industry of this generation should pay the bills of this generation.

I have spoken to you to-day, Gentlemen, upon a single theme, the thorough preparation of the nation to care for its own security and to make sure of entire freedom to play the impartial role in this hemisphere and in the world which we all believe to have been providentially assigned to it. I have had in my mind no thought of any immediate or particular danger arising out of our relations with other nations. We are at peace with all the nations of the world, and there is reason to hope that no question in controversy between this and other Governments will lead to any serious breach of amicable relations, grave as some differences of attitude and policy have been and may yet turn out to be. I am sorry to say that the gravest threats against our national peace and safety have been uttered within our own borders. There are citizens of the United States, I blush to admit, born under other flags but welcomed under our generous naturalization laws to the full freedom and opportunity of America, who have poured the poison of disloyalty into the very arteries of our national life; who have sought to bring the authority and good name of our Government into contempt, to destroy our industries wherever they thought it effective for their vindictive purposes to strike at them, and to debase our politics to the uses of foreign intrigue. Their number is not great as compared with the whole number of those sturdy hosts by which our nation has been enriched in recent generations out of virile foreign stock; but it is great enough to have brought deep disgrace upon us and to have made it necessary that we should promptly make use of processes of law by which we may be purged of their corrupt distempers. America never witnessed anything like this before. It never dreamed it possible that men sworn into its own citizenship, men drawn out of great free stocks such as supplied some of the best and strongest elements of that little, but how heroic, nation that in a high day of old staked its very life to free itself from every entanglement that had darkened the fortunes of the older nations and set up a new standard here,—that men of such origins and such free choices of allegiance would ever turn in malign reaction against the Government and people who had welcomed and nurtured them and seek to make this proud country once more a hotbed of European passion. A little while ago such a thing would have seemed incredible. Because it was incredible we made no preparation for it. We would have been almost ashamed to prepare for it, as if we were suspicious of ourselves, our own comrades and neighbors! But the ugly and incredible thing has actually come about and we are without adequate federal laws to deal with it. I urge you to enact such laws at the earliest possible moment and feel that in doing so I am urging you to do nothing less than save the honor and self-respect of the nation. Such creatures of passion, disloyalty, and anarchy must be crushed out. They are not many, but they are infinitely malignant, and the hand of our power should close over them at once. They have formed plots to destroy property, they have entered into conspiracies against the neutrality of the Government, they have sought to pry into every confidential transaction of the Government in order to serve interests alien to our own. It is possible to deal with these things very effectually. I need not suggest the terms in which they may be dealt with.

I wish that it could be said that only a few men, misled by mistaken sentiments of allegiance to the governments under which they were born, had been guilty of disturbing the self-possession and misrepresenting the temper and principles of the country during these days of terrible war, when it would seem that every man who was truly an American would instinctively make it his duty and his pride to keep the scales of judgment even and prove himself a partisan of no nation but his own. But it cannot. There are some men among us, and many resident abroad who, though born and bred in the United States and calling themselves Americans, have so forgotten themselves and their honor as citizens as to put their passionate sympathy with one or the other side in the great European conflict above their regard for the peace and dignity of the United States. They also preach and practice disloyalty. No laws, I suppose, can reach corruptions of the mind and heart; but I should not speak of others without also speaking of these and expressing the even deeper humiliation and scorn which every self-possessed and thoughtfully patriotic American must feel when he thinks of them and of the discredit they are daily bringing upon us.

While we speak of the preparation of the nation to make sure of her security and her effective power we must not fall into the patent error of supposing that her real strength comes from armaments and mere safeguards of written law. It comes, of course, from her people, their energy, their success in their undertakings, their free opportunity to use the natural resources of our great home land and of the lands outside our continental borders which look to us for protection, for encouragement, and for assistance in their development; from the organization and freedom and vitality of our economic life. The domestic questions which engaged the attention of the last Congress are more vital to the nation in this its time of test than at any other time. We cannot adequately make ready for any trial of our strength unless we wisely and promptly direct the force of our laws into these all-important fields of domestic action.

A matter which it seems to me we should have very much at heart is the creation of the right instrumentalities by which to mobilize our economic resources in any time of national necessity. I take it for granted that I do not need your authority to call into systematic consultation with the directing officers of the army and navy men of recognized leadership and ability from among our citizens who are thoroughly familiar, for example, with the transportation facilities of the country and therefore competent to advise how they may be coordinated when the need arises, those who can suggest the best way in which to bring about prompt cooperation among the manufacturers of the country, should it be necessary, and those who could assist to bring the technical skill of the country to the aid of the Government in the solution of particular problems of defense. I only hope that if I should find it feasible to constitute such an advisory body the Congress would be willing to vote the small sum of money that would be needed to defray the expenses that would probably be necessary to give it the clerical and administrative Machinery with which to do serviceable work.

What is more important is, that the industries and resources of the country should be available and ready for mobilization. It is the more imperatively necessary, therefore, that we should promptly devise means for doing what we have not yet done: that we should give intelligent federal aid and stimulation to industrial and vocational education, as we have long done in the large field of our agricultural industry; that, at the same time that we safeguard and conserve the natural resources of the country we should put them at the disposal of those who will use them promptly and intelligently, as was sought to be done in the admirable bills submitted to the last Congress from its committees on the public lands, bills which I earnestly recommend in principle to your consideration; that we should put into early operation some provision for rural credits which will add to the extensive borrowing facilities already afforded the farmer by the Reserve Bank Act, adequate instrumentalities by which long credits may be obtained on land mortgages; and that we should study more carefully than they have hitherto been studied the right adaptation of our economic arrangements to changing conditions.

Many conditions about which we have repeatedly legislated are being altered from decade to decade, it is evident, under our very eyes, and are likely to change even more rapidly and more radically in the days immediately ahead of us, when peace has returned to the world and the nations of Europe once more take up their tasks of commerce and industry with the energy of those who must bestir themselves to build anew. Just what these changes will be no one can certainly foresee or confidently predict. There are no calculable, because no stable, elements in the problem. The most we can do is to make certain that we have the necessary instrumentalities of information constantly at our service so that we may be sure that we know exactly what we are dealing with when we come to act, if it should be necessary to act at all. We must first certainly know what it is that we are seeking to adapt ourselves to. I may ask the privilege of addressing you more at length on this important matter a little later in your session.

In the meantime may I make this suggestion? The transportation problem is an exceedingly serious and pressing one in this country. There has from time to time of late been reason to fear that our railroads would not much longer be able to cope with it successfully, as at present equipped and coordinated I suggest that it would be wise to provide for a commission of inquiry to ascertain by a thorough canvass of the whole question whether our laws as at present framed and administered are as serviceable as they might be in the solution of the problem. It is obviously a problem that lies at the very foundation of our efficiency as a people. Such an inquiry ought to draw out every circumstance and opinion worth considering and we need to know all sides of the matter if we mean to do anything in the field of federal legislation.

No one, I am sure, would wish to take any backward step. The regulation of the railways of the country by federal commission has had admirable results and has fully justified the hopes and expectations of those by whom the policy of regulation was originally proposed. The question is not what should we undo. It is, whether there is anything else we can do that would supply us with effective means, in the very process of regulation, for bettering the conditions under which the railroads are operated and for making them more useful servants of the country as a whole. It seems to me that it might be the part of wisdom, therefore, before further legislation in this field is attempted, to look at the whole problem of coordination and efficiency in the full light of a fresh assessment of circumstance and opinion, as a guide to dealing with the several parts of it.

For what we are seeking now, what in my mind is the single thought of this message, is national efficiency and security. We serve a great nation. We should serve it in the spirit of its peculiar genius. It is the genius of common men for self-government, industry, justice, liberty and peace. We should see to it that it lacks no instrument, no facility or vigor of law, to make it sufficient to play its part with energy, safety, and assured success. In this we are no partisans but heralds and prophets of a new age.

Woodrow Wilson, 1913–1917

Annual Message to Congress
December 5, 1916

Woodrow Wilson delivered his fourth State of the Union message a month after winning reelection. Wilson defeated Republican nominee Charles Evans Hughes in one of the narrowest presidential elections in U.S. history.

In his 1912 election, Wilson had benefited from a split in the Republican Party, but in 1916 the Republicans united behind Hughes, a former governor of New York and Supreme Court justice—and future chief justice. Wilson won 277 votes in the electoral college to Hughes's 254; the incumbent president took 49.2 percent of the popular vote to his rival's 46.1 percent. Democrats retained control of both houses of Congress.

World War I continued to rage in Europe throughout 1916, and Wilson faced a balancing act as he headed for election day. He had endorsed a program to strengthen and increase the size of the U.S. military, but he continued to profess neutrality. The Democratic platform noted that Wilson had "kept us out of war," and that slogan became a constant theme during the campaign. But U.S. neutrality would not last; the country entered the war on the side of the Allies in April 1917.

This State of the Union address itself was shorter than his previous messages and was one of the shortest ever delivered. Although war was looming, Wilson chose to discuss domestic legislation.

Chief among these was the railroads. Amidst threats of railroad strikes, Congress had passed the Adamson Act earlier in 1916, which established an eight-hour day for railroad workers. In his address, Wilson pushed for additional measures regarding the railroads, including the ability for the executive to take control of them for military reasons. In fact, Wilson did eventually control the railroads after the United States had entered the war.

Wilson had come into office in 1913 espousing a reform platform and had what is considered an extremely productive first term, signing many key pieces of progressive legislation into law. Among them were the Underwood Tariff Act of 1913, which lowered tariffs to pre-Civil War levels; the Federal Reserve Act of 1913, which set up the federal reserve banking system; and the Clayton Anti-Trust Act, which gave the government more power against monopolies.

The president's second term, however, would be dominated by international affairs, as the country entered World War I and faced its uneasy aftermath.

Gentlemen of the Congress:

In fulfilling at this time the duty laid upon me by the Constitution of communicating to you from time to time information of the state of the Union and recommending to your consideration such legislative measures as may be judged necessary and expedient, I shall continue the practice, which I hope has been acceptable to you, of leaving to the reports of the several heads of the executive departments the elaboration of the detailed needs of the public service and confine myself to those matters of more general public policy with which it seems necessary and feasible to deal at the present session of the Congress.

I realize the limitations of time under which you will necessarily act at this session and shall make my suggestions as few as possible; but there were some things left undone at the last session which there will now be time to complete and which it seems necessary in the interest of the public to do at once.

In the first place, it seems to me imperatively necessary that the earliest possible consideration and action should be accorded the remaining measures of the program of settlement and regulation which I had occasion to recommend to you at the close of your last session in view of the public dangers disclosed by the unaccommodated difficulties which then existed, and which still unhappily continue to exist, between the railroads of the country and their locomotive engineers, conductors and trainmen.

I then recommended:

First, immediate provision for the enlargement and administrative reorganization of the Interstate Commerce Commission along the lines embodied in the bill recently passed by the House of Representatives and now awaiting action by the Senate; in order that the Commission may be enabled to deal with the many great and various duties now devolving upon it with a promptness and thoroughness which are, with its present constitution and means of action, practically impossible.

Second, the establishment of an eight-hour day as the legal basis alike of work and wages in the employment of all railway employes who are actually engaged in the work of operating trains in interstate transportation.

Third, the authorization of the appointment by the President of a small body of men to observe actual results in experience of the adoption of the eight-hour day in railway transportation alike for the men and for the railroads.

Fourth, explicit approval by the Congress of the consideration by the Interstate

Commerce Commission of an increase of freight rates to meet such additional expenditures by the railroads as may have been rendered necessary by the adoption of the eight-hour day and which have not been offset by administrative readjustments and economies, should the facts disclosed justify the increase.

Fifth, an amendment of the existing Federal statute which provides for the mediation, conciliation and arbitration of such controversies as the present by adding to it a provision that, in case the methods of accommodation now provided for should fail, a full public investigation of the merits of every such dispute shall be instituted and completed before a strike or lockout may lawfully be attempted.

And, sixth, the lodgment in the hands of the Executive of the power, in case of military necessity, to take control of such portions and such rolling stock of the railways of the country as may be required for military use and to operate them for military purposes, with authority to draft into the military service of the United States such train crews and administrative officials as the circumstances require for their safe and efficient use.

The second and third of these recommendations the Congress immediately acted on: it established the eight-hour day as the legal basis of work and wages in train service and it authorized the appointment of a commission to observe and report upon the practical results, deeming these the measures most immediately needed; but it postponed action upon the other suggestions until an opportunity should be offered for a more deliberate consideration of them.

The fourth recommendation I do not deem it necessary to renew. The power of the Interstate Commerce Commission to grant an increase of rates on the ground referred to is indisputably clear and a recommendation by the Congress with regard to such a matter might seem to draw in question the scope of the commission's authority or its inclination to do justice when there is no reason to doubt either.

The other suggestions—the increase in the Interstate Commerce Commission's membership and in its facilities for performing its manifold duties; the provision for full public investigation and assessment of industrial disputes, and the grant to the Executive of the power to control and operate the railways when necessary in time of war or other like public necessity—I now very earnestly renew.

The necessity for such legislation is manifest and pressing. Those who have entrusted us with the responsibility and duty of serving and safeguarding them in such matters would find it hard, I believe, to excuse a failure to act upon these grave matters or any unnecessary postponement of action upon them.

Not only does the Interstate Commerce Commission now find it practically impossible, with its present membership and organization, to perform its great functions promptly and thoroughly, but it is not unlikely that it may presently be found advisable to add to its duties still others equally heavy and exacting. It must first be perfected as an administrative instrument.

The country cannot and should not consent to remain any longer exposed to profound industrial disturbances for lack of additional means of arbitration and conciliation which the Congress can easily and promptly supply.

And all will agree that there must be no doubt as to the power of the Executive to make immediate and uninterrupted use of the railroads for the concentration of the military forces of the nation wherever they are needed and whenever they are needed.

This is a program of regulation, prevention and administrative efficiency which argues its own case in the mere statement of it. With regard to one of its items, the increase in the efficiency of the Interstate Commerce Commission, the House of Representatives has already acted; its action needs only the concurrence of the Senate.

I would hesitate to recommend, and I dare say the Congress would hesitate to act upon the suggestion should I make it, that any man in any I occupation should be obliged by law to continue in an employment which he desired to leave.

To pass a law which forbade or prevented the individual workman to leave his work before receiving the approval of society in doing so would be to adopt a new principle into our jurisprudence, which I take it for granted we are not prepared to introduce.

But the proposal that the operation of the railways of the country shall not be stopped or interrupted by the concerted action of organized bodies of men until a public investigation shall have been instituted, which shall make the whole question at issue plain for the judgment of the opinion of the nation, is not to propose any such principle.

It is based upon the very different principle that the concerted action of powerful bodies of men shall not be permitted to stop the industrial processes of the nation, at any rate before the nation shall have had an opportunity to acquaint itself with the merits of the case as between employe and employer, time to form its opinion upon an impartial statement of the merits, and opportunity to consider all practicable means of conciliation or arbitration.

I can see nothing in that proposition but the justifiable safeguarding by society of the necessary processes of its very life. There is nothing arbitrary or unjust in it unless it be arbitrarily and unjustly done. It can and should be done with a full and scrupulous regard for the interests and liberties of all concerned as well as for the permanent interests of society itself.

Three matters of capital importance await the action of the Senate which have already been acted upon by the House of Representatives: the bill which seeks to extend greater freedom of combination to those engaged in promoting the foreign commerce of the country than is now thought by some to be legal under the terms of the laws against monopoly; the bill amending the present organic law of Porto Rico; and the bill proposing a more thorough and systematic regulation of the expenditure of money in elections, commonly called the Corrupt Practices Act.

I need not labor my advice that these measures be enacted into law. Their urgency lies in the manifest circumstances which render their adoption at this time not only opportune but necessary. Even delay would seriously jeopard the interests of the country and of the Government.

Immediate passage of the bill to regulate the expenditure of money in elections may seem to be less necessary than the immediate enactment of the other measures to which I refer, because at least two years will elapse before another election in which Federal offices are to be filled; but it would greatly relieve the public mind if this important matter were dealt with while the circumstances and the dangers to the public morals of the present method of obtaining and spending campaign funds stand clear under recent observation, and the methods of expenditure can be frankly studied in the light of present experience; and a delay would have the further very serious disadvantage of postponing action until another election was at hand and some special object connected with it might be thought to be in the mind of those who urged it. Action can be taken now with facts for guidance and without suspicion of partisan purpose.

I shall not argue at length the desirability of giving a freer hand in the matter of combined and concerted effort to those who shall undertake the essential enterprise of building up our export trade. That enterprise will presently, will immediately assume, has indeed already assumed a magnitude unprecedented in our experience. We have not the necessary instrumentalities for its prosecution; it is deemed to be doubtful whether they could be created upon an adequate scale under our present laws.

We should clear away all legal obstacles and create a basis of undoubted law for it which will give freedom without permitting unregulated license. The thing must be done now, because the opportunity is here and may escape us if we hesitate or delay.

The argument for the proposed amendments of the organic law of Porto Rico is brief and conclusive. The present laws governing the island and regulating the rights and privileges of its people are not just. We have created expectations of extended privilege which we have not satisfied. There is uneasiness among the people of the island and even a suspicious doubt with regard to our intentions concerning them which the adoption of the pending measure would happily remove. We do not doubt what we wish to do in any essential particular. We ought to do it at once.

At the last session of the Congress a bill was passed by the Senate which provides for the promotion of vocational and industrial education, which is of vital importance to the whole country because it concerns a matter, too long neglected, upon which the thorough industrial preparation of the country for the critical years of economic development immediately ahead of us in very large measure depends.

May I not urge its early and favorable consideration by the House of Representatives and its early enactment into law? It contains plans which affect all interests and all parts of the country, and I am sure that there is no legislation now pending before the Congress whose passage the country awaits with more thoughtful approval or greater impatience to see a great and admirable thing set in the way of being done.

There are other matters already advanced to the stage of conference between the two houses of which it is not necessary that I should speak. Some practicable basis of agreement concerning them will no doubt be found an action taken upon them.

Inasmuch as this is, gentlemen, probably the last occasion I shall have to address the Sixty-fourth Congress, I hope that you will permit me to say with what genuine pleasure and satisfaction I have co-operated with you in the many measures of constructive policy with which you have enriched the legislative annals of the country. It has been a privilege to labor in such company. I take the liberty of congratulating you upon the completion of a record of rare serviceableness and distinction.

Woodrow Wilson, 1917–1921

Annual Message to Congress
December 4, 1917

Woodrow Wilson's fifth State of the Union message was a wartime address, the first such State of the Union ever delivered in person. After several years of neutrality, the United States had entered World War I on the side of the Allies in April 1917.

On April 2, 1917, Wilson had addressed Congress, asking it for a declaration of war. The United States, he said, would seek to make the world "safe for democracy." After Congress approved the war resolution, the president signed it on April 6.

As of December 4, the United States had been at war with Germany for eight months. Wilson's speech focused entirely on the conflict, including a discussion of why the country was at war and what it hoped to accomplish in the war's aftermath. As was his tendency, Wilson cast the conflict in moral tones, calling it "a war of high, disinterested purpose, in which all the free peoples of the world are banded together for the vindication of right."

The president made it clear that the war would end only after the Allies had defeated Germany. But he also said that, although Germany had committed wrongs during the war, the aftermath of the war should not result in others committing similar wrongs against Germany and its allies. Wilson also urged Congress to declare war on Germany's allies as well, calling it "embarrassing" that the United States had not.

"We are seeking permanent, not temporary, foundations for the peace of the world, and must seek them candidly and fearlessly," Wilson declared. Wilson's efforts to look ahead to the peace to come continued a month later, in January 1918, when he outlined his famous Fourteen Points, which were designed to provide a framework for a peace settlement. They represented a radical reordering of international politics and included such goals as open covenants of peace openly arrived at, self-determination for nations, and a League of Nations.

While Wilson had worked cooperatively with Congress throughout his first term, the dynamic between the two branches changed once the war started. Congress basically ceded much of its power to the executive branch during the war, giving Wilson expanded wartime authority. The president took over the country's communications and transportation systems, controlled mines and plants, and set prices, for example. Congress also approved the Selective Service Act of 1917, which gave Wilson power to draft soldiers for the war effort.

Ultimately, the United States's entry into the war turned the tide for the Allies, Great Britain and France, and by November 1918, they had prevailed.

Gentlemen of the Congress:

Eight months have elapsed since I last had the honor of addressing you. They have been months crowded with events of immense and grave significance for us. I shall not undertake to detail or even to summarize those events. The practical particulars of the part we have played in them will be laid before you in the reports of the executive departments. I shall discuss only our present outlook upon these vast affairs, our present duties, and the immediate means of accomplishing the objects we shall hold always in view.

I shall not go back to debate the causes of the war. The intolerable wrongs done and planned against us by the sinister masters of Germany have long since become too grossly obvious and odious to every true American to need to be rehearsed. But I shall ask you to consider again and with a very grave scrutiny our objectives and the measures by which we mean to attain them; for the purpose of discussion here in this place is action, and our action must move straight toward definite ends. Our object is, of course, to win the war; and we shall not slacken or suffer ourselves to he diverted until it is won. But it is worth while asking and answering the question, When shall we consider the war won?

From one point of view it is not necessary to broach this fundamental matter. I do not doubt that the American people know what the war is about and what sort of an outcome they will regard as a realization of their purpose in it.

As a nation we are united in spirit and intention. I pay little heed to those who tell me otherwise. I hear the voices of dissent—who does not? I bear the criticism and the clamor of the noisily thoughtless and troublesome. I also see men here and there fling themselves in impotent disloyalty against the calm, indomitable power of the Nation. I hear men debate peace who understand neither its nature nor the way in which we may attain it with uplifted eyes and unbroken spirits. But I know that none of these speaks for the Nation. They do not touch the heart of anything. They may safely be left to strut their uneasy hour and be forgotten.

But from another point of view I believe that it is necessary to say plainly what we here at the seat of action consider the war to be for and what part we mean to play in the settlement of its searching issues. We are the spokesmen of the American people, and they have a right to know whether their purpose is ours. They desire peace by the overcoming of evil, by the defeat once for all of the sinister forces that interrupt peace and render it impossible, and they wish to know how closely our thought runs with theirs and what action we propose. They are impatient with those who desire peace by any sort of compromise—deeply and indignantly impatient—but they will be equally impatient with us if we do not make it plain to them what our objectives are and what we are planning for in seeking to make conquest of peace by arms.

I believe that I speak for them when I say two things: First, that this intolerable thing of which the masters of Germany have shown us the ugly face, this menace of combined intrigue and force which we now see so clearly as the German power, a thing without conscience or honor of capacity for covenanted peace, must be crushed and, if it be not utterly brought to an end, at least shut out from the friendly inter-course of the nations; and second, that when this thing and its power are indeed defeated and the time comes that we can discuss peace when the German people have spokesmen whose word we can believe and when those spokesmen are ready in the name of their people to accept the common judgment of the nations as to what shall henceforth be the bases of law and of covenant for the life of the world—we shall be willing and glad to pay the full price for peace, and pay it ungrudgingly.

We know what that price will be. It will be full, impartial justice—justice done at every point and to every nation that the final settlement must affect, our enemies as well as our friends.

You catch, with me, the voices of humanity that are in the air. They grow daily more audible, more articulate, more persuasive, and they come from the hearts of men everywhere. They insist that the war shall not end in vindictive action of any kind; that no nation or people shall be robbed or punished because the irresponsible rulers of a single country have themselves done deep and abominable wrong. It is this thought that has been expressed in the formula, "No annexations, no contributions, no puni-tive indemnities."

Just because this crude formula expresses the instinctive judgment as to right of plain men everywhere, it has been made diligent use of by the masters of German intrigue to lead the people of Russia astray—and the people of every other country their agents could reach—in order that a premature peace might be brought about before autocracy has been taught its final and convincing lesson and the people of the world put in control of their own destinies.

But the fact that a wrong use has been made of a just idea is no reason why a right use should not be made of it. It ought to be brought under the patronage of its real friends. Let it be said again that autocracy must first be shown the utter futility of its claim to power or leadership in the modern world. It is impossible to apply any standard of justice so long as such forces are unchecked and undefeated as the present masters of Germany command. Not until that has been done can right be set up as arbiter and peacemaker among the nations. But when that has been done—as, God willing, it assuredly will be—we shall at last be free to do an unprecedented thing, and this is the time to avow our purpose to do it. We shall be free to base peace on generosity and justice, to the exclusions of all selfish claims to advantage even on the part of the victors.

Let there be no misunderstanding. Our present and immediate task is to win the war and nothing shall turn us aside from it until it is accomplished. Every power and resource we possess, whether of men, of money, or of materials, is being devoted and will continue to be devoted to that purpose until it is achieved. Those who desire to bring peace about before that purpose is achieved I counsel to carry their advice elsewhere. We will not entertain it. We shall regard the war as won only when the German people say to us, through properly accredited representatives, that they are ready to agree to a settlement based upon justice and reparation of the wrongs their rulers have done. They have done a wrong to Belgium which must be repaired. They have established a power over other lands and peoples than their own—over the great empire of Austria-Hungary, over hitherto free Balkan states, over Turkey and within Asia—which must be relinquished.

Germany's success by skill, by industry, by knowledge, by enterprise we did not grudge or oppose, but admired, rather. She had built up for herself a real empire of trade and influence, secured by the peace of the world. We were content to abide by the rivalries of manufacture, science and commerce that were involved for us in her success, and stand or fall as we had or did not have the brains and the initiative to surpass her. But at the moment when she had conspicuously won her triumphs of peace she threw them away, to establish in their stead what the world will no longer permit to be established, military and political domination by arms, by which to oust where she could not excel the rivals she most feared and hated. The peace we make must remedy that wrong. It must deliver the once fair lands and happy peoples of Belgium and Northern France from the Prussian conquest and the Prussian menace, but it must deliver also the peoples of Austria-Hungary, the peoples of the Balkans and the peoples of Turkey, alike in Europe and Asia, from the impudent and alien dominion of the Prussian military and commercial autocracy.

We owe it, however, to ourselves, to say that we do not wish in any way to impair or to rearrange the Austro-Hungarian Empire. It is no affair of ours what they do with their own life, either industrially or politically. We do not purpose or desire to dictate to them in any way. We only desire to see that their affairs are left in their own hands, in all matters, great or small. We shall hope to secure for the peoples of the Balkan peninsula and for the people of the Turkish Empire the right and opportunity to make their own lives safe, their own fortunes secure against oppression or injustice and from the dictation of foreign courts or parties.

And our attitude and purpose with regard to Germany herself are of a like kind. We intend no wrong against the German Empire, no interference with her internal affairs. We should deem either the one or the other absolutely unjustifiable, absolutely contrary to the principles we have professed to live by and to hold most sacred throughout our life as a nation.

The people of Germany are being told by the men whom they now permit to deceive them and to act as their masters that they are fighting for the very life and existence of their empire, a war of desperate self defense against deliberate aggression. Nothing could be more grossly or wantonly false, and we must seek by the utmost openness and candor as to our real aims to convince them of its falseness. We are in fact fighting for their emancipation from the fear, along with our own—from the fear as well as from the fact of unjust attack by neighbors or rivals or schemers after world empire. No one is threatening the existence or the independence of the peaceful enterprise of the German Empire.

The worst that can happen to the detriment the German people is this, that if they should still, after the war is over, continue to be obliged to live under ambitious and intriguing masters interested to disturb the peace of the world, men or classes of men whom the other peoples of the world could not trust, it might be impossible to admit them to the partnership of nations which must henceforth guarantee the world's peace. That partnership must be a partnership of peoples, not a mere partnership of governments. It might be impossible, also, in such untoward circumstances, to admit Germany to the free economic intercourse which must inevitably spring out of the other partnerships of a real peace. But there would be no aggression in that; and such a situation, inevitable, because of distrust, would in the very nature of things sooner or later cure itself, by processes which would assuredly set in.

The wrongs, the very deep wrongs, committed in this war will have to be righted. That, of course. But they cannot and must not be righted by the commission of similar wrongs against Germany and her allies. The world will not permit the commission of similar wrongs as a means of reparation and settlement. Statesmen must by this time have learned that the opinion of the world is everywhere wide awake and fully comprehends the issues involved. No representative of any self-governed nation will dare disregard it by attempting any such covenants of selfishness and compromise as were entered into at the Congress of Vienna. The thought of the plain people here and everywhere throughout the world, the people who enjoy no privilege and have very simple and unsophisticated standards of right and wrong, is the air all governments must henceforth breathe if they would live.

It is in the full disclosing light of that thought that all policies must be received and executed in this midday hour of the world's life. German rulers have been able to upset the peace of the world only because the German people were not suffered under their tutelage to share the comradeship of the other peoples of the world either in thought or in purpose. They were allowed to have no opinion of their own which might be set up as a rule of conduct for those who exercised authority over them. But the Congress that concludes this war will feel the full strength of the tides that run now in the hearts and consciences of free men everywhere. Its conclusions will run with those tides.

All those things have been true from the very beginning of this stupendous war; and I cannot help thinking that if they had been made plain at the very outset the sympathy and enthusiasm of the Russian people might have been once for all enlisted on the side of the Allies, suspicion and distrust swept away, and a real and lasting union of purpose effected. Had they believed these things at the very moment of their revolution, and had they been confirmed in that belief since, the sad reverses which have recently marked the progress of their affairs towards an ordered and stable government of free men might have been avoided. The Russian people have been poisoned by the very same falsehoods that have kept the German people in the dark, and the poison has been administered by the very same hand. The only possible antidote is the truth. It cannot be uttered too plainly or too often.

From every point of view, therefore, it has seemed to be my duty to speak these declarations of purpose, to add these specific interpretations to what I took the liberty of saying to the Senate in January. Our entrance into the war has not altered out attitude towards the settlement that must come when it is over.

When I said in January that the nations of the world were entitled not only to free pathways upon the sea, but also to assured and unmolested access to those—pathways, I was thinking, and I am thinking now, not of the smaller and weaker nations alone which need our countenance and support, but also of the great and powerful nations and of our present enemies as well as our present associates in the war. I was thinking, and am thinking now, of Austria herself, among the rest, as well as of Serbia and of Poland.

Justice and equality of rights can be had only at a great price. We are seeking permanent, not temporary, foundations for the peace of the world, and must seek them candidly and fearlessly. As always, the right will prove to be the expedient.

What shall we do, then, to push this great war of freedom and justice to its righteous conclusion? We must clear away with a thorough hand all impediments to success, and we must make every adjustment of law that will facilitate the full and free use of our whole capacity and force as a fighting unit.

One very embarrassing obstacle that stands in our way is that we are at war with Germany but not with her allies. I, therefore, very earnestly recommend that the Congress immediately declare the United States in a state of war with Austria-Hungary. Does it seem strange to you that this should be the conclusion of the argument I have just addressed to you? It is not. It is in fact the inevitable logic of what I have said. Austria-Hungary is for the time being not her own mistress but simply the vassal of the German Government.

We must face the facts as they are and act upon them without sentiment in this stern business. The Government of Austria and Hungary is not acting upon its own initiative or in response to the wishes and feelings of its own peoples, but as the instrument of another nation. We must meet its force with our own and regard the Central Powers as but one. The war can be successfully conducted in no other way.

The same logic would lead also to a declaration of war against Turkey and Bulgaria. They also are the tools of Germany, but they are mere tools and do not yet stand in the direct path of our necessary action. We shall go wherever the necessities of this war carry us, but it seems to me that we should go only where immediate and practical considerations lead us, and not heed any others.

The financial and military measures which must be adopted will suggest themselves as the war and its undertakings develop, but I will take the liberty of proposing to you certain other acts of legislation which seem to me to be needed for the support of the war and for the release of our whole force and energy.

It will be necessary to extend in certain particulars the legislation of the last session with regard to alien enemies, and also necessary, I believe, to create a very definite and particular control over the entrance and departure of all persons into and from the United States.

Legislation should be enacted defining as a criminal offense every wilful violation of the presidential proclamation relating to alien enemies promulgated under section 4067 of the revised statutes and providing appropriate punishments; and women, as well as men, should be included under the terms of the acts placing restraints upon alien enemies.

It is likely that as time goes on many alien enemies will be willing to be fed and housed at the expense of the Government in the detention camps, and it would be the purpose of the legislation I have suggested to confine offenders among them in the penitentiaries and other similar institutions where they could be made to work as other criminals do.

Recent experience has convinced me that the Congress must go further in authorizing the Government to set limits to prices. The law of supply and demand, I am sorry to say, has been replaced by the law of unrestrained selfishness. While we have eliminated profiteering in several branches of industry, it still runs impudently rampant in others. The farmers, for example, complain with a great deal of justice that, while the regulation of food prices restricts their incomes, no restraints are placed upon the prices of most of the things they must themselves purchase; and similar inequities obtain on all sides.

It is imperatively necessary that the consideration of the full use of the water power of the country, and also of the consideration of the systematic and yet economical development of such of the natural resources of the country as are still under the control of the Federal Government should be immediately resumed and affirmatively and constructively dealt with at the earliest possible moment. The pressing need of such legislation is daily becoming more obvious.

The legislation proposed at the last session with regard to regulated combinations among our exporters in order to provide for our foreign trade a more effective organization and method of co-operation ought by all means to be completed at this session.

And I beg that the members of the House of Representatives will permit me to express the opinion that it will be impossible to deal in any but a very wasteful and extravagant fashion with the enormous appropriations of the public moneys which must continue to be made if the war is to be properly sustained, unless the House will consent to return to its former practice of initiating and preparing all appropriation bills through a single committee, in order that responsibility may be centered, expenditures standardized and made uniform, and waste and duplication as much as possible avoided.

Additional legislation may also become necessary before the present Congress again adjourns in order to effect the most efficient co-ordination and operation of the railways and other transportation systems of the country; but to that I shall, if circumstances should demand, call the attention of Congress upon another occasion.

If I have overlooked anything that ought to be done for the more effective conduct of the war, your own counsels will supply the omission. What I am perfectly clear about is that in the present session of the Congress our whole attention and energy should be concentrated on the vigorous, rapid and successful prosecution of the great task of winning the war.

We can do this with all the greater zeal and enthusiasm because we know that for us this is a war of high principle, debased by no selfish ambition of conquest or spoil-iation; because we know, and all the world knows, that we have been forced into it to save the very institutions we five under from corruption and destruction. The pur-pose of the Central Powers strikes straight at the very heart of everything we believe in; their methods of warfare outrage every principle of humanity and of knightly honor; their intrigue has corrupted the very thought and spirit of many of our people; their sinister and secret diplomacy has sought to take our very territory away from us and disrupt the union of the states. Our safety would be at an end, our honor forever sullied and brought into contempt, were we to permit their triumph. They are strik-ing at the very existence of democracy and liberty.

It is because it is for us a war of high, disinterested purpose, in which all the free peoples of the world are banded together for the vindication of right, a war for the preservation of our nation, of all that it has held dear, of principle and of purpose, that we feel ourselves doubly constrained to propose for its outcome only that which is righteous and of irreproachable intention, for our foes as well as for our friends. The cause being just and holy, the settlement must be of like motive and equality. For this we can fight, but for nothing less noble or less worthy of our traditions. For this cause we entered the war and for this cause will we battle until the last gun is fired.

I have spoken plainly because this seems to me the time when it is most necessary to speak plainly, in order that all the world may know that, even in the heat and ardor of the struggle and when our whole thought is of carrying the war through to its end, we have not forgotten any ideal or principle for which the name of America has been held in honor among the nations and for which it has been our glory to contend in the great generations that went before us. A supreme moment of history has come. The eyes of the people have been opened and they see. The hand of God is laid upon the nations. He will show them favor, I devoutly believe, only if they rise to the clear heights of His own justice and mercy.

Woodrow Wilson, 1917–1921

Annual Message to Congress
December 2, 1918

Woodrow Wilson's sixth State of the Union message was delivered several weeks after the signing of the November 11 armistice that ended the fighting in World War I. Later that month, the president traveled to Europe to participate in peace negotiations.

The president began his address by praising the country for its efforts during the war. He described the massive mobilization of troops required for the war—almost 2 million in the course of the year—and congratulated the military forces from top to bottom for their hard work and courage. He highlighted the role the country's women had played in wartime, advocating women's political rights—a goal that would be achieved when the Nineteenth Amendment was ratified in 1920.

A shift from wartime back to peacetime would prove difficult, and Wilson devoted much of his speech to that subject. During the war, the president had taken on extraordinary powers, controlling much of the country's economy and production. But in his speech, he spoke of releasing the "harness" and gradually allowing industries to return to their normal activities. Wilson also had taken control of the railroads during the war, and sought to work with Congress to figure out the best approach for the railroads now that the war had ended.

Another concern was the return of thousands of soldiers into a peacetime economy. Wilson, in his address, said public works projects would be needed to help these people, many of them unskilled laborers, find work.

While Wilson, a Democrat, had seen his party control both houses of Congress since the start of his presidency in 1913, that situation was about to end. In the midterm congressional elections of 1918, the Republicans had won control of both the House and the Senate. Wilson had urged people to vote Democratic to express support for his wartime leadership, but that plan had backfired. The switch in congressional control would cause immense problems for Wilson in the aftermath of the war as he tried to sell his plan for a League of Nations.

Still, he was welcomed as a hero when he arrived in Europe for the peace talks. Much of the discussion focused around his Fourteen Points—which he had spelled out in an address to Congress the previous January—an idealistic framework for world peace that called not only for a League of Nations, but also for self-determination for nations and open covenants openly arrived at.

Gentlemen of the Congress:

The year that has elapsed since I last stood before you to fulfil my constitutional duty to give to the Congress from time to time information on the state of the Union has been so crowded with great events, great processes, and great results that I cannot hope to give you an adequate picture of its transactions or of the far-reaching changes which have been wrought of our nation and of the world. You have yourselves witnessed these things, as I have. It is too soon to assess them; and we who stand in the midst of them and are part of them are less qualified than men of another generation will be to say what they mean, or even what they have been. But some great outstanding facts are unmistakable and constitute, in a sense, part of the public business with which it is our duty to deal. To state them is to set the stage for the legislative and executive action which must grow out of them and which we have yet to shape and determine.

A year ago we had sent 145,918 men overseas. Since then we have sent 1,950,513, an average of 162,542 each month, the number in fact rising, in May last, to 245,951, in June to 278,760, in July to 307,182, and continuing to reach similar figures in August and September,—in August 289,570 and in September 257,438. No such movement of troops ever took place before, across three thousand miles of sea, followed by adequate equipment and supplies, and carried safely through extraordinary dangers of attack,—dangers which were alike strange and infinitely difficult to guard against. In all this movement only seven hundred and fifty-eight men were lost by enemy attack,—six hundred and thirty of whom were upon a single English transport which was sunk near the Orkney Islands.

I need not tell you what lay back of this great movement of men and material. It is not invidious to say that back of it lay a supporting organization of the industries of the country and of all its productive activities more complete, more thorough in method and effective in result, more spirited and unanimous in purpose and effort than any other great belligerent had been able to effect. We profited greatly by the experience of the nations which had already been engaged for nearly three years in the exigent and exacting business, their every resource and every executive proficiency taxed to the utmost. We were their pupils. But we learned quickly and acted with a promptness and a readiness of cooperation that justify our great pride that we were able to serve the world with unparalleled energy and quick accomplishment.

But it is not the physical scale and executive efficiency of preparation, supply, equipment and despatch that I would dwell upon, but the mettle and quality of the officers and men we sent over and of the sailors who kept the seas, and the spirit of the nation that stood behind them. No soldiers or sailors ever proved themselves more quickly ready for the test of battle or acquitted themselves with more splendid courage and achievement when put to the test. Those of us who played some part in directing the great processes by which the war was pushed irresistibly forward to the final triumph may now forget all that and delight our thoughts with the story of what our men did. Their officers understood the grim and exacting task they had undertaken and performed it with an audacity, efficiency, and unhesitating courage that touch the story of convoy and battle with imperishable distinction at every turn, whether the enterprise were great or small,—from their great chiefs, Pershing and Sims, down to the youngest lieutenant; and their men were worthy of them,—such men as hardly need to be commanded, and go to their terrible adventure blithely and with the quick intelligence of those who know just what it is they would accomplish. I am proud to be the fellow-countryman of men of such stuff and valor. Those of us who stayed at home did our duty; the war could not have been won or the gallant men who fought it given their opportunity to win it otherwise; but for many a long day we shall think ourselves "accurs'd we were not there, and hold our manhoods cheap while any speaks that fought" with these at St. Mihiel or Thierry. The memory of those days of triumphant battle will go with these fortunate men to their graves; and each will have his favorite memory. "Old men forget; yet all shall be forgot, but he'll remember with advantages what feats he did that day!"

What we all thank God for with deepest gratitude is that our men went in force into the line of battle just at the critical moment when the whole fate of the world seemed to hang in the balance and threw their fresh strength into the ranks of freedom in time to turn the whole tide and sweep of the fateful struggle,—turn it once for all, so that thenceforth it was back, back, back for their enemies, always back, never again forward! After that it was only a scant four months before the commanders of the Central Empires knew themselves beaten; and now their very empires are in liquidation!

And throughout it all how fine the spirit of the nation was: what unity of purpose, what untiring zeal! What elevation of purpose ran through all its splendid display of strength, its untiring accomplishment! I have said that those of us who stayed at home to do the work of organization and supply will always wish that we had been with the men whom we sustained by our labor; but we can never be ashamed. It has been an inspiring thing to be here in the midst of fine men who had turned aside from every private interest of their own and devoted the whole of their trained capacity to the tasks that supplied the sinews of the whole great undertaking! The patriotism, the unselfishness, the thoroughgoing devotion and distinguished capacity that marked their toilsome labors, day after day, month after month, have made them fit mates and comrades of the men in the trenches and on the sea. And not the men here in Washington only. They have but directed the vast achievement. Throughout innumerable factories, upon innumerable farms, in the depths of coal mines and iron mines and copper mines, wherever the stuffs of industry were to be obtained and prepared, in the shipyards, on the railways, at the docks, on the sea, in every labor that was needed to sustain the battle lines, men have vied with each other to do their part and do it well. They can look any man-at-arms in the face, and say, We also strove to win and gave the best that was in us to make our fleets and armies sure of their triumph!

And what shall we say of the women,—of their instant intelligence, quickening every task that they touched; their capacity for organization and cooperation, which gave their action discipline and enhanced the effectiveness of everything they attempted; their aptitude at tasks to which they had never before set their hands; their utter self-sacrifice alike in what they did and in what they gave? Their contribution to the great result is beyond appraisal. They have added a new lustre to the annals of American womanhood.

The least tribute we can pay them is to make them the equals of men in political rights as they have proved themselves their equals in every field of practical work they have entered, whether for themselves or for their country. These great days of completed achievement would be sadly marred were we to omit that act of justice. Besides the immense practical services they have rendered the women of the country have been the moving spirits in the systematic economies by which our people have voluntarily assisted to supply the suffering peoples of the world and the armies upon every front with food and everything else that we had that might serve the common cause. The details of such a story can never be fully written, but we carry them at our hearts and thank God that we can say that we are the kinsmen of such.

And now we are sure of the great triumph for which every sacrifice was made. It has come, come in its completeness, and with the pride and inspiration of these days of achievement quick within us, we turn to the tasks of peace again,—a peace secure against the violence of irresponsible monarchs and ambitious military coteries and made ready for a new order, for new foundations of justice and fair dealing.

We are about to give order and organization to this peace not only for ourselves but for the other peoples of the world as well, so far as they will suffer us to serve them. It is international justice that we seek, not domestic safety merely. Our thoughts have dwelt of late upon Europe, upon Asia, upon the near and the far East, very little upon the acts of peace and accommodation that wait to be performed at our own doors. While we are adjusting our relations with the rest of the world is it not of capital importance that we should clear away all grounds of misunderstanding with our immediate neighbors and give proof of the friendship we really feel? I hope that the members of the Senate will permit me to speak once more of the unratified treaty of friendship and adjustment with the Republic of Colombia. I very earnestly urge upon them an early and favorable action upon that vital matter. I believe that they will feel, with me, that the stage of affairs is now set for such action as will be not only just but generous and in the spirit of the new age upon which we have so happily entered.

So far as our domestic affairs are concerned the problem of our return to peace is a problem of economic and industrial readjustment. That problem is less serious for us than it may turn out too he for the nations which have suffered the disarrangements and the losses of war longer than we. Our people, moreover, do not wait to be coached and led. They know their own business, are quick and resourceful at every readjustment, definite in purpose, and self-reliant in action. Any leading strings we might seek to put them in would speedily become hopelessly tangled because they would pay no attention to them and go their own way. All that we can do as their legislative and executive servants is to mediate the process of change here, there, and elsewhere as we may. I have heard much counsel as to the plans that should be formed and personally conducted to a happy consummation, but from no quarter have I seen any general scheme of "reconstruction" emerge which I thought it likely we could force our spirited business men and self-reliant laborers to accept with due pliancy and obedience.

While the war lasted we set up many agencies by which to direct the industries of the country in the services it was necessary for them to render, by which to make sure of an abundant supply of the materials needed, by which to check undertakings that could for the time be dispensed with and stimulate those that were most serviceable in war, by which to gain for the purchasing departments of the Government a certain control over the prices of essential articles and materials, by which to restrain trade with alien enemies, make the most of the available shipping, and systematize financial transactions, both public and private, so that there would be no unnecessary conflict or confusion,—by which, in short, to put every material energy of the country in harness to draw the common load and make of us one team in the accomplishment of a great task. But the moment we knew the armistice to have been signed we took the harness off. Raw materials upon which the Government had kept its hand for fear there should not be enough for the industries that supplied the armies have been released and put into the general market again. Great industrial plants whose whole output and machinery had been taken over for the uses of the Government have been set free to return to the uses to which they were put before the war. It has not been possible to remove so readily or so quickly the control of foodstuffs and of shipping, because the world has still to be fed from our granaries and the ships are still needed to send supplies to our men overseas and to bring the men back as fast as the disturbed conditions on the other side of the water permit; but even there restraints are being relaxed as much as possible and more and more as the weeks go by

Never before have there been agencies in existence in this country which knew so much of the field of supply, of labor, and of industry as the War Industries Board, the War Trade Board, the Labor Department, the Food Administration, and the Fuel Administration have known since their labors became thoroughly systematized; and they have not been isolated agencies; they have been directed by men who represented the permanent Departments of the Government and so have been the centres of unified and cooperative action. It has been the policy of the Executive, therefore, since the armistice was assured (which is in effect a complete submission of the enemy) to put the knowledge of these bodies at the disposal of the business men of the country and to offer their intelligent mediation at every point and in every matter where it was desired. It is surprising how fast the process of return to a peace footing has moved in the three weeks since the fighting stopped. It promises to outrun any inquiry that may be instituted and any aid that may be offered. It will not be easy to direct it any better than it will direct itself. The American business man is of quick initiative.

The ordinary and normal processes of private initiative will not, however, provide immediate employment for all of the men of our returning armies. Those who are of trained capacity, those who are skilled workmen, those who have acquired familiarity with established businesses, those who are ready and willing to go to the farms, all those whose aptitudes are known or will be sought out by employers will find no difficulty, it is safe to say, in finding place and employment. But there will be others who will be at a loss where to gain a livelihood unless pains are taken to guide them and put them in the way of work. There will be a large floating residuum of labor which should not be left wholly to shift for itself. It seems to me important, therefore, that the development of public works of every sort should be promptly resumed, in order that opportunities should be created for unskilled labor in particular, and that plans should be made for such developments of our unused lands and our natural resources as we have hitherto lacked stimulation to undertake.

I particularly direct your attention to the very practical plans which the Secretary of the Interior has developed in his annual report and before your Committees for the reclamation of arid, swamp, and cutover lands which might, if the States were willing and able to cooperate, redeem some three hundred million acres of land for cultivation. There are said to be fifteen or twenty million acres of land in the West, at present arid, for whose reclamation water is available, if properly conserved. There are about two hundred and thirty million acres from which the forests have been cut but which have never yet been cleared for the plow and which lie waste and desolate. These lie scattered all over the Union. And there are nearly eighty million acres of land that lie under swamps or subject to periodical overflow or too wet for anything but grazing, which it is perfectly feasible to drain and protect and redeem. The Congress can at once direct thousands of the returning soldiers to the reclamation of the arid lands which it has already undertaken, if it will but enlarge the plans and appropriations which it has entrusted to the Department of the Interior. It is possible in dealing with our unused land to effect a great rural and agricultural development which will afford the best sort of opportunity to men who want to help themselves; and the Secretary of the Interior has thought the possible methods out in a way which is worthy of your most friendly attention.

I have spoken of the control which must yet for a while, perhaps for a long while, be exercised over shipping because of the priority of service to which our forces overseas are entitled and which should also be accorded the shipments which are to save recently liberated peoples from starvation and many devasted regions from permanent ruin. May I not say a special word about the needs of Belgium and northern France? No sums of money paid by way of indemnity will serve of themselves to save them from hopeless disadvantage for years to come. Something more must be done than merely find the money. If they had money and raw materials in abundance to-morrow they could not resume their place in the industry of the world to-morrow,—the very important place they held before the flame of war swept across them. Many of their factories are razed to the ground. Much of their machinery is destroyed or has been taken away. Their people are scattered and many of their best workmen are dead. Their markets will be taken by others, if they are not in some special way assisted to rebuild their factories and replace their lost instruments of manufacture. They should not be left to the vicissitudes of the sharp competition for materials and for industrial facilities which is now to set in. I hope, therefore, that the Congress will not be unwilling, if it should become necessary, to grant to some such agency as the War Trade Board the right to establish priorities of export and supply for the benefit of these people whom we have been so happy to assist in saving from the German terror and whom we must not now thoughtlessly leave to shift for themselves in a pitiless competitive market.

For the steadying, and facilitation of our own domestic business readjustments nothing is more important than the immediate determination of the taxes that are to be levied for 1918, 1919, and 1920. As much of the burden of taxation must be lifted from business as sound methods of financing the Government will permit, and those who conduct the great essential industries of the country must be told as exactly as possible what obligations to the Government they will be expected to meet in the years immediately ahead of them. It will be of serious consequence to the country to delay removing all uncertainties in this matter a single day longer than the right processes of debate justify. It is idle to talk of successful and confident business reconstruction before those uncertainties are resolved.

If the war had continued it would have been necessary to raise at least eight billion dollars by taxation payable in the year 1919; but the war has ended and I agree with the Secretary of the Treasury that it will be safe to reduce the amount to six billions. An immediate rapid decline in the expenses of the Government is not to be looked for. Contracts made for war supplies will, indeed, be rapidly cancelled and liquidated, but their immediate liquidation will make heavy drains on the Treasury for the months just ahead of us. The maintenance of our forces on the other side of the sea is still necessary. A considerable proportion of those forces must remain in Europe during the period of occupation, and those which are brought home will be transported and demobilized at heavy expense for months to come. The interest on our war debt must of course be paid and provision made for the retirement of the obligations of the Government which represent it. But these demands will of course fall much below what a continuation of military operations would have entailed and six billions should suffice to supply a sound foundation for the financial operations of the year.

I entirely concur with the Secretary of the Treasury in recommending that the two billions needed in addition to the four billions provided by existing law be obtained from the profits which have accrued and shall accrue from war contracts and distinctively war business, but that these taxes be confined to the war profits accruing in 1918, or in 1919 from business originating in war contracts. I urge your acceptance of his recommendation that provision be made now, not subsequently, that the taxes to be paid in 1920 should be reduced from six to four billions. Any arrangements less definite than these would add elements of doubt and confusion to the critical period of industrial readjustment through which the country must now immediately pass, and which no true friend of the nation's essential business interests can afford to be responsible for creating or prolonging. Clearly determined conditions, clearly and simply charted, are indispensable to the economic revival and rapid industrial development which may confidently be expected if we act now and sweep all interrogation points away.

I take it for granted that the Congress will carry out the naval programme which was undertaken before we entered the war. The Secretary of the Navy has submitted to your Committees for authorization that part of the programme which covers the building plans of the next three years. These plans have been prepared along the lines and in accordance with the policy which the Congress established, not under the exceptional conditions of the war, but with the intention of adhering to a definite method of development for the navy. I earnestly recommend the uninterrupted pursuit of that policy. It would clearly be unwise for us to attempt to adjust our programmes to a future world policy as yet undetermined.

The question which causes me the greatest concern is the question of the policy to be adopted towards the railroads. I frankly turn to you for counsel upon it. I have no confident judgment of my own. I do not see how any thoughtful man can have who knows anything of the complexity of the problem. It is a problem which must be studied, studied immediately, and studied without bias or prejudice. Nothing can be gained by becoming partisans of any particular plan of settlement.

It was necessary that the administration of the railways should be taken over by the Government so long as the war lasted. It would have been impossible otherwise to establish and carry through under a single direction the necessary priorities of shipment. It would have been impossible otherwise to combine maximum production at the factories and mines and farms with the maximum possible car supply to take the products to the ports and markets; impossible to route troop shipments and freight shipments without regard to the advantage or disadvantage of the roads employed; impossible to subordinate, when necessary, all questions of convenience to the public necessity; impossible to give the necessary financial support to the roads from the public treasury. But all these necessities have now been served, and the question is, What is best for the railroads and for the public in the future?

Exceptional circumstances and exceptional methods of administration were not needed to convince us that the railroads were not equal to the immense tasks of transportation imposed upon them by the rapid and continuous development of the industries of the country. We knew that already. And we knew that they were unequal to it partly because their full cooperation was rendered impossible by law and their competition made obligatory, so that it has been impossible to assign to them severally the traffic which could best be carried by their respective lines in the interest of expedition and national economy.

We may hope, I believe, for the formal conclusion of the war by treaty by the time Spring has come. The twenty-one months to which the present control of the railways is limited after formal proclamation of peace shall have been made will run at the farthest, I take it for granted, only to the January of 1921. The full equipment of the railways which the federal administration had planned could not be completed within any such period. The present law does not permit the use of the revenues of the several roads for the execution of such plans except by formal contract with their directors, some of whom will consent while some will not, and therefore does not afford sufficient authority to undertake improvements upon the scale upon which it would be necessary to undertake them. Every approach to this difficult subject-matter of decision brings us face to face, therefore, with this unanswered question: What is it right that we should do with the railroads, in the interest of the public and in fairness to their owners?

Let me say at once that I have no answer ready. The only thing that is perfectly clear to me is that it is not fair either to the public or to the owners of the railroads to leave the question unanswered and that it will presently become my duty to relinquish control of the roads, even before the expiration of the statutory period, unless there should appear some clear prospect in the meantime of a legislative solution. Their release would at least produce one element of a solution, namely certainty and a quick stimulation of private initiative.

I believe that it will be serviceable for me to set forth as explicitly as possible the alternative courses that lie open to our choice. We can simply release the roads and go back to the old conditions of private management, unrestricted competition, and multiform regulation by both state and federal authorities; or we can go to the opposite extreme and establish complete government control, accompanied, if necessary, by actual government ownership; or we can adopt an intermediate course of modified private control, under a more unified and affirmative public regulation and under such alterations of the law as will permit wasteful competition to be avoided and a considerable degree of unification of administration to be effected, as, for example, by regional corporations under which the railways of definable areas would be in effect combined in single systems.

The one conclusion that I am ready to state with confidence is that it would be a disservice alike to the country and to the owners of the railroads to return to the old conditions unmodified. Those are conditions of restraint without development. There is nothing affirmative or helpful about them. What the country chiefly needs is that all its means of transportation should be developed, its railways, its waterways, its highways, and its countryside roads. Some new element of policy, therefore, is absolutely necessary—necessary for the service of the public, necessary for the release of credit to those who are administering the railways, necessary for the protection of their security holders. The old policy may be changed much or little, but surely it cannot wisely be left as it was. I hope that the Congress will have a complete and impartial study of the whole problem instituted at once and prosecuted as rapidly as possible. I stand ready and anxious to release the roads from the present control and I must do so at a very early date if by waiting until the statutory limit of time is reached I shall be merely prolonging the period of doubt and uncertainty which is hurtful to every interest concerned.

I welcome this occasion to announce to the Congress my purpose to join in Paris the representatives of the governments with which we have been associated in the war against the Central Empires for the purpose of discussing with them the main features of the treaty of peace. I realize the great inconveniences that will attend my leaving the country, particularly at this time, but the conclusion that it was my paramount duty to go has been forced upon me by considerations which I hope will seem as conclusive to you as they have seemed to me.

The Allied governments have accepted the bases of peace which I outlined to the Congress on the eighth of January last, as the Central Empires also have, and very reasonably desire my personal counsel in their interpretation and application, and it is highly desirable that I should give it in order that the sincere desire of our Government to contribute without selfish purpose of any kind to settlements that will be of common benefit to all the nations concerned may be made fully manifest. The peace settlements which are now to be agreed upon are of transcendent importance both to us and to the rest of the world, and I know of no business or interest which should take precedence of them. The gallant men of our armed forces on land and sea have consciously fought for the ideals which they knew to be the ideals of their country; I have sought to express those ideals; they have accepted my statements of them as the substance of their own thought and purpose, as the associated governments have accepted them; I owe it to them to see to it, so far as in me lies, that no false or mistaken interpretation is put upon them, and no possible effort omitted to realize them. It is now my duty to play my full part in making good what they offered their life's blood to obtain. I can think of no call to service which could transcend this.

I shall be in close touch with you and with affairs on this side the water, and you will know all that I do. At my request, the French and English governments have absolutely removed the censorship of cable news which until within a fortnight they had maintained and there is now no censorship whatever exercised at this end except upon attempted trade communications with enemy countries. It has been necessary to keep an open wire constantly available between Paris and the Department of State and another between France and the Department of War. In order that this might be done with the least possible interference with the other uses of the cables, I have temporarily taken over the control of both cables in order that they may be used as a single system. I did so at the advice of the most experienced cable officials, and I hope that the results will justify my hope that the news of the next few months may pass with the utmost freedom and with the least possible delay from each side of the sea to the other.

May I not hope, Gentlemen of the Congress, that in the delicate tasks I shall have to perform on the other side of the sea, in my efforts truly and faithfully to interpret the principles and purposes of the country we love, I may have the encouragement and the added strength of your united support? I realize the magnitude and difficulty of the duty I am undertaking; I am poignantly aware of its grave responsibilities. I am the servant of the nation. I can have no private thought or purpose of my own in performing such an errand. I go to give the best that is in me to the common settlements which I must now assist in arriving at in conference with the other working heads of the associated governments. I shall count upon your friendly countenance and encouragement. I shall not be inaccessible. The cables and the wireless will render me available for any counsel or service you may desire of me, and I shall be happy in the thought that I am constantly in touch with the weighty matters of domestic policy with which we shall have to deal. I shall make my absence as brief as possible and shall hope to return with the happy assurance that it has been possible to translate into action the great ideals for which America has striven.

Woodrow Wilson, 1917–1921

Annual Message to Congress
December 2, 1919

For the first time in his presidency, Woodrow Wilson, in 1919, did not deliver his State of the Union message to Congress in person. Instead, the message, his seventh, was delivered in written form. Wilson, who had suffered a stroke that fall, was in poor health and would never regain his former strength.

The previous year had been momentous. The president had embarked for Europe in December 1918, a month after hostilities had ceased in World War I, for peace talks. The victorious Allies gave Wilson a hearty welcome, and some of his famed Fourteen Points were used as the basis for the future peace framework.

Wilson, a Democrat, faced a Republican-controlled Congress for the first time in his presidency. When he returned home to try to sell the just-negotiated Treaty of Versailles, which included the internationalist, Wilson-originated idea of a League of Nations, he ran into opposition in the Senate, including from some lawmakers who did not want to become involved in European politics. Wilson traveled around the country making speeches promoting the treaty, but he became ill and had to return to Washington. After suffering a stroke, the president remained in virtual seclusion for some time, seeing almost no one except his wife, Edith.

Wilson's State of the Union message centered on the theme of the country's postwar role. He noted that the United States's international position had shifted, and that it was important for the country—now the "greatest capitalist in the world"— to plunge into the "world market."

On the home front, Wilson noted the "widespread condition of political restlessness in our body politic" and cited a need to return quickly to peacetime conditions.

Among the changes he sought was an improvement in labor conditions, and— still pushing for the treaty and the League of Nations—he tied the issue in with the international situation, arguing that the leaders at Versailles had agreed that changes in workers' conditions must be instituted. The country had seen a series of strikes throughout 1919, including one by 350,000 steelworkers.

Wilson would find the last year of his presidency extremely frustrating. Unable to get the Senate to approve the Versailles Treaty, he also saw his party repudiated in the elections of November 1920, in which Republican Warren G. Harding scored a landslide victory to win the White House and the GOP kept control of both houses of Congress. The elections of 1920 would mark a shift in American politics, as the country turned away from Wilson's idealistic, internationalist views.

To the Senate and House of Representatives:

I sincerely regret that I cannot be present at the opening of this session of the Congress. I am thus prevented from presenting in as direct a way as I could wish the many questions that are pressing for solution at this time. Happily, I have had the advantage of the advice of the heads of the several executive departments who have kept in close touch with affairs in their detail and whose thoughtful recommendations I earnestly second.

In the matter of the railroads and the readjustment of their affairs growing out of Federal control, I shall take the liberty at a later date of addressing you.

I hope that Congress will bring to a conclusion at this session legislation looking to the establishment of a budget system. That there should be one single authority responsible for the making of all appropriations and that appropriations should be made not independently of each other, but with reference to one single comprehensive plan of expenditure properly related to the nation's income, there can be no doubt. I believe the burden of preparing the budget must, in the nature of the case, if the work is to be properly done and responsibility concentrated instead of divided, rest upon the executive. The budget so prepared should be submitted to and approved or amended by a single committee of each House of Congress and no single appropriation should be made by the Congress, except such as may have been included in the budget prepared by the executive or added by the particular committee of Congress charged with the budget legislation.

Another and not less important aspect of the problem is the ascertainment of the economy and efficiency with which the moneys appropriated are expended. Under existing law the only audit is for the purpose of ascertaining whether expenditures have been lawfully made within the appropriations. No one is authorized or equipped to ascertain whether the money has been spent wisely, economically and effectively. The auditors should be highly trained officials with permanent tenure in the Treasury Department, free of obligations to or motives of consideration for this or any subsequent administration, and authorized and empowered to examine into and make report upon the methods employed and the results obtained by the executive departments of the Government. Their reports should be made to the Congress and to the Secretary of the Treasury.

I trust that the Congress will give its immediate consideration to the problem of future taxation. Simplification of the income and profits taxes has become an immediate necessity. These taxes performed indispensable service during the war. They must, however, be simplified, not only to save the taxpayer inconvenience and expense, but in order that his liability may be made certain and definite.

With reference to the details of the Revenue Law, the Secretary of the Treasury and the Commissioner of Internal Revenue will lay before you for your consideration certain amendments necessary or desirable in connection with the administration of the law—recommendations which have my approval and support. It is of the utmost importance that in dealing with this matter the present law should not be disturbed so far as regards taxes for the calendar year 1920 payable in the calendar year 1921. The Congress might well consider whether the higher rates of income and profits taxes can in peace times be effectively productive of revenue, and whether they may not, on the contrary, be destructive of business activity and productive of waste and inefficiency. There is a point at which in peace times high rates of income and profits taxes discourage energy, remove the incentive to new enterprises, encourage extravagant expenditures and produce industrial stagnation with consequent unemployment and other attendant evils.

The problem is not an easy one. A fundamental change has taken place with reference to the position of America in the world's affairs. The prejudice and passions engendered by decades of controversy between two schools of political and economic thought,—the one believers in protection of American industries, the other believers in tariff for revenue only,—must be subordinated to the single consideration of the public interest in the light of utterly changed conditions. Before the war America was heavily the debtor of the rest of the world and the interest payments she had to make to foreign countries on American securities held abroad, the expenditures of American travelers abroad and the ocean freight charges she had to pay to others, about balanced the value of her pre-war favorable balance of trade. During the war America's exports have been greatly stimulated, and increased prices have increased their value. On the other hand, she has purchased a large proportion of the American securities previously held abroad, has loaned some $9,000,000,000 to foreign governments, and has built her own ships. Our favorable balance of trade has thus been greatly increased and Europe has been deprived of the means of meeting it heretofore existing. Europe can have only three ways of meeting the favorable balance of trade in peace times: by imports into this country of gold or of goods, or by establishing new credits. Europe is in no position at the present time to ship gold to us nor could we contemplate large further imports of gold into this country without concern. The time has nearly passed for international governmental loans and it will take time to develop in this country a market for foreign securities. Anything, therefore, which would tend to prevent foreign countries from settling for our exports by shipments of goods into this country could only have the effect of preventing them from paying for our exports and therefore of preventing the exports from being made. The productivity of the country, greatly stimulated by the war, must find an outlet by exports to foreign countries, and any measures taken to prevent imports will inevitably curtail exports, force curtailment of production, load the banking machinery of the country with credits to carry unsold products and produce industrial stagnation and unemployment. If we want to sell, we must be prepared to buy. Whatever, therefore, may have been our views during the period of growth of American business concerning tariff legislation, we must now adjust our own economic life to a changed condition growing out of the fact that American business is full grown and that America is the greatest capitalist in the world.

No policy of isolation will satisfy the growing needs and opportunities of America. The provincial standards and policies of the past, which have held American business as if in a strait-jacket, must yield and give way to the needs and exigencies of the new day in which we live, a day full of hope and promise for American business, if we will but take advantage of the opportunities that are ours for the asking. The recent war has ended our isolation and thrown upon us a great duty and responsibility. The United States must share the expanding world market. The United States desires for itself only equal opportunity with the other nations of the world, and that through the process of friendly cooperation and fair competition the legitimate interests of the nations concerned may be successfully and equitably adjusted.

There are other matters of importance upon which I urged action at the last session of Congress which are still pressing for solution. I am sure it is not necessary for me again to remind you that there is one immediate and very practicable question resulting from the war which we should meet in the most liberal spirit. It is a matter of recognition and relief to our soldiers. I can do no better than to quote from my last message urging this very action:

"We must see to it that our returning soldiers are assisted in every practicable way to find the places for which they are fitted in the daily work of the country. This can be done by developing and maintaining upon an adequate scale the admirable organization created by the Department of Labor for placing men seeking work; and it can also be done, in at least one very great field, by creating new opportunities for individual enterprise. The Secretary of the Interior has pointed out the way by which returning soldiers may be helped to find and take up land in the hitherto undeveloped regions of the country which the Federal Government has already prepared, or can readily prepare, for cultivation and also on many of the cutover or neglected areas which lie within the limits of the older states; and I once more take the liberty of recommending very urgently that his plans shall receive the immediate and substantial support of the Congress."

In the matter of tariff legislation, I beg to call your attention to the statements contained in my last message urging legislation with reference to the establishment of the chemical and dyestuffs industry in America:

Among the industries to which special consideration should be given is that of the manufacture of dyestuffs and related chemicals. Our complete dependence upon German supplies before the war made the interruption of trade a cause of exceptional economic disturbance. The close relation between the manufacture of dyestuffs, on the one hand, and of explosive and poisonous gases, on the other, moreover, has given the industry an exceptional significance and value. Although the United States will gladly and unhesitatingly join in the programme of international disarmament, it will, nevertheless, be a policy of obvious prudence to make certain of the successful maintenance of many strong and well-equipped chemical plants. The German chemical industry, with which we will be brought into competition, was—and may well be again—a thoroughly knit monopoly capable of exercising a competition of a peculiarly insidious and dangerous kind.

During the war the farmer performed a vital and willing service to the nation. By materially increasing the production of his land, he supplied America and the Allies with the increased amounts of food necessary to keep their immense armies in the field. He indispensably helped to win the war. But there is now scarcely less need of increasing the production in food and the necessaries of life. I ask the Congress to consider means of encouraging effort along these lines. The importance of doing everything possible to promote production along economical lines, to improve marketing, and to make rural life more attractive and healthful, is obvious. I would urge approval of the plans already proposed to the Congress by the Secretary of Agriculture, to secure the essential facts required for the proper study of this question, through the proposed enlarged programmes for farm management studies and crop estimates. I would urge, also, the continuance of Federal participation in the building of good roads, under the terms of existing law and under the direction of present agencies; the need of further action on the part of the States and the Federal Government to preserve and develop our forest resources, especially through the practice of better forestry methods on private holdings and the extension of the publicly owned forests; better support for country schools and the more definite direction of their courses of study along lines related to rural problems; and fuller provision for sanitation in rural districts and the building up of needed hospital and medical facilities in these localities. Perhaps the way might be cleared for many of these desirable reforms by a fresh, comprehensive survey made of rural conditions by a conference composed of representatives of the farmers and of the agricultural agencies responsible for leadership.

I would call your attention to the widespread condition of political restlessness in our body politic. The causes of this unrest, while various and complicated, are superficial rather than deep-seated. Broadly, they arise from or are connected with the failure on the part of our Government to arrive speedily at a just and permanent peace permitting return to normal conditions, from the transfusion of radical theories from seething European centers pending such delay, from heartless profiteering resulting in the increase of the cost of living, and lastly from the machinations of passionate and malevolent agitators. With the return to normal conditions, this unrest will rapidly disappear. In the meantime, it does much evil. It seems to me that in dealing with this situation Congress should not be impatient or drastic but should seek rather to remove the causes. It should endeavor to bring our country back speedily to a peace basis, with ameliorated living conditions under the minimum of restrictions upon personal liberty that is consistent with our reconstruction problems. And it should arm the Federal Government with power to deal in its criminal courts with those persons who by violent methods would abrogate our time-tested institutions. With the free expression of opinion and with the advocacy of orderly political change, however fundamental, there must be no interference, but towards passion and malevolence tending to incite crime and insurrection under guise of political evolution there should be no leniency. Legislation to this end has been recommended by the Attorney General and should be enacted. In this direct connection, I would call your attention to my recommendations on August 8th, pointing out legislative measures which would be effective in controlling and bringing down the present cost of living, which contributes so largely to this unrest. On only one of these recommendations has the Congress acted. If the Government's campaign is to be effective, it is necessary that the other steps suggested should be acted on at once.

I renew and strongly urge the necessity of the extension of the present Food Control Act as to the period of time in which it shall remain in operation. The Attorney General has submitted a bill providing for an extension of this Act for a period of six months. As it now stands, it is limited in operation to the period of the war and becomes inoperative upon the formal proclamation of peace. It is imperative that it should be extended at once. The Department of Justice has built up extensive machinery for the purpose of enforcing its provisions; all of which must be abandoned upon the conclusion of peace unless the provisions of this Act are extended.

During this period the Congress will have an opportunity to make similar permanent provisions and regulations with regard to all goods destined for interstate commerce and to exclude them from interstate shipment, if the requirements of the law are not compiled with. Some such regulation is imperatively necessary. The abuses that have grown up in the manipulation of prices by the withholding of foodstuffs and other necessaries of life cannot otherwise be effectively prevented. There can be no doubt of either the necessity of the legitimacy of such measures.

As I pointed out in my last message, publicity can accomplish a great deal in this campaign. The aims of the Government must be clearly brought to the attention of the consuming public, civic organizations and state officials, who are in a position to lend their assistance to our efforts. You have made available funds with which to carry on this campaign, but there is no provision in the law authorizing their expenditure for the purpose of making the public fully informed about the efforts of the Government. Specific recommendation has been made by the Attorney General in this regard. I would strongly urge upon you its immediate adoption, as it constitutes one of the preliminary steps to this campaign.

I also renew my recommendation that the Congress pass a law regulating cold storage as it is regulated, for example, by the laws of the State of New Jersey, which limit the time during which goods may be kept in storage, prescribe the method of disposing of them if kept beyond the permitted period, and require that goods released from storage shall in all cases bear the date of their receipt. It would materially add to the serviceability of the law, for the purpose we now have in view, if it were also prescribed that all goods released from storage for interstate shipment should have plainly marked upon each package the selling or market price at which they went into storage. By this means the purchaser would always be able to learn what profits stood between him and the producer or the wholesale dealer.

I would also renew my recommendation that all goods destined for interstate commerce should in every case, where their form or package makes it possible, be plainly marked with the price at which they left the hands of the producer.

We should formulate a law requiring a Federal license of all corporations engaged in interstate commerce and embodying in the license or in the conditions under which it is to be issued, specific regulations designed to secure competitive selling and prevent unconscionable profits in the method of marketing. Such a law would afford a welcome opportunity to effect other much needed reforms in the business of interstate shipment and in the methods of corporations which are engaged in it; but for the moment I confine my recommendations to the object immediately in hand, which is to lower the cost of living.

No one who has observed the march of events in the last year can fail to note the absolute need of a definite programme to bring about an improvement in the conditions of labor. There can be no settled conditions leading to increased production and a reduction in the cost of living if labor and capital are to be antagonists instead of partners. Sound thinking and an honest desire to serve the interests of the whole nation, as distinguished from the interests of a class, must be applied to the solution of this great and pressing problem. The failure of other nations to consider this matter in a vigorous way has produced bitterness and jealousies and antagonisms, the food of radicalism. The only way to keep men from agitating against grievances is to remove the grievances. An unwillingness even to discuss these matters produces only dissatisfaction and gives comfort to the extreme elements in our country which endeavor to stir up disturbances in order to provoke governments to embark upon a course of retaliation and repression. The seed of revolution is repression. The remedy for these things must not be negative in character. It must be constructive. It must comprehend the general interest. The real antidote for the unrest which manifests itself is not suppression, but a deep consideration of the wrongs that beset our national life and the application of a remedy.

Congress has already shown its willingness to deal with these industrial wrongs by establishing the eight-hour day as the standard in every field of labor. It has sought to find a way to prevent child labor. It has served the whole country by leading the way in developing the means of preserving and safeguarding lives and health in dangerous industries. It must now help in the difficult task of finding a method that will bring about a genuine democratization of industry, based upon the full recognition of the right of those who work, in whatever rank, to participate in some organic way in every decision which directly affects their welfare. It is with this purpose in mind that I called a conference to meet in Washington on December 1st, to consider these problems in all their broad aspects, with the idea of bringing about a better understanding between these two interests.

The great unrest throughout the world, out of which has emerged a demand for an immediate consideration of the difficulties between capital and labor, bids us put our own house in order. Frankly, there can be no permanent and lasting settlements between capital and labor which do not recognize the fundamental concepts for which labor has been struggling through the years. The whole world gave its recognition and endorsement to these fundamental purposes in the League of Nations. The statesmen gathered at Versailles recognized the fact that world stability could not be had by reverting to industrial standards and conditions against which the average workman of the world had revolted. It is, therefore, the task of the statesmen of this new day of change and readjustment to recognize world conditions and to seek to bring about, through legislation, conditions that will mean the ending of age-long antagonisms between capital and labor and that will hopefully lead to the building up of a comradeship which will result not only in greater contentment among the mass of workmen but also bring about a greater production and a greater prosperity to business itself.

To analyze the particulars in the demands of labor is to admit the justice of their complaint in many matters that lie at their basis. The workman demands an adequate wage, sufficient to permit him to live in comfort, unhampered by the fear of poverty and want in his old age. He demands the right to live and the right to work amidst sanitary surroundings, both in home and in workshop, surroundings that develop and do not retard his own health and wellbeing; and the right to provide for his children's wants in the matter of health and education. In other words, it is his desire to make the conditions of his life and the lives of those dear to him tolerable and easy to bear.

The establishment of the principles regarding labor laid down in the covenant of the League of Nations offers us the way to industrial peace and conciliation. No other road lies open to us. Not to pursue this one is longer to invite enmities, bitterness, and antagonisms which in the end only lead to industrial and social disaster. The unwilling workman is not a profitable servant. An employee whose industrial life is hedged about by hard and unjust conditions, which he did not create and over which he has no control, lacks that fine spirit of enthusiasm and volunteer effort which are the necessary ingredients of a great producing entity. Let us be frank about this solemn matter. The evidences of world-wide unrest which manifest themselves in violence throughout the world bid us pause and consider the means to be found to stop the spread of this contagious thing before it saps the very vitality of the nation itself. Do we gain strength by withholding the remedy? Or is it not the business of statesmen to treat these manifestations of unrest which meet us on every hand as evidences of an economic disorder and to apply constructive remedies wherever necessary, being sure that in the application of the remedy we touch not the vital tissues of our industrial and economic life? There can be no recession of the tide of unrest until constructive instrumentalities are set up to stem that tide.

Governments must recognize the right of men collectively to bargain for humane objects that have at their base the mutual protection and welfare of those engaged in all industries. Labor must not be longer treated as a commodity. It must be regarded as the activity of human beings, possessed of deep yearnings and desires. The business man gives his best thought to the repair and replenishment of his machinery, so that its usefulness will not be impaired and its power to produce may always be at its height and kept in full vigor and motion. No less regard ought to be paid to the human machine, which after all propels the machinery of the world and is the great dynamic force that lies back of all industry and progress. Return to the old standards of wage and industry in employment are unthinkable. The terrible tragedy of war which has just ended and which has brought the world to the verge of chaos and disaster would be in vain if there should ensue a return to the conditions of the past. Europe itself, whence has come the unrest which now holds the world at bay, is an example of standpatism in these vital human matters which America might well accept as an example, not to be followed but studiously to be avoided. Europe made labor the differential, and the price of it all is enmity and antagonism and prostrated industry. The right of labor to live in peace and comfort must be recognized by governments and America should be the first to lay the foundation stones upon which industrial peace shall be built.

Labor not only is entitled to an adequate wage, but capital should receive a reasonable return upon its investment and is entitled to protection at the hands of the Government in every emergency. No Government worthy of the name can "play" these elements against each other, for there is a mutuality of interest between them which the Government must seek to express and to safeguard at all cost.

The right of individuals to strike is inviolate and ought not to be interfered with by any process of Government, but there is a predominant right and that is the right of the Government to protect all of its people and to assert its power and majesty against the challenge of any class. The Government, when it asserts that right, seeks not to antagonize a class but simply to defend the right of the whole people as against the irreparable harm and injury that might be done by the attempt by any class to usurp a power that only Government itself has a right to exercise as a protection to all.

In the matter of international disputes which have led to war, statesmen have sought to set up as a remedy arbitration for war. Does this not point the way for the settlement of industrial disputes, by the establishment of a tribunal, fair and just alike to all, which will settle industrial disputes which in the past have led to war and disaster? America, witnessing the evil consequences which have followed out of such disputes between these contending forces, must not admit itself impotent to deal with these matters by means of peaceful processes. Surely, there must be some method of bringing together in a council of peace and amity these two great interests, out of which will come a happier day of peace and cooperation, a day that will make men more hopeful and enthusiastic in their various tasks, that will make for more comfort and happiness in living and a more tolerable condition among all classes of men. Certainly human intelligence can devise some acceptable tribunal for adjusting the differences between capital and labor.

This is the hour of test and trial for America. By her prowess and strength, and the indomitable courage of her soldiers, she demonstrated her power to vindicate on foreign battlefields her conceptions of liberty and justice. Let not her influence as a mediator between capital and labor be weakened and her own failure to settle matters of purely domestic concern be proclaimed to the world. There are those in this country who threaten direct action to force their will, upon a majority. Russia today, with its blood and terror, is a painful object lesson of the power of minorities. It makes little difference what minority it is; whether capital or labor, or any other class; no sort of privilege will ever be permitted to dominate this country. We are a partnership or nothing that is worth while. We are a democracy, where the majority are the masters, or all the hopes and purposes of the men who founded this government have been defeated and forgotten. In America there is but one way by which great reforms can be accomplished and the relief sought by classes obtained, and that is through the orderly processes of representative government. Those who would propose any other method of reform are enemies of this country. America will not be daunted by threats nor lose her composure or calmness in these distressing times. We can afford, in the midst of this day of passion and unrest, to be self-contained and sure. The instrument of all reform in America is the ballot. The road to economic and social reform in America is the straight road of justice to all classes and conditions of men. Men have but to follow this road to realize the full fruition of their objects and purposes. Let those beware who would take the shorter road of disorder and revolution. The right road is the road of justice and orderly process.

Woodrow Wilson, 1917–1921

Annual Message to Congress
December 7, 1920

Woodrow Wilson's last State of the Union message was a lame-duck message from an outgoing president whose health had failed and whose policies had been repudiated in the previous month's presidential election.

Wilson, who had delivered his first six State of the Union addresses before Congress in person—the first president to deliver the address publicly since John Adams—had suffered a stroke in 1919 and ended up submitting his final two addresses in writing.

In this relatively brief State of the Union message, Wilson urged the United States to stand as an example to the world of democracy in action, calling it the nation's "manifest destiny to lead in the attempt to make this spirit [of democracy] prevail."

He also offered a list of suggestions for legislation, including that the country revise its tax laws, improve its services for veterans, and improve agricultural conditions.

The elections of 1920 represented a swing in the national mood away from Wilson, a Democrat, and his high-minded internationalism. The president had run into a roadblock in the Republican-controlled Senate, which refused to approve the postwar Treaty of Versailles and its League of Nations, a concept that Wilson held dear.

Many Americans found themselves exhausted after living through World War I and its chaotic aftermath. In addition to the strikes that had sprung up around the country in 1919, the United States experienced a postwar "Red Scare" targeting alleged radicals.

Although Wilson had urged Americans to make the League of Nations an issue in how they voted in the 1920 elections, voters turned away from the Democratic presidential candidate, James Cox, in favor of Republican Warren G. Harding.

Harding, who promised a return to "normalcy," scored a landslide, winning 404 electoral votes to Cox's 127. Republicans also maintained control of the House and Senate, which they had won in the elections of 1918, scoring big gains in both houses.

Wilson's eight years in office had seen the enactment of major pieces of reform legislation, affecting the country's labor, banking, and tariff laws. He also had served during the Great War and the difficult postwar period. During his time in office, the country had been transformed. Now, with Harding about to take over, it would see a completely different style of president and of governing.

Gentlemen of the Congress:

When I addressed myself to performing the duty laid upon the President by the Constitution to present to you an annual report on the state of the Union, I found my thought dominated by an immortal sentence of Abraham Lincoln's—"Let us have faith that right makes might, and in that faith let us dare to do our duty as we understand it"—a sentence immortal because it embodies in a form of utter simplicity and purity the essential faith of the nation, the faith in which it was conceived, and the faith in which it has grown to glory and power. With that faith and the birth of a nation founded upon it came the hope into the world that a new order would prevail throughout the affairs of mankind, an order in which reason and right would take precedence over covetousness and force; and I believe that I express the wish and purpose of every thoughtful American when I say that this sentence marks for us in the plainest manner the part we should play alike in the arrangement of our domestic affairs and in our exercise of influence upon the affairs of the world.

By this faith, and by this faith alone, can the world be lifted out of its present confusion and despair. It was this faith which prevailed over the wicked force of Germany. You will remember that the beginning of the end of the war came when the German people found themselves face to face with the conscience of the world and realized that right was everywhere arrayed against the wrong that their government was attempting to perpetrate. I think, therefore, that it is true to say that this was the faith which won the war. Certainly this is the faith with which our gallant men went into the field and out upon the seas to make sure of victory.

This is the mission upon which Democracy came into the world. Democracy is an assertion of the right of the individual to live and to be treated justly as against any attempt on the part of any combination of individuals to make laws which will overburden him or which will destroy his equality among his fellows in the matter of right or privilege; and I think we all realize that the day has come when Democracy is being put upon its final test. The Old World is just now suffering from a wanton rejection of the principle of democracy and a substitution of the principle of autocracy as asserted in the name, but without the authority and sanction, of the multitude. This is the time of all others when Democracy should prove its purity and its spiritual power to prevail. It is surely the manifest destiny of the United States to lead in the attempt to make this spirit prevail.

There are two ways in which the United States can assist to accomplish this great object. First, by offering the example within her own borders of the will and power of Democracy to make and enforce laws which are unquestionably just and which are equal in their administration—laws which secure its full right to Labor and yet at the same time safeguard the integrity of property, and particularly of that property which is devoted to the development of industry and the increase of the necessary wealth of the world. Second, by standing for right and justice as toward individual nations. The law of Democracy is for the protection of the weak, and the influence of every democracy in the world should be for the protection of the weak nation, the nation which is struggling toward its right and toward its proper recognition and privilege in the family of nations.

The United States cannot refuse this role of champion without putting the stigma of rejection upon the great and devoted men who brought its government into existence and established it in the face of almost universal opposition and intrigue, even in the face of wanton force, as, for example, against the Orders in Council of Great Britain and the arbitrary Napoleonic decrees which involved us in what we know as the War of 1812.

I urge you to consider that the display of an immediate disposition on the part of the Congress to remedy any injustices or evils that may have shown themselves in our own national life will afford the most effectual offset to the forces of chaos and tyranny which are playing so disastrous a part in the fortunes of the free peoples of more than one part of the world. The United States is of necessity the sample democracy of the world, and the triumph of Democracy depends upon its success.

Recovery from the disturbing and sometimes disastrous effects of the late war has been exceedingly slow on the other side of the water, and has given promise, I venture to say, of early completion only in our own fortunate country; but even with us the recovery halts and is impeded at times, and there are immediately serviceable acts of legislation which it seems to me we ought to attempt, to assist that recovery and prove the indestructible recuperative force of a great government of the people. One of these is to prove that a great democracy can keep house as successfully and in as business-like a fashion as any other government. It seems to me that the first step toward providing this is to supply ourselves with a systematic method of handling our estimates and expenditures and bringing them to the point where they will not be an unnecessary strain upon our income or necessitate unreasonable taxation; in other words, a workable budget system. And I respectfully suggest that two elements are essential to such a system—namely, not only that the proposal of appropriations should be in the hands of a single body, such as a single appropriations committee in each house of the Congress, but also that this body should be brought into such cooperation with the Departments of the Government and with the Treasury of the United States as would enable it to act upon a complete conspectus of the needs of the Government and the resources from which it must draw its income.

I reluctantly vetoed the budget bill passed by the last session of the Congress because of a constitutional objection. The House of Representatives subsequently modified the bill in order to meet this objection. In the revised form, I believe that the bill, coupled with action already taken by the Congress to revise its rules and procedure, furnishes the foundation for an effective national budget system. I earnestly hope, therefore, that one of the first steps to be taken by the present session of the Congress will be to pass the budget bill.

The nation's finances have shown marked improvement during the last year. The total ordinary receipts of $6,694,000,000 for the fiscal year 1920 exceeded those for 1919 by $1,542,000,000, while the total net ordinary expenditures decreased from $18,514,000,000 to $6,403,000,000. The gross public debt, which reached its highest point on August 31, 1919, when it was $26,596,000,000, had dropped on November 30, 1920, to $24,175,000,000.

There has also been a marked decrease in holdings of government war securities by the banking institutions of the country, as well as in the amount of bills held by the Federal Reserve Banks secured by government war obligations. This fortunate result has relieved the banks and left them freer to finance the needs of Agriculture, Industry, and Commerce. It has been due in large part to the reduction of the public debt, especially of the floating debt, but more particularly to the improved distribution of government securities among permanent investors. The cessation of the Government's borrowings, except through short-term certificates of indebtedness, has been a matter of great consequence to the people of the country at large, as well as to the holders of Liberty Bonds and Victory Notes, and has had an important bearing on the matter of effective credit control.

The year has been characterized by the progressive withdrawal of the Treasury from the domestic credit market and from a position of dominant influence in that market. The future course will necessarily depend upon the extent to which economies are practiced and upon the burdens placed upon the Treasury, as well as upon industrial developments and the maintenance of tax receipts at a sufficiently high level. The fundamental fact which at present dominates the Government's financial situation is that seven and a half billions of its war indebtedness mature within the next two and a half years. Of this amount, two and a half billions are floating debt and five billions, Victory Notes and War Savings Certificates. The fiscal program of the Government must be determined with reference to these maturities. Sound policy demands that Government expenditures be reduced to the lowest amount which will permit the various services to operate efficiently and that Government receipts from taxes and salvage be maintained sufficiently high to provide for current requirements, including interest and sinking fund charges on the public debt, and at the same time retire the floating debt and part of the Victory Loan before maturity.

With rigid economy, vigorous salvage operations, and adequate revenues from taxation, a surplus of current receipts over current expenditures can be realized and should be applied to the floating debt. All branches of the Government should cooperate to see that this program is realized. I cannot overemphasize the necessity of economy in Government appropriations and expenditures and the avoidance by the Congress of practices which take money from the Treasury by indefinite or revolving fund appropriations. The estimates for the present year show that over a billion dollars of expenditures were authorized by the last Congress in addition to the amounts shown in the usual compiled statements of appropriations. This strikingly illustrates the importance of making direct and specific appropriations. The relation between the current receipts and current expenditures of the Government during the present fiscal year, as well as during the last half of the last fiscal year, has been disturbed by the extraordinary burdens thrown upon the Treasury by the Transportation Act, in connection with the return of the railroads to private control. Over $600,000,000 has already been paid to the railroads under this act—$350,000,000 during the present fiscal year; and it is estimated that further payments aggregating possibly $650,000,000 must still be made to the railroads during the current year. It is obvious that these large payments have already seriously limited the Government's progress in retiring the floating debt.

Closely connected with this, it seems to me, is the necessity for an immediate consideration of the revision of our tax laws. Simplification of the income and profits taxes has become an immediate necessity. These taxes performed an indispensable service during the war. The need for their simplification, however, is very great, in order to save the taxpayer inconvenience and expense and in order to make his liability more certain and definite. Other and more detailed recommendations with regard to taxes will no doubt be laid before you by the Secretary of the Treasury and the Commissioner of Internal Revenue.

It is my privilege to draw to the attention of Congress for very sympathetic consideration the problem of providing adequate facilities for the care and treatment of former members of the military and naval forces who are sick and disabled as the result of their participation in the war. These heroic men can never be paid in money for the service they patriotically rendered the nation. Their reward will lie rather in realization of the fact that they vindicated the rights of their country and aided in safeguarding civilization. The nation's gratitude must be effectively revealed to them by the most ample provision for their medical care and treatment as well as for their vocational training and placement. The time has come when a more complete program can be formulated and more satisfactorily administered for their treatment and training, and I earnestly urge that the Congress give the matter its early consideration. The Secretary of the Treasury and the Board for Vocational Education will outline in their annual reports proposals covering medical care and rehabilitation which I am sure will engage your earnest study and commend your most generous support.

Permit me to emphasize once more the need for action upon certain matters upon which I dwelt at some length in my message to the second session of the Sixty-sixth Congress. The necessity, for example, of encouraging the manufacture of dyestuffs and related chemicals; the importance of doing everything possible to promote agricultural production along economic lines, to improve agricultural marketing, and to make rural life more attractive and healthful; the need for a law regulating cold storage in such a way as to limit the time during which goods may be kept in storage, prescribing the method of disposing of them if kept beyond the permitted period, and requiring goods released from storage in all cases to bear the date of their receipt. It would also be most serviceable if it were provided that all goods released from cold storage for interstate shipment should have plainly marked upon each package the selling or market price at which they went into storage, in order that the purchaser might be able to learn what profits stood between him and the producer or the wholesale dealer. Indeed, it would be very serviceable to the public if all goods destined for interstate commerce were made to carry upon every packing case whose form made it possible a plain statement of the price at which they left the hands of the producer. I respectfully call your attention also to the recommendations of the message referred to with regard to a federal license for all corporations engaged in interstate commerce.

In brief, the immediate legislative need of the time is the removal of all obstacles to the realization of the best ambitions of our people in their several classes of employment and the strengthening of all instrumentalities by which difficulties are to be met and removed and justice dealt out, whether by law or by some form of mediation and conciliation. I do not feel it to be my privilege at present to suggest the detailed and particular methods by which these objects may be attained, but I have faith that the inquiries of your several committees will discover the way and the method.

In response to what I believe to be the impulse of sympathy and opinion throughout the United States, I earnestly suggest that the Congress authorize the Treasury of the United States to make to the struggling government of Armenia such a loan as was made to several of the Allied governments during the war, and I would also suggest that it would be desirable to provide in the legislation itself that the expenditure of the money thus loaned should be under the supervision of a commission, or at least a commissioner, from the United States in order that revolutionary tendencies within Armenia itself might not be afforded by the loan a further tempting opportunity.

Allow me to call your attention to the fact that the people of the Philippine Islands have succeeded in maintaining a stable government since the last action of the Congress in their behalf, and have thus fulfilled the condition set by the Congress as precedent to a consideration of granting independence to the Islands. I respectfully submit that this condition precedent having been fulfilled, it is now our liberty and our duty to keep our promise to the people of those islands by granting them the independence which they so honorably covet.

I have not so much laid before you a series of recommendations, gentlemen, as sought to utter a confession of faith, of the faith in which I was bred and which it is my solemn purpose to stand by until my last fighting day. I believe this to be the faith of America, the faith of the future, and of all the victories which await national action in the days to come, whether in America or elsewhere.

Warren G. Harding

1921–1923

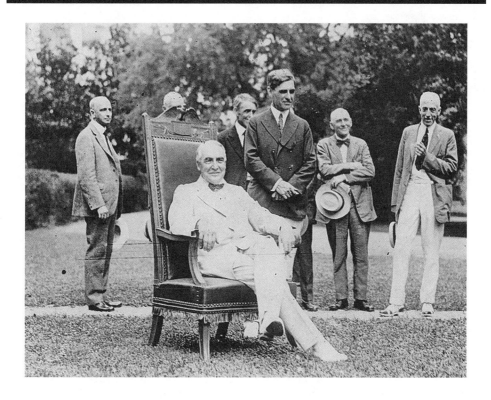

*". . . the contribution of this Republic
to restored normalcy in the world
must come through the initiative of the
executive branch of the Government,
but the best of intentions . . . would fail
utterly if the sanction and the cooperation
of Congress were not cheerfully accorded."*

ANNUAL MESSAGE TO CONGRESS, DECEMBER 6, 1921

Annual Message to Congress

December 6, 1921

President Warren G. Harding continued the practice of his predecessor, Woodrow Wilson, of presenting the State of the Union address in person before Congress. At the time of Harding's first annual message, the new Republican president had been in office for nine months.

Harding's election a year earlier marked a major shift from eight years of Democrat Wilson's policies. Harding moved away from Wilson's internationalist focus and, unlike his predecessor, did not push for the country to join the League of Nations. In his campaign, he had spoken of a return to "normalcy," and voters seemed ready to listen.

In his inaugural address the previous March, Harding had listed higher tariffs among his goals, and the issue of tariff reform was a major theme of this State of the Union message. Congress had approved an emergency tariff measure earlier in the year, but Harding urged them to pass permanent tariff legislation as soon as possible. Indeed, Congress, which was controlled by Republicans during Harding's administration, approved the high-tariff Fordney-McCumber Act in 1922.

Congress already had approved legislation in 1921, previously endorsed by Wilson, creating the Bureau of the Budget, which created a central point for organizing the budget. In his speech, Harding mentioned the new system, remarking that the new budget arrangement, once perfected, would mark a historic change for the government.

Harding also spoke about labor-management relations, stating that both labor and capital had the right to organize themselves but also that both should be regulated for the public good. He compared the negative effects of strikes, lockouts, and boycotts on an industrial society to the negative impact of war and armed revolution in the political sphere.

On the international front, having rejected the League of Nations–Versailles Treaty approach championed by Wilson, the Harding administration had opted to make peace with its World War I opponents through a series of treaties. It also organized the Washington Disarmament Conference, which brought together various nations, including Britain and Japan, in an effort to limit naval armaments. At the end of Harding's speech, he mentioned the ongoing conference, stating that "it is easy to believe a world-hope is centered on this Capital City."

In addition, Harding discussed the ongoing famine in parts of Russia, urging an appropriation to supply food for the stricken population despite the U.S. government's decision not to recognize the revolutionary Russian government.

M

r. Speaker and Members of the Congress:

It is a very gratifying privilege to come to the Congress with the Republic at peace with all the nations of the world. More, it is equally gratifying to report that our country is not only free from every impending, menace of war, but there are growing assurances of the permanency of the peace which we so deeply cherish.

For approximately ten years we have dwelt amid menaces of war or as participants in war's actualities, and the inevitable aftermath, with its disordered conditions, bits added to the difficulties of government which adequately can not be appraised except by, those who are in immediate contact and know the responsibilities. Our tasks would be less difficult if we had only ourselves to consider, but so much of the world was involved, the disordered conditions are so well-nigh universal, even among nations not engaged in actual warfare, that no permanent readjustments can be effected without consideration of our inescapable relationship to world affairs in finance and trade. Indeed, we should be unworthy of our best traditions if we were unmindful of social, moral, and political conditions which are not of direct concern to us, but which do appeal to the human sympathies and the very becoming interest of a people blest with our national good fortune.

It is not my purpose to bring to you a program of world restoration. In the main such a program must be worked out by the nations more directly concerned. They must themselves turn to the heroic remedies for the menacing conditions under which they are struggling, then we can help, and we mean to help. We shall do so unselfishly because there is compensation in the consciousness of assisting, selfishly because the commerce and international exchanges in trade, which marked our high tide of fortunate advancement, are possible only when the nations of all continents are restored to stable order and normal relationship.

In the main the contribution of this Republic to restored normalcy in the world must come through the initiative of the executive branch of the Government, but the best of intentions and most carefully considered purposes would fail utterly if the sanction and the cooperation of Congress were not cheerfully accorded.

I am very sure we shall have no conflict of opinion about constitutional duties or authority. During the anxieties of war, when necessity seemed compelling there were excessive grants of authority and all extraordinary concentration of powers in the Chief Executive. The repeal of war-time legislation and the automatic expirations which attended the peace proclamations have put an end to these emergency excesses but I have the wish to go further than that. I want to join you in restoring, in the most cordial way, the spirit of coordination and cooperation, and that mutuality of confidence and respect which is necessary ill representative popular government.

Encroachment upon the functions of Congress or attempted dictation of its policy are not to be thought of, much less attempted, but there is all insistent call for harmony of purpose and concord of action to speed the solution of the difficult problems confronting both the legislative and executive branches of the Government.

It is worth while to make allusion here to the character of our Clove Government, mindful as one must be that an address to you is no less it message to all our people, for whom you speak most intimately. Ours is a popular Government through political parties. We divide along political lines, and I would ever have it so. I do not mean that partisan preferences should hinder any public servant in the performance of a con-scientious and patriotic official duty. We saw partisan lines utterly obliterated when war imperiled, and our faith in the Republic was riveted anew. We ought not to find these partisan lines obstructing the expeditious solution of the urgent problems of peace.

Granting that we are fundamentally a representative popular Government, with political parties the governing agencies, I believe the political party in power should assume responsibility, determine upon policies ill the conference which supplements conventions and election campaigns, and then strive for achievement through adher-ence to the accepted policy.

There is vastly greater security, immensely more of the national viewpoint, much larger and prompter accomplishment where our divisions are along party lines, in the broader and loftier sense, than to divide geographically, or according to pursuits, or personal following. For a century and a third, parties have been charged with respon-sibility and held to strict accounting. When they fail, they are relieved of authority; and the system has brought us to a national eminence no less than a world example.

Necessarily legislation is a matter of compromise. The full ideal is seldom attained. In that meeting of minds necessary to insure results, there must and will be accom-modations and compromises, but in the estimate of convictions and sincere purposes the supreme responsibility to national interest must not be ignored. The shield to the high-minded public servant who adheres to party policy is manifest, but the higher purpose is the good of the Republic as a whole.

It would be ungracious to withhold acknowledgment of the really large volume and excellent quality of work accomplished by the extraordinary session of Congress which so recently adjourned. I am not unmindful of the very difficult tasks with which you were called to deal, and no one can ignore the insistent conditions which, during recent years, have called for the continued and almost exclusive attention of your member-ship to public work. It would suggest insincerity if I expressed complete accord with every expression recorded in your roll calls, but we are all agreed about the difficulties and the inevitable divergence of opinion in seeking the reduction, amelioration and readjustment of the burdens of taxation. Later on, when other problems are solved, I shall make some recommendations about renewed consideration of our tax program, but for the immediate time before us we must be content with the billion dollar reduc-tion in the tax draft upon the people, and diminished irritations, banished uncertainty and improved methods of collection. By your sustainment of the rigid economies already inaugurated, with hoped-for extension of these economies and added efficien-cies in administration, I believe further reductions may be enacted and hindering bur-dens abolished.

In these urgent economies we shall be immensely assisted by the budget system for which you made provision in the extraordinary session. The first budget is before you. Its preparation is a signal achievement, and the perfection of the system, a thing impos-sible in the few months available for its initial trial, will mark its enactment as the beginning of the greatest reformation in governmental practices since the beginning of the Republic.

There is pending a grant of authority to the administrative branch of the Govern-ment for the funding and settlement of our vast foreign loans growing out of our grant of war credits. With the hands of the executive branch held impotent to deal with these debts we are hindering urgent readjustments among our debtors and accomplishing nothing for ourselves. I think it is fair for the Congress to assume that the executive branch of the Government would adopt no major policy in dealing with these matters which would conflict with the purpose of Congress in authorizing the loans, certainly not without asking congressional approval, but there are minor problems incident to prudent loan transactions and the safeguarding of our interests which can not even be attempted without this authorization. It will be helpful to ourselves and it will improve conditions among our debtors if funding and the settlement of defaulted interest may be negotiated.

The previous Congress, deeply concerned in behalf of our merchant marine, in 1920 enacted the existing shipping law, designed for the upbuilding of the American merchant marine. Among other things provided to encourage our shipping on the world's seas, the Executive was directed to give notice of the termination of all existing commercial treaties in order to admit of reduced duties on imports carried in American bottoms. During the life of the act no Executive has complied with this order of the Congress. When the present administration came into responsibility it began an early inquiry into the failure to execute the expressed purpose of the Jones Act. Only one conclusion has been possible. Frankly, Members of House and Senate, eager as I am to join you in the making of an American merchant marine commensurate with our commerce, the denouncement of our commercial treaties would involve us in a chaos of trade relationships and add indescribably to the confusion of the already disordered commercial world. Our power to do so is not disputed, but power and ships, without comity of relationship, will not give us the expanded trade which is inseparably linked with a great merchant marine. Moreover, the applied reduction of duty, for which the treaty denouncements were necessary, encouraged only the carrying of dutiable imports to our shores, while the tonnage which unfurls the flag on the seas is both free and dutiable, and the cargoes which make it nation eminent in trade are outgoing, rather than incoming.

It is not my thought to lay the problem before you in detail today. It is desired only to say to you that the executive branch of the Government, uninfluenced by the protest of any nation, for none has been made, is well convinced that your proposal, highly intended and heartily supported here, is so fraught with difficulties and so marked by tendencies to discourage trade expansion, that I invite your tolerance of noncompliance for only a few weeks until a plan may be presented which contemplates no greater draft upon the Public Treasury, and which, though yet too crude to offer it to-day, gives such promise of expanding our merchant marine, that it will argue its own approval. It is enough to say to-day that we are so possessed of ships, and the American intention to establish it merchant marine is so unalterable, that a plain of reimbursement, at no other cost than is contemplated in the existing act, will appeal to the pride and encourage the hope of all the American people.

There is before you the completion of the enactment of what has been termed a "permanent" tariff law, the word "permanent" being used to distinguish it from the emergency act which the Congress expedited early in the extraordinary session, and which is the law today. I can not too strongly urge in early completion of this necessary legislation. It is needed to stabilize our industry at home; it is essential to make more definite our trade relations abroad. More, it is vital to the preservation of many of our own industries which contribute so notably to the very lifeblood of our Nation.

There is now, and there always will be, a storm of conflicting opinion about any tariff revision. We can not go far wrong when we base our tariffs on the policy of preserving the productive activities which enhance employment and add to our national prosperity.

Again comes the reminder that we must not be unmindful of world conditions, that peoples are struggling for industrial rehabilitation and that we can not dwell in industrial and commercial exclusion and at the same time do the just thing in aiding world reconstruction and readjustment. We do not seek a selfish aloofness, and we could not profit by it, were it possible. We recognize the necessity of buying wherever we sell, and the permanency of trade lies in its acceptable exchanges. In our pursuit of markets we must give as well as receive. We can not sell to others who do not produce, nor can we buy unless we produce at home. Sensible of every obligation of humanity, commerce and finance, linked as they are in the present world condition, it is not to be argued that we need destroy ourselves to be helpful to others. With all my heart I wish restoration to the peoples blighted by the awful World War, but the process of restoration does not lie in our acceptance of like conditions. It were better to, remain on firm ground, strive for ample employment and high standards of wage at home, and point the way to balanced budgets, rigid economies, and resolute, efficient work as the necessary remedies to cure disaster.

Everything relating to trade, among ourselves and among nations, has been expanded, excessive, inflated, abnormal, and there is a madness in finance which no American policy alone will cure. We are a creditor Nation, not by normal processes, but made so by war. It is not an unworthy selfishness to seek to save ourselves, when the processes of that salvation are not only not denied to others, but commended to them. We seek to undermine for others no industry by which they subsist; we are obligated to permit the undermining of none of our own which make for employment and maintained activities.

Every contemplation, it little matters in which direction one turns, magnifies the difficulty of tariff legislation, but the necessity of the revision is magnified with it. Doubtless we are justified in seeking a more flexible policy than we have provided heretofore. I hope a way will be found to make for flexibility and elasticity, so that rates may be adjusted to meet unusual and changing conditions which can not be accurately anticipated. There are problems incident to unfair practices, and to exchanges which madness in money have made almost unsolvable. I know of no manner in which to effect this flexibility other than the extension of the powers of the Tariff Commission so that it can adapt itself to it scientific and wholly just administration of the law.

I am not unmindful of the constitutional difficulties. These can be met by giving authority to the Chief Executive, who could proclaim additional duties to meet conditions which the Congress may designate.

At this point I must disavow any desire to enlarge the Executive's powers or add to the responsibilities of the office. They are already too large. If there were any other plan I would prefer it.

The grant of authority to proclaim would necessarily bring the Tariff Commission into new and enlarged activities, because no Executive could discharge such a duty except upon the information acquired and recommendations made by this commission. But the plan is feasible, and the proper functioning of the board would give us a better administration of a defined policy than ever can be made possible by tariff duties prescribed without flexibility.

There is a manifest difference of opinion about the merits of American valuation. Many nations have adopted delivery valuation as the basis for collecting duties; that is, they take the cost of the imports delivered at the port of entry as the basis for levying duty. It is no radical departure, in view of varying conditions and the disordered state of money values, to provide for American valuation, but there can not be ignored the danger of such a valuation, brought to the level of our own production costs, making our tariffs prohibitive. It might do so in many instances where imports ought to be encouraged. I believe Congress ought well consider the desirability of the only promising alternative, namely, a provision authorizing proclaimed American valuation, under prescribed conditions, on any given list of articles imported.

In this proposed flexibility, authorizing increases to meet conditions so likely to change, there should also be provision for decreases. A rate may be just to-day, and entirely out of proportion six months from to-day. If our tariffs are to be made equitable, and not necessarily burden our imports and hinder our trade abroad, frequent adjustment will be necessary for years to come. Knowing the impossibility of modification by act of Congress for any one or a score of lines without involving a long array of schedules, I think we shall go a long ways toward stabilization, if there is recognition of the Tariff Commission's fitness to recommend urgent changes by proclamation.

I am sure about public opinion favoring the early determination of our tariff policy. There have been reassuring signs of a business revival from the deep slump which all the world has been experiencing. Our unemployment, which gave its deep concern only a few weeks ago, has grown encouragingly less, and new assurances and renewed confidence will attend the congressional declaration that American industry will be held secure.

Much has been said about the protective policy for ourselves making it impossible for our debtors to discharge their obligations to us. This is a contention not now pressing for decision. If we must choose between a people in idleness pressing for the payment of indebtedness, or a people resuming the normal ways of employment and carrying the credit, let us choose the latter. Sometimes we appraise largest the human ill most vivid in our minds. We have been giving, and are giving now, of our influence and appeals to minimize the likelihood of war and throw off the crushing burdens of armament. It is all very earnest, with a national soul impelling. But a people unemployed, and gaunt with hunger, face a situation quite as disheartening as war, and our greater obligation to-day is to do the Government's part toward resuming productivity and promoting fortunate and remunerative employment.

Something more than tariff protection is required by American agriculture. To the farmer has come the earlier and the heavier burdens of readjustment. There is actual depression in our agricultural industry, while agricultural prosperity is absolutely essential to the general prosperity of the country.

Congress has sought very earnestly to provide relief. It has promptly given such temporary relief as has been possible, but the call is insistent for the permanent solution. It is inevitable that large crops lower the prices and short crops advance them. No legislation can cure that fundamental law. But there must be some economic solution for the excessive variation in returns for agricultural production.

It is rather shocking to be told, and to have the statement strongly supported, that 9,000,000 bales of cotton, raised on American plantations in a given year, will actually be worth more to the producers than 13,000,000 bales would have been. Equally shocking is the statement that 700,000,000 bushels of wheat, raised by American farmers, would bring them more money than a billion bushels. Yet these are not exaggerated statements. In a world where there are tens of millions who need food and clothing which they can not get, such a condition is sure to indict the social system which makes it possible.

In the main the remedy lies in distribution and marketing. Every proper encouragement should be given to the cooperative marketing programs. These have proven very helpful to the cooperating communities in Europe. In Russia the cooperative community has become the recognized bulwark of law and order, and saved individualism from engulfment in social paralysis. Ultimately they will be accredited with the salvation of the Russian State.

There is the appeal for this experiment. Why not try it? No one challenges the right of the farmer to a larger share of the consumer's pay for his product, no one disputes that we can not live without the farmer. Ile is justified in rebelling against the transportation cost. Given a fair return for his labor, he will have less occasion to appeal for financial aid; and given assurance that his labors shall not be in vain, we reassure all the people of a production sufficient to meet our National requirement and guard against disaster.

The base of the pyramid of civilization which rests upon the soil is shrinking through the drift of population from farm to city. For a generation we have been expressing more or less concern about this tendency. Economists have warned and statesmen have deplored. We thought for at time that modern conveniences and the more intimate contact would halt the movement, but it has gone steadily on. Perhaps only grim necessity will correct it, but we ought to find a less drastic remedy.

The existing scheme of adjusting freight rates has been favoring the basing points, until industries are attracted to some centers and repelled from others. A great volume of uneconomic and wasteful transportation has attended, and the cost increased accordingly. The grain-milling and meat-packing industries afford ample illustration, and the attending concentration is readily apparent. The menaces in concentration are not limited to the retarding influences on agriculture. Manifestly the conditions and terms of railway transportation ought not be permitted to increase this undesirable tendency. We have a just pride in our great cities, but we shall find a greater pride in the Nation, which has it larger distribution of its population into the country, where comparatively self-sufficient smaller communities may blend agricultural and manufacturing interests in harmonious helpfulness and enhanced good fortune. Such a movement contemplates no destruction of things wrought, of investments made, or wealth involved. It only looks to a general policy of transportation of distributed industry, and of highway construction, to encourage the spread of our population and restore the proper balance between city and country. The problem may well have your earnest attention.

It has been perhaps the proudest claim of our American civilization that in dealing with human relationships it has constantly moved toward such justice in distributing the product of human energy that it has improved continuously the economic status of the mass of people. Ours has been a highly productive social organization. On the way up from the elemental stages of society we have eliminated slavery and serfdom and are now far on the way to the elimination of poverty.

Through the eradication of illiteracy and the diffusion of education mankind has reached a stage where we may fairly say that in the United States equality of opportunity has been attained, though all are not prepared to embrace it. There is, indeed, a too great divergence between the economic conditions of the most and the least favored classes in the community. But even that divergence has now come to the point where we bracket the very poor and the very rich together as the least fortunate classes. Our efforts may well be directed to improving the status of both.

While this set of problems is commonly comprehended under the general phrase "Capital and labor," it is really vastly broader. It is a question of social and economic organization. Labor has become a large contributor, through its savings, to the stock of capital; while the people who own the largest individual aggregates of capital are themselves often hard and earnest laborers. Very often it is extremely difficult to draw the line of demarcation between the two groups; to determine whether a particular individual is entitled to be set down as laborer or as capitalist. In a very large proportion of cases lie is both, and when lie is both lie is the most useful citizen.

The right of labor to organize is just as fundamental and necessary as is the right of capital to organize. The right of labor to negotiate, to deal with and solve its particular problems in an organized way, through its chosen agents, is just as essential as is the right of capital to organize, to maintain corporations, to limit the liabilities of stockholders. Indeed, we have come to recognize that the limited liability of the citizen as a member of a labor organization closely parallels the limitation of liability of the citizen as a stockholder in a corporation for profit. Along this line of reasoning we shall make the greatest progress toward solution of our problem of capital and labor.

In the case of the corporation which enjoys the privilege of limited liability of stockholders, particularly when engaged in the public service, it is recognized that the outside public has a large concern which must be protected; and so we provide regulations, restrictions, and in some cases detailed supervision. Likewise in the case of labor organizations, we might well apply similar and equally well-defined principles of regulation and supervision in order to conserve the public's interests as affected by their operations.

Just as it is not desirable that a corporation shall be allowed to impose undue exactions upon the public, so it is not desirable that a labor organization shall be permitted to exact unfair terms of employment or subject the public to actual distresses in order to enforce its terms. Finally, just as we are earnestly seeking for procedures whereby to adjust and settle political differences between nations without resort to war, so we may well look about for means to settle the differences between organized capital and organized labor without resort to those forms of warfare which we recognize under the name of strikes, lockouts, boycotts, and the like.

As we have great bodies of law carefully regulating the organization and operations of industrial and financial corporations, as we have treaties and compacts among nations which look to the settlement of differences without the necessity of conflict in arms, so we might well have plans of conference, of common counsel, of mediation, arbitration, and judicial determination in controversies between labor and capital. To accomplish this would involve the necessity to develop a thoroughgoing code of practice in dealing with such affairs. It might be well to frankly set forth the superior interest of the community as a whole to either the labor group or the capital group.

With rights, privileges, immunities, and modes of organization thus carefully defined, it should be possible to set up judicial or quasi judicial tribunals for the consideration and determination of all disputes which menace the public welfare.

In an industrial society such as ours the strike, the lockout, and the boycott are as much out of place and as disastrous in their results as is war or armed revolution in the domain of politics. The same disposition to reasonableness, to conciliation, to recognition of the other side's point of view, the same provision of fair and recognized tribunals and processes, ought to make it possible to solve the one set of questions its easily as the other. I believe the solution is possible.

The consideration of such a policy would necessitate the exercise of care and deliberation in the construction of a code and a charter of elemental rights, dealing with the relations of employer and employee. This foundation in the law, dealing with the modern conditions of social and economic life, would hasten the building of the temple of peace in industry which a rejoicing nation would acclaim.

After each war, until the last, the Government has been enabled to give homes to its returned soldiers, and a large part of our settlement and development has attended this generous provision of land for the Nation's defenders.

There is yet unreserved approximately 200,000,000 acres in the public domain, 20,000,000 acres of which are known to be susceptible of reclamation and made fit for homes by provision for irrigation.

The Government has been assisting in the development of its remaining lands, until the estimated increase in land values in the irrigated sections is full $500,000,000 and the crops of 1920 alone on these lands are estimated to exceed $100,000,000. Under the law authorization these expenditures for development the advances are to be returned and it would be good business for the Government to provide for the reclamation of the remaining 20,000,000 acres, in addition to expediting the completion of projects long under way.

Under what is known as the coal and gas lease law, applicable also to deposits of phosphates and other minerals on the public domain, leases are now being made on the royalty basis, and are producing large revenues to the Government. Under this legislation, 10 per centum of all royalties is to be paid directly to the Federal Treasury, and of the remainder 50 per centum is to be used for reclamation of arid lands by irrigation, and 40 per centum is to be paid to the States, in which the operations are located, to be used by them for school and road purposes.

These resources are so vast, and the development is affording so reliable a basis of estimate, that the Interior Department expresses the belief that ultimately the present law will add in royalties and payments to the treasuries of the Federal Government and the States containing these public lands a total of $12,000,000,000. This means, of course, an added wealth of many times that sum. These prospects seem to afford every justification of Government advances in reclamation and irrigation.

Contemplating the inevitable and desirable increase of population, there is another phase of reclamation full worthy of consideration. There are 79,000,000 acres of swamp and cut-over lands which may be reclaimed and made as valuable as any farm lands we possess. These acres are largely located in Southern States, and the greater proportion is owned by the States or by private citizens. Congress has a report of the survey of this field for reclamation, and the feasibility is established. I gladly commend Federal aid, by way of advances, where State and private participation is assured.

Home making is one of the greater benefits which government can bestow. Measures are pending embodying this sound policy to which we may well adhere. It is easily possible to make available permanent homes which will provide, in turn, for prosperous American families, without injurious competition with established activities, or imposition on wealth already acquired.

While we are thinking of promoting the fortunes of our own people I am sure there is room in the sympathetic thought of America for fellow human beings who are suffering and dying of starvation in Russia. A severe drought in the Valley of the Volga has plunged 15,000,000 people into grievous famine. Our voluntary agencies are exerting themselves to the utmost to save the lives of children in this area, but it is now evident that unless relief is afforded the loss of life will extend into many millions. America can not be deaf to such a call as that.

We do not recognize the government of Russia, nor tolerate the propaganda which emanates therefrom, but we do not forget the traditions of Russian friendship. We may put aside our consideration of all international politics and fundamental differences in government. The big thing is the call of the suffering and the dying. Unreservedly I recommend the appropriation necessary to supply the American Relief Administration with 10,000,000 bushels of corn and 1,000,000 bushels of seed grains, not alone to halt the wave of death through starvation, but to enable spring planting in areas where the seed grains have been exhausted temporarily to stem starvation.

The American Relief Administration is directed in Russia by former officers of our own armies, and has fully demonstrated its ability to transport and distribute relief through American hands without hindrance or loss. The time has come to add the Government's support to the wonderful relief already wrought out of the generosity of the American private purse.

I am not unaware that we have suffering and privation at home. When it exceeds the capacity for the relief within the States concerned, it will have Federal consideration. It seems to me we should be indifferent to our own heart promptings, and out of accord with the spirit which acclaims the Christmastide, if we do not give out of our national abundance to lighten this burden of woe upon a people blameless and helpless in famine's peril.

There are a full score of topics concerning which it would be becoming to address you, and on which I hope to make report at a later time. I have alluded to the things requiring your earlier attention. However, I can not end this limited address without a suggested amendment to the organic law.

Many of us belong to that school of thought which is hesitant about altering the fundamental law. I think our tax problems, the tendency of wealth to seek nontaxable investment, and the menacing increase of public debt, Federal, State and municipal—all justify a proposal to change the Constitution so as to end the issue of nontaxable bonds. No action can change the status of the many billions outstanding, but we can guard against future encouragement of capital's paralysis, while a halt in the growth of public indebtedness would be beneficial throughout our whole land.

Such a change in the Constitution must be very thoroughly considered before submission. There ought to be known what influence it will have on the inevitable refunding of our vast national debt, how it will operate on the necessary refunding of State and municipal debt, how the advantages of Nation over State and municipality, or the contrary, may be avoided. Clearly the States would not ratify to their own apparent disadvantage. I suggest the consideration because the drift of wealth into nontaxable securities is hindering the flow of large capital to our industries, manufacturing, agricultural, and carrying, until we are discouraging the very activities which make our wealth.

Agreeable to your expressed desire and in complete accord with the purposes of the executive branch of the Government, there is in Washington, as you happily know, an International Conference now most earnestly at work on plans for the limitation of armament, a naval holiday, and the just settlement of problems which might develop into causes of international disagreement.

It is easy to believe a world-hope is centered on this Capital City. A most gratifying world-accomplishment is not improbable.

Warren G. Harding, 1921–1923

Annual Message to Congress
December 8, 1922

Warren Harding's second State of the Union message was also his last. He died the following August in San Francisco while on a speaking tour of the country.

In this message, delivered in person before Congress, Harding dwelled on the continuing unrest in the wake of World War I, which had ended four years before, and on the difficulties in moving back to a peacetime economy and way of life.

A series of strikes had disrupted the country in the postwar years. One of these, in 1922, involved 400,000 railway workers. Harding referred to that strike in his speech, stating that among the strike's repercussions were increased difficulties for already troubled American farmers.

Harding's speech underscored the impact of on that strike, and focused on the issue of transportation in general. He called transportation the most important problem facing the country, stating that more needed to be done to coordinate among the network of transportation by rail, highway, and sea. He also said that while railroad workers should be compensated fairly, they should not deliberately disrupt service on the rails.

In 1922, Congress had approved the Fordney–McCumber Act, which raised tariffs—one of Harding's goals when coming into office. In his speech, the president praised the change, saying that it would protect Americans while providing flexibility to readjust the levels if needed.

Another change for the nation was the controversial Eighteenth Amendment to the Constitution, which took effect in January 1920 and prohibited the manufacture, sale, and transportation of alcohol. In his 1922 address, Harding said that the issue of Prohibition was "distracting the public mind and prejudicing the judgment of the electorate." He proposed a conference of federal and state officials to focus on the myriad problems involved in enforcing that law.

In the aftermath of World War I, the country had turned away from the internationalist idealism embodied by Harding's predecessor, Woodrow Wilson. Harding, in his State of the Union message, spoke of his opposition to having an international body determining the course of the country, and he cited the "hostility of the

American people to a supergovernment"; this represented a rejection of Wilson's support for U.S. participation in a League of Nations. But Harding also noted that the country had been involved in international efforts, including a Washington-based naval disarmament conference.

In the congressional midterm elections of 1922, a month before this address, Republicans lost some seats but still retained control of the House and Senate.

Just after Harding's death, a series of scandals, including the "Teapot Dome" bribery fiasco involving Albert Fall, Harding's secretary of the interior, came to public attention and tarnished the reputation of his administration.

Members of the Congress:

So many problems are calling for solution that a recital of all of them, in the face of the known limitations of a short session of Congress, would seem to lack sincerity of purpose. It is four years since the World War ended, but the inevitable readjustment of the social and economic order is not more than barely begun. There is no acceptance of pre-war conditions anywhere in the world. In a very general way humanity harbors individual wishes to go on with war-time compensation for production, with pre-war requirements in expenditure. In short, everyone, speaking broadly, craves readjustment for everybody except himself, while there can be no just and permanent readjustment except when all participate.

The civilization which measured its strength of genius and the power of science and the resources of industries, in addition to testing the limits of man power and the endurance and heroism of men and women—that same civilization is brought to its severest test in restoring a tranquil order and committing humanity to the stable ways of peace.

If the sober and deliberate appraisal of pre-war civilization makes it seem a worthwhile inheritance, then with patience and good courage it will be preserved. There never again will be precisely the old order; indeed, I know of no one who thinks it to be desirable. For out of the old order came the war itself, and the new order, established and made secure, never will permit its recurrence.

It is no figure of speech to say we have come to the test of our civilization. The world has been passing—is today passing through of a great crisis. The conduct of war itself is not more difficult than the solution of the problems which necessarily follow. I am not speaking at this moment of the problem in its wider aspect of world rehabilitation or of international relationships. The reference is to our own social, financial, and economic problems at home. These things are not to be considered solely as problems apart from all international relationship, but every nation must be able to carry on for itself, else its international relationship will have scant importance.

Doubtless our own people have emerged from the World War tumult less impaired than most belligerent powers; probably we have made larger progress toward reconstruction. Surely we have been fortunate in diminishing unemployment, and our industrial and business activities, which are the lifeblood of our material existence, have been restored as in no other reconstruction period of like length in the history of the world. Had we escaped the coal and railway strikes, which had no excuse for their beginning and less justification for their delayed settlement, we should have done infinitely better. But labor was insistent on holding to the war heights, and heedless forces of reaction sought the pre-war levels, and both were wrong. In the folly of conflict our progress was hindered, and the heavy cost has not yet been fully estimated. There can be neither adjustment nor the penalty of the failure to readjust in which all do not somehow participate.

The railway strike accentuated the difficulty of the American farmer. The first distress of readjustment came to the farmer, and it will not be a readjustment fit to abide until he is relieved. The distress brought to the farmer does not affect him alone. Agricultural ill fortune is a national ill fortune. That one-fourth of our population which produces the food of the Republic and adds so largely to our export commerce must participate in the good fortunes of the Nation, else there is none worth retaining.

Agriculture is a vital activity in our national life. In it we had our beginning, and its westward march with the star of the empire has reflected the growth of the Republic. It has its vicissitudes which no legislation will prevent, its hardships for which no law can provide escape. But the Congress can make available to the farmer the financial facilities which have been built up under Government aid and supervision for other commercial and industrial enterprises. It may be done on the same solid fundamentals and make the vitally important agricultural industry more secure, and it must be done.

This Congress already has taken cognizance of the misfortune which precipitate deflation brought to American agriculture. Your measures of relief and the reduction of the Federal reserve discount rate undoubtedly saved the country from widespread disaster. The very proof of helpfulness already given is the strongest argument for the permanent establishment of widened credits, heretofore temporarily extended through the War Finance Corporation.

The Farm Loan Bureau, which already has proven its usefulness through the Federal land banks, may well have its powers enlarged to provide ample farm production credits as well as enlarged land credits. It is entirely practical to create a division in the Federal land banks to deal with production credits, with the limitations of time so adjusted to the farm turnover as the Federal reserve system provides for the turnover in the manufacturing and mercantile world. Special provision must be made for livestock production credits, and the limit of land loans may be safely enlarged. Various measures are pending before you, and the best judgment of Congress ought to be expressed in a prompt enactment at the present session.

But American agriculture needs more than added credit facilities. The credits will help to solve the pressing problems growing out of war-inflated land values and the drastic deflation of three years ago, but permanent and deserved agricultural good fortune depends on better and cheaper transportation.

Here is an outstanding problem, demanding the most rigorous consideration of the Congress and the country. It has to do with more than agriculture. It provides the channel for the flow of the country's commerce. But the farmer is particularly hard hit. His market, so affected by the world consumption, does not admit of the price adjustment to meet carrying charges. In the last half of the year now closing the railways, broken in carrying capacity because of motive power and rolling stock out of order, though insistently declaring to the contrary, embargoed his shipments or denied him cars when fortunate markets were calling. Too frequently transportation failed while perishable products were turning from possible profit to losses counted in tens of millions.

I know of no problem exceeding in importance this one of transportation. In our complex and interdependent modern life transportation is essential to our very existence. Let us pass for the moment the menace in the possible paralysis of such service as we have and note the failure, for whatever reason, to expand our transportation to meet the Nation's needs.

The census of 1880 recorded a population of 50,000,000. In two decades more we may reasonably expect to count thrice that number. In the three decades ending in 1920 the country's freight by rail increased from 631,000,000 tons to 2,234,000,000 tons; that is to say, while our population was increasing less than 70 per cent, the freight movement increased over 250 per cent.

We have built 40 per cent of the world's railroad mileage, and yet find it inadequate to our present requirements. When we contemplate the inadequacy of to-day it is easy to believe that the next few decades will witness the paralysis of our transportation-using social scheme or a complete reorganization on some new basis. Mindful of the tremendous costs of betterments, extensions, and expansions, and mindful of the staggering debts of the world to-day, the difficulty is magnified. Here is a problem demanding wide vision and the avoidance of mere makeshifts. No matter what the errors of the past, no matter how we acclaimed construction and then condemned operations in the past, we have the transportation and the honest investment in the transportation which sped us on to what we are, and we face conditions which reflect its inadequacy to-day, its greater inadequacy to-morrow, and we contemplate transportation costs which much of the traffic can not and will not continue to pay.

Manifestly, we have need to begin on plans to coordinate all transportation facilities. We should more effectively connect up our rail lines with our carriers by sea. We ought to reap some benefit from the hundreds of millions expended on inland waterways, proving our capacity to utilize as well as expend. We ought to turn the motor truck into a railway feeder and distributor instead of a destroying competitor.

It would be folly to ignore that we live in a motor age. The motor car reflects our standard of living and gauges the speed of our present-day life. It long ago ran down Simple Living, and never halted to inquire about the prostrate figure which fell as its victim. With full recognition of motor-car transportation we must turn it to the most practical use. It can not supersede the railway lines, no matter how generously we afford it highways out of the Public Treasury. If freight traffic by motor were charged with its proper and proportionate share of highway construction, we should find much of it wasteful and more costly than like service by rail. Yet we have paralleled the railways, a most natural line of construction, and thereby taken away from the agency of expected service much of its profitable traffic, which the taxpayers have been providing the highways, whose cost of maintenance is not yet realized.

The Federal Government has a right to inquire into the wisdom of this policy, because the National Treasury is contributing largely to this highway construction. Costly highways ought to be made to serve as feeders rather than competitors of the railroads, and the motor truck should become a coordinate factor in our great distributing system.

This transportation problem can not be waived aside. The demand for lowered costs on farm products and basic materials can not be ignored. Rates horizontally increased, to meet increased wage outlays during the war inflation, are not easily reduced. When some very moderate wage reductions were effected last summer there was a 5 per cent horizontal reduction in rates. I sought at that time, in a very informal way, to have the railway managers go before the Interstate Commerce Commission and agree to a heavier reduction on farm products and coal and other basic commodities, and leave unchanged the freight tariffs which a very large portion of the traffic was able to bear. Neither the managers nor the commission saw fit to adopt the suggestion, so we had the horizontal reduction saw fit to adopt too slight to be felt by the higher class cargoes and too little to benefit the heavy tonnage calling most loudly for relief.

Railways are not to be expected to render the most essential service in our social organization without a fair return on capital invested, but the Government has gone so far in the regulation of rates and rules of operation that it has the responsibility of pointing the way to the reduced freight costs so essential to our national welfare.

Government operation does not afford the cure. It was Government operation which brought us to the very order of things against which we now rebel, and we are still liquidating the costs of that supreme folly.

Surely the genius of the railway builders has not become extinct among the railway managers. New economies, new efficiencies in cooperation must be found. The fact that labor takes 50 to 60 per cent of total railway earnings makes limitations within which to effect economies very difficult, but the demand is no less insistent on that account.

Clearly the managers are without that intercarrier, cooperative relationship so highly essential to the best and most economical operation. They could not function in harmony when the strike threatened the paralysis of all railway transportation. The relationship of the service to public welfare, so intimately affected by State and Federal regulation, demands the effective correlation and a concerted drive to meet an insistent and justified public demand.

The merger of lines into systems, a facilitated interchange of freight cars, the economic use of terminals, and the consolidation of facilities are suggested ways of economy and efficiency.

I remind you that Congress provided a Joint Commission of Agricultural Inquiry which made an exhaustive investigation of car service and transportation, and unanimously recommended in its report of October 15, 1921, the pooling of freight cars under a central agency. This report well deserves your serious consideration. I think well of the central agency, which shall be a creation of the railways themselves, to provide, under the jurisdiction of the Interstate Commerce Commission, the means for financing equipment for carriers which are otherwise unable to provide their proportion of car equipment adequate to transportation needs. This same agency ought to point the way to every possible economy in maintained equipment and the necessary interchanges in railway commerce.

In a previous address to the Congress I called to your attention the insufficiency of power to enforce the decisions of the Railroad Labor Board. Carriers have ignored its decisions, on the one hand, railway workmen have challenged its decisions by a strike, on the other hand.

The intent of Congress to establish a tribunal to which railway labor and managers may appeal respecting questions of wages and working conditions can not be too strongly commended. It is vitally important that some such agency should be a guaranty against suspended operation. The public must be spared even the threat of discontinued service.

Sponsoring the railroads as we do, it is an obligation that labor shall be assured the highest justice and every proper consideration of wage and working conditions, but it is an equal obligation to see that no concerted action in forcing demands shall deprive the public of the transportation service essential to its very existence. It is now impossible to safeguard public interest, because the decrees of the board are unenforceable against either employer or employee.

The Labor Board itself is not so constituted as best to serve the public interest. With six partisan members on a board of nine, three partisans nominated by the employees and three by the railway managers, it is inevitable that the partisan viewpoint is maintained throughout hearings and in decisions handed down. Indeed, the few exceptions to a strictly partisan expression in decisions thus far rendered have been followed by accusations of betrayal of the partisan interests represented. Only the public group of three is free to function in unbiased decisions. Therefore the partisan membership may well be abolished, and decisions should be made by an impartial tribunal.

I am well convinced that the functions of this tribunal could be much better carried on here in Washington. Even were it to be continued as a separate tribunal, there ought to be contact with the Interstate Commerce Commission, which has supreme authority in the rate making to which wage cost bears an indissoluble relationship Theoretically, a fair and living wage must be determined quite apart from the employer's earning capacity, but in practice, in the railway service, they are inseparable. The record of advanced rates to meet increased wages, both determined by the Government, is proof enough.

The substitution of a labor division in the Interstate Commerce Commission made up from its membership, to hear and decide disputes relating to wages and working conditions which have failed of adjustment by proper committees created by the railways and their employees, offers a more effective plan.

It need not be surprising that there is dissatisfaction over delayed hearings and decisions by the present board when every trivial dispute is carried to that tribunal. The law should require the railroads and their employees to institute means and methods to negotiate between themselves their constantly arising differences, limiting appeals to the Government tribunal to disputes of such character as are likely to affect the public welfare.

This suggested substitution will involve a necessary increase in the membership of the commission, probably four, to constitute the labor division. If the suggestion appeals to the Congress, it will be well to specify that the labor division shall be constituted of representatives of the four rate-making territories, thereby assuring a tribunal conversant with the conditions which obtain in the different ratemaking sections of the country.

I wish I could bring to you the precise recommendation for the prevention of strikes which threaten the welfare of the people and menace public safety. It is an impotent civilization and an inadequate government which lacks the genius and the courage to guard against such a menace to public welfare as we experienced last summer. You were aware of the Government's great concern and its futile attempt to aid in an adjustment. It will reveal the inexcusable obstinacy which was responsible for so much distress to the country to recall now that, though all disputes are not yet adjusted, the many settlements which have been made were on the terms which the Government proposed in mediation.

Public interest demands that ample power shall be conferred upon the labor tribunal, whether it is the present board or the suggested substitute, to require its rulings to be accepted by both parties to a disputed question.

Let there be no confusion about the purpose of the suggested conferment of power to make decisions effective. There can be no denial of constitutional rights of either railway workmen or railway managers. No man can be denied his right to labor when and how he chooses, or cease to labor when he so elects, but, since the Government assumes to safeguard his interests while employed in an essential public service, the security of society itself demands his retirement from the service shall not be so timed and related as to effect the destruction of that service. This vitally essential public transportation service, demanding so much of brain and brawn, so much for efficiency and security, ought to offer the most attractive working conditions and the highest of wages paid to workmen in any employment.

In essentially every branch, from track repairer to the man at the locomotive throttle, the railroad worker is responsible for the safety of human lives and the care of vast property. His high responsibility might well rate high his pay within the limits the traffic will bear; but the same responsibility, plus governmental protection, may justly deny him and his associates a withdrawal from service without a warning or under circumstances which involve the paralysis of necessary transportation. We have assumed so great a responsibility in necessary regulation that we unconsciously have assumed the responsibility for maintained service; therefore the lawful power for the enforcement of decisions is necessary to sustain the majesty of government and to administer to the public welfare.

During its longer session the present Congress enacted a new tariff law. The protection of the American standards of living demanded the insurance it provides against the distorted conditions of world commerce. The framers of the law made provision for a certain flexibility of customs duties, whereby it is possible to readjust them as developing conditions may require. The enactment has imposed a large responsibility upon the Executive, but that responsibility will be discharged with a broad mindfulness of the whole business situation. The provision itself admits either the possible fallibility of rates or their unsuitableness to changing conditions. I believe the grant of authority may be promptly and discreetly exercised, ever mindful of the intent and purpose to safeguard American industrial activity, and at the same time prevent the exploitation of the American consumer and keep open the paths of such liberal exchanges as do not endanger our own productivity.

No one contemplates commercial aloofness nor any other aloofness contradictory to the best American traditions or loftiest human purposes. Our fortunate capacity for comparative self-containment affords the firm foundation on which to build for our own security, and a like foundation on which to build for a future of influence and importance in world commerce. Our trade expansion must come of capacity and of policies of righteousness and reasonableness in till our commercial relations.

Let no one assume that our provision for maintained good fortune at home, and our unwillingness to assume the correction of all the ills of the world, means a reluctance to cooperate with other peoples or to assume every just obligation to promote human advancement anywhere in the world.

War made us a creditor Nation. We did not seek an excess possession of the world's gold, and we have neither desire to profit unduly by its possession nor permanently retain it. We do not seek to become an international dictator because of its power.

The voice of the United States has a respectful hearing in international councils, because we have convinced the world that we have no selfish ends to serve, no old grievances to avenge, no territorial or other greed to satisfy. But the voice being heard is that of good counsel, not of dictation. It is the voice of sympathy and fraternity and helpfulness, seeking to assist but not assume for the United States burdens which nations must bear for themselves. We would rejoice to help rehabilitate currency systems and facilitate all commerce which does not drag us to the very levels of those we seek to lift up.

While I have everlasting faith in our Republic, it would be folly, indeed, to blind ourselves to our problems at home. Abusing the hospitality of our shores are the advocates of revolution, finding their deluded followers among those who take on the habiliments of an American without knowing an American soul. There is the recrudescence of hyphenated Americanism which we thought to have been stamped out when we committed the Nation, life and soul, to the World War.

There is a call to make the alien respect our institutions while he accepts our hospitality. There is need to magnify the American viewpoint to the alien who seeks a citizenship among us. There is need to magnify the national viewpoint to Americans throughout the land. More there is a demand for every living being in the United States to respect and abide by the laws of the Republic. Let men who are rending the moral fiber of the Republic through easy contempt for the prohibition law, because they think it restricts their personal liberty, remember that they set the example and breed a contempt for law which will ultimately destroy the Republic.

Constitutional prohibition has been adopted by the Nation. It is the supreme law of the land. In plain speaking, there are conditions relating to its enforcement which savor of nation-wide scandal. It is the most demoralizing factor in our public life.

Most of our people assumed that the adoption of the eighteenth amendment meant the elimination of the question from our politics. On the contrary, it has been so intensified as an issue that many voters are disposed to make all political decisions with reference to this single question. It is distracting the public mind and prejudicing the judgment of the electorate.

The day is unlikely to come when the eighteenth amendment will be repealed. The fact may as well be recognized and our course adapted accordingly. If the statutory provisions for its enforcement are contrary to deliberate public opinion, which I do not believe the rigorous and literal enforcement will concentrate public attention on any requisite modification. Such a course, conforms with the law and saves the humiliation of the Government and the humiliation of our people before the world, and challenges the destructive forces engaged in widespread violation, official corruption and individual demoralization.

The eighteenth amendment involves the concurrent authority of State and Federal Governments., for the enforcement of the policy it defines. A certain lack of definiteness, through division of responsibility is thus introduced. In order to bring about a full understanding of duties and responsibilities as thus distributed, I purpose to invite the governors of the States and Territories, at an early opportunity, to a conference with the Federal Executive authority. Out of the full and free considerations which will thus be possible, it is confidently believed, will emerge a more adequate, comprehension of the whole problem, and definite policies of National and State cooperation in administering the laws.

There are pending bills for the registration of the alien who has come to our shores. I wish the passage of such an act might be expedited. Life amid American opportunities is worth the cost of registration if it is worth the seeking, and the Nation has the right to know who are citizens in the making or who live among us anti share our advantages while seeking to undermine our cherished institutions. This provision will enable us to guard against the abuses in immigration, checking the undesirable whose irregular coming is his first violation of our laws. More, it will facilitate the needed Americanizing of those who mean to enroll as fellow citizens.

Before enlarging the immigration quotas we had better provide registration for aliens, those now here or continually pressing for admission, and establish our examination boards abroad, to make sure of desirables only. By the examination abroad we could end the pathos at our ports, when men and women find our doors closed, after long voyages and wasted savings, because they are unfit for admission. It would be kindlier and safer to tell them before they embark.

Our program of admission and treatment of immigrants is very intimately related to the educational policy of the Republic. With illiteracy estimated at front two-tenths of 1 per cent to less than 2 per cent in 10 of the foremost nations of Europe it rivets our attention to it serious problem when we are reminded of a 6 per cent illiteracy in the United States. The figures are based on the test which defines an Illiterate as one having no schooling whatever. Remembering the wide freedom of our public schools with compulsory attendance in many States in the Union, one is convinced that much of our excessive illiteracy comes to us from abroad, and the education of the immigrant becomes it requisite to his Americanization. It must be done if he is fittingly to exercise the duties as well as enjoy the privileges of American citizenship. Here is revealed the Special field for Federal cooperation in furthering education

From the very beginning public education has been left mainly in the hands of the States. So far as schooling youth is concerned the policy has been justified, because no responsibility can be so effective as that of the local community alive to its task. I believe in the cooperation of the national authority to stimulate, encourage, and broaden the Work of the local authorities But it is the especial obligation of the Federal Government to devise means and effectively assist in the education of the newcomer from foreign lands, so that the level of American education may be made the highest that is humanly possible.

Closely related to this problem of education is the abolition of child labor. Twice Congress has attempted the correction of the evils incident to child employment. The decision of the Supreme Court has put this problem outside the proper domain of Federal regulation until the Constitution is so amended as to give the Congress indubitable authority. I recommend the submission of such an amendment.

We have two schools of thought relating to amendment of the Constitution. One need not be committed to the belief that amendment is weakening the fundamental law, or that excessive amendment is essential to meet every ephemeral whim. We ought to amend to meet the demands of the people when sanctioned by deliberate public opinion.

One year ago I suggested the submission of an amendment so that we may lawfully restrict the issues of tax-exempt securities, and I renew that recommendation now. Tax-exempt securities are drying up the sources of Federal taxation and they are encouraging unproductive and extravagant expenditures by States and municipalities. There is more than the menace in mounting public debt, there is the dissipation of capital which should be made available to the needs of productive industry. The proposed amendment will place the State and Federal Governments and all political subdivisions on an exact equality, and will correct the growing menace of public borrowing, which if left unchecked may soon threaten the stability of our institutions.

We are so vast and so varied in our national interests that scores of problems are pressing for attention. I must not risk the wearying of your patience with detailed reference.

Reclamation and irrigation projects, where waste land may be made available for settlement and productivity, are worthy of your favorable consideration.

When it is realized that we are consuming our timber four times as rapidly as we are growing it, we must encourage the greatest possible cooperation between the Federal Government, the various States, and the owners of forest lands, to the end that protection from fire shall be made more effective and replanting encouraged.

The fuel problem is under study now by a very capable fact-finding commission, and any attempt to deal with the coal problem, of such deep concern to the entire Nation, must await the report of the commission.

There are necessary studies of great problems which Congress might well initiate. The wide spread between production costs and prices which consumers pay concerns every citizen of the Republic. It contributes very largely to the unrest in agriculture and must stand sponsor for much against which we inveigh in that familiar term— the high cost of living.

No one doubts the excess is traceable to the levy of the middleman, but it would be unfair to charge him with all responsibility before we appraise what is exacted of him by our modernly complex life. We have attacked the problem on one side by the promotion of cooperative marketing, and we might well inquire into the benefits of cooperative buying. Admittedly, the consumer is much to blame himself, because of his prodigal expenditure and his exaction of service, but Government might well serve to point the way of narrowing the spread of price, especially between the production of food and its consumption.

A superpower survey of the eastern industrial region has recently been completed, looking to unification of steam, water, and electric powers, and to a unified scheme of power distribution. The survey proved that vast economies in tonnage movement of freights, and in the efficiency of the railroads, would be effected if the superpower program were adopted. I am convinced that constructive measures calculated to promote such an industrial development—I am tempted to say, such an industrial revolution—would be well worthy the careful attention and fostering interest of the National Government.

The proposed survey of a plan to draft all the resources of the Republic, human and material, for national defense may well have your approval. I commended such a program in case of future war, in the inaugural address of March 4, 1921, and every experience in the adjustment and liquidation of war claims and the settlement of war obligations persuades me we ought to be prepared for such universal call to armed defense.

I bring you no apprehension of war. The world is abhorrent of it, and our own relations are not only free from every threatening cloud, but we have contributed our larger influence toward making armed conflict less likely.

Those who assume that we played our part in the World War and later took ourselves aloof and apart, unmindful of world obligations, give scant credit to the helpful part we assume in international relationships.

Whether all nations signatory ratify all the treaties growing out of the Washington Conference on Limitation of Armament or some withhold approval, the underlying policy of limiting naval armament has the sanction of the larger naval powers, and naval competition is suspended. Of course, unanimous ratification is much to be desired.

The four-power pact, which abolishes every probability of war on the Pacific, has brought new confidence in a maintained peace, and I can well believe it might be made a model for like assurances wherever in the world any common interests are concerned.

We have had expressed the hostility of the American people to a supergovernment or to any commitment where either a council or an assembly of leagued powers may chart our course. Treaties of armed alliance can have no likelihood of American sanction, but we believe in respecting the rights of nations, in the value of conference and consultation, in the effectiveness of leaders of nations looking each other in the face before resorting to the arbitrament of arms.

It has been our fortune both to preach and promote international understanding. The influence of the United States in bringing near the settlement of an ancient dispute between South American nations is added proof of the glow of peace in ample understanding. In Washington to-day are met the delegates of the Central American nations, gathered at the table of international understanding, to stabilize their Republics and remove every vestige of disagreement. They are met here by our invitation, not in our aloofness, and they accept our hospitality because they have faith in our unselfishness and believe in our helpfulness. Perhaps we are selfish in craving their confidence and friendship, but such a selfishness we proclaim to the world, regardless of hemisphere, or seas dividing.

I would like the Congress and the people of the Nation to believe that in a firm and considerate way we are insistent on American rights wherever they may be questioned, and deny no rights of others in the assertion of our own. Moreover we are cognizant of the world's struggles for full readjustment and rehabilitation, and we have shirked no duty which comes of sympathy, or fraternity, or highest fellowship among nations. Every obligation consonant with American ideals and sanctioned under our form of government is willingly met. When we can not support we do not demand. Our constitutional limitations do not forbid the exercise of a moral influence, the measure of which is not less than the high purposes we have sought to serve.

After all there is less difference about the part this great Republic shall play in furthering peace and advancing humanity than in the manner of playing it. We ask no one to assume responsibility for us; we assume no responsibility which others must bear for themselves, unless nationality is hopelessly swallowed up in internationalism.

Calvin Coolidge

1923–1929

*"Nothing is easier than the expenditure
of public money. It does not appear
to belong to anybody."*

ANNUAL MESSAGE TO CONGRESS, DECEMBER 7, 1926

Annual Message to Congress

December 6, 1923

Calvin Coolidge took office on August 3, 1923, following the sudden death of his predecessor, Warren G. Harding. Coolidge, who had been vice president under Harding, was a former governor of Massachusetts. Coolidge had become famous during a 1919 Boston police strike when he called upon the state militia to keep order. Although both Harding and Coolidge followed conservative Republican agendas, their personalities were different. Harding was seen as a genial man while Coolidge—whose nickname was "Silent Cal"—had a taciturn image.

Coolidge had been in office only four months when he delivered this State of the Union address. It was the first State of the Union message to be broadcast on radio, allowing Americans to hear their president's voice and listen to his assessment of the country's situation. The first U.S. radio station, Pittsburgh's KDKA, had begun operations in 1920, and the new medium was becoming increasingly popular as the decade wore on. Coolidge, despite his silent persona, made good use of the radio to promote his presidency. This 1923 address, though, was the only State of the Union message that Coolidge opted to deliver in person to Congress; his subsequent addresses were sent in writing.

The new president began his speech with praise for his predecessor. Although Harding had been a popular leader, scandals involving several of his cabinet members that came to widespread attention after his death tarnished his reputation. Coolidge, on the other hand, was considered a model of propriety and managed to avoid being tainted by any hint of corruption.

On the foreign policy front, Coolidge followed Harding's model, shunning membership in the League of Nations but seeking to have at least some say in world events. In his speech, for example, Coolidge advocated U.S. membership in the Permanent Court of International Justice, a body with ties to the League of Nations. But Coolidge did not push lawmakers to approve the treaty, and it failed.

In his speech, the president said that domestic concerns were "our main problems" and that tax cuts were at the top of the agenda. Indeed, during Coolidge's presidency, Congress approved a tax-cutting agenda. The country's economy was on the upswing, with the postwar instability finally waning. Although Coolidge had a reputation for being antigovernment and probusiness, he outlined a lengthy program for the government that included enforcement of Prohibition, protection of the rights of black Americans, and civil service reform.

This speech came less than a year before the presidential election of 1924, and Coolidge was running for a full term of his own. He defeated Democrat John W. Davis as well as Progressive candidate Robert LaFollette to win four more years in the White House.

Since the close of the last Congress the Nation has lost President Harding. The world knew his kindness and his humanity, his greatness and his character. He has left his mark upon history. He has made justice more certain and peace more secure. The surpassing tribute paid to his memory as he was borne across the continent to rest at last at home revealed the place he held in the hearts of the American people. But this is not the occasion for extended reference to the man or his work. In this presence, among these who knew and loved him, that is unnecessary. But we who were associated with him could not resume together the functions of our office without pausing for a moment, and in his memory reconsecrating ourselves to the service of our country. He is gone. We remain. It is our duty, under the inspiration of his example, to take up the burdens which he was permitted to lay down, and to develop and support the wise principles of government which he represented.

Foreign Affairs

For us peace reigns everywhere. We desire to perpetuate it always by granting full justice to others and requiring of others full justice to ourselves.

Our country has one cardinal principle to maintain in its foreign policy. It is an American principle. It must be an American policy. We attend to our own affairs, conserve our own strength, and protect the interests of our own citizens; but we recognize thoroughly our obligation to help others, reserving to the decision of our own Judgment the time, the place, and the method. We realize the common bond of humanity. We know the inescapable law of service.

Our country has definitely refused to adopt and ratify the covenant of the League of Nations. We have not felt warranted in assuming the responsibilities which its members have assumed. I am not proposing any change in this policy; neither is the Senate. The incident, so far as we are concerned, is closed. The League exists as a foreign agency. We hope it will be helpful. But the United States sees no reason to limit its own freedom and independence of action by joining it. We shall do well to recognize this basic fact in all national affairs and govern ourselves accordingly.

World Court

Our foreign policy has always been guided by two principles. The one is the avoidance of permanent political alliances which would sacrifice our proper independence. The other is the peaceful settlement of controversies between nations. By example and by treaty we have advocated arbitration. For nearly 25 years we have been a member of The Hague Tribunal, and have long sought the creation of a permanent World Court of Justice. I am in full accord with both of these policies. I favor the establishment of such a court intended to include the whole world. That is, and has long been, an American policy.

Pending before the Senate is a proposal that this Government give its support to the Permanent Court of International Justice, which is a new and somewhat different plan. This is not a partisan question. It should not assume an artificial importance. The court is merely a convenient instrument of adjustment to which we could go, but to which we could not be brought. It should be discussed with entire candor, not by a political but by a judicial method, without pressure and without prejudice. Partisanship has no place in our foreign relations. As I wish to see a court established, and as the proposal presents the only practical plan on which many nations have ever agreed, though it may not meet every desire, I therefore commend it to the favorable consideration of the Senate, with the proposed reservations clearly indicating our refusal to adhere to the League of Nations.

Russia

Our diplomatic relations, lately so largely interrupted, are now being resumed, but Russia presents notable difficulties. We have every desire to see that great people, who are our traditional friends, restored to their position among the nations of the earth. We have relieved their pitiable destitution with an enormous charity. Our Government offers no objection to the carrying on of commerce by our citizens with the people of Russia. Our Government does not propose, however, to enter into relations with another regime which refuses to recognize the sanctity of international obligations. I do not propose to barter away for the privilege of trade any of the cherished rights of humanity. I do not propose to make merchandise of any American principles. These rights and principles must go wherever the sanctions of our Government go.

But while the favor of America is not for sale, I am willing to make very large concessions for the purpose of rescuing the people of Russia. Already encouraging evidences of returning to the ancient ways of society can be detected. But more are needed. Whenever there appears any disposition to compensate our citizens who were despoiled, and to recognize that debt contracted with our Government, not by the Czar, but by the newly formed Republic of Russia; whenever the active spirit of enmity to our institutions is abated; whenever there appear works mete for repentance; our country ought to be the first to go to the economic and moral rescue of Russia. We have every desire to help and no desire to injure. We hope the time is near at hand when we can act.

Debts

The current debt and interest due from foreign Governments, exclusive of the British debt of $4,600,000,000, is about $7,200,000,000. I do not favor the cancellation of this debt, but I see no objection to adjusting it in accordance with the principle adopted for the British debt. Our country would not wish to assume the role of an oppressive creditor, but would maintain the principle that financial obligations between nations are likewise moral obligations which international faith and honor require should be discharged.

Our Government has a liquidated claim against Germany for the expense of the army of occupation of over $255,000,000. Besides this, the Mixed Claims Commission have before them about 12,500 claims of American citizens, aggregating about $1,225,000,000. These claims have already been reduced by a recent decision, but there are valid claims reaching well toward $500,000,000. Our thousands of citizens with credits due them of hundreds of millions of dollars have no redress save in the action of our Government. These are very substantial interests, which it is the duty of our Government to protect as best it can. That course I propose to pursue.

It is for these reasons that we have a direct interest in the economic recovery of Europe. They are enlarged by our desire for the stability of civilization and the welfare of humanity. That we are making sacrifices to that end none can deny. Our deferred interest alone amounts to a million dollars every day. But recently we offered to aid with our advice and counsel. We have reiterated our desire to see France paid and Germany revived. We have proposed disarmament. We have earnestly sought to compose differences and restore peace. We shall persevere in well-doing, not by force, but by reason.

Foreign Papers

Under the law the papers pertaining to foreign relations to be printed are transmitted as a part of this message. Other volumes of these papers will follow.

Foreign Service

The foreign service of our Government needs to be reorganized and improved.

Fiscal Condition

Our main problems are domestic problems. Financial stability is the first requisite of sound government. We can not escape the effect of world conditions. We can not avoid the inevitable results of the economic disorders which have reached all nations. But we shall diminish their harm to us in proportion as we continue to restore our Government finances to a secure and endurable position. This we can and must do. Upon that firm foundation rests the only hope of progress and prosperity. From that source must come relief for the people.

This is being accomplished by a drastic but orderly retrenchment, which is bringing our expenses within our means. The origin of this has been the determination of the American people, the main support has been the courage of those in authority, and the effective method has been the Budget System. The result has involved real sacrifice by department heads, but it has been made without flinching. This system is a law of the Congress. It represents your will. It must be maintained, and ought to be strengthened by the example of your observance. Without a Budget System there can be no fixed responsibility and no constructive scientific economy.

This great concentration of effort by the administration and Congress has brought the expenditures, exclusive of the self-supporting Post Office Department, down to three billion dollars. It is possible, in consequence, to make a large reduction in the taxes of the people, which is the sole object of all curtailment. This is treated at greater length in the Budget message, and a proposed plan has been presented in detail in a statement by the Secretary of the Treasury which has my unqualified approval. I especially commend a decrease on earned incomes, and further abolition of admission, message, and nuisance taxes. The amusement and educational value of moving pictures ought not to be taxed. Diminishing charges against moderate incomes from investment will afford immense relief, while a revision of the surtaxes will not only provide additional money for capital investment, thus stimulating industry and employing more but will not greatly reduce the revenue from that source, and may in the future actually increase it.

Being opposed to war taxes in time of peace, I am not in favor of excess-profits taxes. A very great service could be rendered through immediate enactment of legislation relieving the people of some of the burden of taxation. To reduce war taxes is to give every home a better chance.

For seven years the people have borne with uncomplaining courage the tremendous burden of national and local taxation. These must both be reduced. The taxes of the Nation must be reduced now as much as prudence will permit, and expenditures must be reduced accordingly. High taxes reach everywhere and burden everybody. They bear most heavily upon the poor. They diminish industry and commerce. They make agriculture unprofitable. They increase the rates on transportation. They are a charge on every necessary of life. Of all services which the Congress can render to the country, I have no hesitation in declaring to neglect it, to postpone it, to obstruct it by unsound proposals, is to become unworthy of public confidence and untrue to public trust. The country wants this measure to have the right of way over all others.

Another reform which is urgent in our fiscal system is the abolition of the right to issue tax-exempt securities. The existing system not only permits a large amount of the wealth of the Nation to escape its just burden but acts as a continual stimulant to municipal extravagance. This should be prohibited by constitutional amendment. All the wealth of the Nation ought to contribute its fair share to the expenses of the Nation.

Tariff Law

The present tariff law has accomplished its two main objects. It has secured an abundant revenue and been productive of an abounding prosperity. Under it the country has had a very large export and import trade. A constant revision of the tariff by the Congress is disturbing and harmful. The present law contains an elastic provision authorizing the President to increase or decrease present schedules not in excess of 50 per centum to meet the difference in cost of production at home and abroad. This does not, to my mind, warrant a rewriting of the whole law, but does mean, and will be so administered, that whenever the required investigation shows that inequalities of sufficient importance exist in any schedule, the power to change them should and will be applied.

Shipping

The entire well being of our country is dependent upon transportation by sea and land. Our Government during the war acquired a large merchant fleet which should be transferred, as soon as possible, to private ownership and operation under conditions which would secure two results: First, and of prime importance, adequate means for national defense; second, adequate service to American commerce. Until shipping conditions are such that our fleet can be disposed of advantageously under these conditions, it will be operated as economically as possible under such plans as may be devised from time to time by the Shipping Board. We must have a merchant marine which meets these requirements, and we shall have to pay the cost of its service.

Public Improvements

The time has come to resume in a moderate way the opening of our intracoastal waterways; the control of flood waters of the Mississippi and of the Colorado Rivers; the improvement of the waterways from the Great Lakes toward the Gulf of Mexico; and the development of the great power and navigation project of the St. Lawrence River, for which efforts are now being made to secure the necessary treaty with Canada. These projects can not all be undertaken at once, but all should have the immediate consideration of the Congress and be adopted as fast as plans can be matured and the necessary funds become available. This is not incompatible with economy, for their nature does not require so much a public expenditure as a capital investment which will be reproductive, as evidenced by the marked increase in revenue from the Panama Canal. Upon these projects depend much future industrial and agricultural progress. They represent the protection of large areas from flood and the addition of a great amount of cheap power and cheap freight by use of navigation, chief of which is the bringing of ocean-going ships to the Great Lakes.

Another problem of allied character is the superpower development of the Northeastern States, consideration of which is growing under the direction of the Department of Commerce by joint conference with the local authorities.

Railroads

Criticism of the railroad law has been directed, first, to the section laying down the rule by which rates are fixed, and providing for payment to the Government and use of excess earnings; second, to the method for the adjustment of wage scales; and third, to the authority permitting consolidations.

It has been erroneously assumed that the act undertakes to guarantee railroad earnings. The law requires that rates should be just and reasonable. That has always been the rule under which rates have been fixed. To make a rate that does not yield a fair return results in confiscation, and confiscatory rates are of course unconstitutional. Unless the Government adheres to the rule of making a rate that will yield a fair return, it must abandon rate making altogether. The new and important feature of that part of the law is the recapture and redistribution of excess rates. The constitutionality of this method is now before the Supreme Court for adjudication. Their decision should be awaited before attempting further legislation on this subject. Furthermore, the importance of this feature will not be great if consolidation goes into effect.

The settlement of railroad labor disputes is a matter of grave public concern. The Labor Board was established to protect the public in the enjoyment of continuous service by attempting to insure justice between the companies and their employees. It has been a great help, but is not altogether satisfactory to the public, the employees, or the companies. If a substantial agreement can be reached among the groups interested, there should be no hesitation in enacting such agreement into law. If it is not reached, the Labor Board may very well be left for the present to protect the public welfare.

The law for consolidations is not sufficiently effective to be expeditious. Additional legislation is needed giving authority for voluntary consolidations, both regional and route, and providing Government machinery to aid and stimulate such action, always subject to the approval of the Interstate Commerce Commission. This should authorize the commission to appoint committees for each proposed group, representing the public and the component roads, with power to negotiate with individual security holders for an exchange of their securities for those of the consolidation on such terms and conditions as the commission may prescribe for avoiding any confiscation and preserving fair values. Should this permissive consolidation prove ineffective after a limited period, the authority of the Government will have to be directly invoked.

Consolidation appears to be the only feasible method for the maintenance of an adequate system of transportation with an opportunity so to adjust freight rates as to meet such temporary conditions as now prevail in some agricultural sections. Competent authorities agree that an entire reorganization of the rate structure for freight is necessary. This should be ordered at once by the Congress.

Department of Justice

As no revision of the laws of the United States has been made since 1878, a commission or committee should be created to undertake this work. The Judicial Council reports that two more district judges are needed in the southern district of New York, one in the northern district of Georgia, and two more circuit judges in the Circuit Court of Appeals of the Eighth Circuit. Legislation should be considered for this purpose.

It is desirable to expedite the hearing and disposal of cases. A commission of Federal judges and lawyers should be created to recommend legislation by which the procedure in the Federal trial courts may be simplified and regulated by rules of court, rather than by statute; such rules to be submitted to the Congress and to be in force until annulled or modified by the Congress. The Supreme Court needs legislation revising and simplifying the laws governing review by that court, and enlarging the classes of cases of too little public importance to be subject to review. Such reforms would expedite the transaction of the business of the courts. The administration of justice is likely to fail if it be long delayed.

The National Government has never given adequate attention to its prison problems. It ought to provide employment in such forms of production as can be used by the Government, though not sold to the public in competition with private business, for all prisoners who can be placed at work, and for which they should receive a reasonable compensation, available for their dependents.

Two independent reformatories are needed; one for the segregation of women, and another for the segregation of young men serving their first sentence.

The administration of justice would be facilitated greatly by including in the Bureau of Investigation of the Department of Justice a Division of Criminal Identification, where there would be collected this information which is now indispensable in the suppression of crime.

Prohibition

The prohibition amendment to the Constitution requires the Congress and the President to provide adequate laws to prevent its violation. It is my duty to enforce such laws. For that purpose a treaty is being negotiated with Great Britain with respect to the right of search of hovering vessels. To prevent smuggling, the Coast Guard should be greatly strengthened, and a supply of swift power boats should be provided. The major sources of production should be rigidly regulated, and every effort should be made to suppress interstate traffic. With this action on the part of the National Government, and the cooperation which is usually rendered by municipal and State authorities, prohibition should be made effective. Free government has no greater menace than disrespect for authority and continual violation of law. It is the duty of a citizen not only to observe the law but to let it be known that he is opposed to its violation.

The Negro

Numbered among our population are some 12,000,000 colored people. Under our Constitution their rights are just as sacred as those of any other citizen. It is both a public and a private duty to protect those rights. The Congress ought to exercise all its powers of prevention and punishment against the hideous crime of lynching, of which the negroes are by no means the sole sufferers, but for which they furnish a majority of the victims.

Already a considerable sum is appropriated to give the negroes vocational training in agriculture. About half a million dollars is recommended for medical courses at Howard University to help contribute to the education of 500 colored doctors needed each year. On account of the integration of large numbers into industrial centers, it has been proposed that a commission be created, composed of members from both races, to formulate a better policy for mutual understanding and confidence. Such an effort is to be commended. Everyone would rejoice in the accomplishment of the results which it seeks. But it is well to recognize that these difficulties are to a large extent local problems which must be worked out by the mutual forbearance and human kindness of each community. Such a method gives much more promise of a real remedy than outside interference.

Civil Service

The maintenance and extension of the classified civil service is exceedingly important. There are nearly 550,000 persons in the executive civil service drawing about $700,000,000 of yearly compensation. Four-fifths of these are in the classified service. This method of selection of the employees of the United States is especially desirable for the Post Office Department. The Civil Service Commission has recommended that postmasters at first, second, and third class offices be classified. Such action, accompanied by a repeal of the four-year term of office, would undoubtedly be an improvement. I also recommend that the field force for prohibition enforcement be brought within the classified civil service without covering in the present membership. The best method for selecting public servants is the merit system.

Public Buildings

Many of the departments in Washington need better housing facilities. Some are so crowded that their work is impeded, others are so scattered that they lose their identity. While I do not favor at this time a general public building law, I believe it is now necessary, in accordance with plans already sanctioned for a unified and orderly system for the development of this city, to begin the carrying out of those plans by authorizing the erection of three or four buildings most urgently needed by an annual appropriation of $5,000,000.

Regulatory Legislation

Cooperation with other maritime powers is necessary for complete protection of our coast waters from pollution. Plans for this are under way, but await certain experiments for refuse disposal. Meantime laws prohibiting spreading oil and oil refuse from vessels in our own territorial waters would be most helpful against this menace and should be speedily enacted.

Laws should be passed regulating aviation.

Revision is needed of the laws regulating radio interference.

Legislation and regulations establishing load lines, to provide safe loading of vessels leaving our ports are necessary and recodification of our navigation laws is vital.

Revision of procedure of the Federal Trade Commission will give more constructive purpose to this department.

If our Alaskan fisheries are to be saved from destruction, there must be further legislation declaring a general policy and delegating the authority to make rules and regulations to an administrative body.

Army and Navy

For several years we have been decreasing the personnel of the Army and Navy, and reducing their power to the danger point. Further reductions should not be made. The Army is a guarantee of the security of our citizens at home; the Navy is a guarantee of the security of our citizens abroad. Both of these services should be strengthened rather than weakened. Additional planes are needed for the Army, and additional submarines for the Navy. The defenses of Panama must be perfected. We want no more competitive armaments. We want no more war. But we want no weakness that invites imposition. A people who neglect their national defense are putting in jeopardy their national honor.

Insular Possessions

Conditions in the insular possessions on the whole have been good. Their business has been reviving. They are being administered according to law. That effort has the full support of the administration. Such recommendations as may come from their people or their governments should have the most considerate attention.

Education and Welfare

Our National Government is not doing as much as it legitimately can do to promote the welfare of the people. Our enormous material wealth, our institutions, our whole form of society, can not be considered fully successful until their benefits reach the merit of every individual. This is not a suggestion that the Government should, or could, assume for the people the inevitable burdens of existence. There is no method by which we can either be relieved of the results of our own folly or be guaranteed a successful life. There is an inescapable personal responsibility for the development of character, of industry, of thrift, and of self-control. These do not come from the Government, but from the people themselves. But the Government can and should always be expressive of steadfast determination, always vigilant, to maintain conditions under which these virtues are most likely to develop and secure recognition and reward. This is the American policy.

It is in accordance with this principle that we have enacted laws for the protection of the public health and have adopted prohibition in narcotic drugs and intoxicating liquors. For purposes of national uniformity we ought to provide, by constitutional amendment and appropriate legislation, for a limitation of child labor, and in all cases under the exclusive jurisdiction of the Federal Government a minimum wage law for women, which would undoubtedly find sufficient power of enforcement in the influence of public opinion.

Having in mind that education is peculiarly a local problem, and that it should always be pursued with the largest freedom of choice by students and parents, nevertheless, the Federal Government might well give the benefit of its counsel and encouragement more freely in this direction. If anyone doubts the need of concerted action by the States of the Nation for this purpose, it is only necessary to consider the appalling figures of illiteracy representing a condition which does not vary much in all parts of the Union. I do not favor the making of appropriations from the National Treasury to be expended directly on local education, but I do consider it a fundamental requirement of national activity which, accompanied by allied subjects of welfare, is worthy of a separate department and a place in the Cabinet. The humanitarian side of government should not be repressed, but should be cultivated.

Mere intelligence, however, is not enough. Enlightenment must be accompanied by that moral power which is the product of the home and of rebellion. Real education and true welfare for the people rest inevitably on this foundation, which the Government can approve and commend, but which the people themselves must create.

Immigration

American institutions rest solely on good citizenship. They were created by people who had a background of self-government. New arrivals should be limited to our capacity to absorb them into the ranks of good citizenship. America must be kept American. For this purpose, it is necessary to continue a policy of restricted immigration. It would be well to make such immigration of a selective nature with some inspection at the source, and based either on a prior census or upon the record of naturalization. Either method would insure the admission of those with the largest capacity and best intention of becoming citizens. I am convinced that our present economic and social conditions warrant a limitation of those to be admitted. We should find additional safety in a law requiring the immediate registration of all aliens. Those who do not want to be partakers of the American spirit ought not to settle in America.

Veterans

No more important duty falls on the Government of the United States than the adequate care of its veterans. Those suffering disabilities incurred in the service must have sufficient hospital relief and compensation. Their dependents must be supported. Rehabilitation and vocational training must be completed. All of this service must be clean, must be prompt and effective, and it must be administered in a spirit of the broadest and deepest human sympathy. If investigation reveals any present defects of administration or need of legislation, orders will be given for the immediate correction of administration, and recommendations for legislation should be given the highest preference.

At present there are 9,500 vacant beds in Government hospitals, I recommend that all hospitals be authorized at once to receive and care for, without hospital pay, the veterans of all wars needing such care, whenever there are vacant beds, and that immediate steps be taken to enlarge and build new hospitals to serve all such cases.

The American Legion will present to the Congress a legislative program too extensive for detailed discussion here. It is a carefully matured plan. While some of it I do not favor, with much of it I am in hearty accord, and I recommend that a most painstaking effort be made to provide remedies for any defects in the administration of the present laws which their experience has revealed. The attitude of the Government toward these proposals should be one of generosity. But I do not favor the granting of a bonus.

Coal

The cost of coal has become unbearably high. It places a great burden on our industrial and domestic life. The public welfare requires a reduction in the price of fuel. With the enormous deposits in existence, failure of supply ought not to be tolerated. Those responsible for the conditions in this industry should undertake its reform and free it from any charge of profiteering.

The report of the Coal Commission will be before the Congress. It comprises all the facts. It represents the mature deliberations and conclusions of the best talent and experience that ever made a national survey of the production and distribution of fuel. I do not favor Government ownership or operation of coal mines. The need is for action under private ownership that will secure greater continuity of production and greater public protection. The Federal Government probably has no peacetime authority to regulate wages, prices, or profits in coal at the mines or among dealers, but by ascertaining and publishing facts it can exercise great influence.

The source of the difficulty in the bituminous coal fields is the intermittence of operation which causes great waste of both capital and labor. That part of the report dealing with this problem has much significance, and is suggestive of necessary remedies. By amending the car rules, by encouraging greater unity of ownership, and possibly by permitting common selling agents for limited districts on condition that they accept adequate regulations and guarantee that competition between districts be unlimited, distribution, storage, and continuity ought to be improved.

The supply of coal must be constant. In case of its prospective interruption, the President should have authority to appoint a commission empowered to deal with whatever emergency situation might arise, to aid conciliation and voluntary arbitration, to adjust any existing or threatened controversy between the employer and the employee when collective bargaining fails, and by controlling distribution to prevent profiteering in this vital necessity. This legislation is exceedingly urgent, and essential to the exercise of national authority for the protection of the people. Those who undertake the responsibility of management or employment in this industry do so with the full knowledge that the public interest is paramount, and that to fail through any motive of selfishness in its service is such a betrayal of duty as warrants uncompromising action by the Government.

Reorganization

A special joint committee has been appointed to work out a plan for a reorganization of the different departments and bureaus of the Government more scientific and economical than the present system. With the exception of the consolidation of the War and Navy Departments and some minor details, the plan has the general sanction of the President and the Cabinet. It is important that reorganization be enacted into law at the present session.

Agriculture

Aided by the sound principles adopted by the Government, the business of the country has had an extraordinary revival. Looked at as a whole, the Nation is in the enjoyment of remarkable prosperity. Industry and commerce are thriving. For the most part agriculture is successful, eleven staples having risen in value from about $5,300,000,000 two years ago to about $7,000,000,000 for the current year. But range cattle are still low in price, and some sections of the wheat area, notably Minnesota, North Dakota, and on west, have many cases of actual distress. With his products not selling on a parity with the products of industry, every sound remedy that can be devised should be applied for the relief of the farmer. He represents a character, a type of citizenship, and a public necessity that must be preserved and afforded every facility for regaining prosperity.

The distress is most acute among those wholly dependent upon one crop. Wheat acreage was greatly expanded and has not yet been sufficiently reduced. A large amount is raised for export, which has to meet the competition in the world market of large amounts raised on land much cheaper and much more productive.

No complicated scheme of relief, no plan for Government fixing of prices, no resort to the public Treasury will be of any permanent value in establishing agriculture. Simple and direct methods put into operation by the farmer himself are the only real sources for restoration.

Indirectly the farmer must be relieved by a reduction of national and local taxation. He must be assisted by the reorganization of the freight-rate structure which could reduce charges on his production. To make this fully effective there ought to be railroad consolidations. Cheaper fertilizers must be provided.

He must have organization. His customer with whom he exchanges products on the farm for those of industry is organized, labor is organized, business is organized, and there is no way for agriculture to meet this unless it, too, is organized. The acreage of wheat is too large. Unless we can meet the world market at a profit, we must stop raising for export. Organization would help to reduce acreage. Systems of cooperative marketing created by the farmers themselves, supervised by competent management, without doubt would be of assistance, but they can not wholly solve the problem. Our agricultural schools ought to have thorough courses in the theory of organization and cooperative marketing.

Diversification is necessary. Those farmers who raise their living on their land are not greatly in distress. Such loans as are wisely needed to assist buying stock and other materials to start in this direction should be financed through a Government agency as a temporary and emergency expedient.

The remaining difficulty is the disposition of exportable wheat. I do not favor the permanent interference of the Government in this problem. That probably would increase the trouble by increasing production. But it seems feasible to provide Government assistance to exports, and authority should be given the War Finance Corporation to grant, in its discretion, the most liberal terms of payment for fats and grains exported for the direct benefit of the farm.

Muscle Shoals

The Government is undertaking to develop a great water-power project known as Muscle Shoals, on which it has expended many million dollars. The work is still going on. Subject to the right to retake in time of war, I recommend that this property with a location for auxiliary steam plant and rights of way be sold. This would end the present burden of expense and should return to the Treasury the largest price possible to secure.

While the price is an important element, there is another consideration even more compelling. The agriculture of the Nation needs a greater supply and lower cost of fertilizer. This is now imported in large quantities. The best information I can secure indicates that present methods of power production would not be able profitably to meet the price at which these imports can be sold. To obtain a supply from this water power would require long and costly experimentation to perfect a process for cheap production. Otherwise our purpose would fail completely. It seems desirable, therefore, in order to protect and promote the public welfare, to have adequate covenants that such experimentation be made and carried on to success. The great advantage of low-priced nitrates must be secured for the direct benefit of the farmers and the indirect benefit of the public in time of peace, and of the Government in time of war. If this main object be accomplished, the amount of money received for the property is not a primary or major consideration.

Such a solution will involve complicated negotiations, and there is no authority for that purpose. I therefore recommend that the Congress appoint a small joint committee to consider offers, conduct negotiations, and report definite recommendations.

Reclamation

By reason of many contributing causes, occupants of our reclamation projects are in financial difficulties, which in some cases are acute. Relief should be granted by definite authority of law empowering the Secretary of the Interior in his discretion to suspend, readjust, and reassess all charges against water users. This whole question is being considered by experts. You will have the advantage of the facts and conclusions which they may develop. This situation, involving a Government investment of more than $135,000,000, and affecting more than 30,000 water users, is serious. While relief which is necessary should be granted, yet contracts with the Government which can be met should be met. The established general policy of these projects should not be abandoned for any private control.

Highways and Forests

Highways and reforestation should continue to have the interest and support of the Government. Everyone is anxious for good highways. I have made a liberal proposal in the Budget for the continuing payment to the States by the Federal Government of its share for this necessary public improvement. No expenditure of public money contributes so much to the national wealth as for building good roads.

Reforestation has an importance far above the attention it usually secures. A special committee of the Senate is investigating this need, and I shall welcome a constructive policy based on their report.

It is 100 years since our country announced the Monroe doctrine. This principle has been ever since, and is now, one of the main foundations of our foreign relations. It must be maintained. But in maintaining it we must not be forgetful that a great change has taken place. We are no longer a weak Nation, thinking mainly of defense, dreading foreign imposition. We are great and powerful. New powers bring new responsibilities. Our duty then was to protect ourselves. Added to that, our duty now is to help give stability to the world. We want idealism. We want that vision which lifts men and nations above themselves. These are virtues by reason of their own merit. But they must not be cloistered; they must not be impractical; they must not be ineffective.

The world has had enough of the curse of hatred and selfishness, of destruction and war. It has had enough of the wrongful use of material power. For the healing of the nations there must be good will and charity, confidence and peace. The time has come for a more practical use of moral power, and more reliance upon the principle that right makes its own might. Our authority among the nations must be represented by justice and mercy. It is necessary not only to have faith, but to make sacrifices for our faith. The spiritual forces of the world make all its final determinations. It is with these voices that America should speak. Whenever they declare a righteous purpose there need be no doubt that they will be heard. America has taken her place in the world as a Republic—free, independent, powerful. The best service that can be rendered to humanity is the assurance that this place will be maintained.

Calvin Coolidge, 1923–1925

Annual Message to Congress
December 3, 1924

Calvin Coolidge's second State of the Union message came a month after he was elected president in his own right. Coolidge, a former governor of Massachusetts, had handily defeated Democrat John W. Davis and Progressive candidate Robert LaFollette in the November 1924 elections. Coolidge won 382 votes in the electoral college, while Davis won only 136 and LaFollette 13. Coolidge took 54.1 percent of the popular vote to Davis's 28.8 percent and LaFollette's 16.6 percent. In addition, the president's Republican Party held control of both houses of Congress. Coolidge, who had been vice president, had first assumed the presidency in 1923 after the death of President Warren G. Harding,

Coolidge's message, which he did not deliver in person to Congress but rather sent in writing, enumerated the issues facing the country as Coolidge began his first full term in office. The economy was booming, and Americans appeared to welcome the conservative politics of "Silent Cal."

In his State of the Union message, Coolidge asserted that programs to reduce the debt and lower taxes needed to be continued. The probusiness president remarked in particular that business should be free from tax on excess profits.

Agriculture was one sector of the economy that was not faring as well, but in his message, Coolidge said that it was beginning to return to prosperity. In an example of his hands-off philosophy of governing, the president said that government could not ensure prosperity and that each business at times would have economic difficulties.

By December 1924 it had been six years since the hostilities had ceased in World War I, and Coolidge said in his address that the United States's foreign relations were in better shape than at any time in the past dozen years. Coolidge repeated that the country had no interest in joining the League of Nations—but did call again for U.S. involvement in the Court of International Justice. He voiced support for proposals to outlaw wars of aggression. Toward the end of his presidency, he supported the Kellogg-Briand Pact of 1928, an international effort that sought to outlaw wars among its signatories.

The GOP did not seem to suffer electorally as a result of the scandals that had surfaced in the wake of Harding's death involving several of his cabinet members. Coolidge's upright persona, and the tragedy of his teenage son's death in 1924, fostered sympathy for the new president.

To the Congress of the United States:

The present state of the Union, upon which it is customary for the President to report to the Congress under the provisions of the Constitution, is such that it may be regarded with encouragement and satisfaction by every American. Our country is almost unique in its ability to discharge fully and promptly all its obligations at home and abroad, and provide for all its inhabitants an increase in material resources, in intellectual vigor and in moral power. The Nation holds a position unsurpassed in all former human experience. This does not mean that we do not have any problems. It is elementary that the increasing breadth of our experience necessarily increases the problems of our national life. But it does mean that if all will but apply ourselves industriously and honestly, we have ample powers with which to meet our problems and provide for I heir speedy solution. I do not profess that we can secure an era of perfection in human existence, but we can provide an era of peace and prosperity, attended with freedom and justice and made more and more satisfying by the ministrations of the charities and humanities of life.

Our domestic problems are for the most part economic. We have our enormous debt to pay, and we are paying it. We have the high cost of government to diminish, and we are diminishing it. We have a heavy burden of taxation to reduce, and we are reducing it. But while remarkable progress has been made in these directions, the work is yet far from accomplished. We still owe over $21,000,000,000, the cost of the National Government is still about $3,500,000,000, and the national taxes still amount to about $27 for each one of our inhabitants. There yet exists this enormous field for the application of economy.

In my opinion the Government can do more to remedy the economic ills of the people by a system of rigid economy in public expenditure than can be accomplished through any other action. The costs of our national and local governments combined now stand at a sum close to $100 for each inhabitant of the land. A little less than one-third of this is represented by national expenditure, and a little more than two-thirds by local expenditure. It is an ominous fact that only the National Government is reducing its debt. Others are increasing theirs at about $1,000,000,000 each year.

The depression that overtook business, the disaster experienced in agriculture, the lack of employment and the terrific shrinkage in all values which our country experienced in a most acute form in 1920, resulted in no small measure from the prohibitive taxes which were then levied on all productive effort. The establishment of a system of drastic economy in public expenditure, which has enabled us to pay off about one-fifth of the national debt since 1919, and almost cut in two the national tax burden since 1921, has been one of the main causes in reestablishing a prosperity which has come to include within its benefits almost every one of our inhabitants. Economy reaches everywhere. It carries a blessing to everybody.

The fallacy of the claim that the costs of government are borne by the rich and those who make a direct contribution to the National Treasury can not be too often exposed. No system has been devised, I do not think any system could be devised, under which any person living in this country could escape being affected by the cost of our government. It has a direct effect both upon the rate and the purchasing power of wages. It is felt in the price of those prime necessities of existence, food, clothing, fuel and shelter. It would appear to be elementary that the more the Government expends the more it must require every producer to contribute out of his production to the Public Treasury, and the less he will have for his own benefit. The continuing costs of public administration can be met in only one way—by the work of the people. The higher they become, the more the people must work for the Government. The less they are, the more the people can work for themselves.

The present estimated margin between public receipts and expenditures for this fiscal year is very small. Perhaps the most important work that this session of the Congress can do is to continue a policy of economy and further reduce the cost of government, in order that we may have a reduction of taxes for the next fiscal year. Nothing is more likely to produce that public confidence which is the forerunner and the mainstay of prosperity, encourage and enlarge business opportunity with ample opportunity for employment at good wages, provide a larger market for agricultural products, and put our country in a stronger position to be able to meet the world competition in trade, than a continuing policy of economy. Of course necessary costs must be met, proper functions of the Government performed, and constant investments for capital account and reproductive effort must be carried on by our various departments. But the people must know that their Government is placing upon them no unnecessary burden.

Taxes

Everyone desires a reduction of taxes, and there is a great preponderance of sentiment in favor of taxation reform. When I approved the present tax law, I stated publicly that I did so in spite of certain provisions which I believed unwise and harmful. One of the most glaring of these was the making public of the amounts assessed against different income-tax payers. Although that damage has now been done, I believe its continuation to be detrimental to the public welfare and bound to decrease public revenues, so that it ought to be repealed.

Anybody can reduce taxes, but it is not so easy to stand in the gap and resist the passage of increasing appropriation bills which would make tax reduction impossible. It will be very easy to measure the strength of the attachment to reduced taxation by the power with which increased appropriations are resisted. If at the close of the present session the Congress has kept within the budget which I propose to present, it will then be possible to have a moderate amount of tax reduction and all the tax reform that the Congress may wish for during the next fiscal year. The country is now feeling the direct stimulus which came from the passage of the last revenue bill, and under the assurance of a reasonable system of taxation there is every prospect of an era of prosperity of unprecedented proportions. But it would be idle to expect any such results unless business can continue free from excess profits taxation and be accorded a system of surtaxes at rates which have for their object not the punishment of success or the discouragement of business, but the production of the greatest amount of revenue from large incomes. I am convinced that the larger incomes of the country would actually yield more revenue to the Government if the basis of taxation were scientifically revised downward. Moreover the effect of the present method of this taxation is to increase the cost of interest on productive enterprise and to increase the burden of rent. It is altogether likely that such reduction would so encourage and stimulate investment that it would firmly establish our country in the economic leadership of the world.

Waterways

Meantime our internal development should go on. Provision should be made for flood control of such rivers as the Mississippi and the Colorado, and for the opening up of our inland waterways to commerce. Consideration is due to the project of better navigation from the Great Lakes to the Gulf. Every effort is being made to promote an agreement with Canada to build the St. Lawrence waterway. There are pending before the Congress bills for further development of the Mississippi Basin, for the taking over of the Cape Cod Canal in accordance with a moral obligation which seems to have been incurred during the war, and for the improvement of harbors on both the Pacific and the Atlantic coasts. While this last should be divested of some of its projects and we must proceed slowly, these bills in general have my approval. Such works are productive of wealth and in the long run tend to a reduction of the tax burden.

Reclamation

Our country has a well defined policy of reclamation established under statutory authority. This policy should be continued and made a self-sustaining activity administered in a manner that will meet local requirements and bring our arid lands into a profitable state of cultivation as fast as there is a market for their products. Legislation is pending based on the report of the Fact Finding Commission for the proper relief of those needing extension of time in which to meet their payments on irrigated land, and for additional amendments and reforms of our reclamation laws, which are all exceedingly important and should be enacted at once.

No more important development has taken place in the last year than the beginning of a restoration of agriculture to a prosperous condition. We must permit no division of classes in this country, with one occupation striving to secure advantage over another. Each must proceed under open opportunities and with a fair prospect of economic equality. The Government can not successfully insure prosperity or fix prices by legislative fiat. Every business has its risk and its times of depression. It is well known that in the long run there will be a more even prosperity and a more satisfactory range of prices under the natural working out of economic laws than when the Government undertakes the artificial support of markets and industries. Still we can so order our affairs, so protect our own people from foreign competition, so arrange our national finances, so administer our monetary system, so provide for the extension of credits, so improve methods of distribution, as to provide a better working machinery for the transaction of the business of the Nation with the least possible friction and loss. The Government has been constantly increasing its efforts in these directions for the relief and permanent establishment of agriculture on a sound and equal basis with other business.

It is estimated that the value of the crops for this harvest year may reach $13,000,000,000, which is an increase of over $3,000,000,000 in three years. It compares with $7,100,000,000 in 1913, and if we make deduction from the figures of 1924 for the comparatively decreased value of the dollar, the yield this year still exceeds 1913 in purchasing power by over $1,000,000,000, and in this interval there has been no increase in the number of farmers. Mostly by his own effort the farmer has decreased the cost of production. A marked increase in the price of his products and some decrease in the price of his supplies has brought him about to a parity with the rest of the Nation. The crop area of this season is estimated at 370,000,000 acres, which is a decline of 3,000,000 acres from last year, and 6,000,000 acres from 1919. This has been a normal and natural application of economic laws, which has placed agriculture on a foundation which is undeniably sound and beginning to be satisfactory.

A decrease in the world supply of wheat has resulted in a very large increase in the price of that commodity. The position of all agricultural products indicates a better balanced supply, but we can not yet conclude that agriculture is recovered from the effects of the war period or that it is permanently on a prosperous basis. The cattle industry has not yet recovered and in some sections has been suffering from dry weather. Every effort must be made both by Government activity and by private agencies to restore and maintain agriculture to a complete normal relationship with other industries.

It was on account of past depression, and in spite of present more encouraging conditions, that I have assembled an Agricultural Conference made up of those who are representative of this great industry in both its operating and economic sides. Everyone knows that the great need of the farmers is markets. The country is not suffering on the side of production. Almost the entire difficulty is on the side of distribution. This reaches back, of course, to unit costs and diversification, and many allied subjects. It is exceedingly intricate, for our domestic and foreign trade, transportation and banking, and in fact our entire economic system, are closely related to it. In time for action at this session, I hope to report to the Congress such legislative remedies as the conference may recommend. An appropriation should be made to defray their necessary expenses.

Muscle Shoals

The production of nitrogen for plant food in peace and explosives in war is more and more important. It is one of the chief sustaining elements of life. It is estimated that soil exhaustion each year is represented by about 9,000,000 tons and replenishment by 5,450,000 tons. The deficit of 3,550,000 tons is reported to represent the impairment of 118,000,000 acres of farm lands each year.

To meet these necessities the Government has been developing a water power project at Muscle Shoals to be equipped to produce nitrogen for explosives and fertilizer. It is my opinion that the support of agriculture is the chief problem to consider in connection with this property. It could by no means supply the present needs for nitrogen, but it would help and its development would encourage bringing other water powers into like use.

Several offers have been made for the purchase of this property. Probably none of them represent final terms. Much costly experimentation is necessary to produce commercial nitrogen. For that reason it is a field better suited to private enterprise than to Government operation. I should favor a sale of this property, or long-time lease, tinder rigid guaranties of commercial nitrogen production at reasonable prices for agricultural use. There would be a surplus of power for many years over any possibility of its application to a developing manufacture of nitrogen. It may be found advantageous to dispose of the right to surplus power separately with such reservations as will allow its gradual withdrawal and application to nitrogen manufacture. A subcommittee of the Committees on Agriculture should investigate this field and negotiate with prospective purchasers. If no advantageous offer be made, the development should continue and the plant should be dedicated primarily to the production of materials for the fertilization of the soil.

Railways

The railways during the past year have made still further progress in recuperation from the war, with large gains in efficiency and ability expeditiously to handle the traffic of the country. We have now passed through several periods of peak traffic without the car shortages which so frequently in the past have brought havoc to our agriculture and industries. The condition of many of our great freight terminals is still one of difficulty and results in imposing, large costs on the public for inward-bound freight, and on the railways for outward-bound freight. Owing to the growth of our large cities and the great increase in the volume of traffic, particularly in perishables, the problem is not only difficult of solution, but in some cases not wholly solvable by railway action alone.

In my message last year I emphasized the necessity for further legislation with a view to expediting the consolidation of our railways into larger systems. The principle of Government control of rates and profits, now thoroughly imbedded in our governmental attitude toward natural monopolies such as the railways, at once eliminates the need of competition by small units as a method of rate adjustment. Competition must be preserved as a stimulus to service, but this will exist and can be increased under enlarged systems. Consequently the consolidation of the railways into larger units for the purpose of securing the substantial values to the public which will come from larger operation has been the logical conclusion of Congress in its previous enactments, and is also supported by the best opinion in the country. Such consolidation will assure not only a greater element of competition as to service, but it will afford economy in operation, greater stability in railway earnings, and more economical financing. It opens large possibilities of better equalization of rates between different classes of traffic so as to relieve undue burdens upon agricultural products and raw materials generally, which are now not possible without ruin to small units owing to the lack of diversity of traffic. It would also tend to equalize earnings in such fashion as to reduce the importance of section 15A, at which criticism, often misapplied, has been directed. A smaller number of units would offer less difficulties in labor adjustments and would contribute much to the solution of terminal difficulties.

The consolidations need to be carried out with due regard to public interest and to the rights and established life of various communities in our country. It does not seem to me necessary that we endeavor to anticipate any final plan or adhere to an artificial and unchangeable project which shall stipulate a fixed number of systems, but rather we ought to approach the problem with such a latitude of action that it can be worked out step by step in accordance with a comprehensive consideration of public interest. Whether the number of ultimate systems shall be more or less seems to me can only be determined by time and actual experience in the development of such consolidations.

Those portions of the present law contemplating consolidations are not sufficiently effective in producing expeditious action and need amplification of the authority of the Interstate Commerce Commission, particularly in affording a period for voluntary proposals to the commission and in supplying Government pressure to secure action after the expiration of such a period.

There are other proposals before Congress for amending the transportation acts. One of these contemplates a revision of the method of valuation for rate-making purposes to be followed by a renewed valuation of the railways. The valuations instituted by the Interstate Commerce Commission 10 years ago have not yet been completed. They have cost the Government an enormous sum, and they have imposed great expenditure upon the railways, most of which has in effect come out of the public in increased rates. This work should not be abandoned or supplanted until its results are known and can be considered.

Another matter before the Congress is legislation affecting the labor sections of the transportation act. Much criticism has been directed at the workings of this section and experience has shown that some useful amendment could be made to these provisions.

It would be helpful if a plan could be adopted which, while retaining the practice of systematic collective bargaining with conciliation voluntary arbitration of labor differences, could also provide simplicity in relations and more direct local responsibility of employees and managers. But such legislation will not meet the requirements of the situation unless it recognizes the principle that the public has a right to the uninterrupted service of transportation, and therefore a right to be heard when there is danger that the Nation may suffer great injury through the interruption of operations because of labor disputes. If these elements are not comprehended in proposed legislation, it would be better to gain further experience with the present organization for dealing with these questions before undertaking a change.

Shipping Board

The form of the organization of the Shipping Board was based originally on its functions as a semijudicial body in regulation of rates. During the war it was loaded with enormous administrative duties. It has been demonstrated time and again that this form of organization results in indecision, division of opinion and administrative functions, which make a wholly inadequate foundation for the conduct of a great business enterprise. The first principle in securing the objective set out by Congress in building up the American merchant marine upon the great trade routes and subsequently disposing of it into private operation can not proceed with effectiveness until the entire functions of the board are reorganized. The immediate requirement is to transfer into the Emergency Fleet, Corporation the whole responsibility of operation of the fleet and other property, leaving to the Shipping Board solely the duty of determining certain major policies which require deliberative action.

The procedure under section 28 of the merchant marine act has created great difficulty and threatened friction during the past 12 months. Its attempted application developed not only great opposition from exporters, particularly as to burdens that may be imposed upon agricultural products, but also great anxiety in the different seaports as to the effect upon their relative rate structures. This trouble will certainly recur if action is attempted under this section. It is uncertain in some of its terms and of great difficulty in interpretation.

It is my belief that action under this section should be suspended until the Congress can reconsider the entire question in the light of the experience that has been developed since its enactment.

National Elections

Nothing is so fundamental to the integrity of a republican form of government as honesty in all that relates to the conduct of elections. I am of the opinion that the national laws governing the choice of members of the Congress should be extended to include appropriate representation of the respective parties at the ballot box and equality of representation on the various registration boards, wherever they exist.

The Judiciary

The docket of the Supreme Court is becoming congested. At the opening term last year it had 592 cases, while this year it had 687 cases. Justice long delayed is justice refused. Unless the court be given power by preliminary and summary consideration to determine the importance of cases, and by disposing of those which are not of public moment reserve its time for the more extended consideration of the remainder, the congestion of the docket is likely to increase. It is also desirable that the Supreme Court should have power to improve and reform procedure in suits at law in the Federal courts through the adoption of appropriate rules. The Judiciary Committee of the Senate has reported favorably upon two bills providing for these reforms which should have the immediate favorable consideration of the Congress.

I further recommend that provision be made for the appointment of a commission, to consist of two or three members of the Federal judiciary and as many members of the bar, to examine the present criminal code of procedure and recommend to the Congress measures which may reform and expedite court procedure in the administration and enforcement of our criminal laws.

Prison Reform

Pending before the Congress is a bill which has already passed one House providing for a reformatory to which could be committed first offenders and young men for the purpose of segregating them from contact with banned criminals and providing them with special training in order to reestablish in them the power to pursue a law-abiding existence in the social and economic life of the Nation. This is a matter of so much importance as to warrant the early attention of the present session. Further provision should also be made, for a like reason, for a separate reformatory for women.

National Police Bureau

Representatives of the International Police Conference will bring to the attention of the Congress a proposal for the establishment of a national police bureau. Such action would provide a central point for gathering, compiling, and later distributing to local police authorities much information which would be helpful in the prevention and detection of crime. I believe this bureau is needed, and I recommend favorable consideration of this proposal.

District of Columbia Welfare

The welfare work of the District of Columbia is administered by several different boards dealing with charities and various correctional efforts. It would be an improvement if this work were consolidated and placed under the direction of a single commission.

French Spoliation Claims

During the last session of the Congress legislation was introduced looking to the payment of the remaining claims generally referred to as the French spoliation claims. The Congress has provided for the payment of many similar claims. Those that remain unpaid have been long pending. The beneficiaries thereunder have every reason to expect payment. These claims have been examined by the Court of Claims and their validity and amount determined. The United States ought to pay its debts. I recommend action by the Congress which will permit of the payment of these remaining claims.

The Wage Earner

Two very important policies have been adopted by this country which, while extending their benefits also in other directions, have been of the utmost importance to the wage earners. One of these is the protective tariff, which enables our people to live according to a better standard and receive a better rate of compensation than any people, any time, anywhere on earth, ever enjoyed. This saves the American market for the products of the American workmen. The other is a policy of more recent origin and seeks to shield our wage earners from the disastrous competition of a great influx of foreign peoples. This has been done by the restrictive immigration law. This saves the American job for the American workmen. I should like to see the administrative features of this law rendered a little more humane for the purpose of permitting those already here a greater latitude in securing admission of members of their own families. But I believe this law in principle is necessary and sound, and destined to increase greatly the public welfare. We must maintain our own economic position, we must defend our own national integrity.

It is gratifying to report that the progress of industry, the enormous increase in individual productivity through labor-saving devices, and the high rate of wages have all combined to furnish our people in general with such an abundance not only of the necessaries but of the conveniences of life that we are by a natural evolution solving our problems of economic and social justice.

The Negro

These developments have brought about a very remarkable improvement in the condition of the negro race. Gradually, but surely, with the almost universal sympathy of those among whom they live, the colored people are working out their own destiny. I firmly believe that it is better for all concerned that they should be cheerfully accorded their full constitutional rights, that they should be protected from all of those impositions to which, from their position, they naturally fall a prey, especially from the crime of lynching and that they should receive every encouragement to become full partakers in all the blessings of our common American citizenship.

Civil Service

The merit system has long been recognized as the correct basis for employment in our civil service. I believe that first second, and third class postmasters, and without covering in the present membership the field force of prohibition enforcement, should be brought within the classified service by statute law. Otherwise the Executive order of one administration is changed by the Executive order of another administration, and little real progress is made. Whatever its defects, the merit system is certainly to be preferred to the spoils system.

Departmental Reorganization

One way to save public money would be to pass the pending bill for the reorganization of the various departments. This project has been pending for some time, and has had the most careful consideration of experts and the thorough study of a special congressional committee. This legislation is vital as a companion piece to the Budget law. Legal authority for a thorough reorganization of the Federal structure with some latitude of action to the Executive in the rearrangement of secondary functions would make for continuing economy in the shift of government activities which must follow every change in a developing country. Beyond this many of the independent agencies of the Government must be placed under responsible Cabinet officials, if we are to have safeguards of efficiency, economy, and probity.

Army and Navy

Little has developed in relation to our national defense which needs special attention. Progress is constantly being made in air navigation and requires encouragement and development. Army aviators have made a successful trip around the world, for which I recommend suitable recognition through provisions for promotion, compensation, and retirement. Under the direction of the Navy a new Zeppelin has been successfully brought from Europe across the Atlantic to our own country.

Due to the efficient supervision of the Secretary of War the Army of the United States has been organized with a small body of Regulars and a moderate National Guard and Reserve. The defense test of September 12 demonstrated the efficiency of the operating plans. These methods and operations are well worthy of congressional support.

Under the limitation of armaments treaty a large saving in outlay and a considerable decrease in maintenance of the Navy has been accomplished. We should maintain the policy of constantly working toward the full treaty strength of the Navy. Careful investigation is being made in this department of the relative importance of aircraft, surface and submarine vessels, in order that we may not fail to take advantage of all modern improvements for our national defense. A special commission also is investigating the problem of petroleum oil for the Navy, considering the best policy to insure the future supply of fuel oil and prevent the threatened drainage of naval oil reserves. Legislative action is required to carry on experiments in oil shale reduction, as large deposits of this type have been set aside for the use of the Navy.

We have been constantly besought to engage in competitive armaments. Frequent reports will reach us of the magnitude of the military equipment of other nations. We shall do well to be little impressed by such reports or such actions. Any nation undertaking to maintain a military establishment with aggressive and imperialistic designs will find itself severely handicapped in the economic development of the world. I believe thoroughly in the Army and Navy, in adequate defense and preparation. But I am opposed to any policy of competition in building and maintaining land or sea armaments.

Our country has definitely relinquished the old standard of dealing with other countries by terror and force, and is definitely committed to the new standard of dealing with them through friendship and understanding. This new policy should be constantly kept in mind by the guiding forces of the Army and Navy, by the Congress and by the country at large. I believe it holds a promise of great benefit to humanity. I shall resist any attempt to resort to the old methods and the old standards. I am especially solicitous that foreign nations should comprehend the candor and sincerity with which we have adopted this position. While we propose to maintain defensive and supplementary police forces by land and sea, and to train them through inspections and maneuvers upon appropriate occasions in order to maintain their efficiency, I wish every other nation to understand that this does not express any unfriendliness or convey any hostile intent. I want the armed forces of America to be considered by all peoples not as enemies but as friends as the contribution which is made by this country for the maintenance of the peace and security of the world.

Veterans

With the authorization for general hospitalization of the veterans of all wars provided during the present year, the care and treatment of those who have served their country in time of peril and the attitude of the Government toward them is not now so much one of needed legislation as one of careful, generous and humane administration.

It will ever be recognized that their welfare is of the first concern and always entitled to the most solicitous consideration on the part of their fellow citizens. They are organized in various associations, of which the chief and most representative is the American Legion. Through its officers the Legion will present to the Congress numerous suggestions for legislation. They cover such a wide variety of subjects that it is impossible to discuss them within the scope of this message. With many of the proposals I join in hearty approval and commend them all to the sympathetic investigation and consideration of the Congress.

Foreign Relations

At no period in the past 12 years have our foreign relations been in such a satisfactory condition as they are at the present time. Our actions in the recent months have greatly strengthened the American policy of permanent peace with independence. The attitude which our Government took and maintained toward an adjustment of European reparations, by pointing out that it was not a political but a business problem, has demonstrated its wisdom by its actual results. We desire to see Europe restored that it may resume its productivity in the increase of industry and its support in the advance of civilization. We look with great gratification at the hopeful prospect of recuperation in Europe through the Dawes plan. Such assistance as can be given through the action of the public authorities and of our private citizens, through friendly counsel and cooperation, and through economic and financial support, not for any warlike effort but for reproductive enterprise, not to provide means for unsound government financing but to establish sound business administration should be unhesitatingly provided.

Ultimately nations, like individuals, can not depend upon each other but must depend upon themselves. Each one must work out its own salvation. We have every desire to help. But with all our resources we are powerless to save unless our efforts meet with a constructive response. The situation in our own country and all over the world is one that can be improved only by hard work and self-denial. It is necessary to reduce expenditures, increase savings and liquidate debts. It is in this direction that there lies the greatest hope of domestic tranquility and international peace. Our own country ought to finish the leading example in this effort. Our past adherence to this policy, our constant refusal to maintain a military establishment that could be thought to menace the security of others, our honorable dealings with other nations whether great or small, has left us in the almost constant enjoyment of peace.

It is not necessary to stress the general desire of all the people of this country for the promotion of peace. It is the leading principle of all our foreign relations. We have on every occasion tried to cooperate to this end in all ways that were consistent with our proper independence and our traditional policies. It will be my constant effort to maintain these principles, and to reinforce them by all appropriate agreements and treaties. While we desire always to cooperate and to help, we are equally determined to be independent and free. Right and truth and justice and humanitarian efforts will have the moral support of this country all over the world. But we do not wish to become involved in the political controversies of others. Nor is the country disposed to become a member of the League of Nations or to assume the obligations imposed by its covenant.

International Court

America has been one of the foremost nations in advocating tribunals for the settlement of international disputes of a justiciable character. Our representatives took a leading part in those conferences which resulted in the establishment of The Hague Tribunal, and later in providing for a Permanent Court of International Justice. I believe it would be for the advantage of this country and helpful to the stability of other nations for us to adhere to the protocol establishing that court upon the conditions stated in the recommendation which is now before the Senate, and further that our country shall not be bound by advisory opinions which may be rendered by the court upon questions which we have not voluntarily submitted for its judgment. This court would provide a practical and convenient tribunal before which we could go voluntarily, but to which we could not be summoned, for a determination of justiciable questions when they fail to be resolved by diplomatic negotiations.

Disarmament Conference

Many times I have expressed my desire to see the work of the Washington Conference on Limitation of Armaments appropriately supplemented by further agreements for a further reduction and for the purpose of diminishing the menace and waste of the competition in preparing instruments of international war. It has been and is my expectation that we might hopefully approach other great powers for further conference on this subject as soon as the carrying out of the present reparation plan as the established and settled policy of Europe has created a favorable opportunity. But on account of proposals which have already been made by other governments for a European conference, it will be necessary to wait to see what the outcome of their actions may be. I should not wish to propose or have representatives attend a conference which would contemplate commitments opposed to the freedom of action we desire to maintain unimpaired with respect to our purely domestic policies.

International Law

Our country should also support efforts which are being made toward the codification of international law. We can look more hopefully, in the first instance, for research and studies that are likely to be productive of results, to a cooperation among representatives of the bar and members of international law institutes and societies, than to a conference of those who are technically representative of their respective governments, although, when projects have been developed, they must go to the governments for their approval. These expert professional studies are going on in certain quarters and should have our constant encouragement and approval.

Outlaw of War

Much interest has of late been manifested in this country in the discussion of various proposals to outlaw aggressive war. I look with great sympathy upon the examination of this subject. It is in harmony with the traditional policy of our country, which is against aggressive war and for the maintenance of permanent and honorable peace. While, as I have said, we must safeguard our liberty to deal according to our own judgment with our domestic policies, we can not fail to view with sympathetic interest all progress to this desired end or carefully to study the measures that may be proposed to attain it.

Latin America

While we are desirous of promoting peace in every quarter of the globe, we have a special interest in the peace of this hemisphere. It is our constant desire that all causes of dispute in this area may be tranquilly and satisfactorily adjusted. Along with our desire for peace is the earnest hope for the increased prosperity of our sister republics of Latin America, and our constant purpose to promote cooperation with them which may be mutually beneficial and always inspired by the most cordial friendships.

Foreign Debts

About $12,000,000,000 is due to our Government from abroad, mostly from European Governments. Great Britain, Finland, Hungary, Lithuania and Poland have negotiated settlements amounting close to $5,000,000,000. This represents the funding of over 42 per cent of the debt since the creation of the special Foreign Debt Commission. As the life of this commission is about to expire, its term should be extended. I am opposed to the cancellation of these debts and believe it for the best welfare of the world that they should be liquidated and paid as fast as possible. I do not favor oppressive measures, but unless money that is borrowed is repaid credit can not be secured in time of necessity, and there exists besides a moral obligation which our country can not ignore and no other country can evade. Terms and conditions may have to conform to differences in the financial abilities of the countries concerned, but the principle that each country should meet its obligation admits of no differences and is of universal application.

It is axiomatic that our country can not stand still. It would seem to be perfectly plain from recent events that it is determined to go forward. But it wants no pretenses, it wants no vagaries. It is determined to advance in an orderly, sound and common-sense way. It does not propose to abandon the theory of the Declaration that the people have inalienable rights which no majority and no power of government can destroy. It does not propose to abandon the practice of the Constitution that provides for the protection of these rights. It believes that within these limitations, which are imposed not by the fiat of man but by the law of the Creator, self-government is just and wise. It is convinced that it will be impossible for the people to provide their own government unless they continue to own their own property.

These are the very foundations of America. On them has been erected a Government of freedom and equality, of justice and mercy, of education and charity. Living under it and supporting it the people have come into great possessions on the material and spiritual sides of life. I want to continue in this direction. I know that the Congress shares with me that desire. I want our institutions to be more and more expressive of these principles. I want the people of all the earth to see in the American flag the symbol of a Government which intends no oppression at home and no aggression abroad, which in the spirit of a common brotherhood provides assistance in time of distress.

Annual Message to Congress

December 8, 1925

Calvin Coolidge's third State of the Union message came at a time of economic prosperity for the United States. Coolidge, who became president after Warren G. Harding's death in office in 1923, had won a full term of his own in 1924. As of December 1925, Coolidge had been president for more than two years.

Coolidge, a staunch conservative, adopted somewhat of a minimalist approach to governing, preferring individual initiative to government action. In this State of the Union message, delivered in writing rather than in person, the president stated, "The age of perfection is still in the somewhat distant future, but it is more in danger of being retarded by mistaken Government activity than it is from lack of legislation."

Overall, the country was in a confident mood in the mid-1920s. The economy was thriving, World War I and its uneasy aftermath had receded into the past, and the public seemed content with Coolidge's probusiness politics. The president successfully used the new medium of radio to reach the country, and, although taciturn by nature, he held numerous press conferences.

Among the themes Coolidge highlighted in his 1925 State of the Union address were debt reduction and tax reduction, two of his preoccupations during his presidency. Congress passed tax cuts several times during Coolidge's administration, and the president argued in this message that the reductions benefited not just the wealthy but the entire population.

While this address focused on many of the same issues as his previous State of the Union message, it dealt more with foreign affairs than the 1924 message had. Coolidge advocated that the United States should let European countries solve their own problems, and he used the Locarno agreements of 1925, in which several European nations agreed on various border and other issues growing out of World War I, as a case in point. He favored continued U.S. participation in arms control talks and wanted the country to be involved in the Court of International Justice.

Another issue Coolidge mentioned in his message was immigration. Congress had passed restrictive immigration laws in 1921 and 1924 and would do so again in 1929. In his remarks, Coolidge stated that the restrictions, while still new, seemed helpful but should be monitored in case changes were needed. He also spoke in favor of civil rights for black Americans.

Coolidge would preside over several more years of economic good times, but less than a year after he left office the stock market crashed in October 1929, and the country faced the difficult years of the Great Depression.

Members of the Congress:

In meeting the constitutional requirement of informing the Congress upon the state of the Union, it is exceedingly gratifying to report that the general condition is one of progress and prosperity. Here and there are comparatively small and apparently temporary difficulties needing adjustment and improved administrative methods, such as are always to be expected, but in the fundamentals of government and business the results demonstrate that we are going in the right direction. The country does not appear to require radical departures from the policies already adopted so much as it needs a further extension of these policies and the improvement of details. The age of perfection is still in the somewhat distant future, but it is more in danger of being retarded by mistaken Government activity than it is from lack of legislation. We are by far the most likely to accomplish permanent good if we proceed with moderation.

In our country the people are sovereign and independent, and must accept the resulting responsibilities. It is their duty to support themselves and support the Government. That is the business of the Nation, whatever the charity of the Nation may require. The functions which the Congress are to discharge are not those of local government but of National Government. The greatest solicitude should be exercised to prevent any encroachment upon the rights of the States or their various political subdivisions. Local self-government is one of our most precious possessions. It is the greatest contributing factor to the stability, strength, liberty, and progress of the Nation. It ought not to be in ringed by assault or undermined by purchase. It ought not to abdicate its power through weakness or resign its authority through favor. It does not at all follow that because abuses exist it is the concern of the Federal Government to attempt their reform.

Society is in much more danger from encumbering the National Government beyond its wisdom to comprehend, or its ability to administer, than from leaving the local communities to bear their own burdens and remedy their own evils. Our local habit and custom is so strong, our variety of race and creed is so great, the Federal authority is so tenuous, that the area within which it can function successfully is very limited. The wiser policy is to leave the localities, so far as we can, possessed of their own sources of revenue and charged with their own obligations.

Government Economy

It is a fundamental principle of our country that the people are sovereign. While they recognize the undeniable authority of the state, they have established as its instrument a Government of limited powers. They hold inviolate in their own hands the jurisdiction over their own freedom and the ownership of their own property. Neither of these can be impaired except by due process of law. The wealth of our country is not public wealth, but private wealth. It does not belong to the Government, it belongs to the people. The Government has no justification in taking private Property except for a public purpose. It is always necessary to keep these principles in mind in the laying of taxes and in the making of appropriations. No right exists to levy on a dollar, or to order the expenditure of a dollar, of the money of the people, except for a necessary public purpose duly authorized by the Constitution. The power over the purse is the power over liberty.

That is the legal limitation within which the Congress can act. How it will proceed within this limitation is always a question of policy. When the country is prosperous and free from debt, when the rate of taxation is low, opportunity exists for assuming new burdens and undertaking new enterprises. Such a condition now prevails only to a limited extent. All proposals for assuming new obligations ought to be postponed, unless they are reproductive capital investments or are such as are absolutely necessary at this time. We still have an enormous debt of over $20,000,000,000, on which the interest and sinking-fund requirements are $1,320,000,000. Our appropriations for the Pension Office and the Veterans' Bureau are $600,000,000. The War and Navy Departments call for $642,000,000. Other requirements, exclusive of the Post Office, which is virtually self-sustaining, brought the appropriations for the current year up to almost $3,100,060,000. This shows an expenditure of close to $30 for every inhabitant of our country. For the average family of five it means a tax, directly or indirectly paid, of about $150 for national purposes alone. The local tax adds much more. These enormous expenditures ought not to be increased, but through every possible effort they ought to be reduced.

Only one of these great items can be ultimately extinguished. That is the item of our war debt. Already this has been reduced to about $6,000,000,000, which means an annual saving in interest of close to $250,000,000. The present interest charge is about $820,000,000 yearly. It would seem to be obvious that the sooner this debt can be retired the more the taxpayers will save in interest and the easier it will be to secure funds with which to prosecute needed running expenses, constructions, and improvements. This item of $820,000,000 for interest is a heavy charge on all the people of the country, and it seems to me that we might well consider whether it is not greatly worth while to dispense with it as early as possible by retiring the principal debt which it is required to serve.

It has always been our policy to retire our debts. That of the Revolutionary War period, notwithstanding the additions made in 1812, was paid by 1835, and the Civil War debt within 23 years. Of the amount already paid, over $1,000,000,000 is a reduction in cash balances. That source is exhausted. Over one and two-thirds billions of dollars was derived from excess receipts. Tax reduction eliminates that. The sale of surplus war materials has been another element of our income. That is practically finished. With these eliminated, the reduction of the debt has been only about $500,000,000 each year, not an excessive sum on so large a debt.

Proposals have been made to extend the payment over a period of 62 years. If $1,000,000,000 is paid at the end of 20 years, the cost to the taxpayers is the principal and, if the interest is 4$\frac{1}{4}$ per cent, a total of $1,850,000,000. If the same sum is paid at the end of 62 years, the cost is $3,635,000,000, or almost double. Here is another consideration: Compared with its purchasing power in 1913, the dollar we borrowed represented but 52 cents. As the value of our dollar increases, due to the falling prices of commodities, the burden of our debt increases. It has now risen to 63$\frac{1}{2}$ cents. The taxpayer will be required to produce nearly twice the amount of commodities to pay his debt if the dollar returns to the 1913 value. The more we pay while prices are high, the easier it will be.

Deflation of government after a war period is slower than deflation of business, where curtailment is either prompt and effective or disaster follows. There is room for further economy in the cost of the Federal Government, but a comparison of current expenditures with pre-war expenditures is not unfavorable to the efficiency with which Government business is now being done. The expenditures of 1916, the last pre-war year, were $742,000,000, and in 1925 over $3,500,000,000, or nearly five times as great. If we subtract expenditures for debt retirements and interest, veterans' relief, increase of pensions, and other special outlays, consisting of refunds, trust investments, and like charges, we find that the general expenditures of the Government in 1925 were slightly more than twice as large as in 1916.

As prices in 1925 were approximately 40 per cent higher than in 1916, the cost of the same Government must also have increased. But the Government is not the same. It is more expensive to collect the much greater revenue necessary and to administer our great debt. We have given enlarged and improved services to agriculture and commerce. Above all, America has grown in population and wealth. Government expenditures must always share in this growth. Taking into account the factors I have mentioned, I believe that present Federal expenses are not far out of line with pre-war expenses. We have nearly accomplished the deflation.

This does not mean that further economies will not come. As we reduce our debt our interest charges decline. There are many details yet to correct. The real improvement, however, must come not from additional curtailment of expenses, but by a more intelligent, more ordered spending. Our economy must be constructive. While we should avoid as far as possible increases in permanent current expenditures, oftentimes a capital outlay like internal improvements will result in actual constructive saving. That is economy in its best sense. It is an avoidance of waste that there may be the means for an outlay to-day which will bring larger returns to-morrow. We should constantly engage in scientific studies of our future requirements and adopt an orderly program for their service. Economy is the method by which we prepare to-day to afford the improvements of to-morrow.

A mere policy of economy without any instrumentalities for putting it into operation would be very ineffective. The Congress has wisely set up the Bureau of the Budget to investigate and inform the President what recommendations he ought to make for current appropriations. This gives a centralized authority where a general and comprehensive understanding can be reached of the sources of income and the most equitable distribution of expenditures. How well it has worked is indicated by the fact that the departmental estimates for 1922, before the budget law, were $4,068,000,000 while the Budget estimates for 1927 are $3,156,000,000. This latter figure shows the reductions in departmental estimates for the coming year made possible by the operation of the Budget system that the Congress has provided.

But it is evidently not enough to have care in making appropriations without any restraint upon expenditure. The Congress has provided that check by establishing the office of Comptroller General.

The purpose of maintaining the Budget Director and the Comptroller General is to secure economy and efficiency in Government expenditure. No better method has been devised for the accomplishment of that end. These offices can not be administered in all the various details without making some errors both of fact and of judgment. But the important consideration remains that these are the instrumentalities of the Congress and that no other plan has ever been adopted which was so successful in promoting economy and efficiency. The Congress has absolute authority over the appropriations and is free to exercise its judgment, as the evidence may warrant, in increasing or decreasing budget recommendations. But it ought to resist every effort to weaken or break down this most beneficial system of supervising appropriations and expenditures. Without it all the claim of economy would be a mere pretense.

Taxation

The purpose of reducing expenditures is to secure a reduction in taxes. That purpose is about to be realized. With commendable promptness the Ways and Means Committee of the House has undertaken in advance of the meeting of the Congress to frame a revenue act. As the bill has proceeded through the committee it has taken on a nonpartisan character, and both Republicans and Democrats have joined in a measure which embodies many sound principles of tax reform. The bill will correct substantially the economic defects injected into the revenue act of 1924, as well as many which have remained as war-time legacies. In its present form it should provide sufficient revenue for the Government.

The excessive surtaxes have been reduced, estate tax rates are restored to more reasonable figures, with every prospect of withdrawing from the field when the States have had the opportunity to correct the abuses in their own inheritance tax laws, the gift tax and publicity section are to be repealed, many miscellaneous taxes are lowered or abandoned, and the Board of Tax Appeals and the administrative features of the law are improved and strengthened. I approve of the bill in principle. In so far as income-tax exemptions are concerned, it seems to me the committee has gone as far as it is safe to go and somewhat further than I should have gone. Any further extension along these lines would, in my opinion, impair the integrity of our income-tax system.

I am advised that the bill will be through the House by Christmas. For this prompt action the country can thank the good sense of the Ways and Means Committee in framing an economic measure upon economic considerations. If this attitude continues to be reflected through the Congress, the taxpayer will have his relief by the time his March 15th installment of income taxes is due. Nonpartisan effort means certain, quick action. Determination of a revenue law definitely, promptly and solely as a revenue law, is one of the greatest gifts a legislature can bestow upon its constituents. I commend the example of the Ways and Means Committee. If followed, it will place sound legislation upon the books in time to give the taxpayers the full benefit of tax reduction next year. This means that the bill should reach me prior to March 15.

All these economic results are being sought not to benefit the rich, but to benefit the people. They are for the purpose of encouraging industry in order that employment may be plentiful. They seek to make business good in order that wages may be good. They encourage prosperity in order that poverty may be banished from the home. They seek to lay the foundation which, through increased production, may give the people a more bountiful supply of the necessaries of life, afford more leisure for the improvement of the mind, the appreciation of the arts of music and literature, sculpture and painting, and the beneficial enjoyment of outdoor sports and recreation, enlarge the resources which minister to charity and by all these means attempting to strengthen the spiritual life of the Nation.

Foreign Relations

The policy of our foreign relations, casting aside any suggestion of force, rests solely on the foundation of peace, good will, and good works. We have sought, in our intercourse with other nations, better understandings through conference and exchange of views as befits beings endowed with reason. The results have been the gradual elimination of disputes, the settlement of controversies, and the establishment of a firmer friendship between America and the rest of the world than has ever existed at any previous time.

The example of this attitude has not been without its influence upon other countries. Acting upon it, an adjustment was made of the difficult problem of reparations. This was the second step toward peace in Europe. It paved the way for the agreements which were drawn up at the Locarno Conference. When ratified, these will represent the third step toward peace. While they do not of themselves provide an economic rehabilitation, which is necessary for the progress of Europe, by strengthening the guarantees of peace they diminish the need for great armaments. If the energy which now goes into military effort is transferred to productive endeavor it will greatly assist economic progress.

The Locarno agreements were made by the, European countries directly interested without any formal intervention of America, although on July 3 I publicly advocated such agreements in an address made in Massachusetts. We have consistently refrained from intervening except when our help has been sought and we have felt it could be effectively given, as in the settlement of reparations and the London Conference. These recent Locarno agreements represent the success of this policy which we have been insisting ought to be adopted, of having European countries settle their own political problems without involving this country. This beginning seems to demonstrate that this policy is sound. It is exceedingly gratifying to observe this progress, both in its method and in its result promises so much that is beneficial to the world.

When these agreements are finally adopted, they will provide guarantees of peace that make the present prime reliance upon force in some parts of Europe very much less necessary. The natural corollary to these treaties should be further international contracts for the limitation of armaments. This work was successfully begun at the Washington Conference. Nothing was done at that time concerning land forces because of European objection. Our standing army has been reduced to around 118,000, about the necessary police force for 115,000,000 people. We are not proposing to increase it, nor is it supposable that any foreign country looks with the slightest misapprehension upon our land forces. They do not menace anybody. They are rather a protection to everybody.

The question of disarming upon land is so peculiarly European in its practical aspects that our country would look with particular gratitude upon any action which those countries might take to reduce their own military forces. This is in accordance with our policy of not intervening unless the European powers are unable to agree and make request for our assistance. Whenever they are able to agree of their own accord it is especially gratifying to us, and such agreements may be sure of our sympathetic support.

It seems clear that it is the reduction of armies rather than of navies that is of the first importance to the world at the present time. We shall look with great satisfaction upon that effort and give it our approbation and encouragement. If that can be settled, we may more easily consider further reduction and limitation of naval armaments. For that purpose our country has constantly through its Executive, and through repeated acts of Congress, indicated its willingness to call such a conference. Under congressional sanction it would seem to be wise to participate in any conference of the great powers for naval limitation of armament proposed upon such conditions that it would hold a fair promise of being effective. The general policy of our country is for disarmament, and it ought not to hesitate to adopt any practical plan that might reasonably be expected to succeed. But it would not care to attend a conference which from its location or constituency would in all probability prove futile.

In the further pursuit of strengthening the bonds of peace and good will we have joined with other nations in an international conference held at Geneva and signed an agreement which will be laid before the Senate for ratification providing suitable measures for control and for publicity in international trade in arms, ammunition, and implements of war, and also executed a protocol providing for a prohibition of the use of poison gas in war, in accordance with the principles of Article 5 of the treaty relating thereto signed at the Washington Conference. We are supporting the Pan American efforts that are being made toward the codification of international law, and looking with sympathy on the investigations conducted under philanthropic auspices of the proposal to agreements outlawing war. In accordance with promises made at the Washington Conference, we have urged the calling of and are now represented at the Chinese Customs Conference and on the Commission on Extraterritoriality, where it will be our policy so far as possible to meet the aspirations of China in all ways consistent with the interests of the countries involved.

Court of International Justice

Pending before the Senate for nearly three years is the proposal to adhere to the protocol establishing the Permanent Court of International Justice. A well-established line of precedents mark America's effort to effect the establishment of a court of this nature. We took a leading part in laying the foundation on which it rests in the establishment of The Hague Court of Arbitration. It is that tribunal which nominates the judges who are elected by the Council and Assembly of the League of Nations.

The proposal submitted to the Senate was made dependent upon four conditions, the first of which is that by supporting the court we do not assume any obligations under the league; second, that we may participate upon an equality with other States in the election of judges; third, that the Congress shall determine what part of the expenses we shall bear; fourth, that the statute creating the court shall not be amended without our consent; and to these I have proposed an additional condition to the effect that we are not to be bound by advisory opinions rendered without our consent.

The court appears to be independent of the league. It is true the judges are elected by the Assembly and Council, but they are nominated by the Court of Arbitration, which we assisted to create and of which we are a part. The court was created by a statute, so-called, which is really a treaty made among some forty-eight different countries, that might properly be called a constitution of the court. This statute provides a method by which the judges are chosen, so that when the Court of Arbitration nominates them and the Assembly and Council of the League elect them, they are not acting as instruments of the Court of Arbitration or instruments of the league, but as instruments of the statute.

This will be even more apparent if our representatives sit with the members of the council and assembly in electing the judges. It is true they are paid through the league though not by the league, but by the countries which are members of the league and by our country if we accept the protocol. The judges are paid by the league only in the same sense that it could be said United States judges are paid by the Congress. The court derives all its authority from the statute and is so completely independent of the league that it could go on functioning if the league were disbanded, at least until the terms of the judges expired.

The most careful provisions are made in the statute as to the qualifications of judges. Those who make the nominations are recommended to consult with their highest court of justice, their law schools and academies. The judges must be persons of high moral character, qualified to hold the highest judicial offices in that country, or be jurisconsults of recognized competence in international law. It must be assumed that these requirements will continue to be carefully met, and with America joining the countries already concerned it is difficult to comprehend how human ingenuity could better provide for the establishment of a court which would maintain its independence. It has to be recognized that independence is to a considerable extent a matter of ability, character, and personality. Some effort was made in the early beginnings to interfere with the independence of our Supreme Court. It did not succeed because of the quality of the men who made up that tribunal.

It does not seem that the authority to give advisory opinions interferes with the independence of the court. Advisory opinions in and of themselves are not harmful, but may be used in such a way as to be very beneficial because they undertake to prevent injury rather than merely afford a remedy after the injury has been done. As a principle that only implies that the court shall function when proper application is made to it. Deciding the question involved upon issues submitted for an advisory opinion does not differ materially from deciding the question involved upon issues submitted by contending parties. Up to the present time the court has given an advisory opinion when it judged it had jurisdiction, and refused to give one when it judged it did not have jurisdiction. Nothing in the work of the court has yet been an indication that this is an impairment of its independence or that its practice differs materially from the giving of like opinions under the authority of the constitutions of several of our States.

No provision of the statute seems to me to give this court any authority to be a political rather than a judicial court. We have brought cases in this country before our courts which, when they have been adjudged to be political, have been thereby dismissed. It is not improbable that political questions will be submitted to this court, but again up to the present time the court has refused to pass on political questions and our support would undoubtedly have a tendency to strengthen it in that refusal.

We are not proposing to subject ourselves to any compulsory jurisdiction. If we support the court, we can never be obliged to submit any case which involves our interests for its decision. Our appearance before it would always be voluntary, for the purpose of presenting a case which we had agreed might be presented. There is no more danger that others might bring cases before the court involving our interests which we did not wish to have brought, after we have adhered, and probably not so much, than there would be of bringing such cases if we do not adhere. I think that we would have the same legal or moral right to disregard such a finding in the one case that we would in the other.

If we are going to support any court, it will not be one that we have set up alone or which reflects only our ideals. Other nations have their customs and their institutions, their thoughts and their methods of life. If a court is going to be international, its composition will have to yield to what is good in all these various elements. Neither will it be possible to support a court which is exactly perfect, or under which we assume absolutely no obligations. If we are seeking that opportunity, we might as well declare that we are opposed to supporting any court. If any agreement is made, it will be because it undertakes to set up a tribunal which can do some of the things that other nations wish to have done. We shall not find ourselves bearing a disproportionate share of the world's burdens by our adherence, and we may as well remember that there is absolutely no escape for our country from bearing its share of the world's burdens in any case. We shall do far better service to ourselves and to others if we admit this and discharge our duties voluntarily, than if we deny it and are forced to meet the same obligations unwillingly.

It is difficult to imagine anything that would be more helpful to the world than stability, tranquility and international justice. We may say that we are contributing to these factors independently, but others less fortunately located do not and can not make a like contribution except through mutual cooperation. The old balance of power, mutual alliances, and great military forces were not brought about by any mutual dislike for independence, but resulted from the domination of circumstances. Ultimately they were forced on us. Like all others engaged in the war whatever we said as a matter of fact we joined an alliance, we became a military power, we impaired our independence. We have more at stake than any one else in avoiding a repetition of that calamity. Wars do not spring into existence. They arise from small incidents and trifling irritations which can be adjusted by an international court. We can contribute greatly to the advancement of our ideals by joining with other nations in maintaining such a tribunal.

Foreign Debts

Gradually, settlements have been made which provide for the liquidation of debts due to our Government from foreign governments. Those made with Great Britain, Finland, Hungary Lithuania, and Poland have already been approved by the Congress. Since the adjournment, further agreements have been entered into with Belgium, Czechoslovakia, Latvia, Estonia, Italy, and Rumania. These 11 nations, which have already made settlements, represent $6,419,528,641 of the original principal of the loans. The principal sums without interest, still pending, are the debt of France, of $3,340,000,000; Greece, $15,000,000; Yugoslavia, $51,000,000; Liberia, $26,000; Russia, $192,000,000, which those at present in control have undertaken, openly to repudiate; Nicaragua, $84,000, which is being paid currently; and Austria, $24,000,000, on which by act of Congress a moratorium of 20 years has been granted. The only remaining sum is $12,000,000, due from Armenia, which has now ceased to exist as an independent nation.

In accordance with the settlements made, the amount of principal and interest which is to be paid to the United States under these agreements aggregate $15,200,688,253.93. It is obvious that the remaining settlements, which will undoubtedly be made, will bring this sum up to an amount which will more than equal the principal due on our present national debt. While these settlements are very large in the aggregate, it has been felt that the terms granted were in all cases very generous. They impose no undue burden and are mutually beneficial in the observance of international faith and the improvement of international credit.

Every reasonable effort will be made to secure agreements for liquidation with the remaining countries, whenever they are in such condition that they can be made. Those which have already been negotiated under the bipartisan commission established by the Congress have been made only after the most thoroughgoing and painstaking investigation, continued for a long time before meeting with the representatives of the countries concerned. It is believed that they represent in each instance the best that can be done and the wisest settlement that can be secured. One very important result is the stabilization of foreign currency, making exchange assist rather than embarrass our trade. Wherever sacrifices have been made of money, it will be more than amply returned in better understanding and friendship, while in so far as these adjustments will contribute to the financial stability of the debtor countries, to their good order, prosperity, and progress, they represent hope of improved trade relations and mutual contributions to the civilization of the world.

Alien Problem

Negotiations are progressing among the interested parties in relation to the final distribution of the assets in the hands of the Alien Property Custodian. Our Government and people are interested as creditors; the German Government and people are interested as debtors and owners of the seized property. Pending the outcome of these negotiations, I do not recommend any affirmative legislation. For the present we should continue in possession of this property which we hold as security for the settlement of claims due to our people and our Government.

Immigration

While not enough time has elapsed to afford a conclusive demonstration, such results as have been secured indicate that our immigration law is on the whole beneficial. It is undoubtedly a protection to the wage earners of this country. The situation should however, be carefully surveyed, in order to ascertain whether it is working a needless hardship upon our own inhabitants. If it deprives them of the comfort and society of those bound to them by close family ties, such modifications should be adopted as will afford relief, always in accordance with the principle that our Government owes its first duty to our own people and that no alien, inhabitant of another country, has any legal rights whatever under our Constitution and laws. It is only through treaty, or through residence here that such rights accrue. But we should not, however, be forgetful of the obligations of a common humanity.

While our country numbers among its best citizens many of those of foreign birth, yet those who now enter in violation of our laws by that very act thereby place themselves in a class of undesirables. If investigation reveals that any considerable number are coming here in defiance of our immigration restrictions, it will undoubtedly create the necessity for the registration of all aliens. We ought to have no prejudice against an alien because he is an alien. The standard which we apply to our inhabitants is that of manhood, not place of birth. Restrictive immigration is to a large degree for economic purposes. It is applied in order that we may not have a larger annual increment of good people within our borders than we can weave into our economic fabric in such a way as to supply their needs without undue injury to ourselves.

National Defense

Never before in time of peace has our country maintained so large and effective a military force as it now has. The Army, Navy, Marine Corps, National Guard, and Organized Reserves represent a strength of about 558,400 men. These forces are well trained, well equipped, and high in morale.

A sound selective service act giving broad authority for the mobilization in time of peril of all the resources of the country, both persons and materials, is needed to perfect our defense policy in accordance with our ideals of equality. The provision for more suitable housing to be paid for out of funds derived from the sale of excess lands, pending before the last Congress, ought to be brought forward and passed. Reasonable replacements ought to be made to maintain a sufficient ammunition reserve.

The Navy has the full treaty tonnage of capital ships. Work is going forward in modernizing the older ones, building aircraft carriers, additional fleet submarines, and fast scout cruisers, but we are carefully avoiding anything that might be construed as a competition in armaments with other nations. The joint Army and Navy maneuvers at Hawaii, followed by the cruise of a full Battle Fleet to Australia and New Zealand, were successfully carried out. These demonstrations revealed a most satisfactory condition of the ships and the men engaged.

Last year at my suggestion the General Board of the Navy made an investigation and report on the relation of aircraft to warships. As a result authorizations and appropriations were made for more scout cruisers and fleet submarines and for completing aircraft carriers and equipping them with necessary planes. Additional training in aviation was begun at the Military and Naval Academies. A method of coordination and cooperation of the Army and Navy and the principal aircraft builders is being perfected. At the suggestion of the Secretaries of War and Navy I appointed a special board to make a further study of the problem of aircraft.

The report of the Air Board ought to be reassuring to the country, gratifying to the service and satisfactory to the Congress. It is thoroughly complete and represents the mature thought of the best talent in the country. No radical change in organization of the service seems necessary. The Departments of War, Navy, and Commerce should each be provided with an additional assistant secretary, not necessarily with statutory duties but who would be available under the direction of the Secretary to give especial attention to air navigation. We must have an air strength worthy of America. Provision should be made for two additional brigadier generals for the Army Air Service. Temporary rank corresponding to their duties should be awarded to active flying officers in both Army and Navy.

Aviation is of great importance both for national defense and commercial development. We ought to proceed in its improvement by the necessary experiment and investigation. Our country is not behind in this art. It has made records for speed and for the excellence of its planes. It ought to go on maintaining its manufacturing plants capable of rapid production, giving national assistance to the laying out of airways, equipping itself with a moderate number of planes and keeping an air force trained to the highest efficiency.

While I am a thorough believer in national defense and entirely committed to the policy of adequate preparation, I am just as thoroughly opposed to instigating or participating in a policy of competitive armaments. Nor does preparation mean a policy of militarizing. Our people and industries are solicitous for the cause of our country, and have great respect for the Army and Navy and for the uniform worn by the men who stand ready at all times for our protection to encounter the dangers and perils necessary to military service, but all of these activities are to be taken not in behalf of aggression but in behalf of peace. They are the instruments by which we undertake to do our part to promote good will and support stability among all peoples.

Veterans

If any one desires to estimate the esteem in which the veterans of America are held by their fellow citizens, it is but necessary to remember that the current budget calls for an expenditure of about $650,000,000 in their behalf. This is nearly the amount of the total cost of the National Government, exclusive of the post office, before we entered the last war.

At the two previous sessions of Congress legislation affecting veterans' relief was enacted and the law liberalized. This legislation brought into being a number of new provisions tending more nearly to meet the needs of our veterans, as well as afford the necessary authority to perfect the administration of these laws.

Experience with the new legislation so far has clearly demonstrated its constructive nature. It has increased the benefits received by many and has made eligible for benefits many others. Direct disbursements to the veteran or his dependents exceeding $21,000,000 have resulted, which otherwise would not have been made. The degree of utilization of our hospitals has increased through making facilities available to the incapacitated veteran regardless of service origin of the disability. This new legislation also has brought about a marked improvement of service to the veteran.

The organizations of ex-service men have proposed additional legislative changes which you will consider, but until the new law and the modifications made at the last session of Congress are given a more thorough test further changes in the basic law should be few and made only after careful though sympathetic consideration.

The principal work now before the Veterans' Bureau is the perfection of its organization and further improvements in service. Some minor legislative changes are deemed necessary to enable the bureau to retain that high grade of professional talent essential in handling the problems of the bureau. Such changes as tend toward the improvement of service and the carrying forward to completion of the hospital construction program are recommended for the consideration of the proper committees of Congress.

With the enormous outlay that is now being made in behalf of the veterans and their dependents, with a tremendous war debt still requiring great annual expenditure, with the still high rate of taxation, while every provision should be made for the relief of the disabled and the necessary care of dependents, the Congress may well consider whether the financial condition of the Government is not such that further bounty through the enlargement of general pensions and other emoluments ought not to be postponed.

Agriculture

No doubt the position of agriculture as a whole has very much improved since the depression of three and four years ago. But there are many localities and many groups of individuals, apparently through no fault of their own, sometimes due to climatic conditions and sometimes to the prevailing price of a certain crop, still in a distressing condition. This is probably temporary, but it is none the less acute. National Government agencies, the Departments of Agriculture and Commerce, the Farm Loan Board, the intermediate credit banks, and the Federal Reserve Board are all cooperating to be of assistance and relief. On the other hand, there are localities and individuals who have had one of their most prosperous years. The general price level is fair, but here again there are exceptions both ways, some items being poor while others are excellent. In spite of a lessened production the farm income for this year will be about the same as last year and much above the three preceding years.

Agriculture is a very complex industry. It does not consist of one problem, but of several. They can not be solved at one stroke. They have to be met in different ways, and small gains are not to be despised.

It has appeared from all the investigations that I have been able to make that the farmers as a whole are determined to maintain the independence of their business. They do not wish to have meddling on the part of the Government or to be placed under the inevitable restrictions involved in any system of direct or indirect price-fixing, which would result from permitting the Government to operate in the agricultural markets. They are showing a very commendable skill in organizing themselves to transact their own business through cooperative marketing, which will this year turn over about $2,500,000,000, or nearly one-fifth of the total agricultural business. In this they are receiving help from the Government. The Department of Agriculture should be strengthened in this facility, in order to be able to respond when these marketing associations want help. While it ought not to undertake undue regulation, it should be equipped to give prompt information on crop prospects, supply, demand, current receipts, imports, exports, and prices.

A bill embodying these principles, which has been drafted under the advice and with the approval of substantially all the leaders and managers in the cooperative movement, will be presented to the Congress for its enactment. Legislation should also be considered to provide for leasing the unappropriated public domain for grazing purposes and adopting a uniform policy relative to grazing on the public lands and in the national forests.

A more intimate relation should be established between agriculture and the other business activities of the Nation. They are mutually dependent and can each advance their own prosperity most by advancing the prosperity of the other. Meantime the Government will continue those activities which have resulted in an unprecedented amount of legislation and the pouring out of great sums of money during the last five years. The work for good roads, better land and water transportation, increased support for agricultural education, extension of credit facilities through the Farm Loan Boards and the intermediate credit banks, the encouragement of orderly marketing and a repression of wasteful speculation, will all be continued.

Following every other depression, after a short period the price of farm produce has taken and maintained the lead in the advance. This advance had reached a climax before the war. Everyone will recall the discussion that went on for four or five years prior to 1914 concerning the high cost of living. This history is apparently beginning to repeat itself. While wholesale prices of other commodities have been declining, farm prices have been increasing. There is every reason to suppose that a new era in agricultural prosperity lies just before us, which will probably be unprecedented.

Muscle Shoals

The problem of Muscle Shoals seems to me to have assumed a place all out of proportion with its real importance. It probably does not represent in market value much more than a first-class battleship, yet it has been discussed in the Congress over a period of years and for months at a time. It ought to be developed for the production of nitrates primarily, and incidentally for power purposes. This would serve defensive, agricultural, and industrial purposes. I am in favor of disposing of this property to meet these purposes. The findings of the special commission will be transmitted to the Congress for their information. I am convinced that the best possible disposition can be made by direct authorization of the Congress. As a means of negotiation I recommend the immediate appointment of a small joint special committee chosen from the appropriate general standing committees of the House and Senate to receive bids, which when made should be reported with recommendations as to acceptance, upon which a law should be enacted, effecting a sale to the highest bidder who will agree to carry out these purposes.

If anything were needed to demonstrate the almost utter incapacity of the National Government to deal directly with an industrial and commercial problem, it has been provided by our experience with this property. We have expended vast fortunes, we have taxed everybody, but we are unable to secure results which benefit anybody. This property ought to be transferred to private management under conditions which will dedicate it to the public purpose for which it was conceived.

Reclamation

The National Government is committed to a policy of reclamation and irrigation which it desires to establish on a sound basis and continue in the interest of the localities concerned. Exhaustive studies have recently been made of Federal reclamation, which have resulted in improving the projects and adjusting many difficulties. About one third of the projects is in good financial condition, another third can probably be made profitable, while the other third is under unfavorable conditions. The Congress has already provided for a survey which will soon be embodied in a report. That ought to suggest a method of relief which will make unnecessary further appeals to the Congress. Unless this can be done, Federal reclamation will be considerably retarded. With the greatly increased cost of construction and operation, it has become necessary to plan in advance, by community organization and selective agriculture, methods sufficient to repay these increasing outlays.

The human and economic interests of the farmer citizens suggest that the States should be required to exert some effort and assume some responsibility, especially in the intimate, detailed, and difficult work of securing settlers and developing farms which directly profit them, but only indirectly and remotely can reimburse the Nation. It is believed that the Federal Government should continue to be the agency for planning and constructing the great undertakings needed to regulate and bring into use the rivers of the West, many of which are interstate in character, but the detailed work of creating agricultural communities and a rural civilization on the land made ready for reclamation ought to be either transferred to the State in its entirety or made a cooperative effort of the State and Federal Government.

Shipping

The maintenance of a merchant marine is of the utmost importance for national defense and the service of our commerce. We have a large number of ships engaged in that service. We also have a surplus supply, costly to care for, which ought to be sold. All the investigations that have been made under my direction, and those which have been prosecuted independently, have reached the conclusion that the fleet should be under the direct control of a single executive head, while the Shipping Board should exercise its judicial and regulatory functions in accordance with its original conception. The report of Henry G. Dalton, a business man of broad experience, with a knowledge of shipping, made to me after careful investigation, will be transmitted for the information of the Congress, the studies pursued under the direction of the United States Chamber of Commerce will also be accessible, and added to these will be the report of the special committee of the House.

I do not advocate the elimination of regional considerations, but it has become apparent that without centralized executive action the management of this great business, like the management of any other great business, will flounder in incapacity and languish under a division of council. A plain and unmistakable reassertion of this principle of unified control, which I have always been advised was the intention of the Congress to apply, is necessary to increase the efficiency of our merchant fleet.

Coal

The perennial conflict in the coal industry is still going on to the great detriment of the wage earners, the owners, and especially to the public. With deposits of coal in this country capable of supplying its needs for hundreds of years, inability to manage and control this great resource for the benefit of all concerned is very close to a national economic failure. It has been the subject of repeated investigation and reiterated recommendation. Yet the industry seems never to have accepted modern methods of adjusting differences between employers and employees. The industry could serve the public much better and become subject to a much more effective method of control if regional consolidations and more freedom in the formation of marketing associations, under the supervision of the Department of Commerce, were permitted.

At the present time the National Government has little or no authority to deal with this vital necessity of the life of the country. It has permitted itself to remain so powerless that its only attitude must be humble supplication. Authority should be lodged with the President and the Departments of Commerce and Labor, giving them power to deal with an emergency. They should be able to appoint temporary boards with authority to call for witnesses and documents, conciliate differences, encourage arbitration, and in case of threatened scarcity exercise control over distribution. Making the facts public under these circumstances through a statement from an authoritative source would be of great public benefit. The report of the last coal commission should be brought forward, reconsidered, and acted upon.

Prohibition

Under the orderly processes of our fundamental institutions the Constitution was lately amended providing for national prohibition. The Congress passed an act for its enforcement, and similar acts have been provided by most of the States. It is the law of the land. It is the duty of all who come under its jurisdiction to observe the spirit of that law, and it is the duty of the Department of Justice and the Treasury Department to enforce it. Action to prevent smuggling, illegal transportation in interstate commerce, abuse in the use of permits, and existence of sources of supply for illegal traffic is almost entirely imposed upon the Federal Government.

Through treaties with foreign governments and increased activities of the Coast Guard, revenue agents, district attorneys and enforcement agents effort is being made to prevent these violations. But the Constitution also puts a concurrent duty on the States. We need their active and energetic cooperation, the vigilant action of their police, and the jurisdiction of their courts to assist in enforcement. I request of the people observance, of the public officers continuing efforts for enforcement, and of the Congress favorable action on the budget recommendation for the prosecution of this work.

Waterway Development

For many years our country has been employed in plans and operations for the development of our intracoastal and inland waterways. This work along our coast is an important adjunct to our commerce. It will be carried on, together with the further opening up of our harbors, as our resources permit. The Government made an agreement during the war to take over the Cape Cod Canal, under which the owners made valuable concessions. This pledged faith of the Government ought to be redeemed.

Two other main fields are under consideration. One is the Great Lakes and St. Lawrence, including the Erie Canal. This includes stabilizing the lake level, and is both a waterway and power project. A joint commission of the United States and Canada is working on plans and surveys which will not be completed until next April. No final determination can be made, apparently, except under treaty as to the participation of both countries. The other is the Mississippi River stem. This is almost entirely devoted to navigation. Work on the Ohio River will be completed in about three years. A modern channel connecting Chicago, New Orleans, Kansas City, and Pittsburgh should be laid out and work on the tributaries prosecuted. Some work is being done of a preparatory nature along the Missouri, and large expenditures are being made yearly in the lower reaches of the Mississippi and its tributaries which contribute both to flood control and navigation. Preliminary measures are being taken on the Colorado River project, which is exceedingly important for flood control, irrigation, power development, and water supply to the area concerned. It would seem to be very doubtful, however, whether it is practical to secure affirmative action of the Congress, except under a joint agreement of the several States.

The Government has already expended large sums upon scientific research and engineering investigation in promotion of this Colorado River project. The actual progress has been retarded for many years by differences among the seven States in the basin over their relative water rights and among different groups as to methods. In an attempt to settle the primary difficulty of the water rights, Congress authorized the Colorado River Commission which agreed on November 24, 1922, upon an interstate compact to settle these rights, subject to the ratification of the State legislatures and Congress. All seven States except Arizona at one time ratified, the Arizona Legislature making certain reservations which failed to meet the approval of the governor. Subsequently an attempt was made to establish the compact upon a six-State basis, but in this case California imposed reservations. There appears to be no division of opinion upon the major principles of the compact, but difficulty in separating contentions as to methods of development from the discussion of it. It is imperative that flood control be undertaken for California and Arizona, preparation made for irrigation, for power, and for domestic water.

Some or all of these questions are combined in every proposed development. The Federal Government is interested in some of these phases, State governments and municipalities and irrigation districts in others, and private corporations in still others. Because of all this difference of view it is most desirable that Congress should consider the creation of some agency that will be able to determine methods of improvement solely upon economic and engineering facts, that would be authorized to negotiate and settle, subject to the approval of Congress, the participation, rights, and obligations of each group in any particular works. Only by some such method can early construction be secured.

Water Power

Along with the development of navigation should go every possible encouragement for the development of our water power. While steam still plays a dominant part, this is more and more becoming an era of electricity. Once installed, the cost is moderate, has not tended greatly to increase, and is entirely free from the unavoidable dirt and disagreeable features attendant upon the burning of coal. Every facility should be extended for the connection of the various units into a superpower plant, capable at all times of a current increasing uniformity over the entire system.

Railroads

The railroads throughout the country are in a fair state of prosperity. Their service is good and their supply of cars is abundant. Their condition would be improved and the public better served by a system of consolidations. I recommend that the Congress authorize such consolidations under the supervision of the Interstate Commerce Commission, with power to approve or disapprove when proposed parts are excluded or new parts added. I am informed that the railroad managers and their employees have reached a substantial agreement as to what legislation is necessary to regulate and improve their relationship. Whenever they bring forward such proposals, which seem sufficient also to protect the interests of the public, they should be enacted into law.

It is gratifying to report that both the railroad managers and railroad employees are providing boards for the mutual adjustment of differences in harmony with the principles of conference, conciliation, and arbitration. The solution of their problems ought to be an example to all other industries. Those who ask the protections of civilization should be ready to use the methods of civilization.

A strike in modern industry has many of the aspects of war in the modern world. It injures labor and it injures capital. If the industry involved is a basic one, it reduces the necessary economic surplus and, increasing the cost of living, it injures the economic welfare and general comfort of the whole people. It also involves a deeper cost. It tends to embitter and divide the community into warring classes and thus weakens the unity and power of our national life.

Labor can make no permanent gains at the cost of the general welfare. All the victories won by organized labor in the past generation have been won through the support of public opinion. The manifest inclination of the managers and employees of the railroads to adopt a policy of action in harmony with these principles marks a new epoch in our industrial life.

Outlying Possessions

The time has come for careful investigation of the expenditures and success of the laws by which we have undertaken to administer our outlying possessions. A very large amount of money is being expended for administration in Alaska. It appears so far out of proportion to the number of inhabitants and the amount of production as to indicate cause for thorough investigation. Likewise consideration should be given to the experience under the law which governs the Philippines. From such reports as reach me there are indications that more authority should be given to the Governor General, so that he will not be so dependent upon the local legislative body to render effective our efforts to set an example of the sound administration and good government, which is so necessary for the preparation of the Philippine people for self-government under ultimate independence. If they are to be trained in these arts, it is our duty to provide for them the best that there is.

Retirement of Judges

The act of March 3, 1911, ought to be amended so that the term of years of service of judges of any court of the United States requisite for retirement with pay shall be computed to include not only continuous but aggregate service.

Mothers' Aid

The Government ought always to be alert on the side of the humanities. It ought to encourage provisions for economic justice for the defenseless. It ought to extend its relief through its national and local agencies, as may be appropriate in each case, to the suffering and the needy. It ought to be charitable.

Although more than 40 of our States have enacted measures in aid of motherhood, the District of Columbia is still without such a law. A carefully considered bill will be presented, which ought to have most thoughtful consideration in order that the Congress may adopt a measure which will be hereafter a model for all parts of the Union.

Civil Service

In 1883 the Congress passed the civil service act, which from a modest beginning of 14,000 employees has grown until there are now 425,000 in the classified service. This has removed the clerical force of the Nation from the wasteful effects of the spoils system and made it more stable and efficient. The time has come to consider classifying all postmasters, collectors of customs, collectors of internal revenue, and prohibition agents, by an act covering in those at present in office, except when otherwise provided by Executive order.

The necessary statistics are now being gathered to form the basis of a valuation of the civil service retirement fund based on current conditions of the service. It is confidently expected that this valuation will be completed in time to be made available to the Congress during the present session. It will afford definite knowledge of existing and future liabilities under the present law and determination of liabilities under any proposed change in the present law. We should have this information before creating further obligations for retirement annuities which will become liabilities to be met in the future from the money of the taxpayer.

The classification act of 1923, with the subsequent legislative action providing for adjustment of the compensation of field service positions, has operated materially to improve employment conditions in the Federal service. The administration of the act is in the hands of an impartial board, functioning without the necessity of a direct appropriation. It would be inadvisable at this time to place in other hands the administration of this act.

Federal Trade Commission

The proper function of the Federal Trade Commission is to supervise and correct those practices in commerce which are detrimental to fair competition. In this it performs a useful function and should be continued and supported. It was designed also to be a help to honest business. In my message to the Sixty-eighth Congress I recommended that changes in the procedure then existing be made. Since then the commission by its own action has reformed its rules, giving greater speed and economy in the disposal of its cases and full opportunity for those accused to be heard. These changes are improvements and, if necessary, provision should be made for their permanency.

Reorganization

No final action has yet been taken on the measure providing for the reorganization of the various departments. I therefore suggest that this measure, which will be of great benefit to the efficient and economical administration of the business of the Government, be brought forward and passed.

The Negro

Nearly one-tenth of our population consists of the Negro race. The progress which they have made in all the arts of civilization in the last 60 years is almost beyond belief. Our country has no more loyal citizens. But they do still need sympathy, kindness, and helpfulness. They need reassurance that the requirements of the Government and society to deal out to them even-handed justice will be met. They should be protected from all violence and supported in the peaceable enjoyment of the fruits of their labor. Those who do violence to them should be punished for their crimes. No other course of action is worthy of the American people.

Our country has many elements in its population, many different modes of thinking and living, all of which are striving in their own way to be loyal to the high ideals worthy of the crown of American citizenship. It is fundamental of our institutions that they seek to guarantee to all our inhabitants the right to live their own lives under the protection of the public law. This does not include any license to injure others materially, physically, morally, to incite revolution, or to violate the established customs which have long had the sanction of enlightened society.

But it does mean the full right to liberty and equality before the law without distinction of race or creed. This condition can not be granted to others, or enjoyed by ourselves, except by the application of the principle of broadest tolerance. Bigotry is only another name for slavery. It reduces to serfdom not only those against whom it is directed, but also those who seek to apply it. An enlarged freedom can only be secured by the application of the golden rule. No other utterance ever presented such a practical rule of life.

Conclusion

It is apparent that we are reaching into an era of great general prosperity. It will continue only so long as we shall use it properly. After all, there is but a fixed quantity of wealth in this country at any fixed time. The only way that we can all secure more of it is to create more. The element of time enters into production. If the people have sufficient moderation and contentment to be willing to improve their condition by the process of enlarging production, eliminating waste, and distributing equitably, a prosperity almost without limit lies before us. If the people are to be dominated by selfishness, seeking immediate riches by nonproductive speculation and by wasteful quarreling over the returns from industry, they will be confronted by the inevitable results of depression and privation. If they will continue industrious and thrifty, contented with fair wages and moderate profits, and the returns which accrue from the development of our natural resources, our prosperity will extend itself indefinitely.

In all your deliberations you should remember that the purpose of legislation is to translate principles into action. It is an effort to have our country be better by doing better. Because the thoughts and ways of people are firmly fixed and not easily changed, the field within which immediate improvement can be secured is very narrow. Legislation can provide opportunity. Whether it is taken advantage of or not depends upon the people themselves. The Government of the United States has been created by the people. It is solely responsible to them. It will be most successful if it is conducted solely for their benefit. All its efforts would be of little avail unless they brought more justice, more enlightenment, more happiness and prosperity into the home. This means an opportunity to observe religion, secure education, and earn a living under a reign of law and order. It is the growth and improvement of the material and spiritual life of the Nation. We shall not be able to gain these ends merely by our own action. If they come at all, it will be because we have been willing to work in harmony with the abiding purpose of a Divine Providence.

Calvin Coolidge, 1925–1929

Annual Message to Congress
December 7, 1926

Calvin Coolidge's fourth State of the Union message was, once again, delivered during a time of "general peace and prosperity" for the United States. In the midterm elections of 1926, the president's Republican Party held control of both the House and Senate, retaining the GOP grip on power that characterized the booming 1920s.

Coolidge's mantra was one of government frugality, including tax reductions, debt reduction, and prudent federal spending. In this message, which was written rather than delivered in person to Congress, the president reiterated many of the same themes he had used in previous messages regarding the federal budget. "Nothing is more destructive of the progress of the nation than government extravagance," he said. He urged Congress to make only the most necessary commitments of government money.

One sector of the economy that was not progressing as well was agriculture. In his message, Coolidge listed a series of remedial measures taken during his administration and that of his predecessor, Warren Harding. Among those he cited were cooperative marketing legislation and enlargement of Farm Loan Board loans. He also advocated revisions in the agricultural transportation system. The president, however, would twice veto legislation that would have given farmers parity—representing a certain price level—for various crops.

Another issue the president dwelt on in his message was the regulation of radio. KDKA in Pittsburgh was the first station to begin broadcasting, back in 1920, and Coolidge had made good use of the burgeoning new medium. His State of the Union message of 1923 and his inaugural address of 1925 were the first such events to be broadcast. Coolidge described a chaotic situation sparked by the increasing number of new radio stations. Coolidge noted that Congress had been working on legislation to regulate radio, and in 1927 the Radio Act, which created a Federal Radio Commission, was enacted.

Overall, the 1920s was an era of minimalist government in many ways. Coolidge epitomized that trend. In his message, he argued that local and state governments should take the lead in regulating business, and that federal action should be a last resort. But he did see a number of needs that the federal government should appropriately address. He supported a variety of government programs, including aid to farmers, disaster relief in the wake of a storm in Florida, and water projects.

Coolidge did not approve of an interventionist foreign policy, although he did support U.S. participation in various international negotiations and conferences. In his 1926 address, he discussed the U.S. role in negotiations involving trade relations with China, as well as talks on international disarmament.

M̲embers of the Congress:

In reporting to the Congress the state of the Union, I find it impossible to characterize it other than one of general peace and prosperity. In some quarters our diplomacy is vexed with difficult and as yet unsolved problems, but nowhere are we met with armed conflict. If some occupations and areas are not flourishing, in none does there remain any acute chronic depression. What the country requires is not so much new policies as a steady continuation of those which are already being crowned with such abundant success. It can not be too often repeated that in common with all the world we are engaged in liquidating the war.

In the present short session no great amount of new legislation is possible, but in order to comprehend what is most desirable some survey of our general situation is necessary. A large amount of time is consumed in the passage of appropriation bills. If each Congress in its opening session would make appropriations to continue for two years, very much time would be saved which could either be devoted to a consideration of the general needs of the country or would result in decreasing the work of legislation.

Economy

Our present state of prosperity has been greatly promoted by three important causes, one of which is economy, resulting in reduction and reform in national taxation. Another is the elimination of many kinds of waste. The third is a general raising of the standards of efficiency. This combination has brought the perfectly astonishing result of a reduction in the index price of commodities and an increase in the index rate of wages. We have secured a lowering of the cost to produce and a raising of the ability to consume. Prosperity resulting from these causes rests on the securest of all foundations. It gathers strength from its own progress.

In promoting this progress the chief part which the National Government plays lies in the field of economy. Whatever doubts may have been entertained as to the necessity of this policy and the beneficial results which would accrue from it to all the people of the Nation, its wisdom must now be considered thoroughly demonstrated. It may not have appeared to be a novel or perhaps brilliant conception, but it has turned out to be preeminently sound. It has not failed to work. It has surely brought results. It does not have to be excused as a temporary expedient adopted as the lesser evil to remedy some abuse, it is not a palliative seeking to treat symptoms, but a major operation for the eradication at the source of a large number of social diseases.

Nothing is easier than the expenditure of public money. It does not appear to belong to anybody. The temptation is overwhelming to bestow it on somebody. But the results of extravagance are ruinous. The property of the country, like the freedom of the country, belongs to the people of the country. They have not empowered their Government to take a dollar of it except for a necessary public purpose. But if the Constitution conferred such right, sound economics would forbid it. Nothing is more destructive of the progress of the Nation than government extravagance. It means an increase in the burden of taxation, dissipation of the returns from enterprise, a decrease in the real value of wages, with ultimate stagnation and decay. The whole theory of our institutions is based on the liberty and independence of the individual. He is dependent on himself for support and therefore entitled to the rewards of his own industry. He is not to be deprived of what he earns that others may be benefited by what they do not earn. What he saves through his private effort is not to be wasted by Government extravagance.

Our national activities have become so vast that it is necessary to scrutinize each item of public expenditure if we are to apply the principle of economy. At the last session we made an immediate increase in the annual budget of more than $100,000,000 in benefits conferred on the veterans of three wars, public buildings, and river and harbor improvement. Many projects are being broached requiring further large outlays. I am convinced that it would be greatly for the welfare of the country if we avoid at the present session all commitments except those of the most pressing nature. From a reduction of the debt and taxes will accrue a wider benefit to all the people of this country than from embarking on any new enterprise. When our war debt is decreased we shall have resources for expansion. Until that is accomplished we should confine ourselves to expenditures of the most urgent necessity.

The Department of Commerce has performed a most important function in making plans and securing support of all kinds of national enterprise for the elimination of waste. Efficiency has been greatly promoted through good management and the constantly increasing cooperation of the wage earners throughout the whole realm of private business. It is my opinion that this whole development has been predicated on the foundation of a protective tariff.

Tax Reduction

As a result of economy of administration by the Executive and of appropriation by the Congress, the end of this fiscal year will leave a surplus in the Treasury estimated at $383,000,000. Unless otherwise ordered, such surplus is used for the retirement of the war debt. A bond which can be retired to-day for 100 cents will cost the people 104¼ cents to retire a year from now. While I favor a speedy reduction of the debt as already required by law and in accordance with the promises made to the holders of our Liberty bonds when they were issued, there is no reason why a balanced portion of surplus revenue should not be applied to a reduction of taxation. It can not be repeated too often that the enormous revenues of this Nation could not be collected without becoming a charge on all the people whether or not they directly pay taxes. Everyone who is paying for the bare necessities of food and shelter and clothing, without considering the better things of life, is indirectly paying a national tax. The nearly 20,000,000 owners of securities, the additional scores of millions of holders of insurance policies and depositors in savings banks, are all paying a national tax. Millions of individuals and corporations are making a direct contribution to the National Treasury which runs from 1½ to 25 per cent of their income, besides a number of special requirements, like automobile and admission taxes. Whenever the state of the Treasury will permit, I believe in a reduction of taxation. I think the taxpayers are entitled to it. But I am not advocating tax reduction merely for the benefit of the taxpayer; I am advocating it for the benefit of the country.

If it appeared feasible, I should welcome permanent tax reduction at this time. The estimated surplus, however, for June 30, 1928, is not much larger than is required in a going business of nearly $4,000,000,000. We have had but a few months' experience under the present revenue act and shall need to know what is developed by the returns of income produced under it, which are not required to be made until about the time this session terminates, and what the economic probabilities of the country are in the latter part of 1927, before we can reach any justifiable conclusion as to permanent tax reduction. Moreover the present surplus results from many nonrecurrent items. Meantime, it is possible to grant some real relief by a simple measure making reductions in the payments which accrue on the 15th of March and June, 1927. I am very strongly of the conviction that this is so much a purely business matter that it ought not to be dealt with in a partisan spirit. The Congress has already set the notable example of treating tax problems without much reference to party, which might well be continued. What I desire to advocate most earnestly is relief for the country from unnecessary tax burdens. We can not secure that if we stop to engage in a partisan controversy. As I do not think any change in the special taxes, or tiny permanent reduction is practical, I therefore urge both parties of the House Ways and Means Committee to agree on a bill granting the temporary relief which I have indicated. Such a reduction would directly affect millions of taxpayers, release large sums for investment in new enterprise, stimulating industrial production and agricultural consumption, and indirectly benefiting every family in the whole country. These are my convictions stated with full knowledge that it is for the Congress to decide whether they judge it best to make such a reduction or leave the surplus for the present year to be applied to retirement of the war debt. That also is eventually tax reduction.

Protective Tariff

It is estimated that customs receipts for the present fiscal year will exceed $615,000,000, the largest which were ever secured from that source. The value of our imports for the last fiscal year was $4,466,000,000, an increase of more than 71 per cent since the present tariff law went into effect. Of these imports about 65 per cent, or, roughly, $2,900,000,000, came in free of duty, which means that the United States affords a duty-free market to other countries almost equal in value to the total imports of Germany and greatly exceeding the total imports of France. We have admitted a greater volume of free imports than any other country except England.

We are, therefore, levying duties on about $1,550,000,000 of imports. Nearly half of this, or $700,000,000, is subject to duties for the protection of agriculture and have their origin in countries other than Europe. They substantially increased the prices received by our farmers for their produce. About $300,000,000 more is represented by luxuries such as costly rugs, furs, precious stones, etc. This leaves only about $550,000,000 of our imports under a schedule of duties which is in general under consideration when there is discussion of lowering the tariff. While the duties on this small portion, representing only about 12 per cent of our imports, undoubtedly represent the difference between a fair degree of prosperity or marked depression to many of our industries and the difference between good pay and steady work or wide unemployment to many of our wage earners, it is impossible to conceive how other countries or our own importers could be greatly benefited if these duties are reduced. Those who are starting an agitation for a reduction of tariff duties, partly at least for the benefit of those to whom money has been lent abroad, ought to know that there does not seem to be a very large field within the area of our imports in which probable reductions would be advantageous to foreign goods. Those who wish to benefit foreign producers are much more likely to secure that result by continuing the present enormous purchasing power which comes from our prosperity that has increased our imports over 71 per cent in four years than from any advantages that are likely to accrue from a general tariff reduction.

Agriculture

The important place which agriculture holds in the economic and social life of the Nation can not be overestimated. The National Government is justified in putting forth every effort to make the open country a desirable place to live. No condition meets this requirement which fails to supply a fair return on labor expended and capital invested. While some localities and some particular crops furnish exceptions, in general agriculture is continuing to make progress in recovering from the depression of 1921 and 1922. Animal products and food products are in a more encouraging position, while cotton, due to the high prices of past years supplemented by ideal weather conditions, has been stimulated to a point of temporary over production. Acting on the request of the cotton growing interests, I appointed a committee to assist in carrying out their plans. As a result of this cooperation sufficient funds have been pledged to finance the storage and carrying of 4,000,000 bales of cotton. Whether those who own the cotton are willing to put a part of their stock into this plan depends on themselves. The Federal Government has cooperated in providing ample facilities. No method of meeting the situation would be adequate which does not contemplate a reduction of about one-third in the acreage for the coming year. The responsibility for making the plan effective lies with those who own and finance cotton and cotton lands.

The Department of Agriculture estimates the net income of agriculture for the year 1920–21 at only $375,000,000; for 1924–25, $2,656,000,000; for 1925–26, $2,757,000,000. This increase has been brought about in part by the method already referred to, of Federal tax reduction, the elimination of waste, and increased efficiency in industry. The wide gap that existed a few years ago between the index price of agricultural products and the index price of other products has been gradually closing up, though the recent depression in cotton has somewhat enlarged it. Agriculture had on the whole been going higher while industry had been growing lower. Industrial and commercial activities, being carried on for the most part by corporations, are taxed at a much higher rate than farming, which is carried on by individuals. This will inevitably make industrial commodity costs high while war taxation lasts. It is because of this circumstance that national tax reduction has a very large indirect benefit upon the farmer, though it can not relieve him from the very great burden of the local taxes which he pays directly. We have practically relieved the farmer of any Federal income tax.

There is agreement on all sides that some portions of our agricultural industry have lagged behind other industries in recovery from the war and that further improvement in methods of marketing of agricultural products is most desirable. There is belief also that the Federal Government can further contribute to these ends beyond the many helpful measures taken during the last five years through the different acts of Congress for advancing the interests of the farmers.

The packers and stockyards act,

Establishing of the intermediate credit banks for agricultural purposes,

The Purnell Act for agricultural research,

The Capper-Volstead Cooperative Marketing Act,

The cooperative marketing act of 1926,

Amendments to the warehousing act,

The enlargement of the activities of the Department of Agriculture,

Enlargement of the scope of loans by the Farm Loan Board,

The tariff on agricultural products,

The large Federal expenditure in improvement of waterways and highways,

The reduction of Federal taxes, in all comprise a great series of governmental actions in the advancement of the special interest of agriculture.

In determination of what further measures may be undertaken it seems to me there are certain pitfalls which must be avoided and our test in avoiding them should be to avoid disaster to the farmer himself.

Acting upon my recommendation, the Congress has ordered the interstate Commerce Commission to investigate the freight-rate structure, directing that such changes shall be made in freight rates as will promote freedom of movement of agricultural products. Railroad consolidation which I am advocating would also result in a situation where rates could be made more advantageous for farm produce, as has recently been done in the revision of rates on fertilizers in the South. Additional benefit will accrue from the development of our inland waterways. The Mississippi River system carries a commerce of over 50,000,000 tons at a saving of nearly $18,000,000 annually. The Inland Waterways Corporation operates boats on 2,500 miles of navigable streams and through its relation with 165 railroads carries freight into and out of 45 States of the Union. During the past six months it has handled over 1,000,000 bushels of grain monthly and by its lower freight rates has raised the price of such grain to the farmer probably 2 1/2 cents to 3 cents a bushel. The highway system on which the Federal Government expends about $85,000,000 a year is of vital importance to the rural regions.

The advantages to be derived from a more comprehensive and less expensive system of transportation for agriculture ought to be supplemented by provision for an adequate supply of fertilizer at a lower cost than it is at present obtainable. This advantage we are attempting to secure by the proposed development at Muscle Shoals, and there are promising experiments being made in synthetic chemistry for the production of nitrates.

A survey should be made of the relation of Government grazing lands to the livestock industry. Additional legislation is desirable more definitely to establish the place of grazing in the administration of the national forests, properly subordinated to their functions of producing timber and conserving the water supply. Over 180,000,000 acres of grazing lands are still pastured as commons in the public domain with little or no regulation. This has made their use so uncertain that it has contributed greatly to the instability of the livestock industry. Very little of this land is suited to settlement or private ownership. Some plan ought to be adopted for its use in grazing, corresponding broadly to that already successfully applied to the national forests.

The development of sound and strong cooperative associations is of fundamental importance to our agriculture. It is encouraging to note, therefore, that a vigorous and healthy growth in the cooperative movement is continuing. Cooperative associations reporting to the Department of Agriculture at the end of 1925 had on their membership rolls a total of 2,700,000 producers. Their total business in 1925 amounted to approximately $2,400,000,000, compared with $635,800,000 in 1915. Legislative action to assist cooperative associations and supplement their efforts was passed at the last session of Congress. Important credit measures were also provided by Congress in 1923 which have been of inestimable value to the cooperative associations. Although the Federal credit agencies have served agriculture well, I think it may be possible to broaden and strengthen the service of these institutions.

Attention is again directed to the surplus problem of agriculture by the present cotton situation. Surpluses often affect prices of various farm commodities in a disastrous manner, and the problem urgently demands a solution. Discussions both in and out of Congress during the past few years have given us a better understanding of the subject, and it is my hope that out of the various proposals made the basis will be found for a sound and effective solution upon which agreement can be reached. In my opinion cooperative marketing associations will be important aids to the ultimate solution of the problem. It may well be, however, that additional measures will be needed to supplement their efforts. I believe all will agree that such measures should not conflict with the best interests of the cooperatives, but rather assist and strengthen them. In working out this problem to any sound conclusion it is necessary to avoid putting the Government into the business of production or marketing or attempting to enact legislation for the purpose of price fixing. The farmer does not favor any attempted remedies that partake of these elements. He has a sincere and candid desire for assistance. If matched by an equally sincere and candid consideration of the different remedies proposed, a sound measure of relief ought to result. It is unfortunate that no general agreement has been reached by the various agricultural interests upon any of the proposed remedies. Out of the discussion of various proposals which can be had before the Committees of Agriculture some measure ought to be perfected which would be generally satisfactory.

Due to the emergency arising from a heavy tropical storm in southern Florida, I authorized the Secretary of Agriculture to use certain funds in anticipation of legislation to enable the farmers in that region to plant their crops. The department will present a bill ratifying the loans which were made for this purpose.

Federal legislation has been adopted authorizing the cooperation of the Government with States and private owners in the protection of forest lands from fire. This preventive measure is of such great importance that I have recommended for it an increased appropriation.

Another preventive measure of great economic and sanitary importance is the eradication of tuberculosis in cattle. Active work is now in progress in one-fourth of the counties of the United States to secure this result. Over 12,000,000 cattle have been under treatment, and the average degree of infection has fallen from 4.9 per cent to 2.8 per cent. The Federal Government is making substantial expenditures for this purpose.

Serious damage is threatened to the corn crop by the European corn borer. Since 1917 it has spread from eastern New England westward into Indiana and now covers about 100,000 square miles. It is one of the most formidable pests because it spreads rapidly and is exceedingly difficult of control. It has assumed a menace that is of national magnitude and warrants the Federal Government in extending its cooperation to the State and local agencies which are attempting to prevent its further spread and secure its eradication.

The whole question of agriculture needs most careful consideration. In the past few years the Government has given this subject more attention than any other and has held more consultations in relation to it than on any other subject. While the Government is not to be blamed for failure to perform the impossible, the agricultural regions are entitled to know that they have its constant solicitude and sympathy. Many of the farmers are burdened with debts and taxes which they are unable to carry. We are expending in this country many millions of dollars each year to increase farm production. We ought now to put more emphasis on the question of farm marketing. If a sound solution of a permanent nature can be found for this problem, the Congress ought not to hesitate to adopt it.

Development of Water Resources

In previous messages I have referred to the national importance of the proper development of our water resources. The great projects of extension of the Mississippi system, the protection and development of the lower Colorado River, are before Congress, and I have previously commented upon them. I favor the necessary legislation to expedite these projects. Engineering studies are being made for connecting the Great Lakes with the North Atlantic either through an all-American canal or by way of the St. Lawrence River. These reports will undoubtedly be before the Congress during its present session. It is unnecessary to dwell upon the great importance of such a waterway not only to our mid-continental basin but to the commerce and development of practically the whole Nation. Our river and harbor improvement should be continued in accordance with the present policy. Expenditure of this character is compatible with economy; it is in the nature of capital investment. Work should proceed on the basic trunk lines if this work is to be a success. If the country will be content to be moderate and patient and permit improvements to be made where they will do the greatest general good, rather than insisting on expenditures at this time on secondary projects, our internal Waterways can be made a success. If proposed legislation results in a gross manifestation of local jealousies and selfishness, this program can not be carried out. Ultimately we can take care of extensions, but our first effort should be confined to the main arteries.

Our inland commerce has been put to great inconvenience and expense by reason of the lowering of the water level of the Great Lakes. This is an international problem on which competent engineers are making reports. Out of their study it is expected that a feasible method will be developed for raising the level to provide relief for our commerce and supply water for drainage. Whenever a practical plan is presented it ought to be speedily adopted.

Reclamation

It is increasingly evident that the Federal Government must in the future take a leading part in the impounding of water for conservation with incidental power for the development of the irrigable lands of the and region. The unused waters of the West are found mainly in large rivers. Works to store and distribute these have such magnitude and cost that they are not attractive to private enterprise. Water is the irreplaceable natural resource. Its precipitation can not be increased. Its storage on the higher reaches of streams, to meet growing needs, to be used repeatedly as it flows toward the seas, is a practical and prudent business policy.

The United States promises to follow the course of older irrigation countries, where recent important irrigation developments have been carried out as national undertakings. It is gratifying, therefore, that conditions on Federal reclamation projects have become satisfactory. The gross value of crops grown with water from project works increased from $110,000,000 in 1924 to $131,000,000 in 1925. The adjustments made last year by Congress relieved irrigators from paying construction costs on unprofitable land, and by so doing inspired new hope and confidence in ability to meet the payments required. Construction payments by water users last year were the largest in the history of the bureau.

The anticipated reclamation fund will be fully absorbed for a number of years in the completion of old projects and the construction of projects inaugurated in the past three years. We should, however, continue to investigate and study the possibilities of a carefully planned development of promising projects, logically of governmental concern because of their physical magnitude, immense cost, and the interstate and international problems involved. Only in this way may we be fully prepared to meet intelligently the needs of our fast-growing population in the years to come.

Transportation

It would be difficult to conceive of any modern activity which contributes more to the necessities and conveniences of life than transportation. Without it our present agricultural production and practically all of our commerce would be completely prostrated. One of the large contributing causes to the present highly satisfactory state of our economic condition is the prompt and dependable service, surpassing all our previous records, rendered by the railroads. This power has been fostered by the spirit of cooperation between Federal and State regulatory commissions. To render this service more efficient and effective and to promote a more scientific regulation, the process of valuing railroad properties should be simplified and the primary valuations should be completed as rapidly as possible. The problem of rate reduction would be much simplified by a process of railroad consolidations. This principle has already been adopted as Federal law. Experience has shown that a more effective method must be provided. Studies have already been made and legislation introduced seeking to promote this end. It would be of great advantage if it could be taken up at once and speedily enacted. The railroad systems of the country and the convenience of all the people are waiting on this important decision.

Merchant Marine

It is axiomatic that no agricultural and industrial country can get the full benefit of its own advantages without a merchant marine. We have been proceeding under the act of Congress that contemplates the establishment of trade routes to be ultimately transferred to private ownership and operation. Due to temporary conditions abroad and at home we have a large demand just now for certain types of freight vessels. Some suggestion has been made for new construction. I do not feel that we are yet warranted in entering that field. Such ships as we might build could not be sold after they are launched for anywhere near what they would cost. We have expended over $250,000,000 out of the public Treasury in recent years to make up the losses of operation, not counting the depreciation or any cost whatever of our capital investment. The great need of our merchant marine is not for more ships but for more freight.

Our merchants are altogether too indifferent about using American ships for the transportation of goods which they send abroad or bring home. Some of our vessels necessarily need repairs, which should be made. I do not believe that the operation of our fleet is as economical and efficient as it could be made if placed under a single responsible head, leaving the Shipping Board free to deal with general matters of policy and regulation.

Radio Legislation

The Department of Commerce has for some years urgently presented the necessity for further legislation in order to protect radio listeners from interference between broadcasting stations and to carry out other regulatory functions. Both branches of Congress at the last session passed enactments intended to effect such regulation, but the two bills yet remain to be brought into agreement and final passage.

Due to decisions of the courts, the authority of the department under the law of 1912 has broken down; many more stations have been operating than can be accommodated within the limited number of wave lengths available; further stations are in course of construction; many stations have departed from the scheme of allocation set down by the department, and the whole service of this most important public function has drifted into such chaos as seems likely, if not remedied, to destroy its great value. I most urgently recommend that this legislation should be speedily enacted.

I do not believe it is desirable to set up further independent agencies in the Government. Rather I believe it advisable to entrust the important functions of deciding who shall exercise the privilege of radio transmission and under what conditions, the assigning of wave lengths and determination of power, to a board to be assembled whenever action on such questions becomes necessary. There should be right of appeal to the courts from the decisions of such board. The administration of the decisions of the board and the other features of regulation and promotion of radio in the public interest, together with scientific research, should remain in the Department of Commerce. Such an arrangement makes for more expert, more efficient, and more economical administration that an independent agency or board, whose duties, after initial stages, require but little attention, in which administrative functions are confused with semijudicial functions and from which of necessity there must be greatly increased personnel and expenditure.

The Wage Earner

The great body of our people are made up of wage earners. Several hundred thousands of them are on the pay rolls of the United States Government. Their condition very largely is fixed by legislation. We have recently provided increases in compensation under a method of reclassification and given them the advantage of a liberal retirement system as a support for their declining years. Most of them are under the merit system, which is a guaranty of their intelligence, and the efficiency of their service is a demonstration of their loyalty. The Federal Government should continue to set a good example for all other employers.

In the industries the condition of the wage earner has steadily improved. The 12-hour day is almost entirely unknown. Skilled labor is well compensated. But there are unfortunately a multitude of workers who have not yet come to share in the general prosperity of the Nation. Both the public authorities and private enterprise should be solicitous to advance the welfare of this class. The Federal Government has been seeking to secure this end through a protective tariff, through restrictive immigration, through requiring safety devices for the prevention of accidents, through the granting of workman's compensation, through civilian vocational rehabilitation and education, through employment information bureaus, and through such humanitarian relief as was provided in the maternity and infancy legislation. It is a satisfaction to report that a more general condition of contentment exists among wage earners and the country is more free from labor disputes than it has been for years. While restrictive immigration has been adopted in part for the benefit of the wage earner, and in its entirety for the benefit of the country, it ought not to cause a needless separation of families and dependents from their natural source of support contrary to the dictates of humanity.

Bituminous Coal

No progress appears to have been made within large areas of the bituminous coal industry toward creation of voluntary machinery by which greater assurance can be given to the public of peaceful adjustment of wage difficulties such as has been accomplished in the anthracite industry. This bituminous industry is one of primary necessity and bears a great responsibility to the Nation for continuity of supplies. As the wage agreements in the unionized section of the industry expire on April 1 next, and as conflicts may result which may imperil public interest, and have for many years often called for action of the Executive in protection of the public, I again recommend the passage of such legislation as will assist the Executive in dealing with such emergencies through a special temporary board of conciliation and mediation and through administrative agencies for the purpose of distribution of coal and protection of the consumers of coal from profiteering. At present the Executive is not only without authority to act but is actually prohibited by law from making any expenditure to meet the emergency of a coal famine.

Judiciary

The Federal courts hold a high position in the administration of justice in the world. While individual judicial officers have sometimes been subjected to just criticism, the courts as a whole have maintained an exceedingly high standard. The Congress may well consider the question of supplying fair salaries and conferring upon the Supreme Court the same rule-making power on the law side of the district courts that they have always possessed on the equity side. A bill is also pending providing for retirement after a certain number of years of service, although they have not been consecutive, which should have your favorable consideration. These faithful servants of the Government are about the last that remain to be provided for in the postwar readjustments.

Banking

There has been pending in Congress for nearly three years banking legislation to clarify the national bank act and reasonably to increase the powers of the national banks. I believe that within the limitation of sound banking principles Congress should now and for the future place the national banks upon a fair equality with their competitors, the State banks, and I trust that means may be found so that the differences on branch-banking legislation between the Senate and the House of Representatives may be settled along sound lines and the legislation promptly enacted.

It would be difficult to overestimate the service which the Federal reserve system has already rendered to the country. It is necessary only to recall the chaotic condition of our banking organization at the time the Federal reserve system was put into operation. The old system consisted of a vast number of independent banking units, with scattered bank reserves which never could be mobilized in times of greatest need. In spite of vast banking resources, there was no coordination of reserves or any credit elasticity. As a consequence, a strain was felt even during crop-moving periods and when it was necessary to meet other seasonal and regularly recurring needs.

The Federal reserve system is not a panacea for all economic or financial ills. It can not prevent depression in certain industries which are experiencing overexpansion of production or contraction of their markets. Its business is to furnish adequate credit and currency facilities. This it has succeeded in doing, both during the war and in the more difficult period of deflation and readjustment which followed. It enables us to look to the future with confidence and to make plans far ahead, based on the belief that the Federal reserve system will exercise a steadying influence on credit conditions and thereby prevent tiny sudden or severe reactions from the period of prosperity which we are now enjoying. In order that these plans may go forward, action should be taken at the present session on the question of renewing the banks' charters and thereby insuring a continuation of the policies and present usefulness of the Federal reserve system.

Federal Regulation

I am in favor of reducing, rather than expanding, Government bureaus which seek to regulate and control the business activities of the people. Everyone is aware that abuses exist and will exist so long as we are limited by human imperfections. Unfortunately, human nature can not be changed by an act of the legislature. When practically the sole remedy for many evils lies in the necessity of the people looking out for themselves and reforming their own abuses, they will find that they are relying on a false security if the Government assumes to hold out the promise that it is looking out for them and providing reforms for them. This principle is preeminently applicable to the National Government. It is too much assumed that because an abuse exists it is the business of the National Government to provide a remedy. The presumption should be that it is the business of local and State governments. Such national action results in encroaching upon the salutary independence of the States and by undertaking to supersede their natural authority fills the land with bureaus and departments which are undertaking to do what it is impossible for them to accomplish and brings our whole system of government into disrespect and disfavor. We ought to maintain high standards. We ought to punish wrongdoing. Society has not only the privilege but the absolute duty of protecting itself and its individuals. But we can not accomplish this end by adopting a wrong method. Permanent success lies in local, rather than national action. Unless the locality rises to its own requirements, there is an almost irresistible impulse for the National Government to intervene. The States and the Nation should both realize that such action is to be adopted only as a last resort.

The Negro

The social well-being of our country requires our constant effort for the amelioration of race prejudice and the extension to all elements of equal opportunity and equal protection under the laws which are guaranteed by the Constitution. The Federal Government especially is charged with this obligation in behalf of the colored people of the Nation. Not only their remarkable progress, their devotion and their loyalty, but, our duty to ourselves under our claim that we are an enlightened people requires us to use all our power to protect them from the crime of lynching. Although violence of this kind has very much decreased, while any of it remains we can not justify neglecting to make every effort to eradicate it by law.

The education of the colored race under Government encouragement is proceeding successfully and ought to have continuing support. An increasing need exists for properly educated and trained medical skill to be devoted to the service of this race.

Insular Possessions

This Government holds in sacred trusteeship islands which it has acquired in the East and West Indies. In all of them the people are more prosperous than at any previous time. A system of good roads, education, and general development is in progress. The people are better governed than ever before and generally content.

In the Philippine Islands Maj. Gen. Leonard Wood has been Governor General for five years and has administered his office with tact and ability greatly to the success of the Filipino people. These are a proud and sensitive race, who are making such progress with our cooperation that we can view the results of this experiment with great satisfaction. As we are attempting to assist this race toward self-government, we should look upon their wishes with great respect, granting their requests immediately when they are right, yet maintaining a frank firmness in refusing when they are wrong. We shall measure their progress in no small part by their acceptance of the terms of the organic law under which the islands are governed and their faithful observance of its provisions. Need exists for clarifying the duties of the auditor and declaring them to be what everyone had supposed they were. We have placed our own expenditures under the supervision of the Comptroller General. It is not likely that the expenditures in the Philippine Islands need less supervision than our own. The Governor General is hampered in his selection of subordinates by the necessity of securing a confirmation, which has oftentimes driven him to the expediency of using Army officers in work for which civilian experts would be much better fitted. Means should be provided for this and such other purposes as he may require out of the revenue which this Government now turns back to the Philippine treasury.

In order that these possessions might suffer no seeming neglect, I have recently sent Col. Carmi A. Thompson to the islands to make a survey in cooperation with the Governor General to suggest what might be done to improve conditions. Later, I may make a more extended report including recommendations. The economic development of the islands is very important. They ought not to be turned back to the people until they are both politically fitted for self-government and economically independent. Large areas are adaptable to the production of rubber. No one contemplates any time in the future either under the present or a more independent form of government when we should not assume some responsibility for their defense. For their economic advantage, for the employment of their people, and as a contribution to our power of defense which could not be carried on without rubber, I believe this industry should be encouraged. It is especially adapted to the Filipino people themselves, who might cultivate it individually on a small acreage. It could be carried on extensively by American capital in a way to furnish employment at good wages. I am opposed to the promotion of any policy that does not provide for absolute freedom on the part of the wage earners and do not think we should undertake to give power for large holdings of land in the islands against the opposition of the people of the locality. Any development of the islands must be solely with the first object of benefiting the people of the islands. At an early day, these possessions should be taken out from under all military control and administered entirely on the civil side of government.

National Defense

Our policy of national defense is not one of making war, but of insuring peace. The land and sea force of America, both in its domestic and foreign implications, is distinctly a peace force. It is an arm of the police power to guarantee order and the execution of the law at home and security to our citizens abroad. No self-respecting nation would neglect to provide an army and navy proportionate to its population, the extent of its territory, and the dignity of the place which it occupies in the world. When it is considered that no navy in the world, with one exception, approaches ours and none surpasses it, that our Regular Army of about 115,000 men is the equal of any other like number of troops, that our entire permanent and reserve land and sea force trained and training consists of a personnel of about 610,000, and that our annual appropriations are about $680,000,000 a year, expended under the direction of an exceedingly competent staff, it can not be said that our country is neglecting its national defense. It is true that a cult of disparagement exists, but that candid examination made by the Congress through its various committees has always reassured the country and demonstrated that it is maintaining the most adequate defensive forces in these present years that it has ever supported in time of peace.

This general policy should be kept in effect. Here and there temporary changes may be made in personnel to meet requirements in other directions. Attention should be given to submarines, cruisers, and air forces. Particular points may need strengthening, but as a whole our military power is sufficient.

The one weak place in the whole line is our still stupendous war debt. In any modern campaign the dollars are the shock troops. With a depleted treasury in the rear, no army can maintain itself in the field. A country loaded with debt is a country devoid of the first line of defense. Economy is the handmaid of preparedness. If we wish to be able to defend ourselves to the full extent of our power in the future, we shall discharge as soon as possible the financial burden of the last war. Otherwise we would face a crisis with a part of our capital resources already expended.

The amount and kind of our military equipment is preeminently a question for the decision of the Congress, after giving due consideration to the advice of military experts and the available public revenue. Nothing is more laudable than the cooperation of the agricultural and industrial resources of the country for the purpose of supplying the needs of national defense. In time of peril the people employed in these interests volunteered in a most self-sacrificing way, often at the nominal charge of a dollar a year. But the Army and Navy are not supported for the benefit of supply concerns; supply concerns are supported for the benefit of the Army and Navy. The distribution of orders on what is needed from different concerns for the purpose of keeping up equipment and organization is perfectly justified, but any attempt to prevail upon the Government to purchase beyond its needs ought not to be tolerated. It is eminently fair that those who deal with the Government should do so at a reasonable profit. However, public money is expended not that some one may profit by it, but in order to serve a public purpose.

While our policy of national defense will proceed in order that we may be independent and self-sufficient, I am opposed to engaging in any attempt at competitive armaments. No matter how much or how little some other country may feel constrained to provide, we can well afford to set the example, not of being dictated to by others, but of adopting our own standards. We are strong enough to pursue that method, which will be a most wholesome model for the rest of the world. We are eminently peaceful, but we are by no means weak. While we submit our differences with others, not to the adjudication of force, but of reason, it is not because we are unable to defend our rights. While we are doing our best to eliminate all resort to war for the purpose of settling disputes, we can not but remember that the peace we now enjoy had to be won by the sword and that if the rights of our country are to be defended we can not rely for that purpose upon anyone but ourselves. We can not shirk the responsibility, which is the first requisite of all government, of preserving its own integrity and maintaining the rights of its own citizens. It is only in accordance with these principles that we can establish any lasting foundations for an honorable and permanent peace.

It is for these reasons that our country, like any other country, proposes to provide itself with an army and navy supported by a merchant marine. Yet these are not for competition with any other power. For years we have besought nations to disarm. We have recently expressed our willingness at Geneva to enter into treaties for the limitation of all types of warships according to the ratio adopted at the Washington Conference. This offer is still pending. While we are and shall continue to be armed it is not as a menace, but rather a common assurance of tranquility to all the peace-loving people of the world. For us to do any less would be to disregard our obligations, evade our responsibilities, and jeopardize our national honor.

Veterans

This country, not only because it is bound by honor but because of the satisfaction derived from it, has always lavished its bounty upon its veterans. For years a service pension has been bestowed upon the Grand Army on reaching a certain age. Like provision has been made for the survivors of the Spanish War. A liberal future compensation has been granted to all the veterans of the World War. But it is in the case of the disabled and the dependents that the Government exhibits its greatest solicitude. This work is being well administered by the Veterans' Bureau. The main unfinished feature is that of hospitalization. This requirement is being rapidly met. Various veteran bodies will present to you recommendations which should have your careful consideration. At the last session we increased our annual expenditure for pensions and relief on account of the veterans of three wars. While I approve of proper relief for all suffering, I do not favor any further extension of our pension system at this time.

Alien Property

We still have in the possession of the Government the alien property. It has always been the policy of America to hold that private enemy property should not be confiscated in time of war. This principle we have scrupulously observed. As this property is security for the claims of our citizens and our Government, we can not relinquish it without adequate provision for their reimbursement. Legislation for the return of this property, accompanied by suitable provisions for the liquidation of the claims of our citizens and our Treasury, should be adopted. If our Government releases to foreigners the security which it holds for Americans, it must at the same time provide satisfactory safeguards for meeting American claims.

Prohibition

The duly authorized public authorities of this country have made prohibition the law of the land. Acting under the Constitution, the Congress and the legislatures of practically all the States have adopted legislation for its enforcement. Some abuses have arisen which require reform. Under the law the National Government has entrusted to the Treasury Department the especial duty of regulation and enforcement. Such supplementary legislation as it requires to meet existing conditions should be carefully and speedily enacted. Failure to support the Constitution and observe the law ought not to be tolerated by public opinion. Especially those in public places, who have taken their oath to support the Constitution, ought to be most scrupulous in its observance. Officers of the Department of Justice throughout the country should be vigilant in enforcing the law, but local authorities, which had always been mainly responsible for the enforcement of law in relation to intoxicating liquor, ought not to seek evasion by attempting to shift the burden wholly upon the Federal agencies. Under the Constitution the States are jointly charged with the Nation in providing for the enforcement of the prohibition amendment. Some people do not like the amendment, some do not like other parts of the Constitution, some do not like any of it. Those who entertain such sentiments have a perfect right to seek through legal methods for a change. But for any of our inhabitants to observe such parts of the Constitution as they like, while disregarding others, is a doctrine that would break down all protection of life and property and destroy the American system of ordered liberty.

Foreign Relations

The foreign policy of this Government is well known. It is one of peace based on that mutual respect that arises from mutual regard for international rights and the discharge of international obligations. It is our purpose to promote understanding and good will between ourselves and all other people. The American people are altogether lacking in an appreciation of the tremendous good fortune that surrounds their international position. We have no traditional enemies. We are not embarrassed over any disputed territory. We have no possessions that are coveted by others; they have none that are coveted by us. Our borders are unfortified. We fear no one; no one fears us. All the world knows that the whole extent of our influence is against war and in favor of peace, against the use of force and in favor of negotiation, arbitration, and adjudication as a method of adjusting international differences. We look with disfavor upon all aggressive warfare. We are strong enough so that no one can charge us with weakness if we are slow to anger. Our place is sufficiently established so that we need not be sensitive over trifles. Our resources are large enough so that we can afford to be generous. At the same time we are a nation among nations and recognize a responsibility not only to ourselves, but in the interests of a stable and enlightened civilization, to protect and defend the international rights of our Government and our citizens.

It is because of our historical detachment and the generations of comparative indifference toward it by other nations that our public is inclined to consider altogether too seriously the reports that we are criticized abroad. We never had a larger foreign trade than at the present time. Our good offices were never more sought and the necessity for our assistance and cooperation was never more universally declared in any time of peace. We know that the sentiments which we entertain toward all other nations are those of the most sincere friendship and good will and of all unbounded desire to help, which we are perfectly willing to have judged by their fruits. In our efforts to adjust our international obligations we have met with a response which, when everything is considered, I believe history will record as a most remarkable and gratifying demonstration of the sanctity with which civilized nations undertake to discharge their mutual obligations. Debt settlements have been negotiated with practically all of those who owed us and all finally adjusted but two, which are in process of ratification. When we consider the real sacrifice that will be necessary on the part of other nations, considering all their circumstances, to meet their agreed payments, we ought to hold them in increased admiration and respect. It is true that we have extended to them very generous treatment, but it is also true that they have agreed to repay us all that we loaned to them and some interest.

A special conference on the Chinese customs tariff provided for by the treaty between the nine powers relating to the Chinese customs tariff signed at Washington on February 6, 1922, was called by the Chinese Government to meet at Peking, on October 26, 1925. We participated in this conference through fully empowered delegates and, with good will, endeavored to cooperate with the other participating powers with a view to putting into effect promises made to China at the Washington conference, and considering any reasonable proposal that might be made by the Chinese Government for the revision of the treaties on the subject of China's tariff. With these aims in view the American delegation at the outset of the conference proposed to put into effect the surtaxes provided for by the Washington treaty and to proceed immediately to the negotiation of a treaty, which, among other things, was to make provision for the abolition of taxes collected on goods in transit, remove the tariff restrictions in existing treaties, and put into effect the national tariff law of China.

Early in April of the present year the central Chinese Government was ousted from power by opposing warring factions. It became impossible under the circumstances to continue the negotiations. Finally, on July 3, the delegates of the foreign powers, including those of the United States, issued a statement expressing their unanimous and earnest desire to proceed with the work of the conference at the earliest possible moment when the delegates of the Chinese Government are in a position to resume discussions with the foreign delegates of the problems before the conference. We are prepared to resume the negotiations thus interrupted whenever a Government representing the Chinese people and acting on their behalf presents itself. The fact that constant warfare between contending Chinese factions has rendered it impossible to bring these negotiations to a successful conclusion is a matter of deep regret. Throughout these conflicts we have maintained a position of the most careful neutrality. Our naval vessels in Asiatic waters, pursuant to treaty rights, have been used only for the protection of American citizens.

Silas H. Strawn, Esq., was sent to China as American commissioner to cooperate with commissioners of the other powers in the establishment of a commission to inquire into the present practice of extraterritorial jurisdiction in China, with a view to reporting to the Governments of the several powers their findings of fact in regard to these matters. The commission commenced its work in January, 1926, and agreed upon a joint report which was signed on September 16, 1926. The commission's report has been received and is being studied with a view to determining our future policy in regard to the question of extraterritorial privileges under treaties between the United States and China.

The Preparatory Commission for the Disarmament Conference met at Geneva on May 18 and its work has been proceeding almost continuously since that date. It would be premature to attempt to form a judgment as to the progress that has been made. The commission has had before it a comprehensive list of questions touching upon all aspects of the question of the limitation of armament. In the commission's discussions many differences of opinion have developed. However, I am hopeful that at least some measure of agreement will be reached as the discussions continue. The American representation on the commission has consistently tried to be helpful, and has kept before it the practical objective to which the commission is working, namely, actual agreements for the limitation of armaments. Our representatives will continue their work in that direction.

One of the most encouraging features of the commission's work thus far has been the agreement in principle among the naval experts of a majority of the powers parties to the Washington treaty limiting naval armament upon methods and standards for the comparison and further limitation of naval armament. It is needless to say that at the proper time I shall be prepared to proceed along practical lines to the conclusion of agreements carrying further the work begun at the Washington Conference in 1921.

Department Reports

Many important subjects which it is impossible even to mention in the short space of an annual message you will find fully discussed in the departmental reports. A failure to include them here is not to be taken as indicating any lack of interest, but only a disinclination to state inadequately what has been much better done in other documents.

The Capital City

We are embarking on an ambitious building program for the city of Washington. The Memorial Bridge is under way with all that it holds for use and beauty. New buildings are soon contemplated. This program should represent the best that exists in the art and science of architecture. Into these structures which must be considered as of a permanent nature ought to go the aspirations of the Nation, its ideals expressed in forms of beauty. If our country wishes to compete with others, let it not be in the support of armaments but in the making of a beautiful capital city. Let it express the soul of America. Whenever an American is at the seat of his Government, however traveled and cultured he may be, he ought to find a city of stately proportion, symmetrically laid out and adorned with the best that there is in architecture, which would arouse his imagination and stir his patriotic pride. In the coming years Washington should be not only the art center of our own country but the art center of the world. Around it should center all that is best in science, in learning, in letters, and in art. These are the results that justify the creation of those national resources with which we have been favored.

American Ideals

America is not and must not be a country without ideals. They are useless if they are only visionary; they are only valuable if they are practical. A nation can not dwell constantly on the mountain tops. It has to be replenished and sustained through the ceaseless toil of the less inspiring valleys. But its face ought always to be turned upward, its vision ought always to be fixed on high.

We need ideals that can be followed in daily life, that can be translated into terms of the home. We can not expect to be relieved from toil, but we do expect to divest it of degrading conditions. Work is honorable; it is entitled to an honorable recompense. We must strive mightily, but having striven there is a defect in our political and social system if we are not in general rewarded with success. To relieve the land of the burdens that came from the war, to release to the individual more of the fruits of his own industry, to increase his earning capacity and decrease his hours of labor, to enlarge the circle of his vision through good roads and better transportation, to place before him the opportunity for education both in science and in art, to leave him free to receive the inspiration of religion, all these are ideals which deliver him from the servitude of the body and exalt him to the service of the soul. Through this emancipation from the things that are material, we broaden our dominion over the things that are spiritual.

Calvin Coolidge, 1925–1929

Annual Message to Congress
December 6, 1927

Calvin Coolidge's fifth annual State of the Union message, on December 6, 1927, came just four months after the president, in his usual taciturn fashion, had announced, "I do not choose to run for president in 1928." Some observers have commented that the president had sunk into a depression after the death of one of his two sons in 1924. Coolidge had served as chief executive since August 1923. He had been vice president under Warren G. Harding and succeeded to the presidency upon Harding's death in office; the popular Coolidge won a full term of his own in the 1924 elections.

In his 1927 State of the Union message, delivered in written form rather than in person, Coolidge highlighted many of the same themes of past addresses, including the importance of paying down the national debt and the benefits resulting from tax reductions. However, in discussing the need for debt reduction, he actually argued against further tax reductions and warned against the role of "special interests" in tax legislation. He also noted, once again, that the country, overall, was in the midst of an extremely prosperous period.

One additional topic of discussion in this address was flood control. There had been some disastrous flooding in 1927, first along the lower Mississippi and, later in the year, in New England. Coolidge cited millions of dollars in aid given by the Red Cross and the federal government. While he remarked that the government was "not an insurer of its citizens against the hazards of the elements," and that relief did not equal restoration when it came to disasters, he also said, "No required relief should be refused."

The past year also had seen the first nonstop solo flight across the Atlantic Ocean, made by Charles Lindbergh. While Coolidge did not specifically refer to this feat, he did discuss aviation, noting the growth in aeronautics and the Commerce Department's efforts to construct national airways. In addition, private companies were working to extend air service to Latin America, and Coolidge expressed the administration's interest in working with these companies in this effort.

The president also made mention of Prohibition. The Eighteenth Amendment, which outlawed the manufacture, sale, and transportation of alcohol, had been in effect since 1920. Coolidge urged local governments to become as vigilant as their federal counterparts in their efforts to enforce the law.

On the foreign policy front, Coolidge noted that United States forces had protected American citizens during unrest in both China and Nicaragua in the course of the year. He cited the importance of international law and stated that the United States should promote peace, through the insrument of international treaties against war.

Coolidge would be succeeded by another Republican president, Herbert Hoover. Unfortunately for Hoover, the economic prosperity would end less than a year after his swearing-in, when the stock market crashed in October 1929.

Members of the Congress:

It is gratifying to report that for the fourth consecutive year the state of the Union in general is good. We are at peace. The country as a whole has had a prosperity never exceeded. Wages are at their highest range, employment is plentiful. Some parts of agriculture and industry have lagged; some localities have suffered from storm and flood. But such losses have been absorbed without serious detriment to our great economic structure. Stocks of goods are moderate and a wholesome caution is prevalent. Rates of interest for industry, agriculture, and government have been reduced. Savers and investors are providing capital for new construction in industry and public works. The purchasing power of agriculture has increased. If the people maintain that confidence which they are entitled to have in themselves, in each other, and in America, a comfortable prosperity will continue.

Constructive Economy

Without constructive economy in Government expenditures we should not now be enjoying these results or these prospects. Because we are not now physically at war, some people are disposed to forget that our war debt still remains. The Nation must make financial sacrifices, accompanied by a stern self-denial in public expenditures, until we have conquered the disabilities of our public finance. While our obligation to veterans and dependents is large and continuing, the heavier burden of the national debt is being steadily eliminated. At the end of this fiscal year it will be reduced from about $26,600,000,000 to about $17,975,000,000. Annual interest, including war savings, will have been reduced from $1,055,000,000 to $670,000,000. The sacrifices of the people, the economy of the Government, are showing remarkable results. They should be continued for the purpose of relieving the Nation of the burden of interest and debt and releasing revenue for internal improvements and national development.

Not only the amount, but the rate, of Government interest has been reduced. Callable bonds have been refunded and paid, so that during this year the average rate of interest on the present public debt for the first time fell below 4 per cent. Keeping the credit of the Nation high is a tremendously profitable operation.

Tax Reduction

The immediate fruit of economy and the retirement of the public debt is tax reduction. The annual saving in interest between 1925 and 1929 is $212,000,000. Without this no bill to relieve the taxpayers would be worth proposing. The three measures already enacted leave our Government revenues where they are not oppressive. Exemptions have been increased until 115,000,000 people make but 2,500,000 individual taxable returns, so that further reduction should be mainly for the purpose of removing inequalities. The Secretary of the Treasury has recommended a measure which would give us a much better balanced system of taxation and without oppression produce sufficient revenue. It has my complete support.

Unforeseen contingencies requiring money are always arising. Our probable surplus for June 30, 1929, is small. A slight depression in business would greatly reduce our revenue because of our present method of taxation. The people ought to take no selfish attitude of pressing for removing moderate and fair taxes which might produce a deficit. We must keep our budget balanced for each year. That is the corner stone of our national credit, the trifling price we pay to command the lowest rate of interest of any great power in the world. Any surplus can be applied to debt reduction, and debt reduction is tax reduction. Under the present circumstances it would be far better to leave the rates as they are than to enact a bill carrying the peril of a deficit. This is not a problem to be approached in a narrow or partisan spirit. All of those who participate in finding a reasonable solution will be entitled to participate in any credit that accrues from it without regard to party. The Congress has already demonstrated that tax legislation can be removed from purely political consideration into the realm of patriotic business principles.

Any bill for tax reduction should be written by those who are responsible for raising, managing, and expending the finances of the Government. If special interests, too often selfish, always uninformed of the national needs as a whole, with hired agents using their proposed beneficiaries as engines of propaganda, are permitted to influence the withdrawal of their property from taxation, we shall have a law that is unbalanced and unjust, bad for business, bad for the country, probably resulting in a deficit, with disastrous financial Consequences. The Constitution has given the Members of the Congress sole authority to decide what tax measures shall be presented for approval. While welcoming information from any quarter, the Congress should continue to exercise its own judgment in a matter so vital and important to all the interests of the country as taxation.

National Defense

Being a nation relying not on force, but on fair dealing and good will, to maintain peace with others, we have provided a moderate military force in a form adapted solely to defense. It should be continued with a very generous supply of officers and with the present base of personnel, subject to fluctuations which may be temporarily desirable.

The five-year program for our air forces is in keeping with this same policy and commensurate with the notable contributions of America to the science of aeronautics. The provisions of the law lately enacted are being executed as fast as the practical difficulties of an orderly and stable development permit.

While our Army is small, prudence requires that it should be kept in a high state of efficiency and provided with such supplies as would permit of its immediate expansion. The garrison ration has lately been increased. Recommendations for an appropriation of $6,166,000 for new housing made to the previous Congress failed to pass. While most of the Army is well housed, some of it which is quartered in wartime training camps is becoming poorly housed. In the past three years $12,533,000 have been appropriated for reconstruction and repairs, and an authorization has been approved of $22,301,000 for new housing, under which $8,070,000 has already been appropriated. A law has also been passed, complying with the request of the War Department, allocating funds received from the sale of buildings and land for housing purposes. The work, however, is not completed, so that other appropriations are being recommended.

Our Navy is likewise a weapon of defense. We have a foreign commerce and ocean lines of trade unsurpassed by any other country. We have outlying territory in the two great oceans and long stretches of seacoast studded with the richest cities in the world. We are responsible for the protection of a large population and the greatest treasure ever bestowed upon any people. We are charged with an international duty of defending the Panama Canal. To meet these responsibilities we need a very substantial sea armament. It needs aircraft development, which is being provided under the five-year program. It needs submarines as soon as the department decides upon the best type of construction. It needs airplane carriers and a material addition to its force of cruisers. We can plan for the future and begin a moderate building program.

This country has put away the Old World policy of competitive armaments. It can never be relieved of the responsibility of adequate national defense. We have one treaty secured by an unprecedented attitude of generosity on our part for a limitation in naval armament. After most careful preparation, extending over months, we recently made every effort to secure a three-power treaty to the same end. We were granted much cooperation by Japan, but we were unable to come to an agreement with Great Britain. While the results of the conference were of considerable value, they were mostly of a negative character. We know now that no agreement can be reached which will be inconsistent with a considerable building program on our part. We are ready and willing to continue the preparatory investigations on the general subject of limitation of armaments which have been started under the auspices of the League of Nations.

We have a considerable cruiser tonnage, but a part of it is obsolete. Everyone knew that had a three-power agreement been reached it would have left us with the necessity of continuing our building program. The failure to agree should not cause us to build either more or less than we otherwise should. Any future treaty of limitation will call on us for more ships. We should enter on no competition. We should refrain from no needful program. It should be made clear to all the world that lacking a definite agreement, the attitude of any other country is not to be permitted to alter our own policy. It should especially be demonstrated that propaganda will not cause us to change our course. Where there is no treaty limitation, the size of the Navy which America is to have will be solely for America to determine. No outside influence should enlarge it or diminish it. But it should be known to all that our military power holds no threat of aggrandizement. It is a guaranty of peace and security at home, and when it goes abroad it is an instrument for the protection of the legal rights of our citizens under international law, a refuge in time of disorder, and always the servant of world peace. Wherever our flag goes the rights of humanity increase.

Merchant Marine

The United States Government fleet is transporting a large amount of freight and reducing its drain on the Treasury. The Shipping Board is constantly under pressure, to which it too often yields, to protect private interests, rather than serve the public welfare. More attention should be given to merchant ships as an auxiliary of the Navy. The possibility of including their masters and crews in the Naval Reserve, with some reasonable compensation, should be thoroughly explored as a method of encouraging private operation of shipping. Public operation is not a success. No investigation, of which I have caused several to be made, has failed to report that it could not succeed or to recommend speedy transfer to private ownership. Our exporters and importers are both indifferent about using American ships. It should be our policy to keep our present vessels in repair and dispose of them as rapidly as possible, rather than undertake any new construction. Their operation is a burden on the National Treasury, for which we are not receiving sufficient benefits.

Commercial Aviation

A rapid growth is taking place in aeronautics. The Department of Commerce has charge of the inspection and licensing system and the construction of national airways.

Almost 8,000 miles are already completed and about 4,000 miles more contemplated. Nearly 4,400 miles are now equipped and over 3,000 miles more will have lighting and emergency landing fields by next July. Air mail contracts are expected to cover 24 of these lines. Daily airway flying is nearly 15,000 miles and is expected to reach 25,000 miles early next year.

Flights for other purposes exceed 22,000 miles each day. Over 900 airports, completed and uncompleted, have been laid out. The demand for aircraft has greatly increased. The policy already adopted by the Congress is producing the sound development of this coming industry.

Western Hemisphere Air Mail

Private enterprise is showing much interest in opening up aviation service to Mexico and Central and South America. We are particularly solicitous to have the United States take a leading part in this development. It is understood that the governments of our sister countries would be willing to cooperate. Their physical features, the undeveloped state of their transportation, make an air service especially adaptable to their usage. The Post Office Department should be granted power to make liberal long-term contracts for carrying our mail, and authority should be given to the Army and the Navy to detail aviators and planes to cooperate with private enterprise in establishing such mail service with the consent of the countries concerned. A committee of the Cabinet will later present a report on this subject.

Good Roads

The importance and benefit of good roads is more and more coming to be appreciated. The National Government has been making liberal contributions to encourage their construction. The results and benefits have been very gratifying. National participation, however, should be confined to trunk-line systems. The national tax on automobiles is now nearly sufficient to meet this outlay. This tax is very small, and on low-priced cars is not more than $2 or $3 each year.

While the advantage of having good roads is very large, the desire for improved highways is not limited to our own country. It should and does include all the Western Hemisphere. The principal points in Canada are already accessible. We ought to lend our encouragement in any way we can for more good roads to all the principal points in this hemisphere south of the Rio Grande. It has been our practice to supply these countries with military and naval advisers, when they have requested it, to assist them in national defense. The arts of peace are even more important to them and to us. Authority should be given by law to provide them at their request with engineering advisers for the construction of roads and bridges. In some of these countries already wonderful progress is being made in road building, but the engineering features are often very exacting and the financing difficult. Private interests should look with favor on all reasonable loans sought by these countries to open such main lines of travel.

This general subject has been promoted by the Pan American Congress of Highways, which will convene again at Rio de Janeiro in July, 1928. It is desirable that the Congress should provide for the appointment of delegates to represent the Government of the United States.

Cuban Parcel Post

We have a temporary parcel-post convention with Cuba. The advantage of it is all on our side. During 1926 we shipped twelve times as many parcels, weighing twenty-four times as much, as we received. This convention was made on the understanding that we would repeal an old law prohibiting the importation of cigars and cigarettes in quantities less than 3,000 enacted in 1866 to discourage smuggling, for which it has long been unnecessary. This law unjustly discriminates against an important industry of Cuba. Its repeal has been recommended by the Treasury and Post Office Departments. Unless this is done our merchants and railroads will find themselves deprived of this large parcel-post business after the 1st of next March, the date of the expiration of the convention, which has been extended upon the specific understanding that it would expire at that time unless this legislation was enacted. We purchase large quantities of tobacco made in Cuba. It is not probable that our purchases would be any larger if this law was repealed, while it would be an advantage to many other industries in the United States.

Insular Possessions

Conditions in the Philippine Islands have been steadily improved. Contentment and good order prevail. Roads, irrigation works, harbor improvements, and public buildings are being constructed. Public education and sanitation have been advanced. The Government is in a sound financial condition. These immediate results were especially due to the administration of Gov. Gen. Leonard Wood. The six years of his governorship marked a distinct improvement in the islands and rank as one of the outstanding accomplishments of this distinguished man. His death is a loss to the Nation and the islands.

Greater progress could be made, more efficiency could be put into administration, if the Congress would undertake to expend, through its appropriating power, all or a part of the customs revenues which are now turned over to the Philippine treasury. The powers of the auditor of the islands also need revision and clarification. The government of the islands is about 98 per cent in the hands of the Filipinos. An extension of the policy of self-government will be hastened by the demonstration on their part of their desire and their ability to carry out cordially and efficiently the provisions of the organic law enacted by the Congress for the government of the islands. It would be well for a committee of the Congress to visit the islands every two years.

A fair degree of progress is being made in Porto Rico. Its agricultural products are increasing; its treasury position, which has given much concern, shows improvement. I am advised by the governor that educational facilities are still lacking. Roads are being constructed, which he represents are the first requisite for building schoolhouses. The loyalty of the island to the United States is exceedingly gratifying. A memorial will be presented to you requesting authority to have the governor elected by the people of Porto Rico. This was never done in the case of our own Territories. It is admitted that education outside of the towns is as yet very deficient. Until it has progressed further the efficiency of the government and the happiness of the people may need the guiding hand of an appointed governor. As it is not contemplated that any change should be made immediately, the general subject may well have the thoughtful study of the Congress.

Panama Canal

The number of commercial ships passing through the Panama Canal has increased from 3,967 in 1923 to 5,475 in 1927. The total amount of tolls turned into the Treasury is over $166,000,000, while all the operations of the canal have yielded a surplus of about $80,000,000. In order to provide additional storage of water and give some control over the floods of the Chagres River, it is proposed to erect a dam to cost about $12,000,000 at Alhajuela. It will take some five years to complete this work.

Agriculture

The past year has seen a marked improvement in the general condition of agriculture. Production is better balanced and without acute shortage or heavy surplus. Costs have been reduced and the average output of the worker increased. The level of farm prices has risen while others have fallen, so that the purchasing power of the farmer is approaching a normal figure. The individual farmer is entitled to great credit for the progress made since 1921. He has adjusted his production and through cooperative organizations and other methods improved his marketing. He is using authenticated facts and employing sound methods which other industries are obliged to use to secure stability and prosperity. The old-fashioned haphazard system is being abandoned, economics are being applied to ascertain the best adapted unit of land, diversification is being promoted, and scientific methods are being used in production, and business principles in marketing.

Agriculture has not fully recovered from postwar depression. The fact is that economic progress never marches forward in a straight line. It goes in waves. One part goes ahead, while another halts and another recedes. Everybody wishes agriculture to prosper. Any sound and workable proposal to help the farmer will have the earnest support of the Government. Their interests are not all identical. Legislation should assist as many producers in as many regions as possible. It should be the aim to assist the farmer to work out his own salvation socially and economically. No plan will be of any permanent value to him which does not leave him standing on his own foundation.

In the past the Government has spent vast sums to bring land under cultivation. It is apparent that this has reached temporarily the saturation point. We have had a surplus of production and a poor market for land, which has only lately shown signs of improvement. The main problem which is presented for solution is one of dealing with a surplus of production. It is useless to propose a temporary expedient. What is needed is permanency and stability. Government price fixing is known to be unsound and bound to result in disaster. A Government subsidy would work out in the same way. It can not be sound for all of the people to hire some of the people to produce a crop which neither the producers nor the rest of the people want.

Price fixing and subsidy will both increase the surplus, instead of diminishing it. Putting the Government directly into business is merely a combination of subsidy and price fixing aggravated by political pressure. These expedients would lead logically to telling the farmer by law what and how much he should plant and where he should plant it, and what and how much he should sell and where he should sell it. The most effective means of dealing with surplus crops is to reduce the surplus acreage. While this can not be done by the individual farmer, it can be done through the organizations already in existence, through the information published by the Department of

Agriculture, and especially through banks and others who supply credit refusing to finance an acreage manifestly too large.

It is impossible to provide by law for an assured success and prosperity for all those who engage in farming. If acreage becomes overextended, the Government can not assume responsibility for it. The Government can, however, assist cooperative associations and other organizations in orderly marketing and handling a surplus clearly due to weather and seasonal conditions, in order to save the producer from preventable loss. While it is probably impossible to secure this result at a single step, and much will have to be worked out by trial and rejection, a beginning could be made by setting up a Federal board or commission of able and experienced men in marketing, granting equal advantages under this board to the various agricultural commodities and sections of the country, giving encouragement to the cooperative movement in agriculture, and providing a revolving loan fund at a moderate rate of interest for the necessary financing. Such legislation would lay the foundation for a permanent solution of the surplus problem.

This is not a proposal to lend more money to the farmer, who is already fairly well financed, but to lend money temporarily to experimental marketing associations which will no doubt ultimately be financed by the regularly established banks, as were the temporary operations of the War Finance Corporation. Cooperative marketing especially would be provided with means of buying or building physical properties.

The National Government has almost entirely relieved the farmer from income taxes by successive tax reductions, but State and local taxes have increased, putting on him a grievous burden. A policy of rigid economy should be applied to State and local expenditures. This is clearly within the legislative domain of the States. The Federal Government has also improved our banking structure and system of agricultural credits. The farmer will be greatly benefited by similar action in many States. The Department of Agriculture is undergoing changes in organization in order more completely to separate the research and regulatory divisions, that each may be better administered. More emphasis is being placed on the research program, not only by enlarging the appropriations for State experiment stations but by providing funds for expanding the research work of the department. It is in this direction that much future progress can be expected.

The Protective Tariff

The present tariff rates supply the National Treasury with well over $600,000,000 of annual revenue. Yet, about 65 per cent of our imports come in duty free. Of the remaining 35 per cent of imports on which duties are laid about 23 per cent consists of luxuries and agricultural products, and the balance of about 12 per cent, amounting, to around $560,000,000 is made up of manufactures and merchandise. As no one is advocating any material reduction in the rates on agriculture or luxuries, it is only the comparatively small amount of about $560,000,000 of other imports that are really considered in any discussion of reducing tariff rates. While this amount, duty free, would be large enough seriously to depress many lines of business in our own country, it is of small importance when spread over the rest of the world.

It is often stated that a reduction of tariff rates on industry would benefit agriculture. It would be interesting to know to what commodities it is thought this could be applied. Everything the farmer uses in farming is already on the free list. Nearly everything he sells is protected. It would seem to be obvious that it is better for the country to have the farmer raise food to supply the domestic manufacturer than the foreign manufacturer. In one case our country would have only the farmer; in the other it would have the farmer and the manufacturer. Assuming that Europe would have more money if it sold us larger amounts of merchandise, it is not certain it would consume more food, or, if it did, that its purchases would be made in this country. Undoubtedly it would resort to the cheapest market, which is by no means ours. The largest and best and most profitable market for the farmer in the world is our own domestic market. Any great increase in manufactured imports means the closing of our own plants. Nothing would be worse for agriculture.

Probably no one expects a material reduction in the rates on manufactures while maintaining the rates on agriculture. A material reduction in either would be disastrous to the farmer. It would mean a general shrinkage of values, a deflation of prices, a reduction of wages, a general depression carrying our people down to the low standard of living in our competing countries. It is obvious that this would not improve but destroy our market for imports, which is best served by maintaining our present high purchasing power under which in the past five years imports have increased 63 per cent.

Farm Loan System

It is exceedingly important that the Federal land and joint-stock land banks should furnish the best possible service for agriculture. Certain joint-stock banks have fallen into improper and unsound practices, resulting in the indictment of the officials of three of them. More money has been provided for examinations, and at the instance of the Treasury rules and regulations of the Federal Farm Board have been revised. Early last May three of its members resigned. Their places were filled with men connected with the War Finance Corporation. Eugene Meyer being designated as Farm Loan Commissioner. The new members have demonstrated their ability in the field of agricultural finance in the extensive operations of the War Finance Corporation. Three joint-stock banks have gone into receivership. It is necessary to preserve the public confidence in this system in order to find a market for their bonds. A recent flotation was made at a record low rate of 4 per cent. Careful supervision is absolutely necessary to protect the investor and enable these banks to exercise their chief function in serving agriculture.

Muscle Shoals

The last year has seen considerable changes in the problem of Muscle Shoals. Development of other methods show that nitrates can probably be produced at less cost than by the use of hydroelectric power. Extensive investigation made by the Department of War indicates that the nitrate plants on this project are of little value for national defense and can probably be disposed of within two years. The oxidation part of the plants, however, should be retained indefinitely. This leaves this project mostly concerned with power. It should, nevertheless, continue to be dedicated to agriculture. It is probable that this desire can be best served by disposing of the plant and applying the revenues received from it to research for methods of more economical production of concentrated fertilizer and to demonstrations and other methods of stimulating its use on the farm. But in disposing of the property preference should be given to proposals to use all or part of it for nitrate production and fertilizer manufacturing.

Flood Control

For many years the Federal Government has been building a system of dikes along the Mississippi River for protection against high water. During the past season the lower States were overcome by a most disastrous flood. Many thousands of square miles were inundated a great many lives were lost, much livestock was drowned, and a very heavy destruction of property was inflicted upon the inhabitants. The American Red Cross at once went to the relief of the stricken communities. Appeals for contributions have brought in over $17,000,000. The Federal Government has provided services, equipment, and supplies probably amounting to about $7,000,000 more. Between $5,000,000 and $10,000,000 in addition have been provided by local railroads, the States, and their political units. Credits have been arranged by the Farm Loan Board, and three emergency finance corporations with a total capital of $3,000,000 have insured additional resources to the extent of $12,000,000. Through these means the 700,000 people in the flooded areas have been adequately supported. Provision has been made to care for those in need until after the 1st of January.

The Engineering Corps of the Army has contracted to close all breaks in the dike system before the next season of high water. A most thorough and elaborate survey of the whole situation has been made and embodied in a report with recommendations for future flood control, which will be presented to the Congress. The carrying out of their plans will necessarily extend over a series of years. They will call for a raising and strengthening of the dike system with provision for emergency spillways and improvements for the benefit of navigation.

Under the present law the land adjacent to the dikes has paid one-third of the cost of their construction. This has been a most extraordinary concession from the plan adopted in relation to irrigation, where the general rule has been that the land benefited should bear the entire expense. It is true, of course, that the troublesome waters do not originate on the land to be reclaimed, but it is also true that such waters have a right of way through that section of the country and the land there is charged with that easement. It is the land of this region that is to be benefited. To say that it is unable to bear any expense of reclamation is the same thing as saying that it is not worth reclaiming. Because of expenses incurred and charges already held against this land, it seems probable that some revision will have to be made concerning the proportion of cost which it should bear. But it is extremely important that it should pay enough so that those requesting improvements will be charged with some responsibility for their cost, and the neighborhood where works are constructed have a pecuniary interest in preventing waste and extravagance and securing a wise and economical expenditure of public funds.

It is necessary to look upon this emergency as a national disaster. It has been so treated from its inception. Our whole people have provided with great generosity for its relief. Most of the departments of the Federal Government have been engaged in the same effort. The governments of the afflicted areas, both State and municipal, can not be given too high praise for the courageous and helpful way in which they have come to the rescue of the people. If the sources directly chargeable can not meet the demand, the National Government should not fail to provide generous relief. This, however, does not mean restoration. The Government is not an insurer of its citizens against the hazard of the elements. We shall always have flood and drought, heat and cold, earthquake and wind, lightning and tidal wave, which are all too constant in their afflictions. The Government does not undertake to reimburse its citizens for loss and damage incurred under such circumstances. It is chargeable, however, with the rebuilding of public works and the humanitarian duty of relieving its citizens from distress.

The people in the flooded area and their representatives have approached this problem in the most generous and broad-minded way. They should be met with a like spirit on the part of the National government. This is all one country. The public needs of each part must be provided for by the public at large. No required relief should be refused. An adequate plan should be adopted to prevent a recurrence of this disaster in order that the people may restore to productivity and comfort their fields and their towns.

Legislation by this Congress should be confined to our principal and most pressing problem, the lower Mississippi, considering tributaries only so far as they materially affect the main flood problem. A definite Federal program relating to our waterways was proposed when the last Congress authorized a comprehensive survey of all the important streams of the country in order to provide for their improvement, including flood control, navigation, power, and irrigation. Other legislation should wait pending a report on this survey. The recognized needs of the Mississippi should not be made a vehicle for carrying other projects. All proposals for development should stand on their own merits. Any other method would result in ill-advised conclusions, great waste of money, and instead of promoting would delay the orderly and certain utilization of our water resources.

Very recently several of the New England States have suffered somewhat similarly from heavy rainfall and high water. No reliable estimate of damage has yet been computed, but it is very large to private and public property. The Red Cross is generously undertaking what is needed for immediate relief, repair and reconstruction of houses, restocking of domestic animals, and food, clothing, and shelter. A considerable sum of money will be available through the regular channels in the Department of Agriculture for reconstruction of highways. It may be necessary to grant special aid for this purpose. Complete reports of what is required will undoubtedly be available early in the session.

Inland Navigation

The Congress in its last session authorized the general improvements necessary to provide the Mississippi waterway system with better transportation. Stabilization of the levels of the Great Lakes and their opening to the sea by an effective shipway remain to be considered. Since the last session the Board of Engineers of the War Department has made a report on the proposal for a canal through the State of New York, and the Joint Board of Engineers, representing Canada and the United States, has finished a report on the St. Lawrence River. Both of these boards conclude that the St. Lawrence project is cheaper, affords a more expeditious method of placing western products in European markets, and will cost less to operate. The State Department has requested the Canadian Government to negotiate treaties necessary to provide for this improvement. It will also be necessary to secure an agreement with Canada to put in works necessary to prevent fluctuation in the levels of the Great Lakes.

Legislation is desirable for the construction of a dam at Boulder Canyon on the Colorado River, primarily as a method of flood control and irrigation. A secondary result would be a considerable power development and a source of domestic water supply for southern California. Flood control is clearly a national problem, and water supply is a Government problem, but every other possibility should be exhausted before the Federal Government becomes engaged in the power business. The States which are interested ought to reach mutual agreement. This project is in reality their work. If they wish the Federal Government to undertake it, they should not hesitate to make the necessary concessions to each other. This subject is fully discussed in the annual report of the Secretary of the Interior. The Columbia River Basin project is being studied and will be one to be considered at some future time.

The Inland Waterways Corporation is proving successful and especially beneficial to agriculture. A survey is being made to determine its future needs. It has never been contemplated that if inland rivers were opened to navigation it would then be necessary for the Federal Government to provide the navigation. Such a request is very nearly the equivalent of a declaration that their navigation is not profitable, that the commodities which they are to carry can be taken at a cheaper rate by some other method, in which case the hundreds of millions of dollars proposed to be expended for opening rivers to navigation would be not only wasted, but would entail further constant expenditures to carry the commodities of private persons for less than cost.

The policy is well established that the Government should open public highways on land and on water, but for use of the public in their private capacity. It has put on some demonstration barge lines, but always with the expectation that if they prove profitable they would pass into private hands and if they do not prove profitable they will be withdrawn. The problems of transportation over inland waterways should be taken up by private enterprise, so that the public will have the advantage of competition in service. It is expected that some of our lines can be sold, some more demonstration work done, and that with the completion of the Ohio project a policy of private operation can be fully developed.

Prohibition

After more than two generations of constant debate, our country adopted a system of national prohibition under all the solemnities involved in an amendment to the Federal Constitution. In obedience to this mandate the Congress and the States, with one or two notable exceptions, have passed required laws for its administration and enforcement. This imposes upon the citizenship of the country, and especially on all public officers, not only the duty to enforce, but the obligation to observe the sanctions of this constitutional provision and its resulting laws. If this condition could be secured, all question concerning prohibition would cease. The Federal Government is making every effort to accomplish these results through careful organization, large appropriations, and administrative effort. Smuggling has been greatly cut down, the larger sources of supply for illegal sale have been checked, and by means of injunction and criminal prosecution the process of enforcement is being applied. The same vigilance on the part of local governments would render these efforts much more successful. The Federal authorities propose to discharge their obligation for enforcement to the full extent of their ability.

The Negro

History does not anywhere record so much progress made in the same length of time as that which has been accomplished by the Negro race in the United States since the Emancipation Proclamation. They have come up from slavery to be prominent in education, the professions, art, science, agriculture, banking, and commerce. It is estimated that 50,000 of them are on the Government pay rolls, drawing about $50,000,000 each year. They have been the recipients of presidential appointments and their professional ability has arisen to a sufficiently high plane so that they have been intrusted with the entire management and control of the great veterans' hospital at Tuskegee, where their conduct has taken high rank. They have shown that they have been worthy of all the encouragement which they have received. Nevertheless, they are too often subjected to thoughtless and inconsiderate treatment, unworthy alike of the white or colored races. They have especially been made the target of the foul crime of lynching. For several years these acts of unlawful violence had been diminishing. In the last year they have shown an increase. Every principle of order and law and liberty is opposed to this crime. The Congress should enact any legislation it can under the Constitution to provide for its elimination.

American Indian

The condition of the American Indian has much improved in recent years. Full citizenship was bestowed upon them on June 2, 1924, and appropriations for their care and advancement have been increased. Still there remains much to be done.

Notable increases in appropriations for the several major functions performed by the Department of the Interior on behalf of the Indians have marked the last five years. In that time, successive annual increases in appropriations for their education total $1,804,325; for medical care, $578,000; and for industrial advancement, $205,000; or $2,582,325 more than would have been spent in the same period on the basis of appropriations for 1923 and the preceding years.

The needs along health, educational, industrial and social lines however, are great, and the Budget estimates for 1929 include still further increases for Indian administration.

To advance the time when the Indians may become self-sustaining, it is my belief that the Federal Government should continue to improve the facilities for their care, and as rapidly as possible turn its responsibility over to the States.

Coal

Legislation authorizing a system of fuel administration and the appointment by the President of a Board of Mediation and Conciliation in case of actual or threatened interruption of production is needed. The miners themselves are now seeking information and action from the Government, which could readily be secured through such a board. It is believed that a thorough investigation and reconsideration of this proposed policy by the Congress will demonstrate that this recommendation is sound and should be adopted.

Petroleum Conservation

The National Government is undertaking to join in the formation of a cooperative committee of lawyers, engineers, and public officers, to consider what legislation by the States or by the Congress can be adopted for the preservation and conservation of our supply of petroleum. This has come to be one of the main dependencies for transportation and power so necessary to our agricultural and industrial life. It is expected the report of this committee will be available for later congressional action. Meantime, the requirement that the Secretary of the Interior should make certain leases of land belonging to the Osage Indians, in accordance with the act of March 3, 1921, should be repealed. The authority to lease should be discretionary, in order that the property of the Indians way not be wasted and the public suffer a future lack of supply.

Alien Property

Under treaty the property held by the Alien Property Custodian was to be retained until suitable provision had been made for the satisfaction of American claims. While still protecting the American claimants, in order to afford every possible accommodation to the nationals of the countries whose property was held, the Congress has made liberal provision for the return of a larger part of the property. All trusts under $10,000 were returned in full, and partial returns were made on the others. The total returned was approximately $350,000,000.

There is still retained, however, about $250,000,000. The Mixed Claims Commission has made such progress in the adjudication of claims that legislation can now be enacted providing for the return of the property, which should be done under conditions which will protect our Government and our claimants. Such a measure will be proposed, and I recommend its enactment.

Railroad Consolidation

In order to increase the efficiency of transportation and decrease its cost to the shipper, railroad consolidation must be secured. Legislation is needed to simplify the necessary procedure to secure such agreements and arrangements for consolidation, always under the control and with the approval of the Interstate Commerce Commission. Pending this, no adequate or permanent reorganization can be made of the freight-rate structure. Meantime, both agriculture and industry are compelled to wait for needed relief. This is purely a business question, which should be stripped of all local and partisan bias and decided on broad principles and its merits in order to promote the public welfare. A large amount of new construction and equipment, which will furnish employment for labor and markets for commodities of both factory and farm, wait on the decision of this important question. Delay is holding back the progress of our country.

Many of the same arguments are applicable to the consolidation of the Washington traction companies.

Veterans

The care which this country has lavished on its veterans is known of all men. The yearly outlay for this purpose is about $750,000,000, or about the cost of running the Federal Government, outside of the Post Office Department, before the World War. The Congress will have before it recommendations of the American Legion, the Veterans of Foreign Wars, and other like organizations, which should receive candid consideration. We should continue to foster our system of compensation and rehabilitation, and provide hospitals and insurance. The magnitude of the undertaking is already so large that all requests calling for further expenditure should have the most searching scrutiny. Our present system of pensions is already sufficiently liberal. It was increased by the last Congress for Civil and Spanish War veterans and widows and for some dependents.

It has been suggested that the various governmental agencies now dealing with veterans' relief be consolidated. This would bring many advantages. It is recommended that the proper committees of the Congress make a thorough survey of this subject, in order to determine if legislation to secure such consolidation is desirable.

Education

For many years it has been the policy of the Federal Government to encourage and foster the cause of education. Large sums of money are annually appropriated to carry on vocational training. Many millions go into agricultural schools. The general subject is under the immediate direction of a Commissioner of Education. While this subject is strictly a State and local function, it should continue to have the encouragement of the National Government. I am still of the opinion that much good could be accomplished through the establishment of a Department of Education and Relief, into which would be gathered all of these functions under one directing member of the Cabinet.

Department Of Labor

Industrial relations have never been more peaceful. In recent months they have suffered from only one serious controversy. In all others difficulties have been adjusted, both management and labor wishing to settle controversies by friendly agreement rather than by compulsion. The welfare of women and children is being especially guarded by our Department of Labor. Its Children's Bureau is in cooperation with 26 State boards and 80 juvenile courts.

Through its Bureau of Immigration it bas been found that medical examination abroad has saved prospective immigrants from much hardship. Some further legislation to provide for reuniting families when either the husband or the wife is in this country, and granting more freedom for the migration of the North American Indian tribes is desirable.

The United States Employment Service has enabled about 2,000,000 men and women to gain paying positions in the last fiscal year. Particular attention has been given to assisting men past middle life and in providing field labor for harvesting agricultural crops. This has been made possible in part through the service of the Federal Board for Vocational Education, which is cooperating with the States in a program to increase the technical knowledge and skill of the wage earner.

Public Buildings

Construction is under way in the country and ground has been broken for carrying out a public-building program for Washington. We have reached a time when not only the conveniences but the architectural beauty of the public buildings of the Capital City should be given much attention. It will be necessary to purchase further land and provide the required continuing appropriations.

Historical Celebrations

Provision is being made to commemorate the two hundredth anniversary of the birth of George Washington. Suggestion has been made for the construction of a memorial road leading from the Capital to Mount Vernon, which may well have the consideration of the Congress, and the commission intrusted with preparations for the celebration will undoubtedly recommend publication of the complete writings of Washington and a series of writings by different authors relating to him.

February 25, 1929, is the one hundred and fiftieth anniversary of the capture of Fort Sackville, at Vincennes, in the State of Indiana. This eventually brought into the Union what was known as the Northwest Territory, embracing the region north of the Ohio River between the Alleghenies and the Mississippi River. This expedition was led by George Rogers Clark. His heroic character and the importance of his victory are too little known and understood. They gave us not only this Northwest Territory but by means of that the prospect of reaching the Pacific. The State of Indiana is proposing to dedicate the site of Fort Sackville as a national shrine. The Federal Government may well make some provision for the erection under its own management of a fitting memorial at that point.

Foreign Relations

It is the policy of the United States to promote peace. We are a peaceful people and committed to the settling of disputes by amicable adjustment rather than by force. We have believed that peace can best be secured by a faithful observance on our part of the principles of international law, accompanied by patience and conciliation, and requiring of others a like treatment for ourselves. We have lately had some difference with Mexico relative to the injuries inflicted upon our nationals and their property within that country. A firm adherence to our rights and a scrupulous respect for the sovereignty of Mexico, both in accordance with the law of nations, coupled with patience and forbearance, it is hoped will resolve all our differences without interfering with the friendly relationship between the two Governments.

We have been compelled to send naval and marine forces to China to protect the lives and property of our citizens. Fortunately their simple presence there has been sufficient to prevent any material loss of life. But there has been considerable loss of property. That unhappy country is torn by factions and revolutions which bid fair to last for an indefinite period. Meanwhile we are protecting our citizens and stand ready to cooperate with any government which may emerge in promoting the welfare of the people of China. They have always had our friendship, and they should especially merit our consideration in these days of their distraction and distress.

We were confronted by similar condition on a small scale in Nicaragua. Our marine and naval forces protected our citizens and their property and prevented a heavy sacrifice of life and the destruction of that country by a reversion to a state of revolution. Henry L. Stimson, former Secretary of War, was sent there to cooperate with our diplomatic and military officers in effecting a settlement between the contending parties. This was done on the assurance that we would cooperate in restoring a state of peace where our rights would be protected by giving our assistance in the conduct of the next presidential election, which occurs in a few months. With this assurance the population returned to their peacetime pursuits, with the exception of some small roving bands of outlaws.

In general, our relations with other countries can be said to have improved within the year. While having a due regard for our own affairs, the protection of our own rights, and the advancement of our own people, we can afford to be liberal toward others. Our example has become of great importance in the world. It is recognized that we are independent, detached, and can and do take a disinterested position in relation to international affairs. Our charity embraces the earth. Our trade is far flung. Our financial favors are widespread. Those who are peaceful and law-abiding realize that not only have they nothing to fear from us, but that they can rely on our moral support. Proposals for promoting the peace of the world will have careful consideration. But we are not a people who are always seeking for a sign. We know that peace comes from honesty and fair dealing, from moderation, and a generous regard for the rights of others. The heart of the Nation is more important than treaties. A spirit of generous consideration is a more certain defense than great armaments. We should continue to promote peace by our example, and fortify it by such international covenants against war as we are permitted under our Constitution to make.

American Progress

Our country has made much progress. But it has taken, and will continue to take, much effort. Competition will be keen, the temptation to selfishness and arrogance will be severe, the provocations to deal harshly with weaker peoples will be many. All of these are embraced in the opportunity for true greatness. They will be overbalanced by cooperation by generosity, and a spirit of neighborly kindness. The forces of the universe are taking humanity in that direction. In doing good, in walking humbly, in sustaining its own people in ministering to other nations, America will work out its own mighty destiny.

Calvin Coolidge, 1925–1929

Annual Message to Congress
December 4, 1928

Calvin Coolidge's last State of the Union message came just three months before he left office; the speech followed the electoral triumph of his fellow Republican (and former secretary of commerce) Herbert Hoover. Coolidge had announced in

1927 that he would not seek another term in office, although he remained popular with many Americans.

In his message, delivered in writing to Congress, the president struck a positive note about the country, painting a picture of a prosperous, peaceful nation. "The country can regard the present with satisfaction and anticipate the future with optimism," he declared.

Coolidge had served as president since 1923. He had been vice president under Warren G. Harding, but Harding's untimely death propelled Coolidge into the presidency. A well-liked former governor of Massachusetts, Coolidge easily won a full four-year term in the elections of 1924. While the taciturn New Englander was known as "Silent Cal," his presidency coincided with the growth of radio, and Coolidge made the most of the new technology. His 1923 State of the Union message was the first to be broadcast.

Coolidge's presidency epitomized the probusiness climate of the United States in the 1920s. In his 1928 message, the president focused on many of the same themes found in his previous State of the Union messages, hailing the benefits of low taxation, debt payments, and a balanced budget. "It is desirable that the government continue its helpful attitude toward American business," he said.

He stated that the previous year had seen a reduction in the national debt but remarked that government economies were not made at the expense of "any legitimate public need." He listed a series of government programs underway, including efforts relating to flood control and to public buildings.

In addition, he encouraged the Senate to ratify the Kellogg-Briand Pact, which sought to outlaw war among its signatories, and urged consolidation of veteran-related functions into one government department.

As Coolidge left office and turned the White House reins over to Hoover in March of 1929, the country still seemed in great shape economically. But things were to change, and the boom times of the 1920s were to come crashing to a halt as the stock market plummeted in October 1929, heralding the start of the Great Depression. As a result, the tone of Hoover's presidency would be far different from that of Coolidge.

To the Congress of the United States:

No Congress of the United States ever assembled, on surveying the state of the Union, has met with a more pleasing prospect than that which appears at the present time. In the domestic field there is tranquility and contentment, harmonious relations between management and wage earner, freedom from industrial strife, and the highest record of years of prosperity. In the foreign field there is peace, the good will which comes from mutual understanding, and the knowledge that the problems which a short time ago appeared so ominous are yielding to the touch of manifest friendship. The great wealth created by our enterprise and industry, and saved by our economy, has had the widest distribution among our own people, and has gone out in a steady stream to serve the charity and the business of the world. The requirements of existence have passed beyond the standard of necessity into the region of luxury. Enlarging production is consumed by an increasing demand at home and an expanding commerce abroad. The country can regard the present with satisfaction and anticipate the future with optimism.

The main source of these unexampled blessings lies in the integrity and character of the American people. They have had great faith, which they have supplemented with mighty works. They have been able to put trust in each other and trust in their Government. Their candor in dealing with foreign governments has commanded respect and confidence. Yet these remarkable powers would have been exerted almost in vain without the constant cooperation and careful administration of the Federal Government.

We have been coming into a period which may be fairly characterized as a conservation of our national resources. Wastefulness in public business and private enterprise has been displaced by constructive economy. This has been accomplished by bringing our domestic and foreign relations more and more under a reign of law. A rule of force has been giving way to a rule of reason. We have substituted for the vicious circle of increasing expenditures, increasing tax rates, and diminishing profits the charmed circle of diminishing expenditures, diminishing tax rates, and increasing profits.

Four times we have made a drastic revision of our internal revenue system, abolishing many taxes and substantially reducing almost all others. Each time the resulting stimulation to business has so increased taxable incomes and profits that a surplus has been produced. One-third of the national debt has been paid, while much of the other two-thirds has been refunded at lower rates, and these savings of interest and constant economies have enabled us to repeat the satisfying process of more tax reductions. Under this sound and healthful encouragement the national income has increased nearly 50 per cent, until it is estimated to stand well over $90,000,000,000. It has been a method which has performed the seeming miracle of leaving a much greater percentage of earnings in the hands of the taxpayers with scarcely any diminution of the Government revenue. That is constructive economy in the highest degree. It is the corner stone of prosperity. It should not fail to be continued.

This action began by the application of economy to public expenditure. If it is to be permanent, it must be made so by the repeated application of economy. There is no surplus on which to base further tax revision at this time. Last June the estimates showed a threatened deficit for the current fiscal year of $94,000,000. Under my direction the departments began saving all they could out of their present appropriations. The last tax reduction brought an encouraging improvement in business, beginning early in October, which will also increase our revenue. The combination of economy and good times now indicates a surplus of about $37,000,000. This is a margin of less than 1 percent on our expenditures and makes it obvious that the Treasury is in no condition to undertake increases in expenditures to be made before June 30. It is necessary therefore during the present session to refrain from new appropriations for immediate outlay, or if such are absolutely required to provide for them by new revenue; otherwise, we shall reach the end of the year with the unthinkable result of an unbalanced budget. For the first time during my term of office we face that contingency. I am certain that the Congress would not pass and I should not feel warranted in approving legislation which would involve us in that financial disgrace.

On the whole the finances of the Government are most satisfactory. Last year the national debt was reduced about $906,000,000. The refunding and retirement of the second and third Liberty loans have just been brought to a successful conclusion, which will save about $75,000,000 a year in interest. The unpaid balance has been arranged in maturities convenient for carrying out our permanent debt-paying Program.

The enormous savings made have not been at the expense of any legitimate public need. The Government plant has been kept up and many improvements are under way, while its service is fully manned and the general efficiency of operation has increased. We have been enabled to undertake many new enterprises. Among these are the adjusted compensation of the veterans of the World War, which is costing us $112,000,000 a year; amortizing our liability to the civil service retirement funds, $20,000,000; increase of expenditures for rivers and harbors including flood control, $43,000,000; public buildings, $47,000,000. In 1928 we spent $50,000,000 in the adjustment of war claims and alien property. These are examples of a large list of items.

Foreign Relations

When we turn from our domestic affairs to our foreign relations, we likewise perceive peace and progress. The Sixth International Conference of American States was held at Habana last winter. It contributed to a better understanding and cooperation among the nations. Eleven important conventions were signed and 71 resolutions passed. Pursuant to the plan then adopted, this Government has invited the other 20 nations of this hemisphere to a conference on conciliation and arbitration, which meets in Washington on December 10. All the nations have accepted and the expectation is justified that important progress will be made in methods for resolving international differences by means of arbitration.

During the year we have signed 11 new arbitration treaties, and 22 more are under negotiation.

Nicaragua

When a destructive and bloody revolution lately broke out in Nicaragua, at the earnest and repeated entreaties of its Government I dispatched our Marine forces there to protect the lives and interests of our citizens. To compose the contending parties, I sent there Col. Henry L. Stimson, former Secretary of War and now Governor General of the Philippine Islands, who secured an agreement that warfare should cease, a national election should be held and peace should be restored. Both parties conscientiously carried out this agreement, with the exception of a few bandits who later mostly surrendered or left the country. President Adolfe Diaz appointed Brig. Gen. Frank R. McCoy, United States Army, president of the election board, which included also one member of each political party.

A free and fair election has been held and has worked out so successfully that both parties have joined in requesting like cooperation from this country at the election four years hence, to which I have refrained from making any commitments, although our country must be gratified at such an exhibition of success and appreciation. Nicaragua is regaining its prosperity and has taken a long step in the direction of peaceful self-government.

Tacna-Arica

The long-standing differences between Chile and Peru have been sufficiently composed so that diplomatic relations have been resumed by the exchange of ambassadors.

Negotiations are hopefully proceeding as this is written for the final adjustment of the differences over their disputed territory.

Mexico

Our relations with Mexico are on a more satisfactory basis than at any time since their revolution. Many misunderstandings have been resolved and the most frank and friendly negotiations promise a final adjustment of all unsettled questions. It is exceedingly gratifying that Ambassador Morrow has been able to bring our two neighboring countries, which have so many interests in common, to a position of confidence in each other and of respect for mutual sovereign rights.

China

The situation in China which a few months ago was so threatening as to call for the dispatch of a large additional force has been much composed. The Nationalist Government has established itself over the country and promulgated a new organic law announcing a program intended to promote the political and economic welfare of the people. We have recognized this Government, encouraged its progress, and have negotiated a treaty restoring to China complete tariff autonomy and guaranteeing our citizens against discriminations. Our trade in that quarter is increasing and our forces are being reduced.

Greek and Austrian Debts

Pending before the Congress is a recommendation for the settlement of the Greek debt and the Austrian debt. Both of these are comparatively small and our country can afford to be generous. The rehabilitation of these countries awaits their settlement. There would also be advantages to our trade. We could scarcely afford to be the only nation that refuses the relief which Austria seeks. The Congress has already granted Austria a long-time moratorium, which it is understood will be waived and immediate payments begun on her debt on the same basis which we have extended to other countries.

Peace Treaty

One of the most important treaties ever laid before the Senate of the United States will be that which the 15 nations recently signed at Paris, and to which 44 other nations have declared their intention to adhere, renouncing war as a national policy and agreeing to resort only to peaceful means for the adjustment of international differences. It is the most solemn declaration against war, the most positive adherence to peace, that it is possible for sovereign nations to make. It does not supersede our inalienable sovereign right and duty of national defense or undertake to commit us before the event to any mode of action which the Congress might decide to be wise if ever the treaty should be broken. But it is a new standard in the world around which can rally the informed and enlightened opinion of nations to prevent their governments from being forced into hostile action by the temporary outbreak of international animosities. The observance of this covenant, so simple and so straightforward, promises more for the peace of the world than any other agreement ever negotiated among the nations.

National Defense

The first duty of our Government to its own citizens and foreigners within its borders is the preservation of order. Unless and until that duty is met a government is not even eligible for recognition among the family of nations. The advancement of world civilization likewise is dependent upon that order among the people of different countries which we term peace. To insure our citizens against the infringement of their legal rights at home and abroad, to preserve order, liberty, and peace by making the law supreme, we have an Army and a Navy.

Both of these are organized for defensive purposes. Our Army could not be much reduced, but does not need to be increased. Such new housing and repairs as are necessary are under way and the 6-year program in aviation is being put into effect in both branches of our service.

Our Navy, according to generally accepted standards, is deficient in cruisers. We have 10 comparatively new vessels, 22 that are old, and 8 to be built. It is evident that renewals and replacements must be provided. This matter was thoroughly canvassed at the last session of the Congress and does not need restatement. The bill before the Senate with the elimination of the time clause should be passed. We have no intention of competing with any other country. This building program is for necessary replacements and to meet our needs for defense.

The cost of national defense is stupendous. It has increased $118,000,000 in the past four years. The estimated expenditure for 1930 is $668,000,000. While this is made up of many items it is, after all, mostly dependent upon numbers. Our defensive needs do not call for any increase in the number of men in the Army or the Navy. We have reached the limit of what we ought to expend for that purpose.

I wish to repeat again for the benefit of the timid and the suspicious that this country is neither militaristic nor imperialistic. Many people at home and abroad, who constantly make this charge, are the same ones who are even more solicitous to have us extend assistance to foreign countries. When such assistance is granted, the inevitable result is that we have foreign interests. For us to refuse the customary support and protection of such interests would be in derogation of the sovereignty of this Nation. Our largest foreign interests are in the British Empire, France, and Italy. Because we are constantly solicitous for those interests, I doubt if anyone would suppose that those countries feel we harbor toward them any militaristic or imperialistic design. As for smaller countries, we certainly do not want any of them. We are more anxious than they are to have their sovereignty respected. Our entire influence is in behalf of their independence. Cuba stands as a witness to our adherence to this principle.

The position of this Government relative to the limitation of armaments, the results already secured, and the developments up to the present time are so well known to the Congress that they do not require any restatement.

Veterans

The magnitude of our present system of veterans' relief is without precedent, and the results have been far-reaching. For years a service pension has been granted to the Grand Army and lately to the survivors of the Spanish-American War. At the time we entered the World War however, Congress departed from the usual pension system followed by our Government. Eleven years have elapsed since our laws were first enacted, initiating a system of compensation, rehabilitation, hospitalization, and insurance for the disabled of the World War and their dependents. The administration of all the laws concerning relief has been a difficult task, but it can safely be stated that these measures have omitted nothing in their desire to deal generously and humanely. We should continue to foster this system and provide all the facilities necessary for adequate care. It is the conception of our Government that the pension roll is an honor roll. It should include all those who are justly entitled to its benefits, but exclude all others.

Annual expenditures for all forms of veterans' relief now approximate $765,000,000, and are increasing from year to year. It is doubtful if the peak of expenditures will be reached even under present legislation for some time yet to come. Further amendments to the existing law will be suggested by the American Legion, the Veterans of Foreign Wars of the United States, the Disabled American Veterans of the World War, and other like organizations, and it may be necessary for administrative purposes, or in order to remove some existing inequalities in the present law, to make further changes. I am sure that such recommendations as may be submitted to the Congress will receive your careful consideration. But because of the vast expenditure now being made, each year, with every assurance that it will increase, and because of the great liberality of the existing law, the proposal of any additional legislation dealing with this subject should receive most searching scrutiny from the Congress.

You are familiar with the suggestion that the various public agencies now dealing with matters of veterans' relief be consolidated in one Government department. Some advantages to this plan seem apparent, especially in the simplification of administration and in the opportunity of bringing about a greater uniformity in the application of veterans' relief. I recommend that a survey be made by the proper committees of Congress dealing with this subject, in order to determine whether legislation to secure this consolidation is desirable.

Agriculture

The past year has been marked by notable though not uniform improvement in agriculture. The general purchasing power of farm products and the volume of production have advanced. This means not only further progress, in overcoming the price disparity into which agriculture was plunged in 1920–21, but also increased efficiency on the part of farmers and a well-grounded confidence in the future of agriculture.

The livestock industry has attained the best balance for many years and is prospering conspicuously. Dairymen, beef producers, and poultrymen are receiving substantially larger returns than last year. Cotton, although lower in price than at this time last year, was produced in greater volume and the prospect for cotton incomes is favorable. But progress is never uniform in a vast and highly diversified agriculture or industry. Cash grains, hay, tobacco, and potatoes will bring somewhat smaller returns this year than last. Present indications are, however, that the gross farm income will be somewhat larger than in the crop year 1927–28, when the total was $12,253,000,000. The corresponding figure for 1926–27 was $12,127,000,000, and in 1925–26, $12,670,000,000. Still better results would have been secured this year had there not been an undue increase in the production of certain crops. This is particularly true of potatoes, which have sold at an unremunerative price, or at a loss, as a direct result of overexpansion of acreage.

The present status of agriculture, although greatly improved over that of a few years ago, bespeaks the need of further improvement, which calls for determined effort of farmers themselves, encouraged and assisted by wise public policy. The Government has been, and must continue to be, alive to the needs of agriculture.

In the past eight years more constructive legislation of direct benefit to agriculture has been adopted than during any other period. The Department of Agriculture has been broadened and reorganized to insure greater efficiency. The department is laying greater stress on the economic and business phases of agriculture. It is lending every possible assistance to cooperative marketing associations. Regulatory and research work have been segregated in order that each field may be served more effectively.

I can not too strongly commend, in the field of fact finding, the research work of the Department of Agriculture and the State experiment stations. The department now receives annually $4,000,000 more for research than in 1921. In addition, the funds paid to the States for experimentation purposes under the Purnell Act constitute an annual increase in Federal payments to State agricultural experiment stations of $2,400,000 over the amount appropriated in 1921. The program of support for research may wisely be continued and expanded. Since 1921 we have appropriated nearly an additional $2,000,000 for extension work, and this sum is to be increased next year under authorization by the Capper-Ketcham Act.

The Surplus Problem

While these developments in fundamental research, regulation, and dissemination of agricultural information are of distinct help to agriculture, additional effort is needed. The surplus problem demands attention. As emphasized in my last message, the Government should assume no responsibility in normal times for crop surplus clearly due to overextended acreage. The Government should, however, provide reliable information as a guide to private effort; and in this connection fundamental research on prospective supply and demand, as a guide to production and marketing, should be encouraged. Expenditure of public funds to bring in more new land should have most searching scrutiny, so long as our farmers face unsatisfactory prices for crops and livestock produced on land already under cultivation.

Every proper effort should be made to put land to uses for which it is adapted. The reforestation of land best suited for timber production is progressing and should be encouraged, and to this end the forest taxation inquiry was instituted to afford a practical guide for public policy. Improvement bas been made in grazing regulation in the forest reserves, not only to protect the ranges, but to preserve the soil from erosion. Similar action is urgently needed to protect other public lands which are now overgrazed and rapidly eroding.

Temporary expedients, though sometimes capable of appeasing the demands of the moment, can not permanently solve the surplus problem and might seriously aggravate it. Hence putting the Government directly into business, subsidies, and price fixing, and the alluring promises of political action as a substitute for private initiative, should be avoided.

The Government should aid in promoting orderly marketing and in handling surpluses clearly due to weather and seasonal conditions. As a beginning there should be created a Federal farm board consisting of able and experienced men empowered to advise producers' associations in establishing central agencies or stabilization corporations to handle surpluses, to seek more economical means of merchandising, and to aid the producer in securing returns according to the quality of his product. A revolving loan fund should be provided for the necessary financing until these agencies shall have developed means of financing their operations through regularly constituted credit institutions. Such a bill should carry authority for raising the money, by loans or otherwise, necessary to meet the expense, as the Treasury has no surplus.

Agriculture has lagged behind industry in achieving that unity of effort which modern economic life demands. The cooperative movement, which is gradually building the needed organization, is in harmony with public interest and therefore merits public encouragement.

The Responsibility of the States

Important phases of public policy related to agriculture lie within the sphere of the States. While successive reductions in Federal taxes have relieved most farmers of direct taxes to the National Government, State and local levies have become a serious burden. This problem needs immediate and thorough study with a view to correction at the earliest possible moment. It will have to be made largely by the States themselves.

Commerce

It is desirable that the Government continue its helpful attitude toward American business. The activities of the Department of Commerce have contributed largely to the present satisfactory position in our international trade, which has reached about $9,000,000,000 annually. There should be no slackening of effort in that direction. It is also important that the department's assistance to domestic commerce be continued. There is probably no way in which the Government can aid sound economic progress more effectively than by cooperation with our business men to reduce wastes in distribution.

Commercial Aeronautics

Continued progress in civil aviation is most gratifying. Demands for airplanes and motors have taxed both the industry and the licensing and inspection service of the Department of Commerce to their capacity. While the compulsory licensing provisions of the air commerce act apply only to equipment and personnel engaged in interstate and foreign commerce, a Federal license may be procured by anyone possessing the necessary qualifications. State legislation, local airport regulations, and insurance requirements make such a license practically indispensable. This results in uniformity of regulation and increased safety in operation, which are essential to aeronautical development. Over 17,000 young men and women have now applied for Federal air pilot's licenses or permits. More than 80 per cent of them applied during the past year.

Our national airway system exceeds 14,000 miles in length and has 7,500 miles lighted for night operations. Provision has been made for lighting 4,000 miles more during the current fiscal year and equipping an equal mileage with radio facilities. Three-quarters of our people are now served by these routes. With the rapid growth of air mail, express, and passenger service, this new transportation medium is daily becoming a more important factor in commerce. It is noteworthy that this development has taken place without governmental subsidies. Commercial passenger flights operating on schedule have reached 13,000 miles per day.

During the next fortnight this Nation will entertain the nations of the world in a celebration of the twenty-fifth anniversary of the first successful airplane flight. The credit for this epoch-making achievement belongs to a citizen of our own country, Orville Wright.

Cuban Parcel Post

I desire to repeat my recommendation of an earlier message, that Congress enact the legislation necessary to make permanent the Parcel Post Convention with Cuba, both as a facility to American commerce and as a measure of equity to Cuba in the one class of goods which that country can send here by parcel post without detriment to our own trade.

"Maine" Battleship Memorial

When I attended the Pan American Conference at Habana, the President of Cuba showed me a marble statue made from the original memorial that was overturned by a storm after it was erected on the Cuban shore to the memory of the men who perished in the destruction of the battleship Maine. As a testimony of friendship and appreciation of the Cuban Government and people he most generously offered to present this to the United States, and I assured him of my pleasure in accepting it. There is no location in the White House for placing so large and heavy a structure, and I therefore urge the Congress to provide by law for some locality where it can be set up.

Railroads

In previous annual messages I have suggested the enactment of laws to promote railroad consolidation with the view of increasing the efficiency of transportation and lessening its cost to the public. While consolidations can and should be made under the present law until it is changed, yet the provisions of the act of 1920 have not been found fully adequate to meet the needs of other methods of consolidation. Amendments designed to remedy these defects have been considered at length by the respective committees of Congress and a bill was reported out late in the last session which I understand has the approval in principle of the Interstate Commerce Commission. It is to be hoped that this legislation may be enacted at an early date.

Experience has shown that the interstate commerce law requires definition and clarification in several other respects, some of which have been pointed out by the Interstate Commerce Commission in its annual reports to the Congress. It will promote the public interest to have the Congress give early consideration to the recommendations there made.

Merchant Marine

The cost of maintaining the United States Government merchant fleet has been steadily reduced. We have established American flag lines in foreign trade where they had never before existed as a means of promoting commerce and as a naval auxiliary. There have been sold to private American capital for operation within the past few years 14 of these lines, which, under the encouragement of the recent legislation passed by the Congress, give promise of continued successful operation. Additional legislation from time to time may be necessary to promote future advancement under private control.

Through the cooperation of the Post Office Department and the Shipping Board long-term contracts are being made with American steamship lines for carrying mail, which already promise the construction of 15 to 20 new vessels and the gradual reestablishment of the American merchant marine as a private enterprise. No action of the National Government has been so beneficial to our shipping. The cost is being absorbed to a considerable extent by the disposal of unprofitable lines operated by the Shipping Board, for which the new law has made a market. Meanwhile it should be our policy to maintain necessary strategic lines under the Government operation until they can be transferred to private capital.

Inter-American Highway

In my message last year I expressed the view that we should lend our encouragement for more good roads to all the principal points on this hemisphere south of the Rio Grande. My view has not changed. The Pan American Union has recently indorsed it. In some of the countries to the south a great deal of progress is being made in road building. In others engineering features are often exacting and financing difficult. As those countries enter upon programs for road building we should be ready to contribute from our abundant experience to make their task easier of accomplishment. I prefer not to go into civil life to accomplish this end. We already furnish military and naval advisors, and following this precedent we could draw competent men from these same sources and from the Department of Agriculture.

We should provide our southern neighbors, if they request it, with such engineer advisors for the construction of roads and bridges. Private interests should look with favor upon all reasonable loans sought by these countries to open main lines of travel. Such assistance should be given especially to any project for a highway designed to connect all the countries on this hemisphere and thus facilitate intercourse and closer relations among them.

Air Mail Service

The friendly relations and the extensive commercial intercourse with the Western Hemisphere to the south of us are being further cemented by the establishment and extension of air-mail routes. We shall soon have one from Key West, Fla., over Cuba, Haiti, and Santo Domingo to San Juan, P. R., where it will connect with another route to Trinidad. There will be another route from Key West to the Canal Zone, where connection will be made with a route across the northern coast of South America to Paramaribo. This will give us a circle around the Caribbean under our own control. Additional connections will be made at Colon with a route running down the west coast of South America as far as Conception, Chile, and with the French air mail at Paramaribo running down the eastern coast of South America. The air service already spans our continent, with laterals running to Mexico and Canada, and covering a daily flight of over 28,000 miles, with an average cargo of 15,000 pounds.

Waterways

Our river and harbor improvements are proceeding with vigor. In the past few years we have increased the appropriation for this regular work $28,000,000, besides what is to be expended on flood control. The total appropriation for this year was over $91,000,000. The Ohio River is almost ready for opening; work on the Missouri and other rivers is under way. In accordance with the Mississippi flood law Army engineers are making investigations and surveys on other streams throughout the country with a view to flood control, navigation, waterpower, and irrigation. Our barge lines are being operated under generous appropriations, and negotiations are developing relative to the St. Lawrence waterway. To secure the largest benefits from all these waterways joint rates must be established with the railroads, preferably by agreement, but otherwise as a result of congressional action.

We have recently passed several river and harbor bills. The work ordered by the Congress, not yet completed, will cost about $243,000,000, besides the hundreds of millions to be spent on the Mississippi flood way. Until we can see our way out of this expense no further river and harbor legislation should be passed, as expenditures to put it into effect would be four or five years away.

Irrigation of Arid Lands

For many years the Federal Government has been committed to the wise policy of reclamation and irrigation. While it has met with some failures due to unwise selection of projects and lack of thorough soil surveys, so that they could not be placed on a sound business basis, on the whole the service has been of such incalculable benefit in so many States that no one would advocate its abandonment. The program to which we are already committed, providing for the construction of new projects authorized by Congress and the completion of old projects, will tax the resources of the reclamation fund over a period of years. The high cost of improving and equipping farms adds to the difficulty of securing settlers for vacant farms on federal projects.

Readjustments authorized by the reclamation relief act of May 25, 1926, have given more favorable terms of repayment to settlers. These new financial arrangements and the general prosperity on irrigation projects have resulted in increased collections by the Department of the Interior of charges due the reclamation fund. Nevertheless, the demand for still smaller yearly payments on some projects continues. These conditions should have consideration in connection with any proposed new projects.

Colorado River

For several years the Congress has considered the erection of a dam on the Colorado River for flood-control, irrigation, and domestic water purposes, all of which may properly be considered as Government functions. There would be an incidental creation of water power which could be used for generating electricity. As private enterprise can very well fill this field, there is no need for the Government to go into it. It is unfortunate that the States interested in this water have been unable to agree among themselves. Nevertheless, any legislation should give every possible safeguard to the present and prospective rights of each of them.

The Congress will have before it, the detailed report of a special board appointed to consider the engineering and economic feasibility of this project. From the short summary which I have seen of it, I judge they consider the engineering problems can be met at somewhat increased cost over previous estimates. They prefer the Black Canyon site. On the economic features they are not so clear and appear to base their conclusions on many conditions which can not be established with certainty. So far as I can judge, however, from the summary, their conclusions appear sufficiently favorable, so that I feel warranted in recommending a measure which will protect the rights of the States, discharge the necessary Government functions, and leave the electrical field to private enterprise.

Muscle Shoals

The development of other methods of producing nitrates will probably render this plant less important for that purpose than formerly. But we have it, and I am told it still provides a practical method of making nitrates for national defense and farm fertilizers. By dividing the property into its two component parts of power and nitrate plants it would be possible to dispose of the power, reserving the right to any concern that wished to make nitrates to use any power that might be needed for that purpose. Such a disposition of the power plant can be made that will return in rental about $2,000,000 per year. If the Congress would grant the Secretary of War authority to lease the nitrate plant on such terms as would insure the largest production of nitrates, the entire property could begin to function. Such a division, I am aware, has never seemed to appeal to the Congress. I should also gladly approve a bill granting authority to lease the entire property for the production of nitrates.

I wish to avoid building another dam at public expense. Future operators should provide for that themselves. But if they were to be required to repay the cost of such dam with the prevailing commercial rates for interest, this difficulty will be considerably lessened. Nor do I think this property should be made a vehicle for putting the United States Government indiscriminately into the private and retail field of power distribution and nitrate sales.

Conservation

The practical application of economy to the resources of the country calls for conservation. This does not mean that every resource should not be developed to its full degree, but it means that none of them should be wasted. We have a conservation board working on our oil problem. This is of the utmost importance to the future well-being of our people in this age of oil-burning engines and the general application of gasoline to transportation. The Secretary of the Interior should not be compelled to lease oil lands of the Osage Indians when the market is depressed and the future supply is in jeopardy.

While the area of lands remaining in public ownership is small, compared with the vast area in private ownership, the natural resources of those in public ownership are of immense present and future value. This is particularly true as to minerals and water power. The proper bureaus have been classifying these resources to the end that they may be conserved. Appropriate estimates are being submitted, in the Budget, for the further prosecution of this important work.

Immigration

The policy of restrictive immigration should be maintained. Authority should be granted the Secretary of Labor to give immediate preference to learned professions and experts essential to new industries. The reuniting of families should be expedited. Our immigration and naturalization laws might well be codified.

Wage Earner

In its economic life our country has rejected the long accepted law of a limitation of the wage fund, which led to pessimism and despair because it was the doctrine of perpetual poverty, and has substituted for it the American conception that the only limit to profits and wages is production, which is the doctrine of optimism and hope because it leads to prosperity. Here and there the councils of labor are still darkened by the theory that only by limiting individual production can there be any assurance of permanent employment for increasing numbers, but in general, management and wage earner alike have become emancipated from this doom and have entered a new era in industrial thought which has unleashed the productive capacity of the individual worker with an increasing scale of wages and profits, the end of which is not yet. The application of this theory accounts for our widening distribution of wealth. No discovery ever did more to increase the happiness and prosperity of the people.

Since 1922 increasing production has increased wages in general 12.9 per cent, while in certain selected trades they have run as high as 34.9 per cent and 38 per cent. Even in the boot and shoe shops the increase is over 5 per cent and in woolen mills 8.4 per cent, although these industries have not prospered like others. As the rise in living costs in this period is negligible, these figures represent real wage increases.

The cause of constructive economy requires that the Government should cooperate with private interests to eliminate the waste arising from industrial accidents. This item, with all that has been done to reduce it, still reaches enormous proportions with great suffering to the workman and great loss to the country.

Women and Children

The Federal Government should continue its solicitous care for the 8,500,000 women wage earners and its efforts in behalf of public health, which is reducing infant mortality and improving the bodily and mental condition of our citizens.

Civil Service

The most marked change made in the civil service of the Government in the past eight years relates to the increase in salaries. The Board of Actuaries on the retirement act shows by its report that July 1, 1921, the average salary of the 330,047 employees subject to the act was $1,307, while on June 30, 1927, the average salary of the corresponding 405,263 was $1,969. This was an increase in six years of nearly 53 per cent. On top of this was the generous increase made at the last session of the Congress generally applicable to Federal employees and another bill increasing the pay in certain branches of the Postal Service beyond the large increase which was made three years ago. This raised the average level from $1,969 to $2,092, making an increase in seven years of over 63 per cent. While it is well known that in the upper brackets the pay in the Federal service is much smaller than in private employment, in the lower brackets, ranging well up over $3,000, it is much higher. It is higher not only in actual money paid, but in privileges granted, a vacation of 30 actual working days, or 5 weeks each year, with additional time running in some departments as high as 30 days for sick leave and the generous provisions of the retirement act. No other body of public servants ever occupied such a fortunate position.

Education

Through the Bureau of Education of the Department of the Interior the Federal Government, acting in an informative and advisory capacity, has rendered valuable service. While this province belongs peculiarly to the States, yet the promotion of education and efficiency in educational methods is a general responsibility of the Federal Government. A survey of negro colleges and universities in the United States has just been completed by the Bureau of Education through funds provided by the institutions themselves and through private sources. The present status of negro higher education was determined and recommendations were made for its advancement. This was one of the numerous cooperative undertakings of the bureau. Following the invitation of the Association of Land Grant Colleges and Universities, the Bureau of Education now has under way the survey of agricultural colleges, authorized by Congress. The purpose of the survey is to ascertain the accomplishments, the status, and the future objectives of this type of educational training. It is now proposed to undertake a survey of secondary schools, which educators insist is timely and essential.

Public Buildings

We have laid out a public building program for the District of Columbia and the country at large running into hundreds of millions of dollars. Three important structures and one annex are already under way and one addition has been completed in the City of Washington. In the country sites have been acquired, many buildings are in course of construction, and some are already completed. Plans for all this work are being prepared in order that it may be carried forward as rapidly as possible. This is the greatest building program ever assumed by this Nation. It contemplates structures of utility and of beauty. When it reaches completion the people will be well served and the Federal city will be supplied with the most beautiful and stately public buildings which adorn any capital in the world.

The American Indian

The administration of Indian affairs has been receiving intensive study for several years. The Department of the Interior has been able to provide better supervision of health, education, and industrial advancement of this native race through additional funds provided by the Congress. The present cooperative arrangement existing between the Bureau of Indian Affairs and the Public Health Service should be extended. The Government's responsibility to the American Indian has been acknowledged by annual increases in appropriations to fulfill its obligations to them and to hasten the time when Federal supervision of their affairs may be properly and safely terminated. The movement in Congress and in some of the State legislatures for extending responsibility in Indian affairs to States should be encouraged. A complete participation by the Indian in our economic life is the end to be desired.

The Negro

For 65 years now our negro population has been under the peculiar care and solicitude of the National Government. The progress which they have made in education and the professions, in wealth and in the arts of civilization, affords one of the most remarkable incidents in this period of world history. They have demonstrated their ability to partake of the advantages of our institutions and to benefit by a free and more and more independent existence. Whatever doubt there may have been of their capacity to assume the status granted to them by the Constitution of this Union is being rapidly dissipated. Their cooperation in the life of the Nation is constantly enlarging.

Exploiting the Negro problem for political ends is being abandoned and their protection is being increased by those States in which their percentage of population is largest. Every encouragement should be extended for the development of the race. The colored people have been the victims of the crime of lynching, which has in late years somewhat decreased. Some parts of the South already have wholesome laws for its restraint and punishment. Their example might well be followed by other States, and by such immediate remedial legislation as the Federal Government can extend under the Constitution.

Philippine Islands

Under the guidance of Governor General Stimson the economic and political conditions of the Philippine Islands have been raised to a standard never before surpassed. The cooperation between his administration and the people of the islands is complete and harmonious. It would be an advantage if relief from double taxation could be granted by the Congress to our citizens doing business in the islands.

Porto Rico

Due to the terrific storm that swept Porto Rico last September, the people of that island suffered large losses. The Red Cross and the War Department went to their rescue. The property loss is being retrieved. Sugar, tobacco, citrus fruit, and coffee, all suffered damage. The first three can largely look after themselves. The coffee growers will need some assistance, which should be extended strictly on a business basis, and only after most careful investigation. The people of Porto Rico are not asking for charity.

Department of Justice

It is desirable that all the legal activities of the Government be consolidated under the supervision of the Attorney General. In 1870 it was felt necessary to create the Department of Justice for this purpose. During the intervening period, either through legislation creating law officers or departmental action, additional legal positions not under the supervision of the Attorney General have been provided until there are now over

900. Such a condition is as harmful to the interest of the Government now as it was in 1870, and should be corrected by appropriate legislation.

Special Government Counsel

In order to prosecute the oil cases, I suggested and the Congress enacted a law providing for the appointment of two special counsel. They have pursued their work with signal ability, recovering all the leased lands besides nearly $30,000,000 in money, and nearly $17,000,000 in other property. They find themselves hampered by a statute, which the Attorney General construes as applying to them, prohibiting their appearing for private clients before any department. For this reason, one has been compelled to resign. No good result is secured by the application of this rule to these counsel, and as Mr. Roberts has consented to take reappointment if the rule is abrogated I recommend the passage of an amendment to the law creating their office exempting them from the general rule against taking other cases involving the Government.

Prohibition

The country has duly adopted the eighteenth amendment. Those who object to it have the right to advocate its modification or repeal. Meantime, it is binding upon the National and State Governments and all our inhabitants. The Federal enforcement bureau is making every effort to prevent violations, especially through smuggling, manufacture, and transportation, and to prosecute generally all violations for which it can secure evidence. It is bound to continue this policy. Under the terms of the Constitution, however, the obligation is equally on the States to exercise the power which they have through the executive, legislative, judicial, and police branches of their governments in behalf of enforcement. The Federal Government is doing and will continue to do all it can in this direction and is entitled to the active cooperation of the States.

Conclusion

The country is in the midst of an era of prosperity more extensive and of peace more permanent than it has ever before experienced. But, having reached this position, we should not fail to comprehend that it can easily be lost. It needs more effort for its support than the less exalted places of the world. We shall not be permitted to take our case, but shall continue to be required to spend our days in unremitting toil. The actions of the Government must command the confidence of the country. Without this, our prosperity would be lost. We must extend to other countries the largest measure of generosity, moderation, and patience. In addition to dealing justly, we can well afford to walk humbly.

The end of government is to keep open the opportunity for a more abundant life. Peace and prosperity are not finalities; they are only methods. It is too easy under their influence for a nation to become selfish and degenerate. This test has come to the United States. Our country has been provided with the resources with which it can enlarge its intellectual, moral, and spiritual life. The issue is in the hands of the people. Our faith in man and God is the justification for the belief in our continuing success.

Herbert Hoover

1929–1933

"Economic depression can not be cured by legislative action or executive pronouncement. Economic wounds must be healed by the action of the cells of the economic body: the producers and consumers themselves."

ANNUAL MESSAGE TO CONGRESS, DECEMBER 2, 1930

Annual Message to Congress

December 3, 1929

Herbert Hoover's first State of the Union message was submitted just over a month after the stock market crash of October 1929. The crash heralded the end of the prosperity of the 1920s and the start of the Great Depression of the 1930s.

In his message, which was written rather than delivered to Congress in person, Hoover downplayed the significance of the crash. He cited government safeguards and procedures that had been put in place in recent years, stating that these efforts would help the economy turn around.

Most of his message dealt with other subjects, ranging from a public buildings project in Washington, D.C., to the country's progress in civil aeronautics, to overcrowding in the federal penitentiary system. But he did devote several paragraphs in his lengthy message to the overall economic situation facing the country. He described the crash as "inevitable" and noted that some people had been "thrown temporarily out of employment." He added that the Federal Reserve system had taken precautions for such an event, and that he was working with businesses and with state and local governments to keep business going as usual.

Hoover's approach to dealing with the situation did not help matters, and the depression only deepened. A believer in American self-reliance and in a balanced budget, Hoover chose not to embark on massive welfare programs to aid the unemployed and the poor.

In a section of his State of the Union message devoted to social service, Hoover commented that the federal role in such services involved the sharing of information as well as some temporary subsidies to states. "Any other attitude by the federal government will undermine one of the most precious possessions of the American people: that is, local and individual responsibility," he said. He did, however, approve of such initiatives as an upcoming White House conference on child health—an event that would not result in government expenses, he said.

Hoover's inaugural address the previous March had named crime as the biggest danger facing the country, and he reiterated that point in his State of the Union message. He mentioned that he had appointed a commission to look into the country's law enforcement and judicial systems. He also discussed the problems involved in enforcing the ever-controversial Prohibition—which had posed difficulties for several administrations since it took effect in 1920.

It was clear, however, that the biggest problem facing the Hoover administration would be the increasingly dire economic conditions facing the country.

To the Senate and House of Representatives:

The Constitution requires that the President "shall, from time to time, give to the Congress Information of the state of the Union, and recommend to their consideration such measures as he shall judge necessary and expedient." In complying with that requirement I wish to emphasize that during the past year the Nation has continued to grow in strength; our people have advanced in comfort; we have gained in knowledge; the education of youth has been more widely spread; moral and spiritual forces have been maintained; peace has become more assured. The problems with which we are confronted are the problems of growth and of progress. In their solution we have to determine the facts, to develop the relative importance to be assigned to such facts, to formulate a common judgment upon them, and to realize solutions in spirit of conciliation.

Foreign Relations

We are not only at peace with all the world, but the foundations for future peace are being substantially strengthened. To promote peace is our long-established policy. Through the Kellogg-Briand pact a great moral standard has been raised in the world. By it fifty-four nations have covenanted to renounce war and to settle all disputes by pacific means. Through it a new world outlook has been inaugurated which has profoundly affected the foreign policies of nations. Since its inauguration we have initiated new efforts not only in the organization of the machinery of peace but also to eliminate dangerous forces which produce controversies amongst nations.

In January, 1926, the Senate gave its consent to adherence to the Court of International Justice with certain reservations. In September of this year the statute establishing the court has, by the action of the nations signatory, been amended to meet the Senate's reservations and to go even beyond those reservations to make clear that the court is a true international court of justice. I believe it will be clear to everyone that no controversy or question in which this country has or claims an interest can be passed on by the court without our consent at the time the question arises. The doubt about advisory opinions has been completely safeguarded. Our adherence to the International Court is, as now constituted, not the slightest step toward entry into the League of Nations. As I have before indicated, I shall direct that our signature be affixed to the protocol of adherence and shall submit it for the approval of the Senate with a special message at some time when it is convenient to deal with it.

In the hope of reducing friction in the world, and with the desire that we may reduce the great economic burdens of naval armament, we have joined in conference with Great Britain, France, Italy, and Japan to be held in London in January to consider the further limitation and reduction of naval arms. We hold high hopes that success may attend this effort.

At the beginning of the present administration the neighboring State of Mexico was best with domestic insurrection. We maintained the embargo upon the shipment of arms to Mexico but permitted the duly constituted Government to procure supplies from our surplus war stocks. Fortunately, the Mexican Government by its own strength successfully withstood the insurrection with but slight damage. Opportunity of further peaceful development is given to that country. At the request of the Mexican Government, we have since lifted the embargo on shipment of arms altogether. The two governments have taken further steps to promote friendly relationships and so solve our differences. Conventions prolonging for a period of two years the life of the general and special claims commissions have been concluded.

In South America we are proud to have had part in the settlement of the long-standing dispute between Chile and Peru in the disposal of the question of Tacna-Arica.

The work of the commission of inquiry and conciliation between Bolivia and Paraguay, in which a representative of this Government participated, has successfully terminated an incident which seemed to threaten war. The proposed plan for final settlement as suggested by the neutral governments is still under consideration.

This Government has continued its efforts to act as a mediator in boundary difficulties between Guatemala and Honduras.

A further instance of profound importance in establishing good will was the inauguration of regular air mail service between the United States and Caribbean, Central American, and South American countries.

We still have marines on foreign soil—in Nicaragua, Haiti, and China. In the large sense we do not wish to be represented abroad in such manner. About 1,600 marines remain in Nicaragua at the urgent request of that government and the leaders of all parties pending the training of a domestic constabulary capable of insuring tranquility. We have already reduced these forces materially and we are anxious to withdraw them further as the situation warrants. In Haiti we have about 700 marines, but it is a much more difficult problem, the solution of which is still obscure. If Congress approves, I shall dispatch a commission to Haiti to review and study the matter in an endeavor to arrive at some more definite policy than at present. Our forces in China constitute 2,605 men, which we hope also further to reduce to the normal legation guard.

It is my desire to establish more firmly our understanding and relationships with the Latin American countries by strengthening the diplomatic missions to those countries. It is my hope to secure men long experienced in our Diplomatic Service, who speak the languages of the peoples to whom they are accredited, as chiefs of our diplomatic missions in these States. I shall send to the Senate at an early date the nominations of several such men.

The Congress has by numerous wise and foresighted acts in the past few years greatly strengthened the character of our representation abroad. It has made liberal provision for the establishment of suitable quarters for our foreign staffs in the different countries. In order, however, that we may further develop the most effective force in this, one of the most responsible functions of our Government, I shall recommend to the Congress more liberal appropriations for the work of the State Department. I know of no expenditure of public money from which a greater economic and moral return can come to us than by assuring the most effective conduct of our foreign relations.

National Defense

To preserve internal order and freedom from encroachment is the first purpose of government. Our Army and Navy are being maintained in a most efficient state under officers of high intelligence and zeal. The extent and expansion of their numbers and equipment as at present authorized are ample for this purpose.

We can well be deeply concerned, however, at the growing expense. From a total expenditure for national defense purposes in 1914 of $267,000,000, it naturally rose with the Great War, but receded again to $612,000,000 in 1924, when again it began to rise until during the current fiscal year the expenditures will reach to over $730,000,000, excluding all civilian services of those departments. Programs now authorized will carry it to still larger figures in future years. While the remuneration paid to our soldiers and sailors is justly at a higher rate than that of any other country in the world, and while the cost of subsistence is higher, yet the total of our expenditures is in excess of those of the most highly militarized nations of the world.

Upon the conference shortly to be held in London will depend such moderation as we can make in naval expenditure. If we shall be compelled to undertake the naval construction implied in the Washington arms treaty as well as other construction which would appear to be necessary if no international agreement can be completed, we shall be committed during the next six years to a construction expenditure of upward of $1,200,000,000 besides the necessary further increase in costs for annual upkeep.

After 1914 the various Army contingents necessarily expanded to the end of the Great War and then receded to the low point in 1924, when expansion again began. In 1914 the officers and men in our regular forces, both Army and Navy, were about 164,000, in 1924 there were about 256,000, and in 1929 there were about 250,000. Our citizens' army, however, including the National Guard and other forms of reserves, increase these totals up to about 299,000 in 1914, about 672,000 in 1924, and about 728,000 in 1929.

Under the Kellogg pact we have undertaken never to use war as an instrument of national policy. We have, therefore, undertaken by covenant to use these equipments solely for defensive purposes. From a defense point of view our forces should be proportioned to national need and should, therefore, to some extent be modified by the prospects of peace, which were never brighter than to-day.

It should be borne in mind that the improvement in the National Guard by Federal support begun in 1920 has definitely strengthened our national security by rendering them far more effective than ever heretofore. The advance of aviation has also greatly increased our effectiveness in defense. In addition to the very large program of air forces which we are maintaining in the Army and Navy, there has been an enormous growth of commercial aviation. This has provided unanticipated reserves in manufacturing capacity and in industrial and air personnel, which again adds to our security.

I recommend that Congress give earnest consideration to the possibilities of prudent action which will give relief from our continuously mounting expenditures.

Finances of the Government

The finances of the Government are in sound condition. I shall submit the detailed evidences and the usual recommendations in the special Budget message. I may, however, summarize our position. The public debt on June 30 this year stood at $16,931,000,000, compared to the maximum in August, 1919, of $26,596,000,000. Since June 30 it has been reduced by a further $238,000,000. In the Budget to be submitted the total appropriations recommended for the fiscal year 1931 are $3,830,445,231, as compared to $3,976,141,651 for the present fiscal year. The present fiscal year, however, includes

$150,000,000 for the Federal Farm Board, as to which no estimate can as yet be determined for 1931.

Owing to the many necessary burdens assumed by Congress in previous years which now require large outlays, it is with extreme difficulty that we shall be able to keep the expenditures for the next fiscal year within the bounds of the present year. Economies in many directions have permitted some accommodation of pressing needs, the net result being an increase, as shown above, of about one-tenth of 1 per cent above the present fiscal year. We can not fail to recognize the obligations of the Government in support of the public welfare but we must coincidentally bear in mind the burden of taxes and strive to find relief through some tax reduction. Every dollar so returned fertilizes the soil of prosperity.

Tax Reduction

The estimate submitted to me by the Secretary of the Treasury and the Budget Director indicates that the Government will close the fiscal year 1930 with a surplus of about $225,000,000 and the fiscal year 1931 with a surplus of about $123,000,000. Owing to unusual circumstances, it has been extremely difficult to estimate future revenues with accuracy.

I believe, however, that the Congress will be fully justified in giving the benefits of the prospective surpluses to the taxpayers, particularly as ample provision for debt reduction has been made in both years through the form of debt retirement from ordinary revenues. In view of the uncertainty in respect of future revenues and the comparatively small size of the indicated surplus in 1931, relief should take the form of a provisional revision of tax rates.

I recommend that the normal income tax rates applicable to the incomes of individuals for the calendar year 1929 be reduced from 5, 3, and 1.5 per cent, to 4, 2, and .5 per cent, and that the tax on the income of corporations for the calendar year 1929 be reduced from 12 to 11 per cent. It is estimated that this will result in a reduction of $160,000,000 in income taxes to be collected during the calendar year 1930. The loss in revenue will be divided approximately equally between the fiscal years 1930 and 1931. Such a program will give a measure of tax relief to the maximum number of taxpayers, with relatively larger benefits to taxpayers with small or moderate incomes.

Foreign Debts

The past year has brought us near to completion of settlements of the indebtedness of foreign governments to the United States.

The act of Congress approved February 4, 1929, authorized the settlement with the Government of Austria along lines similar to the terms of settlement offered by that Government to its other relief creditors. No agreement has yet been concluded with that government, but the form of agreement has been settled and its execution only awaits the Government of Austria securing the assent by all the other relief creditors of the terms offered. The act of Congress approved February 14, 1929, authorized the settlement with the Government of Greece, and an agreement was concluded on May 10, 1929.

The Government of France ratified the agreement with us on July 27, 1929. This agreement will shortly be before the Congress and I recommend its approval.

The only indebtedness of foreign governments to the United States now unsettled is that of Russia and Armenia.

During the past year a committee of distinguished experts under American leadership submitted a plan looking to a revision of claims against Germany by the various Governments. The United States denied itself any participation in the war settlement of general reparations and our claims are comparatively small in amount. They arise from costs of the army of occupation and claims of our private citizens for losses under awards from the Mixed Claims Commission established under agreement with the German Government. In finding a basis for settlement it was necessary for the committee of experts to request all the Governments concerned to make some contribution to the adjustment and we have felt that we should share a proportion of the concessions made.

The State and Treasury Departments will be in a position shortly to submit for your consideration a draft of an agreement to be executed between the United States and Germany providing for the payments of these revised amounts. A more extensive statement will be submitted at that time.

The total amount of indebtedness of the various countries to the United States now funded is $11,579,465,885. This sum was in effect provided by the issue of United States Government bonds to our own people. The payments of the various Governments to us on account of principal and interest for 1930 are estimated at a total of about $239,000,000, for 1931 at about $236,000,000, for 1932 at about $246,000,000. The measure of American compromise in these settlements may be appreciated from the fact that our taxpayers are called upon to find annually about $475,000,000 in interest and in addition to redeem the principal of sums borrowed by the United States Government for these purposes.

Alien Enemy Property

The wise determination that this property seized in war should be returned to its owners has proceeded with considerable rapidity. Of the original seized cash and property (valued at a total of about $625,000,000), all but $111,566,700 has been returned. Most of the remainder should be disposed of during the next year.

General Economic Situation

The country has enjoyed a large degree of prosperity and sound progress during the past year with a steady improvement in methods of production and distribution and consequent advancement in standards of living. Progress has, of course, been unequal among industries, and some, such as coal, lumber, leather, and textiles, still lag behind. The long upward trend of fundamental progress, however, gave rise to over-optimism as to profits, which translated itself into a wave of uncontrolled speculation in securities, resulting in the diversion of capital from business to the stock market and the inevitable crash. The natural consequences have been a reduction in the consumption of luxuries and semi-necessities by those who have met with losses, and a number of persons thrown temporarily out of employment. Prices of agricultural products dealt in upon the great markets have been affected in sympathy with the stock crash.

Fortunately, the Federal reserve system had taken measures to strengthen the position against the day when speculation would break, which together with the strong position of the banks has carried the whole credit system through the crisis without impairment. The capital which has been hitherto absorbed in stock-market loans for speculative purposes is now returning to the normal channels of business. There has been no inflation in the prices of commodities; there has been no undue accumulation of goods, and foreign trade has expanded to a magnitude which exerts a steadying influence upon activity in industry and employment.

The sudden threat of unemployment and especially the recollection of the economic consequences of previous crashes under a much less secured financial system created unwarranted pessimism and fear. It was recalled that past storms of similar character had resulted in retrenchment of construction, reduction of wages, and laying off of workers. The natural result was the tendency of business agencies throughout the country to pause in their plans and proposals for continuation and extension of their businesses, and this hesitation unchecked could in itself intensify into a depression with widespread unemployment and suffering.

I have, therefore, instituted systematic, voluntary measures of cooperation with the business institutions and with State and municipal authorities to make certain that fundamental businesses of the country shall continue as usual, that wages and therefore consuming power shall not be reduced, and that a special effort shall be made to expand construction work in order to assist in equalizing other deficits in employment. Due to the enlarged sense of cooperation and responsibility which has grown in the business world during the past few years the response has been remarkable and satisfactory. We have canvassed the Federal Government and instituted measures of prudent expansion in such work that should be helpful, and upon which the different departments will make some early recommendations to Congress.

I am convinced that through these measures we have reestablished confidence. Wages should remain stable. A very large degree of industrial unemployment and suffering which would otherwise have occurred has been prevented. Agricultural prices have reflected the returning confidence. The measures taken must be vigorously pursued until normal conditions are restored.

Agriculture

The agricultural situation is improving. The gross farm income as estimated by the Department of Agriculture for the crop season 1926–27 was $12,100,000,000; for 1927–28 it was $12,300,000,000; for 1928–29 it was $12,500,000,000; and estimated on the basis of prices since the last harvest the value of the 1929–30 crop would be over $12,650,000,000. The slight decline in general commodity prices during the past few years naturally assists the farmers' buying power.

The number of farmer bankruptcies is very materially decreased below previous years. The decline in land values now seems to be arrested and rate of movement from the farm to the city has been reduced. Not all sections of agriculture, of course, have fared equally, and some areas have suffered from drought. Responsible farm leaders have assured me that a large measure of confidence is returning to agriculture and that a feeling of optimism pervades that industry.

The most extensive action for strengthening the agricultural industry ever taken by any government was inaugurated through the farm marketing act of June 15 last. Under its provisions the Federal Farm Board has been established, comprised of men long and widely experienced in agriculture and sponsored by the farm organizations of the country. During its short period of existence the board has taken definite steps toward a more efficient organization of agriculture, toward the elimination of waste in marketing, and toward the upbuilding of farmers' marketing organizations on sounder and more efficient lines. Substantial headway has been made in the organization of four of the basic commodities—grain, cotton, livestock, and wool. Support by the board to cooperative marketing organizations and other board activities undoubtedly have served to steady the farmers' market during the recent crisis and have operated also as a great stimulus to the cooperative organization of agriculture. The problems of the industry are most complex, and the need for sound organization is imperative. Yet the board is moving rapidly along the lines laid out for it in the act, facilitating the creation by farmers of farmer-owned and farmer-controlled organizations and federating them into central institutions, with a view to increasing the bargaining power of agriculture, preventing and controlling surpluses, and mobilizing the economic power of agriculture.

The Tariff

The special session of Congress was called to expedite the fulfillment of party pledges of agricultural relief and the tariff. The pledge of farm relief has been carried out. At that time I stated the principles upon which I believed action should be taken in respect to the tariff:

"An effective tariff upon agricultural products, that will compensate the farmer's higher costs and higher standards of living, has a dual purpose. Such a tariff not only protects the farmer in our domestic market but it also stimulates him to diversify his crops and to grow products that he could not otherwise produce, and thus lessens his dependence upon exports to foreign markets. The great expansion of production abroad under the conditions I have mentioned renders foreign competition in our export markets increasingly serious. It seems but natural, therefore, that the American farmer, having been greatly handicapped in his foreign market by such competition from the younger expanding countries, should ask that foreign access to our domestic market should be regulated by taking into account the differences in our costs of production.

"In considering the tariff for other industries than agriculture, we find that there have been economic shifts necessitating a readjustment of some of the tariff schedules. Seven years of experience under the tariff bill enacted in 1922 have demonstrated the wisdom of Congress in the enactment of that measure. On the whole it has worked well. In the main our wages have been maintained at high levels; our exports and imports have steadily increased; with some exceptions our manufacturing industries have been prosperous. Nevertheless, economic changes have taken place during that time which have placed certain domestic products at a disadvantage and new industries have come into being, all of which create the necessity for some limited changes in the schedules and in the administrative clauses of the laws as written in 1922.

"It would seem to me that the test of necessity for revision is, in the main, whether there has been a substantial slackening of activity in an industry during the past few years, and a consequent decrease of employment due to insurmountable competition in the products of that industry. It is not as if we were setting up a new basis of protective duties. We did that seven years ago. What we need to remedy now is whatever substantial loss of employment may have resulted from shifts since that time.

"In determining changes in our tariff we must not fail to take into account the broad interests of the country as a whole, and such interests include our trade relations with other countries."

No condition has arisen in my view to change these principles stated at the opening of the special session. I am firmly of the opinion that their application to the pending revision will give the country the kind of a tariff law it both needs and wants. It would be most helpful if action should be taken at an early moment, more especially at a time when business and agriculture are both cooperating to minimize future uncertainties. It is just that they should know what the rates are to be.

Even a limited revision requires the consideration and readjustment of many items. The exhaustive inquiries and valuable debate from men representative of all parts of the country which is needed to determine the detailed rates must necessarily be accomplished in the Congress. However perfectly this rate structure may be framed at any given time, the shifting of economic forces which inevitably occurs will render changes in some items desirable between the necessarily long intervals of congressional revision. Injustices are bound to develop, such as were experienced by the dairymen, the flaxseed producers, the glass industry, and others, under the 1922 rates. For this reason, I have been most anxious that the broad principle of the flexible tariff as provided in the existing law should be preserved and its delays in action avoided by more expeditious methods of determining the costs of production at home and abroad, with executive authority to promulgate such changes upon recommendation of the Tariff Commission after exhaustive investigation. Changes by the Congress in the isolated items such as those to which I have referred would have been most unlikely both because of the concentrations of oppositions in the country, who could see no advantage to their own industry or State, and because of the difficulty of limiting consideration by the Congress to such isolated cases.

There is no fundamental conflict between the interests of the farmer and the worker. Lowering of the standards of living of either tends to destroy the other. The prosperity of one rests upon the well-being of the other. Nor is there any real conflict between the East and the West or the North and the South in the United States. The complete interlocking of economic dependence, the common striving for social and spiritual progress, our common heritage as Americans, and the infinite web of national sentiment, have created a solidarity in a great people unparalleled in all human history. These invisible bonds should not and can not be shattered by differences of opinion growing out of discussion of a tariff.

Public Buildings

Under the provisions of various acts of Congress $300,000,000 has been authorized for public buildings and the land upon which to construct them, being $75,000,000 for the District of Columbia and $225,000,000 for the country at large. Excluding $25,000,000 which is for the acquisition of land in the so-called "triangle" in this city, this public building legislation provides for a five-year program for the District of Columbia and between an eight and nine year program for the country at large. Of this sum approximately $27,400,000 was expended up to June 30 last, of which $11,400,000 has been expended in the District and $16,000,000 outside.

Even this generous provision for both the District of Columbia and the country is insufficient for most pressing governmental needs. Expensive rents and inadequate facilities are extravagance and not economy. In the District even after the completion of these projects we shall have fully 20,000 clerks housed in rented and temporary war buildings which can last but a little longer.

I therefore recommend that consideration should be given to the extension of authorizations both for the country at large and for the District of Columbia again distributed over a term of years. A survey of the need in both categories has been made by the Secretary of the Treasury and the Postmaster General. It would be helpful in the present economic situation if such steps were taken as would enable early construction work.

An expedition and enlargement of the program in the District would bring about direct economies in construction by enabling the erection of buildings in regular sequence. By maintaining a stable labor force in the city, contracts can be made on more advantageous terms.

The earlier completion of this program which is an acknowledged need would add dignity to the celebration in 1932 of the two hundredth anniversary of the birth of President Washington.

In consideration of these projects which contribute so much to dignify the National Capital I should like to renew the suggestion that the Fine Arts Commission should be required to pass upon private buildings which are proposed for sites facing upon public buildings and parks. Without such control much of the effort of the Congress in beautification of the Capital will be minimized.

The Waterways and Flood Control

The development of inland waterways has received new impulse from the completion during this year of the canalization of the Ohio to a uniform 9-foot depth. The development of the other segments of the Mississippi system should be expedited and with this in view I am recommending an increase in appropriations for rivers and harbors from $50,000,000 to $55,000,000 per annum which, together with about $4,000,000 per annum released by completion of the Ohio, should make available after providing for other river and harbor works a sum of from $25,000,000 to $30,000,000 per annum for the Mississippi system and thus bring it to early completion.

Conflict of opinion which has arisen over the proposed floodway from the Arkansas River to the Gulf of Mexico via the Atchafalaya River has led me to withhold construction upon this portion of the Mississippi flood control plan until it could be again reviewed by the engineers for any further recommendation to Congress. The other portions of the project are being vigorously prosecuted and I have recommended an increase in appropriations for this from $30,000,000 of the present year to $35,000,000 during the next fiscal year.

Expansion of our intracoastal waterways to effective barge depths is well warranted. We are awaiting the action of Canada upon the St. Lawrence waterway project.

Highways

There are over 3,000,000 miles of legally established highways in the United States, of which about 10 per cent are included in the State highway systems, the remainder being county and other local roads. About 626,000 miles have been improved with some type of surfacing, comprising some 63 per cent of the State highway systems and 16 per cent of the local roads. Of the improved roads about 102,000 miles are hard surfaced, comprising about 22 per cent of the State highway systems and about 8 per cent of the local roads.

While proper planning should materially reduce the listed mileage of public roads, particularly in the agricultural districts, and turn these roads back to useful purposes, it is evident that road construction must be a long-continued program. Progress in improvement is about 50,000 miles of all types per annum, of which some 12,000 miles are of the more durable types. The total expenditures of Federal, State, and local governments last year for construction and maintenance assumed the huge total of $1,660,000,000.

Federal aid in the construction of the highway systems in conjunction with the States has proved to be beneficial and stimulating. We must ultimately give consideration to the increase of our contribution to these systems, particularly with a view to stimulating the improvement of farm-to-market roads.

Post Office

Our Post Office deficit has now increased to over $80,000,000 a year, of which perhaps $14,000,000 is due to losses on ocean mail and air mail contracts. The department is making an exhaustive study of the sources of the deficit with view to later recommendation to Congress in respect to it.

The Post Office quarters are provided in part by the Federal construction, in part by various forms of rent and lease arrangements. The practice has grown up in recent years of contracting long term leases under which both rent and amortization principal cost of buildings is included. I am advised that fully 40 per cent could be saved from many such rent and lease agreements even after allowing interest on the capital required at the normal Government rate. There are also many objectionable features to some of these practices. The provision of adequate quarters for the Post Office should be put on a sound basis.

A revision of air mail rates upon a more systematic and permanent footing is necessary. The subject is under study, and if legislation should prove necessary the subject will be presented to the Congress. In the meantime I recommend that the Congress should consider the desirability of authorizing further expansion of the South American services.

Commercial Aviation

During the past year progress in civil aeronautics has been remarkable. This is to a considerable degree due to the wise assistance of the Federal Government through the establishment and maintenance of airways by the Department of Commerce and the mail contracts from the Post Office Department. The Government-improved airways now exceed 25,000 miles—more than 14,000 miles of which will be lighted and equipped for night-flying operations by the close of the current year. Airport construction through all the States is extremely active. There are now 1,000 commercial and municipal airports in operation with an additional 1,200 proposed for early development.

Through this assistance the Nation is building a sound aviation system, operated by private enterprise. Over 6,400 planes are in commercial use, and 9,400 pilots are licensed by the Government. Our manufacturing capacity has risen to 7,500 planes per annum. The aviation companies have increased regular air transportation until it now totals 90,000 miles per day—one-fourth of which is flown by night. Mail and express services now connect our principal cities, and extensive services for passenger transportation have been inaugurated, and others of importance are imminent. American air lines now reach into Canada and Mexico, to Cuba, Porto Rico, Central America, and most of the important countries of South America.

Railways

As a whole, the railroads never were in such good physical and financial condition, and the country has never been so well served by them. The greatest volume of freight traffic ever tendered is being carried at a speed never before attained and with satisfaction to the shippers. Efficiencies and new methods have resulted in reduction in the cost of providing freight transportation, and freight rates show a continuous descending line from the level enforced by the World War.

We have, however, not yet assured for the future that adequate system of transportation through consolidations which was the objective of the Congress in the transportation act. The chief purpose of consolidation is to secure well-balanced systems with more uniform and satisfactory rate structure, a more stable financial structure, more equitable distribution of traffic, greater efficiency, and single-line instead of multiple-line hauls. In this way the country will have the assurance of better service and ultimately at lower and more even rates than would otherwise be attained. Legislation to simplify and expedite consolidation methods and better to protect public interest should be enacted.

Consideration should also be given to relief of the members of the Commission from the necessity of detailed attention to comparatively inconsequential matters which, under the existing law, must receive their direct and personal consideration. It is in the public interest that the members of the Commission should not be so pressed by minor matters that they have inadequate time for investigation and consideration of the larger questions committed to them for solution. As to many of these minor matters, the function of the Commission might well be made revisory, and the primary responsibility delegated to subordinate officials after the practice long in vogue in the executive departments.

Merchant Marine

Under the impulse of the merchant marine act of 1928 the transfer to private enterprise of the Government-owned steamship lines is going forward with increasing success. The Shipping Board now operates about 18 lines, which is less than half the number originally established, and the estimate of expenditures for the coming fiscal year is based upon reduction in losses on Government lines by approximately one-half. Construction loans have been made to the amount of approximately $75,000,000 out of the revolving fund authorized by Congress and have furnished an additional aid to American shipping and further stimulated the building of vessels in American yards.

Desirous of securing the full values to the Nation of the great effort to develop our merchant marine by the merchant marine act soon after the inauguration of the present administration, I appointed an interdepartmental committee, consisting of the Secretary of Commerce, as chairman, the Secretary of the Navy, the Postmaster General, and the chairman of the Shipping Board, to make a survey of the policies being pursued under the act of 1928 in respect of mail contracts; to inquire into its workings and to advise the Postmaster General in the administration of the act.

In particular it seemed to me necessary to determine if the result of the contracts already let would assure the purpose expressed in the act, "to further develop an American merchant marine, to assure its permanence in the transportation of the foreign trade of the United States, and for other purposes," and to develop a coordinated policy by which these purposes may be translated into actualities.

In review of the mail contracts already awarded it was found that they aggregated 25 separate awards imposing a governmental obligation of a little over $12,000,000 per annum. Provision had been imposed in five of the contracts for construction of new vessels with which to replace and expand services. These requirements come to a total of 12 vessels in the 10-year period, aggregating 122,000 tons. Some other conditions in the contracts had not worked out satisfactorily.

That study has now been substantially completed and the committee has advised the desirability and the necessity of securing much larger undertakings as to service and new construction in future contracts. The committee at this time is recommending the advertising of 14 additional routes, making substantial requirements for the construction of new vessels during the life of each contract recommended. A total of 40 new vessels will be required under the contracts proposed, about half of which will be required to be built during the next three years. The capital cost of this new construction will be approximately $250,000,000, involving approximately 460,000 gross tons. Should bidders be found who will make these undertakings, it will be necessary to recommend to Congress an increase in the authorized expenditure by the Post Office of about $5,500,000 annually. It will be most advantageous to grant such an authority.

A conflict as to the administration of the act has arisen in the contention of persons who have purchased Shipping Board vessels that they are entitled to mail contracts irrespective of whether they are the lowest bidder, the Post Office, on the other hand, being required by law to let contracts in that manner. It is urgent that Congress should clarify this situation.

The Banking System

It is desirable that Congress should consider the revision of some portions of the banking law.

The development of "group" and "chain" banking presents many new problems. The question naturally arises as to whether if allowed to expand without restraint these methods would dangerously concentrate control of credit, and whether they would not in any event seriously threaten one of the fundamentals of the American credit system—which is that credit which is based upon banking deposits should be controlled by persons within those areas which furnish these deposits and thus be subject to the restraints of local interest and public opinion in those areas. To some degree, however, this movement of chain or group banking is a groping for stronger support to the banks and a more secure basis for these institutions.

The growth in size and stability of the metropolitan banks is in marked contrast to the trend in the country districts, with its many failures and the losses these failures have imposed upon the agricultural community.

The relinquishment of charters of national banks in great commercial centers in favor of State charters indicates that some conditions surround the national banks which render them unable to compete with State banks; and their withdrawal results in weakening our national banking system.

It has been proposed that permission should be granted to national banks to engage in branch banking of a nature that would preserve within limited regions the local responsibility and the control of such credit institutions.

All these subjects, however, require careful investigation, and it might be found advantageous to create a joint commission embracing Members of the Congress and other appropriate Federal officials for subsequent report.

Electrical Power Regulation

The Federal Power Commission is now comprised of three Cabinet officers, and the duties involved in the competent conduct of the growing responsibilities of this commission far exceed the time and attention which these officials can properly afford from other important duties. I recommended that authority be given for the appointment of full-time commissioners to replace them.

It is also desirable that the authority of the commission should be extended to certain phases of power regulation. The nature of the electric utilities industry is such that about 90 per cent of all power generation and distribution is intrastate in character, and most of the States have developed their own regulatory systems as to certificates of convenience, rates, and profits of such utilities. To encroach upon their authorities and responsibilities would be an encroachment upon the rights of the States. There are cases, however, of interstate character beyond the jurisdiction of the States. To meet these cases it would be most desirable if a method could be worked out by which initial action may be taken between the commissions of the States whose joint action should be made effective by the Federal Power Commission with a reserve to act on its own motion in case of disagreement or nonaction by the States.

The Radio Commission

I recommend the reorganization of the Radio Commission into a permanent body from its present temporary status. The requirement of the present law that the commissioners shall be appointed from specified zones should be abolished and a general provision made for their equitable selection from different parts of the country. Despite the effort of the commissioners, the present method develops a public insistence that the commissioners are specially charged with supervision of radio affairs in the zone from which each is appointed. As a result there is danger that the system will degenerate from a national system into five regional agencies with varying practices, varying policies, competitive tendencies, and consequent failure to attain its utmost capacity for service to the people as a whole.

Muscle Shoals

It is most desirable that this question should be disposed of. Under present conditions the income from these plants is less than could otherwise be secured for its use, and more especially the public is not securing the full benefits which could be obtained from them.

It is my belief that such parts of these plants as would be useful and the revenues from the remainder should be dedicated for all time to the farmers of the United States for investigation and experimentation on a commercial scale in agricultural chemistry. By such means advancing discoveries of science can be systematically applied to agricultural need, and development of the chemical industry of the Tennessee Valley can be assured.

I do not favor the operation by the Government of either power or manufacturing business except as an unavoidable by-product of some other major public purpose.

Any form of settlement of this question will imply entering upon a contract or contracts for the lease of the plants either as a whole or in parts and the reservation of facilities, products, or income for agricultural purposes. The extremely technical and involved nature of such contracts dealing with chemical and electrical enterprises, added to the unusual difficulties surrounding these special plants, and the rapid commercial changes now in progress in power and synthetic nitrogen manufacture, lead me to suggest that Congress create a special commission, not to investigate and report as in the past, but with authority to negotiate and complete some sort of contract or contracts on behalf of the Government, subject, of course, to such general requirements as Congress may stipulate.

Boulder Dam

The Secretary of the Interior is making satisfactory progress in negotiation of the very complex contracts required for the sale of the power to be generated at this project. These contracts must assure the return of all Government outlays upon the project. I recommend that the necessary funds be appropriated for the initiation of this work as soon as the contracts are in the hands of Congress.

Conservation

Conservation of national resources is a fixed policy of the Government. Three important questions bearing upon conservation of the public lands have become urgent.

Conservation of our oil and gas resources against future need is a national necessity. The working of the oil permit system in development of oil and gas resources on the public domain has been subject to great abuse. I considered it necessary to suspend the issuance of such permits and to direct the review of all outstanding permits as to compliance of the holders with the law. The purpose was not only to end such abuse but to place the Government in position to review the entire subject.

We are also confronted with a major problem in conservation due to the overgrazing on public lands. The effect of overgrazing (which has now become general) is not only to destroy the ranges but by impairing the ground coverage seriously to menace the water supply in many parts of the West through quick run-off, spring floods, and autumn drought.

We have a third problem of major dimensions in the reconsideration of our reclamation policy. The inclusion of most of the available lands of the public domain in existing or planned reclamation projects largely completes the original purpose of the Reclamation Service. There still remains the necessity for extensive storage of water in the arid States which renders it desirable that we should give a wider vision and purpose to this service.

To provide for careful consideration of these questions and also of better division of responsibilities in them as between the State and Federal Governments, including the possible transfer to the States for school purposes of the lands unreserved for forests, parks, power, minerals, etc., I have appointed a Commission on Conservation of the Public Domain, with a membership representing the major public land States and at the same time the public at large. I recommend that Congress should authorize a moderate sum to defray their expenses.

Social Service

The Federal Government provides for an extensive and valuable program of constructive social service, in education, home building, protection to women and children, employment, public health, recreation, and many other directions.

In a broad sense Federal activity in these directions has been confined to research and dissemination of information and experience, and at most to temporary subsidies to the States in order to secure uniform advancement in practice and methods. Any other attitude by the Federal Government will undermine one of the most precious possessions of the American people; that is, local and individual responsibility. We should adhere to this policy.

Federal officials can, however, make a further and most important contribution by leadership in stimulation of the community and voluntary agencies, and by extending Federal assistance in organization of these forces and bringing about cooperation among them.

As an instance of this character, I have recently, in cooperation with the Secretaries of Interior and Labor, laid the foundations of an exhaustive inquiry into the facts precedent to a nation-wide White House conference on child health and protection. This cooperative movement among interested agencies will impose no expense upon the Government. Similar nation-wide conferences will be called in connection with better housing and recreation at a later date.

In view of the considerable difference of opinion as to the policies which should be pursued by the Federal Government with respect to education, I have appointed a committee representative of the important educational associations and others to investigate and present recommendations. In cooperation with the Secretary of the Interior, I have also appointed a voluntary committee of distinguished membership to assist in a nation-wide movement for abolition of illiteracy.

I have recommended additional appropriations for the Federal employment service in order that it may more fully cover its cooperative work with State and local services.

I have also recommended additional appropriations for the Women's and Children's Bureaus for much needed research as to facts which I feel will prove most helpful.

Public Health

The advance in scientific discovery as to disease and health imposes new considerations upon us. The Nation as a whole is vitally interested in the health of all the people; in protection from spread of contagious disease; in the relation of physical and mental disabilities to criminality; and in the economic and moral advancement which is fundamentally associated with sound body and mind. The organization of preventive measures and health education in its personal application is the province of public health service. Such organization should be as universal as public education. Its support is a proper burden upon the taxpayer. It can not be organized with success, either in its sanitary or educational phases, except under public authority. It should be based upon local and State responsibility, but I consider that the Federal Government has an obligation of contribution to the establishment of such agencies.

In the practical working out of organization, exhaustive experiment and trial have demonstrated that the base should be competent organization of the municipality, county, or other local unit. Most of our municipalities and some 400 rural counties out of 3,000 now have some such unit organization. Where highly developed, a health unit comprises at least a physician, sanitary engineer, and community nurse with the addition, in some cases, of another nurse devoted to the problems of maternity and children. Such organization gives at once a fundamental control of preventive measures and assists in community instruction. The Federal Government, through its interest in control of contagion, acting through the United States Public Health Service and the State agencies, has in the past and should in the future concern itself with this development, particularly in the many rural sections which are unfortunately far behind in progress. Some parts of the funds contributed under the Sheppard-Towner Act through the Children's Bureau of the Department of Labor have also found their way into these channels.

I recommend to the Congress that the purpose of the Sheppard Towner Act should be continued through the Children's Bureau for a limited period of years; and that the Congress should consider the desirability of confining the use of Federal funds by the States to the building up of such county or other local units, and that such outlay should be positively coordinated with the funds expended through the United States Public Health Service directed to other phases of the same county or other local unit organization. All funds appropriated should of course be applied through the States, so that the public health program of the county or local unit will be efficiently coordinated with that of the whole State.

Federal Prisons

Closely related to crime conditions is the administration of the Federal prison system. Our Federal penal institutions are overcrowded, and this condition is daily becoming worse. The parole and probation systems are inadequate. These conditions make it impossible to perform the work of personal reconstruction of prisoners so as to prepare them for return to the duties of citizenship. In order to relieve the pressing evils I have directed the temporary transfer of the Army Disciplinary Barracks at

Leavenworth to the Department of Justice for use as a Federal prison. Not only is this temporary but it is inadequate for present needs.

We need some new Federal prisons and a reorganization of our probation and parole systems; and there should be established in the Department of Justice a Bureau of Prisons with a sufficient force to deal adequately with the growing activities of our prison institutions. Authorization for the improvements should be given speedily, with initial appropriations to allow the construction of the new institutions to be undertaken at once.

Immigration

Restriction of immigration has from every aspect proved a sound national policy. Our pressing problem is to formulate a method by which the limited number of immigrants whom we do welcome shall be adapted to our national setting and our national needs.

I have been opposed to the basis of the quotas now in force and I have hoped that we could find some practical method to secure what I believe should be our real national objective; that is, fitness of the immigrant as to physique, character, training, and our need of service. Perhaps some system of priorities within the quotas could produce these results and at the same time enable some hardships in the present system to be cleared up. I recommend that the Congress should give the subject further study, in which the executive departments will gladly cooperate with the hope of discovering such method as will more fully secure our national necessities.

Veterans

It has been the policy of our Government almost from its inception to make provision for the men who have been disabled in defense of our country. This policy should be maintained. Originally it took the form of land grants and pensions. This system continued until our entry into the World War. The Congress at that time inaugurated a new plan of compensation, rehabilitation, hospitalization, medical care and treatment, and insurance, whereby benefits were awarded to those veterans and their immediate dependents whose disabilities were attributable to their war service. The basic principle in this legislation is sound.

In a desire to eliminate all possibilities of injustice due to difficulties in establishing service connection of disabilities, these principles have been to some degree extended. Veterans whose diseases or injuries have become apparent within a brief period after the war are now receiving compensation; insurance benefits have been liberalized. Emergency officers are now receiving additional benefits. The doors of the Government's hospitals have been opened to all veterans, even though their diseases or injuries were not the result of their war service. In addition adjusted service certificates have been issued to 3,433,300 veterans. This in itself will mean an expenditure of nearly $3,500,000,000 before 1945, in addition to the $600,000,000 which we are now appropriating annually for our veterans' relief.

The administration of all laws concerning the veterans and their dependents has been upon the basis of dealing generously, humanely, and justly. While some inequalities have arisen, substantial and adequate care has been given and justice administered. Further improvement in administration may require some amendment from time to time to the law, but care should be taken to see that such changes conform to the basic principles of the legislation.

I am convinced that we will gain in efficiency, economy, and more uniform administration and better definition of national policies if the Pension Bureau, the National Home for Volunteer Soldiers, and the Veterans' Bureau are brought together under a single agency. The total appropriations to these agencies now exceed $800,000,000 per annum.

Civil Service

Approximately four-fifths of all the employees in the executive civil service now occupy positions subject to competitive examination under the civil service law.

There are, however, still commanding opportunities for extending the system. These opportunities lie within the province of Congress and not the President. I recommend that a further step be taken by authorization that appointments of third-class postmasters be made under the civil service law.

Departmental Reorganization

This subject has been under consideration for over 20 years. It was promised by both political parties in the recent campaign. It has been repeatedly examined by committees and commissions—congressional, executive, and voluntary. The conclusions of these investigations have been unanimous that reorganization is a necessity of sound administration; of economy; of more effective governmental policies and of relief to the citizen from unnecessary harassment in his relations with a multitude of scattered governmental agencies. But the presentation of any specific plan at once enlivens opposition from every official whose authority may be curtailed or who fears his position is imperiled by such a result; of bureaus and departments which wish to maintain their authority and activities; of citizens and their organizations who are selfishly interested, or who are inspired by fear that their favorite bureau may, in a new setting, be less subject to their influence or more subject to some other influence.

It seems to me that the essential principles of reorganization are two in number. First, all administrative activities of the same major purpose should be placed in groups under single-headed responsibility; second, all executive and administrative functions should be separated from boards and commissions and placed under individual responsibility, while quasi-legislative and quasi-judicial and broadly advisory functions should be removed from individual authority and assigned to boards and commissions. Indeed, these are the fundamental principles upon which our Government was founded, and they are the principles which have been adhered to in the whole development of our business structure, and they are the distillation of the common sense of generations.

For instance, the conservation of national resources is spread among eight agencies in five departments. They suffer from conflict and overlap. There is no proper development and adherence to broad national policies and no central point where the searchlight of public opinion may concentrate itself. These functions should be grouped under the direction of some such official as an assistant secretary of conservation. The particular department or cabinet officer under which such a group should be placed is of secondary importance to the need of concentration. The same may be said of educational services, of merchant marine aids, of public works, of public health, of veterans' services, and many others, the component parts of which are widely scattered in the various departments and independent agencies. It is desirable that we first have experience with these different groups in action before we create new departments. These may be necessary later on.

With this background of all previous experience I can see no hope for the development of a sound reorganization of the Government unless Congress be willing to delegate its authority over the problem (subject to defined principles) to the Executive, who should act upon approval of a joint committee of Congress or with the reservation of power of revision by Congress within some limited period adequate for its consideration.

Prohibition

The first duty of the President under his oath of office is to secure the enforcement of the laws. The enforcement of the laws enacted to give effect to the eighteenth amendment is far from satisfactory and this is in part due to the inadequate organization of the administrative agencies of the Federal Government. With the hope of expediting such reorganization, I requested on June 6 last that Congress should appoint a joint committee to collaborate with executive agencies in preparation of legislation. It would be helpful if it could be so appointed. The subject has been earnestly considered by the Law Enforcement Commission and the administrative officials of the Government. Our joint conclusions are that certain steps should be taken at once. First, there should be an immediate concentration of responsibility and strengthening of enforcement agencies of the Federal Government by transfer to the Department of Justice of the Federal functions of detection and to a considerable degree of prosecution, which are now lodged in the Prohibition Bureau in the Treasury; and at the same time the control of the distribution of industrial alcohol and legalized beverages should remain in the Treasury. Second, provision should be made for relief of congestion in the Federal courts by modifying and simplifying the procedure for dealing with the large volume of petty prosecutions under various Federal acts. Third, there should be a codification of the laws relating to prohibition to avoid the necessity which now exists of resorting to more than 25 statutes enacted at various times over 40 years. Technical defects in these statutes that have been disclosed should be cured. I would add to these recommendations the desirability of reorganizing the various services engaged in the prevention of smuggling into one border patrol under the Coast Guard. Further recommendations upon the subject as a whole will be developed after further examination by the Law Enforcement Commission, but it is not to be expected that any criminal law will ever be fully enforced so long as criminals exist.

The District of Columbia should be the model of city law enforcement in the Nation. While conditions here are much better than in many other cities, they are far from perfect, and this is due in part to the congestion of criminal cases in the Supreme Court of the District, resulting in long delays. Furthermore, there is need for legislation in the District supplementing the national prohibition act, more sharply defining and enlarging the duties and powers of the District Commissioners and the police of the District, and opening the way for better cooperation in the enforcement of prohibition between the District officials and the prohibition officers of the Federal Government. It is urgent that these conditions be remedied.

Law Enforcement and Observance

No one will look with satisfaction upon the volume of crime of all kinds and the growth of organized crime in our country. We have pressing need so to organize our system of administering criminal justice as to establish full vigor and effectiveness. We need to reestablish faith that the highest interests of our country are served by insistence upon the swift and even-handed administration of justice to all offenders, whether they be rich or poor. That we shall effect improvement is vital to the preservation of our institutions. It is the most serious issue before our people.

Under the authority of Congress I have appointed a National Commission on Law Observance and Enforcement, for an exhaustive study of the entire problem of the enforcement of our laws and the improvement of our judicial system, including the special problems and abuses growing out of the prohibition laws. The commission has been invited to make the widest inquiry into the shortcomings of the administration of justice and into the causes and remedies for them. It has organized its work under subcommittees dealing with the many contributory causes of our situation and has enlisted the aid of investigators in fields requiring special consideration. I am confident that as a result of its studies now being carried forward it will make a notable contribution to the solution of our pressing problems.

Pending further legislation, the Department of Justice has been striving to weed out inefficiency wherever it exists, to stimulate activity on the part of its prosecuting officers, and to use increasing care in examining into the qualifications of those appointed to serve as prosecutors. The department is seeking systematically to strengthen the law enforcement agencies week by week and month by month, not by dramatic displays but by steady pressure; by removal of negligent officials and by encouragement and assistance to the vigilant. During the course of these efforts it has been revealed that in some districts causes contributing to the congestion of criminal dockets, and to delays and inefficiency in prosecutions, have been lack of sufficient forces in the offices of United States attorneys, clerks of courts, and marshals. These conditions tend to clog the machinery of justice. The last conference of senior circuit judges has taken note of them and indorsed the department's proposals for improvement. Increases in appropriations are necessary and will be asked for in order to reinforce these offices.

The orderly administration of the law involves more than the mere machinery of law enforcement. The efficient use of that machinery and a spirit in our people in support of law are alike essential. We have need for improvement in both. However much we may perfect the mechanism, still if the citizen who is himself dependent upon some laws for the protection of all that he has and all that he holds dear, shall insist on selecting the particular laws which he will obey, he undermines his own safety and that of his country. His attitude may obscure, but it can not conceal, the ugly truth that the lawbreaker, whoever he may be, is the enemy of society. We can no longer gloss over the unpleasant reality which should be made vital in the consciousness of every citizen, that he who condones or traffics with crime, who is indifferent to it and to the punishment of the criminal, or to the lax performance of official duty, is himself the most effective agency for the breakdown of society.

Law can not rise above its source in good citizenship—in what right-minded men most earnestly believe and desire. If the law is upheld only by Government officials, then all law is at an end. Our laws are made by the people themselves; theirs is the right to work for their repeal; but until repeal it is an equal duty to observe them and demand their enforcement.

I have been gratified at the awakening sense of this responsibility in our citizens during the past few months, and gratified that many instances have occurred which refuted the cynicism which has asserted that our system could not convict those who had defied the law and possessed the means to resist its execution. These things reveal a moral awakening both in the people and in officials which lies at the very foundation of the rule of law.

Conclusion

The test of the rightfulness of our decisions must be whether we have sustained and advanced the ideals of the American people; self-government in its foundations of local government; justice whether to the individual or to the group; ordered liberty; freedom from domination; open opportunity and equality of opportunity; the initiative and individuality of our people; prosperity and the lessening of poverty; freedom of public opinion; education; advancement of knowledge; the growth of religious spirit; the tolerance of all faiths; the foundations of the home and the advancement of peace.

Herbert Hoover, 1929–1933

Annual Message to Congress
December 2, 1930

Herbert Hoover's second State of the Union message dealt in large part with the economic problems facing the country. It had been more than a year since the stock market crash of October 1929, and the Great Depression had begun.

While Hoover's previous annual message, delivered just over a month after the crash, had downplayed its impact, this message—also made in writing rather than in person—struck a more somber note. Hoover, who had been trained as an engineer and had vast experience dealing with international relief efforts, discussed the impact of the economic crisis and described efforts by the federal government to alleviate its impact.

The president explained that the Great Depression was caused not just by overspeculation in U.S. securities, but also by a host of worldwide factors, including overproduction of commodities such as wheat, rubber, and coffee; political instability in Asia, South America, and Europe; and international financial crises. These circumstances, he argued, served to prolong the Depression.

One factor that many historians see as exacerbating the international instability was the Hawley-Smoot tariff law, which Congress passed in 1930. Initially envisioned as a way to help American farmers by slapping high tariffs on a variety of agricultural products, the law ended up including other commodities as well.

Hoover's governing philosophy, as expressed in this 1930 message and elsewhere, involved the virtues of self-reliance and voluntarism. While he was willing to undertake some temporary measures to alleviate the economic situation, he did not see the federal government as an ongoing source of massive relief for the poor and unemployed. The president expounded upon methods by which the government encouraged various voluntary cooperation measures, including efforts to keep wages intact, retain as many employees as possible, and provide construction jobs.

Another mantra for Hoover, as it had been for his predecessor, Calvin Coolidge, was a balanced budget. Hoover noted that the Great Depression had negatively affected the federal budget by turning a projected surplus into a deficit.

Republicans had effective control over the federal government in the 1920s, with Republicans residing in the White House and maintaining majorities in both houses of Congress, but this was starting to change. Just weeks before this message was delivered, Democrats won control of the House of Representatives in the 1930 midterm elections. This change would become complete two years later, when the Democrats would also win both the White House and the Senate, effectively repudiating Hoover and his management of the Great Depression.

To the Senate and House of Representatives:

I have the honor to comply with the requirement of the Constitution that I should lay before the Congress information as to the state of the Union, and recommend consideration of such measures as are necessary and expedient.

Substantial progress has been made during the year in national peace and security; the fundamental strength of the Nation's economic life is unimpaired; education and scientific discovery have made advances; our country is more alive to its problems of moral and spiritual welfare.

Economic Situation

During the past 12 months we have suffered with other Nations from economic depression.

The origins of this depression lie to some extent within our own borders through a speculative period which diverted capital and energy into speculation rather than constructive enterprise. Had overspeculation in securities been the only force operating, we should have seen recovery many months ago, as these particular dislocations have generally readjusted themselves.

Other deep-seated causes have been in action, however, chiefly the world-wide overproduction beyond even the demand of prosperous times for such important basic commodities as wheat, rubber, coffee, sugar, copper, silver, zinc, to some extent cotton, and other raw materials. The cumulative effects of demoralizing price falls of these important commodities in the process of adjustment of production to world consumption have produced financial crises in many countries and have diminished the buying power of these countries for imported goods to a degree which extended the difficulties farther afield by creating unemployment in all the industrial nations. The political agitation in Asia; revolutions in South America and political unrest in some European States; the methods of sale by Russia of her increasing agricultural exports to European markets; and our own drought—have all contributed to prolong and deepen the depression.

In the larger view the major forces of the depression now lie outside of the United States, and our recuperation has been retarded by the unwarranted degree of fear and apprehension created by these outside forces.

The extent of the depression is indicated by the following approximate percentages of activity during the past three months as compared with the highly prosperous year of 1928:

Value of department-store sales	93% of 1928
Volume of manufacturing production	80% of 1928
Volume of mineral production	90% of 1928
Volume of factory employment	84% of 1928
Total of bank deposits	105% of 1928
Wholesale prices—all commodities	83% of 1928
Cost of living	94% of 1928

Various other indexes indicate total decrease of activity from 1928 of from 15 to 20 per cent.

There are many factors which give encouragement for the future. The fact that we are holding from 80 to 85 per cent of our normal activities and incomes; that our major financial and industrial institutions have come through the storm unimpaired; that price levels of major commodities have remained approximately stable for some time; that a number of industries are showing signs of increasing demand; that the world at large is readjusting itself to the situation; all reflect grounds for confidence. We should remember that these occasions have been met many times before, that they are but temporary, that our country is to-day stronger and richer in resources, in equipment, in skill, than ever in its history. We are in an extraordinary degree self-sustaining, we will overcome world influences and will lead the march of prosperity as we have always done hitherto.

Economic depression can not be cured by legislative action or executive pronouncement. Economic wounds must be healed by the action of the cells of the economic body—the producers and consumers themselves. Recovery can be expedited and its effects mitigated by cooperative action. That cooperation requires that every individual should sustain faith and courage; that each should maintain his self-reliance; that each and every one should search for methods of improving his business or service; that the vast majority whose income is unimpaired should not hoard out of fear but should pursue their normal living and recreations; that each should seek to assist his neighbors who may be less fortunate; that each industry should assist its own employees; that each community and each State should assume its full responsibilities for organization of employment and relief of distress with that sturdiness and independence which built a great Nation.

Our people are responding to these impulses in remarkable degree. The best contribution of government lies in encouragement of this voluntary cooperation in the community. The Government, National, State, and local, can join with the community in such programs and do its part. A year ago I, together with other officers of the Government, initiated extensive cooperative measures throughout the country.

The first of these measures was an agreement of leading employers to maintain the standards of wages and of labor leaders to use their influence against strife. In a large sense these undertakings have been adhered to and we have not witnessed the usual reductions of wages which have always heretofore marked depressions. The index of union wage scales shows them to be today fully up to the level of any of the previous three years. In consequence the buying power of the country has been much larger than would otherwise have been the case. Of equal importance the Nation has had unusual peace in industry and freedom from the public disorder which has characterized previous depressions.

The second direction of cooperation has been that our governments, National, State, and local, the industries and business so distribute employment as to give work to the maximum number of employees.

The third direction of cooperation has been to maintain and even extend construction work and betterments in anticipation of the future. It has been the universal experience in previous depressions that public works and private construction have fallen off rapidly with the general tide of depression. On this occasion, however, the increased authorization and generous appropriations by the Congress and the action of States and municipalities have resulted in the expansion of public construction to an amount even above that in the most prosperous years. In addition the cooperation of public utilities, railways, and other large organizations has been generously given in construction and betterment work in anticipation of future need. The Department of Commerce advises me that as a result, the volume of this type of construction work, which amounted to roughly $6,300,000,000 in 1929, instead of decreasing will show a total of about $7,000,000,000 for 1930. There has, of course, been a substantial decrease in the types of construction which could not be undertaken in advance of need.

The fourth direction of cooperation was the organization in such States and municipalities, as was deemed necessary, of committees to organize local employment, to provide for employment agencies, and to effect relief of distress.

The result of magnificent cooperation throughout the country has been that actual suffering has been kept to a minimum during the past 12 months, and our unemployment has been far less in proportion than in other large industrial countries. Some time ago it became evident that unemployment would continue over the winter and would necessarily be added to from seasonal causes and that the savings of workpeople would be more largely depleted. We have as a Nation a definite duty to see that no deserving person in our country suffers from hunger or cold. I therefore set up a more extensive organization to stimulate more intensive cooperation throughout the country. There has been a most gratifying degree of response, from governors, mayors, and other public officials, from welfare organizations, and from employers in concerns both large and small. The local communities through their voluntary agencies have assumed the duty of relieving individual distress and are being generously supported by the public.

The number of those wholly out of employment seeking for work was accurately determined by the census last April as about 2,500,000. The Department of Labor index of employment in the larger trades shows some decrease in employment since that time. The problem from a relief point of view is somewhat less than the published estimates of the number of unemployed would indicate. The intensive community and individual efforts in providing special employment outside the listed industries are not reflected in the statistical indexes and tend to reduce such published figures. Moreover, there is estimated to be a constant figure at all times of nearly 1,000,000 unemployed who are not without annual income but temporarily idle in the shift from one job to another. We have an average of about three breadwinners to each two families, so that every person unemployed does not represent a family without income. The view that the relief problems are less than the gross numbers would indicate is confirmed by the experience of several cities, which shows that the number of families in distress represents from 10 to 20 per cent of the number of the calculated unemployed. This is not said to minimize the very real problem which exists but to weigh its actual proportions.

As a contribution to the situation the Federal Government is engaged upon the greatest program of waterway, harbor, flood control, public building, highway, and airway improvement in all our history. This, together with loans to merchant ship-builders, improvement of the Navy and in military aviation, and other construction work of the Government will exceed $520,000,000 for this fiscal year. This compares with $253,000,000 in the fiscal year 1928. The construction works already authorized and the continuation of policies in Government aid will require a continual expenditure upwards of half a billion dollars annually.

I favor still further temporary expansion of these activities in aid to unemployment during this winter. The Congress will, however, have presented to it numbers of projects, some of them under the guise of, rather than the reality of, their usefulness in the increase of employment during the depression. There are certain commonsense limitations upon any expansions of construction work. The Government must not undertake works that are not of sound economic purpose and that have not been subject to searching technical investigation, and which have not been given adequate consideration by the Congress. The volume of construction work in the Government is already at the maximum limit warranted by financial prudence as a continuing policy. To increase taxation for purposes of construction work defeats its own purpose, as such taxes directly diminish employment in private industry. Again any kind of construction requires, after its authorization, a considerable time before labor can be employed in which to make engineering, architectural, and legal preparations. Our immediate problem is the increase of employment for the next six months, and new plans which do not produce such immediate result or which extend commitments beyond this period are not warranted.

The enlarged rivers and harbors, public building, and highway plans authorized by the Congress last session, however, offer an opportunity for assistance by the temporary acceleration of construction of these programs even faster than originally planned, especially if the technical requirements of the laws which entail great delays could be amended in such fashion as to speed up acquirements of land and the letting of contracts.

With view, however, to the possible need for acceleration, we, immediately upon receiving those authorities from the Congress five months ago, began the necessary technical work in preparation for such possible eventuality. I have canvassed the departments of the Government as to the maximum amount that can be properly added to our present expenditure to accelerate all construction during the next six months, and I feel warranted in asking the Congress for an appropriation of from $100,000,000 to $150,000,000 to provide such further employment in this emergency. In connection therewith we need some authority to make enlarged temporary advances of Federal-highway aid to the States.

I recommend that this appropriation be made distributable to the different departments upon recommendation of a committee of the Cabinet and approval by the President. Its application to works already authorized by the Congress assures its use in directions of economic importance and to public welfare. Such action will imply an expenditure upon construction of all kinds of over $650,000,000 during the next twelve months.

Agriculture

The world-wide depression has affected agriculture in common with all other industries. The average price of farm produce has fallen to about 80 per cent of the levels of 1928. This average is, however, greatly affected by wheat and cotton, which have participated in world-wide overproduction and have fallen to about 60 per cent of the average price of the year 1928. Excluding these commodities, the prices of all other agricultural products are about 84 per cent of those of 1928. The average wholesale prices of other primary goods, such as nonferrous metals, have fallen to 76 per cent of 1928.

The price levels of our major agricultural commodities are, in fact, higher than those in other principal producing countries, due to the combined result of the tariff and the operations of the Farm Board. For instance, wheat prices at Minneapolis are about 30 per cent higher than at Winnipeg, and at Chicago they are about 20 per cent higher than at Buenos Aires. Corn prices at Chicago are over twice as high as at Buenos Aires. Wool prices average more than 80 per cent higher in this country than abroad, and butter is 30 per cent higher in New York City than in Copenhagen.

Aside from the misfortune to agriculture of the world-wide depression we have had the most severe drought. It has affected particularly the States bordering on the Potomac, Ohio, and Lower Mississippi Rivers, with some areas in Montana, Kansas, Oklahoma, and Texas. It has found its major expression in the shortage of pasturage and a shrinkage in the corn crop from an average of about 2,800,000,000 bushels to about 2,090,000,000 bushels.

On August 14 I called a conference of the governors of the most acutely affected States, and as a result of its conclusions I appointed a national committee comprising the heads of the important Federal agencies under the chairmanship of the Secretary of Agriculture. The governors in turn have appointed State committees representative of the farmers, bankers, business men, and the Red Cross, and subsidiary committees have been established in most of the acutely affected counties. Railway rates were reduced on feed and livestock in and out of the drought areas, and over 50,000 cars of such products have been transported under these reduced rates. The Red Cross established a preliminary fund of $5,000,000 for distress relief purposes and established agencies for its administration in each county. Of this fund less than $500,000 has been called for up to this time as the need will appear more largely during the winter. The Federal Farm Loan Board has extended its credit facilities, and the Federal Farm Board has given financial assistance to all affected cooperatives.

In order that the Government may meet its full obligation toward our countrymen in distress through no fault of their own, I recommend that an appropriation should be made to the Department of Agriculture to be loaned for the purpose of seed and feed for animals. Its application should as hitherto in such loans be limited to a gross amount to any one individual, and secured upon the crop.

The Red Cross can relieve the cases of individual distress by the sympathetic assistance of our people.

Finances of the Government

I shall submit the detailed financial position of the Government with recommendations in the usual Budget message. I will at this time, however, mention that the Budget estimates of receipts and expenditures for the current year were formulated by the Treasury and the Budget Bureau at a time when it was impossible to forecast the severity of the business depression and have been most seriously affected by it. At that time a surplus of about $123,000,000 was estimated for this fiscal year and tax reduction which affected the fiscal year to the extent of $75,000,000 was authorized by the Congress, thus reducing the estimated surplus to about $48,000,000. Closely revised estimates now made by the Treasury and the Bureau of the Budget of the tax, postal, and other receipts for the current fiscal year indicate a decrease of about $430,000,000 from the estimate of a year ago, of which about $75,000,000 is due to tax reduction, leaving about $355,000,000 due to the depression. Moreover, legislation enacted by Congress subsequent to the submission of the Budget enlarging Federal construction work to expand employment and for increase in veterans' services and other items, have increased expenditures during the current fiscal year by about $225,000,000.

Thus the decrease of $430,000,000 in revenue and the increase of $225,000,000 in expenditure adversely change the original Budget situation by about $655,000,000. This large sum is offset by the original estimated surplus a year ago of about $123,000,000, by the application of $185,000,000 of interest payments upon the foreign debt to current expenditures, by arrangements of the Farm Board through repayments, etc., in consequence of which they reduced their net cash demands upon the Treasury by $100,000,000 in this period, and by about $67,000,000 economies and deferments brought about in the Government, thus reducing the practical effect of the change in the situation to an estimated deficit of about $180,000,000 for the present fiscal year. I shall make suggestions for handling the present-year deficit in the Budget message, but I do not favor encroachment upon the statutory reduction of the public debt.

While it will be necessary in public interest to further increase expenditures during the current fiscal year in aid to unemployment by speeding up construction work and aid to the farmers affected by the drought, I can not emphasize too strongly the absolute necessity to defer any other plans for increase of Government expenditures. The Budget for 1932 fiscal year indicates estimated expenditure of about $4,054,000,000, including postal deficit. The receipts are estimated at about $4,085,000,000 if the temporary tax reduction of last year be discontinued, leaving a surplus of only about $30,000,000. Most rigid economy is therefore necessary to avoid increase in taxes.

National Defense

Our Army and Navy are being maintained at a high state of efficiency, under officers of high training and intelligence, supported by a devoted personnel of the rank and file. The London naval treaty has brought important economies in the conduct of the Navy. The Navy Department will lay before the committees of the Congress recommendations for a program of authorization of new construction which should be initiated in the fiscal year of 1932.

Legislation

This is the last session of the Seventy-first Congress. During its previous sittings it has completed a very large amount of important legislation, notably: The establishment of the Federal Farm Board; fixing congressional reapportionment; revision of the tariff, including the flexible provisions and a reorganization of the Tariff Commission; reorganization of the Radio Commission; reorganization of the Federal Power Commission; expansion of Federal prisons; reorganization of parole and probation system in Federal prisons; expansion of veterans' hospitals; establishment of disability allowances to veterans; consolidation of veteran activities; consolidation and strengthening of prohibition enforcement activities in the Department of Justice; organization of a Narcotics Bureau; large expansion of rivers and harbors improvements; substantial increase in Federal highways; enlargement of public buildings construction program; and the ratification of the London naval treaty.

The Congress has before it legislation partially completed in the last sitting in respect to Muscle Shoals, bus regulation, relief of congestion in the courts, reorganization of border patrol in prevention of smuggling, law enforcement in the District of Columbia, and other subjects.

It is desirable that these measures should be completed.

The short session does not permit of extensive legislative programs, but there are a number of questions which, if time does not permit action, I recommend should be placed in consideration by the Congress, perhaps through committees cooperating in some instances with the Federal departments, with view to preparation for subsequent action. Among them are the following subjects:

Electrical Power

I have in a previous message recommended effective regulation of interstate electrical power. Such regulation should preserve the independence and responsibility of the States.

Railways

We have determined upon a national policy of consolidation of the railways as a necessity of more stable and more economically operated transportation. Further legislation is necessary to facilitate such consolidation. In the public interest we should strengthen the railways that they may meet our future needs.

Antitrust Laws

I recommend that the Congress institute an inquiry into some aspects of the economic working of these laws. I do not favor repeal of the Sherman Act. The prevention of monopolies is of most vital public importance. Competition is not only the basis of protection to the consumer but is the incentive to progress. However, the interpretation of these laws by the courts, the changes in business, especially in the economic effects upon those enterprises closely related to the use of the natural resources of the country, make such an inquiry advisable. The producers of these materials assert that certain unfortunate results of wasteful and destructive use of these natural resources together with a destructive competition which impoverishes both operator and worker can not be remedied because of the prohibitive interpretation of the antitrust laws. The well-known condition of the bituminous coal industry is an illustration. The people have a vital interest in the conservation of their natural resources; in the prevention of wasteful practices; in conditions of destructive competition which may impoverish the producer and the wage earner; and they have an equal interest in maintaining adequate competition. I therefore suggest that an inquiry be directed especially to the effect of the workings of the antitrust laws in these particular fields to determine if these evils can be remedied without sacrifice of the fundamental purpose of these laws.

Capital-Gains Tax

It is urged by many thoughtful citizens that the peculiar economic effect of the income tax on so-called capital gains at the present rate is to enhance speculative inflation and likewise impede business recovery. I believe this to be the case and I recommend that a study be made of the economic effects of this tax and of its relation to the general structure of our income tax law.

Immigration

There is need for revision of our immigration laws upon a more limited and more selective basis, flexible to the needs of the country.

Under conditions of current unemployment it is obvious that persons coming to the United States seeking work would likely become either a direct or indirect public charge. As a temporary measure the officers issuing visas to immigrants have been, in pursuance of the law, instructed to refuse visas to applicants likely to fall into this class. As a result the visas issued have decreased from an average of about 24,000 per month prior to restrictions to a rate of about 7,000 during the last month. These are largely preferred persons under the law. Visas from Mexico are about 250 per month compared to about 4,000 previous to restrictions. The whole subject requires exhaustive reconsideration.

Deportation of Alien Criminals

I urge the strengthening of our deportation laws so as to more fully rid ourselves of criminal aliens. Furthermore, thousands of persons have entered the country in violation of the immigration laws. The very method of their entry indicates their objectionable character, and our law-abiding foreign-born residents suffer in consequence. I recommend that the Congress provide methods of strengthening the Government to correct this abuse.

Post Office

Due to deferment of Government building over many years, previous administrations had been compelled to enter upon types of leases for secondary facilities in large cities, some of which were objectionable as representing too high a return upon the value of the property. To prevent the occasion for further uneconomic leasing I recommend that the Congress authorize the building by the Government of its own facilities.

Veterans

The Nation has generously expanded its care for veterans. The consolidation of all veterans' activities into the Veterans' Administration has produced substantial administrative economies. The consolidation also brings emphasis to the inequalities in service and allowances. The whole subject is under study by the administrator, and I recommend it should also be examined by the committees of the Congress.

Social Service

I urge further consideration by the Congress of the recommendations I made a year ago looking to the development through temporary Federal aid of adequate State and local services for the health of children and the further stamping out of communicable disease, particularly in the rural sections. The advance of scientific discovery, methods, and social thought imposes a new vision in these matters. The drain upon the Federal Treasury is comparatively small. The results both economic and moral are of the utmost importance.

General

It is my belief that after the passing of this depression, when we can examine it in retrospect, we shall need to consider a number of other questions as to what action may be taken by the Government to remove Possible governmental influences which make for instability and to better organize mitigation of the effect of depression. It is as yet too soon to constructively formulate such measures.

There are many administrative subjects, such as departmental reorganization, extension of the civil service, readjustment of the postal rates, etc., which at some appropriate time require the attention of the Congress.

Foreign Relations

Our relations with foreign countries have been maintained upon a high basis of cordiality and good will.

During the past year the London naval pact was completed, approved by the Senate, and ratified by the governments concerned. By this treaty we have abolished competition in the building of warships, have established the basis of parity of the United States with the strongest of foreign powers, and have accomplished a substantial reduction in war vessels.

During the year there has been an extended political unrest in the world. Asia continues in disturbed condition, and revolutions have taken place in Brazil, Argentina, Peru, and Bolivia. Despite the jeopardy to our citizens and their property which naturally arises in such circumstances, we have, with the cooperation of the governments concerned, been able to meet all such instances without friction.

We have resumed normal relations with the new Governments of Brazil, Argentina, Peru, and Bolivia immediately upon evidence that they were able to give protection to our citizens and their property, and that they recognized their international obligations.

A commission which was supported by the Congress has completed its investigation and reported upon our future policies in respect to Haiti and proved of high value in securing the acceptance of these policies. An election has been held and a new government established. We have replaced our high commissioner by a minister and have begun the gradual withdrawal of our activities with view to complete retirement at the expiration of the present treaty in 1935.

A number of arbitration and conciliation treaties have been completed or negotiated during the year, and will be presented for approval by the Senate.

I shall, in a special message, lay before the Senate the protocols covering the statutes of the World Court which have been revised to accord with the sense of previous Senate reservations.

Herbert Hoover, 1929–1933

Annual Message to Congress
December 8, 1931

Herbert Hoover's third State of the Union message, which was written rather than delivered in person, focused on the Great Depression and what policies his administration would employ to reverse it. Unfortunately for Hoover, his particular approach did not turn the country's economy around, and he would lose the White House to Franklin D. Roosevelt in a landslide less than a year after this address.

As can be seen in this message and the two that preceded it, Hoover's philosophy of governing involved voluntarism and self-reliance, as well as a balanced budget—a difficult goal during this period. He did not approve of massive ongoing federal programs designed to help the unemployed and the poor, although he did mention some temporary measures, such as assistance to farmers and banks, designed to assist people affected by the Great Depression.

One of the themes Hoover highlighted in this address was international instability. In contrast to the relatively peaceful world situation in the years before the economic crash, the worldwide depression had sparked political turmoil in various countries, including Germany. These international economic and political problems hindered any U.S. recovery, Hoover said.

He also discussed the measures his government had taken to try to face the economic emergency at home, measures that fit with his view of the limited role of the federal government. "There has been the least possible government entry into the economic field, and that only in temporary and emergency form," he said.

One of the programs he called for in this message was a federal emergency Reconstruction Finance Corporation, designed to loan money to various businesses. Congress approved legislation creating this relatively large-scale entity in early 1932. But even it was dwarfed by the scope of the relief measures enacted once Roosevelt took office in 1933.

Because Hoover believed that a balanced budget was necessary to instill confidence, and because the country faced a deficit due to increased spending during the economic emergency, he called for a temporary tax increase. Congress approved the Revenue Act of 1932 that next year. Even that shift from the tax cuts of the 1920s did not solve the country's economic problems, however.

Despite Hoover's efforts, it appeared that the Great Depression was worsening, resulting in diminishing public support for the president. Collections of shanties housing the poor would become known as "Hoovervilles," for example. The president faced reelection in a very unpromising political climate, to say the least. The victory of his Democratic opponent in 1932 would usher in the New Deal era.

To the Senate and House of Representatives:

It is my duty under the Constitution to transmit to the Congress information on the state of the Union and to recommend for its consideration necessary and expedient measures.

The chief influence affecting the state of the Union during the past year has been the continued world-wide economic disturbance. Our national concern has been to meet the emergencies it has created for us and to lay the foundations for recovery.

If we lift our vision beyond these immediate emergencies we find fundamental national gains even amid depression. In meeting the problems of this difficult period, we have witnessed a remarkable development of the sense of cooperation in the community. For the first time in the history of our major economic depressions there has been a notable absence of public disorders and industrial conflict. Above all there is an enlargement of social and spiritual responsibility among the people. The strains and stresses upon business have resulted in closer application, in saner policies, and in better methods. Public improvements have been carried out on a larger scale than even in normal times. The country is richer in physical property, in newly discovered resources, and in productive capacity than ever before. There has been constant gain in knowledge and education; there has been continuous advance in science and invention; there has been distinct gain in public health. Business depressions have been recurrent in the life of our country and are but transitory. The Nation has emerged from each of them with increased strength and virility because of the enlightenment they have brought, the readjustments and the larger understanding of the realities and obligations of life and work which come from them.

National Defense

Both our Army and Navy have been maintained in a high state of efficiency. The ability and devotion of both officers and men sustain the highest traditions of the service. Reductions and postponements in expenditure of these departments to meet the present emergency are being made without reducing existing personnel or impairing the morale of either establishment.

The agreement between the leading naval powers for limitation of naval armaments and establishment of their relative strength and thus elimination of competitive building also implies for ourselves the gradual expansion of the deficient categories in our Navy to the parities provided in those treaties. However, none of the other nations, parties to these agreements, is to-day maintaining the full rate of construction which the treaty size of fleets would imply.

Although these agreements secured the maximum reduction of fleets which it was at that time possible to attain, I am hopeful that the naval powers, party to these agreements, will realize that establishment of relative strength in itself offers opportunity for further reduction without injury to any of them. This would be the more possible if pending negotiations are successful between France and Italy. If the world is to regain its standards of life, it must further decrease both naval and other arms. The subject will come before the General Disarmament Conference which meets in Geneva on February 2.

Foreign Affairs

We are at peace with the world. We have cooperated with other nations to preserve peace. The rights of our citizens abroad have been protected.

The economic depression has continued and deepened in every part of the world during the past year. In many countries political instability, excessive armaments, debts, governmental expenditures, and taxes have resulted in revolutions, in unbalanced budgets and monetary collapse and financial panics, in dumping of goods upon world markets, and in diminished consumption of commodities.

Within two years there have been revolutions or acute social disorders in 19 countries, embracing more than half the population of the world. Ten countries have been unable to meet their external obligations. In 14 countries, embracing a quarter of the world's population, former monetary standards have been temporarily abandoned. In a number of countries there have been acute financial panics or compulsory restraints upon banking. These disturbances have many roots in the dislocations from the World War. Every one of them has reacted upon us. They have sharply affected the markets and prices of our agricultural and industrial products. They have increased unemployment and greatly embarrassed our financial and credit system.

As our difficulties during the past year have plainly originated in large degree from these sources, any effort to bring about our own recuperation has dictated the necessity of cooperation by us with other nations in reasonable effort to restore world confidence and economic stability.

Cooperation of our Federal reserve system and our banks with the central banks in foreign countries has contributed to localize and ameliorate a number of serious financial crises or moderate the pressures upon us and thus avert disasters which would have affected us.

The economic crisis in Germany and Central Europe last June rose to the dimensions of a general panic from which it was apparent that without assistance these nations must collapse. Apprehensions of such collapse had demoralized our agricultural and security markets and so threatened other nations as to impose further dangers upon us. But of highest importance was the necessity of cooperation on our part to relieve the people of Germany from imminent disasters and to maintain their important relations to progress and stability in the world. Upon the initiative of this Government a year's postponement of reparations and other intergovernmental debts was brought about. Upon our further initiative an agreement was made by Germany's private creditors providing for an extension of such credits until the German people can develop more permanent and definite forms of relief.

We have continued our policy of withdrawing our marines from Haiti and Nicaragua.

The difficulties between China and Japan have given us great concern, not alone for the maintenance of the spirit of the Kellogg-Briand Pact, but for the maintenance of the treaties to which we are a party assuring the territorial integrity of China. It is our purpose to assist in finding solutions sustaining the full spirit of those treaties.

I shall deal at greater length with our foreign relations in a later message.

The Domestic Situation

Many undertakings have been organized and forwarded during the past year to meet the new and changing emergencies which have constantly confronted us.

Broadly the community has cooperated to meet the needs of honest distress, and to take such emergency measures as would sustain confidence in our financial system and would cushion the violence of liquidation in industry and commerce, thus giving time for orderly readjustment of costs, inventories, and credits without panic and widespread bankruptcy. These measures have served those purposes and will promote recovery.

In these measures we have striven to mobilize and stimulate private initiative and local and community responsibility. There has been the least possible Government entry into the economic field, and that only in temporary and emergency form. Our citizens and our local governments have given a magnificent display of unity and action, initiative and patriotism in solving a multitude of difficulties and in cooperating with the Federal Government.

For a proper understanding of my recommendations to the Congress it is desirable very briefly to review such activities during the past year.

The emergencies of unemployment have been met by action in many directions. The appropriations for the continued speeding up of the great Federal construction program have provided direct and indirect aid to employment upon a large scale. By organized unity of action, the States and municipalities have also maintained large programs of public improvement. Many industries have been prevailed upon to anticipate and intensify construction. Industrial concerns and other employers have been organized to spread available work amongst all their employees, instead of discharging a portion of them. A large majority have maintained wages at as high levels as the safe conduct of their business would permit. This course has saved us from industrial conflict and disorder which have characterized all previous depressions. Immigration has been curtailed by administrative action. Upon the basis of normal immigration the decrease amounts to about 300,000 individuals who otherwise would have been added to our unemployment. The expansion of Federal employment agencies under appropriations by the Congress has proved most effective. Through the President's organization for unemployment relief, public and private agencies were successfully mobilized last winter to provide employment and other measures against distress. Similar organization gives assurance against suffering during the coming winter. Committees of leading citizens are now active at practically every point of unemployment. In the large majority they have been assured the funds necessary which, together with local government aids, will meet the situation. A few exceptional localities will be further organized. The evidence of the Public Health Service shows an actual decrease of sickness and infant and general mortality below normal years. No greater proof could be adduced that our people have been protected from hunger and cold and that the sense of social responsibility in the Nation has responded to the need of the unfortunate.

To meet the emergencies in agriculture the loans authorized by Congress for rehabilitation in the drought areas have enabled farmers to produce abundant crops in those districts. The Red Cross undertook and magnificently administered relief for over 2,500,000 drought sufferers last winter. It has undertaken this year to administer relief to 100,000 sufferers in the new drought area of certain Northwest States. The action of the Federal Farm Board in granting credits to farm cooperatives saved many of them from bankruptcy and increased their purpose and strength. By enabling farm cooperatives to cushion the fall in prices of farm products in 1930 and 1931 the Board secured higher prices to the farmer than would have been obtained otherwise, although the benefits of this action were partially defeated by continued world overproduction. Incident to this action the failure of a large number of farmers and of country banks was averted which could quite possibly have spread into a major disaster. The banks in the South have cooperated with the Farm Board in creation of a pool for the better marketing of accumulated cotton. Growers have been materially assisted by this action. Constant effort has been made to reduce overproduction in relief of agriculture and to promote the foreign buying of agricultural products by sustaining economic stability abroad.

To meet our domestic emergencies in credit and banking arising from the reaction to acute crisis abroad the National Credit Association was set up by the banks with resources of $500,000,000 to support sound banks against the frightened withdrawals and hoarding. It is giving aid to reopen solvent banks which have been closed. Federal officials have brought about many beneficial unions of banks and have employed other means which have prevented many bank closings. As a result of these measures the hoarding withdrawals which had risen to over $250,000,000 per week after the British crisis have substantially ceased.

Further Measures

The major economic forces and weaknesses at home and abroad have now been exposed and can be appraised, and the time is ripe for forward action to expedite our recovery.

Although some of the causes of our depression are due to speculation, inflation of securities and real estate, unsound foreign investments, and mismanagement of financial institutions, yet our self-contained national economy, with its matchless strength and resources, would have enabled us to recover long since but for the continued dislocations, shocks, and setbacks from abroad.

Whatever the causes may be, the vast liquidation and readjustments which have taken place have left us with a large degree of credit paralysis, which together with the situation in our railways and the conditions abroad, are now the outstanding obstacles to recuperation. If we can put our financial resources to work and can ameliorate the financial situation in the railways, I am confident we can make a large measure of recovery independent of the rest of the world. A strong America is the highest contribution to world stability.

One phase of the credit situation is indicated in the banks. During the past year banks, representing 3 per cent of our total deposits have been closed. A large part of these failures have been caused by withdrawals for hoarding, as distinguished from the failures early in the depression where weakness due to mismanagement was the larger cause of failure. Despite their closing, many of them will pay in full. Although such withdrawals have practically ceased, yet $1,100,000,000 of currency was previously withdrawn which has still to return to circulation. This represents a large reduction of the ability of our banks to extend credit which would otherwise fertilize industry and agriculture. Furthermore, many of our bankers, in order to prepare themselves to meet possible withdrawals, have felt compelled to call in loans, to refuse new credits, and to realize upon securities, which in turn has demoralized the markets. The paralysis has been further augmented by the steady increase in recent years of the proportion of bank assets invested in long-term securities, such as mortgages and bonds. These securities tend to lose their liquidity in depression or temporarily to fall in value so that the ability of the banks to meet the shock of sudden withdrawal is greatly lessened and the restriction of all kinds of credit is thereby increased. The continuing credit paralysis has operated to accentuate the deflation and liquidation of commodities, real estate, and securities below any reasonable basis of values.

All of this tends to stifle business, especially the smaller units, and finally expresses itself in further depression of prices and values, in restriction on new enterprise, and in increased unemployment.

The situation largely arises from an unjustified lack of confidence. We have enormous volumes of idle money in the banks and in hoarding. We do not require more money or working capital—we need to put what we have to work.

The fundamental difficulties which have brought about financial strains in foreign countries do not exist in the United States. No external drain on our resources can threaten our position, because the balance of international payments is in our favor; we owe less to foreign countries than they owe to us; our industries are efficiently organized; our currency and bank deposits are protected by the greatest gold reserve in history.

Our first step toward recovery is to reestablish confidence and thus restore the flow of credit which is the very basis of our economic life. We must put some steel beams in the foundations of our credit structure. It is our duty to apply the full strength of our Government not only to the immediate phases, but to provide security against shocks and the repetition of the weaknesses which have been proven.

The recommendations which I here lay before the Congress are designed to meet these needs by strengthening financial, industrial, and agricultural life through the medium of our existing institutions, and thus to avoid the entry of the Government into competition with private business.

Federal Government Finance

The first requirement of confidence and of economic recovery is financial stability of the United States Government. I shall deal with fiscal questions at greater length in the Budget message. But I must at this time call attention to the magnitude of the deficits which have developed and the resulting necessity for determined and courageous policies. These deficits arise in the main from the heavy decrease in tax receipts due to the depression and to the increase in expenditure on construction in aid to unemployment, aids to agriculture, and upon services to veterans.

During the fiscal year ending June 30 last we incurred a deficit of about $903,000,000, which included the statutory reduction of the debt and represented an increase of the national debt by $616,000,000. Of this, however, $153,000,000 is offset by increased cash balances.

In comparison with the fiscal year 1928 there is indicated a fall in Federal receipts for the present fiscal year amounting to $1,683,000,000, of which $1,034,000,000 is in individual and corporate income taxes alone. During this fiscal year there will be an increased expenditure, as compared to 1928, on veterans of $255,000,000, and an increased expenditure on construction work which may reach $520,000,000. Despite large economies in other directions, we have an indicated deficit, including the statutory retirement of the debt, of $2,123,000,000, and an indicated net debt increase of about $1,711,000,000.

The Budget for the fiscal year beginning July 1 next, after allowing for some increase of taxes under the present laws and after allowing for drastic reduction in expenditures, still indicates a deficit of $1,417,000,000. After offsetting the statutory debt retirements this would indicate an increase in the national debt for the fiscal year 1933 of about $921,000,000.

Several conclusions are inevitable. We must have insistent and determined reduction in Government expenses. We must face a temporary increase in taxes. Such increase should not cover the whole of these deficits or it will retard recovery. We must partially finance the deficit by borrowing. It is my view that the amount of taxation should be fixed so as to balance the Budget for 1933 except for the statutory debt retirement. Such Government receipts would assure the balance of the following year's budget including debt retirement. It is my further view that the additional taxation should be imposed solely as an emergency measure terminating definitely two years from July 1 next. Such a basis will give confidence in the determination of the Government to stabilize its finance and will assure taxpayers of its temporary character. Even with increased taxation, the Government will reach the utmost safe limit of its borrowing capacity by the expenditures for which we are already obligated and the recommendations here proposed. To go further than these limits in either expenditures, taxes, or borrowing will destroy confidence, denude commerce and industry of its resources, jeopardize the financial system, and actually extend unemployment and demoralize agriculture rather than relieve it.

Federal Land Banks

I recommend that the Congress authorize the subscription by the Treasury of further capital to the Federal land banks to be retired as provided in the original act, or when funds are available, and that repayments of such capital be treated as a fund available for further subscriptions in the same manner. It is urgent that the banks be supported so as to stabilize the market values of their bonds and thus secure capital for the farmers at low rates, that they may continue their services to agriculture and that they may meet the present situation with consideration to the farmers.

Deposits in Closed Banks

A method should be devised to make available quickly to depositors some portion of their deposits in closed banks as the assets of such banks may warrant. Such provision would go far to relieve distress in a multitude of families, would stabilize values in many communities, and would liberate working capital to thousands of concerns. I recommend that measures be enacted promptly to accomplish these results and I suggest that the Congress should consider the development of such a plan through the Federal Reserve Banks.

Home-Loan Discount Banks

I recommend the establishment of a system of home-loan discount banks as the necessary companion in our financial structure of the Federal Reserve Banks and our Federal Land Banks. Such action will relieve present distressing pressures against home and farm property owners. It will relieve pressures upon and give added strength to building and loan associations, savings banks, and deposit banks, engaged in extending such credits. Such action would further decentralize our credit structure. It would revive residential construction and employment. It would enable such loaning institutions more effectually to promote home ownership. I discussed this plan at some length in a statement made public November 14, last. This plan has been warmly indorsed by the recent National Conference upon Home Ownership and Housing, whose members were designated by the governors of the States and the groups interested.

Reconstruction Finance Corporation

In order that the public may be absolutely assured and that the Government may be in position to meet any public necessity, I recommend that an emergency Reconstruction Corporation of the nature of the former War Finance Corporation should be established. It may not be necessary to use such an instrumentality very extensively. The very existence of such a bulwark will strengthen confidence. The Treasury should be authorized to subscribe a reasonable capital to it, and it should be given authority to issue its own debentures. It should be placed in liquidation at the end of two years. Its purpose is that by strengthening the weak spots to thus liberate the full strength of the Nation's resources. It should be in position to facilitate exports by American agencies; make advances to agricultural credit agencies where necessary to protect and aid the agricultural industry; to make temporary advances upon proper securities to established industries, railways, and financial institutions which can not otherwise secure credit, and where such advances will protect the credit structure and stimulate employment. Its functions would not overlap those of the National Credit Corporation.

Federal Reserve Eligibility

On October 6th I issued a statement that I should recommend to the Congress an extension during emergencies of the eligibility provisions in the Federal reserve act. This statement was approved by a representative gathering of the Members of both Houses of the Congress, including members of the appropriate committees. It was approved by the officials of the Treasury Department, and I understand such an extension has been approved by a majority of the governors of the Federal reserve banks. Nothing should be done which would lower the safeguards of the system.

The establishment of the mortgage-discount banks herein referred to will also contribute to further reserve strength in the banks without inflation.

Banking Laws

Our people have a right to a banking system in which their deposits shall be safeguarded and the flow of credit less subject to storms. The need of a sounder system is plainly shown by the extent of bank failures. I recommend the prompt improvement of the banking laws. Changed financial conditions and commercial practices must be met. The Congress should investigate the need for separation between different kinds of banking; an enlargement of branch banking under proper restrictions; and the methods by which enlarged membership in the Federal reserve system may be brought about.

Postal Savings Banks

The Postal Savings deposits have increased from about $200,000,000 to about $550,000,000 during the past year. This experience has raised important practical questions in relation to deposits and investments which should receive the attention of the Congress.

Railways

The railways present one of our immediate and pressing problems. They are and must remain the backbone of our transportation system. Their prosperity is interrelated with the prosperity of all industries. Their fundamental service in transportation, the volume of their employment, their buying power for supplies from other industries, the enormous investment in their securities, particularly their bonds, by insurance companies, savings banks, benevolent and other trusts, all reflect their partnership in the whole economic fabric. Through these institutions the railway bonds are in a large sense the investment of every family. The well-maintained and successful operation and the stability of railway finances are of primary importance to economic recovery. They should have more effective opportunity to reduce operating costs by proper consolidation. As their rates must be regulated in public interest, so also approximate regulation should be applied to competing services by some authority. The methods of their regulation should be revised. The Interstate Commerce Commission has made important and far-reaching recommendations upon the whole subject, which I commend to the early consideration of the Congress.

Antitrust Laws

In my message of a year ago I commented on the necessity of congressional inquiry into the economic action of the antitrust laws. There is wide conviction that some change should be made especially in the procedure under these laws. I do not favor their repeal. Such action would open wide the door to price fixing, monopoly, and destruction of healthy competition. Particular attention should be given to the industries rounded upon natural resources, especially where destructive competition produces great wastes of these resources and brings great hardships upon operators, employees, and the public. In recent years there has been continued demoralization in the bituminous coal, oil, and lumber industries. I again commend the matter to the consideration of the Congress.

Unemployment

As an aid to unemployment the Federal Government is engaged in the greatest program of public-building, harbor, flood-control, highway, waterway, aviation, merchant and naval ship construction in all history. Our expenditures on these works during this calendar year will reach about $780,000,000 compared with $260,000,000 in

1928. Through this increased construction, through the maintenance of a full complement of Federal employees, and through services to veterans it is estimated that the Federal taxpayer is now directly contributing to the livelihood of 10,000,000 of our citizens.

We must avoid burdens upon the Government which will create more unemployment in private industry than can be gained by further expansion of employment by the Federal Government. We can now stimulate employment and agriculture more effectually and speedily through the voluntary measures in progress, through the thawing out of credit, through the building up of stability abroad, through the home loan discount banks, through an emergency finance corporation and the rehabilitation of the railways and other such directions.

I am opposed to any direct or indirect Government dole. The breakdown and increased unemployment in Europe is due in part to such practices. Our people are providing against distress from unemployment in true American fashion by a magnificent response to public appeal and by action of the local governments.

General Legislation

There are many other subjects requiring legislative action at this session of the Congress. I may list the following among them:

Veterans' Services

The law enacted last March authorizing loans of 50 per cent upon adjusted-service certificates has, together with the loans made under previous laws, resulted in payments of about $1,260,000,000. Appropriations have been exhausted. The Administrator of Veterans' Affairs advises that a further appropriation of $200,000,000 is required at once to meet the obligations made necessary by existing legislation.

There will be demands for further veterans' legislation; there are inequalities in our system of veterans' relief; it is our national duty to meet our obligations to those who have served the Nation. But our present expenditure upon these services now exceeds $1,000,000,000 per annum. I am opposed to any extension of these expenditures until the country has recovered from the present situation.

Electrical-Power Regulation

I have recommended in previous messages the effective regulation of interstate electrical power as the essential function of the reorganized Federal Power Commission. I renew the recommendation. It is urgently needed in public protection.

Muscle Shoals

At my suggestion, the Governors and Legislatures of Alabama and Tennessee selected three members each for service on a committee to which I appointed a representative of the farm organizations and two representatives of the War Department for the purpose of recommending a plan for the disposal of these properties which would be in the interest of the people of those States and the agricultural industry throughout the country. I shall transmit the recommendations to the Congress.

Reorganization of Federal Departments

I have referred in previous messages to the profound need of further reorganization and consolidation of Federal administrative functions to eliminate overlap and waste, and to enable coordination and definition of Government policies now wholly impossible in scattered and conflicting agencies which deal with parts of the same major function. I shall lay before the Congress further recommendations upon this subject, particularly in relation to the Department of the Interior. There are two directions of such reorganization, however, which have an important bearing upon the emergency problems with which we are confronted.

Shipping Board

At present the Shipping Board exercises large administrative functions independent of the Executive. These administrative functions should be transferred to the Department of Commerce, in keeping with that single responsibility which has been the basis of our governmental structure since its foundation. There should be created in that department a position of Assistant Secretary for Merchant Marine, under whom this work and the several bureaus having to do with merchant marine may be grouped.

The Shipping Board should be made a regulatory body acting also in advisory capacity on loans and policies, in keeping with its original conception. Its regulatory powers should be amended to include regulation of coastwise shipping so as to assure stability and better service. It is also worthy of consideration that the regulation of rates and services upon the inland waterways should be assigned to such a reorganized board.

Reorganization of Public Works Administration

I recommend that all building and construction activities of the Government now carried on by many departments be consolidated into an independent establishment under the President to be known as the "Public Works Administration" directed by a Public Works Administrator. This agency should undertake all construction work in service to the different departments of the Government (except naval and military work). The services of the Corps of Army Engineers should be delegated in rotation for military duty to this administration in continuation of their supervision of river and harbor work. Great economies, sounder policies, more effective coordination to employment, and expedition in all construction work would result from this consolidation.

Law Enforcement

I shall present some recommendations in a special message looking to the strengthening of criminal-law enforcement and improvement in judicial procedure connected therewith.

Inland Waterway and Harbor Improvement

These improvements are now proceeding upon an unprecedented scale. Some indication of the volume of work in progress is conveyed by the fact that during the current year over 380,000,000 cubic yards of material have been moved—an amount equal to the entire removal in the construction of the Panama Canal. The Mississippi waterway system, connecting Chicago, Kansas City, Pittsburgh, and New Orleans, will be in full operation during 1933. Substantial progress is being made upon the projects of the upper Missouri, upper Mississippi, etc.

Negotiations are now in progress with Canada for the construction of the St. Lawrence Waterway.

The Tariff

Wages and standards of living abroad have been materially lowered during the past year. The temporary abandonment of the gold standard by certain countries has also reduced their production costs compared to ours. Fortunately any increases in the tariff which may be necessary to protect agriculture and industry from these lowered foreign costs, or decreases in items which may prove to be excessive, may be undertaken at any time by the Tariff Commission under authority which it possesses by virtue of the tariff act of 1930. The commission during the past year has reviewed the rates upon over 254 items subject to tariff. As a result of vigorous and industrious action, it is up to date in the consideration of pending references and is prepared to give prompt attention to any further applications. This procedure presents an orderly method for correcting inequalities. I am opposed to any general congressional revision of the tariff. Such action would disturb industry, business, and agriculture. It would prolong the depression.

Immigration and Deportation

I recommend that immigration restriction now in force under administrative action be placed upon a more definite basis by law. The deportation laws should be strengthened. Aliens lawfully in the country should be protected by the issuance of a certificate of residence.

Public Health

I again call attention to my previous recommendations upon this subject, particularly in its relation to children. The moral results are of the utmost importance.

Conclusion

It is inevitable that in these times much of the legislation proposed to the Congress and many of the recommendations of the Executive must be designed to meet emergencies. In reaching solutions we must not jeopardize those principles which we have found to be the basis of the growth of the Nation. The Federal Government must not encroach upon nor permit local communities to abandon that precious possession of local initiative and responsibility. Again, just as the largest measure of responsibility in the government of the Nation rests upon local self-government, so does the largest measure of social responsibility in our country rest upon the individual. If the individual surrenders his own initiative and responsibilities, he is surrendering his own freedom and his own liberty. It is the duty of the National Government to insist that both the local governments and the individual shall assume and bear these responsibilities as a fundamental of preserving the very basis of our freedom.

Many vital changes and movements of vast proportions are taking place in the economic world. The effect of these changes upon the future can not be seen clearly as yet. Of this, however, we are sure: Our system, based upon the ideals of individual initiative and of equality of opportunity, is not an artificial thing. Rather it is the outgrowth of the experience of America, and expresses the faith and spirit of our people. It has carried us in a century and a half to leadership of the economic world. If our economic system does not match our highest expectations at all times, it does not require revolutionary action to bring it into accord with any necessity that experience may prove. It has successfully adjusted itself to changing conditions in the past. It will do so again. The mobility of our institutions, the richness of our resources, and the abilities of our people enable us to meet them unafraid. It is a distressful time for many of our people, but they have shown qualities as high in fortitude, courage, and resourcefulness as ever in our history. With that spirit, I have faith that out of it will come a sounder life, a truer standard of values, a greater recognition of the results of honest effort, and a healthier atmosphere in which to rear our children. Ours must be a country of such stability and security as can not fail to carry forward and enlarge among all the people that abundant life of material and spiritual opportunity which it has represented among all nations since its beginning.

Herbert Hoover, 1929–1933

Annual Message to Congress
December 6, 1932

Herbert Hoover's fourth and last State of the Union message was submitted while he remained in office as a "lame duck." A month earlier, Hoover, deeply unpopular with the American public and associated with the despair of the Great Depression, had lost his reelection bid in a landslide to Democrat Franklin D. Roosevelt.

Roosevelt, in contrast to the dour Hoover, projected an image of optimism. A victim of polio who used a wheelchair—although, at the time, the public was not aware of the extent of his disability—Roosevelt traveled through the country during the campaign, proving his vigor, and he made good use of the radio as he did so.

Roosevelt swamped Hoover, winning 57.4 percent of the vote and 472 of 531 electoral votes. In addition to Roosevelt's win, the Senate went Democratic and the House—which had shifted two years earlier—remained Democratic, giving the Democrats control of the nation's capital for the first time in more than a decade.

Hoover mentioned the election results in his December 6 message—like his others, it was delivered in writing rather than in person—stating that acceptance of the results was evidence of the country's strength.

The outgoing president praised the generosity of the American people during the difficult winter then under way, mentioning contributions to assist those in need from private agencies and governments at all levels. Remaining consistent with the ideology evident in his first three messages, he suggested ways in which the government could restore confidence among the public: balancing the budget through reduction of expenditures, reorganization of the nation's banking system, and working with other countries on economic issues.

With the Great Depression showing no signs of ending, 1932 had been a particularly difficult year. One incident that drew negative public attention was a march on Washington that summer by the so-called Bonus Army, a group of World War I veterans who demanded that a promised bonus—set for 1945—be paid immediately. With the veterans camped out in the capital, the Hoover administration ordered the police and then the army to move in on the protestors. The situation turned violent, and images of the unrest contributed to Hoover's unpopularity.

Herbert Hoover's four years in office ended ignominiously. The defeated president handed the reins over to Roosevelt in March 1933, marking a major shift in American political history. While Hoover believed in voluntarism and self-reliance, and therefore was unwilling to unleash the full potential power of the federal government on the problems of the Depression, Roosevelt had no such qualms. Roosevelt's accession to the White House would begin what many see as the modern presidency.

T o the Senate and House of Representatives:

In accord with my constitutional duty, I transmit herewith to the Congress information upon the state of the Union together with recommendation of measures for its consideration.

Our country is at peace. Our national defense has been maintained at a high state of effectiveness. All of the executive departments of the Government have been conducted during the year with a high devotion to public interest. There has been a far larger degree of freedom from industrial conflict than hitherto known. Education and science have made further advances. The public health is to-day at its highest known level. While we have recently engaged in the aggressive contest of a national election, its very tranquility and the acceptance of its results furnish abundant proof of the strength of our institutions.

In the face of widespread hardship our people have demonstrated daily a magnificent sense of humanity, of individual and community responsibility for the welfare of the less fortunate. They have grown in their conceptions and organization for cooperative action for the common welfare.

In the provision against distress during this winter, the great private agencies of the country have been mobilized again; the generosity of our people has again come into evidence to a degree in which all America may take great pride. Likewise the local authorities and the States are engaged everywhere in supplemental measures of relief. The provisions made for loans from the Reconstruction Finance Corporation, to States that have exhausted their own resources, guarantee that there should be no hunger or suffering from cold in the country. The large majority of States are showing a sturdy cooperation in the spirit of the Federal aid.

The Surgeon General, in charge of the Public Health Service, furnishes me with the following information upon the state of public health:

MORTALITY RATE PER 1,000 OF POPULATION ON AN ANNUAL BASIS
FROM REPRESENTATIVE STATES

	General	Infant
First 9 months of		
1928	11.9	67.8
1929	12.0	65.8
1930	11.4	62.0
1931	11.2	60.0
1932	10.6	55.0

The sickness rates from data available show the same trends. These facts indicate the fine endeavor of the agencies which have been mobilized for care of those in distress.

Economic Situation

The unparalleled world-wide economic depression has continued through the year. Due to the European collapse, the situation developed during last fall and winter into a series of most acute crises. The unprecedented emergency measures enacted and policies adopted undoubtedly saved the country from economic disaster. After serving to defend the national security, these measures began in July to show their weight and influence toward improvement of conditions in many parts of the country. The following tables of current business indicators show the general economic movement during the past eleven months.

MONTHLY BUSINESS INDICES WITH SEASONAL VARIATIONS ELIMINATED
[MONTHLY AVERAGE 1923–1925 = 100]

Year and Month	Industrial Production	Factory Employment	Freight Car Loadings	Department Store Sales, Value	Exports, Value	Imports, Value	Building Contracts, All Types	Industrial Electric Power Consumption
1931								
Dec.	74	69.4	69	81	46	48	38	89.1
1932								
Jan.	72	68.1	64	78	39	42	31	93.9
Feb.	69	67.8	62	78	45	41	27	98.8
March	67	66.4	61	72	41	37	26	88.0
April	63	64.3	59	80	38	36	27	82.2
May	60	62.1	54	73	37	34	26	82.0
June	59	60.0	52	71	34	36	27	78.1
July	58	58.3	51	67	32	27	27	79.2
Aug.	60	58.8	51	66	31	29	30	73.5
Sept.	66	60.3	54	70	33	32	30	84.0
Oct.	66	61.1	57	70	33	32	30	84.4

The measures and policies which have procured this turn toward recovery should be continued until the depression is passed, and then the emergency agencies should be promptly liquidated. The expansion of credit facilities by the Federal Reserve System and the Reconstruction Finance Corporation has been of incalculable value.

The loans of the latter for reproductive works, and to railways for the creation of employment; its support of the credit structure through loans to banks, insurance companies, railways, building and loan associations, and to agriculture has protected the savings and insurance policies of millions of our citizens and has relieved millions of borrowers from duress; they have enabled industry and business to function and expand. The assistance given to Farm Loan Banks, the establishment of the Home Loan Banks and Agricultural Credit Associations—all in their various ramifications have placed large sums of money at the disposal of the people in protection and aid. Beyond this, the extensive organization of the country in voluntary action has produced profound results.

The following table indicates direct expenditures of the Federal Government in aid to unemployment, agriculture, and financial relief over the past four years. The sums applied to financial relief multiply themselves many fold, being in considerable measure the initial capital supplied to the Reconstruction Finance Corporation, Farm Loan Banks, etc., which will be recovered to the Treasury.

Fiscal year ending June 30—	Public works[1]	Agricultural relief and financial loans
1930	$410,420,000	$156,100,000
1931	574,870,000	196,700,000
1932	655,880,000	772,700,000
1933	717,260,000	52,000,000
Total	2,358,430,000	1,177,500,000

[1] Public Building, Highways, Rivers and Harbors and their maintenance, naval and other vessels construction, hospitals, etc.

Continued constructive policies promoting the economic recovery of the country must be the paramount duty of the Government. The result of the agencies we have created and the policies we have pursued has been to buttress our whole domestic financial structure and greatly to restore credit facilities. But progress in recovery requires another element as well—that is fully restored confidence in the future. Institutions and men may have resources and credit but unless they have confidence progress is halting and insecure.

There are three definite directions in which action by the Government at once can contribute to strengthen further the forces of recovery by strengthening of confidence. They are the necessary foundations to any other action, and their accomplishment would at once promote employment and increase prices.

The first of these directions of action is the continuing reduction of all Government expenditures, whether national, State, or local. The difficulties of the country demand undiminished efforts toward economy in government in every direction. Embraced in this problem is the unquestioned balancing of the Federal Budget. That is the first necessity of national stability and is the foundation of further recovery. It must be balanced in an absolutely safe and sure manner if full confidence is to be inspired.

The second direction for action is the complete reorganization at once of our banking system. The shocks to our economic life have undoubtedly been multiplied by the weakness of this system, and until they are remedied recovery will be greatly hampered.

The third direction for immediate action is vigorous and whole souled cooperation with other governments in the economic field. That our major difficulties find their origins in the economic weakness of foreign nations requires no demonstration. The first need to-day is strengthening of commodity prices. That can not be permanently accomplished by artificialities. It must be accomplished by expansion in consumption of goods through the return of stability and confidence in the world at large and that in turn can not be fully accomplished without cooperation with other nations.

Balancing the Budget

I shall in due course present the Executive Budget to the Congress. It will show proposed reductions in appropriations below those enacted by the last session of the Congress by over $830,000,000. In addition I shall present the necessary Executive orders under the recent act authorizing the reorganization of the Federal Government which, if permitted to go into force, will produce still further substantial economies. These sums in reduction of appropriations will, however, be partially offset by an increase of about $250,000,000 in uncontrollable items such as increased debt services, etc.

In the Budget there is included only the completion of the Federal public works projects already undertaken or under contract. Speeding up of Federal public works during the past four years as an aid to employment has advanced many types of such improvements to the point where further expansion can not be justified in their usefulness to the Government or the people. As an aid to unemployment we should beyond the normal constructive programs substitute reproductive or so-called self-liquidating works. Loans for such purposes have been provided for through the Reconstruction Finance Corporation. This change in character of projects directly relieves the taxpayer and is capable of expansion into a larger field than the direct Federal works. The reproductive works constitute an addition to national wealth and to future employment, whereas further undue expansion of Federal public works is but a burden upon the future.

The Federal construction program thus limited to commitments and work in progress under the proposed appropriations contemplates expenditures for the next fiscal year, including naval and other vessel construction, as well as other forms of public works and maintenance, of a total of $442,769,000, as compared with $717,262,000 for the present year.

The expenditure on such items over the four years ending June 30 next will amount to $2,350,000,000, or an amount of construction work eight times as great as the cost of the Panama Canal and, except for completion of certain long-view projects, places the Nation in many directions well ahead of its requirements for some years to come. A normal program of about $200,000,000 per annum should hereafter provide for the country's necessities and will permit substantial future reduction in Federal expenditures.

I recommend that the furlough system installed last year be continued not only because of the economy produced but because, being tantamount to the "5-day week," it sets an example which should be followed by the country and because it embraces within its workings the "spread work" principle and thus serves to maintain a number of public servants who would otherwise be deprived of all income. I feel, however, in view of the present economic situation and the decrease in the cost of living by over 20 per cent, that some further sacrifice should be made by salaried officials of the Government over and above the 8⅓ per cent reduction under the furlough system. I will recommend that after exempting the first $1,000 of salary there should be a temporary reduction for one year of 11 per cent of that part of all Government salaries in excess of the $1,000 exemption, the result of which, combined with the furlough system, will average about 14.8 per cent reduction in pay to those earning more than $1,000.

I will recommend measures to eliminate certain payments in the veterans' services. I conceive these outlays were entirely beyond the original intentions of Congress in building up veterans' allowances. Many abuses have grown up from ill-considered legislation. They should be eliminated. The Nation should not ask for a reduction in allowances to men and dependents whose disabilities rise out of war service nor to those veterans with substantial service who have become totally disabled from non-war-connected causes and who are at the same time without other support. These latter veterans are a charge on the community at some point, and I feel that in view of their service to the Nation as a whole the responsibility should fall upon the Federal Government.

Many of the economies recommended in the Budget were presented at the last session of the Congress but failed of adoption. If the Economy and Appropriations Committees of the Congress in canvassing these proposed expenditures shall find further reductions which can be made without impairing essential Government services, it will be welcomed both by the country and by myself. But under no circumstances do I feel that the Congress should fail to uphold the total of reductions recommended.

Some of the older revenues and some of the revenues provided under the act passed during the last session of the Congress, particularly those generally referred to as the nuisance taxes, have not been as prolific of income as had been hoped. Further revenue is necessary in addition to the amount of reductions in expenditures recommended. Many of the manufacturers' excise taxes upon selected industries not only failed to produce satisfactory revenue, but they are in many ways unjust and discriminatory. The time has come when, if the Government is to have an adequate basis of revenue to assure a balanced Budget, this system of special manufacturers' excise taxes should be extended to cover practically all manufactures at a uniform rate, except necessary food and possibly some grades of clothing.

At the last session the Congress responded to my request for authority to reorganize the Government departments. The act provides for the grouping and consolidation of executive and administrative agencies according to major purpose, and thereby reducing the number and overlap and duplication of effort. Executive orders issued for these purposes are required to be transmitted to the Congress while in session and do not become effective until after the expiration of 60 calendar days after such transmission, unless the Congress shall sooner approve.

I shall issue such Executive orders within a few days grouping or consolidating over fifty executive and administrative agencies including a large number of commissions and "independent" agencies.

The second step, of course, remains that after these various bureaus and agencies are placed cheek by jowl into such groups, the administrative officers in charge of the groups shall eliminate their overlap and still further consolidate these activities. Therein lie large economies.

The Congress must be warned that a host of interested persons inside and outside the Government whose vision is concentrated on some particular function will at once protest against these proposals. These same sorts of activities have prevented reorganization of the Government for over a quarter of a century. They must be disregarded if the task is to be accomplished.

Banking

The basis of every other and every further effort toward recovery is to reorganize at once our banking system. The shocks to our economic system have undoubtedly multiplied by the weakness of our financial system. I first called attention of the Congress in 1929 to this condition, and I have unceasingly recommended remedy since that time. The subject has been exhaustively investigated both by the committees of the Congress and the officers of the Federal Reserve System.

The banking and financial system is presumed to serve in furnishing the essential lubricant to the wheels of industry, agriculture, and commerce, that is, credit. Its diversion from proper use, its improper use, or its insufficiency instantly brings hardship and dislocation in economic life. As a system our banking has failed to meet this great emergency. It can be said without question of doubt that our losses and distress have been greatly augmented by its wholly inadequate organization. Its inability as a system to respond to our needs is to-day a constant drain upon progress toward recovery. In this statement I am not referring to individual banks or bankers. Thousands of them have shown distinguished courage and ability. On the contrary, I am referring to the system itself, which is so organized, or so lacking in organization, that in an emergency its very mechanism jeopardizes or paralyzes the action of sound banks and its instability is responsible for periodic dangers to our whole economic system.

Bank failures rose in 1931 to 10½ per cent of all the banks as compared to 1½ per cent of the failures of all other types of enterprise. Since January 1, 1930, we have had 4,665 banks suspend, with $3,300,000,000 in deposits. Partly from fears and drains from abroad, partly from these failures themselves (which indeed often caused closing of sound banks), we have witnessed hoarding of currency to an enormous sum, rising during the height of the crisis to over $1,600,000,000. The results from interreaction of cause and effect have expressed themselves in strangulation of credit which at times has almost stifled the Nation's business and agriculture. The losses, suffering, and tragedies of our people are incalculable. Not alone do they lie in the losses of savings to millions of homes, injury by deprival of working capital to thousands of small businesses, but also, in the frantic pressure to recall loans to meet pressures of hoarding and in liquidation of failed banks, millions of other people have suffered in the loss of their homes and farms, businesses have been ruined, unemployment increased, and farmers' prices diminished.

That this failure to function is unnecessary and is the fault of our particular system is plainly indicated by the fact that in Great Britain, where the economic mechanism has suffered far greater shocks than our own, there has not been a single bank failure during the depression. Again in Canada, where the situation has been in large degree identical with our own, there have not been substantial bank failures.

The creation of the Reconstruction Finance Corporation and the amendments to the Federal Reserve Act served to defend the Nation in a great crisis. They are not remedies; they are relief. It is inconceivable that the Reconstruction Corporation, which has extended aid to nearly 6,000 institutions and is manifestly but a temporary device, can go on indefinitely.

It is to-day a matter of satisfaction that the rate of bank failures, of hoarding, and the demands upon the Reconstruction Corporation have greatly lessened. The acute phases of the crisis have obviously passed and the time has now come when this national danger and this failure to respond to national necessities must be ended and the measures to end them can be safely undertaken. Methods of reform have been exhaustively examined. There is no reason now why solution should not be found at the present session of the Congress. Inflation of currency or governmental conduct of banking can have no part in these reforms. The Government must abide within the field of constructive organization, regulation, and the enforcement of safe practices only.

Parallel with reform in the banking laws must be changes in the Federal Farm Loan Banking system and in the Joint Stock Land Banks. Some of these changes should be directed to permanent improvement and some to emergency aid to our people where they wish to fight to save their farms and homes.

I wish again to emphasize this view—that these widespread banking reforms are a national necessity and are the first requisites for further recovery in agriculture and business. They should have immediate consideration as steps greatly needed to further recovery.

Economic Cooperation with Other Nations

Our major difficulties during the past two years find their origins in the shocks from economic collapse abroad which in turn are the aftermath of the Great War. If we are to secure rapid and assured recovery and protection for the future we must cooperate with foreign nations in many measures.

We have actively engaged in a World Disarmament Conference where, with success, we should reduce our own tax burdens and the tax burdens of other major nations. We should increase political stability of the world. We should lessen the danger of war by increasing defensive powers and decreasing offensive powers of nations. We would thus open new vistas of economic expansion for the world.

We are participating in the formulation of a World Economic Conference, successful results from which would contribute much to advance in agricultural prices, employment, and business. Currency depreciation and correlated forces have contributed greatly to decrease in price levels. Moreover, from these origins rise most of the destructive trade barriers now stifling the commerce of the world. We could by successful action increase security and expand trade through stability in international exchange and monetary values. By such action world confidence could be restored. It would bring courage and stability, which will reflect into every home in our land.

The European governments, obligated to us in war debts, have requested that there should be suspension of payments due the United States on December 15 next, to be accompanied by exchange of views upon this debt question. Our Government has informed them that we do not approve of suspension of the December 15 payments.

I have stated that I would recommend to the Congress methods to overcome temporary exchange difficulties in connection with this payment from nations where it may be necessary.

In the meantime I wish to reiterate that here are three great fields of international action which must be considered not in part but as a whole. They are of most vital interest to our people. Within them there are not only grave dangers if we fail in right action but there also tie immense opportunities for good if we shall succeed. Within success there lie major remedies for our economic distress and major progress in stability and security to every fireside in our country.

The welfare of our people is dependent upon successful issue of the great causes of world peace, world disarmament, and organized world recovery. Nor is it too much to say that to-day as never before the welfare of mankind and the preservation of civilization depend upon our solution of these questions. Such solutions can not be attained except by honest friendship, by adherence to agreements entered upon until mutually revised and by cooperation amongst nations in a determination to find solutions which will be mutually beneficial.

Other Legislation

I have placed various legislative needs before the Congress in previous messages, and these views require no amplification on this occasion. I have urged the need for reform in our transportation and power regulation, in the antitrust laws as applied to our national resource industries, western range conservation, extension of Federal aid to child health services, membership in the World Court, the ratification of the Great Lakes-St. Lawrence Seaway Treaty, revision of the bankruptcy acts, revision of Federal court procedure, and many other pressing problems.

These and other special subjects I shall where necessary deal with by special communications to the Congress.

The activities of our Government are so great, when combined with the emergency activities which have arisen out of the world crisis, that even the briefest review of them would render the annual message unduly long. I shall therefore avail myself of the fact that every detail of the Government is covered in the reports to the Congress by each of the departments and agencies of the Government.

Conclusion

It seems to me appropriate upon this occasion to make certain general observations upon the principles which must dominate the solution of problems now pressing upon the Nation. Legislation in response to national needs will be effective only if every such act conforms to a complete philosophy of the people's purposes and destiny. Ours is a distinctive government with a unique history and background, consciously dedicated to specific ideals of liberty and to a faith in the inviolable sanctity of the individual human spirit. Furthermore, the continued existence and adequate functioning of our government in preservation of ordered liberty and stimulation of progress depends upon the maintenance of State, local, institutional, and individual sense of responsibility. We have builded a system of individualism peculiarly our own which must not be forgotten in any governmental acts, for from it have grown greater accomplishments than those of any other nation.

On the social and economic sides, the background of our American system and the motivation of progress is essentially that we should allow free play of social and economic forces as far as will not limit equality of opportunity and as will at the same time stimulate the initiative and enterprise of our people. In the maintenance of this balance the Federal Government can permit of no privilege to any person or group. It should act as a regulatory agent and not as a participant in economic and social life. The moment the Government participates, it becomes a competitor with the people. As a competitor it becomes at once a tyranny in whatever direction it may touch. We have around us numerous such experiences, no one of which can be found to have justified itself except in cases where the people as a whole have met forces beyond their control, such as those of the Great War and this great depression, where the full powers of the Federal Government must be exerted to protect the people. But even these must be limited to an emergency sense and must be promptly ended when these dangers are overcome.

With the free development of science and the consequent multitude of inventions, some of which are absolutely revolutionary in our national life, the Government must not only stimulate the social and economic responsibility of individuals and private institutions but it must also give leadership to cooperative action amongst the people which will soften the effect of these revolutions and thus secure social transformations in an orderly manner. The highest form of self-government is the voluntary cooperation within our people for such purposes.

But I would emphasize again that social and economic solutions, as such, will not avail to satisfy the aspirations of the people unless they conform with the traditions of our race deeply grooved in their sentiments through a century and a half of struggle for ideals of life that are rooted in religion and fed from purely spiritual springs.

Franklin D. Roosevelt

1933–1945

*"Once I prophesied that this generation
of Americans had a rendezvous with destiny.
That prophecy comes true.
To us much is given; more is expected."*

ANNUAL MESSAGE TO CONGRESS, JANUARY 4, 1939

Annual Message to Congress

January 3, 1934

Franklin Delano Roosevelt's first annual message followed an extraordinarily productive year that saw the enactment of a host of laws designed to combat the Great Depression.

Roosevelt, a master at the art of communication, chose to revive the tradition of delivering the State of the Union address in person to Congress. Woodrow Wilson, in 1913, had been the first president to do so since John Adams, but the tradition subsequently had died with Calvin Coolidge's second message; Herbert Hoover chose to submit all four of his in writing.

Another innovation was a change in the timing of the annual message. It had been delivered in December but was moved to early January after the passage of the Twentieth Amendment in early 1933. That amendment set January 3 as the start of a new Congress, and January 20 as the presidential inauguration day, moving both events up in the calendar.

In this relatively brief address, Roosevelt congratulated Congress for its work the previous year, comparing it to the tasks undertaken by the first Congress in 1789. Among the new measures he referred to were the National Industrial Recovery Act, an effort to involve industry and trade unions as well as the government in an economic stimulus program; the Agricultural Adjustment Act, which set out a national agriculture policy; and the Tennessee Valley Authority Act, which, among other things, provided power to that region. Roosevelt, a Democrat, was working with a Democratic House and Senate, giving the party control of all the levers of power in Washington for the first time in over a decade.

The president also mentioned the Twenty-first Amendment, ratified December 5, 1933, which repealed the Eighteenth Amendment, or Prohibition, which had made illegal the manufacture, sale, or transportation of alcohol. Roosevelt had backed the repeal of Prohibition and said that the new amendment should help remove crime connected to the illegal liquor trade.

The president's first ten months in office marked the start of the New Deal, Roosevelt's signature plan designed to move the country back to firmer economic ground. In addition, Roosevelt's tenure in office—which lasted until 1945, the longest in the country's history—saw a huge expansion both in the powers of the presidency and of the federal government.

M r. President, Mr. Speaker, Senators and Representatives in Congress:

I come before you at the opening of the Regular Session of the 73d Congress, not to make requests for special or detailed items of legislation; I come, rather, to counsel with you, who, like myself, have been selected to carry out a mandate of the whole people, in order that without partisanship you and I may cooperate to continue the restoration of our national wellbeing and, equally important, to build on the ruins of the past a new structure designed better to meet the present problems of modern civilization.

Such a structure includes not only the relations of industry and agriculture and finance to each other but also the effect which all of these three have on our individual citizens and on the whole people as a Nation.

Now that we are definitely in the process of recovery, lines have been rightly drawn between those to whom this recovery means a return to old methods—and the number of these people is small—and those for whom recovery means a reform of many old methods, a permanent readjustment of many of our ways of thinking and therefore of many of our social and economic arrangements. . . .

Civilization cannot go back; civilization must not stand still. We have undertaken new methods. It is our task to perfect, to improve, to alter when necessary, but in all cases to go forward. To consolidate what we are doing, to make our economic and social structure capable of dealing with modern life is the joint task of the legislative, the judicial, and the executive branches of the national Government.

Without regard to party, the overwhelming majority of our people seek a greater opportunity for humanity to prosper and find happiness. They recognize that human welfare has not increased and does not increase through mere materialism and luxury, but that it does progress through integrity, unselfishness, responsibility and justice.

In the past few months, as a result of our action, we have demanded of many citizens that they surrender certain licenses to do as they please, in their business relationships; but we have asked this in exchange for the protection which the State can give against exploitation by their fellow men or by combinations of their fellow men.

I congratulate this Congress upon the courage, the earnestness and the efficiency with which you met the crisis at the Special Session. It was your fine understanding of the national problem that furnished the example which the country has so splendidly followed. I venture to say that the task confronting the First Congress of 1789 was no greater than your own.

I shall not attempt to set forth either the many phases of the crisis which we experienced last March, or the many measures which you and I undertook during the Special Session that we might initiate recovery and reform.

It is sufficient that I should speak in broad terms of the results of our common counsel. The credit of the Government has been fortified by drastic reduction in the cost of its permanent agencies through the Economy Act.

With the twofold purpose of strengthening the whole financial structure and of arriving eventually at a medium of exchange which over the years will have less variable purchasing and debt paying power for our people than that of the past, I have used the authority granted me to purchase all American-produced gold and silver and to buy additional gold in the world markets. Careful investigation and constant study prove that in the matter of foreign exchange rates certain of our sister Nations find themselves so handicapped by internal and other conditions that they feel unable at this time to enter into stabilization discussion based on permanent and world-wide objectives.

The overwhelming majority of the banks, both national and State, which reopened last spring, are in sound condition and have been brought within the protection of Federal insurance. In the case of those banks which were not permitted to reopen, nearly six hundred million dollars of frozen deposits are being restored to the depositors through the assistance of the national Government.

We have made great strides toward the objectives of the National Industrial Recovery Act, for not only have several millions of our unemployed been restored to work, but industry is organizing itself with a greater understanding that reasonable profits can be earned while at the same time protection can be assured to guarantee to labor adequate pay and proper conditions of work. Child labor is abolished. Uniform standards of hours and wages apply today to 95 percent of industrial employment within the field of the National Industrial Recovery Act. We seek the definite end of preventing combinations in furtherance of monopoly and in restraint of trade, while at the same time we seek to prevent ruinous rivalries within industrial groups which in many cases resemble the gang wars of the underworld and in which the real victim in every case is the public itself.

Under the authority of this Congress, we have brought the component parts of each industry together around a common table, just as we have brought problems affecting labor to a common meeting ground. Though the machinery, hurriedly devised, may need readjustment from time to time, nevertheless I think you will agree with me that we have created a permanent feature of our modernized industrial structure and that it will continue under the supervision but not the arbitrary dictation of Government itself.

You recognized last spring that the most serious part of the debt burden affected those who stood in danger of losing their farms and their homes. I am glad to tell you that refinancing in both of these cases is proceeding with good success and in all probability within the financial limits set by the Congress.

But agriculture had suffered from more than its debts. Actual experience with the operation of the Agricultural Adjustment Act leads to my belief that thus far the experiment of seeking a balance between production and consumption is succeeding and has made progress entirely in line with reasonable expectations toward the restoration of farm prices to parity. I continue in my conviction that industrial progress and prosperity can only be attained by bringing the purchasing power of that portion of our population which in one form or another is dependent upon agriculture up to a level which will restore a proper balance between every section of the country and between every form of work.

In this field, through carefully planned flood control, power development and land-use policies in the Tennessee Valley and in other, great watersheds, we are seeking the elimination of waste, the removal of poor lands from agriculture and the encouragement of small local industries, thus furthering this principle of a better balanced national life. We recognize the great ultimate cost of the application of this rounded policy to every part of the Union. Today we are creating heavy obligations to start the work because of the great unemployment needs of the moment. I look forward, however, to the time in the not distant future, when annual appropriations, wholly covered by current revenue, will enable the work to proceed under a national plan. Such a national plan will, in a generation or two, return many times the money spent on it; more important, it will eliminate the use of inefficient tools, conserve and increase natural resources, prevent waste, and enable millions of our people to take better advantage of the opportunities which God has given our country.

I cannot, unfortunately, present to you a picture of complete optimism regarding world affairs.

The delegation representing the United States has worked in close cooperation with the other American Republics assembled at Montevideo to make that conference an outstanding success. We have, I hope, made it clear to our neighbors that we seek with them future avoidance of territorial expansion and of interference by one Nation in the internal affairs of another. Furthermore, all of us are seeking the restoration of commerce in ways which will preclude the building up of large favorable trade balances by any one Nation at the expense of trade debits on the part of other Nations.

In other parts of the world, however, fear of immediate or future aggression and with it the spending of vast sums on armament and the continued building up of defensive trade barriers prevent any great progress in peace or trade agreements. I have made it clear that the United States cannot take part in political arrangements in Europe but that we stand ready to cooperate at any time in practicable measures on a world basis looking to immediate reduction of armaments and the lowering of the barriers against commerce.

I expect to report to you later in regard to debts owed the Government and people of this country by the Governments and peoples of other countries. Several Nations, acknowledging the debt, have paid in small part; other Nations have failed to pay. One Nation—Finland—has paid the installments due this country in full.

Returning to home problems, we have been shocked by many notorious examples of injuries done our citizens by persons or groups who have been living off their neighbors by the use of methods either unethical or criminal.

In the first category—a field which does not involve violations of the letter of our laws—practices have been brought to light which have shocked those who believed that we were in the past generation raising the ethical standards of business. They call for stringent preventive or regulatory measures. I am speaking of those individuals who have evaded the spirit and purpose of our tax laws, of those high officials of banks or corporations who have grown rich at the expense of their stockholders or the public, of those reckless speculators with their own or other people's money whose operations have injured the values of the farmers' crops and the savings of the poor.

In the other category, crimes of organized banditry, coldblooded shooting, lynching and kidnapping have threatened our security.

These violations of ethics and these violations of law call on the strong arm of Government for their immediate suppression; they call also on the country for an aroused public opinion.

The adoption of the Twenty-first Amendment should give material aid to the elimination of those new forms of crime which came from the illegal traffic in liquor.

I shall continue to regard it as my duty to use whatever means may be necessary to supplement State, local and private agencies for the relief of suffering caused by unemployment. With respect to this question, I have recognized the dangers inherent in the direct giving of relief and have sought the means to provide not mere relief, but the opportunity for useful and remunerative work. We shall, in the process of recovery, seek to move as rapidly as possible from direct relief to publicly supported work and from that to the rapid restoration of private employment.

It is to the eternal credit of the American people that this tremendous readjustment of our national life is being accomplished peacefully, without serious dislocation, with only a minimum of injustice and with a great, willing spirit of cooperation throughout the country.

Disorder is not an American habit. Self-help and self-control are the essence of the American tradition—not of necessity the form of that tradition, but its spirit. The program itself comes from the American people.

It is an integrated program, national in scope. Viewed in the large, it is designed to save from destruction and to keep for the future the genuinely important values created by modern society. The vicious and wasteful parts of that society we could not save if we wished; they have chosen the way of self-destruction. We would save useful mechanical invention, machine production, industrial efficiency, modern means of communication, broad education. We would save and encourage the slowly growing impulse among consumers to enter the industrial market place equipped with sufficient organization to insist upon fair prices and honest sales.

But the unnecessary expansion of industrial plants, the waste of natural resources, the exploitation of the consumers of natural monopolies, the accumulation of stagnant surpluses, child labor, and the ruthless exploitation of all labor, the encouragement of speculation with other people's money, these were consumed in the fires that they themselves kindled; we must make sure that as we reconstruct our life there be no soil in which such weeds can grow again.

We have plowed the furrow and planted the good seed; the hard beginning is over. If we would reap the full harvest, we must cultivate the soil where this good seed is sprouting and the plant is reaching up to mature growth.

A final personal word. I know that each of you will appreciate that. I am speaking no mere politeness when I assure you how much I value the fine relationship that we have shared during these months of hard and incessant work. Out of these friendly contacts we are, fortunately, building a strong and permanent tie between the legislative and executive branches of the Government. The letter of the Constitution wisely declared a separation, but the impulse of common purpose declares a union. In this spirit we join once more in serving the American people.

Franklin D. Roosevelt, 1933–1937

Annual Message to Congress
January 4, 1935

Franklin D. Roosevelt's inauguration as president in 1933 had launched the start of the New Deal. During his first hundred days in office, Congress passed a historic number of laws designed to assist the country in starting to recover from the Great Depression, which already had been under way for several years.

The president, a Democrat, had the political good fortune of working with a heavily Democratic Congress. While many midterm congressional elections favor the opposition party, this was not the case in the 1934 contests. Democrats, who already controlled both the House and Senate, racked up even more wins, creating lopsided majorities in both houses.

In his second annual State of the Union message, delivered before Congress, the president gave notice that he wanted to continue his efforts. Among other proposals, he called for additional measures that would provide work for unemployed Americans.

Roosevelt and his New Deal enjoyed another landmark year in 1935. Social Security, the government entitlement program into which workers pay a portion of their wages and from which they eventually receive benefits, was created in 1935. In addition, the Works Progress Administration, a government program that set up public works and other jobs for the unemployed, began in 1935.

Roosevelt, in his message, stated that inequality was still a huge problem for the United States. "We have not weeded out the over privileged and we have not effectively lifted up the underprivileged," he argued. He called for three types of security for Americans—the ability to obtain a livelihood through better use of natural resources, protection from hazards of life such as illness, and decent homes—and said that he had a broad program in mind that would address all three.

The bulk of his message, though, focused on how to get more people working. He said that the direct relief many unemployed Americans had been receiving was not the best approach to take, as it would destroy their spirit. Work, rather than relief, would be the correct answer to the problem of massive unemployment, he said.

He set out a plan that would create projects that would be useful for the country but would not compete with private enterprises. Among the types of work he cited were slum clearance, rural electrification, and reforestation. The program Roosevelt outlined strongly resembled what became the Works Progress Administration.

Mr. President, Mr. Speaker, Members of the Senate and of the House of Representatives:

The Constitution wisely provides that the Chief Executive shall report to the Congress on the state of the Union, for through you, the chosen legislative representatives, our citizens everywhere may fairly judge the progress of our governing. I am confident that today, in the light of the events of the past two years, you do not consider it merely a trite phrase when I tell you that I am truly glad to greet you and that I look forward to common counsel, to useful cooperation, and to genuine friendships between us.

We have undertaken a new order of things; yet we progress to it under the framework and in the spirit and intent of the American Constitution. We have proceeded throughout the Nation a measurable distance on the road toward this new order. Materially, I can report to you substantial benefits to our agricultural population, increased industrial activity, and profits to our merchants. Of equal moment, there is evident a restoration of that spirit of confidence and faith which marks the American character. Let him, who, for speculative profit or partisan purpose, without just warrant would seek to disturb or dispel this assurance, take heed before he assumes responsibility for any act which slows our onward steps.

Throughout the world, change is the order of the day. In every Nation economic problems, long in the making, have brought crises of many kinds for which the masters of old practice and theory were unprepared. In most Nations social justice, no longer a distant ideal, has become a definite goal, and ancient Governments are beginning to heed the call.

Thus, the American people do not stand alone in the world in their desire for change. We seek it through tested liberal traditions, through processes which retain all of the deep essentials of that republican form of representative government first given to a troubled world by the United States.

As the various parts in the program begun in the Extraordinary Session of the 73rd Congress shape themselves in practical administration, the unity of our program reveals itself to the Nation. The outlines of the new economic order, rising from the disinte-gration of the old, are apparent. We test what we have done as our measures take root in the living texture of life. We see where we have built wisely and where we can do still better.

The attempt to make a distinction between recovery and reform is a narrowly con-ceived effort to substitute the appearance of reality for reality itself. When a man is convalescing from illness, wisdom dictates not only cure of the symptoms, but also removal of their cause.

It is important to recognize that while we seek to outlaw specific abuses, the Amer-ican objective of today has an infinitely deeper, finer and more lasting purpose than mere repression. Thinking people in almost every country of the world have come to realize certain fundamental difficulties with which civilization must reckon. Rapid changes—the machine age, the advent of universal and rapid communication and many other new factors—have brought new problems. Succeeding generations have attempted to keep pace by reforming in piecemeal fashion this or that attendant abuse. As a result, evils overlap and reform becomes confused and frustrated. We lose sight, from time to time, of our ultimate human objectives.

Let us, for a moment, strip from our simple purpose the confusion that results from a multiplicity of detail and from millions of written and spoken words.

We find our population suffering from old inequalities, little changed by vast spo-radic remedies. In spite of our efforts and in spite of our talk, we have not weeded out the over privileged and we have not effectively lifted up the underprivileged. Both of these manifestations of injustice have retarded happiness. No wise man has any intention of destroying what is known as the profit motive; because by the profit motive we mean the right by work to earn a decent livelihood for ourselves and for our families.

We have, however, a clear mandate from the people, that Americans must forswear that conception of the acquisition of wealth which, through excessive profits, creates undue private power over private affairs and, to our misfortune, over public affairs as well. In building toward this end we do not destroy ambition, nor do we seek to divide our wealth into equal shares on stated occasions. We continue to recognize the greater ability of some to earn more than others. But we do assert that the ambition of the individual to obtain for him and his a proper security, a reasonable leisure, and a decent living throughout life, is an ambition to be preferred to the appetite for great wealth and great power.

I recall to your attention my message to the Congress last June in which I said: "among our objectives I place the security of the men, women and children of the Nation first." That remains our first and continuing task; and in a very real sense every major legislative enactment of this Congress should be a component part of it.

In defining immediate factors which enter into our quest, I have spoken to the Con-gress and the people of three great divisions:

1. The security of a livelihood through the better use of the national resources of the land in which we live.

2. The security against the major hazards and vicissitudes of life.

3. The security of decent homes.

I am now ready to submit to the Congress a broad program designed ultimately to establish all three of these factors of security—a program which because of many lost years will take many future years to fulfill.

A study of our national resources, more comprehensive than any previously made, shows the vast amount of necessary and practicable work which needs to be done for the development and preservation of our natural wealth for the enjoyment and advantage of our people in generations to come. The sound use of land and water is far more comprehensive than the mere planting of trees, building of dams, distributing of electricity or retirement of sub-marginal land. It recognizes that stranded populations, either in the country or the city, cannot have security under the conditions that now surround them.

To this end we are ready to begin to meet this problem—the intelligent care of population throughout our Nation, in accordance with an intelligent distribution of the means of livelihood for that population. A definite program for putting people to work, of which I shall speak in a moment, is a component part of this greater program of security of livelihood through the better use of our national resources.

Closely related to the broad problem of livelihood is that of security against the major hazards of life. Here also, a comprehensive survey of what has been attempted or accomplished in many Nations and in many States proves to me that the time has come for action by the national Government. I shall send to you, in a few days, definite recommendations based on these studies. These recommendations will cover the broad subjects of unemployment insurance and old age insurance, of benefits for children, form others, for the handicapped, for maternity care and for other aspects of dependency and illness where a beginning can now be made.

The third factor—better homes for our people—has also been the subject of experimentation and study. Here, too, the first practical steps can be made through the proposals which I shall suggest in relation to giving work to the unemployed.

Whatever we plan and whatever we do should be in the light of these three clear objectives of security. We cannot afford to lose valuable time in haphazard public policies which cannot find a place in the broad outlines of these major purposes. In that spirit I come to an immediate issue made for us by hard and inescapable circumstance—the task of putting people to work. In the spring of 1933 the issue of destitution seemed to stand apart; today, in the light of our experience and our new national policy, we find we can put people to work in ways which conform to, initiate and carry forward the broad principles of that policy.

The first objectives of emergency legislation of 1933 were to relieve destitution, to make it possible for industry to operate in a more rational and orderly fashion, and to put behind industrial recovery the impulse of large expenditures in Government undertakings. The purpose of the National Industrial Recovery Act to provide work for more people succeeded in a substantial manner within the first few months of its life, and the Act has continued to maintain employment gains and greatly improved working conditions in industry.

The program of public works provided for in the Recovery Act launched the Federal Government into a task for which there was little time to make preparation and little American experience to follow. Great employment has been given and is being given by these works.

More than two billions of dollars have also been expended in direct relief to the destitute. Local agencies of necessity determined the recipients of this form of relief. With inevitable exceptions the funds were spent by them with reasonable efficiency and as a result actual want of food and clothing in the great majority of cases has been overcome.

But the stark fact before us is that great numbers still remain unemployed.

A large proportion of these unemployed and their dependents have been forced on the relief rolls. The burden on the Federal Government has grown with great rapidity. We have here a human as well as an economic problem. When humane considerations are concerned, Americans give them precedence. The lessons of history, confirmed by the evidence immediately before me, show conclusively that continued dependence upon relief induces a spiritual and moral disintegration fundamentally destructive to the national fibre. To dole out relief in this way is to administer a narcotic, a subtle destroyer of the human spirit. It is inimical to the dictates of sound policy. It is in violation of the traditions of America. Work must be found for able-bodied but destitute workers.

The Federal Government must and shall quit this business of relief.

I am not willing that the vitality of our people be further sapped by the giving of cash, of market baskets, of a few hours of weekly work cutting grass, raking leaves or picking up papers in the public parks. We must preserve not only the bodies of the unemployed from destitution but also their self-respect, their self-reliance and courage and determination. This decision brings me to the problem of what the Government should do with approximately five million unemployed now on the relief rolls.

About one million and a half of these belong to the group which in the past was dependent upon local welfare efforts. Most of them are unable for one reason or another to maintain themselves independently—for the most part, through no fault of their own. Such people, in the days before the great depression, were cared for by local efforts—by States, by counties, by towns, by cities, by churches and by private welfare agencies. It is my thought that in the future they must be cared for as they were before. I stand ready through my own personal efforts, and through the public influence of the office that I hold, to help these local agencies to get the means necessary to assume this burden.

The security legislation which I shall propose to the Congress will, I am confident, be of assistance to local effort in the care of this type of cases. Local responsibility can and will be resumed, for, after all, common sense tells us that the wealth necessary for this task existed and still exists in the local community, and the dictates of sound administration require that this responsibility be in the first instance a local one. There are, however, an additional three and one half million employable people who are on relief. With them the problem is different and the responsibility is different. This group was the victim of a nation-wide depression caused by conditions which were not local but national. The Federal Government is the only governmental agency with sufficient power and credit to meet this situation. We have assumed this task and we shall not shrink from it in the future. It is a duty dictated by every intelligent consideration of national policy to ask you to make it possible for the United States to give employment to all of these three and one half million employable people now on relief, pending their absorption in a rising tide of private employment.

It is my thought that with the exception of certain of the normal public building operations of the Government, all emergency public works shall be united in a single new arid greatly enlarged plan.

With the establishment of this new system we can supersede the Federal Emergency Relief Administration with a coordinated authority which will be charged with the orderly liquidation of our present relief activities and the substitution of a national chart for the giving of work.

This new program of emergency public employment should be governed by a number of practical principles.

1. All work undertaken should be useful—not just for a day, or a year, but useful in the sense that it affords permanent improvement in living conditions or that it creates future new wealth for the Nation.

2. Compensation on emergency public projects should be in the form of security payments which should be larger than the amount now received as a relief dole, but at the same time not so large as to encourage the rejection of opportunities for private employment or the leaving of private employment to engage in Government work.

3. Projects should be undertaken on which a large percentage of direct labor can be used.

4. Preference should be given to those projects which will be self-liquidating in the sense that there is a reasonable expectation that the Government will get its money back at some future time.

5. The projects undertaken should be selected and planned so as to compete as little as possible with private enterprises. This suggests that if it were not for the necessity of giving useful work to the unemployed now on relief, these projects in most instances would not now be undertaken.

6. The planning of projects would seek to assure work during the coming fiscal year to the individuals now on relief, or until such time as private employment is available. In order to make adjustment to increasing private employment, work should be planned with a view to tapering it off in proportion to the speed with which the emergency workers are offered positions with private employers.

7. Effort should be made to locate projects where they will serve the greatest unemployment needs as shown by present relief rolls, and the broad program of the National Resources Board should be freely used for guidance in selection. Our ultimate objective being the enrichment of human lives, the Government has the primary duty to use its emergency expenditures as much as possible to serve those who cannot secure the advantages of private capital.

Ever since the adjournment of the 73d Congress, the Administration has been studying from every angle the possibility and the practicability of new forms of employment.

As a result of these studies I have arrived at certain very definite convictions as to the amount of money that will be necessary for the sort of public projects that I have described. I shall submit these figures in my budget message. I assure you now they will be within the sound credit of the Government.

The work itself will cover a wide field including clearance of slums, which for adequate reasons cannot be undertaken by private capital; in rural housing of several kinds, where, again, private capital is unable to function; in rural electrification; in the reforestation of the great watersheds of the Nation; in an intensified program to prevent soil erosion and to reclaim blighted areas; in improving existing road systems and in constructing national highways designed to handle modern traffic; in the elimination of grade crossings; in the extension and enlargement of the successful work of the Civilian Conservation Corps; in non-Federal works, mostly self-liquidating and highly useful to local divisions of Government; and on many other projects which the Nation needs and cannot afford to neglect.

This is the method which I propose to you in order that we may better meet this present-day problem of unemployment. Its greatest advantage is that it fits logically and usefully into the long-range permanent policy of providing the three types of security which constitute as a whole an American plan for the betterment of the future of the American people.

I shall consult with you from time to time concerning other measures of national importance. Among the subjects that lie immediately before us are the consolidation of Federal regulatory administration over all forms of transportation, the renewal and clarification of the general purposes of the National Industrial Recovery Act, the strengthening of our facilities for the prevention, detection and treatment of crime and criminals, the restoration of sound conditions in the public utilities field through abolition of the evil features of holding companies, the gradual tapering off of the emergency credit activities of Government, and improvement in our taxation forms and methods.

We have already begun to feel the bracing effect upon our economic system of a restored agriculture. The hundreds of millions of additional income that farmers are receiving are finding their way into the channels of trade. The farmers' share of the national income is slowly rising. The economic facts justify the widespread opinion of those engaged in agriculture that our provisions for maintaining a balanced production give at this time the most adequate remedy for an old and vexing problem. For the present, and especially in view of abnormal world conditions, agricultural adjustment with certain necessary improvements in methods should continue.

It seems appropriate to call attention at this time to the fine spirit shown during the past year by our public servants. I cannot praise too highly the cheerful work of the Civil Service employees, and of those temporarily working for the Government. As for those thousands in our various public agencies spread throughout the country who, without compensation, agreed to take over heavy responsibilities in connection with our various loan agencies and particularly in direct relief work, I cannot say too much. I do not think any country could show a higher average of cheerful and even enthusiastic team-work than has been shown by these men and women.

I cannot with candor tell you that general international relationships outside the borders of the United States are improved. On the surface of things many old jealousies are resurrected, old passions aroused; new strivings for armament and power, in more than one land, rear their ugly heads. I hope that calm counsel and constructive leadership will provide the steadying influence and the time necessary for the coming of new and more practical forms of representative government throughout the world wherein privilege and power will occupy a lesser place and world welfare a greater.

I believe, however, that our own peaceful and neighborly attitude toward other Nations is coming to be understood and appreciated. The maintenance of international peace is a matter in which we are deeply and unselfishly concerned. Evidence of our persistent and undeniable desire to prevent armed conflict has recently been more than once afforded.

There is no ground for apprehension that our relations with any Nation will be otherwise than peaceful. Nor is there ground for doubt that the people of most Nations seek relief from the threat and burden attaching to the false theory that extravagant armament cannot be reduced and limited by international accord.

The ledger of the past year shows many more gains than losses. Let us not forget that, in addition to saving millions from utter destitution, child labor has been for the moment outlawed, thousands of homes saved to their owners and most important of all, the morale of the Nation has been restored. Viewing the year 1934 as a whole, you and I can agree that we have a generous measure of reasons for giving thanks.

It is not empty optimism that moves me to a strong hope in the coming year. We can, if we will, make 1935 a genuine period of good feeling, sustained by a sense of purposeful progress. Beyond the material recovery, I sense a spiritual recovery as well. The people of America are turning as never before to those permanent values that are not limited to the physical objectives of life. There are growing signs of this on every hand. In the face of these spiritual impulses we are sensible of the Divine Providence to which Nations turn now, as always, for guidance and fostering care.

Franklin D. Roosevelt, 1933–1937

Annual Message to Congress
January 3, 1936

Franklin D. Roosevelt's third State of the Union message resembled a fiery campaign speech. The president was looking ahead to November, when he would seek reelection to a second term. In his address, he highlighted many of the changes wrought by his New Deal program and asked the country whether it wanted to go back to a pre–New Deal system.

He painted a picture of the United States in the years before his inauguration as a nation dominated by a small group of industrial and financial groups, and stated that he and Congress had worked together to return control to Washington. In so doing, he said, "we have earned the hatred of entrenched greed." And now, those forces were trying to regain power, he argued.

The president then launched into a litany of examples of what the New Deal had accomplished for various groups—farmers, homeowners, the unemployed—asking whether they would be better off under the old ways.

Roosevelt did not mention his foe by name—a useful political tactic—but said he was confident that Congress would fight on against those who would use "the weapon of fear" to frighten the public.

Indeed, Roosevelt had his enemies. A wealthy man himself, from an aristocratic family, the president was despised by many in his own social class, but he remained popular with most Americans and ended up scoring a landslide victory in November over Republican nominee Alf Landon.

While the bulk of Roosevelt's 1936 address dealt with his record in office and his attack on the moneyed interests, he began the speech with a look at international affairs. He stated that, in both Europe and Asia, warlike conditions were increasing, and he spoke of the potential danger for the world and for the United States. He said the country and the rest of the Western Hemisphere should take a stance of "well-ordered neutrality" if the situation worsened.

Roosevelt did not mention specific countries. But in 1939, just a few years after this address, World War II was to begin—a massive conflict that pitted the Allies, including Britain, against the Axis, whose primary members were Germany, Japan, and Italy. The United States would not enter the war until 1941, on the side of the Allies, but international issues would become an increasingly important part of Roosevelt's presidency.

M r. President, Mr. Speaker, Members of the Senate and of the House of Representatives:

We are about to enter upon another year of the responsibility which the electorate of the United States has placed in our hands. Having come so far, it is fitting that we should pause to survey the ground which we have covered and the path which lies ahead.

On the fourth day of March, 1933, on the occasion of taking the oath of office as President of the United States, I addressed the people of our country. Need I recall either the scene or the national circumstances attending the occasion? The crisis of that moment was almost exclusively a national one. In recognition of that fact, so obvious to the millions in the streets and in the homes of America, I devoted by far the greater part of that address to what I called, and the Nation called, critical days within our own borders.

You will remember that on that fourth of March, 1933, the world picture was an image of substantial peace. International consultation and widespread hope for the bettering of relations between the Nations gave to all of us a reasonable expectation that the barriers to mutual confidence, to increased trade, and to the peaceful settlement of disputes could be progressively removed. In fact, my only reference to the field of world policy in that address was in these words: "I would dedicate this Nation to the policy of the good neighbor—the neighbor who resolutely respects himself and, because he does so, respects the rights of others—a neighbor who respects his obligations and respects the sanctity of his agreements in and with a world of neighbors."

In the years that have followed, that sentiment has remained the dedication of this Nation. Among the Nations of the great Western Hemisphere the policy of the good neighbor has happily prevailed. At no time in the four and a half centuries of modern civilization in the Americas has there existed—in any year, in any decade, in any generation in all that time—a greater spirit of mutual understanding, of common helpfulness, and of devotion to the ideals of serf-government than exists today in the twenty-one American Republics and their neighbor, the Dominion of Canada. This policy of the good neighbor among the Americas is no longer a hope, no longer an objective remaining to be accomplished. It is a fact, active, present, pertinent and effective. In this achievement, every American Nation takes an understanding part. There is neither war, nor rumor of war, nor desire for war. The inhabitants of this vast area, two hundred and fifty million strong, spreading more than eight thousand miles from the Arctic to the Antarctic, believe in, and propose to follow, the policy of the good neighbor. They wish with all their heart that the rest of the world might do likewise.

The rest of the world—Ah! There is the rub.

Were I today to deliver an Inaugural Address to the people of the United States, I could not limit my comments on world affairs to one paragraph. With much regret I should be compelled to devote the greater part to world affairs. Since the summer of that same year of 1933, the temper and the purposes of the rulers of many of the great populations in Europe and in Asia have not pointed the way either to peace or to good-will among men. Not only have peace and good-will among men grown more remote in those areas of the earth during this period, but a point has been reached where the people of the Americas must take cognizance of growing ill-will, of marked trends toward aggression, of increasing armaments, of shortening tempers—a situation which has in it many of the elements that lead to the tragedy of general war.

On those other continents many Nations, principally the smaller peoples, if left to themselves, would be content with their boundaries and willing to solve within themselves and in cooperation with their neighbors their individual problems, both economic and social. The rulers of those Nations, deep in their hearts, follow these peaceful and reasonable aspirations of their peoples. These rulers must remain ever vigilant against the possibility today or tomorrow of invasion or attack by the rulers of other peoples who fail to subscribe to the principles of bettering the human race by peaceful means.

Within those other Nations—those which today must bear the primary, definite responsibility for jeopardizing world peace—what hope lies? To say the least, there are grounds for pessimism. It is idle for us or for others to preach that the masses of the people who constitute those Nations which are dominated by the twin spirits of autocracy and aggression, are out of sympathy with their rulers, that they are allowed no opportunity to express themselves, that they would change things if they could.

That, unfortunately, is not so clear. It might be true that the masses of the people in those Nations would change the policies of their Governments if they could be allowed full freedom and full access to the processes of democratic government as we understand them. But they do not have that access; lacking it they follow blindly and fervently the lead of those who seek autocratic power.

Nations seeking expansion, seeking the rectification of injustices springing from former wars, or seeking outlets for trade, for population or even for their own peaceful contributions to the progress of civilization, fail to demonstrate that patience necessary to attain reasonable and legitimate objectives by peaceful negotiation or by an appeal to the finer instincts of world justice.

They have therefore impatiently reverted to the old belief in the law of the sword, or to the fantastic conception that they, and they alone, are chosen to fulfill a mission and that all the others among the billion and a half of human beings in the world must and shall learn from and be subject to them.

I recognize and you will recognize that these words which I have chosen with deliberation will not prove popular in any Nation that chooses to fit this shoe to its foot. Such sentiments, however, will find sympathy and understanding in those Nations where the people themselves are honestly desirous of peace but must constantly align themselves on one side or the other in the kaleidoscopic jockeying for position which is characteristic of European and Asiatic relations today. For the peace-loving Nations, and there are many of them, find that their very identity depends on their moving and moving again on the chess board of international politics.

I suggested in the spring of 1933 that 85 or 90 percent of all the people in the world were content with the territorial limits of their respective Nations and were willing further to reduce their armed forces if every other Nation in the world would agree to do likewise.

That is equally true today, and it is even more true today that world peace and world good-will are blocked by only 10 or 15 percent of the world's population. That is why efforts to reduce armies have thus far not only failed, but have been met by vastly increased armaments on land and in the air. That is why even efforts to continue the existing limits on naval armaments into the years to come show such little current success.

But the policy of the United States has been clear and consistent. We have sought with earnestness in every possible way to limit world armaments and to attain the peaceful solution of disputes among all Nations.

We have sought by every legitimate means to exert our moral influence against repression, against intolerance, against autocracy and in favor of freedom of expression, equality before the law, religious tolerance and popular rule.

In the field of commerce we have undertaken to encourage a more reasonable interchange of the world's goods. In the field of international finance we have, so far as we are concerned, put an end to dollar diplomacy, to money grabbing, to speculation for the benefit of the powerful and the rich, at the expense of the small and the poor.

As a consistent part of a clear policy, the United States is following a twofold neutrality toward any and all Nations which engage in wars that are not of immediate concern to the Americas. First, we decline to encourage the prosecution of war by permitting belligerents to obtain arms, ammunition or implements of war from the United States. Second, we seek to discourage the use by belligerent Nations of any and all American products calculated to facilitate the prosecution of a war in quantities over and above our normal exports of them in time of peace.

I trust that these objectives thus clearly and unequivocally stated will be carried forward by cooperation between this Congress and the President.

I realize that I have emphasized to you the gravity of the situation which confronts the people of the world. This emphasis is justified because of its importance to civilization and therefore to the United States. Peace is jeopardized by the few and not by the many. Peace is threatened by those who seek selfish power. The world has witnessed similar eras—as in the days when petty kings and feudal barons were changing the map of Europe every fortnight, or when great emperors and great kings were engaged in a mad scramble for colonial empire. We hope that we are not again at the threshold of such an era. But if face it we must, then the United States and the rest of the Americas can play but one role: through a well-ordered neutrality to do naught to encourage the contest, through adequate defense to save ourselves from embroilment and attack, and through example and all legitimate encouragement and assistance to persuade other Nations to return to the ways of peace and good-will.

The evidence before us clearly proves that autocracy in world affairs endangers peace and that such threats do not spring from those Nations devoted to the democratic ideal. If this be true in world affairs, it should have the greatest weight in the determination of domestic policies.

Within democratic Nations the chief concern of the people is to prevent the continuance or the rise of autocratic institutions that beget slavery at home and aggression abroad. Within our borders, as in the world at large, popular opinion is at war with a power-seeking minority.

That is no new thing. It was fought out in the Constitutional Convention of 1787. From time to time since then, the battle has been continued, under Thomas Jefferson, Andrew Jackson, Theodore Roosevelt and Woodrow Wilson.

In these latter years we have witnessed the domination of government by financial and industrial groups, numerically small but politically dominant in the twelve years that succeeded the World War. The present group of which I speak is indeed numerically small and, while it exercises a large influence and has much to say in the world of business, it does not, I am confident, speak the true sentiments of the less articulate but more important elements that constitute real American business.

In March, 1933, I appealed to the Congress of the United States and to the people of the United States in a new effort to restore power to those to whom it rightfully belonged. The response to that appeal resulted in the writing of a new chapter in the history of popular government. You, the members of the Legislative branch, and I, the Executive, contended for and established a new relationship between Government and people.

What were the terms of that new relationship? They were an appeal from the clamor of many private and selfish interests, yes, an appeal from the clamor of partisan interest, to the ideal of the public interest. Government became the representative and the trustee of the public interest. Our aim was to build upon essentially democratic institutions, seeking all the while the adjustment of burdens, the help of the needy, the protection of the weak, the liberation of the exploited and the genuine protection of the people's property.

It goes without saying that to create such an economic constitutional order, more than a single legislative enactment was called for. We, you in the Congress and I as the Executive, had to build upon a broad base. Now, after thirty-four months of work, we contemplate a fairly rounded whole. We have returned the control of the Federal Government to the City of Washington.

To be sure, in so doing, we have invited battle. We have earned the hatred of entrenched greed. The very nature of the problem that we faced made it necessary to drive some people from power and strictly to regulate others. I made that plain when I took the oath of office in March, 1933. I spoke of the practices of the unscrupulous money-changers who stood indicted in the court of public opinion. I spoke of the rulers of the exchanges of mankind's goods, who failed through their own stubbornness and their own incompetence. I said that they had admitted their failure and had abdicated.

Abdicated? Yes, in 1933, but now with the passing of danger they forget their damaging admissions and withdraw their abdication.

They seek the restoration of their selfish power. They offer to lead us back round the same old corner into the same old dreary street.

Yes, there are still determined groups that are intent upon that very thing. Rigorously held up to popular examination, their true character presents itself. They steal the livery of great national constitutional ideals to serve discredited special interests. As guardians and trustees for great groups of individual stockholders they wrongfully seek to carry the property and the interests entrusted to them into the arena of partisan politics. They seek—this minority in business and industry—to control and often do control and use for their own purposes legitimate and highly honored business associations; they engage in vast propaganda to spread fear and discord among the people—they would "gang up" against the people's liberties.

The principle that they would instill into government if they succeed in seizing power is well shown by the principles which many of them have instilled into their own affairs: autocracy toward labor, toward stockholders, toward consumers, toward public sentiment. Autocrats in smaller things, they seek autocracy in bigger things. "By their fruits ye shall know them."

If these gentlemen believe, as they say they believe, that the measures adopted by this Congress and its predecessor, and carried out by this Administration, have hindered rather than promoted recovery, let them be consistent. Let them propose to this Congress the complete repeal of these measures. The way is open to such a proposal.

Let action be positive and not negative. The way is open in the Congress of the United States for an expression of opinion by yeas and nays. Shall we say that values are restored and that the Congress will, therefore, repeal the laws under which we have been bringing them back? Shall we say that because national income has grown with rising prosperity, we shall repeal existing taxes and thereby put off the day of approaching a balanced budget and of starting to reduce the national debt? Shall we abandon the reasonable support and regulation of banking? Shall we restore the dollar to its former gold content?

Shall we say to the farmer, "The prices for your products are in part restored. Now go and hoe your own row?"

Shall we say to the home owners, "We have reduced your rates of interest. We have no further concern with how you keep your home or what you pay for your money. That is your affair?"

Shall we say to the several millions of unemployed citizens who face the very problem of existence, of getting enough to eat, "We will withdraw from giving you work. We will turn you back to the charity of your communities and those men of selfish power who tell you that perhaps they will employ you if the Government leaves them strictly alone?"

Shall we say to the needy unemployed, "Your problem is a local one except that perhaps the Federal Government, as an act of mere generosity, will be willing to pay to your city or to your county a few grudging dollars to help maintain your soup kitchens?"

Shall we say to the children who have worked all day in the factories, "Child labor is a local issue and so are your starvation wages; something to be solved or left unsolved by the jurisdiction of forty-eight States?"

Shall we say to the laborer, "Your right to organize, your relations with your employer have nothing to do with the public interest; if your employer will not even meet with you to discuss your problems and his, that is none of our affair?"

Shall we say to the unemployed and the aged, "Social security lies not within the province of the Federal Government; you must seek relief elsewhere?"

Shall we say to the men and women who live in conditions of squalor in country and in city, "The health and the happiness of you and your children are no concern of ours?"

Shall we expose our population once more by the repeal of laws which protect them against the loss of their honest investments and against the manipulations of dishonest speculators? Shall we abandon the splendid efforts of the Federal Government to raise the health standards of the Nation and to give youth a decent opportunity through such means as the Civilian Conservation Corps?

Members of the Congress, let these challenges be met. If this is what these gentlemen want, let them say so to the Congress of the United States. Let them no longer hide their dissent in a cowardly cloak of generality. Let them define the issue. We have been specific in our affirmative action. Let them be specific in their negative attack.

But the challenge faced by this Congress is more menacing than merely a return to the past—bad as that would be. Our resplendent economic autocracy does not want to return to that individualism of which they prate, even though the advantages under that system went to the ruthless and the strong. They realize that in thirty-four months we have built up new instruments of public power. In the hands of a people's Government this power is wholesome and proper. But in the hands of political puppets of an economic autocracy such power would provide shackles for the liberties of the people. Give them their way and they will take the course of every autocracy of the past—power for themselves, enslavement for the public.

Their weapon is the weapon of fear. I have said, "The only thing we have to fear is fear itself." That is as true today as it was in 1933. But such fear as they instill today is not a natural fear, a normal fear; it is a synthetic, manufactured, poisonous fear that is being spread subtly, expensively and cleverly by the same people who cried in those other days, "Save us, save us, lest we perish."

I am confident that the Congress of the United States well understands the facts and is ready to wage unceasing warfare against those who seek a continuation of that spirit of fear. The carrying out of the laws of the land as enacted by the Congress requires protection until final adjudication by the highest tribunal of the land. The Congress has the right and can find the means to protect its own prerogatives.

We are justified in our present confidence. Restoration of national income, which shows continuing gains for the third successive year, supports the normal and logical policies under which agriculture and industry are returning to full activity. Under these policies we approach a balance of the national budget. National income increases; tax receipts, based on that income, increase without the levying of new taxes. That is why I am able to say to this, the Second Session of the 74th Congress, that it is my belief based on existing laws that no new taxes, over and above the present taxes, are either advisable or necessary.

National income increases; employment increases. Therefore, we can look forward to a reduction in the number of those citizens who are in need. Therefore, also, we can anticipate a reduction in our appropriations for relief.

In the light of our substantial material progress, in the light of the increasing effectiveness of the restoration of popular rule, I recommend to the Congress that we advance; that we do not retreat. I have confidence that you will not fail the people of the Nation whose mandate you have already so faithfully fulfilled.

I repeat, with the same faith and the same determination, my words of March 4, 1933: "We face the arduous days that lie before us in the warm courage of national unity; with a clear consciousness of seeking old and precious moral values; with a clean satisfaction that comes from the stern performance of duty by old and young alike. We aim at the assurance of a rounded and permanent national life. We do not distrust the future of essential democracy."

I cannot better end this message on the state of the Union than by repeating the words of a wise philosopher at whose feet I sat many, many years ago.

"What great crises teach all men whom the example and counsel of the brave inspire is the lesson: Fear not, view all the tasks of life as sacred, have faith in the triumph of the ideal, give daily all that you have to give, be loyal and rejoice whenever you find yourselves part of a great ideal enterprise. You, at this moment, have the honor to belong to a generation whose lips are touched by fire. You live in a land that now enjoys the blessings of peace. But let nothing human be wholly alien to you. The human race now passes through one of its great crises. New ideas, new issues—a new call for men to carry on the work of righteousness, of charity, of courage, of patience, and of loyalty. . . . However memory brings back this moment to your minds, let it be able to say to you: That was a great moment. It was the beginning of a new era. . . . This world in its crisis called for volunteers, for men of faith in life, of patience in service, of charity and of in-sight. I responded to the call however I could. I volunteered to give myself to my Master—the cause of humane and brave living. I studied, I loved, I labored, unsparingly and hopefully, to be worthy of my generation."

Franklin D. Roosevelt, 1933–1937

Annual Message to Congress

January 6, 1937

Franklin D. Roosevelt delivered his fourth State of the Union message two weeks before his second presidential inauguration. Roosevelt, a Democrat, had scored a huge landslide win in the presidential election of the previous November, triumphing over Republican Alfred M. Landon.

Roosevelt took 60.8 percent of the vote and 523 of 531 electoral votes; Landon, the governor of Kansas, won only Maine and Vermont. Democrats padded their margins in Congress as well; in the new Congress, they would hold 75 of 96 Senate seats and 333 of 435 House seats.

The president's first term had been historic. Working with Congress, Roosevelt had completely changed the role of the federal government. Dozens of new laws created dozens of new government entities, from Social Security to the Tennessee Valley Authority. Along with the increase in federal government responsibilities, the power of the presidency had increased as well.

In his State of the Union message, Roosevelt surveyed the events of his first four years in office, declaring that the federal government had met the challenges it faced when he first took office in 1933, in the depths of the Depression.

Roosevelt warned that more work needed to be done to solve the remaining problems. He cited the need for improvements in housing standards, in assistance to tenant farmers, in the Social Security program, and in the overall unemployment picture.

Since the start of the New Deal, some of Roosevelt's programs—such as the National Industrial Recovery Act and the Agricultural Adjustment Act—had been ruled unconstitutional by the Supreme Court. In his speech, Roosevelt addressed that issue, stating that while the Recovery Act had been "outlawed," the problems it addressed were still there. He defended the act, stating that its objectives were good but that it "tried to do too much."

Roosevelt's frustration with the Supreme Court would become more obvious shortly after the start of his second presidential term, when he floated a plan that would have increased the size of the Court—and allowed him to make some new appointments of justices more sympathetic to his views.

The president also discussed the international situation, stating that at a time when much of the world seemed preoccupied with war, he had attended an inter-American conference in Buenos Aires that sought to foster peace in the hemisphere.

M r. President, Mr. Speaker, Members of the Congress of the United States:

For the first time in our national history a President delivers his Annual Message to a new Congress within a fortnight of the expiration of his term of office. While there is no change in the Presidency this year, change will occur in future years. It is my belief that under this new constitutional practice, the President should in every fourth year, in so far as seems reasonable, review the existing state of our national affairs and outline broad future problems, leaving specific recommendations for future legislation to be made by the President about to be inaugurated.

At this time, however, circumstances of the moment compel me to ask your immediate consideration of: First, measures extending the life of certain authorizations and powers which, under present statutes, expire within a few weeks; second, an addition to the existing Neutrality Act to cover specific points raised by the unfortunate civil strife in Spain; and, third, a deficiency appropriation bill for which I shall submit estimates this week.

In March, 1933, the problems which faced our Nation and which only our national Government had the resources to meet were more serious even than appeared on the surface.

It was not only that the visible mechanism of economic life had broken down. More disturbing was the fact that long neglect of the needs of the underprivileged had brought too many of our people to the verge of doubt as to the successful adaptation of our historic traditions to the complex modern world. In that lay a challenge to our democratic form of Government itself.

Ours was the task to prove that democracy could be made to function in the world of today as effectively as in the simpler world of a hundred years ago. Ours was the task to do more than to argue a theory. The times required the confident answer of performance to those whose instinctive faith in humanity made them want to believe that in the long run democracy would prove superior to more extreme forms of Government as a process of getting action when action was wisdom, without the spiritual sacrifices which those other forms of Government exact.

That challenge we met. To meet it required unprecedented activities under Federal leadership to end abuses, to restore a large measure of material prosperity, to give new faith to millions of our citizens who had been traditionally taught to expect that democracy would provide continuously wider opportunity and continuously greater security in a world where science was continuously making material riches more available to man.

In the many methods of attack with which we met these problems, you and I, by mutual understanding and by determination to cooperate, helped to make democracy succeed by refusing to permit unnecessary disagreement to arise between two of our branches of Government. That spirit of cooperation was able to solve difficulties of extraordinary magnitude and ramification with few important errors, and at a cost cheap when measured by the immediate necessities and the eventual results.

I look forward to a continuance of that cooperation in the next four years. I look forward also to a continuance of the basis of that cooperation—mutual respect for each other's proper sphere of functioning in a democracy which is working well, and a common-sense realization of the need for play in the joints of the machine.

On that basis, it is within the right of the Congress to determine which of the many new activities shall be continued or abandoned, increased or curtailed.

On that same basis, the President alone has the responsibility for their administration. I find that this task of Executive management has reached the point where our administrative machinery needs comprehensive overhauling. I shall, therefore, shortly address the Congress more fully in regard to modernizing and improving the Executive branch of the Government.

That cooperation of the past four years between the Congress and the President has aimed at the fulfillment of a twofold policy: first, economic recovery through many kinds of assistance to agriculture, industry and banking; and, second, deliberate improvement in the personal security and opportunity of the great mass of our people.

The recovery we sought was not to be merely temporary. It was to be a recovery protected from the causes of previous disasters. With that aim in view—to prevent a future similar crisis—you and I joined in a series of enactments—safe banking and sound currency, the guarantee of bank deposits, protection for the investor in securities, the removal of the threat of agricultural surpluses, insistence on collective bargaining, the outlawing of sweat shops, child labor and unfair trade practices, and the beginnings of security for the aged and the worker.

Nor was the recovery we sought merely a purposeless whirring of machinery. It is important, of course, that every man and woman in the country be able to find work, that every factory run, that business and farming as a whole earn profits. But Government in a democratic Nation does not exist solely, or even primarily, for that purpose.

It is not enough that the wheels turn. They must carry us in the direction of a greater satisfaction in life for the average man. The deeper purpose of democratic government is to assist as many of its citizens as possible, especially those who need it most, to improve their conditions of life, to retain all personal liberty which does not adversely affect their neighbors, and to pursue the happiness which comes with security and an opportunity for recreation and culture.

Even with our present recovery we are far from the goal of that deeper purpose. There are far-reaching problems still with us for which democracy must find solutions if it is to consider itself successful.

For example, many millions of Americans still live in habitations which not only fail to provide the physical benefits of modern civilization but breed disease and impair the health of future generations. The menace exists not only in the slum areas of the very large cities, but in many smaller cities as well. It exists on tens of thousands of farms, in varying degrees, in every part of the country.

Another example is the prevalence of an un-American type of tenant farming. I do not suggest that every farm family has the capacity to earn a satisfactory living on its own farm. But many thousands of tenant farmers, indeed most of them, with some financial assistance and with some advice and training, can be made self-supporting on land which can eventually belong to them. The Nation would be wise to offer them that chance instead of permitting them to go along as they do now, year after year, with neither future security as tenants nor hope of ownership of their homes nor expectation of bettering the lot of their children.

Another national problem is the intelligent development of our social security system, the broadening of the services it renders, and practical improvement in its operation. In many Nations where such laws are in effect, success in meeting the expectations of the community has come through frequent amendment of the original statute.

And, of course, the most far-reaching and the most inclusive problem of all is that of unemployment and the lack of economic balance of which unemployment is at once the result and the symptom. The immediate question of adequate relief for the needy unemployed who are capable of performing useful work, I shall discuss with the Congress during the coming months. The broader task of preventing unemployment is a matter of long-range evolutionary policy. To that we must continue to give our best thought and effort. We cannot assume that immediate industrial and commercial activity which mitigates present pressures justifies the national Government at this time in placing the unemployment problem in a filing cabinet of finished business.

Fluctuations in employment are tied to all other wasteful fluctuations in our mechanism of production and distribution. One of these wastes is speculation. In securities or commodities, the larger the volume of speculation, the wider become the upward and downward swings and the more certain the result that in the long run there will be more losses than gains in the underlying wealth of the community.

And, as is now well known to all of us, the same net loss to society comes from reckless overproduction and monopolistic underproduction of natural and manufactured commodities.

Overproduction, underproduction and speculation are three evil sisters who distill the troubles of unsound inflation and disastrous deflation. It is to the interest of the Nation to have Government help private enterprise to gain sound general price levels and to protect those levels from wide perilous fluctuations. We know now that if early in 1931 Government had taken the steps which were taken two and three years later, the depression would never have reached the depths of the beginning of 1933.

Sober second thought confirms most of us in the belief that the broad objectives of the National Recovery Act were sound. We know now that its difficulties arose from the fact that it tried to do too much. For example, it was unwise to expect the same agency to regulate the length of working hours, minimum wages, child labor and collective bargaining on the one hand and the complicated questions of unfair trade practices and business controls on the other.

The statute of N.R.A. has been outlawed. The problems have not. They are still with us.

That decent conditions and adequate pay for labor, and just return for agriculture, can be secured through parallel and simultaneous action by forty-eight States is a proven impossibility. It is equally impossible to obtain curbs on monopoly, unfair trade practices and speculation by State action alone. There are those who, sincerely or insincerely, still cling to State action as a theoretical hope. But experience with actualities makes it clear that Federal laws supplementing State laws are needed to help solve the problems which result from modern invention applied in an industrialized Nation which conducts its business with scant regard to State lines.

During the past year there has been a growing belief that there is little fault to be found with the Constitution of the United States as it stands today. The vital need is not an alteration of our fundamental law, but an increasingly enlightened view with reference to it. Difficulties have grown out of its interpretation; but rightly considered, it can be used as an instrument of progress, and not as a device for prevention of action.

It is worth our while to read and reread the preamble of the Constitution, and Article I thereof which confers the legislative powers upon the Congress of the United States. It is also worth our while to read again the debates in the Constitutional Convention of one hundred and fifty years ago. From such reading, I obtain the very definite thought that the members of that Convention were fully aware that civilization would raise problems for the proposed new Federal Government, which they themselves could not even surmise; and that it was their definite intent and expectation that a liberal interpretation in the years to come would give to the Congress the same relative powers over new national problems as they themselves gave to the Congress over the national problems of their day.

In presenting to the Convention the first basic draft of the Constitution, Edmund Randolph explained that it was the purpose "to insert essential principles only, lest the operation of government should be clogged by rendering those provisions permanent and unalterable which ought to be accommodated to times and events."

With a better understanding of our purposes, and a more intelligent recognition of our needs as a Nation, it is not to be assumed that there will be prolonged failure to bring legislative and judicial action into closer harmony. Means must be found to adapt our legal forms and our judicial interpretation to the actual present national needs of the largest progressive democracy in the modern world.

That thought leads to a consideration of world problems. To go no further back than the beginning of this century, men and women everywhere were seeking conditions of life very different from those which were customary before modern invention and modern industry and modern communications had come into being. The World war, for all of its tragedy, encouraged these demands, and stimulated action to fulfill these new desires.

Many national Governments seemed unable adequately to respond; and, often with the improvident assent of the masses of the people themselves, new forms of government were set up with oligarchy taking the place of democracy. In oligarchies, militarism has leapt forward, while in those Nations which have retained democracy, militarism has waned.

I have recently visited three of our sister Republics in South America. The very cordial receptions with which I was greeted were in tribute to democracy. To me the outstanding observation of that visit was that the masses of the peoples of all the Americas are convinced that the democratic form of government can be made to succeed and do not wish to substitute for it any other form of government. They believe that democracies are best able to cope with the changing problems of modern civilization within themselves, and that democracies are best able to maintain peace among themselves.

The Inter-American Conference, operating on these fundamental principles of democracy, did much to assure peace in this Hemisphere. Existing peace machinery was improved. New instruments to maintain peace and eliminate causes of war were adopted. Wider protection of the interests of the American Republics in the event of war outside the Western Hemisphere was provided. Respect for, and observance of, international treaties and international law were strengthened. Principles of liberal trade policies, as effective aids to the maintenance of peace, were reaffirmed. The intellectual and cultural relationships among American Republics were broadened as a part of the general peace program.

In a world unhappily thinking in terms of war, the representatives of twenty-one Nations sat around a table, in an atmosphere of complete confidence and understanding, sincerely discussing measures for maintaining peace. Here was a great and a permanent achievement directly affecting the lives and security of the two hundred and fifty million human beings who dwell in this Western Hemisphere. Here was an example which must have a wholesome effect upon the rest of the world.

In a very real sense, the Conference in Buenos Aires sent forth a message on behalf of all the democracies of the world to those Nations which live otherwise. Because such other Governments are perhaps more spectacular, it was high time for democracy to assert itself.

Because all of us believe that our democratic form of government can cope adequately with modern problems as they arise, it is patriotic as well as logical for us to prove that we can meet new national needs with new laws consistent with an historic constitutional framework clearly intended to receive liberal and not narrow interpretation.

The United States of America, within itself, must continue the task of making democracy succeed.

In that task the Legislative branch of our Government will, I am confident, continue to meet the demands of democracy whether they relate to the curbing of abuses, the extension of help to those who need help, or the better balancing of our interdependent economies.

So, too, the Executive branch of the Government must move forward in this task, and, at the same time, provide better management for administrative action of all kinds.

The Judicial branch also is asked by the people to do its part in making democracy successful. We do not ask the Courts to call non-existent powers into being, but we have a right to expect that conceded powers or those legitimately implied shall be made effective instruments for the common good.

The process of our democracy must not be imperiled by the denial of essential powers of free government.

Your task and mine is not ending with the end of the depression. The people of the United States have made it clear that they expect us to continue our active efforts in behalf of their peaceful advancement.

In that spirit of endeavor and service I greet the 75th Congress at the beginning of this auspicious New Year.

Franklin D. Roosevelt, 1937–1941

Annual Message to Congress
January 3, 1938

Franklin D. Roosevelt's fifth annual message followed a tough year for the president. While 1936 had ended on a triumphant note for Roosevelt—he won reelection by a landslide that November—1937 would prove more difficult.

First, the country, which had been pulling itself out of the mire of the Great Depression, slipped back into recession. The recession, which was the backdrop to this January 3 speech, continued into 1938.

Second, Roosevelt chose to launch an ill-fated attack on the Supreme Court in February 1937. The conservative-minded Court had struck down several pieces of New Deal legislation, which infuriated Roosevelt. He proposed legislation that would increase the size of the Court. Congress was less than thrilled with this "court-packing" idea, and Roosevelt battled unsuccessfully with lawmakers for much of the year.

So, as the president spoke before Congress on January 3, he had a great deal on his mind. In a relatively lengthy address, Roosevelt discoursed upon various domestic issues facing the country.

In regards to agricultural policy, Roosevelt spoke in favor of a system designed to avoid the huge surpluses that hurt the farm economy. He noted that Congress was working on farming legislation, and, indeed, lawmakers did produce a new agriculture bill that year. Among other provisions, it sought to set up quotas for certain crops.

The president also backed additional wage-and-hour laws for industrial workers. Later that year, Congress approved what was considered a relatively weak, watered-down wage-and-hours bill.

Roosevelt also discussed balancing the budget, arguing that it should be brought into balance under three conditions: that the government continue to provide work for the needy; that Congress and the executive work together to eliminate unnecessary programs without harming the government or the country; and that the country's purchasing power be increased such that income taxes were enough to meet the government's expenses.

In addition, the president listed various "wrongful business practices" that he believed should end, including tax avoidance and price-rigging.

He did not say much about the ongoing recession, although he commented that the public attitude about it was far different than "the terror and despair" he had seen five years earlier—now, there was "more perplexity than fear," he said.

Roosevelt talked only briefly about international relations in this speech. His highlighting of domestic concerns would change as World War II loomed, however. The world situation would play a large role in Roosevelt's remaining State of the Union messages.

Mr. President, Mr. Speaker, Members of the Senate and of the House of Representatives:

In addressing the Congress on the state of the Union present facts and future hazards demand that I speak clearly and earnestly of the causes which underlie events of profound concern to all.

In spite of the determination of this Nation for peace, it has become clear that acts and policies of nations in other parts of the world have far-reaching effects not only upon their immediate neighbors but also on us.

I am thankful that I can tell you that our Nation is at peace. It has been kept at peace despite provocations which in other days, because of their seriousness, could well have engendered war. The people of the United States and the Government of the United States have shown capacity for restraint and a civilized approach to the purposes of peace, while at the same time we maintain the integrity inherent in the sovereignty of 130,000,000 people, lest we weaken or destroy our influence for peace and jeopardize the sovereignty itself.

It is our traditional policy to live at peace with other nations. More than that, we have been among the leaders in advocating the use of pacific methods of discussion and conciliation in international differences. We have striven for the reduction of military forces.

But in a world of high tension and disorder, in a world where stable civilization is actually threatened, it becomes the responsibility of each nation which strives for peace at home and peace with and among others to be strong enough to assure the observance of those fundamentals of peaceful solution of conflicts which are the only ultimate basis for orderly existence.

Resolute in our determination to respect the rights of others, and to command respect for the rights of ourselves, we must keep ourselves adequately strong in self-defense.

There is a trend in the world away from the observance both of the letter and the spirit of treaties. We propose to observe, as we have in the past, our own treaty obligations to the limit; but we cannot be certain of reciprocity on the part of others.

Disregard for treaty obligations seems to have followed the surface trend away from the democratic representative form of government. It would seem, therefore, that world peace through international agreements is most safe in the hands of democratic representative governments—or, in other words, peace is most greatly jeopardized in and by those nations where democracy has been discarded or has never developed.

I have used the words "surface trend," for I still believe that civilized man increasingly insists and in the long run will insist on genuine participation in his own government. Our people believe that over the years democracies of the world will survive, and that democracy will be restored or established in those nations which today know it not. In that faith lies the future peace of mankind.

At home, conditions call for my equal candor. Events of recent months are new proof that we cannot conduct a national government after the practice of 1787, or

1837 or 1887, for the obvious reason that human needs and human desires are infinitely greater, infinitely more difficult to meet than in any previous period in the life of our Republic. Hitherto it has been an acknowledged duty of government to meet these desires and needs: nothing has occurred of late to absolve the Congress, the Courts or the President from that task. It faces us as squarely, as insistently, as in March, 1933.

Much of trouble in our own lifetime has sprung from a long period of inaction—from ignoring what fundamentally was happening to us, and from a time-serving unwillingness to face facts as they forced themselves upon us.

Our national life rests on two nearly equal producing forces, agriculture and industry, each employing about one-third of our citizens. The other third transports and distributes the products of the first two, or performs special services for the whole.

The first great force, agriculture—and with it the production of timber, minerals and other natural resources—went forward feverishly and thoughtlessly until nature rebelled and we saw deserts encroach, floods destroy, trees disappear and soil exhausted.

At the same time we have been discovering that vast numbers of our farming population live in a poverty more abject than that of many of the farmers of Europe whom we are wont to call peasants; that the prices of our products of agriculture are too often dependent on speculation by non-farming groups; and that foreign nations, eager to become self-sustaining or ready to put virgin land under the plough are no longer buying our surpluses of cotton and wheat and lard and tobacco and fruit as they had before.

Since 1933 we have knowingly faced a choice of three remedies. First, to cut our cost of farm production below that of other nations—an obvious impossibility in many crops today unless we revert to human slavery or its equivalent.

Second, to make the government the guarantor of farm prices and the underwriter of excess farm production without limit—a course which would bankrupt the strongest government in the world in a decade.

Third, to place the primary responsibility directly on the farmers themselves, under the principle of majority rule, so that they may decide, with full knowledge of the facts of surpluses, scarcities, world markets and domestic needs, what the planting of each crop should be in order to maintain a reasonably adequate supply which will assure a minimum adequate price under the normal processes of the law of supply and demand.

That means adequacy of supply but not glut. It means adequate reserves against the day of drought. It is shameless misrepresentation to call this a policy of scarcity. It is in truth insurance before the fact, instead of government subsidy after the fact.

Any such plan for the control of excessive surpluses and the speculation they bring has two enemies. There are those well meaning theorists who harp on the inherent right of every free born American to do with his land what he wants—to cultivate it well—or badly; to conserve his timber by cutting only the annual increment thereof—or to strip it clean, let fire burn the slash, and erosion complete the ruin; to raise only one crop—and if that crop fails, to look for food and support from his neighbors or his government.

That, I assert is not an inherent right of citizenship. For if a man farms his land to the waste of the soil or the trees, he destroys not only his own assets but the Nation's assets as well. Or if by his methods he makes himself, year after year, a financial hazard of the community and the government, he becomes not only a social problem but an economic menace. The day has gone by when it could be claimed that government has no interest in such ill-considered practices and no right through representative methods to stop them.

The other group of enemies is perhaps less well-meaning. It includes those who for partisan purposes oppose each and every practical effort to help the situation, and also those who make money from undue fluctuations in crop prices.

I gladly note that measures which seek to initiate a government program for a balanced agriculture are now in conference between the two Houses of the Congress. In their final consideration, I hope for a sound consistent measure which will keep the cost of its administration within the figure of current government expenditures in aid of agriculture. The farmers of this Nation know that a balanced output can be put into effect without excessive cost and with the cooperation of the great majority of them.

If this balance can be created by an all-weather farm program, our farm population will soon be assured of relatively constant purchasing power. From this will flow two other practical results: the consuming public will be protected against excessive food and textile prices, and the industries of the Nation and their workers will find a steadier demand for wares sold to the agricultural third of our people.

To raise the purchasing power of the farmer is, however, not enough. It will not stay raised if we do not also raise the purchasing power of that third of the Nation which receives its income from industrial employment. Millions of industrial workers receive pay so low that they have little buying power. Aside from the undoubted fact that they thereby suffer great human hardship, they are unable to buy adequate food and shelter, to maintain health or to buy their share of manufactured goods.

We have not only seen minimum wage and maximum hour provisions prove their worth economically and socially under government auspices in 1933, 1934 and 1935, but the people of this country, by an overwhelming vote, are in favor of having the Congress—this Congress—put a floor below which industrial wages shall not fall, and a ceiling beyond which the hours of industrial labor shall not rise.

Here again let us analyze the opposition. A part of it is sincere in believing that an effort thus to raise the purchasing power of lowest paid industrial workers is not the business of the Federal Government. Others give "lip service" to a general objective, but do not like any specific measure that is proposed. In both cases it is worth our while to wonder whether some of these opponents are not at heart opposed to any program for raising the wages of the underpaid or reducing the hours of the overworked.

Another group opposes legislation of this type on the ground that cheap labor will help their locality to acquire industries and outside capital, or to retain industries which today are surviving only because of existing low wages and long hours. It has been my thought that, especially during these past five years, this Nation has grown away from local or sectional selfishness and toward national patriotism and unity. I am disappointed by some recent actions and by some recent utterances which sound like the philosophy of half a century ago.

There are many communities in the United States where the average family income is pitifully low. It is in those communities that we find the poorest educational facilities and the worst conditions of health. Why? It is not because they are satisfied to live as they do. It is because those communities have the lowest per capita wealth and income; therefore, the lowest ability to pay taxes; and, therefore, inadequate functioning of local government.

Such communities exist in the East, in the Middle West, in the Far West, and in the South. Those who represent such areas in every part of the country do their constituents ill service by blocking efforts to raise their incomes, their property values and, therefore, their whole scale of living. In the long run, the profits from Child labor, low pay and overwork enure not to the locality or region where they exist but to the absentee owners who have sent their capital into these exploited communities to gather larger profits for themselves. Indeed, new enterprises and new industries which bring permanent wealth will come more readily to those communities which insist on good pay and reasonable hours, for the simple reason that there they will find a greater industrial efficiency and happier workers.

No reasonable person seeks a complete uniformity in wages in every part of the United States; nor does any reasonable person seek an immediate and drastic change from the lowest pay to the highest pay. We are seeking, of course, only legislation to end starvation wages and intolerable hours; more desirable wages are and should continue to be the product of collective bargaining.

Many of those who represent great cities have shown their understanding of the necessity of helping the agricultural third of the Nation. I hope that those who represent constituencies primarily agricultural will not underestimate the importance of extending like aid to the industrial third.

Wage and hour legislation, therefore, is a problem which is definitely before this Congress for action. It is an essential part of economic recovery. It has the support of an overwhelming majority of our people in every walk of life. They have expressed themselves through the ballot box.

Again I revert to the increase of national purchasing power as an underlying necessity of the day. If you increase that purchasing power for the farmers and for the industrial workers, especially for those in both groups who have least of it today, you will increase the purchasing power of the final third of our population—those who transport and distribute the products of farm and factory, and those of the professions who serve all groups. I have tried to make clear to you, and through you to the people of the United States, that this is an urgency which must be met by complete and not by partial action.

If it is met, if the purchasing power of the Nation as a whole—in other words, the total of the Nation's income—can be still further increased, other happy results will flow from such increase.

We have raised the Nation's income from thirty-eight billion dollars in the year 1932 to about sixty-eight billion dollars in the year 1937. Our goal, our objective is to raise it to ninety or one hundred billion dollars.

We have heard much about a balanced budget, and it is interesting to note that many of those who have pleaded for a balanced budget as the sole need now come to me to plead for additional government expenditures at the expense of unbalancing the budget. As the Congress is fully aware, the annual deficit, large for several years, has been declining the last fiscal year and this. The proposed budget for 1939, which I shall shortly send to the Congress, will exhibit a further decrease in the deficit, though not a balance between income and outgo.

To many who have pleaded with me for an immediate balancing of the budget, by a sharp curtailment or even elimination of government functions, I have asked the question: "What present expenditures would you reduce or eliminate?" And the invariable answer has been "that is not my business—I know nothing of the details, but I am sure that it could be done." That is not what you or I would call helpful citizenship.

On only one point do most of them have a suggestion. They think that relief for the unemployed by the giving of work is wasteful, and when I pin them down I discover that at heart they are actually in favor of substituting a dole in place of useful work. To that neither I nor, I am confident, the Senators and Representatives in the Congress will ever consent.

I am as anxious as any banker or industrialist or business man or investor or economist that the budget of the United States Government be brought into balance as quickly as possible. But I lay down certain conditions which seem reasonable and which I believe all should accept.

The first condition is that we continue the policy of not permitting any needy American who can and is willing to work to starve because the Federal Government does not provide the work.

The second is that the Congress and the Executive join hands in eliminating or curtailing any Federal activity which can be eliminated or curtailed or even postponed without harming necessary government functions or the safety of the Nation from a national point of view.

The third is to raise the purchasing power of the Nation to the point that the taxes on this purchasing power—or, in other words, on the Nation's income—will be sufficient to meet the necessary expenditures of the national government.

I have hitherto stated that, in my judgment, the expenditures of the national government cannot be cut much below seven billion dollars a year without destroying essential functions or letting people starve. That sum can be raised and will be cheerfully provided by the American people, if we can increase the Nation's income to a point well beyond the present level.

This does not mean that as the Nation's income goes up the Federal expenditures should rise in proportion. On the contrary, the Congress and the Executive should use every effort to hold the normal Federal expenditures to approximately the present level, thus making it possible, with an increase in the Nation's income and the resulting increase in tax receipts, not only to balance future budgets but to reduce the debt.

In line with this policy fall my former recommendations for the reorganization and improvement of the administrative structure of the government, both for immediate Executive needs and for the planning of future national needs. I renew those recommendations.

In relation to tax changes, three things should be kept in mind. First, the total sum to be derived by the Federal Treasury must not be decreased as a result of any changes in schedules. Second, abuses by individuals or corporations designed to escape tax-paying by using various methods of doing business, corporate and otherwise—abuses which we have sought, with great success, to end—must not be restored. Third, we should rightly change certain provisions where they are proven to work definite hardship, especially on the small business men of the Nation. But, speculative income should not be favored over earned income.

It is human nature to argue that this or that tax is responsible for every ill. It is human nature on the part of those who pay graduated taxes to attack all taxes based on the principle of ability to pay. These are the same complainants who for a generation blocked the imposition of a graduated income tax. They are the same complainants who would impose the type of flat sales tax which places the burden of government more on those least able to pay and less on those most able to pay.

Our conclusion must be that while proven hardships should be corrected, they should not be corrected in such a way as to restore abuses already terminated or to shift a greater burden to the less fortunate.

This subject leads naturally into the wider field of the public attitude toward business. The objective of increasing the purchasing power of the farming third, the industrial third and the service third of our population presupposes the cooperation of what we call capital and labor.

Capital is essential; reasonable earnings on capital are essential; but misuse of the powers of capital or selfish suspension of the employment of capital must be ended, or the capitalistic system will destroy itself through its own abuses.

The overwhelming majority of business men and bankers intend to be good citizens. Only a small minority have displayed poor citizenship by engaging in practices which are dishonest or definitely harmful to society. This statement is straightforward and true. No person in any responsible place in the Government of the United States today has ever taken any position contrary to it.

But, unfortunately for the country, when attention is called to, or attack is made on specific misuses of capital, there has been a deliberate purpose on the part of the condemned minority to distort the criticism into an attack on all capital. That is willful deception but it does not long deceive.

If attention is called to, or attack made on, certain wrongful business practices, there are those who are eager to call it "an attack on all business." That, too, is willful deception that will not long deceive. Let us consider certain facts:

There are practices today which most people believe should be ended. They include tax avoidance through corporate and other methods, which I have previously mentioned; excessive capitalization, investment write-ups and security manipulations; price rigging and collusive bidding in defiance of the spirit of the antitrust laws by methods which baffle prosecution under the present statutes. They include high-pressure salesmanship which creates cycles of overproduction within given industries and consequent recessions in production until such time as the surplus is consumed; the use of patent laws to enable larger corporations to maintain high prices and withhold from the public the advantages of the progress of science; unfair competition which drives the smaller producer out of business locally, regionally or even on a national scale; intimidation of local or state government to prevent the enactment of laws for the protection of labor by threatening to move elsewhere; the shifting of actual production from one locality or region to another in pursuit of the cheapest wage scale.

The enumeration of these abuses does not mean that business as a whole is guilty of them. Again, it is deception that will not long deceive to tell the country that an attack on these abuses is an attack on business.

Another group of problems affecting business, which cannot be termed specific abuses, gives us food for grave thought about the future. Generically such problems arise out of the concentration of economic control to the detriment of the body politic—control of other people's money, other people's labor, other people's lives.

In many instances such concentrations cannot be justified on the ground of operating efficiency, but have been created for the sake of securities profits, financial control, the suppression of competition and the ambition for power over others. In some lines of industry a very small numerical group is in such a position of influence that its actions are of necessity followed by the other units operating in the same field.

That such influences operate to control banking and finance is equally true, in spite of the many efforts, through Federal legislation, to take such control out of the hands of a small group. We have but to talk with hundreds of small bankers throughout the United States to realize that irrespective of local conditions, they are compelled in practice to accept the policies laid down by a small number of the larger banks in the Nation. The work undertaken by Andrew Jackson and Woodrow Wilson is not finished yet.

The ownership of vast properties or the organization of thousands of workers creates a heavy obligation of public service. The power should not be sought or sanctioned unless the responsibility is accepted as well. The man who seeks freedom from such responsibility in the name of individual liberty is either fooling himself or trying to cheat his fellow men. He wants to eat the fruits of orderly society without paying for them.

As a Nation we have rejected any radical revolutionary program. For a permanent correction of grave weaknesses in our economic system we have relied on new applications of old democratic processes. It is not necessary to recount what has been accomplished in preserving the homes and livelihood of millions of workers on farms and in cities, in reconstructing a sound banking and credit system, in reviving trade and industry, in reestablishing security of life and property. All we need today is to look upon the fundamental, sound economic conditions to know that this business recession causes more perplexity than fear on the part of most people and to contrast our prevailing mental attitude with the terror and despair of five years ago.

Furthermore, we have a new moral climate in America. That means that we ask business and finance to recognize that fact, to cure such inequalities as they can cure without legislation but to join their government in the enactment of legislation where the ending of abuses and the steady functioning of our economic system calls for government assistance. The Nation has no obligation to make America safe either for incompetent business men or for business men who fail to note the trend of the times and continue the use of machinery of economics and practices of finance as outworn as the cotton spindle of 1870.

Government can be expected to cooperate in every way with the business of the Nation provided the component parts of business abandon practices which do not belong to this day and age, and adopt price and production policies appropriate to the times.

In regard to the relationship of government to certain processes of business, to which I have referred, it seems clear to me that existing laws undoubtedly require reconstruction. I expect, therefore, to address the Congress in a special message on this subject, and I hope to have the help of business in the efforts of government to help business.

I have spoken of labor as another essential in the three great groups of the population in raising the Nation's income. Definite strides in collective bargaining have been made and the right of labor to organize has been nationally accepted. Nevertheless in the evolution of the process difficult situations have arisen in localities and among groups. Unfortunate divisions relating to jurisdiction among the workers themselves have retarded production within given industries and have, therefore, affected related industries. The construction of homes and other buildings has been hindered in some localities not only by unnecessarily high prices for materials but also by certain hourly wage scales.

For economic and social reasons our principal interest for the near future lies along two lines: first, the immediate desirability of increasing the wages of the lowest paid groups in all industry; and, second, in thinking in terms of regularizing the work of the individual worker more greatly through the year—in other words, in thinking more in terms of the worker's total pay for a period of a whole year rather than in terms of his remuneration by the hour or by the day.

In the case of labor as in the case of capital, misrepresentation of the policy of the government of the United States is deception which will not long deceive. In both cases we seek cooperation. In every case power and responsibility must go hand in hand.

I have spoken of economic causes which throw the Nation's income out of balance; I have spoken of practices and abuses which demand correction through the cooperation of capital and labor with the government. But no government can help the destinies of people who insist in putting sectional and class consciousness ahead of general wealth. There must be proof that sectional and class interests are prepared more greatly than they are today to be national in outlook.

A government can punish specific acts of spoliation; but no government can conscript cooperation. We have improved some matters by way of remedial legislation. But where in some particulars that legislation has failed we cannot be sure whether it fails because some of its details are unwise or because it is being sabotaged. At any rate, we hold our objectives and our principles to be sound. We will never go back on them.

Government has a final responsibility for the well-being of its citizenship. If private cooperative endeavor fails to provide work for willing hands and relief for the unfortunate, those suffering hardship from no fault of their own have a right to call upon the Government for aid; and a government worthy of its name must make fitting response.

It is the opportunity and the duty of all those who have faith in democratic methods as applied in industry, in agriculture and in business, as well as in the field of politics, to do their utmost to cooperate with government—without regard to political affiliation, special interests or economic prejudices—in whatever program may be sanctioned by the chosen representatives of the people.

That presupposes on the part of the representatives of the people, a program, its enactment and its administration.

Not because of the pledges of party programs alone, not because of the clear policies of the past five years, but chiefly because of the need of national unity in ending mistakes of the past and meeting the necessities of today, we must carry on. I do not propose to let the people down.

I am sure the Congress of the United States will not let the people down.

Annual Message to Congress

January 4, 1939

Franklin D. Roosevelt's sixth State of the Union message was delivered against a backdrop of looming world war. In his speech, the president tried to prepare Americans for the possibility that the conflicts in other parts of the world would affect them, one way or another.

As of early 1939, the three countries that would form the Axis powers of World War II—Nazi Germany under Adolf Hitler, Japan, and Italy—each had embarked on aggressive moves against other nations. In 1938, Great Britain and France agreed to let Hitler take over part of Czechoslovakia if he agreed not to go further; he was quick to break the agreement. In the end, war would break out in September 1939, when Hitler attacked Poland—and Britain and France, in response, declared war on Germany.

The U.S. Congress, seeking to keep the country out of another world war, had passed a series of neutrality laws beginning in 1935, prohibiting the country from selling arms to belligerents. While some Americans were fervent isolationists, believing that the United States should stay away from other countries' problems, others strongly disagreed, believing the United States had a duty to act.

Roosevelt was walking a political tightrope. It took until December 1941, when Japan attacked Pearl Harbor, for the United States to enter the war. But the president, as seen in this speech, was paving the way for some sort of action.

The president declared that there were international threats to three major American institutions: religion, democracy, and international good faith. He said that even if the United States did not choose to intervene with arms against aggression, the country should not ignore the aggression. "There are many methods short of war, but stronger and more effective than mere words," for dealing with aggressive countries, the president stated.

Neutrality laws can end up helping an aggressor, Roosevelt argued, adding that the possibility of an attack is lessened when a country is well defended. The United States needed strong enough defenses to ward off a sudden attack, he said.

In his speech, Roosevelt sought to link the country's domestic agenda to its defense preparedness, stating that the reforms adopted since his first inauguration had brought the country closer together and made it stronger. He also called for a greater effort to increase the country's national income from sixty billion to eighty billion dollars.

Mr. Vice President, Mr. Speaker, Members of the Senate and the Congress:

In Reporting on the state of the nation, I have felt it necessary on previous occasions to advise the Congress of disturbance abroad and of the need of putting our own house in order in the face of storm signals from across the seas. As this Seventy-sixth Congress opens there is need for further warning.

A war which threatened to envelop the world in flames has been averted; but it has become increasingly clear that world peace is not assured.

All about us rage undeclared wars—military and economic. All about us grow more deadly armaments—military and economic. All about us are threats of new aggression—military and economic.

Storms from abroad directly challenge three institutions indispensable to Americans, now as always. The first is religion. It is the source of the other two—democracy and international good faith.

Religion, by teaching man his relationship to God, gives the individual a sense of his own dignity and teaches him to respect himself by respecting his neighbors.

Democracy, the practice of self-government, is a covenant among free men to respect the rights and liberties of their fellows.

International good faith, a sister of democracy, springs from the will of civilized nations of men to respect the rights and liberties of other nations of men.

In a modern civilization, all three—religion, democracy and international good faith—complement and support each other.

Where freedom of religion has been attacked, the attack has come from sources opposed to democracy. Where democracy has been overthrown, the spirit of free worship has disappeared. And where religion and democracy have vanished, good faith and reason in international affairs have given way to strident ambition and brute force.

An ordering of society which relegates religion, democracy and good faith among nations to the background can find no place within it for the ideals of the Prince of Peace. The United States rejects such an ordering, and retains its ancient faith.

There comes a time in the affairs of men when they must prepare to defend, not their homes alone, but the tenets of faith and humanity on which their churches, their governments and their very civilization are founded. The defense of religion, of democracy and of good faith among nations is all the same fight. To save one we must now make up our minds to save all.

We know what might happen to us of the United States if the new philosophies of force were to encompass the other continents and invade our own. We, no more than other nations, can afford to be surrounded by the enemies of our faith and our humanity. Fortunate it is, therefore, that in this Western Hemisphere we have, under a common ideal of democratic government, a rich diversity of resources and of peoples functioning together in mutual respect and peace.

That Hemisphere, that peace, and that ideal we propose to do our share in protecting against storms from any quarter. Our people and our resources are pledged to secure that protection. From that determination no American flinches.

This by no means implies that the American Republics disassociate themselves from the nations of other continents. It does not mean the Americas against the rest of the world. We as one of the Republics reiterate our willingness to help the cause of world peace. We stand on our historic offer to take counsel with all other nations of the world to the end that aggression among them be terminated, that the race of armaments cease and that commerce be renewed.

But the world has grown so small and weapons of attack so swift that no nation can be safe in its will to peace so long as any other powerful nation refuses to settle its grievances at the council table.

For if any government bristling with implements of war insists on policies of force, weapons of defense give the only safety.

In our foreign relations we have learned from the past what not to do. From new wars we have learned what we must do.

We have learned that effective timing of defense, and the distant points from which attacks may be launched are completely different from what they were twenty years ago.

We have learned that survival cannot be guaranteed by arming after the attack begins—for there is new range and speed to offense.

We have learned that long before any overt military act, aggression begins with preliminaries of propaganda, subsidized penetration, the loosening of ties of good will, the stirring of prejudice and the incitement to disunion.

We have learned that God-fearing democracies of the world which observe the sanctity of treaties and good faith in their dealings with other nations cannot safely be indifferent to international lawlessness anywhere. They cannot forever let pass, without effective protest, acts of aggression against sister nations—acts which automatically undermine all of us.

Obviously they must proceed along practical, peaceful lines. But the mere fact that we rightly decline to intervene with arms to prevent acts of aggression does not mean that we must act as if there were no aggression at all. Words may be futile, but war is not the only means of commanding a decent respect for the opinions of mankind. There are many methods short of war, but stronger and more effective than mere words, of bringing home to aggressor governments the aggregate sentiments of our own people.

At the very least, we can and should avoid any action, or any lack of action, which will encourage, assist or build up an aggressor. We have learned that when we deliberately try to legislate neutrality, our neutrality laws may operate unevenly and unfairly—may actually give aid to an aggressor and deny it to the victim. The instinct of self-preservation should warn us that we ought not to let that happen any more.

And we have learned something else—the old, old lesson that probability of attack is mightily decreased by the assurance of an ever ready defense. Since 1931, nearly eight years ago, world events of thunderous import have moved with lightning speed. During these eight years many of our people clung to the hope that the innate decency of mankind would protect the unprepared who showed their innate trust in mankind. Today we are all wiser—and sadder.

Under modern conditions what we mean by "adequate defense"—a policy subscribed to by all of us—must be divided into three elements. First, we must have armed forces and defenses strong enough to ward off sudden attack against strategic positions and key facilities essential to ensure sustained resistance and ultimate victory. Secondly, we must have the organization and location of those key facilities so that they may be immediately utilized and rapidly expanded to meet all needs without danger of serious interruption by enemy attack.

In the course of a few days I shall send you a special message making recommendations for those two essentials of defense against danger which we cannot safely assume will not come.

If these first two essentials are reasonably provided for, we must be able confidently to invoke the third element, the underlying strength of citizenship—the self-confidence, the ability, the imagination and the devotion that give the staying power to see things through.

A strong and united nation may be destroyed if it is unprepared against sudden attack. But even a nation well armed and well organized from a strictly military standpoint may, after a period of time, meet defeat if it is unnerved by self-distrust, endangered by class prejudice, by dissension between capital and labor, by false economy and by other unsolved social problems at home.

In meeting the troubles of the world we must meet them as one people—with a unity born of the fact that for generations those who have come to our shores, representing many kindreds and tongues, have been welded by common opportunity into a united patriotism. If another form of government can present a united front in its attack on a democracy, the attack must and will be met by a united democracy. Such a democracy can and must exist in the United States.

A dictatorship may command the full strength of a regimented nation. But the united strength of a democratic nation can be mustered only when its people, educated by modern standards to know what is going on and where they are going, have conviction that they are receiving as large a share of opportunity for development, as large a share of material success and of human dignity, as they have a right to receive.

Our nation's program of social and economic reform is therefore a part of defense, as basic as armaments themselves.

Against the background of events in Europe, in Africa and in Asia during these recent years, the pattern of what we have accomplished since 1933 appears in even clearer focus.

For the first time we have moved upon deep-seated problems affecting our national strength and have forged national instruments adequate to meet them.

Consider what the seemingly piecemeal struggles of these six years add up to in terms of realistic national preparedness.

We are conserving and developing natural resources—land, water power, forests.

We are trying to provide necessary food, shelter and medical care for the health of our population.

We are putting agriculture—our system of food and fibre supply—on a sounder basis.

We are strengthening the weakest spot in our system of industrial supply—its long smouldering labor difficulties.

We have cleaned up our credit system so that depositor and investor alike may more readily and willingly make their capital available for peace or war.

We are giving to our youth new opportunities for work and education.

We have sustained the morale of all the population by the dignified recognition of our obligations to the aged, the helpless and the needy.

Above all, we have made the American people conscious of their interrelationship and their interdependence. They sense a common destiny and a common need of each other. Differences of occupation, geography, race and religion no longer obscure the nation's fundamental unity in thought and in action.

We have our difficulties, true—but we are a wiser and a tougher nation than we were in 1929, or in 1932.

Never have there been six years of such far-flung internal preparedness in our history. And this has been done without any dictator's power to command, without conscription of labor or confiscation of capital, without concentration camps and without a scratch on freedom of speech, freedom of the press or the rest of the Bill of Rights.

We see things now that we could not see along the way. The tools of government which we had in 1933 are outmoded. We have had to forge new tools for a new role of government operating in a democracy—a role of new responsibility for new needs and increased responsibility for old needs, long neglected.

Some of these tools had to be roughly shaped and still need some machining down. Many of those who fought bitterly against the forging of these new tools welcome their use today. The American people, as a whole, have accepted them. The Nation looks to the Congress to improve the new machinery which we have permanently installed, provided that in the process the social usefulness of the machinery is not destroyed or impaired.

All of us agree that we should simplify and improve laws if experience and operation clearly demonstrate the need. For instance, all of us want better provision for our older people under our social security legislation. For the medically needy we must provide better care.

Most of us agree that for the sake of employer and employee alike we must find ways to end factional labor strife and employer-employee disputes.

Most of us recognize that none of these tools can be put to maximum effectiveness unless the executive processes of government are revamped—reorganized, if you will— into more effective combination. And even after such reorganization it will take time to develop administrative personnel and experience in order to use our new tools with a minimum of mistakes. The Congress, of course, needs no further information on this.

With this exception of legislation to provide greater government efficiency, and with the exception of legislation to ameliorate our railroad and other transportation problems, the past three Congresses have met in part or in whole the pressing needs of the new order of things.

We have now passed the period of internal conflict in the launching of our program of social reform. Our full energies may now be released to invigorate the processes of recovery in order to preserve our reforms, and to give every man and woman who wants to work a real job at a living wage.

But time is of paramount importance. The deadline of danger from within and from without is not within our control. The hour-glass may be in the hands of other nations. Our own hour-glass tells us that we are off on a race to make democracy work, so that we may be efficient in peace and therefore secure in national defense.

This time element forces us to still greater efforts to attain the full employment of our labor and our capital.

The first duty of our statesmanship is to bring capital and man-power together.

Dictatorships do this by main force. By using main force they apparently succeed at it—for the moment. However we abhor their methods, we are compelled to admit that they have obtained substantial utilization of all their material and human resources. Like it or not, they have solved, for a time at least, the problem of idle men and idle capital. Can we compete with them by boldly seeking methods of putting idle men and idle capital together and, at the same time, remain within our American way of life, within the Bill of Rights, and within the bounds of what is, from our point of view, civilization itself?

We suffer from a great unemployment of capital. Many people have the idea that as a nation we are overburdened with debt and are spending more than we can afford. That is not so. Despite our Federal Government expenditures the entire debt of our national economic system, public and private together, is no larger today than it was in 1929, and the interest thereon is far less than it was in 1929.

The object is to put capital—private as well as public—to work.

We want to get enough capital and labor at work to give us a total turnover of business, a total national income, of at least eighty billion dollars a year. At that figure we shall have a substantial reduction of unemployment; and the Federal Revenues will be sufficient to balance the current level of cash expenditures on the basis of the existing tax structure. That figure can be attained, working within the framework of our traditional profit system.

The factors in attaining and maintaining that amount of national income are many and complicated.

They include more widespread understanding among business men of many changes which world conditions and technological improvements have brought to our economy over the last twenty years—changes in the interrelationship of price and volume and employment, for example—changes of the kind in which business men are now educating themselves through excellent opportunities like the so-called "monopoly investigation."

They include a perfecting of our farm program to protect farmers' income and consumers' purchasing power from alternate risks of crop gluts and crop shortages.

They include wholehearted acceptance of new standards of honesty in our financial markets.

They include reconcilement of enormous, antagonistic interests—some of them long in litigation—in the railroad and general transportation field.

They include the working out of new techniques—private, state and federal—to protect the public interest in and to develop wider markets for electric power.

They include a revamping of the tax relationships between federal, state and local units of government, and consideration of relatively small tax increases to adjust inequalities without interfering with the aggregate income of the American people.

They include the perfecting of labor organization and a universal ungrudging attitude by employers toward the labor movement, until there is a minimum of interruption of production and employment because of disputes, and acceptance by labor of the truth that the welfare of labor itself depends on increased balanced out-put of goods.

To be immediately practical, while proceeding with a steady evolution in the solving of these and like problems, we must wisely use instrumentalities, like Federal investment, which are immediately available to us.

Here, as elsewhere, time is the deciding factor in our choice of remedies.

Therefore, it does not seem logical to me, at the moment we seek to increase production and consumption, for the Federal Government to consider a drastic curtailment of its own investments.

The whole subject of government investing and government income is one which may be approached in two different ways.

The first calls for the elimination of enough activities of government to bring the expenses of government immediately into balance with income of government. This school of thought maintains that because our national income this year is only sixty billion dollars, ours is only a sixty billion dollar country; that government must treat it as such; and that without the help of government, it may some day, somehow, happen to become an eighty billion dollar country.

If the Congress decides to accept this point of view, it will logically have to reduce the present functions or activities of government by one-third. Not only will the Congress have to accept the responsibility for such reduction; but the Congress will have to determine which activities are to be reduced.

Certain expenditures we cannot possibly reduce at this session, such as the interest on the public debt. A few million dollars saved here or there in the normal or in curtailed work of the old departments and commissions will make no great saving in the Federal budget. Therefore, the Congress would have to reduce drastically some of certain large items, very large items, such as aids to agriculture and soil conservation, veterans' pensions, flood control, highways, waterways and other public works, grants for social and health security, Civilian Conservation Corps activities, relief for the unemployed, or national defense itself.

The Congress alone has the power to do all this, as it is the appropriating branch of the government.

The other approach to the question of government spending takes the position that this Nation ought not to be and need not be only a sixty billion dollar nation; that at this moment it has the men and the resources sufficient to make it at least an eighty billion dollar nation. This school of thought does not believe that it can become an eighty billion dollar nation in the near future if government cuts its operations by one-third. It is convinced that if we were to try it, we would invite disaster—and that we would not long remain even a sixty billion dollar nation. There are many complicated factors with which we have to deal, but we have learned that it is unsafe to make abrupt reductions at any time in our net expenditure program.

By our common sense action of resuming government activities last spring, we have reversed a recession and started the new rising tide of prosperity and national income which we are now just beginning to enjoy.

If government activities are fully maintained, there is a good prospect of our becoming an eighty billion dollar country in a very short time. With such a national income, present tax laws will yield enough each year to balance each year's expenses.

It is my conviction that down in their hearts the American public—industry, agriculture, finance—want this Congress to do whatever needs to be done to raise our national income to eighty billion dollars a year.

Investing soundly must preclude spending wastefully. To guard against opportunist appropriations, I have on several occasions addressed the Congress on the importance of permanent long-range planning. I hope, therefore, that following my recommendation of last year, a permanent agency will be set up and authorized to report on the urgency and desirability of the various types of government investment.

Investment for prosperity can be made in a democracy.

I hear some people say, "This is all so complicated. There are certain advantages in a dictatorship. It gets rid of labor trouble, of unemployment, of wasted motion and of having to do your own thinking."

My answer is, "Yes, but it also gets rid of some other things which we Americans intend very definitely to keep—and we still intend to do our own thinking."

It will cost us taxes and the voluntary risk of capital to attain some of the practical advantages which other forms of government have acquired.

Dictatorship, however, involves costs which the American people will never pay: The cost of our spiritual values. The cost of the blessed right of being able to say what we please. The cost of freedom of religion. The cost of seeing our capital confiscated. The cost of being cast into a concentration camp. The cost of being afraid to walk down the street with the wrong neighbor. The cost of having our children brought up, not as free and dignified human beings, but as pawns molded and enslaved by a machine.

If the avoidance of these costs means taxes on my income; if avoiding these costs means taxes on my estate at death, I would bear those taxes willingly as the price of my breathing and my children breathing the free air of a free country, as the price of a living and not a dead world.

Events abroad have made it increasingly clear to the American people that dangers within are less to be feared than dangers from without. If, therefore, a solution of this problem of idle men and idle capital is the price of preserving our liberty, no formless selfish fears can stand in the way.

Once I prophesied that this generation of Americans had a rendezvous with destiny. That prophecy comes true. To us much is given; more is expected.

This generation will "nobly save or meanly lose the last best hope of earth. . . . The way is plain, peaceful, generous, just—a way which if followed the world will forever applaud and God must forever bless."

Franklin D. Roosevelt, 1937–1941

Annual Message to Congress
January 3, 1940

Franklin D. Roosevelt delivered his sevventh State of the Union message four months after the start of World War II. The United States would not enter the conflict until December 1941, after the Japanese attack on Pearl Harbor, but the president's speech focused on the international crisis and the U.S. response to it.

The war had begun in September 1939 following several years of aggressive actions taken by Germany, Japan and Italy—the Axis powers of World War II. Germany had taken over Austria and Czechoslovakia, and when it attacked Poland, Britain and France declared war on Germany.

After the start of the war, the president had urged a special session of Congress to revise the Neutrality Acts that had been passed starting in 1935. Those laws had prohibited U.S. weapons sales to belligerents. The new law extended the "cash-and-carry" concept, under which belligerents had to pay cash and ship their own purchases of American non-military goods, to military goods as well.

In his January 3 speech, Roosevelt stressed the point that Americans were affected by the events going on in other parts of the world. He compared those people who were unrealistic about international events to ostriches, saying, "I hope that we shall have fewer American ostriches in our midst."

Still, the president was not willing to concede that American forces would end up participating in the war in Europe. "Nobody expects such an undertaking," he said.

But he did call for a continued strengthening of the country's defenses, asking Congress for increases in the budgets of the Army and the Navy. He also said that national unity was important during such a time of crisis, calling it "the fundamental safeguard of all democracy."

As 1940 continued, Germany attacked Denmark, Norway, the Netherlands, Belgium, and France. Roosevelt began to work more closely with British Prime Minister Winston Churchill to provide assistance.

Not only was 1940 a time of international turmoil, it also was a presidential election year in the United States. At the start of the year, Roosevelt, a Democrat, was pondering whether to seek an unprecedented third term as president. The president did not withdraw from the contest, although he did not make a big public push to win the nomination. Ultimately, Roosevelt was nominated for a third term, and won four more years in the White House.

Mr. Vice President, Mr. Speaker, Members of the Senate and the House of Representatives:

I wish each and every one of you a very happy New Year.

As the Congress reassembles, the impact of war abroad makes it natural to approach "the state of the union" through a discussion of foreign affairs.

But it is important that those who hear and read this message should in no way confuse that approach with any thought that our Government is abandoning, or even overlooking, the great significance of its domestic policies.

The social and economic forces which have been mismanaged abroad until they have resulted in revolution, dictatorship and war are the same as those which we here are struggling to adjust peacefully at home.

You are well aware that dictatorships—and the philosophy of force that justifies and accompanies dictatorships—have originated in almost every case in the necessity for drastic action to improve internal conditions in places where democratic action for one reason or another has failed to respond to modern needs and modern demands.

It was with far-sighted wisdom that the framers of our Constitution brought together in one magnificent phrase three great concepts—"common defense," "general welfare" and "domestic tranquility."

More than a century and a half later we, who are here today, still believe with them that our best defense is the promotion of our general welfare and domestic tranquility.

In previous messages to the Congress I have repeatedly warned that, whether we like it or not, the daily lives of American citizens will, of necessity, feel the shock of events on other continents. This is no longer mere theory; because it has been definitely proved to us by the facts of yesterday and today.

To say that the domestic well-being of one hundred and thirty million Americans is deeply affected by the well-being or the ill-being of the populations of other nations is only to recognize in world affairs the truth that we all accept in home affairs.

If in any local unit—a city, county, State or region—low standards of living are permitted to continue, the level of the civilization of the entire nation will be pulled downward.

The identical principle extends to the rest of the civilized world. But there are those who wishfully insist, in innocence or ignorance or both, that the United States of America as a self-contained unit can live happily and prosperously, its future secure, inside a high wall of isolation while, outside, the rest of Civilization and the commerce and culture of mankind are shattered.

I can understand the feelings of those who warn the nation that they will never again consent to the sending of American youth to fight on the soil of Europe. But, as I remember, nobody has asked them to consent—for nobody expects such an undertaking.

The overwhelming majority of our fellow citizens do not abandon in the slightest their hope and their expectation that the United States will not become involved in military participation in these wars.

I can also understand the wishfulness of those who oversimplify the whole situation by repeating that all we have to do is to mind our own business and keep the nation out of war. But there is a vast difference between keeping out of war and pretending that this war is none of our business.

We do not have to go to war with other nations, but at least we can strive with other nations to encourage the kind of peace that will lighten the troubles of the world, and by so doing help our own nation as well.

I ask that all of us everywhere think things through with the single aim of how best to serve the future of our own nation. I do not mean merely its future relationship with the outside world. I mean its domestic future as well—the work, the security, the prosperity, the happiness, the life of all the boys and girls in the United States, as they are inevitably affected by such world relationships. For it becomes clearer and clearer that the future world will be a shabby and dangerous place to live in—yes, even for Americans to live in—if it is ruled by force in the hands of a few.

Already the crash of swiftly moving events over the earth has made us all think with a longer view. Fortunately, that thinking cannot be controlled by partisanship. The time is long past when any political party or any particular group can curry or capture public favor by labeling itself the "peace party" or the "peace bloc." That label belongs to the whole United States and to every right thinking man, woman and child within it.

For out of all the military and diplomatic turmoil, out of all the propaganda, and counter-propaganda of the present conflicts, there are two facts which stand out, and which the whole world acknowledges.

The first is that never before has the Government of the United States of America done so much as in our recent past to establish and maintain the policy of the Good Neighbor with its sister nations.

The second is that in almost every nation in the world today there is a true public belief that the United States has been, and will continue to be, a potent and active factor in seeking the reestablishment of world peace.

In these recent years we have had a clean record of peace and good-will. It is an open book that cannot be twisted or defamed. It is a record that must be continued and enlarged.

So I hope that Americans everywhere will work out for themselves the several alternatives which lie before world civilization, which necessarily includes our own.

We must look ahead and see the possibilities for our children if the rest of the world comes to be dominated by concentrated force alone—even though today we are a very great and a very powerful nation.

We must look ahead and see the effect on our own future if all the small nations of the world have their independence snatched from them or become mere appendages to relatively vast and powerful military systems.

We must look ahead and see the kind of lives our children would have to lead if a large part of the rest of the world were compelled to worship a god imposed by a military ruler, or were forbidden to worship God at all; if the rest of the world were forbidden to read and hear the facts—the daily news of their own and other nations—if they were deprived of the truth that makes men free.

We must look ahead and see the effect on our future generations if world trade is controlled by any nation or group of nations which sets up that control through military force.

It is, of course, true that the record of past centuries includes destruction of many small nations, the enslavement of peoples, and the building of empires on the foundation of force. But wholly apart from the greater international morality which we seek today, we recognize the practical fact that with modern weapons and modern conditions, modern man can no longer lead a civilized life if we are to go back to the practice of wars and conquests of the seventeenth and eighteenth centuries.

Summing up this need of looking ahead, and in words of common sense and good American citizenship, I hope that we shall have fewer American ostriches in our midst. It is not good for the ultimate health of ostriches to bury their heads in the sand.

Only an ostrich would look upon these wars through the eyes of cynicism or ridicule.

Of course, the peoples of other nations have the right to choose their own form of Government. But we in this nation still believe that such choice should be predicated on certain freedoms which we think are essential everywhere. We know that we ourselves shall never be wholly safe at home unless other governments recognize such freedoms.

Twenty-one American Republics, expressing the will of two hundred and fifty million people to preserve peace and freedom in this Hemisphere, are displaying a unanimity of ideals and practical relationships which gives hope that what is being done here can be done on other continents. We in all the Americas are coming to the realization that we can retain our respective nationalities without, at the same time, threatening the national existence of our neighbors.

Such truly friendly relationships, for example, permit us to follow our own domestic policies with reference to our agricultural products, while at the same time we have the privilege of trying to work out mutual assistance arrangements for a world distribution of world agricultural surpluses.

And we have been able to apply the same simple principle to many manufactured products—surpluses of which must be sold in the world export markets if we intend to continue a high level of production and employment.

For many years after the World War blind economic selfishness in most countries, including our own, resulted in a destructive mine-field of trade restrictions which blocked the channels of commerce among nations. Indeed, this policy was one of the contributing causes of existing wars. It dammed up vast unsalable surpluses, helping to bring about unemployment and suffering in the United States and everywhere else.

To point the way to break up that log-jam our Trade Agreements Act was passed—

based upon a policy of equality of treatment among nations and of mutually profitable arrangements of trade.

It is not correct to infer that legislative powers have been transferred from the Congress to the Executive Branch of the Government. Everyone recognizes that general tariff legislation is a Congressional function; but we know that, because of the stupendous task involved in the fashioning and the passing of a general tariff law, it is advisable to provide at times of emergency some flexibility to make the general law adjustable to quickly changing conditions.

We are in such a time today. Our present trade agreement method provides a temporary flexibility and is, therefore, practical in the best sense. It should be kept alive to serve our trade interests—agricultural and industrial—in many valuable ways during the existing wars.

But what is more important, the Trade Agreements Act should be extended as an indispensable part of the foundation of any stable and enduring peace.

The old conditions of world trade made for no enduring peace; and when the time comes, the United States must use its influence to open up the trade channels of the world, in all nations, in order that no one nation need feel compelled in later days to seek by force of arms what it can well gain by peaceful conference. For that purpose, too, we need the Trade Agreements Act even more today than when it was passed.

I emphasize the leadership which this nation can take when the time comes for a renewal of world peace. Such an influence will be greatly weakened if this Government becomes a dog in the manger of trade selfishness.

The first President of the United States warned us against entangling foreign alliances. The present President of the United States subscribes to and follows that precept.

I hope that most of you will agree that trade cooperation with the rest of the world does not violate that precept in any way.

Even as through these trade agreements we prepare to cooperate in a world that wants peace, we must likewise be prepared to take care of ourselves if the world cannot attain peace.

For several years past we have been compelled to strengthen our own national defense. That has created a very large portion of our Treasury deficits. This year in the light of continuing world uncertainty, I am asking the Congress for Army and Navy increases which are based not on panic but on common sense. They are not as great as enthusiastic alarmists seek. They are not as small as unrealistic persons claiming superior private information would demand.

As will appear in the annual budget tomorrow, the only important increase in any part of the budget is the estimate for national defense. Practically all other important items show a reduction. But you know, you can't eat your cake and have it too. Therefore, in the hope that we can continue in these days of increasing economic prosperity to reduce the Federal deficit, I am asking the Congress to levy sufficient additional taxes to meet the emergency spending for national defense.

Behind the Army and Navy, of course, lies our ultimate line of defense—"the general welfare" of our people. We cannot report, despite all the progress that we have made in our domestic problems—despite the fact that production is back to 1929 levels—that all our problems are solved. The fact of unemployment of millions of men and women remains a symptom of a number of difficulties in our economic system not yet adjusted.

While the number of the unemployed has decreased very greatly, while their immediate needs for food and clothing—as far as the Federal Government is concerned—have been largely met, while their morale has been kept alive by giving them useful public work, we have not yet found a way to employ the surplus of our labor which the efficiency of our industrial processes has created.

We refuse the European solution of using the unemployed to build up excessive armaments which eventually result in dictatorships and war. We encourage an American way—through an increase of national income which is the only way we can be sure will take up the slack. Much progress has been made; much remains to be done.

We recognize that we must find an answer in terms of work and opportunity.

The unemployment problem today has become very definitely a problem of youth as well as of age. As each year has gone by hundreds of thousands of boys and girls have come of working age. They now form an army of unused youth. They must be an especial concern of democratic Government.

We must continue, above all things, to look for a solution of their special problem. For they, looking ahead to life, are entitled to action on our part and not merely to admonitions of optimism or lectures on economic laws.

Some in our midst have sought to instill a feeling of fear and defeatism in the minds of the American people about this problem.

To face the task of finding jobs faster than invention can take them away—is not defeatism. To warble easy platitudes that if we would only go back to ways that have failed, everything would be all right—is not courage.

In 1933 we met a problem of real fear and real defeatism. We faced the facts—with action and not with words alone.

The American people will reject the doctrine of fear, confident that in the 'thirties we have been building soundly a new order of things, different from the order of the 'twenties. In this dawn of the decade of the 'forties, with our program of social improvement started, we will continue to carry on the processes of recovery, so as to preserve our gains and provide jobs at living wages.

There are, of course, many other items of great public interest which could be enumerated in this message—the continued conservation of our natural resources, the improvement of health and of education, the extension of social security to larger groups, the freeing of large areas from restricted transportation discriminations, the extension of the merit system and many others.

Our continued progress in the social and economic field is important not only for the significance of each part of it but for the total effect which our program of domestic betterment has upon that most valuable asset of a nation in dangerous times—its national unity.

The permanent security of America in the present crisis does not lie in armed force alone. What we face is a set of world-wide forces of disintegration—vicious, ruthless, destructive of all the moral, religious and political standards which mankind, after centuries of struggle, has come to cherish most.

In these moral values, in these forces which have made our nation great, we must actively and practically reassert our faith.

These words—"national unity"—must not be allowed to become merely a high-sounding phrase, a vague generality, a pious hope, to which everyone can give lip-service. They must be made to have real meaning in terms of the daily thoughts and acts of every man, woman and child in our land during the coming year and during the years that lie ahead.

For national unity is, in a very real and a very deep sense, the fundamental safeguard of all democracy.

Doctrines that set group against group, faith against faith, race against race, class against class, fanning the fires of hatred in men too despondent, too desperate to think for themselves, were used as rabble-rousing slogans on which dictators could ride to power. And once in power they could saddle their tyrannies on whole nations and on their weaker neighbors.

This is the danger to which we in America must begin to be more alert. For the apologists for foreign aggressors, and equally those selfish and partisan groups at home who wrap themselves in a false mantle of Americanism to promote their own economic, financial or political advantage, are now trying European tricks upon us, seeking to muddy the stream of our national thinking, weakening us in the face of danger, by trying to set our own people to fighting among themselves. Such tactics are what have helped to plunge Europe into war. We must combat them, as we would the plague, if American integrity and American security are to be preserved. We cannot afford to face the future as a disunited people.

We must as a united people keep ablaze on this continent the flames of human liberty, of reason, of democracy and of fair play as living things to be preserved for the better world that is to come.

Overstatement, bitterness, vituperation, and the beating of drums have contributed mightily to ill-feeling and wars between nations. If these unnecessary and unpleasant actions are harmful in the international field, if they have hurt in other parts of the world, they are also harmful in the domestic scene. Peace among ourselves would seem to have some of the advantage of peace between us and other nations. In the long run history amply demonstrates that angry controversy surely wins less than calm discussion.

In the spirit, therefore, of a greater unselfishness, recognizing that the world—including the United States of America—passes through perilous times, I am very hopeful that the closing session of the Seventy-sixth Congress will consider the needs of the nation and of humanity with calmness, with tolerance and with cooperative wisdom.

May the year 1940 be pointed to by our children as another period when democracy justified its existence as the best instrument of government yet devised by mankind.

Franklin D. Roosevelt, 1937–1941

Annual Message to Congress
January 6, 1941

Franklin D. Roosevelt's State of the Union message for 1941 is one of his best-known speeches. In this address, he enumerated "four essential human freedoms"—freedom of speech, freedom of worship, freedom from want, and freedom from fear—on which a future world order should be founded.

"Freedom means the supremacy of human rights everywhere," he said. "Our support goes to those who struggle to gain those rights or keep them."

The president delivered this address eleven months before the United States would enter World War II, which had begun in 1939. Roosevelt focused the speech on the dangers facing the world and the United States, and described what the country needed to do to be prepared.

The president, gearing his fellow Americans up for the conflict to come, stated that the country had never before faced such an external security threat as it did at that moment. And he said that while Americans may be proud of being "soft-hearted," they should not be "soft-headed" when it came to the world situation.

Roosevelt called for an increase in the country's armament production, stating that the United States should be "an arsenal" for those countries at war with aggressors. He urged a shift in how those countries should pay for these armaments, arguing that the nations would not be able to pay in cash.

In March 1941, Congress approved the Lend-Lease Act, which basically gave Roosevelt the power to help the Allies without actually using the U.S. armed forces. The president already had given Britain fifty "overage" destroyers, in September 1940. Also in 1940, Congress had approved a selective service bill instituting the first peacetime draft in U.S. history.

Roosevelt had just been elected to an unprecedented third term in November 1940; his third inaugural would be two weeks after this State of the Union speech. Throughout much of 1940, the president did not publicly seek another term, nor did he pull out of the race. He waited, in effect, for his party to draft him. Indeed, the Democratic convention of 1940 did nominate him for a third term.

The president's Republican opponent in 1940 was Wendell Willkie, a business executive. The president won 54.7 percent of the popular vote and 449 electoral votes to Willkie's 44.8 percent and 82 electoral votes. In addition, Democrats continued their hold on both houses of Congress.

In the course of the campaign, Roosevelt had promised not to get the country involved in "foreign wars." Ultimately, Japan attacked the U.S. naval base at Pearl Harbor in Hawaii on December 7, 1941—"a date which will live in infamy," as Roosevelt subsequently described it—leading the United States to enter the war.

M r. President, Mr. Speaker, Members of the Seventy-seventh Congress:

I address you, the Members of the Seventy-seventh Congress, at a moment unprecedented in the history of the Union. I use the word "unprecedented," because at no previous time has American security been as seriously threatened from without as it is today.

Since the permanent formation of our Government under the Constitution, in 1789, most of the periods of crisis in our history have related to our domestic affairs. Fortunately, only one of these—the four-year War Between the States—ever threatened our national unity. Today, thank God, one hundred and thirty million Americans, in forty-eight States, have forgotten points of the compass in our national unity.

It is true that prior to 1914 the United States often had been disturbed by events in other Continents. We had even engaged in two wars with European nations and in a number of undeclared wars in the West Indies, in the Mediterranean and in the Pacific for the maintenance of American rights and for the principles of peaceful commerce. But in no case had a serious threat been raised against our national safety or our continued independence.

What I seek to convey is the historic truth that the United States as a nation has at all times maintained clear, definite opposition, to any attempt to lock us in behind an ancient Chinese wall while the procession of civilization went past. Today, thinking of our children and of their children, we oppose enforced isolation for ourselves or for any other part of the Americas.

That determination of ours, extending over all these years, was proved, for example, during the quarter century of wars following the French Revolution.

While the Napoleonic struggles did threaten interests of the United States because of the French foothold in the West Indies and in Louisiana, and while we engaged in the War of 1812 to vindicate our right to peaceful trade, it is nevertheless clear that neither France nor Great Britain, nor any other nation, was aiming at domination of the whole world.

In like fashion from 1815 to 1914—ninety-nine years—no single war in Europe or in Asia constituted a real threat against our future or against the future of any other American nation.

Except in the Maximilian interlude in Mexico, no foreign power sought to establish itself in this Hemisphere; and the strength of the British fleet in the Atlantic has been a friendly strength. It is still a friendly strength.

Even when the World War broke out in 1914, it seemed to contain only small threat of danger to our own American future. But, as time went on, the American people began to visualize what the downfall of democratic nations might mean to our own democracy.

We need not overemphasize imperfections in the Peace of Versailles. We need not harp on failure of the democracies to deal with problems of world reconstruction. We should remember that the Peace of 1919 was far less unjust than the kind of "pacification" which began even before Munich, and which is being carried on under the new order of tyranny that seeks to spread over every continent today. The American people have unalterably set their faces against that tyranny.

Every realist knows that the democratic way of life is at this moment being directly assailed in every part of the world—assailed either by arms, or by secret spreading of poisonous propaganda by those who seek to destroy unity and promote discord in nations that are still at peace.

During sixteen long months this assault has blotted out the whole pattern of democratic life in an appalling number of independent nations, great and small. The assailants are still on the march, threatening other nations, great and small.

Therefore, as your President, performing my constitutional duty to "give to the Congress information of the state of the Union," I find it, unhappily, necessary to report that the future and the safety of our country and of our democracy are overwhelmingly involved in events far beyond our borders.

Armed defense of democratic existence is now being gallantly waged in four continents. If that defense fails, all the population and all the resources of Europe, Asia, Africa and Australasia will be dominated by the conquerors. Let us remember that the total of those populations and their resources in those four continents greatly exceeds the sum total of the population and the resources of the whole of the Western Hemisphere—many times over.

In times like these it is immature—and incidentally, untrue—for anybody to brag that an unprepared America, single-handed, and with one hand tied behind its back, can hold off the whole world.

No realistic American can expect from a dictator's peace international generosity, or return of true independence, or world disarmament, or freedom of expression, or freedom of religion—or even good business.

Such a peace would bring no security for us or for our neighbors. "Those, who would give up essential liberty to purchase a little temporary safety, deserve neither liberty nor safety."

As a nation, we may take pride in the fact that we are softhearted; but we cannot afford to be soft-headed.

We must always be wary of those who with sounding brass and a tinkling cymbal preach the "ism" of appeasement.

We must especially beware of that small group of selfish men who would clip the wings of the American eagle in order to feather their own nests.

I have recently pointed out how quickly the tempo of modern warfare could bring into our very midst the physical attack which we must eventually expect if the dictator nations win this war.

There is much loose talk of our immunity from immediate and direct invasion from across the seas. Obviously, as long as the British Navy retains its power, no such danger exists. Even if there were no British Navy, it is not probable that any enemy would be stupid enough to attack us by landing troops in the United States from across thousands of miles of ocean, until it had acquired strategic bases from which to operate.

But we learn much from the lessons of the past years in Europe—particularly the lesson of Norway, whose essential seaports were captured by treachery and surprise built up over a series of years.

The first phase of the invasion of this Hemisphere would not be the landing of regular troops. The necessary strategic points would be occupied by secret agents and their dupes—and great numbers of them are already here, and in Latin America.

As long as the aggressor nations maintain the offensive, they—not we—will choose the time and the place and the method of their attack.

That is why the future of all the American Republics is today in serious danger.

That is why this Annual Message to the Congress is unique in our history.

That is why every member of the Executive Branch of the Government and every member of the Congress faces great responsibility and great accountability.

The need of the moment is that our actions and our policy should be devoted primarily—almost exclusively—to meeting this foreign peril. For all our domestic problems are now a part of the great emergency.

Just as our national policy in internal affairs has been based upon a decent respect for the rights and the dignity of all our fellow men within our gates, so our national policy in foreign affairs has been based on a decent respect for the rights and dignity of all nations, large and small. And the justice of morality must and will win in the end.

Our national policy is this:

First, by an impressive expression of the public will and without regard to partisanship, we are committed to all-inclusive national defense.

Second, by an impressive expression of the public will and without regard to partisanship, we are committed to full support of all those resolute peoples, everywhere, who are resisting aggression and are thereby keeping war away from our Hemisphere. By this support, we express our determination that the democratic cause shall prevail; and we strengthen the defense and the security of our own nation.

Third, by an impressive expression of the public will and without regard to partisanship, we are committed to the proposition that principles of morality and considerations for our own security will never permit us to acquiesce in a peace dictated by aggressors and sponsored by appeasers. We know that enduring peace cannot be bought at the cost of other people's freedom.

In the recent national election there was no substantial difference between the two great parties in respect to that national policy. No issue was fought out on this line before the American electorate. Today it is abundantly evident that American citizens everywhere are demanding and supporting speedy and complete action in recognition of obvious danger.

Therefore, the immediate need is a swift and driving increase in our armament production.

Leaders of industry and labor have responded to our summons. Goals of speed have been set. In some cases these goals are being reached ahead of time; in some cases we are on schedule; in other cases there are slight but not serious delays; and in some cases—and I am sorry to say very important cases—we are all concerned by the slowness of the accomplishment of our plans.

The Army and Navy, however, have made substantial progress during the past year. Actual experience is improving and speeding up our methods of production with every passing day. And today's best is not good enough for tomorrow.

I am not satisfied with the progress thus far made. The men in charge of the program represent the best in training, in ability, and in patriotism. They are not satisfied with the progress thus far made. None of us will be satisfied until the job is done.

No matter whether the original goal was set too high or too low, our objective is quicker and better results. To give you two illustrations:

We are behind schedule in turning out finished airplanes; we are working day and night to solve the innumerable problems and to catch up.

We are ahead of schedule in building warships but we are working to get even further ahead of that schedule.

To change a whole nation from a basis of peacetime production of implements of peace to a basis of wartime production of implements of war is no small task. And the greatest difficulty comes at the beginning of the program, when new tools, new plant facilities, new assembly lines, and new ship ways must first be constructed before the actual materiel begins to flow steadily and speedily from them.

The Congress, of course, must rightly keep itself informed at all times of the progress of the program. However, there is certain information, as the Congress itself will readily recognize, which, in the interests of our own security and those of the nations that we are supporting, must of needs be kept in confidence.

New circumstances are constantly begetting new needs for our safety. I shall ask this Congress for greatly increased new appropriations and authorizations to carry on what we have begun.

I also ask this Congress for authority and for funds sufficient to manufacture additional munitions and war supplies of many kinds, to be turned over to those nations which are now in actual war with aggressor nations.

Our most useful and immediate role is to act as an arsenal for them as well as for ourselves. They do not need man power, but they do need billions of dollars worth of the weapons of defense.

The time is near when they will not be able to pay for them all in ready cash. We cannot, and we will not, tell them that they must surrender, merely because of present inability to pay for the weapons which we know they must have.

I do not recommend that we make them a loan of dollars with which to pay for these weapons—a loan to be repaid in dollars.

I recommend that we make it possible for those nations to continue to obtain war materials in the United States, fitting their orders into our own program. Nearly all their materiel would, if the time ever came, be useful for our own defense.

Taking counsel of expert military and naval authorities, considering what is best for our own security, we are free to decide how much should be kept here and how much should be sent abroad to our friends who by their determined and heroic resistance are giving us time in which to make ready our own defense.

For what we send abroad, we shall be repaid within a reasonable time following the close of hostilities, in similar materials, or, at our option, in other goods of many kinds, which they can produce and which we need.

Let us say to the democracies: "We Americans are vitally concerned in your defense of freedom. We are putting forth our energies, our resources and our organizing powers to give you the strength to regain and maintain a free world. We shall send you, in ever-increasing numbers, ships, planes, tanks, guns. This is our purpose and our pledge."

In fulfillment of this purpose we will not be intimidated by the threats of dictators that they will regard as a breach of international law or as an act of war our aid to the democracies which dare to resist their aggression. Such aid is not an act of war, even if a dictator should unilaterally proclaim it so to be.

When the dictators, if the dictators, are ready to make war upon us, they will not wait for an act of war on our part. They did not wait for Norway or Belgium or the Netherlands to commit an act of war.

Their only interest is in a new one-way international law, which lacks mutuality in its observance, and, therefore, becomes an instrument of oppression.

The happiness of future generations of Americans may well depend upon how effective and how immediate we can make our aid felt. No one can tell the exact character of the emergency situations that we may be called upon to meet. The Nation's hands must not be tied when the Nation's life is in danger.

We must all prepare to make the sacrifices that the emergency—almost as serious as war itself—demands. Whatever stands in the way of speed and efficiency in defense preparations must give way to the national need.

A free nation has the right to expect full cooperation from all groups. A free nation has the right to look to the leaders of business, of labor, and of agriculture to take the lead in stimulating effort, not among other groups but within their own groups.

The best way of dealing with the few slackers or trouble makers in our midst is, first, to shame them by patriotic example, and, if that fails, to use the sovereignty of Government to save Government.

As men do not live by bread alone, they do not fight by armaments alone. Those who man our defenses, and those behind them who build our defenses, must have the stamina and the courage which come from unshakable belief in the manner of life which they are defending. The mighty action that we are calling for cannot be based on a disregard of all things worth fighting for.

The Nation takes great satisfaction and much strength from the things which have been done to make its people conscious of their individual stake in the preservation of democratic life in America. Those things have toughened the fibre of our people, have renewed their faith and strengthened their devotion to the institutions we make ready to protect.

Certainly this is no time for any of us to stop thinking about the social and economic problems which are the root cause of the social revolution which is today a supreme factor in the world.

For there is nothing mysterious about the foundations of a healthy and strong democracy. The basic things expected by our people of their political and economic systems are simple. They are:

Equality of opportunity for youth and for others.

Jobs for those who can work.

Security for those who need it.

The ending of special privilege for the few.

The preservation of civil liberties for all.

The enjoyment of the fruits of scientific progress in a wider and constantly rising standard of living.

These are the simple, basic things that must never be lost sight of in the turmoil and unbelievable complexity of our modern world. The inner and abiding strength of our economic and political systems is dependent upon the degree to which they fulfill these expectations.

Many subjects connected with our social economy call for immediate improvement. As examples:

We should bring more citizens under the coverage of old-age pensions and unemployment insurance.

We should widen the opportunities for adequate medical care.

We should plan a better system by which persons deserving or needing gainful employment may obtain it.

I have called for personal sacrifice. I am assured of the willingness of almost all Americans to respond to that call.

A part of the sacrifice means the payment of more money in taxes. In my Budget Message I shall recommend that a greater portion of this great defense program be paid for from taxation than we are paying today. No person should try, or be allowed, to get rich out of this program; and the principle of tax payments in accordance with ability to pay should be constantly before our eyes to guide our legislation.

If the Congress maintains these principles, the voters, putting patriotism ahead of pocketbooks, will give you their applause.

In the future days, which we seek to make secure, we look forward to a world founded upon four essential human freedoms.

The first is freedom of speech and expression—everywhere in the world.

The second is freedom of every person to worship God in his own way—everywhere in the world.

The third is freedom from want—which, translated into world terms, means economic understandings which will secure to every nation a healthy peacetime life for its inhabitants—everywhere in the world.

The fourth is freedom from fear—which, translated into world terms, means a world-wide reduction of armaments to such a point and in such a thorough fashion that no nation will be in a position to commit an act of physical aggression against any neighbor—anywhere in the world.

That is no vision of a distant millennium. It is a definite basis for a kind of world attainable in our own time and generation. That kind of world is the very antithesis of the so-called new order of tyranny which the dictators seek to create with the crash of a bomb.

To that new order we oppose the greater conception—the moral order. A good society is able to face schemes of world domination and foreign revolutions alike without fear.

Since the beginning of our American history, we have been engaged in change—in a perpetual peaceful revolution—a revolution which goes on steadily, quietly adjusting itself to changing conditions—without the concentration camp or the quick-lime in the ditch. The world order which we seek is the cooperation of free countries, working together in a friendly, civilized society.

This nation has placed its destiny in the hands and heads and hearts of its millions of free men and women; and its faith in freedom under the guidance of God. Freedom means the supremacy of human rights everywhere. Our support goes to those who struggle to gain those rights or keep them. Our strength is our unity of purpose. To that high concept there can be no end save victory.

Franklin D. Roosevelt, 1941–1945

State of the Union Address

January 6, 1942

Franklin D. Roosevelt's speech of January 6, 1942, was his first wartime State of the Union address. The United States had entered World War II on December 7, 1941, following the Japanese attack on the U.S. naval base at Pearl Harbor, Hawaii.

In his State of the Union address a year earlier, Roosevelt had spoken of the "Four Freedoms"—freedom of speech, freedom of religion, freedom from want, and freedom from fear. In this address, he said that one major objective for the United States and its allies was to establish these freedoms around the world.

Roosevelt called for an "overwhelming" superiority in armaments on the side of the United States and its allies, or the "United Nations," as he called them. He said the arms should be used for U.S. forces, allied forces, and those in conquered countries who sought to rebel against Germany and Japan.

The president said that production of airplanes, tanks, anti-aircraft guns, and merchant ships needed to be increased, and he provided specific numbers as goals. He called on workers to be prepared for long hours and for plants to be converted to war production. And he said civilians would need to cut back on use of materials such as steel, copper and tin.

In terms of the budget, the president stated that "war costs money." The percentage of the national income devoted to national defense would jump from 15 percent to more than 50 percent, meaning "taxes and bonds and bonds and taxes," he told his listeners.

The U.S. entry into the war came after months of increasing U.S. involvement on behalf of Great Britain and in opposition to Germany. In August 1941, Roosevelt and British Prime Minister Winston Churchill agreed on the Atlantic Charter, which set out "common principles" that basically served as a set of war aims.

In addition, the United States was facing increasingly difficult problems in Asia, where Japan was seeking to take over not only China but various Asian territories held by European countries. After diplomatic efforts failed, it became clear that a Japanese attack on the United States would occur soon. The day after the attack on Pearl Harbor, Roosevelt addressed Congress, calling December 7 "a date which will live in infamy." The United States joined the Allied cause, and Roosevelt's last years in office would be dominated by the war.

In fulfilling my duty to report upon the State of the Union, I am proud to say to you that the spirit of the American people was never higher than it is today—the Union was never more closely knit together—this country was never more deeply determined to face the solemn tasks before it.

The response of the American people has been instantaneous, and it will be sustained until our security is assured.

Exactly one year ago today I said to this Congress: "When the dictators . . . are ready to make war upon us, they will not wait for an act of war on our part. . . . They—not we—will choose the time and the place and the method of their attack."

We now know their choice of the time: a peaceful Sunday morning—December 7, 1941.

We know their choice of the place: an American outpost in the Pacific.

We know their choice of the method: the method of Hitler himself.

Japan's scheme of conquest goes back half a century. It was not merely a policy of seeking living room: it was a plan which included the subjugation of all the peoples in the Far East and in the islands of the Pacific, and the domination of that ocean by Japanese military and naval control of the western coasts of North, Central, and South America.

The development of this ambitious conspiracy was marked by the war against China in 1894; the subsequent occupation of Korea; the war against Russia in 1904; the illegal fortification of the mandated Pacific islands following 1920; the seizure of Manchuria in 1931; and the invasion of China in 1937.

A similar policy of criminal conquest was adopted by Italy. The Fascists first revealed their imperial designs in Libya and Tripoli. In 1935 they seized Abyssinia. Their goal was the domination of all North Africa, Egypt, parts of France, and the entire Mediterranean world.

But the dreams of empire of the Japanese and Fascist leaders were modest in comparison with the gargantuan aspirations of Hitler and his Nazis. Even before they came to power in 1933, their plans for that conquest had been drawn. Those plans provided for ultimate domination, not of any one section of the world, but of the whole earth and all the oceans on it.

When Hitler organized his Berlin-Rome-Tokyo alliance, all these plans of conquest became a single plan. Under this, in addition to her own schemes of conquest, Japan's role was obviously to cut off our supply of weapons of war to Britain, and Russia and China—weapons which increasingly were speeding the day of Hitler's doom. The act of Japan at Pearl Harbor was intended to stun us—to terrify us to such an extent that we would divert our industrial and military strength to the Pacific area, or even to our own continental defense.

The plan has failed in its purpose. We have not been stunned. We have not been terrified or confused. This very reassembling of the Seventy-seventh Congress today is proof of that; for the mood of quiet, grim resolution which here prevails bodes ill for those who conspired and collaborated to murder world peace.

That mood is stronger than any mere desire for revenge. It expresses the will of the American people to make very certain that the world will never so suffer again.

Admittedly, we have been faced with hard choices. It was bitter, for example, not to be able to relieve the heroic and historic defenders of Wake Island. It was bitter for us not to be able to land a million men in a thousand ships in the Philippine Islands.

But this adds only to our determination to see to it that the Stars and Stripes will fly again over Wake and Guam. Yes, see to it that the brave people of the Philippines will be rid of Japanese imperialism; and will live in freedom, security, and independence.

Powerful and offensive actions must and will be taken in proper time. The consolidation of the United Nations' total war effort against our common enemies is being achieved.

That was and is the purpose of conferences which have been held during the past two weeks in Washington, and Moscow and Chungking. That is the primary objective of the declaration of solidarity signed in Washington on January 1, 1942, by 26 Nations united against the Axis powers.

Difficult choices may have to be made in the months to come. We do not shrink from such decisions. We and those united with us will make those decisions with courage and determination.

Plans have been laid here and in the other capitals for coordinated and cooperative action by all the United Nations—military action and economic action. Already we have established, as you know, unified command of land, sea, and air forces in the southwestern Pacific theater of war. There will be a continuation of conferences and consultations among military staffs, so that the plans and operations of each will fit into the general strategy designed to crush the enemy. We shall not fight isolated wars—each Nation going its own way. These 26 Nations are united—not in spirit and determination alone, but in the broad conduct of the war in all its phases.

For the first time since the Japanese and the Fascists and the Nazis started along their blood-stained course of conquest they now face the fact that superior forces are assembling against them. Gone forever are the days when the aggressors could attack and destroy their victims one by one without unity of resistance. We of the United Nations will so dispose our forces that we can strike at the common enemy wherever the greatest damage can be done him.

The militarists of Berlin and Tokyo started this war. But the massed, angered forces of common humanity will finish it.

Destruction of the material and spiritual centers of civilization—this has been and still is the purpose of Hitler and his Italian and Japanese chessmen. They would wreck the power of the British Commonwealth and Russia and China and the Netherlands—and then combine all their forces to achieve their ultimate goal, the conquest of the United States.

They know that victory for us means victory for freedom.

They know that victory for us means victory for the institution of democracy—the ideal of the family, the simple principles of common decency and humanity.

They know that victory for us means victory for religion. And they could not tolerate that. The world is too small to provide adequate "living room" for both Hitler and God. In proof of that, the Nazis have now announced their plan for enforcing their new German, pagan religion all over the world—a plan by which the Holy Bible and the Cross of Mercy would be displaced by Mein Kampf and the swastika and the naked sword.

Our own objectives are clear: the objective of smashing the militarism imposed by war lords upon their enslaved peoples—the objective of liberating the subjugated Nations—the objective of establishing and securing freedom of speech, freedom of religion, freedom from want, and freedom from fear everywhere in the world.

We shall not stop short of these objectives—nor shall we be satisfied merely to gain them and then call it a day. I know that I speak for the American people—and I have good reason to believe that I speak also for all the other peoples who fight with us—when I say that this time we are determined not only to win the war, but also to maintain the security of the peace that will follow.

But we know that modern methods of warfare make it a task, not only of shooting and fighting, but an even more urgent one of working and producing.

Victory requires the actual weapons of war and the means of transporting them to a dozen points of combat.

It will not be sufficient for us and the other United Nations to produce a slightly superior supply of munitions to that of Germany, Japan, Italy, and the stolen industries in the countries which they have overrun.

The superiority of the United Nations in munitions and ships must be overwhelming—so overwhelming that the Axis Nations can never hope to catch up with it. And so, in order to attain this overwhelming superiority the United States must build planes and tanks and guns and ships to the utmost limit of our national capacity. We have the ability and capacity to produce arms not only for our own forces, but also for the armies, navies, and air forces fighting on our side.

And our overwhelming superiority of armament must be adequate to put weapons of war at the proper time into the hands of those men in the conquered Nations who stand ready to seize the first opportunity to revolt against their German and Japanese oppressors, and against the traitors in their own ranks, known by the already infamous name of "Quislings." And I think that it is a fair prophecy to say that, as we get guns to the patriots in those lands, they too will fire shots heard 'round the world.

This production of ours in the United States must be raised far above present levels, even though it will mean the dislocation of the lives and occupations of millions of our own people. We must raise our sights all along the production line. Let no man say it cannot be done. It must be done—and we have undertaken to do it.

I have just sent a letter of directive to the appropriate departments and agencies of our Government, ordering that immediate steps be taken:

First, to increase our production rate of airplanes so rapidly that in this year, 1942, we shall produce 60,000 planes, 10,000 more than the goal that we set a year and a half ago. This includes 45,000 combat planes—bombers, dive bombers, pursuit planes. The rate of increase will be maintained and continued so that next year, 1943, we shall produce 125,000 airplanes, including 100,000 combat planes.

Second, to increase our production rate of tanks so rapidly that in this year, 1942, we shall produce 45,000 tanks; and to continue that increase so that next year, 1943, we shall produce 75,000 tanks.

Third, to increase our production rate of anti-aircraft guns so rapidly that in this year, 1942, we shall produce 20,000 of them; and to continue that increase so that next year, 1943, we shall produce 35,000 anti-aircraft guns.

And fourth, to increase our production rate of merchant ships so rapidly that in this year, 1942, we shall build 6,000,000 deadweight tons as compared with a 1941 completed production of 1,100,000. And finally, we shall continue that increase so that next year, 1943, we shall build 10,000,000 tons of shipping.

These figures and similar figures for a multitude of other implements of war will give the Japanese and the Nazis a little idea of just what they accomplished in the attack at Pearl Harbor.

And I rather hope that all these figures which I have given will become common knowledge in Germany and Japan.

Our task is hard—our task is unprecedented—and the time is short. We must strain every existing armament-producing facility to the utmost. We must convert every available plant and tool to war production. That goes all the way from the greatest plants to the smallest—from the huge automobile industry to the village machine shop.

Production for war is based on men and women—the human hands and brains which collectively we call Labor. Our workers stand ready to work long hours; to turn out more in a day's work; to keep the wheels turning and the fires burning twenty-four hours a day, and seven days a week. They realize well that on the speed and efficiency of their work depend the lives of their sons and their brothers on the fighting fronts.

Production for war is based on metals and raw materials—steel, copper, rubber, aluminum, zinc, tin. Greater and greater quantities of them will have to be diverted to war purposes. Civilian use of them will have to be cut further and still further—and, in many cases, completely eliminated.

War costs money. So far, we have hardly even begun to pay for it. We have devoted only 15 percent of our national income to national defense. As will appear in my Budget Message tomorrow, our war program for the coming fiscal year will cost 56 billion dollars or, in other words, more than half of the estimated annual national income. That means taxes and bonds and bonds and taxes. It means cutting luxuries and other non-essentials. In a word, it means an "all-out" war by individual effort and family effort in a united country.

Only this all-out scale of production will hasten the ultimate all-out victory. Speed will count. Lost ground can always be regained—lost time never. Speed will save lives;

speed will save this Nation which is in peril; speed will save our freedom and our civilization—and slowness has never been an American characteristic.

As the United States goes into its full stride, we must always be on guard against misconceptions which will arise, some of them naturally, or which will be planted among us by our enemies.

We must guard against complacency. We must not underrate the enemy. He is powerful and cunning—and cruel and ruthless. He will stop at nothing that gives him a chance to kill and to destroy. He has trained his people to believe that their highest perfection is achieved by waging war. For many years he has prepared for this very conflict—planning, and plotting, and training, arming, and fighting. We have already tasted defeat. We may suffer further setbacks. We must face the fact of a hard war, a long war, a bloody war, a costly war.

We must, on the other hand, guard against defeatism. That has been one of the chief weapons of Hitler's propaganda machine—used time and again with deadly results. It will not be used successfully on the American people.

We must guard against divisions among ourselves and among all the other United Nations. We must be particularly vigilant against racial discrimination in any of its ugly forms. Hitler will try again to breed mistrust and suspicion between one individual and another, one group and another, one race and another, one Government and another. He will try to use the same technique of falsehood and rumor-mongering with which he divided France from Britain. He is trying to do this with us even now. But he will find a unity of will and purpose against him, which will persevere until the destruction of all his black designs upon the freedom and safety of the people of the world.

We cannot wage this war in a defensive spirit. As our power and our resources are fully mobilized, we shall carry the attack against the enemy—we shall hit him and hit him again wherever and whenever we can reach him.

We must keep him far from our shores, for we intend to bring this battle to him on his own home grounds.

American armed forces must be used at any place in all the world where it seems advisable to engage the forces of the enemy. In some cases these operations will be defensive, in order to protect key positions. In other cases, these operations will be offensive, in order to strike at the common enemy, with a view to his complete encirclement and eventual total defeat.

American armed forces will operate at many points in the Far East.

American armed forces will be on all the oceans—helping to guard the essential communications which are vital to the United Nations.

American land and air and sea forces will take stations in the British Isles—which constitute an essential fortress in this great world struggle.

American armed forces will help to protect this hemisphere—and also help to protect bases outside this hemisphere, which could be used for an attack on the Americas.

If any of our enemies, from Europe or from Asia, attempt long-range raids by "suicide" squadrons of bombing planes, they will do so only in the hope of terrorizing our people and disrupting our morale. Our people are not afraid of that. We know that we may have to pay a heavy price for freedom. We will pay this price with a will. Whatever the price, it is a thousand times worth it. No matter what our enemies, in their desperation, may attempt to do to us—we will say, as the people of London have said, "We can take it." And what's more we can give it back and we will give it back—with compound interest.

When our enemies challenged our country to stand up and fight, they challenged each and every one of us. And each and every one of us has accepted the challenge—for himself and for his Nation.

There were only some 400 United States Marines who in the heroic and historic defense of Wake Island inflicted such great losses on the enemy. Some of those men were killed in action; and others are now prisoners of war. When the survivors of that great fight are liberated and restored to their homes, they will learn that a hundred and thirty million of their fellow citizens have been inspired to render their own full share of service and sacrifice.

We can well say that our men on the fighting fronts have already proved that Americans today are just as rugged and just as tough as any of the heroes whose exploits we celebrate on the Fourth of July.

Many people ask, "When will this war end?" There is only one answer to that. It will end just as soon as we make it end, by our combined efforts, our combined strength, our combined determination to fight through and work through until the end—the end of militarism in Germany and Italy and Japan. Most certainly we shall not settle for less.

That is the spirit in which discussions have been conducted during the visit of the British Prime Minister to Washington. Mr. Churchill and I understand each other, our motives and our purposes. Together, during the past two weeks, we have faced squarely the major military and economic problems of this greatest world war.

All in our Nation have been cheered by Mr. Churchill's visit. We have been deeply stirred by his great message to us. He is welcome in our midst, and we unite in wishing him a safe return to his home.

For we are fighting on the same side with the British people, who fought alone for long, terrible months, and withstood the enemy with fortitude and tenacity and skill.

We are fighting on the same side with the Russian people who have seen the Nazi hordes swarm up to the very gates of Moscow, and who with almost superhuman will and courage have forced the invaders back into retreat.

We are fighting on the same side as the brave people of China—those millions who for four and a half long years have withstood bombs and starvation and have whipped the invaders time and again in spite of the superior Japanese equipment and arms. Yes, we are fighting on the same side as the indomitable Dutch. We are fighting on the same side as all the other Governments in exile, whom Hitler and all his armies and all his Gestapo have not been able to conquer.

But we of the United Nations are not making all this sacrifice of human effort and human lives to return to the kind of world we had after the last world war.

We are fighting today for security, for progress, and for peace, not only for ourselves but for all men, not only for one generation but for all generations. We are fighting to cleanse the world of ancient evils, ancient ills.

Our enemies are guided by brutal cynicism, by unholy contempt for the human race. We are inspired by a faith that goes back through all the years to the first chapter of the Book of Genesis: "God created man in His own image."

We on our side are striving to be true to that divine heritage. We are fighting, as our fathers have fought, to uphold the doctrine that all men are equal in the sight of

God. Those on the other side are striving to destroy this deep belief and to create a world in their own image—a world of tyranny and cruelty and serfdom.

That is the conflict that day and night now pervades our lives.

No compromise can end that conflict. There never has been—there never can be—successful compromise between good and evil. Only total victory can reward the champions of tolerance, and decency, and freedom, and faith.

State of the Union Address

January 7, 1943

When Franklin D. Roosevelt delivered his tenth State of the Union message, the country had been at war for just over a year. Roosevelt summarized the progress of the war over the course of 1942 and looked ahead to the type of peace he hoped would emerge after the war's end.

The United States had entered World War II after the Japanese attacked the U.S. naval base at Pearl Harbor in Hawaii on December 7, 1941—a date that "will live in infamy," as Roosevelt called it. The country was faced with a war not just against Japan in the Pacific, but also against Japan's Axis allies, Germany and Italy, in Europe and also North Africa.

Roosevelt painted a picture of gradually improving fortunes for America's allies, Great Britain, the Soviet Union, and China. One turning point, in early June 1942, was the battle of Midway Island in the Pacific, which Roosevelt termed "our most important victory in 1942" on the Pacific front. On the European front, in 1942 the Allies had launched what would ultimately become a successful campaign in North Africa, which preceded their 1943 attack on Sicily. "Yes, the Nazis and the Fascists have asked for it—and they are going to get it," Roosevelt declared.

At the start of the war, the United States needed to increase the size of its armed forces and its production of war equipment and supplies. In his address, Roosevelt spoke of the progress in both those areas. "I think the arsenal of democracy is making good," he said of the country's production.

In his 1941 State of the Union address, Roosevelt had spoken of "four freedoms"—of speech, of religion, from want, and from fear. In this address, the president returned to that theme, and focused specifically on freedom from want. Once the war ended, the returning troops and those who had been working in war production would need jobs, and he vowed that in postwar America, the government would provide "assurance against the evils of all major economic hazards."

He also urged a greater emphasis on worldwide economic stability, and said that while victory in war was the current goal, victory in peacetime would come next. Germany and Japan should "be disarmed and kept disarmed" after the war, he said.

The midterm congressional elections of 1942 had followed a typical pattern in that the president's party—in this case, the Democrats—had lost seats in both houses of Congress. While Democrats still formed a majority, conservative Southern Democrats combined with Republicans would make the president's life difficult over the next couple of years when it came to reform-minded legislation.

Mr. Vice President, Mr. Speaker, Members of the Seventy-eighth Congress:

This Seventy-eighth Congress assembles in one of the great moments in the history of the Nation. The past year was perhaps the most crucial for modern civilization; the coming year will be filled with violent conflicts—yet with high promise of better things.

We must appraise the events of 1942 according to their relative importance; we must exercise a sense of proportion.

First in importance in the American scene has been the inspiring proof of the great qualities of our fighting men. They have demonstrated these qualities in adversity as well as in victory. As long as our flag flies over this Capitol, Americans will honor the soldiers, sailors, and marines who fought our first battles of this war against over-whelming odds the heroes, living and dead, of Wake and Bataan and Guadalcanal, of the Java Sea and Midway and the North Atlantic convoys. Their unconquerable spirit will live forever.

By far the largest and most important developments in the whole world-wide strategic picture of 1942 were the events of the long fronts in Russia: first, the implacable defense of Stalingrad; and, second, the offensives by the Russian armies at various points that started in the latter part of November and which still roll on with great force and effectiveness.

The other major events of the year were: the series of Japanese advances in the Philippines, the East Indies, Malaya, and Burma; the stopping of that Japanese advance in the mid-Pacific, the South Pacific, and the Indian Oceans; the successful defense of the Near East by the British counterattack through Egypt and Libya; the American-British occupation of North Africa. Of continuing importance in the year 1942 were the unending and bitterly contested battles of the convoy routes, and the gradual passing of air superiority from the Axis to the United Nations.

The Axis powers knew that they must win the war in 1942—or eventually lose everything. I do not need to tell you that our enemies did not win the war in 1942.

In the Pacific area, our most important victory in 1942 was the air and naval battle off Midway Island. That action is historically important because it secured for our use communication lines stretching thousands of miles in every direction. In placing this emphasis on the Battle of Midway, I am not unmindful of other successful actions in the Pacific, in the air and on land and afloat—especially those on the Coral Sea and New Guinea and in the Solomon Islands. But these actions were essentially defensive. They were part of the delaying strategy that characterized this phase of the war.

During this period we inflicted steady losses upon the enemy—great losses of Japanese planes and naval vessels, transports and cargo ships. As early as one year ago, we set as a primary task in the war of the Pacific a day-by-day and week-by-week and month-by-month destruction of more Japanese war materials than Japanese industry could replace. Most certainly, that task has been and is being performed by our fighting ships and planes. And a large part of this task has been accomplished by the gallant crews of our American submarines who strike on the other side of the Pacific at Japanese ships—right up at the very mouth of the harbor of Yokohama.

We know that as each day goes by, Japanese strength in ships and planes is going down and down, and American strength in ships and planes is going up and up. And so I sometimes feel that the eventual outcome can now be put on a mathematical basis. That will become evident to the Japanese people themselves when we strike at their own home islands, and bomb them constantly from the air.

And in the attacks against Japan, we shall be joined with the heroic people of China—that great people whose ideals of peace are so closely akin to our own. Even today we are flying as much lend-lease material into China as ever traversed the Burma Road, flying it over mountains 17,000 feet high, flying blind through sleet and snow. We shall overcome all the formidable obstacles, and get the battle equipment into China to shatter the power of our common enemy. From this war, China will realize the security, the prosperity and the dignity, which Japan has sought so ruthlessly to destroy.

The period of our defensive attrition in the Pacific is drawing to a close. Now our aim is to force the Japanese to fight. Last year, we stopped them. This year, we intend to advance.

Turning now to the European theater of war, during this past year it was clear that our first task was to lessen the concentrated pressure on the Russian front by compelling Germany to divert part of her manpower and equipment to another theater of war. After months of secret planning and preparation in the utmost detail, an enormous amphibious expedition was embarked for French North Africa from the United States and the United Kingdom in literally hundreds of ships. It reached its objectives with very small losses, and has already produced an important effect upon the whole situation of the war. It has opened to attack what Mr. Churchill well described as "the under-belly of the Axis," and it has removed the always dangerous threat of an Axis attack through West Africa against the South Atlantic Ocean and the continent of South America itself.

The well-timed and splendidly executed offensive from Egypt by the British Eighth Army was a part of the same major strategy of the United Nations.

Great rains and appalling mud and very limited communications have delayed the final battles of Tunisia. The Axis is reinforcing its strong positions. But I am confident that though the fighting will be tough, when the final Allied assault is made, the last vestige of Axis power will be driven from the whole of the south shores of the Mediterranean.

Any review of the year 1942 must emphasize the magnitude and the diversity of the military activities in which this Nation has become engaged. As I speak to you, approximately one and a half million of our soldiers, sailors, marines, and fliers are in service outside of our continental limits, all through the world. Our merchant seamen, in addition, are carrying supplies to them and to our allies over every sea lane.

Few Americans realize the amazing growth of our air strength, though I am sure our enemy does. Day in and day out our forces are bombing the enemy and meeting him in combat on many different fronts in every part of the world. And for those who question the quality of our aircraft and the ability of our fliers, I point to the fact that, in Africa, we are shooting down two enemy planes to every one we lose, and in the Pacific and the Southwest Pacific we are shooting them down four to one.

We pay great tribute—the tribute of the United States of America—to the fighting men of Russia and China and Britain and the various members of the British Commonwealth—the millions of men who through the years of this war have fought our common enemies, and have denied to them the world conquest which they sought.

We pay tribute to the soldiers and fliers and seamen of others of the United Nations whose countries have been overrun by Axis hordes.

As a result of the Allied occupation of North Africa, powerful units of the French Army and Navy are going into action. They are in action with the United Nations forces. We welcome them as allies and as friends. They join with those Frenchmen who, since the dark days of June, 1940, have been fighting valiantly for the liberation of their stricken country.

We pay tribute to the fighting leaders of our allies, to Winston Churchill, to Joseph Stalin, and to the Generalissimo Chiang Kai-shek. Yes, there is a very great unanimity between the leaders of the United Nations. This unity is effective in planning and carrying out the major strategy of this war and in building up and in maintaining the lines of supplies.

I cannot prophesy. I cannot tell you when or where the United Nations are going to strike next in Europe. But we are going to strike—and strike hard. I cannot tell you whether we are going to hit them in Norway, or through the Low Countries, or in France, or through Sardinia or Sicily, or through the Balkans, or through Poland—or at several points simultaneously. But I can tell you that no matter where and when we strike by land, we and the British and the Russians will hit them from the air heavily and relentlessly. Day in and day out we shall heap tons upon tons of high explosives on their war factories and utilities and seaports.

Hitler and Mussolini will understand now the enormity of their miscalculations—that the Nazis would always have the advantage of superior air power as they did when they bombed Warsaw, and Rotterdam, and London and Coventry. That superiority has gone—forever.

Yes, the Nazis and the Fascists have asked for it—and they are going to get it.

Our forward progress in this war has depended upon our progress on the production front.

There has been criticism of the management and conduct of our war production. Much of this self-criticism has had a healthy effect. It has spurred us on. It has reflected a normal American impatience to get on with the job. We are the kind of people who are never quite satisfied with anything short of miracles.

But there has been some criticism based on guesswork and even on malicious falsification of fact. Such criticism creates doubts and creates fears, and weakens our total effort.

I do not wish to suggest that we should be completely satisfied with our production progress today, or next month, or ever. But I can report to you with genuine pride on what has been accomplished in 1942.

A year ago we set certain production goals for 1942 and for 1943. Some people, including some experts, thought that we had pulled some big figures out of a hat just to frighten the Axis. But we had confidence in the ability of our people to establish new records. And that confidence has been justified.

Of course, we realized that some production objectives would have to be changed—some of them adjusted upward, and others downward; some items would be taken out of the program altogether, and others added. This was inevitable as we gained battle experience, and as technological improvements were made.

Our 1942 airplane production and tank production fell short, numerically—stress the word numerically of the goals set a year ago. Nevertheless, we have plenty of reason to be proud of our record for 1942. We produced 48,000 military planes—more than the airplane production of Germany, Italy, and Japan put together. Last month, in December, we produced 5,500 military planes and the rate is rapidly rising. Furthermore, we must remember that as each month passes by, the averages of our types weigh more, take more man-hours to make, and have more striking power.

In tank production, we revised our schedule—and for good and sufficient reasons. As a result of hard experience in battle, we have diverted a portion of our tank-producing capacity to a stepped-up production of new, deadly field weapons, especially self-propelled artillery.

Here are some other production figures:

In 1942, we produced 56,000 combat vehicles, such as tanks and self-propelled artillery.

In 1942, we produced 670,000 machine guns, six times greater than our production in 1941 and three times greater than our total production during the year and a half of our participation in the first World War.

We produced 21,000 anti-tank guns, six times greater than our 1941 production.

We produced ten and a quarter billion rounds of small-arms ammunition, five times greater than our 1941 production and three times greater than our total production in the first World War.

We produced 181 million rounds of artillery ammunition, twelve times greater than our 1941 production and ten times greater than our total production in the first World War.

I think the arsenal of democracy is making good.

These facts and figures that I have given will give no great aid and comfort to the enemy. On the contrary, I can imagine that they will give him considerable discomfort. I suspect that Hitler and Tojo will find it difficult to explain to the German and Japanese people just why it is that "decadent, inefficient democracy" can produce such phenomenal quantities of weapons and munitions—and fighting men.

We have given the lie to certain misconceptions—which is an extremely polite word—especially the one which holds that the various blocs or groups within a free country cannot forego their political and economic differences in time of crisis and work together toward a common goal.

While we have been achieving this miracle of production, during the past year our armed forces have grown from a little over 2,000,000 to 7,000,000. In other words, we have withdrawn from the labor force and the farms some 5,000,000 of our younger workers. And in spite of this, our farmers have contributed their share to the common effort by producing the greatest quantity of food ever made available during a single year in all our history.

I wonder is there any person among us so simple as to believe that all this could have been done without creating some dislocations in our normal national life, some inconveniences, and even some hardships?

Who can have hoped to have done this without burdensome Government regulations which are a nuisance to everyone—including those who have the thankless task of administering them?

We all know that there have been mistakes—mistakes due to the inevitable process of trial and error inherent in doing big things for the first time. We all know that there have been too many complicated forms and questionnaires. I know about that. I have had to fill some of them out myself.

But we are determined to see to it that our supplies of food and other essential civilian goods are distributed on a fair and just basis—to rich and poor, management and labor, farmer and city dweller alike. We are determined to keep the cost of living at a stable level. All this has required much information. These forms and questionnaires represent an honest and sincere attempt by honest and sincere officials to obtain this information.

We have learned by the mistakes that we have made.

Our experience will enable us during the coming year to improve the necessary mechanisms of wartime economic controls, and to simplify administrative procedures. But we do not intend to leave things so lax that loopholes will be left for cheaters, for chiselers, or for the manipulators of the black market.

Of course, there have been disturbances and inconveniences—and even hardships. And there will be many, many more before we finally win. Yes, 1943 will not be an easy year for us on the home front. We shall feel in many ways in our daily lives the sharp pinch of total war.

Fortunately, there are only a few Americans who place appetite above patriotism. The overwhelming majority realize that the food we send abroad is for essential military purposes, for our own and Allied fighting forces, and for necessary help in areas that we occupy.

We Americans intend to do this great job together. In our common labors we must build and fortify the very foundation of national unity—confidence in one another.

It is often amusing, and it is sometimes politically profitable, to picture the City of Washington as a madhouse, with the Congress and the Administration disrupted with confusion and indecision and general incompetence.

However—what matters most in war is results. And the one pertinent fact is that after only a few years of preparation and only one year of warfare, we are able to engage, spiritually as well as physically, in the total waging of a total war.

Washington may be a madhouse—but only in the sense that it is the Capital City of a Nation which is fighting mad. And I think that Berlin and Rome and Tokyo, which had such contempt for the obsolete methods of democracy, would now gladly use all they could get of that same brand of madness.

And we must not forget that our achievements in production have been relatively no greater than those of the Russians and the British and the Chinese who have developed their own war industries under the incredible difficulties of battle conditions. They have had to continue work through bombings and blackouts. And they have never quit.

We Americans are in good, brave company in this war, and we are playing our own, honorable part in the vast common effort.

As spokesmen for the United States Government, you and I take off our hats to those responsible for our American production—to the owners, managers, and supervisors, to the draftsmen and the engineers, and to the workers—men and women—in factories and arsenals and shipyards and mines and mills and forests—and railroads and on highways.

We take off our hats to the farmers who have faced an unprecedented task of feeding not only a great Nation but a great part of the world.

We take off our hats to all the loyal, anonymous, untiring men and women who have worked in private employment and in Government and who have endured rationing and other stringencies with good humor and good will.

Yes, we take off our hats to all Americans who have contributed so magnificently to our common cause.

I have sought to emphasize a sense of proportion in this review of the events of the war and the needs of the war.

We should never forget the things we are fighting for. But, at this critical period of the war, we should confine ourselves to the larger objectives and not get bogged down in argument over methods and details.

We, and all the United Nations, want a decent peace and a durable peace. In the years between the end of the first World War and the beginning of the second World War, we were not living under a decent or a durable peace.

I have reason to know that our boys at the front are concerned with two broad aims beyond the winning of the war; and their thinking and their opinion coincide with what most Americans here back home are mulling over. They know, and we know, that it would be inconceivable—it would, indeed, be sacrilegious—if this Nation and the world did not attain some real, lasting good out of all these efforts and sufferings and bloodshed and death.

The men in our armed forces want a lasting peace, and, equally, they want permanent employment for themselves, their families, and their neighbors when they are mustered out at the end of the war.

Two years ago I spoke in my Annual Message of four freedoms. The blessings of two of them—freedom of speech and freedom of religion—are an essential part of the very life of this Nation; and we hope that these blessings will be granted to all men everywhere.

The people at home, and the people at the front, are wondering a little about the third freedom—freedom from want. To them it means that when they are mustered out, when war production is converted to the economy of peace, they will have the right to expect full employment—full employment for themselves and for all able-bodied men and women in America who want to work.

They expect the opportunity to work, to run their farms, their stores, to earn decent wages. They are eager to face the risks inherent in our system of free enterprise.

They do not want a postwar America which suffers from undernourishment or slums—or the dole. They want no get-rich-quick era of bogus "prosperity" which will end for them in selling apples on a street corner, as happened after the bursting of the boom in 1929.

When you talk with our young men and our young women, you will find they want to work for themselves and for their families; they consider that they have the right to work; and they know that after the last war their fathers did not gain that right.

When you talk with our young men and women, you will find that with the opportunity for employment they want assurance against the evils of all major economic hazards—assurance that will extend from the cradle to the grave. And this great Government can and must provide this assurance.

I have been told that this is no time to speak of a better America after the war. I am told it is a grave error on my part.

I dissent.

And if the security of the individual citizen, or the family, should become a subject of national debate, the country knows where I stand.

I say this now to this Seventy-eighth Congress, because it is wholly possible that freedom from want—the right of employment, the right of assurance against life's hazards—will loom very large as a task of America during the coming two years.

I trust it will not be regarded as an issue—but rather as a task for all of us to study sympathetically, to work out with a constant regard for the attainment of the objective, with fairness to all and with injustice to none.

In this war of survival we must keep before our minds not only the evil things we fight against but the good things we are fighting for. We fight to retain a great past—and we fight to gain a greater future.

Let us remember, too, that economic safety for the America of the future is threatened unless a greater economic stability comes to the rest of the world. We cannot make America an island in either a military or an economic sense. Hitlerism, like any other form of crime or disease, can grow from the evil seeds of economic as well as military feudalism.

Victory in this war is the first and greatest goal before us. Victory in the peace is the next. That means striving toward the enlargement of the security of man here and throughout the world—and, finally, striving for the fourth freedom—freedom from fear.

It is of little account for any of us to talk of essential human needs, of attaining security, if we run the risk of another World War in ten or twenty or fifty years. That is just plain common sense. Wars grow in size, in death and destruction, and in the inevitability of engulfing all Nations, in inverse ratio to the shrinking size of the world as a result of the conquest of the air. I shudder to think of what will happen to humanity, including ourselves, if this war ends in an inconclusive peace, and another war breaks out when the babies of today have grown to fighting age.

Every normal American prays that neither he nor his sons nor his grandsons will be compelled to go through this horror again.

Undoubtedly a few Americans, even now, think that this Nation can end this war comfortably and then climb back into an American hole and pull the hole in after them.

But we have learned that we can never dig a hole so deep that it would be safe against predatory animals. We have also learned that if we do not pull the fangs of the predatory animals of this world, they will multiply and grow in strength—and they will be at our throats again once more in a short generation.

Most Americans realize more clearly than ever before that modern war equipment in the hands of aggressor Nations can bring danger overnight to our own national existence or to that of any other Nation—or island—or continent.

It is clear to us that if Germany and Italy and Japan—or any one of them—remain armed at the end of this war, or are permitted to rearm, they will again, and inevitably, embark upon an ambitious career of world conquest. They must be disarmed and kept disarmed, and they must abandon the philosophy, and the teaching of that philosophy, which has brought so much suffering to the world.

After the first World War we tried to achieve a formula for permanent peace, based on a magnificent idealism. We failed. But, by our failure, we have learned that we cannot maintain peace at this stage of human development by good intentions alone.

Today the United Nations are the mightiest military coalition in all history. They represent an overwhelming majority of the population of the world. Bound together in solemn agreement that they themselves will not commit acts of aggression or conquest against any of their neighbors, the United Nations can and must remain united for the maintenance of peace by preventing any attempt to rearm in Germany, in Japan, in Italy, or in any other Nation which seeks to violate the Tenth Commandment—"Thou shalt not covet."

There are cynics, there are skeptics who say it cannot be done. The American people and all the freedom-loving peoples of this earth are now demanding that it must be done. And the will of these people shall prevail.

The very philosophy of the Axis powers is based on a profound contempt for the human race. If, in the formation of our future policy, we were guided by the same cynical contempt, then we should be surrendering to the philosophy of our enemies, and our victory would turn to defeat.

The issue of this war is the basic issue between those who believe in mankind and those who do not—the ancient issue between those who put their faith in the people and those who put their faith in dictators and tyrants. There have always been those who did not believe in the people, who attempted to block their forward movement across history, to force them back to servility and suffering and silence.

The people have now gathered their strength. They are moving forward in their might and power—and no force, no combination of forces, no trickery, deceit, or violence, can stop them now. They see before them the hope of the world—a decent, secure, peaceful life for men everywhere.

I do not prophesy when this war will end.

But I do believe that this year of 1943 will give to the United Nations a very substantial advance along the roads that lead to Berlin and Rome and Tokyo.

I tell you it is within the realm of possibility that this Seventy-eight Congress may have the historic privilege of helping greatly to save the world from future fear.

Therefore, let us all have confidence, let us redouble our efforts.

A tremendous, costly, long-enduring task in peace as well as in war is still ahead of us.

But, as we face that continuing task, we may know that the state of this Nation is good—the heart of this Nation is sound—the spirit of this Nation is strong—the faith of this Nation is eternal.

Franklin D. Roosevelt, 1941–1945

State of the Union Message
January 11, 1944

Franklin D. Roosevelt's 1944 State of the Union address was delivered in the midst of a war—and at the start of a presidential election year. In the address, the president discussed his goals for a future peace and also laid out a bold agenda for an "economic bill of rights" for Americans.

Roosevelt already had been in office for three terms—more than any other president—but it was clear as 1944 progressed that he would seek another term. Because he was suffering from the flu, Roosevelt sent a written message to Congress on January 11, but later addressed the nation via radio stating that he was, "anxious that the American people be given an opportunity to hear what I have recommended to the Congress for this very fateful year in our history."

The president stated that "the one supreme objective for the future" was security—physical, economic, social, and moral—and added that for a peaceful future world, a decent standard of living in all countries was a prerequisite.

At home, Roosevelt called for an "all out" effort to win the war, while also creating economic stability and fairness. The economic bill of rights that Roosevelt unveiled included taxes on "unreasonable profits" and a national service law that would make "every able-bodied adult" in the country "available for war production or for any other essential services." He also called for legislation that would give troops serving away from home the right to vote.

Although Congress was controlled by Roosevelt's Democratic Party, he often faced difficulties with lawmakers; the combination of Republicans and conservative Southern Democrats was a powerful force, one that did not see eye-to-eye with the president on much of his domestic agenda.

Roosevelt, who had called for tax legislation in his speech, ended up vetoing a tax bill that called for far less revenue than he had sought; Congress overrode his veto. Congress did not approve national-service legislation. It did pass legislation giving troops the right to vote, but the bill was far weaker than Roosevelt would have wanted; it became law without his signature.

Roosevelt did win another term in 1944, defeating Republican nominee Thomas E. Dewey, the forty-two-year-old governor of New York. One issue in the campaign was the president's health, but the sixty-two-year-old Roosevelt overcame that concern with a show of strength. He won 432 electoral votes to Dewey's 99, and 53.4 percent of the popular vote to Dewey's 45.9 percent. However, the president died in April 1945, less than three months into his fourth term, and did not live to see the end of World War II.

To the Congress:

This Nation in the past two years has become an active partner in the world's greatest war against human slavery.

We have joined with like-minded people in order to defend ourselves in a world that has been gravely threatened with gangster rule.

But I do not think that any of us Americans can be content with mere survival. Sacrifices that we and our allies are making impose upon us all a sacred obligation to see to it that out of this war we and our children will gain something better than mere survival.

We are united in determination that this war shall not be followed by another interim which leads to new disaster—that we shall not repeat the tragic errors of ostrich isolationism—that we shall not repeat the excesses of the wild twenties when this Nation went for a joy ride on a roller coaster which ended in a tragic crash.

When Mr. [Cordell] Hull went to Moscow in October, and when I went to Cairo and Teheran in November, we knew that we were in agreement with our allies in our common determination to fight and win this war. But there were many vital questions concerning the future peace, and they were discussed in an atmosphere of complete candor and harmony.

In the last war such discussions, such meetings, did not even begin until the shooting had stopped and the delegates began to assemble at the peace table. There had been no previous opportunities for man-to-man discussions which lead to meetings of minds. The result was a peace which was not a peace.

That was a mistake which we are not repeating in this war.

And right here I want to address a word or two to some suspicious souls who are fearful that Mr. Hull or I have made "commitments" for the future which might pledge this Nation to secret treaties, or to enacting the role of Santa Claus.

To such suspicious souls—using a polite terminology—I wish to say that Mr. Churchill, and Marshal Stalin, and Generalissimo Chiang Kai-shek are all thoroughly conversant with the provisions of our Constitution. And so is Mr. Hull. And so am I.

Of course we made some commitments. We most certainly committed ourselves to very large and very specific military plans which require the use of all Allied forces to bring about the defeat of our enemies at the earliest possible time.

But there were no secret treaties or political or financial commitments.

The one supreme objective for the future, which we discussed for each Nation individually, and for all the United Nations, can be summed up in one word: Security.

And that means not only physical security which provides safety from attacks by aggressors. It means also economic security, social security, moral security—in a family of Nations.

In the plain down-to-earth talks that I had with the Generalissimo and Marshal Stalin and Prime Minister Churchill, it was abundantly clear that they are all most deeply interested in the resumption of peaceful progress by their own peoples—progress toward a better life. All our allies want freedom to develop their lands and resources, to build up industry, to increase education and individual opportunity, and to raise standards of living.

All our allies have learned by bitter experience that real development will not be possible if they are to be diverted from their purpose by repeated wars—or even threats of war.

China and Russia are truly united with Britain and America in recognition of this essential fact:

The best interests of each Nation, large and small, demand that all freedom-loving Nations shall join together in a just and durable system of peace. In the present world situation, evidenced by the actions of Germany, Italy, and Japan, unquestioned military control over disturbers of the peace is as necessary among Nations as it is among citizens in a community. And an equally basic essential to peace is a decent standard of living for all individual men and women and children in all Nations. Freedom from fear is eternally linked with freedom from want.

There are people who burrow through our Nation like unseeing moles, and attempt to spread the suspicion that if other Nations are encouraged to raise their standards of living, our own American standard of living must of necessity be depressed.

The fact is the very contrary. It has been shown time and again that if the standard of living of any country goes up, so does its purchasing power—and that such a rise encourages a better standard of living in neighboring countries with whom it trades. That is just plain common sense—and it is the kind of plain common sense that provided the basis for our discussions at Moscow, Cairo, and Teheran.

Returning from my journeyings, I must confess to a sense of "let-down" when I found many evidences of faulty perspective here in Washington. The faulty perspective consists in overemphasizing lesser problems and thereby underemphasizing the first and greatest problem.

The overwhelming majority of our people have met the demands of this war with magnificent courage and understanding. They have accepted inconveniences; they have accepted hardships; they have accepted tragic sacrifices. And they are ready and eager to make whatever further contributions are needed to win the war as quickly as possible—if only they are given the chance to know what is required of them.

However, while the majority goes on about its great work without complaint, a noisy minority maintains an uproar of demands for special favors for special groups. There are pests who swarm through the lobbies of the Congress and the cocktail bars of Washington, representing these special groups as opposed to the basic interests of the Nation as a whole. They have come to look upon the war primarily as a chance to make profits for themselves at the expense of their neighbors—profits in money or in terms of political or social preferment.

Such selfish agitation can be highly dangerous in wartime. It creates confusion. It damages morale. It hampers our national effort. It muddies the waters and therefore prolongs the war.

If we analyze American history impartially, we cannot escape the fact that in our past we have not always forgotten individual and selfish and partisan interests in time of war—we have not always been united in purpose and direction. We cannot overlook the serious dissensions and the lack of unity in our war of the Revolution, in our War of 1812, or in our War Between the States, when the survival of the Union itself was at stake.

In the first World War we came closer to national unity than in any previous war. But that war lasted only a year and a half, and increasing signs of disunity began to appear during the final months of the conflict.

In this war, we have been compelled to learn how interdependent upon each other are all groups and sections of the population of America.

Increased food costs, for example, will bring new demands for wage increases from all war workers, which will in turn raise all prices of all things including those things which the farmers themselves have to buy. Increased wages or prices will each in turn produce the same results. They all have a particularly disastrous result on all fixed income groups.

And I hope you will remember that all of us in this Government represent the fixed income group just as much as we represent business owners, workers, and farmers. This group of fixed income people includes: teachers, clergy, policemen, firemen, widows and minors on fixed incomes, wives and dependents of our soldiers and sailors, and old-age pensioners. They and their families add up to one-quarter of our one hundred and thirty million people. They have few or no high pressure representatives at the Capitol. In a period of gross inflation they would be the worst sufferers.

If ever there was a time to subordinate individual or group selfishness to the national good, that time is now. Disunity at home—bickerings, self-seeking partisanship, stoppages of work, inflation, business as usual, politics as usual, luxury as usual—these are the influences which can undermine the morale of the brave men ready to die at the front for us here.

Those who are doing most of the complaining are not deliberately striving to sabotage the national war effort. They are laboring under the delusion that the time is past when we must make prodigious sacrifices—that the war is already won and we can begin to slacken off. But the dangerous folly of that point of view can be measured by the distance that separates our troops from their ultimate objectives in Berlin and Tokyo—and by the sum of all the perils that lie along the way.

Overconfidence and complacency are among our deadliest enemies. Last spring—after notable victories at Stalingrad and in Tunisia and against the U-boats on the high seas—overconfidence became so pronounced that war production fell off. In two months, June and July, 1943, more than a thousand airplanes that could have been made and should have been made were not made. Those who failed to make them were not on strike. They were merely saying, "The war's in the bag—so let's relax."

That attitude on the part of anyone—Government or management or labor—can lengthen this war. It can kill American boys.

Let us remember the lessons of 1918. In the summer of that year the tide turned in favor of the allies. But this Government did not relax. In fact, our national effort was stepped up. In August, 1918, the draft age limits were broadened from 21–31 to 18–45. The President called for "force to the utmost," and his call was heeded. And in November, only three months later, Germany surrendered.

That is the way to fight and win a war—all out—and not with half-an-eye on the battlefronts abroad and the other eye-and-a-half on personal, selfish, or political interests here at home.

Therefore, in order to concentrate all our energies and resources on winning the war, and to maintain a fair and stable economy at home, I recommend that the Congress adopt:

(1) A realistic tax law—which will tax all unreasonable profits, both individual and corporate, and reduce the ultimate cost of the war to our sons and daughters. The tax bill now under consideration by the Congress does not begin to meet this test.

(2) A continuation of the law for the renegotiation of war contracts—which will prevent exorbitant profits and assure fair prices to the Government. For two long years I have pleaded with the Congress to take undue profits out of war.

(3) A cost of food law—which will enable the Government (a) to place a reasonable floor under the prices the farmer may expect for his production; and (b) to place a ceiling on the prices a consumer will have to pay for the food he buys. This should apply to necessities only; and will require public funds to carry out. It will cost in appropriations about one percent of the present annual cost of the war.

(4) Early reenactment of the stabilization statute of October, 1942. This expires June 30, 1944, and if it is not extended well in advance, the country might just as well expect price chaos by summer.

We cannot have stabilization by wishful thinking. We must take positive action to maintain the integrity of the American dollar.

(5) A national service law—which, for the duration of the war, will prevent strikes, and, with certain appropriate exceptions, will make available for war production or for any other essential services every able-bodied adult in this Nation.

These five measures together form a just and equitable whole. I would not recommend a national service law unless the other laws were passed to keep down the cost of living, to share equitably the burdens of taxation, to hold the stabilization line, and to prevent undue profits.

The Federal Government already has the basic power to draft capital and property of all kinds for war purposes on a basis of just compensation.

As you know, I have for three years hesitated to recommend a national service act. Today, however, I am convinced of its necessity. Although I believe that we and our allies can win the war without such a measure, I am certain that nothing less than total mobilization of all our resources of manpower and capital will guarantee an earlier victory, and reduce the toll of suffering and sorrow and blood.

I have received a joint recommendation for this law from the heads of the War Department, the Navy Department, and the Maritime Commission. These are the men who bear responsibility for the procurement of the necessary arms and equipment, and for the successful prosecution of the war in the field. They say:

"When the very life of the Nation is in peril the responsibility for service is common to all men and women. In such a time there can be no discrimination between the men and women who are assigned by the Government to its defense at the battlefront and the men and women assigned to producing the vital materials essential to successful military operations. A prompt enactment of a National Service Law would be merely an expression of the universality of this responsibility."

I believe the country will agree that those statements are the solemn truth.

National service is the most democratic way to wage a war. Like selective service for the armed forces, it rests on the obligation of each citizen to serve his Nation to his utmost where he is best qualified.

It does not mean reduction in wages. It does not mean loss of retirement and seniority rights and benefits. It does not mean that any substantial numbers of war workers will be disturbed in their present jobs. Let these facts be wholly clear.

Experience in other democratic Nations at war—Britain, Canada, Australia, and New Zealand—has shown that the very existence of national service makes unnecessary the widespread use of compulsory power. National service has proven to be a unifying moral force based on an equal and comprehensive legal obligation of all people in a Nation at war.

There are millions of American men and women who are not in this war at all. It is not because they do not want to be in it. But they want to know where they can best do their share. National service provides that direction. It will be a means by which every man and woman can find that inner satisfaction which comes from making the fullest possible contribution to victory.

I know that all civilian war workers will be glad to be able to say many years hence to their grandchildren: "Yes, I, too, was in service in the great war. I was on duty in an airplane factory, and I helped make hundreds of fighting planes. The Government told me that in doing that I was performing my most useful work in the service of my country."

It is argued that we have passed the stage in the war where national service is necessary. But our soldiers and sailors know that this is not true. We are going forward on a long, rough road—and, in all journeys, the last miles are the hardest. And it is for that final effort—for the total defeat of our enemies—that we must mobilize our total resources. The national war program calls for the employment of more people in 1944 than in 1943.

It is my conviction that the American people will welcome this win-the-war measure which is based on the eternally just principle of "fair for one, fair for all."

It will give our people at home the assurance that they are standing four-square behind our soldiers and sailors. And it will give our enemies demoralizing assurance that we mean business—that we, 130,000,000 Americans, are on the march to Rome, Berlin, and Tokyo.

I hope that the Congress will recognize that, although this is a political year, national service is an issue which transcends politics. Great power must be used for great purposes.

As to the machinery for this measure, the Congress itself should determine its nature—but it should be wholly nonpartisan in its make-up.

Our armed forces are valiantly fulfilling their responsibilities to our country and our people. Now the Congress faces the responsibility for taking those measures which are essential to national security in this the most decisive phase of the Nation's greatest war.

Several alleged reasons have prevented the enactment of legislation which would preserve for our soldiers and sailors and marines the fundamental prerogative of citizenship—the right to vote. No amount of legalistic argument can becloud this issue in the eyes of these ten million American citizens. Surely the signers of the Constitution did not intend a document which, even in wartime, would be construed to take away the franchise of any of those who are fighting to preserve the Constitution itself.

Our soldiers and sailors and marines know that the overwhelming majority of them will be deprived of the opportunity to vote, if the voting machinery is left exclusively to the States under existing State laws—and that there is no likelihood of these laws being changed in time to enable them to vote at the next election. The Army and Navy have reported that it will be impossible effectively to administer forty-eight different soldier voting laws. It is the duty of the Congress to remove this unjustifiable discrimination against the men and women in our armed forces—and to do it as quickly as possible.

It is our duty now to begin to lay the plans and determine the strategy for the winning of a lasting peace and the establishment of an American standard of living higher than ever before known. We cannot be content, no matter how high that general standard of living may be, if some fraction of our people—whether it be one-third or one-fifth or one-tenth—is ill-fed, ill-clothed, ill housed, and insecure.

This Republic had its beginning, and grew to its present strength, under the protection of certain inalienable political rights—among them the right of free speech, free press, free worship, trial by jury, freedom from unreasonable searches and seizures. They were our rights to life and liberty.

As our Nation has grown in size and stature, however—as our industrial economy expanded—these political rights proved inadequate to assure us equality in the pursuit of happiness.

We have come to a clear realization of the fact that true individual freedom cannot exist without economic security and independence. "Necessitous men are not free men." People who are hungry and out of a job are the stuff of which dictatorships are made.

In our day these economic truths have become accepted as self-evident. We have accepted, so to speak, a second Bill of Rights under which a new basis of security and prosperity can be established for all regardless of station, race, or creed.

Among these are:

The right to a useful and remunerative job in the industries or shops or farms or mines of the Nation;

The right to earn enough to provide adequate food and clothing and recreation;

The right of every farmer to raise and sell his products at a return which will give him and his family a decent living;

The right of every businessman, large and small, to trade in an atmosphere of freedom from unfair competition and domination by monopolies at home or abroad;

The right of every family to a decent home;

The right to adequate medical care and the opportunity to achieve and enjoy good health;

The right to adequate protection from the economic fears of old age, sickness, accident, and unemployment;

The right to a good education.

All of these rights spell security. And after this war is won we must be prepared to move forward, in the implementation of these rights, to new goals of human happiness and well-being.

America's own rightful place in the world depends in large part upon how fully these and similar rights have been carried into practice for our citizens. For unless there is security here at home there cannot be lasting peace in the world.

One of the great American industrialists of our day—a man who has rendered yeoman service to his country in this crisis—recently emphasized the grave dangers of "rightist reaction" in this Nation. All clear-thinking businessmen share his concern. Indeed, if such reaction should develop—if history were to repeat itself and we were to return to the so-called "normalcy" of the 1920's—then it is certain that even though we shall have conquered our enemies on the battlefields abroad, we shall have yielded to the spirit of Fascism here at home.

I ask the Congress to explore the means for implementing this economic bill of rights—for it is definitely the responsibility of the Congress so to do. Many of these problems are already before committees of the Congress in the form of proposed legislation. I shall from time to time communicate with the Congress with respect to these and further proposals. In the event that no adequate program of progress is evolved, I am certain that the Nation will be conscious of the fact.

Our fighting men abroad—and their families at home—expect such a program and have the right to insist upon it. It is to their demands that this Government should pay heed rather than to the whining demands of selfish pressure groups who seek to feather their nests while young Americans are dying.

The foreign policy that we have been following—the policy that guided us at Moscow, Cairo, and Teheran—is based on the common sense principle which was best expressed by Benjamin Franklin on July 4, 1776: "We must all hang together, or assuredly we shall all hang separately."

I have often said that there are no two fronts for America in this war. There is only one front. There is one line of unity which extends from the hearts of the people at home to the men of our attacking forces in our farthest outposts. When we speak of our total effort, we speak of the factory and the field, and the mine as well as of the battleground—we speak of the soldier and the civilian, the citizen and his Government.

Each and every one of us has a solemn obligation under God to serve this Nation in its most critical hour—to keep this Nation great—to make this Nation greater in a better world.

Franklin D. Roosevelt, 1941–1945

State of the Union Message
January 6, 1945

Franklin D. Roosevelt's last State of the Union message was written at the end of his third term as president, just two weeks before he was sworn in for a fourth term. It was a lengthy message, which Roosevelt did not deliver in person before Congress. Instead, he addressed the nation via radio with a summary of his key points.

World War II was still ongoing in January 1945. In his address, Roosevelt vowed that the Allies would continue fighting until "ultimate total victory" was achieved. The president summarized the war to date, including actions in Europe and the Pacific, and sought to reassure the nation that the United States and its allies had successfully overcome the adversity of German counterattacks the previous month.

Roosevelt also urged still more increases in production of war materials, and called for 20,000 more nurses to enter the armed forces. And as he had in his 1944 message, he called for a national service law that would mobilize workers for war production efforts.

A month after this 1945 State of the Union message, the president met in Yalta, in the Crimea, with British prime minister Winston Churchill and Soviet leader Joseph Stalin, to discuss wartime and postwar aims. The three leaders also had met in 1943 in Tehran. In his 1945 message, Roosevelt discussed the type of peace he sought, which included the principles of the Atlantic Charter, which he and Churchill had signed in 1941. These included political self-determination of nations, as well as international cooperation. Roosevelt noted that differences among the soon-to-be victors already were present; he presaged the coming of the Cold War, which pitted the United States against the Soviet Union, one of its World War II allies.

The president also spoke in favor of full employment in a postwar America, and he downplayed differences between the Executive and Congress; the president had faced some difficulties with Congress on domestic issues, although both the House and Senate were controlled by Democrats, Roosevelt's party.

Roosevelt would die just three months after writing this speech. On April 12, while at his vacation home in Warm Springs, Georgia, he had a cerebral hemorrhage. He remains the longest-serving U.S. President, and his administration, which lasted from 1933 to 1945, spanned both the Great Depression of the 1930s and World War II. During his time in the White House, the size and scope of the federal government increased immensely, as did the power of the presidency itself.

To the Congress:

In considering the State of the Union, the war and the peace that is to follow are naturally uppermost in the minds of all of us.

This war must be waged—it is being waged—with the greatest and most persistent intensity. Everything we are and have is at stake. Everything we are and have will be given. American men, fighting far from home, have already won victories which the world will never forget.

We have no question of the ultimate victory. We have no question of the cost. Our losses will be heavy.

We and our allies will go on fighting together to ultimate total victory.

We have seen a year marked, on the whole, by substantial progress toward victory, even though the year ended with a setback for our arms, when the Germans launched a ferocious counter-attack into Luxembourg and Belgium with the obvious objective of cutting our line in the center.

Our men have fought with indescribable and unforgettable gallantry under most difficult conditions, and our German enemies have sustained considerable losses while failing to obtain their objectives.

The high tide of this German effort was reached two days after Christmas. Since then we have reassumed the offensive, rescued the isolated garrison at Bastogne, and forced a German withdrawal along the whole line of the salient. The speed with which we recovered from this savage attack was largely possible because we have one supreme commander in complete control of all the Allied armies in France. General Eisenhower has faced this period of trial with admirable calm and resolution and with steadily increasing success. He has my complete confidence.

Further desperate attempts may well be made to break our lines, to slow our progress. We must never make the mistake of assuming that the Germans are beaten until the last Nazi has surrendered.

And I would express another most serious warning against the poisonous effects of enemy propaganda.

The wedge that the Germans attempted to drive in western Europe was less dangerous in actual terms of winning the war than the wedges which they are continually attempting to drive between ourselves and our allies.

Every little rumor which is intended to weaken our faith in our allies is like an actual enemy agent in our midst—seeking to sabotage our war effort. There are, here and there, evil and baseless rumors against the Russians—rumors against the British—rumors against our own American commanders in the field.

When you examine these rumors closely, you will observe that every one of them bears the same trade-mark—"Made in Germany."

We must resist this divisive propaganda—we must destroy it—with the same strength and the same determination that our fighting men are displaying as they resist and destroy the panzer divisions.

In Europe, we shall resume the attack and—despite temporary setbacks here or there—we shall continue the attack relentlessly until Germany is completely defeated.

It is appropriate at this time to review the basic strategy which has guided us through three years of war, and which will lead, eventually, to total victory.

The tremendous effort of the first years of this war was directed toward the concentration of men and supplies in the various theaters of action at the points where they could hurt our enemies most.

It was an effort—in the language of the military men—of deployment of our forces. Many battles—essential battles—were fought; many victories—vital victories—were won. But these battles and these victories were fought and won to hold back the attacking enemy, and to put us in positions from which we and our allies could deliver the final, decisive blows.

In the beginning our most important military task was to prevent our enemies— the strongest and most violently aggressive powers that ever have threatened civilization—from winning decisive victories. But even while we were conducting defensive, delaying actions, we were looking forward to the time when we could wrest the initiative from our enemies and place our superior resources of men and materials into direct competition with them.

It was plain then that the defeat of either enemy would require the massing of overwhelming forces—ground, sea, and air—in positions from which we and our allies could strike directly against the enemy homelands and destroy the Nazi and Japanese war machines.

In the case of Japan, we had to await the completion of extensive preliminary operations—operations designed to establish secure supply lines through the Japanese outer-zone defenses. This called for overwhelming sea power and air power—supported by ground forces strategically employed against isolated outpost garrisons.

Always—from the very day we were attacked—it was right militarily as well as morally to reject the arguments of those shortsighted people who would have had us throw Britain and Russia to the Nazi wolves and concentrate against the Japanese. Such people urged that we fight a purely defensive war against Japan while allowing the domination of all the rest of the world by Nazism and Fascism.

In the European theater the necessary bases for the massing of ground and air power against Germany were already available in Great Britain. In the Mediterranean area we could begin ground operations against major elements of the German Army as rapidly as we could put troops in the field, first in North Africa and then in Italy.

Therefore, our decision was made to concentrate the bulk of our ground and air forces against Germany until her utter defeat. That decision was based on all these factors; and it was also based on the realization that, of our two enemies, Germany would be more able to digest quickly her conquests, the more able quickly to convert the manpower and resources of her conquered territory into a war potential.

We had in Europe two active and indomitable allies—Britain and the Soviet Union—and there were also the heroic resistance movements in the occupied countries, constantly engaging and harassing the Germans. We cannot forget how Britain held the line, alone, in 1940 and 1941; and at the same time, despite ferocious bombardment from the air, built up a tremendous armaments industry which enabled her to take the offensive at El Alamein in 1942.

We cannot forget the heroic defense of Moscow and Leningrad and Stalingrad, or the tremendous Russian offensives of 1943 and 1944 which destroyed formidable German armies.

Nor can we forget how, for more than seven long years, the Chinese people have been sustaining the barbarous attacks of the Japanese and containing large enemy forces on the vast areas of the Asiatic mainland.

In the future we must never forget the lesson that we have learned—that we must have friends who will work with us in peace as they have fought at our side in war.

As a result of the combined effort of the Allied forces, great military victories were achieved in 1944: The liberation of France, Belgium, Greece, and parts of The Netherlands, Norway, Poland, Yugoslavia, and Czechoslovakia; the surrender of Rumania and Bulgaria; the invasion of Germany itself and Hungary; the steady march through the Pacific islands to the Philippines, Guam, and Saipan; and the beginnings of a mighty air offensive against the Japanese islands.

Now, as this Seventy-ninth Congress meets, we have reached the most critical phase of the war.

The greatest victory of the last year was, of course, the successful breach on June 6, 1944, of the German "impregnable" seawall of Europe and the victorious sweep of the Allied forces through France and Belgium and Luxembourg—almost to the Rhine itself.

The cross-channel invasion of the Allied armies was the greatest amphibious operation in the history of the world. It overshadowed all other operations in this or any other war in its immensity. Its success is a tribute to the fighting courage of the soldiers who stormed the beaches—to the sailors and merchant seamen who put the soldiers ashore and kept them supplied—and to the military and naval leaders who achieved a real miracle of planning and execution. And it is also a tribute to the ability of two Nations, Britain and America, to plan together, and work together, and fight together in perfect cooperation and perfect harmony.

This cross-channel invasion was followed in August by a second great amphibious operation, landing troops in southern France. In this, the same cooperation and the same harmony existed between the American, French, and other Allied forces based in North Africa and Italy.

The success of the two invasions is a tribute also to the ability of many men and women to maintain silence, when a few careless words would have imperiled the lives of hundreds of thousands, and would have jeopardized the whole vast undertakings.

These two great operations were made possible by success in the Battle of the Atlantic.

Without this success over German submarines, we could not have built up our invasion forces or air forces in Great Britain, nor could we have kept a steady stream of supplies flowing to them after they had landed in France.

The Nazis, however, may succeed in improving their submarines and their crews. They have recently increased their U-boat activity. The Battle of the Atlantic—like all campaigns in this war—demands eternal vigilance. But the British, Canadian, and other Allied navies, together with our own, are constantly on the alert.

The tremendous operations in western Europe have overshadowed in the public mind the less spectacular but vitally important Italian front. Its place in the strategic conduct of the war in Europe has been obscured, and—by some people unfortunately—underrated.

It is important that any misconception on that score be corrected—now.

What the Allied forces in Italy are doing is a well-considered part in our strategy in Europe, now aimed at only one objective—the total defeat of the Germans. These valiant forces in Italy are continuing to keep a substantial portion of the German Army under constant pressure—including some 20 first-line German divisions and the necessary supply and transport and replacement troops—all of which our enemies need so badly elsewhere.

Over very difficult terrain and through adverse weather conditions, our Fifth Army and the British Eighth Army—reinforced by units from other United Nations, including a brave and well equipped unit of the Brazilian Army—have, in the past year, pushed north through bloody Cassino and the Anzio beachhead, and through Rome until now they occupy heights overlooking the valley of the Po.

The greatest tribute which can be paid to the courage and fighting ability of these splendid soldiers in Italy is to point out that although their strength is about equal to that of the Germans they oppose, the Allies have been continuously on the offensive.

That pressure, that offensive, by our troops in Italy will continue.

The American people—and every soldier now fighting in the Apennines—should remember that the Italian front has not lost any of the importance which it had in the days when it was the only Allied front in Europe.

In the Pacific during the past year, we have conducted the fastest-moving offensive in the history of modern warfare. We have driven the enemy back more than 3,000 miles across the Central Pacific. A year ago, our conquest of Tarawa was a little more than a month old.

A year ago, we were preparing for our invasion of Kwajalein, the second of our great strides across the Central Pacific to the Philippines.

A year ago, General MacArthur was still fighting in New Guinea almost 1,500 miles from his present position in the Philippine Islands.

We now have firmly established bases in the Mariana Islands, from which our Super fortresses bomb Tokyo itself—and will continue to blast Japan in ever-increasing numbers.

Japanese forces in the Philippines have been cut in two. There is still hard fighting ahead—costly fighting. But the liberation of the Philippines will mean that Japan has been largely cut off from her conquests in the East Indies.

The landing of our troops on Leyte was the largest amphibious operation thus far conducted in the Pacific.

Moreover, these landings drew the Japanese Fleet into the first great sea battle which Japan has risked in almost two years. Not since the night engagements around Guadalcanal in November–December, 1942, had our Navy been able to come to grips with major units of the Japanese Fleet. We had brushed against their fleet in the first battle of the Philippine Sea in June, 1944, but not until last October were we able really to engage a major portion of the Japanese Navy in actual combat. The naval engagement which raged for three days was the heaviest blow ever struck against Japanese sea power.

As a result of that battle, much of what is left of the Japanese Fleet has been driven behind the screen of islands that separates the Yellow Sea, the China Sea, and the Sea of Japan from the Pacific.

Our Navy looks forward to any opportunity which the lords of the Japanese Navy will give us to fight them again.

The people of this Nation have a right to be proud of the courage and fighting ability of the men in the armed forces—on all fronts. They also have a right to be proud of American leadership which has guided their sons into battle.

The history of the generalship of this war has been a history of teamwork and cooperation, of skill and daring. Let me give you one example out of last year's operations in the Pacific.

Last September Admiral Halsey led American naval task forces into Philippine waters and north to the East China Sea, and struck heavy blows at Japanese air and sea power.

At that time it was our plan to approach the Philippines by further stages, taking islands which we may call A, C, and E. However, Admiral Halsey reported that a direct attack on Leyte appeared feasible. When General MacArthur received the reports from Admiral Halsey's task forces, he also concluded that it might be possible to attack the Japanese in the Philippines directly—bypassing islands A, C, and E.

Admiral Nimitz thereupon offered to make available to General MacArthur several divisions which had been scheduled to take the intermediate objectives. These discussions, conducted at great distances, all took place in one day.

General MacArthur immediately informed the Joint Chiefs of Staff here in Washington that he was prepared to initiate plans for an attack on Leyte in October. Approval of the change in plan was given on the same day.

Thus, within the space of 24 hours, a major change of plans was accomplished which involved Army and Navy forces from two different theaters of operations—a change which hastened the liberation of the Philippines and the final day of victory—a change which saved lives which would have been expended in the capture of islands which are now neutralized far behind our lines.

Our over-all strategy has not neglected the important task of rendering all possible aid to China. Despite almost insuperable difficulties, we increased this aid during 1944. At present our aid to China must be accomplished by air transport—there is no other way. By the end of 1944, the Air Transport Command was carrying into China a tonnage of supplies three times as great as that delivered a year ago, and much more, each month, than the Burma Road ever delivered at its peak.

Despite the loss of important bases in China, the tonnage delivered by air transport has enabled General Chennault's Fourteenth Air Force, which includes many Chinese flyers, to wage an effective and aggressive campaign against the Japanese. In 1944 aircraft of the Fourteenth Air Force flew more than 35,000 sorties against the Japanese and sank enormous tonnage of enemy shipping, greatly diminishing the usefulness of the China Sea lanes.

British, Dominion, and Chinese forces together with our own have not only held the line in Burma against determined Japanese attacks but have gained bases of considerable importance to the supply line into China.

The Burma campaigns have involved incredible hardship, and have demanded exceptional fortitude and determination. The officers and men who have served with so much devotion in these far distant jungles and mountains deserve high honor from their countrymen.

In all of the far-flung operations of our own armed forces—on land, and sea and in the air—the final job, the toughest job, has been performed by the average, easy-going, hard-fighting young American, who carries the weight of battle on his own shoulders.

It is to him that we and all future generations of Americans must pay grateful tribute.

But—it is of small satisfaction to him to know that monuments will be raised to him in the future. He wants, he needs, and he is entitled to insist upon, our full and active support—now.

Although unprecedented production figures have made possible our victories, we shall have to increase our goals even more in certain items.

Peak deliveries of supplies were made to the War Department in December, 1943. Due in part to cutbacks, we have not produced as much since then. Deliveries of Army supplies were down by 15 percent by July, 1944, before the upward trend was once more resumed.

Because of increased demands from overseas, the Army Service Forces in the month of October, 1944, had to increase its estimate of required production by 10 percent. But in November, one month later, the requirements for 1945 had to be increased another 10 percent, sending the production goal well above anything we have yet attained. Our armed forces in combat have steadily increased their expenditure of medium and heavy artillery ammunition. As we continue the decisive phases of this war, the munitions that we expend will mount day by day.

In October, 1944, while some were saying the war in Europe was over, the Army was shipping more men to Europe than in any previous month of the war.

One of the most urgent immediate requirements of the armed forces is more nurses. Last April the Army requirement for nurses was set at 50,000. Actual strength in nurses was then 40,000. Since that time the Army has tried to raise the additional 10,000. Active recruiting has been carried on, but the net gain in eight months has been only 2,000. There are now 42,000 nurses in the Army.

Recent estimates have increased the total number needed to 60,000. That means that 18,000 more nurses must be obtained for the Army alone and the Navy now requires 2,000 additional nurses.

The present shortage of Army nurses is reflected in undue strain on the existing force. More than a thousand nurses are now hospitalized, and part of this is due to overwork. The shortage is also indicated by the fact that 11 Army hospital units have been sent overseas without their complement of nurses. At Army hospitals in the United States there is only 1 nurse to 26 beds, instead of the recommended 1 to 15 beds.

It is tragic that the gallant women who have volunteered for service as nurses should be so overworked. It is tragic that our wounded men should ever want for the best possible nursing care.

The inability to get the needed nurses for the Army is not due to any shortage of nurses; 280,000 registered nurses are now practicing in this country. It has been estimated by the War Manpower Commission that 27,000 additional nurses could be made available to the armed forces without interfering too seriously with the needs of the civilian population for nurses.

Since volunteering has not produced the number of nurses required, I urge that the Selective Service Act be amended to provide for the induction of nurses into the armed forces. The need is too pressing to await the outcome of further efforts at recruiting.

The care and treatment given to our wounded and sick soldiers have been the best known to medical science. Those standards must be maintained at all costs. We cannot tolerate a lowering of them by failure to provide adequate nursing for the brave men who stand desperately in need of it.

In the continuing progress of this war we have constant need for new types of weapons, for we cannot afford to fight the war of today or tomorrow with the weapons of yesterday. For example, the American Army now has developed a new tank with a gun more powerful than any yet mounted on a fast-moving vehicle. The Army will need many thousands of these new tanks in 1945.

Almost every month finds some new development in electronics which must be put into production in order to maintain our technical superiority—and in order to save lives. We have to work every day to keep ahead of the enemy in radar. On D-Day, in France, with our superior new equipment, we located and then put out of operation every warning set which the Germans had along the French coast.

If we do not keep constantly ahead of our enemies in the development of new weapons, we pay for our backwardness with the life's blood of our sons.

The only way to meet these increased needs for new weapons and more of them is for every American engaged in war work to stay on his war job—for additional American civilians, men and women, not engaged in essential work, to go out and get a war job. Workers who are released because their production is cut back should get another job where production is being increased. This is no time to quit or change to less essential jobs.

There is an old and true saying that the Lord hates a quitter. And this Nation must pay for all those who leave their essential jobs—or all those who lay down on their essential jobs for nonessential reasons. And—again—that payment must be made with the life's blood of our sons.

Many critical production programs with sharply rising needs are now seriously hampered by manpower shortages. The most important Army needs are artillery ammunition, cotton duck, bombs, tires, tanks, heavy trucks, and even B-29's. In each of these vital programs, present production is behind requirements.

Navy production of bombardment ammunition is hampered by manpower shortages; so is production for its huge rocket program. Labor shortages have also delayed its cruiser and carrier programs, and production of certain types of aircraft.

There is critical need for more repair workers and repair parts; this lack delays the return of damaged fighting ships to their places in the fleet, and prevents ships now in the fighting line from getting needed overhauling.

The pool of young men under 26 classified as I-A is almost depleted. Increased replacements for the armed forces will take men now deferred who are at work in war industry. The armed forces must have an assurance of a steady flow of young men for replacements. Meeting this paramount need will be difficult, and will also make it progressively more difficult to attain the 1945 production goals.

Last year, after much consideration, I recommended that the Congress adopt a national service act as the most efficient and democratic way of insuring full production for our war requirements. This recommendation was not adopted.

I now again call upon the Congress to enact this measure for the total mobilization of all our human resources for the prosecution of the war. I urge that this be done at the earliest possible moment.

It is not too late in the war. In fact, bitter experience has shown that in this kind of mechanized warfare where new weapons are constantly being created by our enemies and by ourselves, the closer we come to the end of the war, the more pressing becomes the need for sustained war production with which to deliver the final blow to the enemy.

There are three basic arguments for a national service law:

First, it would assure that we have the right numbers of workers in the right places at the right times.

Second, it would provide supreme proof to all our fighting men that we are giving them what they are entitled to, which is nothing less than our total effort.

And, third, it would be the final, unequivocal answer to the hopes of the Nazis and the Japanese that we may become halfhearted about this war and that they can get from us a negotiated peace.

National service legislation would make it possible to put ourselves in a position to assure certain and speedy action in meeting our manpower needs.

It would be used only to the extent absolutely required by military necessities. In fact, experience in Great Britain and in other Nations at war indicates that use of the compulsory powers of national service is necessary only in rare instances.

This proposed legislation would provide against loss of retirement and seniority rights and benefits. It would not mean reduction in wages.

In adopting such legislation, it is not necessary to discard the voluntary and cooperative processes which have prevailed up to this time. This cooperation has already produced great results. The contribution of our workers to the war effort has been beyond measure. We must build on the foundations that have already been laid and supplement the measures now in operation, in order to guarantee the production that may be necessary in the critical period that lies ahead.

At the present time we are using the inadequate tools at hand to do the best we can by such expedients as manpower ceilings, and the use of priority and other powers, to induce men and women to shift from non-essential to essential war jobs.

I am in receipt of a joint letter from the Secretary of War and the Secretary of the Navy, dated January 3, 1945, which says:

"With the experience of three years of war and after the most thorough consideration, we are convinced that it is now necessary to carry out the statement made by the Congress in the joint resolutions declaring that a state of war existed with Japan and Germany: That 'to bring the conflict to a successful conclusion, all of the resources of the country are hereby pledged by the Congress of the United States.'

"In our considered judgment, which is supported by General Marshall and Admiral King, this requires total mobilization of our manpower by the passage of a national war service law. The armed forces need this legislation to hasten the day of final victory, and to keep to a minimum the cost in lives.

"National war service, the recognition by law of the duty of every citizen to do his or her part in winning the war, will give complete assurance that the need for war equipment will be filled. In the coming year we must increase the output of many weapons and supplies on short notice. Otherwise we shall not keep our production abreast of the swiftly changing needs of war. At the same time it will be necessary to draw progressively many men now engaged in war production to serve with the armed forces, and their places in war production must be filled promptly. These developments will require the addition of hundreds of thousands to those already working in war industry. We do not believe that these needs can be met effectively under present methods.

"The record made by management and labor in war industry has been a notable testimony to the resourcefulness and power of America. The needs are so great, nevertheless, that in many instances we have been forced to recall soldiers and sailors from military duty to do work of a civilian character in war production, because of the urgency of the need for equipment and because of inability to recruit civilian labor."

Pending action by the Congress on the broader aspects of national service, I recommend that the Congress immediately enact legislation which will be effective in using the services of the 4,000,000 men now classified as IV-F in whatever capacity is best for the war effort.

In the field of foreign policy, we propose to stand together with the United Nations not for the war alone but for the victory for which the war is fought.

It is not only a common danger which unites us but a common hope. Ours is an association not of Governments but of peoples—and the peoples' hope is peace. Here, as in England; in England, as in Russia; in Russia, as in China; in France, and through the continent of Europe, and throughout the world; wherever men love freedom, the hope and purpose of the people are for peace—a peace that is durable and secure.

It will not be easy to create this peoples' peace. We delude ourselves if we believe that the surrender of the armies of our enemies will make the peace we long for. The unconditional surrender of the armies of our enemies is the first and necessary step—but the first step only.

We have seen already, in areas liberated from the Nazi and the Fascist tyranny, what problems peace will bring. And we delude ourselves if we attempt to believe wishfully that all these problems can be solved overnight.

The firm foundation can be built—and it will be built. But the continuance and assurance of a living peace must, in the long run, be the work of the people themselves.

We ourselves, like all peoples who have gone through the difficult processes of liberation and adjustment, know of our own experience how great the difficulties can be. We know that they are not difficulties peculiar to any continent or any Nation. Our own Revolutionary War left behind it, in the words of one American historian, "an eddy of lawlessness and disregard of human life." There were separatist movements of one kind or another in Vermont, Pennsylvania, Virginia, Tennessee, Kentucky, and Maine. There were insurrections, open or threatened, in Massachusetts and New Hampshire. These difficulties we worked out for ourselves as the peoples of the liberated areas of Europe, faced with complex problems of adjustment, will work out their difficulties for themselves.

Peace can be made and kept only by the united determination of free and peace-loving peoples who are willing to work together—willing to help one another—willing to respect and tolerate and try to understand one another's opinions and feelings.

The nearer we come to vanquishing our enemies the more we inevitably become conscious of differences among the victors.

We must not let those differences divide us and blind us to our more important common and continuing interests in winning the war and building the peace.

International cooperation on which enduring peace must be based is not a one-way street.

Nations like individuals do not always see alike or think alike, and international cooperation and progress are not helped by any Nation assuming that it has a monopoly of wisdom or of virtue.

In the future world the misuse of power, as implied in the term "power politics," must not be a controlling factor in international relations. That is the heart of the principles to which we have subscribed. We cannot deny that power is a factor in world politics any more than we can deny its existence as a factor in national politics. But in a democratic world, as in a democratic Nation, power must be linked with responsibility, and obliged to defend and justify itself within the framework of the general good.

Perfectionism, no less than isolationism or imperialism or power politics, may obstruct the paths to international peace. Let us not forget that the retreat to isolationism a quarter of a century ago was started not by a direct attack against international cooperation but against the alleged imperfections of the peace.

In our disillusionment after the last war we preferred international anarchy to international cooperation with Nations which did not see and think exactly as we did. We gave up the hope of gradually achieving a better peace because we had not the courage to fulfill our responsibilities in an admittedly imperfect world.

We must not let that happen again, or we shall follow the same tragic road again—the road to a third world war.

We can fulfill our responsibilities for maintaining the security of our own country only by exercising our power and our influence to achieve the principles in which we believe and for which we have fought.

In August, 1941, Prime Minister Churchill and I agreed to the principles of the Atlantic Charter, these being later incorporated into the Declaration by United Nations of January 1, 1942. At that time certain isolationists protested vigorously against our right to proclaim the principles—and against the very principles themselves. Today, many of the same people are protesting against the possibility of violation of the same principles.

It is true that the statement of principles in the Atlantic Charter does not provide rules of easy application to each and every one of this war-torn world's tangled situations. But it is a good and a useful thing—it is an essential thing—to have principles toward which we can aim.

And we shall not hesitate to use our influence—and to use it now—to secure so far as is humanly possible the fulfillment of the principles of the Atlantic Charter. We have not shrunk from the military responsibilities brought on by this war. We cannot and will not shrink from the political responsibilities which follow in the wake of battle.

I do not wish to give the impression that all mistakes can be avoided and that many disappointments are not inevitable in the making of peace. But we must not this time lose the hope of establishing an international order which will be capable of maintaining peace and realizing through the years more perfect justice between Nations.

To do this we must be on our guard not to exploit and exaggerate the differences between us and our allies, particularly with reference to the peoples who have been liberated from Fascist tyranny. That is not the way to secure a better settlement of those differences or to secure international machinery which can rectify mistakes which may be made.

I should not be frank if I did not admit concern about many situations—the Greek and Polish for example. But those situations are not as easy or as simple to deal with as some spokesmen, whose sincerity I do not question, would have us believe. We have obligations, not necessarily legal, to the exiled Governments, to the underground leaders, and to our major allies who came much nearer the shadows than we did.

We and our allies have declared that it is our purpose to respect the right of all peoples to choose the form of government under which they will live and to see sovereign rights and self-government restored to those who have been forcibly deprived of them. But with internal dissension, with many citizens of liberated countries still prisoners of war or forced to labor in Germany, it is difficult to guess the kind of self-government the people really want.

During the interim period, until conditions permit a genuine expression of the people's will, we and our allies have a duty, which we cannot ignore, to use our influence to the end that no temporary or provisional authorities in the liberated countries block the eventual exercise of the peoples' right freely to choose the government and institutions under which, as freemen, they are to live.

It is only too easy for all of us to rationalize what we want to believe, and to consider those leaders we like responsible and those we dislike irresponsible. And our task is not helped by stubborn partisanship, however understandable on the part of opposed internal factions.

It is our purpose to help the peace-loving peoples of Europe to live together as good neighbors, to recognize their common interests and not to nurse their traditional grievances against one another.

But we must not permit the many specific and immediate problems of adjustment connected with the liberation of Europe to delay the establishment of permanent machinery for the maintenance of peace. Under the threat of a common danger, the United Nations joined together in war to preserve their independence and their freedom. They must now join together to make secure the independence and freedom of all peace-loving states, so that never again shall tyranny be able to divide and conquer.

International peace and well-being, like national peace and well-being, require constant alertness, continuing cooperation, and organized effort.

International peace and well-being, like national peace and well-being, can be secured only through institutions capable of life and growth.

Many of the problems of the peace are upon us even now while the conclusion of the war is still before us. The atmosphere of friendship and mutual understanding and determination to find a common ground of common understanding, which surrounded the conversations at Dumbarton Oaks, gives us reason to hope that future discussions will succeed in developing the democratic and fully integrated world security system toward which these preparatory conversations were directed.

We and the other United Nations are going forward, with vigor and resolution, in our efforts to create such a system by providing for it strong and flexible institutions of joint and cooperative action.

The aroused conscience of humanity will not permit failure in this supreme endeavor.

We believe that the extraordinary advances in the means of intercommunication between peoples over the past generation offer a practical method of advancing the mutual understanding upon which peace and the institutions of peace must rest, and it is our policy and purpose to use these great technological achievements for the common advantage of the world.

We support the greatest possible freedom of trade and commerce.

We Americans have always believed in freedom of opportunity, and equality of opportunity remains one of the principal objectives of our national life. What we believe in for individuals, we believe in also for Nations. We are opposed to restrictions, whether by public act or private arrangement, which distort and impair commerce, transit, and trade.

We have house-cleaning of our own to do in this regard. But it is our hope, not only in the interest of our own prosperity but in the interest of the prosperity of the world, that trade and commerce and access to materials and markets may be freer after this war than ever before in the history of the world.

One of the most heartening events of the year in the international field has been the renaissance of the French people and the return of the French Nation to the ranks of the United Nations. Far from having been crushed by the terror of Nazi domination, the French people have emerged with stronger faith than ever in the destiny of their country and in the soundness of the democratic ideals to which the French Nation has traditionally contributed so greatly.

During her liberation, France has given proof of her unceasing determination to fight the Germans, continuing the heroic efforts of the resistance groups under the occupation and of all those Frenchmen throughout the world who refused to surrender after the disaster of 1940.

Today, French armies are again on the German frontier, and are again fighting shoulder to shoulder with our sons.

Since our landings in Africa, we have placed in French hands all the arms and material of war which our resources and the military situation permitted. And I am glad to say that we are now about to equip large new French forces with the most modern weapons for combat duty.

In addition to the contribution which France can make to our common victory, her liberation likewise means that her great influence will again be available in meeting the problems of peace.

We fully recognize France's vital interest in a lasting solution of the German problem and the contribution which she can make in achieving international security. Her formal adherence to the declaration by United Nations a few days ago and the proposal at the Dumbarton Oaks discussions, whereby France would receive one of the five permanent seats in the proposed Security Council, demonstrate the extent to which France has resumed her proper position of strength and leadership.

I am clear in my own mind that, as an essential factor in the maintenance of peace in the future, we must have universal military training after this war, and I shall send a special message to the Congress on this subject.

An enduring peace cannot be achieved without a strong America—strong in the social and economic sense as well as in the military sense.

In the State of the Union message last year I set forth what I considered to be an American economic bill of rights.

I said then, and I say now, that these economic truths represent a second bill of rights under which a new basis of security and prosperity can be established for all—regardless of station, race, or creed.

Of these rights the most fundamental, and one on which the fulfillment of the others in large degree depends, is the "right to a useful and remunerative job in the industries or shops or farms or mines of the Nation." In turn, others of the economic rights of American citizenship, such as the right to a decent home, to a good education, to good medical care, to social security, to reasonable farm income, will, if fulfilled, make major contributions to achieving adequate levels of employment.

The Federal Government must see to it that these rights become realities—with the help of States, municipalities, business, labor, and agriculture.

We have had full employment during the war. We have had it because the Government has been ready to buy all the materials of war which the country could produce—and this has amounted to approximately half our present productive capacity.

After the war we must maintain full employment with Government performing its peacetime functions. This means that we must achieve a level of demand and purchasing power by private consumers—farmers, businessmen, workers, professional men, housewives—which is sufficiently high to replace wartime Government demands; and it means also that we must greatly increase our export trade above the prewar level.

Our policy is, of course, to rely as much as possible on private enterprise to provide jobs. But the American people will not accept mass unemployment or mere makeshift work. There will be need for the work of everyone willing and able to work—and that means close to 60,000,000 jobs.

Full employment means not only jobs—but productive jobs. Americans do not regard jobs that pay substandard wages as productive jobs.

We must make sure that private enterprise works as it is supposed to work—on the basis of initiative and vigorous competition, without the stifling presence of monopolies and cartels.

During the war we have guaranteed investment in enterprise essential to the war effort. We should also take appropriate measures in peacetime to secure opportunities for new small enterprises and for productive business expansion for which finance would otherwise be unavailable.

This necessary expansion of our peacetime productive capacity will require new facilities, new plants, and new equipment.

It will require large outlays of money which should be raised through normal investment channels. But while private capital should finance this expansion program, the Government should recognize its responsibility for sharing part of any special or abnormal risk of loss attached to such financing.

Our full-employment program requires the extensive development of our natural resources and other useful public works. The undeveloped resources of this continent are still vast. Our river-watershed projects will add new and fertile territories to the United States. The Tennessee Valley Authority, which was constructed at a cost of $750,000,000—the cost of waging this war for less than 4 days—was a bargain. We have similar opportunities in our other great river basins. By harnessing the resources of these river basins, as we have in the Tennessee Valley, we shall provide the same kind of stimulus to enterprise as was provided by the Louisiana Purchase and the new discoveries in the West during the nineteenth century.

If we are to avail ourselves fully of the benefits of civil aviation, and if we are to use the automobiles we can produce, it will be necessary to construct thousands of airports and to overhaul our entire national highway system.

The provision of a decent home for every family is a national necessity, if this country is to be worthy of its greatness—and that task will itself create great employment opportunities. Most of our cities need extensive rebuilding. Much of our farm plant is in a state of disrepair. To make a frontal attack on the problems of housing and urban reconstruction will require thoroughgoing cooperation between industry and labor, and the Federal, State, and local Governments.

An expanded social security program, and adequate health and education programs, must play essential roles in a program designed to support individual productivity and mass purchasing power. I shall communicate further with the Congress on these subjects at a later date.

The millions of productive jobs that a program of this nature could bring are jobs in private enterprise. They are jobs based on the expanded demand for the output of our economy for consumption and investment. Through a program of this character we can maintain a national income high enough to provide for an orderly retirement of the public debt along with reasonable tax reduction.

Our present tax system geared primarily to war requirements must be revised for peacetime so as to encourage private demand.

While no general revision of the tax structure can be made until the war ends on all fronts, the Congress should be prepared to provide tax modifications at the end of the war in Europe, designed to encourage capital to invest in new enterprises and to provide jobs. As an integral part of this program to maintain high employment, we must, after the war is over, reduce or eliminate taxes which bear too heavily on consumption.

The war will leave deep disturbances in the world economy, in our national economy, in many communities, in many families, and in many individuals. It will require determined effort and responsible action of all of us to find our way back to peacetime, and to help others to find their way back to peacetime—a peacetime that holds the values of the past and the promise of the future.

If we attack our problems with determination we shall succeed. And we must succeed. For freedom and peace cannot exist without security.

During the past year the American people, in a national election, reasserted their democratic faith.

In the course of that campaign various references were made to "strife" between this Administration and the Congress, with the implication, if not the direct assertion, that this Administration and the Congress could never work together harmoniously in the service of the Nation.

It cannot be denied that there have been disagreements between the legislative and executive branches—as there have been disagreements during the past century and a half.

I think we all realize too that there are some people in this Capital City whose task is in large part to stir up dissension, and to magnify normal healthy disagreements so that they appear to be irreconcilable conflicts.

But—I think that the over-all record in this respect is eloquent: The Government of the United States of America—all branches of it—has a good record of achievement in this war.

The Congress, the Executive, and the Judiciary have worked together for the common good.

I myself want to tell you, the Members of the Senate and of the House of Representatives, how happy I am in our relationships and friendships. I have not yet had the pleasure of meeting some of the new Members in each House, but I hope that opportunity will offer itself in the near future.

We have a great many problems ahead of us and we must approach them with realism and courage.

This new year of 1945 can be the greatest year of achievement in human history.

Nineteen forty-five can see the final ending of the Nazi-Fascist reign of terror in Europe.

Nineteen forty-five can see the closing in of the forces of retribution about the center of the malignant power of imperialistic Japan.

Most important of all—1945 can and must see the substantial beginning of the organization of world peace. This organization must be the fulfillment of the promise for which men have fought and died in this war. It must be the justification of all the sacrifices that have been made—of all the dreadful misery that this world has endured.

We Americans of today, together with our allies, are making history—and I hope it will be better history than ever has been made before.

We pray that we may be worthy of the unlimited opportunities that God has given us.

Harry S. Truman

1945–1953

*"Above all, we have the vigor of free men
in a free society. We have our liberties.
And while we keep them, while we retain
our democratic faith, the ultimate advantage
in this hard competition lies with us,
not with the communists."*

MESSAGE TO CONGRESS ON THE STATE OF THE UNION, JANUARY 7, 1953

Message to Congress
on the State of the Union

January 21, 1946

Harry Truman's first State of the Union message came after an extremely eventful year. In the course of 1945, Franklin D. Roosevelt died, and World War II ended. The country faced a double transition: to a new president, Truman, and to a peacetime society.

Truman's written message, dated January 14 but released January 21, was lengthy; it combined the State of the Union and budget messages. In his message, the president discussed a wide range of issues, including the establishment—then under way—of the United Nations, postwar inflation at home, and labor strikes.

Truman, a former senator from Missouri who had served as Roosevelt's vice president for less than three months when Roosevelt died on April 12, found himself leading a country that was concluding a monumental war. The war in Europe ended May 8, when Germany surrendered; the war in Asia concluded when Japan surrendered August 14, following Truman's decision to drop atomic bombs on Hiroshima and Nagasaki.

Truman signaled early in his presidency that he would continue the social reforms that Roosevelt had championed during the New Deal. On September 6, 1945, the new president outlined a twenty-one-point program, which came to be called the Fair Deal. It included an increase in the minimum wage, an extension of Social Security, and full employment; these themes were among those discussed in this State of the Union message.

However, Congress did not go along with much of Truman's program, especially after the midterm congressional elections of November 1946, which saw Republicans win control of both houses of Congress.

As World War II was ending, the United States already was heading toward the beginnings of the Cold War with the communist Soviet Union, a conflict between two divergent ideologies that would dominate U.S. foreign policy for more than forty years. In this State of the Union message, Truman spoke of the importance of international cooperation, stating that the United Nations should become "the representative of the world as one society." But that goal, as Truman came to see as his presidency progressed, proved elusive.

Truman's message also included information on the federal budget; the president stated that for the first time since fiscal 1930, there would be no increase needed in the national debt. His overall budget reflected the shift from wartime to peacetime, and much of the budget-related section of the address dealt with that subject.

To the Congress of the United States:

A quarter century ago the Congress decided that it could no longer consider the financial programs of the various departments on a piecemeal basis. Instead it has called on the President to present a comprehensive Executive Budget. The Congress has shown its satisfaction with that method by extending the budget system and tightening its controls. The bigger and more complex the Federal Program, the more necessary it is for the Chief Executive to submit a single budget for action by the Congress.

At the same time, it is clear that the budgetary program and the general program of the Government are actually inseparable. The president bears the responsibility for recommending to the Congress a comprehensive set of proposals on all Government activities and their financing. In formulating policies, as in preparing budgetary estimates, the Nation and the Congress have the right to expect the President to adjust and coordinate the views of the various departments and agencies to form a unified program. And that program requires consideration in connection with the Budget, which is the annual work program of the Government.

Since our programs for this period which combines war liquidation with reconversion to a peacetime economy are inevitably large and numerous it is imperative that they be planned and executed with the utmost efficiency and the utmost economy. We have cut the war program to the maximum extent consistent with national security. We have held our peacetime programs to the level necessary to our national well-being and the attainment of our postwar objectives. Where increased programs have been recommended, the increases have been held as low as is consistent with these goals. I can assure the Congress of the necessity of these programs. I can further assure the Congress that the program as a whole is well within our capacity to finance it. All the programs I have recommended for action are included in the Budget figures.

For these reasons I have chosen to combine the customary Message on the State of the Union with the annual Budget Message, and to include in the Budget not only estimates for functions authorized by the Congress, but also for those which I recommend for its action.

I am also transmitting herewith the Fifth Quarterly Report of the Director of War Mobilization and Reconversion. It is a comprehensive discussion of the present state of the reconversion program and of the immediate and long-range needs and recommendations.

This constitutes, then, as complete a report as I find it possible to prepare now. It constitutes a program of government in relation to the Nation's needs.

With the growing responsibility of modern government to foster economic expansion and to promote conditions that assure full and steady employment opportunities, it has become necessary to formulate and determine the Government program in the light of national economic conditions as a whole. In both the executive and the legislative branches we must make arrangements which will permit us to formulate the Government program in that light. Such an approach has become imperative if the American political and economic system is to succeed under the conditions of economic instability and uncertainty which we have to face. The Government needs to assure business, labor, and agriculture that Government policies will take due account of the requirements of a full employment economy. The lack of that assurance would, I believe, aggravate the economic instability.

With the passage of a full employment bill which I confidently anticipate for the very near future, the executive and legislative branches of government will be empowered to devote their best talents and resources in subsequent years to preparing and acting on such a program.

I. From War to Peace—The Year of Decision

In his last Message on the State of the Union, delivered one year ago, President Roosevelt said:

> "This new year of 1945 can be the greatest year of achievement in human history.

> "1945 can see the final ending of the Nazi-Fascist reign of terror in Europe.

> "1945 can see the closing in of the forces of retribution about the center of the malignant power of imperialistic Japan.

> "Most important of all—1945 can and must see the substantial beginning of the organization of world peace."

All those hopes, and more, were fulfilled in the year 1945. It was the greatest year of achievement in human history. It saw the end of the Nazi-Fascist terror in Europe, and also the end of the malignant power of Japan. And it saw the substantial beginning of world organization for peace. These momentous events became realities because of the steadfast purpose of the United Nations and of the forces that fought for freedom under their flags. The plain fact is that civilization was saved in 1945 by the United Nations.

Our own part in this accomplishment was not the product of any single service. Those who fought on land, those who fought on the sea, and those who fought in the air deserve equal credit. They were supported by other millions in the armed forces who through no fault of their own could not go overseas and who rendered indispensable service in this country. They were supported by millions in all levels of government, including many volunteers, whose devoted public service furnished basic organization and leadership. They were also supported by the millions of Americans in private life—men and women in industry, in commerce, on the farms, and in all manner of activity on the home front—who contributed their brains and their brawn in arming, equipping, and feeding them. The country was brought through four years of peril by an effort that was truly national in character.

Everlasting tribute and gratitude will be paid by all Americans to those brave men who did not come back, who will never come back—the 330,000 who died that the Nation might live and progress. All Americans will also remain deeply conscious of the obligation owed to that larger number of soldiers, sailors, and marines who suffered wounds and sickness in their service. They may be certain that their sacrifice will never be forgotten or their needs neglected.

The beginning of the year 1946 finds the United States strong and deservedly confident. We have a record of enormous achievements as a democratic society in solving problems and meeting opportunities as they developed. We find ourselves possessed of immeasurable advantages—vast and varied natural resources; great plants, institutions, and other facilities; unsurpassed technological and managerial skills; an alert, resourceful, and able citizenry. We have in the United States Government rich resources in information, perspective, and facilities for doing whatever may be found necessary to do in giving support and form to the widespread and diversified efforts of all our people.

And for the immediate future the business prospects are generally so favorable that there is danger of such feverish and opportunistic activity that our grave postwar problems may be neglected. We need to act now with full regard for pitfalls; we need to act with foresight and balance. We should not be lulled by the immediate alluring prospects into forgetting the fundamental complexity of modern affairs, the catastrophe that can come in this complexity, or the values that can be wrested from it.

But the long-range difficulties we face should no more lead to despair than our immediate business prospects should lead to the optimism which comes from the present short-range prospect. On the foundation of our victory we can build a lasting peace, with greater freedom and security for mankind in our country and throughout the world. We will more certainly do this if we are constantly aware of the fact that we face crucial issues and prepare now to meet them.

To achieve success will require both boldness in setting our sights and caution in steering our way on an uncharted course. But we have no luxury of choice. We must move ahead. No return to the past is possible.

Our Nation has always been a land of great opportunities for those people of the world who sought to become part of us. Now we have become a land of great responsibilities to all the people of all the world. We must squarely recognize and face the fact of those responsibilities. Advances in science, in communication, in transportation, have compressed the world into a community. The economic and political health of each member of the world community bears directly on the economic and political health of each other member.

The evolution of centuries has brought us to a new era in world history in which manifold relationships between nations must be formalized and developed in new and intricate ways.

The United Nations Organization now being established represents a minimum essential beginning. It must be developed rapidly and steadily. Its work must be amplified to fill in the whole pattern that has been outlined. Economic collaboration, for example, already charted, now must be carried on as carefully and as comprehensively as the political and security measures.

It is important that the nations come together as States in the Assembly and in the Security Council and in the other specialized assemblies and councils that have been and will be arranged. But this is not enough. Our ultimate security requires more than a process of consultation and compromise.

It requires that we begin now to develop the United Nations Organization as the representative of the world as one society. The United Nations Organization, if we have the will adequately to staff it and to make it work as it should, will provide a great voice to speak constantly and responsibly in terms of world collaboration and world well-being.

There are many new responsibilities for us as we enter into this new international era. The whole power and will and wisdom of our Government and of our people should be focused to contribute to and to influence international action. It is intricate, continuing business. Many concessions and adjustments will be required.

The spectacular progress of science in recent years makes these necessities more vivid and urgent. That progress has speeded internal development and has changed world relationships so fast that we must realize the fact of a new era. It is an era in which affairs have become complex and rich in promise. Delicate and intricate relationships, involving us all in countless ways, must be carefully considered.

On the domestic scene, as well as on the international scene, we must lay a new and better foundation for cooperation. We face a great peacetime venture; the challenging venture of a free enterprise economy making full and effective use of its rich resources and technical advances. This is a venture in which business, agriculture, and labor have vastly greater opportunities than heretofore. But they all also have vastly greater responsibilities. We will not measure up to those responsibilities by the simple return to "normalcy" that was tried after the last war.

The general objective, on the contrary, is to move forward to find the way in time of peace to the full utilization and development of our physical and human resources that were demonstrated so effectively in the war.

To accomplish this, it is not intended that the Federal Government should do things that can be done as well for the Nation by private enterprise, or by State and local governments. On the contrary, the war has demonstrated how effectively we can organize our productive system and develop the potential abilities of our people by aiding the efforts of private enterprise.

As we move toward one common objective there will be many and urgent problems to meet.

Industrial peace between management and labor will have to be achieved—through the process of collective bargaining—with Government assistance but not Government compulsion. This is a problem which is the concern not only of management, labor, and the Government, but also the concern of every one of us.

Private capital and private management are entitled to adequate reward for efficiency, but business must recognize that its reward results from the employment of the resources of the Nation. Business is a public trust and must adhere to national standards in the conduct of its affairs. These standards include as a minimum the establishment of fair wages and fair employment practices.

Labor also has its own new peacetime responsibilities. Under our collective bargaining system, which must become progressively more secure, labor attains increasing political as well as economic power, and this, as with all power, means increased responsibility.

The lives of millions of veterans and war workers will be greatly affected by the success or failure of our program of war liquidation and reconversion. Their transition to peacetime pursuits will be determined by our efforts to break the bottlenecks in key items of production, to make surplus property immediately available where it is needed, to maintain an effective national employment service, and many other reconversion policies. Our obligations to the people who won the war will not be paid if we fail to prevent inflation and to maintain employment opportunities.

While our peacetime prosperity will be based on the private enterprise the government can and must assist in many ways. It is the Government's responsibility to see that our economic system remains competitive, that new businesses have adequate opportunities, and that our national resources are restored and improved. Government must realize the effect of its operations on the whole economy. It is the responsibility of Government to gear its total program to the achievement of full production and full employment.

Our basic objective—toward which all others lead—is to improve the welfare of the American people. In addition to economic prosperity, this means that we use social security in the fullest sense of the word. And people must be protected from excessive want during old age, sickness, and unemployment. Opportunities for a good economy and adequate medical care must be readily available. Every family should build a decent home. The new economic rights to which I have referred on previous occasions is a charter of economic freedom which seeks to assure that all who will may work toward their own security and the general advancement; that we become a well-housed people, a well-nourished people, an educated people, a people socially and economically secure, an alert and responsible people.

These and other problems which may face us can be met by the cooperation of all of us in furthering a positive and well-balanced Government program—a program which will further national and international well-being.

II. The Federal Program—International Affairs

1. Foreign Policy

The year 1945 brought with it the final defeat of our enemies. There lies before us now the work of building a just and enduring peace.

Our most immediate task toward that end is to deprive our enemies completely and forever of their power to start another war. Of even greater importance to the preservation of international peace is the need to preserve the wartime agreement of the United Nations and to direct it into the ways of peace.

Long before our enemies surrendered, the foundations had been laid on which to continue this unity in the peace to come. The Atlantic meeting in 1941 and the conferences at Casablanca, Quebec, Moscow, Cairo, Tehran, and Dumbarton Oaks each added a stone to the structure.

Early in 1945, at Yalta, the three major powers broadened and solidified this base of understanding. There fundamental decisions were reached concerning the occupation and control of Germany. There also a formula was arrived at for the interim government of the areas in Europe which were rapidly being wrested from Nazi control. This formula was based on the policy of the United States that people be permitted to choose their own form of government by their own freely expressed choice without interference from any foreign source.

At Potsdam, in July 1945, Marshal Stalin, Prime Ministers Churchill and Attlee, and I met to exchange views primarily with respect to Germany. As a result, agreements were reached which outlined broadly the policy to be executed by the Allied Control Council. At Potsdam there was also established a Council of Foreign Ministers which convened for the first time in London in September. The Council is about to resume its primary assignment of drawing up treaties of peace with Italy, Rumania, Bulgaria, Hungary, and Finland.

In addition to these meetings, and, in accordance with the agreement at Yalta, the Foreign Ministers of Great Britain, the Soviet Union, and the United States conferred together in San Francisco last spring, in Potsdam in July, in London in September, and in Moscow in December. These meetings have been useful in promoting understanding and agreement among the three governments.

Simply to name all the international meetings and conferences is to suggest the size and complexity of the undertaking to prevent international war in which the United States has now enlisted for the duration of history.

It is encouraging to know that the common effort of the United Nations to learn to live together did not cease with the surrender of our enemies.

When difficulties arise among us, the United States does not propose to remove them by sacrificing its ideals or its vital interests. Neither do we propose, however, to ignore the ideals and vital interests of our friends.

Last February and March an Inter-American Conference on Problems of War and Peace was held in Mexico City. Among the many significant accomplishments of that Conference was an understanding that an attack by any country against any one of the sovereign American republics would be considered an act of aggression against all of them; and that if such an attack were made or threatened, the American republics would decide jointly, through consultations in which each republic has equal representation, what measures they would take for their mutual protection. This agreement stipulates that its execution shall be in full accord with the Charter of the United Nations Organization.

The first meeting of the General Assembly of the United Nations now in progress in London marks the real beginning of our bold adventure toward the preservation of world peace, to which is bound the clearest hope of men.

We have solemnly dedicated ourselves and all our will to the success of the United Nations Organization. For this reason we have sought to insure that in the peace-making the smaller nations shall have a voice as well as the larger states. The agreement reached at Moscow last month preserves this opportunity in the making of peace with Italy, Rumania, Bulgaria, Hungary, and Finland. The United States intends to preserve it when the treaties with Germany and Japan are drawn.

It will be the continuing policy of the United States to use all its influence to foster, support, and develop the United Nations Organization in its purpose of preventing international war. If peace is to endure it must rest upon justice no less than upon power. The question is how justice among nations is best achieved. We know from day-to-day experience that the chance for a just solution is immeasurably increased when everyone directly interested is given a voice. That does not mean that each must enjoy an equal voice, but it does mean that each must be heard.

Last November, Prime Minister Attlee, Prime Minister MacKenzie King, and I announced our proposal that a commission be established within the framework of the United Nations to explore the problems of effective international control of atomic energy.

The Soviet Union, France, and China have joined us in the purpose of introducing in the General Assembly a resolution for the establishment of such a commission. Our earnest wish is that the work of this commission go forward carefully and thoroughly, but with the greatest dispatch. I have great hope for the development of mutually effective safeguards which will permit the fullest international control of this new atomic force.

I believe it possible that effective means can be developed through the United Nations Organization to prohibit, outlaw, and prevent the use of atomic energy for destructive purposes.

The power which the United States demonstrated during the war is the fact that underlies every phase of our relations with other countries. We cannot escape the responsibility which it thrusts upon us. What we think, plan, say, and do is of profound significance to the future of every corner of the world.

The great and dominant objective of United States foreign policy is to build and preserve a just peace. The peace we seek is not peace for twenty years. It is permanent peace. At a time when massive changes are occurring with lightning speed throughout the world, it is often difficult to perceive how this central objective is best served in one isolated complex situation or another. Despite this very real difficulty, there are certain basic propositions to which the United States adheres and to which we shall continue to adhere.

One proposition is that lasting peace requires genuine understanding and active cooperation among the most powerful nations. Another is that even the support of the strongest nations cannot guarantee a peace unless it is infused with the quality of justice for all nations.

On October 27, 1945, I made, in New York City, the following public statement of my understanding of the fundamental foreign policy of the United States. I believe that policy to be in accord with the opinion of the Congress and of the people of the United States. I believe that that policy carries out our fundamental objectives.

1. We seek no territorial expansion or selfish advantage. We have no plans for aggression against any other state, large or small. We have no objective which need clash with the peaceful aims of any other nation.

2. We believe in the eventual return of sovereign rights and self-government to all peoples who have been deprived of them by force.

3. We shall approve no territorial changes in any friendly part of the world unless they accord with the freely expressed wishes of the people concerned.

4. We believe that all peoples who are prepared for self-government should be permitted to choose their own form of government by their own freely expressed choice, without interference from any foreign source. That is true in Europe, in Asia, in Africa, as well as in the Western Hemisphere.

5. By the combined and cooperative action of our war allies, we shall help the defeated enemy states establish peaceful democratic governments of their own free choice. And we shall try to attain a world in which nazism, fascism, and military aggression cannot exist.

6. We shall refuse to recognize any government imposed upon any nation by the force of any foreign power. In some cases it may be impossible to prevent forceful imposition of such a government. But the United States will not recognize any such government.

7. We believe that all nations should have the freedom of the seas and equal rights to the navigation of boundary rivers and waterways and of rivers and waterways which pass through more than one country.

8. We believe that all states which are accepted in the society of nations should have access on equal terms to the trade and the raw materials of the world.

9. We believe that the sovereign states of the Western Hemisphere, without interference from outside the Western Hemisphere, must work together as good neighbors in the solution of their common problems.

10. We believe that full economic collaboration between all nations, great and small, is essential to the improvement of living conditions all over the world, and to the establishment of freedom from fear and freedom from want.

11. We shall continue to strive to promote freedom of expression and freedom of religion throughout the peace-loving areas of the world.

12. We are convinced that the preservation of peace between nations requires a United Nations Organization composed of all the peace-loving nations of the world who are willing jointly to use force, if necessary, to insure peace.

That is our foreign policy.

We may not always fully succeed in our objectives. There may be instances where the attainment of those objectives is delayed. But we will not give our full sanction and approval to actions which fly in the face of these ideals.

The world has a great stake in the political and economic future of Germany. The Allied Control Council has now been in operation there for a substantial period of time. It has not met with unqualified success. The accommodation of varying views of four governments in the day-to-day civil administration of occupied territory is a challenging task. In my judgment, however, the Council has made encouraging progress in the face of most serious difficulties. It is my purpose at the earliest practicable date to transfer from military to civilian personnel the execution of United States participation in the government of occupied territory in Europe. We are determined that effective control shall be maintained in Germany until we are satisfied that the German people have regained the right to a place of honor and respect.

On the other side of the world, a method of international cooperation has recently been agreed upon for the treatment of Japan. In this pattern of control, the United States, with the full approval of its partners, has retained primary authority and primary responsibility. It will continue to do so until the Japanese people, by their own freely expressed choice, choose their own form of government.

Our basic policy in the Far East is to encourage the development of a strong, independent, united, and democratic China. That has been the traditional policy of the United States.

At Moscow the United States, the Union of Soviet Socialist Republics, and Great Britain agreed to further this development by supporting the efforts of the national government and nongovernmental Chinese political elements in bringing about cessation of civil strife and in broadening the basis of representation in the Government. That is the policy which General Marshall is so ably executing today.

It is the purpose of the Government of the United States to proceed as rapidly as is practicable toward the restoration of the sovereignty of Korea and the establishment of a democratic government by the free choice of the people of Korea.

At the threshold of every problem which confronts us today in international affairs is the appalling devastation, hunger, sickness, and pervasive human misery that mark so many areas of the world.

By joining and participating in the work of the United Nations Relief and Rehabilitation Administration the United States has directly recognized and assumed an obligation to give such relief assistance as is practicable to millions of innocent and helpless victims of the war. The Congress has earned the gratitude of the world by generous financial contributions to the United Nations Relief and Rehabilitation Administration.

We have taken the lead, modest though it is, in facilitating under our existing immigration quotas the admission to the United States of refugees and displaced persons from Europe.

We have joined with Great Britain in the organization of a commission to study the problem of Palestine. The Commission is already at work and its recommendations will be made at an early date.

The members of the United Nations have paid us the high compliment of choosing the United States as the site of the United Nations headquarters. We shall be host in spirit as well as in fact, for nowhere does there abide a fiercer determination that this peace shall live than in the hearts of the American people.

It is the hope of all Americans that in time future historians will speak not of World War I and World War II, but of the first and last world wars.

2. Foreign Economic Policy

The foreign economic policy of the United States is designed to promote our own prosperity, and at the same time to aid in the restoration and expansion of world markets and to contribute thereby to world peace and world security. We shall continue our efforts to provide relief from the devastation of war, to alleviate the sufferings of displaced persons, to assist in reconstruction and development, and to promote the expansion of world trade.

We have already joined the International Monetary Fund and the International Bank for Reconstruction and Development. We have expanded the Export-Import Bank and provided it with additional capital. The Congress has renewed the Trade Agreements Act which provides the necessary framework within which to negotiate a reduction of trade barriers on a reciprocal basis. It has given our support to the United Nations Relief and Rehabilitation Administration.

In accordance with the intentions of the Congress, lend-lease, except as to continuing military lend-lease in China, was terminated upon the surrender of Japan. The first of the lend-lease settlement agreements has been completed with the United Kingdom. Negotiations with other lend-lease countries are in progress. In negotiating these agreements, we intend to seek settlements which will not encumber world trade through war debts of a character that proved to be so detrimental to the stability of the world economy after the last war.

We have taken steps to dispose of the goods which on VJ-day were in the lend-lease pipe line to the various lend-lease countries and to allow them long-term credit for the purpose where necessary. We are also making arrangements under which those countries may use the lend-lease inventories in their possession and acquire surplus property abroad to assist in their economic rehabilitation and reconstruction. These goods will be accounted for at fair values.

The proposed loan to the United Kingdom, which I shall recommend to the Congress in a separate message, will contribute to easing the transition problem of one of our major partners in the war. It will enable the whole sterling area and other countries affiliated with it to resume trade on a multilateral basis. Extension of this credit will enable the United Kingdom to avoid discriminatory trade arrangements of the type which destroyed freedom of trade during the 1930's. I consider the progress toward multilateral trade which will be achieved by this agreement to be in itself sufficient warrant for the credit.

The view of this Government is that, in the longer run, our economic prosperity and the prosperity of the whole world are best served by the elimination of artificial barriers to international trade, whether in the form of unreasonable tariffs or tariff preferences or commercial quotas or embargoes or the restrictive practices of cartels.

The United States Government has issued proposals for the expansion of world trade and employment to which the Government of the United Kingdom has given its support on every important issue. These proposals are intended to form the basis for a trade and employment conference to be held in the middle of this year. If that conference is a success, I feel confident that the way will have been adequately prepared for an expanded and prosperous world trade.

We shall also continue negotiations looking to the full and equitable development of facilities for transportation and communications among nations.

The vast majority of the nations of the world have chosen to work together to achieve, on a cooperative basis, world security and world prosperity. The effort cannot succeed without full cooperation of the United States. To play our part, we must not only resolutely carry out the foreign policies we have adopted but also follow a domestic policy which will maintain full production and employment in the United States. A serious depression here can disrupt the whole fabric of the world economy.

3. Occupied Countries

The major tasks of our Military Establishment in Europe following VE-day, and in the Pacific since the surrender of Japan, have been those of occupation and military government. In addition we have given much needed aid to the peoples of the liberated countries.

The end of the war in Europe found Germany in a chaotic condition. Organized government had ceased to exist, transportation systems had been wrecked, cities and industrial facilities had been bombed into ruins. In addition to the tasks of occupation we had to assume all of the functions of government. Great progress has been made in the repatriation of displaced persons and of prisoners of war. Of the total of 3,500,000 displaced persons found in the United States zone only 460,000 now remain.

The extensive complications involved by the requirement of dealing with three other governments engaged in occupation and with the governments of liberated countries require intensive work and energetic cooperation. The influx of some 2 million German refugees into our zone of occupation is a pressing problem, making exacting demands upon an already overstrained internal economy.

Improvements in the European economy during 1945 have made it possible for our military authorities to relinquish to the governments of all liberated areas, or to the United Nations Relief and Rehabilitation Administration, the responsibility for the provision of food and other civilian relief supplies. The Army's responsibilities in Europe extend now only to our zones of occupation in Germany and Austria and to two small areas in northern Italy.

By contrast with Germany, in Japan we have occupied a country still possessing an organized and operating governmental system. Although severely damaged, the Japanese industrial and transportation systems have been able to insure at least a survival existence for the population. The repatriation of Japanese military and civilian personnel from overseas is proceeding as rapidly as shipping and other means permit.

In order to insure that neither Germany nor Japan will again be in a position to wage aggressive warfare, the armament making potential of these countries is being dismantled and fundamental changes in their social and political structures are being effected. Democratic systems are being fostered to the end that the voice of the common man may be heard in the councils of his government.

For the first time in history the legal culpability of war makers is being determined. The trials now in progress in Nurnberg—and those soon to begin in Tokyo—bring before the bar of international justice those individuals who are charged with the responsibility for the sufferings of the past six years. We have high hope that this public portrayal of the guilt of these evildoers will bring wholesale and permanent revulsion on the part of the masses of our former enemies against war, militarism, aggression, and notions of race superiority.

4. Demobilization of Our Armed Forces

The cessation of active campaigning does not mean that we can completely disband our fighting forces. For their sake and for the sake of their loved ones at home, I wish that we could. But we still have the task of clinching the victories we have won—of making certain that Germany and Japan can never again wage aggressive warfare, that they will not again have the means to bring on another world war. The performance of that task requires that, together with our allies, we occupy the hostile areas, complete the disarmament of our enemies, and take the necessary measures to see to it that they do not rearm.

As quickly as possible, we are bringing about the reduction of our armed services to the size required for these tasks of occupation and disarmament. The Army and the Navy are following both length-of-service and point systems as far as possible in releasing men and women from the service. The points are based chiefly on length and character of service, and on the existence of dependents.

Over 5 million from the Army have already passed through the separation centers.

The Navy, including the Marine Corps and the Coast Guard, has discharged over one and a half million.

Of the 12 million men and women serving in the Army and Navy at the time of the surrender of Germany, one-half have already been released. The greater part of these had to be brought back to this country from distant parts of the world.

Of course there are cases of individual hardship in retention of personnel in the service. There will be in the future. No system of such size can operate to perfection. But the systems are founded on fairness and justice, and they are working at full speed. We shall try to avoid mistakes, injustices, and hardship—as far as humanly possible.

We have already reached the point where shipping is no longer the bottleneck in the return of troops from the European theater. The governing factor now has become the requirement for troops in sufficient strength to carry out their missions.

In a few months the same situation will exist in the Pacific. By the end of June, 9 out of 10 who were serving in the armed forces on VE-day will have been released. Demobilization will continue thereafter, but at a slower rate, determined by our military responsibilities.

Our national safety and the security of the world will require substantial armed forces, particularly in overseas service. At the same time it is imperative that we relieve those who have already done their duty, and that we relieve them as fast as we can. To do that, the Army and the Navy are conducting recruiting drives with considerable success.

The Army has obtained nearly 400,000 volunteers in the past four months, and the Navy has obtained 80,000. Eighty percent of these volunteers for the regular service have come from those already with the colors. The Congress has made it possible to offer valuable inducements to those who are eligible for enlistment. Every effort will be made to enlist the required number of young men.

The War and Navy Departments now estimate that by a year from now we still will need a strength of about 2 million including officers, for the armed forces—Army, Navy, and Air. I have reviewed their estimates and believe that the safety of the Nation will require the maintenance of an armed strength of this size for the calendar year that is before us.

In case the campaign for volunteers does not produce that number, it will be necessary by additional legislation to extend the Selective Service Act beyond May 16, the date of expiration under existing law. That is the only way we can get the men and bring back our veterans. There is no other way. Action along this line should not be postponed beyond March, in order to avoid uncertainty and disruption.

Domestic Affairs

1. The Economic Outlook

Prophets of doom predicted that the United States could not escape a runaway inflation during the war and an economic collapse after the war. These predictions have not been borne out. On the contrary, the record of economic stabilization during the war and during the period of reconversion has been an outstanding accomplishment.

We know, however, that nothing is as dangerous as overconfidence, in war or in peace. We have had to fight hard to hold the line. We have made strenuous efforts to speed reconversion. But neither the danger of a postwar inflation nor of a subsequent collapse in production and employment is yet overcome. We must base our policies not on unreasoning optimism or pessimism but upon a candid recognition of our objectives and upon a careful analysis of foreseeable trends.

Any precise appraisal of the economic outlook at this time is particularly difficult. The period of demobilization and reconversion is fraught with uncertainties. There are also serious gaps in our statistical information. Certain tendencies are, however, fairly clear and recognition of them should serve as background for the consideration of next year's Federal Program. In general, the outlook for business is good, and it is likely to continue to be good—provided we control inflation and achieve peace in management-labor relations.

Civilian production and employment can be expected to increase throughout the next year. This does not mean, however, that continuing full employment is assured. It is probable that demobilization of the armed forces will proceed faster than the increase in civilian employment opportunities. Even if substantial further withdrawals from the labor market occur, unemployment will increase temporarily. The extent to which this unemployment will persist depends largely on the speed of industrial expansion and the effectiveness of the policies of the Federal Government.

Along with extraordinary demand there are still at this time many critical shortages resulting from the war. These extraordinary demands and shortages may lead to a speculative boom, especially in the price of securities, real estate, and inventories.

Therefore, our chief worry still is inflation. While we control this inflationary pressure we must look forward to the time when this extraordinary demand will subside. It will be years before we catch up with the demand for housing. The extraordinary demand for other durable goods, for the replenishment of inventories, and for exports may be satisfied earlier. No backlog of demand can exist very long in the face of our tremendous productive capacity. We must expect again to face the problem of shrinking demand and consequent slackening in sales, production, and employment. This possibility of a deflationary spiral in the future will exist unless we now plan and adopt an effective full employment program.

2. General Policies—Immediate and Long-Range

During the war, production for civilian use was limited by war needs and available manpower. Economic stabilization required measures, to spread limited supplies equitably by rationing, price controls, increased taxes, savings bond campaigns, and credit controls. Now, with the surrender of our enemies, economic stabilization requires that policies be directed toward promoting an increase in supplies at low unit prices.

We must encourage the development of resources and enterprises in all parts of the country, particularly in underdeveloped areas. For example, the establishment of new peacetime industries in the Western States and in the South would, in my judgment, add to existing production and markets rather than merely bring about a shifting of production. I am asking the Secretaries of Agriculture, Commerce, and Labor to explore jointly methods for stimulating new industries, particularly in areas with surplus agricultural labor.

We must also aid small businessmen and particularly veterans who are competent to start their own businesses. The establishment and development of efficient small business ventures, I believe, will not take away from, but rather will add to, the total business of all enterprises.

Even with maximum encouragement of Production, we cannot hope to remove scarcities within a short time. The most serious deficiencies will persist in the fields of residential housing, building materials, and consumers' durable goods. The critical situation makes continued rent control, price control, and priorities, allocations, and inventory controls absolutely essential. Continued control of consumer credit will help to reduce the pressure on prices of durable goods and will also prolong the period during which the backlog demand will be effective.

While we are meeting these immediate needs we must look forward to a long-range program of security and increased standard of living.

The best protection of purchasing power is a policy of full production and full employment opportunities. Obviously, an employed worker is a better customer than an unemployed worker. There always will be, however, some frictional unemployment. In the present period of transition we must deal with such temporary unemployment as results from the fact that demobilization will proceed faster than reconversion or industrial expansion. Such temporary unemployment is probably unavoidable in a period of rapid change. The unemployed worker is a victim of conditions beyond his control. He should be enabled to maintain a reasonable standard of living for himself and his family.

The most serious difficulty in the path of reconversion and expansion is the establishment of a fair wage structure.

The ability of labor and management to work together, and the wage and price policies which they develop, are social and economic issues of first importance.

Both labor and management have a special interest. Labor's interest is very direct and personal because working conditions, wages, and prices affect the very life and happiness of the worker and his family.

Management has a no less direct interest because on management rests the responsibility for conducting a growing and prosperous business.

But management and labor have identical interests in the long run. Good wages mean good markets. Good business means more jobs and better wages. In this age of cooperation and in our highly organized economy the problems of one very soon become the problems of all.

Better human relationships are an urgent need to which organized labor and management should address themselves. No government policy can make men understand each other, agree, and get along unless they conduct themselves in a way to foster mutual respect and good will.

The Government can, however, help to develop machinery which, with the backing of public opinion, will assist labor and management to resolve their disagreements in a peaceful manner and reduce the number and duration of strikes.

All of us realize that productivity—increased output per man—is in the long run the basis of our standard of living. Management especially must realize that if labor is to work wholeheartedly for an increase in production, workers must be given a just share of increased output in higher wages.

Most industries and most companies have adequate leeway within which to grant substantial wage increases. These increases will have a direct effect in increasing consumer demand to the high levels needed. Substantial wage increases are good business for business because they assure a large market for their products; substantial wage increases are good business for labor because they increase labor's standard of living; substantial wage increases are good business for the country as a whole because capacity production means an active, healthy, friendly citizenry enjoying the benefits of democracy under our free enterprise system.

Labor and management in many industries have been operating successfully under the Government's wage-price policy. Upward revisions of wage scales have been made in thousands of establishments throughout the Nation since VJ-day. It is estimated that about 6 million workers, or more than 20 percent of all employees in nonagricultural and nongovernmental establishments, have received wage increases since August 18, 1945. The amounts of increases given by individual employers concentrate between 10 and 15 percent, but range from less than 5 percent to over 30 percent.

The United States Conciliation Service since VJ-day has settled over 3,000 disputes affecting over 1,300,000 workers without a strike threat and has assisted in settling about 1,300 disputes where strikes were threatened which involved about 500,000 workers. Only workers directly involved, and not those in related industries who might have been indirectly affected, are included in these estimates.

Many of these adjustments have occurred in key industries and would have seemed to us major crises if they had not been settled peaceably.

Within the framework of the wage-price policy there has been definite success, and it is to be expected that this success will continue in a vast majority of the cases arising in the months ahead.

However, everyone who realizes the extreme need for a swift and orderly reconversion must feel a deep concern about the number of major strikes now in progress. If long continued, these strikes could put a heavy brake on our program.

I have already made recommendations to the Congress as to the procedure best adapted to meeting the threat of work stoppages in Nation-wide industries without sacrificing the fundamental rights of labor to bargain collectively and ultimately to strike in support of their position.

If we manage our economy properly, the future will see us on a level of production half again as high as anything we have ever accomplished in peacetime. Business can in the future pay higher wages and sell for lower prices than ever before. This is not true now for all companies, nor will it ever be true for all, but for business generally it is true.

We are relying on all concerned to develop, through collective bargaining, wage structures that are fair to labor, allow for necessary business incentives, and conform with a policy designed to "hold the line" on prices.

Production and more production was the byword during the war and still is during the transition from war to peace. However, when deferred demand slackens, we shall once again face the deflationary dangers which beset this and other countries during the 1930's. Prosperity can be assured only by a high level of demand supported by high current income; it cannot be sustained by deferred needs and use of accumulated savings.

If we take the right steps in time we can certainly avoid the disastrous excesses of runaway booms and headlong depressions. We must not let a year or two of prosperity lull us into a false feeling of security and a repetition of the mistakes of the 1920's that culminated in the crash of 1929.

During the year ahead the Government will be called upon to act in many important fields of economic policy from taxation and foreign trade to social security and housing. In every case there will be alternatives. We must choose the alternatives which will best measure up to our need for maintaining production and employment in the future. We must never lose sight of our long-term objectives: the broadening of markets—the maintenance of steadily rising demand. This demand can come from only three sources: consumers, businesses, or government.

In this country the job of production and distribution is in the hands of businessmen, farmers, workers, and professional people—in the hands of our citizens. We want to keep it that way. However, it is the Government's responsibility to help business, labor, and farmers do their jobs.

There is no question in my mind that the Government, acting on behalf of all the people, must assume the ultimate responsibility for the economic health of the Nation. There is no other agency that can. No other organization has the scope or the authority, nor is any other agency accountable, to all the people. This does not mean that the Government has the sole responsibility, nor that it can do the job alone, nor that it can do the job directly.

All of the policies of the Federal Government must be geared to the objective of sustained full production and full employment—to raise consumer purchasing power and to encourage business investment. The programs we adopt this year and from now on will determine our ability to achieve our objectives. We must continue to pay particular attention to our fiscal, monetary, and tax policy, programs to aid business—

especially small business—and transportation, labor-management relations and wage-price policy, social security and health, education, the farm program, public works, housing and resource development, and economic foreign policy.

For example, the kinds of tax measures we have at different times—whether we raise our revenue in a way to encourage consumer spending and business investment or to discourage it—have a vital bearing on this question. It is affected also by regulations on consumer credit and by the money market, which is strongly influenced by the rate of interest on Government securities. It is affected by almost every step we take.

In short, the way we handle the proper functions of government, the way we time the exercise of our traditional and legitimate governmental functions, has a vital bearing on the economic health of the Nation.

These policies are discussed in greater detail in the accompanying Fifth Quarterly Report of the Director of War Mobilization and Reconversion.

3. Legislation Heretofore Recommended and Still Pending

To attain some of these objectives and to meet the other needs of the United States in the reconversion and postwar period, I have from time to time made various recommendations to the Congress.

In making these recommendations I have indicated the reasons why I deemed them essential for progress at home and abroad. A few—a very few—of these recommendations have been enacted into law by the Congress. Most of them have not. I here reiterate some of them, and discuss others later in this Message. I urge upon the Congress early consideration of them. Some are more urgent than others, but all are necessary.

(1) Legislation to authorize the President to create fact-finding boards for the prevention of stoppages of work in Nationwide industries after collective bargaining and conciliation and voluntary arbitration have failed—as recommended by me on December 3, 1945.

(2) Enactment of a satisfactory full employment bill such as the Senate bill now in conference between the Senate and the House—as recommended by me on September 6, 1945.

(3) Legislation to supplement the unemployment insurance benefits for unemployed workers now provided by the different States—as recommended by me on May 28, 1945.

(4) Adoption of a permanent Fair Employment Practice Act—as recommended by me on September 6, 1945.

(5) Legislation substantially raising the amount of minimum wages now provided by law—as recommended by me on September 6, 1945.

(6) Legislation providing for a comprehensive program for scientific research—as recommended by me on September 6, 1945.

(7) Legislation enacting a health and medical care program—as recommended by me on November 19, 1945.

(8) Legislation adopting the program of universal training—as recommended by me on October 23, 1945.

(9) Legislation providing an adequate salary scale for all Government employees in all branches of the Government—as recommended by me on September 6, 1945.

(10) Legislation making provision for succession to the Presidency in the event of the death or incapacity or disqualification of the President and Vice President—as recommended by me on June 19, 1945.

(11) Legislation for the unification of the armed services—as recommended by me on December 19, 1945.

(12) Legislation for the domestic use and control of atomic energy—as recommended by me on October 3, 1945.

(13) Retention of the United States Employment Service in the Federal Government for a period at least up to June 30, 1947—as recommended by me on September 6, 1945.

(14) Legislation to increase unemployment allowances for veterans in line with increases for civilians—as recommended by me on September 6, 1945.

(15) Social security coverage for veterans for their period of military service—as recommended by me on September 6, 1945.

(16) Extension of crop insurance—as recommended by me on September 6, 1945.

(17) Legislation permitting the sale of ships by the Maritime Commission at home and abroad—as recommended by me on September 6, 1945. I further recommend that this legislation include adequate authority for chartering vessels both here and abroad.

(18) Legislation to take care of the stock piling of materials in which the United States is naturally deficient—as recommended by me on September 6, 1945.

(19) Enactment of Federal airport legislation—as recommended by me on September 6, 1945.

(20) Legislation repealing the Johnson Act on foreign loans—as recommended by me on September 6, 1945.

(21) Legislation for the development of the Great Lakes-St. Lawrence River Basin—as recommended by me on October 3, 1945.

4. Policies in Specific Fields
(a) Extension of Price Control Act.

Today inflation is our greatest immediate domestic problem. So far the fight against inflation has been waged successfully. Since May 1943, following President Roosevelt's "hold the line" order and in the face of the greatest pressures which this country has ever seen, the cost of living index has risen only three percent. Wholesale prices in this same period have been held to an increase of two and one-half percent.

This record has been made possible by the vigorous efforts of the agencies responsible for this program. But their efforts would have been fruitless if they had not had the solid support of the great masses of our people. The Congress is to be congratulated for its role in providing the legislation under which this work has been carried out.

On VJ-day it was clear to all thinking people that the danger of inflation was by no means over. Many of us can remember vividly our disastrous experience following World War I. Then the very restricted wartime controls were lifted too quickly, and as a result prices and rents moved more rapidly upward. In the year and a half following the armistice, rents, food, and clothing shot to higher and still higher levels.

When the inevitable crash occurred less than two years after the end of the war, business bankruptcies were widespread. Profits were wiped out. Inventory losses amounted to billions of dollars. Farm income dropped by one-half. Factory pay rolls dropped 40 percent, and nearly one-fifth of all our industrial workers were walking the streets in search of jobs. This was a grim greeting, indeed, to offer our veterans who had just returned from overseas.

When I addressed the Congress in September, I emphasized that we must continue to hold the price line until the production of goods caught up with the tremendous demands. Since then we have seen demonstrated the strength of the inflationary pressures which we have to face.

Retail sales in the closing months of 1945 ran 12 percent above the previous peak for that season, which came in 1944. Prices throughout the entire economy have been pressing hard against the price ceilings. The prices of real estate, which cannot now be controlled under the law, are rising rapidly. Commercial rents are not included in the present price control law and, where they are not controlled by State law, have been increasing, causing difficulties to many businessmen.

It will be impossible to maintain a high purchasing power or an expanding production unless we can keep prices at levels which can be met by the vast majority of our people. Full production is the greatest weapon against inflation, but until we can produce enough goods to meet the threat of inflation the Government will have to exercise its wartime control over prices.

I am sure that the people of the United States are disturbed by the demands made by several business groups with regard to price and rent control.

I am particularly disturbed at the effect such thinking may have on production and employment. If manufacturers continue to hold back goods and decline to submit bids when invited—as I am informed some are doing—in anticipation of higher prices which would follow the end of price controls, we shall inevitably slow down production and create needless unemployment. On the other hand, there are the vast majority of American businessmen who are not holding back goods, but who need certainty about the Government pricing policy in order to fix their own long-range pricing policies.

Businessmen are entitled therefore to a clear statement of the policy of the Government on the subject. Tenants and housewives, farmers and workers—consumers in general—have an equal right.

We are all anxious to eliminate unnecessary controls just as rapidly as we can do so. The steps that we have already taken in many directions toward that end are a clear indication of our policy.

The present Price Control Act expires on June 30, 1946. If we expect to maintain a steady economy we shall have to maintain price and rent control for many months to come. The inflationary pressures on prices and rents, with relatively few exceptions, are now at an all-time peak. Unless the Price Control Act is renewed there will be no limit to which our price levels would soar. Our country would face a national disaster.

We cannot wait to renew the act until immediately before it expires. Inflation results from psychological as well as economic conditions. The country has a clear right to know where the Congress stands on this all-important problem. Any uncertainty now as to whether the act will be extended gives rise to price speculation, to withholding of goods from the market in anticipation of rising prices, and to delays in achieving maximum production.

I do not doubt that the Congress will be beset by many groups who will urge that the legislation that I have proposed should either be eliminated or modified to the point where it is nearly useless. The Congress has a clear responsibility to meet this challenge with courage and determination. I have every confidence that it will do so.

I strongly urge that the Congress now resolve all doubts and as soon as possible adopt legislation continuing rent and price control in effect for a full year from June 30, 1946.

(b) Food Subsidies.

If the price line is to be held, if our people are to be protected against the inflationary dangers which confront us, we must do more than extend the Price Control Act. In September we were hopeful that the inflationary pressures would by this time have begun to diminish. We were particularly hopeful on food. Indeed, it was estimated that food prices at retail would drop from 3 to 5 percent in the first six months following the end of the war.

In anticipation of this decline in food prices, it was our belief that food subsidies could be removed gradually during the winter and spring months, and eliminated almost completely by June 30 of this year. It was our feeling that the food subsidies could be dropped without an increase to the consumer in the present level of food prices or in the over-all cost of living.

As matters stand today, however, food prices are pressing hard against the ceilings. The expected decline in food prices has not occurred, nor is it likely to occur for many months to come. This brings me to the reluctant conclusion that food subsidies must be continued beyond June 30, 1946.

If we fail to take this necessary step, meat prices on July 1 will be from 3 to 5 cents higher than their average present levels; butter will be at least 12 cents a pound higher, in addition to the 5 cents a pound increase of last fall; milk will increase from 1 to 2 cents a quart; bread will increase about 1 cent a loaf; sugar will increase over 1 cent a pound; cheese, in addition to the increase of 4 cents now planned for the latter part of this month, will go up an additional 8 cents. In terms of percentages we may find the cost-of-living index for food increased by more than 8 percent, which in turn would result in more than a 3-percent increase in the cost of living.

If prices of food were allowed to increase by these amounts, I must make it clear to the Congress that, in my opinion, it would become extremely difficult for us to control the forces of inflation.

None of us likes subsidies. Our farmers, in particular, have always been opposed to them.

But I believe our farmers are as deeply conscious as any group in the land of the havoc which inflation can create. Certainly in the past eighteen months there has been no group which has fought any harder in support of the Government's price control program. I am confident that, if the facts are placed before them and if they see clearly the evils between which we are forced to choose, they will understand the reasons why subsidies must be continued.

The legislation continuing the use of food subsidies into the new fiscal year should be tied down specifically to certain standards. A very proper requirement, in my opinion, would be that subsidies be removed as soon as it is indicated that the cost of living will decline below the present levels.

(c) **Extension of War Powers Act.**

The Second War Powers Act has recently been extended by the Congress for six months instead of for a year. It will now expire, unless further extended, on June 30, 1946. This act is the basis for priority and inventory controls governing the use of scarce materials, as well as for other powers essential to orderly reconversion.

I think that this Administration has given adequate proof of the fact that it desires to eliminate wartime controls as quickly and as expeditiously as possible. However, we know that there will continue to be shortages of certain materials caused by the war even after June 30, 1946. It is important that businessmen know now that materials in short supply are going to be controlled and distributed fairly as long as these war-born shortages continue.

I, therefore, urge the Congress soon to extend the Second War Powers Act. We cannot afford to wait until just before the act expires next June. To wait would cause the controls to break down in a short time, and would hamper our production and employment program.

(d) **Small Business and Competition.**

A rising birth rate for small business, and a favorable environment for its growth, are not only economic necessities but also important practical demonstrations of opportunity in a democratic free society. A great many veterans and workers with new skills and experience will want to start in for themselves. The opportunity must be afforded them to do so. They are the small businessmen of the future.

Actually when we talk about small business we are talking about almost all of the Nation's individual businesses. Nine out of every ten concerns fall into this category, and 45 percent of all workers are employed by them. Between 30 and 40 percent of the total value of all business transactions are handled by small business.

It is obvious national policy to foster the sound development of small business. It helps to maintain high levels of employment and national income and consumption of the goods and services that the Nation can produce. It encourages the competition that keeps our free enterprise economy vigorous and expanding. Small business, because of its flexibility, assists in the rapid exploitation of scientific and technological discoveries. Investment in small business can absorb a large volume of savings that might otherwise not be tapped.

The Government should encourage and is encouraging small-business initiative and originality to stimulate progress through competition.

During the war, the Smaller War Plants Corporation assisted small concerns to make a maximum contribution to victory. The work of the Smaller War Plants Corporation is being carried on in peacetime by the Federal Loan Agency and the Department of Commerce. The fundamental approach to the job of encouraging small concerns must be based on:

1. Arrangements for making private and public financial resources available on reasonable terms.

2. Provision of technical advice and assistance to business as a whole on production, research, and management problems. This will help equalize competitive relationships between large and small companies, for many of the small companies cannot afford expensive technical research, accounting, and tax advice.

3. Elimination of trade practices and agreements which reduce competition and discriminate against new or small enterprises.

We speak a great deal about the free enterprise economy of our country. It is competition that keeps it free. It is competition that keeps it growing and developing. The truth is that we need far more competition in the future than we have had in the immediate past.

By strangling competition, monopolistic activity prevents or deters investment in new or expanded production facilities. This lessens the opportunity for employment and chokes off new outlets for idle savings. Monopoly maintains prices at artificially high levels and reduces consumption which, with lower prices, would rise and support larger production and higher employment. Monopoly, not being subject to competitive pressure, is slow to take advantage of technical advances which would lower prices or improve quality. All three of these monopolistic activities very directly lower the standard of living—through higher prices and lower quality of product—which free competition would improve.

The Federal Government must protect legitimate business and consumers from predatory and monopolistic practices by the vigilant enforcement of regulatory legislation. The program will be designed to have a maximum impact upon monopolistic bottlenecks and unfair competitive practices hindering expansion in employment.

During the war, enforcement of antimonopoly laws was suspended in a number of fields. The Government must now take major steps not only to maintain enforcement of antitrust laws but to encourage new and competing enterprises in every way. The deferred demand of the war years and the large accumulations of liquid assets provide ample incentive for expansion. Equalizing of business opportunity, under full and free competition, must be a prime responsibility in the reconversion period and in the years that follow. Many leading businessmen have recognized the importance of such action both to themselves and to the economy as a whole.

But we must do more than break up trusts and monopolies after they have begun to strangle competition. We must take positive action to foster new, expanding enterprises. By legislation and by administration we must take specific steps to discourage the formation or the strengthening of competition-restricting business. We must have an overall antimonopoly policy which can be applied by all agencies of the Government in exercising the functions assigned to them—a policy designed to encourage the formation and growth of new and freely competitive enterprises.

Among the many departments and agencies which have parts in the program affecting business and competition, the Department of Commerce has a particularly important role. That is why I have recommended a substantial increase in appropriations for the next fiscal year for this Department.

In its assistance to industry, the Department of Commerce will concentrate its efforts on these primary objectives: Promotion of a large and well-balanced foreign trade; provision of improved technical assistance and management aids, especially for small enterprises; and strengthening of basic statistics on business operations, both by industries and by regions. To make new inventions and discoveries available more promptly to all businesses, small and large, the Department proposes to expand its own research activities, promote research by universities, improve Patent Office procedures, and develop a greatly expanded system of field offices readily accessible to the businesses they serve.

Many gaps exist in the private financial mechanism, especially in the provision of long-term funds for small- and medium-sized enterprises. In the peacetime economy the Reconstruction Finance Corporation will take the leadership in assuring adequate financing for small enterprises which cannot secure funds from other sources. Most of the funds should and will be provided by private lenders; but the Reconstruction Finance Corporation will share any unusual risks through guarantees of private loans, with direct loans only when private capital is unwilling to participate on a reasonable basis.

(e) Minimum Wage.

Full employment and full production may be achieved only by maintaining a level of consumer income far higher than that of the prewar period. A high level of consumer income will maintain the market for the output of our mills, farms, and factories, which we have demonstrated during the war years that we can produce. One of the basic steps which the Congress can take to establish a high level of consumer income is to amend the Fair Labor Standards Act to raise substandard wages to a decent minimum and to extend similar protection to additional workers who are not covered by the present act.

Substandard wages are bad for business and for the farmer. Substandard wages provide only a substandard market for the goods and services produced by American industry and agriculture.

At the present time the Fair Labor Standards Act prescribes a minimum wage of 40 cents an hour for those workers who are covered by the act. The present minimum wage represents an annual income of about $800 to those continuously employed for 50 weeks—clearly a wholly inadequate budget for an American family. I am in full accord with the proposal now pending in the Congress that the statutory minimum be raised immediately to 65 cents an hour, with further increases to 70 cents after one year and to 75 cents after two years. I also favor the proposal that the industry committee procedure be used to set rates higher than 65 cents per hour during the two-year interval before the 75-cent basic wage would otherwise become applicable.

The proposed minimum wage of 65 cents an hour would assure the worker an annual income of about $1,300 a year in steady employment. This amount is clearly a modest goal. After considering cost-of-living increases in recent years, it is little more than a 10-cent increase over the present legal minimum. In fact, if any large number of workers earn less than this amount, we will find it impossible to maintain the levels of purchasing power needed to sustain the stable prosperity which we desire. Raising the minimum to 75 cents an hour will provide the wage earner with an annual income of $1,500 if he is fully employed.

The proposed higher minimum wage levels are feasible without involving serious price adjustments or serious geographic dislocations.

Today about 20 percent of our manufacturing wage earners—or about 2 million—earn less than 65 cents an hour. Because wages in most industries have risen during the war, this is about the same as the proportion—17 percent—who were earning less than 40 cents an hour in 1941.

I also recommend that minimum wage protection be extended to several groups of workers not now covered. The need for a decent standard of living is by no means limited to those workers who happen to be covered by the act as it now stands. It is particularly vital at this period of readjustment in the national economy and readjustment in employment of labor to extend minimum wage protection as far as possible.

Lifting the basic minimum wage is necessary, it is justified as a matter of simple equity to workers, and it will prove not only feasible but also directly beneficial to the Nation's employers.

(f) Agricultural Programs.

The farmers of America generally are entering the crop year of 1946 in better financial condition than ever before. Farm mortgage debt is the lowest in 30 years. Farmers' savings are the largest in history. Our agricultural plant is in much better condition than after World War I. Farm machinery and supplies are expected to be available in larger volume, and farm labor problems will be less acute.

The demand for farm products will continue strong during the next year or two because domestic purchases will be supplemented by a high level of exports and foreign relief shipments. It is currently estimated that from 7 to 10 percent of the total United States food supply may be exported in the calendar year 1946.

Farm prices are expected to remain at least at their present levels in the immediate future, and for at least the next 12 months they are expected to yield a net farm income double the 1935–39 average and higher than in any year prior to 1943.

We can look to the future of agriculture with greater confidence than in many a year in the past. Agriculture itself is moving confidently ahead, planning for another year of big production, taking definite and positive steps to lead the way toward an economy of abundance.

Agricultural production goals for 1946 call for somewhat greater acreage than actually was planted in 1945. Agriculture is prepared to demonstrate that it can make a peacetime contribution as great as its contribution toward the winning of the war.

In spite of supplying our armed forces and our allies during the war with a fifth to a fourth of our total food output, farmers were still able to provide our civilians with 8 percent more food per capita than the average for the five years preceding the war. Since the surrender of Japan, civilian food consumption has risen still further. By the end of 1945 the amount of the increase in food consumption was estimated to be as high as 15 percent over the prewar average. The record shows that the people of this country want and need more food and that they will buy more food if only they have the jobs and the purchasing power. The first essential therefore in providing fully for the welfare of agriculture is to maintain full employment and a high level of purchasing power throughout the Nation.

For the period immediately ahead we shall still have the problem of supplying enough food. If we are to do our part in aiding the war-stricken and starving countries some of the food desires of our own people will not be completely satisfied, at least until these nations have had an opportunity to harvest another crop. During the next few months the need for food in the world will be more serious than at any time during the war. And, despite the large shipments we have already made, and despite what we shall send, there remain great needs abroad.

Beyond the relief feeding period, there will still be substantial foreign outlets for our farm commodities. The chief dependence of the farmer, however, as always, must be upon the buying power of our own people.

The first obligation of the Government to agriculture for the reconversion period is to make good on its price-support commitments. This we intend to do, with realistic consideration for the sound patterns of production that will contribute most to the long-time welfare of agriculture and the whole Nation. The period during which prices are supported will provide an opportunity for farmers individually to strengthen their position in changing over from a wartime to a peacetime basis of production. It will provide an opportunity for the Congress to review the needs of agriculture and make changes in national legislation where experience has shown changes to be needed. In this connection, the Congress will wish to consider legislation to take the place of the 1937 Sugar Act which expires at the end of this year. During this period we must do a thorough job of basic planning to the end that agriculture shall be able to contribute its full share toward a healthy national economy.

Our long-range agricultural policies should have two main objectives: First, to assure the people on the farms a fair share of the national income; and, second, to encourage an agricultural production pattern that is best fitted to the Nation's needs. To accomplish this second objective we shall have to take into consideration changes that have taken place and will continue to take place in the production of farm commodities—changes that affect costs and efficiency and volume.

What we seek ultimately is a high level of food production and consumption that will provide good nutrition for everyone. This cannot be accomplished by agriculture alone. We can be certain of our capacity to produce food, but we have often failed to distribute it as well as we should and to see that our people can afford to buy it. The way to get good nutrition for the whole Nation is to provide employment opportunities and purchasing power for all groups that will enable them to buy full diets at market prices.

Wherever purchasing power fails to reach this level we should see that they have some means of getting adequate food at prices in line with their ability to buy. Therefore, we should have available supplementary programs that will enable all our people to have enough of the right kind of food.

For example, one of the best possible contributions toward building a stronger, healthier Nation would be a permanent school-lunch program on a scale adequate to assure every school child a good lunch at noon. The Congress, of course, has recognized this need for a continuing school-lunch program and legislation to that effect has been introduced and hearings held. The plan contemplates the attainment of this objective with a minimum of Federal expenditures. I hope that the legislation will be enacted in time for a permanent program to start with the beginning of the school year next fall.

We have the technical knowledge and the productive capacity to provide plenty of good food for every man, woman, and child in the United States. It is time we made that possibility a reality.

(g) Resource Development.

The strength of our Nation and the welfare of the people rest upon the natural resources of the country. We have learned that proper conservation of our lands, including our forests and minerals, and wise management of our waters will add immensely to our national wealth.

The first step in the Government's conservation program must be to find out just what are our basic resources, and how they should be used. We need to take, as soon as possible, an inventory of the lands, the minerals, and the forests of the Nation.

During the war it was necessary to curtail some of our long-range plans for development of our natural resources, and to emphasize programs vital to the prosecution of the war. Work was suspended on a number of flood control and reclamation projects and on the development of our national forests and parks. This work must now be resumed, and new projects must be undertaken to provide essential services and to assist in the process of economic development.

The rivers of America offer a great opportunity to our generation in the management of the national wealth. By a wise use of Federal funds, most of which will be repaid into the Treasury, the scourge of floods and drought can be curbed, water can be brought to arid lands, navigation can be extended, and cheap power can be brought alike to the farms and to the industries of our land.

Through the use of the waters of the Columbia River, for example, we are creating a rich agricultural area as large as the State of Delaware. At the same time, we are producing power at Grand Coulee and at Bonneville which played a mighty part in winning the war and which will found a great peacetime industry in the Northwest. The Tennessee Valley Authority will resume its peacetime program of promoting full use of the resources of the Valley. We shall continue our plans for the development of the Missouri Valley, the Arkansas Valley, and the Central Valley of California.

The Congress has shown itself alive to the practical requirements for a beneficial use of our water resources by providing that preference in the sale of power be given to farmers' cooperatives and public agencies. The public power program thus authorized must continue to be made effective by building the necessary generating and transmission facilities to furnish the maximum of firm power needed at the wholesale markets, which are often distant from the dam sites.

These great developmental projects will open the frontiers of agriculture, industry, and commerce. The employment opportunities thus offered will also go far to ease the transition from war to peace.

(h) Public Works.

During the war even urgently needed Federal, State, and local construction projects were deferred in order to release sources for war production. In resuming public works construction, it is desirable to proceed only at a moderate rate, since demand for private construction will be abnormally high for some time. Our public works program should be timed to reach its peak after demand for private construction has begun to taper off. Meanwhile, however, plans should be prepared if we are to act promptly when the present extraordinary private demand begins to run out.

The Congress made money available to Federal agencies for their public works planning in the fiscal year 1946. I strongly recommend that this policy be continued and extended in the fiscal year 1947.

State and local governments also have an essential role to play in a national public works program. In my message of September 6, 1945, I recommended that the Congress vote such grants to State and local governments as will insure that each level of government makes its proper contribution to a balanced public construction program.

Specifically, the Federal Government should aid State and local governments in planning their own public works programs, in undertaking projects related to Federal programs of regional development, and in constructing such public works as are necessary to carry out the various policies of the Federal Government.

Early in 1945 the Congress made available advances to State and local governments for planning public works projects, and recently made additional provision to continue these advances through the fiscal year 1946. I believe that further appropriations will be needed for the same purpose for the fiscal year 1947.

The Congress has already made provision for highway programs. It is now considering legislation which would expand Federal grants and loans in several other fields, including construction of airports, hospital and health centers, housing, water pollution control facilities, and educational plant facilities. I hope that early action will be taken to authorize these Federal programs.

With respect to public works of strictly local importance, State and local governments should proceed without Federal assistance except in planning. This rule should be subject to review when and if the prospect of highly adverse general economic developments warrants it.

All loans and grants for public works should be planned and administered in such a way that they are brought into accord with the other elements of the Federal Program.

Our long-run objective is to achieve a program of direct Federal and Federally assisted public works which is planned in advance and synchronized with business conditions. In this way it can make its greatest contribution to general economic stability.

(i) National Housing Program.

Last September I stated in my message to the Congress that housing was high on the list of matters calling for decisive action.

Since then the housing shortage in countless communities, affecting millions of families, has magnified this call to action.

Today we face both an immediate emergency and a major postwar problem.

Since VJ-day the wartime housing shortage has been growing steadily worse and pressure on real estate values has increased. Returning veterans often cannot find a satisfactory place for their families to live, and many who buy have to pay exorbitant prices. Rapid demobilization inevitably means further overcrowding.

A realistic and practical attack on the emergency will require aggressive action by local governments, with Federal aid, to exploit all opportunities and to give the veterans as far as possible first chance at vacancies. It will require continuation of rent control in shortage areas as well as legislation to permit control of sales prices. It will require maximum conversion of temporary war units for veterans' housing and their transportation to communities with the most pressing needs; the Congress has already appropriated funds for this purpose.

The inflation in the price of housing is growing daily.

As a result of the housing shortage, it is inevitable that the present dangers of inflation in home values will continue unless the Congress takes action in the immediate future.

Legislation is now pending in the Congress which would provide for ceiling prices for old and new houses. The authority to fix such ceilings is essential. With such authority, our veterans and other prospective home owners would be protected against a skyrocketing of home prices. The country would be protected from the extension of the present inflation in home values which, if allowed to continue, will threaten not only the stabilization program but our opportunities for attaining a sustained high level of home construction.

Such measures are necessary stopgaps—but only stopgaps. This emergency action, taken alone, is good—but not enough. The housing shortage did not start with the war or with demobilization; it began years before that and has steadily accumulated. The speed with which the Congress establishes the foundation for a permanent, long-range housing program will determine how effectively we grasp the immense opportunity to achieve our goal of decent housing and to make housing a major instrument of continuing prosperity and full employment in the years ahead. It will determine whether we move forward to a stable and healthy housing enterprise and toward providing a decent home for every American family.

Production is the only fully effective answer. To get the wheels turning, I have appointed an emergency housing expediter. I have approved establishment of priorities designed to assure an ample share of scarce materials to builders of houses for which veterans will have preference. Additional price and wage adjustments will be made where necessary, and other steps will be taken to stimulate greater production of bottleneck items. I recommend consideration of every sound method for expansion in facilities for insurance of privately financed housing by the Federal Housing Administration and resumption of previously authorized low-rent public housing projects suspended during the war.

In order to meet as many demands of the emergency situation as possible, a program of emergency measures is now being formulated for action. These will include steps in addition to those already taken. As quickly as this program can be formulated, announcement will be made.

Last September I also outlined to the Congress the basic principles for the kind of decisive, permanent legislation necessary for a long-range housing program.

These principles place paramount the fact that housing construction and financing for the overwhelming majority of our citizens should be done by private enterprise. They contemplate also that we afford governmental encouragement to privately financed house construction for families of moderate income, through extension of the successful system of insurance of housing investment; that research be undertaken to develop better and cheaper methods of building homes; that communities be assisted in appraising their housing needs; that we commence a program of Federal aid, with fair local participation, to stimulate and promote the rebuilding and redevelopment of slums and blighted areas—with maximum use of private capital. It is equally essential that we use public funds to assist families of low income who could not otherwise enjoy adequate housing, and that we quicken our rate of progress in rural housing.

Legislation now under consideration by the Congress provides for a comprehensive attack jointly by private enterprise, State and local authorities, and the Federal Government. This legislation would make permanent the National Housing Agency and give it authority and funds for much needed technical and economic research. It would provide additional stimulus for privately financed housing construction. This stimulus consists of establishing a new system of yield insurance to encourage large-scale investment in rental housing and broadening the insuring powers of the Federal Housing Administration and the lending powers of the Federal savings and loan associations.

Where private industry cannot build, the Government must step in to do the job. The bill would encourage expansion in housing available for the lowest income groups by continuing to provide direct subsidies for low-rent housing and rural housing. It would facilitate land assembly for urban redevelopment by loans and contributions to local public agencies where the localities do their share.

Prompt enactment of permanent housing legislation along these lines will not interfere with the emergency action already under way. On the contrary, it would lift us out of a potentially perpetual state of housing emergency. It would offer the best hope and prospect to millions of veterans and other American families that the American system can offer more to them than temporary makeshifts.

I have said before that the people of the United States can be the best housed people in the world. I repeat that assertion, and I welcome the cooperation of the Congress in achieving that goal.

(j) Social Security and Health.

Our Social Security System has just celebrated its tenth anniversary. During the past decade this program has supported the welfare and morale of a large part of our people by removing some of the hazards and hardships of the aged, the unemployed, and widows and dependent children.

But, looking back over 10 years' experience and ahead to the future, we cannot fail to see defects and serious inadequacies in our system as it now exists. Benefits are in many cases inadequate; a great many persons are excluded from coverage; and provision has not been made for social insurance to cover the cost of medical care and the earnings lost by the sick and the disabled.

In the field of old-age security, there seems to be no adequate reason for excluding such groups as the self-employed, agricultural and domestic workers, and employees of nonprofit organizations. Since many of these groups earn wages too low to permit significant savings for old age, they are in special need of the assured income that can be provided by old-age insurance.

We must take urgent measures for the readjustment period ahead. The Congress for some time has been considering legislation designed to supplement at Federal expense, during the immediate reconversion period, compensation payments to the unemployed. Again I urge the Congress to enact legislation liberalizing unemployment compensation benefits and extending the coverage. Providing for the sustained consumption by the unemployed persons and their families is more than a welfare policy; it is sound economic policy. A sustained high level of consumer purchases is a basic ingredient of a prosperous economy.

During the war, nearly 5 million men were rejected for military service because of physical or mental defects which in many cases might have been prevented or corrected. This is shocking evidence that large sections of the population are at substandard levels of health. The need for a program that will give everyone opportunity for medical care is obvious. Nor can there be any serious doubt of the Government's responsibility for helping in this human and social problem.

The comprehensive health program which I recommended on November 19, 1945, will require substantial additions to the Social Security System and, in conjunction with other changes that need to be made, will require further consideration of the financial basis for social security. The system of prepaid medical care which I have recommended is expected eventually to require amounts equivalent to 4 percent of earnings up to $3,600 a year, which is about the average of present expenditures by individuals for medical care. The pooling of medical costs, under a plan which permits each individual to make a free choice of doctor and hospital, would assure that individuals receive adequate treatment and hospitalization when they are faced with emergencies for which they cannot budget individually. In addition, I recommended insurance benefits to replace part of the earnings lost through temporary sickness and permanent disability.

Even without these proposed major additions, it would now be time to undertake a thorough reconsideration of our social security laws. The structure should be expanded and liberalized. Provision should be made for extending coverage credit to veterans for the period of their service in the armed forces. In the financial provisions we must reconcile the actuarial needs of social security, including health insurance, with the requirements of a revenue system that is designed to promote a high level of consumption and full employment.

(k) Education.

Although the major responsibility for financing education rests with the States, some assistance has long been given by the Federal Government. Further assistance is desirable and essential. There are many areas and some whole States where good schools cannot be provided without imposing an undue local tax burden on the citizens. It is essential to provide adequate elementary and secondary schools everywhere, and additional educational opportunities for large numbers of people beyond the secondary level. Accordingly, I repeat the proposal of last year's Budget Message that the Federal Government provide financial aid to assist the States in assuring more nearly equal opportunities for a good education. The proposed Federal grants for current educational expenditures should be made for the purpose of improving the educational system where improvement is most needed. They should not be used to replace existing non-Federal expenditures, or even to restore merely the situation which existed before the war.

In the future we expect incomes considerably higher than before the war. Higher incomes should make it possible for State and local governments and for individuals to support higher and more nearly adequate expenditures for education. But inequality among the States will still remain, and Federal help will still be needed.

As a part of our total public works program, consideration should be given to the need for providing adequate buildings for schools and other educational institutions. In view of current arrears in the construction of educational facilities, I believe that legislation to authorize grants for educational facilities, to be matched by similar expenditures by State and local authorities, should receive the favorable consideration of the Congress.

The Federal Government has not sought, and will not seek, to dominate education in the States. It should continue its historic role of leadership and advice and, for the purpose of equalizing educational opportunity, it should extend further financial support to the cause of education in areas where this is desirable.

(l) Federal Government Personnel.

The rapid reconversion of the Federal Government from war to peace is reflected in the demobilization of its civilian personnel. The number of these employees in continental United States has been reduced by more than 500,000 from the total of approximately 2,900,000 employed in the final months of the war. I expect that by next June we shall have made a further reduction of equal magnitude and that there will be continuing reductions during the next fiscal year. Of the special wartime agencies now remaining, only a few are expected to continue actively into the next fiscal year.

At the same time that we have curtailed the number of employees, we have shortened the workweek by one-sixth or more throughout the Government and have restored holidays. The process of readjustment has been complicated and costs have been increased by a heavy turn-over in the remaining personnel—particularly by the loss of some of our best administrators. Thousands of war veterans have been reinstated or newly employed in the civil service. Many civilians have been transferred from war agencies to their former peacetime agencies. Recruitment standards, which had to be relaxed during the war, are now being tightened.

The elimination last autumn of overtime work for nearly all Federal employees meant a sharp cut in their incomes. For salaried workers, the blow was softened but by no means offset by the increased rates of pay which had become effective July 1. Further adjustments to compensate for increased living costs are required. Moreover, we have long needed a general upward revision of Federal Government salary scales at all levels in all branches—legislative, judicial, and executive. Too many in Government have had to sacrifice too much in economic advantage to serve the Nation.

Adequate salaries will result in economies and improved efficiency in the conduct of Government business—gains that will far outweigh the immediate costs. I hope the Congress will expedite action on salary legislation for all Federal employees in all branches of the Government. The only exception I would make is in the case of workers whose pay rates are established by wage boards; a blanket adjustment would destroy the system by which their wages are kept aligned with prevailing rates in particular localities. The wage boards should be sensitive now, as they were during the war, to changes in local prevailing wage rates and should make adjustments accordingly.

I hope also that the Congress may see fit to enact legislation for the adequate protection of the health and safety of Federal employees, for their coverage under a system of unemployment compensation, and for their return at Government expense to their homes after separation from wartime service.

(m) Territories, Insular Possessions, and the District of Columbia.

The major governments of the world face few problems as important and as perplexing as those relating to dependent peoples. This Government is committed to the democratic principle that it is for the dependent peoples themselves to decide what their status shall be. To this end I asked the Congress last October to provide a means by which the people of Puerto Rico might choose their form of government and ultimate status with respect to the United States. I urge, too, that the Congress promptly accede to the wishes of the people of Hawaii that the Territory be admitted to statehood in our Union, and that similar action be taken with respect to Alaska as soon as it is certain that this is the desire of the people of that great Territory. The people of the Virgin Islands should be given an increasing measure of self-government.

We have already determined that the Philippine Islands are to be independent on July 4, 1946. The ravages of war and enemy occupation, however, have placed a heavy responsibility upon the United States. I urge that the Congress complete, as promptly and as generously as may be possible, legislation which will aid economic rehabilitation for the Philippines. This will be not only a just acknowledgment of the loyalty of the people of the Philippines, but it will help to avoid the economic chaos which otherwise will be their heritage from our common war. Perhaps no event in the long centuries of colonialism gives more hope for the pattern of the future than the independence of the Philippines.

The District of Columbia, because of its special relation to the Federal Government, has been treated since 1800 as a dependent area. We should move toward a greater measure of local self-government consistent with the constitutional status of the District. We should take adequate steps to assure that citizens of the United States are not denied their franchise merely because they reside at the Nation's Capital.

We have won a great war—we, the nations of plain people who hate war. In the test of that war we found a strength of unity that brought us through—a strength that crushed the power of those who sought by force to deny our faith in the dignity of man.

During this trial the voices of disunity among us were silent or were subdued to an occasional whine that warned us that they were still among us. Those voices are beginning to cry aloud again. We must learn constantly to turn deaf ears to them. They are voices which foster fear and suspicion and intolerance and hate. They seek to destroy our harmony, our understanding of each other, our American tradition of "live and let live." They have become busy again, trying to set race against race, creed against creed, farmer against city dweller, worker against employer, people against their own governments. They seek only to do us mischief. They must not prevail.

It should be impossible for any man to contemplate without a sense of personal humility the tremendous events of the 12 months since the last annual Message, the great tasks that confront us, the new and huge problems of the coming months and years. Yet these very things justify the deepest confidence in the future of this Nation of free men and women.

The plain people of this country found the courage and the strength, the self-discipline, and the mutual respect to fight and to win, with the help of our allies, under God. I doubt if the tasks of the future are more difficult. But if they are, then I say that our strength and our knowledge and our understanding will be equal to those tasks.

Harry S. Truman, 1945–1949

Address to Congress on the State of the Union
January 6, 1947

Harry Truman's second State of the Union message was delivered before a Republican-controlled Congress—the first GOP Congress since the early years of the Great Depression. In his address, the Democratic president urged Congress to work with him despite their party differences. This 80th Congress, which came to be known as the "Do-Nothing" Congress, stymied the president's domestic agenda but also provided a target for Truman's presidential campaign in 1948.

In this State of the Union address, the first to be televised, the president discussed five economic programs he sought: revision of labor-management relations, restrictions on monopolies, construction of more housing, balancing the budget, and management of farm production. He also touched on the issue of civil rights and talked about the difficulties of coming to postwar agreements with the Soviet Union.

The country had faced some major strikes in the months after World War II ended, including in the spring of 1946 when both the United Mine Workers and many railroad-related workers went on strike. Truman, stating that both sides, not just labor, bore responsibility for these work stoppages, called in his State of the Union message for a commission to study labor-management relations.

The president was to clash with Congress in 1947 over the issue of labor-management relations when lawmakers passed the Labor-Management Relations Act of 1947, known as the Taft-Hartley Act. Truman, who believed the bill hurt unions' bargaining power, vetoed the legislation, only to have Congress override his veto. This battle was just one that Truman would have with Congress, which was not inclined to approve many of the president's domestic proposals.

Truman also became the first president to call for a national health insurance program. He had mentioned the issue in his written speech from a year earlier, but this was his first rhetorical effort to put the topic on the national agenda.

On the issue of civil rights, Truman had established a month earlier a presidential committee to look into federal enforcement of civil rights, which was to report to Congress on its findings. In his speech, the president spoke against "racial and religious bigotry" that infringed upon the constitutional rights of individual Americans.

When it came to international relations, the United States already had been feuding with the communist Soviet Union over the shape of the post-World War II international picture. Truman noted in his speech that delays in reaching peace treaties relating to Italy, Bulgaria, Romania, and Hungary were due to "the difficulty of reaching agreement with the Soviet Union on the terms of settlement."

In March 1947 Truman spoke before Congress, stating that U.S. policy should support "free people" resisting subjugation; this came to be known as the Truman Doctrine. Later that year, Secretary of State George C. Marshall announced what came to be known as the Marshall Plan: a huge economic aid package for European countries devastated by the war and vulnerable to communist pressure.

Mr. President, Mr. Speaker, Members of the Congress of the United States:

It looks like a good many of you have moved over to the left since I was here last!

I come before you today to report on the State of the Union and, in the words of the Constitution, to recommend such measures as I judge necessary and expedient.

I come also to welcome you as you take up your duties and to discuss with you the manner in which you and I should fulfill our obligations to the American people during the next 2 years.

The power to mold the future of this Nation lies in our hands—yours and mine, and they are joined together by the Constitution.

If in this year, and in the next, we can find the right course to take as each issue arises, and if, in spite of all difficulties, we have the courage and the resolution to take that course, then we shall achieve a state of well-being for our people without precedent in history. And if we continue to work with the other nations of the world earnestly, patiently, and wisely, we can—granting a will for peace on the part of our neighbors—make a lasting peace for the world.

But, if we are to realize these ends, the Congress and the President, during the next 2 years, must work together. It is not unusual in our history that the majority of the Congress represents a party in opposition to the President's party. I am the twentieth President of the United States who, at some time during his term of office, has found his own party to be in the minority in one or both Houses of Congress. The first one was George Washington. Wilson was number eighteen, and Hoover was number nineteen.

I realize that on some matters the Congress and the President may have honest differences of opinion. Partisan differences, however, did not cause material disagreements as to the conduct of the war. Nor, in the conduct of our international relations, during and since the war, have such partisan differences been material.

On some domestic issues we may, and probably shall, disagree. That in itself is not to be feared. It is inherent in our form of Government. But there are ways of disagreeing; men who differ can still work together sincerely for the common good. We shall be risking the Nation's safety and destroying our opportunities for progress if we do not settle any disagreements in this spirit, without thought of partisan advantage.

The General Domestic Economy

As the year 1947 begins, the state of our national economy presents great opportunities for all. We have virtually full employment. Our national production of goods and services is 50 percent higher than in any year prior to the war emergency. The national income in 1946 was higher than in any peacetime year. Our food production is greater than it has ever been. During the last 5 years our productive facilities have been expanded in almost every field. The American standard of living is higher now than ever before, and when the housing shortage can be overcome it will be even higher.

During the past few months we have removed at a rapid rate the emergency controls that the Federal Government had to exercise during the war. The remaining controls will be retained only as long as they are needed to protect the public. Private enterprise must be given the greatest possible freedom to continue the expansion of economy.

In my proclamation of December 31, 1946 I announced the termination of hostilities. This automatically ended certain temporary legislation and certain executive powers.

Two groups of temporary laws still remain: the first are those which by Congressional mandate are to last during the "emergency"; the second are those which are to continue until the "termination of the war."

I shall submit to the Congress recommendations for the repeal of certain of the statutes which by their terms continue for the duration of the "emergency." I shall at the same time recommend that others within this classification be extended until the state of war has been ended by treaty or by legislative action. As to those statutes which continue until the state of war has been terminated, I urge that the Congress promptly consider each statute individually, and repeal such emergency legislation where it is advisable.

Now that nearly all wartime controls have been removed, the operation of our industrial system depends to a greater extent on the decisions of businessmen, farmers, and workers. These decisions must be wisely made with genuine concern for public welfare. The welfare of businessmen, farmers, and workers depends upon the economic well-being of those who buy their products.

An important present source of danger to our economy is the possibility that prices might be raised to such an extent that the consuming public could not purchase the tremendous volume of goods and services which will be produced during 1947.

We all know that recent price increases have denied to many of our workers much of the value of recent wage increases. Farmers have found that a large part of their increased income has been absorbed by increased prices. While some of our people have received raises in income which exceed price increases, the great majority have not. Those persons who live on modest fixed incomes—retired persons living on pensions, for example—and workers whose incomes are relatively inflexible, such as teachers and other civil servants—have suffered hardship.

In the effort to bring about a sound and equitable price structure, each group of our population has its own responsibilities.

It is up to industry not only to hold the line on existing prices, but to make reductions whenever profits justify such action.

It is up to labor to refrain from pressing for unjustified wage increases that will force increases in the price level.

And it is up to Government to do everything in its power to encourage high-volume Production, for that is what makes possible good wages, low prices, and reasonable profits.

In a few days there will be submitted to the Congress the Economic Report of the President, and also the Budget Message. Those messages will contain many recommendations. Today I shall outline five major economic policies which I believe the Government should pursue during 1947. These policies are designed to meet our immediate needs and, at the same time, to provide for the long-range welfare of our free enterprise system:

First, the promotion of greater harmony between labor and management.

Second, restriction of monopoly and unfair business practices; assistance to small business; and the promotion of the free competitive system of private enterprise.

Third, continuation of an aggressive program of home construction.

Fourth, the balancing of the budget in the next fiscal year and the achieving of a substantial surplus to be applied to the reduction of the public debt.

Fifth, protection of a fair level of return to farmers in post-war agriculture.

Labor and Management

The year just past—like the year after the first World War—was marred by labor management strife.

Despite this outbreak of economic warfare in 1946, we are today producing goods and services in record volume. Nevertheless, it is essential to improve the methods for reaching agreement between labor and management and to reduce the number of strikes and lockouts.

We must not, however, adopt punitive legislation. We must not in order to punish a few labor leaders, pass vindictive laws which will restrict the proper rights of the rank and file of labor. We must not, under the stress of emotion, endanger our American freedoms by taking ill-considered action which will lead to results not anticipated or desired.

We must remember, in reviewing the record of disputes in 1946, that management shares with labor the responsibility for failure to reach agreements which would have averted strikes. For that reason, we must realize that industrial peace cannot be achieved merely by laws directed against labor unions.

During the last decade and a half, we have established a national labor policy in this country based upon free collective bargaining as the process for determining wages and working conditions.

That is still the national policy.

And it should continue to be the national policy!

But as yet, not all of us have learned what it means to bargain freely and fairly. Nor have all of us learned to carry the mutual responsibilities that accompany the right to bargain. There have been abuses and harmful practices which limit the effectiveness of our system of collective bargaining. Furthermore, we have lacked sufficient governmental machinery to aid labor and management in resolving their differences.

Certain labor-management problems need attention at once and certain others, by reason of their complexity, need exhaustive investigation and study.

We should enact legislation to correct certain abuses and to provide additional governmental assistance in bargaining. But we should also concern ourselves with the basic causes of labor-management difficulties.

In the light of these considerations, I propose to you and urge your cooperation in effecting the following four-point program to reduce industrial strife:

Point number one is the early enactment of legislation to prevent certain unjustifiable practices.

First, under this point, are jurisdictional strikes. In such strikes the public and the employer are innocent bystanders who are injured by a collision between rival unions. This type of dispute hurts production, industry, and the public—and labor itself. I consider jurisdictional strikes indefensible.

The National Labor Relations Act provides procedures for determining which union represents employees of a particular employer. In some jurisdictional disputes, however, minority unions strike to compel employers to deal with them despite a legal duty to bargain with the majority union. Strikes to compel an employer to violate the law are inexcusable. Legislation to prevent such strikes is clearly desirable.

Another form of inter-union disagreement is the jurisdictional strike involving the question of which labor union is entitled to perform a particular task. When rival unions are unable to settle such disputes themselves, provision must be made for peaceful and binding determination of the issues.

A second unjustifiable practice is the secondary boycott, when used to further jurisdictional disputes or to compel employers to violate the National Labor Relations Act.

Not all secondary boycotts are unjustified. We must judge them on the basis of their objectives. For example, boycotts intended to protect wage rates and working conditions should be distinguished from those in furtherance of jurisdictional disputes. The structure of industry sometimes requires unions, as a matter of self-preservation, to extend the conflict beyond a particular employer. There should be no blanket prohibition against boycotts. The appropriate goal is legislation which prohibits secondary boycotts in pursuance of unjustifiable objectives, but does not impair the union's right to preserve its own existence and the gains made in genuine collective bargaining.

A third practice that should be corrected is the use of economic force, by either labor or management, to decide issues arising out of the interpretation of existing contracts.

Collective bargaining agreements, like other contracts, should be faithfully adhered to by both parties. In the most enlightened union-management relationships, disputes over the interpretation of contract terms are settled peaceably by negotiation or arbitration. Legislation should be enacted to provide machinery whereby unsettled disputes concerning the interpretation of an existing agreement may be referred by either party to final and binding arbitration.

Point number two is the extension of facilities within the Department of Labor for assisting collective bargaining.

One of our difficulties in avoiding labor strife arises from a lack of order in the collective bargaining process. The parties often do not have a clear understanding of their responsibility for settling disputes through their own negotiations. We constantly see instances where labor or management resorts to economic force without exhausting the possibilities for agreement through the bargaining process. Neither the parties nor the Government have a definite yardstick for determining when and how Government assistance should be invoked. There is need for integrated governmental machinery to provide the successive steps of mediation, voluntary arbitration, and—ultimately in appropriate cases—ascertainment of the facts of the dispute and the reporting of the facts to the public. Such machinery would facilitate and expedite the settlement of disputes.

Point number three is the broadening of our program of social legislation to alleviate the causes of workers' insecurity.

On June 11, 1946, in my message vetoing the Case Bill, I made a comprehensive statement of my views concerning labor-management relations. I said then, and I repeat now, that the solution of labor-management difficulties is to be found not only in legislation dealing directly with labor relations, but also in a program designed to remove the causes of insecurity felt by many workers in our industrial society. In this connection, for example, the Congress should consider the extension and broadening of our social security system, better housing, a comprehensive national health program, and provision for a fair minimum wage.

Point number four is the appointment of a Temporary Joint Commission to inquire into the entire field of labor-management relations.

I recommend that the Congress provide for the appointment of a Temporary Joint Commission to undertake this broad study.

The President, the Congress, and management and labor have a continuing responsibility to cooperate in seeking and finding the solution of these problems. I therefore recommend that the Commission be composed as follows: twelve to be chosen by the Congress from members of both parties in the House and the Senate, and eight representing the public, management and labor, to be appointed by the President.

The Commission should be charged with investigating and making recommendations upon certain major subjects, among others:

First, the special and unique problem of nationwide strikes in vital industries affecting the public interest. In particular, the Commission should examine into the question of how to settle or prevent such strikes without endangering our general democratic freedoms.

Upon a proper solution of this problem may depend the whole industrial future of the United States. The paralyzing effects of a nationwide strike in such industries as transportation, coal, oil, steel, or communications can result in national disaster. We have been able to avoid such disaster, in recent years, only by the use of extraordinary war powers. All those powers will soon be gone. In their place there must be created an adequate system and effective machinery in these vital fields. This problem will require careful study and a bold approach, but an approach consistent with the preservation of the rights of our people. The need is pressing. The Commission should give this its earliest attention.

Second, the best methods and procedures for carrying out the collective bargaining process. This should include the responsibilities of labor and management to negotiate freely and fairly with each other, and to refrain from strikes or lockouts until all possibilities of negotiation have been exhausted.

Third, the underlying causes of labor management disputes.

Some of the subjects presented here for investigation involve long-range study. Others can be considered immediately by the Commission and its recommendations can be submitted to the Congress in the near future.

I recommend that this Commission make its first report, including specific legislative recommendations, not later than March 15, 1947.

Restriction of Monopoly and Promotion of Private Enterprise

The second major policy I desire to lay before you has to do with the growing concentration of economic power and the threat to free competitive private enterprise. In 1941 the Temporary National Economic Committee completed a comprehensive investigation into the workings of the national economy. The Committee's study showed that, despite a half century of anti-trust law enforcement, one of the gravest threats to our welfare lay in the increasing concentration of power in the hands of a small number of giant organizations.

During the war, this long-standing tendency toward economic concentration was accelerated. As a consequence, we now find that to a greater extent than ever before, whole industries are dominated by one or a few large organizations which can restrict production in the interest of higher profits and thus reduce employment and purchasing power.

In an effort to assure full opportunity and free competition to business we will vigorously enforce the anti-trust laws. There is much the Congress can do to cooperate and assist in this program.

To strengthen and enforce the laws that regulate business practices is not enough. Enforcement must be supplemented by positive measures of aid to new enterprises. Government assistance, research programs, and credit powers should be designed and used to promote the growth of new firms and new industries. Assistance to small business is particularly important at this time when thousands of veterans who are potential business and industrial leaders are beginning their careers.

We should also give special attention to the decentralization of industry and the development of areas that are now under-industrialized.

Housing

The third major policy is also of great importance to the national economy: an aggressive program to encourage housing construction. The first federal program to relieve the veterans' housing shortage was announced in February 1946. In 1946 one million family housing units have been put under construction and more than 665,000 units have already been completed. The rate of expansion in construction has broken all records.

In the coming year the number of dwelling units built will approach, if not surpass, the top construction year of 1926. The primary responsibility to deliver housing at reasonable prices that veterans can afford rests with private industry and with labor. The Government will continue to expedite the flow of key building materials, to limit nonresidential construction, and to give financial support where it will do the most good. Measures to stimulate rental housing and new types of housing construction will receive special emphasis.

To reach our long-range goal of adequate housing for all our people, comprehensive housing legislation is urgently required, similar to the non-partisan bill passed by the Senate last year. At a minimum, such legislation should open the way for rebuilding the blighted areas of our cities and should establish positive incentives for the investment of billions of dollars of private capital in large-scale rental housing projects. It should provide for improvement of housing in rural areas and for the construction, over a 4-year period, of half a million units of public low-rental housing. It should authorize a single peacetime federal housing agency to assure efficient use of our resources on the vast housing front.

Fiscal Affairs

The fourth major policy has to do with the balancing of the budget. In a prosperous period such as the present one, the budget of the Federal Government should be balanced. Prudent management of public finance requires that we begin the process of reducing the public debt. The budget which I shall submit to you this week has a small margin of surplus. In the Budget Message I am making recommendations which, if accepted, will result in a substantially larger surplus which should be applied to debt retirement. One of these recommendations is that the Congress take early action to continue throughout the next fiscal year the war excise tax rates which, under the present law, will expire on June 30, 1947.

Expenditures relating to the war are still high. Considerable sums are required to alleviate world famine and suffering. Aid to veterans will continue at peak level. The world situation is such that large military expenditures are required. Interest on the public debt and certain other costs are irreducible. For these reasons I have had to practice stringent economy in preparing the budget; and I hope that the Congress will cooperate in this program of economy.

Agriculture

The fifth major policy has to do with the welfare of our farm population.

Production of food reached record heights in 1946. Much of our tremendous grain crop can readily be sold abroad and thus will become no threat to our domestic markets. But in the next few years American agriculture can face the same dangers it did after World War I. In the early twenties the Nation failed to maintain outlets for the new productive capacity of our agricultural plant. It failed to provide means to protect the farmer while he adjusted his acreage to peacetime demands.

The result we all remember too well. Farm production stayed up while demand and prices fell, in contrast with industry where prices stayed up and output declined, farm surpluses piled up, and disaster followed.

We must make sure of meeting the problems which we failed to meet after the first World War. Present laws give considerable stability to farm prices for 1947 and 1948, and these 2 years must be utilized to maintain and develop markets for our great productive power.

The purpose of these laws was to permit an orderly transition from war to peace. The Government plan of support prices was not designed to absorb, at great cost, the unlimited surpluses of a highly productive agriculture.

We must not wait until the guarantees expire to set the stage for permanent farm welfare.

The farmer is entitled to a fair income.

Ways can be found to utilize his new skills and better practices, to expand his markets at home and abroad, and to carry out the objectives of a balanced pattern of peacetime production without either undue sacrifice by farm people or undue expense to the Government.

Health and General Welfare

Of all our national resources, none is of more basic value than the health of our people. Over a year ago I presented to the Congress my views on a national health program. The Congress acted on several of the recommendations in this program—mental health, the health of mothers and children, and hospital construction. I urge this Congress to complete the work begun last year and to enact the most important recommendation of the program—to provide adequate medical care to all who need it, not as charity but on the basis of payments made by the beneficiaries of the program.

One administrative change would help greatly to further our national program in the fields of health, education, and welfare. I again recommend the establishment of a well-integrated Department of Welfare.

Veterans

Fourteen million World War II servicemen have returned to civil life. The great majority have found their places as citizens of their communities and their Nation. It is a tribute to the fiber of our servicemen and to the flexibility of our economy that these adjustments have been made so rapidly and so successfully.

More than two million of these veterans are attending schools or acquiring job skills through the financial assistance of the Federal Government. Thousands of sick and wounded veterans are daily receiving the best of medical and hospital care. Half a million have obtained loans, with Government guarantees, to purchase homes or farms or to embark upon new businesses. Compensation is being paid in almost two million cases for disabilities or death. More than three million are continuing to maintain their low-cost National Service Life Insurance policies. Almost seven million veterans have been aided by unemployment and self-employment allowances.

Exclusive of mustering-out payments and terminal leave pay, the program for veterans of all wars is costing over seven billion dollars a year—one-fifth of our total federal budget. This is the most far-reaching and complete veterans program ever conceived by any nation.

Except for minor adjustments, I believe that our program of benefits for veterans is now complete. In the long run, the success of the program will not be measured by the number of veterans receiving financial aid or by the number of dollars we spend. History will judge us not by the money we spend, but by the further contribution we enable our veterans to make to their country. In considering any additional legislation, that must be our criterion.

Civil Rights

We have recently witnessed in this country numerous attacks upon the constitutional rights of individual citizens as a result of racial and religious bigotry. Substantial segments of our people have been prevented from exercising fully their right to participate in the election of public officials, both locally and nationally. Freedom to engage in lawful callings has been denied.

The will to fight these crimes should be in the hearts of every one of us.

For the Federal Government that fight is now being carried on by the Department of Justice to the full extent of the powers that have been conferred upon it. While the Constitution withholds from the Federal Government the major task of preserving peace in the several States, I am not convinced that the present legislation reached the limit of federal power to protect the civil rights of its citizens.

I have, therefore, by Executive Order, established the President's Committee on Civil Rights to study and report on the whole problem of federally-secured civil rights, with a view to making recommendations to the Congress.

Natural Resources

In our responsibility to promote the general welfare of the people, we have always to consider the natural resources of our country. They are the foundation of our life. In the development of the great river systems of America there is the major opportunity of our generation to contribute to the increase of the national wealth. This program is already well along; it should be pushed with full vigor.

I must advise the Congress that we are rapidly becoming a "have not" Nation as to many of our minerals. The economic progress and the security of our country depend upon an expanding return of mineral discovery and upon improved methods of recovery. The Federal Government must do its part to meet this need.

Foreign Affairs

Progress in reaching our domestic goals is closely related to our conduct of foreign affairs. All that I have said about maintaining a sound and prosperous economy and improving the welfare of our people has greater meaning because of the world leadership of the United States. What we do, or fail to do, at home affects not only ourselves but millions throughout the world. If we are to fulfill our responsibilities to ourselves and to other peoples, we must make sure that the United States is sound economically, socially, and politically. Only then will we be able to help bring about the elements of peace in other countries—political stability, economic advancement, and social progress.

Peace treaties for Italy, Bulgaria, Rumania, and Hungary have finally been prepared. Following the signing of these treaties next month in Paris, they will be submitted to the Senate for ratification. This Government does not regard the treaties as completely satisfactory. Whatever their defects, however, I am convinced that they are as good as we can hope to obtain by agreement among the principal wartime Allies. Further dispute and delay would gravely jeopardize political stability in the countries concerned for many years.

During the long months of debate on these treaties, we have made it clear to all nations that the United States will not consent to settlements at the expense of principles we regard as vital to a just and enduring peace. We have made it equally clear that we will not retreat to isolationism. Our policies will be the same during the forthcoming negotiations in Moscow on the German and Austrian treaties, and during the future conferences on the Japanese treaty.

The delay in arriving at the first peace settlements is due partly to the difficulty of reaching agreement with the Soviet Union on the terms of settlement. Whatever differences there may have been between us and the Soviet Union, however, should not be allowed to obscure the fact that the basic interests of both nations lie in the early making of a peace under which the peoples of all countries may return, as free men and women, to the essential tasks of production and reconstruction. The major concern of each of us should be the promotion of collective security, not the advancement of individual security.

Our policy toward the Soviet Union is guided by the same principles which determine our policies toward all nations. We seek only to uphold the principles of international justice which have been embodied in the Charter of the United Nations.

We must now get on with the peace settlements. The occupying powers should recognize the independence of Austria and withdraw their troops. The Germans and the Japanese cannot be left in doubt and fear as to their future; they must know their national boundaries, their resources, and what reparations they must pay. Without trying to manage their internal affairs, we can insure that these countries do not re-arm.

International Relief and Displaced Persons

The United States can be proud of its part in caring for the peoples reduced to want by the ravages of war, and in aiding nations to restore their national economies. We have shipped more supplies to the hungry peoples of the world since the end of the war than all other countries combined!

However, insofar as admitting displaced persons is concerned, I do not feel that the United States has done its part. Only about 5,000 of them have entered this country since May, 1946. The fact is that the executive agencies are now doing all that is reasonably possible under the limitation of the existing law and established quotas. Congressional assistance in the form of new legislation is needed. I urge the Congress to turn its attention to this world problem, in an effort to find ways whereby we can fulfill our responsibilities to these thousands of homeless and suffering refugees of all faiths.

International Trade

World economic cooperation is essential to world political cooperation. We have made a good start on economic cooperation through the International Bank, the International Monetary fund, and the Export-Import Bank. We must now take other steps for the reconstruction of world trade and we should continue to strive for an international trade system as free from obstructions as possible.

Atomic Energy

The United States has taken the lead in the endeavor to put atomic energy under effective international control. We seek no monopoly for ourselves or for any group of nations. We ask only that there be safeguards sufficient to insure that no nation will be able to use this power for military purposes. So long as all governments are not agreed on means of international control of atomic energy, the shadow of fear will obscure the bright prospects for the peaceful use of this enormous power.

In accordance with the Atomic Energy Act of 1946, the Commission established under that law is assuming full jurisdiction over domestic atomic energy enterprise. The program of the Commission will, of course, be worked out in close collaboration with the military services in conformity with the wish of the Congress, but it is my fervent hope that the military significance of atomic energy will steadily decline. We look to the Commission to foster the development of atomic energy for industrial use and scientific and medical research. In the vigorous and effective development of peaceful uses of atomic energy rests our hope that this new force may ultimately be turned into a blessing for all nations.

Military Policy

In 1946 the Army and Navy completed the demobilization of their wartime forces. They are now maintaining the forces which we need for national defense and to fulfill our international obligations.

We live in a world in which strength on the part of peace-loving nations is still the greatest deterrent to aggression. World stability can be destroyed when nations with great responsibilities neglect to maintain the means of discharging those responsibilities.

This is an age when unforeseen attack could come with unprecedented speed. We must be strong enough to defeat, and thus forestall, any such attack. In our steady Progress toward a more rational world order, the need for large armed forces is progressively declining; but the stabilizing force of American military strength must not be weakened until our hopes are fully realized. When a system of collective security under the United Nations has been established, we shall be willing to lead in collective disarmament, but, until such a system becomes a reality, we must not again allow ourselves to become weak and invite attack.

For those reasons, we need well-equipped, well-trained armed forces and we must be able to mobilize rapidly our resources in men and material for our own defense, should the need arise.

The Army will be reduced to 1,070,000 officers and men by July 1, 1947. Half of the Army will be used for occupation duties abroad and most of the remainder will be employed at home in the support of these overseas forces.

The Navy is supporting the occupation troops in Europe and in the Far East. Its fundamental mission—to support our national interests wherever required—is unchanged. The Navy, including the Marine Corps, will average 571,000 officers and men during the fiscal year 1948.

We are encountering serious difficulties in maintaining our forces at even these reduced levels. Occupation troops are barely sufficient to carry out the duties which our foreign policy requires. Our forces at home are at a point where further reduction is impracticable. We should like an Army and a Navy composed entirely of long-term volunteers, but in spite of liberal inducements the basic needs of the Army are not now being met by voluntary enlistments.

The War Department has advised me that it is unable to make an accurate forecast at the present time as to whether it will be possible to maintain the strength of the Army by relying exclusively on volunteers. The situation will be much clearer in a few weeks, when the results of the campaign for volunteers are known. The War Department will make its recommendations as to the need for the extension of Selective Service in sufficient time to enable the Congress to take action prior to the expiration of the present law on March 31st. The responsibility for maintaining our armed forces at the strength necessary for our national safety rests with the Congress.

The development of a trained citizen reserve is also vital to our national security. This can best be accomplished through universal training. I have appointed an Advisory Commission on Universal Training to study the various plans for a training program, and I expect that the recommendations of the Commission will be of benefit to the Congress and to me in reaching decisions on this problem.

The cost of the military establishment is substantial. There is one certain way by which we can cut costs and at the same time enhance our national security. That is by the establishment of a single Department of National Defense. I shall communicate with the Congress in the near future with reference to the establishment of a single Department of National Defense.

National security does not consist only of an army, a navy, and an air force. It rests on a much broader basis. It depends on a sound economy of prices and wages, on prosperous agriculture, on satisfied and productive workers, on a competitive private enterprise free from monopolistic repression, on continued industrial harmony and production, on civil liberties and human freedoms—on all the forces which create in our men and women a strong moral fiber and spiritual stamina.

But we have a higher duty and a greater responsibility than the attainment of our own national security. Our goal is collective security for all mankind.

If we can work in a spirit of understanding and mutual respect, we can fulfill this solemn obligation which rests upon us.

The spirit of the American people can set the course of world history. If we maintain and strengthen our cherished ideals, and if we share our great bounty with war-stricken people over the world, then the faith of our citizens in freedom and democracy will be spread over the whole earth and free men everywhere will share our devotion to those ideals.

Let us have the will and the patience to do this job together.

May the Lord strengthen us in our faith.

May He give us wisdom to lead the peoples of the world in His ways of peace.

Address to Congress on the State of the Union

January 7, 1948

Harry Truman's third State of the Union message came at the start of a presidential election year, one in which the president—who had taken office after the death of Franklin D. Roosevelt—successfully sought a full four-year term of his own.

The president was fighting an uphill battle with the 80th Congress, which came to be known as the "Do-Nothing" Congress. Controlled by Republicans, with a sizeable group of conservative Democrats as well, the legislature was not willing to embrace Truman's "Fair Deal" domestic agenda.

In his address, delivered before Congress, Truman outlined five goals for the country—both international and domestic—and also stated that inflation needed to be curbed for any of those goals to succeed.

The first goal was to secure human rights for all Americans. In this context, Truman referred to the President's Committee on Civil Rights, which he had established in late 1946 and which had recently reported its findings. The president was to deliver a separate speech the following month to Congress specifically on that topic, in which he called for civil rights legislation; Congress would not go along. Truman also would sign an executive order in 1948 calling for desegregation of the armed forces.

Other goals included protecting and developing the country's human resources. Truman called for an extension of Social Security and for a national health program that would provide payment for medical care, conserving natural resources and using them effectively, strengthening the country's economic system and raising living standards, and "achiev[ing] world peace based on principles of freedom and justice and the equality of all nations."

In terms of international relations, Truman referred to the passage of the National Security Act, adopted the previous year, which created the Defense Department. He focused on helping the countries of Europe recover from World War II, which at this point had been over for more than two years. He urged Congress to provide funding for what is now known as the Marshall Plan, part of a doctrine of containment designed to block Soviet aggression; eventually, lawmakers agreed.

Truman, a Democrat, faced a difficult challenge from Republican Thomas E. Dewey, who had lost to Franklin D. Roosevelt in the 1944 presidential election. In addition, Democratic factions to the left and right split from the party and ran their own presidential candidates. In the end, Truman won with 303 electoral votes to Dewey's 189.

M r. President, Mr. Speaker, and Members of the 80th Congress:
We are here today to consider the state of the Union.

On this occasion, above all others, the Congress and the President should concentrate their attention, not upon party but upon the country; not upon things which divide us but upon those which bind us together—the enduring principles of our American system, and our common aspirations for the future welfare and security of the people of the United States.

The United States has become great because we, as a people, have been able to work together for great objectives even while differing about details.

The elements of our strength are many. They include our democratic government, our economic system, our great natural resources. But these are only partial explanations.

The basic source of our strength is spiritual. For we are a people with a faith. We believe in the dignity of man. We believe that he was created in the image of the Father of us all.

We do not believe that men exist merely to strengthen the state or to be cogs in the economic machine. We do believe that governments are created to serve the people and that economic systems exist to minister to their wants. We have a profound devotion to the welfare and rights of the individual as a human being.

The faith of our people has particular meaning at this time in history because of the unsettled and changing state of the world.

The victims of war in many lands are striving to rebuild their lives, and are seeking assurance that the tragedy of war will not occur again. Throughout the world new ideas are challenging the old. Men of all nations are reexamining the beliefs by which they live. Great scientific and industrial changes have released new forces which will affect the future course of civilization.

The state of our Union reflects the changing nature of the modern world. On all sides there is heartening evidence of great energy—of capacity for economic development—and even more important, capacity for spiritual growth. But accompanying this great activity there are equally great questions, great anxieties, and great aspirations. They represent the concern of an enlightened people that conditions should be so arranged as to make life more worthwhile.

We must devote ourselves to finding answers to these anxieties and aspirations. We seek answers which will embody the moral and spiritual elements of tolerance, unselfishness, and brotherhood upon which true freedom and opportunity must rest.

As we examine the state of our Union today, we can benefit from viewing it on a basis of the accomplishments of the last decade and of our goals for the next. How far have we come during the last 10 years and how far can we go in the next 10?

It was 10 years ago that the determination of dictators to wage war upon mankind became apparent. The years that followed brought untold death and destruction.

We shared in the human suffering of the war, but we were fortunate enough to escape most of war's destruction. We were able through these 10 years to expand the productive strength of our farms and factories.

More important, however, is the fact that these years brought us new courage, new confidence in the ideals of our free democracy. Our deep belief in freedom and justice was reinforced in the crucible of war.

On the foundations of our greatly strengthened economy and our renewed confidence in democratic values, we can continue to move forward.

There are some who look with fear and distrust upon planning for the future. Yet our great national achievements have been attained by those with vision. Our Union was formed, our frontiers were pushed back, and our great industries were built by men who looked ahead.

I propose that we look ahead today toward those goals for the future which have the greatest bearing upon the foundations of our democracy and the happiness of our people.

I do so, confident in the thought that with clear objectives and with firm determination, we can, in the next 10 years, build upon the accomplishments of the past decade to achieve a glorious future. Year by year, beginning now, we must make a substantial part of this progress.

Our first goal is to secure fully the essential human rights of our citizens.

The United States has always had a deep concern for human rights. Religious freedom, free speech, and freedom of thought are cherished realities in our land. Any denial of human rights is a denial of the basic beliefs of democracy and of our regard for the worth of each individual.

Today, however, some of our citizens are still denied equal opportunity for education, for jobs and economic advancement, and for the expression of their views at the polls. Most serious of all, some are denied equal protection under laws. Whether discrimination is based on race, or creed, or color, or land of origin, it is utterly contrary to American ideals of democracy.

The recent report of the President's Committee on Civil Rights points the way to corrective action by the Federal Government and by State and local governments. Because of the need for effective Federal action, I shall send a special message to the Congress on this important subject.

We should also consider our obligation to assure the fullest possible measure of civil rights to the people of our territories and possessions. I believe that the time has come for Alaska and Hawaii to be admitted to the Union as States.

Our second goal is to protect and develop our human resources.

The safeguarding of the rights of our citizens must be accompanied by an equal regard for their opportunities for development and their protection from economic insecurity. In this Nation the ideals of freedom and equality can be given specific meaning in terms of health, education, social security, and housing.

Over the past 12 years we have erected a sound framework of social security legislation. Many millions of our citizens are now protected against the loss of income which can come with unemployment, old age, or the death of wage earners. Yet our system has gaps and inconsistencies; it is only half finished.

We should now extend unemployment compensation, old age benefits, and survivors' benefits to millions who are not now protected. We should also raise the level of benefits.

The greatest gap in our social security structure is the lack of adequate provision for the Nation's health. We are rightly proud of the high standards of medical care we know how to provide in the United States. The fact is, however, that most of our people cannot afford to pay for the care they need.

I have often and strongly urged that this condition demands a national health program. The heart of the program must be a national system of payment for medical care based on well-tried insurance principles. This great Nation cannot afford to allow its citizens to suffer needlessly from the lack of proper medical care.

Our ultimate aim must be a comprehensive insurance system to protect all our people equally against insecurity and ill health.

Another fundamental aim of our democracy is to provide an adequate education for every person.

Our educational systems face a financial crisis. It is deplorable that in a Nation as rich as ours there are millions of children who do not have adequate schoolhouses or enough teachers for a good elementary or secondary education. If there are educational inadequacies in any State, the whole Nation suffers. The Federal Government has a responsibility for providing financial aid to meet this crisis.

In addition, we must make possible greater equality of opportunity to all our citizens for education. Only by so doing can we insure that our citizens will be capable of understanding and sharing the responsibilities of democracy.

The Government's programs for health, education, and security are of such great importance to our democracy that we should now establish an executive department for their administration.

Health and education have their beginning in the home. No matter what our hospitals or schools are like, the youth of our Nation are handicapped when millions of them live in city slums and country shacks. Within the next decade, we must see that every American family has a decent home. As an immediate step we need the long-range housing program which I have recommended on many occasions to this Congress. This should include financial aids designed to yield more housing at lower prices. It should provide public housing for low-income families, and vigorous development of new techniques to lower the cost of building.

Until we can overcome the present drastic housing shortage, we must extend and strengthen rent control.

We have had, and shall continue to have, a special interest in the welfare of our veterans. Over 14 million men and women who served in the armed forces in World War II have now returned to civilian life. Over 2 million veterans are being helped through school. Millions have been aided while finding jobs, and have been helped in buying homes, in obtaining medical care, and in adjusting themselves to physical handicaps.

All but a very few veterans have successfully made the transition from military life to their home communities. The success of our veterans' program is proved by this fact. This Nation is proud of the eagerness shown by our veterans to become self-reliant and self-supporting citizens.

Our third goal is to conserve and use our natural resources so that they can contribute most effectively to the welfare of our people.

The resources given by nature to this country are rich and extensive. The material foundations of our growth and economic development are the bounty of our fields, the wealth of our mines and forests, and the energy of our waters. As a Nation, we are coming to appreciate more each day the close relationship between the conservation of these resources and the preservation of our national strength.

We are doing far less than we know how to do to make use of our resources without destroying them. Both the public and private use of these resources must have the primary objective of maintaining and increasing these basic supports for an expanding future.

We must continue to take specific steps toward this goal. We must vigorously defend our natural wealth against those who would misuse it for selfish gain.

We need accurate and comprehensive knowledge of our mineral resources and must intensify our efforts to develop new supplies and to acquire stockpiles of scarce materials.

We need to protect and restore our land—public and private—through combating erosion and rebuilding the fertility of the soil.

We must expand our reclamation program to bring millions of acres of arid land into production, and to improve water supplies for additional millions of acres. This will provide new opportunities for veterans and others, particularly in the West, and aid in providing a rising living standard for a growing population.

We must protect and restore our forests by sustained-yield forestry and by planting new trees in areas now slashed and barren.

We must continue to erect multiple-purpose dams on our great rivers—not only to reclaim land, but also to prevent floods, to extend our inland waterways and to provide hydroelectric power. This public power must not be monopolized for private gain. Only through well-established policies of transmitting power directly to its market and thus encouraging widespread use at low rates can the Federal Government assure the people of their full share of its benefits. Additional power—public and private—is needed to raise the ceilings now imposed by power shortages on industrial and agricultural development.

We should achieve the wise use of resources through the integrated development of our great river basins. We can learn much from our Tennessee Valley experience. We should no longer delay in applying the lessons of that vast undertaking to our other great river basins.

Our fourth goal is to lift the standard of living for all our people by strengthening our economic system and sharing more broadly among our people the goods we produce.

The amazing economic progress of the past 10 years points the way for the next 10.

Today 14 million more people have jobs than in 1938.

Our yearly output of goods and services has increased by two-thirds.

The average income of our people, measured in dollars of equal purchasing power, has increased—after taxes—by more than 50 percent.

In no other 10 years have farmers, businessmen, and wage earners made such great gains.

We may not be able to expand as rapidly in the next decade as in the last, because we are now starting from full employment and very high production. But we can increase our annual output by at least one-third above the present level. We can lift our standard of living to nearly double what it was 10 years ago.

If we distribute these gains properly, we can go far toward stamping out poverty in our generation.

To do this, agriculture, business, and labor must move forward together.

Permanent farm prosperity and agricultural abundance will be achieved only as our whole economy grows and prospers. The farmer can sell more food at good prices when the incomes of wage earners are high and when there is full employment. Adequate diets for every American family, and the needs of our industries at full production, will absorb a farm output well above our present levels.

Although the average farmer is now better off than ever before, farm families as a whole have only begun to catch up with the standards of living enjoyed in the cities. In 1946, the average income of farm people was $779, contrasted with an average income of $1,288 for nonfarm people. Within the next decade, we should eliminate elements of inequality in these living standards.

To this end our farm program should enable the farmer to market his varied crops at fair price levels and to improve his standard of living.

We need to continue price supports for major farm commodities on a basis which will afford reasonable protection against fluctuations in the levels of production and demand. The present price support program must be reexamined and modernized.

Crop insurance should be strengthened and its benefits extended in order to protect the farmer against the special hazards to which he is subject.

We also need to improve the means for getting farm products into markets and into the hands of consumers. Cooperatives which directly or indirectly serve this purpose must be encouraged—not discouraged. The school lunch program should be continued and adequately financed.

We need to go forward with the rural electrification program to bring the benefits of electricity to all our farm population.

We can, and must, aid and encourage farmers to conserve their soil resources and restore the fertility of the land that has suffered from neglect or unwise use.

All these are practical measures upon which we should act immediately to enable agriculture to make its full contribution to our prosperity.

We must also strengthen our economic system within the next decade by enlarging our industrial capacity within the framework of our free enterprise system.

We are today far short of the industrial capacity we need for a growing future. At least $50 billion should be invested by industry to improve and expand our productive facilities over the next few years. But this is only the beginning. The industrial application of atomic energy and other scientific advances will constantly open up further opportunities for expansion. Farm prosperity and high employment will call for an immensely increased output of goods and services.

Growth and vitality in our economy depend on vigorous private enterprise. Free competition is the key to industrial development, full production and employment, fair prices, and an ever improving standard of living. Competition is seriously limited today in many industries by the concentration of economic power and other elements of monopoly. The appropriation of sufficient funds to permit proper enforcement of the present antitrust laws is essential. Beyond that we should go on to strengthen our legislation to protect competition.

Another basic element of a strong economic system is the well-being of the wage earners.

We have learned that the well-being of workers depends on high production and consequent high employment. We have learned equally well that the welfare of industry and agriculture depends on high incomes for our workers.

The Government has wisely chosen to set a floor under wages. But our 40-cent minimum wage is inadequate and obsolete. I recommend the lifting of the minimum wage to 75 cents an hour.

In general, however, we must continue to rely on our sound system of collective bargaining to set wage scales. Workers' incomes should increase at a rate consistent with the maintenance of sound price, profit, and wage relationships and with increase of productivity.

The Government's part in labor-management relations is now largely controlled by the terms of the Labor-Management Relations Act of 1947. I made my attitude clear on this act in my veto message to the Congress last June. Nothing has occurred since to change my opinion of this law. As long as it remains the law of the land, however, I shall carry out my constitutional duty and administer it.

As we look ahead we can understand the crucial importance of restraint and wisdom in arriving at new labor-management contracts. Work stoppages would result in a loss of production—a loss which could bring higher prices for our citizens and could also deny the necessities of life to the hard-pressed peoples of other lands. It is my sincere hope that the representatives of labor and of industry will bear in mind that the Nation as a whole has a vital stake in the success of their bargaining efforts.

If we surmount our current economic difficulties, we can move ahead to a great increase in our national income which will enable all our people to enjoy richer and fuller lives.

All of us must advance together. One-fifth of our families now have average annual incomes of less than $850. We must see that our gains in national income are made more largely available to those with low incomes, whose need is greatest. This will benefit us all through providing a stable foundation of buying power to maintain prosperity.

Business, labor, agriculture, and Government, working together, must develop the policies which will make possible the realization of the full benefits of our economic system.

Our fifth goal is to achieve world peace based on principles of freedom and justice and the equality of all nations.

Twice within our generation, world wars have taught us that we cannot isolate ourselves from the rest of the world.

We have learned that the loss of freedom in any area of the world means a loss of freedom to ourselves—that the loss of independence by any nation adds directly to the insecurity of the United States and all free nations.

We have learned that a healthy world economy is essential to world peace—that economic distress is a disease whose evil effects spread far beyond the boundaries of the afflicted nation.

For these reasons the United States is vigorously following policies designed to achieve a peaceful and prosperous world.

We are giving, and will continue to give, our full support to the United Nations. While that organization has encountered unforeseen and unwelcome difficulties, I am confident of its ultimate success. We are also devoting our efforts toward world economic recovery and the revival of world trade. These actions are closely related and mutually supporting.

We believe that the United States can be an effective force for world peace only if it is strong. We look forward to the day when nations will decrease their armaments. Yet so long as there remains serious opposition to the ideals of a peaceful world, we must maintain strong armed forces.

The passage of the National Security Act by the Congress at its last session was a notable step in providing for the security of this country. A further step which I consider of even greater importance is the early provision for universal training. There are many elements in a balanced national security program, all interrelated and necessary, but universal training should be the foundation for them all. A favorable decision by the Congress at an early date is of world importance. I am convinced that such action is vital to the security of this Nation and to the maintenance of its leadership.

The United States is engaged today in many international activities directed toward the creation of lasting peaceful relationships among nations.

We have been giving substantial aid to Greece and Turkey to assist those nations in preserving their integrity against foreign pressures. Had it not been for our aid, their situation today might well be radically different. The continued integrity of those countries will have a powerful effect upon other nations in the Middle East and in Europe struggling to maintain their independence while they repair the damages of war.

The United States has special responsibilities with respect to the countries in which we have occupation forces: Germany, Austria, Japan, and Korea. Our efforts to reach agreements on peace settlements for these countries have so far been blocked. But we shall continue to exert our utmost efforts to obtain satisfactory settlements for each of these nations.

Many thousands of displaced persons, still living in camps overseas, should be allowed entry into the United States. I again urge the Congress to pass suitable legislation at once so that this Nation may do its share in caring for the homeless and suffering refugees of all faiths. I believe that the admission of these persons will add to the strength and energy of this Nation.

We are moving toward our goal of world peace in many ways. But the most important efforts which we are now making are those which support world economic reconstruction. We are seeking to restore the world trading system which was shattered by the war and to remedy the economic paralysis which grips many countries.

To restore world trade we have recently taken the lead in bringing about the greatest reduction of world tariffs that the world has ever seen. The extension of the provisions of the Reciprocal Trade Agreements Act, which made this achievement possible, is of extreme importance. We must also go on to support the International Trade Organization, through which we hope to obtain worldwide agreement on a code of fair conduct in international trade.

Our present major effort toward economic reconstruction is to support the program for recovery developed by the countries of Europe. In my recent message to the Congress, I outlined the reasons why it is wise and necessary for the United States to extend this support.

I want to reaffirm my belief in the soundness and the promise of this proposal. When the European economy is strengthened, the product of its industry will be of benefit to many other areas of economic distress. The ability of free men to overcome hunger and despair will be a moral stimulus to the entire world.

We intend to work also with other nations in achieving world economic recovery. We shall continue our cooperation with the nations of the Western Hemisphere. A special program of assistance to China, to provide urgent relief needs and to speed reconstruction, will be submitted to the Congress.

Unfortunately, not all governments share the hope of the people of the United States that economic reconstruction in many areas of the world can be achieved through cooperative effort among nations. In spite of these differences we will go forward with our efforts to overcome economic paralysis.

No nation by itself can carry these programs to success; they depend upon the cooperative and honest efforts of all participating countries. Yet the leadership is inevitably ours.

I consider it of the highest importance that the Congress should authorize support for the European recovery program for the period from April 1, 1948, to June 30, 1952, with an initial amount for the first 15 months of $6.8 billion. I urge the Congress to act promptly on this vital measure of our foreign policy—on this decisive contribution to world peace.

We are following a sound, constructive, and practical course in carrying out our determination to achieve peace.

We are fighting poverty, hunger, and suffering.

This leads to peace—not war.

We are building toward a world where all nations, large and small alike, may live free from the fear of aggression. This leads to peace—not war.

Above all else, we are striving to achieve a concord among the peoples of the world based upon the dignity of the individual and the brotherhood of man.

This leads to peace—not war.

We can go forward with confidence that we are following sound policies, both at home and with other nations, which will lead us toward our great goals for economic, social and moral achievement.

As we enter the new year, we must surmount one major problem which affects all our goals. That is the problem of inflation.

Already inflation in this country is undermining the living standards of millions of families. Food costs too much. Housing has reached fantastic price levels. Schools and hospitals are in financial distress. Inflation threatens to bring on disagreement and strife between labor and management.

Worst of all, inflation holds the threat of another depression, just as we had a depression after the unstable boom following the First World War.

When I announced last October that the Congress was being called into session, I described the price increases which had taken place since June 1946. Wholesale prices had increased 40 percent; retail prices had increased 23 percent.

Since October prices have continued to rise. Wholesale prices have gone up at an annual rate of 18 percent. Retail prices have gone up at an annual rate of 10 percent.

The events which have occurred since I presented my 10-point anti-inflation program to the Congress in November have made it even clearer that all 10 points are essential.

High prices must not be our means of rationing.

We must deal effectively and at once with the high cost of living.

We must stop the spiral of inflation.

I trust that within the shortest possible time the Congress will make available to the Government the weapons that are so desperately needed in the fight against inflation.

One of the most powerful anti-inflationary factors in our economy today is the excess of Government revenues over expenditures.

Government expenditures have been and must continue to be held at the lowest safe levels. Since V-J day Federal expenditures have been sharply reduced. They have been cut from more than $63 billion in the fiscal year 1946 to less than $38 billion in the present fiscal year. The number of civilian employees has been cut nearly in half—from 3 3/4 million down to 2 million.

On the other hand, Government revenues must not be reduced. Until inflation has been stopped there should be no cut in taxes that is not offset by additions at another point in our tax structure.

Certain adjustments should be made within our existing tax structure that will not affect total receipts, yet will adjust the tax burden so that those least able to pay will have their burden lessened by the transfer of a portion of it to those best able to pay.

Many of our families today are suffering hardship because of the high cost of living. At the same time profits of corporations have reached an all-time record in 1947. Corporate profits total $17 billion after taxes. This compared with $12.5 billion in 1946, the previous high year.

Because of this extraordinarily high level of profits, corporations can well afford to carry a larger share of the taxload at this time.

During this period in which the high cost of living is bearing down on so many of our families, tax adjustments should be made to ease their burden. The low-income group particularly is being pressed very hard. To this group a tax adjustment would result in a saving that could be used to buy the necessities of life.

I recommend therefore that, effective January 1, 1948, a cost of living tax credit be extended to our people consisting of a credit of $40 to each individual taxpayer and an additional credit of $40 for each dependent. Thus the income tax of a man with a wife and two children would be reduced $160. The credit would be extended to all taxpayers, but it would be particularly helpful to those in the low-income group.

It is estimated that such a tax credit would reduce Federal revenue by $3.2 billion. This reduction should be made up by increasing the tax on corporate profits in an amount that will produce this sum—with appropriate adjustments for small corporations.

This is the proper method of tax relief at this time. It gives relief to those who need it most without cutting the total tax revenue of the Government.

When the present danger of inflation has passed we should consider tax reduction based upon a revision of our entire tax structure.

When we have conquered inflation, we shall be in a position to move forward toward our chosen goals.

As we do so, let us keep ever before us our high purposes. We are determined that every citizen of this Nation shall have an equal right and an equal opportunity to grow in wisdom and in stature and to take his place in the control of his Nation's destiny.

We are determined that the productive resources of this Nation shall be used wisely and fully for the benefit of all.

We are determined that the democratic faith of our people and the strength of our resources shall contribute their full share to the attainment of enduring peace in the world.

It is our faith in human dignity that underlies these purposes. It is this faith that keeps us a strong and vital people.

This is a time to remind ourselves of these fundamentals. For today the whole world looks to us for leadership.

This is the hour to rededicate ourselves to the faith in mankind that makes us strong.

This is the hour to rededicate ourselves to the faith in God that gives us confidence as we face the challenge of the years ahead.

Address to Congress on the State of the Union

January 5, 1949

Harry Truman delivered his fourth State of the Union message two months after winning his own four-year term as president. Truman had served almost four years at this point, having taken over after the death of Franklin D. Roosevelt in April 1945.

The 1948 election had been difficult for Truman, whose chief opponent was Republican Thomas E. Dewey. In addition, two factions of Democrats, representing the ideological right and left of the party, each had run their own presidential candidates. But the president prevailed, running an underdog-style campaign that often featured barbs against the Republican-controlled "Do-Nothing" 80th Congress, which had stymied much of his domestic agenda. Truman won 303 electoral votes and 49.51 percent of the popular vote; Dewey took 189 electoral votes and 45.12 percent. In addition, Democrats won control of Congress.

In his speech, Truman defended the record of the Roosevelt-Truman years, and stated that the election results meant that the public wanted to continue in the same vein. He said that every American had the right to a "fair deal" from the government—a term by which his domestic reform agenda has come to be known.

Although the 81st Congress was controlled by Democrats, it remained difficult for Truman to achieve much of his domestic agenda. Many senior Democrats were conservatives, who had not been fans of either Roosevelt's New Deal or Truman's Fair Deal.

One major point of conflict between Truman and the previous Congress had been the Labor-Management Relations Act of 1947, otherwise known as Taft-Hartley, which Truman believed was unfair to labor. Congress had passed it over Truman's veto. "That act should be repealed," he declared in his 1949 State of the Union speech; Congress did not go along with his idea.

While many of Truman's proposals failed to progress in Congress, lawmakers did approve the Housing Act of 1949, which sought to provide "a decent home and a suitable living environment for every American family." Affordable housing was one of the goals Truman cited in his 1949 State of the Union message.

Truman did not focus a great deal on international relations in his speech, but he linked the country's foreign and domestic policies together, stating that "our domestic programs are the foundation of our foreign policy" and that the country epitomized for the world the "benefits of democratic government."

Mr. President, Mr. Speaker, Members of the Congress:

I am happy to report to this 81st Congress that the state of the Union is good. Our Nation is better able than ever before to meet the needs of the American people, and to give them their fair chance in the pursuit of happiness. This great Republic is foremost among the nations of the world in the search for peace.

During the last 16 years, our people have been creating a society which offers new opportunities for every man to enjoy his share of the good things of life.

In this society, we are conservative about the values and principles which we cherish; but we are forward-looking in protecting those values and principles and in extending their benefits. We have rejected the discredited theory that the fortunes of the Nation should be in the hands of a privileged few. We have abandoned the "trickledown" concept of national prosperity. Instead, we believe that our economic system should rest on a democratic foundation and that wealth should be created for the benefit of all.

The recent election shows that the people of the United States are in favor of this kind of society and want to go on improving it.

The American people have decided that poverty is just as wasteful and just as unnecessary as preventable disease. We have pledged our common resources to help one another in the hazards and struggles of individual life. We believe that no unfair prejudice or artificial distinction should bar any citizen of the United States of America from an education, or from good health, or from a job that he is capable of performing.

The attainment of this kind of society demands the best efforts of every citizen in every walk of life, and it imposes increasing responsibilities on the Government.

The Government must work with industry, labor, and the farmers in keeping our economy running at full speed. The Government must see that every American has a chance to obtain his fair share of our increasing abundance. These responsibilities go hand in hand.

We cannot maintain prosperity unless we have a fair distribution of opportunity and a widespread consumption of the products of our factories and farms.

Our Government has undertaken to meet these responsibilities.

We have made tremendous public investments in highways, hydroelectric power projects, soil conservation, and reclamation. We have established a system of social security. We have enacted laws protecting the rights and the welfare of our working people and the income of our farmers. These Federal policies have paid for themselves many times over. They have strengthened the material foundations of our democratic ideals. Without them, our present prosperity would be impossible.

Reinforced by these policies, our private enterprise system has reached new heights of production. Since the boom year of 1929, while our population has increased by only 20 percent, our agricultural production has increased by 45 percent, and our industrial production has increased by 75 percent. We are turning out far more goods and more wealth per worker than we have ever done before.

This progress has confounded the gloomy prophets—at home and abroad—who predicted the downfall of American capitalism. The people of the United States, going their own way, confident in their own powers, have achieved the greatest prosperity the world has even seen.

But, great as our progress has been, we still have a long way to go.

As we look around the country, many of our shortcomings stand out in bold relief.

We are suffering from excessively high prices.

Our production is still not large enough to satisfy our demands.

Our minimum wages are far too low.

Small business is losing ground to growing monopoly.

Our farmers still face an uncertain future. And too many of them lack the benefits of our modern civilization.

Some of our natural resources are still being wasted.

We are acutely short of electric power, although the means for developing such power are abundant.

Five million families are still living in slums and firetraps. Three million families share their homes with others.

Our health is far behind the progress of medical science. Proper medical care is so expensive that it is out of the reach of the great majority of our citizens.

Our schools, in many localities, are utterly inadequate.

Our democratic ideals are often thwarted by prejudice and intolerance.

Each of these shortcomings is also an opportunity—an opportunity for the Congress and the President to work for the good of the people.

Our first great opportunity is to protect our economy against the evils of "boom and bust."

This objective cannot be attained by government alone. Indeed, the greater part of the task must be performed by individual efforts under our system of free enterprise. We can keep our present prosperity, and increase it, only if free enterprise and free government work together to that end.

We cannot afford to float along ceaselessly on a postwar boom until it collapses. It is not enough merely to prepare to weather a recession if it comes. Instead, government and business must work together constantly to achieve more and more jobs and more and more production—which mean more and more prosperity for all the people.

The business cycle is man-made; and men of good will, working together, can smooth it out.

So far as business is concerned, it should plan for steady, vigorous expansion—seeking always to increase its output, lower its prices, and avoid the vices of monopoly and restriction. So long as business does this, it will be contributing to continued prosperity, and it will have the help and encouragement of the Government.

The Employment Act of 1946 pledges the Government to use all its resources to promote maximum employment, production, and purchasing power. This means that the Government is firmly committed to protect business and the people against the dangers of recession and against the evils of inflation. This means that the Government must adapt its plans and policies to meet changing circumstances.

At the present time, our prosperity is threatened by inflationary pressures at a number of critical points in our economy. And the Government must be in a position to take effective action at these danger spots. To that end, I recommend that the Congress enact legislation for the following purposes:

First, to continue the power to control consumer credit and enlarge the power to control bank credit.

Second, to grant authority to regulate speculation on the commodity exchanges.

Third, to continue export control authority and to provide adequate machinery for its enforcement.

Fourth, to continue the priorities and allocation authority in the field of transportation.

Fifth, to authorize priorities and allocations for key materials in short supply.

Sixth, to extend and strengthen rent control.

Seventh, to provide standby authority to impose price ceilings for scarce commodities which basically affect essential industrial production or the cost of living, and to limit unjustified wage adjustments which would force a break in an established price ceiling.

Eighth, to authorize an immediate study of the adequacy of production facilities for materials in critically short supply, such as steel; and, if found necessary, to authorize Government loans for the expansion of production facilities to relieve such shortages, and to authorize the construction of such facilities directly, if action by private industry fails to meet our needs.

The Economic Report, which I shall submit to the Congress shortly, will discuss in detail the economic background for these recommendations.

One of the most important factors in maintaining prosperity is the Government's fiscal policy. At this time, it is essential not only that the Federal budget be balanced, but also that there be a substantial surplus to reduce inflationary pressures, and to permit a sizable reduction in the national debt, which now stands at $252 billion. I recommend, therefore, that the Congress enact new tax legislation to bring in an additional $4 billion of Government revenue. This should come principally from additional corporate taxes. A portion should come from revised estate and gift taxes. Consideration should be given to raising personal income rates in the middle and upper brackets.

If we want to keep our economy running in high gear, we must be sure that every group has the incentive to make its full contribution to the national welfare. At present, the working men and women of the Nation are unfairly discriminated against by a statute that abridges their rights, curtails their constructive efforts, and hampers our system of free collective bargaining. That statute is the Labor-Management Relations Act of 1947, sometimes called the Taft-Hartley Act.

That act should be repealed!

The Wagner Act should be reenacted. However, certain improvements, which I recommended to the Congress 2 years ago, are needed. Jurisdictional strikes and unjustified secondary boycotts should be prohibited. The use of economic force to decide issues arising out of the interpretation of existing contracts should be prevented. Without endangering our democratic freedoms, means should be provided for setting up machinery for preventing strikes in vital industries which affect the public interest.

The Department of Labor should be rebuilt and strengthened and those units properly belonging within that department should be placed in it.

The health of our economy and its maintenance at high levels further require that the minimum wage fixed by law should be raised to at least 75 cents an hour.

If our free enterprise economy is to be strong and healthy, we must reinvigorate the forces of competition. We must assure small business the freedom and opportunity to grow and prosper. To this purpose, we should strengthen our antitrust laws by closing those loopholes that permit monopolistic mergers and consolidations.

Our national farm program should be improved—not only in the interest of the farmers, but for the lasting prosperity of the whole Nation. Our goals should be abundant farm production and parity income for agriculture. Standards of living on the farm should be just as good as anywhere else in the country.

Farm price supports are an essential part of our program to achieve these ends. Price supports should be used to prevent farm price declines which are out of line with general price levels, to facilitate adjustments in production to consumer demands, and to promote good land use. Our price support legislation must be adapted to these objectives. The authority of the Commodity Credit Corporation to provide adequate storage space for crops should be restored.

Our program for farm prosperity should also seek to expand the domestic market for agricultural products, particularly among low-income groups, and to increase and stabilize foreign markets.

We should give special attention to extending modern conveniences and services to our farms. Rural electrification should be pushed forward. And in considering legislation relating to housing, education, health, and social security, special attention should be given to rural problems.

Our growing population and the expansion of our economy depend upon the wise management of our land, water, forest, and mineral wealth. In our present dynamic economy, the task of conservation is not to lockup our resources but to develop and improve them. Failure, today, to make the investments which are necessary to support our progress in the future would be false economy.

We must push forward the development of our rivers for power, irrigation, navigation, and flood control. We should apply the lessons of our Tennessee Valley experience to our other great river basins.

I again recommend action be taken by the Congress to approve the St. Lawrence Seaway and Power project. This is about the fifth time I have recommended it.

We must adopt a program for the planned use of the petroleum reserves under the sea, which are—and must remain—vested in the Federal Government. We must extend our programs of soil conservation. We must place our forests on a sustained yield basis, and encourage the development of new sources of vital minerals.

In all this we must make sure that the benefits of these public undertakings are directly available to the people. Public power should be carried to consuming areas by public transmission lines where necessary to provide electricity at the lowest possible rates. Irrigation waters should serve family farms and not land speculators.

The Government has still other opportunities—to help raise the standard of living of our citizens. These opportunities lie in the fields of social security, health, education, housing, and civil rights.

The present coverage of the social security laws is altogether inadequate; the benefit payments are too low. One-third of our workers are not covered. Those who receive old-age and survivors insurance benefits receive an average payment of only $25 a month. Many others who cannot work because they are physically disabled are left to the mercy of charity. We should expand our social security program, both as to the size of the benefits and the extent of coverage, against the economic hazards due to unemployment, old age, sickness, and disability.

We must spare no effort to raise the general level of health in this country. In a nation as rich as ours, it is a shocking fact that tens of millions lack adequate medical care. We are short of doctors, hospitals, nurses. We must remedy these shortages. Moreover, we need—and we must have without further delay—a system of prepaid medical insurance which will enable every American to afford good medical care.

It is equally shocking that millions of our children are not receiving a good education. Millions of them are in overcrowded, obsolete buildings. We are short of teachers, because teachers' salaries are too low to attract new teachers, or to hold the ones we have. All these school problems will become much more acute as a result of the tremendous increase in the enrollment in our elementary schools in the next few years. I cannot repeat too strongly my desire for prompt Federal financial aid to the States to help them operate and maintain their school systems.

The governmental agency which now administers the programs of health, education, and social security should be given full departmental status.

The housing shortage continues to be acute. As an immediate step, the Congress should enact the provisions for low-rent public housing, slum clearance, farm housing, and housing research which I have repeatedly recommended. The number of low rent public housing units provided for in the legislation should be increased to 1 million units in the next 7 years. Even this number of units will not begin to meet our need for new housing.

Most of the houses we need will have to be built by private enterprise, without public subsidy. By producing too few rental units and too large a proportion of high-priced houses, the building industry is rapidly pricing itself out of the market. Building costs must be lowered.

The Government is now engaged in a campaign to induce all segments of the building industry to concentrate on the production of lower priced housing. Additional legislation to encourage such housing will be submitted.

The authority which I have requested, to allocate materials in short supply and to impose price ceilings on such materials, could be used, if found necessary, to channel more materials into homes large enough for family life at prices which wage earners can afford.

The driving force behind our progress is our faith in our democratic institutions. That faith is embodied in the promise of equal rights and equal opportunities which the founders of our Republic proclaimed to their countrymen and to the whole world.

The fulfillment of this promise is among the highest purposes of government. The civil rights proposals I made to the 80th Congress, I now repeat to the 81st Congress. They should be enacted in order that the Federal Government may assume the leadership and discharge the obligations clearly placed upon it by the Constitution.

I stand squarely behind those proposals.

Our domestic programs are the foundation of our foreign policy. The world today looks to us for leadership because we have so largely realized, within our borders, those benefits of democratic government for which most of the peoples of the world are yearning.

We are following a foreign policy which is the outward expression of the democratic faith we profess. We are doing what we can to encourage free states and free peoples throughout the world, to aid the suffering and afflicted in foreign lands, and to strengthen democratic nations against aggression.

The heart of our foreign policy is peace. We are supporting a world organization to keep peace and a world economic policy to create prosperity for mankind. Our guiding star is the principle of international cooperation. To this concept we have made a national commitment as profound as anything in history.

To it we have pledged our resources and our honor.

Until a system of world security is established upon which we can safely rely, we cannot escape the burden of creating and maintaining armed forces sufficient to deter aggression. We have made great progress in the last year in the effective organization of our Armed Forces, but further improvements in our national security legislation are necessary. Universal training is essential to the security of the United States.

During the course of this session I shall have occasion to ask the Congress to consider several measures in the field of foreign policy. At this time, I recommend that we restore the Reciprocal Trade Agreements Act to full effectiveness, and extend it for 3 years. We should also open our doors to displaced persons without unfair discrimination.

It should be clear by now to all citizens that we are not seeking to freeze the status quo. We have no intention of preserving the injustices of the past. We welcome the constructive efforts being made by many nations to achieve a better life for their citizens. In the European recovery program, in our good-neighbor policy and in the United Nations, we have begun to batter down those national walls which block the economic growth and the social advancement of the peoples of the world.

We believe that if we hold resolutely to this course, the principle of international cooperation will eventually command the approval even of those nations which are now seeking to weaken or subvert it.

We stand at the opening of an era which can mean either great achievement or terrible catastrophe for ourselves and for all mankind.

The strength of our Nation must continue to be used in the interest of all our people rather than a privileged few. It must continue to be used unselfishly in the struggle for world peace and the betterment of mankind the world over.

This is the task before us.

It is not an easy one. It has many complications, and there will be strong opposition from selfish interests.

I hope for cooperation from farmers, from labor, and from business. Every segment of our population and every individual has a right to expect from our Government a fair deal.

In 1945, when I came down before the Congress for the first time on April 16, I quoted to you King Solomon's prayer that he wanted wisdom and the ability to govern his people as they should be governed. I explained to you at that time that the task before me was one of the greatest in the history of the world, and that it was necessary to have the complete cooperation of the Congress and the people of the United States.

Well now, we are taking a new start with the same situation. It is absolutely essential that your President have the complete cooperation of the Congress to carry out the great work that must be done to keep the peace in this world, and to keep this country prosperous.

The people of this great country have a right to expect that the Congress and the President will work in closest cooperation with one objective—the welfare of the people of this Nation as a whole.

In the months ahead I know that I shall be able to cooperate with this Congress.

Now, I am confident that the Divine Power which has guided us to this time of fateful responsibility and glorious opportunity will not desert us now.

With that help from Almighty God which we have humbly acknowledged at every turning point in our national life, we shall be able to perform the great tasks which He now sets before us.

Harry S. Truman, 1949–1953

Address to Congress on the State of the Union

January 4, 1950

Harry Truman delivered his fifth State of the Union message at a time of concern for the country. The Soviet Union had succeeded in testing an atomic bomb in September 1949, and in October of that year a communist government under Mao Tse-tung had taken control of China. Unbeknownst to Truman and the nation at the time was that six months following the speech, communist North Korea would invade South Korea.

The president focused about half his speech on international matters, such as the ongoing U.S. aid to European countries under the Marshall Plan, the effort to increase security cooperation between the United States and Western Europe under the North Atlantic Treaty Organization, and strong U.S. backing for the activities of the United Nations. He declared that at the century's midpoint, the United States had become a leading world force, in contrast to its position fifty years earlier. "Among all the great changes that have occurred in the last fifty years, none is more important than the change in the position of the United States in world affairs," Truman said. He also remarked, "Our objective in the world is peace."

The president mentioned the Far East in his speech, stating that it was important for people there in particular to experience scientific and economic advances that would lead to freedom and representative government. While the president did not speak of China, it was a major world issue at the time. And the United States would become embroiled in two wars in Asia in the next two decades: the Korean and Vietnam conflicts.

Truman stated that the United States and other industrial countries would have to participate in this scientific and economic effort; he said that the undertaking "has nothing in common with either the old imperialism of the last century or the new imperialism of the Communists."

The president also discussed domestic matters, including his pleas, repeated from earlier State of the Union messages, to curb monopolies; repeal the 1947 Taft-Hartley labor law, which he saw as unfair to labor unions; and enact civil rights legislation. Truman's domestic agenda generally tended to fare badly in Congress, where a combination of conservative Democrats and Republicans opposed his reform legislation.

Truman had been in office almost five years at the time of this speech. The last three years of his presidency would, even more than the first five, be focused on international events, as the country entered the Korean War. It would last through the rest of Truman's time in the White House and be concluded under an armistice in 1953, after Dwight D. Eisenhower became president.

M r. President, Mr. Speaker, Members of the Congress:

A year ago I reported to this Congress that the state of the Union was good. I am happy to be able to report to you today that the state of the Union continues to be good. Our Republic continues to increase in the enjoyment of freedom within its borders, and to offer strength and encouragement to all those who love freedom throughout the world.

During the past year we have made notable progress in strengthening the foundations of peace and freedom, abroad and at home.

We have taken important steps in securing the North Atlantic community against aggression. We have continued our successful support of European recovery. We have returned to our established policy of expanding international trade through reciprocal agreement. We have strengthened our support of the United Nations.

While great problems still confront us, the greatest danger has receded—the possibility which faced us 3 years ago that most of Europe and the Mediterranean area might collapse under totalitarian pressure. Today, the free peoples of the world have new vigor and new hope for the cause of peace.

In our domestic affairs, we have made notable advances toward broader opportunity and a better life for all our citizens.

We have met and reversed the first significant downturn in economic activity since the war. In accomplishing this, Government programs for maintaining employment and purchasing power have been of tremendous benefit. As the result of these programs, and the wisdom and good judgment of our businessmen and workers, major readjustments have been made without widespread suffering.

During the past year, we have also made a good start in providing housing for low-income groups; we have raised minimum wages; we have gone forward with the development of our natural resources; we have given a greater assurance of stability to the farmer; and we have improved the organization and efficiency of our Government.

Today, by the grace of God, we stand a free and prosperous nation with greater possibilities for the future than any people ever had before in the history of the world.

We are now, in this year of 1950, nearing the midpoint of the 20th century.

The first half of this century will be known as the most turbulent and eventful period in recorded history. The swift pace of events promises to make the next 50 years decisive in the history of man on this planet.

The scientific and industrial revolution which began two centuries ago has, in the last 50 years, caught up the peoples of the globe in a common destiny. Two world-shattering wars have proved that no corner of the earth can be isolated from the affairs of mankind.

The human race has reached a turning point. Man has opened the secrets of nature and mastered new powers. If he uses them wisely, he can reach new heights of civilization. If he uses them foolishly, they may destroy him.

Man must create the moral and legal framework for the world which will insure that his new powers are used for good and not for evil. In shaping the outcome, the people of the United States will play a leading role.

Among all the great changes that have occurred in the last 50 years, none is more important than the change in the position of the United States in world affairs. Fifty years ago we were a country devoted largely to our own internal affairs. Our industry was growing, and we had new interests in the Far East and in the Caribbean, but we were primarily concerned with the development of vast areas of our own continental territory.

Today, our population has doubled. Our national production has risen from about $50 billion, in terms of today's prices, to the staggering figure of $255 billion a year. We have a more productive economic system and a greater industrial potential than any other nation on the globe. Our standard of living is an inspiration for all other peoples. Even the slightest changes in our economic and social life have their effect on other countries all around the world.

Our tremendous strength has brought with it tremendous responsibilities. We have moved from the outer edge to the center of world affairs. Other nations look to us for a wise exercise of our economic and military strength, and for vigorous support of the ideals of representative government and a free society. We will not fail them.

Our objective in the world is peace. Our country has joined with others in the task of achieving peace. We know now that this is not an easy task, or a short one. But we are determined to see it through. Both of our great political parties are committed to working together—and I am sure they will continue to work together—to achieve this end. We are prepared to devote our energy and our resources to this task, because we know that our own security and the future of mankind are at stake.

Right here, I want to say that no one appreciates more than I the bipartisan cooperation in foreign affairs which has been enjoyed by this administration.

Our success in working with other nations to achieve peace depends largely on what we do at home. We must preserve our national strength. Strength is not simply a matter of arms and force. It is a matter of economic growth, and social health, and vigorous institutions, public and private. We can achieve peace only if we maintain our productive energy, our democratic institutions, and our firm belief in individual freedom.

Our surest guide in the days that lie ahead will be the spirit in which this great Republic was founded. We must make our decisions in the conviction that all men are created equal, that they are equally entitled to life, liberty, and the pursuit of happiness, and that the duty of government is to serve these ends.

This country of ours has experienced many blessings, but none greater than its dedication to these principles. At every point in our history, these ideals have served to correct our failures and shortcomings, to spur us on to greater efforts, and to keep clearly before us the primary purpose of our existence as a nation. They have enshrined for us, a principle of government, the moral imperative to do justice, and the divine command to men to love one another.

These principles give meaning to all that we do.

In foreign policy, they mean that we can never be tolerant of oppression or tyranny. They mean that we must throw our weight on the side of greater freedom and a better life for all peoples. These principles confirm us in carrying out the specific programs for peace which we have already begun.

We shall continue to give our wholehearted support to the United Nations. We believe that this organization can ultimately provide the framework of international law and morality without which mankind cannot survive. It has already set up new standards for the conduct of nations in the Declaration of Human Rights and the

Convention on Genocide. It is moving ahead to give meaning to the concept of world brotherhood through a wide variety of cultural, economic, and technical activities.

The events of the past year again showed the value of the United Nations in bringing about the peaceful adjustment of tense international controversies. In Indonesia and in Palestine the efforts of the United Nations have put a stop to bloodshed and paved the way to peaceful settlements.

We are working toward the time when the United Nations will control weapons of mass destruction and will have the forces to preserve international law and order. While the world remains unsettled, however, and as long as our own security and the security of the free world require, we will maintain a strong and well-balanced defense organization. The Selective Service System is an essential part of our defense plans, and it must be continued.

Under the principles of the United Nations Charter we must continue to share in the common defense of free nations against aggression. At the last session this Congress laid the basis for this joint effort. We now must put into effect the common defense plans that are being worked out.

We shall continue our efforts for world economic recovery, because world prosperity is the only sure foundation of a permanent peace.

As an immediate means to this end we must continue our support of the European recovery program. This program has achieved great success in the first 2 years of its operation, but it has not yet been completed. If we were to stop this program now, or cripple it, just because it is succeeding, we should be doing exactly what the enemies of democracy want us to do. We should be just as foolish as a man who, for reasons of false economy, failed to put a roof on his house after building the foundation and the walls.

World prosperity also requires that we do all we can to expand world trade. As a major step in this direction we should promptly join the International Trade Organization. The purpose of this organization, which the United States has been foremost in creating, is to establish a code of fair practice, and an international authority for adjusting differences in international commercial relations. It is an effort to prevent the kind of anarchy and irresponsibility in world trade which did so much to bring about the world depression of the 1930's. An expanding world economy requires the improvement of living standards and the development of resources in areas where human poverty and misery now prevail. Without such improvement the recovery of Europe and the future of our own economy will not be secure. I urge that the Congress adopt the legislation now before it to provide for increasing the flow of technical assistance and capital investment in underdeveloped regions.

It is more essential now than ever, if the ideals of freedom and representative government are to prevail in these areas, and particularly in the Far East, that their peoples experience, in their own lives, the benefits of scientific and economic advances. This program will require the movement of large amounts of capital from the industrial nations, and particularly from the United States, to productive uses in the underdeveloped areas of the world. Recent world events make prompt action imperative.

This program is in the interest of all peoples—and has nothing in common with either the old imperialism of the last century or the new imperialism of the Communists.

Our aim for a peaceful, democratic world of free peoples will be achieved in the long run, not by force of arms, but by an appeal to the minds and hearts of men. If the peace policy of the democratic nations is to be successful, they must demonstrate that the benefits of their way of life can be increased and extended to all nations and all races.

In the world today we are confronted with the danger that the rising demand of people everywhere for freedom and a better life may be corrupted and betrayed by the false promises of communism. In its ruthless struggle for power, communism seizes upon our imperfections, and takes advantage of the delays and setbacks which the democratic nations experience in their effort to secure a better life for their citizens. This challenge to us is more than a military challenge. It is a challenge to the honesty of our profession of the democratic faith; it is a challenge to the efficiency and stability of our economic system; it is a challenge to the willingness to work with other peoples for world peace and for world prosperity.

For my part I welcome that challenge. I believe that our country, at this crucial point in world history, will meet that challenge successfully. I believe that, in cooperation with the other free nations of the world, we shall extend the full benefits of the democratic way of life to millions who do not now enjoy them, and preserve mankind from dictatorship and tyranny.

I believe that we shall succeed in our struggle for this peace, because I have seen the success we have had in our own country in following the principles of freedom. Over the last 50 years, the ideals of liberty and equal opportunity to which this Nation is dedicated have been increasingly realized in the lives of our people.

The ideal of equal opportunity no longer means simply the opportunity which a man has to advance beyond his fellows. Some of our citizens do achieve greater success than others as a reward for individual merit and effort, and this is as it should be. At the same time our country must be more than a land of opportunity for a select few. It must be a land of opportunity for all of us. In such a land we can grow and prosper together.

The simple truth that we can all go forward together is often questioned by selfish or shortsighted persons. It is strange that this is so, for this proposition is so clearly demonstrated by our national history. During the last 50 years, for example, our Nation has grown enormously in material well-being. This growth has come about, not by concentrating the benefits of our progress in the hands of a few, but by increasing the wealth of the great body of our Nation and our citizens.

In the last 50 years the income of the average family has increased so greatly that its buying power has doubled. The average hours of work have declined from 60 to 40 a week, the whole hourly production of the average worker has tripled. Average wages, allowing for price changes, have increased from about 45 cents an hour to $1.40 an hour.

We have accomplished what to earlier ages of mankind would have been a miracle—we work shorter hours, we produce more, and we live better.

Increasing freedom from poverty and drudgery has given a fuller meaning to American life. Our people are better educated; we have more opportunities for travel and recreation and enjoyment of the arts. We enjoy more personal liberty in the United States today than ever before.

If we can continue in the spirit of cooperative adventure which has marked the recent years of our progress, we can expect further scientific advances, further increases in our standard of living, and a still wider enjoyment of democratic freedom.

No one, of course, can foretell the future exactly. However, if we assume that we shall grow as fast in the future as we have grown in the past, we can get a good idea of how much our country should grow in the next 50 years.

At present our total national production is $255 billion a year. Our working population and our output per worker are increasing. If our productive power continues to increase at the same rate as it has increased over the past 50 years, our total national production 50 years from now will be nearly four times as much as it is today. Allowing for the expected growth in population, this would mean that the real income of the average family in the year 2000 A.D. would be about three times what it is today.

These are estimates of what we can do in the future, but we can reach these heights only if we follow the right policies. We have learned by bitter experience that progress is not automatic—that wrong policies lead to depression and disaster. We cannot achieve these gains unless we have a stable economy and avoid the catastrophes of boom and bust that have set us back in the past.

These gains cannot be achieved unless our businessmen maintain their spirit of initiative and enterprise and operate in a competitive economy. They cannot be achieved unless our workingmen and women and their unions help to increase productivity and obtain for labor a fair share of the benefits of our economic system. They cannot be achieved unless we have a stable and prosperous agriculture. They cannot be achieved unless we conserve and develop our natural resources in the public interest. Our system will not work unless our people are healthy, well-educated, and confident of the future. It will not work unless all citizens can participate fully in our national life.

In achieving these gains the Government has a special responsibility to help create and maintain the conditions which will permit the growth we know is possible. Foremost among these conditions is the need for a fair distribution of our increasing prosperity among all the great groups of our population who help to bring it about—labor, business, agriculture.

Businessmen must continue to have the incentives necessary for investment and for the development of new lines of enterprise. In the future growth of this country, lie possibilities for hundreds of thousands of new and independent businesses. As our national production increases, as it doubles and redoubles in the next 50 years, the number of independent and competing enterprises should also increase. If the number does not increase, our constantly growing economy will fall under the control of a few dominant economic groups whose powers will be so great that they will be a challenge to democratic institutions.

To avoid this danger, we must curb monopoly and provide aids to independent business so that it may have the credit and capital to compete in a system of free enterprise. I recommend that the Congress complete action at this session on the pending bill to close the loopholes in the Clayton Act which now permit monopolistic mergers. I also hope before this session is over to transmit to the Congress a series of proposals to strengthen the antimonopoly laws, to assist small business, and to encourage the growth of new enterprises.

In the case of labor, free collective bargaining must be protected and encouraged. Collective bargaining is not only a fundamental economic freedom for labor. It is also a strengthening and stabilizing influence for our whole economy.

The Federal statute now governing labor relations is punitive in purpose and one-sided in operation. This statute is, and always has been, inconsistent with the practice of true and effective collective bargaining. It should be repealed and replaced by a law that is fair to all and in harmony with our democratic ideals.

A full understanding of the problems of modern labor relations is of such importance that I recommend the establishment of a labor extension service to encourage educational activities in this field.

Another essential for our continued growth is a stable and prosperous agriculture. For many years we have been building a program to give the farmer a reasonable measure of protection against the special hazards to which he is exposed. That program was improved at the last session of the Congress. However, our farm legislation is still not adequate.

Although the Congress has properly declared as a matter of national policy that safeguards must be maintained against slumps in farm prices, there are serious shortcomings in the methods now available for carrying out this policy. Mandatory price supports should be provided for the commodities not now covered which are major sources of farm income.

Moreover, we should provide a method of supporting farm income at fair levels which will, at the same time, avoid piling up unmanageable surpluses and allow consumers to obtain the full benefit of our abundant agricultural production. A system of production payments gives the greatest promise of accomplishing this purpose. I recommend that the use of such a system be authorized.

One of the most important factors in our continued growth is the construction of more good, up-to-date housing. In a country such as ours there is no reason why decent homes should not be within the reach of all. With the help of various Government programs we have made great progress in the last few years in increasing the number of homes.

Despite this increase, there is still an acute shortage of housing for the lower and middle-income groups, especially in large metropolitan areas. We have laid the groundwork for relieving the plight of lower-income families in the Housing Act of 1949. To aid the middle-income families, I recommend that the Congress enact new legislation authorizing a vigorous program to help cooperatives and other nonprofit groups build housing which these families can afford.

Rent control has done a great deal to prevent the housing shortage from having had worse effects during this postwar period of adjustment. Rent control is still necessary to prevent widespread hardship and sharp curtailment of the buying power of millions of consumers in metropolitan areas. I recommend, therefore, that rent control be continued for another year.

If we are to achieve a better life for all, the natural resources of the country must be regarded as a public trust. We must use our precious assets of soil, water, and forest, and grassland in such a way that they become constantly more productive and more valuable. Government investment in the conservation and development of our resources is necessary to the future economic expansion of the country.

We need to enlarge the production and transmission of public power. That is true not only in those regions which have already received great benefits from Federal power projects, but also in regions such as New England where the benefits of large-scale public power development have not yet been experienced.

In our hydroelectric and irrigation undertakings, as well as in our other resource programs, we must continue policies to assure that their benefits will be spread among the many and not restricted to the favored few.

Important resource legislation which should be passed at this session includes the authorization of the St. Lawrence seaway and power project and the establishment of the Columbia Valley Administration—the establishment of the Columbia Valley Administration, I don't want you to miss that.

Through wise Government policies and Government expenditures for the conservation and development of our natural resources, we can be sure of transmitting to our children and our children's children a country far richer and more productive than the one we know today.

The value of our natural resources is constantly being increased by the progress of science. Research is finding new ways of using such natural assets as minerals, sea water, and plant life. In the peaceful development of atomic energy, particularly, we stand on the threshold of new wonders. The first experimental machines for producing useful power from atomic energy are now under construction. We have made only the first beginnings in this field, but in the perspective of history they may loom larger than the first airplane, or even the first tools that started man on the road to civilization.

To take full advantage of the increasing possibilities of nature we must equip ourselves with increasing knowledge. Government has a responsibility to see that our country maintains its position in the advance of science. As a step toward this end, the Congress should complete action on the measure to create a National Science Foundation.

Another duty of the Government is to promote the economic security, the health, and the education of its citizens. By so doing, we strengthen both our economy and the structure of our society. In a nation as rich as ours, all citizens should be able to live in decency and health.

Our Social Security System should be developed into the main reliance of our people for basic protection against the economic hazards of old-age, unemployment, and illness. I earnestly hope that the Congress will complete action at this session on legislation to increase the benefits and extend the coverage of old-age and survivors' insurance. The widespread movement to provide pensions in private industry dramatizes the need for improvements in the public insurance system.

I also urge that the Congress strengthen our unemployment compensation law to meet present-day needs more adequately. The economic downturn of the past year was the first real test that our system of unemployment insurance has had to meet. That test has proved the wisdom of the system, but it has also made strikingly apparent the need for improving its operation and increasing its coverage and its benefits.

In the field of health there are immense opportunities to extend to more of our people the benefits of the amazing advances in medical science. We have made a good beginning in expanding our hospitals, but we must also go on to remedy the shortages of doctors, nurses, and public health services, and to establish a system of medical insurance which will enable all Americans to afford good medical care.

We must take immediate steps to strengthen our educational system. In many parts of our country, young people are being handicapped for life because of a poor education. The rapidly increasing number of children of school age, coupled with the shortage of qualified teachers, makes this problem more critical each year. I believe that the Congress should no longer delay in providing Federal assistance to the States so that they can maintain adequate schools.

As we go forward in achieving greater economic security and greater opportunity for all our people, we should make every effort to extend the benefits of our democratic institutions to every citizen. The religious ideals which we profess, and the heritage of freedom which we have received from the past, clearly place that duty upon us. I again urge the Congress to enact the civil rights proposals I made in February 1948. These proposals are for the enactment of Federal statutes which will protect all our people in the exercise of their democratic rights and their search for economic opportunity, grant statehood to Alaska and Hawaii, provide a greater measure of self-government for our island possessions, and accord home rule to the District of Columbia. Some of those proposals have been before the Congress for a long time. Those who oppose them, as well as those who favor them, should recognize that it is the duty of the elected representatives of the people to let these proposals come to a vote.

Our democratic ideals, as well as our best interests, require that we do our fair share in providing homes for the unfortunate victims of war and tyranny. In so doing, we shall add strength to our democracy through the abilities and skills which these men and women will bring here. I urge the prompt enactment by the Congress of the legislation now before it to extend and broaden the existing displaced persons law and remove its discriminatory features.

The measures I am recommending to the Congress concerning both our foreign and our domestic policies represent a carefully considered program to meet our national needs. It is a program which necessarily requires large expenditures of funds. More than 70 percent of the Government's expenditures are required to meet the costs of past wars and to work for world peace. This is the dominant factor in our fiscal policy. At the same time, the Government must make substantial expenditures which are necessary to the growth and expansion of the domestic economy.

At present, largely because of the ill-considered tax reduction of the 80th Congress, the Government is not receiving enough revenue to meet its necessary expenditures.

To meet this situation, I am proposing that Federal expenditures be held to the lowest levels consistent with our international requirements and the essential needs of economic growth, and the well-being of our people. I think I had better read that over; you interrupted me in the middle.

To meet this situation, I am proposing that Federal expenditures be held to the lowest levels consistent with our international requirements and the essential needs of economic growth, and the well-being of our people. Don't forget that last phrase. At the same time, we must guard against the folly of attempting budget slashes which would impair our prospects for peace or cripple the programs essential to our national strength.

The budget recommendations I shall shortly transmit to the Congress show that we can expect a substantial improvement in our fiscal position over the next few years, as the cost of some of our extraordinary postwar programs declines, and as the Government revenue rises as a result of growth in employment and national income. To further improve our fiscal outlook, we should make some changes in our tax system which will reduce present inequities, stimulate business activity, and yield a moderate amount of additional revenue. I expect to transmit specific recommendations to the Congress on this subject at a very early date.

The fiscal policy I am recommending is the quickest and safest way of achieving a balanced budget.

As we move forward into the second half of the 20th century, we must always bear in mind the central purpose of our national life. We do not seek material prosperity for ourselves because we love luxury; we do not aid other nations because we wish to increase our power. We have not devised programs for the security and well-being of our people because we are afraid or unwilling to take risks. This is not the meaning of our past history or our present course.

We work for a better life for all, so that all men may put to good use the great gifts with which they have been endowed by their Creator. We seek to establish those material conditions of life in which, without exception, men may live in dignity, perform useful work, serve their communities, and worship God as they see fit.

These may seem simple goals, but they are not little ones. They are worth a great deal more than all the empires and conquests of history. They are not to be achieved by military aggression or political fanaticism. They are to be achieved by humbler means—by hard work, by a spirit of self-restraint in our dealings with one another, and by a deep devotion to the principles of justice and equality.

It should make us truly thankful, as we look back to the beginnings of this country, that we have come so far along the road to a better life for all. It should make us humble to think, as we look ahead, how much farther we have to go to accomplish, at home and abroad, the objectives that were set out for us at the founding of this great Nation.

As we approach the halfway mark of the 20th century, we should ask for continued strength and guidance from that Almighty Power who has placed before us such great opportunities for the good of mankind in the years to come.

Harry S. Truman, 1949–1953

Address to Congress on the State of the Union

January 8, 1951

The United States was embroiled in the Korean War when Harry Truman delivered his sixth State of the Union address. His speech before Congress focused on the country's battle against Soviet communism, using the Korean conflict as just one example of this worldwide struggle.

The Korean War started when North Korea attacked South Korea on June 25, 1950. The United States, together with United Nations forces, entered the war on the side of South Korea, while communist China entered the conflict later that year on the side of its ally, North Korea. Before the introduction of thousands of Chinese troops into the battle, the United States and its allies had succeeded in pushing the North Koreans out of the South and into the North almost to the Chinese border, but by the end of the year, the Chinese had reversed the tide of the war and had pushed far into South Korea.

Truman told the newly elected 82nd Congress—still controlled by Democrats, but with an increase in the number of Republicans—that it "faces as grave a task as any Congress in the history of our Republic," and that he expected the country to meet its challenge. He described the war in Korea as "part of the attempt of the Russian Communist dictatorship to take over the world, step by step."

The president stated that the Soviets had two methods: subversion within a country and aggression from without. The United States, he said, as the world's most powerful "free nation," had a "special responsibility" to combat this challenge. He cited economic assistance, including the Marshall Plan of U.S. aid to Europe, as one approach, and military assistance, as seen in the North Atlantic Treaty, as another.

Truman noted that Dwight D. Eisenhower, the U.S. general of World War II fame—and future president—had gone to Europe the previous week to command the North Atlantic Treaty forces.

On the home front, the president called for a war production drive and an increase in training of reserve forces. He also briefly mentioned several longtime goals, including more effective social insurance programs and equal rights for all citizens.

While gains would be made in Korea over the course of 1951, and the U.N. troops would reverse the Chinese progress, Truman would run into problems with General Douglas MacArthur, whom he fired for insubordination that April after the general had called for a larger-scale war against China itself. It would take until Eisenhower became president in 1953 for an armistice to be concluded in Korea that split the country with a demilitarized zone near the original border at the 38th parallel.

Mr. President, Mr. Speaker, Members of the Congress:

This 82d Congress faces as grave a task as any Congress in the history of our Republic. The actions you take will be watched by the whole world. These actions will measure the ability of a free people, acting through their chosen representatives and their free institutions, to meet a deadly challenge to their way of life.

We can meet this challenge foolishly or wisely. We can meet it timidly or bravely, shamefully or honorably.

I know that the 82d Congress will meet this challenge in a way worthy of our great heritage. I know that your debates will be earnest, responsible, constructive, and to the point. I know that from these debates there will come the great decisions needed to carry us forward.

At this critical time, I am glad to say that our country is in a healthy condition. Our democratic institutions are sound and strong. We have more men and women at work than ever before. We are able to produce more than ever before—in fact, far more than any country ever produced in the history of the world.

I am confident that we can succeed in the great task that lies before us. We will succeed, but we must all do our part. We must all act together as citizens of this great Republic.

As we meet here today, American soldiers are fighting a bitter campaign in Korea. We pay tribute to their courage, devotion, and gallantry.

Our men are fighting, alongside their United Nations allies, because they know, as we do, that the aggression in Korea is part of the attempt of the Russian Communist dictatorship to take over the world, step by step.

Our men are fighting a long way from home, but they are fighting for our lives and our liberties. They are fighting to protect our right to meet here today—our right to govern ourselves as a free nation.

The threat of world conquest by Soviet Russia endangers our liberty and endangers the kind of world in which the free spirit of man can survive. This threat is aimed at all peoples who strive to win or defend their own freedom and national independence.

Indeed, the state of our Nation is in great part the state of our friends and allies throughout the world. The gun that points at them points at us, also. The threat is a total threat and the danger is a common danger.

All free nations are exposed and all are in peril. Their only security lies in banding together. No one nation can find protection in a selfish search for a safe haven from the storm.

The free nations do not have any aggressive purpose. We want only peace in the world—peace for all countries. No threat to the security of any nation is concealed in our plans and programs.

We had hoped that the Soviet Union, with its security assured by the Charter of the United Nations, would be willing to live and let live. But I am sorry to say that has not been the case.

The imperialism of the czars has been replaced by the even more ambitious, more crafty, and more menacing imperialism of the rulers of the Soviet Union.

This new imperialism has powerful military forces. It is keeping millions of men under arms. It has a large air force and a strong submarine force. It has complete control of the men and equipment of its satellites. It has kept its subject peoples and its economy in a state of perpetual mobilization.

The present rulers of the Soviet Union have shown that they are willing to use this power to destroy the free nations and win domination over the whole world.

The Soviet imperialists have two ways of going about their destructive work. They use the method of subversion and internal revolution, and they use the method of external aggression. In preparation for either of these methods of attack, they stir up class strife and disorder. They encourage sabotage. They put out poisonous propaganda. They deliberately try to prevent economic improvement.

If their efforts are successful, they foment a revolution, as they did in Czechoslovakia and China, and as they tried, unsuccessfully, to do in Greece. If their methods of subversion are blocked, and if they think they can get away with outright warfare, they resort to external aggression. This is what they did when they loosed the armies of their puppet states against the Republic of Korea, in an evil war by proxy.

We of the free world must be ready to meet both of these methods of Soviet action. We must not neglect one or the other.

The free world has power and resources to meet these two forms of aggression—resources that are far greater than those of the Soviet dictatorship. We have skilled and vigorous peoples, great industrial strength, and abundant sources of raw materials. And above all, we cherish liberty. Our common ideals are a great part of our strength. These ideals are the driving force of human progress.

The free nations believe in the dignity and the worth of man.

We believe in independence for all nations.

We believe that free and independent nations can band together into a world order based on law. We have laid the cornerstone of such a peaceful world in the United Nations.

We believe that such a world order can and should spread the benefits of modern science and industry, better health and education, more food and rising standards of living—throughout the world.

These ideals give our cause a power and vitality that Russian communism can never command.

The free nations, however, are bound together by more than ideals. They are a real community bound together also by the ties of self-interest and self-preservation. If they should fall apart, the results would be fatal to human freedom.

Our own national security is deeply involved with that of the other free nations. While they need our support, we equally need theirs. Our national safety would be gravely prejudiced if the Soviet Union were to succeed in harnessing to its war machine the resources and the manpower of the free nations on the borders of its empire.

If Western Europe were to fall to Soviet Russia, it would double the Soviet supply of coal and triple the Soviet supply of steel. If the free countries of Asia and Africa should fall to Soviet Russia, we would lose the sources of many of our most vital raw materials, including uranium, which is the basis of our atomic power. And Soviet command of the manpower of the free nations of Europe and Asia would confront us with military forces which we could never hope to equal.

In such a situation, the Soviet Union could impose its demands on the world, without resort to conflict, simply through the preponderance of its economic and military power. The Soviet Union does not have to attack the United States to secure domination of the world. It can achieve its ends by isolating us and swallowing up all our allies. Therefore, even if we were craven enough I do not believe we could be—but, I say, even if we were craven enough to abandon our ideals, it would be disastrous for us to withdraw from the community of free nations.

We are the most powerful single member of this community, and we have a special responsibility. We must take the leadership in meeting the challenge to freedom and in helping to protect the rights of independent nations.

This country has a practical, realistic program of action for meeting this challenge.

First, we shall have to extend economic assistance, where it can be effective. The best way to stop subversion by the Kremlin is to strike at the roots of social injustice and economic disorder. People who have jobs, homes, and hopes for the future will defend themselves against the underground agents of the Kremlin. Our programs of economic aid have done much to turn back Communism.

In Europe the Marshall plan has had an electrifying result. As European recovery progressed, the strikes led by the Kremlin's agents in Italy and France failed. All over Western Europe the Communist Party took worse and worse beatings at the polls.

The countries which have received Marshall plan aid have been able, through hard work, to expand their productive strength—in many cases, to levels higher than ever before in their history. Without this strength they would be completely incapable of defending themselves today. They are now ready to use this strength in helping to build a strong combined defense against aggression.

We shall need to continue some economic aid to European countries. This aid should now be specifically related to the building of their defenses.

In other parts of the world our economic assistance will need to be more broadly directed toward economic development. In the Near East, in Africa, in Asia, we must do what we can to help people who are striving to advance from misery, poverty, and hunger. We must also continue to help the economic growth of our good neighbors in this hemisphere. These actions will bring greater strength for the free world. They will give many people a real stake in the future and reason to defend their freedom. They will mean increased production of goods they need and materials we need.

Second, we shall need to continue our military assistance to countries which want to defend themselves.

The heart of our common defense effort is the North Atlantic community. The defense of Europe is the basis for the defense of the whole free world—ourselves included. Next to the United States, Europe is the largest workshop in the world. It is also a homeland of the great religious beliefs shared by many of our citizens beliefs which are now threatened by the tide of atheistic communism.

Strategically, economically, and morally, the defense of Europe is a part of our own defense. That is why we have joined with the countries of Europe in the North Atlantic Treaty, pledging ourselves to work with them.

There has been much discussion recently over whether the European countries are willing to defend themselves. Their actions are answering this question.

Our North Atlantic Treaty partners have strict systems of universal military training. Several have recently increased the term of service. All have taken measures to improve the quality of training. Forces are being trained and expanded as rapidly as the necessary arms and equipment can be supplied from their factories and ours. Our North Atlantic Treaty partners, together, are building armies bigger than our own.

None of the North Atlantic Treaty countries, including our own country, has done enough yet. But real progress is being made. Together, we have worked out defense plans. The military leaders of our own country took part in working out these plans, and are agreed that they are sound and within our capabilities.

To put these plans into action, we sent to Europe last week one of our greatest military commanders, General Dwight D. Eisenhower.

General Eisenhower went to Europe to assume command of the united forces of the North Atlantic Treaty countries, including our own forces in Germany.

The people of Europe have confidence in General Eisenhower. They know his ability to put together a fighting force of allies. His mission is vital to our security. We should all stand behind him, and give him every bit of help we can.

Part of our job will be to reinforce the military strength of our European partners by sending them weapons and equipment as our military production expands.

Our program of military assistance extends to the nations in the Near East and the Far East which are trying to defend their freedom. Soviet communism is trying to make these nations into colonies, and to use their people as cannon fodder in new wars of conquest. We want their people to be free men and to enjoy peace.

Our country has always stood for freedom for the peoples of Asia. Long, long ago it stood for the freedom of the peoples of Asia. Our history shows this. We have demonstrated it in the Philippines. We have demonstrated it in our relations with

Indonesia, India, and with China. We hope to join in restoring the people of Japan to membership in the community of free nations.

It is in the Far East that we have taken up arms, under the United Nations, to preserve the principle of independence for free nations. We are fighting to keep the forces of Communist aggression from making a slave state out of Korea.

Korea has tremendous significance for the world. It means that free nations, acting through the United Nations, are fighting together against aggression.

We will understand the importance of this best if we look back into history. If the democracies had stood up against the invasion of Manchuria in 1931, or the attack on Ethiopia in 1935, or the seizure of Austria in 1938, if they had stood together against aggression on those occasions as the United Nations has done in Korea, the whole history of our time would have been different.

The principles for which we are fighting in Korea are right and just. They are the foundations of collective security and of the future of free nations. Korea is not only a country undergoing the torment of aggression; it is also a symbol. It stands for right and justice in the world against oppression and slavery. The free world must always stand for these principles—and we will stand with the free world.

As the third part of our program, we will continue to work for peaceful settlements in international disputes. We will support the United Nations and remain loyal to the great principles of international cooperation laid down in its charter.

We are willing, as we have always been, to negotiate honorable settlements with the Soviet Union. But we will not engage in appeasement.

The Soviet rulers have made it clear that we must have strength as well as right on our side. If we build our strength—and we are building it—the Soviet rulers may face the facts and lay aside their plans to take over the world.

That is what we hope will happen, and that is what we are trying to bring about. That is the only realistic road to peace.

These are the main elements of the course our Nation must follow as a member of the community of free nations. These are the things we must do to preserve our security and help create a peaceful world. But they will be successful only if we increase the strength of our own country.

Here at home we have some very big jobs to do. We are building much stronger military forces—and we are building them fast. We are preparing for full wartime mobilization, if that should be necessary. And we are continuing to build a strong and growing economy, able to maintain whatever effort may be required for as long as necessary.

We are building our own Army, Navy, and Air Force to an active strength of nearly 3 1/2 million men and women. We are stepping up the training of the reserve forces, and establishing more training facilities, so that we can rapidly increase our active forces far more on short notice.

We are going to produce all the weapons and equipment that such an armed force will need. Furthermore, we will make weapons for our allies, and weapons for our own reserve supplies. On top of this, we will build the capacity to turn out on short notice arms and supplies that may be needed for a full-scale war.

Fortunately, we have a good start on this because of our enormous plant capacity and because of the equipment on hand from the last war. For example, many combat ships are being returned to active duty from the "mothball fleet" and many others can be put into service on very short notice. We have large reserves of arms and ammunition and thousands of workers skilled in arms production.

In many cases, however, our stocks of weapons are low. In other cases, those on hand are not the most modern. We have made remarkable technical advances. We have developed new types of jet planes and powerful new tanks. We are concentrating on producing the newest types of weapons and producing them as fast as we can.

This production drive is more selective than the one we had during World War II, but it is just as urgent and intense. It is a big program and it is a costly one.

Let me give you two concrete examples. Our present program calls for expanding the aircraft industry so that it will have the capacity to produce 50,000 modern military planes a year. We are preparing the capacity to produce 35,000 tanks a year. We are not now ordering that many planes or that many tanks, and we hope that we never have to, but we mean to be able to turn them out if we need them.

The planes we are producing now are much bigger, much better, and much more expensive than the planes we had during the last war.

We used to think that the B-17 was a huge plane, and the blockbuster it carried a huge load. But the B-36 can carry five of these blockbusters in its belly, and it can carry them five times as far. Of course, the B-36 is much more complicated to build than the B-17, and far more expensive. One B-17 costs $275,000, while now one B-36 costs $3 million.

I ask you to remember that what we are doing is to provide the best and most modern military equipment in the world for our fighting forces.

This kind of defense production program has two parts.

The first part is to get our defense production going as fast as possible. We have to convert plants and channel materials to defense production. This means heavy cuts in civilian uses of copper, aluminum, rubber, and other essential materials. It means shortages in various consumer goods.

The second part is to increase our capacity to produce and to keep our economy strong for the long pull. We do not know how long Communist aggression will threaten the world.

Only by increasing our output can we carry the burden of preparedness for an indefinite period in the future. This means that we will have to build more power plants and more steel mills, grow more cotton, mine more copper, and expand our capacity in many other ways.

First, appropriations for our military buildup.

Second, extension and revision of the Selective Service Act.

Third, military and economic aid to help build up the strength of the free world.

Fourth, revision and extension of the authority to expand production and to stabilize prices, wages, and rents.

Fifth, improvement of our agricultural laws to help obtain the kinds of farm products we need for the defense effort.

Sixth, improvement of our labor laws to help provide stable labor-management relations and to make sure that we have steady production in this emergency.

Seventh, housing and training of defense workers and the full use of all our manpower resources.

Eighth, means for increasing the supply of doctors, nurses, and other trained medical personnel critically needed for the defense effort.

Ninth, aid to the States to meet the most urgent needs of our elementary and secondary schools. Some of our plans will have to be deferred for the time being. But we should do all we can to make sure our children are being trained as good and useful citizens in the critical times ahead.

Tenth, a major increase in taxes to meet the cost of the defense effort.

The Economic Report and the Budget Message will discuss these subjects further. In addition, I shall send to the Congress special messages containing detailed recommendations on legislation needed at this Session.

In the months ahead the Government must give priority to activities that are urgent—like military procurement and atomic energy and power development. It must practice rigid economy in its nondefense activities. Many of the things we would normally do must be curtailed or postponed.

But in a long-term defense effort like this one, we cannot neglect the measures needed to maintain a strong economy and a healthy democratic society.

The Congress, therefore, should give continued attention to the measures which our country will need for the long pull. And it should act upon such legislation as promptly as circumstances permit.

To take just one example—we need to continue and complete the work of rounding out our system of social insurance. We still need to improve our protection against unemployment and old age. We still need to provide insurance against the loss of earnings through sickness, and against the high costs of modern medical care.

And above all, we must remember that the fundamentals of our strength rest upon the freedoms of our people. We must continue our efforts to achieve the full realization of our democratic ideals. We must uphold the freedom of speech and the freedom of conscience in our land. We must assure equal rights and equal opportunities to all our citizens.

As we go forward this year in the defense of freedom, let us keep clearly before us the nature of our present effort.

We are building up our strength, in concert with other free nations, to meet the danger of aggression that has been turned loose on the world. The strength of the free nations is the world's best hope of peace.

I ask the Congress for unity in these crucial days.

Make no mistake about my meaning. I do not ask, or expect, unanimity. I do not ask for an end to debate. Only by debate can we arrive at decisions which are wise, and which reflect the desires of the American people. We do not have a dictatorship in this country, and we never will have one in this country.

When I request unity, what I am really asking for is a sense of responsibility on the part of every Member of this Congress. Let us debate the issues, but let every man among us weigh his words and his deeds. There is a sharp difference between harmful criticism and constructive criticism. If we are truly responsible as individuals, I am sure that we will be unified as a government.

Let us keep our eyes on the issues and work for the things we all believe in.

Let each of us put our country ahead of our party, and ahead of our own personal interests.

I had the honor to be a Member of the Senate during World War II, and I know from experience that unity of purpose and of effort is possible in the Congress without any lessening of the vitality of our two-party system.

Let us all stand together as Americans. Let us stand together with all men everywhere who believe in human liberty.

Peace is precious to us. It is the way of life we strive for with all the strength and wisdom we possess. But more precious than peace are freedom and justice. We will fight, if fight we must, to keep our freedom and to prevent justice from being destroyed.

These are the things that give meaning to our lives, and which we acknowledge to be greater than ourselves.

This is our cause—peace, freedom, justice. We will pursue this cause with determination and humility, asking divine guidance that in all we do we may follow the will of God.

Harry S. Truman, 1949–1953

Address to Congress on the State of the Union

January 9, 1952

Harry Truman's seventh State of the Union address was delivered at the start of a presidential election year, and while the Korean War was still under way. At the start of his speech, the president made a plea for balance between the needs of an election campaign and the importance of maintaining a bipartisan foreign policy during troubled times, saying, "all of us—Republicans and Democrats alike—all of us are Americans; and we are all going to sink or swim together."

The country was in the midst of the Cold War, pitting democratic values against the communist system of the Soviet Union. Truman summarized the high and low points of the year just ended, 1951. Among the positives were the gains made in the Korean conflict by the United States and its allies in reversing the advances of the communist Chinese; among the negatives were the continued increases in the overall military power of the Soviet Union.

The president asked the country to be prepared for difficult times and warned that world war was still a threat, that the country could not stand alone in a Soviet-dominated world, and that American values were under attack. "This is a time for courage, not for grumbling and mumbling," Truman stated.

The president also urged increases in the size of the armed forces, particularly air power, and stated that shortages of some consumer goods—although on a smaller scale than during World War II—could be coming. In addition, he said that inflation must be controlled, and that the country should prepare for high taxes over the next several years. He also mentioned several of his perennial pleas, including for the repeal of the Taft-Hartley labor-management law and for additional efforts to advance civil rights.

Truman would announce in March 1952 that he would not seek another term as president, making the 1952 presidential election the first since 1928 without an incumbent running for reelection.

The president's popularity was suffering. For example, one episode that angered many Americans took place in April 1951, when he fired well-liked General

Douglas MacArthur from his command in Korea, for insubordination. A Gallup Poll taken on April 14, three days after the firing, found 58.64 percent of respondents disagreeing with the president's decision and only 20.68 percent approving.

The Korean conflict, in which more than 150,000 Americans were killed or wounded, was in a stalemate in 1952; it would take until 1953, during the presidency of Dwight D. Eisenhower, for an armistice to be reached.

Mr. President, Mr. Speaker, Members of the Congress:

I have the honor to report to the Congress on the state of the Union.

At the outset, I should like to speak of the necessity for putting first things first as we work together this year for the good of our country.

The United States and the whole free world are passing through a period of grave danger. Every action you take here in Congress, and every action that I take as President, must be measured against the test of whether it helps to meet that danger.

This will be a presidential election year—the year in which politics plays a large part in our lives—a larger part than usual. That is perfectly proper. But we have a greater responsibility to conduct our political fights in a manner that does not harm the national interest.

We can find plenty of things to differ about without destroying our free institutions and without abandoning our bipartisan foreign policy for peace.

When everything is said and done, all of us—Republicans and Democrats alike—all of us are Americans; and we are all going to sink or swim together.

We are moving through a perilous time. Faced with a terrible threat of aggression, our Nation has embarked upon a great effort to help establish the kind of world in which peace shall be secure. Peace is our goal—not peace at any price, but a peace based on freedom and justice. We are now in the midst of our effort to reach that goal. On the whole, we have been doing very well.

Last year, 1951, was a year in which we threw back aggression, added greatly to our military strength, and improved the chances for peace and freedom in many parts of the world.

This year, 1952, is a critical year in the defense effort of the whole free world. If we falter we can lose all the gains we have made. If we drive ahead, with courage and vigor and determination, we can by the end of 1952 be in a position of much greater security. The way will be dangerous for the years ahead, but if we put forth our best efforts this year—and next year—we can be "over the hump" in our effort to build strong defenses.

When we look at the record of the past year, 1951, we find important things on both the credit and the debit side of the ledger. We have made great advances. At the same time we have run into new problems which must be overcome.

Now let us look at the credit side first.

Peace depends upon the free nations sticking together, and making a combined effort to check aggression and prevent war. In this respect, 1951 was a year of great achievement.

In Korea the forces of the United Nations turned hack the Chinese Communist invasion—and did it without widening the area of conflict. The action of the United

Nations in Korea has been a powerful deterrent to a third world war. However, the situation in Korea remains very hazardous. The outcome of the armistice negotiation still remains uncertain.

In Indochina and Malaya, our aid has helped our allies to hold back the Communist advance, although there are signs of further trouble in that area.

In 1951 we strengthened the chances of peace in the Pacific region by the treaties with Japan and the defense arrangements with Australia, New Zealand, and the Philippines.

In Europe combined defense has become a reality. The free nations have created a real fighting force. This force is not yet as strong as it needs to be; but it is already a real obstacle to any attempt by hostile forces to sweep across Europe to the Atlantic.

In 1951 we also moved to strengthen the security of Europe by the agreement to bring Greece and Turkey into the North Atlantic Treaty.

The United Nations, the world's greatest hope for peace, has come through a year of trial stronger and more useful than ever. The free nations have stood together in blocking Communist attempts to tear up the charter.

At the present session of the United Nations in Paris, we, together with the British and the French, offered a plan to reduce and control all armaments under a foolproof inspection system. This is a concrete, practical proposal for disarmament.

But what happened? Vishinsky laughed at it. Listen to what he said: "I could hardly sleep at all last night. . . . I could not sleep because I kept laughing." The world will be a long time forgetting the spectacle of that fellow laughing at disarmament.

Disarmament is not a joke. Vishinsky's laughter met with shock and anger from the people all over the world. And, as a result, Mr. Stalin's representative received orders to stop laughing and start talking.

If the Soviet leaders were to accept this proposal, it would lighten the burden of armaments, and permit the resources of the earth to be devoted to the good of mankind. But until the Soviet Union accepts a sound disarmament proposal, and joins in peaceful settlements, we have no choice except to build up our defenses.

During this past year we added more than a million men and women to our Armed Forces. The total is now nearly 3½ million. We have made rapid progress in the field of atomic weapons. We have turned out $16 billion worth of military supplies and equipment, three times as much as the year before.

Economic conditions in the country are good. There are 61 million people on the job; wages, farm incomes, and business profits are at high levels. Total production of goods and services in our country has increased 8 percent over last year—about twice the normal rate of growth.

Perhaps the most amazing thing about our economic progress is the way we are increasing our basic capacity to produce. For example, we are now in the second year of a 3-year program which will double our output of aluminum, increase our electric power supply by 40 percent, and increase our steelmaking capacity by 15 percent. We can then produce 120 million tons of steel a year, as much as all the rest of the world put together.

This expansion will mean more jobs and higher standards of living for all of us in the years ahead. At the present time it means greater strength for us and for the rest of the free world in the fight for peace.

Now, I must turn to the debit side of the ledger for the past year.

The outstanding fact to note on the debit side of the ledger is that the Soviet Union, in 1951, continued to expand its military production and increase its already excessive military power.

It is true that the Soviets have run into increasing difficulties. Their hostile policies have awakened stern resistance among free men throughout the world. And behind the Iron Curtain the Soviet rule of force has created growing political and economic stresses in the satellite nations.

Nevertheless, the grim fact remains that the Soviet Union is increasing its armed might. It is still producing more war planes than the free nations. It has set off two more atomic explosions. The world still walks in the shadow of another world war.

And here at home, our defense preparations are far from complete.

During 1951 we did not make adequate progress in building up civil defense against atomic attack. This is a major weakness in our plans for peace, since inadequate civilian defense is an open invitation to a surprise attack. Failure to provide adequate civilian defense has the same effect as adding to the enemy's supply of atomic bombs.

In the field of defense production we have run into difficulties and delays in designing and producing the latest types of airplanes and tanks. Some machine tools and metals are still in extremely short supply.

In other free countries the defense buildup has created severe economic problems. It has increased inflation in Europe and has endangered the continued recovery of our allies.

In the Middle East political tensions and the oil controversy in Iran are keeping the region in a turmoil. In the Far East the dark threat of Communist imperialism still hangs over many nations.

This, very briefly, is the good side and the bad side of the picture.

Taking the good and bad together, we have made real progress this last year along the road to peace. We have increased the power and unity of the free world. And while we were doing this, we have avoided world war on the one hand, and appeasement on the other. This is a hard road to follow, but the events of the last year show that it is the right road to peace.

We cannot expect to complete the job overnight. The free nations may have to maintain for years the larger military forces needed to deter aggression. We must build steadily, over a period of years, toward political solidarity and economic progress among the free nations in all parts of the world.

Our task will not be easy; but if we go at it with a will, we can look forward to steady progress. On our side are all the great resources of freedom—the ideals of religion and democracy, the aspiration of people for a better life, and the industrial and technical power of a free civilization.

These advantages outweigh anything the slave world can produce. The only thing that can defeat us is our own state of mind. We can lose if we falter.

The middle period of a great national effort like this is a very difficult time. The way seems long and hard. The goal seems far distant. Some people get discouraged. That is only natural.

But if there are any among us who think we ought to ease up in the fight for peace, I want to remind them of three things—just three things.

First: The threat of world war is still very real. We had one Pearl Harbor—let's not get caught off guard again. If you don't think the threat of Communist armies is real, talk to some of our men back from Korea.

Second: If the United States had to try to stand alone against a Soviet-dominated world, it would destroy the life we know and the ideals we hold dear. Our allies are essential to us, just as we are essential to them. The more shoulders there are to bear the burden the lighter that burden will be.

Third: The things we believe in most deeply are under relentless attack. We have the great responsibility of saving the basic moral and spiritual values of our civilization. We have started out well—with a program for peace that is unparalleled in history. If we believe in ourselves and the faith we profess, we will stick to that job until it is victoriously finished.

This is a time for courage, not for grumbling and mumbling.

Now, let us take a look at the things we have to do.

The thing that is uppermost in the minds of all of us is the situation in Korea. We must, and we will, keep up the fight there until we get the kind of armistice that will put an end to the aggression and protect the safety of our forces and the security of the Republic of Korea. Beyond that we shall continue to work for a settlement in Korea that upholds the principles of the United Nations.

We went into Korea because we knew that Communist aggression had to be met firmly if freedom was to be preserved in the world. We went into the fight to save the Republic of Korea, a free country, established under the United Nations. These are our aims. We will not give up until we attain them.

Meanwhile, we must continue to strengthen the forces of freedom throughout the world.

I hope the Senate will take early and favorable action on the Japanese peace treaty, on our security pacts with the Pacific countries, and on the agreement to bring Greece and Turkey into the North Atlantic Treaty.

We are also negotiating an agreement with the German Federal Republic under which it can play an honorable and equal part among nations and take its place in the defense of Western Europe.

But treaties and plans are only the skeleton of our defense structure. The sinew and muscle of defense are the forces and equipment which must be provided.

In Europe we must go on helping our friends and allies to build up their military forces. This means we must send weapons in large volume to our European allies. I have directed that weapons for Europe be given a very high priority. Economic aid is necessary, too, to supply the margin of difference between success and failure in making Europe a strong partner in our joint defense.

In the long run we want to see Europe freed from any dependence on our aid. Our European allies want that just as bad as we do. The steps that are now being taken to build European unity should help bring that about. Six European countries are pooling their coal and steel production under the Schuman plan. Work is going forward on the merger of European national forces on the Continent into a single army. These great projects should become realities in 1952.

We should do all we can to help and encourage the move toward a strong and united Europe.

In Asia the new Communist empire is a daily threat to millions of people. The peoples of Asia want to be free to follow their own way of life. They want to preserve their culture and their traditions against communism, just as much as we want to preserve ours. They are laboring under terrific handicaps—poverty, ill health, feudal systems of land ownership, and the threat of internal subversion or external attack. We can and we must increase our help to them.

This means military aid, especially to those places like Indochina which might be hardest hit by some new Communist attack.

It also means economic aid, both technical know-how and capital investment.

This last year we made available millions of bushels of wheat to relieve famine in India. But far more important, in the long run, is the work Americans are doing in India to help the Indian farmers themselves raise more grain. With the help of our technicians, Indian farmers, using simple, inexpensive means, have been able since 1948 to double the crops in one area in India. One farmer there raised 63 bushels of wheat to the acre, where 13 bushels had been the average before.

This is point 4—our point 4 program at work. It is working—not only in India but in Iran, Paraguay, Liberia—in 33 countries around the globe. Our technical missionaries are out there. We need more of them. We need more funds to speed their efforts, because there is nothing of greater importance in all our foreign policy. There is nothing that shows more clearly what we stand for, and what we want to achieve.

My friends of the Congress, less than one-third of the expenditure for the cost of World War II would have created the developments necessary to feed the whole world so we wouldn't have to stomach communism. That is what we have got to fight, and unless we fight that battle and win it, we can't win the cold war or a hot one either.

We have recently lost a great public servant who was leading this effort to bring opportunity and hope to the people of half the world. Dr. Henry Bennett and his associates died in line of duty on a point 4 mission. It is up to us to carry on the great work for which they gave their lives.

During the coming year we must not forget the suffering of the people who live behind the Iron Curtain. In those areas minorities are being oppressed, human rights violated, religions persecuted. We should continue to expose those wrongs. We should continue and expand the activities of the Voice of America, which brings our message of hope and truth to those peoples and other peoples throughout the world.

I have just had an opportunity to discuss many of these world problems with Prime Minister Churchill. We have had a most satisfactory series of meetings. We thoroughly reviewed the situation in Europe, the Middle East, and the Far East. We both look forward to steady progress toward peace through the cooperative action and teamwork of the free nations.

Turning from our foreign policies, let us consider the jobs we have here at home as a part of our program for peace.

The first of these jobs is to move ahead full steam on the defense program.

Our objective is to have a well-equipped active defense force large enough—in concert with the forces of our allies—to deter aggression and to inflict punishing losses on the enemy immediately if we should be attacked. This active force must be backed by adequate reserves, and by the plants and tools to turn out the tremendous quantities of new weapons that would be needed if war came. We are not building an active force adequate to carry on full scale war, but we are putting ourselves in a position to mobilize very rapidly if we have to.

This year I shall recommend some increases in the size of the active force we are building, with particular emphasis on air power. This means we shall have to continue large-scale production of planes and other equipment for a longer period of time than we had originally planned.

Planes and tanks and other weapons—what the military call "hard goods"—are now beginning to come off the production lines in volume. Deliveries of hard goods now amount to about a billion and a half dollars worth a month. A year from now, we expect that rate to be doubled.

We shall have to hold to a high rate of military output for about a year after that. In 1954 we hope to have enough equipment so that we can reduce the production of most military items substantially. The next 2 years should therefore be the peak period of defense production.

Defense needs will take a lot of steel, aluminum, copper, nickel, and other scarce materials. This means smaller production of some civilian goods. The cutbacks will be nothing like those during World War II, when most civilian production was completely stopped. But there will be considerably less of some goods than we have been used to these past 2 or 3 years.

The very critical part of our defense job this year is to keep down inflation.

We can control inflation if we make up our minds to do it.

On the executive side of the Government, we intend to hold the line on prices just as tightly as the law allows. We will permit only those wage increases which are clearly justified under sound stabilization policies; and we will see to it that industries absorb cost increases out of earnings wherever feasible, before they are authorized to raise prices. We will do that, at any rate, except where the recent amendments to the law specifically require us to give further price increases.

Congress has a tremendous responsibility in this matter. Our stabilization law was shot full of holes at the last session. This year, it will be one of the main tasks before the Congress to repair the damage and enact a strong anti-inflation law.

As a part of our program to keep our country strong, we are determined to preserve the financial strength of the Government. This means high taxes over the next few years. We must see to it that these taxes are shared among the people as fairly as possible. I expect to discuss these matters in the Economic Report and the Budget Message which will soon be presented to the Congress.

Our tax laws must be fair. And we must make absolutely certain they are administered fairly, without fear or favor of any kind for anybody. To this end, steps have already been taken to remedy weaknesses which have been disclosed in the administration of the tax laws. In addition, I hope the Congress will approve my reorganization plan for the Bureau of Internal Revenue. We must do everything necessary in order to make just as certain as is humanly possible that every taxpayer receives equal treatment under the law.

To carry the burden of defense we must have a strong, productive, and expanding economy here at home. We cannot neglect those things that have made us the great and powerful nation we are today.

Our strength depends upon the health, the morale, the freedom of our people. We can take on the burden of leadership in the fight for world peace because, for nearly 20 years, the Government and the people have been working together for the general welfare. We have given more and more of our citizens a fair chance at decent, useful, productive lives. That is the reason we are as strong as we are today.

This Government of ours—the Congress and the executive both—must keep on working to bring about a fair deal for all the American people. Some people will say that we haven't the time or the money this year for measures for the welfare of the people. But if we want to win the fight for peace, this is a part of the job we cannot ignore.

We will have to give up some things, we will have to go forward on others at a slower pace. But, so far as I am concerned, I do not think we can give up the things that are vital to our national strength.

I believe most people in this country will agree with me on that.

I think most farmers understand that soil conservation and rural electrification and agricultural research are not frills or luxuries, but real necessities in order to boost our farm production.

I think most workers understand that decent housing and good working conditions are not luxuries, but necessities if the working men and women of this country are to continue to out-produce the rest of the world.

I think our businessmen know that scientific research and transportation services and more steel mills and power projects are not luxuries, but necessities to keep our business and our industry in the forefront of industrial progress.

I think everybody knows that social insurance and better schools and health services are not frills, but necessities in helping all Americans to be useful and productive citizens, who can contribute their full share in the national effort to protect and advance our way of life.

We cannot do all we want to in times like these—we have to choose the things that will contribute most to defense—but we must continue to make progress if we are to be a strong nation in the years ahead.

Let me give you some examples.

We are going right ahead with the urgently needed work to develop our natural resources, to conserve our soil, and to prevent floods. We are going to produce essential power and build the lines that are necessary and that we have to have to transmit it to our farms and factories. We are going to encourage exploration for new mineral deposits.

We are going to keep on building essential highways and taking any other steps that will assure the Nation an adequate transportation system—on land, on the sea, and in the air.

We must move right ahead this year to see that defense workers and soldiers' families get decent housing at rents they can afford to pay.

We must begin our long deferred program of Federal aid to education—to help the States meet the present crisis in the operation of our schools. And we must help with the construction of schools in areas where they are critically needed because of the defense effort.

We urgently need to train more doctors and other health personnel, through aid to medical education. We also urgently need to expand the basic public health services in our home communities—especially in defense areas. The Congress should go ahead with these two measures immediately.

I have set up an impartial commission to make a thorough study of the Nation's health needs. One of the things this commission is looking into is how to bring the cost of modern medical care within the reach of all the people. I have repeatedly recommended national health insurance as the best way to do this. So far as I know, it is still the best way. If there are any better answers, I hope this commission will find them. But of one thing I am sure: something must be done, and done soon.

This year we ought to make a number of urgently needed improvements in our social security law. For one thing, benefits under old-age and survivors insurance should be raised $5 a month above the present average of $42. For another thing, the States should be given special aid to help them increase public assistance payments. By doing these things now, we can ease the pressure of living costs for people who depend on those fixed payments.

We should also make some cost-of-living adjustments for those receiving veterans' compensation for death or disability incurred in the service of our country. In addition, now is the time to start a sensible program of readjustment benefits for our veterans who have seen service since the fighting broke out in Korea.

Another thing the Congress should do at this session is to strengthen our system of farm price supports to meet the defense emergency. The "sliding scale" in the price support law should not be allowed to penalize farmers for increasing production to meet defense needs. We should also find a new and less costly method for supporting perishable commodities than the law now provides.

We need to act promptly to improve our labor law. The Taft-Hartley Act has many serious and far-reaching defects. Experience has demonstrated this so clearly that even the sponsors of the act now admit that it needs to be changed. A fair law, fair to both management and labor, is indispensable to sound labor relations and to full, uninterrupted production. I intend to keep on working for a fair law until we get one.

As we build our strength to defend the freedom in the world, we ourselves must extend the benefits of freedom more widely among all our own people. We need to take action toward the wider enjoyment of civil rights. Freedom is the birthright of every American.

The executive branch has been making real progress toward full equality of treatment and opportunity—in the Armed Forces, in the civil service, and in private firms working for the Government. Further advances require action by Congress, and I hope that means will be provided to give the Members of the Senate and the House a chance to vote on them.

I am glad to hear that home rule for the District of Columbia will be the first item of business before the Senate. I hope that it, as well as statehood for Hawaii and Alaska, will be adopted promptly.

All these measures I have been talking about—measures to advance the well-being of our people—demonstrate to the world the forward movement of our free society.

This demonstration of the way free men govern themselves has a more powerful influence on the people of the world—on both sides of the Iron Curtain—than all the trick slogans and pie-in-the-sky promises of the Communists.

But our shortcomings, as well as our progress, are watched from abroad. And there is one shortcoming I want to speak about plainly.

Our kind of government above all others cannot tolerate dishonesty among public servants.

Some dishonest people worm themselves into almost every human organization. It is all the more shocking, however, when they make their way into a Government such as ours, which is based on the principle of justice for all. Such unworthy public servants must be weeded out. I intend to see to it that Federal employees who have been guilty of misconduct are punished for it. I also intend to see to it that the honest and hard-working great majority of our Federal employees are protected against partisan slander and malicious attack.

I have already made some recommendations to the Congress to help accomplish these purposes. I intend to submit further recommendations to this end. I will welcome the wholehearted cooperation of the Congress in this effort.

I also think that the Congress can do a great deal to strengthen confidence in our institutions by applying rigorous standards of moral integrity to its own operations, and by finding an effective way to control campaign expenditures, and by protecting the rights of individuals in congressional investigations.

To meet the crisis which now hangs over the world, we need many different kinds of strength—military, economic, political, and moral. And of all these, I am convinced that moral strength is the most vital.

When you come right down to it, it is the courage and the character of our Nation—and of each one of us as individuals—that will really decide how well we meet this challenge.

We are engaged in a great undertaking at home and abroad—the greatest, in fact, that any nation has ever been privileged to embark upon. We are working night and day to bring peace to the world and to spread the democratic ideals of justice and self-government to all people. Our accomplishments are already remarkable. We ought to be full of pride in what we are doing, and full of confidence and hope in the outcome. No nation ever had greater resources, or greater energy, or nobler traditions to inspire it.

And yet, day in and day out, we see a long procession of timid and fearful men who wring their hands and cry out that we have lost the way, that we don't know what we are doing, that we are bound to fail. Some say we should give up the struggle for peace, and others say we should have a war and get it over with. That's a terrible statement. I had heard it made, but they want us to forget the great objective of preventing another world war—the objective for which our soldiers have been fighting in the hills of Korea.

If we are to be worthy of all that has been done for us by our soldiers in the field, we must be true to the ideals for which they are fighting. We must reject the counsels of defeat and despair. We must have the determination to complete the great work for which our men have laid down their lives.

In all we do, we should remember who we are and what we stand for. We are Americans. Our forefathers had far greater obstacles than we have, and much poorer chances of success. They did not lose heart, or turn aside from their goals. In the darkest of all winters in American history, at Valley Forge, George Washington said: "We must not, in so great a contest, expect to meet with nothing but sunshine." With that spirit they won their fight for freedom.

We must have that same faith and vision. In the great contest in which we are engaged today, we cannot expect to have fair weather all the way. But it is a contest just as important for this country and for all men, as the desperate struggle that George Washington fought through to victory.

Let us prove, again, that we are not merely sunshine patriots and summer soldiers. Let us go forward, trusting in the God of Peace, to win the goals we seek.

Message to Congress on the State of the Union

January 7, 1953

Harry Truman's last State of the Union message, which was written rather than delivered in person before Congress, summed up his eight years in office. While the Twenty-second Amendment, which set term limits for the office of president, did not take effect until the next president took office, Truman decided not to run for reelection and his last months in office were those of a lame-duck leader.

Truman's message reflected the huge changes that had come about since 1945. When Truman first took office, World War II was still under way; it would end later that year. At the time of his departure from office, the Cold War between the United States and the Soviet Union was in full swing. U.S. troops, along with their allies, were involved in the Korean War, against communist China and North Korea. For this reason, much of Truman's address dealt with international relations and foreign policy. The president summed up the U.S.-Soviet conflict as a struggle between freedom and tyranny. He discussed how the two countries had been allies in World War II, but instead of working together after the war, he said, the Soviets "violated, one by one, the solemn agreements they had made with us in wartime."

He painted a picture of the communist world—including the Soviet Union and its satellite countries, as well as China—as "trying to expand the boundaries of their world, whenever and wherever they can."

Truman cited military security as one weapon with which to fight back, and he listed a series of steps taken during his presidency, including support for Greece, Turkey, the North Atlantic countries, and, finally, South Korea. But he added that military security had to be combined with economic measures, and he mentioned the Marshall Plan, the U.S. initiative that pumped billions of dollars into the postwar economies of the democracies of Western Europe.

He spoke of the dangers of living in the atomic age, and of the importance of the American role in the world. He warned his fellow Americans not to be afraid of the challenges ahead of them. "To beat back fear, we must hold fast to our heritage as free men," he stated.

Truman was succeeded by Dwight D. Eisenhower, the famous World War II general who had sought the presidency as a Republican; Eisenhower's eight years in office also would be dominated by the Cold War. For his part, Truman, a former senator from Missouri, retired to his home state; he lived until 1972.

To the Congress of the United States:

I have the honor to report to the Congress on the state of the Union.

This is the eighth such report that, as President, I have been privileged to present to you and to the country. On previous occasions, it has been my custom to set forth proposals for legislative action in the coming year. But that is not my purpose today. The presentation of a legislative program falls properly to my successor, not to me, and I would not infringe upon his responsibility to chart the forward course. Instead, I wish to speak of the course we have been following the past eight years and the position at which we have arrived.

In just two weeks, General Eisenhower will be inaugurated as President of the United States and I will resume—most gladly—my place as a private citizen of this Republic. The Presidency last changed hands eight years ago this coming April. That was a tragic time: a time of grieving for President Roosevelt—the great and gallant human being who had been taken from us; a time of unrelieved anxiety to his successor, thrust so suddenly into the complexities and burdens of the Presidential office.

Not so this time. This time we see the normal transition under our democratic system. One President, at the conclusion of his term, steps back to private life; his successor, chosen by the people, begins his tenure of the office. And the Presidency of the United States continues to function without a moment's break.

Since the election, I have done my best to assure that the transfer from one Administration to another shall be smooth and orderly. From General Eisenhower and his associates, I have had friendly and understanding collaboration in this endeavor. I have not sought to thrust upon him—nor has he sought to take—the responsibility which must be mine until twelve o'clock noon on January twentieth. But together, I hope and believe we have found means whereby the incoming President can obtain the full and detailed information he will need to assume the responsibility the moment he takes the oath of office.

The President-elect is about to take up the greatest burdens, the most compelling responsibilities, given to any man. And I, with you and all Americans, wish for him all possible success in undertaking the tasks that will so soon be his.

What are these tasks? The President is Chief of State, elected representative of all the people, national spokesman for them and to them. He is Commander-in-Chief of our armed forces. He is charged with the conduct of our foreign relations. He is Chief Executive of the Nation's largest civilian organization. He must select and nominate all top officials of the Executive Branch and all Federal judges. And on the legislative side, he has the obligation and the opportunity to recommend, and to approve or veto legislation. Besides all this, it is to him that a great political party turns naturally for leadership, and that, too, he must provide as President.

This bundle of burdens is unique; there is nothing else like it on the face of the earth. Each task could be a full-time job. Together, they would be a tremendous undertaking in the easiest of times.

But our times are not easy; they are hard—as hard and complex, perhaps as any in our history. Now, the President not only has to carry on these tasks in such a way that our democracy may grow and flourish and our people prosper, but he also has to lead the whole free world in overcoming the communist menace—and all this under the shadow of the atomic bomb.

This is a huge challenge to the human being who occupies the Presidential office. But it is not a challenge to him alone, for in reality he cannot meet it alone. The challenge runs not just to him but to his whole Administration, to the Congress, to the country.

Ultimately, no President can master his responsibilities, save as his fellow citizens—indeed, the whole people—comprehend the challenge of our times and move, with him, to meet it.

It has been my privilege to hold the Presidential office for nearly eight years now, and much has been done in which I take great pride. But this is not personal pride. It is pride in the people, in the Nation. It is pride in our political system and our form of government—balky sometimes, mechanically deficient perhaps, in many ways—but enormously alive and vigorous; able through these years to keep the Republic on the right course, rising to the great occasions, accomplishing the essentials, meeting the basic challenge of our times.

There have been misunderstandings and controversies these past eight years, but through it all the President of the United States has had that measure of support and understanding without which no man could sustain the burdens of the Presidential office, or hope to discharge its responsibilities.

For this I am profoundly grateful—grateful to my associates in the Executive Branch—most of them non-partisan civil servants; grateful—despite our disagreements—to the Members of the Congress on both sides of the aisle; grateful especially to the American people, the citizens of this Republic, governors of us all.

We are still so close to recent controversies that some of us may find it hard to understand the accomplishments of these past eight years. But the accomplishments are real and very great, not as the President's, not as the Congress', but as the achievements of our country and all the people in it.

Let me remind you of some of the things we have done since I first assumed my duties as President of the United States.

I took the oath of office on April 12, 1945. In May of that same year, the Nazis surrendered. Then, in July, that great white flash of light, man-made at Alamogordo, heralded swift and final victory in World War II—and opened the doorway to the atomic age.

Consider some of the great questions that were posed for us by sudden, total victory in World War II. Consider also, how well we as a Nation have responded.

Would the American economy collapse, after the war? That was one question. Would there be another depression here—a repetition of 1921 or 1929? The free world feared and dreaded it. The communists hoped for it and built their policies upon that hope.

We answered that question—answered it with a resounding "no."

Our economy has grown tremendously. Free enterprise has flourished as never fore. Sixty-two million people are now gainfully employed, compared with 51 million seven years ago. Private businessmen and farmers have invested more than 200 billion dollars in new plant and equipment since the end of World War II. Prices have risen further than they should have done—but incomes, by and large, have risen even more, so that real living standards are now considerably higher than seven years ago. Aided by sound government policies, our expanding economy has shown the strength and flexibility for swift and almost painless reconversion from war to peace, in 1945 and 1946; for quick reaction and recovery—well before Korea—from the beginnings of recession in 1949. Above all, this live and vital economy of ours has now shown the remarkable capacity to sustain a great mobilization program for defense, a vast outpouring of aid to friends and allies all around the world—and still to produce more goods and services for peaceful use at home than we have ever known before.

This has been our answer, up to now, to those who feared or hoped for a depression in this country.

How have we handled our national finances? That was another question arising at war's end. In the administration of the Government, no problem takes more of the President's time, year in and year out, than fashioning the Budget, and the related problem of managing the public debt.

Financing World War II left us with a tremendous public debt, which reached 279 billion dollars at its peak in February, 1946.

Beginning in July, 1946, when war and reconversion financing had ended, we have held quite closely to the sound standard that in times of high employment and high national income, the Federal Budget should be balanced and the debt reduced.

For the four fiscal years from July 1, 1946, to June 30, 1950, we had a net surplus of 4.3 billion dollars. Using this surplus, and the Treasury's excess cash reserves, the debt was reduced substantially, reaching a low point of 251 billion dollars in June, 1949, and ending up at 257 billion dollars on June 30, 1950.

In July of 1950, we began our rapid rearmament, and for two years held very close to a pay-as-we-go policy. But in the current fiscal year and the next, rising expenditures for defense will substantially outrun receipts. This will pose an immediate and serious problem for the new Congress.

Now let me turn to another question we faced at the war's end. Would we take up again, and carry forward, the great projects of social welfare—so badly needed, so long overdue—that the New Deal had introduced into our national life? Would our Government continue to have a heart for the people, or was the progress of the New Deal to be halted in the aftermath of war as decisively as the progress of Woodrow Wilson's New Freedom had been halted after the first world war?

This question, too, we have answered. We have answered it by doubling old age insurance benefits and extending coverage to ten million more people. We have answered it by increasing our minimum wage. We have answered by the three million privately constructed homes that the Federal Government has helped finance since the war—and the 155 thousand units of low rent public housing placed under construction since 1949.

We have answered with the 42 thousand new hospital beds provided since 1946 through the joint efforts of the Federal Government and local communities.

We have answered by helping eight million veterans of World War II to obtain advanced education, 196 thousand to start in business, and 64 thousand to buy farms.

We have answered by continuing to help farmers obtain electric power, until today nearly 90 per cent of our farms have power line electric service.

In these and other ways, we have demonstrated, up to now, that our democracy has not forgotten how to use the powers of the Government to promote the people's welfare and security.

Another of the big post-war questions was this: What we would do with the Nation's natural resources—its soils and water, forests and grasslands. Would we continue the strong conservation movement of the 1930's, or would we, as we did after the First World War, slip back into the practices of monopoly, exploitation, and waste?

The answer is plain. All across our country, the soil conservation movement has spread, aided by Government programs, enriching private and public lands, preserving them from destruction, improving them for future use. In our river basins, we have invested nearly 5 billion dollars of public funds in the last eight years—invested them in projects to control floods, irrigate farmlands, produce low-cost power and get it to the housewives and farmers and businessmen who need it. We have been vigilant in protecting the people's property—lands and forests and oil and minerals.

We have had to fight hard against those who would use our resources for private greed; we have met setbacks; we have had to delay work because of defense priorities, but on the whole we can be proud of our record in protecting our natural heritage, and in using our resources for the public good.

Here is another question we had to face at the war's close: Would we continue, in peace as well as war, to promote equality of opportunity for all our citizens, seeking ways and means to guarantee for all of them the full enjoyment of their civil rights?

During the war we achieved great economic and social gains for millions of our fellow citizens who had been held back by prejudice. Were we prepared, in peacetime, to keep on moving toward full realization of the democratic promise? Or would we let it be submerged, wiped out, in post-war riots and reaction, as after World War I?

We answered these questions in a series of forward steps at every level of government and in many spheres of private life. In our armed forces, our civil service, our universities, our railway trains, the residential districts of our cities—in stores and factories all across the Nation—in the polling booths as well—the barriers are coming down. This is happening, in part, at the mandate of the courts; in part, at the insistence of Federal, State and local governments; in part, through the enlightened action of private groups and persons in every region and every walk of life.

There has been a great awakening of the American conscience on the issues of civil rights. And all this progress—still far from complete but still continuing—has been our answer, up to now, to those who questioned our intention to live up to the promises of equal freedom for us all.

There was another question posed for us at the war's end, which equally concerned the future course of our democracy: Could the machinery of government and politics in this Republic be changed, improved, adapted rapidly enough to carry through, responsibly and well, the vast, new complicated undertakings called for in our time?

We have answered this question, too, answered it by tackling the most urgent, most specific, problems which the war experience itself had brought into sharp focus. The reorganization of the Congress in 1946; the unification of our armed services, beginning in 1947; the closer integration of foreign and military policy through the National Security Council created that same year; and the Executive reorganizations, before and after the Hoover-Acheson Commission Report in 1949—these are landmarks in our continuing endeavor to make government an effective instrument of service to the people.

I come now to the most vital question of all, the greatest of our concerns: Could there be built in the world a durable structure of security, a lasting peace for all the nations, or would we drift, as after World War I, toward another terrible disaster—a disaster which this time might be the holocaust of atomic war?

That is still the overriding question of our time. We cannot know the answer yet; perhaps we will not know it finally for a long time to come. But day and night, these past eight years, we have been building for peace, searching out the way that leads most surely to security and freedom and justice in the world for us and all mankind.

This, above all else, has been the task of our Republic since the end of World War II, and our accomplishment so far should give real pride to all Americans. At the very least, a total war has been averted, each day up to this hour. And at the most, we may already have succeeded in establishing conditions which can keep that kind of war from happening, for as far ahead as man can see.

The Second World War radically changed the power relationships of the world. Nations once great were left shattered and weak, channels of communication, routes of trade, political and economic ties of many kinds were ripped apart.

And in this changed, disrupted, chaotic situation, the United States and the Soviet Union emerged as the two strongest powers of the world. Each had tremendous human and natural resources, actual or potential, on a scale unmatched by any other nation.

Nothing could make plainer why the world is in its present state—and how that came to pass—than an understanding of the diametrically opposite principles and policies of these two great powers in a war-ruined world.

For our part, we in this Republic were—and are—free men, heirs of the American Revolution, dedicated to the truths of our Declaration of Independence:

" . . . That all men are created equal, that they are endowed by their Creator with certain unalienable rights. . . . That to secure these rights, governments are instituted among men, deriving their just powers from the consent of the governed."

Our post-war objective has been in keeping with this great idea. The United States has sought to use its pre-eminent position of power to help other nations recover from the damage and dislocation of the war. We held out a helping hand to enable them to restore their national lives and to regain their positions as independent, self-supporting members of the great family of nations. This help was given without any attempt on our part to dominate or control any nation. We did not want satellites but partners.

The Soviet Union, however, took exactly the opposite course.

Its rulers saw in the weakened condition of the world not an obligation to assist in the great work of reconstruction, but an opportunity to exploit misery and suffering for the extension of their power. Instead of help, they brought subjugation. They extinguished, blotted out, the national independence of the countries that the military operations of World War II had left within their grasp.

The difference stares at us from the map of Europe today. To the west of the line that tragically divides Europe we see nations continuing to act and live in the light of their own traditions and principles. On the other side, we see the dead uniformity of a tyrannical system imposed by the rulers of the Soviet Union. Nothing could point up more clearly what the global struggle between the free world and the communists is all about.

It is a struggle as old as recorded history; it is freedom versus tyranny.

For the dominant idea of the Soviet regime is the terrible conception that men do not have rights but live at the mercy of the state.

Inevitably this idea of theirs—and all the consequences flowing from it—collided with the efforts of free nations to build a just and peaceful world. The "cold war" between the communists and the free world is nothing more or less than the Soviet attempt to checkmate and defeat our peaceful purposes, in furtherance of their own dread objective.

We did not seek this struggle, God forbid. We did our utmost to avoid it. In World War II, we and the Russians had fought side by side, each in our turn attacked and forced to combat by the aggressors. After the war, we hoped that our wartime collaboration could be maintained, that the frightful experience of Nazi invasion, of devastation in the heart of Russia, had turned the Soviet rulers away from their old proclaimed allegiance to world revolution and communist dominion. But instead, they violated, one by one, the solemn agreements they had made with us in wartime. They sought to use the rights and privileges they had obtained in the United Nations, to frustrate its purposes and cut down its powers as an effective agent of world progress and the keeper of the world's peace.

Despite this outcome, the efforts we made toward peaceful collaboration are a source of our present strength. They demonstrated that we believed what we proclaimed, that we actually sought honest agreements as the way to peace. Our whole moral position, our leadership in the free world today, is fortified by that fact.

The world is divided, not through our fault or failure, but by Soviet design. They, not we, began the cold war. And because the free world saw this happen because men know we made the effort and the Soviet rulers spurned it—the free nations have accepted leadership from our Republic, in meeting and mastering the Soviet offensive.

It seems to me especially important that all of us be clear, in our own thinking, about the nature of the threat we have faced—and will face for a long time to come. The measures we have devised to meet it take shape and pattern only as we understand what we were—and are—up against.

The Soviet Union occupies a territory of 8 million square miles. Beyond its borders, East and West, are the nearly five million square miles of the satellite states—virtually incorporated into the Soviet Union—and of China, now its close partner. This vast land mass contains an enormous store of natural resources sufficient to support an economic development comparable to our own.

That is the Stalinist world. It is a world of great natural diversity in geography and climate, in distribution of resources, in population, language, and living standards, in economic and cultural development. It is a world whose people are not all convinced communists by any means. It is a world where history and national traditions, particularly in its borderlands, tend more toward separation than unification, and run counter to the enforced combination that has been made of these areas today.

But it is also a world of great man-made uniformities, a world that bleeds its population white to build huge military forces; a world in which the police are everywhere and their authority unlimited; a world where terror and slavery are deliberately administered both as instruments of government and as means of production; a world where all effective social power is the state's monopoly—yet the state itself is the creature of the communist tyrants.

The Soviet Union, with its satellites, and China are held in the tight grip of communist party chieftains. The party dominates all social and political institutions. The party regulates and centrally directs the whole economy. In Moscow's sphere, and in Peiping's, all history, philosophy, morality and law are centrally established by rigid dogmas, incessantly drummed into the whole population and subject to interpretation—or to change by none except the party's own inner circle.

And lest their people learn too much of other ways of life, the communists have walled off their world, deliberately and uniformly, from the rest of human society.

That is the communist base of operation in their cold war. In addition, they have at their command hundreds and thousands of dedicated foreign communists, people in nearly every free country who will serve Moscow's ends. Thus the masters of the Kremlin are provided with deluded followers all through the free world whom they can manipulate, cynically and quite ruthlessly, to serve the purposes of the Soviet state.

Given their vast internal base of operations, and their agents in foreign lands, what are the communist rulers trying to do?

Inside their homeland, the communists are trying to maintain and modernize huge military forces. And simultaneously, they are endeavoring to weld their whole vast area and population into a completely self-contained, advanced industrial society. They aim, some day, to equal or better the production levels of Western Europe and North America combined—thus shifting the balance of world economic power, and war potential, to their side.

They have a long way to go and they know it. But they are prepared to levy upon living generations any sacrifice that helps strengthen their armed power, or speed industrial development.

Externally, the communist rulers are trying to expand the boundaries of their world, whenever and wherever they can. This expansion they have pursued steadfastly since the close of World War II, using any means available to them.

Where the Soviet army was present, as in the countries of Eastern Europe, they have gradually squeezed free institutions to death.

Where post-war chaos existed in industrialized nations, as in Western Europe, the local Stalinists tried to gain power through political processes, politically-inspired strikes, and every available means for subverting free institutions to their evil ends.

Where conditions permitted, the Soviet rulers have stimulated and aided armed insurrection by communist-led revolutionary forces, as in Greece, Indo-China, the Philippines, and China, or outright aggression by one of their satellites, as in Korea.

Where the forces of nationalism, independence, and economic change were at work throughout the great sweep of Asia and Africa, the communists tried to identify themselves with the cause of progress, tried to picture themselves as the friends of freedom and advancement—surely one of the most cynical efforts of which history offers record.

Thus, everywhere in the free world, the communists seek to fish in troubled waters, to seize more countries, to enslave more millions of human souls. They were, and are, ready to ally themselves with any group, from the extreme left to the extreme right, that offers them an opportunity to advance their ends.

Geography gives them a central position. They are both a European and an Asian power, with borders touching many of the most sensitive and vital areas in the free world around them. So situated, they can use their armies and their economic power to set up simultaneously a whole series of threats—or inducements—to such widely dispersed places as Western Germany, Iran, and Japan. These pressures and attractions can be sustained at will, or quickly shifted from place to place.

Thus the communist rulers are moving, with implacable will, to create greater strength in their vast empire, and to create weakness and division in the free world, preparing for the time their false creed teaches them must come: the time when the whole world outside their sway will be so torn by strife and contradictions that it will be ripe for the communist plucking.

This is the heart of the distorted Marxist interpretation of history. This is the glass through which Moscow and Peiping look out upon the world, the glass through which they see the rest of us. They seem really to believe that history is on their side. And they are trying to boost "history" along, at every opportunity, in every way they can.

I have set forth here the nature of the communist menace confronting our Republic and the whole free world. This is the measure of the challenge we have faced since World War II—a challenge partly military and partly economic, partly moral and partly intellectual, confronting us at every level of human endeavor and all around the world.

It has been and must be the free world's purpose not only to organize defenses against aggression and subversion, not only to build a structure of resistance and salvation for the community of nations outside the iron curtain, but in addition to give expression and opportunity to the forces of growth and progress in the free world, to so organize and unify the cooperative community of free men that we will not crumble but grow stronger over the years, and the Soviet empire, not the free world, will eventually have to change its ways or fall.

Our whole program of action to carry out this purpose has been directed to meet two requirements.

The first of these had to do with security. Like the pioneers who settled this great continent of ours, we have had to carry a musket while we went about our peaceful business. We realized that if we and our allies did not have military strength to meet the growing Soviet military threat, we would never have the opportunity to carry forward our efforts to build a peaceful world of law and order—the only environment in which our free institutions could survive and flourish.

Did this mean we had to drop everything else and concentrate on armies and weapons? Of course it did not: side-by-side with this urgent military requirement, we had to continue to help create conditions of economic and social progress in the world. This work had to be carried forward alongside the first, not only in order to meet the non-military aspects of the communist drive for power, but also because this creative effort toward human progress is essential to bring about the kind of world we as free men want to live in.

These two requirements—military security and human progress—are more closely related in action than we sometimes recognize. Military security depends upon a strong economic underpinning and a stable and hopeful political order; conversely, the confidence that makes for economic and political progress does not thrive in areas that are vulnerable to military conquest.

These requirements are related in another way. Both of them depend upon unity of action among the free nations of the world. This, indeed, has been the foundation of our whole effort, for the drawing together of the free people of the world has become a condition essential not only to their progress, but to their survival as free people.

This is the conviction that underlies all the steps we have been taking to strengthen and unify the free nations during the past seven years.

What have these steps been? First of all, how have we gone about meeting the requirement of providing for our security against this world-wide challenge?

Our starting point, as I have said on many occasions, has been and remains the United Nations.

We were prepared, and so were the other nations of the free world, to place our reliance on the machinery of the United Nations to safeguard peace. But before the

United Nations could give full expression to the concept of international security embodied in the Charter, it was essential that the five permanent members of the Security Council honor their solemn pledge to cooperate to that end. This the Soviet Union has not done.

I do not need to outline here the dreary record of Soviet obstruction and veto and the unceasing efforts of the Soviet representatives to sabotage the United Nations. It is important, however, to distinguish clearly between the principle of collective security embodied in the Charter and the mechanisms of the United Nations to give that principle effect. We must frankly recognize that the Soviet Union has been able, in certain instances, to stall the machinery of collective security. Yet it has not been able to impair the principle of collective security. The free nations of the world have retained their allegiance to that idea. They have found the means to act despite the Soviet veto, both through the United Nations itself and through the application of this principle in regional and other security arrangements that are fully in harmony with the Charter and give expression to its purposes.

The free world refused to resign itself to collective suicide merely because of the technicality of a Soviet veto.

The principle of collective measures to forestall aggression has found expression in the Treaty of Rio de Janeiro, the North Atlantic Treaty, now extended to include Greece and Turkey, and the several treaties we have concluded to reinforce security in the Pacific area.

But the free nations have not this time fallen prey to the dangerous illusion that treaties alone will stop an aggressor. By a series of vigorous actions, as varied as the nature of the threat, the free nations have successfully thwarted aggression or the threat of aggression in many different parts of the world.

Our country has led or supported these collective measures. The aid we have given to people determined to act in defense of their freedom has often spelled the difference between success and failure.

We all know what we have done, and I shall not review in detail the steps we have taken. Each major step was a milepost in the developing unity, strength and resolute will of the free nations.

The first was the determined and successful effort made through the United Nations to safeguard the integrity and independence of Iran in 1945 and 1946.

Next was our aid and support to embattled Greece, which enabled her to defeat the forces threatening her national independence.

In Turkey, cooperative action resulted in building up a bulwark of military strength for an area vital to the defenses of the entire free world.

In 1949, we began furnishing military aid to our partners in the North Atlantic Community and to a number of other free countries.

The Soviet Union's threats against Germany and Japan, its neighbors to the West and to the East, have been successfully withstood. Free Germany is on its way to becoming a member of the peaceful community of nations, and a partner in the common defense. The Soviet effort to capture Berlin by blockade was thwarted by the courageous Allied airlift. An independent and democratic Japan has been brought back into the community of free nations.

In the Far East, the tactics of communist imperialism have reached heights of violence unmatched elsewhere—and the problem of concerted action by the free nations has been at once more acute and more difficult.

Here, in spite of outside aid and support, the free government of China succumbed to the communist assault. Our aid has enabled the free Chinese to rebuild and strengthen their forces on the island of Formosa. In other areas of the Far East—in Indo-China, Malaya, and the Philippines—our assistance has helped sustain a staunch resistance against communist insurrectionary attacks.

The supreme test, up to this point, of the will and determination of the free nations came in Korea, when communist forces invaded the Republic of Korea, a state that was in a special sense under the protection of the United Nations. The response was immediate and resolute. Under our military leadership, the free nations for the first time took up arms, collectively, to repel aggression.

Aggression was repelled, driven back, punished. Since that time, communist strategy has seen fit to prolong the conflict, in spite of honest efforts by the United Nations to reach an honorable truce. The months of deadlock have demonstrated that the communists cannot achieve by persistence, or by diplomatic trickery, what they failed to achieve by sneak attack. Korea has demonstrated that the free world has the will and the endurance to match the communist effort to overthrow international order through local aggression.

It has been a bitter struggle and it has cost us much in brave lives and human suffering, but it has made it plain that the free nations will fight side by side, that they will not succumb to aggression or intimidation, one by one. This, in the final analysis, is the only way to halt the communist drive to world power.

At the heart of the free world's defense is the military strength of the United States.

From 1945 to 1949, the United States was sole possessor of the atomic bomb. That was a great deterrent and protection in itself.

But when the Soviets produced an atomic explosion—as they were bound to do in time—we had to broaden the whole basis of our strength. We had to endeavor to keep our lead in atomic weapons. We had to strengthen our armed forces generally and to enlarge our productive capacity—our mobilization base. Historically, it was the Soviet atomic explosion in the fall of 1949, nine months before the aggression in Korea, which stimulated the planning for our program of defense mobilization.

What we needed was not just a central force that could strike back against aggression. We also needed strength along the outer edges of the free world, defenses for our allies as well as for ourselves, strength to hold the line against attack as well as to retaliate.

We have made great progress on this task of building strong defenses. In the last two and one half years, we have more than doubled our own defenses, and we have helped to increase the protection of nearly all the other free nations.

All the measures of collective security, resistance to aggression, and the building of defenses, constitute the first requirement for the survival and progress of the free world. But, as I have pointed out, they are interwoven with the necessity of taking steps to create and maintain economic and social progress in the free nations. There can be no military strength except where there is economic capacity to back it. There can be no freedom where there is economic chaos or social collapse. For these reasons, our national policy has included a wide range of economic measures.

In Europe, the grand design of the Marshall Plan permitted the people of Britain and France and Italy and a half dozen other countries, with help from the United States, to lift themselves from stagnation and find again the path of rising production, rising incomes, rising standards of living. The situation was changed almost overnight by the Marshall Plan; the people of Europe have a renewed hope and vitality, and they are able to carry a share of the military defense of the free world that would have been impossible a few years ago.

Now the countries of Europe are moving rapidly towards political and economic unity, changing the map of Europe in more hopeful ways than it has been changed for 500 years. Customs unions, European economic institutions like the Schuman Plan, the movement toward European political integration, the European Defense Community—all are signs of practical and effective growth toward greater common strength and unity. The countries of Western Europe, including the free Republic of Germany are working together, and the whole free world is the gainer.

It sometimes happens, in the course of history, that steps taken to meet an immediate necessity serve an ultimate purpose greater than may be apparent at the time. This, I believe, is the meaning of what has been going on in Europe under the threat of aggression. The free nations there, with our help, have been drawing together in defense of their free institutions. In so doing, they have laid the foundations of a unity that will endure as a major creative force beyond the exigencies of this period of history. We may, at this close range, be but dimly aware of the creative surge this movement represents, but I believe it to be of historic importance. I believe its benefits will survive long after communist tyranny is nothing but an unhappy memory.

In Asia and Africa, the economic and social problems are different but no less urgent. There hundreds of millions of people are in ferment, exploding into the twentieth century, thrusting toward equality and independence and improvement in the hard conditions of their lives.

Politically, economically, socially, things cannot and will not stay in their pre-war mold in Africa and Asia. Change must come—is coming—fast. Just in the years I have been President, 12 free nations, with more than 600 million people, have become independent: Burma, Indonesia, the Philippines, Korea, Israel, Libya, India, Pakistan and Ceylon, and the three Associated States of Indo-China, now members of the French Union. These names alone are testimony to the sweep of the great force which is changing the face of half the world.

Working out new relationships among the peoples of the free world would not be easy in the best of times. Even if there were no Communist drive for expansion, there would be hard and complex problems of transition from old social forms, old political arrangements, old economic institutions to the new ones our century demands—problems of guiding change into constructive channels, of helping new nations grow strong and stable. But now, with the Soviet rulers striving to exploit this ferment for their own purposes, the task has become harder and more urgent—terribly urgent.

In this situation, we see the meaning and the importance of the Point IV program, through which we can share our store of know-how and of capital to help these people develop their economies and reshape their societies. As we help Iranians to raise more grain, Indians to reduce the incidence of malaria, Liberians to educate their children better, we are at once helping to answer the desires of the people for advancement, and demonstrating the superiority of freedom over communism. There will be no quick solution for any of the difficulties of the new nations of Asia and Africa—but there may be no solution at all if we do not press forward with full energy to help these countries grow and flourish in freedom and in cooperation with the rest of the free world.

Our measures of economic policy have already had a tremendous effect on the course of events. Eight years ago, the Kremlin thought post-war collapse in Western Europe and Japan—with economic dislocation in America—might give them the signal to advance. We demonstrated they were wrong. Now they wait with hope that the economic recovery of the free world has set the stage for violent and disastrous rivalry among the economically developed nations, struggling for each other's markets and a greater share of trade. Here is another test that we shall have to meet and master in the years immediately ahead. And it will take great ingenuity and effort—and much time—before we prove the Kremlin wrong again. But we can do it. It is true that economic recovery presents its problems, as does economic decline, but they are problems of another order. They are the problems of distributing abundance fairly, and they can be solved by the process of international cooperation that has already brought us so far.

These are the measures we must continue. This is the path we must follow. We must go on, working with our free associates, building an international structure for military defense, and for economic, social, and political progress. We must be prepared for war, because war may be thrust upon us. But the stakes in our search for peace are immensely higher than they have ever been before.

For now we have entered the atomic age, and war has undergone a technological change which makes it a very different thing from what it used to be. War today between the Soviet empire and the free nations might dig the grave not only of our Stalinist opponents, but of our own society, our world as well as theirs.

This transformation has been brought to pass in the seven years from Alamogordo to Eniwetok. It is only seven years, but the new force of atomic energy has turned the world into a very different kind of place.

Science and technology have worked so fast that war's new meaning may not yet be grasped by all the peoples who would be its victims; nor, perhaps, by the rulers in the Kremlin. But I have been President of the United States, these seven years, responsible for the decisions which have brought our science and our engineering to their present place. I know what this development means now. I know something of what it will come to mean in the future.

We in this Government realized, even before the first successful atomic explosion, that this new force spelled terrible danger for all mankind unless it were brought under international control. We promptly advanced proposals in the United Nations to take this new source of energy out of the arena of national rivalries, to make it impossible to use it as a weapon of war. These proposals, so pregnant with benefit for all humanity, were rebuffed by the rulers of the Soviet Union.

The language of science is universal, the movement of science is always forward into the unknown. We could not assume that the Soviet Union would not develop the same weapon, regardless of all our precautions, nor that there were not other and even more terrible means of destruction lying in the unexplored field of atomic energy.

We had no alternative, then, but to press on, to probe the secrets of atomic power to the uttermost of our capacity, to maintain, if we could, our initial superiority in the atomic field. At the same time, we sought persistently for some avenue, some formula, for reaching an agreement with the Soviet rulers that would place this new form of power under effective restraints—that would guarantee no nation would use it in war. I do not have to recount here the proposals we made, the steps taken in the United Nations, striving at least to open a way to ultimate agreement. I hope and believe that we will continue to make these efforts so long as there is the slightest possibility of progress. All civilized nations are agreed on the urgency of the problem, and have shown their willingness to agree on effective measures of control—all save the Soviet Union and its satellites. But they have rejected every reasonable proposal.

Meanwhile, the progress of scientific experiment has outrun our expectations. Atomic science is in the full tide of development; the unfolding of the innermost secrets of matter is uninterrupted and irresistible. Since Alamogordo we have developed atomic weapons with many times the explosive force of the early models, and we have produced them in substantial quantities. And recently, in the thermonuclear tests at Eniwetok, we have entered another stage in the world-shaking development of atomic energy. From now on, man moves into a new era of destructive power, capable of creating explosions of a new order of magnitude, dwarfing the mushroom clouds of Hiroshima and Nagasaki.

We have no reason to think that the stage we have now reached in the release of atomic energy will be the last. Indeed, the speed of our scientific and technical progress over the last seven years shows no signs of abating. We are being hurried forward, in our mastery of the atom, from one discovery to another, toward yet unforeseeable peaks of destructive power.

Inevitably, until we can reach international agreement, this is the path we must follow. And we must realize that no advance we make is unattainable by others, that no advantage in this race can be more than temporary.

The war of the future would be one in which man could extinguish millions of lives at one blow, demolish the great cities of the world, wipe out the cultural achievements of the past—and destroy the very structure of a civilization that has been slowly and painfully built up through hundreds of generations.

Such a war is not a possible policy for rational men. We know this, but we dare not assume that others would not yield to the temptation science is now placing in their hands.

With that in mind, there is something I would say, to Stalin: You claim belief in Lenin's prophecy that one stage in the development of communist society would be war between your world and ours. But Lenin was a pre-atomic man, who viewed society and history with pre-atomic eyes. Something profound has happened since he wrote. War has changed its shape and its dimension. It cannot now be a "stage" in the development of anything save ruin for your regime and your homeland.

I do not know how much time may elapse before the communist rulers bring themselves to recognize this truth. But when they do, they will find us eager to reach understandings that will protect the world from the danger it faces today.

It is no wonder that some people wish that we had never succeeded in splitting the atom. But atomic power, like any other force of nature, is not evil in itself. Properly used, it is an instrumentality for human betterment. As a source of power, as a tool of scientific inquiry, it has untold possibilities. We are already making good progress in the constructive use of atomic power. We could do much more if we were free to concentrate on its peaceful uses exclusively.

Atomic power will be with us all the days of our lives. We cannot legislate it out of existence. We cannot ignore the dangers or the benefits it offers.

I believe that man can harness the forces of the atom to work for the improvement of the lot of human beings everywhere. That is our goal. As a nation, as a people, we must understand this problem, we must handle this new force wisely through our democratic processes. Above all, we must strive, in all earnestness and good faith, to bring it under effective international control. To do this will require much wisdom and patience and firmness. The awe-inspiring responsibility in this field now falls on a new Administration and a new Congress. I will give them my support, as I am sure all our citizens will, in whatever constructive steps they may take to make this newest of man's discoveries a source of good and not of ultimate destruction.

We cannot tell when or whether the attitude of the Soviet rulers may change. We do not know how long it may be before they show a willingness to negotiate effective control of atomic energy and honorable settlements of other world problems. We cannot measure how deep-rooted are the Kremlin's illusions about us. We can be sure, however, that the rulers of the communist world will not change their basic objectives lightly or soon.

The communist rulers have a sense of time about these things wholly unlike our own. We tend to divide our future into short spans, like the two-year life of this Congress, or the four years of the next Presidential term. They seem to think and plan in terms of generations. And there is, therefore, no easy, short-run way to make them see that their plans cannot prevail.

This means there is ahead of us a long hard test of strength and stamina, between the free world and the communist domain—our politics and our economy, our science and technology against the best they can do—our liberty against their slavery—our voluntary concert of free nations against their forced amalgam of "people's republics"—our strategy against their strategy—our nerve against their nerve.

Above all, this is a test of the will and the steadiness of the people of the United States.

There has been no challenge like this in the history of our Republic. We are called upon to rise to the occasion, as no people before us.

What is required of us is not easy. The way we must learn to live, the world we have to live in, cannot be so pleasant, safe or simple as most of us have known before, or confidently hoped to know.

Already we have had to sacrifice a number of accustomed ways of working and of living, much nervous energy, material resources, even human life. Yet if one thing is certain in our future, it is that more sacrifice still lies ahead.

Were we to grow discouraged now, were we to weaken and slack off, the whole structure we have built, these past eight years, would come apart and fall away. Never then, no matter by what stringent means, could our free world regain the ground, the time, the sheer momentum, lost by such a move. There can and should be changes and improvements in our programs, to meet new situations, serve new needs. But to desert the spirit of our basic policies, to step back from them now, would surely start the free world's slide toward the darkness that the communists have prophesied—toward the moment for which they watch and wait.

If we value our freedom and our way of life and want to see them safe, we must meet the challenge and accept its implications, stick to our guns and carry out our policies.

I have set out the basic conditions, as I see them, under which we have been working in the world, and the nature of our basic policies. What, then, of the future? The answer, I believe, is this: As we continue to confound Soviet expectations, as our world grows stronger, more united, more attractive to men on both sides of the iron curtain, then inevitably there will come a time of change within the communist world. We do not know how that change will come about, whether by deliberate decision in the Kremlin, by coup d'etat, by revolution, by defection of satellites, or perhaps by some unforeseen combination of factors such as these.

But if the communist rulers understand they cannot win by war, and if we frustrate their attempts to win by subversion, it is not too much to expect their world to change its character, moderate its aims, become more realistic and less implacable, and recede from the cold war they began.

Do not be deceived by the strong face, the look of monolithic power that the communist dictators wear before the outside world. Remember their power has no basis in consent. Remember they are so afraid of the free world's ideas and ways of life, they do not dare to let their people know about them. Think of the massive effort they put forth to try to stop our Campaign of Truth from reaching their people with its message of freedom.

The masters of the Kremlin live in fear their power and position would collapse were their own people to acquire knowledge, information, comprehension about our free society. Their world has many elements of strength, but this one fatal flaw: the weakness represented by their iron curtain and their police state. Surely, a social order at once so insecure and so fearful, must ultimately lose its competition with our free society.

Provided just one thing—and this I urge you to consider carefully—provided that the free world retains the confidence and the determination to outmatch the best our adversary can accomplish and to demonstrate for uncertain millions on both sides of the iron curtain the superiority of the free way of life.

That is the test upon all the free nations; upon none more than our own Republic.

Our resources are equal to the task. We have the industry, the skills, the basic economic strength. Above all, we have the vigor of free men in a free society. We have our liberties. And while we keep them, while we retain our democratic faith, the ultimate advantage in this hard competition lies with us, not with the communists.

But there are some things that could shift the advantage to their side. One of the things that could defeat us is fear—fear of the task we face, fear of adjusting to it, fear that breeds more fear, sapping our faith, corroding our liberties, turning citizen against citizen, ally against ally. Fear could snatch away the very values we are striving to defend.

Already the danger signals have gone up. Already the corrosive process bas begun. And every diminution of our tolerance, each new act of enforced conformity, each idle accusation, each demonstration of hysteria—each new restrictive law—is one more sign that we can lose the battle against fear.

The communists cannot deprive us of our liberties—fear can. The communists cannot stamp out our faith in human dignity—fear can. Fear is an enemy within ourselves, and if we do not root it out, it may destroy the very way of life we are so anxious to protect.

To beat back fear, we must hold fast to our heritage as free men. We must renew our confidence in one another, our tolerance, our sense of being neighbors, fellow citizens. We must take our stand on the Bill of Rights. The inquisition, the star chamber, have no place in a free society.

Our ultimate strength lies, not alone in arms, but in the sense of moral values and moral truths that give meaning and vitality to the purposes of free people. These values are our faith, our inspiration, the source of our strength and our indomitable determination.

We face hard tasks, great dangers. But we are Americans and we have faced hardships and uncertainty before, we have adjusted before to changing circumstances. Our whole history has been a steady training for the work it is now ours to do.

No one can lose heart for the task, none can lose faith in our free ways, who stops to remember where we began, what we have sought, and what accomplished, all together as Americans.

I have lived a long time and seen much happen in our country. And I know out of my own experience, that we can do what must be done.

When I think back to the country I grew up in—and then look at what our country has become—I am quite certain that having done so much, we can do more.

After all, it has been scarcely fifteen years since most Americans rejected out-of-hand the wise counsel that aggressors must be "quarantined". The very concept of collective security, the foundation-stone of all our actions now, was then strange doctrine, shunned and set aside. Talk about adapting; talk about adjusting; talk about responding as a people to the challenge of changed times and circumstances—there has never been a more spectacular example than this great change in America's outlook on the world.

Let all of us pause now, think back, consider carefully the meaning of our national experience. Let us draw comfort from it and faith, and confidence in our future as Americans.

The Nation's business is never finished. The basic questions we have been dealing with, these eight years past, present themselves anew. That is the way of our society. Circumstances change and current questions take on different forms, new complications, year by year. But underneath, the great issues remain the same—prosperity, welfare, human rights, effective democracy, and above all, peace.

Now we turn to the inaugural of our new President. And in the great work he is called upon to do he will have need for the support of a united people, a confident people, with firm faith in one another and in our common cause. I pledge him my support as a citizen of our Republic, and I ask you to give him yours.

To him, to you, to all my fellow citizens, I say, Godspeed.

May God bless our country and our cause.

Dwight D. Eisenhower

1953–1961

*"The threat we face is not sporadic or dated:
It is continuous. Hence we must not be swayed
in our calculations either by groundless fear
or by complacency."*

ADDRESS TO CONGRESS ON THE STATE OF THE UNION, JANUARY 9, 1958

Address to Congress on the State of the Union

February 2, 1953

Dwight D. Eisenhower delivered his first State of the Union address less than two weeks after his swearing-in as president on January 20, 1953. His lengthy speech served as a blueprint for what the new president hoped to accomplish and how he hoped to govern.

Eisenhower, a Republican, had won a landslide victory in November 1952 and, in the process, swept the GOP into control of the House and Senate. A former military hero in World War II who had served as supreme commander of Allied forces in Europe, Eisenhower—who used the slogan "I like Ike"—won 442 electoral votes and 55.1 percent of the popular vote to Democrat Adlai Stevenson's 89 electoral votes and 44.4 percent. The election of 1952 marked a sea-change in American politics; Democrats had been in the White House since 1933 and had controlled Congress for most of that time.

The new president referred to the election as a "summons to governmental responsibility" and gave four "ruling purposes" under which the new leadership would operate: deterring aggression and securing peace, establishing integrity within the administration, encouraging a productive economy, and seeking equality of opportunity for all Americans.

He stated that while Americans had expected a peaceful world after the end of World War II, that was not the case due to "aggressive communism." The Cold War, which had started in the later half of the 1940s, was in full force during the eight years of Eisenhower's presidency. The president called for cooperation between the executive and legislative branches—something that had not always been the case during the presidency of his predecessor, Harry Truman. He also stated that the country would defend freedom around the world.

Eisenhower devoted part of his speech to the war in Korea, calling it "the most painful phase of communist aggression throughout the world" for Americans. It had begun in 1950, and pitted U.S., South Korean, and United Nations troops against communist North Korean and Chinese armies. The conflict had reached a point of stalemate, and an armistice finally would be reached in July 1953. Among the other subjects he discussed were balancing the budget, attempting to end discrimination, and updating immigration legislation.

Overall, Eisenhower's presidency, which lasted eight years, was a prosperous time for the United States, but also one of great international tension due to the Cold War rivalry between the United States and the Soviet Union. By 1955, both countries were in possession of stockpiles of nuclear weapons, which created a balance of terror.

Mr. President, Mr. Speaker, Members of the Eighty-third Congress:

I welcome the honor of appearing before you to deliver my first message to the Congress.

It is manifestly the joint purpose of the congressional leadership and of this administration to justify the summons to governmental responsibility issued last November by the American people. The grand labors of this leadership will involve:

Application of America's influence in world affairs with such fortitude and such foresight that it will deter aggression and eventually secure peace;

Establishment of a national administration of such integrity and such efficiency that its honor at home will ensure respect abroad;

Encouragement of those incentives that inspire creative initiative in our economy, so that its productivity may fortify freedom everywhere; and

Dedication to the well-being of all our citizens and to the attainment of equality of opportunity for all, so that our Nation will ever act with the strength of unity in every task to which it is called.

The purpose of this message is to suggest certain lines along which our joint efforts may immediately be directed toward realization of these four ruling purposes.

The time that this administration has been in office has been too brief to permit preparation of a detailed and comprehensive program of recommended action to cover all phases of the responsibilities that devolve upon our country's new leaders. Such a program will be filled out in the weeks ahead as, after appropriate study, I shall submit additional recommendations for your consideration. Today can provide only a sure and substantial beginning.

II.

Our country has come through a painful period of trial and disillusionment since the victory of 1945. We anticipated a world of peace and cooperation. The calculated pressures of aggressive communism have forced us, instead, to live in a world of turmoil.

From this costly experience we have learned one clear lesson. We have learned that the free world cannot indefinitely remain in a posture of paralyzed tension, leaving forever to the aggressor the choice of time and place and means to cause greatest hurt to us at least cost to himself.

This administration has, therefore, begun the definition of a new, positive foreign policy. This policy will be governed by certain fixed ideas. They are these:

(1) Our foreign policy must be clear, consistent, and confident. This means that it must be the product of genuine, continuous cooperation between the executive and the legislative branches of this Government. It must be developed and directed in the spirit of true bipartisanship.

(2) The policy we embrace must be a coherent global policy. The freedom we cherish and defend in Europe and in the Americas is no different from the freedom that is imperiled in Asia.

(3) Our policy, dedicated to making the free world secure, will envision all peaceful methods and devices—except breaking faith with our friends. We shall never acquiesce in the enslavement of any people in order to purchase fancied gain for ourselves. I shall ask the Congress at a later date to join in an appropriate resolution making clear that this Government recognizes no kind of commitment contained in secret understandings of the past with foreign governments which permit this kind of enslavement.

(4) The policy we pursue will recognize the truth that no single country, even one so powerful as ours, can alone defend the liberty of all nations threatened by Communist aggression from without or subversion within. Mutual security means effective mutual cooperation. For the United States, this means that, as a matter of common sense and national interest, we shall give help to other nations in the measure that they strive earnestly to do their full share of the common task. No wealth of aid could compensate for poverty of spirit. The heart of every free nation must be honestly dedicated to the preserving of its own independence and security.

(5) Our policy will be designed to foster the advent of practical unity in Western Europe. The nations of that region have contributed notably to the effort of sustaining the security of the free world. From the jungles of Indochina and Malaya to the northern shores of Europe, they have vastly improved their defensive strength. Where called upon to do so, they have made costly and bitter sacrifices to hold the line of freedom.

But the problem of security demands closer cooperation among the nations of Europe than has been known to date. Only a more closely integrated economic and political system can provide the greatly increased economic strength needed to maintain both necessary military readiness and respectable living standards.

Europe's enlightened leaders have long been aware of these facts. All the devoted work that has gone into the Schuman plan, the European Army, and the Strasbourg Conference has testified to their vision and determination. These achievements are the more remarkable when we realize that each of them has marked a victory—for France and for Germany alike over the divisions that in the past have brought such tragedy to these two great nations and to the world.

The needed unity of Western Europe manifestly cannot be manufactured from without; it can only be created from within. But it is right and necessary that we encourage Europe's leaders by informing them of the high value we place upon the earnestness of their efforts toward this goal. Real progress will be conclusive evidence to the American people that our material sacrifices in the cause of collective security are matched by essential political, economic, and military accomplishments in Western Europe.

(6) Our foreign policy will recognize the importance of profitable and equitable world trade.

A substantial beginning can and should be made by our friends themselves. Europe, for example, is now marked by checkered areas of labor surplus and labor shortage, of agricultural areas needing machines and industrial areas needing food. Here and elsewhere we can hope that our friends will take the initiative in creating broader markets and more dependable currencies, to allow greater exchange of goods and services among themselves.

Action along these lines can create an economic environment that will invite vital help from us.

This help includes:

First: Revising our customs regulations to remove procedural obstacles to profitable trade. I further recommend that the Congress take the Reciprocal Trade Agreements Act under immediate study and extend it by appropriate legislation. This objective must not ignore legitimate safeguarding of domestic industries, agriculture, and labor standards. In all executive study and recommendations on this problem labor and management and farmers alike will be earnestly consulted.

Second: Doing whatever Government properly can to encourage the flow of private American investment abroad. This involves, as a serious and explicit purpose of our foreign policy, the encouragement of a hospitable climate for such investment in foreign nations.

Third: Availing ourselves of facilities overseas for the economical production of manufactured articles which are needed for mutual defense and which are not seriously competitive with our own normal peacetime production.

Fourth: Receiving from the rest of the world, in equitable exchange for what we supply, greater amounts of important raw materials which we do not ourselves possess in adequate quantities.

III.

In this general discussion of our foreign policy, I must make special mention of the war in Korea.

This war is, for Americans, the most painful phase of Communist aggression throughout the world. It is clearly a part of the same calculated assault that the aggressor is simultaneously pressing in Indochina and in Malaya, and of the strategic situation that manifestly embraces the island of Formosa and the Chinese Nationalist forces there. The working out of any military solution to the Korean war will inevitably affect all these areas.

The administration is giving immediate increased attention to the development of additional Republic of Korea forces. The citizens of that country have proved their capacity as fighting men and their eagerness to take a greater share in the defense of their homeland. Organization, equipment, and training will allow them to do so. Increased assistance to Korea for this purpose conforms fully to our global policies.

In June 1950, following the aggressive attack on the Republic of Korea, the United States Seventh Fleet was instructed both to prevent attack upon Formosa and also to insure that Formosa should not be used as a base of operations against the Chinese Communist mainland.

This has meant, in effect, that the United States Navy was required to serve as a defensive arm of Communist China. Regardless of the situation in 1950, since the date of that order the Chinese Communists have invaded Korea to attack the United Nations forces there. They have consistently rejected the proposals of the United Nations Command for an armistice. They recently joined with Soviet Russia in rejecting the armistice proposal sponsored in the United Nations by the Government of India. This proposal had been accepted by the United States and 53 other nations.

Consequently there is no longer any logic or sense in a condition that required the United States Navy to assume defensive responsibilities on behalf of the Chinese

Communists, thus permitting those Communists, with greater impunity, to kill our soldiers and those of our United Nations allies in Korea.

I am, therefore, issuing instructions that the Seventh Fleet no longer be employed to shield Communist China. This order implies no aggressive intent on our part. But we certainly have no obligation to protect a nation fighting us in Korea.

IV.

Our labor for peace in Korea and in the world imperatively demands the maintenance by the United States of a strong fighting service ready for any contingency.

Our problem is to achieve adequate military strength within the limits of endurable strain upon our economy. To amass military power without regard to our economic capacity would be to defend ourselves against one kind of disaster by inviting another.

Both military and economic objectives demand a single national military policy, proper coordination of our armed services, and effective consolidation of certain logistics activities.

We must eliminate waste and duplication of effort in the armed services.

We must realize clearly that size alone is not sufficient. The biggest force is not necessarily the best—and we want the best.

We must not let traditions or habits of the past stand in the way of developing an efficient military force. All members of our forces must be ever mindful that they serve under a single flag and for a single cause.

We must effectively integrate our armament programs and plan them in such careful relation to our industrial facilities that we assure the best use of our manpower and our materials.

Because of the complex technical nature of our military organization and because of the security reasons involved, the Secretary of Defense must take the initiative and assume the responsibility for developing plans to give our Nation maximum safety at minimum cost. Accordingly, the new Secretary of Defense and his civilian and military associates will, in the future, recommend such changes in present laws affecting our defense activities as may be necessary to clarify responsibilities and improve the total effectiveness of our defense effort.

This effort must always conform to policies laid down in the National Security Council.

The statutory function of the National Security Council is to assist the President in the formulation and coordination of significant domestic, foreign, and military policies required for the security of the Nation. In these days of tension it is essential that this central body have the vitality to perform effectively its statutory role. I propose to see that it does so.

Careful formulation of policies must be followed by clear understanding of them by all peoples. A related need, therefore, is to make more effective all activities of the Government related to international information.

I have recently appointed a committee of representative and informed citizens to survey this subject and to make recommendations in the near future for legislative, administrative, or other action.

A unified and dynamic effort in this whole field is essential to the security of the United States and of the other peoples in the community of free nations. There is but one sure way to avoid total war—and that is to win the cold war.

While retaliatory power is one strong deterrent to a would-be aggressor, another powerful deterrent is defensive power. No enemy is likely to attempt an attack foredoomed to failure.

Because the building of a completely impenetrable defense against attack is still not possible, total defensive strength must include civil defense preparedness. Because we have incontrovertible evidence that Soviet Russia possesses atomic weapons, this kind of protection becomes sheer necessity.

Civil defense responsibilities primarily belong to the State and local governments—recruiting, training, and organizing volunteers to meet any emergency. The immediate job of the Federal Government is to provide leadership, to supply technical guidance, and to continue to strengthen its civil defense stockpile of medical, engineering, and related supplies and equipment. This work must go forward without lag.

V.

I have referred to the inescapable need for economic health and strength if we are to maintain adequate military power and exert influential leadership for peace in the world.

Our immediate task is to chart a fiscal and economic policy that can:

(1) Reduce the planned deficits and then balance the budget, which means, among other things, reducing Federal expenditures to the safe minimum;

(2) Meet the huge costs of our defense;

(3) Properly handle the burden of our inheritance of debt and obligations;

(4) Check the menace of inflation;

(5) Work toward the earliest possible reduction of the tax burden;

(6) Make constructive plans to encourage the initiative of our citizens.

It is important that all of us understand that this administration does not and cannot begin its task with a clean slate. Much already has been written on the record, beyond our power quickly to erase or to amend. This record includes our inherited burden of indebtedness and obligations and deficits.

The current year's budget, as you know, carries a 5.9 billion dollar deficit; and the budget, which was presented to you before this administration took office, indicates a budgetary deficit of 9.9 billion for the fiscal year ending June 30, 1954. The national debt is now more than 265 billion dollars. In addition, the accumulated obligational authority of the Federal Government for future payment totals over 80 billion dollars. Even this amount is exclusive of large contingent liabilities, so numerous and extensive as to be almost beyond description.

The bills for the payment of nearly all of the 80 billion dollars of obligations will be presented during the next 4 years. These bills, added to the current costs of government we must meet, make a formidable burden.

The present authorized Government-debt limit is 275 billion dollars. The forecast presented by the outgoing administration with the fiscal year 1954 budget indicates that—before the end of the fiscal year and at the peak of demand for payments during the year—the total Government debt may approach and even exceed that limit. Unless budgeted deficits are checked, the momentum of past programs will force an increase of the statutory debt limit.

Permit me this one understatement: to meet and to correct this situation will not be easy.

Permit me this one assurance: every department head and I are determined to do everything we can to resolve it.

The first order of business is the elimination of the annual deficit. This cannot be achieved merely by exhortation. It demands the concerted action of all those in responsible positions in the Government and the earnest cooperation of the Congress.

Already, we have begun an examination of the appropriations and expenditures of all departments in an effort to find significant items that may be decreased or canceled without damage to our essential requirements.

Getting control of the budget requires also that State and local governments and interested groups of citizens restrain themselves in their demands upon the Congress that the Federal Treasury spend more and more money for all types of projects.

A balanced budget is an essential first measure in checking further depreciation in the buying power of the dollar. This is one of the critical steps to be taken to bring an end to planned inflation. Our purpose is to manage the Government's finances so as to help and not hinder each family in balancing its own budget.

Reduction of taxes will be justified only as we show we can succeed in bringing the budget under control. As the budget is balanced and inflation checked, the tax burden that today stifles initiative can and must be eased.

Until we can determine the extent to which expenditures can be reduced, it would not be wise to reduce our revenues.

Meanwhile, the tax structure as a whole demands review. The Secretary of the Treasury is undertaking this study immediately. We must develop a system of taxation which will impose the least possible obstacle to the dynamic growth of the country. This includes particularly real opportunity for the growth of small businesses. Many readjustments in existing taxes will be necessary to serve these objectives and also to remove existing inequities. Clarification and simplification in the tax laws as well as the regulations will be undertaken.

In the entire area of fiscal policy—which must, in its various aspects, be treated in recommendations to the Congress in coming weeks—there can now be stated certain basic facts and principles.

First. It is axiomatic that our economy is a highly complex and sensitive mechanism. Hasty and ill-considered action of any kind could seriously upset the subtle equation that encompasses debts, obligations, expenditures, defense demands, deficits, taxes, and the general economic health of the Nation. Our goals can be clear, our start toward them can be immediate—but action must be gradual.

Second. It is clear that too great a part of the national debt comes due in too short a time. The Department of the Treasury will undertake at suitable times a program of extending part of the debt over longer periods and gradually placing greater amounts in the hands of longer-term investors.

Third. Past differences in policy between the Treasury and the Federal Reserve Board have helped to encourage inflation. Henceforth, I expect that their single purpose shall be to serve the whole Nation by policies designed to stabilize the economy and encourage the free play of our people's genius for individual initiative.

In encouraging this initiative, no single item in our current problems has received more thoughtful consideration by my associates, and by the many individuals called into our counsels, than the matter of price and wage control by law.

The great economic strength of our democracy has developed in an atmosphere of freedom. The character of our people resists artificial and arbitrary controls of any kind. Direct controls, except those on credit, deal not with the real causes of inflation but only with its symptoms. In times of national emergency, this kind of control has a role to play. Our whole system, however, is based upon the assumption that, normally, we should combat wide fluctuations in our price structure by relying largely on the effective use of sound fiscal and monetary policy, and upon the natural workings of economic law.

Moreover, American labor and American business can best resolve their wage problems across the bargaining table. Government should refrain from sitting in with them unless, in extreme cases, the public welfare requires protection.

We are, of course, living in an international situation that is neither an emergency demanding full mobilization, nor is it peace. No one can know how long this condition will persist. Consequently, we are forced to learn many new things as we go along-clinging to what works, discarding what does not.

In all our current discussions on these and related facts, the weight of evidence is clearly against the use of controls in their present forms. They have proved largely unsatisfactory or unworkable. They have not prevented inflation; they have not kept down the cost of living. Dissatisfaction with them is wholly justified. I am convinced that now—as well as in the long run—free and competitive prices will best serve the interests of all the people, and best meet the changing, growing needs of our economy.

Accordingly, I do not intend to ask for a renewal of the present wage and price controls on April 30, 1953, when present legislation expires. In the meantime, steps will be taken to eliminate controls in an orderly manner, and to terminate special agencies no longer needed for this purpose. It is obviously to be expected that the removal of these controls will result in individual price changes—some up, some down. But a maximum of freedom in market prices as well as in collective bargaining is characteristic of a truly free people.

I believe also that material and product controls should be ended, except with respect to defense priorities and scarce and critical items essential for our defense. I shall recommend to the Congress that legislation be enacted to continue authority for such remaining controls of this type as will be necessary after the expiration of the existing statute on June 30, 1953.

I recommend the continuance of the authority for Federal control over rents in those communities in which serious housing shortages exist. These are chiefly the so-called defense areas. In these and all areas the Federal Government should withdraw from the control of rents as soon as practicable. But before they are removed entirely, each legislature should have full opportunity to take over, within its own State, responsibility for this function.

It would be idle to pretend that all our problems in this whole field of prices will solve themselves by mere Federal withdrawal from direct controls.

We shall have to watch trends closely. If the freer functioning of our economic system, as well as the indirect controls which can be appropriately employed, prove insufficient during this period of strain and tension, I shall promptly ask the Congress to enact such legislation as may be required.

In facing all these problems—wages, prices, production, tax rates, fiscal policy, deficits—everywhere we remain constantly mindful that the time for sacrifice has not ended. But we are concerned with the encouragement of competitive enterprise and individual initiative precisely because we know them to be our Nation's abiding sources of strength.

VI.

Our vast world responsibility accents with urgency our people's elemental right to a government whose clear qualities are loyalty, security, efficiency, economy, and integrity.

The safety of America and the trust of the people alike demand that the personnel of the Federal Government be loyal in their motives and reliable in the discharge of their duties. Only a combination of both loyalty and reliability promises genuine security.

To state this principle is easy; to apply it can be difficult. But this security we must and shall have. By way of example, all principal new appointees to departments and agencies have been investigated at their own request by the Federal Bureau of Invest igation.

Confident of your understanding and cooperation, I know that the primary responsibility for keeping out the disloyal and the dangerous rests squarely upon the executive branch. When this branch so conducts itself as to require policing by another branch of the Government, it invites its own disorder and confusion.

I am determined to meet this responsibility of the Executive. The heads of all executive departments and agencies have been instructed to initiate at once effective programs of security with respect to their personnel. The Attorney General will advise and guide the departments and agencies in the shaping of these programs, designed at once to govern the employment of new personnel and to review speedily any derogatory information concerning incumbent personnel.

To carry out these programs, I believe that the powers of the executive branch under existing law are sufficient. If they should prove inadequate, the necessary legislation will be requested.

These programs will be both fair to the rights of the individual and effective for the safety of the Nation. They will, with care and justice, apply the basic principle that public employment is not a right but a privilege.

All these measures have two clear purposes: Their first purpose is to make certain that this Nation's security is not jeopardized by false servants. Their second purpose is to clear the atmosphere of that unreasoned suspicion that accepts rumor and gossip as substitutes for evidence.

Our people, of course, deserve and demand of their Federal Government more than security of personnel. They demand, also, efficient and logical organization, true to constitutional principles.

I have already established a Committee on Government Organization. The Committee is using as its point of departure the reports of the Hoover Commission and subsequent studies by several independent agencies. To achieve the greater efficiency and economy which the Committee analyses show to be possible, I ask the Congress to extend the present Government Reorganization Act for a period of 18 months or 2 years beyond its expiration date of April 1, 1953.

There is more involved here than realigning the wheels and smoothing the gears of administrative machinery. The Congress rightfully expects the Executive to take the initiative in discovering and removing outmoded functions and eliminating duplication.

One agency, for example, whose head has promised early and vigorous action to provide greater efficiency is the Post Office. One of the oldest institutions of our Federal Government, its service should be of the best. Its employees should merit and receive the high regard and esteem of the citizens of the Nation. There are today in some areas of the postal service, both waste and incompetence to be corrected. With the cooperation of the Congress, and taking advantage of its accumulated experience in postal affairs, the Postmaster General will institute a program directed at improving service while at the same time reducing costs and decreasing deficits.

In all departments, dedication to these basic precepts of security and efficiency, integrity, and economy can and will produce an administration deserving of the trust the people have placed in it.

Our people have demanded nothing less than good, efficient government. They shall get nothing less.

VII.

Vitally important are the water and minerals, public lands and standing timber, forage and wildlife of this country. A fast-growing population will have vast future needs in these resources. We must more than match the substantial achievements in the half-century since President Theodore Roosevelt awakened the Nation to the problem of conservation.

This calls for a strong Federal program in the field of resource development. Its major projects should be timed, where possible to assist in leveling off peaks and valleys in our economic life. Soundly planned projects already initiated should be carried out. New ones will be planned for the future.

The best natural resources program for America will not result from exclusive dependence on Federal bureaucracy. It will involve a partnership of the States and local communities, private citizens, and the Federal Government, all working together. This combined effort will advance the development of the great river valleys of our Nation and the power that they can generate. Likewise, such a partnership can be effective in the expansion throughout the Nation of upstream storage; the sound use of public lands; the wise conservation of minerals; and the sustained yield of our forests.

There has been much criticism, some of it apparently justified, of the confusion resulting from overlapping Federal activities in the entire field of resource-conservation. This matter is being exhaustively studied and appropriate reorganization plans will be developed.

Most of these particular resource problems pertain to the Department of the Interior. Another of its major concerns is our country's island possessions. Here, one matter deserves attention. The platforms of both political parties promised immediate statehood to Hawaii. The people of that Territory have earned that status. Statehood should be granted promptly with the first election scheduled for 1954.

VIII.

One of the difficult problems which face the new administration is that of the slow, irregular decline of farm prices. This decline, which has been going on for almost 2 years, has occurred at a time when most nonfarm prices and farm costs of production are extraordinarily high.

Present agricultural legislation provides for the mandatory support of the prices of basic farm commodities at 90 percent of parity. The Secretary of Agriculture and his associates will, of course, execute the present act faithfully and thereby seek to mitigate the consequences of the downturn in farm income.

This price-support legislation will expire at the end of 1954.

So we should begin now to consider what farm legislation we should develop for 1955 and beyond. Our aim should be economic stability and full parity of income for American farmers. But we must seek this goal in ways that minimize governmental interference in the farmers' affairs, that permit desirable shifts in production, and that encourage farmers themselves to use initiative in meeting changing economic conditions.

A continuing study reveals nothing more emphatically than the complicated nature of this subject. Among other things, it shows that the prosperity of our agriculture depends directly upon the prosperity of the whole country—upon the purchasing power of American consumers. It depends also upon the opportunity to ship abroad large surpluses of particular commodities, and therefore upon sound economic relationships between the United States and many foreign countries. It involves research and scientific investigation, conducted on an extensive scale. It involves special credit mechanisms and marketing, rural electrification, soil conservation, and other programs. The whole complex of agricultural programs and policies will be studied by a Special Agricultural Advisory Commission, as I know it will by appropriate committees of the Congress. A nonpartisan group of respected authorities in the field of agriculture has already been appointed as an interim advisory group.

The immediate changes needed in agricultural programs are largely budgetary and administrative in nature. New policies and new programs must await the completion of the far-reaching studies which have already been launched.

IX.

The determination of labor policy must be governed not by the vagaries of political expediency but by the firmest principles and convictions. Slanted partisan appeals to American workers, spoken as if they were a group apart, necessitating a special language and treatment, are an affront to the fullness of their dignity as American citizens.

The truth in matters of labor policy has become obscured in controversy. The very meaning of economic freedom as it affects labor has become confused. This misunderstanding has provided a climate of opinion favoring the growth of governmental paternalism in labor relations. This tendency, if left uncorrected, could end only by producing a bureaucratic despotism. Economic freedom is, in fact, the requisite of greater prosperity for every American who earns his own living.

In the field of labor legislation, only a law that merits the respect and support of both labor and management can help reduce the loss of wages and of production through strikes and stoppages, and thus add to the total economic strength of our Nation.

We have now had 5 years' experience with the Labor Management Act of 1947, commonly known as the Taft-Hartley Act. That experience has shown the need for some corrective action, and we should promptly proceed to amend that act.

I know that the Congress is already proceeding with renewed studies of this subject. Meanwhile, the Department of Labor is at once beginning work to devise further specific recommendations for your consideration.

In the careful working out of legislation, I know you will give thoughtful consideration—as will we in the executive branch—to the views of labor, and of management, and of the general public. In this process, it is only human that each of us should bring forward the arguments of self-interest. But if all conduct their arguments in the overpowering light of national interest—which is enlightened self-interest—we shall get the right answers. I profoundly hope that every citizen of our country will follow with understanding your progress in this work. The welfare of all of us is involved.

Especially must we remember that the institutions of trade unionism and collective bargaining are monuments to the freedom that must prevail in our industrial life. They have a century of honorable achievement behind them. Our faith in them is proven, firm, and final.

Government can do a great deal to aid the settlement of labor disputes without allowing itself to be employed as an ally of either side. Its proper role in industrial strife is to encourage the processes of mediation and conciliation. These processes can successfully be directed only by a government free from the taint of any suspicion that it is partial or punitive.

The administration intends to strengthen and to improve the services which the Department of Labor can render to the worker and to the whole national community. This Department was created—just 40 years ago—to serve the entire Nation. It must aid, for example, employers and employees alike in improving training programs that will develop skilled and competent workers. It must enjoy the confidence and respect of labor and industry in order to play a significant role in the planning of America's economic future. To that end, I am authorizing the Department of Labor to establish promptly a tripartite advisory committee consisting of representatives of employers, labor, and the public.

X.

Our civil and social rights form a central part of the heritage we are striving to defend on all fronts and with all our strength. I believe with all my heart that our vigilant guarding of these rights is a sacred obligation binding upon every citizen. To be true to one's own freedom is, in essence, to honor and respect the freedom of all others. A cardinal ideal in this heritage we cherish is the equality of rights of all citizens of every race and color and creed.

We know that discrimination against minorities persists despite our allegiance to this ideal. Such discrimination—confined to no one section of the Nation—is but the outward testimony to the persistence of distrust and of fear in the hearts of men.

This fact makes all the more vital the fighting of these wrongs by each individual, in every station of life, in his every deed.

Much of the answer lies in the power of fact, fully publicized; of persuasion, honestly pressed; and of conscience, justly aroused. These are methods familiar to our way of life, tested and proven wise.

I propose to use whatever authority exists in the office of the President to end segregation in the District of Columbia, including the Federal Government, and any segregation in the Armed Forces.

Here in the District of Columbia, serious attention should be given to the proposal to develop and authorize, through legislation, a system to provide an effective voice in local self-government. While consideration of this proceeds, I recommend an immediate increase of two in the number of District Commissioners to broaden representation of all elements of our local population. This will be a first step toward insuring that this Capital provide an honored example to all communities of our Nation. In this manner, and by the leadership of the office of the President exercised through friendly conferences with those in authority in our States and cities, we expect to make true and rapid progress in civil rights and equality of employment opportunity.

There is one sphere in which civil rights are inevitably involved in Federal legislation. This is the sphere of immigration.

It is a manifest right of our Government to limit the number of immigrants our Nation can absorb. It is also a manifest right of our Government to set reasonable requirements on the character and the numbers of the people who come to share our land and our freedom.

It is well for us, however, to remind ourselves occasionally of an equally manifest fact: we are—one and all—immigrants or sons and daughters of immigrants.

Existing legislation contains injustices. It does, in fact, discriminate. I am informed by Members of the Congress that it was realized, at the time of its enactment, that future study of the basis of determining quotas would be necessary.

I am therefore requesting the Congress to review this legislation and to enact a statute that will at one and the same time guard our legitimate national interests and be faithful to our basic ideas of freedom and fairness to all.

In another but related area—that of social rights—we see most clearly the new application of old ideas of freedom.

This administration is profoundly aware of two great needs born of our living in a complex industrial economy. First, the individual citizen must have safeguards against personal disaster inflicted by forces beyond his control; second, the welfare of the people demands effective and economical performance by the Government of certain indispensable social services.

In the light of this responsibility, certain general purposes and certain concrete measures are plainly indicated now.

There is urgent need for greater effectiveness in our programs, both public and private, offering safeguards against the privations that too often come with unemployment, old age, illness, and accident. The provisions of the old-age and survivors insurance law should promptly be extended to cover millions of citizens who have been left out of the social-security system. No less important is the encouragement of privately sponsored pension plans. Most important of all, of course, is renewed effort to check the inflation which destroys so much of the value of all social-security payments.

Our school system demands some prompt, effective help. During each of the last 9 years, more than 1½ million children have swelled the elementary and secondary school population of the country. Generally, the school population is proportionately higher in States with low per capita income. This whole situation calls for careful congressional study and action. I am sure that you share my conviction that the firm conditions of Federal aid must be proved need and proved lack of local income.

One phase of the school problem demands special action. The school population of many districts has been greatly increased by the swift growth of defense activities. These activities have added little or nothing to the tax resources of the communities affected. Legislation aiding construction of schools in the districts expires on June 30.

This law should be renewed; and likewise, the partial payments for current operating expenses for these particular school districts should be made, including the deficiency requirement of the current fiscal year.

Public interest similarly demands one prompt specific action in protection of the general consumer. The Food and Drug Administration should be authorized to continue its established and necessary program of factory inspections. The invalidation of these inspections by the Supreme Court of December 8, 1952, was based solely on the fact that the present law contained inconsistent and unclear provisions. These must be promptly corrected.

I am well aware that beyond these few immediate measures there remains much to be done. The health and housing needs of our people call for intelligently planned programs. Involved are the solvency of the whole security system; and its guarding against exploitation by the irresponsible.

To bring clear purpose and orderly procedure into this field, I anticipate a thorough study of the proper relationship among Federal, State, and local programs. I shall shortly send you specific recommendations for establishing such an appropriate commission, together with a reorganization plan defining new administrative status for all Federal activities in health, education, and social security.

I repeat that there are many important subjects of which I make no mention today. Among these is our great and growing body of veterans. America has traditionally been generous in caring for the disabled—and the widow and the orphan of the fallen. These millions remain close to all our hearts. Proper care of our uniformed citizens and appreciation of the past service of our veterans are part of our accepted governmental responsibilities.

XI.

We have surveyed briefly some problems of our people and a portion of the tasks before us.

The hope of freedom itself depends, in real measure, upon our strength, our heart, and our wisdom.

We must be strong in arms. We must be strong in the source of all our armament, our productivity. We all—workers and farmers, foremen and financiers, technicians and builders—all must produce, produce more, and produce yet more.

We must be strong, above all, in the spiritual resources upon which all else depends. We must be devoted with all our heart to the values we defend. We must know that each of these values and virtues applies with equal force at the ends of the earth and in our relations with our neighbor next door. We must know that freedom expresses itself with equal eloquence in the right of workers to strike in the nearby factory, and in the yearnings and sufferings of the peoples of Eastern Europe.

As our heart summons our strength, our wisdom must direct it.

There is, in world affairs, a steady course to be followed between an assertion of strength that is truculent and a confession of helplessness that is cowardly.

There is, in our affairs at home, a middle way between untrammeled freedom of the individual and the demands for the welfare of the whole Nation. This way must avoid government by bureaucracy as carefully as it avoids neglect of the helpless.

In every area of political action, free men must think before they can expect to win.

In this spirit must we live and labor: confident of our strength, compassionate in our heart, clear in our mind.

In this spirit, let us together turn to the great tasks before us.

Address to Congress on the State of the Union

January 7, 1954

Dwight D. Eisenhower delivered his second State of the Union address in person before Congress on January 7, 1954. The Korean War had finally been concluded with an armistice in 1953, but the Cold War between the United States and the Soviet Union—between democracy and communism—still continued and would do so for more than three decades.

In his speech, the president cited three areas on which American policy should focus: protecting Americans' freedom, maintaining a strong economy, and being concerned with "the human problems of the individual citizen." He organized the speech around those themes.

On the theme of freedom, Eisenhower stated that freedom was under threat by "the world communist conspiracy." He linked American freedom to that of people in other countries, and stated that the United States, being a strong nation, had a great deal of responsibility when it came to preserving freedom. Eisenhower mentioned various parts of the world, including the Far East and Western Europe, where the United States was cooperating with allies.

In terms of the economy, Eisenhower pointed out that the country was in transition from wartime to peacetime, and that it must be prepared economically for that task. He sought a balanced budget, and—unlike many of his successors who failed to achieve that goal—ended up balancing the budget in three of his eight years in office. He also mentioned the importance of working on the interstate highway system, which would become one of his legacies.

When it came to the third area, human problems, Eisenhower went through a variety of subjects, including Social Security, health care and suffrage. He repeated an earlier call for additional people to be covered under Social Security, declared himself "flatly opposed to the socialization of medicine," and called for the right to vote for overseas military personnel.

Although Eisenhower was the first Republican to serve as president since Herbert Hoover's 1929–1933 term, his attitude toward the federal government was far different from that of Hoover and other GOP presidents earlier in the century. In the interim, the New Deal of Franklin D. Roosevelt and the Fair Deal espoused by Harry Truman had vastly increased the scope of federal government power and also had given more power to the president himself. Eisenhower did not choose to dismantle the federal system set up under his two immediate predecessors, although he was more conservative politically than they had been. Thus the larger-scale federal government became a lasting feature of American democracy.

M r. President, Mr. Speaker, Members of the Eighty-third Congress:

It is a high honor again to present to the Congress my views on the state of the Union and to recommend measures to advance the security, prosperity, and well-being of the American people.

All branches of this Government—and I venture to say both of our great parties— can support the general objective of the recommendations I make today, for that objective is the building of a stronger America. A nation whose every citizen has good reason for bold hope; where effort is rewarded and prosperity is shared; where freedom expands and peace is secure—that is what I mean by a stronger America.

Toward this objective a real momentum has been developed during this Administration's first year in office. We mean to continue that momentum and to increase it. We mean to build a better future for this nation.

Much for which we may be thankful has happened during the past year.

First of all we are deeply grateful that our sons no longer die on the distant mountains of Korea. Although they are still called from our homes to military service, they are no longer called to the field of battle.

The nation has just completed the most prosperous year in its history. The damaging effect of inflation on the wages, pensions, salaries and savings of us all has been brought under control. Taxes have begun to go down. The cost of our government has been reduced and its work proceeds with some 183,000 fewer employees; thus the discouraging trend of modern governments toward their own limitless expansion has in our case been reversed. The cost of armaments becomes less oppressive as we near our defense goals; yet we are militarily stronger every day. During the year, creation of the new Cabinet Department of Health, Education, and Welfare symbolized the government's permanent concern with the human problems of our citizens.

Segregation in the armed forces and other Federal activities is on the way out. We have also made progress toward its elimination in the District of Columbia. These are steps in the continuing effort to eliminate inter-racial difficulty.

Some developments beyond our shores have been equally encouraging. Communist aggression, halted in Korea, continues to meet in Indo-china the vigorous resistance of France and the Associated States, assisted by timely aid from our country. In West Germany, in Iran, and in other areas of the world, heartening political victories have been won by the forces of stability and freedom. Slowly but surely, the free world gathers strength. Meanwhile, from behind the iron curtain, there are signs that tyranny is in trouble and reminders that its structure is as brittle as its surface is hard.

There has been in fact a great strategic change in the world during the past year. That precious intangible, the initiative, is becoming ours. Our policy, not limited to mere reaction against crises provoked by others, is free to develop along lines of our choice not only abroad, but also at home. As a major theme for American policy during the coming year, let our joint determination be to hold this new initiative and to use it.

We shall use this initiative to promote three broad purposes: First, to protect the freedom of our people; second, to maintain a strong, growing economy; third, to concern ourselves with the human problems of the individual citizen.

Only by active concern for each of these purposes can we be sure that we are on the forward road to a better and a stronger America. All my recommendations today are in furtherance of these three purposes.

I. Foreign Affairs

American freedom is threatened so long as the world Communist conspiracy exists in its present scope, power and hostility. More closely than ever before, American freedom is interlocked with the freedom of other people. In the unity of the free world lies our best chance to reduce the Communist threat without war. In the task of maintaining this unity and strengthening all its parts, the greatest responsibility falls naturally on those who, like ourselves, retain the most freedom and strength.

We shall, therefore, continue to advance the cause of freedom on foreign fronts.

In the Far East, we retain our vital interest in Korea. We have negotiated with the Republic of Korea a mutual security pact, which develops our security system for the Pacific and which I shall promptly submit to the Senate for its consent to ratification. We are prepared to meet any renewal of armed aggression in Korea. We shall maintain indefinitely our bases in Okinawa. I shall ask the Congress to authorize continued material assistance to hasten the successful conclusion of the struggle in Indochina. This assistance will also bring closer the day when the Associated States may enjoy the independence already assured by France. We shall also continue military and economic aid to the Nationalist Government of China.

In South Asia, profound changes are taking place in free nations which are demonstrating their ability to progress through democratic methods. They provide an inspiring contrast to the dictatorial methods and backward course of events in Communist China. In these continuing efforts, the free peoples of South Asia can be assured of the support of the United States.

In the Middle East, where tensions and serious problems exist, we will show sympathetic and impartial friendship.

In Western Europe our policy rests firmly on the North Atlantic Treaty. It will remain so based as far ahead as we can see. Within its organization, the building of a united European community, including France and Germany, is vital to a free and self-reliant Europe. This will be promoted by the European Defense Community which offers assurance of European security. With the coming of unity to Western Europe, the assistance this Nation can render for the security of Europe and the free world will be multiplied in effectiveness.

In the Western Hemisphere we shall continue to develop harmonious and mutually beneficial cooperation with our neighbors. Indeed, solid friendship with all our American neighbors is a cornerstone of our entire policy.

In the world as a whole, the United Nations, admittedly still in a state of evolution, means much to the United States. It has given uniquely valuable services in many places where violence threatened. It is the only real world forum where we have the opportunity for international presentation and rebuttal. It is a place where the nations of the world can, if they have the will, take collective action for peace and justice. It is a place where the guilt can be squarely assigned to those who fail to take all necessary steps to keep the peace. The United Nations deserves our continued firm support.

Foreign Assistance and Trade

In the practical application of our foreign policy, we enter the field of foreign assistance and trade.

Military assistance must be continued. Technical assistance must be maintained. Economic assistance can be reduced. However, our economic programs in Korea and in a few other critical places of the world are especially important, and I shall ask Congress to continue them in the next fiscal year.

The forthcoming Budget Message will propose maintenance of the Presidential power of transferability of all assistance funds and will ask authority to merge these funds with the regular defense funds. It will also propose that the Secretary of Defense have primary responsibility for the administration of foreign military assistance in accordance with the policy guidance of the Secretary of State.

The fact that we can now reduce our foreign economic assistance in many areas is gratifying evidence that its objectives are being achieved. By continuing to surpass her prewar levels of economic activity, Western Europe gains self-reliance. Thus our relationship enters a new phase which can bring results beneficial to our taxpayers and our allies alike, if still another step is taken.

This step is the creation of a healthier and freer system of trade and payments within the free world—a system in which our allies can earn their own way and our own economy can continue to flourish. The free world can no longer afford the kinds of arbitrary restraints on trade that have continued ever since the war. On this problem I shall submit to the Congress detailed recommendations, after our Joint Commission on Foreign Economic Policy has made its report.

Atomic Energy Proposal

As we maintain our military strength during the coming year and draw closer the bonds with our allies, we shall be in an improved position to discuss outstanding issues with the Soviet Union. Indeed we shall be glad to do so whenever there is a reasonable prospect of constructive results. In this spirit the atomic energy proposals of the United States were recently presented to the United Nations General Assembly. A truly constructive Soviet reaction will make possible a new start toward an era of peace, and away from the fatal road toward atomic war.

Defense

Since our hope is peace, we owe ourselves and the world a candid explanation of the military measures we are taking to make that peace secure.

As we enter this new year, our military power continues to grow. This power is for our own defense and to deter aggression. We shall not be aggressors, but we and our allies have and will maintain a massive capability to strike back.

Here are some of the considerations in our defense planning:

First, while determined to use atomic power to serve the usages of peace, we take into full account our great and growing number of nuclear weapons and the most effective means of using them against an aggressor if they are needed to preserve our freedom. Our defense will be stronger if, under appropriate security safeguards, we share with our allies certain knowledge of the tactical use of our nuclear weapons. I urge the Congress to provide the needed authority.

Second, the usefulness of these new weapons creates new relationships between men and materials. These new relationships permit economies in the use of men as we build forces suited to our situation in the world today. As will be seen from the Budget Message on January 21, the airpower of our Navy and Air Force is receiving heavy emphasis.

Third, our armed forces must regain maximum mobility of action. Our strategic reserves must be centrally placed and readily deployable to meet sudden aggression against ourselves and our allies.

Fourth, our defense must rest on trained manpower and its most economical and mobile use. A professional corps is the heart of any security organization. It is necessarily the teacher and leader of those who serve temporarily in the discharge of the obligation to help defend the Republic. Pay alone will not retain in the career service of our armed forces the necessary numbers of long-term personnel. I strongly urge, therefore, a more generous use of other benefits important to service morale. Among these are more adequate living quarters and family housing units and medical care for dependents.

Studies of military manpower have just been completed by the National Security Training Commission and a Committee appointed by the Director of the Office of Defense Mobilization. Evident weaknesses exist in the state of readiness and organization of our reserve forces. Measures to correct these weaknesses will be later submitted to the Congress.

Fifth, the ability to convert swiftly from partial to all-out mobilization is imperative to our security. For the first time, mobilization officials know what the requirements are for 1,000 major items needed for military uses. These data, now being related to civilian requirements and our supply potential, will show us the gaps in our mobilization base. Thus we shall have more realistic plant-expansion and stockpiling goals. We shall speed their attainment. This Nation is at last to have an up-to-date mobilization base—the foundation of a sound defense program.

Another part of this foundation is, of course, our continental transport system. Some of our vital heavy materials come increasingly from Canada. Indeed our relations with Canada, happily always close, involve more and more the unbreakable ties of strategic interdependence. Both nations now need the St. Lawrence Seaway for security as well as for economic reasons. I urge the Congress promptly to approve our participation in its construction.

Sixth, military and non-military measures for continental defense must be and are being strengthened. In the current fiscal year we are allocating to these purposes an increasing portion of our effort, and in the next fiscal year we shall spend nearly a billion dollars more for them than in 1953.

An indispensable part of our continental security is our civil defense effort. This will succeed only as we have the complete cooperation of State Governors, Mayors, and voluntary citizen groups. With their help we can advance a cooperative program which, if an attack should come, would save many lives and lessen destruction.

The defense program recommended in the 1955 Budget is consistent with all of the considerations which I have just discussed. It is based on a new military program unanimously recommended by the Joint Chiefs of Staff and approved by me following consideration by the National Security Council. This new program will make and keep America strong in an age of peril. Nothing should bar its attainment.

The international and defense policies which I have outlined will enable us to negotiate from a position of strength as we hold our resolute course toward a peaceful world. We now turn to matters which are normally characterized as domestic, well realizing that what we do abroad affects every problem at home—from the amount of taxes to our very state of mind.

Internal Security

Under the standards established for the new employee security program, more than 2,200 employees have been separated from the Federal government. Our national security demands that the investigation of new employees and the evaluation of derogatory information respecting present employees be expedited and concluded at the earliest possible date. I shall recommend that the Congress provide additional funds where necessary to speed these important procedures.

From the special employment standards of the Federal government I turn now to a matter relating to American citizenship. The subversive character of the Communist Party in the United States has been clearly demonstrated in many ways, including court proceedings. We should recognize by law a fact that is plain to all thoughtful citizens—that we are dealing here with actions akin to treason—that when a citizen knowingly participates in the Communist conspiracy he no longer holds allegiance to the United States.

I recommend that Congress enact legislation to provide that a citizen of the United States who is convicted in the courts of hereafter conspiring to advocate the overthrow of this government by force or violence be treated as having, by such act, renounced his allegiance to the United States and forfeited his United States citizenship.

In addition, the Attorney General will soon appear before your Committees to present his recommendations for needed additional legal weapons with which to combat subversion in our country and to deal with the question of claimed immunity.

II. Strong Economy

I turn now to the second great purpose of our government: Along with the protection of freedom, the maintenance of a strong and growing economy.

The American economy is one of the wonders of the world. It undergirds our international position, our military security, and the standard of living of every citizen. This Administration is determined to keep our economy strong and to keep it growing.

At this moment we are in transition from a wartime to a peacetime economy. I am confident that we can complete this transition without serious interruption in our economic growth. But we shall not leave this vital matter to chance. Economic preparedness is fully as important to the nation as military preparedness.

Subsequent special messages and the economic report on January 28 will set forth plans of the Administration and its recommendations for Congressional action. These will include flexible credit and debt management policies; tax measures to stimulate consumer and business spending; suitable lending, guaranteeing, insuring, and grant-in-aid activities; strengthened old-age and unemployment insurance measures; improved agricultural programs; public-works plans laid well in advance; enlarged opportunities for international trade and investment. This mere enumeration of these subjects implies the vast amount of study, coordination, and planning, to say nothing of authorizing legislation, that altogether make our economic preparedness complete.

If new conditions arise that require additional administrative or legislative action, the Administration will still be ready. A government always ready, as this is, to take well-timed and vigorous action, and a business community willing, as ours is, to plan, boldly and with confidence, can between them develop a climate assuring steady economic growth.

The Budget

I shall submit to the Congress on January 21 the first budget prepared by this Administration, for the period July 1, 1954, through June 1955. This budget is adequate to the current needs of the government. It recognizes that a Federal budget should be a stabilizing factor in the economy. Its tax and expenditure programs will foster individual initiative and economic growth.

Pending the transmittal of my Budget Message, I shall mention here only a few points about our budgetary situation.

First, one of our initial acts was to revise, with the cooperation of the Congress, the Budget prepared before this Administration took office. Requests for new appropriations were greatly reduced. In addition, the spending level provided in that Budget for the current fiscal year has been reduced by about $7,000,000,000. In the next fiscal year we estimate a further reduction in expenditures of more than $5,000,000,000. This will reduce the spending level over the two fiscal years by more than $12,000,000,000. We are also reducing further our requests for new appropriations.

Second, despite the substantial loss of revenue in the coming fiscal year, resulting from tax reductions now in effect and tax adjustments which I shall propose, our reduced spending will move the new budget closer to a balance.

Third, by keeping new appropriation requests below estimated revenues, we continue to reduce the tremendous accumulation of unfinanced obligations incurred by the Government under past appropriations.

Fourth, until those claims on our Government's revenues are further reduced, the growth in the public debt cannot be entirely stopped. Because of this—because the government's bills have to be paid every month, while the tax money to pay them comes in with great unevenness within the fiscal year—and because of the need for flexibility to manage this enormous debt, I find it necessary to renew my request for an increase in the statutory debt limit.

Taxes

The new budget provides for a lower level of taxation than has prevailed in preceding years. Six days ago individual income taxes were reduced and the excess profits tax expired. These tax reductions are justified only because of the substantial reductions we already have made and are making in governmental expenditures. As additional reductions in expenditures are brought gradually but surely into sight, further reductions in taxes can and will be made. When budget savings and sound governmental financing are assured, tax burdens should be reduced so that taxpayers may spend their own money in their own way.

While we are moving toward lower levels of taxation we must thoroughly revise our whole tax system. The groundwork for this revision has already been laid by the Committee on Ways and Means of the House of Representatives, in close consultation with the Department of the Treasury. We should now remove the more glaring tax inequities, particularly on small taxpayers; reduce restraints on the growth of small business; and make other changes that will encourage initiative, enterprise and production. Twenty-five recommendations toward these ends will be contained in my budget message.

Without attempting to summarize these manifold reforms, I can here illustrate their tendency. For example, we propose more liberal tax treatment for dependent children who work, for widows or widowers with dependent children, and for medical expenses. For the business that wants to expand or modernize its plant, we propose liberalized tax treatment of depreciation, research and development expenses, and retained earnings.

Because of the present need for revenue the corporation income tax should be kept at the current rate of 52 percent for another year, and the excise taxes scheduled to be reduced on April first, including those on liquor, tobacco, gasoline and automobiles, should be continued at present rates.

Immediate extension of the Renegotiation Act of 1951 is also needed to eliminate excessive profits and to prevent waste of public funds in the purchase of defense materials.

Agriculture

The well being of our 160 million people demands a stable and prosperous agriculture. Conversely, every farmer knows he cannot prosper unless all America prospers. As we seek to promote increases in our standard of living, we must be sure that the farmer fairly shares in that increase. Therefore, a farm program promoting stability and prosperity in all elements of our agriculture is urgently needed.

Agricultural laws now in effect successfully accomplished their wartime purpose of encouraging maximum production of many crops. Today, production of these crops at such levels far exceeds present demand. Yet the laws encouraging such production are still in effect. The storage facilities of the Commodity Credit Corporation bulge with surplus stocks of dairy products, wheat, cotton, corn, and certain vegetable oils; and the Corporation's presently authorized borrowing authority—$6,750,000,000—is nearly exhausted. Some products, priced out of domestic markets, and others, priced out of world markets, have piled up in government hands. In a world in which millions of people are hungry, destruction of food would, of course, be unconscionable. Yet surplus stocks continue to threaten the market and in spite of the acreage controls authorized by present law, surpluses will continue to accumulate.

We confront two alternatives. The first is to impose still greater acreage reductions for some crops and apply rigid Federal controls over the use of the diverted acres. This will regiment the production of every basic agricultural crop. It will place every producer of those crops under the domination and control of the Federal government in Washington. This alternative is contrary to the fundamental interests, not only of the farmer, but of the Nation as a whole. Nor is it a real solution to the problem facing us.

The second alternative is to permit the market price for these agricultural products gradually to have a greater influence on the planning of production by farmers, while continuing the assistance of the government. This is the sound approach. To make it effective, surpluses existing when the new program begins must be insulated from the normal channels of trade for special uses. These uses would include school lunch programs, disaster relief, emergency assistance to foreign friends, and of particular importance the stockpiling of reserves for a national emergency.

Building on the agricultural laws of 1948 and 1949, we should establish a price support program with enough flexibility to attract the production of needed supplies of essential commodities and to stimulate the consumption of those commodities that are flooding American markets. Transition to modernized parity must be accomplished gradually. In no case should there be an abrupt downward change in the dollar level or in the percentage level of price supports.

Next Monday I shall transmit to the Congress my detailed recommendations embodying this approach. They have been developed through the cooperation of innumerable individuals vitally interested in agriculture. My special message on Monday will briefly describe the consultative and advisory processes to which this whole program has been subjected during the past ten months.

I have chosen this farm program because it will build markets, protect the consumers' food supply, and move food into consumption instead of into storage. It is a program that will remove the threat to the farmer of these overhanging surpluses, a program, also, that will stimulate production when a commodity is scarce and encourage consumption when nature is bountiful. Moreover, it will promote the individual freedom, responsibility, and initiative which distinguish American agriculture. And, by helping our agriculture achieve full parity in the market, it promises our farmers a higher and steadier financial return over the years than any alternative plan.

Conservation

Part of our Nation's precious heritage is its natural resources. It is the common responsibility of Federal, state, and local governments to improve and develop them, always working in the closest harmony and partnership.

All Federal conservation and resource development projects are being reappraised. Sound projects now under way will be continued. New projects in which the Federal Government has a part must be economically sound, with local sharing of cost wherever appropriate and feasible. In the next fiscal year work will be started on twenty-three projects that meet these standards. The Federal Government will continue to construct and operate economically sound flood control, power, irrigation and water supply projects wherever these projects are beyond the capacity of local initiative, public or private, and consistent with the needs of the whole Nation.

Our conservation program will also take into account the important role played by farmers in protecting our soil resources. I recommend enactment of legislation to strengthen agricultural conservation and upstream flood prevention work, and to achieve a better balance with major flood control structures in the down-stream areas.

Recommendations will be made from time to time for the adoption of:

A uniform and consistent water resources policy;

A revised public lands policy; and

A sound program for safeguarding the domestic production of critical and strategic metals and minerals.

In addition we shall continue to protect and improve our national forests, parks, monuments and other natural and historic sites, as well as our fishery and wildlife resources.

I hope that pending legislation to improve the conservation and management of publicly-owned grazing lands in national forests will soon be approved by the Congress.

National Highways

To protect the vital interest of every citizen in a safe and adequate highway system, the Federal Government is continuing its central role in the Federal Aid Highway Program. So that maximum progress can be made to overcome present inadequacies in the Interstate Highway System, we must continue the Federal gasoline tax at two cents per gallon. This will require cancellation of the $1/2¢$ decrease which otherwise will become effective April 1st, and will maintain revenues so that an expanded highway program can be undertaken.

When the Commission on Intergovernmental Relations completes its study of the present system of financing highway construction, I shall promptly submit it for consideration by the Congress and the governors of the states.

Post Office

It is apparent that the substantial savings already made, and to be made, by the Post Office Department cannot eliminate the postal deficit. I recommend, therefore, that the Congress approve the bill now pending in the House of Representatives providing for the adjustment of certain postal rates. To handle the long term aspects of this, I also recommend that the Congress create a permanent commission to establish fair and reasonable postal rates from time to time in the future.

III. Human Problems

Along with the protection of freedom and maintenance of a strong and growing economy, this Administration recognizes a third great purpose of government: concern for the human problems of our citizens. In a modern industrial society, banishment of destitution and cushioning the shock of personal disaster on the individual are proper concerns of all levels of government, including the federal government. This is especially true where remedy and prevention alike are beyond the individual's capacity.

Labor and Welfare

Of the many problems in this area, those I shall first discuss are of particular concern to the members of our great labor force, who with their heads, hearts and hands produce so much of the wealth of our country.

Protection against the hazards of temporary unemployment should be extended to some $6 1/2$ millions of workers, including civilian Federal workers, who now lack this safeguard. Moreover, the Secretary of Labor is making available to the states studies and recommendations in the fields of weekly benefits, periods of protection and extension of coverage. The Economic Report will consider the related matter of minimum wages and their coverage.

The Labor Management Relations Act of 1947 is basically a sound law. However, six years of experience have revealed that in some respects it can be improved. On January 11, I shall forward to the Congress suggestions for changes designed to reinforce the basic objectives of the Act.

Our basic social security program, the Old-Age and Survivors Insurance system, to which individuals contribute during their productive years and receive benefits based on previous earnings, is designed to shield them from destitution. Last year I recommended extension of the social insurance system to include more than 10,000,000 additional persons. I ask that this extension soon be accomplished. This and other major improvements in the insurance system will bring substantial benefit increases and broaden the membership of the insurance system, thus diminishing the need for Federal grants-in-aid for such purposes. A new formula will therefore be proposed, permitting progressive reduction in such grants as the need for them declines.

Federal grant-in-aid welfare programs, now based on widely varying formulas, should be simplified. Concrete proposals on fourteen of them will be suggested to the appropriate Committees.

The program for rehabilitation of the disabled especially needs strengthening. Through special vocational training, this program presently returns each year some 60,000 handicapped individuals to productive work. Far more disabled people can be saved each year from idleness and dependence if this program is gradually increased. My more detailed recommendations on this and the other social insurance problems I have mentioned will be sent to the Congress on January 14th.

Health

I am flatly opposed to the socialization of medicine. The great need for hospital and medical services can best be met by the initiative of private plans. But it is unfortunately a fact that medical costs are rising and already impose severe hardships on many families. The Federal Government can do many helpful things and still carefully avoid the socialization of medicine.

The Federal Government should encourage medical research in its battle with such mortal diseases as cancer and heart ailments, and should continue to help the states in their health and rehabilitation programs. The present Hospital Survey and Construction Act should be broadened in order to assist in the development of adequate facilities for the chronically ill, and to encourage the construction of diagnostic centers, rehabilitation facilities, and nursing homes. The war on disease also needs a better working relationship between Government and private initiative. Private and non-profit hospital and medical insurance plans are already in the field, soundly based on the experience and initiative of the people in their various communities.

A limited Government reinsurance service would permit the private and non-profit insurance companies to offer broader protection to more of the many families which want and should have it. On January 18 I shall forward to the Congress a special message presenting this Administration's health program in its detail.

Education

Youth—our greatest resource—is being seriously neglected in a vital respect. The nation as a whole is not preparing teachers or building schools fast enough to keep up with the increase in our population.

The preparation of teachers as, indeed, the control and direction of public education policy, is a state and local responsibility. However, the Federal Government should stand ready to assist states which demonstrably cannot provide sufficient school buildings. In order to appraise the needs, I hope that this year a conference on education will be held in each state, culminating in a national conference. From these conferences on education, every level of government—from the Federal Government to each local school board—should gain the information with which to attack this serious problem.

Housing

The details of a program to enlarge and improve the opportunities for our people to acquire good homes will be presented to the Congress by special message on January 25.

This program will include:

Modernization of the home mortgage insurance program of the Federal Government;

Redirection of the present system of loans and grants-in-aid to cities for slum clearance and redevelopment;

Extension of the advantages of insured lending to private credit engaged in this task of rehabilitating obsolete neighborhoods;

Insurance of long-term, mortgage loans, with small down payment for low-income families; and, until alternative programs prove more effective.

Continuation of the public housing program adopted in the Housing Act of 1949.

If the individual, the community, the State and federal governments will alike apply themselves, every American family can have a decent home.

Veterans Administration

The internal reorganization of the Veterans Administration is proceeding with my full approval. When completed, it will afford a single agency whose services, including medical facilities, will be better adapted to the needs of those 20,000,000 veterans to whom this Nation owes so much.

Suffrage

My few remaining recommendations all relate to a basic right of our citizens—that of being represented in the decisions of the government.

I hope that the States will cooperate with the Congress in adopting uniform standards in their voting laws that will make it possible for our citizens in the armed forces overseas to vote.

In the District of Columbia the time is long overdue for granting national suffrage to its citizens and also applying the principle of local self-government to the Nation's Capital. I urge the Congress to move promptly in this direction and also to revise District revenue measures to provide needed public works improvements.

The people of Hawaii are ready for statehood. I renew my request for this legislation in order that Hawaii may elect its State officials and its representatives in Washington along with the rest of the country this fall.

For years our citizens between the ages of 18 and 21 have, in time of peril, been summoned to fight for America. They should participate in the political process that produces this fateful summons. I urge Congress to propose to the States a constitutional amendment permitting citizens to vote when they reach the age of 18.

Conclusion

I want to add one final word about the general purport of these many recommendations.

Our government's powers are wisely limited by the Constitution; but quite apart from those limitations, there are things which no government can do or should try to do.

A government can strive, as ours is striving, to maintain an economic system whose doors are open to enterprise and ambition—those personal qualities on which economic growth largely depends. But enterprise and ambition are qualities which no government can supply. Fortunately no American government need concern itself on this score; our people have these qualities in good measure.

A government can sincerely strive for peace, as ours is striving, and ask its people to make sacrifices for the sake of peace. But no government can place peace in the hearts of foreign rulers. It is our duty then to ourselves and to freedom itself to remain strong in all those ways—spiritual, economic, military—that will give us maximum safety against the possibility of aggressive action by others.

No government can inoculate its people against the fatal materialism that plagues our age. Happily, our people, though blessed with more material goods than any people in history, have always reserved their first allegiance to the kingdom of the spirit, which is the true source of that freedom we value above all material things.

But a government can try, as ours tries, to sense the deepest aspirations of the people, and to express them in political action at home and abroad. So long as action and aspiration humbly and earnestly seek favor in the sight of the Almighty, there is no end to America's forward road; there is no obstacle on it she will not surmount in her march toward a lasting peace in a free and prosperous world.

Dwight D. Eisenhower, 1953–1957

Address to Congress on the State of the Union

January 6, 1955

Dwight D. Eisenhower delivered his third State of the Union address in person to a Congress newly controlled by the opposition Democrats. As often is the case in a midterm election, the opposition party had won seats in the House and Senate in November 1954—in this case, enough to win back control from the Republicans, who had held control for the previous two years.

In his speech, Eisenhower made a plea for bipartisan cooperation, warning that in the past political divisions had led to "paralyzing indecision."

Eisenhower's address was delivered against the continuing backdrop of the Cold War between the United States and the Soviet Union, and, once again, the speech focused on that struggle. The president called the conflict one that "goes to the roots of the human spirit," stating that "at issue is the true nature of man."

As he had in his 1954 State of the Union address, Eisenhower referred to three main emphases of his administration: to champion freedom, keep the economy strong, and focus on "human problems" such as health.

Eisenhower stated that the world was at peace, but he warned of the ongoing efforts by the communist Soviet Union "to communize the world." He cited a series of international agreements designed to combat this effort, including in the Western Hemisphere, the Middle East, and Asia. He also called for an extension of the Selective Service draft law, which was to expire that June.

Eisenhower's eight years in office represented a generally prosperous period for the country, and in this 1955 State of the Union speech the president called for increased economic expansion. He sought a balanced budget, and noted that the previous year there had been a tax cut and a revision in the country's tax laws.

The president also called for a modern highway system, something he also had mentioned in the previous year's speech. Eisenhower would be known for presiding over the creation of the national interstate highway system, an idea that had been in the works for years but was to reach its initial launch in 1956.

When it came to "human problems," the president recommended an increase in the minimum wage to 90 cents, called for statehood for Hawaii and eventual statehood for Alaska, and called for a Federal Advisory Commission on the Arts.

One historic event that had occurred since Eisenhower's last speech was the Supreme Court's anti-segregation decision in *Brown v. Board of Education,* which was handed down in May 1954. Eisenhower did not mention the decision in his address.

Mr. President, Mr. Speaker, Members of the Congress:

First, I extend cordial greetings to the 84th Congress. We shall have much to do together; I am sure that we shall get it done—and, that we shall do it in harmony and good will.

At the outset, I believe it would be well to remind ourselves of this great fundamental in our national life: our common belief that every human being is divinely endowed with dignity and worth and inalienable rights. This faith, with its corollary—that to grow and flourish people must be free—shapes the interests and aspirations of every American.

From this deep faith have evolved three main purposes of our Federal Government:

First, to maintain justice and freedom among ourselves and to champion them for others so that we may work effectively for enduring peace;

Second, to help keep our economy vigorous and expanding, thus sustaining our international strength and assuring better jobs, better living, better opportunities for every citizen;

And third, to concern ourselves with the human problems of our people so that every American may have the opportunity to lead a healthy, productive and rewarding life.

Foremost among these broad purposes of government is our support of freedom, justice and peace.

It is of the utmost importance, that each of us understand the true nature of the struggle now taking place in the world.

It is not a struggle merely of economic theories, or of forms of government, or of military power. At issue is the true nature of man. Either man is the creature whom the Psalmist described as "a little lower than the angels," crowned with glory and honor, holding "dominion over the works" of his Creator; or man is a soulless, animated machine to be enslaved, used and consumed by the state for its own glorification.

It is, therefore, a struggle which goes to the roots of the human spirit, and its shadow falls across the long sweep of man's destiny. This prize, so precious, so fraught with ultimate meaning, is the true object of the contending forces in the world.

In the past year, there has been progress justifying hope, both for continuing peace and for the ultimate rule of freedom and justice in the world. Free nations are collectively stronger than at any time in recent years.

Just as nations of this Hemisphere, in the historic Caracas and Rio conferences, have closed ranks against imperialistic Communism and strengthened their economic ties, so free nations elsewhere have forged new bonds of unity.

Recent agreements between Turkey and Pakistan have laid a foundation for increased strength in the Middle East. With our understanding support, Egypt and Britain, Yugoslavia and Italy, Britain and Iran have resolved dangerous differences. The security of the Mediterranean has been enhanced by an alliance among Greece, Turkey and Yugoslavia. Agreements in Western Europe have paved the way for unity to replace past divisions which have undermined Europe's economic and military vitality. The defense of the West appears likely at last to include a free, democratic Germany participating as an equal in the councils of NATO.

In Asia and the Pacific, the pending Manila Pact supplements our treaties with Australia, New Zealand, the Philippines, Korea and Japan and our prospective treaty with the Republic of China. These pacts stand as solemn warning that future military aggression and subversion against the free nations of Asia will meet united response. The Pacific Charter, also adopted at Manila, is a milestone in the development of human freedom and self-government in the Pacific area.

Under the auspices of the United Nations, there is promise of progress in our country's plan for the peaceful use of atomic energy.

Finally, today the world is at peace. It is, to be sure, a secure peace. Yet all humanity finds hope in the simple fact that for an appreciable time there has been no active major battlefield on earth. This same fact inspires us to work all the more effectively with other nations for the well-being, the freedom, the dignity, of every human on earth.

These developments are heartening indeed, and we are hopeful of continuing progress. But sobering problems remain.

The massive military machines and ambitions of the Soviet-Communist bloc still create uneasiness in the world. All of us are aware of the continuing reliance of the Soviet Communists on military force, of the power of their weapons, of their present resistance to realistic armament limitation, and of their continuing effort to dominate or intimidate free nations on their periphery. Their steadily growing power includes an increasing strength in nuclear weapons. This power, combined with the proclaimed intentions of the Communist leaders to communize the world, is the threat confronting us today.

To protect our nations and our peoples from the catastrophe of a nuclear holocaust, free nations must maintain countervailing military power to persuade the Communists of the futility of seeking their ends through aggression. If Communist rulers understand that America's response to aggression will be swift and decisive—that never shall we buy peace at the expense of honor or faith—they will be powerfully deterred from launching a military venture engulfing their own peoples and many others in disaster. This, of course, is merely world stalemate. But in this stalemate each of us may and must exercise his high duty to strive in every honorable way for enduring peace.

The military threat is but one menace to our freedom and security. We must not only deter aggression; we must also frustrate the effort of Communists to gain their goals by subversion. To this end, free nations must maintain and reinforce their cohesion, their internal security, their political and economic vitality, and their faith in freedom.

In such a world, America's course is clear:

We must tirelessly labor to make the peace more just and durable.

We must strengthen the collective defense under the United Nations Charter and gird ourselves with sufficient military strength and productive capacity to discourage resort to war and protect our nation's vital interests.

We must continue to support and strengthen the United Nations. At this very moment, by vote of the United Nations General Assembly, its Secretary-General is in Communist China on a mission of deepest concern to all Americans: seeking the release of our never-to-be-forgotten American aviators and all other United Nations prisoners wrongfully detained by the Communist regime.

We must also encourage the efforts being made in the United Nations to limit armaments and to harness the atom to peaceful use.

We must expand international trade and investment and assist friendly nations whose own best efforts are still insufficient to provide the strength essential to the security of the free world.

We must be willing to use the processes of negotiation whenever they will advance the cause of just and secure peace to which the United States and other free nations are dedicated.

In respect to all these matters, we must, through a vigorous information program, keep the peoples of the world truthfully advised of our actions and purposes. This problem has been attacked with new vigor during the past months. I urge that the Congress give its earnest consideration to the great advantages that can accrue to our country through the successful operations of this program.

We must also carry forward our educational exchange program. This sharing of knowledge and experience between our citizens and those of free countries is a powerful factor in the development and maintenance of true partnership among free peoples.

To advance these many efforts, the Congress must act in this session on appropriations, legislation, and treaties. Today I shall mention especially our foreign economic and military programs.

The recent economic progress in many free nations has been most heartening. The productivity of labor and the production of goods and services are increasing in ever-widening areas. There is a growing will to improve the living standards of all men. This progress is important to all our people. It promises us allies who are strong and self-reliant; it promises a growing world market for the products of our mines, our factories, and our farms.

But only through steady effort can we hope to continue this progress. Barriers still impede trade and the flow of capital needed to develop each nation's human and material resources. Wise reduction of these barriers is a long-term objective of our foreign economic policy—a policy of an evolutionary and selective nature, assuring broad benefits to our own and other peoples.

We must gradually reduce certain tariff obstacles to trade. These actions should, of course, be accompanied by a similar lowering of trade barriers by other nations, so that we may move steadily toward greater economic advantage for all. We must further simplify customs administration and procedures. We must facilitate the flow of capital and continue technical assistance, both directly and through the United Nations, to less developed countries to strengthen their independence and raise their living standards. Many another step must be taken in and among the nations of the free world to release forces of private initiative. In our own nation, these forces have brought strength and prosperity; once released, they will generate rising incomes in these other countries with which to buy the products of American industry, labor and agriculture.

On January 10, by special message, I shall submit specific recommendations for carrying forward the legislative phases of our foreign economic policy.

Our many efforts to build a better world include the maintenance of our military strength. This is a vast undertaking. Major national security programs consume two-thirds of the entire Federal budget. Over four million Americans—servicemen and civilians—are on the rolls of the defense establishment. During the past two years, by eliminating duplication and overstaffing, by improved procurement and inventory controls, and by concentrating on the essentials, many billions of dollars have been saved in our defense activities. I should like to mention certain fundamentals underlying this vast program.

First, a realistic limitation of armaments and an enduring, just peace remain our national goals; we maintain powerful military forces because there is no present alternative—forces designed for deterrent and defensive purposes alone but able instantly to strike back with destructive power in response to an attack.

Second, we must stay alert to the fact that undue reliance on one weapon or preparation for only one kind of warfare simply invites an enemy to resort to another. We must, therefore, keep in our armed forces balance and flexibility adequate for our purposes and objectives.

Third, to keep our armed forces abreast of the advances of science, our military planning must be flexible enough to utilize the new weapons and techniques which flow ever more speedily from our research and development programs. The forthcoming military budget therefore emphasizes modern airpower in the Air Force, Navy and Marine Corps and increases the emphasis on new weapons, especially those of rapid and destructive striking power. It assures the maintenance of effective, retaliatory force as the principal deterrent to overt aggression. It accelerates the continental defense program and the build-up of ready military reserve forces. It continues a vigorous program of stockpiling strategic and critical materials and strengthening our mobilization base. The budget also contemplates the strategic concentration of our strength through redeployment of certain forces. It provides for reduction of forces in certain categories and their expansion in others, to fit them to the military realities of our time. These emphases in our defense planning have been made at my personal direction after long and thoughtful study. In my judgment, they will give our nation a defense accurately adjusted to the national need.

Fourth, pending a world agreement on armament limitation, we must continue to improve and expand our supplies of nuclear weapons for our land, naval and air forces, while, at the same time, continuing our encouraging progress in the peaceful use of atomic power.

And fifth, in the administration of these costly programs, we must demand the utmost in efficiency and ingenuity. We must assure our people not only of adequate protection but also of a defense that can be carried forward from year to year until the threat of aggression has disappeared.

To help maintain this kind of armed strength and improve its efficiency, I must urge the enactment of several important measures in this session.

The first concerns the selective service act which expires next June 30th. For the foreseeable future, our standing forces must remain much larger than voluntary methods can sustain. We must, therefore, extend the statutory authority to induct men for two years of military service.

The second kind of measure concerns the rapid turnover of our most experienced servicemen. This process seriously weakens the combat readiness of our armed forces and is exorbitantly expensive. To encourage more trained servicemen to remain in uniform, I shall, on the thirteenth of this month, propose a number of measures to increase the attractions of a military career. These measures will include more adequate medical care for dependents, survivors' benefits, more and better housing, and selective adjustments in military pay and other allowances.

And third—also on January 13—I shall present a program to rebuild and strengthen the civilian components of our armed forces. This is a comprehensive program, designed to make better use of our manpower of military age. Because it will go far in assuring fair and equitable participation in military training and service, it is of particular importance to our combat veterans. In keeping with the historic military policy of our Republic, this program is designed to build and maintain powerful civilian reserves immediately capable of effective military service in an emergency in lieu of maintaining active duty forces in excess of the nation's immediate need.

Maintenance of an effective defense requires continuance of our aggressive attack on subversion at home. In this effort we have, in the past two years, made excellent progress. FBI investigations have been powerfully reinforced by a new Internal Security Division in the Department of Justice; the security activities of the Immigration and Naturalization Service have been revitalized; an improved and strengthened security system is in effect throughout the government; the Department of Justice and the FBI have been armed with effective new legal weapons forged by the 83rd Congress.

We shall continue to ferret out and to destroy Communist subversion.

We shall, in the process, carefully preserve our traditions and the basic rights of our citizens.

Our civil defense program is also a key element in the protection of our country. We are developing cooperative methods with State Governors, Mayors, and voluntary citizen groups, as well as among Federal agencies, in building the civil defense organization. Its significance in time of war is obvious; its swift assistance in disaster areas last year proved its importance in time of peace.

An industry capable of rapid expansion and essential materials and facilities swiftly available in time of emergency are indispensable to our defense. I urge, therefore, a two-year extension of the Defense Production Act and Title II of the First War Powers Act of 1941. These are cornerstones of our program for the development and maintenance of an adequate mobilization base. At this point, I should like to make this additional observation. Our quest for peace and freedom necessarily presumes that we who hold positions of public trust must rise above self and section—that we must subordinate to the general good our partisan, our personal pride and prejudice. Tirelessly, with united purpose, we must fortify the material and spiritual foundations of this land of freedom and of free nations throughout the world. As never before, there is need for unhesitating cooperation among the branches of our government.

At this time the executive and legislative branches are under the management of different political parties. This fact places both parties on trial before the American people.

In less perilous days of the past, division of governmental responsibility among our great parties has produced a paralyzing indecision. We must not let this happen in our time. We must avoid a paralysis of the will for peace and international security.

In the traditionally bipartisan areas—military security and foreign relations—I can report to you that I have already, with the leaders of this Congress, expressed assurances of unreserved cooperation. Yet, the strength of our country requires more than mere maintenance of military strength and success in foreign affairs; these vital matters are in turn dependent upon concerted and vigorous action in a number of supporting programs. I say, therefore, to the 84th Congress:

In all areas basic to the strength of America, there will be—to the extent I can insure them—cooperative, constructive relations between the Executive and Legislative Branches of this government. Let the general good be our yardstick on every great issue of our time.

Our efforts to defend our freedom and to secure a just peace are, of course, inseparable from the second great purpose of our government: to help maintain a strong, growing economy—an economy vigorous and free, in which there are ever-increasing opportunities, just rewards for effort, and a stable prosperity that is widely shared.

In the past two years, many important governmental Actions helped our economy adjust to conditions of peace; these and other actions created a climate for renewed economic growth. Controls were removed from wages, prices and materials. Tax revisions encouraged increased private spending and employment. Federal expenditures were sharply reduced, making possible a record tax cut. These actions, together with flexible monetary and debt management policies, helped to halt inflation and stabilize the value of the dollar. A program of cooperation and partnership in resource development was begun. Social security and unemployment insurance laws were broadened and strengthened. New laws started the long process of balancing farm production with farm markets. Expanded shipbuilding and stockpiling programs strengthened key sectors of the economy, while improving our mobilization base. A comprehensive new housing law brought impressive progress in an area fundamental to our economic strength and closed loopholes in the old laws permitting dishonest manipulation. Many of these programs are just beginning to exert their main stimulating effect upon the economy generally and upon specific communities and industries throughout the country.

The past year—1954—was one of the most prosperous years in our history. Business activity now surges with new strength. Production is rising. Employment is high. Toward the end of last year average weekly wages in manufacturing were higher than ever before. Personal income after taxes is at a record level. So is consumer spending. Construction activity is reaching new peaks. Export demand for our goods is strong. State and local government expenditures on public works are rising. Savings are high, and credit is readily available.

So, today, the transition to a peacetime economy is largely behind us.

The economic outlook is good.

The many promising factors I have mentioned do not guarantee sustained economic expansion; however, they do give us a strong position from which to carry forward our economic growth. If we as a people act wisely, within ten years our annual national output can rise from its present level of about $360 billion to $500 billion, measured in dollars of stable buying power.

My Budget Message on January 17, the Economic Report on the 20th of this month, and several special messages will set forth in detail major programs to foster the growth of our economy and to protect the integrity of the people's money. Today I shall discuss these programs only in general terms.

Government efficiency and economy remain essential to steady progress toward a balanced budget. More than ten billion dollars were cut from the spending program proposed in the budget of January 9, 1953. Expenditures of that year were six and a half billion below those of the previous year. In the current fiscal year, government spending will be nearly four and a half billion dollars less than in the fiscal year which ended last June 30. New spending authority has been held below expenditures, reducing government obligations accumulated over the years.

Last year we had a large tax cut and, for the first time in seventy-five years a basic revision of Federal tax laws. It is now clear that defense and other essential government costs must remain at a level precluding further tax reductions this year. Although excise and corporation income taxes must, therefore, be continued at their present rates, further tax cuts will be possible when justified by lower expenditures and by revenue increases arising from the nation's economic growth. I am hopeful that such reductions can be made next year.

At the foundation of our economic growth are the raw materials and energy produced from our minerals and fuels, lands and forests, and water resources. With respect to them, I believe that the nation must adhere to three fundamental policies: first, to develop, wisely use and conserve basic resources from generation to generation; second, to follow the historic pattern of developing these resources primarily by private citizens under fair provisions of law, including restraints for proper conservation; and third, to treat resource development as a partnership undertaking—a partnership in which the participation of private citizens and State and local governments is as necessary as Federal participation.

This policy of partnership and cooperation is producing good results, most immediately noticeable in respect to water resources. First, it has encouraged local public bodies and private citizens to plan their own power sources. Increasing numbers of applications to the Federal Power Commission to conduct surveys and prepare plans for power development, notably in the Columbia River Basin, are evidence of local response.

Second, the Federal Government and local and private organizations have been encouraged to coordinate their developments. This is important because Federal hydroelectric developments supply but a small fraction of the nation's power needs. Such partnership projects as Priest Rapids in Washington, the Coosa River development in Alabama, and Markham Ferry in Oklahoma already have the approval of the Congress. This year justifiable projects of a similar nature will again have Administration support.

Third, the Federal Government must shoulder its own partnership obligations by undertaking projects of such complexity and size that their success requires Federal development. In keeping with this principle, I again urge the Congress to approve the development of the Upper Colorado River Basin to conserve and assure better use of precious water essential to the future of the West.

In addition, the 1956 budget will recommend appropriations to start six new reclamation and more than thirty new Corps of Engineers projects of varying size. Going projects and investigations of potential new resource developments will be continued.

Although this partnership approach is producing encouraging results, its full success requires a nation-wide comprehensive water resources policy firmly based in law. Such a policy is under preparation and when completed will be submitted to the Congress.

In the interest of their proper conservation, development and use, continued vigilance will be maintained over our fisheries, wildlife resources, the national parks and forests, and the public lands; and we shall continue to encourage an orderly development of the nation's mineral resources.

A modern, efficient highway system is essential to meet the needs of our growing population, our expanding economy, and our national security. We are accelerating our highway improvement program as rapidly as possible under existing State and Federal laws and authorizations. However, this effort will not in itself assure our people of an adequate highway system. On my recommendation, this problem has been carefully considered by the Conference of State Governors and by a special Advisory Committee on a National Highway Program, composed of leading private citizens. I have received the recommendations of the Governors' Conference and will shortly receive the views of the special Advisory Committee. Aided by their findings, I shall submit on January 27th detailed recommendations which will meet our most pressing national highway needs.

In further recognition of the importance of transportation to our economic strength and security, the Administration, through a Cabinet committee, is thoroughly examining existing Federal transportation policies to determine their effect on the adequacy of transportation services. This is the first such comprehensive review directly undertaken by the Executive Branch of the government in modern times. We are not only examining major problems facing the various modes of transport; we are also studying closely the inter-relationships of civilian and government requirements for transportation. Legislation will be recommended to correct policy deficiencies which we may find.

The nation's public works activities are tremendous in scope. It is expected that more than $12 billion will be expended in 1955 for the development of land, water and other resources; control of floods, and navigation and harbor improvements; construction of roads, schools, and municipal water supplies, and disposal of domestic and industrial wastes. Many of the Federal, State and local agencies responsible for this work are, in their separate capacities, highly efficient. But public works activities are closely inter-related and have a substantial influence on the growth of the country. Moreover, in times of threatening economic contraction, they may become a valuable sustaining force. To these ends, efficient planning and execution of the nation's public works require both the coordination of Federal activities and effective cooperation with State and local governments.

The Council of Economic Advisers, through its public works planning section, has made important advances during the past year in effecting this coordination and cooperation. In view of the success of these initial efforts, and to give more emphasis and continuity to this essential coordination, I shall request the Congress to appropriate funds for the support of an Office of Coordinator of Public Works in the Executive Office of the President.

A most significant element in our growing economy is an agriculture that is stable, prosperous and free. The problems of our agriculture have evolved over many years and cannot be solved overnight; nevertheless, governmental actions last year hold great promise of fostering a better balance between production and markets and, consequently, a better and more stable income for our farmers.

Through vigorous administration and through new authority provided by the 83rd Congress, surplus farm products are now moving into consumption. From February 1953 through November 1954, the rate of increase of government-held surpluses has been reduced by our moving into use more than 2.3 billion dollars' worth of government-owned farm commodities; this amount is equal to more than seven percent of a year's production of all our farms and ranches. Domestic consumption remains high, and farm exports will be higher than last year. As a result of the flexibility provided by the Agricultural Act of 1954, we can move toward less restrictive acreage controls.

Thus, farm production is gradually adjusting to markets, markets are being expanded, and stocks are moving into use. We can now look forward to an easing of the influences depressing farm prices, to reduced government expenditures for purchase of surplus products, and to less Federal intrusion into the lives and plans of our farm people. Agricultural programs have been redirected toward better balance, greater stability and sustained prosperity. We are headed in the right direction. I urgently recommend to the Congress that we continue resolutely on this road.

Greater attention must be directed to the needs of low-income farm families. Twenty-eight per cent of our farm-operator families have net cash incomes of less than $1,000 per year. Last year, at my request, careful studies were made of the problems of these farm people. I shall later submit recommendations designed to assure the steady alleviation of their most pressing concerns.

Because drought also remains a serious agricultural problem, I shall recommend legislation to strengthen Federal disaster assistance programs. This legislation will prescribe an improved appraisal of need, better adjustment of the various programs to local conditions, and a more equitable sharing of costs between the States and the Federal Government.

The prosperity of our small business enterprises is an indispensable element in the maintenance of our economic strength. Creation of the Small Business Administration and recently enacted tax laws facilitating small business expansion are but two of many important steps we have taken to encourage our smaller enterprises. I recommend that the Congress extend the Small Business Act of 1953 which is due to expire next June.

We come now to the third great purpose of our government—its concern for the health, productivity and well-being of all our people.

Every citizen wants to give full expression to his God-given talents and abilities and to have the recognition and respect accorded under our religious and political traditions. Americans also want a good material standard of living—not simply to accumulate possessions, but to fulfill a legitimate aspiration for an environment in which their families may live meaningful and happy lives. Our people are committed, therefore, to the creation and preservation of opportunity for every citizen to lead a more rewarding life. They are equally committed to the alleviation of misfortune and distress among their fellow citizens.

The aspirations of most of our people can best be fulfilled through their own enterprise and initiative, without government interference. This Administration, therefore, follows two simple rules: first, the Federal Government should perform an essential task only when it cannot otherwise be adequately performed; and second, in performing that task, our government must not impair the self-respect, freedom and incentive of the individual. So long as these two rules are observed, the government can fully meet its obligation without creating a dependent population or a domineering bureaucracy.

During the past two years, notable advances were made in these functions of government. Protection of old-age and survivors' insurance was extended to an additional ten million of our people, and the benefits were substantially increased. Legislation was enacted to provide unemployment insurance protection to some four million additional Americans. Stabilization of living costs and the halting of inflation protected the value of pensions and savings. A broad program now helps to bring good homes within the reach of the great majority of our people. With the States, we are providing rehabilitation facilities and more clinics, hospitals, and nursing homes for patients with chronic illnesses. Also with the States, we have begun a great and fruitful expansion in the restoration of disabled persons to employment and useful lives. In the areas of Federal responsibility, we have made historic progress in eliminating from among our people demeaning practices based on race or color.

All of us may be proud of these achievements during the past two years. Yet essential Federal tasks remain to be done.

As part of our efforts to provide decent, safe and sanitary housing for low-income families, we must carry forward the housing program authorized during the 83rd Congress. We must also authorize contracts for a firm program of 35,000 additional public housing units in each of the next two fiscal years. This program will meet the most pressing obligations of the Federal Government into the 1958 fiscal year for planning and building public housing. By that time the private building industry, aided by the Housing Act of 1954, will have had the opportunity to assume its full role in providing adequate housing for our low income families.

The health of our people is one of our most precious assets. Preventable sickness should be prevented; knowledge available to combat disease and disability should be fully used. Otherwise, we as a people are guilty not only of neglect of human suffering but also of wasting our national strength.

Constant advances in medical care are not available to enough of our citizens. Clearly our nation must do more to reduce the impact of accident and disease. Two fundamental problems confront us: first, high and ever-rising costs of health services; second, serious gaps and shortages in these services.

By special message on January 24, I shall propose a coordinated program to strengthen and improve existing health services. This program will continue to reject socialized medicine. It will emphasize individual and local responsibility. Under it the Federal Government will neither dominate nor direct, but serve as a helpful partner. Within this framework, the program can be broad in scope.

My recommendations will include a Federal health reinsurance service to encourage the development of more and better voluntary health insurance coverage by private organizations. I shall also recommend measures to improve the medical care of that group of our citizens who, because of need, receive Federal-State public assistance. These two proposals will help more of our people to meet the costs of health services. To reduce the gaps in these services, I shall propose:

New measures to facilitate construction of needed health facilities and help reduce shortages of trained health personnel;

Vigorous steps to combat the misery and national loss involved in mental illness;

Improved services for crippled children and for maternal and child health;

Better consumer protection under our existing pure food and drug laws; and, finally,

Strengthened programs to combat the increasingly serious pollution of our rivers and streams and the growing problem of air pollution.

These measures together constitute a comprehensive program holding rich promise for better health for all of our people.

Last year's expansion of social security coverage and our new program of improved medical care for public assistance recipients together suggest modification of the formula for Federal sharing in old age assistance payments. I recommend modification of the formula where such payments will, in the future, supplement benefits received under the old age and survivors insurance system.

It is the inalienable right of every person, from childhood on, to have access to knowledge. In our form of society, this right of the individual takes on a special meaning, for the education of all our citizens is imperative to the maintenance and invigoration of America's free institutions.

Today, we face grave educational problems. Effective and up-to-date analyses of these problems and their solutions are being carried forward through the individual State conferences and the White House Conference to be completed this year.

However, such factors as population growth, additional responsibilities of schools, and increased and longer school attendance have produced an unprecedented classroom shortage. This shortage is of immediate concern to all of our people. Positive, affirmative action must be taken now.

Without impairing in any way the responsibilities of our States, localities, communities, or families, the Federal government can and should serve as an effective-catalyst in dealing with this problem. I shall forward a special message to the Congress on February 15, presenting an affirmative program dealing with this shortage.

To help the States do a better and more timely job, we must strengthen their resources for preventing and dealing with juvenile delinquency. I shall propose Federal legislation to assist the States to promote concerted action in dealing with this nationwide problem. I shall carry forward the vigorous efforts of the Administration to improve the international control of the traffic in narcotics and, in cooperation with State and local agencies, to combat narcotic addiction in our country.

I should like to speak now of additional matters of importance to all our people and especially to our wage earners.

During the past year certain industrial changes and the readjustment of the economy to conditions of peace brought unemployment and other difficulties to various localities and industries. These problems are engaging our most earnest attention. But for the overwhelming majority of our working people, the past year has meant good jobs. Moreover, the earnings and savings of our wage earners are no longer depreciating in value. Because of cooperative relations between labor and management, fewer working days were lost through strikes in 1954 than in any year in the past decade.

The outlook for our wage earners can be made still more promising by several legislative actions.

First, in the past five years we have had economic growth which will support an increase in the Federal minimum wage. In the light of present economic conditions, I recommend its increase to ninety cents an hour. I also recommend that many others, at present excluded, be given the protection of a minimum wage.

Second, I renew my recommendation of last year for amendment of the Labor Management Relations Act of 1947 to further the basic objectives of this statute. I especially call to the attention of the Congress amendments dealing with the right of economic strikers to vote in representation elections and the need for equalizing the obligation under the Act to file disclaimers of Communist affiliation.

Third, the Administration will propose other important measures including occupational safety, workmen's compensation for longshoremen and harbor workers, and the "Eight Hour Laws" applicable to Federal contractors. Legislation will also be proposed respecting nonoccupational disability insurance and unemployment compensation in the District of Columbia.

In considering human needs, the Federal Government must take special responsibility for citizens in its direct employ. On January 11 I shall propose a pay adjustment plan for civilian employees outside the Postal Field Service to correct inequities and increase individual pay rates. I shall also recommend voluntary health insurance on a contributory basis for Federal employees and their dependents. In keeping with the Group Life Insurance Act passed in the 83rd Congress, this protection should be provided on the group insurance principle and purchased from private facilities. Also on January 11 I shall recommend a modern pay plan, including pay increases, for postal field employees. As part of this program, and to carry forward our progress toward elimination of the large annual postal deficit. I shall renew my request for an increase in postal rates. Again I urge that in the future the fixing of rates be delegated to an impartial, independent body.

More adequate training programs to equip career employees of the government to render improved public service will be recommended, as will improvements in the laws affecting employees serving on foreign assignments.

Needed improvements in survivor, disability, and retirement benefits for Federal civilian and military personnel have been extensively considered by the Committee on Retirement Policy for Federal personnel. The Committee's proposals would strengthen and improve benefits for our career people in government, and I endorse their broad objectives. Full contributory coverage under old-age and survivors' insurance should be made available to all Federal personnel, just as in private industry. For career military personnel, the protection of the old-age and survivors' insurance system would be an important and long-needed addition, especially to their present unequal and inadequate survivorship protection. The military retirement pay system should remain separate and unchanged. Certain adjustments in the present civilian personnel retirement systems will be needed to reflect the additional protection of old-age and survivors' insurance. However, these systems also are a basic part of a total compensation and should be separately and independently retained.

I also urge the Congress to approve a long overdue increase in the salaries of Members of the Congress and of the Federal judiciary to a level commensurate with their heavy responsibilities.

Our concern for the individual in our country requires that we consider several additional problems.

We must continue our program to help our Indian citizens improve their lot and make their full contribution to national life. Two years ago I advised the Congress of injustices under existing immigration laws. Through humane administration, the Department of Justice is doing what it legally can to alleviate hardships. Clearance of aliens before arrival has been initiated, and except for criminal offenders, the imprisonment of aliens awaiting admission or deportation has been stopped. Certain provisions of law, however, have the effect of compelling action in respect to aliens which are inequitable in some instances and discriminatory in others. These provisions should be corrected in this session of the Congress.

As the complex problems of Alaska are resolved, that Territory should expect to achieve statehood. In the meantime, there is no justification for deferring the admission to statehood of Hawaii. I again urge approval of this measure.

We have three splendid opportunities to demonstrate the strength of our belief in the right of suffrage. First, I again urge that a Constitutional amendment be submitted to the States to reduce the voting age for Federal elections. Second, I renew my request that the principle of self-government be extended and the right of suffrage granted to the citizens of the District of Columbia. Third, I again recommend that we work with the States to preserve the voting rights of citizens in the nation's service overseas.

In our determination to keep faith with those who in the past have met the highest call of citizenship, we now have under study the system of benefits for veterans and for surviving dependents of deceased veterans and servicemen. Studies will be undertaken to determine the need for measures to ease the readjustment to civilian life of men required to enter the armed forces for two years of service.

In the advancement of the various activities which will make our civilization endure and flourish, the Federal Government should do more to give official recognition to the importance of the arts and other cultural activities. I shall recommend the establishment of a Federal Advisory Commission on the Arts within the Department of Health, Education and Welfare, to advise the Federal Government on ways to encourage artistic endeavor and appreciation. I shall also propose that awards of merit be established whereby we can honor our fellow citizens who make great contribution to the advancement of our civilization.

Every citizen rightly expects efficient and economical administration of these many government programs I have outlined today. I strongly recommend extension of the Reorganization Act and the law establishing the Commission on Intergovernmental Relations, both of which expire this spring. Thus the Congress will assure continuation of the excellent progress recently made in improving government organization and administration. In this connection we are looking forward with great interest to the reports which will soon be going to the Congress from the Commission on Organization of the Executive Branch of the Government. I am sure that these studies, made under the chairmanship of former President Herbert Hoover with the assistance of more than two hundred distinguished citizens, will be of great value in paving the way toward more efficiency and economy in the government.

And now, I return to the point at which I began—the faith of our people. The many programs here summarized are, I believe, in full keeping with their needs, interests and aspirations. The obligations upon us are clear:

To labor earnestly, patiently, prayerfully, for peace, for freedom, for justice, throughout the world;

To keep our economy vigorous and free, that our people may lead fuller, happier lives;

To advance, not merely by our words but by our acts, the determination of our government that every citizen shall have opportunity to develop to his fullest capacity.

As we do these things, before us is a future filled with opportunity and hope. That future will be ours if in our time we keep alive the patience, the courage, the confidence in tomorrow, the deep faith, of the millions who, in years past, made and preserved us this nation.

A decade ago, in the death and desolation of European battlefields, I saw the courage and resolution, I felt the inspiration, of American youth. In these young men I felt America's buoyant confidence and irresistible will-to-do. In them I saw, too, a devout America, humble before God.

And so, I know with all my heart—and I deeply believe that all Americans know—that, despite the anxieties of this divided world, our faith, and the cause in which we all believe, will surely prevail.

Dwight D. Eisenhower, 1953–1957

Message to Congress on the State of the Union
January 5, 1956

Dwight D. Eisenhower's fourth State of the Union address came at the start of a presidential election year. Although he had suffered a heart attack in 1955, Eisenhower opted to run again, and—as he had in 1952—trounced Democrat Adlai Stevenson on election day.

Due to his heart attack, Eisenhower did not deliver his address in person at the Capitol but instead broadcast a summary of it. As had been the case in his two previous State of the Union addresses, the president divided his speech into three major themes: world affairs; the economy; and human concerns facing Americans, such as health issues.

On the world front, the Cold War between the United States and the Soviet Union was still under way. The president discussed this ongoing struggle and stressed that the country needed to continue its connections with other democratic countries in opposition to communism. He noted that the United States had security pacts with more than forty countries, and he cited the importance of the United Nations in helping countries work together.

He also mentioned the summit meeting the previous year with the Soviet leaders, stating that they all agreed that nuclear war would be "an intolerable disaster."

Eisenhower urged economic assistance to less developed countries to help them remain free of "communist threats and enticements." He also mentioned various national security initiatives that were under way, including efforts to work with Canada on improved early warning systems.

President Eisenhower believed in the benefits of a balanced budget and projected that the budget would come into balance during the fiscal year ending in June. Taxes, he said, "should be reduced when we prudently can."

The national highway system was one of the domestic issues Eisenhower discussed. As he had before, he pushed for the interstate highway system to be funded. In 1956 legislation finally passed that funded the massive highway project; Eisenhower signed the landmark $25 billion measure into law that June.

The president also mentioned issues relating to Americans' "human concerns," including increased attention to child welfare services and help for the elderly. He called for a bipartisan commission to look into voting rights violations against black Americans.

In addition to his heart attack in 1955, Eisenhower would suffer an attack of ileitis, or small intestine inflammation, in June 1956 that sent him to the hospital for an operation. But the president's health issues did not pose a problem as he sought a second term that November; he won 457 electoral votes and 57.4 percent of the popular vote to Stevenson's 73 electoral votes and 42 percent of the vote.

To the Congress of the United States:

The opening of this new year must arouse in us all grateful thanks to a kind Providence whose protection has been ever present and whose bounty has been manifold and abundant. The State of the Union today demonstrates what can be accomplished under God by a free people; by their vision, their understanding of national problems, their initiative, their self-reliance, their capacity for work—and by their willingness to sacrifice whenever sacrifice is needed.

In the past three years, responding to what our people want their Government to do, the Congress and the Executive have done much in building a stronger, better America. There has been broad progress in fostering the energies of our people, in providing greater opportunity for the satisfaction of their needs, and in fulfilling their demands for the strength and security of the Republic.

Our country is at peace. Our security posture commands respect. A spiritual vigor marks our national life. Our economy, approaching the 400 billion dollar mark, is at an unparalleled level of prosperity. The national income is more widely and fairly distributed than ever before. The number of Americans at work has reached an all-time high. As a people, we are achieving ever higher standards of living—earning more, producing more, consuming more, building more and investing more than ever before.

Virtually all sectors of our society are sharing in these good times. Our farm families, if we act wisely, imaginatively and promptly to strengthen our present farm programs, can also look forward to sharing equitably in the prosperity they have helped to create.

War in Korea ended two and a half years ago. The collective security system has been powerfully strengthened. Our defenses have been reinforced at sharply reduced costs. Programs to expand world trade and to harness the atom for the betterment of mankind have been carried forward. Our economy has been freed from governmental wage and price controls. Inflation has been halted; the cost of living stabilized.

Government spending has been cut by more than ten billion dollars. Nearly three hundred thousand positions have been eliminated from the Federal payroll. Taxes have been substantially reduced. A balanced budget is in prospect. Social security has been extended to ten million more Americans and unemployment insurance to four million more. Unprecedented advances in civil rights have been made. The long-standing and deep-seated problems of agriculture have been forthrightly attacked.

This record of progress has been accomplished with a self imposed caution against unnecessary and unwise interference in the private affairs of our people, of their communities and of the several States.

If we of the Executive and Legislative Branches, keeping this caution ever in mind, address ourselves to the business of the year before us—and to the unfinished business of last year—with resolution, the outlook is bright with promise.

Many measures of great national importance recommended last year to the Congress still demand immediate attention legislation for school and highway construction; health and immigration legislation; water resources legislation; legislation to complete the implementation of our foreign economic policy; such labor legislation as amendments of the Labor-Management Relations Act, extension of the Fair Labor Standards Act to additional groups not now covered, and occupational safety legislation; and legislation for construction of an atomic-powered exhibit vessel.

Many new items of business likewise require our attention—measures that will further promote the release of the energies of our people; that will broaden opportunity for all of them; that will advance the Republic in its leadership toward a just peace; measures, in short, that are essential to the building of an ever-stronger, ever-better America.

Every political and economic guide supports a valid confidence that wise effort will be rewarded by an even more plentiful harvest of human benefit than we now enjoy. Our resources are too many, our principles too dynamic, our purposes too worthy and the issues at stake too immense for us to entertain doubt or fear. But our responsibilities require that we approach this year's business with a sober humility.

A heedless pride in our present strength and position would blind us to the facts of the past, to the pitfalls of the future. We must walk ever in the knowledge that we are enriched by a heritage earned in the labor and sacrifice of our forebears; that, for our children's children, we are trustees of a great Republic and a time-tested political system; that we prosper as a cooperating member of the family of nations.

In this light the Administration has continued work on its program for the Republic, begun three years ago. Because the vast spread of national and human interests is involved within it, I shall not in this Message attempt its detailed delineation. Instead, from time to time during this Session, there will be submitted to the Congress specific recommendations within specific fields. In the comprehensive survey required for their preparation, the Administration is guided by enduring objectives. The first is:

The Discharge of Our World Responsibility

Our world policy and our actions are dedicated to the achievement of peace with justice for all nations.

With this purpose, we move in a wide variety of ways and through many agencies to remove the pall of fear; to strengthen the ties with our partners and to improve the cooperative cohesion of the free world; to reduce the burden of armaments, and to stimulate and inspire action among all nations for a world of justice and prosperity and peace. These national objectives are fully supported by both our political parties.

In the past year, our search for a more stable and just peace has taken varied forms. Among the most important were the two Conferences at Geneva, in July and in the fall of last year. We explored the possibilities of agreement on critical issues that jeopardize the peace.

The July meeting of Heads of Government held out promise to the world of moderation in the bitterness, of word and action, which tends to generate conflict and war. All were in agreement that a nuclear war would be an intolerable disaster which must not be permitted to occur. But in October, when the Foreign Ministers met again, the results demonstrated conclusively that the Soviet leaders are not yet willing to create the indispensable conditions for a secure and lasting peace.

Nevertheless, it is clear that the conflict between international communism and freedom has taken on a new complexion.

We know the Communist leaders have often practiced the tactics of retreat and zigzag. We know that Soviet and Chinese communism still poses a serious threat to the free world. And in the Middle East recent Soviet moves are hardly compatible with the reduction of international tension.

Yet Communist tactics against the free nations have shifted in emphasis from reliance on violence and the threat of violence to reliance on division, enticement and duplicity. We must be well prepared to meet the current tactics which pose a dangerous though less obvious threat. At the same time, our policy must be dynamic as well as flexible, designed primarily to forward the achievement of our own objectives rather than to meet each shift and change on the Communist front. We must act in the firm assurance that the fruits of freedom are more attractive and desirable to mankind in the pursuit of happiness than the record of Communism.

In the face of Communist military power, we must, of course, continue to maintain an effective system of collective security. This involves two things—a system which gives clear warning that armed aggression will be met by joint action of the free nations, and deterrent military power to make that warning effective. Moreover, the awesome power of the atom must be made to serve as a guardian of the free community and of the peace.

In the last year, the free world has seen major gains for the system of collective security: the accession to the North Atlantic Treaty Organization and Western European Union of the sovereign Federal German Republic; the developing cooperation under the Southeast Asia Collective Defense Treaty; and the formation in the Middle East of the Baghdad Pact among Turkey, Iraq, Iran, Pakistan and the United Kingdom. In our own hemisphere, the inter-American system has continued to show its vitality in maintaining peace and a common approach to world problems. We now have security pacts with more than 40 other nations.

In the pursuit of our national purposes, we have been steadfast in our support of the United Nations, now entering its second decade with a wider membership and ever-increasing influence and usefulness. In the release of our fifteen fliers from Communist China, an essential prelude was the world opinion mobilized by the General Assembly, which condemned their imprisonment and demanded their liberation. The successful Atomic Energy Conference held in Geneva under United Nations auspices and our Atoms for Peace program have been practical steps toward the world-wide use of this new energy source. Our sponsorship of such use has benefited our relations with other countries. Active negotiations are now in progress to create an International Agency to foster peaceful uses of atomic energy.

During the past year the crucial problem of disarmament has moved to the forefront of practical political endeavor. At Geneva, I declared the readiness of the United States to exchange blueprints of the military establishments of our nation and the USSR, to be confirmed by reciprocal aerial reconnaissance. By this means, I felt mutual suspicions could be allayed and an atmosphere developed in which negotiations looking toward limitation of arms would have improved chances of success.

In the United Nations Subcommittee on Disarmament last fall, this proposal was explored and the United States also declared itself willing to include reciprocal ground inspection of key points. By the overwhelming vote of 56 to 7, the United Nations on December 16 endorsed these proposals and gave them a top priority. Thereby, the issue is placed squarely before the bar of world opinion. We shall persevere in seeking a general reduction of armaments under effective inspection and control which are essential safeguards to ensure reciprocity and protect the security of all.

In the coming year much remains to be done.

While maintaining our military deterrent, we must intensify our efforts to achieve a just peace. In Asia we shall continue to give help to nations struggling to maintain their freedom against the threat of Communist coercion or subversion. In Europe we shall endeavor to increase not only the military strength of the North Atlantic Alliance but also its political cohesion and unity of purpose. We shall give such assistance as is feasible to the recently renewed effort of Western European nations to achieve a greater measure of integration, such as in the field of peaceful uses of atomic energy.

In the Near East we shall spare no effort in seeking to promote a fair solution of the tragic dispute between the Arab States and Israel, all of whom we want as our friends. The United States is ready to do its part to assure enduring peace in that area. We hope that both sides will make the contributions necessary to achieve that purpose. In Latin America, we shall continue to cooperate vigorously in trade and other measures designed to assist economic progress in the area.

Strong economic ties are an essential element in our free world partnership. Increasing trade and investment help all of us prosper together. Gratifying progress has been made in this direction, most recently by the three-year extension of our trade agreements legislation.

I most earnestly request that the Congress approve our membership in the Organization for Trade Cooperation, which would assist the carrying out of the General Agreement on Tariffs and Trade to which we have been a party since 1948. Our membership in the OTC will provide the most effective and expeditious means for removing discriminations and restrictions against American exports and in making our trade agreements truly reciprocal. United States membership in the Organization will evidence our continuing desire to cooperate in promoting an expanded trade among the free nations. Thus the Organization, as proposed, is admirably suited to our own interests and to those of like-minded nations in working for steady expansion of trade and closer economic cooperation. Being strictly an administrative entity, the Organization for Trade Cooperation cannot, of course, alter the control by Congress of the tariff, import, and customs policies of the United States.

We need to encourage investment overseas by avoiding unfair tax duplications, and to foster foreign trade by further simplification and improvement of our customs legislation.

We must sustain and fortify our Mutual Security Program. Because the conditions of poverty and unrest in less developed areas make their people a special target of international communism, there is a need to help them achieve the economic growth and stability necessary to preserve their independence against communist threats and enticements.

In order that our friends may better achieve the greater strength that is our common goal, they need assurance of continuity in economic assistance for development projects and programs which we approve and which require a period of years for planning and completion. Accordingly, I ask Congress to grant limited authority to make longer-term commitments for assistance to such projects, to be fulfilled from appropriations to be made in future fiscal years.

These various steps will powerfully strengthen the economic foundation of our foreign policy. Together with constructive action abroad, they will maintain the present momentum toward general economic progress and vitality of the free world.

In all things, change is the inexorable law of life. In much of the world the ferment of change is working strongly; but grave injustices are still uncorrected. We must not, by any sanction of ours, help to perpetuate these wrongs. I have particularly in mind the oppressive division of the German people, the bondage of millions elsewhere, and the exclusion of Japan from United Nations membership.

We shall keep these injustices in the forefront of human consciousness and seek to maintain the pressure of world opinion to fight these vast wrongs in the interest both of justice and secure peace.

Injustice thrives on ignorance. Because an understanding of the truth about America is one of our most powerful forces, I am recommending a substantial increase in budgetary support of the United States Information Agency.

The sum of our international effort should be this: the waging of peace, with as much resourcefulness, with as great a sense of dedication and urgency, as we have ever mustered in defense of our country in time of war. In this effort, our weapon is not force. Our weapons are the principles and ideas embodied in our historic traditions, applied with the same vigor that in the past made America a living promise of freedom for all mankind.

To accomplish these vital tasks, all of us should be concerned with the strength, effectiveness and morale of our State Department and our Foreign Service.

Another guide in the preparation of the Administration's program is:

The Constant Improvement of Our National Security

Because peace is the keystone of our national policy, our defense program emphasizes an effective flexible type of power calculated to deter or repulse any aggression and to preserve the peace. Short of war, we have never had military strength better adapted to our needs with improved readiness for emergency use. The maintenance of this strong military capability for the indefinite future will continue to call for a large share of our national budget. Our military programs must meet the needs of today. To build less would expose the nation to aggression. To build excessively, under the influence of fear, could defeat our purposes and impair or destroy the very freedom and economic system our military defenses are designed to protect.

We have improved the effectiveness and combat readiness of our forces by developing and making operational new weapons and by integrating the latest scientific developments, including new atomic weapons, into our military plans. We continue to push the production of the most modern military aircraft. The development of long-range missiles has been on an accelerated basis for some time. We are moving as rapidly as practicable toward nuclear-powered aircraft and ships. Combat capability, especially in terms of firepower, has been substantially increased. We have made the adjustments in personnel permitted by the cessation of the Korean War, the buildup of our allies and the introduction of new weapons. The services are all planning realistically on a long-term basis.

To strengthen our continental defenses the United States and Canada, in the closest cooperation, have substantially augmented early warning networks. Great progress is being made in extending surveillance of the Arctic, the Atlantic and the Pacific approaches to North America.

In the last analysis our real strength lies in the caliber of the men and women in our Armed Forces, active and Reserve. Much has been done to attract and hold capable military personnel, but more needs to be done. This year, I renew my request of last year for legislation to provide proper medical care for military dependents and a more equitable survivors' benefit program. The Administration will prepare additional recommendations designed to achieve the same objectives, including career incentives for medical and dental officers and nurses, and increases in the proportion of regular officers.

Closely related to the mission of the Defense Department is the task of the Federal Civil Defense Administration. A particular point of relationship arises from the fact that the key to civil defense is the expanded continental defense program, including the distant early warning system. Our Federal civil defense authorities have made progress in their program, and now comprehensive studies are being conducted jointly by the Federal Civil Defense Administration, the States, and critical target cities to determine the best procedures that can be adopted in case of an atomic attack. We must strengthen Federal assistance to the States and cities in devising the most effective common defense.

We have a broad and diversified mobilization base. We have the facilities, materials, skills and knowledge rapidly to expand the production of things we need for our defense whenever they are required. But mobilization base requirements change with changing technology and strategy. We must maintain flexibility to meet new requirements. I am requesting, therefore, that the Congress once again extend the Defense Production Act.

Of great importance to our nation's security is a continuing alertness to internal subversive activity within or without our government. This Administration will not relax its efforts to deal forthrightly and vigorously in protection of this government and its citizens against subversion, at the same time fully protecting the constitutional rights of all citizens.

A third objective of the Administration is:

Fiscal Integrity

A public office is, indeed, a public trust. None of its aspects is more demanding than the proper management of the public finances. I refer now not only to the indispensable virtues of plain honesty and trustworthiness but also to the prudent, effective and conscientious use of tax money. I refer also to the attitude of mind that makes efficient and economical service to the people a watchword in our government.

Over the long term, a balanced budget is a sure index to thrifty management—in a home, in a business or in the Federal Government. When achievement of a balanced budget is for long put off in a business or home, bankruptcy is the result. But in similar circumstances a government resorts to inflation of the money supply. This inevitably results in depreciation of the value of the money, and an increase in the cost of living. Every investment in personal security is threatened by this process of inflation, and the real values of the people's savings, whether in the form of insurance, bonds, pension and retirement funds or savings accounts are thereby shriveled.

We have made long strides these past three years in bringing our Federal finances under control. The deficit for fiscal year 1953 was almost 9½ billion dollars. Larger deficits seemed certain—deficits which would have depreciated the value of the dollar and pushed the cost of living still higher. But government waste and extravagance were searched out. Nonessential activities were dropped. Government expenses were carefully scrutinized. Total spending was cut by 14 billion dollars below the amount planned by the previous Administration for the fiscal year 1954.

This made possible—and it was appropriate in the existing circumstances of transition to a peacetime economy—the largest tax cut in any year in our history. Almost 7½ billion dollars were released and every taxpayer in the country benefited. Almost two-thirds of the savings went directly to individuals. This tax cut also helped to build up the economy, to make jobs in industry and to increase the production of the many things desired to improve the scale of living for the great majority of Americans.

The strong expansion of the economy, coupled with a constant care for efficiency in government operations and an alert guard against waste and duplication, has brought us to a prospective balance between income and expenditure. This is being done while we continue to strengthen our military security.

I expect the budget to be in balance during the fiscal year ending June 30, 1956.

I shall propose a balanced budget for the next fiscal year ending June 30, 1957.

But the balance we are seeking cannot be accomplished without the continuing every-day effort of the Executive and Legislative Branches to keep expenditures under control. It will also be necessary to continue all of the present excise taxes without any reduction and the corporation income taxes at their present rates for another year beyond next April 1st.

It is unquestionably true that our present tax level is very burdensome and, in the interest of long term and continuous economic growth, should be reduced when we prudently can. It is essential, in the sound management of the Government's finances, that we be mindful of our enormous national debt and of the obligation we have toward future Americans to reduce that debt whenever we can appropriately do so. Under conditions of high peacetime prosperity, such as now exist, we can never justify going further into debt to give ourselves a tax cut at the expense of our children. So, in the present state of our financial affairs, I earnestly believe that a tax cut can be deemed justifiable only when it will not unbalance the budget, a budget which makes provision for some reduction, even though modest, in our national debt. In this way we can best maintain fiscal integrity.

A fourth aim of our program is:

To Foster a Strong Economy

Our competitive enterprise system depends on the energy of free human beings, limited by prudent restraints in law, using free markets to plan, organize and distribute production, and spurred by the prospect of reward for successful effort. This system has developed our resources. It has marvelously expanded our productive capacity. Against the record of all other economic systems devised through the ages, this competitive system has proved the most creative user of human skills in the development of physical resources, and the richest rewarder of human effort.

This is still true in this era when improved living standards and rising national requirements are accompanied by swift advances in technology and rapid obsolescence in machines and methods. Typical of these are the strides made in construction of plants to produce electrical energy from atomic power and of laboratories and installations for the application of this new force in industry, agriculture and the healing arts. These developments make it imperative—to assure effective functioning of our enterprise system—that the Federal Government concern itself with certain broad areas of our economic life. Most important of these is:

Agriculture

Our farm people are not sharing as they should in the general prosperity. They alone of all major groups have seen their incomes decline rather than rise. They are caught between two millstones—rising production costs and declining prices. Such harm to a part of the national economy so vitally important to everyone is of great concern to us all. No other resource is so indispensable as the land that feeds and clothes us. No group is more fundamental to our national life than our farmers.

In successful prosecution of the war, the nation called for the utmost effort of its farmers. Their response was superb, their contribution unsurpassed. Farmers are not now to be blamed for the mountainous, price-depressing surpluses produced in response to wartime policies and laws that were too long continued. War markets are not the markets of peacetime. Failure to recognize that basic fact by a timely adjustment of wartime legislation brought its inevitable result in peacetime—surpluses, lower prices and lower incomes for our farmers.

The dimensions of government responsibility are as broad and complex as the farm problem itself. We are here concerned not only with our essential continuing supplies of food and fiber, but also with a way of life. Both are indispensable to the well-being and strength of the nation. Consideration of these matters must be above and beyond politics. Our national farm policy, so vital to the welfare of farm people and all of us, must not become a field for political warfare. Too much is at stake.

Our farm people expect of us, who have responsibility for their government, understanding of their problems and the will to help solve them. Our objective must be to help bring production into balance with existing and new markets, at prices that yield farmers a return for their work in line with what other Americans get.

To reach this goal, deep-seated problems must be subjected to a stepped-up attack. There is no single easy solution. Rather, there must be a many-sided assault on the stubborn problems of surpluses, prices, costs, and markets; and a steady, persistent, imaginative advance in the relationship between farmers and their government.

In a few days, by special message, I shall lay before the Congress my detailed recommendations for new steps that should be taken promptly to speed the transition in agriculture and thus assist our farmers to achieve their fair share of the national income.

Basic to this program will be a new attack on the surplus problem—for even the best-conceived farm program cannot work under a multi-billion dollar weight of accumulated stocks.

I shall urge authorization of a soil bank program to alleviate the problem of diverted acres and an overexpanded agricultural plant. This will include an acreage reserve to reduce current and accumulated surpluses of crops in most serious difficulty, and a conservation reserve to achieve other needed adjustments in the use of agricultural resources. I shall urge measures to strengthen our surplus disposal activities.

I shall propose measures to strengthen individual commodity programs, to remove controls where possible, to reduce carryovers, and to stop further accumulations of surpluses. I shall ask the Congress to provide substantial new funds for an expanded drive on the research front, to develop new markets, new crops, and new uses. The Rural Development Program to better the lot of low-income farm families deserves full Congressional support. The Great Plains Program must go forward vigorously. Advances on these and other fronts will pull down the price-depressing surpluses and raise farm income.

In this time of testing in agriculture, we should all together, regardless of party, carry forward resolutely with a sound and forward looking program on which farm people may confidently depend, now and for years to come.

I shall briefly mention four other subjects directly related to the well-being of the economy, preliminary to their fuller discussion in the Economic Report and later communications.

Resources Conservation

I wish to re-emphasize the critical importance of the wise use and conservation of our great natural resources of land, forests, minerals and water and their long-range development consistent with our agricultural policy. Water in particular now plays an increasing role in industrial processes, in the irrigation of land, in electric power, as well as in domestic uses. At the same time, it has the potential of damage and disaster.

A comprehensive legislative program for water conservation will be submitted to the Congress during the Session. The development of our water resources cannot be accomplished overnight. The need is such that we must make faster progress and without delay. Therefore, I strongly recommend that action be taken at this Session on such wholly Federal projects as the Colorado River Storage Project and the Frying-pan-Arkansas Project; on the John Day partnership project, and other projects which provide for cooperative action between the Federal Government and non-Federal interests; and on legislation, which makes provision for Federal participation in small projects under the primary sponsorship of agencies of State and local government.

During the past year the areas of our National Parks have been expanded, and new wildlife refuges have been created. The visits of our people to the Parks have increased much more rapidly than have the facilities to care for them. The Administration will submit recommendations to provide more adequate facilities to keep abreast of the increasing interest of our people in the great outdoors.

Disaster Assistance

A modern community is a complex combination of skills, specialized buildings, machines, communications and homes. Most importantly, it involves human lives. Disaster in many forms—by flood, frost, high winds, for instance—can destroy on a massive scale in a few hours the labor of many years.

Through the past three years the Administration has repeatedly moved into action wherever disaster struck. The extent of State participation in relief activities, however, has been far from uniform and, in many cases, has been either inadequate or nonexistent. Disaster assistance legislation requires overhauling and an experimental program of flood-damage indemnities should be undertaken. The Administration will make detailed recommendations on these subjects.

Area Redevelopment

We must help deal with the pockets of chronic unemployment that here and there mar the nation's general industrial prosperity. Economic changes in recent years have been often so rapid and far-reaching that areas committed to a single local resource or industrial activity have found themselves temporarily deprived of their markets and their livelihood.

Such conditions mean severe hardship for thousands of people as the slow process of adaptation to new circumstances goes on. This process can be speeded up. Last year I authorized a major study of the problem to find additional steps to supplement existing programs for the redevelopment of areas of chronic unemployment. Recommendations will be submitted, designed to supplement, with Federal technical and loan assistance local efforts to get on with this vital job. Improving such communities must, of course, remain the primary responsibility of the people living there and of their States. But a soundly conceived Federal partnership program can be of real assistance to them in their efforts.

Highway Legislation

Legislation to provide a modern, interstate highway system is even more urgent this year than last, for 12 months have now passed in which we have fallen further behind in road construction needed for the personal safety, the general prosperity, the national security of the American people. During the year, the number of motor vehicles has increased from 58 to 61 million. During the past year over 38,000 persons lost their lives in highway accidents, while the fearful toll of injuries and property damage has gone on unabated.

In my message of February 22, 1955, I urged that measures be taken to complete the vital 40,000 mile interstate system over a period of 10 years at an estimated Federal cost of approximately 25 billion dollars. No program was adopted.

If we are ever to solve our mounting traffic problem, the whole interstate system must be authorized as one project, to be completed approximately within the specified time. Only in this way can industry efficiently gear itself to the job ahead. Only in this way can the required planning and engineering be accomplished without the confusion and waste unavoidable in a piecemeal approach. Furthermore, as I pointed out last year, the pressing nature of this problem must not lead us to solutions outside the bounds of sound fiscal management. As in the case of other pressing problems, there must be an adequate plan of financing. To continue the drastically needed improvement in other national highway systems, I recommend the continuation of the Federal Aid Highway Program.

Aside from agriculture and the four subjects specifically mentioned, an integral part of our efforts to foster a strong and expanding free economy is keeping open the door of opportunity to new and small enterprises, checking monopoly, and preserving a competitive environment. In this past year the steady improvement in the economic health of small business has reinforced the vitality of our competitive economy. We shall continue to help small business concerns to obtain access to adequate financing and to competent counsel on management, production, and marketing problems.

Through measures already taken, opportunities for small business participation in government procurement programs, including military procurement, are greatly improved. The effectiveness of these measures will become increasingly apparent. We shall continue to make certain that small business has a fair opportunity to compete and has an economic environment in which it may prosper.

In my message last year I referred to the appointment of an advisory committee to appraise and report to me on the deficiencies as well as the effectiveness of existing Federal transportation policies. I have commended the fundamental purposes and objectives of the committee's report. I earnestly recommend that the Congress give prompt attention to the committee's proposals.

Essential to a prosperous economic environment for all business, small and large— for agriculture and industry and commerce—is efficiency in Government. To that end, exhaustive studies of the entire governmental structure were made by the Commission on Intergovernmental Relations and the Commission on the Organization of the Executive Branch of the Government—the reports of these Commissions are now under intensive review and already in the process of implementation in important areas.

One specific and most vital governmental function merits study and action by the Congress. As part of our program of promoting efficiency in Government and getting the fiscal situation in hand, the Post Office Department in the past three years has been overhauled. Nearly one thousand new post offices have been provided. Financial practices have been modernized, and transportation and operating methods are being constantly improved. A new wage and incentive plan for the half million postal employees has been established. Never before has the postal system handled so much mail so quickly and so economically.

The Post Office Department faces two serious problems. First, much of its physical plant—post offices and other buildings—is obsolete and inadequate. Many new buildings and the modernization of present ones are essential if we are to have improved mail service. The second problem is the Department's fiscal plight. It now faces an annual deficit of one-half billion dollars.

Recommendations on postal facilities and on additional postal revenues will be submitted to the Congress.

A final consideration in our program planning is:

The Response to Human Concerns

A fundamental belief shines forth in this Republic. We believe in the worth and dignity of the individual. We know that if we are to govern ourselves wisely—in the tradition of America—we must have the opportunity to develop our individual capacities to the utmost.

To fulfill the individual's aspirations in the American way of life, good education is fundamental. Good education is the outgrowth of good homes, good communities, good churches, and good schools. Today our schools face pressing problems—problems which will not yield to swift and easy solutions, or to any single action. They will yield only to a continuing, active, formed effort by the people toward achieving better schools.

This kind of effort has been spurred by the thousands of conferences held in recent months by half a million citizens and educators in all parts of the country, culminating in the White House Conference on Education. In that Conference, some two thousand delegates, broadly representative of the nation, studied together the problems of the nation's schools.

They concluded that the people of the United States must make a greater effort through their local, State, and Federal Governments to improve the education of our youth. This expression from the people must now be translated into action at all levels of government.

So far as the Federal share of responsibility is concerned, I urge that the Congress move promptly to enact an effective program of Federal assistance to help erase the existing deficit of school classrooms. Such a program, which should be limited to a five-year period, must operate to increase rather than decrease local and State support of schools and to give the greatest help to the States and localities with the least financial resources. Federal aid should in no way jeopardize the freedom of local school systems. There will be presented to the Congress a recommended program of Federal assistance for school construction.

Such a program should be accompanied by action to increase services to the nation's schools by the Office of Education and by legislation to provide continuation of payments to school districts where Federal activities have impaired the ability of those districts to provide adequate schools.

Under the 1954 Amendments to the old-age and survivors' insurance program, protection was extended to some 10 million additional workers and benefits were increased. The system now helps protect 9 out of 10 American workers and their families against loss of income in old age or on the death of the breadwinner. The system is sound. It must be kept so. In developing improvements in the system, we must give the most careful consideration to population and social trends, and to fiscal requirements. With these considerations in mind, the Administration will present its recommendations for further expansion of coverage and other steps which can be taken wisely at this time.

Other needs in the area of social welfare include increased child welfare services, extension of the program of aid to dependent children, intensified attack on juvenile delinquency, and special attention to the problems of mentally retarded children. The training of more skilled workers for these fields and the quest for new knowledge through research in social welfare are essential. Similarly the problems of our aged people need our attention.

The nation has made dramatic progress in conquering disease—progress of profound human significance which can be greatly accelerated by an intensified effort in medical research. A well-supported, well-balanced program of research, including basic research, can open new frontiers of knowledge, prevent and relieve suffering, and prolong life. Accordingly I shall recommend a substantial increase in Federal funds for the support of such a program. As an integral part of this effort, I shall recommend a new plan to aid construction of non-Federal medical research and teaching facilities and to help provide more adequate support for the training of medical research manpower.

Finally, we must aid in cushioning the heavy and rising costs of illness and hospitalization to individuals and families. Provision should be made, by Federal reinsurance or otherwise, to foster extension of voluntary health insurance coverage to many more persons, especially older persons and those in rural areas. Plans should be evolved to improve protection against the costs of prolonged or severe illness. These measures will help reduce the dollar barrier between many Americans and the benefits of modern medical care.

The Administration health program will be submitted to the Congress in detail.

The response of government to human concerns embraces, of course, other measures of broad public interest, and of special interest to our working men and women. The need still exists for improvement of the Labor Management Relations Act. The recommendations I submitted to the Congress last year take into account not only the interests of labor and management but also the public welfare. The needed amendments should be enacted without further delay.

We must also carry forward the job of improving the wage hour law. Last year I requested the Congress to broaden the coverage of the minimum wage. I repeat that recommendation, and I pledge the full resources of the Executive Branch to assist the Congress in finding ways to attain this goal. Moreover, as requested last year, legislation should be passed to clarify and strengthen the eight-hour laws for the benefit of workers who are subject to Federal wage standards on Federal and Federally assisted construction and other public works.

The Administration will shortly propose legislation to assure adequate disclosure of the financial affairs of each employee pension and welfare plan and to afford substantial protection to their beneficiaries in accordance with the objectives outlined in my message of January 11, 1954. Occupational safety still demands attention, as I pointed out last year, and legislation to improve the Longshoremen's and Harbor Workers' Compensation Act is still needed. The improvement of the District of Columbia

Unemployment Insurance Law and legislation to provide employees in the District with non-occupational disability insurance are no less necessary now than 12 months ago. Legislation to apply the principle of equal pay for equal work without discrimination because of sex is a matter of simple justice. I earnestly urge the Congress to move swiftly to implement these needed labor measures.

In the field of human needs, we must carry forward the housing program, which is contributing so greatly to the well-being of our people and the prosperity of our economy. Home ownership is now advanced to the point where almost three of every five families in our cities, towns, and suburbs own the houses they live in.

For the housing program, most of the legislative authority already exists. However, a firm program of public housing is essential until the private building industry has found ways to provide more adequate housing for low-income families. The Administration will propose authority to contract for 35 thousand additional public housing units in each of the next 2 fiscal years for communities which will participate in an integrated attack on slums and blight.

To meet the needs of the growing number of older people, several amendments to the National Housing Act will be proposed to assist the private homebuilding industry as well as charitable and non-profit organizations.

With so large a number of the American people desiring to modernize and improve existing dwellings, I recommend that the Title 1 program for permanent improvements in the home be liberalized.

I recommend increases in the general FHA mortgage insurance authority; the extension of the FHA military housing program; an increase in the authorization for Urban Planning grants; in the special assistance authority of the Federal National Mortgage Association; and continued support of the college housing program in a way that will not discourage private capital from helping to meet the needs of our colleges.

The legislation I have recommended for workers in private industry should be accompanied by a parallel effort for the welfare of Government employees. We have accomplished much in this field, including a contributory life insurance program; equitable pay increases and a fringe benefits program, covering many needed personnel policy changes, from improved premium pay to a meaningful incentive award program.

Additional personnel management legislation is needed in this Session. As I stated last year, an executive pay increase is essential to efficient governmental management. Such an increase, together with needed adjustments in the pay for the top career positions, is also necessary to the equitable completion of the Federal pay program initiated last year. Other legislation will be proposed, including legislation for prepaid group health insurance for employees and their dependents and to effect major improvements in the Civil Service retirement system.

All of us share a continuing concern for those who have served this nation in the Armed Forces. The Commission on Veterans Pensions is at this time conducting a study of the entire field of veterans' benefits and will soon submit proposed improvements.

We are proud of the progress our people have made in the field of civil rights. In Executive Branch operations throughout the nation, elimination of discrimination and segregation is all but completed. Progress is also being made among contractors engaged in furnishing Government services and requirements. Every citizen now has the opportunity to fit himself for and to hold a position of responsibility in the service of his country. In the District of Columbia, through the voluntary cooperation of the people, discrimination and segregation are disappearing from hotels, theaters, restaurants and other facilities.

It is disturbing that in some localities allegations persist that Negro citizens are being deprived of their right to vote and are likewise being subjected to unwarranted economic pressures. I recommend that the substance of these charges be thoroughly examined by a Bipartisan Commission created by the Congress. It is hoped that such a commission will be established promptly so that it may arrive at findings which can receive early consideration.

The stature of our leadership in the free world has increased through the past three years because we have made more progress than ever before in a similar period to assure our citizens equality in justice, in opportunity and in civil rights. We must expand this effort on every front. We must strive to have every person judged and measured by what he is, rather than by his color, race or religion. There will soon be recommended to the Congress a program further to advance the efforts of the Government, within the area of Federal responsibility, to accomplish these objectives.

One particular challenge confronts us. In the Hawaiian Islands, East meets West. To the Islands, Asia and Europe and the Western Hemisphere, all the continents, have contributed their peoples and their cultures to display a unique example of a community that is a successful laboratory in human brotherhood.

Statehood, supported by the repeatedly expressed desire of the Islands' people and by our traditions, would be a shining example of the American way to the entire earth. Consequently, I urgently request this Congress to grant statehood for Hawaii. Also, in harmony with the provisions I last year communicated to the Senate and House Committees on Interior and Insular Affairs, I trust that progress toward statehood for Alaska can be made in this Session.

Progress is constant toward full integration of our Indian citizens into normal community life. During the past two years the Administration has provided school facilities for thousands of Indian children previously denied this opportunity. We must continue to meet the needs of increased numbers of Indian children. Provision should also be made for the education of adult Indians whose schooling in earlier years was neglected.

In keeping with our responsibility of world leadership and in our own self interest, I again point out to the Congress the urgent need for revision of the immigration and nationality laws. Our nation has always welcomed immigrants to our shores. The wisdom of such a policy is clearly shown by the fact that America has been built by immigrants and the descendants of immigrants. That policy must be continued realistically with present day conditions in mind.

I recommend that the number of persons admitted to this country annually be based not on the 1920 census but on the latest, the 1950 census. Provision should be made to allow for greater flexibility in the use of quotas so if one country does not use its share, the vacancies may be made available for the use of qualified individuals from other countries.

The law should be amended to permit the Secretary of State and the Attorney General to waive the requirements of fingerprinting on a reciprocal basis for persons coming to this country for temporary visits. This and other changes in the law are long overdue and should be taken care of promptly. Detailed recommendations for revision of the immigration laws will be submitted to the Congress.

I am happy to report substantial progress in the flow of immigrants under the Refugee Relief Act of 1953; however, I again request this Congress to approve without further delay the urgently needed amendments to that act which I submitted in the last Session. Because of the high prosperity in Germany and Austria, the number of immigrants from those countries will be reduced. This will make available thousands of unfilled openings which I recommend be distributed to Greece and Italy and to escapees from behind the Iron Curtain.

Once again I ask the Congress to join with me in demonstrating our belief in the right of suffrage. I renew my request that the principle of self-government be extended and the right of suffrage granted to the citizens of the District of Columbia.

To conclude: the vista before us is bright. The march of science, the expanding economy, the advance in collective security toward a just peace—in this threefold movement our people are creating new standards by which the future of the Republic may be judged.

Progress, however, will be realized only as it is more than matched by a continuing growth in the spiritual strength of the nation. Our dedication to moral values must be complete in our dealings abroad and in our relationships among ourselves. We have single-minded devotion to the common good of America. Never must we forget that this means the well-being, the prosperity, the security of all Americans in every walk of life.

To the attainment of these objectives, I pledge full energies of the Administration, as in the Session ahead, it works on a program for submission to you, the Congress of the United States.

Dwight D. Eisenhower, 1953–1957

Address to Congress on the State of the Union
January 10, 1957

President Dwight D. Eisenhower delivered his 1957 State of the Union address just a few months after having been triumphantly reelected to a second term. In his address, Eisenhower cited three governing principles on which the United States was founded: "a vigilant regard for human liberty," "a wise concern for human welfare," and "a ceaseless effort for human progress."

Among the domestic issues the president mentioned was civil rights. He repeated a call for various civil rights measures to be undertaken, including voting-rights legislation. The 1950s marked the start of the civil rights movement, including the arrest in 1955 of Rosa Parks, who would not relinquish her seat on a Montgomery, Alabama, bus to a white passenger. In 1957 Congress approved a civil rights bill that set up a civil rights section in the Justice Department and included some federal protections for voting rights. The legislation was considered weak, but it was the first civil rights bill since Reconstruction.

On the international front, Eisenhower once again discussed the need for the United States to work with other countries to ensure security. "The world has so shrunk that all free nations are our neighbors," he declared. He had stated what is known as the Eisenhower Doctrine in a message to Congress five days earlier; under that doctrine, the United States pledged to help countries in the Middle East against any communist aggression.

Later that year, in October, the Soviets would launch Sputnik, the first satellite in space; the event shocked the United States and pushed the country to increase its focus on science.

The president, despite having suffered a heart attack in 1955 and undergoing an operation for an intestinal problem in 1956, had easily defeated Democrat Adlai Stevenson, who also had been his 1952 opponent, in the November 1956 election. Eisenhower took 457 electoral votes and 57.4 percent of the popular vote, compared with Stevenson's 73 electoral votes and 42 percent of the popular vote. But the Congress remained in Democratic hands.

The president's first term had been a time of economic prosperity. Eisenhower—who had served as supreme commander of Allied forces in Europe during World War II—had presided over the end of the Korean War in 1953. But his eight years in office were also dominated by the ongoing Cold War with the communist Soviet Union.

To the Congress of the United States:

I appear before the Congress today to report on the State of the Union and the relationships of the Union to the other nations of the world. I come here, firmly convinced that at no time in the history of the Republic have circumstances more emphatically underscored the need, in all echelons of government, for vision and wisdom and resolution.

You meet in a season of stress that is testing the fitness of political systems and the validity of political philosophies. Each stress stems in part from causes peculiar to itself. But every stress is a reflection of a universal phenomenon.

In the world today, the surging and understandable tide of nationalism is marked by widespread revulsion and revolt against tyranny, injustice, inequality and poverty. As individuals, joined in a common hunger for freedom, men and women and even children pit their spirit against guns and tanks. On a larger scale, in an ever more persistent search for the self-respect of authentic sovereignty and the economic base on which national independence must rest, peoples sever old ties; seek new alliances; experiment—sometimes dangerously—in their struggle to satisfy these human aspirations.

Particularly, in the past year, this tide has changed the pattern of attitudes and thinking among millions. The changes already accomplished foreshadow a world transformed by the spirit of freedom. This is no faint and pious hope. The forces now at work in the minds and hearts of men will not be spent through many years. In the main, today's expressions of nationalism are, in spirit, echoes of our forefathers' struggle for independence.

This Republic cannot be aloof to these events heralding a new epoch in the affairs of mankind.

Our pledged word, our enlightened self-interest, our character as a Nation commit us to a high role in world affairs: a role of vigorous leadership, ready strength, sympathetic understanding.

The State of the Union, at the opening of the 85th Congress continues to vindicate the wisdom of the principles on which this Republic is founded. Proclaimed in the Constitution of the Nation and in many of our historic documents, and founded in devout religious convictions, these principles enunciate:

A vigilant regard for human liberty.

A wise concern for human welfare.

A ceaseless effort for human progress.

Fidelity to these principles, in our relations with other peoples, has won us new friendships and has increased our opportunity for service within the family of nations. The appeal of these principles is universal, lighting fires in the souls of men everywhere. We shall continue to uphold them, against those who deny them and in counselling with our friends.

At home, the application of these principles to the complex problems of our national life has brought us to an unprecedented peak in our economic prosperity and has exemplified in our way of life the enduring human values of mind and spirit.

Through the past four years these principles have guided the legislative programs submitted by the Administration to the Congress. As we attempt to apply them to current events, domestic and foreign, we must take into account the complex entity that is the United States of America; what endangers it; what can improve it.

The visible structure is our American economy itself. After more than a century and a half of constant expansion, it is still rich in a wide variety of natural resources. It is first among nations in its people's mastery of industrial skills. It is productive beyond our own needs of many foodstuffs and industrial products. It is rewarding to all our citizens in opportunity to earn and to advance in self-realization and in self-expression. It is fortunate in its wealth of educational and cultural and religious centers. It is vigorously dynamic in the limitless initiative and willingness to venture that characterize free enterprise. It is productive of a widely shared prosperity.

Our economy is strong, expanding, and fundamentally sound. But in any realistic appraisal, even the optimistic analyst will realize that in a prosperous period the principal threat to efficient functioning of a free enterprise system is inflation. We look back on four years of prosperous activities during which prices, the cost of living, have been relatively stable—that is, inflation has been held in check. But it is clear that the danger is always present, particularly if the government might become profligate in its expenditures or private groups might ignore all the possible results on our economy of unwise struggles for immediate gain.

This danger requires a firm resolution that the Federal Government shall utilize only a prudent share of the Nation's resources, that it shall live within its means, carefully measuring against need alternative proposals for expenditures.

Through the next four years, I shall continue to insist that the executive departments and agencies of Government search out additional ways to save money and manpower. I urge that the Congress be equally watchful in this matter.

We pledge the Government's share in guarding the integrity of the dollar. But the Government's efforts cannot be the entire campaign against inflation, the thief that can rob the individual of the value of the pension and social security he has earned during his productive life. For success, Government's efforts must be paralleled by the attitudes and actions of individual citizens.

I have often spoken of the purpose of this Administration to serve the national interest of 170 million people. The national interest must take precedence over temporary advantages which may be secured by particular groups at the expense of all the people.

In this regard I call on leaders in business and in labor to think well on their responsibility to the American people. With all elements of our society, they owe the Nation a vigilant guard against the inflationary tendencies that are always at work in a dynamic economy operating at today's high levels. They can powerfully help counteract or accentuate such tendencies by their wage and price policies.

Business in its pricing policies should avoid unnecessary price increases especially at a time like the present when demand in so many areas presses hard on short supplies. A reasonable profit is essential to the new investments that provide more jobs in an expanding economy. But business leaders must, in the national interest, studiously avoid those price rises that are possible only because of vital or unusual needs of the whole nation.

If our economy is to remain healthy, increases in wages and other labor benefits, negotiated by labor and management, must be reasonably related to improvements in productivity. Such increases are beneficial, for they provide wage earners with greater purchasing power. Except where necessary to correct obvious injustices, wage increases that outrun productivity, however, are an inflationary factor. They make for higher prices for the public generally and impose a particular hardship on those whose welfare depends on the purchasing power of retirement income and savings. Wage negotiations should also take cognizance of the right of the public generally to share in the benefits of improvements in technology.

Freedom has been defined as the opportunity for self-discipline. This definition has a special application to the areas of wage and price policy in a free economy. Should we persistently fail to discipline ourselves, eventually there will be increasing pressure on government to redress the failure. By that process freedom will step by step disappear. No subject on the domestic scene should more attract the concern of the friends of American working men and women and of free business enterprise than the forces that threaten a steady depreciation of the value of our money.

Concerning developments in another vital sector of our economy—agriculture—I am gratified that the long slide in farm income has been halted and that further improvement is in prospect. This is heartening progress. Three tools that we have developed—improved surplus disposal, improved price support laws, and the soil bank—are working to reduce price-depressing government stocks of farm products. Our concern for the well-being of farm families demands that we constantly search for new ways by which they can share more fully in our unprecedented prosperity. Legislative recommendations in the field of agriculture are contained in the Budget Message.

Our soil, water, mineral, forest, fish, and wildlife resources are being conserved and improved more effectively. Their conservation and development are vital to the present and future strength of the Nation. But they must not be the concern of the

Federal Government alone. State and local entities, and private enterprise should be encouraged to participate in such projects.

I would like to make special mention of programs for making the best uses of water, rapidly becoming our most precious natural resource, just as it can be, when neglected, a destroyer of both life and wealth. There has been prepared and published a comprehensive water report developed by a Cabinet Committee and relating to all phases of this particular problem.

In the light of this report, there are two things I believe we should keep constantly in mind. The first is that each of our great river valleys should be considered as a whole. Piecemeal operations within each lesser drainage area can be self-defeating or, at the very least, needlessly expensive. The second is that the domestic and industrial demands for water grow far more rapidly than does our population.

The whole matter of making the best use of each drop of water from the moment it touches our soil until it reaches the oceans, for such purposes as irrigation, flood control, power production, and domestic and industrial uses clearly demands the closest kind of cooperation and partnership between municipalities, States and the Federal Government. Through partnership of Federal, state and local authorities in these vast projects we can obtain the economy and efficiency of development and operation that springs from a lively sense of local responsibility.

Until such partnership is established on a proper and logical basis of sharing authority, responsibility and costs, our country will never have both the fully productive use of water that it so obviously needs and protection against disastrous flood.

If we fail in this, all the many tasks that need to be done in America could be accomplished only at an excessive cost, by the growth of a stifling bureaucracy, and eventually with a dangerous degree of centralized control over our national life.

In all domestic matters, I believe that the people of the United States will expect of us effective action to remedy past failure in meeting critical needs.

High priority should be given the school construction bill. This will benefit children of all races throughout the country—and children of all races need schools now. A program designed to meet emergency needs for more classrooms should be enacted without delay. I am hopeful that this program can be enacted on its own merits, uncomplicated by provisions dealing with the complex problems of integration. I urge the people in all sections of the country to approach these problems with calm and reason, with mutual understanding and good will, and in the American tradition of deep respect for the orderly processes of law and justice.

I should say here that we have much reason to be proud of the progress our people are making in mutual understanding—the chief buttress of human and civil rights. Steadily we are moving closer to the goal of fair and equal treatment of citizens without regard to race or color. But unhappily much remains to be done.

Last year the Administration recommended to the Congress a four-point program to reinforce civil rights. That program included:

(1) creation of a bipartisan commission to investigate asserted violations of civil rights and to make recommendations;
(2) creation of a civil rights division in the Department of Justice in charge of an Assistant Attorney General;

(3) enactment by the Congress of new laws to aid in the enforcement of voting rights; and

(4) amendment of the laws so as to permit the Federal Government to seek from the civil courts preventive relief in civil rights cases.

I urge that the Congress enact this legislation.

Essential to the stable economic growth we seek is a system of well-adapted and efficient financial institutions. I believe the time has come to conduct a broad national inquiry into the nature, performance and adequacy of our financial system, both in terms of its direct service to the whole economy and in terms of its function as the mechanism through which monetary and credit policy takes effect. I believe the Congress should authorize the creation of a commission of able and qualified citizens to undertake this vital inquiry. Out of their findings and recommendations the Administration would develop and present to the Congress any legislative proposals that might be indicated for the purpose of improving our financial machinery.

In this message it seems unnecessary that I should repeat recommendations involving our domestic affairs that have been urged upon the Congress during the past four years, but which, in some instances, did not reach the stage of completely satisfactory legislation.

The Administration will, through future messages either directly from me or from heads of the departments and agencies, transmit to the Congress specific recommendations. These will involve our financial and fiscal affairs, our military and civil defenses; the administration of justice; our agricultural economy; our domestic and foreign commerce; the urgently needed increase in our postal rates; the development of our natural resources; our labor laws, including our labor-management relations legislation, and vital aspects of the health, education and welfare of our people. There will be special recommendations dealing with such subjects as atomic energy, the furthering of public works, the continued efforts to eliminate government competition with the businesses of tax-paying citizens.

A number of legislative recommendations will be mentioned specifically in my forthcoming Budget Message, which will reach you within the week. That message will also recommend such sums as are needed to implement the proposed action.

Turning to the international scene:

The existence of a strongly armed imperialistic dictatorship poses a continuing threat to the free world's and thus to our own Nation's security and peace. There are certain truths to be remembered here.

First, America alone and isolated cannot assure even its own security. We must be joined by the capability and resolution of nations that have proved themselves dependable defenders of freedom. Isolation from them invites war. Our security is also enhanced by the immeasurable interest that joins us with all peoples who believe that peace with justice must be preserved, that wars of aggression are crimes against humanity.

Another truth is that our survival in today's world requires modern, adequate, dependable military strength. Our Nation has made great strides in assuring a modern defense, so armed in new weapons, so deployed, so equipped, that today our security force is the most powerful in our peacetime history. It can punish heavily any enemy who undertakes to attack us. It is a major deterrent to war.

By our research and development more efficient weapons—some of amazing capabilities—are being constantly created. These vital efforts we shall continue. Yet we must not delude ourselves that safety necessarily increases as expenditures for military research or forces in being go up. Indeed, beyond a wise and reasonable level, which is always changing and is under constant study, money spent on arms may be money wasted on sterile metal or inflated costs, thereby weakening the very security and strength we seek.

National security requires far more than military power. Economic and moral factors play indispensable roles. Any program that endangers our economy could defeat us. Any weakening of our national will and resolution, any diminution of the vigor and initiative of our individual citizens, would strike a blow at the heart of our defenses.

The finest military establishment we can produce must work closely in cooperation with the forces of our friends. Our system of regional pacts, developed within the Charter of the United Nations, serves to increase both our own security and the security of other nations.

This system is still a recent introduction on the world scene. Its problems are many and difficult, because it insists on equality among its members and brings into association some nations traditionally divided. Repeatedly in recent months, the collapse of these regional alliances has been predicted. The strains upon them have been at times indeed severe. Despite these strains our regional alliances have proved durable and strong, and dire predictions of their disintegration have proved completely false.

With other free nations, we should vigorously prosecute measures that will promote mutual strength, prosperity and welfare within the free world. Strength is essentially a product of economic health and social well-being. Consequently, even as we continue our programs of military assistance, we must emphasize aid to our friends in building more productive economies and in better satisfying the natural demands of their people for progress. Thereby we shall move a long way toward a peaceful world.

A sound and safeguarded agreement for open skies, unarmed aerial sentinels, and reduced armament would provide a valuable contribution toward a durable peace in the years ahead. And we have been persistent in our effort to reach such an agreement. We are willing to enter any reliable agreement which would reverse the trend toward ever more devastating nuclear weapons; reciprocally provide against the possibility of surprise attack; mutually control the outer space missile and satellite development; and make feasible a lower level of armaments and armed forces and an easier burden of military expenditures. Our continuing negotiations in this field are a major part of our quest for a confident peace in this atomic age.

This quest requires as well a constructive attitude among all the nations of the free world toward expansion of trade and investment, that can give all of us opportunity to work out economic betterment.

An essential step in this field is the provision of an administrative agency to insure the orderly and proper operation of existing arrangements trader which multilateral trade is now carried on. To that end I urge Congressional authorization for United States membership in the proposed Organization for Trade Cooperation, an action which will speed removal of discrimination against our export trade.

We welcome the efforts of a number of our European friends to achieve an integrated community to develop a common market. We likewise welcome their cooperative effort in the field of atomic energy.

To demonstrate once again our unalterable purpose to make of the atom a peaceful servant of humanity, I shortly shall ask the Congress to authorize full United States participation in the International Atomic Energy Agency.

World events have magnified both the responsibilities and the opportunities of the United States Information Agency. Just as, in recent months, the voice of communism has become more shaken and confused, the voice of truth must be more clearly heard. To enable our Information Agency to cope with these new responsibilities and opportunities, I am asking the Congress to increase appreciably the appropriations for this program and for legislation establishing a career service for the Agency's overseas foreign service officers.

The recent historic events in Hungary demand that all free nations share to the extent of their capabilities in the responsibility of granting asylum to victims of Communist persecution. I request the Congress promptly to enact legislation to regularize the status in the United States of Hungarian refugees brought here as parolees. I shall shortly recommend to the Congress by special message the changes in our immigration laws that I deem necessary in the light of our world responsibilities.

The cost of peace is something we must face boldly, fearlessly. Beyond money, it involves changes in attitudes, the renunciation of old prejudices, even the sacrifice of some seeming self-interest.

Only five days ago I expressed to you the grave concern of your Government over the threat of Soviet aggression in the Middle East. I asked for Congressional authorization to help counter this threat. I say again that this matter is of vital and immediate importance to the Nation's and the free world's security and peace. By our proposed programs in the Middle East, we hope to assist in establishing a climate in which constructive and long-term solutions to basic problems of the area may be sought.

From time to time, there will be presented to the Congress requests for other legislation in the broad field of international affairs. All requests will reflect the steadfast purpose of this Administration to pursue peace, based on justice. Although in some cases details will be new, the underlying purpose and objectives will remain the same.

All proposals made by the Administration in this field are based on the free world's unity. This unity may not be immediately obvious unless we examine link by link the chain of relationships that binds us to every area and to every nation. In spirit the free world is one because its people uphold the right of independent existence for all nations. I have already alluded to their economic interdependence. But their interdependence extends also into the field of security.

First of all, no reasonable man will question the absolute need for our American neighbors to be prosperous and secure. Their security and prosperity are inextricably bound to our own. And we are, of course, already joined with these neighbors by historic pledges.

Again, no reasonable man will deny that the freedom and prosperity and security of Western Europe are vital to our own prosperity and security. If the institutions, the skills, the manpower of its peoples were to fall under the domination of an aggressive imperialism, the violent change in the balance of world power and in the pattern of world commerce could not be fully compensated for by any American measures, military or economic.

But these people, whose economic strength is largely dependent on free and uninterrupted movement of oil from the Middle East, cannot prosper—indeed, their economies would be severely impaired—should that area be controlled by an enemy and the movement of oil be subject to its decisions.

Next, to the Eastward, are Asiatic and Far Eastern peoples, recently returned to independent control of their own affairs or now emerging into sovereign statehood. Their potential strength constitutes new assurance for stability and peace in the world—if they can retain their independence. Should they lose freedom and be dominated by an aggressor, the world-wide effects would imperil the security of the free world.

In short, the world has so shrunk that all free nations are our neighbors. Without cooperative neighbors, the United States cannot maintain its own security and welfare, because:

First, America's vital interests are world-wide, embracing both hemispheres and every continent.

Second, we have community of interest with every nation in the free world.

Third, interdependence of interests requires a decent respect for the rights and the peace of all peoples.

These principles motivate our actions within the United Nations. There, before all the world, by our loyalty to them, by our practice of them, let us strive to set a standard to which all who seek justice and who hunger for peace can rally.

May we at home, here at the Seat of Government, in all the cities and towns and farmlands of America, support these principles in a personal effort of dedication. Thereby each of us can help establish a secure world order in which opportunity for freedom and justice will be more widespread, and in which the resources now dissipated on the armaments of war can be released for the life and growth of all humanity.

When our forefathers prepared the immortal document that proclaimed our independence, they asserted that every individual is endowed by his Creator with certain inalienable rights. As we gaze back through history to that date, it is clear that our nation has striven to live up to this declaration, applying it to nations as well as to individuals.

Today we proudly assert that the government of the United States is still committed to this concept, both in its activities at home and abroad.

The purpose is Divine; the implementation is human.

Our country and its government have made mistakes—human mistakes. They have been of the head—not of the heart. And it is still true that the great concept of the dignity of all men, alike created in the image of the Almighty, has been the compass by which we have tried and are trying to steer our course.

So long as we continue by its guidance, there will be true progress in human affairs, both among ourselves and among those with whom we deal.

To achieve a more perfect fidelity to it, I submit, is a worthy ambition as we meet together in these first days of this, the first session of the 85th Congress.

Dwight D. Eisenhower, 1957–1961

Address to Congress on the State of the Union

January 9, 1958

Dwight D. Eisenhower opted to devote his sixth State of the Union address to two major themes: ensuring U.S. safety through strength and working to build a genuine peace. He declared, "I am here to state what I believe to be right and what I believe to be wrong; and to propose action for correcting what I think wrong!"

The eight years of Eisenhower's presidency coincided with some of the most difficult years of the Cold War, which pitted the United States against the communist Soviet Union and lasted for more than four decades. As a result, many of Eisenhower's State of the Union addresses focused at least in part on world troubles. In this 1958 address the president cited "communist imperialism" as the threat to the United States and the world. "The Soviets are, in short, waging total cold war," he declared. So the United States, he said, must "wage total peace."

Eisenhower, who had been a top U.S. general in World War II, spent some time discussing the United States' military strength as compared with that of the Soviet Union—a topic of great concern in the nuclear era. He mentioned ballistic missiles, noting that since the end of the Korean War in 1953, the United States had spent $225 billion on its defensive shield.

In 1957 the Soviets had launched the first satellite into space, which had taken the United States by surprise. Eisenhower stated in his address that the country should not be taken by surprise on another front: Soviet economic initiatives. He commented that the United States should be focused on long-term economic aid and foreign trade initiatives.

The president also called for a reorganization of the Defense Department, which had been created in 1947 under the National Security Act. In 1958 the Department of Defense Reorganization Act was approved, which gave the defense secretary control over the military command system.

Eisenhower also stated that warning equipment was becoming increasingly important as long-range missiles were readied, and that the country must be ready in case of attack. He stressed the importance of U.S. economic aid to fight communism.

Toward the end of his speech he called for "a real first step toward disarmament," mentioning a United Nations General Assembly vote the previous August on a disarmament plan; the United States had supported the plan, he said, but the Soviet Union had rejected it. "[W]e will always go the extra mile with anyone on earth if it will bring us nearer a genuine peace," he said.

Mr. President, Mr. Speaker, Members of the 85th Congress:

It is again my high privilege to extend personal greetings to the members of the 85th Congress.

All of us realize that, as this new session begins, many Americans are troubled about recent world developments which they believe may threaten our nation's safety. Honest men differ in their appraisal of America's material and intellectual strength, and the dangers that confront us. But all know these dangers are real.

The purpose of this message is to outline the measures that can give the American people a confidence—just as real—in their own security.

I am not here to justify the past, gloss over the problems of the present, or propose easy solutions for the future.

I am here to state what I believe to be right and what I believe to be wrong; and to propose action for correcting what I think wrong!

I.

There are two tasks confronting us that so far outweigh all others that I shall devote this year's message entirely to them. The first is to ensure our safety through strength.

As to our strength, I have repeatedly voiced this conviction: We now have a broadly based and efficient defensive strength, including a great deterrent power, which is, for the present, our main guarantee against war; but, unless we act wisely and promptly, we could lose that capacity to deter attack or defend ourselves.

My profoundest conviction is that the American people will say, as one man: No matter what the exertions or sacrifices, we shall maintain that necessary strength!

But we could make no more tragic mistake than merely to concentrate on military strength.

For if we did only this, the future would hold nothing for the world but an Age of Terror.

And so our second task is to do the constructive work of building a genuine peace. We must never become so preoccupied with our desire for military strength that we neglect those areas of economic development, trade, diplomacy, education, ideas and principles where the foundations of real peace must be laid.

II.

The threat to our safety, and to the hope of a peaceful world, can be simply stated. It is communist imperialism.

This threat is not something imagined by critics of the Soviets. Soviet spokesmen, from the beginning, have publicly and frequently declared their aim to expand their power, one way or another, throughout the world.

The threat has become increasingly serious as this expansionist aim has been reinforced by an advancing industrial, military and scientific establishment.

But what makes the Soviet threat unique in history is its all-inclusiveness. Every human activity is pressed into service as a weapon of expansion. Trade, economic development, military power, arts, science, education, the whole world of ideas—all are harnessed to this same chariot of expansion.

The Soviets are, in short, waging total cold war.

The only answer to a regime that wages total cold war is to wage total peace.

This means bringing to bear every asset of our personal and national lives upon the task of building the conditions in which security and peace can grow.

III.

Among our assets, let us first briefly glance at our military power.

Military power serves the cause of security by making prohibitive the cost of any aggressive attack.

It serves the cause of peace by holding up a shield behind which the patient constructive work of peace can go on.

But it can serve neither cause if we make either of two mistakes. The one would be to overestimate our strength, and thus neglect crucially important actions in the period just ahead. The other would be to underestimate our strength. Thereby we might be tempted to become irresolute in our foreign relations, to dishearten our friends, and to lose our national poise and perspective in approaching the complex problems ahead.

Any orderly balance-sheet of military strength must be in two parts. The first is the position as of today. The second is the position in the period ahead.

As of today: our defensive shield comprehends a vast complex of ground, sea, and air units, superbly equipped and strategically deployed around the world. The most powerful deterrent to war in the world today lies in the retaliatory power of our Strategic Air Command and the aircraft of our Navy. They present to any potential attacker who would unleash war upon the world the prospect of virtual annihilation of his own country.

Even if we assume a surprise attack on our bases, with a marked reduction in our striking power, our bombers would immediately be on their way in sufficient strength to accomplish this mission of retaliation. Every informed government knows this. It is no secret.

Since the Korean Armistice, the American people have spent $225 billion in maintaining and strengthening this overall defensive shield. This is the position as of today.

Now as to the period ahead: Every part of our military establishment must and will be equipped to do its defensive job with the most modern weapons and methods. But it is particularly important to our planning that we make a candid estimate of the effect of long-range ballistic missiles on the present deterrent power I have described.

At this moment, the consensus of opinion is that we are probably somewhat behind the Soviets in some areas of long-range ballistic missile development. But it is my conviction, based on close study of all relevant intelligence, that if we make the necessary effort, we will have the missiles, in the needed quantity and in time, to sustain and strengthen the deterrent power of our increasingly efficient bombers. One encouraging fact evidencing this ability is the rate of progress we have achieved since we began to concentrate on these missiles.

The intermediate ballistic missiles, Thor and Jupiter, have already been ordered into production. The parallel progress in the intercontinental ballistic missile effort will be advanced by our plans for acceleration. The development of the submarine-based Polaris missile system has progressed so well that its future procurement schedules are being moved forward markedly.

When it is remembered that our country has concentrated on the development of ballistic missiles for only about a third as long as the Soviets, these achievements show a rate of progress that speaks for itself. Only a brief time back, we were spending at the rate of only about one million dollars a year on long range ballistic missiles. In 1957 we spent more than one billion dollars on the Arias, Titan, Thor, Jupiter, and Polaris programs alone.

But I repeat, gratifying though this rate of progress is, we must still do more!

Our real problem, then, is not our strength today; it is rather the vital necessity of action today to ensure our strength tomorrow.

What I have just said applies to our strength as a single country. But we are not alone. I have returned from the recent NATO meeting with renewed conviction that, because we are a part of a world-wide community of free and peaceful nations, our own security is immeasurably increased.

By contrast, the Soviet Union has surrounded itself with captive and sullen nations. Like a crack in the crust of an uneasily sleeping volcano, the Hungarian uprising revealed the depth and intensity of the patriotic longing for liberty that still burns within these countries.

The world thinks of us as a country which is strong, but which will never start a war. The world also thinks of us as a land which has never enslaved anyone and which is animated by humane ideals. This friendship, based on common ideals, is one of our greatest sources of strength.

It cements into a cohesive security arrangement the aggregate of the spiritual, military and economic strength of all those nations which, with us, are allied by treaties and agreements.

Up to this point, I have talked solely about our military strength to deter a possible future war.

I now want to talk about the strength we need to win a different kind of war—one that has already been launched against us.

It is the massive economic offensive that has been mounted by the communist imperialists against free nations.

The communist imperialist regimes have for some time been largely frustrated in their attempts at expansion based directly on force. As a result, they have begun to concentrate heavily on economic penetration, particularly of newly-developing countries, as a preliminary to political domination.

This non-military drive, if underestimated, could defeat the free world regardless of our military strength. This danger is all the greater precisely because many of us fail or refuse to recognize it. Thus, some people may be tempted to finance our extra military effort by cutting economic assistance. But at the very time when the economic threat is assuming menacing proportions, to fail to strengthen our own effort would be nothing less than reckless folly!

Admittedly, most of us did not anticipate the psychological impact upon the world of the launching of the first earth satellite. Let us not make the same kind of mistake in another field, by failing to anticipate the much more serious impact of the Soviet economic offensive.

As with our military potential, our economic assets are more than equal to the task. Our independent farmers produce an abundance of food and fibre. Our free workers are versatile, intelligent, and hardworking. Our businessmen are imaginative and resourceful. The productivity, the adaptability of the American economy is the solid foundation-stone of our security structure.

We have just concluded another prosperous year. Our output was once more the greatest in the nation's history. In the latter part of the year, some decline in employment and output occurred, following the exceptionally rapid expansion of recent years. In a free economy, reflecting as it does the independent judgments of millions of people, growth typically moves forward unevenly. But the basic forces of growth remain unimpaired. There are solid grounds for confidence that economic growth will be resumed without an extended interruption. Moreover, the Federal government, constantly alert to signs of weakening in any part of our economy, always stands ready, with its full power, to take any appropriate further action to promote renewed business expansion.

If our history teaches us anything, it is this lesson: so far as the economic potential of our nation is concerned, the believers in the future of America have always been the realists. I count myself as one of this company.

Our long-range problem, then, is not the stamina of our enormous engine of production. Our problem is to make sure that we use these vast economic forces confidently and creatively, not only in direct military defense efforts, but likewise in our foreign policy, through such activities as mutual economic aid and foreign trade.

In much the same way, we have tremendous potential resources on other non-military fronts to help in countering the Soviet threat: education, science, research, and, not least, the ideas and principles by which we live. And in all these cases the task ahead is to bring these resources more sharply to bear upon the new tasks of security and peace in a swiftly-changing world.

IV.

There are many items in the Administration's program, of a kind frequently included in a State of the Union Message, with which I am not dealing today. They are important to us and to our prosperity. But I am reserving them for treatment in separate communications because of my purpose today of speaking only about matters bearing directly upon our security and peace.

I now place before you an outline of action designed to focus our resources upon the two tasks of security and peace.

In this special category I list eight items requiring action. They are not merely desirable. They are imperative.

1. Defense Reorganization

The first need is to assure ourselves that military organization facilitates rather than hinders the functioning of the military establishment in maintaining the security of the nation.

Since World War II, the purpose of achieving maximum organizational efficiency in a modern defense establishment has several times occasioned action by the Congress and by the Executive.

The advent of revolutionary new devices, bringing with them the problem of over-all continental defense, creates new difficulties, reminiscent of those attending the advent of the airplane half a century ago.

Some of the important new weapons which technology has produced do not fit into any existing service pattern. They cut across all services, involve all services, and transcend all services, at every stage from development to operation. In some instances they defy classification according to branch of service.

Unfortunately, the uncertainties resulting from such a situation, and the jurisdictional disputes attending upon it, tend to bewilder and confuse the public and create the impression that service differences are damaging the national interest.

Let us proudly remember that the members of the Armed Forces give their basic allegiance solely to the United States. Of that fact all of us are certain. But pride of service and mistaken zeal in promoting particular doctrine has more than once occasioned the kind of difficulty of which I have just spoken.

I am not attempting today to pass judgment on the charge of harmful service rivalries. But one thing is sure. Whatever they are, America wants them stopped.

Recently I have had under special study the never-ending problem of efficient organization, complicated as it is by new weapons. Soon my conclusions will be finalized. I shall promptly take such Executive action as is necessary and, in a separate message, I shall present appropriate recommendations to the Congress.

Meanwhile, without anticipating the detailed form that a reorganization should take, I can state its main lines in terms of objectives:

A major purpose of military organization is to achieve real unity in the Defense establishment in all the principal features of military activities. Of all these, one of the most important to our nation's security is strategic planning and control. This work must be done under unified direction.

The defense structure must be one which, as a whole, can assume, with top efficiency and without friction, the defense of America. The Defense establishment must therefore plan for a better integration of its defensive resources, particularly with respect to the newer weapons now building and under development. These obviously require full coordination in their development, production and use. Good organization can help assure this coordination.

In recognition of the need for single control in some of our most advanced development projects, the Secretary of Defense has already decided to concentrate into one organization all the anti-missile and satellite technology undertaken within the Department of Defense.

Another requirement of military organization is a clear subordination of the military services to duly constituted civilian authority. This control must be real; not merely on the surface.

Next there must be assurance that an excessive number of compartments in organization will not create costly and confusing compartments in our scientific and industrial effort.

Finally, to end inter-service disputes requires clear organization and decisive central direction, supported by the unstinted cooperation of every individual in the defense establishment, civilian and military.

2. Accelerated Defense Effort

The second major action item is the acceleration of the defense effort in particular areas affected by the fast pace of scientific and technological advance.

Some of the points at which improved and increased effort are most essential are these:

We must have sure warning in case of attack. The improvement of warning equipment is becoming increasingly important as we approach the period when long-range missiles will come into use.

We must protect and disperse our striking forces and increase their readiness for instant reaction. This means more base facilities and standby crews.

We must maintain deterrent retaliatory power. This means, among other things, stepped-up long range missile programs; accelerated programs for other effective missile systems; and, for some years, more advanced aircraft.

We must maintain freedom of the seas. This means nuclear submarines and cruisers; improved anti-submarine weapons; missile ships; and the like.

We must maintain all necessary types of mobile forces to deal with local conflicts, should there be need. This means further improvements in equipment, mobility, tactics and fire power.

Through increases in pay and incentive, we must maintain in the armed forces the skilled manpower modern military forces require.

We must be forward-looking in our research and development to anticipate and achieve the unimagined weapons of the future.

With these and other improvements, we intend to assure that our vigilance, power, and technical excellence keep abreast of any realistic threat we face.

3. Mutual Aid

Third: We must continue to strengthen our mutual security efforts. Most people now realize that our programs of military aid and defense support are an integral part of our own defense effort. If the foundations of the Free World structure were progressively allowed to crumble under the pressure of communist imperialism, the entire house of freedom would be in danger of collapse.

As for the mutual economic assistance program, the benefit to us is threefold. First, the countries receiving this aid become bulwarks against communist encroachment as their military defenses and economies are strengthened. Nations that are conscious of a steady improvement in their industry, education, health and standard of living are not apt to fall prey to the blandishments of communist imperialists.

Second, these countries are helped to reach the point where mutually profitable trade can expand between them and us.

Third, the mutual confidence that comes from working together on constructive projects creates an atmosphere in which real understanding and peace can flourish.

To help bring these multiple benefits, our economic aid effort should be made more effective.

In proposals for future economic aid, I am stressing a greater use of repayable loans, through the Development Loan Fund, through funds generated by sale of surplus farm products, and through the Export-Import Bank.

While some increase in Government funds will be required, it remains our objective to encourage shifting to the use of private capital sources as rapidly as possible.

One great obstacle to the economic aid program in the past has been, not a rational argument against it on the merits, but a catchword: "give-away program."

The real fact is that no investment we make in our own security and peace can pay us greater dividends than necessary amounts of economic aid to friendly nations. This is no "give-away."

Let's stick to facts!

We cannot afford to have one of our most essential security programs shot down with a slogan!

4. Mutual Trade

Fourth: Both in our national interest, and in the interest of world peace, we must have a five-year extension of the Trade Agreements Act with broadened authority to negotiate.

World trade supports a significant segment of American industry and agriculture. It provides employment for four and one-half million American workers. It helps supply our ever increasing demand for raw materials. It provides the opportunity for American free enterprise to develop on a worldwide scale. It strengthens our friends and increases their desire to be friends. World trade helps to lay the groundwork for peace by making all free nations of the world stronger and more self-reliant.

America is today the world's greatest trading nation. If we use this great asset wisely to meet the expanding demands of the world, we shall not only provide future opportunities for our own business, agriculture, and labor, but in the process strengthen our security posture and other prospects for a prosperous, harmonious world.

As President McKinley said, as long ago as 1901: "Isolation is no longer possible or desirable. . . . The period of exclusiveness is past."

5. Scientific Cooperation with Our Allies

Fifth: It is of the highest importance that the Congress enact the necessary legislation to enable us to exchange appropriate scientific and technical information with friendly countries as part of our effort to achieve effective scientific cooperation.

It is wasteful in the extreme for friendly allies to consume talent and money in solving problems that their friends have already solved—all because of artificial barriers to sharing. We cannot afford to cut ourselves off from the brilliant talents and minds of scientists in friendly countries. The task ahead will be hard enough without handcuffs of our own making.

The groundwork for this kind of cooperation has already been laid in discussions among NATO countries. Promptness in following through with legislation will be the best possible evidence of American unity of purpose in cooperating with our friends.

6. Education and Research

Sixth: In the area of education and research, I recommend a balanced program to improve our resources, involving an investment of about a billion dollars over a four year period. This involves new activities by the Department of Health, Education and Welfare designed principally to encourage improved teaching quality and student opportunities in the interests of national security. It also provides a five-fold increase in sums available to the National Science Foundation for its special activities in stimulating and improving science education.

Scrupulous attention has been paid to maintaining local control of educational policy, spurring the maximum amount of local effort, and to avoiding undue stress on the physical sciences at the expense of other branches of learning.

In the field of research, I am asking for substantial increases in basic research funds, including a doubling of the funds available to the National Science Foundation for this purpose.

But Federal action can do only a part of the job. In both education and research, redoubled exertions will be necessary on the part of all Americans if we are to rise to the demands of our times. This means hard work on the part of state and local governments, private industry, schools and colleges, private organizations and foundations, teachers, parents, and—perhaps most important of all—the student himself, with his bag of books and his homework.

With this kind of all-inclusive campaign, I have no doubt that we can create the intellectual capital we need for the years ahead, invest it in the right places—and do all this, not as regimented pawns, but as free men and women!

7. Spending and Saving

Seventh: To provide for this extra effort for security, we must apply stern tests of priority to other expenditures, both military and civilian. This extra effort involves, most immediately, the need for a supplemental defense appropriation of $1.3 billion for fiscal year 1958.

In the 1959 budget, increased expenditures for missiles, nuclear ships, atomic energy, research and development, science and education, a special contingency fund to deal with possible new technological discoveries, and increases in pay and incentives to obtain and retain competent manpower add up to a total increase over the comparable figures in the 1957 budget of about $4 billion.

I believe that, in spite of these necessary increases, we should strive to finance the 1959 security effort out of expected revenues. While we now believe that expected revenues and expenditures will roughly balance, our real purpose will be to achieve adequate security, but always with the utmost regard for efficiency and careful management.

This purpose will require the cooperation of Congress in making careful analysis of estimates presented, reducing expenditure on less essential military programs and installations, postponing some new civilian programs, transferring some to the states, and curtailing or eliminating others.

Such related matters as the national debt ceiling and tax revenues will be dealt with in later messages.

8. Works of Peace

My last call for action is not primarily addressed to the Congress and people of the United States. Rather, it is a message from the people of the United States to all other peoples, especially those of the Soviet Union.

This is the spirit of what we would like to say:

"In the last analysis, there is only one solution to the grim problems that lie ahead. The world must stop the present plunge toward more and more destructive weapons of war, and turn the corner that will start our steps firmly on the path toward lasting peace.

"Our greatest hope for success lies in a universal fact: the people of the world, as people, have always wanted peace and want peace now.

"The problem, then, is to find a way of translating this universal desire into action.

"This will require more than words of peace. It requires works of peace."

Now, may I try to give you some concrete examples of the kind of works of peace that might make a beginning in the new direction.

For a start our people should learn to know each other better. Recent negotiations in Washington have provided a basis in principle for greater freedom of communication and exchange of people. I urge the Soviet government to cooperate in turning principle into practice by prompt and tangible actions that will break down the unnatural barriers that have blocked the flow of thought and understanding between our people.

Another kind of work of peace is cooperation on projects of human welfare. For example, we now have it within our power to eradicate from the face of the earth that age-old scourge of mankind: malaria. We are embarking with other nations in an all-out five-year campaign to blot out this curse forever. We invite the Soviets to join with us in this great work of humanity.

Indeed, we would be willing to pool our efforts with the Soviets in other campaigns against the diseases that are the common enemy of all mortals—such as cancer and heart disease.

If people can get together on such projects, is it not possible that we could then go on to a full-scale cooperative program of Science for Peace?

We have as a guide and inspiration the success of our Atoms-for-Peace proposal, which in only a few years, under United Nations auspices, became a reality in the International Atomic Energy Agency.

A program of Science for Peace might provide a means of funneling into one place the results of research from scientists everywhere and from there making it available to all parts of the world.

There is almost no limit to the human betterment that could result from such cooperation. Hunger and disease could increasingly be driven from the earth. The age-old dream of a good life for all could, at long last, be translated into reality.

But of all the works of peace, none is more needed now than a real first step toward disarmament.

Last August the United Nations General Assembly, by an overwhelming vote, approved a disarmament plan that we and our allies sincerely believed to be fair and practical. The Soviets have rejected both the plan, and the negotiating procedure set up by the United Nations. As a result, negotiation on this supremely important issue is now at a stand-still.

But the world cannot afford to stand still on disarmament! We must never give up the search for a basis of agreement.

Our allies from time to time develop differing ideas on how to proceed. We must concert these convictions among ourselves. Thereafter, any reasonable proposal that holds promise for disarmament and reduction of tension must be heard, discussed, and, if possible, negotiated.

But a disarmament proposal, to hold real promise, must at the minimum have one feature: reliable means to ensure compliance by all. It takes actions and demonstrated integrity on both sides to create and sustain confidence. And confidence in a genuine disarmament agreement is vital, not only to the signers of the agreement, but also to the millions of people all over the world who are weary of tensions and armaments.

I say once more, to all peoples, that we will always go the extra mile with anyone on earth if it will bring us nearer a genuine peace.

Conclusion

These, then, are the ways in which we must funnel our energies more efficiently into the task of advancing security and peace.

These actions demand and expect two things of the American people: sacrifice, and a high degree of understanding. For sacrifice to be effective it must be intelligent. Sacrifice must be made for the right purpose and in the right place—even if that place happens to come close to home!

After all, it is no good demanding sacrifice in general terms one day, and the next day, for local reasons, opposing the elimination of some unneeded Federal facility.

It is pointless to condemn Federal spending in general, and the next moment condemn just as strongly an effort to reduce the particular Federal grant that touches one's own interest.

And it makes no sense whatever to spend additional billions on military strength to deter a potential danger, and then, by cutting aid and trade programs, let the world succumb to a present danger in economic guise.

My friends of the Congress: The world is waiting to see how wisely and decisively a free representative government will now act.

I believe that this Congress possesses and will display the wisdom promptly to do its part in translating into law the actions demanded by our nation's interests. But, to make law effective, our kind of government needs the full voluntary support of millions of Americans for these actions.

I am fully confident that the response of the Congress and of the American people will make this time of test a time of honor. Mankind then will see more clearly than ever that the future belongs, not to the concept of the regimented atheistic state, but to the people—the God-fearing, peace-loving people of all the world.

Dwight D. Eisenhower, 1957–1961

Address to Congress on the State of the Union

January 9, 1959

President Dwight D. Eisenhower delivered his seventh State of the Union address to Congress on January 9, 1959. In this address, the president focused once again on the conflict between the United States and the Soviet Union. The Cold War had been under way for more than a decade at this point and would continue for another three decades.

Eisenhower, appealing to Americans' reliance on faith to meet their challenges, stated that, in the Cold War battle, "for us the answer has always been found, and is still found in the devotion, the vision, the courage and the fortitude of our people."

One flashpoint in the hostile relationship between the two countries was Berlin. The former German capital had been divided into two segments in the wake of World War II; West Berlin was part of democratic West Germany while East Berlin was part of communist East Germany. The entire city was located inside East Germany.

In 1958 tensions over Berlin had increased; the Soviets had announced that they wanted the Western powers out of West Berlin. The Western countries refused. In his address, Eisenhower referred to this crisis, stating that the communists had "disdain" for international treaties and giving Berlin as an example. The United States would work with other allies to protect West Berlin, he said, linking its fate to those of "all free peoples." He declared in his speech that "there can be no such thing as Fortress America."

Eisenhower noted that national security expenses accounted for almost 60 percent of the federal budget and stated that his defense budget for the upcoming year would maintain a sensible defense and avoid waste.

The economy had been strong overall during his presidency, with an exception occurring during a recession in 1958. In his address, Eisenhower stated that while that recession had been under way a year earlier, it now was "fading into history." The president warned of the dangers of inflation and urged Congress to work with him on keeping federal spending in line.

Eisenhower, a Republican, had worked for the first two years of his presidency, 1953 and 1954, with a Republican-controlled Congress. But Democrats had won control of the House and Senate in the 1954 elections and had held on even during Eisenhower's landslide presidential election victory of 1956; his personal popularity apparently did not carry over to congressional elections. In the 1958 midterm elections, Democrats had scored major victories—as a result of the election they held 283 of 436 House seats and 64 of 98 Senate seats—to retain control in both houses for Eisenhower's last two years in office.

M r. President, Mr. Speaker, Members of the 86th Congress, my fellow citizens:

This is the moment when Congress and the Executive annually begin their cooperative work to build a better America.

One basic purpose unites us: To promote strength and security, side by side with liberty and opportunity.

As we meet today, in the 170th year of the Republic, our Nation must continue to provide—as all other free governments have had to do throughout time—a satisfactory answer to a question as old as history. It is: Can Government based upon liberty and the God-given rights of man, permanently endure when ceaselessly challenged by a dictatorship, hostile to our mode of life, and controlling an economic and military power of great and growing strength?

For us the answer has always been found, and is still found in the devotion, the vision, the courage and the fortitude of our people.

Moreover, this challenge we face, not as a single powerful nation, but as one that has in recent decades reached a position of recognized leadership in the Free World.

We have arrived at this position of leadership in an era of remarkable productivity and growth. It is also a time when man's power of mass destruction has reached fearful proportions.

Possession of such capabilities helps create world suspicion and tension. We, on our part, know that we seek only a just peace for all, with aggressive designs against no one. Yet we realize that there is uneasiness in the world because of a belief on the part of peoples that through arrogance, miscalculation or fear of attack, catastrophic war could be launched. Keeping the peace in today's world more than ever calls for the utmost in the nation's resolution, wisdom, steadiness and unremitting effort.

We cannot build peace through desire alone. Moreover, we have learned the bitter lesson that international agreements, historically considered by us as sacred, are regarded in Communist doctrine and in practice to be mere scraps of paper. The most recent proof of their disdain of international obligations, solemnly undertaken, is their announced intention to abandon their responsibilities respecting Berlin.

As a consequence, we can have no confidence in any treaty to which Communists are a party except where such a treaty provides within itself for self-enforcing mechanisms. Indeed, the demonstrated disregard of the Communists of their own pledges is one of the greatest obstacles to success in substituting the Rule of Law for rule by force.

Yet step by step we must strengthen the institutions of peace—a peace that rests upon justice—a peace that depends upon a deep knowledge and dear understanding by all peoples of the cause and consequences of possible failure in this great purpose.

To achieve this peace we seek to prevent war at any place and in any dimension. If, despite our best efforts, a local dispute should flare into armed hostilities, the next problem would be to keep the conflict from spreading, and so compromising freedom. In support of these objectives we maintain forces of great power and flexibility.

Our formidable air striking forces are a powerful deterrent to general war. Large and growing portions of these units can depart from their bases in a matter of minutes.

Similar forces are included in our naval fleets.

Ground and other tactical formations can move with swiftness and precision, when requested by friendly and responsible governments, to help curb threatened aggression. The stabilizing influence of this capacity has been dramatically demonstrated more than once over the past year.

Our military and related scientific progress has been highly gratifying.

Great strides have been made in the development of ballistic missiles. Intermediate range missiles are now being deployed in operational units. The Arias intercontinental ballistic missile program has been marked by rapid development as evidenced by recent successful tests. Missile training units have been established and launching sites are far along in construction.

New aircraft that fly at twice the speed of sound are entering our squadrons.

We have successfully placed five satellites in orbit, which have gathered information of scientific importance never before available. Our latest satellite illustrates our steady advance in rocketry and foreshadows new developments in world-wide communications.

Warning systems constantly improve.

Our atomic submarines have shattered endurance records and made historic voyages under the North Polar Sea.

A major segment of our national scientific and engineering community is working intensively to achieve new and greater developments. Advance in military technology requires adequate financing but, of course, even more, it requires talent and time.

All this is given only as a matter of history; as a record of our progress in space and ballistic missile fields in no more than four years of intensive effort. At the same time we clearly recognize that some of the recent Soviet accomplishments in this particular technology are indeed brilliant.

Under the law enacted last year the Department of Defense is being reorganized to give the Secretary of Defense full authority over the military establishment. Greater efficiency, more cohesive effort and speedier reaction to emergencies are among the many advantages we are already noting from these changes.

These few highlights point up our steady military gains. We are rightfully gratified by the achievements they represent. But we must remember that these imposing armaments are purchased at great cost.

National Security programs account for nearly sixty percent of the entire Federal budget for this coming fiscal year.

Modern weapons are exceedingly expensive.

The overall cost of introducing Atlas into our armed forces will average $35 million per missile on the firing line.

This year we are investing an aggregate of close to $7 billion in missile programs alone.

Other billions go for research, development, test and evaluation of new weapons systems.

Our latest atomic submarines will cost $50 millions each, while some special types will cost three times as much.

We are now ordering fighter aircraft which are priced at fifty times as much as the fighters of World War II.

We are buying certain bombers that cost their weight in gold.

These sums are tremendous, even when compared with the marvelous resiliency and capacity of our economy.

Such expenditures demand both balance and perspective in our planning for defense. At every turn, we must weigh, judge and select. Needless duplication of weapons and forces must be avoided.

We must guard against feverish building of vast armaments to meet glibly predicted moments of so-called "maximum peril." The threat we face is not sporadic or dated: It is continuous. Hence we must not be swayed in our calculations either by groundless fear or by complacency. We must avoid extremes, for vacillation between extremes is inefficient, costly, and destructive of morale. In these days of unceasing technological advance, we must plan our defense expenditures systematically and with care, fully recognizing that obsolescence compels the never-ending replacement of older weapons with new ones.

The defense budget for the coming year has been planned on the basis of these principles and considerations. Over these many months I have personally participated in its development.

The aim is a sensible posture of defense. The secondary aim is increased efficiency and avoidance of waste. Both are achieved by this budgetary plan.

Working by these guide lines I believe with all my heart that America can be as sure of the strength and efficiency of her armed forces as she is of their loyalty. I am equally sure that the nation will thus avoid useless expenditures which, in the name of security, might tend to undermine the economy and, therefore, the nation's safety.

Our own vast strength is only a part of that required for dependable security. Because of this we have joined with nearly 50 other nations in collective security arrangements. In these common undertakings each nation is expected to contribute what it can in sharing the heavy load. Each supplies part of a strategic deployment to protect the forward boundaries of freedom.

Constantly we seek new ways to make more effective our contribution to this system of collective security. Recently I have asked a Committee of eminent Americans of both parties to re-appraise our military assistance programs and the relative emphasis which should be placed on military and economic aid.

I am hopeful that preliminary recommendations of this Committee will be available in time to assist in shaping the Mutual Security program for the coming fiscal year.

Any survey of the free world's defense structure cannot fail to impart a feeling of regret that so much of our effort and resources must be devoted to armaments. At Geneva and elsewhere we continue to seek technical and other agreements that may help to open up, with some promise, the issues of international disarmament. America will never give up the hope that eventually all nations can, with mutual confidence, drastically reduce these non-productive expenditures.

II.

The material foundation of our national safety is a strong and expanding economy. This we have—and this we must maintain. Only with such an economy can we be secure and simultaneously provide for the well-being of our people.

A year ago the nation was experiencing a decline in employment and output. Today that recession is fading into history, and this without gigantic, hastily-improvised public works projects or untimely tax reductions. A healthy and vigorous recovery has been under way since last May. New homes are being built at the highest rate in several years. Retail sales are at peak levels. Personal income is at an all-time high.

The marked forward thrust of our economy reaffirms our confidence in competitive enterprise. But—clearly—wisdom and prudence in both the public and private sectors of the economy are always necessary.

Our outlook is this: 1960 commitments for our armed forces, the Atomic Energy Commission and Military Assistance exceed 47 billion dollars. In the foreseeable future they are not likely to be significantly lower. With an annual population increase of three million, other governmental costs are bound to mount.

After we have provided wisely for our military strength, we must judge how to allocate our remaining government resources most effectively to promote our well-being and economic growth.

Federal programs that will benefit all citizens are moving forward.
Next year we will be spending increased amounts on health programs; on Federal assistance to science and education; on the development of the nation's water resources; on the renewal of urban areas; and on our vast system of Federal-aid highways.

Each of these additional outlays is being made necessary by the surging growth of America.

Let me illustrate. Responsive to this growth, Federal grants and long term loans to assist 14 major types of capital improvements in our cities will total over 2 billion dollars in 1960—double the expenditure of two years ago. The major responsibility for development in these fields rests in the localities, even though the Federal Government will continue to do its proper part in meeting the genuine needs of a burgeoning population.

But the progress of our economy can more than match the growth of our needs. We need only to act wisely and confidently.

Here, I hope you will permit me to digress long enough to express something that is much on my mind.

The basic question facing us today is more than mere survival—the military defense of national life and territory. It is the preservation of a way of life.

We must meet the world challenge and at the same time permit no stagnation in America.

Unless we progress, we regress.

We can successfully sustain security and remain true to our heritage of freedom if we clearly visualize the tasks ahead and set out to perform them with resolution and fervor. We must first define these tasks and then understand what we must do to perform them.

If progress is to be steady we must have long term guides extending far ahead, certainly five, possibly even ten years. They must reflect the knowledge that before the end of five years we will have a population of over 190 million. They must be goals that stand high, and so inspire every citizen to climb always toward mounting levels of moral, intellectual and material strength. Every advance toward them must stir pride in individual and national achievements.

To define these goals, I intend to mobilize help from every available source.

We need more than politically ordained national objectives to challenge the best efforts of free men and women. A group of selfless and devoted individuals, outside of government, could effectively participate in making the necessary appraisal of the potentials of our future. The result would be establishment of national goals that would not only spur us on to our finest efforts, but would meet the stern test of practicality.

The Committee I plan will comprise educators and representatives of labor, management, finance, the professions and every other kind of useful activity.

Such a study would update and supplement, in the light of continuous changes in our society and its economy, the monumental work of the Committee on Recent Social Trends which was appointed in 1931 by President Hoover. Its report has stood the test of time and has had a beneficial influence on national development. The new Committee would be concerned, among other things, with the acceleration of our economy's growth and the living standards of our people, their health and education, their better assurance of life and liberty and their greater opportunities. It would also be concerned with methods to meet such goals and what levels of government—Local, State, or Federal—might or should be particularly concerned.

As one example, consider our schools, operated under the authority of local communities and states. In their capacity and in their quality they conform to no recognizable standards. In some places facilities are ample, in others meager. Pay of teachers ranges between wide limits, from the adequate to the shameful. As would be expected, quality of teaching varies just as widely. But to our teachers we commit the most valuable possession of the nation and of the family—our children.

We must have teachers of competence. To obtain and hold them we need standards. We need a National Goal. Once established I am certain that public opinion would compel steady progress toward its accomplishment.

Such studies would be helpful, I believe, to government at all levels and to all individuals. The goals so established could help us see our current needs in perspective. They will spur progress.

We do not forget, of course, that our nation's progress and fiscal integrity are interdependent and inseparable. We can afford everything we clearly need, but we cannot afford one cent of waste. We must examine every item of governmental expense critically. To do otherwise would betray our nation's future. Thrift is one of the characteristics that has made this nation great. Why should we ignore it now?

We must avoid any contribution to inflationary processes, which could disrupt sound growth in our economy.

Prices have displayed a welcome stability in recent months and, if we are wise and resolute, we will not tolerate inflation in the years to come. But history makes clear the risks inherent in any failure to deal firmly with the basic causes of inflation. Two of the most important of these causes are the wage-price spiral and continued deficit financing.

Inflation would reduce job opportunities, price us out of world markets, shrink the value of savings and penalize the thrift so essential to finance a growing economy.

Inflation is not a Robin Hood, taking from the rich to give to the poor. Rather, it deals most cruelly with those who can least protect themselves. It strikes hardest those millions of our citizens whose incomes do not quickly rise with the cost of living. When prices soar, the pensioner and the widow see their security undermined, the man of thrift sees his savings melt away; the white collar worker, the minister, and the teacher see their standards of living dragged down.

Inflation can be prevented. But this demands statesmanship on the part of business and labor leaders and of government at all levels.

We must encourage the self-discipline, the restraint necessary to curb the wage-price spiral and we must meet current costs from current revenue.

To minimize the danger of future soaring prices and to keep our economy sound and expanding, I shall present to the Congress certain proposals.

First, I shall submit a balanced budget for the next year, a year expected to be the most prosperous in our history. It is a realistic budget with wholly attainable objectives.

If we cannot live within our means during such a time of rising prosperity, the hope for fiscal integrity will fade. If we persist in living beyond our means, we make it difficult for every family in our land to balance its own household budget. But to live within our means would be a tangible demonstration of the self-discipline needed to assure a stable dollar.

The Constitution entrusts the Executive with many functions, but the Congress—and the Congress alone—has the power of the purse. Ultimately upon Congress rests responsibility for determining the scope and amount of Federal spending.

By working together, the Congress and the Executive can keep a balance between income and outgo. If this is done there is real hope that we can look forward to a time in the foreseeable future when needed tax reforms can be accomplished.

In this hope, I am requesting the Secretary of the Treasury to prepare appropriate proposals for revising, at the proper time, our tax structure, to remove inequities and to enhance incentives for all Americans to work, to save, and to invest. Such recommendations will be made as soon as our fiscal condition permits. These prospects will be brightened if 1960 expenditures do not exceed the levels recommended.

Second, I shall recommend to the Congress that the Chief Executive be given the responsibility either to approve or to veto specific items in appropriations and authorization bills. This would save tax dollars.

I assure you gentlemen that I know this recommendation has been made time and again by every President that has appeared in this hall for many years, but I say this, it still is one of the most important corrections that could be made in our annual expenditure program, because this would save tax dollars.

Third, to reduce Federal operations in an area where private enterprise can do the job, I shall recommend legislation for greater flexibility in extending Federal credit, and in improving the procedures under which private credits are insured or guaranteed. Present practices have needlessly added large sums to Federal expenditures.

Fourth, action is required to make more effective use of the large Federal expenditures for agriculture and to achieve greater fiscal control in this area.

Outlays of the Department of Agriculture for the current fiscal year for the support of farm prices on a very few farm products will exceed five billion dollars. That is a sum equal to approximately two-fifths of the net income of all farm operators in the entire United States.

By the end of this fiscal year it is estimated that there will be in Government hands surplus farm products worth about nine billion dollars. And by July 1, 1959, Government expenditures for storage, interest, and handling of its agricultural inventory will reach a rate of one billion dollars a year.

This level of expenditure for farm products could be made willingly for a temporary period if it were leading to a sound solution of the problem. But unfortunately this is not true. We need new legislation.

In the past I have sent messages to the Congress requesting greater freedom for our farmers to manage their own farms and greater freedom for markets to reflect the wishes of producers and consumers. Legislative changes that followed were appropriate in direction but did not go far enough.

The situation calls for prompt and forthright action. Recommendation for action will be contained in a message to be transmitted to the Congress shortly.

These fiscal and related actions will help create an environment of price stability for economic growth. However, certain additional measures are needed.

I shall ask Congress to amend the Employment Act of 1946 to make it clear that Government intends to use all appropriate means to protect the buying power of the dollar.

I am establishing a continuing Cabinet group on Price Stability for Economic Growth to study governmental and private policies affecting costs, prices, and economic growth. It will strive also to build a better public understanding of the conditions necessary for maintaining growth and price stability.

Studies are being undertaken to improve our information on prices, wages, and productivity.

I believe all citizens in all walks of life will support this program of action to accelerate economic growth and promote price stability.

III.

I take up next certain aspects of our international situation and our programs to strengthen it.

America's security can be assured only within a world community of strong, stable, independent nations, in which the concepts of freedom, justice and human dignity can flourish.

There can be no such thing as Fortress America. If ever we were reduced to the isolation implied by that term, we would occupy a prison, not a fortress. The question whether we can afford to help other nations that want to defend their freedom but cannot fully do so from their own means, has only one answer: we can and we must, we have been doing so since 1947.

Our foreign policy has long been dedicated to building a permanent and just peace.

During the past six years our free world security arrangements have been bolstered and the bonds of freedom have been more closely knit. Our friends in Western Europe are experiencing new internal vitality, and are increasingly more able to resist external threats.

Over the years the world has come to understand clearly that it is our firm policy not to countenance aggression. In Lebanon, Taiwan, and Berlin—our stand has been clear, right, and expressive of the determined will of a united people.

Acting with other free nations we have undertaken the solemn obligation to defend the people of free Berlin against any effort to destroy their freedom. In the meantime we shall constantly seek meaningful agreements to settle this and other problems, knowing full well that not only the integrity of a single city, but the hope of all free peoples is at stake.

We need, likewise, to continue helping to build the economic base so essential to the Free World's stability and strength.

The International Monetary Fund and the World Bank have both fully proven their worth as instruments of international financial cooperation. Their Executive Directors have recommended an increase in each member country's subscription. I am requesting the Congress for immediate approval of our share of these increases.

We are now negotiating with representatives of the twenty Latin American Republics for the creation of an inter-American financial institution. Its purpose would be to join all the American Republics in a common institution which would promote and finance development in Latin America, and make more effective the use of capital from the World Bank, the Export-Import Bank, and private sources.

Private enterprise continues to make major contributions to economic development in all parts of the world. But we have not yet marshalled the full potential of American business for this task, particularly in countries which have recently attained their independence. I shall present to this Congress a program designed to encourage greater participation by private enterprise in economic development abroad.

Further, all of us know that to advance the cause of freedom we must do much more than help build sound economies. The spiritual, intellectual, and physical strength of people throughout the world will in the last analysis determine their willingness and their ability to resist Communism.

To give a single illustration of our many efforts in these fields: We have been a participant in the effort that has been made over the past few years against one of the great scourges of mankind—disease. Through the Mutual Security program public health officials are being trained by American universities to serve in less developed countries. We are engaged in intensive malaria eradication projects in many parts of the world. America's major successes in our own country prove the feasibility of success everywhere.

By these and other means we shall continue and expand our campaign against the afflictions that now bring needless suffering and death to so many of the world's people. We wish to be part of a great shared effort toward the triumph of health.

IV.

America is best described by one word, freedom.

If we hope to strengthen freedom in the world we must be ever mindful of how our own conduct reacts elsewhere. No nation has ever been so floodlighted by world opinion as the United States is today. Everything we do is carefully scrutinized by other peoples throughout the world. The bad is seen along with the good.

Because we are human we err. But as free men we are also responsible for correcting the errors and imperfections of our ways.

Last January I made comprehensive recommendations to the Congress for legislation in the labor-management field. To my disappointment, Congress failed to act. The McClellan Committee disclosures of corruption, racketeering, and abuse of trust and power in labor-management affairs have aroused America and amazed other peoples. They emphasize the need for improved local law enforcement and the enactment of effective Federal legislation to protect the public interest and to insure the rights and economic freedoms of millions of American workers. Halfhearted measures will not do. I shall recommend prompt enactment of legislation designed:

To safeguard workers' funds in union treasuries against misuse of any kind whatsoever.

To protect the rights and freedoms of individual union members, including the basic right to free and secret elections of officers.

To advance true and responsible collective bargaining.

To protect the public and innocent third parties from unfair and coercive practices such as boycotting and blackmail picketing.

The workers and the public must have these vital protections.

In other areas of human rights—freedom from discrimination in voting, in public education, in access to jobs, and in other respects—the world is likewise watching our conduct.

The image of America abroad is not improved when school children, through closing of some of our schools and through no fault of their own, are deprived of their opportunity for an education.

The government of a free people has no purpose more noble than to work for the maximum realization of equality of opportunity under law. This is not the sole responsibility of any one branch of our government. The judicial arm, which has the ultimate authority for interpreting the Constitution, has held that certain state laws and practices discriminate upon racial grounds and are unconstitutional. Whenever the supremacy of the Constitution of the United States is challenged I shall continue to take every action necessary to uphold it.

One of the fundamental concepts of our constitutional system is that it guarantees to every individual, regardless of race, religion, or national origin, the equal protection of the laws. Those of us who are privileged to hold public office have a solemn obligation to make meaningful this inspiring objective. We can fulfill that obligation by our leadership in teaching, persuading, demonstrating, and in enforcing the law.

We are making noticeable progress in the field of civil rights—we are moving forward toward achievement of equality of opportunity for all people everywhere in the United States. In the interest of the nation and of each of its citizens, that progress must continue.

Legislative proposals of the Administration in this field will be submitted to the Congress early in the session. All of us should help to make clear that the government is united in the common purpose of giving support to the law and the decisions of the Courts.

By moving steadily toward the goal of greater freedom under law, for our own people, we shall be the better prepared to work for the cause of freedom under law throughout the world.

All peoples are solely tired of the fear, destruction, and the waste of war. As never before, the world knows the human and material costs of war and seeks to replace force with a genuine role of law among nations.

It is my purpose to intensify efforts during the coming two years in seeking ways to supplement the procedures of the United Nations and other bodies with similar objectives, to the end that the rule of law may replace the rule of force in the affairs of nations. Measures toward this end will be proposed later, including a re-examination of our own relation to the International Court of Justice.

Finally—let us remind ourselves that Marxist scripture is not new; it is not the gospel of the future. Its basic objective is dictatorship, old as history. What is new is the shining prospect that man can build a world where all can live in dignity.

We seek victory—not over any nation or people—but over the ancient enemies of us all; victory over ignorance, poverty, disease, and human degradation wherever they may be found. We march in the noblest of causes—human freedom.

If we make ourselves worthy of America's ideals, if we do not forget that our nation was founded on the premise that all men are creatures of God's making, the world will come to know that it is free men who carry forward the true promise of human progress and dignity.

Dwight D. Eisenhower, 1957–1961

Address to Congress on the State of the Union
January 7, 1960

Dwight D. Eisenhower delivered his eighth State of the Union address in an election year. Eisenhower, a Republican who was at the end of his second term, was a lame-duck president. As the first president inaugurated after passage of the 22nd Amendment in 1951, he was limited to two terms. His vice president, Richard Nixon, would face Democratic senator John F. Kennedy in November, ultimately losing in one of the closest elections in U.S. history.

As he had in past State of the Union addresses, Eisenhower focused at least in part on the world situation. The United States and the Soviet Union were still embroiled in the Cold War, and the arms race between the two was a major pre-occupation. The president stated that the most important fact facing the world was that "mankind approaches a state where mutual annihilation becomes a possibil-ity." As a result, the country needed to achieve appropriate levels of security, while also seeking "a just peace," he said.

Eisenhower voiced hope that a "somewhat less strained period" in the U.S.-Soviet rivalry could be approaching; he called for increased communication between the American and Russian people, as well as continued negotiations on a weapons-testing ban.

World politics were undergoing major shifts in this period, with many new coun-tries gaining independence from former colonial powers; Eisenhower noted that over the previous fifteen years, twenty countries had become independent. He stated that these countries would progress more effectively with technical and finan-cial assistance from the United States and its allies.

On the domestic front, one big change for the United States in 1959 had been the addition of two new states, Alaska and Hawaii. In his State of the Union address, Eisenhower referred to this development, stating that "we salute these two western stars proudly." The new states brought the total to fifty.

For most of his presidency, Eisenhower had worked with a Democratic Con-gress, a fact he mentioned in this address; he expressed gratitude to lawmakers and pledged cooperation for the remainder of his term.

Eisenhower, who was sixty-nine at the time of this speech, had been president for most of the 1950s, and his eight years in office were marked by the continuing Cold War as well as a generally prosperous economy. The election of 1960 would usher in both a new generation of presidential leadership and a new tone in Amer-ican politics.

Mr. President, Mr. Speaker, Members of the 86th Congress:

Seven years ago I entered my present office with one long-held resolve overriding all others. I was then, and remain now, determined that the United States shall become an ever more potent resource for the cause of peace—realizing that peace cannot be for ourselves alone, but for peoples everywhere. This determination is shared by the entire Congress—indeed, by all Americans.

My purpose today is to discuss some features of America's position, both at home and in her relations to others.

First, I point out that for us, annual self-examination is made a definite necessity by the fact that we now live in a divided world of uneasy equilibrium, with our side committed to its own protection and against aggression by the other.

With both sides of this divided world in possession of unbelievably destructive weapons, mankind approaches a state where mutual annihilation becomes a possibil-ity. No other fact of today's world equals this in importance—it colors everything we say, plan, and do.

There is demanded of us, vigilance, determination, and the dedication of whatever portion of our resources that will provide adequate security, especially a real deterrent to aggression. These things we are doing.

All these facts emphasize the importance of striving incessantly for a just peace.

Only through the strengthening of the spiritual, intellectual, economic and defensive resources of the Free World can we, in confidence, make progress toward this goal.

Second, we note that recent Soviet deportment and pronouncements suggest the possible opening of a somewhat less strained period in the relationships between the Soviet Union and the Free World. If these Pronouncements be genuine, there is brighter hope of diminishing the intensity of past rivalry and eventually of substituting persuasion for coercion. Whether this is to become an era of lasting promise remains to be tested by actions.

Third, we now stand in the vestibule of a vast new technological age—one that, despite its capacity for human destruction, has an equal capacity to make poverty and human misery obsolete. If our efforts are wisely directed—and if our unremitting efforts for dependable peace begin to attain some success—we can surely become participants in creating an age characterized by justice and rising levels of human well-being.

Over the past year the Soviet Union has expressed an interest in measures to reduce the common peril of war.

While neither we nor any other Free World nation can permit ourselves to be misled by pleasant promises until they are tested by performance, yet we approach this apparently new opportunity with the utmost seriousness. We must strive to break the calamitous cycle of frustrations and crises which, if unchecked, could spiral into nuclear disaster; the ultimate insanity.

Though the need for dependable agreements to assure against resort to force in settling disputes is apparent to both sides yet as in other issues dividing men and nations, we cannot expect sudden and revolutionary results. But we must find some place to begin.

One obvious road on which to make a useful start is in the widening of communication between our two peoples. In this field there are, both sides willing, countless opportunities—most of them well known to us all—for developing mutual understanding, the true foundation of peace.

Another avenue may be through the reopening, on January twelfth, of negotiations looking to a controlled ban on the testing of nuclear weapons. Unfortunately, the closing statement from the Soviet scientists who met with our scientists at Geneva in an unsuccessful effort to develop an agreed basis for a test ban, gives the clear impression that their conclusions have been politically guided. Those of the British and American scientific representatives are their own freely-formed, individual and collective opinion. I am hopeful that as new negotiations begin, truth—not political opportunism—will be the guiding light of the deliberations.

Still another avenue may be found in the field of disarmament, in which the Soviets have professed a readiness to negotiate seriously. They have not, however, made clear the plans they may have, if any, for mutual inspection and verification—the essential condition for any extensive measure of disarmament.

There is one instance where our initiative for peace has recently been successful. A multi-lateral treaty signed last month provides for the exclusively peaceful use of

Antarctica, assured by a system of inspection. It provides for free and cooperative scientific research in that continent, and prohibits nuclear explosions there pending general international agreement on the subject. The Treaty is a significant contribution toward peace, international cooperation, and the advancement of science. I shall transmit its text to the Senate for consideration and approval in the near future.

The United States is always ready to participate with the Soviet Union in serious discussion of these or any other subjects that may lead to peace with justice.

Certainly it is not necessary to repeat that the United States has no intention of interfering in the internal affairs of any nation; likewise we reject any attempt to impose its system on us or on other peoples by force or subversion.

This concern for the freedom of other peoples is the intellectual and spiritual cement which has allied us with more than forty other nations in a common defense effort. Not for a moment do we forget that our own fate is firmly fastened to that of these countries; we will not act in any way which would jeopardize our solemn commitments to them.

We and our friends are, of course, concerned with self-defense. Growing out of this concern is the realization that all people of the Free World have a great stake in the progress, in freedom, of the uncommitted and newly emerging nations. These peoples, desperately hoping to lift themselves to decent levels of living must not, by our neglect, be forced to seek help from, and finally become virtual satellites of, those who proclaim their hostility to freedom.

Their natural desire for a better life must not be frustrated by withholding from them necessary technical and investment assistance. This is a problem to be solved not by America alone, but also by every nation cherishing the same ideals and in position to provide help.

In recent years America's partners and friends in Western Europe and Japan have made great economic progress. Their newly found economic strength is eloquent testimony to the striking success of the policies of economic cooperation which we and they have pursued.

The international economy of 1960 is markedly different from that of the early postwar years. No longer is the United States the only major industrial country capable of providing substantial amounts of the resources so urgently needed in the newly-developing countries.

To remain secure and prosperous themselves, wealthy nations must extend the kind of cooperation to the less fortunate members that will inspire hope, confidence and progress. A rich nation can for a time, without noticeable damage to itself, pursue a course of self-indulgence, making its single goal the material ease and comfort of its own citizens—thus repudiating its own spiritual and material stake in a peaceful and prosperous society of nations. But the enmities it will incur, the isolation into which it will descend, and the internal moral and physical softness that will be engendered, will, in the long term, bring it to disaster.

America did not become great through softness and self-indulgence. Her miraculous progress and achievements flow from other qualities far more worthy and substantial—

—adherence to principles and methods consonant with our religious philosophy

—a satisfaction in hard work

—the readiness to sacrifice for worthwhile causes

—the courage to meet every challenge to her progress

—the intellectual honesty and capacity to recognize the true path of her own best interests.

To us and to every nation of the Free World, rich or poor, these qualities are necessary today as never before if we are to march together to greater security, prosperity and peace.

I believe the industrial countries are ready to participate actively in supplementing the efforts of the developing countries to achieve progress.

The immediate need for this kind of cooperation is underscored by the strain in our international balance of payments. Our surplus from foreign business transactions has in recent years fallen substantially short of the expenditures we make abroad to maintain our military establishments overseas, to finance private investment, and to provide assistance to the less developed nations. In 1959 our deficit in balance of payments approached $4 billion.

Continuing deficits of anything like this magnitude would, over time, impair our own economic growth and check the forward progress of the Free World.

We must meet this situation by promoting a rising volume of exports and world trade. Further, we must induce all industrialized nations of the Free World to work together in a new cooperative endeavor to help lift the scourge of poverty from less fortunate nations. This will provide for better sharing of this burden and for still further profitable trade.

New nations, and others struggling with the problems of development, will progress only if they demonstrate faith in their own destiny and possess the will and use their own resources to fulfill it. Moreover, progress in a national transformation can be only gradually earned; there is no easy and quick way to follow from the oxcart to the jet plane. But, just as we drew on Europe for assistance in our earlier years, so now do those new and emerging nations that have this faith and determination deserve help.

Over the last fifteen years, twenty nations have gained political independence. Others are doing so each year. Most of them are woefully lacking in technical capacity and in investment capital; without Free World support in these matters they cannot effectively progress in freedom.

Respecting their need, one of the major focal points of our concern is the South Asian region. Here, in two nations alone, are almost five hundred million people, all working, and working hard, to raise their standards, and in doing so, to make of themselves a strong bulwark against the spread of an ideology that would destroy liberty.

I cannot express to you the depth of my conviction that, in our own and Free World interests, we must cooperate with others to help these people achieve their legitimate ambitions, as expressed in their different multi-year plans. Through the World Bank and other instrumentalities, as well as through individual action by every nation in position to help, we must squarely face this titanic challenge.

All of us must realize, of course, that development in freedom by the newly emerging nations, is no mere matter of obtaining outside financial assistance. An indispensable element in this process is a strong and continuing determination on the part of these nations to exercise the national discipline necessary for any sustained development period. These qualities of determination are particularly essential because of the fact that the process of improvement will necessarily be gradual and laborious rather than revolutionary. Moreover, everyone should be aware that the development process is no short term phenomenon. Many years are required for even the most favorably situated countries.

I shall continue to urge the American people, in the interests of their own security, prosperity and peace, to make sure that their own part of this great project be amply and cheerfully supported. Free World decisions in this matter may spell the difference between world disaster and world progress in freedom.

Other countries, some of which I visited last month, have similar needs.

A common meeting ground is desirable for those nations which are prepared to assist in the development effort. During the past year I have discussed this matter with the leaders of several Western Nations.

Because of its wealth of experience, the Organization for European Economic Cooperation could help with initial studies. The goal is to enlist all available economic resources in the industrialized Free World—especially private investment capital. But I repeat that this help, no matter how great, can be lastingly effective only if it is used as a supplement to the strength of spirit and will of the people of the newly-developing nations.

By extending this help we hope to make possible the enthusiastic enrollment of these nations under freedom's banner. No more startling contrast to a system of sullen satellites could be imagined.

If we grasp this opportunity to build an age of productive partnership between the less fortunate nations and those that have already achieved a high state of economic advancement, we will make brighter the outlook for a world order based upon security, freedom and peace. Otherwise, the outlook could be dark indeed. We face what may be a turning point in history, and we must act decisively.

As a nation we can successfully pursue these objectives only from a position of broadly based strength.

No matter how earnest is our quest for guaranteed peace, we must maintain a high degree of military effectiveness at the same time we are engaged in negotiating the issue of arms reduction. Until tangible and mutually enforceable arms reduction measures are worked out, we will not weaken the means of defending our institutions.

America possesses an enormous defense power. It is my studied conviction that no nation will ever risk general war against us unless we should be so foolish as to neglect the defense forces we now so powerfully support. It is world-wide knowledge that any nation which might be tempted today to attack the United States, even though our country might sustain great losses, would itself promptly suffer a terrible destruction. But I once again assure all peoples and all nations that the United States, except in defense, will never turn loose this destructive power.

During the past year, our long-range striking power, unmatched today in manned bombers, has taken on new strength as the Atlas intercontinental ballistic missile has entered the operational inventory. In fourteen recent test launchings, at ranges of over 5,000 miles, Atlas has been striking on an average within two miles of the target. This is less than the length of a jet runway—well within the circle of total destruction. Such performance is a great tribute to American scientists and engineers, who in the past five years have had to telescope time and technology to develop these long-range ballistic missiles, where America had none before.

This year, moreover, growing numbers of nuclear-powered submarines will enter our active forces, some to be armed with Polaris missiles. These remarkable ships and weapons, ranging the oceans, will be capable of accurate fire on targets virtually anywhere on earth. Impossible to destroy by surprise attack, they will become one of our most effective sentinels for peace.

To meet situations of less than general nuclear war, we continue to maintain our carrier forces, our many service units abroad, our always ready Army strategic forces and Marine Corps divisions, and the civilian components. The continuing modernization of these forces is a costly but necessary process, and is scheduled to go forward at a rate which will steadily add to our strength.

The deployment of a portion of these forces beyond our shores, on land and sea, is persuasive demonstration of our determination to stand shoulder-to-shoulder with our allies for collective security. Moreover, I have directed that steps be taken to program our military assistance to these allies on a longer range basis. This is necessary for a sounder collective defense system.

Next I refer to our effort in space exploration, which is often mistakenly supposed to be an integral part of defense research and development.

First, America has made great contributions in the past two years to the world's fund of knowledge of astrophysics and space science. These discoveries are of present interest chiefly to the scientific community; but they are important foundation-stones for more extensive exploration of outer space for the ultimate benefit of all mankind.

Second, our military missile program, going forward so successfully, does not suffer from our present lack of very large rocket engines, which are so necessary in distant space exploration. I am assured by experts that the thrust of our present missiles is fully adequate for defense requirements.

Third, the United States is pressing forward in the development of large rocket engines to place much heavier vehicles into space for exploration purposes.

Fourth, in the meantime, it is necessary to remember that we have only begun to probe the environment immediately surrounding the earth. Using launch systems presently available, we are developing satellites to scout the world's weather; satellite relay stations to facilitate and extend communications over the globe; for navigation aids to give accurate bearings to ships and aircraft; and for perfecting instruments to collect and transmit the data we seek. This is the area holding the most promise for early and useful applications of space technology.

Fifth, we have just completed a year's experience with our new space law. I believe it deficient in certain particulars and suggested improvements will be submitted shortly.

The accomplishment of the many tasks I have alluded to requires the continuous strengthening of the spiritual, intellectual, and economic sinews of American life. The steady purpose of our society is to assure justice, before God, for every individual. We must be ever alert that freedom does not wither through the careless amassing of restrictive controls or the lack of courage to deal boldly with the giant issues of the day.

A year ago, when I met with you, the nation was emerging from an economic downturn, even though the signs of resurgent prosperity were not then sufficiently convincing to the doubtful. Today our surging strength is apparent to everyone. 1960 promises to be the most prosperous year in our history.

Yet we continue to be afflicted by nagging disorders.

Among current problems that require solution are:

—the need to protect the public interest in situations of prolonged labor-management stalemate;

—the persistent refusal to come to grips with a critical problem in one sector of American agriculture;

—the continuing threat of inflation, together with the persisting tendency toward fiscal irresponsibility;

—in certain instances the denial to some of our citizens of equal protection of the law.

Every American was disturbed by the prolonged dispute in the steel industry and the protracted delay in reaching a settlement.

We are all relieved that a settlement has at last been achieved in that industry. Percentagewise, by this settlement the increase to the steel companies in employment costs is lower than in any prior wage settlement since World War II. It is also gratifying to note that despite the increase in wages and benefits several of the major steel producers have announced that there will be no increase in steel prices at this time. The national interest demands that in the period of industrial peace which has been assured by the new contract both management and labor make every possible effort to increase efficiency and productivity in the manufacture of steel so that price increases can be avoided.

One of the lessons of this story is that the potential danger to the entire Nation of longer and greater strikes must be met. To insure against such possibilities we must of course depend primarily upon the good commonsense of the responsible individuals. It is my intention to encourage regular discussions between management and labor outside the bargaining table, to consider the interest of the public as well as their mutual interest in the maintenance of industrial peace, price stability and economic growth.

To me, it seems almost absurd for the United States to recognize the need, and so earnestly to seek, for cooperation among the nations unless we can achieve voluntary, dependable, abiding cooperation among the important segments of our own free society.

Failure to face up to basic issues in areas other than those of labor-management can cause serious strains on the firm freedom supports of our society.

I refer to agriculture as one of these areas.

Our basic farm laws were written 27 years ago, in an emergency effort to redress hardship caused by a world-wide depression. They were continued—and their economic distortions intensified—during World War II in order to provide incentives for production of food needed to sustain a war-torn free world.

Today our farm problem is totally different. It is that of effectively adjusting to the changes caused by a scientific revolution. When the original farm laws were written, an hour's farm labor produced only one fourth as much wheat as at present. Farm legislation is woefully out-of-date, ineffective, and expensive.

For years we have gone on with an outmoded system which not only has failed to protect farm income, but also has produced soaring, threatening surpluses. Our farms have been left producing for war while America has long been at peace.

Once again I urge Congress to enact legislation that will gear production more closely to markets, make costly surpluses more manageable, provide greater freedom in farm operations, and steadily achieve increased net farm incomes.

Another issue that we must meet squarely is that of living within our means. This requires restraint in expenditure, constant reassessment of priorities, and the maintenance of stable prices.

We must prevent inflation. Here is an opponent of so many guises that it is sometimes difficult to recognize. But our clear need is to stop continuous and general price rises—a need that all of us can see and feel.

To prevent steadily rising costs and prices calls for stern self-discipline by every citizen. No person, city, state, or organized group can afford to evade the obligation to resist inflation, for every American pays its crippling tax.

Inflation's ravages do not end at the water's edge. Increases in prices of the goods we sell abroad threaten to drive us out of markets that once were securely ours. Whether domestic prices, so high as to be noncompetitive, result from demands for too-high profit margins or from increased labor costs that outrun growth in productivity, the final result is seriously damaging to the nation.

We must fight inflation as we would a fire that imperils our home. Only by so doing can we prevent it from destroying our salaries, savings, pensions and insurance, and from gnawing away the very roots of a free, healthy economy and the nation's security.

One major method by which the Federal government can counter inflation and rising prices is to insure that its expenditures are below its revenues. The debt with which we are now confronted is about 290 billion dollars. With interest charges alone now costing taxpayers about 9$\frac{1}{2}$ billions, it is clear that this debt growth must stop. You will be glad to know that despite the unsettling influences of the recent steel strike, we estimate that our accounts will show, on June 30, this year, a favorable balance of approximately $200 million.

I shall present to the Congress for 1961 a balanced budget. In the area of defense, expenditures continue at the record peace-time levels of the last several years. With a single exception, expenditures in every major category of Health, Education and Welfare will be equal or greater than last year. In Space expenditures the amounts are practically doubled. But the over-all guiding goal of this budget is national need—not response to specific group, local or political insistence.

Expenditure increases, other than those I have indicated, are largely accounted for by the increased cost of legislation previously enacted.

I repeat, this budget will be a balanced one. Expenditures will be 79 billion 8 hundred million. The amount of income over outgo, described in the budget as a Surplus, to be applied against our national debt, is 4 billion 2 hundred million. Personally, I do not feel that any amount can be properly called a "Surplus" as long as the nation is in debt. I prefer to think of such an item as "reduction on our children's inherited mortgage." Once we have established such payments as normal practice, we can profitably make improvements in our tax structure and thereby truly reduce the heavy burdens of taxation.

In any event, this one reduction will save taxpayers, each year, approximately 2 hundred million dollars in interest costs.

This budget will help ease pressures in our credit and capital markets. It will enhance the confidence of people all over the world in the strength of our economy and our currency and in our individual and collective ability to be fiscally responsible.

In the management of the huge public debt the Treasury is unfortunately not free of artificial barriers. Its ability to deal with the difficult problems in this field has been weakened greatly by the unwillingness of the Congress to remove archaic restrictions. The need for a freer hand in debt management is even more urgent today because the costs of the undesirable financing practices which the Treasury has been forced into are mounting. Removal of this roadblock has high priority in my legislative recommendations.

Still another issue relates to civil rights.

In all our hopes and plans for a better world we all recognize that provincial and racial prejudices must be combated. In the long perspective of history, the right to vote has been one of the strongest pillars of a free society. Our first duty is to protect this right against all encroachment. In spite of constitutional guarantees, and notwithstanding much progress of recent years, bias still deprives some persons in this country of equal protection of the laws.

Early in your last session I recommended legislation which would help eliminate several practices discriminating against the basic rights of Americans. The Civil Rights Commission has developed additional constructive recommendations. I hope that these will be among the matters to be seriously considered in the current session. I trust that Congress will thus signal to the world that our Government is striving for equality under law for all our people.

Each year and in many ways our nation continues to undergo profound change and growth.

In the past 18 months we have hailed the entry of two more States of the Union— Alaska and Hawaii. We salute these two western stars proudly.

Our vigorous expansion, which we all welcome as a sign of health and vitality, is many-sided. We are, for example, witnessing explosive growth in metropolitan areas.

By 1975 the metropolitan areas of the United States will occupy twice the territory they do today. The roster of urban problems with which they must cope is staggering. They involve water supply, cleaning the air, adjusting local tax systems, providing for essential educational, cultural, and social services, and destroying those conditions which breed delinquency and crime.

In meeting these, we must, if we value our historic freedoms, keep within the traditional framework of our Federal system with powers divided between the national and state governments. The uniqueness of this system may confound the casual observer, but it has worked effectively for nearly 200 years.

I do not doubt that our urban and other perplexing problems can be solved in the traditional American method. In doing so we must realize that nothing is really solved and ruinous tendencies are set in motion by yielding to the deceptive bait of the "easy" Federal tax dollar.

Our educational system provides a ready example. All recognize the vital necessity of having modern school plants, well-qualified and adequately compensated teachers, and of using the best possible teaching techniques and curricula.

We cannot be complacent about educating our youth.

But the route to better trained minds is not through the swift administration of a

Federal hypodermic or sustained financial transfusion. The educational process, essentially a local and personal responsibility, cannot be made to leap ahead by crash, centralized governmental action.

The Administration has proposed a carefully reasoned program for helping eliminate current deficiencies. It is designed to stimulate classroom construction, not by substitution of Federal dollars for state and local funds, but by incentives to extend and encourage state and local efforts. This approach rejects the notion of Federal domination or control. It is workable, and should appeal to every American interested in advancement of our educational system in the traditional American way. I urge the Congress to take action upon it.

There is one other subject concerning which I renew a recommendation I made in my State of the Union Message last January. I then advised the Congress of my purpose to intensify our efforts to replace force with a rule of law among nations. From many discussions abroad, I am convinced that purpose is widely and deeply shared by other peoples and nations of the world.

In the same Message I stated that our efforts would include a reexamination of our own relation to the International Court of Justice. The Court was established by the United Nations to decide international legal disputes between nations. In 1946 we accepted the Court's jurisdiction, but subject to a reservation of the right to determine unilaterally whether a matter lies essentially within domestic jurisdiction. There is pending before the Senate, a Resolution which would repeal our present self-judging reservation. I support that Resolution and urge its prompt passage. If this is done, I intend to urge similar acceptance of the Court's jurisdiction by every member of the United Nations.

Here perhaps it is not amiss for me to say to the Members of the Congress, in this my final year of office, a word about the institutions we respectively represent and the meaning which the relationships between our two branches has for the days ahead.

I am not unique as a President in having worked with a Congress controlled by the opposition party—except that no other President ever did it for quite so long! Yet in both personal and official relationships we have weathered the storms of the past five years. For this I am grateful.

My deep concern in the next twelve months, before my successor takes office, is with our joint Congressional-Executive duty to our own and to other nations. Acting upon the beliefs I have expressed here today, I shall devote my full energies to the tasks at hand, whether these involve travel for promoting greater world understanding, negotiations to reduce international discord, or constant discussions and communications with the Congress and the American people on issues both domestic and foreign.

In pursuit of these objectives, I look forward to, and shall dedicate myself to, a close and constructive association with the Congress.

Every minute spent in irrelevant interbranch wrangling is precious time taken from the intelligent initiation and adoption of coherent policies for our national survival and progress.

We seek a common goal—brighter opportunity for our own citizens and a world peace with justice for all.

Before us and our friends is the challenge of an ideology which, for more than four decades, has trumpeted abroad its purpose of gaining ultimate victory over all forms of government at variance with its own.

We realize that however much we repudiate the tenets of imperialistic Communism, it represents a gigantic enterprise grimly pursued by leaders who compel its subjects to subordinate their freedom of action and spirit and personal desires for some hoped-for advantage in the future.

The Communists can present an array of material accomplishments over the past fifteen years that lends a false persuasiveness to many of their glittering promises to the uncommitted peoples.

The competition they provide is formidable.

But in our scale of values we place freedom first—our whole national existence and development have been geared to that basic concept and are responsible for the position of free world leadership to which we have succeeded. It is the highest prize that any nation can possess; it is one that Communism can never offer. And America's record of material accomplishment in freedom is written not only in the unparalleled prosperity of our own nation, but in the many billions we have devoted to the reconstruction of Free World economics wrecked by World War II and in the effective help of many more billions we have given in saving the independence of many others threatened by outside domination. Assuredly we have the capacity for handling the problems in the new era of the world's history we are now entering.

But we must use that capacity intelligently and tirelessly, regardless of personal sacrifice.

The fissure that divides our political planet is deep and wide.

We live, moreover, in a sea of semantic disorder in which old labels no longer faithfully describe.

Police states are called "people's democracies."

Armed conquest of free people is called "liberation."

Such slippery slogans make more difficult the problem of communicating true faith, facts and beliefs.

We must make clear our peaceful intentions, our aspirations for a better world. So doing, we must use language to enlighten the mind, not as the instrument of the studied innuendo and distorter of truth.

And we must live by what we say.

On my recent visit to distant lands I found one statesman after another eager to tell me of the elements of their government that had been borrowed from our American Constitution, and from the indestructible ideals set forth in our Declaration of Independence.

As a nation we take pride that our own constitutional system, and the ideals which sustain it, have been long viewed as a fountainhead of freedom.

By our every action we must strive to make ourselves worthy of this trust, ever mindful that an accumulation of seemingly minor encroachments upon freedom gradually could break down the entire fabric of a free society.

So persuaded, we shall get on with the task before us.

So dedicated, and with faith in the Almighty, humanity shall one day achieve the unity in freedom to which all men have aspired from the dawn of time.

Dwight D. Eisenhower, 1957–1961

Message to Congress on the State of the Union

January 12, 1961

Dwight D. Eisenhower's ninth and last State of the Union address was not delivered in person before Congress but was written. The address came just eight days before Eisenhower, a Republican, would turn the reins of power over to Democrat John F. Kennedy, who had narrowly defeated Eisenhower's vice president, Richard Nixon, in the presidential election the previous November.

This address is not the same as Eisenhower's famous "Farewell Address," which was delivered on January 17. In that speech, he warned of the potential for "unwarranted influence" on government by the "military-industrial complex."

In his State of the Union address, the outgoing president summed up his eight years in office; he had been inaugurated in January 1953. He termed the period one of "profound change," with problems growing and scientific advances increasing.

One constant throughout Eisenhower's eight years in office was the Cold War struggle between the United States and the communist-run Soviet Union. Eisenhower's State of the Union addresses tended to dwell at least in part on this conflict, which dominated foreign policy. The president devoted one section to international relations, including efforts during his time in office to develop and strengthen security pacts with nations in Europe, Southeast Asia, and the Western Hemisphere.

Eisenhower also focused on the defense of the country, particularly the vast technological increases in missiles, including long-range ballistic missiles; nuclear-powered ships; and planes that flew at twice the speed of sound.

On the domestic front, the president noted that the country's output of goods and services was almost 25 percent higher than it had been in 1952, the year before he took office. He mentioned a variety of other domestic initiatives, including the national highway system; 25 percent of the system was now open to traffic, he said. He also spoke of the civil rights legislation passed in 1957 and 1960—the first civil rights laws since Reconstruction—and called for increased efforts in that area.

Eisenhower left office on January 20, 1961, at the age of seventy, having led the nation for most of the decade of the 1950s. He retired to his Gettysburg, Pennsylvania, farm; wrote his memoirs; and died in 1969 of a heart attack. His successor, Kennedy, only forty-three when he was elected, represented a new generation of American politicians and would usher in a new spirit in U.S. politics.

To the Congress of the United States:

Once again it is my Constitutional duty to assess the state of the Union.

On each such previous occasion during these past eight years I have outlined a forward course designed to achieve our mutual objective—a better America in a world of peace. This time my function is different.

The American people, in free election, have selected new leadership which soon will be entrusted with the management of our government. A new President shortly will lay before you his proposals to shape the future of our great land. To him, every citizen, whatever his political beliefs, prayerfully extends best wishes for good health and for wisdom and success in coping with the problems that confront our Nation.

For my part, I should like, first, to express to you of the Congress, my appreciation of your devotion to the common good and your friendship over these difficult years. I will carry with me pleasant memories of this association in endeavors profoundly significant to all our people.

We have been through a lengthy period in which the control over the executive and legislative branches of government has been divided between our two great political parties. Differences, of course, we have had, particularly in domestic affairs. But in a united determination to keep this Nation strong and free and to utilize our vast resources for the advancement of all mankind, we have carried America to unprecedented heights.

For this cooperative achievement I thank the American people and those in the Congress of both parties who have supported programs in the interest of our country.

I should also like to give special thanks for the devoted service of my associates in the Executive Branch and the hundreds of thousands of career employees who have implemented our diverse government programs.

My second purpose is to review briefly the record of these past eight years in the hope that, out of the sum of these experiences, lessons will emerge that are useful to our Nation. Supporting this review are detailed reports from the several agencies and departments, all of which are now or will shortly be available to the Congress.

Throughout the world the years since 1953 have been a period of profound change. The human problems in the world grow more acute hour by hour; yet new gains in science and technology continually extend the promise of a better life. People yearn to be free, to govern themselves; yet a third of the people of the world have no freedom, do not govern themselves. The world recognizes the catastrophic nature of nuclear war; yet it sees the wondrous potential of nuclear peace.

During the period, the United States has forged ahead under a constructive foreign policy. The continuing goal is peace, liberty, and well-being—for others as well as ourselves. The aspirations of all peoples are one—peace with justice in freedom. Peace can only be attained collectively as peoples everywhere unite in their determination that liberty and well-being come to all mankind.

Yet while we have worked to advance national aspirations for freedom, a divisive force has been at work to divert that aspiration into dangerous channels. The Communist movement throughout the world exploits the natural striving of all to be free and attempts to subjugate men rather than free them. These activities have caused and are continuing to cause grave troubles in the world.

Here at home these have been times for careful adjustment of our economy from the artificial impetus of a hot war to constructive growth in a precarious peace. While building a new economic vitality without inflation, we have also increased public expenditures to keep abreast of the needs of a growing population and its attendant new problems, as well as our added international responsibilities. We have worked toward these ends in a context of shared responsibility—conscious of the need for maximum scope to private effort and for State and local, as well as Federal, governmental action.

Success in designing and executing national purposes, domestically and abroad, can only come from a steadfast resolution that integrity in the operation of government and in our relations with each other be fully maintained. Only in this way could our spiritual goals be fully advanced.

Foreign Policy

On January 20, 1953, when I took office, the United States was at war. Since the signing of the Korean Armistice in 1953, Americans have lived in peace in highly troubled times.

During the 1956 Suez crisis, the United States government strongly supported United Nations' action—resulting in the ending of the hostilities in Egypt.

Again in 1958, peace was preserved in the Middle East despite new discord. Our government responded to the request of the friendly Lebanese Government for military help, and promptly withdrew American forces as soon as the situation was stabilized.

In 1958 our support of the Republic of China during the all-out bombardment of Quemoy restrained the Communist Chinese from attempting to invade the off-shore islands.

Although, unhappily, Communist penetration of Cuba is real and poses a serious threat, Communist dominated regimes have been deposed in Guatemala and Iran. The occupation of Austria has ended and the Trieste question has been settled.

Despite constant threats to its integrity, West Berlin has remained free.

Important advances have been made in building mutual security arrangements—which lie at the heart of our hopes for future peace and security in the world. The Southeast Asia Treaty Organization has been established; the NATO alliance has been militarily strengthened; the Organization of American States has been further developed as an instrument of inter-American cooperation; the Anzus treaty has strengthened ties with Australia and New Zealand, and a mutual security treaty with Japan has been signed. In addition, the CENTO pact has been concluded, and while we are not officially a member of this alliance we have participated closely in its deliberations.

The "Atoms for Peace" proposal to the United Nations led to the creation of the International Atomic Energy Agency. Our policy has been to push for enforceable programs of inspection against surprise attack, suspension of nuclear testing, arms reduction, and peaceful use of outer space.

The United Nations has been vigorously supported in all of its actions, including the condemnations of the wholesale murder of the people of Tibet by the Chinese Communists and the brutal Soviet repression of the people of Hungary, as well as the more recent UN actions in the Congo.

The United States took the initiative in negotiating the significant treaty to guarantee the peaceful use of vast Antarctica.

The United States Information Agency has been transformed into a greatly improved medium for explaining our policies and actions to audiences overseas, answering the lies of communist propaganda, and projecting a clearer image of American life and culture.

Cultural, technological and educational exchanges with the Soviet Union have been encouraged, and a comprehensive agreement was made which authorized, among other things, the distribution of our Russian language magazine *Amerika* and the highly successful American Exhibition in Moscow.

This country has continued to withhold recognition of Communist China and to oppose vigorously the admission of this belligerent and unrepentant nation into the United Nations. Red China has yet to demonstrate that it deserves to be considered a "peace-loving" nation.

With communist imperialism held in check, constructive actions were undertaken to strengthen the economies of free world nations. The United States government has given sturdy support to the economic and technical assistance activities of the UN. This country stimulated a doubling of the capital of the World Bank and a 50 percent capital increase in the International Monetary Fund. The Development Loan Fund and the International Development Association were established. The United States also took the lead in creating the Inter-American Development Bank.

Vice President Nixon, Secretaries of State Dulles and Herter and I travelled extensively through the world for the purpose of strengthening the cause of peace, freedom, and international understanding. So rewarding were these visits that their very success became a significant factor in causing the Soviet Union to wreck the planned Summit Conference of 1960.

These vital programs must go on. New tactics will have to be developed, of course, to meet new situations, but the underlying principles should be constant. Our great moral and material commitments to collective security, deterrence of force, international law, negotiations that lead to self-enforcing agreements, and the economic interdependence of free nations should remain the cornerstone of a foreign policy that will ultimately bring permanent peace with justice in freedom to all mankind. The continuing need of all free nations today is for each to recognize clearly the essentiality of an unbreakable bond among themselves based upon a complete dedication to the principles of collective security, effective cooperation and peace with justice.

National Defense

For the first time in our nation's history we have consistently maintained in peacetime, military forces of a magnitude sufficient to deter and if need be to destroy predatory forces in the world.

Tremendous advances in strategic weapons systems have been made in the past eight years. Not until 1953 were expenditures on long-range ballistic missile programs even as much as a million dollars a year; today we spend ten times as much each day on these programs as was spent in all of 1952.

No guided ballistic missiles were operational at the beginning of 1953. Today many types give our armed forces unprecedented effectiveness. The explosive power of our weapons systems for all purposes is almost inconceivable.

Today the United States has operational ATLAS missiles which can strike a target 5000 miles away in a half-hour. The POLARIS weapons system became operational last fall and the TITAN is scheduled to become so this year. Next year, more than a year ahead of schedule, a vastly improved ICBM, the solid propellant MINUTEMAN, is expected to be ready.

Squadrons of accurate Intermediate Range Ballistic Missiles are now operational. The THOR and JUPITER IRBMs based in forward areas can hit targets 1500 miles away in 18 minutes.

Aircraft which fly at speeds faster than sound were still in a developmental stage eight years ago. Today American fighting planes go twice the speed of sound. And either our B-58 Medium Range Jet Bomber or our B-52 Long Range Jet Bomber can carry more explosive power than was used by all combatants in World War II—Allies and Axis combined.

Eight years ago we had no nuclear-powered ships. Today 49 nuclear warships have been authorized. Of these, 14 have been commissioned, including three of the revolutionary POLARIS submarines. Our nuclear submarines have cruised under the North Pole and circumnavigated the earth while submerged. Sea warfare has been revolutionized, and the United States is far and away the leader.

Our tactical air units overseas and our aircraft carriers are alert; Army units, guarding the frontiers of freedom in Europe and the Far East, are in the highest state of readiness in peacetime history; our Marines, a third of whom are deployed in the Far East, are constantly prepared for action; our Reserve establishment has maintained high standards of proficiency, and the Ready Reserve now numbers over 2$\frac{1}{2}$ million citizen-soldiers.

The Department of Defense, a young and still evolving organization, has twice been improved and the line of command has been shortened in order to meet the demands of modern warfare. These major reorganizations have provided a more effective structure for unified planning and direction of the vast defense establishment. Gradual improvements in its structure and procedures are to be expected.

United States civil defense and nonmilitary defense capacity has been greatly strengthened and these activities have been consolidated in one Federal agency.

The defense forces of our Allies now number five million men, several thousand combatant ships, and over 25,000 aircraft. Programs to strengthen these allies have been consistently supported by the Administration. U.S. military assistance goes almost exclusively to friendly nations on the rim of the communist world. This American contribution to nations who have the will to defend their freedom, but insufficient means, should be vigorously continued. Combined with our Allies, the free world now has a far stronger shield than we could provide alone.

Since 1953, our defense policy has been based on the assumption that the international situation would require heavy defense expenditures for an indefinite period to come, probably for years. In this protracted struggle, good management dictates that we resist overspending as resolutely as we oppose under-spending. Every dollar uselessly spent on military mechanisms decreases our total strength and, therefore, our security. We must not return to the "crash-program" psychology of the past when each new feint by the Communists was responded to in panic. The "bomber gap" of several years ago was always a fiction, and the "missile gap" shows every sign of being the same.

The nation can ill afford to abandon a national policy which provides for a fully adequate and steady level of effort, designed for the long pull; a fast adjustment to new scientific and technological advances; a balanced force of such strength as to deter general war, to effectively meet local situations and to retaliate to attack and destroy the attacker; and a strengthened system of free world collective security.

The Economy

The expanding American economy passed the half-trillion dollar mark in gross national product early in 1960. The Nation's output of goods and services is now nearly 25 percent higher than in 1952.

In 1959, the average American family had an income of $6,520, 15 percent higher in dollars of constant buying power than in 1952, and the real wages of American factory workers have risen 20 percent during the past eight years. These facts reflect the rising standard of individual and family well-being enjoyed by Americans.

Our Nation benefits also from a remarkable improvement in general industrial peace through strengthened processes of free collective bargaining. Time lost since 1952 because of strikes has been half that lost in the eight years prior to that date. Legislation now requires that union members have the opportunity for full participation in the affairs of their unions. The Administration supported the Landrum-Griffin Act, which I believe is greatly helpful to the vast bulk of American Labor and its leaders, and also is a major step in getting racketeers and gangsters out of labor-management affairs.

The economic security of working men and women has been strengthened by an extension of unemployment insurance coverage to 2.5 million ex-servicemen, 2.4 million Federal employees, and 1.2 million employees of small businesses, and by a strengthening of the Railroad Unemployment Insurance Act. States have been encouraged to improve their unemployment compensation benefits, so that today average weekly benefits are 40 percent higher than in 1953.

Determined efforts have improved workers' safety standards. Enforceable safety standards have been established for longshoremen and ship repair workers; Federal Safety Councils have been increased from 14 to over 100; safety awards have been initiated, and a national construction safety program has been developed.

A major factor in strengthening our competitive enterprise system, and promoting economic growth, has been the vigorous enforcement of antitrust laws over the last eight years and a continuing effort to reduce artificial restraints on competition and trade and enhance our economic liberties. This purpose was also significantly advanced in 1953 when, as one of the first acts of this Administration, restrictive wage and price controls were ended.

An additional measure to strengthen the American system of competitive enterprise was the creation of the Small Business Administration in 1953 to assist existing small businesses and encourage new ones. This agency has approved over $1 billion in loans, initiated a new program to provide long-term capital for small businesses, aided in setting aside $3½ billion in government contracts for award to small business concerns, and brought to the attention of individual businessmen, through programs of information and education, new developments in management and production techniques. Since 1952, important tax revisions have been made to encourage small businesses.

Many major improvements in the Nation's transportation system have been made:

—After long years of debate, the dream of a great St. Lawrence Seaway, opening the heartland of America to ocean commerce, has been fulfilled.
—The new Federal Aviation Agency is fostering greater safety in air travel.
—The largest public construction program in history—the 41,000 mile national system of Interstate and Defense highways—has been pushed rapidly forward. Twenty-five percent of this system is now open to traffic.

Efforts to help every American build a better life have included also a vigorous program for expanding our trade with other nations. A 4-year renewal of the Reciprocal Trade Agreements Act was passed in 1958, and a continuing and rewarding effort has been made to persuade other countries to remove restrictions against our exports. A new export expansion program was launched in 1960, inaugurating improvement of export credit insurance and broadening research and information programs to awaken Americans to business opportunities overseas. These actions and generally prosperous conditions abroad have helped push America's export trade to a level of $20 billion in 1960.

Although intermittent declines in economic activity persist as a problem in our enterprise system, recent downturns have been moderate and of short duration. There is, however, little room for complacency. Currently our economy is operating at high levels, but unemployment rates are higher than any of us would like, and chronic pockets of high unemployment persist. Clearly, continued sound and broadly shared economic growth remains a major national objective toward which we must strive through joint private and public efforts.

If government continues to work to assure every American the fullest opportunity to develop and utilize his ability and talent, it will be performing one of its most vital functions, that of advancing the welfare and protecting the dignity, rights, and freedom of all Americans.

Government Finance and Administration

In January 1953, the consumer's dollar was worth only 52 cents in terms of the food, clothing, shelter and other items it would buy compared to 1939. Today, the inflationary spiral which had raised the cost of living by 36 percent between 1946 and 1952 has all but ceased and the value of the dollar virtually stabilized.

In 1954 we had the largest tax cut in history, amounting to $7.4 billion annually, of which over 62 percent went to individuals mostly in the small income brackets.

This Administration has directed constant efforts toward fiscal responsibility. Balanced budgets have been sought when the economy was advancing, and a rigorous evaluation of spending programs has been maintained at all times. Resort to deficit financing in prosperous times could easily erode international confidence in the dollar and contribute to inflation at home. In this belief, I shall submit a balanced budget for fiscal 1962 to the Congress next week.

There has been a firm policy of reducing government competition with private enterprise. This has resulted in the discontinuance of some 2,000 commercial industrial installations and in addition the curtailment of approximately 550 industrial installations operated directly by government agencies.

Also an aggressive surplus disposal program has been carried on to identify and dispose of unneeded government-owned real property. This has resulted in the addition of a substantial number of valuable properties to local tax rolls, and a significant monetary return to the government.

Earnest and persistent attempts have been made to strengthen the position of State and local governments and thereby to stop the dangerous drift toward centralization of governmental power in Washington.

Significant strides have been made in increasing the effectiveness of government. Important new agencies have been established, such as the Department of Health, Education, and Welfare, the Federal Aviation Agency, and the National Aeronautics and Space Administration. The Council of Economic Advisers was reconstituted.

The operation of our postal system has been modernized to get better and more efficient service. Modernized handling of local mail now brings next-day delivery to 168 million people in our population centers, expanded carrier service now accommodates 9.3 million families in the growing suburbs, and 1.4 million families have been added to the rural delivery service. Common sense dictates that the Postal Service should be on a self-financing basis.

The concept of a trained and dedicated government career service has been strengthened by the provision of life and health insurance benefits, a vastly improved retirement system, a new merit promotion program, and the first effective incentive awards program. With no sacrifice in efficiency, Federal civilian employment since 1953 has been reduced by over a quarter of a million persons.

I am deeply gratified that it was under the urging of this Administration that Alaska and Hawaii became our 49th and 50th States.

Agriculture

Despite the difficulties of administering Congressional programs which apply outmoded prescriptions and which aggravate rather than solve problems, the past eight years brought notable advances in agriculture.

Total agricultural assets are approximately $200 billion—up $36 billion in eight years.

Farm owner equities are at the near record high of $174 billion.

Farm ownership is at a record high with fewer farmers in a tenant and sharecropper status than at any time in our nation's history.

The "Food-for-Peace" program has demonstrated how surplus of American food and fiber can be effectively used to feed and clothe the needy abroad. Aided by this humanitarian program, total agricultural exports have grown from $2.8 billion in 1953 to an average of about $4 billion annually for the past three years. For 1960, exports are estimated at $4.5 billion, the highest volume on record. Under the Food-for-Peace program, the largest wheat transaction in history was consummated with India in 1960.

The problems of low-income farm families received systematic attention for the first time in the Rural Development Program. This program has gone forward in 39 States, yielding higher incomes and a better living for rural people most in need.

The Rural Electrification Administration has helped meet the growing demand for power and telephones in agricultural areas. Ninety-seven percent of all farms now have central station electric power. Dependence upon Federal financing should no longer be necessary.

The Farm Credit Administration has been made an independent agency more responsive to the farmer's needs.

The search for new uses for our farm abundance and to develop new crops for current needs has made major progress. Agricultural research appropriations have increased by 171 percent since 1953.

Farmers are being saved approximately $80 million a year by the repeal in 1956 of Federal taxes on gasoline used in tractors and other machinery.

Since 1953, appropriations have been doubled for county agents, home agents and the Extension Service.

Eligibility for Social Security benefits has been extended to farmers and their families.

Yet in certain aspects our agricultural surplus situation is increasingly grave. For example, our wheat stocks now total 1.3 billion bushels. If we did not harvest one bushel of wheat in this coming year, we would still have all we could eat, all we could sell abroad, all we could give away, and still have a substantial carryover. Extraordinary costs are involved just in management and disposal of this burdensome surplus. Obviously important adjustments must still come. Congress must enact additional legislation to permit wheat and other farm commodities to move into regular marketing channels in an orderly manner and at the same time afford the needed price protection to the farmer. Only then will agriculture again be free, sound, and profitable.

Natural Resources

New emphasis has been placed on the care of our national parks. A ten year development program of our National Park System—Mission 66—was initiated and 633,000 acres of park land have been added since 1953.

Appropriations for fish and wildlife operations have more than doubled. Thirty-five new refuges, containing 11,342,000 acres, have been added to the national wildlife management system.

Our Nation's forests have been improved at the most rapid rate in history.

The largest sustained effort in water resources development in our history has taken place. In the field of reclamation alone, over 50 new projects, or project units, have been authorized since 1953—including the billion dollar Colorado River Storage Project. When all these projects have been completed they will have a storage capacity of nearly 43 million acre-feet—an increase of 50 percent over the Bureau of Reclamation's storage capacity in mid-1953. In addition, since 1953 over 450 new navigation flood control and multiple purpose projects of the Corps of Engineers have been started, costing nearly 6 billion dollars.

Soil and water conservation has been advanced as never before. One hundred forty-one projects are now being constructed under the Watershed Protection Program.

Hydroelectric power has been impressively developed through a policy which recognizes that the job to be done requires comprehensive development by Federal, State, and local governments and private enterprise. Teamwork is essential to achieve this objective.

The Federal Columbia River power system has grown from two multipurpose dams with a 2.6 million kilowatt capacity to 17 multipurpose projects completed or under construction with an ultimate installed capacity of 8.1 million kilowatts. After years of negotiation, a Columbia River Storage Development agreement with Canada now opens the way for early realization of unparalleled power, flood control and resource conservation benefits for the Pacific Northwest. A treaty implementing this agreement will shortly be submitted to the Senate.

A farsighted and highly successful program for meeting urgent water needs is being carded out by converting salt water to fresh water. A 75 percent reduction in the cost of this process has already been realized.

Continuous resource development is essential for our expanding economy. We must continue vigorous, combined Federal, State and private programs, at the same time preserving to the maximum extent possible our natural and scenic heritage for future generations.

Education, Science, and Technology

The National Defense Education Act of 1958 is already a milestone in the history of American education. It provides broad opportunities for the intellectual development of all children by strengthening courses of study in science, mathematics, and foreign languages, by developing new graduate programs to train additional teachers, and by providing loans for young people who need financial help to go to college.

The Administration proposed on numerous occasions a broad new five-year program of Federal aid to help overcome the classroom shortage in public elementary and secondary schools. Recommendations were also made to give assistance to colleges and universities for the construction of academic and residential buildings to meet future enrollment increases.

This Administration greatly expanded Federal loans for building dormitories for students, teachers, and nurses training, a program assisting in the construction of approximately 200,000 living accommodations during the past 8 years.

There has been a vigorous acceleration of health, resource and education programs designed to advance the role of the American Indian in our society. Last fall, for example, 91 percent of the Indian children between the ages of 6 and 18 on reservations were enrolled in school. This is a rise of 12 percent since 1953.

In the field of science and technology, startling strides have been made by the new National Aeronautics and Space Administration. In little more than two years, NASA has successfully launched meteorological satellites, such as Tiros I and Tiros II, that promise to revolutionize methods of weather forecasting; demonstrated the feasibility of satellites for global communications by the successful launching of Echo I; produced an enormous amount of valuable scientific data, such as the discovery of the Van Allen Radiation Belt; successfully launched deep-space probes that maintained communication over the greatest range man has ever tracked; and made real progress toward the goal of manned space flights.

These achievements unquestionably make us preeminent today in space exploration for the betterment of mankind. I believe the present organizational arrangements in this area, with the revisions proposed last year, are completely adequate for the tasks ahead.

Americans can look forward to new achievements in space exploration. The near future will hold such wonders as the orbital flight of an astronaut, the landing of instruments on the moon, the launching of the powerful giant Saturn rocket vehicles, and the reconnaissance of Mars and Venus by unmanned vehicles.

The application of atomic energy to industry, agriculture, and medicine has progressed from hope and experiment to reality. American industry and agriculture are making increasing use of radioisotopes to improve manufacturing, testing, and crop-raising. Atomic energy has improved the ability of the healing professions to combat disease, and holds promise for an eventual increase in man's life span.

Education, science, technology and balanced programs of every kind-these are the roadways to progress. With appropriate Federal support, the States and localities can assure opportunities for achieving excellence at all levels of the educational system; and with the Federal government continuing to give wholehearted support to basic scientific research and technology, we can expect to maintain our position of leadership in the world.

Civil Rights

The first consequential Federal Civil Rights legislation in 85 years was enacted by Congress on recommendation of the Administration in 1957 and 1960.

A new Civil Rights Division in the Department of Justice has already moved to enforce constitutional rights in such areas as voting and the elimination of Jim Crow laws.

Greater equality of job opportunity in Federal employment and employment with Federal contractors has been effectively provided through the President's Committees on Government Contracts and Government Employment Practices.

The Civil Rights Commission has undertaken important surveys in the fields of housing, voting, and education.

Segregation has been abolished in the Armed Forces, in Veterans' Hospitals, in all Federal employment, and throughout the District of Columbia—administratively accomplished progress in this field that is unmatched in America's recent history.

This pioneering work in civil rights must go on. Not only because discrimination is morally wrong, but also because its impact is more than national—it is world-wide.

Health and Welfare

Federal medical research expenditures have increased more than fourfold since 1954.

A vast variety of the approaches known to medical science has been explored to find better methods of treatment and prevention of major diseases, particularly heart diseases, cancer, and mental illness.

The control of air and water pollution has been greatly strengthened.

Americans now have greater protection against harmful, unclean, or misrepresented foods, drugs, or cosmetics through a strengthened Food and Drug Administration and by new legislation which requires that food additives be proved safe for human consumption before use.

A newly established Federal Radiation Council, along with the Department of Health, Education, and Welfare, analyzes and coordinates information regarding radiological activities which affect the public health.

Medical manpower has been increased by Federal grants for teaching and research.

Construction of new medical facilities has been stepped up and extended to include nursing homes, diagnostic and treatment centers, and rehabilitation facilities.

The vocational rehabilitation program has been significantly expanded. About 90,000 handicapped people are now being rehabilitated annually so they are again able to earn their own living with self-respect and dignity.

New legislation provides for better medical care for the needy aged, including those older persons, who, while otherwise self-sufficient, need help in meeting their health care costs. The Administration recommended a major expansion of this effort.

The coverage of the Social Security Act has been broadened since 1953 to make 11 million additional people eligible for retirement, disability or survivor benefits for themselves or their dependents, and the Social Security benefits have been substantially improved.

Grants to the States for maternal and child welfare services have been increased.

The States, aided by Federal grants, now assist some 6 million needy people through the programs of Old Age Assistance, Aid to Dependent Children, Aid to the Blind, and Aid to the Totally and Permanently Disabled.

Housing and Urban Development

More houses have been built during the past eight years—over nine million—than during any previous eight years in history.

An historic new approach—Urban Renewal—now replaces piecemeal thrusts at slum pockets and urban blight. Communities engaged in urban renewal have doubled and renewal projects have more than tripled since 1953. An estimated 68 projects in 50 cities will be completed by the end of the current fiscal year; another 577 projects will be underway, and planning for 310 more will be in process. A total of $2 billion in Federal grants will ultimately be required to finance these 955 projects.

New programs have been initiated to provide more and better housing for elderly people. Approximately 25,000 units especially designed for the elderly have been built, started, or approved in the past three years.

For the first time, because of Federal help and encouragement, 90 metropolitan areas and urban regions and 1140 smaller towns throughout the country are making comprehensive development plans for their future growth and development.

American communities have been helped to plan water and sanitation systems and schools through planning advances for 1600 public works projects with a construction cost of nearly $2 billion.

Mortgage insurance on individual homes has been greatly expanded. During the past eight years, the Federal Housing Administration alone insured over 2½ million home mortgages valued at $27 billion, and in addition, insured more than ten million property improvement loans.

The Federal government must continue to provide leadership in order to make our cities and communities better places in which to live, work, and raise families, but without usurping rightful local authority, replacing individual responsibility, or stifling private initiative.

Immigration

Over 32,000 victims of Communist tyranny in Hungary were brought to our shores, and at this time our country is working to assist refugees from tyranny in Cuba.

Since 1953, the waiting period for naturalization applicants has been reduced from 18 months to 45 days.

The Administration also has made legislative recommendations to liberalize existing restrictions upon immigration while still safeguarding the national interest. It is imperative that our immigration policy be in the finest American tradition of providing a haven for oppressed peoples and fully in accord with our obligation as a leader of the free world.

Veterans

In discharging the nation's obligation to our veterans, during the past eight years there have been:

The readjustment of World War II veterans was completed, and the five million Korean conflict veterans were assisted in achieving successful readjustment to civilian life;

Increases in compensation benefits for all eligible veterans with service connected disabilities;

Higher non-service connected pension benefits for needy veterans;

Greatly improved benefits to survivors of veterans dying in or as a result of service;

Authorization, by Presidential directive, of an increase in the number of beds available for sick and disabled veterans;

Development of a 12-year, $900 million construction program to modernize and improve our veterans hospitals;

New modern techniques brought into the administration of Veterans Affairs to provide the highest quality service possible to those who have defended us.

Conclusion

In concluding my final message to the Congress, it is fitting to look back to my first—to the aims and ideals I set forth on February 2, 1953: To use America's influence in world affairs to advance the cause of peace and justice, to conduct the affairs of the Executive Branch with integrity and efficiency, to encourage creative initiative in our economy, and to work toward the attainment of the well-being and equality of opportunity of all citizens.

Equally, we have honored our commitment to pursue and attain specific objectives. Among them, as stated eight years ago: strengthening of the mutual security program; development of world trade and commerce; ending of hostilities in Korea; creation of a powerful deterrent force; practicing fiscal responsibility; checking the menace of inflation; reducing the tax burden; providing an effective internal security program; developing and conserving our natural resources; reducing governmental interference in the affairs of the farmer; strengthening and improving services by the Department of Labor, and the vigilant guarding of civil and social fights.

I do not close this message implying that all is well—that all problems are solved. For progress implies both new and continuing problems and, unlike Presidential administrations, problems rarely have terminal dates.

Abroad, there is the continuing Communist threat to the freedom of Berlin, an explosive situation in Laos, the problems caused by Communist penetration of Cuba, as well as the many problems connected with the development of the new nations in Africa. These areas, in particular, call for delicate handling and constant review.

At home, several conspicuous problems remain: promoting higher levels of employment, with special emphasis on areas in which heavy unemployment has persisted; continuing to provide for steady economic growth and preserving a sound currency; bringing our balance of payments into more reasonable equilibrium and continuing a high level of confidence in our national and international systems; eliminating heavily excessive surpluses of a few farm commodities; and overcoming deficiencies in our health and educational programs.

Our goal always has been to add to the spiritual, moral, and material strength of our nation. I believe we have done this. But it is a process that must never end. Let us pray that leaders of both the near and distant future will be able to keep the nation strong and at peace, that they will advance the well-being of all our people, that they will lead us on to still higher moral standards, and that, in achieving these goals, they will maintain a reasonable balance between private and governmental responsibility.

John F. Kennedy

1961–1963

*". . . On the Presidential Coat of Arms,
the American eagle holds in his right talon
the olive branch, while in his left he holds
a bundle of arrows. We intend to give
equal attention to both."*

ADDRESS TO CONGRESS ON THE STATE OF THE UNION, JANUARY 30, 1961

Address to Congress on the State of the Union

January 30, 1961

John F. Kennedy's first State of the Union address was delivered before Congress just ten days after Kennedy was inaugurated. The new president, a Democrat, had narrowly defeated incumbent vice president Richard Nixon the previous November. Kennedy's inaugural address, one of the most famous political speeches in American history, called upon his fellow Americans to serve their country. The State of the Union message, a far longer address, spoke in greater specifics about Kennedy's plan. His platform, known as the New Freedom, was reform-minded and marked a change from the stay-the-course political philosophy of his predecessor, Dwight D. Eisenhower.

Kennedy painted a dire picture of the American economy, stating that it was "in trouble" and had been in recession for seven months. He also commented that the federal budget for fiscal year 1961 was "almost certain to show a net deficit." In addition, he declared that the nation's "cities are being engulfed in squalor."

But, he said, these domestic problems were minor in comparison to the problems facing America around the world. The country was still in the throes of the Cold War, pitting it against the communist Soviet Union and communist China. Kennedy mentioned South Vietnam, which was to loom larger as a foreign policy crisis as his administration progressed.

Another country he mentioned was Cuba, which, since its 1959 revolution, had been led by Fidel Castro. The Cuban leader started to ally himself with the Soviets, which caused great consternation to the Eisenhower, and then the Kennedy, administrations. Kennedy stated that "communist domination in this hemisphere can never be negotiated." That April, a CIA plan known as the Bay of Pigs invasion, which sought to overthrow Castro, failed miserably, constituting what is considered Kennedy's biggest foreign policy mistake.

Kennedy also referred in his State of the Union speech to a "National Peace Corps." He would go on to establish the Peace Corps that year, tapping into a deep American vein of idealism by sending Americans to various underdeveloped nations to perform humanitarian missions.

At the end of this speech, the new president quoted Franklin D. Roosevelt, whose birthday anniversary was marked on January 30: "We pray that we may be worthy of the unlimited opportunities that God has given us."

Kennedy's administration lasted only about a thousand days; he would be assassinated on November 22, 1963, while on a trip to Dallas, Texas. But his presidency, often referred to as "Camelot" because of its glamour, would become one of the more memorable in recent history.

M r. Speaker, Mr. Vice President, Members of the Congress:

It is a pleasure to return from whence I came. You are among my oldest friends in Washington—and this House is my oldest home. It was here, more than 14 years ago, that I first took the oath of Federal office. It was here, for 14 years, that I gained both knowledge and inspiration from members of both parties in both Houses—from your wise and generous leaders—and from the pronouncements which I can vividly recall, sitting where you now sit—including the programs of two great Presidents, the undimmed eloquence of [Winston] Churchill, the soaring idealism of [Jawaharlal] Nehru, the steadfast words of General [Charles] de Gaulle. To speak from this same historic rostrum is a sobering experience. To be back among so many friends is a happy one.

I am confident that that friendship will continue. Our Constitution wisely assigns both joint and separate roles to each branch of the government; and a President and a Congress who hold each other in mutual respect will neither permit nor attempt any trespass. For my part, I shall withhold from neither the Congress nor the people any fact or report, past, present, or future, which is necessary for an informed judgment of our conduct and hazards. I shall neither shift the burden of executive decisions to the Congress, nor avoid responsibility for the outcome of those decisions.

I speak today in an hour of national peril and national opportunity. Before my term has ended, we shall have to test anew whether a nation organized and governed such as ours can endure. The outcome is by no means certain. The answers are by no means clear. All of us together—this Administration, this Congress, this nation—must forge those answers.

But today, were I to offer—after little more than a week in office—detailed legislation to remedy every national ill, the Congress would rightly wonder whether the desire for speed had replaced the duty of responsibility.

My remarks, therefore, will be limited. But they will also be candid. To state the facts frankly is not to despair the future nor indict the past. The prudent heir takes careful inventory of his legacies, and gives a faithful accounting to those whom he owes an obligation of trust. And, while the occasion does not call for another recital of our blessings and assets, we do have no greater asset than the willingness of a free and determined people, through its elected officials, to face all problems frankly and meet all dangers free from panic or fear.

I.

The present state of our economy is disturbing. We take office in the wake of seven months of recession, three and one-half years of slack, seven years of diminished economic growth, and nine years of falling farm income.

Business bankruptcies have reached their highest level since the Great Depression. Since 1951 farm income has been squeezed down by 25 percent. Save for a brief period in 1958, insured unemployment is at the highest peak in our history. Of some five and one-half million Americans who are without jobs, more than one million have been searching for work for more than four months. And during each month some 150,000 workers are exhausting their already meager jobless benefit rights.

Nearly, one-eighth of those who are without jobs live almost without hope in nearly one hundred especially depressed and troubled areas. The rest include new school graduates unable to use their talents, farmers forced to give up their part-time jobs which helped balance their family budgets, skilled and unskilled workers laid off in such important industries as metals, machinery, automobiles and apparel.

Our recovery from the 1958 recession, moreover, was anemic and incomplete. Our Gross National Product never regained its full potential. Unemployment never returned to normal levels. Maximum use of our national industrial capacity was never restored.

In short, the American economy is in trouble. The most resourceful industrialized country on earth ranks among the last in the rate of economic growth. Since last spring our economic growth rate has actually receded. Business investment is in a decline. Profits have fallen below predicted levels. Construction is off. A million unsold automobiles are in inventory. Fewer people are working—and the average work week has shrunk well below 40 hours. Yet prices have continued to rise—so that now too many Americans have less to spend for items that cost more to buy.

Economic prophecy is at best an uncertain art—as demonstrated by the prediction one year ago from this same podium that 1960 would be, and I quote, "the most prosperous year in our history." Nevertheless, forecasts of continued slack and only slightly reduced unemployment through 1961 and 1962 have been made with alarming unanimity—and this Administration does not intend to stand helplessly by.

We cannot afford to waste idle hours and empty plants while awaiting the end of the recession. We must show the world what a free economy can do—to reduce unemployment, to put unused capacity to work, to spur new productivity, and to foster higher economic growth within a range of sound fiscal policies and relative price stability.

I will propose to the Congress within the next 14 days measures to improve unemployment compensation through temporary increases in duration on a self-supporting basis—to provide more food for the families of the unemployed, and to aid their needy children—to redevelop our areas of chronic labor surplus—to expand the services of the U.S. Employment Offices—to stimulate housing and construction—to secure more purchasing power for our lowest paid workers by raising and expanding the minimum wage—to offer tax incentives for sound plant investment—to increase the development of our natural resources—to encourage price stability—and to take other steps aimed at insuring a prompt recovery and paving the way for increased long-range growth. This is not a partisan program concentrating on our weaknesses—it is, I hope, a national program to realize our national strength.

II.

Efficient expansion at home, stimulating the new plant and technology that can make our goods more competitive, is also the key to the international balance of payments problem. Laying aside all alarmist talk and panicky solutions, let us put that knotty problem in its proper perspective.

It is true that, since 1958, the gap between the dollars we spend or invest abroad and the dollars returned to us has substantially widened. This overall deficit in our balance of payments increased by nearly $11 billion in the 3 years—and holders of dollars abroad converted them to gold in such a quantity as to cause a total outflow of nearly $5 billion of gold from our reserve. The 1959 deficit was caused in large part by the failure of our exports to penetrate foreign markets—the result both of restrictions on our goods and our own uncompetitive prices. The 1960 deficit, on the other hand, was more the result of an increase in private capital outflow seeking new opportunity, higher return or speculative advantage abroad.

Meanwhile this country has continued to bear more than its share of the West's military and foreign aid obligations. Under existing policies, another deficit of $2 billion is predicted for 1961—and individuals in those countries whose dollar position once depended on these deficits for improvement now wonder aloud whether our gold reserves will remain sufficient to meet our own obligations.

All this is cause for concern—but it is not cause for panic. For our monetary and financial position remains exceedingly strong. Including our drawing rights in the International Monetary Fund and the gold reserve held as backing for our currency and Federal Reserve deposits, we have some $22 billion in total gold stocks and other international monetary reserves available—and I now pledge that their full strength stands behind the value of the dollar for use if needed.

Moreover, we hold large assets abroad—the total owed this nation far exceeds the claims upon our reserves—and our exports once again substantially exceed our imports.

In short, we need not—and we shall not—take any action to increase the dollar price of gold from $35 an ounce—to impose exchange controls—to reduce our anti-recession efforts—to fall back on restrictive trade policies—or to weaken our commitments around the world.

This Administration will not distort the value of the dollar in any fashion. And this is a commitment.

Prudence and good sense do require, however, that new steps be taken to ease the payments deficit and prevent any gold crisis. Our success in world affairs has long depended in part upon foreign confidence in our ability to pay. A series of executive orders, legislative remedies and cooperative efforts with our allies will get underway immediately—aimed at attracting foreign investment and travel to this country—promoting American exports, at stable prices and with more liberal government guarantees and financing—curbing tax and customs loopholes that encourage undue spending of private dollars abroad—and (through OECD [Organization for Economic Co-operation and Development], NATO [North Atlantic Treaty Organization] and otherwise) sharing with our allies all efforts to provide for the common defense of the free world and the hopes for growth of the less developed lands. While the current deficit lasts, ways will be found to ease our dollar outlays abroad without placing the full burden on the families of men whom we have asked to serve our Flag overseas.

In short, whatever is required will be done to back up all our efforts abroad, and to make certain that, in the future as in the past, the dollar is as "sound as a dollar."

III.

But more than our exchange of international payments is out of balance. The current Federal budget for fiscal 1961 is almost certain to show a net deficit. The budget already submitted for fiscal 1962 will remain in balance only if the Congress enacts all the revenue measures requested—and only if an earlier and sharper up-turn in the economy than my economic advisers now think likely produces the tax revenues estimated. Nevertheless, a new Administration must of necessity build on the spending and revenue estimates already submitted. Within that framework, barring the development of urgent national defense needs or a worsening of the economy, it is my current intention to advocate a program of expenditures which, including revenues from a stimulation of the economy, will not of and by themselves unbalance the earlier Budget.

However, we will do what must be done. For our national household is cluttered with unfinished and neglected tasks. Our cities are being engulfed in squalor. Twelve long years after Congress declared our goal to be "a decent home and a suitable environment for every American family," we still have 25 million Americans living in substandard homes. A new housing program under a new Housing and Urban Affairs Department will be needed this year.

Our classrooms contain 2 million more children than they can properly have room for, taught by 90,000 teachers not properly qualified to teach. One third of our most promising high school graduates are financially unable to continue the development of their talents. The war babies of the 1940's, who overcrowded our schools in the 1950's, are now descending in 1960 upon our colleges—with two college students for every one, ten years from now—and our colleges are ill prepared. We lack the scientists, the engineers and the teachers our world obligations require. We have neglected oceanography, saline water conversion, and the basic research that lies at the root of all progress. Federal grants for both higher and public school education can no longer be delayed.

Medical research has achieved new wonders—but these wonders are too often beyond the reach of too many people, owing to a lack of income (particularly among the aged), a lack of hospital beds, a lack of nursing homes and a lack of doctors and dentists. Measures to provide health care for the aged under Social Security, and to increase the supply of both facilities and personnel, must be undertaken this year.

Our supply of clean water is dwindling. Organized and juvenile crimes cost the taxpayers millions of dollars each year, making it essential that we have improved enforcement and new legislative safeguards. The denial of constitutional rights to some of our fellow Americans on account of race—at the ballot box and elsewhere—disturbs the national conscience, and subjects us to the charge of world opinion that our democracy is not equal to the high promise of our heritage. Morality in private business has not been sufficiently spurred by morality in public business. A host of problems and projects in all 50 States, though not possible to include in this Message, deserves—and will receive—the attention of both the Congress and the Executive Branch. On most of these matters, Messages will be sent to the Congress within the next two weeks.

IV.

But all these problems pale when placed beside those which confront us around the world. No man entering upon this office, regardless of his party, regardless of his previous service in Washington, could fail to be staggered upon learning—even in this brief 10 day period—the harsh enormity of the trials through which we must pass in the next four years. Each day the crises multiply. Each day their solution grows more difficult. Each day we draw nearer the hour of maximum danger, as weapons spread and hostile forces grow stronger. I feel I must inform the Congress that our analyses over the last ten days make it clear that—in each of the principal areas of crisis—the tide of events has been running out and time has not been our friend.

In Asia, the relentless pressures of the Chinese Communists menace the security of the entire area—from the borders of India and South Viet Nam to the jungles of Laos, struggling to protect its newly-won independence. We seek in Laos what we seek in all Asia, and, indeed, in all of the world—freedom for the people and independence for the government. And this Nation shall persevere in our pursuit of these objectives. In Africa, the Congo has been brutally torn by civil strife, political unrest and public disorder. We shall continue to support the heroic efforts of the United Nations to restore peace and order—efforts which are now endangered by mounting tensions, unsolved problems, and decreasing support from many member states.

In Latin America, Communist agents seeking to exploit that region's peaceful revolution of hope have established a base on Cuba, only 90 miles from our shores. Our objection with Cuba is not over the people's drive for a better life. Our objection is to their domination by foreign and domestic tyrannies. Cuban social and economic reform should be encouraged. Questions of economic and trade policy can always be negotiated. But Communist domination in this Hemisphere can never be negotiated.

We are pledged to work with our sister republics to free the Americas of all such foreign domination and all tyranny, working toward the goal of a free hemisphere of free governments, extending from Cape Horn to the Arctic Circle.

In Europe our alliances are unfulfilled and in some disarray. The unity of NATO has been weakened by economic rivalry and partially eroded by national interest. It has not yet fully mobilized its resources nor fully achieved a common outlook. Yet no Atlantic power can meet on its own the mutual problems now facing us in defense, foreign aid, monetary reserves, and a host of other areas; and our close ties with those whose hopes and interests we share are among this Nation's most powerful assets.

Our greatest challenge is still the world that lies beyond the Cold War—but the first great obstacle is still our relations with the Soviet Union and Communist China. We must never be lulled into believing that either power has yielded its ambitions for world domination—ambitions which they forcefully restated only a short time ago. On the contrary, our task is to convince them that aggression and subversion will not be profitable routes to pursue these ends. Open and peaceful competition—for prestige, for markets, for scientific achievement, even for men's minds—is something else again. For if Freedom and Communism were to compete for man's allegiance in a world at peace, I would look to the future with ever increasing confidence.

To meet this array of challenges—to fulfill the role we cannot avoid on the world scene—we must reexamine and revise our whole arsenal of tools: military, economic and political.

One must not overshadow the other: On the Presidential Coat of Arms, the American eagle holds in his right talon the olive branch, while in his left he holds a bundle of arrows. We intend to give equal attention to both.

First, we must strengthen our military tools. We are moving into a period of uncertain risk and great commitment in which both the military and diplomatic possibilities require a Free World force so powerful as to make any aggression clearly futile. Yet in the past, lack of a consistent, coherent military strategy, the absence of basic assumptions about our national requirements and the faulty estimates and duplication arising from inter-service rivalries have all made it difficult to assess accurately how adequate—or inadequate—our defenses really are.

I have, therefore, instructed the Secretary of Defense to reappraise our entire defense strategy—our ability to fulfill our commitments—the effectiveness, vulnerability, and dispersal of our strategic bases, forces and warning systems—the efficiency and economy of our operation and organization—the elimination of obsolete bases and installations—and the adequacy, modernization and mobility of our present conventional and nuclear forces and weapons systems in the light of present and future dangers. I have asked for preliminary conclusions by the end of February—and I then shah recommend whatever legislative, budgetary or executive action is needed in the light of these conclusions.

In the meantime, I have asked the Defense Secretary to initiate immediately three new steps most clearly needed now:

First, I have directed prompt attention to increase our air-lift capacity. Obtaining additional air transport mobility—and obtaining it now—will better assure the ability of our conventional forces to respond, with discrimination and speed, to any problem at any spot on the globe at any moment's notice. In particular it will enable us to meet any deliberate effort to avoid or divert our forces by starting limited wars in widely scattered parts of the globe.

(b) I have directed prompt action to step up our Polaris submarine program. Using unobligated ship-building funds now (to let contracts originally scheduled for the next fiscal year) will build and place on station—at least nine months earlier than planned—substantially more units of a crucial deterrent—a fleet that will never attack first, but possess sufficient powers of retaliation, concealed beneath the seas, to discourage any aggressor from launching an attack upon our security.

(c) I have directed prompt action to accelerate our entire missile program. Until the Secretary of Defense's reappraisal is completed, the emphasis here will be largely on improved organization and decision making—on cutting down the wasteful duplications and the time-lag that have handicapped our whole family of missiles. If we are to keep the peace, we need an invulnerable missile force powerful enough to deter any aggressor from even threatening an attack that he would know could not destroy enough of our force to prevent his own destruction. For as I said upon taking the oath of office: "Only when our arms are sufficient beyond doubt can we be certain beyond doubt that they will never be employed."

Secondly, we must improve our economic tools. Our role is essential and unavoidable in the construction of a sound and expanding economy for the entire noncommunist world, helping other nations build the strength to meet their own problems, to satisfy their own aspirations—to surmount their own dangers. The problems in achieving this goal are towering and unprecedented—the response must be towering and unprecedented as well, much as Lend-Lease and the Marshall Plan were in earlier years, which brought such fruitful results.

(a) I intend to ask the Congress for authority to establish a new and more effective program for assisting the economic, educational and social development of other countries and continents. That program must stimulate and take more effectively into account the contributions of our allies, and provide central policy direction for all our own programs that now so often overlap, conflict or diffuse our energies and resources.

Such a program, compared to past programs, will require

—more flexibility for short run emergencies

—more commitment to long term development

—new attention to education at all levels

—greater emphasis on the recipient nation's role, their effort, their purpose, with greater social justice for their people, broader distribution and participation by their people and more efficient public administration and more efficient tax systems of their own

—and orderly planning for national and regional development instead of a piece-meal approach.

I hope the Senate will take early action approving the Convention establishing the Organization for Economic Cooperation and Development. This will be an important instrument in sharing with our allies this development effort—working toward the time when each nation will contribute in proportion to its ability to pay. For, while we are prepared to assume our full share of these huge burdens, we cannot and must not be expected to bear them alone.

To our sister republics to the south, we have pledged a new alliance for progress— *alianza para progreso*. Our goal is a free and prosperous Latin America, realizing for all its states and all its citizens a degree of economic and social progress that matches their historic contributions of culture, intellect and liberty. To start this nation's role at this time in that alliance of neighbors, I am recommending the following:

—That the Congress appropriate in full the $500 million fund pledged by the Act of Bogota, to be used not as an instrument of the Cold War, but as a first step in the sound development of the Americas.

—That a new Inter-Departmental Task Force be established under the leadership of the Department of State, to coordinate at the highest level all policies and pro-grams of concern to the Americas.

—That our delegates to the OAS, working with those of other members, strengthen that body as an instrument to preserve the peace and to prevent foreign domina-tion anywhere in the Hemisphere.

—That, in cooperation with other nations, we launch a new hemispheric attack on illiteracy and inadequate educational opportunities to all levels; and, finally,

—That a Food-for-Peace mission be sent immediately to Latin America to explore ways in which our vast food abundance can be used to help end hunger and malnutrition in certain areas of suffering in our own hemisphere.

This Administration is expanding its Food-for-Peace Program in every possible way. The product of our abundance must be used more effectively to relieve hunger and help economic growth in all corners of the globe. And I have asked the Director of this Program to recommend additional ways in which these surpluses can advance the interests of world peace—including the establishment of world food reserves.

An even more valuable national asset is our reservoir of dedicated men and women—not only on our college campuses but in every age group—who have indicated their desire to contribute their skills, their efforts, and a part of their lives to the fight for world order. We can mobilize this talent through the formation of a National Peace Corps, enlisting the services of all those with the desire and capacity to help foreign lands meet their urgent needs for trained personnel.

Finally, while our attention is centered on the development of the noncommunist world, we must never forget our hopes for the ultimate freedom and welfare of the Eastern European peoples. In order to be prepared to help re-establish historic ties of friendship, I am asking the Congress for increased discretion to use economic tools in this area whenever this is found to be clearly in the national interest. This will require amendment of the Mutual Defense Assistance Control Act along the lines I proposed as a member of the Senate, and upon which the Senate voted last summer. Meanwhile, I hope to explore with the Polish government the possibility of using our frozen Polish funds on projects of peace that will demonstrate our abiding friendship for and interest in the people of Poland.

Third, we must sharpen our political and diplomatic tools—the means of cooperation and agreement on which an enforceable world order must ultimately rest.

I have already taken steps to coordinate and expand our disarmament effort—to increase our programs of research and study—and to make arms control a central goal of our national policy under my direction. The deadly arms race, and the huge resources it absorbs, have too long overshadowed all else we must do. We must prevent that arms race from spreading to new nations, to new nuclear powers and to the reaches of outer space. We must make certain that our negotiators are better informed and better prepared—to formulate workable proposals of our own and to make sound judgments about the proposals of others.

I have asked the other governments concerned to agree to a reasonable delay in the talks on a nuclear test ban—and it is our intention to resume negotiations prepared to reach a final agreement with any nation that is equally willing to agree to an effective and enforceable treaty.

We must increase our support of the United Nations as an instrument to end the Cold War instead of an arena in which to fight it. In recognition of its increasing importance and the doubling of its membership

—we are enlarging and strengthening our own mission to the U.N.

—we shall help insure that it is properly financed.

—we shall work to see that the integrity of the office of the Secretary-General is maintained.

—And I would address a special plea to the smaller nations of the world—to join with us in strengthening this organization, which is far more essential to their security than it is to ours—the only body in the world where no nation need be powerful to be secure, where every nation has an equal voice, and where any nation can exert influence not according to the strength of its armies but according to the strength of its ideas. It deserves the support of all.

Finally, this Administration intends to explore promptly all possible areas of cooperation with the Soviet Union and other nations "to invoke the wonders of science instead of its terrors." Specifically, I now invite all nations—including the Soviet

Union—to join with us in developing a weather prediction program, in a new communications satellite program and in preparation for probing the distant planets of Mars and Venus, probes which may someday unlock the deepest secrets of the universe.

Today this country is ahead in the science and technology of space, while the Soviet Union is ahead in the capacity to lift large vehicles into orbit. Both nations would help themselves as well as other nations by removing these endeavors from the bitter and wasteful competition of the Cold War. The United States would be willing to join with the Soviet Union and the scientists of all nations in a greater effort to make the fruits of this new knowledge available to all—and, beyond that, in an effort to extend farm technology to hungry nations—to wipe out disease—to increase the exchanges of scientists and. their knowledge—and to make our own laboratories available to technicians of other lands who lack the facilities to pursue their own work. Where nature makes natural allies of us all, we can demonstrate that beneficial relations are possible even with those with whom we most deeply disagree—and this must someday be the basis of world peace and world law.

V.

I have commented on the state of the domestic economy, our balance of payments, our Federal and social budget and the state of the world. I would like to conclude with a few remarks about the state of the Executive branch. We have found it full of honest and useful public servants—but their capacity to act decisively at the exact time action is needed has too often been muffled in the morass of committees, timidities and fictitious theories which have created a growing gap between decision and execution, between planning and reality. In a time of rapidly deteriorating situations at home and abroad, this is bad for the public service and particularly bad for the country; and we mean to make a change.

I have pledged myself and my colleagues in the cabinet to a continuous encouragement of initiative, responsibility and energy in serving the public interest. Let every public servant know, whether his post is high or low, that a man's rank and reputation in this Administration will be determined by the size of the job he does, and not by the size of his staff, his office or his budget. Let it be clear that this Administration recognizes the value of dissent and daring—that we greet healthy controversy as the hallmark of healthy change. Let the public service be a proud and lively career. And let every man and woman who works in any area of our national government, in any branch, at any level, be able to say with pride and with honor in future years: "I served the United States government in that hour of our nation's need."

For only with complete dedication by us all to the national interest can we bring our country through the troubled years that lie ahead. Our problems are critical. The tide is unfavorable. The news will be worse before it is better. And while hoping and working for the best, we should prepare ourselves now for the worst.

We cannot escape our dangers—neither must we let them drive us into panic or narrow isolation. In many areas of the world where the balance of power already rests with our adversaries, the forces of freedom are sharply divided. It is one of the ironies of our time that the techniques of a harsh and repressive system should be able to instill discipline and ardor in its servants. While the blessings of liberty have too often stood for privilege, materialism and a life of case.

But I have a different view of liberty.

Life in 1961 will not be easy. Wishing it, predicting it, even asking for it, will not make it so. There will be further setbacks before the tide is turned. But turn it we must. The hopes of all mankind rest upon us—not simply upon those of us in this chamber, but upon the peasant in Laos, the fisherman in Nigeria, the exile from Cuba, the spirit that moves every man and Nation who shares our hopes for freedom and the future. And in the final analysis, they rest most of all upon the pride and perseverance of our fellow citizens of the great Republic.

In the words of a great President, whose birthday we honor today, closing his final State of the Union Message sixteen years ago, "We pray that we may be worthy of the unlimited opportunities that God has given us."

John F. Kennedy, 1961–1963

Address to Congress on the State of the Union
January 11, 1962

John F. Kennedy split his second State of the Union speech between domestic and international concerns, and urged his fellow Americans to rise to the challenges of a difficult world, stating, "if we cannot fulfill our own ideals here, we cannot expect others to accept them."

On the domestic front, Kennedy said that despite improving economic conditions, more needed to be done. He called for legislation to train workers in new skills, to train and place young workers, and to strengthen the country's unemployment compensation program, among others. He urged the creation of a "new Department of Urban Affairs and Housing." That cabinet department—housing and urban development—eventually would be created in 1965, after Kennedy's death.

During his brief administration, Kennedy sought progress on the issue of civil rights. He named many African Americans to public positions, called for school desegregation, and set up a plan to encourage black voter participation. In this 1962 State of the Union address, the president called for the abolition of such tactics as poll taxes that inhibited African Americans from voting and mentioned that the one hundredth anniversary of the Emancipation Proclamation would be the following January. Major civil rights legislation would end up being passed after Kennedy's assassination, during the presidency of Lyndon B. Johnson.

When it came to the international scene, Kennedy's administration, like those of its two predecessors, faced the difficulties of dealing with Cold War tensions between the United States and its allies, and the communist world—a situation Kennedy described in this address as "a global civil war." Kennedy did not specifically mention Cuba, which the previous year had been the site of the Bay of Pigs disaster—a failed CIA plan that sought to overthrow Fidel Castro's communist government.

Kennedy praised the Peace Corps, a new program initiated the previous year that sent volunteers to less-developed countries, noting that the program was now operating in fourteen nations.

He also commented that the United States had made a commitment the previous year to focus on the exploration of outer space. In a May 25, 1961, speech entitled, "Special Message to the Congress on Urgent National Needs," Kennedy had pledged to send a man to the moon by the end of the 1960s. The Soviets had been ahead of the United States in the space race, but the United States succeeded in 1969 in becoming the first country to land a man on the moon.

Kennedy also mentioned Vietnam. It already was a trouble spot for the United States, which was backing the South Vietnamese regime against the communist North Vietnamese and their southern Viet Cong allies. "It is a war of attempted subjugation—and it will be resisted," the president declared.

Mr. Vice President, my old colleague from Massachusetts and your new Speaker, John McCormack, Members of the 87th Congress, ladies and gentlemen:

This week we begin anew our joint and separate efforts to build the American future. But, sadly, we build without a man who linked a long past with the present and looked strongly to the future. "Mister Sam" Rayburn is gone. Neither this House nor the Nation is the same without him.

Members of the Congress, the Constitution makes us not rivals for power but partners for progress. We are all trustees for the American people, custodians of the American heritage. It is my task to report the State of the Union—to improve it is the task of us all.

In the past year, I have traveled not only across our own land but to other lands—to the North and the South, and across the seas. And I have found—as I am sure you have, in your travels—that people everywhere, in spite of occasional disappointments, look to us—not to our wealth or power, but to the splendor of our ideals. For our Nation is commissioned by history to be either an observer of freedom's failure or the cause of its success. Our overriding obligation in the months ahead is to fulfill the world's hopes by fulfilling our own faith.

I. Strengthening the Economy

That task must begin at home. For if we cannot fulfill our own ideals here, we cannot expect others to accept them. And when the youngest child alive today has grown to the cares of manhood, our position in the world will be determined first of all by what provisions we make today—for his education, his health, and his opportunities for a good home and a good job and a good life.

At home, we began the year in the valley of recession—we completed it on the high road of recovery and growth. With the help of new congressionally approved or administratively increased stimulants to our economy, the number of major surplus labor u areas has declined from 101 to 60; nonagricultural employment has increased by more than a million jobs; and the average factory work-week has risen to well over 40 hours. At year's end the economy which Mr. Khrushchev once called a "stumbling horse" was racing to new records in consumer spending, labor income, and industrial production.

We are gratified—but we are not satisfied. Too many unemployed are still looking for the blessings of prosperity. As those who leave our schools and farms demand new jobs, automation takes old jobs away. To expand our growth and job opportunities, I urge on the Congress three measures:

First, the Manpower Training and Development Act, to stop the waste of able-bodied men and women who want to work, but whose only skill has been replaced by a machine, or moved with a mill, or shut down with a mine;

Second, the Youth Employment Opportunities Act, to help train and place not only the one million young Americans who are both out of school and out of work, but the twenty-six million young Americans entering the labor market in this decade; and

Third, the 8 percent tax credit for investment in machinery and equipment, which, combined with planned revisions of depreciation allowances, will spur our modernization, our growth, and our ability to compete abroad.

Moreover—pleasant as it may be to bask in the warmth of recovery—let us not forget that we have suffered three recessions in the last 7 years. The time to repair the roof is when the sun is shining—by filling three basic gaps in our anti-recession protection. We need:

First, presidential standby authority, subject to congressional veto, to adjust personal income tax rates downward within a specified range and time, to slow down an economic decline before it has dragged us all down;

Second, presidential standby authority, upon a given rise in the rate of unemployment, to accelerate Federal and federally-aided capital improvement programs; and

Third, a permanent strengthening of our unemployment compensation system—to maintain for our fellow citizens searching for a job who cannot find it, their purchasing power and their living standards without constant resort—as we have seen in recent years by the Congress and the administrations—to temporary supplements.

If we enact this six-part program, we can show the whole world that a free economy need not be an unstable economy—that a free system need not leave men unemployed—and that a free society is not only the most productive but the most stable form of organization yet fashioned by man.

II. Fighting Inflation

But recession is only one enemy of a free economy—inflation is another. Last year, 1961, despite rising production and demand, consumer prices held almost steady—and wholesale prices declined. This is the best record of overall price stability of any comparable period of recovery since the end of World War II.

Inflation too often follows in the shadow of growth—while price stability is made easy by stagnation or controls. But we mean to maintain both stability and growth in a climate of freedom.

Our first line of defense against inflation is the good sense and public spirit of business and labor—keeping their total increases in wages and profits in step with productivity. There is no single statistical test to guide each company and each union. But I strongly urge them—for their country's interest, and for their own—to apply the test of the public interest to these transactions.

Within this same framework of growth and wage-price stability:

—This administration has helped keep our economy competitive by widening the access of small business to credit and Government contracts, and by stepping up the drive against monopoly, price-fixing, and racketeering;

—We will submit a Federal Pay Reform bill aimed at giving our classified, postal, and other employees new pay scales more comparable to those of private industry;

—We are holding the fiscal 1962 budget deficit far below the level incurred after the last recession in 1958; and, finally,

—I am submitting for fiscal 1963 a balanced Federal Budget.

This is a joint responsibility, requiring Congressional cooperation on appropriations, and on three sources of income in particular:

First, an increase in postal rates, to end the postal deficit;

Secondly, passage of the tax reforms previously urged, to remove unwarranted tax preferences, and to apply to dividends and to interest the same withholding requirements we have long applied to wages; and

Third, extension of the present excise and corporation tax rates, except for those changes—which will be recommended in a message—affecting transportation.

III. Getting America Moving

But a stronger nation and economy require more than a balanced Budget. They require progress in those programs that spur our growth and fortify our strength.

Cities

A strong America depends on its cities—America's glory, and sometimes America's shame. To substitute sunlight for congestion and progress for decay, we have stepped up existing urban renewal and housing programs, and launched new ones—redoubled the attack on water pollution—speeded aid to airports, hospitals, highways, and our declining mass transit systems—and secured new weapons to combat organized crime, racketeering, and youth delinquency, assisted by the coordinated and hard-hitting efforts of our investigative services: the FBI, the Internal Revenue, the Bureau of Narcotics, and many others. We shall need further anti-crime, mass transit, and transportation legislation—and new tools to fight air pollution. And with all this effort under way, both equity and commonsense require that our nation's urban areas—containing three-fourths of our population—sit as equals at the Cabinet table. I urge a new Department of Urban Affairs and Housing.

Agriculture and Resources

A strong America also depends on its farms and natural resources. American farmers took heart in 1961—from a billion dollar rise in farm income—and from a hopeful start on reducing the farm surpluses. But we are still operating under a patchwork accumulation of old laws, which cost us $1 billion a year in CCC [Commodity Credit Coprporation] carrying charges alone, yet fail to halt rural poverty or boost farm earnings.

Our task is to master and turn to fully fruitful ends the magnificent productivity of our farms and farmers. The revolution on our own countryside stands in the sharpest contrast to the repeated farm failures of the Communist nations and is a source of pride to us all. Since 1950 our agricultural output per man-hour has actually doubled! Without new, realistic measures, it will someday swamp our farmers and our taxpayers in a national scandal or a farm depression.

I will, therefore, submit to the Congress a new comprehensive farm program— tailored to fit the use of our land and the supplies of each crop to the long-range needs of the sixties—and designed to prevent chaos in the sixties with a program of commonsense.

We also need for the sixties—if we are to bequeath our full national estate to our heirs—a new long-range conservation and recreation program—expansion of our superb national parks and forests—preservation of our authentic wilderness areas—new starts on water and power projects as our population steadily increases—and expanded REA generation and transmission loans.

Civil Rights

But America stands for progress in human rights as well as economic affairs, and a strong America requires the assurance of full and equal rights to all its citizens, of any race or of any color. This administration has shown as never before how much could be done through the full use of Executive powers—through the enforcement of laws already passed by the Congress—through persuasion, negotiation, and litigation, to secure the constitutional rights of all: the right to vote, the right to travel without hindrance across State lines, and the right to free public education.

I issued last March a comprehensive order to guarantee the right to equal employment opportunity in all Federal agencies and contractors. The Vice President's Committee thus created has done much, including the voluntary "Plans for progress" which, in all sections of the country, are achieving a quiet but striking success in opening up to all races new professional, supervisory, and other job opportunities.

But there is much more to be done—by the Executive, by the courts, and by the Congress. Among the bills now pending before you, on which the executive departments will comment in detail, are appropriate methods of strengthening these basic rights which have our full support. The right to vote, for example, should no longer be denied through such arbitrary devices on a local level, sometimes abused, such as literacy tests and poll taxes. As we approach the 100th anniversary, next January, of the Emancipation Proclamation, let the acts of every branch of the Government—and every citizen—portray that "righteousness does exalt a nation."

Health and Welfare

Finally, a strong America cannot neglect the aspirations of its citizens—the welfare of the needy, the health care of the elderly, the education of the young. For we are not developing the Nation's wealth for its own sake. Wealth is the means—and people are the ends. All our material riches will avail us little if we do not use them to expand the opportunities of our people.

Last year, we improved the diet of needy people—provided more hot lunches and fresh milk to school children built more college dormitories—and, for the elderly, expanded private housing, nursing homes, heath services, and social security. But we have just begun.

To help those least fortunate of all, I am recommending a new public welfare program, stressing services instead of support, rehabilitation instead of relief, and training for useful work instead of prolonged dependency.

To relieve the critical shortage of doctors and dentists—and this is a matter which should concern us all—and expand research, I urge action to aid medical and dental colleges and scholarships and to establish new National Institutes of Health.

To take advantage of modern vaccination achievements, I am proposing a mass immunization program, aimed at the virtual elimination of such ancient enemies of our children as polio, diphtheria, whooping cough, and tetanus.

To protect our consumers from the careless and the unscrupulous, I shall recommend improvements in the Food and Drug laws—strengthening inspection and standards, halting unsafe and worthless products, preventing misleading labels, and cracking down on the illicit sale of habit-forming drugs.

But in matters of health, no piece of unfinished business is more important or more urgent than the enactment under the social security system of health insurance for the aged.

For our older citizens have longer and more frequent illnesses, higher hospital and medical bills and too little income to pay them. Private health insurance helps very few—for its cost is high and its coverage limited. Public welfare cannot help those too proud to seek relief but hard-pressed to pay their own bills. Nor can their children or grandchildren always sacrifice their own health budgets to meet this constant drain.

Social security has long helped to meet the hardships of retirement, death, and disability. I now urge that its coverage be extended without further delay to provide health insurance for the elderly.

Education

Equally important to our strength is the quality of our education. Eight million adult Americans are classified as functionally illiterate. This is a disturbing figure—reflected in Selective Service rejection rates—reflected in welfare rolls and crime rates. And I shall recommend plans for a massive attack to end this adult illiteracy.

I shall also recommend bills to improve educational quality, to stimulate the arts, and, at the college level, to provide Federal loans for the construction of academic facilities and federally financed scholarships.

If this Nation is to grow in wisdom and strength, then every able high school graduate should have the opportunity to develop his talents. Yet nearly half lack either the funds or the facilities to attend college. Enrollments are going to double in our colleges in the short space of 10 years. The annual cost per student is skyrocketing to astronomical levels—now averaging $1,650 a year, although almost half of our families earn less than $5,000. They cannot afford such costs—but this Nation cannot afford to maintain its military power and neglect its brainpower.

But excellence in education must begin at the elementary level. I sent to the Congress last year a proposal for Federal aid to public school construction and teachers' salaries. I believe that bill, which passed the Senate and received House Committee approval, offered the minimum amount required by our needs and—in terms of across-the-board aid—the maximum scope permitted by our Constitution. I therefore see no reason to weaken or withdraw that bill: and I urge its passage at this session.

"Civilization," said H. G. Wells, "is a race between education and catastrophe." It is up to you in this Congress to determine the winner of that race.

These are not unrelated measures addressed to specific gaps or grievances in our national life. They are the pattern of our intentions and the foundation of our hopes. "I believe in democracy," said Woodrow Wilson, "because it releases the energy of every human being." The dynamic of democracy is the power and the purpose of the individual, and the policy of this administration is to give to the individual the opportunity to realize his own highest possibilities.

Our program is to open to all the opportunity for steady and productive employment, to remove from all the handicap of arbitrary or irrational exclusion, to offer to all the facilities for education and health and welfare, to make society the servant of the individual and the individual the source of progress, and thus to realize for all the full promise of American life.

IV. Our Goals Abroad

All of these efforts at home give meaning to our efforts abroad. Since the close of the Second World War, a global civil war has divided and tormented mankind. But it is not our military might, or our higher standard of living, that has most distinguished us from our adversaries. It is our belief that the state is the servant of the citizen and not his master.

This basic clash of ideas and wills is but one of the forces reshaping our globe—swept as it is by the tides of hope and fear, by crises in the headlines today that become mere footnotes tomorrow. Both the successes and the setbacks of the past year remain on our agenda of unfinished business. For every apparent blessing contains the seeds of danger—every area of trouble gives out a ray of hope—and the one unchangeable certainty is that nothing is certain or unchangeable.

Yet our basic goal remains the same: a peaceful world community of free and independent states—free to choose their own future and their own system, so long as it does not threaten the freedom of others.

Some may choose forms and ways that we would not choose for ourselves—but it is not for us that they are choosing. We can welcome diversity—the Communists cannot. For we offer a world of choice—they offer the world of coercion. And the way of the past shows clearly that freedom, not coercion, is the wave of the future. At times our goal has been obscured by crisis or endangered by conflict—but it draws sustenance from five basic sources of strength:

—the moral and physical strength of the United States;

—the united strength of the Atlantic Community;

—the regional strength of our Hemispheric relations;

—the creative strength of our efforts in the new and developing nations; and

—the peace-keeping strength of the United Nations.

V. Our Military Strength

Our moral and physical strength begins at home as already discussed. But it includes our military strength as well. So long as fanaticism and fear brood over the affairs of men, we must arm to deter others from aggression.

In the past 12 months our military posture has steadily improved. We increased the previous defense budget by 15 percent—not in the expectation of war but for the preservation of peace. We more than doubled our acquisition rate of Polaris submarines—we doubled the production capacity for Minuteman missiles—and increased by 50 percent the number of manned bombers standing ready on a 15 minute alert. This year the combined force levels planned under our new Defense budget—including nearly three hundred additional Polaris and Minuteman missiles—have been precisely calculated to insure the continuing strength of our nuclear deterrent.

But our strength may be tested at many levels. We intend to have at all times the capacity to resist non-nuclear or limited attacks—as a complement to our nuclear capacity, not as a substitute. We have rejected any all-or-nothing posture which would leave no choice but inglorious retreat or unlimited retaliation.

Thus we have doubled the number of ready combat divisions in the Army's strategic reserve—increased our troops in Europe—built up the Marines—added new sealift and airlift capacity—modernized our weapons and ammunition—expanded our anti-guerrilla forces—and increased the active fleet by more than 70 vessels and our tactical air forces by nearly a dozen wings.

Because we needed to reach this higher long-term level of readiness more quickly, 155,000 members of the Reserve and National Guard were activated under the Act of this Congress. Some disruptions and distress were inevitable. But the overwhelming majority bear their burdens—and their Nation's burdens—with admirable and traditional devotion.

In the coming year, our reserve programs will be revised—two Army Divisions will, I hope, replace those Guard Divisions on duty—and substantial other increases will boost our Air Force fighter units, the procurement of equipment, and our continental defense and warning efforts. The Nation's first serious civil defense shelter program is under way, identifying, marking, and stocking 50 million spaces; and I urge your approval of Federal incentives for the construction of public fall-out shelters in schools and hospitals and similar centers.

VI. The United Nations

But arms alone are not enough to keep the peace—it must be kept by men. Our instrument and our hope is the United Nations—and I see little merit in the impatience of those who would abandon this imperfect world instrument because they dislike our imperfect world. For the troubles of a world organization merely reflect the troubles of the world itself. And if the organization is weakened, these troubles can only increase. We may not always agree with every detailed action taken by every officer of the United Nations, or with every voting majority. But as an institution, it should have in the future, as it has had in the past since its inception, no stronger or more faithful member than the United States of America.

In 1961 the peace-keeping strength of the United Nations was reinforced. And those who preferred or predicted its demise, envisioning a troika in the seat of Hammarskjöld—or Red China inside the Assembly—have seen instead a new vigor, under a new Secretary General and a fully independent Secretariat. In making plans for a new forum and principles on disarmament for peace-keeping in outer space—for a decade of development effort—the UN fulfilled its Charter's lofty aim.

Eighteen months ago the tangled and turbulent Congo presented the UN with its gravest challenge. The prospect was one of chaos—or certain big-power confrontation, with all of its hazards and all of its risks, to us and to others. Today the hopes have improved for peaceful conciliation within a united Congo. This is the objective of our policy in this important area.

No policeman is universally popular—particularly when he uses his stick to restore law and order on his beat. Those members who are willing to contribute their votes and their views—but very little else—have created a serious deficit by refusing to pay their share of special UN assessments. Yet they do pay their annual assessments to retain their votes—and a new UN Bond issue, financing special operations for the next 18 months, is to be repaid with interest from these regular assessments. This is clearly in our interest. It will not only keep the UN solvent, but require all voting members to pay their fair share of its activities. Our share of special operations has long been much higher than our share of the annual assessment—and the bond issue will in effect reduce our disproportionate obligation, and for these reasons, I am urging Congress to approve our participation.

With the approval of this Congress, we have undertaken in the past year a great new effort in outer space. Our aim is not simply to be first on the moon, any more than Charles Lindbergh's real aim was to be the first to Paris. His aim was to develop the techniques of our own country and other countries in the field of air and the atmosphere, and our objective in making this effort, which we hope will place one of our citizens on the moon, is to develop in a new frontier of science, commerce and cooperation, the position of the United States and the Free World.

This Nation belongs among the first to explore it, and among the first—if not the first—we shall be. We are offering our know-how and our cooperation to the United Nations. Our satellites will soon be providing other nations with improved weather observations. And I shall soon send to the Congress a measure to govern the financing and operation of an International Communications Satellite system, in a manner consistent with the public interest and our foreign policy.

But peace in space will help us naught once peace on earth is gone. World order will be secured only when the whole world has laid down these weapons which seem to offer us present security but threaten the future survival of the human race. That armistice day seems very far away. The vast resources of this planet are being devoted more and more to the means of destroying, instead of enriching, human life.

But the world was not meant to be a prison in which man awaits his execution. Nor has mankind survived the tests and trials of thousands of years to surrender everything—including its existence—now. This Nation has the will and the faith to make a supreme effort to break the log jam on disarmament and nuclear tests—and we will persist until we prevail, until the rule of law has replaced the ever dangerous use of force.

VII. Latin America

I turn now to a prospect of great promise: our Hemispheric relations. The Alliance for Progress is being rapidly transformed from proposal to program. Last month in Latin America I saw for myself the quickening of hope, the revival of confidence, the new trust in our country—among workers and farmers as well as diplomats. We have pledged our help in speeding their economic, educational, and social progress. The Latin American Republics have in turn pledged a new and strenuous effort of self-help and self-reform.

To support this historic undertaking, I am proposing—under the authority contained in the bills of the last session of the Congress—a special long-term Alliance for Progress fund of $3 billion. Combined with our Food for Peace, Export-Import Bank, and other resources, this will provide more than $1 billion a year in new support for the Alliance. In addition, we have increased twelve-fold our Spanish and Portuguese language broadcasting in Latin America, and improved Hemispheric trade and defense.

And while the blight of communism has been increasingly exposed and isolated in the Americas, liberty has scored a gain. The people of the Dominican Republic, with our firm encouragement and help, and those of our sister Republics of this Hemisphere are safely passing through the treacherous course from dictatorship through disorder towards democracy.

VIII. The New and Developing Nations

Our efforts to help other new or developing nations, and to strengthen their stand for freedom, have also made progress. A newly unified Agency for International Development is reorienting our foreign assistance to emphasize long-term development loans instead of grants, more economic aid instead of military, individual plans to meet the individual needs of the nations, and new standards on what they must do to marshal their own resources.

A newly conceived Peace Corps is winning friends and helping people in fourteen countries—supplying trained and dedicated young men and women, to give these new nations a hand in building a society, and a glimpse of the best that is in our country. If there is a problem here, it is that we cannot supply the spontaneous and mounting demand.

A newly-expanded Food for Peace Program is feeding the hungry of many lands with the abundance of our productive farms—providing lunches for children in school, wages for economic development, relief for the victims of flood and famine, and a better diet for millions whose daily bread is their chief concern.

These programs help people; and, by helping people, they help freedom. The views of their governments may sometimes be very different from ours—but events in Africa, the Middle East, and Eastern Europe teach us never to write off any nation as lost to the Communists. That is the lesson of our time. We support the independence of those newer or weaker states whose history, geography, economy or lack of power impels them to remain outside "entangling alliances"—as we did for more than a century. For the independence of nations is a bar to the Communists' "grand design"— it is the basis of our own.

In the past year, for example, we have urged a neutral and independent Laos— regained there a common policy with our major allies—and insisted that a cease-fire precede negotiations. While a workable formula for supervising its independence is still to be achieved, both the spread of war—which might have involved this country also— and a Communist occupation have thus far been prevented.

A satisfactory settlement in Laos would also help to achieve and safeguard the peace in Viet-Nam—where the foe is increasing his tactics of terror—where our own efforts have been stepped up—and where the local government has initiated new programs and reforms to broaden the base of resistance. The systematic aggression now bleeding that country is not a "war of liberation"—for Viet-Nam is already free. It is a war of attempted subjugation—and it will be resisted.

IX. The Atlantic Community

Finally, the united strength of the Atlantic Community has flourished in the last year under severe tests. NATO has increased both the number and the readiness of its air, ground, and naval units—both its nuclear and non-nuclear capabilities. Even greater efforts by all its members are still required. Nevertheless our unity of purpose and will has been, I believe, immeasurably strengthened.

The threat to the brave city of Berlin remains. In these last 6 months the Allies have made it unmistakably clear that our presence in Berlin, our free access thereto, and the freedom of two million West Berliners would not be surrendered either to force or through appeasement—and to maintain those rights and obligations, we are prepared to talk, when appropriate, and to fight, if necessary. Every member of NATO stands with us in a common commitment to preserve this symbol of free man's will to remain free.

I cannot now predict the course of future negotiations over Berlin. I can only say that we are sparing no honorable effort to find a peaceful and mutually acceptable resolution of this problem. I believe such a resolution can be found, and with it an improvement in our relations with the Soviet Union, if only the leaders in the Kremlin will recognize the basic rights and interests involved, and the interest of all mankind in peace.

But the Atlantic Community is no longer concerned with purely military aims. As its common undertakings grow at an ever-increasing pace, we are, and increasingly will be, partners in aid, trade, defense, diplomacy, and monetary affairs.

The emergence of the new Europe is being matched by the emergence of new ties across the Atlantic. It is a matter of undramatic daily cooperation in hundreds of workaday tasks: of currencies kept in effective relation, of development loans meshed together, of standardized weapons, and concerted diplomatic positions. The Atlantic Community grows, not like a volcanic mountain, by one mighty explosion, but like a coral reef, from the accumulating activity of all.

Thus, we in the free world are moving steadily toward unity and cooperation, in the teeth of that old Bolshevik prophecy, and at the very time when extraordinary rumbles of discord can be heard across the Iron Curtain. It is not free societies which bear within them the seeds of inevitable disunity.

X. Our Balance of Payments

On one special problem, of great concern to our friends, and to us, I am proud to give the Congress an encouraging report. Our efforts to safeguard the dollar are progressing. In the 11 months preceding last February 1, we suffered a net loss of nearly $2 billion in gold. In the 11 months that followed, the loss was just over half a billion dollars. And our deficit in our basic transactions with the rest of the world—trade, defense, foreign aid, and capital, excluding volatile short-term flows—has been reduced from $2 billion for 1960 to about one-third that amount for 1961. Speculative fever against the dollar is ending—and confidence in the dollar has been restored.

We did not—and could not—achieve these gains through import restrictions, troop withdrawals, exchange controls, dollar devaluation or choking off domestic recovery. We acted not in panic but in perspective. But the problem is not yet solved. Persistently large deficits would endanger our economic growth and our military and defense commitments abroad. Our goal must be a reasonable equilibrium in our balance of payments. With the cooperation of the Congress, business, labor, and our major allies, that goal can be reached.

We shall continue to attract foreign tourists and investments to our shores, to seek increased military purchases here by our allies, to maximize foreign aid procurement from American firms, to urge increased aid from other fortunate nations to the less fortunate, to seek tax laws which do not favor investment in other industrialized nations or tax havens, and to urge coordination of allied fiscal and monetary policies so as to discourage large and disturbing capital movements.

Trade

Above all, if we are to pay for our commitments abroad, we must expand our exports. Our businessmen must be export conscious and export competitive. Our tax policies must spur modernization of our plants—our wage and price gains must be consistent with productivity to hold the line on prices—our export credit and promotion campaigns for American industries must continue to expand.

But the greatest challenge of all is posed by the growth of the European Common Market. Assuming the accession of the United Kingdom, there will arise across the Atlantic a trading partner behind a single external tariff similar to ours with an economy which nearly equals our own. Will we in this country adapt our thinking to these new prospects and patterns—or will we wait until events have passed us by?

This is the year to decide. The Reciprocal Trade Act is expiring. We need a new law—a wholly new approach—a bold new instrument of American trade policy. Our decision could well affect the unity of the West, the course of the Cold War, and the economic growth of our Nation for a generation to come.

If we move decisively, our factories and farms can increase their sales to their richest, fastest-growing market. Our exports will increase. Our balance of payments position will improve. And we will have forged across the Atlantic a trading partnership with vast resources for freedom.

If, on the other hand, we hang back in deference to local economic pressures, we will find ourselves cut off from our major allies. Industries—and I believe this is most vital—industries will move their plants and jobs and capital inside the walls of the Common Market, and jobs, therefore, will be lost here in the United States if they cannot otherwise compete for its consumers. Our farm surpluses—our balance of trade, as you all know, to Europe, the Common Market, in farm products, is nearly three or four to one in our favor, amounting to one of the best earners of dollars in our balance of payments structure, and without entrance to this Market, without the ability to enter it, our farm surpluses will pile up in the Middle West, tobacco in the South, and other commodities, which have gone through Western Europe for 15 years. Our balance of payments position will worsen. Our consumers will lack a wider choice of goods at lower prices. And millions of American workers—whose jobs depend on the sale or the transportation or the distribution of exports or imports, or whose jobs will be endangered by the movement of our capital to Europe, or whose jobs can be maintained only in. an expanding economy—these millions of workers in your home States and mine will see their real interests sacrificed.

Members of the Congress: The United States did not rise to greatness by waiting for others to lead. This Nation is the world's foremost manufacturer, farmer, banker, consumer, and exporter. The Common Market is moving ahead at an economic growth rate twice ours. The Communist economic offensive is under way. The opportunity is ours—the initiative is up to us—and I believe that 1962 is the time.

To seize that initiative, I shall shortly send to the Congress a new five-year Trade Expansion Action, far-reaching in scope but designed with great care to make certain that its benefits to our people far outweigh any risks. The bill will permit the gradual elimination of tariffs here in the United States and in the Common Market on those items in which we together supply 80 percent of the world's trade—mostly items in which our own ability to compete is demonstrated by the fact that we sell abroad, in these items, substantially more than we import. This step will make it possible for our major industries to compete with their counterparts in Western Europe for access to European consumers.

On other goods the bill will permit a gradual reduction of duties up to 50 percent—permitting bargaining by major categories—and provide for appropriate and tested forms of assistance to firms and employees adjusting to import competition. We are not neglecting the safeguards provided by peril points, an escape clause, or the National Security Amendment. Nor are we abandoning our non-European friends or our traditional "most-favored nation" principle. On the contrary, the bill will provide new encouragement for their sale of tropical agricultural products, so important to our friends in Latin America, who have long depended upon the European market, who now find themselves faced with new challenges which we must join with them in overcoming.

Concessions, in this bargaining, must of course be reciprocal, not unilateral. The Common Market will not fulfill its own high promise unless its outside tariff walls are low. The dangers of restriction or timidity in our own policy have counterparts for our friends in Europe. For together we face a common challenge: to enlarge the prosperity of free men everywhere—to build in partnership a new trading community in which all free nations may gain from the productive energy of free competitive effort.

These various elements in our foreign policy lead, as I have said, to a single goal—the goal of a peaceful world of free and independent states. This is our guide for the present and our vision for the future—a free community of nations, independent but interdependent, uniting north and south, east and west, in one great family of man, outgrowing and transcending the hates and fears that rend our age.

We will not reach that goal today, or tomorrow. We may not reach it in our own lifetime. But the quest is the greatest adventure of our century. We sometimes chafe at the burden of our obligations, the complexity of our decisions, the agony of our choices. But there is no comfort or security for us in evasion, no solution in abdication, no relief in irresponsibility.

A year ago, in assuming the tasks of the Presidency, I said that few generations, in all history, had been granted the role of being the great defender of freedom in its hour of maximum danger. This is our good fortune; and I welcome it now as I did a year ago. For it is the fate of this generation—of you in the Congress and of me as President—to live with a struggle we did not start, in a world we did not make. But the pressures of life are not always distributed by choice. And while no nation has ever faced such a challenge, no nation has ever been so ready to seize the burden and the glory of freedom.

And in this high endeavor, may God watch over the United States of America.

John F. Kennedy, 1961–1963

Address to Congress on the State of the Union

January 14, 1963

John F. Kennedy's third—and last—State of the Union address was delivered in January 1963. The previous October, the United States had faced a major show-down with the Soviet Union over the presence of missiles in Cuba and had emerged with a Cold War triumph: the Soviets had agreed to remove the missiles from the island. Kennedy referred indirectly to the Cuban Missile Crisis at the start of his address, noting "the courageous calm of a united people in a perilous hour."

Kennedy, once again, called for continued commitment on the part of Americans to keep pushing forward on both the domestic and international fronts. "This is the side of the hill, not the top," the president stated.

On the domestic side, Kennedy called for a major tax cut that would affect both individuals and businesses, calling it the most important task for the new Congress. Both the House and Senate had remained in Democratic hands as a result of the 1962 midterm elections. But it would take until after Kennedy's death, during the presidency of his successor, Lyndon Johnson, for the tax cut to pass.

When it came to the larger world picture, Kennedy commented that the United States would continue to need "the best defense in the world," one that would mean a larger defense budget. He noted that there were "increasing strains and tensions within the communist bloc" between the two major communist powers, the Soviet Union and China. Vietnam was not a major part of the president's speech, but he did mention it, at one point stating that the "spearpoint of aggression has been blunted in Vietnam." That year, however, the United States would come to be more involved in the conflict in the Southeast Asian country—a conflict that would come to dominate Johnson's presidency.

Kennedy's administration would come to a shocking close on November 22, 1963. The president was on a trip to Dallas, Texas, and, as his motorcade drove along, he was shot and mortally wounded; he died later that day. Lee Harvey Oswald was apprehended for the crime; he would be assassinated several days later by Jack Ruby. The country was plunged into a period of mourning, with Americans glued to the television coverage of the tragic events. The Kennedy era, with its romantic, glamorous image, would become known as "Camelot."

Mr. Vice President, Mr. Speaker, Members of the 88th Congress:

I.

I congratulate you all—not merely on your electoral victory but on your selected role in history. For you and I are privileged to serve the great Republic in what could be the most decisive decade in its long history. The choices we make, for good or ill, may well shape the state of the Union for generations yet to come.

Little more than 100 weeks ago I assumed the office of President of the United States. In seeking the help of the Congress and our countrymen, I pledged no easy answers. I pledged—and asked—only toil and dedication. These the Congress and the people have given in good measure. And today, having witnessed in recent months a heightened respect for our national purpose and power—having seen the courageous calm of a united people in a perilous hour—and having observed a steady improvement in the opportunities and well-being of our citizens—I can report to you that the state of this old but youthful Union, in the 175th year of its life, is good.

In the world beyond our borders, steady progress has been made in building a world of order. The people of West Berlin remain both free and secure. A settlement, though still precarious, has been reached in Laos. The spearpoint of aggression has been blunted in Viet-Nam. The end of agony may be in sight in the Congo. The doctrine of troika is dead. And, while danger continues, a deadly threat has been removed in Cuba.

At home, the recession is behind us. Well over a million more men and women are working today than were working 2 years ago. The average factory workweek is once again more than 40 hours; our industries are turning out more goods than ever before; and more than half of the manufacturing capacity that lay silent and wasted 100 weeks ago is humming with activity.

In short, both at home and abroad, there may now be a temptation to relax. For the road has been long, the burden heavy, and the pace consistently urgent.

But we cannot be satisfied to rest here. This is the side of the hill, not the top. The mere absence of war is not peace. The mere absence of recession is not growth. We have made a beginning—but we have only begun.

Now the time has come to make the most of our gains—to translate the renewal of our national strength into the achievement of our national purpose.

II.

America has enjoyed 22 months of uninterrupted economic recovery. But recovery is not enough. If we are to prevail in the long run, we must expand the long-run strength of our economy. We must move along the path to a higher rate of growth and full employment.

For this would mean tens of billions of dollars more each year in production, profits, wages, and public revenues. It would mean an end to the persistent slack which has kept our unemployment at or above 5 percent for 61 out of the past 62 months—and an end to the growing pressures for such restrictive measures as the 35-hour week, which alone could increase hourly labor costs by as much as 14 percent, start a new wage-price spiral of inflation, and undercut our efforts to compete with other nations.

To achieve these greater gains, one step, above all, is essential—the enactment this year of a substantial reduction and revision in Federal income taxes.

For it is increasingly clear—to those in Government, business, and labor who are responsible for our economy's success—that our obsolete tax system exerts too heavy a drag on private purchasing power, profits, and employment. Designed to check inflation in earlier years, it now checks growth instead. It discourages extra effort and risk. It distorts the use of resources. It invites recurrent recessions, depresses our Federal revenues, and causes chronic budget deficits.

Now, when the inflationary pressures of the war and the post-war years no longer threaten, and the dollar commands new respect—now, when no military crisis strains our resources—now is the time to act. We cannot afford to be timid or slow. For this is the most urgent task confronting the Congress in 1963.

In an early message, I shall propose a permanent reduction in tax rates which will lower liabilities by $13.5 billion. Of this, $11 billion results from reducing individual tax rates, which now range between 20 and 91 percent, to a more sensible range of 14 to 65 percent, with a split in the present first bracket. Two and one-half billion dollars results from reducing corporate tax rates, from 52 percent—which gives the Government today a majority interest in profits—to the permanent pre-Korean level of 47 percent. This is in addition to the more than $2 billion cut in corporate tax liabilities resulting from last year's investment credit and depreciation reform.

To achieve this reduction within the limits of a manageable budgetary deficit, I urge: first, that these cuts be phased over 3 calendar years, beginning in 1963 with a cut of some $6 billion at annual rates; second, that these reductions be coupled with selected structural changes, beginning in 1964, which will broaden the tax base, end unfair or unnecessary preferences, remove or lighten certain hardships, and in the net offset some $3.5 billion of the revenue loss; and third, that budgetary receipts at the outset be increased by $1.5 billion a year, without any change in tax liabilities, by gradually shifting the tax payments of large corporations to a more current time schedule. This combined program, by increasing the amount of our national income, will in time result in still higher Federal revenues. It is a fiscally responsible program—the surest and the soundest way of achieving in time a balanced budget in a balanced full employment economy.

This net reduction in tax liabilities of $10 billion will increase the purchasing power of American families and business enterprises in every tax bracket, with greatest increase going to our low-income consumers. It will, in addition, encourage the initiative and risk-taking on which our free system depends—induce more investment, production, and capacity use—help provide the 2 million new jobs we need every year—and reinforce the American principle of additional reward for additional effort.

I do not say that a measure for tax reduction and reform is the only way to achieve these goals.

—No doubt a massive increase in Federal spending could also create jobs and growth—but, in today's setting, private consumers, employers, and investors should be given a full opportunity first.

—No doubt a temporary tax cut could provide a spur to our economy—but a long-run problem compels a long-run solution.

—No doubt a reduction in either individual or corporation taxes alone would be of great help—but corporations need customers and job seekers need jobs.

—No doubt tax reduction without reform would sound simpler and more attractive to many—but our growth is also hampered by a host of tax inequities and special preferences which have distorted the flow of investment.

—And, finally, there are no doubt some who would prefer to put off a tax cut in the hope that ultimately an end to the cold war would make possible an equivalent cut in expenditures—but that end is not in view and to wait for it would be costly and self-defeating.

In submitting a tax program which will, of course, temporarily increase the deficit but can ultimately end it—and in recognition of the need to control expenditures—I will shortly submit a fiscal 1964 administrative budget which, while allowing for needed rises in defense, space, and fixed interest charges, holds total expenditures for all other purposes below this year's level.

This requires the reduction or postponement of many desirable programs, the absorption of a large part of last year's Federal pay raise through personnel and other economies, the termination of certain installations and projects, and the substitution in several programs of private for public credit. But I am convinced that the enactment this year of tax reduction and tax reform overshadows all other domestic problems in this Congress. For we cannot for long lead the cause of peace and freedom, if we ever cease to set the pace here at home.

III.

Tax reduction alone, however, is not enough to strengthen our society, to provide opportunities for the four million Americans who are born every year, to improve the lives of 32 million Americans who live on the outskirts of poverty.

The quality of American life must keep pace with the quantity of American goods. This country cannot afford to be materially rich and spiritually poor.

Therefore, by holding down the budgetary cost of existing programs to keep within the limitations I have set, it is both possible and imperative to adopt other new measures that we cannot afford to postpone.

These measures are based on a series of fundamental premises, grouped under four related headings:

First, we need to strengthen our Nation by investing in our youth:

—The future of any country which is dependent upon the will and wisdom of its citizens is damaged, and irreparably damaged, whenever any of its children is not educated to the full extent of his talent, from grade school through graduate school. Today, an estimated 4 out of every 10 students in the 5th grade will not even finish high school—and that is a waste we cannot afford.

—In addition, there is no reason why one million young Americans, out of school and out of work, should all remain unwanted and often untrained on our city streets when their energies can be put to good use.

—Finally, the overseas success of our Peace Corps volunteers, most of them young men and women carrying skills and ideas to needy people, suggests the merit of a similar corps serving our own community needs: in mental hospitals, on Indian reservations, in centers for the aged or for young delinquents, in schools for the illiterate or the handicapped. As the idealism of our youth has served world peace, so can it serve the domestic tranquility.

Second, we need to strengthen our Nation by safeguarding its health:

—Our working men and women, instead of being forced to beg for help from public charity once they are old and ill, should start contributing now to their own retirement health program through the Social Security System.

—Moreover, all our miracles of medical research will count for little if we cannot reverse the growing nationwide shortage of doctors, dentists, and nurses, and the widespread shortages of nursing homes and modern urban hospital facilities. Merely to keep the present ratio of doctors and dentists from declining any further, we must over the next 10 years increase the capacity of our medical schools by 50 percent and our dental schools by 100 percent.

—Finally, and of deep concern, I believe that the abandonment of the mentally ill and the mentally retarded to the grim mercy of custodial institutions too often inflicts on them and on their families a needless cruelty which this Nation should not endure. The incidence of mental retardation in this country is three times as high as that of Sweden, for example—and that figure can and must be reduced.

Third, we need to strengthen our Nation by protecting the basic rights of its citizens:

—The right to competent counsel must be assured to every man accused of crime in Federal court, regardless of his means.

—And the most precious and powerful right in the world, the right to vote in a free American election, must not be denied to any citizen on grounds of his race or color. I wish that all qualified Americans permitted to vote were willing to vote, but surely in this centennial year of Emancipation all those who are willing to vote should always be permitted.

Fourth, we need to strengthen our Nation by making the best and the most economical use of its resources and facilities:

—Our economic health depends on healthy transportation arteries; and I believe the way to a more modern, economical choice of national transportation service is through increased competition and decreased regulation. Local mass transit, faring even worse, is as essential a community service as hospitals and highways. Nearly three-fourths of our citizens live in urban areas, which occupy only 2 percent of our land—and if local transit is to survive and relieve the congestion of these cities, it needs Federal stimulation and assistance.

—Next, this Government is in the storage and stockpile business to the melancholy tune of more than $16 billion. We must continue to support farm income, but we should not pile more farm surpluses on top of the $7.5 billion we already own. We must maintain a stockpile of strategic materials, but the $8.5 billion we have acquired—for reasons both good and bad—is much more than we need; and we should be empowered to dispose of the excess in ways which will not cause market disruption.

—Finally, our already overcrowded national parks and recreation areas will have twice as many visitors 10 years from now as they do today. If we do not plan today for the future growth of these and other great natural assets—not only parks and forests but wildlife and wilderness preserves, and water projects of all kinds—our children and their children will be poorer in every sense of the word.

These are not domestic concerns alone. For upon our achievement of greater vitality and strength here at home hang our fate and future in the world: our ability to sustain and supply the security of free men and nations, our ability to command their respect for our leadership, our ability to expand our trade without threat to our balance of payments, and our ability to adjust to the changing demands of cold war competition and challenge.

We shall be judged more by what we do at home than by what we preach abroad. Nothing we could do to help the developing countries would help them half as much as a booming U.S. economy. And nothing our opponents could do to encourage their own ambitions would encourage them half as much as a chronic lagging U.S. economy. These domestic tasks do not divert energy from our security—they provide the very foundation for freedom's survival and success.

IV.

Turning to the world outside, it was only a few years ago—in Southeast Asia, Africa, Eastern Europe, Latin America, even outer space—that communism sought to convey the image of a unified, confident, and expanding empire, closing in on a sluggish America and a free world in disarray. But few people would hold to that picture today.

In these past months we have reaffirmed the scientific and military superiority of freedom. We have doubled our efforts in space, to assure us of being first in the future. We have undertaken the most far-reaching defense improvements in the peacetime history of this country. And we have maintained the frontiers of freedom from Viet-Nam to West Berlin.

But complacency or self-congratulation can imperil our security as much as the weapons of tyranny. A moment of pause is not a promise of peace. Dangerous problems remain from Cuba to the South China Sea. The world's prognosis prescribes, in short, not a year's vacation for us, but a year of obligation and opportunity.

Four special avenues of opportunity stand out: the Atlantic Alliance, the developing nations, the new Sino-Soviet difficulties, and the search for worldwide peace.

V.

First, how fares the grand alliance? Free Europe is entering into a new phase of its long and brilliant history. The era of colonial expansion has passed; the era of national rivalries is fading; and a new era of interdependence and unity is taking shape. Defying the old prophecies of Marx, consenting to what no conqueror could ever compel, the free nations of Europe are moving toward a unity of purpose and power and policy in every sphere of activity.

For 17 years this movement has had our consistent support, both political and economic. Far from resenting the new Europe, we regard her as a welcome partner, not a rival. For the road to world peace and freedom is still long, and there are burdens which only full partners can share—in supporting the common defense, in expanding world trade, in aligning our balance of payments, in aiding the emergent nations, in concerting political and economic policies, and in welcoming to our common effort other industrialized nations, notably Japan, whose remarkable economic and political development of the 1950's permits it now to play on the world scene a major constructive role.

No doubt differences of opinion will continue to get more attention than agreements on action, as Europe moves from independence to more formal interdependence. But these are honest differences among honorable associates—more real and frequent, in fact, among our Western European allies than between them and the United States. For the unity of freedom has never relied on uniformity of opinion. But the basic agreement of this alliance on fundamental issues continues.

The first task of the alliance remains the common defense. Last month Prime Minister Macmillan and I laid plans for a new stage in our long cooperative effort, one which aims to assist in the wider task of framing a common nuclear defense for the whole alliance.

The Nassau agreement recognizes that the security of the West is indivisible, and so must be our defense. But it also recognizes that this is an alliance of proud and sovereign nations, and works best when we do not forget it. It recognizes further that the nuclear defense of the West is not a matter for the present nuclear powers alone—that France will be such a power in the future—and that ways must be found without increasing the hazards of nuclear diffusion, to increase the role of our other partners in planning, manning, and directing a truly multilateral nuclear force within an increasingly intimate NATO alliance. Finally, the Nassau agreement recognizes that nuclear defense is not enough, that the agreed NATO levels of conventional strength must be met, and that the alliance cannot afford to be in a position of having to answer every threat with nuclear weapons or nothing.

We remain too near the Nassau decisions, and too far from their full realization, to know their place in history. But I believe that, for the first time, the door is open for the nuclear defense of the alliance to become a source of confidence, instead of a cause of contention.

The next most pressing concern of the alliance is our common economic goals of trade and growth. This Nation continues to be concerned about its balance-of-payments deficit, which, despite its decline, remains a stubborn and troublesome problem. We believe, moreover, that closer economic ties among all free nations are essential to prosperity and peace. And neither we nor the members of the European Common Market are so affluent that we can long afford to shelter high cost farms or factories from the winds of foreign competition, or to restrict the channels of trade with other nations of the free world. If the Common Market should move toward protectionism and restrictionism, it would undermine its, own basic principles. This Government means to use the authority conferred on it last year by the Congress to encourage trade expansion on both sides of the Atlantic and around the world.

VI.

Second, what of the developing and nonaligned nations? They were shocked by the Soviets' sudden and secret attempt to transform Cuba into a nuclear striking base— and by Communist China's arrogant invasion of India. They have been reassured by our prompt assistance to India, by our support through the United Nations of the Congo's unification, by our patient search for disarmament, and by the improvement in our treatment of citizens and visitors whose skins do not happen to be white. And as the older colonialism recedes, and the neocolonialism of the Communist powers stands out more starkly than ever, they realize more clearly that the issue in the world struggle is not communism versus capitalism, but coercion versus free choice.

They are beginning to realize that the longing for independence is the same the world over, whether it is the independence of West Berlin or Viet-Nam. They are beginning to realize that such independence runs athwart all Communist ambitions but is in keeping with our own—and that our approach to their diverse needs is resilient and resourceful, while the Communists are still relying on ancient doctrines and dogmas.

Nevertheless it is hard for any nation to focus on an external or subversive threat to its independence when its energies are drained in daily combat with the forces of poverty and despair. It makes little sense for us to assail, in speeches and resolutions, the horrors of communism, to spend $50 billion a year to prevent its military advance—and then to begrudge spending, largely on American products, less than one-tenth of that amount to help other nations strengthen their independence and cure the social chaos in which communism always has thrived.

I am proud—and I think most Americans are proud—of a mutual defense and assistance program, evolved with bipartisan support in three administrations, which has, with all its recognized problems, contributed to the fact that not a single one of the nearly fifty U.N. members to gain independence since the Second World War has succumbed to Communist control.

I am proud of a program that has helped to arm and feed and clothe millions of people who live on the front lines of freedom.

I am especially proud that this country has put forward for the 60's a vast cooperative effort to achieve economic growth and social progress throughout the Americas—the Alliance for Progress.

I do not underestimate the difficulties that we face in this mutual effort among our close neighbors, but the free states of this hemisphere, working in close collaboration, have begun to make this alliance a living reality. Today it is feeding one out of every four school age children in Latin America an extra food ration from our farm surplus. It has distributed 1.5 million school books and is building 17,000 classrooms. It has helped resettle tens of thousands of farm families on land they can call their own. It is stimulating our good neighbors to more self-help and self-reform—fiscal, social, institutional, and land reforms. It is bringing new housing and hope, new health and dignity, to millions who were forgotten. The men and women of this hemisphere know that the alliance cannot succeed if it is only another name for United States handouts—that it can succeed only as the Latin American nations themselves devote their best effort to fulfilling its goals.

This story is the same in Africa, in the Middle East, and in Asia. Wherever nations are willing to help themselves, we stand ready to help them build new bulwarks of freedom. We are not purchasing votes for the cold war; we have gone to the aid of imperiled nations, neutrals and allies alike. What we do ask—and all that we ask—is that our help be used to best advantage, and that their own efforts not be diverted by needless quarrels with other independent nations.

Despite all its past achievements, the continued progress of the mutual assistance program requires a persistent discontent with present performance. We have been reorganizing this program to make it a more effective, efficient instrument—and that process will continue this year.

But free world development will still be an uphill struggle. Government aid can only supplement the role of private investment, trade expansion, commodity stabilization, and, above all, internal self-improvement. The processes of growth are gradual—bearing fruit in a decade, not a day. Our successes will be neither quick nor dramatic. But if these programs were ever to be ended, our failures in a dozen countries would be sudden and certain.

Neither money nor technical assistance, however, can be our only weapon against poverty. In the end, the crucial effort is one of purpose, requiring the fuel of finance but also a torch of idealism. And nothing carries the spirit of this American idealism more effectively to the far corners of the earth than the American Peace Corps.

A year ago, less than 900 Peace Corps volunteers were on the job. A year from now they will number more than 9,000—men and women, aged 18 to 79, willing to give 2 years of their lives to helping people in other lands.

There are, in fact, nearly a million Americans serving their country and the cause of freedom in overseas posts, a record no other people can match. Surely those of us who stay at home should be glad to help indirectly: by supporting our aid programs; by opening our doors to foreign visitors and diplomats and students; and by proving, day by day, by deed as well as word, that we are a just and generous people.

VII.

Third, what comfort can we take from the increasing strains and tensions within the Communist bloc? Here hope must be tempered with caution. For the Soviet-Chinese disagreement is over means, not ends. A dispute over how best to bury the free world is no grounds for Western rejoicing.

Nevertheless, while a strain is not a fracture, it is clear that the forces of diversity are at work inside the Communist camp, despite all the iron disciplines of regimentation and all the iron dogmatism's of ideology. Marx is proven wrong once again: for it is the closed Communist societies, not the free and open societies which carry within themselves the seeds of internal disintegration.

The disarray of the Communist empire has been heightened by two other formidable forces. One is the historical force of nationalism—and the yearning of all men to be free. The other is the gross inefficiency of their economies. For a closed society is not open to ideas of progress—and a police state finds that it cannot command the grain to grow.

New nations asked to choose between two competing systems need only compare conditions in East and West Germany, Eastern and Western Europe, North and South Viet-Nam. They need only compare the disillusionment of Communist Cuba with the promise of the Alliance for Progress. And all the world knows that no successful system builds a wall to keep its people in and freedom out—and the wall of shame dividing Berlin is a symbol of Communist failure.

VIII.

Finally, what can we do to move from the present pause toward enduring peace? Again I would counsel caution. I foresee no spectacular reversal in Communist methods or goals. But if all these trends and developments can persuade the Soviet Union to walk the path of peace, then let her know that all free nations will journey with her. But until that choice is made, and until the world can develop a reliable system of international security, the free peoples have no choice but to keep their arms nearby.

This country, therefore, continues to require the best defense in the world—a defense which is suited to the sixties. This means, unfortunately, a rising defense budget—for there is no substitute for adequate defense, and no "bargain basement" way of achieving it. It means the expenditure of more than $15 billion this year on nuclear weapons systems alone, a sum which is about equal to the combined defense budgets of our European Allies.

But it also means improved air and missile defenses, improved civil defense, a strengthened anti-guerrilla capacity and, of prime importance, more powerful and flexible non-nuclear forces. For threats of massive retaliation may not deter piecemeal aggression—and a line of destroyers in a quarantine, or a division of well-equipped men on a border, may be more useful to our real security than the multiplication of awesome weapons beyond all rational need.

But our commitment to national safety is not a commitment to expand our military establishment indefinitely. We do not dismiss disarmament as merely an idle dream. For we believe that, in the end, it is the only way to assure the security of all without impairing the interests of any. Nor do we mistake honorable negotiation for appeasement. While we shall never weary in the defense of freedom, neither shall we ever abandon the pursuit of peace.

In this quest, the United Nations requires our full and continued support. Its value in serving the cause of peace has been shown anew in its role in the West New Guinea settlement, in its use as a forum for the Cuban crisis, and in its task of unification in the Congo. Today the United Nations is primarily the protector of the small and the weak, and a safety valve for the strong. Tomorrow it can form the framework for a world of law—a world in which no nation dictates the destiny of another, and in which the vast resources now devoted to destructive means will serve constructive ends.

In short, let our adversaries choose. If they choose peaceful competition, they shall have it. If they come to realize that their ambitions cannot succeed—if they see their "wars of liberation" and subversion will ultimately fail—if they recognize that there is more security in accepting inspection than in permitting new nations to master the black arts of nuclear war—and if they are willing to turn their energies, as we are, to the great unfinished tasks of our own peoples—then, surely, the areas of agreement can be very wide indeed: a clear understanding about Berlin, stability in Southeast Asia, an end to nuclear testing, new checks on surprise or accidental attack, and, ultimately, general and complete disarmament.

IX.

For we seek not the worldwide victory of one nation or system but a worldwide victory of man. The modern globe is too small, its weapons are too destructive, and its disorders are too contagious to permit any other kind of victory.

To achieve this end, the United States will continue to spend a greater portion of its national production than any other people in the free world. For 15 years no other free nation has demanded so much of itself. Through hot wars and cold, through recession and prosperity, through the ages of the atom and outer space, the American people have never faltered and their faith has never flagged. If at times our actions seem to make life difficult for others, it is only because history has made life difficult for us all.

But difficult days need not be dark. I think these are proud and memorable days in the cause of peace and freedom. We are proud, for example, of Major Rudolf Anderson who gave his life over the island of Cuba. We salute Specialist James Allen Johnson who died on the border of South Korea. We pay honor to Sergeant Gerald Pendell who was killed in Viet-Nam. They are among the many who in this century, far from home, have died for our country. Our task now, and the task of all Americans is to live up to their commitment.

My friends: I close on a note of hope. We are not lulled by the momentary calm of the sea or the somewhat clearer skies above. We know the turbulence that lies below, and the storms that are beyond the horizon this year. But now the winds of change appear to be blowing more strongly than ever, in the world of communism as well as our own. For 175 years we have sailed with those winds at our back, and with the tides of human freedom in our favor. We steer our ship with hope, as Thomas Jefferson said, "leaving Fear astern."

Today we still welcome those winds of change—and we have every reason to believe that our tide is running strong. With thanks to Almighty God for seeing us through a perilous passage, we ask His help anew in guiding the "Good Ship Union."

Lyndon B. Johnson

1963–1969

". . . the war against poverty will not be won here in Washington. It must be won in the field, in every private home, in every public office, from the courthouse to the White House."

<small>ADDRESS TO CONGRESS ON THE STATE OF THE UNION, JANUARY 8, 1964</small>

Address to Congress on the State of the Union

January 8, 1964

Lyndon B. Johnson's first State of the Union address came just a month and a half into his presidency. He had succeeded to the office after the assassination on November 22, 1963, of his predecessor, John F. Kennedy. The nation was still in a state of shock over the assassination, and Johnson, who had been Kennedy's vice president, referred early on in his address to the slain president, asking lawmakers to put partisanship aside and enact JFK's proposals.

For Johnson, and for the country, 1964 also was a election year, one in which the new president, a Democrat, would successfully seek his own four-year term in the White House; he defeated Republican Barry Goldwater in a landslide. Johnson, a Texan who had served as Senate majority leader before being selected to run on Kennedy's ticket in 1960, succeeded in pushing Kennedy's tax cut and a major civil rights bill through Congress in 1964.

Johnson opened his speech by urging Congress to make this session "the best in the nation's history" when it came to civil rights, a tax cut, and a variety of other issues. He made a special plea for the tax cut, which Kennedy had proposed. He also stated that "all racial discrimination" must end under federal law.

The new president also called for an "unconditional war on poverty in America"—an issue that would be featured in his Great Society program enacted with Congress's help once Johnson was elected to a four-year term. Among the specific proposals he mentioned in this State of the Union address were assisting poverty-stricken areas of Appalachia, enacting youth employment laws, broadening the food stamp program, and creating a National Service Corps.

When it came to international matters, Johnson spoke of defending freedom from aggressors and from "infiltration practiced by those in Hanoi and Havana"—a reference to problems in Vietnam and Cuba. He also mentioned space exploration, referring to Kennedy's goal of reaching the moon in the 1960s. Although Vietnam was not a focus of Johnson's speech, the conflict there eventually would overwhelm his presidency, which would end in January 1969.

Johnson concluded his speech with a plea against hatred, calling Kennedy "a victim of hate" but also a "builder of faith" and urging Americans to express that faith and help create a world free from hate.

M r. Speaker, Mr. President, Members of the House and Senate, my fellow Americans:

I will be brief, for our time is necessarily short and our agenda is already long.

Last year's congressional session was the longest in peacetime history. With that foundation, let us work together to make this year's session the best in the Nation's history.

Let this session of Congress be known as the session which did more for civil rights than the last hundred sessions combined; as the session which enacted the most far-reaching tax cut of our time; as the session which declared all-out war on human poverty and unemployment in these United States; as the session which finally recognized the health needs of all our older citizens; as the session which reformed our tangled transportation and transit policies; as the session which achieved the most effective, efficient foreign aid program ever; and as the session which helped to build more homes, more schools, more libraries, and more hospitals than any single session of Congress in the history of our Republic.

All this and more can and must be done. It can be done by this summer, and it can be done without any increase in spending. In fact, under the budget that I shall shortly submit, it can be done with an actual reduction in Federal expenditures and Federal employment.

We have in 1964 a unique opportunity and obligation—to prove the success of our system; to disprove those cynics and critics at home and abroad who question our purpose and our competence. If we fail, if we fritter and fumble away our opportunity in needless, senseless quarrels between Democrats and Republicans, or between the House and the Senate, or between the South and North, or between the Congress and the administration, then history will rightfully judge us harshly. But if we succeed, if we can achieve these goals by forging in this country a greater sense of union, then, and only then, can we take full satisfaction in the State of the Union.

II.

Here in the Congress you can demonstrate effective legislative leadership by discharging the public business with clarity and dispatch, voting each important proposal up, or voting it down, but at least bringing it to a fair and a final vote.

Let us carry forward the plans and programs of John Fitzgerald Kennedy—not because of our sorrow or sympathy, but because they are right.

In his memory today, I especially ask all members of my own political faith, in this election year, to put your country ahead of your party, and to always debate principles; never debate personalities.

For my part, I pledge a progressive administration which is efficient, and honest and frugal. The budget to be submitted to the Congress shortly is in full accord with this pledge.

It will cut our deficit in half—from $10 billion to $4,900 million. It will be, in proportion to our national output, the smallest budget since 1951.

It will call for a substantial reduction in Federal employment, a feat accomplished only once before in the last 10 years. While maintaining the full strength of our combat defenses, it will call for the lowest number of civilian personnel in the Department of Defense since 1950.

It will call for total expenditures of $97,900 million—compared to $98,400 million for the current year, a reduction of more than $500 million. It will call for new obligational authority of $103,800 million—a reduction of more than $4 billion below last year's request of $107,900 million.

But it is not a standstill budget, for America cannot afford to stand still. Our population is growing. Our economy is more complex. Our people's needs are expanding.

But by closing down obsolete installations, by curtailing less urgent programs, by cutting back where cutting back seems to be wise, by insisting on a dollar's worth for a dollar spent, I am able to recommend in this reduced budget the most Federal support in history for education, for health, for retraining the unemployed, and for helping the economically and the physically handicapped.

This budget, and this year's legislative program, are designed to help each and every American citizen fulfill his basic hopes—his hopes for a fair chance to make good; his hopes for fair play from the law; his hopes for a full-time job on full-time pay; his hopes for a decent home for his family in a decent community; his hopes for a good school for his children with good teachers; and his hopes for security when faced with sickness or unemployment or old age.

III.

Unfortunately, many Americans live on the outskirts of hope—some because of their poverty, and some because of their color, and all too many because of both. Our task is to help replace their despair with opportunity.

This administration today, here and now, declares unconditional war on poverty in America. I urge this Congress and all Americans to join with me in that effort.

It will not be a short or easy struggle, no single weapon or strategy will suffice, but we shall not rest until that war is won. The richest Nation on earth can afford to win it. We cannot afford to lose it. One thousand dollars invested in salvaging an unemployable youth today can return $40,000 or more in his lifetime.

Poverty is a national problem, requiring improved national organization and support. But this attack, to be effective, must also be organized at the State and the local level and must be supported and directed by State and local efforts.

For the war against poverty will not be won here in Washington. It must be won in the field, in every private home, in every public office, from the courthouse to the White House.

The program I shall propose will emphasize this cooperative approach to help that one-fifth of all American families with incomes too small to even meet their basic needs.

Our chief weapons in a more pinpointed attack will be better schools, and better health, and better homes, and better training, and better job opportunities to help more Americans, especially young Americans, escape from squalor and misery and unemployment rolls where other citizens help to carry them.

Very often a lack of jobs and money is not the cause of poverty, but the symptom. The cause may lie deeper in our failure to give our fellow citizens a fair chance to develop their own capacities, in a lack of education and training, in a lack of medical care and housing, in a lack of decent communities in which to live and bring up their children.

But whatever the cause, our joint Federal-local effort must pursue poverty, pursue it wherever it exists—in city slums and small towns, in sharecropper shacks or in migrant worker camps, on Indian Reservations, among whites as well as Negroes, among the young as well as the aged, in the boom towns and in the depressed areas.

Our aim is not only to relieve the symptom of poverty, but to cure it and, above all, to prevent it. No single piece of legislation, however, is going to suffice.

We will launch a special effort in the chronically distressed areas of Appalachia.

We must expand our small but our successful area redevelopment program.

We must enact youth employment legislation to put jobless, aimless, hopeless youngsters to work on useful projects.

We must distribute more food to the needy through a broader food stamp program.

We must create a National Service Corps to help the economically handicapped of our own country as the Peace Corps now helps those abroad.

We must modernize our unemployment insurance and establish a high-level commission on automation. If we have the brain power to invent these machines, we have the brain power to make certain that they are a boon and not a bane to humanity.

We must extend the coverage of our minimum wage laws to more than 2 million workers now lacking this basic protection of purchasing power.

We must, by including special school aid funds as part of our education program, improve the quality of teaching, training, and counseling in our hardest hit areas.

We must build more libraries in every area and more hospitals and nursing homes under the Hill-Burton Act, and train more nurses to staff them.

We must provide hospital insurance for our older citizens financed by every worker and his employer under Social Security, contributing no more than $1 a month during the employee's working career to protect him in his old age in a dignified manner without cost to the Treasury, against the devastating hardship of prolonged or repeated illness.

We must, as a part of a revised housing and urban renewal program, give more help to those displaced by slum clearance, provide more housing for our poor and our elderly, and seek as our ultimate goal in our free enterprise system a decent home for every American family.

We must help obtain more modern mass transit within our communities as well as low-cost transportation between them.

Above all, we must release $11 billion of tax reduction into the private spending stream to create new jobs and new markets in every area of this land.

IV.

These programs are obviously not for the poor or the underprivileged alone. Every American will benefit by the extension of social security to cover the hospital costs of their aged parents. Every American community will benefit from the construction or modernization of schools, libraries, hospitals, and nursing homes, from the training of more nurses and from the improvement of urban renewal in public transit. And every individual American taxpayer and every corporate taxpayer will benefit from the earliest possible passage of the pending tax bill from both the new investment it will bring and the new jobs that it will create.

That tax bill has been thoroughly discussed for a year. Now we need action. The new budget clearly allows it. Our taxpayers surely deserve it. Our economy strongly demands it. And every month of delay dilutes its benefits in 1964 for consumption, for investment, and for employment.

For until the bill is signed, its investment incentives cannot be deemed certain, and the withholding rate cannot be reduced—and the most damaging and devastating thing you can do to any businessman in America is to keep him in doubt and to keep him guessing on what our tax policy is. And I say that we should now reduce to 14 percent instead of 15 percent our withholding rate.

I therefore urge the Congress to take final action on this bill by the first of February, if at all possible. For however proud we may be of the unprecedented progress of our free enterprise economy over the last 3 years, we should not and we cannot permit it to pause.

In 1963, for the first time in history, we crossed the 70 million job mark, but we will soon need more than 75 million jobs. In 1963 our gross national product reached the $600 billion level—$100 billion higher than when we took office. But it easily could and it should be still $30 billion higher today than it is.

Wages and profits and family income are also at their highest levels in history—but I would remind you that 4 million workers and 13 percent of our industrial capacity are still idle today.

We need a tax cut now to keep this country moving.

V.

For our goal is not merely to spread the work. Our goal is to create more jobs. I believe the enactment of a 35-hour week would sharply increase costs, would invite inflation, would impair our ability to compete, and merely share instead of creating employment. But I am equally opposed to the 45- or 50-hour week in those industries where consistently excessive use of overtime causes increased unemployment.

So, therefore, I recommend legislation authorizing the creation of a tripartite industry committee to determine on an industry-by-industry basis as to where a higher penalty rate for overtime would increase job openings without unduly increasing costs, and authorizing the establishment of such higher rates.

VI.

Let me make one principle of this administration abundantly clear: All of these increased opportunities—in employment, in education, in housing, and in every field—must be open to Americans of every color. As far as the writ of Federal law will run, we must abolish not some, but all racial discrimination. For this is not merely an economic issue, or a social, political, or international issue. It is a moral issue, and it must be met by the passage this session of the bill now pending in the House.

All members of the public should have equal access to facilities open to the public. All members of the public should be equally eligible for Federal benefits that are financed by the public. All members of the public should have an equal chance to vote for public officials and to send their children to good public schools and to contribute their talents to the public good.

Today, Americans of all races stand side by side in Berlin and in Viet Nam. They died side by side in Korea. Surely they can work and eat and travel side by side in their own country.

VII.

We must also lift by legislation the bars of discrimination against those who seek entry into our country, particularly those who have much needed skills and those joining their families.

In establishing preferences, a nation that was built by the immigrants of all lands can ask those who now seek admission: "What can you do for our country?" But we should not be asking: "In what country were you born?"

VIII.

For our ultimate goal is a world without war, a world made safe for diversity, in which all men, goods, and ideas can freely move across every border and every boundary. We must advance toward this goal in 1964 in at least 10 different ways, not as partisans, but as patriots.

First, we must maintain—and our reduced defense budget will maintain—that margin of military safety and superiority obtained through 3 years of steadily increasing both the quality and the quantity of our strategic, our conventional, and our anti-guerilla forces. In 1964 we will be better prepared than ever before to defend the cause of freedom, whether it is threatened by outright aggression or by the infiltration practiced by those in Hanoi and Havana, who ship arms and men across international borders to foment insurrection. And we must continue to use that strength as John Kennedy used it in the Cuban crisis and for the test ban treaty—to demonstrate both the futility of nuclear war and the possibilities of lasting peace.

Second, we must take new steps—and we shall make new proposals at Geneva—toward the control and the eventual abolition of arms. Even in the absence of agreement, we must not stockpile arms beyond our needs or seek an excess of military power that could be provocative as well as wasteful.

It is in this spirit that in this fiscal year we are cutting back our production of enriched uranium by 25 percent. We are shutting down four plutonium piles. We are closing many nonessential military installations. And it is in this spirit that we today call on our adversaries to do the same.

Third, we must make increased use of our food as an instrument of peace—making it available by sale or trade or loan or donation—to hungry people in all nations which tell us of their needs and accept proper conditions of distribution.

Fourth, we must assure our pre-eminence in the peaceful exploration of outer space, focusing on an expedition to the moon in this decade—in cooperation with other powers if possible, alone if necessary.

Fifth, we must expand world trade. Having recognized in the Act of 1962 that we must buy as well as sell, we now expect our trading partners to recognize that we must sell as well as buy. We are willing to give them competitive access to our market, asking only that they do the same for us.

Sixth, we must continue, through such measures as the interest equalization tax, as well as the cooperation of other nations, our recent progress toward balancing our international accounts.

This administration must and will preserve the present gold value of the dollar.

Seventh, we must become better neighbors with the free states of the Americas, working with the councils of the OAS, with a stronger Alliance for Progress, and with all the men and women of this hemisphere who really believe in liberty and justice for all.

Eighth, we must strengthen the ability of free nations everywhere to develop their independence and raise their standard of living, and thereby frustrate those who prey on poverty and chaos. To do this, the rich must help the poor—and we must do our part. We must achieve a more rigorous administration of our development assistance, with larger roles for private investors, for other industrialized nations, and for international agencies and for the recipient nations themselves.

Ninth, we must strengthen our Atlantic and Pacific partnerships, maintain our alliances and make the United Nations a more effective instrument for national independence and international order.

Tenth, and finally, we must develop with our allies new means of bridging the gap between the East and the West, facing danger boldly wherever danger exists, but being equally bold in our search for new agreements which can enlarge the hopes of all, while violating the interests of none.

In short, I would say to the Congress that we must be constantly prepared for the worst, and constantly acting for the best. We must be strong enough to win any war, and we must be wise enough to prevent one.

We shall neither act as aggressors nor tolerate acts of aggression. We intend to bury no one, and we do not intend to be buried.

We can fight, if we must, as we have fought before, but we pray that we will never have to fight again.

IX.

My good friends and my fellow Americans: In these last 7 sorrowful weeks, we have learned anew that nothing is so enduring as faith, and nothing is so degrading as hate. John Kennedy was a victim of hate, but he was also a great builder of faith—faith in our fellow Americans, whatever their creed or their color or their station in life; faith in the future of man, whatever his divisions and differences.

This faith was echoed in all parts of the world. On every continent and in every land to which Mrs. Johnson and I traveled, we found faith and hope and love toward this land of America and toward our people.

So I ask you now in the Congress and in the country to join with me in expressing and fulfilling that faith in working for a nation, a nation that is free from want and a world that is free from hate—a world of peace and justice, and freedom and abundance, for our time and for all time to come.

Address to Congress on the State of the Union
January 4, 1965

Lyndon B. Johnson delivered his second State of the Union address under circumstances very different from those under which he had given his first the year before. In early January 1964 Johnson had been president for just over a month, having succeeded to the office after John F. Kennedy was assassinated on November 22, 1963. The country was still mourning the late president.

On January 4, 1965, when Johnson gave this speech, he had just been elected, in a landslide the previous November, to his own four-year term in the White House. Johnson, a Democrat, had defeated Republican senator Barry Goldwater of Arizona; the president took 61 percent of the popular vote to Goldwater's 38 percent and 486 electoral college votes to Goldwater's 52. In the process, Democrats won even larger majorities in the House and Senate.

Johnson, a Texan who before serving as Kennedy's vice president had been Senate majority leader, campaigned in 1964 on the platform of a reform-minded "Great Society." Working with Congress, Johnson succeeded in 1965 in enacting vast quantities of new legislation; Congress approved 80 of 83 of the president's plans. Among them were Medicare, which provided health insurance for senior citizens; Medicaid, a health plan for the poor; the Voting Rights Act, which aimed to assist minorities in voting; the Elementary and Secondary Education Act, which helped provide funds for disadvantaged children; and the War on Poverty.

In his State of the Union message, Johnson listed a series of goals under the rubric of the Great Society. He stated that the country's task involved three goals: keeping the economy growing, opening opportunities for all Americans, and improving their quality of life.

The president began this message with a look at the international situation. The Cold War between the United States and the communist world was continuing, and the president stated that Americans and Soviets should "come to know each other better" to live in peace.

One area that was becoming a greater concern—and before long would dominate Johnson's presidency—was the fighting in Vietnam, where the United States was assisting South Vietnam in its struggle against communist North Vietnam. "Why are we there?" Johnson asked rhetorically, and he provided two answers. The first was that the United States had made a commitment to help an ally fight communism, a commitment that had been honored by three presidents. The second was that if the United States ignored the situation, it would end up increasing the likelihood of a larger conflict. "Our goal is peace in southeast Asia," he declared.

M r. Speaker, Mr. President, Members of the Congress, my fellow Americans: On this Hill which was my home, I am stirred by old friendships.

Though total agreement between the Executive and the Congress is impossible, total respect is important.

I am proud to be among my colleagues of the Congress whose legacy to their trust is their loyalty to their Nation.

I am not unaware of the inner emotions of the new Members of this body tonight.

Twenty-eight years ago, I felt as you do now. You will soon learn that you are among men whose first love is their country, men who try each day to do as best they can what they believe is right.

We are entering the third century of the pursuit of American union.

Two hundred years ago, in 1765, nine assembled colonies first joined together to demand freedom from arbitrary power.

For the first century we struggled to hold together the first continental union of democracy in the history of man. One hundred years ago, in 1865, following a terrible test of blood and fire, the compact of union was finally sealed.

For a second century we labored to establish a unity of purpose and interest among the many groups which make up the American community.

That struggle has often brought pain and violence. It is not yet over. But we have achieved a unity of interest among our people that is unmatched in the history of freedom.

And so tonight, now, in 1965, we begin a new quest for union. We seek the unity of man with the world that he has built—with the knowledge that can save or destroy him—with the cities which can stimulate or stifle him—with the wealth and the machines which can enrich or menace his spirit.

We seek to establish a harmony between man and society which will allow each of us to enlarge the meaning of his life and all of us to elevate the quality of our civilization. This is the search that we begin tonight.

State of the World

But the unity we seek cannot realize its full promise in isolation. For today the state of the Union depends, in large measure, upon the state of the world.

Our concern and interest, compassion and vigilance, extend to every corner of a dwindling planet.

Yet, it is not merely our concern but the concern of all free men. We will not, and we should not, assume that it is the task of Americans alone to settle all the conflicts of a torn and troubled world.

Let the foes of freedom take no comfort from this. For in concert with other nations, we shall help men defend their freedom.

Our first aim remains the safety and the well-being of our own country.

We are prepared to live as good neighbors with all, but we cannot be indifferent to acts designed to injure our interests, or our citizens, or our establishments abroad. The community of nations requires mutual respect. We shall extend it—and we shall expect it.

In our relations with the world we shall follow the example of Andrew Jackson who said: "I intend to ask for nothing that is not clearly right and to submit to nothing that is wrong." And he promised, that "the honor of my country shall never be stained by an apology from me for the statement of truth or for the performance of duty." That was this Nation's policy in the 1830's and that is this Nation's policy in the 1960's.

Our own freedom and growth have never been the final goal of the American dream.

We were never meant to be an oasis of liberty and abundance in a worldwide desert of disappointed dreams. Our Nation was created to help strike away the chains of ignorance and misery and tyranny wherever they keep man less than God means him to be.

We are moving toward that destiny, never more rapidly than we have moved in the last 4 years.

In this period we have built a military power strong enough to meet any threat and destroy any adversary. And that superiority will continue to grow so long as this office is mine—and you sit on Capitol Hill.

In this period no new nation has become Communist, and the unity of the Communist empire has begun to crumble.

In this period we have resolved in friendship our disputes with our neighbors of the hemisphere, and joined in an Alliance for Progress toward economic growth and political democracy.

In this period we have taken more steps toward peace—including the test ban treaty—than at any time since the cold war began.

In this period we have relentlessly pursued our advances toward the conquest of space.

Most important of all, in this period, the United States has reemerged into the fullness of its self-confidence and purpose. No longer are we called upon to get America moving. We are moving. No longer do we doubt our strength or resolution. We are strong and we have proven our resolve.

No longer can anyone wonder whether we are in the grip of historical decay. We know that history is ours to make. And if there is great danger, there is now also the excitement of great expectations.

America and the Communist Nations

Yet we still live in a troubled and perilous world. There is no longer a single threat. There are many. They differ in intensity and in danger. They require different attitudes and different answers.

With the Soviet Union we seek peaceful understandings that can lessen the danger to freedom.

Last fall I asked the American people to choose that course. I will carry forward their command.

If we are to live together in peace, we must come to know each other better.

I am sure that the American people would welcome a chance to listen to the Soviet leaders on our television—as I would like the Soviet people to hear our leaders on theirs.

I hope the new Soviet leaders can visit America so they can learn about our country at firsthand.

In Eastern Europe restless nations are slowly beginning to assert their identity. Your Government, assisted by the leaders in American labor and business, is now exploring ways to increase peaceful trade with these countries and with the Soviet Union. I will report our conclusions to the Congress.

In Asia, communism wears a more aggressive face. We see that in Viet-Nam. Why are we there?

We are there, first, because a friendly nation has asked us for help against the Communist aggression. Ten years ago our President pledged our help. Three Presidents have supported that pledge. We will not break it now.

Second, our own security is tied to the peace of Asia. Twice in one generation we have had to fight against aggression in the Far East. To ignore aggression now would only increase the danger of a much larger war.

Our goal is peace in southeast Asia. That will come only when aggressors leave their neighbors in peace.

What is at stake is the cause of freedom and in that cause America will never be found wanting.

The Non-Communist World

But communism is not the only source of trouble and unrest. There are older and deeper sources—in the misery of nations and in man's irrepressible ambition for liberty and a better life.

With the free Republics of Latin America I have always felt—and my country has always felt—very special ties of interest and affection. It will be the purpose of my administration to strengthen these ties. Together we share and shape the destiny of the new world. In the coming year I hope to pay a visit to Latin America. And I will steadily enlarge our commitment to the Alliance for Progress as the instrument of our war against poverty and injustice in this hemisphere.

In the Atlantic community we continue to pursue our goal of 20 years—a Europe that is growing in strength, unity, and cooperation with America. A great unfinished task is the reunification of Germany through self-determination.

This European policy is not based on any abstract design. It is based on the realities of common interests and common values, common dangers and common expectations. These realities will continue to have their way—especially, I think, in our expanding trade and especially in our common defense.

Free Americans have shaped the policies of the United States. And because we know these realities, those policies have been, and will be, in the interest of Europe.

Free Europeans must shape the course of Europe. And, for the same reasons, that course has been, and will be, in our interest and in the interest of freedom.

I found this truth confirmed in my talks with European leaders in the last year. I hope to repay these visits to some of our friends in Europe this year.

In Africa and Asia we are witnessing the turbulent unfolding of new nations and continents.

We welcome them to the society of nations.

We are committed to help those seeking to strengthen their own independence, and to work most closely with those governments dedicated to the welfare of all of their people.

We seek not fidelity to an iron faith, but a diversity of belief as varied as man himself. We seek not to extend the power of America but the progress of humanity. We seek not to dominate others but to strengthen the freedom of all people.

I will seek new ways to use our knowledge to help deal with the explosion in world population and the growing scarcity in world resources.

Finally, we renew our commitment to the continued growth and the effectiveness of the United Nations. The frustrations of the United Nations are a product of the world that we live in, and not of the institution which gives them voice. It is far better to throw these differences open to the assembly of nations than to permit them to fester in silent danger.

These are some of the goals of the American Nation in the world in which we live.

For ourselves we seek neither praise nor blame, neither gratitude nor obedience.

We seek peace.

We seek freedom.

We seek to enrich the life of man.

For that is the world in which we will flourish and that is the world that we mean for all men to ultimately have.

Toward the Great Society

World affairs will continue to call upon our energy and our courage.

But today we can turn increased attention to the character of American life.

We are in the midst of the greatest upward surge of economic well-being in the history of any nation.

Our flourishing progress has been marked by price stability that is unequalled in the world. Our balance of payments deficit has declined and the soundness of our dollar is unquestioned. I pledge to keep it that way and I urge business and labor to cooperate to that end.

We worked for two centuries to climb this peak of prosperity. But we are only at the beginning of the road to the Great Society. Ahead now is a summit where freedom from the wants of the body can help fulfill the needs of the spirit.

We built this Nation to serve its people.

We want to grow and build and create, but we want progress to be the servant and not the master of man.

We do not intend to live in the midst of abundance, isolated from neighbors and nature, confined by blighted cities and bleak suburbs, stunted by a poverty of learning and an emptiness of leisure.

The Great Society asks not how much, but how good; not only how to create wealth but how to use it; not only how fast we are going, but where we are headed.

It proposes as the first test for a nation: the quality of its people.

This kind of society will not flower spontaneously from swelling riches and surging power.

It will not be the gift of government or the creation of presidents. It will require of every American, for many generations, both faith in the destination and the fortitude to make the journey.

And like freedom itself, it will always be challenge and not fulfillment. And tonight we accept that challenge.

A National Agenda

I propose that we begin a program in education to ensure every American child the fullest development of his mind and skills.

I propose that we begin a massive attack on crippling and killing diseases.

I propose that we launch a national effort to make the American city a better and a more stimulating place to live.

I propose that we increase the beauty of America and end the poisoning of our rivers and the air that we breathe.

I propose that we carry out a new program to develop regions of our country that are now suffering from distress and depression.

I propose that we make new efforts to control and prevent crime and delinquency.

I propose that we eliminate every remaining obstacle to the right and the opportunity to vote.

I propose that we honor and support the achievements of thought and the creations of art.

I propose that we make an all-out campaign against waste and inefficiency.

The Task

Our basic task is threefold:

First, to keep our economy growing;
—to open for all Americans the opportunity that is now enjoyed by most Americans;
—and to improve the quality of life for all.

In the next 6 weeks I will submit special messages with detailed proposals for national action in each of these areas.

Tonight I would like just briefly to explain some of my major recommendations in the three main areas of national need.

I. A GROWING ECONOMY

Basic Policies

First, we must keep our Nation prosperous. We seek full employment opportunity for every American citizen. I will present a budget designed to move the economy forward. More money will be left in the hands of the consumer by a substantial cut in excise taxes. We will continue along the path toward a balanced budget in a balanced economy.

I confidently predict—what every economic sign tells us tonight—the continued flourishing of the American economy.

But we must remember that fear of a recession can contribute to the fact of a recession. The knowledge that our Government will, and can, move swiftly will strengthen the confidence of investors and business.

Congress can reinforce this confidence by insuring that its procedures permit rapid action on temporary income tax cuts. And special funds for job-creating public programs should be made available for immediate use if recession threatens.

Our continued prosperity demands continued price stability. Business, labor, and the consumer all have a high stake in keeping wages and prices within the framework of the guideposts that have already served the Nation so well.

Finding new markets abroad for our goods depends on the initiative of American business. But we stand ready—with credit and other help—to assist the flow of trade which will benefit the entire Nation.

On the Farms

Our economy owes much to the efficiency of our farmers. We must continue to assure them the opportunity to earn a fair reward. I have instructed the Secretary of Agriculture to lead a major effort to find new approaches to reduce the heavy cost of our farm programs and to direct more of our effort to the small farmer who needs the help the most.

Increased Prosperity

We can help insure continued prosperity through:

—a regional recovery program to assist the development of stricken areas left behind by our national progress;

—further efforts to provide our workers with the skills demanded by modern technology, for the laboring-man is an indispensable force in the American system;

—the extension of the minimum wage to more than 2 million unprotected workers;

—the improvement and the modernization of the unemployment compensation system.

And as pledged in our 1960 and 1964 Democratic platforms, I will propose to Congress changes in the Taft-Hartley Act including section 14(b). I will do so hoping to reduce the conflicts that for several years have divided Americans in various States of our Union.

In a country that spans a continent modern transportation is vital to continued growth.

Transportation for Growth
I will recommend heavier reliance on competition in transportation and a new policy for our merchant marine.

I will ask for funds to study high-speed rail transportation between urban centers. We will begin with test projects between Washington and Boston. On high-speed trains, passengers could travel this distance in less than 4 hours.

II. Opportunity for All

Second, we must open opportunity to all our people.

Most Americans enjoy a good life. But far too many are still trapped in poverty and idleness and fear.

Let a just nation throw open to them the city of promise:

—to the elderly, by providing hospital care under social security and by raising benefit payments to those struggling to maintain the dignity of their later years;

—to the poor and the unfortunate, through doubling the war against poverty this year;

—to Negro Americans, through enforcement of the civil rights law and elimination of barriers to the right to vote;

—to those in other lands that are seeking the promise of America, through an immigration law based on the work a man can do and not where he was born or how he spells his name.

III. To Enrich the Life of All

Our third goal is to improve the quality of American life.

Through Education
We begin with learning.

Every child must have the best education that this Nation can provide.

Thomas Jefferson said that no nation can be both ignorant and free. Today no nation can be both ignorant and great.

In addition to our existing programs, I will recommend a new program for schools and students with a first year authorization of $1,500 million.

It will help at every stage along the road to learning.

For the preschool years we will help needy children become aware of the excitement of learning.

For the primary and secondary school years we will aid public schools serving low-income families and assist students in both public and private schools.

For the college years we will provide scholarships to high school students of the greatest promise and the greatest need and we will guarantee low-interest loans to students continuing their college studies.

New laboratories and centers will help our schools—help them lift their standards of excellence and explore new methods of teaching. These centers will provide special training for those who need and those who deserve special treatment.

Through Better Health

Greatness requires not only an educated people but a healthy people.

Our goal is to match the achievements of our medicine to the afflictions of our people.

We already carry on a large program in this country for research and health.

In addition, regional medical centers can provide the most advanced diagnosis and treatment for heart disease and cancer and stroke and other major diseases.

New support for medical and dental education will provide the trained people to apply our knowledge.

Community centers can help the mentally ill and improve health care for school-age children from poor families, including services for the mentally retarded.

Through Improving the World We Live In

The City. An educated and healthy people require surroundings in harmony with their hopes. In our urban areas the central problem today is to protect and restore man's satisfaction in belonging to a community where he can find security and significance. The first step is to break old patterns—to begin to think and work and plan for the development of the entire metropolitan areas. We will take this step with new programs of help for the basic community facilities and for neighborhood centers of health and recreation.

New and existing programs will be open to those cities which work together to develop unified long-range policies for metropolitan areas.

We must also make some very important changes in our housing programs if we are to pursue these same basic goals.

So a Department of Housing and Urban Development will be needed to spearhead this effort in our cities.

Every citizen has the right to feel secure in his home and on the streets of his community.

To help control crime, we will recommend programs:

—to train local law enforcement officers;

—to put the best techniques of modern science at their disposal;

—to discover the causes of crime and better ways to prevent it.

I will soon assemble a panel of outstanding experts of this Nation to search out answers to the national problem of crime and delinquency, and I welcome the recommendations and the constructive efforts of the Congress.

The Beauty of America. For over three centuries the beauty of America has sustained our spirit and has enlarged our vision. We must act now to protect this heritage. In a fruitful new partnership with the States and the cities the next decade should be a conservation milestone. We must make a massive effort to save the countryside and to establish—as a green legacy for tomorrow—more large and small parks, more seashores and open spaces than have been created during any other period in our national history.

A new and substantial effort must be made to landscape highways to provide places of relaxation and recreation wherever our roads run,

Within our cities imaginative programs are needed to landscape streets and to transform open areas into places of beauty and recreation.

We will seek legal power to prevent pollution of our air and water before it happens. We will step up our effort to control harmful wastes, giving first priority to the cleanup of our most contaminated rivers. We will increase research to learn much more about the control of pollution.

We hope to make the Potomac a model of beauty here in the Capital, and preserve unspoiled stretches of some of our waterways with a Wild Rivers bill.

More ideas for a beautiful America will emerge from a White House Conference on Natural Beauty which I will soon call.

Art and Science. We must also recognize and encourage those who can be pathfinders for the Nation's imagination and understanding.

To help promote and honor creative achievements, I will propose a National Foundation on the Arts.

To develop knowledge which will enrich our lives and ensure our progress, I will recommend programs to encourage basic science, particularly in the universities—and to bring closer the day when the oceans will supply our growing need for fresh water.

IV. The Government

For government to serve these goals it must be modern in structure, efficient in action, and ready for any emergency.

I am busy, currently, reviewing the structure of the entire executive branch of this Government. I hope to reshape it and to reorganize it to meet more effectively the tasks of the 20th century.

Wherever waste is found, I will eliminate it.

Last year we saved almost $3,500 million by eliminating waste in the National Government.

And I intend to do better this year.

And very soon I will report to you on our progress and on new economies that your Government plans to make.

Even the best of government is subject to the worst of hazards.

I will propose laws to insure the necessary continuity of leadership should the President become disabled or die.

In addition, I will propose reforms in the electoral college—leaving undisturbed the vote by States—but making sure that no elector can substitute his will for that of the people.

Last year, in a sad moment, I came here and I spoke to you after 33 years of public service, practically all of them here on this Hill.

This year I speak after 1 year as President of the United States.

Many of you in this Chamber are among my oldest friends. We have shared many happy moments and many hours of work, and we have watched many Presidents together. Yet, only in the White House can you finally know the full weight of this Office.

The greatest burden is not running the huge operations of government—or meeting daily troubles, large and small—or even working with the Congress.

A President's hardest task is not to do what is right, but to know what is right.

Yet the Presidency brings no special gift of prophecy or foresight. You take an oath, you step into an office, and you must then help guide a great democracy.

The answer was waiting for me in the land where I was born.

It was once barren land. The angular hills were covered with scrub cedar and a few large live oaks. Little would grow in that harsh caliche soil of my country. And each spring the Pedernales River would flood our valley.

But men came and they worked and they endured and they built.

And tonight that country is abundant; abundant with fruit and cattle and goats and sheep, and there are pleasant homes and lakes and the floods are gone.

Why did men come to that once forbidding land?

Well, they were restless, of course, and they had to be moving on. But there was more than that. There was a dream—a dream of a place where a free man could build for himself, and raise his children to a better life—a dream of a continent to be conquered, a world to be won, a nation to be made.

Remembering this, I knew the answer.

A President does not shape a new and personal vision of America.

He collects it from the scattered hopes of the American past.

It existed when the first settlers saw the coast of a new world, and when the first pioneers moved westward.

It has guided us every step of the way.

It sustains every President. But it is also your inheritance and it belongs equally to all the people that we all serve.

It must be interpreted anew by each generation for its own needs; as I have tried, in part, to do tonight.

It shall lead us as we enter the third century of the search for "a more perfect union?

This, then, is the state of the Union: Free and restless, growing and full of hope.

So it was in the beginning.

So it shall always be, while God is willing, and we are strong enough to keep the faith.

Address to Congress
on the State of the Union

January 12, 1966

During his presidency, Lyndon B. Johnson sought to achieve a host of reform goals while also pursuing a growing war in Vietnam. His third State of the Union message, delivered January 12, 1966, demonstrated his desire to have both his aims met at the same time.

Johnson had succeeded to the presidency upon the death of John F. Kennedy, who was slain by an assassin on November 22, 1963. After less than a year as president, Johnson won a full four-year term as president, defeating Republican Barry Goldwater in a landslide. The Texan and former senator worked with a heavily Democratic Congress to push through a variety of landmark pieces of legislation in 1965, including laws creating the Medicare and Medicaid programs as well as the Voting Rights Act.

But 1965 also saw an increase in the American commitment in Vietnam—to assist the South Vietnamese government against the communist North Vietnamese and its allies—that had slowly been building through three presidencies but only reached critical mass during Johnson's. In 1964 Congress passed the Tonkin Gulf Resolution, which gave the president broad authority over conducting war in Vietnam; in 1965 Johnson sent the first regular U.S. combat troops to that country.

In his State of the Union address, Johnson called Vietnam "the center of our concerns." But he urged Congress to press ahead on his domestic Great Society programs, such as the War on Poverty and civil rights efforts. "I believe that we can continue the Great Society while we fight in Vietnam," he declared; he followed that remark with a discussion of the Great Society, stating that it "leads us along three roads—growth and justice and liberation."

When it came to Vietnam, Johnson provided a historical explanation for the U.S. presence there, calling it "not an isolated episode" but part of a pattern in U.S. foreign policy since World War II. He mentioned other examples of actions pitting the United States against communist forces in the previous two decades, including in Korea and Cuba.

He called "support of national independence" the most important principle in American foreign policy, citing South Vietnam as an example. "We will stay until aggression is stopped," he stated.

By 1968, toward the end of Johnson's presidency, there were 500,000 U.S. troops in Vietnam, and the conflict was growing increasingly unpopular with the American public. Johnson pulled out of the 1968 presidential race that March after facing a stiff primary challenge from antiwar senator Eugene McCarthy.

Mr. Speaker, Mr. President, Members of the House and the Senate, my fellow Americans:

I come before you tonight to report on the State of the Union for the third time.

I come here to thank you and to add my tribute, once more, to the Nation's gratitude for this, the 89th Congress. This Congress has already reserved for itself an honored chapter in the history of America.

Our Nation tonight is engaged in a brutal and bitter conflict in Vietnam. Later on I want to discuss that struggle in some detail with you. It just must be the center of our concerns.

But we will not permit those who fire upon us in Vietnam to win a victory over the desires and the intentions of all the American people. This Nation is mighty enough, its society is healthy enough, its people are strong enough, to pursue our goals in the rest of the world while still building a Great Society here at home.

And that is what I have come here to ask of you tonight.

I recommend that you provide the resources to carry forward, with full vigor, the great health and education programs that you enacted into law last year.

I recommend that we prosecute with vigor and determination our war on poverty.

I recommend that you give a new and daring direction to our foreign aid program, designed to make a maximum attack on hunger and disease and ignorance in those countries that are determined to help themselves, and to help those nations that are trying to control population growth.

I recommend that you make it possible to expand trade between the United States and Eastern Europe and the Soviet Union.

I recommend to you a program to rebuild completely, on a scale never before attempted, entire central and slum areas of several of our cities in America.

I recommend that you attack the wasteful and degrading poisoning of our rivers, and, as the cornerstone of this effort, clean completely entire large river basins.

I recommend that you meet the growing menace of crime in the streets by building up law enforcement and by revitalizing the entire Federal system from prevention to probation.

I recommend that you take additional steps to insure equal justice to all of our people by effectively enforcing nondiscrimination in Federal and State jury selection, by making it a serious Federal crime to obstruct public and private efforts to secure civil rights, and by outlawing discrimination in the sale and rental of housing.

I recommend that you help me modernize and streamline the Federal Government by creating a new Cabinet level Department of Transportation and reorganizing several existing agencies. In turn, I will restructure our civil service in the top grades so that men and women can easily be assigned to jobs where they are most needed, and ability will be both required as well as rewarded.

I will ask you to make it possible for Members of the House of Representatives to work more effectively in the service of the Nation through a constitutional amendment extending the term of a Congressman to 4 years, concurrent with that of the President.

Because of Vietnam we cannot do all that we should, or all that we would like to do. We will ruthlessly attack waste and inefficiency. We will make sure that every dollar is spent with the thrift and with the commonsense which recognizes how hard the taxpayer worked in order to earn it.

We will continue to meet the needs of our people by continuing to develop the Great Society.

Last year alone the wealth that we produced increased $47 billion, and it will soar again this year to a total over $720 billion.

Because our economic policies have produced rising revenues, if you approve every program that I recommend tonight, our total budget deficit will be one of the lowest in many years. It will be only $1.8 billion next year. Total spending in the administrative budget will be $112.8 billion. Revenues next year will be $111 billion.

On a cash basis—which is the way that you and I keep our family budget—the Federal budget next year will actually show a surplus. That is to say, if we include all the money that your Government will take in and all the money that your Government will spend, your Government next year will collect one-half billion dollars more than it will spend in the year 1967.

I have not come here tonight to ask for pleasant luxuries or for idle pleasures. I have come here to recommend that you, the representatives of the richest Nation on earth, you, the elected servants of a people who live in abundance unmatched on this globe, you bring the most urgent decencies of life to all of your fellow Americans.

There are men who cry out: We must sacrifice. Well, let us rather ask them: Who will they sacrifice? Are they going to sacrifice the children who seek the learning, or the sick who need medical care, or the families who dwell in squalor now brightened by the hope of home? Will they sacrifice opportunity for the distressed, the beauty of our land, the hope of our poor?

Time may require further sacrifices. And if it does, then we will make them.

But we will not heed those who wring it from the hopes of the unfortunate here in a land of plenty.

I believe that we can continue the Great Society while we fight in Vietnam. But if there are some who do not believe this, then, in the name of justice, let them call for the contribution of those who live in the fullness of our blessing, rather than try to strip it from the hands of those that are most in need.

And let no one think that the unfortunate and the oppressed of this land sit stifled and alone in their hope tonight. Hundreds of their servants and their protectors sit before me tonight here in this great Chamber.

The Great Society leads us along three roads—growth and justice and liberation.

First is growth—the national prosperity which supports the well-being of our people and which provides the tools of our progress.

I can report to you tonight what you have seen for yourselves already—in every city and countryside. This Nation is flourishing.

Workers are making more money than ever—with after-tax income in the past 5 years up 33 percent; in the last year alone, up 8 percent.

More people are working than ever before in our history—an increase last year of 2½ million jobs.

Corporations have greater after-tax earnings than ever in history. For the past 5 years those earnings have been up over 65 percent, and last year alone they had a rise of 20 percent.

Average farm income is higher than ever. Over the past 5 years it is up 40 percent, and over the past year it is up 22 percent alone.

I was informed this afternoon by the distinguished Secretary of the Treasury that his preliminary estimates indicate that our balance of payments deficit has been reduced from $2.8 billion in 1964 to $1.3 billion, or less, in 1965. This achievement has been made possible by the patriotic voluntary cooperation of businessmen and bankers working with your Government.

We must now work together with increased urgency to wipe out this balance of payments deficit altogether in the next year.

And as our economy surges toward new heights we must increase our vigilance against the inflation which raises the cost of living and which lowers the savings of every family in this land. It is essential, to prevent inflation, that we ask both labor and business to exercise price and wage restraint, and I do so again tonight.

I believe it desirable, because of increased military expenditures, that you temporarily restore the automobile and certain telephone excise tax reductions made effective only 12 days ago. Without raising taxes—or even increasing the total tax bill paid—we should move to improve our withholding system so that Americans can more realistically pay as they go, speed up the collection of corporate taxes, and make other necessary simplifications of the tax structure at an early date.

I hope these measures will be adequate. But if the necessities of Vietnam require it, I will not hesitate to return to the Congress for additional appropriations, or additional revenues if they are needed.

The second road is justice. Justice means a man's hope should not be limited by the color of his skin.

I propose legislation to establish unavoidable requirements for nondiscriminatory jury selection in Federal and State courts—and to give the Attorney General the power necessary to enforce those requirements.

I propose legislation to strengthen authority of Federal courts to try those who murder, attack, or intimidate either civil rights workers or others exercising their constitutional rights—and to increase penalties to a level equal to the nature of the crime.

Legislation, resting on the fullest constitutional authority of the Federal Government, to prohibit racial discrimination in the sale or rental of housing.

For that other nation within a Nation—the poor—whose distress has now captured the conscience of America, I will ask the Congress not only to continue, but to speed up the war on poverty. And in so doing, we will provide the added energy of achievement with the increased efficiency of experience.

To improve the life of our rural Americans and our farm population, we will plan for the future through the establishment of several new Community Development Districts, improved education through the use of Teacher Corps teams, better health measures, physical examinations, and adequate and available medical resources.

For those who labor, I propose to improve unemployment insurance, to expand minimum wage benefits, and by the repeal of section 14(b) of the Taft-Hartley Act to make the labor laws in all our States equal to the laws of the 31 States which do not have tonight right-to-work measures.

And I also intend to ask the Congress to consider measures which, without improperly invading State and local authority, will enable us effectively to deal with strikes which threaten irreparable damage to the national interest.

The third path is the path of liberation. It is to use our success for the fulfillment of our lives. A great nation is one which breeds a great people. A great people flower not from wealth and power, but from a society which spurs them to the fullness of their genius. That alone is a Great Society.

Yet, slowly, painfully, on the edge of victory, has come the knowledge that shared prosperity is not enough. In the midst of abundance modern man walks oppressed by forces which menace and confine the quality of his life, and which individual abundance alone will not overcome.

We can subdue and we can master these forces—bring increased meaning to our lives—if all of us, Government and citizens, are bold enough to change old ways, daring enough to assault new dangers, and if the dream is dear enough to call forth the limitless capacities of this great people.

This year we must continue to improve the quality of American life.

Let us fulfill and improve the great health and education programs of last year, extending special opportunities to those who risk their lives in our Armed Forces.

I urge the House of Representatives to complete action on three programs already passed by the Senate—the Teacher Corps, rent assistance, and home rule for the District of Columbia.

In some of our urban areas we must help rebuild entire sections and neighborhoods containing, in some cases, as many as 100,000 people. Working together, private enterprise and government must press forward with the task of providing homes and shops, parks and hospitals, and all the other necessary parts of a flourishing community where our people can come to live the good life.

I will offer other proposals to stimulate and to reward planning for the growth of entire metropolitan areas.

Of all the reckless devastations of our national heritage, none is really more shameful than the continued poisoning of our rivers and our air.

We must undertake a cooperative effort to end pollution in several river basins, making additional funds available to help draw the plans and construct the plants that are necessary to make the waters of our entire river systems clean, and make them a source of pleasure and beauty for all of our people.

To attack and to overcome growing crime and lawlessness, I think we must have a stepped-up program to help modernize and strengthen our local police forces.

Our people have a right to feel secure in their homes and on their streets—and that right just must be secured.

Nor can we fail to arrest the destruction of life and property on our highways.

I will propose a Highway Safety Act of 1966 to seek an end to this mounting tragedy.

We must also act to prevent the deception of the American consumer—requiring all packages to state clearly and truthfully their contents—all interest and credit charges to be fully revealed—and keeping harmful drugs and cosmetics away from our stores.

It is the genius of our Constitution that under its shelter of enduring institutions and rooted principles there is ample room for the rich fertility of American political invention. We must change to master change.

I propose to take steps to modernize and streamline the executive branch, to modernize the relations between city and State and Nation.

A new Department of Transportation is needed to bring together our transportation activities. The present structure—35 Government agencies, spending $5 billion yearly—makes it almost impossible to serve either the growing demands of this great Nation or the needs of the industry, or the right of the taxpayer to full efficiency and real frugality.

I will propose in addition a program to construct and to flight-test a new supersonic transport airplane that will fly three times the speed of sound—in excess of 2,000 miles per hour.

I propose to examine our Federal system—the relation between city, State, Nation, and the citizens themselves. We need a commission of the most distinguished scholars and men of public affairs to do this job. I will ask them to move on to develop a creative federalism to best use the wonderful diversity of our institutions and our people to solve the problems and to fulfill the dreams of the American people.

As the process of election becomes more complex and more costly, we must make it possible for those without personal wealth to enter public life without being obligated to a few large contributors.

Therefore, I will submit legislation to revise the present unrealistic restriction on contributions—to prohibit the endless proliferation of committees, bringing local and State committees under the act—to attach strong teeth and severe penalties to the requirement of full disclosure of contributions—and to broaden the participation of the people, through added tax incentives, to stimulate small contributions to the party and to the candidate of their choice.

To strengthen the work of Congress I strongly urge an amendment to provide a 4-year term for Members of the House of Representatives—which should not begin before 1972.

The present 2-year term requires most Members of Congress to divert enormous energies to an almost constant process of campaigning—depriving this Nation of the fullest measure of both their skill and their wisdom. Today, too, the work of government is far more complex than in our early years, requiring more time to learn and more time to master the technical tasks of legislating. And a longer term will serve to attract more men of the highest quality to political life. The Nation, the principle of democracy, and, I think, each congressional district, will all be better served by a 4-year term for Members of the House. And I urge your swift action.

Tonight the cup of peril is full in Vietnam. That conflict is not an isolated episode, but another great event in the policy that we have followed with strong consistency since World War II.

The touchstone of that policy is the interest of the United States—the welfare and the freedom of the people of the United States. But nations sink when they see that interest only through a narrow glass.

In a world that has grown small and dangerous, pursuit of narrow aims could bring decay and even disaster.

An America that is mighty beyond description—yet living in a hostile or despairing world—would be neither safe nor free to build a civilization to liberate the spirit of man.

In this pursuit we helped rebuild Western Europe. We gave our aid to Greece and Turkey, and we defended the freedom of Berlin.

In this pursuit we have helped new nations toward independence. We have extended the helping hand of the Peace Corps and carried forward the largest program of economic assistance in the world.

And in this pursuit we work to build a hemisphere of democracy and of social justice.

In this pursuit we have defended against Communist aggression—in Korea under President Truman—in the Formosa Straits under President Eisenhower—in Cuba under President Kennedy—and again in Vietnam.

Tonight Vietnam must hold the center of our attention, but across the world problems and opportunities crowd in on the American Nation. I will discuss them fully in the months to come, and I will follow the five continuing lines of policy that America has followed under its last four Presidents.

The first principle is strength. Tonight I can tell you that we are strong enough to keep all of our commitments. We will need expenditures of $58.3 billion for the next fiscal year to maintain this necessary defense might.

While special Vietnam expenditures for the next fiscal year are estimated to increase by $5.8 billion, I can tell you that all the other expenditures put together in the entire Federal budget will rise this coming year by only $.6 billion. This is true because of the stringent cost-conscious economy program inaugurated in the Defense Department, and followed by the other departments of Government.

A second principle of policy is the effort to control, and to reduce, and to ultimately eliminate the modern engines of destruction.

We will vigorously pursue existing proposals—and seek new ones—to control arms and to stop the spread of nuclear weapons.

A third major principle of our foreign policy is to help build those associations of nations which reflect the opportunities and the necessities of the modern world.

By strengthening the common defense, by stimulating world commerce, by meeting new hopes, these associations serve the cause of a flourishing world.

We will take new steps this year to help strengthen the Alliance for Progress, the unity of Europe, the community of the Atlantic, the regional organizations of developing continents, and that supreme association—the United Nations.

We will work to strengthen economic cooperation, to reduce barriers to trade, and to improve international finance.

A fourth enduring strand of policy has been to help improve the life of man.

From the Marshall plan to this very moment tonight, that policy has rested on the claims of compassion, and the certain knowledge that only a people advancing in expectation will build secure and peaceful lands.

This year I propose major new directions in our program of foreign assistance to help those countries who will help themselves.

We will conduct a worldwide attack on the problems of hunger and disease and ignorance.

We will place the matchless skill and the resources of our own great America, in farming and in fertilizers, at the service of those countries committed to develop a modern agriculture.

We will aid those who educate the young in other lands, and we will give children in other continents the same head start that we are trying to give our own children. To advance these ends I will propose the International Education Act of 1966.

I will also propose the International Health Act of 1966 to strike at disease by a new effort to bring modern skills and knowledge to the uncared-for, those suffering in the world, and by trying to wipe out smallpox and malaria and control yellow fever over most of the world during this next decade; to help countries trying to control population growth, by increasing our research—and we will earmark funds to help their efforts.

In the next year, from our foreign aid sources, we propose to dedicate $1 billion to these efforts, and we call on all who have the means to join us in this work in the world.

The fifth and most important principle of our foreign policy is support of national independence—the right of each people to govern themselves—and to shape their own institutions.

For a peaceful world order will be possible only when each country walks the way that it has chosen to walk for itself.

We follow this principle by encouraging the end of colonial rule.

We follow this principle, abroad as well as at home, by continued hostility to the rule of the many by the few—or the oppression of one race by another.

We follow this principle by building bridges to Eastern Europe. And I will ask the Congress for authority to remove the special tariff restrictions which are a barrier to increasing trade between the East and the West.

The insistent urge toward national independence is the strongest force of today's world in which we live.

In Africa and Asia and Latin America it is shattering the designs of those who would subdue others to their ideas or their will.

It is eroding the unity of what was once a Stalinist empire.

In recent months a number of nations have cast out those who would subject them to the ambitions of mainland China.

History is on the side of freedom and is on the side of societies shaped from the genius of each people. History does not favor a single system or belief—unless force is used to make it so.

That is why it has been necessary for us to defend this basic principle of our policy, to defend it in Berlin, in Korea, in Cuba—and tonight in Vietnam.

For tonight, as so many nights before, young Americans struggle and young Americans die in a distant land.

Tonight, as so many nights before, the American Nation is asked to sacrifice the blood of its children and the fruits of its labor for the love of its freedom.

How many times—in my lifetime and in yours—have the American people gathered, as they do now, to hear their President tell them of conflict and tell them of danger?

Each time they have answered. They have answered with all the effort that the security and the freedom of this Nation required.

And they do again tonight in Vietnam. Not too many years ago Vietnam was a peaceful, if troubled, land. In the North was an independent Communist government. In the South a people struggled to build a nation, with the friendly help of the United States.

There were some in South Vietnam who wished to force Communist rule on their own people. But their progress was slight. Their hope of success was dim. Then, little more than 6 years ago, North Vietnam decided on conquest. And from that day to this, soldiers and supplies have moved from North to South in a swelling stream that is swallowing the remnants of revolution in aggression.

As the assault mounted, our choice gradually became clear. We could leave, abandoning South Vietnam to its attackers and to certain conquest, or we could stay and fight beside the people of South Vietnam. We stayed.

And we will stay until aggression has stopped.

We will stay because a just nation cannot leave to the cruelties of its enemies a people who have staked their lives and independence on America's solemn pledge—a pledge which has grown through the commitments of three American Presidents.

We will stay because in Asia and around the world are countries whose independence rests, in large measure, on confidence in America's word and in America's protection. To yield to force in Vietnam would weaken that confidence, would undermine the independence of many lands, and would whet the appetite of aggression. We would have to fight in one land, and then we would have to fight in another—or abandon much of Asia to the domination of Communists.

And we do not intend to abandon Asia to conquest.

Last year the nature of the war in Vietnam changed again. Swiftly increasing numbers of armed men from the North crossed the borders to join forces that were already in the South. Attack and terror increased, spurred and encouraged by the belief that the United States lacked the will to continue and that their victory was near.

Despite our desire to limit conflict, it was necessary to act: to hold back the mounting aggression, to give courage to the people of the South, and to make our firmness clear to the North. Thus we began limited air action against military targets in North Vietnam. We increased our fighting force to its present strength tonight of 190,000 men.

These moves have not ended the aggression but they have prevented its success. The aims of the enemy have been put out of reach by the skill and the bravery of Americans and their allies—and by the enduring courage of the South Vietnamese who, I can tell you, have lost eight men last year for every one of ours.

The enemy is no longer close to victory. Time is no longer on his side. There is no cause to doubt the American commitment.

Our decision to stand firm has been matched by our desire for peace.

In 1965 alone we had 300 private talks for peace in Vietnam, with friends and adversaries throughout the world.

Since Christmas your Government has labored again, with imagination and endurance, to remove any barrier to peaceful settlement. For 20 days now we and our Vietnamese allies have dropped no bombs in North Vietnam.

Able and experienced spokesmen have visited, in behalf of America, more than 40 countries. We have talked to more than a hundred governments, all 113 that we have relations with, and some that we don't. We have talked to the United Nations and we have called upon all of its members to make any contribution that they can toward helping obtain peace.

In public statements and in private communications, to adversaries and to friends, in Rome and Warsaw, in Paris and Tokyo, in Africa and throughout this hemisphere, America has made her position abundantly clear.

We seek neither territory nor bases, economic domination or military alliance in Vietnam. We fight for the principle of self-determination—that the people of South Vietnam should be able to choose their own course, choose it in free elections without violence, without terror, and without fear.

The people of all Vietnam should make a free decision on the great question of reunification.

This is all we want for South Vietnam. It is all the people of South Vietnam want. And if there is a single nation on this earth that desires less than this for its own people, then let its voice be heard.

We have also made it clear—from Hanoi to New York—that there are no arbitrary limits to our search for peace. We stand by the Geneva Agreements of 1954 and 1962. We will meet at any conference table, we will discuss any proposals—four points or fourteen or forty—and we will consider the views of any group. We will work for a cease-fire now or once discussions have begun. We will respond if others reduce their use of force, and we will withdraw our soldiers once South Vietnam is securely guaranteed the right to shape its own future.

We have said all this, and we have asked—and hoped—and we have waited for a response.

So far we have received no response to prove either success or failure.

We have carried our quest for peace to many nations and peoples because we share this planet with others whose future, in large measure, is tied to our own action, and whose counsel is necessary to our own hopes.

We have found understanding and support. And we know they wait with us tonight for some response that could lead to peace.

I wish tonight that I could give you a blueprint for the course of this conflict over the coming months, but we just cannot know what the future may require. We may have to face long, hard combat or a long, hard conference, or even both at once.

Until peace comes, or if it does not come, our course is clear. We will act as we must to help protect the independence of the valiant people of South Vietnam. We will strive to limit the conflict, for we wish neither increased destruction nor do we want to invite increased danger.

But we will give our fighting men what they must have: every gun, and every dollar, and every decision—whatever the cost or whatever the challenge.

And we will continue to help the people of South Vietnam care for those that are ravaged by battle, create progress in the villages, and carry forward the healing hopes of peace as best they can amidst the uncertain terrors of war.

And let me be absolutely clear: The days may become months, and the months may become years, but we will stay as long as aggression commands us to battle.

There may be some who do not want peace, whose ambitions stretch so far that war in Vietnam is but a welcome and convenient episode in an immense design to subdue history to their will. But for others it must now be clear—the choice is not between peace and victory, it lies between peace and the ravages of a conflict from which they can only lose.

The people of Vietnam, North and South, seek the same things: the shared needs of man, the needs for food and shelter and education—the chance to build and work and till the soil, free from the arbitrary horrors of battle—the desire to walk in the dignity of those who master their own destiny. For many painful years, in war and revolution and infrequent peace, they have struggled to fulfill those needs.

It is a crime against mankind that so much courage, and so much will, and so many dreams, must be flung on the fires of war and death.

To all of those caught up in this conflict we therefore say again tonight: Let us choose peace, and with it the wondrous works of peace, and beyond that, the time when hope reaches toward consummation, and life is the servant of life.

In this work, we plan to discharge our duty to the people whom we serve.

This is the State of the Union.

But over it all—wealth, and promise, and expectation—lies our troubling awareness of American men at war tonight.

How many men who listen to me tonight have served their Nation in other wars? How very many are not here to listen?

The war in Vietnam is not like these other wars. Yet, finally, war is always the same. It is young men dying in the fullness of their promise. It is trying to kill a man that you do not even know well enough to hate.

Therefore, to know war is to know that there is still madness in this world.

Many of you share the burden of this knowledge tonight with me. But there is a difference. For finally I must be the one to order our guns to fire, against all the most inward pulls of my desire. For we have children to teach, and we have sick to be cured, and we have men to be freed. There are poor to be lifted up, and there are cities to be built, and there is a world to be helped.

Yet we do what we must.

I am hopeful, and I will try as best I can, with everything I have got, to end this battle and to return our sons to their desires.

Yet as long as others will challenge America's security and test the clearness of our beliefs with fire and steel, then we must stand or see the promise of two centuries tremble. I believe tonight that you do not want me to try that risk. And from that belief your President summons his strength for the trials that lie ahead in the days to come.

The work must be our work now. Scarred by the weaknesses of man, with whatever guidance God may offer us, we must nevertheless and alone with our mortality, strive to ennoble the life of man on earth.

Thank you, and goodnight.

Lyndon B. Johnson, 1965–1969

Address to Congress on the State of the Union

January 10, 1967

Lyndon B. Johnson delivered his fourth State of the Union message before Congress at a time when the country was embroiled in the Vietnam War. Johnson had worked with Congress to push through his ambitious Great Society agenda, which included laws creating the Medicare and Medicaid programs as well as major civil rights legislation.

The president sought to continue his efforts on both the home front and the international front, and he urged Congress and the country to forge ahead with both domestic programs and Vietnam.

Johnson summarized various accomplishments of his administration so far, including the preschool Head Start program, which had started in 1965, and Medicare. He listed five alliterative themes under which he hoped the country could continue: programs, partnerships, priorities, prosperity, and peace.

One program he focused on was the war on poverty, which he had declared in his 1964 State of the Union speech. He compared it to the war in Vietnam, stating that neither was simple. In terms of partnership, he sought not just cooperation with Congress—both houses had remained Democratic, although somewhat less so, as a result of the previous November's elections—but efforts on all levels of government to work together. He listed a long agenda of priorities, including strengthening Head Start.

One priority to which he devoted greater attention in his speech was a bill designed to provide federal assistance to states and cities for combating crime. The crime bill eventually was passed in 1968, and Johnson signed it into law that June.

On the issue of prosperity, the president praised the national economy, citing high wages and low unemployment. But he called for a 6 percent surcharge for two years on corporate and individual income taxes to help pay for the Vietnam War; a surcharge finally would be enacted the following year.

When it came to peace, the president said that he hoped to end the Cold War with the Soviet Union and slow down the arms race between the two superpowers. He devoted the end of his address to the situation in Vietnam, listing several reasons why U.S. troops were fighting there. Among them was his statement that the "limited war" was an attempt to stop a larger war that would occur if the communists took over South Vietnam. He made comparisons with World War II and the Korean War and pledged to "stand firm in Vietnam."

Mr. Speaker, Mr. Vice President, distinguished Members of the Congress:

I share with all of you the grief that you feel at the death today of one of the most beloved, respected, and effective Members of this body, the distinguished Representative from Rhode Island, Mr. [John] Fogarty.

I have come here tonight to report to you that this is a time of testing for our Nation.

At home, the question is whether we will continue working for better opportunities for all Americans, when most Americans are already living better than any people in history.

Abroad, the question is whether we have the staying power to fight a very costly war, when the objective is limited and the danger to us is seemingly remote.

So our test is not whether we shrink from our country's cause when the dangers to us are obvious and close at hand, but, rather, whether we carry on when they seem obscure and distant—and some think that it is safe to lay down our burdens.

I have come tonight m ask this Congress and this Nation to resolve that issue: to meet our commitments at home and abroad—to continue to build a better America—and to reaffirm this Nation's allegiance to freedom.

As President Abraham Lincoln said, "We must ask where we are, and whither we are tending."

I.

The last 3 years bear witness to our determination to make this a better country.

We have struck down legal barriers to equality.

We have improved the education of 7 million deprived children and this year alone we have enabled almost 1 million students to go to college.

We have brought medical care to older people who were unable to afford it. Three and one-half million Americans have already received treatment under Medicare since July.

We have built a strong economy that has put almost 3 million more Americans on the payrolls in the last year alone.

We have included more than 9 million new workers under a higher minimum wage.

We have launched new training programs to provide job skills for almost 1 million Americans.

We have helped more than a thousand local communities to attack poverty in the neighborhoods of the poor. We have set out to rebuild our cities on a scale that has never been attempted before. We have begun to rescue our waters from the menace of pollution and to restore the beauty of our land and our countryside, our cities and our towns.

We have given 1 million young Americans a chance to earn through the Neighborhood Youth Corps—or through Head Start, a chance to learn.

So together we have tried to meet the needs of our people. And, we have succeeded in creating a better life for the many as well as the few. Now we must answer whether our gains shall be the foundations of further progress, or whether they shall be only monuments to what might have been—abandoned now by a people who lacked the will to see their great work through.

I believe that our people do not want to quit—though the task is great, the work hard, often frustrating, and success is a matter not of days or months, but of years—and sometimes it may be even decades.

II.

I have come here tonight to discuss with you five ways of carrying forward the progress of these last 3 years. These five ways concern programs, partnerships, priorities, prosperity, and peace.

First, programs. We must see to it, I think, that these new programs that we have passed work effectively and are administered in the best possible way.

Three years ago we set out to create these new instruments of social progress. This required trial and error—and it has produced both. But as we learn, through success and failure, we are changing our strategy and we are trying to improve our tactics. In the long run, these starts—some rewarding, others inadequate and disappointing—are crucial to success.

One example is the struggle to make life better for the less fortunate among us.

On a similar occasion, at this rostrum in 1949, I heard a great American President, Harry S. Truman, declare this: "The American people have decided that poverty is just as wasteful and just as unnecessary as preventable disease."

Many listened to President Truman that day here in this Chamber, but few understood what was required and did anything about it. The executive branch and the Congress waited 15 long years before ever taking any action on that challenge, as it did on many other challenges that great President presented. And when, 3 years ago, you here in the Congress joined with me in a declaration of war on poverty, then I warned, "It will not be a short or easy struggle—no single weapon . . . will suffice—but we shall not rest until that war is won."

And I have come here to renew that pledge tonight.

I recommend that we intensify our efforts to give the poor a chance to enjoy and to join in this Nation's progress.

I shall propose certain administrative changes suggested by the Congress—as well as some that we have learned from our own trial and error.

I shall urge special methods and special funds to reach the hundreds of thousands of Americans that are now trapped in the ghettos of our big cities and, through Head Start, to try to reach out to our very young, little children. The chance to learn is their brightest hope and must command our full determination. For learning brings skills; and skills bring jobs; and jobs bring responsibility and dignity, as well as taxes.

This war—like the war in Vietnam—is not a simple one. There is no single battleline which you can plot each day on a chart. The enemy is not easy to perceive, or to isolate, or to destroy. There are mistakes and there are setbacks. But we are moving, and our direction is forward.

This is true with other programs that are making and breaking new ground. Some do not yet have the capacity to absorb well or wisely all the money that could be put into them. Administrative skills and trained manpower are just as vital to their success as dollars. And I believe those skills will come. But it will take time and patience and hard work. Success cannot be forced at a single stroke. So we must continue to strengthen the administration of every program if that success is to come—as we know it must.

We have done much in the space of 2 short years, working together.

I have recommended, and you, the Congress, have approved, 10 different reorganization plans, combining and consolidating many bureaus of this Government, and creating two entirely new Cabinet departments.

I have come tonight to propose that we establish a new department—a Department of Business and Labor.

By combining the Department of Commerce with the Department of Labor and other related agencies, I think we can create a more economical, efficient, and streamlined instrument that will better serve a growing nation.

This is our goal throughout the entire Federal Government. Every program will be thoroughly evaluated. Grant-in-aid programs will be improved and simplified as desired by many of our local administrators and our Governors.

Where there have been mistakes, we will try very hard to correct them.

Where there has been progress, we will try to build upon it.

Our second objective is partnership—to create an effective partnership at all levels of government. And I should treasure nothing more than to have that partnership begin between the executive and the Congress.

The 88th and the 89th Congresses passed more social and economic legislation than any two single Congresses in American history. Most of you who were Members of those Congresses voted to pass most of those measures. But your efforts will come to nothing unless it reaches the people.

Federal energy is essential. But it is not enough. Only a total working partnership among Federal, State, and local governments can succeed. The test of that partnership will be the concern of each public organization, each private institution, and each responsible citizen.

Each State, county, and city needs to examine its capacity for government in today's world, as we are examining ours in the executive department, and as I see you are examining yours. Some will need to reorganize and reshape their methods of administration—as we are doing. Others will need to revise their constitutions and their laws to bring them up to date—as we are doing. Above all, I think we must work together and find ways in which the multitudes of small jurisdictions can be brought together more efficiently.

During the past 3 years we have returned to State and local governments about $40 billion in grants-in-aid. This year alone, 70 percent of our Federal expenditures for domestic programs will be distributed through the State and local governments. With Federal assistance, State and local governments by 1970 will be spending close to $110 billion annually. These enormous sums must be used wisely, honestly, and effectively. We intend to work closely with the States and the localities to do exactly that.

Our third objective is priorities, to move ahead on the priorities that we have established within the resources that are available.

I wish, of course, that we could do all that should be done—and that we could do it now. But the Nation has many commitments and responsibilities which make heavy demands upon our total resources. No administration would more eagerly utilize for these programs all the resources they require than the administration that started them.

So let us resolve, now, to do all that we can, with what we have—knowing that it is far, far more than we have ever done before, and far, far less than our problems will ultimately require.

Let us create new opportunities for our children and our young Americans who need special help.

We should strengthen the Head Start program, begin it for children 3 years old, and maintain its educational momentum by following through in the early years.

We should try new methods of child development and care from the earliest years, before it is too late to correct.

And I will propose these measures to the 90th Congress.

Let us insure that older Americans, and neglected Americans, share in their Nation's progress.

We should raise social security payments by an overall average of 20 percent. That will add $4 billion 100 million to social security payments in the first year. I will recommend that each of the 23 million Americans now receiving payments get an increase of at least 15 percent.

I will ask that you raise the minimum payments by 59 percent—from $44 to $70 a month, and to guarantee a minimum benefit of $100 a month for those with a total of 25 years of coverage. We must raise the limits that retired workers can earn without losing social security income.

We must eliminate by law unjust discrimination in employment because of age.

We should embark upon a major effort to provide self-help assistance to the forgotten in our midst—the American Indians and the migratory farm workers. And we should reach with the hand of understanding to help those who live in rural poverty.

And I will propose these measures to the 90th Congress.

So let us keep on improving the quality of life and enlarging the meaning of justice for all of our fellow Americans.

We should transform our decaying slums into places of decency through the landmark Model Cities program. I intend to seek for this effort, this year, the full amount that you in Congress authorized last year.

We should call upon the genius of private industry and the most advanced technology to help rebuild our great cities.

We should vastly expand the fight for clean air with a total attack on pollution at its sources, and—because air, like water, does not respect manmade boundaries—we should set up "regional airsheds" throughout this great land.

We should continue to carry to every corner of the Nation our campaign for a beautiful America—to dean up our towns, to make them more beautiful, our cities, our countryside, by creating more parks, and more seashores, and more open spaces for our children to play in, and for the generations that come after us to enjoy.

We should continue to seek equality and justice for each citizen—before a jury, in seeking a job, in exercising his civil rights. We should find a solution to fair housing, so that every American, regardless of color, has a decent home of his choice.

We should modernize our Selective Service System. The National Commission on Selective Service will shortly submit its report. I will send you new recommendations to meet our military manpower needs. But let us resolve that this is to be the Congress that made our draft laws as fair and as effective as possible.

We should protect what Justice Brandeis called the "right most valued by civilized men"—the right to privacy. We should outlaw all wiretapping—public and private—wherever and whenever it occurs, except when the security of this Nation itself is at stake—and only then with the strictest governmental safeguards. And we should exercise the full reach of our constitutional powers to outlaw electronic "bugging" and "snooping."

I hope this Congress will try to help me do more for the consumer. We should demand that the cost of credit be clearly and honestly expressed where average citizens can understand it. We should immediately take steps to prevent massive power failures, to safeguard the home against hazardous household products, and to assure safety in the pipelines that carry natural gas across our Nation.

We should extend Medicare benefits that are now denied to 1,300,000 permanently and totally disabled Americans under 65 years of age.

We should improve the process of democracy by passing our election reform and financing proposals, by tightening our laws regulating lobbying, and by restoring a reasonable franchise to Americans who move their residences.

We should develop educational television into a vital public resource to enrich our homes, educate our families, and to provide assistance in our classrooms. We should insist that the public interest be fully served through the public's airwaves.

And I will propose these measures to the 90th Congress.

Now we come to a question that weighs very heavily on all our minds—on yours and mine. This Nation must make an all-out effort to combat crime.

The 89th Congress gave us a new start in the attack on crime by passing the Law Enforcement Assistance Act that I recommended. We appointed the National Crime Commission to study crime in America and to recommend the best ways to carry that attack forward.

And while we do not have all the answers, on the basis of its preliminary recommendations we are ready to move.

This is not a war that Washington alone can win. The idea of a national police force is repugnant to the American people. Crime must be rooted out in local communities by local authorities. Our policemen must be better trained, must be better paid, and must be better supported by the local citizens that they try to serve and to protect.

The National Government can and expects to help.

And so I will recommend to the 90th Congress the Safe Streets and Crime Control Act of 1967. It will enable us to assist those States and cities that try to make their streets and homes safer, their police forces better, their corrections systems more effective, and their courts more efficient.

When the Congress approves, the Federal Government will be able to provide a substantial percentage of the cost:

—90 percent of the cost of developing the State and local plans, master plans, to combat crime in their area;

—60 percent of the cost of training new tactical units, developing instant communications and special alarm systems, and introducing the latest equipment and techniques so that they can become weapons in the war on crime;

—50 percent of the cost of building crime laboratories and police academy-type centers so that our citizens can be protected by the best trained and served by the best equipped police to be found anywhere.

We will also recommend new methods to prevent juvenile delinquents from becoming adult delinquents. We will seek new partnerships with States and cities in order to deal with this hideous narcotics problem. And we will recommend strict controls on the sale of firearms.

At the heart of this attack on crime must be the conviction that a free America—as Abraham Lincoln once said—must "let reverence for the laws . . . become the political religion of the Nation."

Our country's laws must be respected. Order must be maintained. And I will support—with all the constitutional powers the President possesses—our Nation's law enforcement officials in their attempt to control the crime and the violence that tear the fabric of our communities.

Many of these priority proposals will be built on foundations that have already been laid. Some will necessarily be small at first, but "every beginning is a consequence." If we postpone this urgent work now, it will simply have to be done later, and later we will pay a much higher price.

Our fourth objective is prosperity, to keep our economy moving ahead, moving ahead steadily and safely.

We have now enjoyed 6 years of unprecedented and rewarding prosperity. Last year, in 1966:

—Wages were the highest in history—and the unemployment rate, announced yesterday, reached the lowest point in 13 years;

—Total after-tax income of American families rose nearly 5 percent;

—Corporate profits after taxes rose a little more than 5 percent;

—Our gross national product advanced 5.5 percent, to about $740 billion;

—Income per farm went up 6 percent.

Now we have been greatly concerned because consumer prices rose 4.5 percent over the 18 months since we decided to send troops to Vietnam. This was more than we had expected—and the Government tried to do everything that we knew how to do to hold it down. Yet we were not as successful as we wished to be. In the 18 months after we entered World War II, prices rose not 4.5 percent, but 13.5 percent. In the first 18 months after Korea, after the conflict broke out there, prices rose not 4.5 percent, but 11 percent. During those two periods we had OPA price control that the Congress gave us and War Labor Board wage controls.

Since Vietnam we have not asked for those controls and we have tried to avoid imposing them. We believe that we have done better, but we make no pretense of having been successful or doing as well as we wished.

Our greatest disappointment in the economy during 1966 was the excessive rise in interest rates and the tightening of credit. They imposed very severe and very unfair burdens on our home buyers and on our home builders, and all those associated with the home industry.

Last January, and again last September, I recommended fiscal and moderate tax measures to try to restrain the unbalanced pace of economic expansion. Legislatively and administratively we took several billions out of the economy. With these measures, in both instances, the Congress approved most of the recommendations rather promptly.

As 1966 ended, price stability was seemingly being restored. Wholesale prices are lower tonight than they were in August. So are retail food prices. Monetary conditions are also easing. Most interest rates have retreated from their earlier peaks. More money now seems to be available.

Given the cooperation of the Federal Reserve System, which I so earnestly seek, I am confident that this movement can continue. I pledge the American people that I will do everything in a President's power to lower interest rates and to ease money in this country. The Federal Home Loan Bank Board tomorrow morning will announce that it will make immediately available to savings and loan associations an additional $1 billion, and will lower from 6 percent to $5\,^{3}/_{4}$ percent the interest rate charged on those loans.

We shall continue on a sensible course of fiscal and budgetary policy that we believe will keep our economy growing without new inflationary spirals; that will finance responsibly the needs of our men in Vietnam and the progress of our people at home; that will support a significant improvement in our export surplus, and will press forward toward easier credit and toward lower interest rates.

I recommend to the Congress a surcharge of 6 percent on both corporate and individual income taxes—to last for 2 years or for so long as the unusual expenditures associated with our efforts in Vietnam continue. I will promptly recommend an earlier termination date if a reduction in these expenditures permits it. This surcharge will raise revenues by some $4.5 billion in the first year. For example, a person whose tax payment, the tax he owes, is $1,000, will pay, under this proposal, an extra $60 over the 12-month period, or $5 a month. The overwhelming majority of Americans who pay taxes today are below that figure and they will pay substantially less than $5 a month. Married couples with two children, with incomes up to $5,000 per year, will be exempt from this tax—as will single people with an income of up to $1,900 a year.

Now if Americans today still paid the income and excise tax rates in effect when I came into the Presidency, in the year 1964, their annual taxes would have been over $20 billion more than at present tax rates. So this proposal is that while we have this problem and this emergency in Vietnam, while we are trying to meet the needs of our people at home, your Government asks for slightly more than one-fourth of that tax cut each year in order to try to hold our budget deficit in fiscal 1968 within prudent limits and to give our country and to give our fighting men the help they need in this hour of trial.

For fiscal 1967, we estimate the budget expenditures to be $126.7 billion and revenues of $117 billion. That will leave us a deficit this year of $9.7 billion.

For fiscal 1968, we estimate budget expenditures of $135 billion. And with the tax measures recommended, and a continuing strong economy, we estimate revenues will be $126.9 billion. The deficit then will be $8.1 billion.

I will very soon forward all of my recommendations to the Congress. Yours is the responsibility to discuss and to debate them—to approve or modify or reject them.

I welcome your views, as I have welcomed working with you for 30 years as a colleague and as Vice President and President.

I should like to say to the Members of the opposition—whose numbers, if I am not mistaken, seem to have increased somewhat—that the genius of the American political system has always been best expressed through creative debate that offers choices and reasonable alternatives. Throughout our history, great Republicans and Democrats have seemed to understand this. So let there be light and reason in our relations. That is the way to a responsible session and a responsive government.

Let us be remembered as a President and a Congress who tried to improve the quality of life for every American—not just the rich, not just the poor, but every man, woman, and child in this great Nation of ours.

We all go to school—to good schools or bad schools. We all take air into our lungs—clean air or polluted air. We all drink water—pure water or polluted water. We all face sickness someday, and some more often than we wish, and old age as well. We all have a stake in this Great Society—in its economic growth, in reduction of civil strife—a great stake in good government.

We just must not arrest the pace of progress we have established in this country in these years. Our children's children will pay the price if we are not wise enough, and courageous enough, and determined enough to stand up and meet the Nation's needs as well as we can in the time allotted us.

III.

Abroad, as at home, there is also risk in change. But abroad, as at home, there is a greater risk in standing still. No part of our foreign policy is so sacred that it ever remains beyond review. We shall be flexible where conditions in the world change—and where man's efforts can change them for the better.

We are in the midst of a great transition—a transition from narrow nationalism to international partnership; from the harsh spirit of the cold war to the hopeful spirit of common humanity on a troubled and a threatened planet.

In Latin America, the American chiefs of state will be meeting very shortly to give our hemispheric policies new direction.

We have come a long way in this hemisphere since the inter-American effort in economic and social development was launched by the conference at Bogota in 1960 under the leadership of President Eisenhower. The Alliance for Progress moved dramatically forward under President Kennedy. There is new confidence that the voice of the people is being heard; that the dignity of the individual is stronger than ever in this hemisphere, and we are facing up to and meeting many of the hemispheric problems together. In this hemisphere that reform under democracy can be made to happen—because it has happened. So together, I think, we must now move to strike down the barriers to full cooperation among the American nations, and to free the energies and the resources of two great continents on behalf of all of our citizens.

Africa stands at an earlier stage of development than Latin America. It has yet to develop the transportation, communications, agriculture, and, above all, the trained men and women without which growth is impossible. There, too, the job will best be done if the nations and peoples of Africa cooperate on a regional basis. More and more our programs for Africa are going to be directed toward self-help.

The future of Africa is shadowed by unsolved racial conflicts. Our policy will continue to reflect our basic commitments as a people to support those who are prepared to work towards cooperation and harmony between races, and to help those who demand change but reject the fool's gold of violence.

In the Middle East the spirit of good will toward all, unfortunately, has not yet taken hold. An already tortured peace seems to be constantly threatened. We shall try to use our influence to increase the possibilities of improved relations among the nations of that region. We are working hard at that task.

In the great subcontinent of South Asia live more than a sixth of the earth's population. Over the years we—and others—have invested very heavily in capital and food for the economic development of India and Pakistan.

We are not prepared to see our assistance wasted, however, in conflict. It must strengthen their capacity to help themselves. It must help these two nations—both our friends—to overcome poverty, to emerge as self-reliant leaders, and find terms for reconciliation and cooperation.

In Western Europe we shall maintain in NATO an integrated common defense. But we also look forward to the time when greater security can be achieved through measures of arms control and disarmament, and through other forms of practical agreement.

We are shaping a new future of enlarged partnership in nuclear affairs, in economic and technical cooperation, in trade negotiations, in political consultation, and in working together with the governments and peoples of Eastern Europe and the Soviet Union.

The emerging spirit of confidence is precisely what we hoped to achieve when we went to work a generation ago to put our shoulder to the wheel and try to help rebuild Europe. We faced new challenges and opportunities then and there—and we faced also some dangers. But I believe that the peoples on both sides of the Atlantic, as well as both sides of this Chamber, wanted to face them together.

Our relations with the Soviet Union and Eastern Europe are also in transition. We have avoided both the acts and the rhetoric of the cold war. When we have differed with the Soviet Union, or other nations, for that matter, I have tried to differ quietly and with courtesy, and without venom.

Our objective is not to continue the cold war, but to end it.

We have reached an agreement at the United Nations on the peaceful uses of outer space.

We have agreed to open direct air flights with the Soviet Union.

We have removed more than 400 nonstrategic items from export control.

We are determined that the Export-Import Bank can allow commercial credits to Poland, Hungary, Bulgaria, and Czechoslovakia, as well as to Romania and Yugoslavia.

We have entered into a cultural agreement with the Soviet Union for another 2 years.

We have agreed with Bulgaria and Hungary to upgrade our legations to embassies.

We have started discussions with international agencies on ways of increasing contacts with Eastern European countries.

This administration has taken these steps even as duty compelled us to fulfill and execute alliances and treaty obligations throughout the world that were entered into before I became President.

So tonight I now ask and urge this Congress to help our foreign and our commercial trade policies by passing an East-West trade bill and by approving our consular convention with the Soviet Union.

The Soviet Union has in the past year increased its long-range missile capabilities. It has begun to place near Moscow a limited antimissile defense. My first responsibility to our people is to assure that no nation can ever find it rational to launch a nuclear attack or to use its nuclear power as a credible threat against us or against our allies.

I would emphasize that that is why an important link between Russia and the United States is in our common interest, in arms control and in disarmament. We have the solemn duty to slow down the arms race between us, if that is at all possible, in both conventional and nuclear weapons and defenses. I thought we were making some progress in that direction the first few months I was in office. I realize that any additional race would impose on our peoples, and on all mankind, for that matter, an additional waste of resources with no gain in security to either side.

I expect in the days ahead to closely consult and seek the advice of the Congress about the possibilities of international agreements bearing directly upon this problem.

Next to the pursuit of peace, the really greatest challenge to the human family is the race between food supply and population increase. That race tonight is being lost.

The time for rhetoric has clearly passed. The time for concerted action is here and we must get on with the job.

We believe that three principles must prevail if our policy is to succeed:

First, the developing nations must give highest priority to food production, including the use of technology and the capital of private enterprise.

Second, nations with food deficits must put more of their resources into voluntary family planning programs.

And third, the developed nations must all assist other nations to avoid starvation in the short run and to move rapidly towards the ability to feed themselves.

Every member of the world community now bears a direct responsibility to help bring our most basic human account into balance.

IV.

I come now finally to Southeast Asia—and to Vietnam in particular. Soon I will submit to the Congress a detailed report on that situation. Tonight I want to just review the essential points as briefly as I can.

We are in Vietnam because the United States of America and our allies are committed by the SEATO [Southeast Asia Treaty Organization] Treaty to "act to meet the common danger" of aggression in Southeast Asia.

We are in Vietnam because an international agreement signed by the United States, North Vietnam, and others in 1962 is being systematically violated by the Communists. That violation threatens the independence of all the small nations in Southeast Asia, and threatens the peace of the entire region and perhaps the world.

We are there because the people of South Vietnam have as much right to remain non-Communist—if that is what they choose—as North Vietnam has to remain Communist.

We are there because the Congress has pledged by solemn vote to take all necessary measures to prevent further aggression.

No better words could describe our present course than those once spoken by the great Thomas Jefferson: "It is the melancholy law of human societies to be compelled sometimes to choose a great evil in order to ward off a greater."

We have chosen to fight a limited war in Vietnam in an attempt to prevent a larger war—a war almost certain to follow, I believe, if the Communists succeed in overrunning and taking over South Vietnam by aggression and by force. I believe, and I am supported by some authority, that if they are not checked now the world can expect to pay a greater price to check them later.

That is what our statesmen said when they debated this treaty, and that is why it was ratified 82 to 1 by the Senate many years ago.

You will remember that we stood in Western Europe 20 years ago. Is there anyone in this Chamber tonight who doubts that the course of freedom was not changed for the better because of the courage of that stand?

Sixteen years ago we and others stopped another kind of aggression—this time it was in Korea. Imagine how different Asia might be today if we had failed to act when the Communist army of North Korea marched south. The Asia of tomorrow will be far different because we have said in Vietnam, as we said 16 years ago in Korea: "This far and no further."

I think I reveal no secret when I tell you that we are dealing with a stubborn adversary who is committed to the use of force and terror to settle political questions.

I wish I could report to you that the conflict is almost over. This I cannot do. We face more cost, more loss, and more agony. For the end is not yet. I cannot promise you that it will come this year—or come next year. Our adversary still believes, I think, tonight, that he can go on fighting longer than we can, and longer than we and our allies will be prepared to stand up and resist.

Our men in that area—there are nearly 500,000 now—have borne well "the burden and the heat of the day." Their efforts have deprived the Communist enemy of the victory that he sought and that he expected a year ago. We have steadily frustrated his main forces. General Westmoreland reports that the enemy can no longer succeed on the battlefield.

So I must say to you that our pressure must be sustained—and will be sustained— until he realizes that the war he started is costing him more than he can ever gain.

I know of no strategy more likely to attain that end than the strategy of "accumulating slowly, but inexorably, every kind of material resource"—of "laboriously teaching troops the very elements of their trade." That, and patience—and I mean a great deal of patience.

Our South Vietnamese allies are also being tested tonight. Because they must provide real security to the people living in the countryside. And this means reducing the terrorism and the armed attacks which kidnapped and killed 26,900 civilians in the last 32 months, to levels where they can be successfully controlled by the regular South Vietnamese security forces. It means bringing to the villagers an effective civilian government that they can respect, and that they can rely upon and that they can participate in, and that they can have a personal stake in. We hope that government is now beginning to emerge.

While I cannot report the desired progress in the pacification effort, the very distinguished and able Ambassador, Henry Cabot Lodge, reports that South Vietnam is turning to this task with a new sense of urgency. We can help, but only they can win this part of the war. Their task is to build and protect a new life in each rural province.

One result of our stand in Vietnam is already clear.

It is this: The peoples of Asia now know that the door to independence is not going to be slammed shut. They know that it is possible for them to choose their own national destinies—without coercion.

The performance of our men in Vietnam—backed by the American people—has created a feeling of confidence and unity among the independent nations of Asia and the Pacific. I saw it in their faces in the 19 days that I spent in their homes and in their countries. Fear of external Communist conquest in many Asian nations is already subsiding—and with this, the spirit of hope is rising. For the first time in history, a common outlook and common institutions are already emerging.

This forward movement is rooted in the ambitions and the interests of Asian nations themselves. It was precisely this movement that we hoped to accelerate when I spoke at Johns Hopkins in Baltimore in April 1965, and I pledged "a much more massive effort to improve the life of man" in that part of the world, in the hope that we could take some of the funds that we were spending on bullets and bombs and spend it on schools and production.

Twenty months later our efforts have produced a new reality: The doors of the billion dollar Asian Development Bank that I recommended to the Congress, and you endorsed almost unanimously, I am proud to tell you are already open. Asians are engaged tonight in regional efforts in a dozen new directions. Their hopes are high. Their faith is strong. Their confidence is deep.

And even as the war continues, we shall play our part in carrying forward this constructive historic development. As recommended by the Eugene Black mission, and if other nations will join us, I will seek a special authorization from the Congress of $200 million for East Asian regional programs.

We are eager to turn our resources to peace. Our efforts in behalf of humanity I think need not be restricted by any parallel or by any boundary line. The moment that peace comes, as I pledged in Baltimore, I will ask the Congress for funds to join in an international program of reconstruction and development for all the people of Vietnam—and their deserving neighbors who wish our help.

We shall continue to hope for a reconciliation between the people of Mainland China and the world community—including working together in all the tasks of arms control, security, and progress on which the fate of the Chinese people, like their fellow men elsewhere, depends.

We would be the first to welcome a China which decided to respect her neighbors' rights. We would be the first to applaud her were she to apply her great energies and intelligence to improving the welfare of her people. And we have no intention of trying to deny her legitimate needs for security and friendly relations with her neighboring countries.

Our hope that all of this will someday happen rests on the conviction that we, the American people and our allies, will and are going to see Vietnam through to an honorable peace.

We will support all appropriate initiatives by the United Nations, and others, which can bring the several parties together for unconditional discussions of peace—anywhere, any time. And we will continue to take every possible initiative ourselves to constantly probe for peace.

Until such efforts succeed, or until the infiltration ceases, or until the conflict subsides, I think the course of wisdom for this country is that we just must firmly pursue our present course. We will stand firm in Vietnam.

I think you know that our fighting men there tonight bear the heaviest burden of all. With their lives they serve their Nation. We must give them nothing less than our full support—and we have given them that—nothing less than the determination that Americans have always given their fighting men. Whatever our sacrifice here, even if it is more than $5 a month, it is small compared to their own.

How long it will take I cannot prophesy. I only know that the will of the American people, I think, is tonight being tested.

Whether we can fight a war of limited objectives over a period of time, and keep alive the hope of independence and stability for people other than ourselves; whether we can continue to act with restraint when the temptation to "get it over with" is inviting but dangerous; whether we can accept the necessity of choosing "a great evil in order to ward off a greater"; whether we can do these without arousing the hatreds and the passions that are ordinarily loosed in time of war—on all these questions so much turns.

The answers will determine not only where we are, but "whither we are tending."

A time of testing—yes. And a time of transition. The transition is sometimes slow; sometimes unpopular; almost always very painful; and often quite dangerous.

But we have lived with danger for a long time before, and we shall live with it for a long time yet to come. We know that "man is born unto trouble." We also know that this Nation was not forged and did not survive and grow and prosper without a great deal of sacrifice from a great many men.

For all the disorders that we must deal with, and all the frustrations that concern us, and all the anxieties that we are called upon to resolve, for all the issues we must face with the agony that attends them, let us remember that "those who expect to reap the blessings of freedom must, like men, undergo the fatigues of supporting it."

But let us also count not only our burdens but our blessings—for they are many. And let us give thanks to the One who governs us all.

Let us draw encouragement from the signs of hope—for they, too, are many.

Let us remember that we have been tested before and America has never been found wanting.

So with your understanding, I would hope your confidence, and your support, we are going to persist—and we are going to succeed.

Lyndon B. Johnson, 1965–1969

Address to Congress on the State of the Union
January 17, 1968

Lyndon B. Johnson's fifth State of the Union message came at the start of a presidential election year, one in which Johnson seemed prepared to seek another term in the White House. But, to the country's surprise, the president, battered by the Vietnam War, would pull out of the contest on March 31.

In this speech, Johnson began with a discussion of the war, stating that the United States would "persevere" in the conflict while also seeking a peaceful resolution. He went on to discuss other international issues, including the relationship with the Soviet Union. He declared that progress had been made in recent years in dealing with the Cold War and listed a series of treaties, including the first commercial air agreement between the two countries.

But Johnson chose to devote most of his speech to domestic issues. Here, too, as with unrest over Vietnam, the country was going through some turmoil, with race riots plaguing major cities. The president commented in his speech on those incidents, stating that they showed that some Americans faced a wide disparity between "the promise and the reality of our society." He proposed more jobs, especially focusing on the "hard-core unemployed"; additional housing for low- and middle-income families; and a child health program for prenatal and infant care.

He urged Congress, as he had in his previous State of the Union address the year before, to pass the Safe Streets Act, which would provide federal assistance to states and localities for crime-fighting efforts. It finally would pass later that year. Johnson urged action on his tax bill, which also would pass in 1968; he had called in his previous State of the Union message for a two-year tax surcharge to help pay for the war in Vietnam.

The war was not going well, and the Tet Offensive—a communist offensive that failed militarily and took a huge psychological toll on U.S. morale—only made the situation worse for Johnson. In addition, he was challenged in the Democratic primaries by antiwar senator Eugene McCarthy. The eventual Democratic nominee, Vice President Hubert Humphrey, would lose a close election to Republican Richard Nixon, the former vice president under Dwight D. Eisenhower. The Southeast Asian conflict would drag on for several more years, with U.S. troops finally withdrawing from Vietnam in January 1973; the South Vietnamese government in Saigon fell to the communists in 1975, during the presidency of Gerald R. Ford.

Mr. Speaker, Mr. President, Members of the Congress, and my fellow Americans:

I was thinking as I was walking down the aisle tonight of what Sam Rayburn told me many years ago: The Congress always extends a very warm welcome to the President—as he comes in.

Thank all of you very, very much.

I have come once again to this Chamber—the home of our democracy—to give you, as the Constitution requires, "Information of the State of the Union."

I report to you that our country is challenged, at home and abroad:

—that it is our will that is being tried, not our strength; our sense of purpose, not our ability to achieve a better America;

—that we have the strength to meet our every challenge; the physical strength to hold the course of decency and compassion at home; and the moral strength to support the cause of peace in the world.

And I report to you that I believe, with abiding conviction, that this people—nurtured by their deep faith, tutored by their hard lessons, moved by their high aspirations—have the will to meet the trials that these times impose.

Since I reported to you last January:

—Three elections have been held in Vietnam—in the midst of war and under the constant threat of violence.

—A President, a Vice President, a House and Senate, and village officials have been chosen by popular, contested ballot.

—The enemy has been defeated in battle after battle.

—The number of South Vietnamese living in areas under Government protection tonight has grown by more than a million since January of last year.

These are all marks of progress. Yet:

—The enemy continues to pour men and material across frontiers and into battle, despite his continuous heavy losses.

—He continues to hope that America's will to persevere can be broken. Well—he is wrong. America will persevere. Our patience and our perseverance will match our power. Aggression will never prevail.

But our goal is peace—and peace at the earliest possible moment.

Right now we are exploring the meaning of Hanoi's recent statement. There is no mystery about the questions which must be answered before the bombing is stopped.

We believe that any talks should follow the San Antonio formula that I stated last September, which said:

—The bombing would stop immediately if talks would take place promptly and with reasonable hopes that they would be productive.

—And the other side must not take advantage of our restraint as they have in the past. This Nation simply cannot accept anything less without jeopardizing the lives of our men and of our allies.

If a basis for peace talks can be established on the San Antonio foundations—and it is my hope and my prayer that they can—we would consult with our allies and with the other side to see if a complete cessation of hostilities—a really true cease-fire—could be made the first order of business. I will report at the earliest possible moment the results of these explorations to the American people.

I have just recently returned from a very fruitful visit and talks with His Holiness the Pope and I share his hope—as he expressed it earlier today—that both sides will extend themselves in an effort to bring an end to the war in Vietnam. I have today assured him that we and our allies will do our full part to bring this about.

Since I spoke to you last January, other events have occurred that have major consequences for world peace.

—The Kennedy Round achieved the greatest reduction in tariff barriers in all the history of trade negotiations.

—The nations of Latin America at Punta del Este resolved to move toward economic integration.

—In Asia, the nations from Korea and Japan to Indonesia and Singapore worked behind America's shield to strengthen their economies and to broaden their political cooperation.

—In Africa, from which the distinguished Vice President has just returned, he reports to me that there is a spirit of regional cooperation that is beginning to take hold in very practical ways.

These events we all welcomed. Yet since I last reported to you, we and the world have been confronted by a number of crises:

—During the Arab-Israeli war last June, the hot line between Washington and Moscow was used for the first time in our history. A cease-fire was achieved without a major power confrontation. Now the nations of the Middle East have the opportunity to cooperate with Ambassador [Gunnar] Jarring's U.N. mission and they have the responsibility to find the terms of living together in stable peace and dignity, and we shall do all in our power to help them achieve that result.

—Not far from this scene of conflict, a crisis flared on Cyprus involving two peoples who are America's friends: Greece and Turkey. Our very able representative, Mr. Cyrus Vance, and others helped to ease this tension.

—Turmoil continues on the mainland of China after a year of violent disruption. The radical extremism of their Government has isolated the Chinese people behind their own borders. The United States, however, remains willing to permit the travel of journalists to both our countries; to undertake cultural and educational exchanges; and to talk about the exchange of basic food crop materials.

Since I spoke to you last, the United States and the Soviet Union have taken several important steps toward the goal of international cooperation.

As you will remember, I met with Chairman Kosygin at Glassboro and we achieved if not accord, at least a clearer understanding of our respective positions after 2 days of meeting.

Because we believe the nuclear danger must be narrowed, we have worked with the Soviet Union and with other nations to reach an agreement that will halt the spread of nuclear weapons. On the basis of communications from Ambassador Fisher in Geneva this afternoon, I am encouraged to believe that a draft treaty can be laid before the conference in Geneva in the very near future. I hope to be able to present that treaty to the Senate this year for the Senate's approval.

We achieved, in 1967, a consular treaty with the Soviets, the first commercial air agreement between the two countries, and a treaty banning weapons in outer space. We shall sign, and submit to the Senate shortly, a new treaty with the Soviets and with others for the protection of astronauts.

Serious differences still remain between us, yet in these relations, we have made some progress since Vienna, the Berlin Wall, and the Cuban missile crisis.

But despite this progress, we must maintain a military force that is capable of deterring any threat to this Nation's security, whatever the mode of aggression. Our choices must not be confined to total war—or to total acquiescence.

We have such a military force today. We shall maintain it.

I wish—with all of my heart—that the expenditures that are necessary to build and to protect our power could all be devoted to the programs of peace. But until world conditions permit, and until peace is assured, America's might—and America's bravest sons who wear our Nation's uniform—must continue to stand guard for all of us—as they gallantly do tonight in Vietnam and other places in the world.

Yet neither great weapons nor individual courage can provide the conditions of peace.

For two decades America has committed itself against the tyranny of want and ignorance in the world that threatens the peace. We shall sustain that commitment. This year I shall propose:

—That we launch, with other nations, an exploration of the ocean depths to tap its wealth, and its energy, and its abundance.

—That we contribute our fair share to a major expansion of the International Development Association, and to increase the resources of the Asian Development Bank.

—That we adopt a prudent aid program, rooted in the principle of self-help.

—That we renew and extend the food for freedom program.

Our food programs have already helped millions avoid the horrors of famine.

But unless the rapid growth of population in developing countries is slowed, the gap between rich and poor will widen steadily.

Governments in the developing countries must take such facts into consideration. We in the United States are prepared to help assist them in those efforts.

But we must also improve the lives of children already born in the villages and towns and cities on this earth. They can be taught by great teachers through space communications and the miracle of satellite television—and we are going to bring to bear every resource of mind and technology to help make this dream come true.

Let me speak now about some matters here at home.

Tonight our Nation is accomplishing more for its people than has ever been accomplished before. Americans are prosperous as men have never been in recorded history. Yet there is in the land a certain restlessness—a questioning.

The total of our Nation's annual production is now above $800 billion. For 83 months this Nation has been on a steady upward trend of growth.

All about them, most American families can see the evidence of growing abundance: higher paychecks, humming factories, new cars moving down new highways. More and more families own their own homes, equipped with more than 70 million television sets.

A new college is founded every week. Today more than half of the high school graduates go on to college.

There are hundreds of thousands of fathers and mothers who never completed grammar school—who will see their children graduate from college.

Why, then, this restlessness?

Because when a great ship cuts through the sea, the waters are always stirred and troubled.

And our ship is moving. It is moving through troubled and new waters; it is moving toward new and better shores.

We ask now, not how can we achieve abundance?—but how shall we use our abundance? Not, is there abundance enough for all?—but, how can all share in our abundance?

While we have accomplished much, much remains for us to meet and much remains for us to master.

—In some areas, the jobless rate is still three or four times the national average.

—Violence has shown its face in some of our cities.

—Crime increases on our streets.

—Income for farm workers remains far behind that for urban workers; and parity for our farmers who produce our food is still just a hope—not an achievement.

—New housing construction is far less than we need—to assure decent shelter for every family.

—Hospital and medical costs are high, and they are rising.

—Many rivers—and the air in many cities—remain badly polluted. And our citizens suffer from breathing that air.

We have lived with conditions like these for many, many years. But much that we once accepted as inevitable, we now find absolutely intolerable.

In our cities last summer, we saw how wide is the gulf for some Americans between the promise and the reality of our society.

We know that we cannot change all of this in a day. It represents the bitter consequences of more than three centuries.

But the issue is not whether we can change this; the issue is whether we will change this.

Well, I know we can. And I believe we will.

This then is the work we should do in the months that are ahead of us in this Congress.

The first essential is more jobs, useful jobs for tens of thousands who can become productive and can pay their own way.

Our economy has created 7½ million new jobs in the past 4 years. It is adding more than a million and a half new jobs this year.

Through programs passed by the Congress, job training is being given tonight to more than a million Americans in this country.

This year, the time has come when we must get to those who are last in line—the hard-core unemployed—the hardest to reach.

Employment officials estimate that 500,000 of these persons are now unemployed in the major cities of America. Our objective is to place these 500,000 in private industry jobs within the next 3 years.

To do this, I propose a $2.1 billion manpower program in the coming fiscal year—a 25 percent increase over the current year. Most of this increase will be used to start a new partnership between government and private industry to train and to hire the hard-core unemployed persons. I know of no task before us of more importance to us, to the country, or to our future.

Another essential is to rebuild our cities.

Last year the Congress authorized $662 million for the Model Cities program. I requested the full amount of that authorization to help meet the crisis in the cities of America. But the Congress appropriated only $312 million—less than half.

This year I urge the Congress to honor my request for model cities funds to rebuild the centers of American cities by granting us the full amount that you in the Congress authorized—$1 billion.

The next essential is more housing—and more housing now.

Surely a nation that can go to the moon can place a decent home within the reach of its families.

Therefore we must call together the resources of industry and labor, to start building 300,000 housing units for low- and middle-income families next year—that is three times more than this year. We must make it possible for thousands of families to become homeowners, not rent-payers.

I propose, for the consideration of this Congress, a 10-year campaign to build 6 million new housing units for low and middle-income families. Six million units in the next 10 years. We have built 530,000 the last 10 years.

Better health for our children—all of our children—is essential if we are to have a better America.

Last year, Medicare, Medicaid, and other new programs that you passed in the Congress brought better health to more than 25 million Americans.

American medicine—with the very strong support and cooperation of public resources—has produced a phenomenal decline in the death rate from many of the dread diseases.

But it is a shocking fact that, in saving the lives of babies, America ranks 15th among the nations of the world. And among children, crippling defects are often discovered too late for any corrective action. This is a tragedy that Americans can, and Americans should, prevent.

I shall, therefore, propose to the Congress a child health program to provide, over the next 5 years, for families unable to afford it—access to health services from prenatal care of the mother through the child's first year.

When we do that you will find it is the best investment we ever made because we will get these diseases in their infancy and we will find a cure in a great many instances that we can never find by overcrowding our hospitals when they are grown.

Now when we act to advance the consumer's cause I think we help every American.

Last year, with very little fanfare the Congress and the executive branch moved in that field.

We enacted the Wholesome Meat Act, the Flammable Fabrics Act, the Product Safety Commission, and a law to improve clinical laboratories.

And now, I think, the time has come to complete our unfinished work. The Senate has already passed the truth-in-lending bill, the fire safety bill, and the pipeline safety laws.

Tonight I plead with the House to immediately act upon these measures and I hope take favorable action upon all of them. I call upon the Congress to enact, without delay, the remainder of the 12 vital consumer protection laws that I submitted to the Congress last year.

I also urge final action on a measure that is already passed by the House to guard against fraud and manipulation in the Nation's commodity exchange market.

These measures are a pledge to our people—to keep them safe in their homes and at work, and to give them a fair deal in the marketplace.

And I think we must do more. I propose:

—New powers for the Federal Trade Commission to stop those who defraud and who swindle our public.

—New safeguards to insure the quality of fish and poultry, and the safety of our community water supplies.

—A major study of automobile insurance.

—Protection against hazardous radiation from television sets and other electronic equipment.

And to give the consumer a stronger voice, I plan to appoint a consumer counsel in the Justice Department—a lawyer for the American consumer—to work directly under the Attorney General, to serve the President's Special Assistant for Consumer Affairs, and to serve the consumers of this land.

This Congress—Democrats and Republicans—can earn the thanks of history. We can make this truly a new day for the American consumer, and by giving him this protection we can live in history as the consumer-conscious Congress.

So let us get on with the work. Let us act soon.

We, at every level of the government, State, local, Federal, know that the American people have had enough of rising crime and lawlessness in this country.

They recognize that law enforcement is first the duty of local police and local government.

They recognize that the frontline headquarters against crime is in the home, the church, the city hall and the county courthouse and the statehouse—not in the far-removed National Capital of Washington.

But the people also recognize that the National Government can and the National Government should help the cities and the States in their war on crime to the full extent of its resources and its constitutional authority. And this we shall do.

This does not mean a national police force. It does mean help and financial support:

—to develop State and local master plans to combat crime,

—to provide better training and better pay for police, and

—to bring the most advanced technology to the war on crime in every city and every county in America.

There is no more urgent business before this Congress than to pass the Safe Streets Act this year that I proposed last year. That law will provide these required funds. They are so critically needed that I have doubled my request under this act to $100 million in fiscal 1969.

And I urge the Congress to stop the trade in mail-order murder, to stop it this year by adopting a proper gun control law.

This year, I will propose a Drug Control Act to provide stricter penalties for those who traffic in LSD and other dangerous drugs with our people.

I will ask for more vigorous enforcement of all of our drug laws by increasing the number of Federal drug and narcotics control officials by more than 30 percent. The time has come to stop the sale of slavery to the young. I also request you to give us funds to add immediately 100 assistant United States attorneys throughout the land to help prosecute our criminal laws. We have increased our judiciary by 40 percent and we have increased our prosecutors by 16 percent. The dockets are full of cases because we don't have assistant district attorneys to go before the Federal judge and handle them. We start these young lawyers at $8,200 a year. And the docket is clogged because we don't have authority to hire more of them.

I ask the Congress for authority to hire 100 more. These young men will give special attention to this drug abuse, too.

Finally, I ask you to add 100 FBI agents to strengthen law enforcement in the Nation and to protect the individual rights of every citizen.

A moment ago I spoke of despair and frustrated hopes in the cities where the fires of disorder burned last summer. We can—and in time we will—change that despair into confidence, and change those frustrations into achievements. But violence will never bring progress.

We can make progress only by attacking the causes of violence and only where there is civil order founded on justice.

Today we are helping local officials improve their capacity to deal promptly with disorders.

Those who preach disorder and those who preach violence must know that local authorities are able to resist them swiftly, to resist them sternly, and to resist them decisively.

I shall recommend other actions:

—To raise the farmers' income by establishing a security commodity reserve that will protect the market from price-depressing stocks and protect the consumer from food scarcity.

—I shall recommend programs to help farmers bargain more effectively for fair prices.

—I shall recommend programs for new air safety measures.

—Measures to stem the rising costs of medical care.

—Legislation to encourage our returning veterans to devote themselves to careers in community service such as teaching, and being firemen, and joining our police force, and our law enforcement officials.

—I shall recommend programs to strengthen and finance our anti-pollution efforts.

—Fully funding all of the $2.18 billion poverty program that you in the Congress had just authorized in order to bring opportunity to those who have been left far behind.

—I shall recommend an Educational Opportunity Act to speed up our drive to break down the financial barriers that are separating our young people from college.

I shall also urge the Congress to act on several other vital pending bills—especially the civil rights measures—fair jury trials, protection of Federal rights, enforcement of equal employment opportunity, and fair housing.

The unfinished work of the first session must be completed—the Higher Education Act, the Juvenile Delinquency Act, conservation measures to save the redwoods of California, and to preserve the wonders of our scenic rivers, the Highway Beautification Act—and all the other measures for a cleaner, and for a better, and for a more beautiful America.

Next month we'll begin our 8th year of uninterrupted prosperity. The economic outlook for this year is one of steady growth—if we are vigilant.

True, there are some clouds on the horizon. Prices are rising. Interest rates have passed the peak of 1966; and if there is continued inaction on the tax bill, they will climb even higher.

I warn the Congress and the Nation tonight that this failure to act on the tax bill will sweep us into an accelerating spiral of price increases, a slump in homebuilding, and a continuing erosion of the American dollar.

This would be a tragedy for every American family. And I predict that if this happens, they will all let us know about it.

We—those of us in the executive branch, in the Congress, and the leaders of labor and business—must do everything we can to prevent that kind of misfortune.

Under the new budget, the expenditures for 1969 will increase by $10.4 billion. Receipts will increase by $22.3 billion including the added tax revenues. Virtually all of this expenditure increase represents the mandatory cost of our defense efforts, $3 billion; increased interest, almost $1 billion; or mandatory payments under laws passed by Congress—such as those provided in the Social Security Act that you passed in 1967, and to Medicare and Medicaid beneficiaries, veterans, and farmers, of about $4½ billion; and the additional $1 billion 600 million next year for the pay increases that you passed in military and civilian pay. That makes up the $10 billion that is added to the budget. With few exceptions, very few, we are holding the fiscal 1969 budget to last year's level, outside of those mandatory and required increases.

A Presidential commission composed of distinguished congressional fiscal leaders and other prominent Americans recommended this year that we adopt a new budget approach. I am carrying out their recommendations in this year's budget. This budget, therefore, for the first time accurately covers all Federal expenditures and all Federal receipts, including for the first time in one budget $47 billion from the social security, Medicare, highway, and other trust funds.

The fiscal 1969 budget has expenditures of approximately $186 billion, with total estimated revenues, including the tax bill, of about $178 billion.

If the Congress enacts the tax increase, we will reduce the budget deficit by some $12 billion. The war in Vietnam is costing us about $25 billion and we are asking for about $12 billion in taxes—and if we get that $12 billion tax bill we will reduce the deficit from about $20 billion in 1968 to about $8 billion in 1969.

Now, this is a tight budget. It follows the reduction that I made in cooperation with the Congress—a reduction made after you had reviewed every appropriations bill and reduced the appropriations by some $5 or $6 billion and expenditures by $1.5 billion. We conferred together and I recommended to the Congress and you subsequently approved taking 2 percent from payrolls and 10 percent from controllable expenditures. We therefore reduced appropriations almost $10 billion last session and expenditures over $4 billion. Now, that was in the budget last year.

I ask the Congress to recognize that there are certain selected programs that meet the Nation's most urgent needs and they have increased. We have insisted that decreases in very desirable but less urgent programs be made before we would approve any increases. So I ask the Congress tonight:

—to hold its appropriations to the budget requests, and

—to act responsibly early this year by enacting the tax surcharge which for the average American individual amounts to about a penny out of each dollar's income.

This tax increase would yield about half of the $23 billion per year that we returned to the people in the tax reduction bills of 1964 and 1965.

This must be a temporary measure, which expires in less than 2 years. Congress can repeal it sooner if the need has passed. But Congress can never repeal inflation.

The leaders of American business and the leaders of American labor—those who really have power over wages and prices—must act responsibly, and in their Nation's interest by keeping increases in line with productivity. If our recognized leaders do not do this, they and those for whom they speak and all of us are going to suffer very serious consequences.

On January 1st, I outlined a program to reduce our balance of payments deficit sharply this year. We will ask the Congress to help carry out those parts of the program which require legislation. We must restore equilibrium to our balance of payments.

We must also strengthen the international monetary system. We have assured the world that America's full gold stock stands behind our commitment to maintain the price of gold at $35 an ounce. We must back this commitment by legislating now to free our gold reserves.

Americans, traveling more than any other people in history, took $4 billion out of their country last year in travel costs. We must try to reduce the travel deficit that we have of more than $2 billion. We are hoping that we can reduce it by $500 million—without unduly penalizing the travel of teachers, students, business people who have essential and necessary travel, or people who have relatives abroad whom they want to see. Even with this reduction of $500 million, the American people will still be traveling more overseas than they did in 1967, 1966, or 1965 or any other year in their history.

If we act together as I hope we can, I believe we can continue our economic expansion which has already broken all past records. And I hope that we can continue that expansion in the days ahead.

Each of these questions I have discussed with you tonight is a question of policy for our people. Therefore, each of them should be—and doubtless will be—debated by candidates for public office this year.

I hope those debates will be marked by new proposals and by a seriousness that matches the gravity of the questions themselves.

These are not appropriate subjects for narrow partisan oratory. They go to the heart of what we Americans are all about—all of us, Democrats and Republicans.

Tonight I have spoken of some of the goals I should like to see America reach. Many of them can be achieved this year—others by the time we celebrate our Nation's 200th birthday—the bicentennial of our independence.

Several of these goals are going to be very hard to reach. But the State of our Union will be much stronger 8 years from now on our 200th birthday if we resolve to reach these goals now. They are more important—much more important—than the identity of the party or the President who will then be in office.

These goals are what the fighting and our alliances are really meant to protect.

Can we achieve these goals?

Of course we can—if we will.

If ever there was a people who sought more than mere abundance, it is our people.

If ever there was a nation that was capable of solving its problems, it is this Nation.

If ever there were a time to know the pride and the excitement and the hope of being an American—it is this time.

So this, my friends, is the State of our Union: seeking, building, tested many times in this past year—and always equal to the test.

Thank you and good night.

Address to Congress on the State of the Union

January 14, 1969

In Lyndon B. Johnson's last State of the Union message he looked back at his presidency and suggested approaches for the future. Johnson, who had been president since the assassination of John F. Kennedy in 1963, had presided over a tumultuous time in American history, with a war raging in Vietnam and civil unrest erupting in cities all over the nation.

So this State of the Union message was delivered at a difficult moment for the country. The president spoke of the accomplishments of his presidency, including Medicare and voting rights legislation. He also called for continued action on some of his Great Society programs, asking for additional housing for the needy and increases in Social Security benefits.

During his presidency, Johnson, a Democrat, had pushed through a huge number of reform-minded bills, known under the general description of the Great Society. But the country also was dealing with increased crime and race rioting, and 1968 had seen the assassinations of two major leaders, civil rights leader Martin Luther King and Democratic presidential candidate and senator Robert F. Kennedy, the late president's brother.

When it came to Vietnam, Johnson stated in his speech, "I regret more than any of you know that it has not been possible to restore peace to South Vietnam." But he did maintain that the prospects for peace were better than at any point in the previous four years.

Johnson had sent U.S. combat troops to Vietnam, numbering 500,000 by 1968, to help the South Vietnamese government fight communist forces. But the war was going badly, and as more Americans turned against it, Johnson's frustrations grew.

The president concluded his remarks on a sentimental note, reminiscing about his years in the House and Senate and the leaders with whom he had worked. And he urged Congress to work together with incoming Republican president Richard Nixon. Johnson's address marked the first lame-duck State of the Union message delivered in person rather than in writing.

Johnson, to the astonishment of many, had given a speech on March 31, 1968, in which he pulled out of the race for president. The eventual Democratic nominee was his vice president, Hubert Humphrey. In one of the closest contests the country had seen, Humphrey lost narrowly to Nixon. Nixon won 43.4 percent of the popular vote and 301 electoral votes; Humphrey took 42.7 percent and 191 electoral votes.

Johnson would retire to his ranch in Texas; he died of a heart attack in January 1973.

Mr. Speaker, Mr. President, Members of the Congress and my fellow Americans:

For the sixth and the last time, I present to the Congress my assessment of the State of the Union.

I shall speak to you tonight about challenge and opportunity—and about the commitments that all of us have made together that will, if we carry them out, give America our best chance to achieve the kind of great society that we all want. Every President lives, not only with what is, but with what has been and what could be.

Most of the great events in his Presidency are part of a larger sequence extending back through several years and extending back through several other administrations.

Urban unrest, poverty, pressures on welfare, education of our people, law enforcement and law and order, the continuing crisis in the Middle East, the conflict in Vietnam, the dangers of nuclear war, the great difficulties of dealing with the Communist powers, all have this much in common: They and their causes—the causes that gave rise to them—all of these have existed with us for many years. Several Presidents have already sought to try to deal with them. One or more Presidents will try to resolve them or try to contain them in the years that are ahead of us.

But if the Nation's problems are continuing, so are this great Nation's assets:

—our economy,

—the democratic system,

—our sense of exploration, symbolized most recently by the wonderful flight of the Apollo 8, in which all Americans took great pride,

—the good commonsense and sound judgment of the American people, and

—their essential love of justice.

We must not ignore our problems. But neither should we ignore our strengths. Those strengths are available to sustain a President of either party—to support his progressive efforts both at home and overseas.

Unfortunately, the departure of an administration does not mean the end of the problems that this administration has faced. The effort to meet the problems must go on, year after year, if the momentum that we have all mounted together in these past years is not to be lost.

Although the struggle for progressive change is continuous, there are times when a watershed is reached—when there is—if not really a break with the past—at least the fulfillment of many of its oldest hopes, and a stepping forth into a new environment, to seek new goals. I think the past 5 years have been such a time.

We have finished a major part of the old agenda.

Some of the laws that we wrote have already, in front of our eyes, taken on the flesh of achievement.

Medicare that we were unable to pass for so many years is now a part of American life.

Voting rights and the voting booth that we debated so long back in the riffles, and the doors to public service, are open at last to all Americans regardless of their color.

Schools and school children all over America tonight are receiving Federal assistance to go to good schools.

Preschool education—Head Start—is already here to stay and, I think, so are the Federal programs that tonight are keeping more than a million and a half of the cream of our young people in the colleges and the universities of this country.

Part of the American earth—not only in description on a map, but in the reality of our shores, our hills, our parks, our forests, and our mountains—has been permanently set aside for the American public and for their benefit. And there is more that will be set aside before this administration ends.

Five million Americans have been trained for jobs in new Federal programs.

I think it is most important that we all realize tonight that this Nation is close to full employment—with less unemployment than we have had at any time in almost 20 years. That is not in theory; that is in fact. Tonight, the unemployment rate is down to 3.3 percent. The number of jobs has grown more than 8½ million in the last 5 years. That is more than in all the preceding 12 years.

These achievements completed the full cycle, from idea to enactment and, finally, to a place in the lives of citizens all across this country.

I wish it were possible to say that everything that this Congress and the administration achieved during this period had already completed that cycle. But a great deal of what we have committed needs additional funding to become a tangible realization.

Yet the very existence of these commitments—these promises to the American people, made by this Congress and by the executive branch of the Government—are achievements in themselves, and failure to carry through on our commitments would be a tragedy for this Nation.

This much is certain: No one man or group of men made these commitments alone. Congress and the executive branch, with their checks and balances, reasoned together and finally wrote them into the law of the land. They now have all the moral force that the American political system can summon when it acts as one.

They express America's common determination to achieve goals. They imply action.

In most cases, you have already begun that action—but it is not fully completed, of course.

Let me speak for a moment about these commitments. I am going to speak in the language which the Congress itself spoke when it passed these measures. I am going to quote from your words.

In 1966, Congress declared that "improving the quality of urban life is the most critical domestic problem facing the United States." Two years later it affirmed the historic goal of "a decent home . . . for every American family." That is your language.

Now to meet these commitments, we must increase our support for the model cities program, where blueprints of change are already being prepared in more than 150 American cities.

To achieve the goals of the Housing Act of 1968 that you have already passed, we should begin this year more than 500,000 homes for needy families in the coming fiscal year. Funds are provided in the new budget to do just this. This is almost 10 times—10 times—the average rate of the past 10 years.

Our cities and our towns are being pressed for funds to meet the needs of their growing populations. So I believe an urban development bank should be created by the Congress. This bank could obtain resources through the issuance of taxable bonds and it could then lend these resources at reduced rates to the communities throughout the land for schools, hospitals, parks, and other public facilities.

Since we enacted the Social Security Act back in 1935, Congress has recognized the necessity to "make more adequate provision for aged persons . . . through maternal and child welfare . . . and public health." Those are the words of the Congress—"more adequate."

The time has come, I think, to make it more adequate. I believe we should increase social security benefits, and I am so recommending tonight.

I am suggesting that there should be an overall increase in benefits of at least 13 percent. Those who receive only the minimum of $55 should get $80 a month.

Our Nation, too, is rightfully proud of our medical advances. But we should remember that our country ranks 15th among the nations of the world in its infant mortality rate.

I think we should assure decent medical care for every expectant mother and for their children during the first year of their life in the United States of America.

I think we should protect our children and their families from the costs of catastrophic illness.

As we pass on from medicine, I think nothing is clearer to the Congress than the commitment that the Congress made to end poverty. Congress expressed it well, I think, in 1964, when they said: "It is the policy of the United States to eliminate the paradox of poverty in the midst of plenty in this nation."

This is the richest nation in the world. The antipoverty program has had many achievements. It also has some failures. But we must not cripple it after only 3 years of trying to solve the human problems that have been with us and have been building up among us for generations.

I believe the Congress this year will want to improve the administration of the poverty program by reorganizing portions of it and transferring them to other agencies. I believe, though, it will want to continue, until we have broken the back of poverty, the efforts we are now making throughout this land.

I believe, and I hope the next administration—I believe they believe—that the key to success in this effort is jobs. It is work for people who want to work.

In the budget for fiscal 1970, I shall recommend a total of $3.5 billion for our job training program, and that is five times as much as we spent in 1964 trying to prepare Americans where they can work to earn their own living.

The Nation's commitment in the field of civil rights began with the Declaration of Independence. They were extended by the 13th, 14th, and 15th amendments. They have been powerfully strengthened by the enactment of three far-reaching civil rights laws within the past 5 years, that this Congress, in its wisdom, passed.

On January 1 of this year, the Fair Housing Act of 1968 covered over 20 million American homes and apartments. The prohibition against racial discrimination in that act should be remembered and it should be vigorously enforced throughout this land.

I believe we should also extend the vital provisions of the Voting Rights Act for another 5 years.

In the Safe Streets Act of 1968, Congress determined "To assist state and local governments in reducing the incidence of crime."

This year I am proposing that the Congress provide the full $300 million that the Congress last year authorized to do just that.

I hope the Congress will put the money where the authorization is.

I believe this is an essential contribution to justice and to public order in the United States. I hope these grants can be made to the States and they can be used effectively to reduce the crime rate in this country.

But all of this is only a small part of the total effort that must be made—I think chiefly by the local governments throughout the Nation—if we expect to reduce the toll of crime that we all detest.

Frankly, as I leave the Office of the Presidency, one of my greatest disappointments is our failure to secure passage of a licensing and registration act for firearms. I think if we had passed that act, it would have reduced the incidence of crime. I believe that the Congress should adopt such a law, and I hope that it will at a not too distant date.

In order to meet our long-standing commitment to make government as efficient as possible, I believe that we should reorganize our postal system along the lines of the Kappel report.

I hope we can all agree that public service should never impose an unreasonable financial sacrifice on able men and women who want to serve their country.

I believe that the recommendations of the Commission on Executive, Legislative and Judicial Salaries are generally sound. Later this week, I shall submit a special message which I reviewed with the leadership this evening containing a proposal that has been reduced and has modified the Commission's recommendation to some extent on the congressional salaries.

For Members of Congress, I will recommend the basic compensation not of the $50,000 unanimously recommended by the Kappel Commission and the other distinguished Members, but I shall reduce that $50,000 to $42,500. I will suggest that Congress appropriate a very small additional allowance for official expenses, so that Members will not be required to use their salary increase for essential official business.

I would have submitted the Commission's recommendations, except the advice that I received from the leadership—and you usually are consulted about matters that affect the Congress—was that the Congress would not accept the $50,000 recommendation, and if I expected my recommendation to be seriously considered, I should make substantial reductions. That is the only reason I didn't go along with the Kappel report.

In 1967 I recommended to the Congress a fair and impartial random selection system for the draft. I submit it again tonight for your most respectful consideration.

I know that all of us recognize that most of the things we do to meet all of these commitments I talk about will cost money. If we maintain the strong rate of growth that we have had in this country for the past 8 years, I think we shall generate the resources that we need to meet these commitments.

We have already been able to increase our support for major social programs—although we have heard a lot about not being able to do anything on the home front because of Vietnam; but we have been able in the last 5 years to increase our commitments for such things as health and education from $30 billion in 1964 to $68 billion in the coming fiscal year. That is more than double. That is more than it has ever been increased in the 188 years of this Republic, notwithstanding Vietnam.

We must continue to budget our resources and budget them responsibly in a way that will preserve our prosperity and will strengthen our dollar.

Greater revenues and the reduced Federal spending required by Congress last year have changed the budgetary picture dramatically since last January when we made our estimates. At that time, you will remember that we estimated we would have a deficit of $8 billion. Well, I am glad to report to you tonight that the fiscal year ending June 30, 1969, this June, we are going to have not a deficit, but we are going to have a $2.4 billion surplus.

You will receive the budget tomorrow. The budget for the next fiscal year, that begins July 1—which you will want to examine very carefully in the days ahead—will provide a $3.4 billion surplus.

This budget anticipates the extension of the surtax that Congress enacted last year. I have communicated with the President-elect, Mr. Nixon, in connection with this policy of continuing the surtax for the time being.

I want to tell you that both of us want to see it removed just as soon as circumstances will permit, but the President-elect has told me that he has concluded that until his administration, and this Congress, can examine the appropriation bills, and each item in the budget, and can ascertain that the facts justify permitting the surtax to expire or to be reduced, he, Mr. Nixon, will support my recommendation that the surtax be continued.

Americans, I believe, are united in the hope that the Paris talks will bring an early peace to Vietnam. And if our hopes for an early settlement of the war are realized, then our military expenditures can be reduced and very substantial savings can be made to be used for other desirable purposes, as the Congress may determine.

In any event, I think it is imperative that we do all that we responsibly can to resist inflation while maintaining our prosperity. I think all Americans know that our prosperity is broad and it is deep, and it has brought record profits, the highest in our history, and record wages.

Our gross national product has grown more in the last 5 years than any other period in our Nation's history. Our wages have been the highest. Our profits have been the best. This prosperity has enabled millions to escape the poverty that they would have otherwise had the last few years.

I think also you will be very glad to hear that the Secretary of the Treasury informs me tonight that in 1968 in our balance of payments we have achieved a surplus. It appears that we have, in fact, done better this year than we have done in any year in this regard since the year 1957.

The quest for a durable peace, I think, has absorbed every administration since the end of World War II. It has required us to seek a limitation of arms races not only among the superpowers, but among the smaller nations as well. We have joined in the test ban treaty of 1963, the outer space treaty of 1967, and the treaty against the spread of nuclear weapons in 1968.

This latter agreement—the nonproliferation treaty—is now pending in the Senate and it has been pending there since last July. In my opinion, delay in ratifying it is not going to be helpful to the cause of peace. America took the lead in negotiating this treaty and America should now take steps to have it approved at the earliest possible date.

Until a way can be found to scale down the level of arms among the superpowers, mankind cannot view the future without fear and great apprehension. So, I believe that we should resume the talks with the Soviet Union about limiting offensive and defensive missile systems. I think they would already have been resumed except for Czechoslovakia and our election this year.

It was more than 20 years ago that we embarked on a program of trying to aid the developing nations. We knew then that we could not live in good conscience as a rich enclave on an earth that was seething in misery.

During these years there have been great advances made under our program, particularly against want and hunger, although we are disappointed at the appropriations last year. We thought they were woefully inadequate. This year I am asking for adequate funds for economic assistance in the hope that we can further peace throughout the world.

I think we must continue to support efforts in regional cooperation. Among those efforts, that of Western Europe has a very special place in America's concern.

The only course that is going to permit Europe to play the great world role that its resources permit is to go forward to unity. I think America remains ready to work with a united Europe, to work as a partner on the basis of equality.

For the future, the quest for peace, I believe, requires:

—that we maintain the liberal trade policies that have helped us become the leading nation in world trade,

—that we strengthen the international monetary system as an instrument of world prosperity, and

—that we seek areas of agreement with the Soviet Union where the interests of both nations and the interests of world peace are properly served.

The strained relationship between us and the world's leading Communist power has not ended—especially in the light of the brutal invasion of Czechoslovakia. But totalitarianism is no less odious to us because we are able to reach some accommodation that reduces the danger of world catastrophe.

What we do, we do in the interest of peace in the world. We earnestly hope that time will bring a Russia that is less afraid of diversity and individual freedom.

The quest for peace tonight continues in Vietnam, and in the Paris talks.

I regret more than any of you know that it has not been possible to restore peace to South Vietnam.

The prospects, I think, for peace are better today than at any time since North Vietnam began its invasion with its regular forces more than 4 years ago.

The free nations of Asia know what they were not sure of at that time: that America cares about their freedom, and it also cares about America's own vital interests in Asia and throughout the Pacific.

The North Vietnamese know that they cannot achieve their aggressive purposes by force. There may be hard fighting before a settlement is reached; but, I can assure you, it will yield no victory to the Communist cause.

I cannot speak to you tonight about Vietnam without paying a very personal tribute to the men who have carried the battle out there for all of us. I have been honored to be their Commander in Chief. The Nation owes them its unstinting support while the battle continues—and its enduring gratitude when their service is done.

Finally, the quest for stable peace in the Middle East goes on in many capitals tonight. America fully supports the unanimous resolution of the U.N. Security Council which points the way. There must be a settlement of the armed hostility that exists in that region of the world today. It is a threat not only to Israel and to all the Arab States, but it is a threat to every one of us and to the entire world as well.

Now, my friends in Congress, I want to conclude with a few very personal words to you.

I rejected and rejected and then finally accepted the congressional leadership's invitation to come here to speak this farewell to you in person tonight.

I did that for two reasons. One was philosophical. I wanted to give you my judgment, as I saw it, on some of the issues before our Nation, as I view them, before I leave.

The other was just pure sentimental. Most all of my life as a public official has been spent here in this building. For 38 years—since I worked on that gallery as a doorkeeper in the House of Representatives—I have known these halls, and I have known most of the men pretty well who walked them.

I know the questions that you face. I know the conflicts that you endure. I know the ideals that you seek to serve.

I left here first to become Vice President, and then to become, in a moment of tragedy, the President of the United States.

My term of office has been marked by a series of challenges, both at home and throughout the world.

In meeting some of these challenges, the Nation has found a new confidence. In meeting others, it knew turbulence and doubt, and fear and hate.

Throughout this time, I have been sustained by my faith in representative democracy—a faith that I had learned here in this Capitol Building as an employee and as a Congressman and as a Senator.

I believe deeply in the ultimate purposes of this Nation—described by the Constitution, tempered by history, embodied in progressive laws, and given life by men and women that have been elected to serve their fellow citizens.

Now for 5 most demanding years in the White House, I have been strengthened by the counsel and the cooperation of two great former Presidents, Harry S. Truman and Dwight David Eisenhower. I have been guided by the memory of my pleasant and close association with the beloved John F. Kennedy, and with our greatest modern legislator, Speaker Sam Rayburn.

I have been assisted by my friend every step of the way, Vice President Hubert Humphrey. I am so grateful that I have been supported daily by the loyalty of Speaker [John] McCormack and Majority Leader [Carl] Albert.

I have benefited from the wisdom of Senator Mike Mansfield, and I am sure that I have avoided many dangerous pitfalls by the good commonsense counsel of the President Pro Tem of the Senate, Senator Richard Brevard Russell.

I have received the most generous cooperation from the leaders of the Republican Party in the Congress of the United States, Senator [Everett] Dirksen and Congressman Gerald Ford, the Minority Leader.

No President should ask for more, although I did upon occasions. But few Presidents have ever been blessed with so much.

President-elect Nixon, in the days ahead, is going to need your understanding, just as I did. And he is entitled to have it. I hope every Member will remember that the burdens he will bear as our President, will be borne for all of us. Each of us should try not to increase these burdens for the sake of narrow personal or partisan advantage.

Now, it is time to leave. I hope it may be said, a hundred years from now, that by working together we helped to make our country more just, more just for all of its people, as well as to insure and guarantee the blessings of liberty for all of our posterity.

That is what I hope. But I believe that at least it will be said that we tried.

Richard Nixon

1969–1974

"... I will soon be visiting the People's Republic
of China and the Soviet Union. I go there
with no illusions. ... But peace depends on the
ability of great powers to live together on the
same planet despite their differences."

ADDRESS TO CONGRESS ON THE STATE OF THE UNION, JANUARY 20, 1972

Address to Congress on the State of the Union

January 22, 1970

Richard M. Nixon delivered his first State of the Union address a year after being sworn into office. The president focused much of the address on domestic issues, stating that he would submit a separate report on foreign policy to Congress.

Early in the address he noted that the "major immediate goal" of the country's foreign policy was to end the Vietnam War with a "just peace." He stated that progress was being made to achieve such a peace, but it would be another three years before the United States would end its presence in Vietnam. Nixon's policy involved "Vietnamization" of the war, which meant making gradual reductions in U.S. troops and shifting greater responsibility to South Vietnam. At the same time, Nixon also expanded the U.S. role in the war to Vietnam's neighbor, Cambodia.

The president cited a goal of having America at peace with all other countries, and he referred to what became known as the Nixon Doctrine, which he had first unveiled the previous year. He stated in this address that "neither the defense nor the development of other nations can be exclusively or primarily an American undertaking." He pledged that the United States would reduce its involvement in the affairs of other countries.

Nixon's years in office marked a period of "détente" with the Soviet Union, the country's longtime Cold War enemy. Nixon remarked in his speech that the relationship between the two was moving from "confrontation" to "negotiation." In addition, he mentioned talks with communist China; he would make a ground-breaking trip to China in 1972. On the domestic front, Nixon proposed various changes. One was a reform of the welfare system. Nixon stated that he had suggested a new plan to Congress the year before, including "income support, job training, and work incentives." In the end, the plan did not pass.

He also called for efforts to create a "new federalism," which would reorder the relationship between the federal government and the states, sending more of the power back to the states and the people—a shift from the approach espoused by his two immediate predecessors, Lyndon Johnson and John F. Kennedy.

In addition, Nixon called for a balanced budget, with an increase in money to fight crime; he criticized Congress for failing to pass various pieces of crime-related legislation the previous year. He also called for efforts to protect the environment, including a clean water program, and a plan for national growth and development.

Mr. Speaker, Mr. President, my colleagues in the Congress, our distinguished guests and my fellow Americans:

To address a joint session of the Congress in this great Chamber in which I was once privileged to serve is an honor for which I am deeply grateful.

The State of the Union Address is traditionally an occasion for a lengthy and detailed account by the President of what he has accomplished in the past, what he wants the Congress to do in the future, and, in an election year, to lay the basis for the political issues which might be decisive in the fall.

Occasionally there comes a time when profound and far-reaching events command a break with tradition. This is such a time.

I say this not only because 1970 marks the beginning of a new decade in which America will celebrate its 200th birthday. I say it because new knowledge and hard experience argue persuasively that both our programs and our institutions in America need to be reformed.

The moment has arrived to harness the vast energies and abundance of this land to the creation of a new American experience, an experience richer and deeper and more truly a reflection of the goodness and grace of the human spirit.

The seventies will be a time of new beginnings, a time of exploring both on the earth and in the heavens, a time of discovery. But the time has also come for emphasis on developing better ways of managing what we have and of completing what man's genius has begun but left unfinished.

Our land, this land that is ours together, is a great and a good land. It is also an unfinished land, and the challenge of perfecting it is the summons of the seventies.

It is in that spirit that I address myself to those great issues facing our Nation which are above partisanship.

When we speak of America's priorities the first priority must always be peace for America and the world.

The major immediate goal of our foreign policy is to bring an end to the war in Vietnam in a way that our generation will be remembered not so much as the generation that suffered in war, but more for the fact that we had the courage and character to win the kind of a just peace that the next generation was able to keep.

We are making progress toward that goal.

The prospects for peace are far greater today than they were a year ago.

A major part of the credit for this development goes to the Members of this Congress who, despite their differences on the conduct of the war, have overwhelmingly indicated their support of a just peace. By this action, you have completely demolished the enemy's hopes that they can gain in Washington the victory our fighting men have denied them in Vietnam.

No goal could be greater than to make the next generation the first in this century in which America was at peace with every nation in the world.

I shall discuss in detail the new concepts and programs designed to achieve this goal in a separate report on foreign policy, which I shall submit to the Congress at a later date.

Today, let me describe the directions of our new policies.

We have based our policies on an evaluation of the world as it is, not as it was 25 years ago at the conclusion of World War II. Many of the policies which were necessary and fight then are obsolete today.

Then, because of America's overwhelming military and economic strength, because of the weakness of other major free world powers and the inability of scores of newly independent nations to defend, or even govern, themselves, America had to assume the major burden for the defense of freedom in the world.

In two wars, first in Korea and now in Vietnam, we furnished most of the money, most of the arms, most of the men to help other nations defend their freedom.

Today the great industrial nations of Europe, as well as Japan, have regained their economic strength; and the nations of Latin America—and many of the nations who acquired their freedom from colonialism after World War II in Asia and Africa—have a new sense of pride and dignity and a determination to the responsibility for their own defense.

We shall be faithful to our treaty commitments, but we shall reduce our involvement and our presence in other nations' affairs.

To insist that other nations play a role is not a retreat from responsibility; it is a sharing of responsibility.

The result of this new policy has been not to weaken our alliances, but to give them new life, new strength, a new sense of common purpose.

Relations with our European allies are once again strong and healthy, based on mutual consultation and mutual responsibility.

We have initiated a new approach to Latin America in which we deal with those nations as partners rather than patrons.

The new partnership concept has been welcomed in Asia. We have developed an historic new basis for Japanese-American friendship and cooperation, which is the linchpin for peace in the Pacific.

If we are to have peace in the last third of the century, a major factor will be the development of a new relationship between the United States and the Soviet Union.

I would not underestimate our differences, but we are moving with precision and purpose from an era of confrontation to an era of negotiation.

Our negotiations on strategic arms limitations and in other areas will have far greater chance for success if both sides enter them motivated by mutual self-interest rather than naive sentimentality.

It is with this same spirit that we have resumed discussions with Communist China in our talks at Warsaw.

Our concern in our relations with both these nations is to avoid a catastrophic collision and to build a solid basis for peaceful settlement of our differences.

I would be the last to suggest that the road to peace is not difficult and dangerous, but I believe our new policies have contributed to the prospect that America may have the best chance since World War II to enjoy a generation of uninterrupted peace. And that chance will be enormously increased if we continue to have a relationship between Congress and the Executive in which, despite differences in detail, where the security of America and the peace of mankind are concerned, we act not as Republicans, not as Democrats, but as Americans.

As we move into the decade of the seventies, we have the greatest opportunity for progress at home of any people in world history.

Our gross national product will increase by $500 billion in the next 10 years. This increase alone is greater than the entire growth of the American economy from 1790 to 1950.

The critical question is not whether we will grow, but how we will use that growth.

The decade of the sixties was also a period of great growth economically. But in that same 10-year period we witnessed the greatest growth of crime, the greatest increase in inflation, the greatest social unrest in America in 100 years. Never has a nation seemed to have had more and enjoyed it less.

At heart, the issue is the effectiveness of government.

Ours has become—as it continues to be, and should remain—a society of large expectations. Government helped to generate these expectations. It undertook to meet them. Yet, increasingly, it proved unable to do so.

As a people, we had too many visions—and too little vision.

Now, as we enter the seventies, we should enter also a great age of reform of the institutions of American government.

Our purpose in this period should not be simply better management of the programs of the past. The time has come for a new quest—a quest not for a greater quantity of what we have, but for a new quality of life in America.

A major part of the substance for an unprecedented advance in this Nation's approach to its problems and opportunities is contained in more than two score legislative proposals which I sent to the Congress last year and which still await enactment.

I will offer at least a dozen more major programs in the course of this session.

At this point I do not intend to through a detailed listing of what I have proposed or will propose, but I would like to mention three areas in which urgent priorities demand that we move and move now:

First, we cannot delay longer in accomplishing a total reform of our welfare system. When a system penalizes work, breaks up homes, robs recipients of dignity, there is no alternative to abolishing that system and adopting in its place the program of income support, job training, and work incentives which I recommended to the Congress last year.

Second, the time has come to assess and reform all of our institutions of government at the Federal, State, and local level. It is time for a New Federalism, in which, after 190 years of power flowing from the people and local and State governments to Washington, D.C., it will begin to flow from Washington back to the States and to the people of the United States.

Third, we must adopt reforms which will expand the range of opportunities for all Americans. We can fulfill the American dream only when each person has a fair chance to fulfill his own dreams. This means equal voting rights, equal employment opportunity, and new opportunities for expanded ownership. Because in order to be secure in their human rights, people need access to property rights.

I could give similar examples of the need for reform in our programs for health, education, housing, transportation, as well as other critical areas which directly affect the well-being of millions of Americans.

The people of the United States should wait no longer for these reforms that would so deeply enhance the quality of their life.

When I speak of actions which would be beneficial to the American people, I can think of none more important than for the Congress to join this administration in the battle to stop the rise in the cost of living.

Now, I realize it is tempting to blame someone else for inflation. Some blame business for raising prices. Some blame unions for asking for more wages.

But a review of the stark fiscal facts of the 1960's clearly demonstrates where the primary blame for rising prices must be placed.

In the decade of the sixties the Federal Government spent $57 billion more than it took in taxes.

In that same decade the American people paid the bill for that deficit in price increases which raised the cost of living for the average family of four by $200 per month in America.

Now millions of Americans are forced to go into debt today because the Federal Government decided to go into debt yesterday. We must balance our Federal budget so that American families will have a better chance to balance their family budgets.

Only with the cooperation of the Congress can we meet this highest priority objective of responsible government. We are on the right track.

We had a balanced budget in 1969. This administration cut more than $7 billion out of spending plans in order to produce a surplus in 1970, and in spite of the fact that Congress reduced revenues by $3 billion, I shall recommend a balanced budget for 1971.

But I can assure you that not only to present, but to stay within, a balanced budget requires some very hard decisions. It means rejecting spending programs which would benefit some of the people when their net effect would result in price increases for all the people.

It is time to quit putting good money into bad programs. Otherwise, we will end up with bad money and bad programs.

I recognize the political popularity of spending programs, and particularly in an election year. But unless we stop the rise in prices, the cost of living for millions of American families will become unbearable and government's ability to plan programs for progress for the future will become impossible.

In referring to budget cuts, there is one area where I have ordered an increase rather than a cut—and that is the requests of those agencies with the responsibilities for law enforcement.

We have heard a great deal of overblown rhetoric during the sixties in which the word "war" has perhaps too often been used—the war on poverty, the war on misery, the war on disease, the war on hunger. But if there is one area where the word "war" is appropriate it is in the fight against crime. We must declare and win the war against the criminal elements which increasingly threaten our cities, our homes, and our lives.

We have a tragic example of this problem in the Nation's Capital, for whose safety the Congress and the Executive have the primary responsibility. I doubt if many Members of this Congress who live more than a few blocks from here would dare leave their cars in the Capitol garage and walk home alone tonight.

Last year this administration sent to the Congress 13 separate pieces of legislation dealing with organized crime, pornography, street crime, narcotics, crime in the District of Columbia.

None of these bills has reached my desk for signature.

I am confident that the Congress will act now to adopt the legislation I placed before you last year. We in the Executive have done everything we can under existing law, but new and stronger weapons are needed in that fight.

While it is true that State and local law enforcement agencies are the cutting edge in the effort to eliminate street crime, burglaries, murder, my proposals to you have embodied my belief that the Federal Government should play a greater role in working in partnership with these agencies.

That is why 1971 Federal spending for local law enforcement will double that budgeted for 1970.

The primary responsibility for crimes that affect individuals is with local and State rather than with Federal Government. But in the field of organized crime, narcotics, pornography, the Federal Government has a special responsibility it should fulfill. And we should make Washington, D.C., where we have the primary responsibility, an example to the Nation and the world of respect for law rather than lawlessness.

I now turn to a subject which, next to our desire for peace, may well become the major concern of the American people in the decade of the seventies.

In the next 10 years we shall increase our wealth by 50 percent. The profound question is: Does this mean we will be 50 percent richer in a real sense, 50 percent better off, 50 percent happier?

Or does it mean that in the year 1980 the President standing in this place will look back on a decade in which 70 percent of our people lived in metropolitan areas choked by traffic, suffocated by smog, poisoned by water, deafened by noise, and terrorized by crime?

These are not the great questions that concern world leaders at summit conferences. But people do not live at the summit. They live in the foothills of everyday experience, and it is time for all of us to concern ourselves with the way real people live in real life.

The great question of the seventies is, shall we surrender to our surroundings, or shall we make our peace with nature and begin to make reparations for the damage we have done to our air, to our land, and to our water?

Restoring nature to its natural state is a cause beyond party and beyond factions. It has become a common cause of all the people of this country. It is a cause of particular concern to young Americans, because they more than we will reap the grim consequences of our failure to act on programs which are needed now if we are to prevent disaster later.

Clean air, clean water, open spaces—these should once again be the birthright of every American. If we act now, they can be.

We still think of air as free. But clean air is not free, and neither is clean water. The price tag on pollution control is high. Through our years of past carelessness we incurred a debt to nature, and now that debt is being called.

The program I shall propose to Congress will be the most comprehensive and costly program in this field in America's history.

It is not a program for just one year. A year's plan in this field is no plan at all. This is a time to look ahead not a year, but 5 years or 10 years—whatever time is required to do the job.

I shall propose to this Congress a $10 billion nationwide clean waters program to put modern municipal waste treatment plants in every place in America where they are needed to make our waters clean again, and do it now. We have the industrial capacity, if we begin now, to build them all within 5 years. This program will get them built within 5 years.

As our cities and suburbs relentlessly expand, those priceless open spaces needed for recreation areas accessible to their people are swallowed up—often forever. Unless we preserve these spaces while they are still available, we will have none to preserve. Therefore, I shall propose new financing methods for purchasing open space and parklands now, before they are lost to us.

The automobile is our worst polluter of the air. Adequate control requires further advances in engine design and fuel composition. We shall intensify our research, set increasingly strict standards, and strengthen enforcement procedures—and we shall do it now.

We can no longer afford to consider air and water common property, free to be abused by anyone without regard to the consequences. Instead, we should begin now to treat them as scarce resources, which we are no more free to contaminate than we are free to throw garbage into our neighbor's yard.

This requires comprehensive new regulations. It also requires that, to the extent possible, the price of goods should be made to include the costs of producing and disposing of them without damage to the environment.

Now, I realize that the argument is often made that there is a fundamental contradiction between economic growth and the quality of life, so that to have one we must forsake the other.

The answer is not to abandon growth, but to redirect it. For example, we should turn toward ending congestion and eliminating smog the same reservoir of inventive genius that created them in the first place.

Continued vigorous economic growth provides us with the means to enrich life itself and to enhance our planet as a place hospitable to man.

Each individual must enlist in this fight if it is to be won.

It has been said that no matter how many national parks and historical monuments we buy and develop, the truly significant environment for each of us is that in which we spend 80 percent of our time—in our homes, in our places of work, the streets over which we travel.

Street litter, rundown parking strips and yards, dilapidated fences, broken windows, smoking automobiles, dingy working places, all should be the object of our fresh view.

We have been too tolerant of our surroundings and too willing to leave it to others to clean up our environment. It is time for those who make massive demands on society to make some minimal demands on themselves. Each of us must resolve that each day he will leave his home, his property, the public places of the city or town a little cleaner, a little better, a little more pleasant for himself and those around him.

With the help of people we can do anything, and without their help, we can do nothing. In this spirit, together, we can reclaim our land for ours and generations to come.

Between now and the year 5000, over 100 million children will be born in the United States. Where they grow up—and how will, more than any one thing, measure the quality of American life in these years ahead.

This should be a warning to us.

For the past 30 years our population has also been growing and shifting. The result is exemplified in the vast areas of rural America emptying out of people and of promise—a third of our counties lost population in the sixties.

The violent and decayed central cities of our great metropolitan complexes are the most conspicuous area of failure in American life today.

I propose that before these problems become insoluble, the Nation develop a national growth policy.

In the future, government decisions as to where to build highways, locate airports, acquire land, or sell land should be made with a clear objective of aiding a balanced growth for America.

In particular, the Federal Government must be in a position to assist in the building of new cities and the rebuilding of old ones.

At the same time, we will carry our concern with the quality of life in America to the farm as well as the suburb, to the village as well as to the city. What rural America needs most is a new kind of assistance. It needs to be dealt with, not as a separate nation, but as part of an overall growth policy for America. We must create a new rural environment which will not only stem the migration to urban centers, but reverse it. If we seize our growth as a challenge, we can make the 1970's an historic period when by conscious choice we transformed our land into what we want it to become.

America, which has pioneered in the new abundance, and in the new technology, is called upon today to pioneer in meeting the concerns which have followed in their wake—in turning the wonders of science to the service of man.

In the majesty of this great Chamber we hear the echoes of America's history, of debates that rocked the Union and those that repaired it, of the summons to war and the search for peace, of the uniting of the people, the building of a nation.

Those echoes of history remind us of our roots and our strengths.

They remind us also of that special genius of American democracy, which at one critical turning point after another has led us to spot the new road to the future and given us the wisdom and the courage to take it.

As I look down that new road which I have tried to map out today, I see a new America as we celebrate our 200th anniversary 6 years from now.

I see an America in which we have abolished hunger, provided the means for every family in the Nation to obtain a minimum income, made enormous progress in providing better housing, faster transportation, improved health, and superior education.

I see an America in which we have checked inflation, and waged a winning war against crime.

I see an America in which we have made great strides in stopping the pollution of our air, cleaning up our water, opening up our parks, continuing to explore in space.

Most important, I see an America at peace with all the nations of the world.

This is not an impossible dream. These goals are all within our reach.

In times past, our forefathers had the vision but not the means to achieve such goals.

Let it not be recorded that we were the first American generation that had the means but not the vision to make this dream come true.

But let us, above all, recognize a fundamental truth. We can be the best clothed, best fed, best housed people in the world, enjoying clean air, clean water, beautiful parks, but we could still be the unhappiest people in the world without an indefinable spirit—the lift of a driving dream which has made America, from its beginning, the hope of the world.

Two hundred years ago this was a new nation of 3 million people, weak militarily, poor economically. But America meant something to the world then which could not be measured in dollars, something far more important than military might.

Listen to President Thomas Jefferson in 1802: We act not "for ourselves alone, but for the whole human race."

We had a spiritual quality then which caught the imagination of millions of people in the world.

Today, when we are the richest and strongest nation in the world, let it not be recorded that we lack the moral and spiritual idealism which made us the hope of the world at the time of our birth.

The demands of us in 1976 are even greater than in 1776.

It is no longer enough to live and let live. Now we must live and help live.

We need a fresh climate in America, one in which a person can breathe freely and breathe in freedom.

Our recognition of the truth that wealth and happiness are not the same thing requires us to measure success or failure by new criteria.

Even more than the programs I have described today, what this Nation needs is an example from its elected leaders in providing the spiritual and moral leadership which no programs for material progress can satisfy.

Above all, let us inspire young Americans with a sense of excitement, a sense of destiny, a sense of involvement, in meeting the challenges we face in this great period of our history. Only then are they going to have any sense of satisfaction in their lives.

The greatest privilege an individual can have is to serve in a cause bigger than himself. We have such a cause.

How we seize the opportunities I have described today will determine not only our future, but the future of peace and freedom in this world in the last third of the century.

May God give us the wisdom, the strength and, above all, the idealism to be worthy of that challenge, so that America can fulfill its destiny of being the world's best hope for liberty, for opportunity, for progress and peace for all peoples.

Richard Nixon, 1969–1973

Address to Congress on the State of the Union

January 22, 1971

Richard Nixon chose to focus his second State of the Union message around six domestic issues; he stated that he would discuss foreign policy in a separate report.

The first issue was welfare reform. Nixon had urged an overhaul of the country's welfare system, a subject he also had discussed in the previous year's State of the Union message and elsewhere. He described the current system as "a monstrous, consuming outrage" that needed to be abolished. Among the new proposals he sought were work incentives and "an effective work requirement." This welfare overhaul did not end up passing.

Nixon's second goal was "full prosperity in peacetime"—something he said the country had not had since 1957. He pledged to reduce inflation, which had been increasing in recent years, and stated that his budget for the next year would help stimulate the economy and create new job opportunities.

His third topic was environmental protection. He had discussed this issue the previous year, too, and had called for a clean water program. This time he promised to propose new initiatives on clean water, clean air, and noise pollution, as well as expansion of the national park system. Concern for the environment was a growing cause; the U.S. Environmental Protection Agency had been created in 1970, and the first Earth Day celebration took place that year.

The fourth goal was health care; the president asked for an additional $100 million to fight cancer. He called for the same type of effort that had sent a man to the moon—which had occurred in 1969. Nixon signed the National Cancer Act in December 1971, which sought to increase support for cancer research.

Nixon's fifth topic was strengthening state and local governments. He also had referred to this subject in his previous State of the Union message, calling for a New Federalism that gave more power back to the people and the localities from the federal government. This time, he spoke in favor of a revenue-sharing plan that would provide money for such programs as urban development, rural development, and education—"more money and less interference" from the federal government, Nixon said.

His last goal was a reorganization of the federal government. Under this plan, he called for reducing the twelve cabinet departments to eight; his reduction plan did not end up taking place. Nixon termed his government-renewal plan a "new American revolution," linking it to the events of almost 200 years earlier.

Mr. Speaker, Mr. President, my colleagues in the Congress, our distinguished guests, my fellow Americans:

As this 92d Congress begins its session, America has lost a great Senator, and all of us who had the privilege to know him have lost a loyal friend. I had the privilege of visiting Senator [Richard] Russell in the hospital just a few days before he died. He never spoke about himself. He only spoke eloquently about the need for a strong national defense.

In tribute to one of the most magnificent Americans of all time, I respectfully ask that all those here will rise in silent prayer for Senator Russell.

Thank you.

Mr. Speaker, before I begin my formal address, I want to use this opportunity to congratulate all of those who were winners in the rather spirited contest for leadership positions in the House and the Senate and, also, to express my condolences to the losers. I know how both of you feel.

And I particularly want to join with all of the Members of the House and the Senate as well in congratulating the new Speaker of the United States Congress.

To those new Members of this House who may have some doubts about the possibilities for advancement in the years ahead, I would remind you that the Speaker and I met just 24 years ago in this Chamber as freshmen Members of the 80th Congress. As you see, we both have come up in the world a bit since then.

Mr. Speaker, this 92d Congress has a chance to be recorded as the greatest Congress in America's history.

In these troubled years just past, America has been going through a long nightmare of war and division, of crime and inflation. Even more deeply, we have gone through a long, dark night of the American spirit. But now that night is ending. Now we must let our spirits soar again. Now we are ready for the lift of a driving dream.

The people of this Nation are eager to get on with the quest for new greatness. They see challenges, and they are prepared to meet those challenges. It is for us here to open the doors that will set free again the real greatness of this Nation—the genius of the American people.

How shall we meet this challenge? How can we truly open the doors, and set free the full genius of our people?

The way in which the 92d Congress answers these questions will determine its place in history. More importantly, it can determine this Nation's place in history as we enter the third century of our independence.

Tonight I shall present to the Congress six great goals. I shall ask not simply for more new programs in the old framework. I shall ask to change the framework of government itself—to reform the entire structure of American government so we can make it again fully responsive to the needs and the wishes of the American people.

If we act boldly—if we seize this moment and achieve these goals—we can close the gap between promise and performance in American government. We can bring together the resources of this Nation and the spirit of the American people.

In discussing these great goals, I shall deal tonight only with matters on the domestic side of the Nation's agenda. I shall make a separate report to the Congress and the Nation next month on developments in foreign policy.

The first of these great goals is already before the Congress.

I urge that the unfinished business of the 91st Congress be made the first priority business of the 92d Congress.

Over the next 2 weeks, I will call upon Congress to take action on more than 35 pieces of proposed legislation on which action was not completed last year.

The most important is welfare reform.

The present welfare system has become a monstrous, consuming outrage—an outrage against the community, against the taxpayer, and particularly against the children it is supposed to help.

We may honestly disagree, as we do, on what to do about it. But we can all agree that we must meet the challenge, not by pouring more money into a bad program, but by abolishing the present welfare system and adopting a new one.

So let us place a floor under the income of every family with children in America—and without those demeaning, soul-stifling affronts to human dignity that so blight the lives of welfare children today. But let us also establish an effective work incentive and an effective work requirement.

Let us provide the means by which more can help themselves. This shall be our goal.

Let us generously help those who are not able to help themselves. But let us stop helping those who are able to help themselves but refuse to do so.

The second great goal is to achieve what Americans have not enjoyed since 1957—full prosperity in peacetime.

The tide of inflation has turned. The rise in the cost of living, which had been gathering dangerous momentum in the late sixties, was reduced last year. Inflation will be further reduced this year.

But as we have moved from runaway inflation toward reasonable price stability and at the same time as we have been moving from a wartime economy to a peacetime economy, we have paid a price in increased unemployment.

We should take no comfort from the fact that the level of unemployment in this transition from a wartime to a peacetime economy is lower than in any peacetime year of the sixties.

This is not good enough for the man who is unemployed in the seventies. We must do better for workers in peacetime and we will do better.

To achieve this, I will submit an expansionary budget this year—one that will help stimulate the economy and thereby open up new job opportunities for millions of Americans.

It will be a full employment budget, a budget designed to be in balance if the economy were operating at its peak potential. By spending as if we were at full employment, we will help to bring about full employment.

I ask the Congress to accept these expansionary policies—to accept the concept of a full employment budget. At the same time, I ask the Congress to cooperate in resisting expenditures that go beyond the limits of the full employment budget. For as we wage a campaign to bring about a widely shared prosperity, we must not reignite the fires of inflation and so undermine that prosperity.

With the stimulus and the discipline of a full employment budget, with the commitment of the independent Federal Reserve System to provide fully for the monetary needs of a growing economy, and with a much greater effort on the part of labor and management to make their wage and price decisions in the light of the national interest and their own self-interest—then for the worker, the farmer, the consumer, for Americans everywhere we shall gain the goal of a new prosperity: more jobs, more income, more profits, without inflation and without war.

This is a great goal, and one that we can achieve together.

The third great goal is to continue the effort so dramatically begun last year: to restore and enhance our natural environment.

Building on the foundation laid in the 37-point program that I submitted to Congress last year, I will propose a strong new set of initiatives to clean up our air and water, to combat noise, and to preserve and restore our surroundings.

I will propose programs to make better use of our land, to encourage a balanced national growth—growth that will revitalize our rural heartland and enhance the quality of life in America.

And not only to meet today's needs but to anticipate those of tomorrow, I will put forward the most extensive program ever proposed by a President of the United States to expand the Nation's parks, recreation areas, open spaces, in a way that truly brings parks to the people where the people are. For only if we leave a legacy of parks will the next generation have parks to enjoy.

As a fourth great goal, I will offer a far-reaching set of proposals for improving America's health care and making it available more fairly to more people.

I will propose:

- A program to insure that no American family will be prevented from obtaining basic medical care by inability to pay.

- I will propose a major increase in and redirection of aid to medical schools, to greatly increase the number of doctors and other health personnel.

- Incentives to improve the delivery of health services, to get more medical care resources into those areas that have not been adequately served, to make greater use of medical assistants, and to slow the alarming rise in the costs of medical care.

- New programs to encourage better preventive medicine, by attacking the causes of disease and injury, and by providing incentives to doctors to keep people well rather than just to treat them when they are sick.

I will also ask for an appropriation of an extra $100 million to launch an intensive campaign to find a cure for cancer, and I will ask later for whatever additional funds can effectively be used. The time has come in America when the same kind of concentrated effort that split the atom and took man to the moon should be turned toward conquering this dread disease. Let us make a total national commitment to achieve this goal.

America has long been the wealthiest nation in the world. Now it is time we became the healthiest nation in the world.

The fifth great goal is to strengthen and to renew our State and local governments.

As we approach our 200th anniversary in 1976, we remember that this Nation launched itself as a loose confederation of separate States, without a workable central government. At that time, the mark of its leaders' vision was that they quickly saw the need to balance the separate powers of the States with a government of central powers.

And so they gave us a constitution of balanced powers, of unity with diversity—and so clear was their vision that it survives today as the oldest written constitution still in force in the world.

For almost two centuries since—and dramatically in the 1930's—at those great turning points when the question has been between the States and the Federal Government, that question has been resolved in favor of a stronger central Federal Government.

During this time the Nation grew and the Nation prospered. But one thing history tells us is that no great movement goes in the same direction forever. Nations change, they adapt, or they slowly die.

The time has now come in America to reverse the flow of power and resources from the States and communities to Washington, and start power and resources flowing back from Washington to the States and communities and, more important, to the people all across America.

The time has come for a new partnership between the Federal Government and the States and localities—a partnership in which we entrust the States and localities with a larger share of the Nation's responsibilities, and in which we share our Federal revenues with them so that they can meet those responsibilities.

To achieve this goal, I propose to the Congress tonight that we enact a plan of revenue sharing historic in scope and bold in concept.

All across America today, States and cities are confronted with a financial crisis. Some have already been cutting back on essential services—for example, just recently San Diego and Cleveland cut back on trash collections. Most are caught between the prospects of bankruptcy on the one hand and adding to an already crushing tax burden on the other.

As one indication of the rising costs of local government, I discovered the other day that my home town of Whittier, California—which has a population of 67,000—has a larger budget for 1971 than the entire Federal budget was in 1791.

Now the time has come to take a new direction, and once again to introduce a new and more creative balance to our approach to government.

So let us put the money where the needs are. And let us put the power to spend it where the people are.

I propose that the Congress make a $16 billion investment in renewing State and local government. Five billion dollars of this will be in new and unrestricted funds to be used as the States and localities see fit. The other $11 billion will be provided by allocating $1 billion of new funds and converting one-third of the money going to the present narrow-purpose aid programs into Federal revenue sharing funds for six broad purposes for urban development, rural development, education, transportation, job training, and law enforcement but with the States and localities making their own decisions on how it should be spent within each category.

For the next fiscal year, this would increase total Federal aid to the States and localities more than 25 percent over the present level.

The revenue sharing proposals I send to the Congress will include the safeguards against discrimination that accompany all other Federal funds allocated to the States. Neither the President nor the Congress nor the conscience of this Nation can permit money which comes from all the people to be used in a way which discriminates against some of the people.

The Federal Government will still have a large and vital role to play in achieving our national progress. Established functions that are clearly and essentially Federal in nature will still be performed by the Federal Government. New functions that need to be sponsored or performed by the Federal Government—such as those I have urged tonight in welfare and health—will be added to the Federal agenda. Whenever it makes the best sense for us to act as a whole nation, the Federal Government should and will lead the way. But where States or local governments can better do what needs to be done, let us see that they have the resources to do it there.

Under this plan, the Federal Government will provide the States and localities with more money and less interference—and by cutting down the interference the same amount of money will go a lot further.

Let us share our resources.

Let us share them to rescue the States and localities from the brink of financial crisis.

Let us share them to give homeowners and wage earners a chance to escape from ever-higher property taxes and sales taxes.

Let us share our resources for two other reasons as well.

The first of these reasons has to do with government itself, and the second has to do it, h each of us, with the individual.

Let's face it. Most Americans today are simply fed up with government at all levels. They will not—and they should not—continue to tolerate the gap between promise and performance in government.

The fact is that we have made the Federal Government so strong it grows muscle-bound and the States and localities so weak they approach impotence.

If we put more power in more places, we can make government more creative in more places. That way we multiply the number of people with the ability to make things happen—and we can open the way to a new burst of creative energy throughout America.

The final reason I urge this historic shift is much more personal, for each and for every one of us.

As everything seems to have grown bigger and more complex in America, as the forces that shape our lives seem to have grown more distant and more impersonal, a great feeling of frustration has crept across this land.

Whether it is the workingman who feels neglected, the black man who feels oppressed, or the mother concerned about her children, there has been a growing feeling that "Things are in the saddle, and ride mankind."

Millions of frustrated young Americans today are crying out—asking not what will government do for me, but what can I do, how can I contribute, how can I matter?

And so let us answer them. Let us say to them and let us say to all Americans, "We hear you. We will give you a chance. We are going to give you a new chance to have more to say about the decisions that affect your future—a chance to participate in government—because we are going to provide more centers of power where what you do can make a difference that you can see and feel in your own life and the life of your whole community."

The further away government is from people, the stronger government becomes and the weaker people become. And a nation with a strong government and a weak people is an empty shell.

I reject the patronizing idea that government in Washington, D.C., is inevitably more wise, more honest, and more efficient than government at the local or State level. The honesty and efficiency of government depends on people. Government at all levels has good people and bad people. And the way to get more good people into government is to give them more opportunity to do good things.

The idea that a bureaucratic elite in Washington knows best what is best for people everywhere and that you cannot trust local governments is really a contention that you cannot trust people to govern themselves. This notion is completely foreign to the American experience. Local government is the government closest to the people, it is most responsive to the individual person. It is people's government in a far more intimate way than the Government in Washington can ever be.

People came to America because they wanted to determine their own future rather than to live in a country where others determined their future for them.

What this change means is that once again in America we are placing our trust in people.

I have faith in people. I trust the judgment of people. Let us give the people of America a chance, a bigger voice in deciding for themselves those questions that so greatly affect their lives.

The sixth great goal is a complete reform of the Federal Government itself.

Based on a long and intensive study with the aid of the best advice obtainable, I have concluded that a sweeping reorganization of the executive branch is needed if the Government is to keep up with the times and with the needs of the people.

I propose, therefore, that we reduce the present 12 Cabinet Departments to eight.

I propose that the Departments of State, Treasury, Defense, and Justice remain, but that all the other departments be consolidated into four: Human Resources, Community Development, Natural Resources, and Economic Development.

Let us look at what these would be:

- First, a department dealing with the concerns of people—as individuals, as members of a family—a department focused on human needs.

- Second, a department concerned with the community—rural communities and urban communities—and with all that it takes to make a community function as a community.

- Third, a department concerned with our physical environment, with the preservation and balanced use of those great natural resources on which our Nation depends.

- And fourth, a department concerned with our prosperity—with our jobs, our businesses, and those many activities that keep our economy running smoothly and well.

Under this plan, rather than dividing up our departments by narrow subjects, we would organize them around the great purposes of government. Rather than scattering responsibility by adding new levels of bureaucracy, we would focus and concentrate the responsibility for getting problems solved.

With these four departments, when we have a problem we will know where to go—and the department will have the authority and the resources to do something about it.

Over the years we have added departments and created agencies at the Federal level, each to serve a new constituency, to handle a particular task—and these have grown and multiplied in what has become a hopeless confusion of form and function.

The time has come to match our structure to our purposes—to look with a fresh eye, to organize the Government by conscious, comprehensive design to meet the new needs of a new era.

One hundred years ago, Abraham Lincoln stood on a battlefield and spoke of a "government of the people, by the people, for the people." Too often since then, we have become a nation of the Government, by the Government, for the Government.

By enacting these reforms, we can renew that principle that Lincoln stated so simply and so well.

By giving everyone's voice a chance to be heard, we will have government that truly is of the people.

By creating more centers of meaningful power, more places where decisions that really count can be made, by giving more people a chance to do something, we can have government that truly is by the people.

And by setting up a completely modern, functional system of government at the national level, we in Washington will at last be able to provide government that is truly for the people.

I realize that what I am asking is that not only the executive branch in Washington but that even this Congress will have to change by giving up some of its power.

Change is hard. But without change there can be no progress. And for each of us the question then becomes, not "Will change cause me inconvenience?" but "Will change bring progress for America?"

Giving up power is hard. But I would urge all of you, as leaders of this country, to remember that the truly revered leaders in world history are those who gave power to people, and not those who took it away.

As we consider these reforms we will be acting, not for the next 2 years or for the next 10 years, but for the next 100 years.

So let us approach these six great goals with a sense not only of this moment in history but also of history itself.

Let us act with the willingness to work together and the vision and the boldness and the courage of those great Americans who met in Philadelphia almost 190 years ago to write a constitution.

Let us leave a heritage as they did—not just for our children but for millions yet unborn—of a nation where every American will have a chance not only to live in peace and to enjoy prosperity and opportunity but to participate in a system of government where he knows not only his votes but his ideas count—a system of government which will provide the means for America to reach heights of achievement undreamed of before.

Those men who met at Philadelphia left a great heritage because they had a vision—not only of what the Nation was but of what it could become.

As I think of that vision, I recall that America was founded as the land of the open door—as a haven for the oppressed, a land of opportunity, a place of refuge, of hope.

When the first settlers opened the door of America three and a half centuries ago, they came to escape persecution and to find opportunity—and they left wide the door of welcome for others to follow.

When the Thirteen Colonies declared their independence almost two centuries ago, they opened the door to a new vision of liberty and of human fulfillment—not just for an elite but for all.

To the generations that followed, America's was the open door that beckoned millions from the old world to the new in search of a better life, a freer life, a fuller life, and in which, by their own decisions, they could shape their own destinies.

For the black American, the Indian, the Mexican-American, and for those others in our land who have not had an equal chance, the Nation at last has begun to confront the need to press open the door of full and equal opportunity, and of human dignity.

For all Americans, with these changes I have proposed tonight we can open the door to a new era of opportunity. We can open the door to full and effective participation in the decisions that affect their lives. We can open the door to a new partnership among governments at all levels, between those governments and the people themselves. And by so doing, we can open wide the doors of human fulfillment for millions of people here in America now and in the years to come.

In the next few weeks I will spell out in greater detail the way I propose that we achieve these six great goals. I ask this Congress to be responsive. If it is, then the 92d Congress, your Congress, our Congress, at the end of its term, will be able to look back on a record more splendid than any in our history.

This can be the Congress that helped us end the longest war in the Nation's history, and end it in a way that will give us at last a genuine chance to enjoy what we have not had in this century: a full generation of peace.

This can be the Congress that helped achieve an expanding economy, with full employment and without inflation—and without the deadly stimulus of war.

This can be the Congress that reformed a welfare system that has robbed recipients of their dignity and robbed States and cities of their resources.

This can be the Congress that pressed forward the rescue of our environment, and established for the next generation an enduring legacy of parks for the people.

This can be the Congress that launched a new era in American medicine, in which the quality of medical care was enhanced while the costs were made less burdensome.

But above all, what this Congress can be remembered for is opening the way to a new American revolution—a peaceful revolution in which power was turned back to the people—in which government at all levels was refreshed and renewed and made truly responsive. This can be a revolution as profound, as far-reaching, as exciting as that first revolution almost 200 years ago—and it can mean that just 5 years from now America will enter its third century as a young nation new in spirit, with all the vigor and the freshness with which it began its first century.

My colleagues in the Congress, these are great goals. They can make the sessions of this Congress a great moment for America. So let us pledge together to go forward together—by achieving these goals to give America the foundation today for a new greatness tomorrow and in all the years to come, and in so doing to make this the greatest Congress in the history of this great and good country.

Address to Congress on the State of the Union

January 20, 1972

Richard Nixon's 1972 State of the Union address was delivered before Congress at the start of a presidential election year. Nixon would seek, and win, reelection that November, only to find his presidency brought down during his second term by the Watergate scandal. He would resign from office in August 1974.

Early in his State of the Union address, the president noted that there were many presidential candidates present in the House chamber—possibly more than ever before. He urged lawmakers on both sides of the aisle to join together and "transcend partisanship" when it came to the country's problems. Congress was controlled by Democrats while Nixon was a Republican.

Nixon focused primarily on domestic issues in his message. He also sent a longer, 15,000-word version of the speech to Congress in writing. On the international front, he mentioned briefly that the country's involvement in Vietnam was coming to an end. The United States would pull its troops out of that controversial conflict in early 1973, a year after Nixon's speech; South Vietnam would fall to the communists in 1975. The president also mentioned his upcoming trips to China—a landmark visit that marked a shift in U.S. relations with the communist power—and to the Soviet Union; Nixon was the first incumbent president to go to Moscow, where he would sign a major nuclear arms treaty with the Soviet Union.

In his previous State of the Union message, delivered in January 1971, Nixon had spoken of six goals: welfare reform, economic prosperity, environmental protection, expanded health care, revenue sharing, and government reorganization. He again urged Congress to take action in these areas. In addition, he called for changes in the system under which property taxes served as a key source for school funding; he stated that high property taxes were hurting the elderly and retired in particular. And he sought a new program to increase technological research and development.

While Republicans praised Nixon's speech, Democrats voiced criticism, saying it was not substantive enough.

Nixon's 1972 opponent was Senator George McGovern of South Dakota, who beat out a large field of Democrats to win the party's nomination. McGovern, known for his stance against the Vietnam War, won only Massachusetts and the District of Columbia, as Nixon scored a landslide victory. The president won 520 electoral votes to McGovern's 17; he took 60.7 percent of the popular vote.

Mr. Speaker, Mr. President, my colleagues in the Congress, our distinguished guests, my fellow Americans:

Twenty-five years ago I sat here as a freshman Congressman—along with Speaker Albert—and listened for the first time to the President address the State of the Union.

I shall never forget that moment. The Senate, the diplomatic corps, the Supreme Court, the Cabinet entered the Chamber, and then the President of the United States. As all of you are aware, I had some differences with President Truman. He had some with me. But I remember that on that day—the day he addressed that joint session of the newly elected Republican 80th Congress, he spoke not as a partisan, but as President of all the people—calling upon the Congress to put aside partisan considerations in the national interest.

The Greek-Turkish aid program, the Marshall Plan, the great foreign policy initiatives which have been responsible for avoiding a world war for over 25 years were approved by the Both Congress, by a bipartisan majority of which I was proud to be a part.

Nineteen hundred seventy-two is now before us. It holds precious time in which to accomplish good for the Nation. We must not waste it. I know the political pressures in this session of the Congress will be great. There are more candidates for the Presidency in this Chamber today than there probably have been at any one time in the whole history of the Republic. And there is an honest difference of opinion, not only between the parties, but within each party, on some foreign policy issues and on some domestic policy issues.

However, there are great national problems that are so vital that they transcend partisanship. So let us have our debates. Let us have our honest differences. But let us join in keeping the national interest first. Let us join in making sure that legislation the Nation needs does not become hostage to the political interests of any party or any person.

There is ample precedent, in this election year, for me to present you with a huge list of new proposals, knowing full well that there would not be any possibility of your passing them if you worked night and day.

I shall not do that.

I have presented to the leaders of the Congress today a message of 15,000 words discussing in some detail where the Nation stands and setting forth specific legislative items on which I have asked the Congress to act. Much of this is legislation which I proposed in 1969, in 1970, and also in the first session of this 92d Congress and on which I feel it is essential that action be completed this year.

I am not presenting proposals which have attractive labels but no hope of passage. I am presenting only vital programs which are within the capacity of this Congress to enact, within the capacity of the budget to finance, and which I believe should be above partisanship—programs which deal with urgent priorities for the Nation, which should and must be the subject of bipartisan action by this Congress in the interests of the country in 1972.

When I took the oath of office on the steps of this building just 3 years ago today, the Nation was ending one of the most tortured decades in its history.

The 1960's were a time of great progress in many areas. But as we all know, they were also times of great agony—the agonies of war, of inflation, of rapidly rising crime, of deteriorating titles, of hopes raised and disappointed, and of anger and frustration that led finally to violence and to the worst civil disorder in a century.

I recall these troubles not to point any fingers of blame. The Nation was so torn in those final years of the sixties that many in both parties questioned whether America could be governed at all.

The Nation has made significant progress in these first years of the seventies:

Our cities are no longer engulfed by civil disorders.

Our colleges and universities have again become places of learning instead of battlegrounds.

A beginning has been made in preserving and protecting our environment.

The rate of increase in crime has been slowed—and here in the District of Columbia, the one city where the Federal Government has direct jurisdiction, serious crime in 1971 was actually reduced by 13 percent from the year before.

Most important, because of the beginnings that have been made, we can say today that this year 1972 can be the year in which America may make the greatest progress in 25 years toward achieving our goal of being at peace with all the nations of the world.

As our involvement in the war in Vietnam comes to an end, we must now go on to build a generation of peace.

To achieve that goal, we must first face realistically the need to maintain our defense.

In the past 3 years, we have reduced the burden of arms. For the first time in 20 years, spending on defense has been brought below spending on human resources.

As we look to the future, we find encouraging progress in our negotiations with the Soviet Union on limitation of strategic arms. And looking further into the future, we hope there can eventually be agreement on the mutual reduction of arms. But until there is such a mutual agreement, we must maintain the strength necessary to deter war.

And that is why, because of rising research and development costs, because of increases in military and civilian pay, because of the need to proceed with new weapons systems, my budget for the coming fiscal year will provide for an increase in defense spending.

Strong military defenses are not the enemy of peace; they are the guardians of peace.

There could be no more misguided set of priorities than one which would tempt others by weakening America, and thereby endanger the peace of the world.

In our foreign policy, we have entered a new era. The world has changed greatly in the 11 years since President John Kennedy said in his Inaugural Address, ". . . we shall pay any price, bear any burden, meet any hardship, support any friend, oppose any foe to assure the survival and the success of liberty."

Our policy has been carefully and deliberately adjusted to meet the new realities of the new world we live in. We make today only those commitments we are able and prepared to meet.

Our commitment to freedom remains strong and unshakable. But others must bear their share of the burden of defending freedom around the world.

And so this, then, is our policy:

- We will maintain a nuclear deterrent adequate to meet any threat to the security of the United States or of our allies.
- We will help other nations develop the capability of defending themselves.
- We will faithfully honor all of our treaty commitments.
- We will act to defend our interests, whenever and wherever they are threatened anyplace in the world.
- But where our interests or our treaty commitments are not involved, our role will be limited.
- We will not intervene militarily.
- But we will use our influence to prevent war.
- If war comes, we will use our influence to stop it.
- Once it is over, we will do our share in helping to bind up the wounds of those who have participated in it.

As you know, I will soon be visiting the People's Republic of China and the Soviet Union. I go there with no illusions. We have great differences with both powers. We shall continue to have great differences. But peace depends on the ability of great powers to live together on the same planet despite their differences.

We would not be true to our obligation to generations yet unborn if we failed to seize this moment to do everything in our power to insure that we will be able to talk about those differences, rather than to fight about them, in the future.

As we look back over this century, let us, in the highest spirit of bipartisanship, recognize that we can be proud of our Nation's record in foreign affairs.

America has given more generously of itself toward maintaining freedom, preserving peace, alleviating human suffering around the globe, than any nation has ever done in the history of man.

We have fought four wars in this century, but our power has never been used to break the peace, only to keep it; never been used to destroy freedom, only to defend it. We now have within our reach the goal of insuring that the next generation can be the first generation in this century to be spared the scourges of war.

Turning to our problems at home, we are making progress toward our goal of a new prosperity without war.

Industrial production, consumer spending, retail sales, personal income all have been rising. Total employment, real income are the highest in history. New home building starts this past year reached the highest level ever. Business and consumer confidence have both been rising. Interest rates are down. The rate of inflation is down. We can look with confidence to 1972 as the year when the back of inflation will be broken.

Now, this a good record, but it is not good enough—not when we still have an unemployment rate of 6 percent.

It is not enough to point out that this was the rate of the early peacetime years of the sixties, or that if the more than 2 million men released from the Armed Forces and defense-related industries were still in their wartime jobs, unemployment would be far lower.

Our goal in this country is full employment in peacetime. We intend to meet that goal, and we can.

The Congress has helped to meet that goal by passing our job-creating tax program last month.

The historic monetary agreements, agreements that we have reached with the major European nations, Canada, and Japan, will help meet it by providing new markets for American products, new jobs for American workers.

Our budget will help meet it by being expansionary without being inflationary—a job-producing budget that will help take up the gap as the economy expands to full employment.

Our program to raise farm income will help meet it by helping to revitalize rural America, by giving to America's farmers their fair share of America's increasing productivity.

We also will help meet our goal of full employment in peacetime with a set of major initiatives to stimulate more imaginative use of America's great capacity for technological advance, and to direct it toward improving the quality of life for every American.

In reaching the moon, we demonstrated what miracles American technology is capable of achieving. Now the time has come to move more deliberately toward making full use of that technology here on earth, of harnessing the wonders of science to the service of man.

I shall soon send to the Congress a special message proposing a new program of Federal partnership in technological research and development—with Federal incentives to increase private research, federally supported research on projects designed to improve our everyday lives in ways that will range from improving mass transit to developing new systems of emergency health care that could save thousands of lives annually.

Historically, our superior technology, and high productivity have made it possible for American workers to be the highest paid in the world by far, and yet for our goods still to compete in world markets.

Now we face a new situation. As other nations move rapidly forward in technology, the answer to the new competition is not to build a wall around America, but rather to remain competitive by improving our own technology still further and by increasing productivity in American industry.

Our new monetary and trade agreements will make it possible for American goods to compete fairly in the world's markets—but they still must compete. The new technology program will put to use the skills of many highly trained Americans, skills that might otherwise be wasted. It will also meet the growing technological challenge from abroad, and it will thus help to create new industries, as well as creating more jobs for America's workers in producing for the world's markets.

This second session of the 92d Congress already has before it more than 90 major Administration proposals which still await action.

I have discussed these in the extensive written message that I have presented to the Congress today.

They include, among others, our programs to improve life for the aging; to combat crime and drug abuse; to improve health services and to ensure that no one will be denied needed health care because of inability to pay; to protect workers' pension rights; to promote equal opportunity for members of minorities, and others who have been left behind; to expand consumer protection; to improve the environment; to revitalize rural America; to help the cities; to launch new initiatives in education; to improve transportation, and to put an end to costly labor tie-ups in transportation.

The west coast dock strike is a case in point. This Nation cannot and will not tolerate that kind of irresponsible labor tie-up in the future.

The messages also include basic reforms which are essential if our structure of government is to be adequate in the decades ahead.

They include reform of our wasteful and outmoded welfare system—substitution of a new system that provides work requirements and work incentives for those who can help themselves, income support for those who cannot help themselves, and fairness to the working poor.

They include a $17 billion program of Federal revenue sharing with the States and localities as an investment in their renewal, an investment also of faith in the American people.

They also include a sweeping reorganization of the executive branch of the Federal Government so that it will be more efficient, more responsive, and able to meet the challenges of the decades ahead.

One year ago, standing in this place, I laid before the opening session of this Congress six great goals. One of these was welfare reform. That proposal has been before the Congress now for nearly 2½ years.

My proposals on revenue sharing, government reorganization, health care, and the environment have now been before the Congress for nearly a year. Many of the other major proposals that I have referred to have been here that long or longer.

Now, 1971, we can say, was a year of consideration of these measures. Now let us join in making 1972 a year of action on them, action by the Congress, for the Nation and for the people of America.

Now, in addition, there is one pressing need which I have not previously covered, but which must be placed on the national agenda.

We long have looked in this Nation to the local property tax as the main source of financing for public primary and secondary education.

As a result, soaring school costs, soaring property tax rates now threaten both our communities and our schools. They threaten communities because property taxes, which more than doubled in the 10 years from 1960 to '70, have become one of the most oppressive and discriminatory of all taxes, hitting most cruelly at the elderly and the retired; and they threaten schools, as hard-pressed voters understandably reject new bond issues at the polls.

The problem has been given even greater urgency by four recent court decisions, which have held that the conventional method of financing schools through local property taxes is discriminatory and unconstitutional.

Nearly 2 years ago, I named a special Presidential commission to study the problems of school finance, and I also directed the Federal departments to look into the same problems. We are developing comprehensive proposals to meet these problems.

This issue involves two complex and interrelated sets of problems: support of the schools and the basic relationships of Federal, State, and local governments in any tax reforms.

Under the leadership of the Secretary of the Treasury, we are carefully reviewing all of the tax aspects, and I have this week enlisted the Advisory Commission on Intergovernmental Relations in addressing the intergovernmental relations aspects.

I have asked this bipartisan Commission to review our proposals for Federal action to cope with the gathering crisis of school finance and property taxes. Later in the year, when both Commissions have completed their studies, I shall make my final recommendations for relieving the burden of property taxes and providing both fair and adequate financing for our children's education.

These recommendations will be revolutionary. But all these recommendations, however, will be rooted in one fundamental principle with which there can be no compromise: Local school boards must have control over local schools.

As we look ahead over the coming decades, vast new growth and change are not only certainties, they will be the dominant reality of this world, and particularly of our life in America.

Surveying the certainty of rapid change, we can be like a fallen rider caught in the stirrups—or we can sit high in the saddle, the masters of change, directing it on a course we choose.

The secret of mastering change in today's world is to reach back to old and proven principles, and to adapt them with imagination and intelligence to the new realities of a new age.

That is what we have done in the proposals that I have laid before the Congress. They are rooted in basic principles that are as enduring as human nature, as robust as the American experience; and they are responsive to new conditions. Thus they represent a spirit of change that is truly renewal.

As we look back at those old principles, we find them as timely as they are timeless. We believe in independence, and self-reliance, and the creative value of the competitive spirit.

We believe in full and equal opportunity for all Americans and in the protection of individual rights and liberties.

We believe in the family as the keystone of the community, and in the community as the keystone of the Nation.

We believe in compassion toward those in need.

We believe in a system of law, justice, and order as the basis of a genuinely free society.

We believe that a person should get what he works for—and that those who can, should work for what they get.

We believe in the capacity of people to make their own decisions in their own lives, in their own communities—and we believe in their right to make those decisions.

In applying these principles, we have done so with the full understanding that what we seek in the seventies, what our quest is, is not merely for more, but for better for a better quality of life for all Americans.

Thus, for example, we are giving a new measure of attention to cleaning up our air and water, making our surroundings more attractive. We are providing broader support for the arts, helping stimulate a deeper appreciation of what they can contribute to the Nation's activities and to our individual lives.

But nothing really matters more to the quality of our lives than the way we treat one another, than our capacity to live respectfully together as a unified society, with a full, generous regard for the rights of others and also for the feelings of others.

As we recover from the turmoil and violence of recent years, as we learn once again to speak with one another instead of shouting at one another, we are regaining that capacity.

As is customary here, on this occasion, I have been talking about programs. Programs are important. But even more important than programs is what we are as a Nation—what we mean as a Nation, to ourselves and to the world.

In New York Harbor stands one of the most famous statues in the world—the Statue of Liberty, the gift in 1886 of the people of France to the people of the United States. This statue is more than a landmark; it is a symbol—a symbol of what America has meant to the world.

It reminds us that what America has meant is not its wealth, and not its power, but its spirit and purpose—a land that enshrines liberty and opportunity, and that has held out a hand of welcome to millions in search of a better and a fuller and, above all, a freer life.

The world's hopes poured into America, along with its people. And those hopes, those dreams, that have been brought here from every corner of the world, have become a part of the hope that we now hold out to the world.

Four years from now, America will celebrate the 200th anniversary of its founding as a Nation. There are those who say that the old Spirit of '76 is dead—that we no longer have the strength of character, the idealism, the faith in our founding purposes that that spirit represents.

Those who say this do not know America.

We have been undergoing self-doubts and self-criticism. But these are only the other side of our growing sensitivity to the persistence of want in the midst of plenty, of our impatience with the slowness with which age-old ills are being overcome.

If we were indifferent to the shortcomings of our society, or complacent about our institutions, or blind to the lingering inequities—then we would have lost our way.

But the fact that we have those concerns is evidence that our ideals, deep down, are still strong. Indeed, they remind us that what is really best about America is its compassion. They remind us that in the final analysis, America is great not because it is strong, not because it is rich, but because this is a good country.

Let us reject the narrow visions of those who would tell us that we are evil because we are not yet perfect, that we are corrupt because we are not yet pure, that all the sweat and toil and sacrifice that have gone into the building of America were for naught because the building is not yet done.

Let us see that the path we are traveling is wide, with room in it for all of us, and that its direction is toward a better Nation and a more peaceful world.

Never has it mattered more that we go forward together.

Look at this Chamber. The leadership of America is here today—the Supreme Court, the Cabinet, the Senate, the House of Representatives.

Together, we hold the future of the Nation, and the conscience of the Nation in our hands.

Because this year is an election year, it will be a time of great pressure.

If we yield to that pressure and fail to deal seriously with the historic challenges that we face, we will have failed the trust of millions of Americans and shaken the confidence they have a right to place in us, in their Government.

Never has a Congress had a greater opportunity to leave a legacy of a profound and constructive reform for the Nation than this Congress.

If we succeed in these tasks, there will be credit enough for all—not only for doing what is right, but doing it in the right way, by rising above partisan interest to serve the national interest.

And if we fail, more than any one of us, America will be the loser.

That is why my call upon the Congress today is for a high statesmanship, so that in the years to come Americans will look back and say because it withstood the intense pressures of a political year, and achieved such great good for the American people and for the future of this Nation, this was truly a great Congress.

State of the Union Message to Congress: Overview and Goals
February 2, 1973

Richard Nixon's 1973 State of the Union message was historically unique. Generally, presidents throughout most of the twentieth century had either delivered one speech to Congress, or submitted a written message. The previous year, Nixon had done both, but in 1973, believing his recent second Inaugural Address would suffice as a general address to the nation, he sent six messages to Congress over the course of February and March of 1973. He also delivered five radio addresses over that same period, dealing with the same subjects.

The first message served as an overview for what the president hoped to discuss. He stated that a single message "would not appear to be adequate," given the changes he contemplated.

He planned a series of messages representing what he called "a fresh approach to government." The subjects would be economic affairs, natural resources, human resources, community development and foreign and defense policy. He ended up substituting a message on law enforcement for the one on foreign policy.

Nixon commented that the country was at peace. On January 27, the United States had signed a treaty with North Vietnam ending direct U.S. participation in the Vietnam War, which had cost more than 50,000 American lives. He declared that the United States had achieved "peace with honor" in Vietnam and that American credibility had been strengthened—a statement that not all Americans, in a country polarized by the war, did not necessarily agree with.

On the domestic side, Nixon stated that the nation should reject the concept that "ever bigger government is the answer to every problem." He said that heavy taxation and high government spending were not a "cure-all," and that the country needed to "draw the line."

The previous November, Nixon, a Republican, had won a landslide victory over Democratic Senator George McGovern to claim a second term in the White House; both houses of Congress would remain Democratic, however. But Nixon's second term would be cut short by the Watergate scandal, and he would resign as president in August 1974.

To the Congress of the United States:

The traditional form of the President's annual report giving "to the Congress Information of the State of the Union" is a single message or address. As the affairs and concerns of our Union have multiplied over the years, however, so too have the subjects that require discussion in State of the Union Messages.

This year in particular, with so many changes in Government programs under consideration—and with our very philosophy about the relationship between the individual and the State at an historic crossroads—a single, all-embracing State of the Union Message would not appear to be adequate.

I have therefore decided to present my 1973 State of the Union report in the form of a series of messages during these early weeks of the 93rd Congress. The purpose of this first message in the series is to give a concise overview of where we stand as a people today, and to outline some of the general goals that I believe we should pursue over the next year and beyond. In coming weeks, I will send to the Congress further State of the Union reports on specific areas of policy including economic affairs, natural resources, human resources, community development and foreign and defense policy.

The new course these messages will outline represents a fresh approach to Government: an approach that addresses the realities of the 1970s, not those of the 1930s or of the 1960s. The role of the Federal Government as we approach our third century of independence should not be to dominate any facet of American life, but rather to aid and encourage people, communities and institutions to deal with as many of the difficulties and challenges facing them as possible, and to help see to it that every American has a full and equal opportunity to realize his or her potential.

If we were to continue to expand the Federal Government at the rate of the past several decades, it soon would consume us entirely. The time has come when we must make clear choices—choices between old programs that set worthy goals but failed to reach them and new programs that provide a better way to realize those goals; and choices, too, between competing programs—all of which may be desirable in themselves but only some of which we can afford with the finite resources at our command.

Because our resources are not infinite, we also face a critical choice in 1973 between holding the line in Government spending and adopting expensive programs which will surely force up taxes and refuel inflation.

Finally, it is vital at this time that we restore a greater sense of responsibility at the State and local level, and among individual Americans.

Where We Stand

The basic state of our Union today is sound, and full of promise.

We enter 1973 economically strong, militarily secure and, most important of all, at peace after a long and trying war.

America continues to provide a better and more abundant life for more of its people than any other nation in the world. We have passed through one of the most difficult periods in our history without surrendering to despair and without dishonoring our ideals as a people.

Looking back, there is a lesson in all this for all of us. The lesson is one that we sometimes had to learn the hard way over the past few years. But we did learn it. That lesson is that even potentially destructive forces can be converted into positive forces when we know how to channel them, and when we use common sense and common decency to create a climate of mutual respect and goodwill.

By working together and harnessing the forces of nature, Americans have unlocked some of the great mysteries of the universe.

Men have walked the surface of the moon and soared to new heights of discovery.

This same spirit of discovery is helping us to conquer disease and suffering that have plagued our own planet since the dawn of time.

By working together with the leaders of other nations, we have been able to build a new hope for lasting peace—for a structure of world order in which common interest outweighs old animosities, and in which a new generation of the human family can grow up at peace in a changing world.

At home, we have learned that by working together we can create prosperity without fanning inflation; we can restore order without weakening freedom.

The Challenges We Face

These first years of the 1970s have been good years for America.

Our job—all of us together—is to make 1973 and the years to come even better ones. I believe that we can. I believe that we can make the years leading to our Bicentennial the best four years in American history.

But we must never forget that nothing worthwhile can be achieved without the will to succeed and the strength to sacrifice.

Hard decisions must be made, and we must stick by them.

In the field of foreign policy, we must remember that a strong America—an America whose word is believed and whose strength is respected—is essential to continued peace and understanding in the world. The peace with honor we have achieved in Vietnam has strengthened this basic American credibility. We must act in such a way in coming years that this credibility will remain intact, and with it, the world stability of which it is so indispensable a part.

At home, we must reject the mistaken notion—a notion that has dominated too much of the public dialogue for too long—that ever bigger Government is the answer to every problem.

We have learned only too well that heavy taxation and excessive Government spending are not a cure-all. In too many cases, instead of solving the problems they were aimed at, they have merely placed an ever heavier burden on the shoulders of the American taxpayer, in the form of higher taxes and a higher cost of living. At the same time they have deceived our people because many of the intended beneficiaries received far less than was promised, thus undermining public faith in the effectiveness of Government as a whole.

The time has come for us to draw the line. The time has come for the responsible leaders of both political parties to take a stand against overgrown Government and for the American taxpayer. We are not spending the Federal Government's money, we are spending the taxpayer's money, and it must be spent in a way which guarantees his money's worth and yields the fullest possible benefit to the people being helped.

The answer to many of the domestic problems we face is not higher taxes and more spending. It is less waste, more results and greater freedom for the individual American to earn a rightful place in his own community—and for States and localities to address their own needs in their own ways, in the light of their own priorities.

By giving the people and their locally elected leaders a greater voice through changes such as revenue sharing, and by saying "no" to excessive Federal spending and higher taxes, we can help achieve this goal.

Coming Messages

The policies which I will outline to the Congress in the weeks ahead represent a reaffirmation, not an abdication, of Federal responsibility. They represent a pragmatic rededication to social compassion and national excellence, in place of the combination of good intentions and fuzzy follow-through which too often in the past was thought sufficient.

In the field of economic affairs, our objectives will be to hold down taxes, to continue controlling inflation, to promote economic growth, to increase productivity, to encourage foreign trade, to keep farm income high, to bolster small business, and to promote better labor-management relations.

In the area of natural resources, my recommendations will include programs to preserve and enhance the environment, to advance science and technology, and to assure balanced use of our irreplaceable natural resources.

In developing human resources, I will have recommendations to advance the Nation's health and education, to improve conditions of people in need, to carry forward our increasingly successful attacks on crime, drug abuse and injustice, and to deal with such important areas of special concern as consumer affairs. We will continue and improve our Nation's efforts to assist those who have served in the Armed Services in Vietnam through better job and training opportunities.

We must do a better job in community development—in creating more livable communities, in which all of our children can grow up with fuller access to opportunity and greater immunity to the social evils and blights which now plague so many of our towns and cities. I shall have proposals to help us achieve this.

I shall also deal with our defense and foreign policies, and with our new approaches to the role and structure of Government itself.

Considered as a whole, this series of messages will be a blueprint for modernizing the concept and the functions of American Government to meet the needs of our people.

Converting it into reality will require a spirit of cooperation and shared commitment on the part of all branches of the Government, for the goals we seek are not those of any single party or faction, they are goals for the betterment of all Americans. As President, I recognize that I cannot do this job alone. The Congress must help, and I pledge to do my part to achieve a constructive working relationship with the Congress. My sincere hope is that the executive and legislative branches can work together in this great undertaking in a positive spirit of mutual respect and cooperation.

Working together—the Congress, the President and the people—I am confident that we can translate these proposals into an action program that can reform and revitalize American Government and, even more important, build a better life for all Americans.

State of the Union Message to Congress on Natural Resources and the Environment

February 15, 1973

Nixon's second of six written State of the Union messages in 1973 dealt with natural resources and the environment. Nixon proclaimed the country "well on the way to making our peace with nature." He criticized Congress for not acting on 19 administration proposals relating to the environment, but declared himself pleased with bills he had signed, including air quality legislation. Nixon also mentioned the creation of the Environmental Protection Agency in 1970, as well as the Council on Environmental Quality and the National Oceanic and Atmospheric Administration.

To the Congress of the United States:

With the opening of a new Congress and the beginning of a new Presidential term come fresh opportunities for achievement in America. To help us consider more adequately the very special challenges of this new year, I am presenting my 1973 State of the Union Message in a number of sections.

Two weeks ago I sent the first of those sections to the Congress—an overview reporting that "the basic state of our Union today is sound, and full of promise."

Today I wish to report to the Congress on the state of our natural resources and environment. It is appropriate that this topic be first of our substantive policy discussions in the State of the Union presentation, since nowhere in our national affairs do we have more gratifying progress—nor more urgent, remaining problems.

There was a time when Americans took our natural resources largely for granted. For example, President Lincoln observed in his State of the Union message for 1862 that "A nation may be said to consist of its territory, its people, and its laws. The territory is the only part which is of certain durability."

In recent years, however, we have come to realize that our "territory"—that is, our land, air, water, minerals, and the like—is not of "certain durability" after all. We have learned that these natural resources are fragile and finite, and that many have been seriously damaged or despoiled.

When we came to office in 1969, we tackled this problem with all the power at our command. Now there is encouraging evidence that the United States has moved away from the environmental crisis that could have been and toward a new era of restoration and renewal. Today, in 1973, I can report to the Congress that we are well on the way to winning the war against environmental degradation—well on the way to making our peace with nature.

Years of Progress

While I am disappointed that the 92nd Congress failed to act upon 19 of my key natural resources and environment proposals, I am pleased to have signed many of the proposals I supported into law during the past four years. They have included air quality legislation, strengthened water quality and pesticide control legislation, new authorities to control noise and ocean dumping, regulations to prevent oil and other spills in our ports and waterways, and legislation establishing major national recreation areas at America's Atlantic and Pacific gateways, New York and San Francisco.

On the organizational front, the National Environmental Policy Act of 1969 has reformed programs and decision-making processes in our Federal agencies and has given citizens a greater opportunity to contribute as decisions are made. In 1970 I appointed the first Council on Environmental Quality—a group which has provided active leadership in environmental policies. In the same year, I established the Environmental Protection Agency and the National Oceanic and Atmospheric Administration to provide more coordinated and vigorous environmental management. Our natural resource programs still need to be consolidated, however, and I will again submit legislation to the Congress to meet this need.

The results of these efforts are tangible and measurable. Day by day, our air is getting cleaner; in virtually every one of our major cities the levels of air pollution are declining. Month by month, our water pollution problems are also being conquered, our noise and pesticide problems are coming under control, our parklands and protected wilderness areas are increasing.

Year by year, our commitment of public funds for environmental programs continues to grow; it has increased four-fold in the last four years. In the area of water quality alone, it has grown fifteen-fold. In fact, we are now buying new facilities nearly as fast as the construction industry can build them. Spending still more money would not buy us more pollution control facilities but only more expensive ones.

In addition to what Government is doing in the battle against pollution, our private industries are assuming a steadily growing share of responsibility in this field. Last year industrial spending for pollution control jumped by 50 percent, and this year it could reach as much as $5 billion.

All nations, regardless of their economic systems, share to some extent in the environmental problem—but with vigorous United States leadership, joint efforts to solve this global problem are showing results. The United Nations has adopted the American proposal for a special U.N. environmental fund to coordinate and support international environmental programs.

Some 92 nations have concluded an international convention to control the ocean dumping of wastes. An agreement is now being forged in the Intergovernmental Maritime Consultative Organization to end the intentional discharge of oil from ships into the ocean. This objective, first recommended by my Administration, was adopted by the NATO Committee on the Challenges of Modern Society.

Representatives of almost 70 countries are meeting in Washington this week at our initiative to draft a treaty to protect endangered species of plant and animal wildlife. The U.S.-USSR environmental cooperation agreement which I signed in Moscow last year makes two of the world's greatest industrial powers allies against pollution. Another agreement which we concluded last year with Canada will help to clean up the Great Lakes.

Domestically, we can also be proud of the steady progress being made in improving the quality of life in rural and agricultural America. We are beginning to break away from the old rigid system of controls which eroded the farmer's freedom through Government intrusion in the marketplace. The new flexibility permitted by the Agricultural Act of 1970 has enabled us to help expand farm markets and take advantage of the opportunity to increase exports by almost 60 percent in just three years. Net farm income is at an all-time high, up from $16.1 billion in 1971 to $19 billion in 1972.

Principles To Guide Us

A record is not something to stand on; it is something to build on. And in this field of natural resources and the environment, we intend to build diligently and well.

As we strive to transform our concern into action, our efforts will be guided by five basic principles:

The first principle is that we must strike a balance so that the protection of our irreplaceable heritage becomes as important as its use. The price of economic growth need not and will not be deterioration in the quality of our lives and our surroundings.

Second, because there are no local or State boundaries to the problems of our environment, the Federal Government must play an active, positive role. We can and will set standards and exercise leadership. We are providing necessary funding support. And we will provide encouragement and incentive for others to help with the job. But Washington must not displace State and local initiative, and we shall expect the State and local governments—along with the private sector—to play the central role in making the difficult, particular decisions which lie ahead.

Third, the costs of pollution should be more fully met in the free marketplace, not in the Federal budget. For example, the price of pollution control devices for automobiles should be borne by the owner and the user and not by the general taxpayer. The costs of eliminating pollution should be reflected in the costs of goods and services.

Fourth, we must realize that each individual must take the responsibility for looking after his own home and workplace. These daily surroundings are the environment where most Americans spend most of their time. They reflect people's pride in themselves and their consideration for their communities. A person's backyard is not the domain of the Federal Government.

Finally, we must remain confident that America's technological and economic ingenuity will be equal to our environmental challenges. We will not look upon these challenges as insurmountable obstacles.

Instead, we shall convert the so-called crisis of the environment into an opportunity for unprecedented progress.

Controlling Pollution

We have made great progress in developing the laws and institutions to clean up pollution. We now have formidable new tools to protect against air, water and noise pollution and the special problem of pesticides. But to protect ourselves fully from harmful contaminants, we must still close several gaps in governmental authority.

I was keenly disappointed when the last Congress failed to take action on many of my legislative requests related to our natural resources and environment. In the coming weeks I shall once again send these urgently needed proposals to the Congress so that the unfinished environmental business of the 92nd Congress can become the environmental achievements of the 93rd.

Among these 19 proposals are eight whose passage would give us much greater control over the sources of pollution:

- Toxic Substances. Many new chemicals can pose hazards to humans and the environment and are not well regulated. Authority is now needed to provide adequate testing standards for chemical substances and to restrict or prevent their distribution if testing confirms a hazard.

- Hazardous Wastes. Land disposal of hazardous wastes has always been widely practiced but is now becoming more prevalent because of strict air and water pollution control programs. The disposal of the extremely hazardous wastes which endanger the health of humans and other organisms is a problem requiring direct Federal regulation. For other hazardous wastes, Federal standards should be established with guidelines for State regulatory programs to carry them out.

- Safe Drinking Water. Federal action is also needed to stimulate greater State and local action to ensure high standards for our drinking water. We should establish national drinking water standards, with primary enforcement and monitoring powers retained by the State and local agencies, as well as a Federal requirement that suppliers notify their customers of the quality of their water.

- Sulfur Oxides Emissions Charge. We now have national standards to help curtail sulfur emitted into the atmosphere from combustion, refining, smelting and other processes, but sulfur oxides continue to be among our most harmful air pollutants. For that reason, I favor legislation which would allow the Federal Government to impose a special financial charge on those who produce sulfur oxide emissions. This legislation would also help to ensure that low-sulfur fuels are allocated to areas where they are most urgently needed to protect the public health.

- Sediment Control. Sediment from soil erosion and runoff continues to be a pervasive pollutant of our waters. Legislation is needed to ensure that the States make the control of sediment from new construction a vital part of their water quality programs.

- Controlling Environmental Impacts of Transportation. As we have learned in recent years, we urgently need a mass transportation system not only to relieve urban congestion but also to reduce the concentrations of pollution that are too often the result of our present methods of transportation. Thus I will continue to place high priority upon my request to permit use of the Highway Trust Fund for mass transit purposes and to help State and local governments achieve air quality, conserve energy, and meet other environmental objectives.

- United Nations Environmental Fund. Last year the United Nations adopted my proposal to establish a fund to coordinate and support international environmental programs. My 1974 budget includes a request for $10 million as our initial contribution toward the Fund's five-year goal of $100 million, and I recommend authorizing legislation for this purpose.

- Ocean Dumping Convention. Along with 91 other nations, the United States recently concluded an international convention calling for regulation of ocean dumping. I am most anxious to obtain the advice and consent of the Senate for this convention as soon as possible. Congressional action is also needed on several other international conventions and amendments to control oil pollution from ships in the oceans.

Managing the Land

As we steadily bring our pollution problems under control, more effective and sensible use of our land is rapidly emerging as among the highest of our priorities. The land is our Nation's basic natural resource, and our stewardship of this resource today will affect generations to come.

America's land once seemed inexhaustible. There was always more of it beyond the horizon. Until the twentieth century we displayed a carelessness about our land, born of our youthful innocence and desire to expand. But our land is no longer an open frontier.

Americans not only need, but also very much want to preserve diverse and beautiful landscapes, to maintain essential farm lands, to save wetlands and wildlife habitats, to keep open recreational space near crowded population centers, and to protect our shorelines and beaches. Our goal is to harmonize development with environmental quality and to add creatively to the beauty and long-term worth of land already being used.

Land use policy is a basic responsibility of State and local governments. They are closer to the problems and closer to the people. Some localities are already reforming land use regulation—a trend I hope will accelerate. But because land is a national heritage, the Federal Government must exercise leadership in land use decision processes, and I am today again proposing that we provide it. In the coming weeks, I will ask the Congress to enact a number of legislative initiatives which will help us achieve this goal:

- National Land Use Policy. Our greatest need is for comprehensive new legislation to stimulate State land use controls. We especially need a National Land Use Policy Act authorizing Federal assistance to encourage the States, in cooperation with local governments, to protect lands of critical environmental concern and to regulate the siting of key facilities such as airports, highways and major private developments. Appropriate Federal funds should be withheld from States that fail to act.

- Power Plant Siting. An open, long-range planning process is needed to help meet our power needs while also protecting the environment. We can avoid unnecessary delays with a power plant siting law which assures that electric power facilities are constructed on a timely basis, but with early and thorough review of long-range plans and specific provisions to protect the environment.

- Protection of Wetlands. Our coastal wetlands are increasingly threatened by residential and commercial development. To increase their protection, I believe we should use the Federal tax laws to discourage unwise development in wetlands.

- Historic Preservation and Rehabilitation. An important part of our national heritage are those historic structures in our urban areas which should be rehabilitated and preserved, not demolished. To help meet this goal, our tax laws should be revised to encourage rehabilitation of older buildings, and we should provide Federal insurance of loans to restore historic buildings for residential purposes.

• Management of Public Lands. Approximately one-fifth of the Nation's land is considered "public domain", and lacks the protection of an overall management policy with environmental safeguards. Legislation is required to enable the Secretary of the Interior to protect our environmental interest on those lands.

• Legacy of Parks. Under the Legacy of Parks program which I initiated in 1971, 257 separate parcels of parklands and underused Federal lands in all 50 States have been turned over to local control for park and recreational purposes. Most of these parcels are near congested urban areas, so that millions of citizens can now have easy access to parklands. I am pleased to announce today that 16 more parcels of Federal land will soon be made available under this same program.

We must not be content, however, with just the Legacy of Parks program. New authority is needed to revise the formula for allocating grant funds to the States from the Land and Water Conservation Fund. More of these funds should be channelled to States with large urban populations.

• Mining on Public Lands. Under a statute now over a century old, public lands must be transferred to private ownership at the request of any person who discovers minerals on them. We thus have no effective control over mining on these properties. Because the public lands belong to all Americans, this 1872 Mining Act should be repealed and replaced with new legislation which I shall send to the Congress.

• Mined Area Protection. Surface and underground mining can too often cause serious air and water pollution as well as unnecessary destruction of wildlife habitats and aesthetic and recreational areas. New legislation with stringent performance standards is required to regulate abuses of surface and underground mining in a manner compatible with the environment.

American Agriculture a Basic National Resource

Nearly three-fifths of America's land is in the stewardship of the farmer and the rancher. We can be grateful that farmers have been among our best conservationists over the years. Farmers know better than most that sound conservation means better long-term production and improved land values. More importantly, no one respects and understands our soil and land better than those who make their living by the land.

But Americans know their farmers and ranchers best for all they have done to keep us the best-fed and best-clothed people in the history of mankind. A forward-looking agricultural economy is not only essential for environmental progress, but also to provide for our burgeoning food and fiber needs.

My Administration is not going to express its goal for farmers in confusing terms. Our goal, instead, is very simple. The farmer wants, has earned, and deserves more freedom to make his own decisions. The Nation wants and needs expanded supplies of reasonably priced goods and commodities.

These goals are complementary. Both have been advanced by the basic philosophy of the Agricultural Act of 1970. They must be further advanced by Congressional action this year.

The Agricultural Act of 1970 expires with the 1973 crop. We now face the fundamental challenge of developing legislation appropriate to the economy of the 1970's. Over the next several months, the future direction of the farm program must he discussed, debated and written into law. The outcome of this process will be crucial not only to farmers and ranchers, but to consumers and taxpayers as well.

My Administration's fundamental approach to farm policy is to build on the forward course set by the 1970 Act. These principles should guide us in enacting new farm legislation:

- Farmers must be provided with greater freedom to make production and marketing decisions. I have never known anyone in Washington who knows better than a farmer what is in his own best interest.

- Government influence in the farm commodity marketplace must be reduced. Old fashioned Federal intrusion is as inappropriate to today's farm economy as the old McCormick reaper would be on a highly sophisticated modern farm.

- We must allow farmers the opportunity to produce for expanding domestic demands and to continue our vigorous competition in export markets. We will not accomplish that goal by telling the farmer how much he can grow or the rancher how much livestock he can raise. Fidelity to this principle will have the welcome effect of encouraging both fair food prices for consumers and growing income from the marketplace for farmers.

- We must reduce the farmer's dependence on Government payments through increased returns from sales of farm products at home and abroad. Because some of our current methods of handling farm problems are outmoded, the farmer has been unfairly saddled with the unflattering image of drinking primarily at the Federal well. Let us remember that more than 93 percent of gross farm income comes directly through the marketplace. Farmers and ranchers are strong and independent businessmen; we should expand their opportunity to exercise their strength and independence.

- Finally, we need a program that will put the United States in a good posture for forthcoming trade negotiations.

In pursuing all of these goals, we will work closely through the Secretary of Agriculture with the Senate Committee on Agriculture and Forestry and the House Committee on Agriculture to formulate and enact new legislation in areas where it is needed.

I believe, for example, that dairy support systems, wheat, feed grains and cotton allotments and bases—some established decades ago—are drastically outdated. They tend to be discriminatory for many farm operators.

It would be desirable to establish, after a reasonable transition period, a more equitable basis for production adjustment in the agricultural economy should such adjustment be needed in the years ahead. Direct Federal payments should, at the end of the transition period, be limited to the amounts necessary to compensate farmers for withholding unneeded land from crop production.

As new farm legislation is debated in the months ahead, I hope the Congress will address this important subject with a deep appreciation of the need to keep the Government off the farm as well as keeping the farmer on.

Protecting, Our Natural Heritage

An important measure of our true commitment to environmental quality is our dedication to protecting the wilderness and its inhabitants. We must recognize their ecological significance and preserve them as sources of inspiration and education. And we need them as places of quiet refuge and reflection.

Important progress has been made in recent years, but still further action is needed in the Congress. Specifically, I will ask the 93rd Congress to direct its attention to the following areas of concern:

- Endangered Species. The limited scope of existing laws requires new authority to identify and protect endangered species before they are so depleted that it is too late. New legislation must also make the taking of an endangered animal a Federal offense.

- Predator Control. The widespread use of highly toxic poisons to kill coyotes and other predatory animals has spread persistent poisons to range and forest lands without adequate foresight of environmental effects. I believe Federal assistance is now required so that we can find better means of controlling predators without endangering other wildlife.

- Wilderness Areas. Historically, Americans have always looked westward to enjoy wilderness areas. Today we realize that we must also preserve the remaining areas of wilderness in the East, if the majority of our people are to have the full benefit of our natural glories. Therefore I will ask the Congress to amend the legislation that established the Wilderness Preservation System so that more of our Eastern lands can be included.

- Wild and Scenic Rivers. New legislation is also needed to continue our expansion of the national system of wild and scenic rivers. Funding authorization must be increased by $20 million to complete acquisitions in seven areas, and we must extend the moratorium on Federal licensing for water resource projects on those rivers being considered for inclusion in the system.

- Big Cypress National Fresh Water Preserve. It is our great hope that we can create a reserve of Florida's Big Cypress Swamp in order to protect the outstanding wildlife in that area, preserve the water supply of Everglades National Park and provide the Nation with an outstanding recreation area. Prompt passage of Federal legislation would allow the Interior Department to forestall private or commercial development and inflationary pressures that will build if we delay.

- Protecting Marine Fisheries. Current regulation of fisheries off U.S. coasts is inadequate to conserve and manage these resources. Legislation is needed to authorize U.S. regulation of foreign fishing off U.S. coasts to the fullest extent authorized by international agreements. In addition, domestic fishing should be regulated in the U.S. fisheries zone and in the high seas beyond that zone.

- World Heritage Trust. The United States has endorsed an international convention for a World Heritage Trust embodying our proposals to accord special recognition and protection to areas of the world which are of such unique natural, historical, or cultural value that they are a part of the heritage of all mankind. I am hopeful that this convention will be ratified early in 1973.

- Weather Modification. Our capacity to affect the weather has grown considerably in sophistication and predictability, but with this advancement has also come a new potential for endangering lives and property and causing adverse environmental effects. With additional Federal regulations, I believe that we can minimize these dangers.

Meeting Our Energy Needs

One of the highest priorities of my Administration during the coming year will be a concern for energy supplies—a concern underscored this winter by occasional fuel shortages. We must face up to a stark fact in America: we are now consuming more energy than we produce.

A year and a half ago I sent to the Congress the first Presidential message ever devoted to the energy question. I shall soon submit a new and far more comprehensive energy message containing wide-ranging initiatives to ensure necessary supplies of energy at acceptable economic and environmental costs. In the meantime, to help meet immediate needs, I have temporarily suspended import quotas on home heating oil east of the Rocky Mountains.

As we work to expand our supplies of energy, we should also recognize that we must balance those efforts with our concern to preserve our environment. In the past, as we have sought new energy sources, we have too often damaged or despoiled our land. Actions to avoid such damage will probably aggravate our energy problems to some extent and may lead to higher prices. But all development and use of energy sources carry environmental risks, and we must find ways to minimize those risks while also providing adequate supplies of energy. I am fully confident that we can satisfy both of these imperatives.

Going Forward in Confidence

The environmental awakening of recent years has triggered substantial progress in the fight to preserve and renew the great legacies of nature. Unfortunately, it has also triggered a certain tendency to despair. Some people have moved from complacency to the opposite extreme of alarmism, suggesting that our pollution problems were hopeless and predicting impending ecological disaster. Some have suggested that we could never reconcile environmental protection with continued economic growth.

I reject this doomsday mentality—and I hope the Congress will also reject it. I believe that we can meet our environmental challenges without turning our back on progress. What we must do is to stop the hand-wringing, roll up our sleeves and get on with the job.

The advocates of defeatism warn us of all that is wrong. But I believe they underestimate this Nation's genius for responsive adaptability and its enormous reservoir of spirit.

I believe there is always a sensible middle ground between the Cassandras and the Pollyannas. We must take our stand upon that ground.

I have profound respect for the enormous challenge ahead, but I have even stronger respect for the capacity and character of the American people. Many of us have heard the adage that the last letters of the word, "American," say "I can." I am confident that we can, and we will, meet our natural resource challenges.

State of the Union Message to Congress on the Economy

February 22, 1973

Nixon's third of six written State of the Union addresses for 1973 focused on the economy. The president called for a series of policies, including restraint in federal spending, reasonableness in labor-management relations, and vigilance in efforts to hold down food prices.

To the Congress of the United States:

Today, in this third section of my 1973 State of the Union Message, I wish to report on the state of our economy and to urge the Congress to join with me in building the foundations for a new era of prosperity in the United States.

The state of our Union depends fundamentally on the state of our economy. I am pleased to report that our economic prospects are very bright. For the first time in nearly 20 years, we can look forward to a period of genuine prosperity in a time of peace. We can, in fact, achieve the most bountiful prosperity that this Nation has ever known.

That goal can only be attained, however, if we discipline ourselves and unite on certain basic policies:

- We must be restrained in Federal spending.
- We must show reasonableness in labor-management relations.
- We must comply fully with the new Phase III requirements of our economic stabilization program.
- We must continue our battle to hold down the price of food.
- And we must vigorously meet the challenge of foreign trading competition.

It is clear to me that the American people stand firmly together in support of these policies. Their President stands with them. And as Members of the 93rd Congress consider the alternatives before us this year, I am confident that they, too, will join in this great endeavor.

Impact of the Economy on People's Lives

This message will present my basic economic recommendations and priorities and will indicate some areas in which further detailed plans will be submitted later. But I also want to discuss our economic situation in less formal terms: how do statistical measurements, comparisons and projections affect the daily lives of individual Americans and their families?

We build our economy, after all, not to create cold, impersonal statistics for the record books but to better the lives of our people.

Basically, the economy affects people in three ways.

First, it affects their jobs—how plentiful they are, how secure they are, how good they are.

Second, it affects what people are paid on their jobs—and how much they can buy with that income.

Finally, it affects how much people have to pay back to the Government in taxes.

Job Picture Encouraging

To begin with, the job picture today is very encouraging.

The number of people at work in this country rose by 2.3 million during 1972—the largest increase in 25 years. Unemployment fell from the 6 percent level in 1971 to 5 percent last month.

The reason jobs have grown so rapidly is that the economy grew in real terms by 6½ percent last year, one of the best performances in the past quarter century,. Our economic advisers expect a growth rate of nearly 7 percent in 1973. That would bring unemployment down to around the 4½ percent level by the end of the year.

Five percent unemployment is too high. Nevertheless, it is instructive to examine that 5 percent figure more closely. For example:

- Only 40 percent of those now counted as unemployed are in that status because they lost their last job. The rate of layoffs at the end of last year was lower than it has been since the Korean War.

- The other 60 percent either left their last job voluntarily, are seeking jobs for the first time or are re-entering the labor force after being out of it for a period of time.

- About 45 percent of the unemployed have been unemployed for less than five weeks.

- As compared with earlier periods when the overall unemployment rate was about what it is now, the unemployment rate is significantly lower for adult males, household heads and married men. Among married men it is only 2.4 percent. Unemployment among these groups should decline even further during 1973.

This employment gain is even more remarkable since so many more people have been seeking jobs than usual. For example, nearly three million Americans have been released from defense-related jobs since 1969—including over one million veterans.

The unemployment rate for veterans of the Vietnam War now stands at 5.9 percent, above the general rate of unemployment but slightly below the rate for other males in the 20-to-29-year-old age bracket. While much better than the 8.5 percent of a year ago, this 5.9 percent rate is still too high. The employment problems of veterans, who have given so much for their country, will remain high on my list of concerns for the coming year.

Women and young people have also been seeking work in record numbers. Yet, as in the case of veterans, jobs for these groups have been increasing even faster. Unemployment among women and young people has thus declined—but it is also much too high and constitutes a great waste for our Nation.

As we move into a new era of peacetime prosperity, our economic system is going to have room—indeed, is going to have need—for nearly every available hand.

The role of women in our economy thus is bound to grow. And it should—not only because the expansion of opportunities for women is right, but also because America will not be able to achieve its full economic potential unless every woman who wants to work can find a job that provides fair compensation and equal opportunity for advancement.

This Administration is committed to the promotion of this goal. We support the Equal Rights Amendment. We have opened the doors of employment to qualified women in the Federal service. We have called for similar efforts in businesses and institutions which receive Federal contracts or assistance.

Just last year, we established the Advisory Committee on the Economic Role of Women. This Committee will provide leadership in helping to identify economic problems facing women and helping to change the attitudes which create unjust and illogical barriers to their employment.

Pay and Purchasing Power

The second great question is what people are paid on their jobs and how much it will buy for them.

Here the news is also good. Not only are more people working, but they are getting more for their work. Average per capita income rose by 7.7 percent during 1972, well above the average gain during the previous ten years.

The most important thing, however, is that these gains were not wiped out by rising prices—as they often were in the 1960's. The Federal Government spent too much, too fast in that period and the result was runaway inflation.

While wages may have climbed very rapidly during those years, purchasing power did not. Instead, purchasing power stalled, or even moved backward. Inflation created an economic treadmill that sometimes required a person to achieve a 6 percent salary increase every year just to stay even.

Now that has changed. The inflation rate last year was cut nearly in half from what it was four years ago. The purchasing power of the average worker's takehome pay rose more last year than in any year since 1955; it went up by 4.3 percent—the equivalent of two extra weekly paychecks.

We expect inflation to be reduced even further in 1973—for several reasons.

A fundamental reason is the Nation's growing opposition to runaway Federal spending. The public increasingly perceives what such spending does to prices and taxes. As a result, we have a good chance now, the best in years, to curb the growth of the Federal budget. That will do more than anything else to protect the family budget.

Other forces are working for us too. Productivity increased sharply last year—which means the average worker is producing more and can therefore earn more without driving prices higher. In addition, the fact that real spendable earnings rose so substantially last year will encourage reasonable wage demands this year. Workers will not have to catch up from an earlier slump in earnings.

Finally, we now have a new system of wage and price controls—one that is the right kind of system for 1973.

Firm Controls in Force; Food Prices Fought

Any idea that controls have virtually been ended is totally wrong. We still have firm controls. We are still enforcing them firmly. All that has changed is our method of enforcing them.

The old system depended on a Washington bureaucracy to approve major wage and price increases in advance. Although it was effective while it lasted, this system was beginning to produce inequities and to get tangled in red tape. The new system will avoid these dangers. Like most of our laws, it relies largely on self-administration, on the voluntary cooperation of the American people.

But if some people should fail to cooperate, we still have the will and the means to crack down on them.

To any economic interests which might feel that the new system will permit them, openly or covertly, to achieve gains beyond the safety limits we shall prescribe, let me deliver this message in clear and unmistakable terms:

We will regard any flouting of our anti-inflationary rules and standards as nothing less than attempted economic arson threatening our national economic stability—and we shall act accordingly.

We would like Phase III to be as voluntary as possible. But we will make it as mandatory as necessary.

Our new system of controls has broad support from business and labor—the keystone for any successful program. It will prepare us for the day when we no longer need controls. It will allow us to concentrate on those areas where inflation has been most troublesome—construction, health care and especially food prices.

We are focusing particular attention and action on the tough problem of food prices. These prices have risen sharply at the wholesale level in recent months, so that figures for retail prices in January and February will inevitably show sharp increases. In fact, we will probably see increases in food prices for some months to come.

The underlying cause of this problem is that food supplies have not risen fast enough to keep up with the rapidly rising demand.

But we must not accept rising food prices as a permanent feature of American life. We must halt this inflationary spiral by attacking the causes of rising food prices on all fronts. Our first priority must be to increase supplies of food to meet the increasing demand.

We are moving vigorously to expand our food supplies:

- We are encouraging farmers to put more acreage into production of both crops and livestock.
- We are allowing more meat and dried milk to come in from abroad.
- We have ended subsidies for agricultural exports.
- And we are reducing the Government's agricultural stockpiles and encouraging farmers to sell the stock they own.

Measures such as these will stop the rise of wholesale food prices and will slow the rise of retail food prices. Unfortunately, nothing we can do will have a decisive effect in the next few months. But the steps I have taken will have a powerful effect in the second half of the year.

These steps will also help our farmers to improve their incomes by producing more without corresponding price increases. We anticipate that farm prices will be no higher at the end of this year than they were at the beginning.

For all of these reasons, we have a good chance to reduce the overall inflation rate to 2½ percent by the end of 1973.

Holding the Line on Taxes

The third important economic question concerns how much money people pay out in taxes and how much they have left to control themselves. Here, too, the picture is promising.

Since 1950, the share of the average family's income taken for taxes in the United States has nearly doubled—to more than 20 percent. The average person worked less than one hour out of each eight-hour day to pay his taxes in 1950; today he works nearly two hours each day for the tax collector.

In fact, if tax cut proposals had not been adopted during our first term, the average worker's pay increase last year would have been wiped out completely by increased taxes and the taxpayers would have to pay out an additional $25 billion in personal income taxes this year.

The only way to hold the line on taxes is to hold the line on Federal spending.

This is why we are cutting back, eliminating or reforming Federal programs that waste the taxpayers' money.

My Administration has now had four years of experience with all of our Federal programs. We have conducted detailed studies comparing their costs and results. On the basis of that experience I am convinced that the cost of many Federal programs can no longer be justified. Among them are:

- housing programs that benefit the well-to-do but short-change the poor;
- health programs that build more hospitals when hospital beds are now in surplus;
- educational fellowships designed to attract more people into teaching when tens of thousands of teachers already cannot find teaching jobs;
- programs that subsidize education for the children of Federal employees who already pay enough local taxes to support their local schools;
- programs that blindly continue welfare payments to those who are ineligible or overpaid.

Such programs may have appealing names; they may sound like good causes. But behind a fancy label can lie a dismal failure. And unless we cut back now on the programs that have failed, we will soon run out of money for the programs that succeed.

It has been charged that our budget cuts show a lack of compassion for the disadvantaged. The best answer to this charge is to look at the facts. We are budgeting 66 percent more to help the poor next year than was the case four years ago; 67 percent more to help the sick; 71 percent more to help older Americans and 242 percent more to help the hungry and malnourished. Altogether, our human resources budget is a record $125 billion—nearly double that of four years ago when I came into office.

We have already shifted our spending priorities from defense programs to human resource programs. Now we must also switch our spending priorities from programs which give us a bad return on the dollar to programs that pay off. That is how to show we truly care about the needy.

The question is not whether we help but how we help. By eliminating programs that are wasteful, we can concentrate on programs that work.

Our recent round of budget cuts can save $11 billion in this fiscal year, $19 billion next fiscal year, and $24 billion the year after. That means an average saving of $700 over the next three years for each of America's 75 million taxpayers.

Without the savings I have achieved through program reductions and reforms, those spending totals respectively would be $261 billion, $288 billion and $312 billion—figures which would spell either higher taxes, a new surge of crippling inflation, or both.

To hold the line on Federal spending, it is absolutely vital that we have the full cooperation of the Congress. I urge the Congress, as one of its most pressing responsibilities, to adopt an overall spending ceiling for each fiscal year. I also ask that it establish a regular procedure for ensuring that the ceiling is maintained.

The International Challenge

In recent years, the attention of Americans has increasingly turned to the serious questions confronting us in international trade and in the monetary arena.

This is no longer the era in which the United States, preeminent in science, marketing and services, can dominate world markets with the advanced products of our technology and our advanced means of production.

This is no longer the era in which the United States can automatically sell more abroad than we purchase from foreign countries.

We face new challenges in international competition and are thus in a period of substantial adjustment in our relations with our trading partners.

One consequence of these developments was the step we took last week to change the relative value of the dollar in trading abroad.

We took this step because of a serious trade imbalance which could threaten the mounting prosperity of our people. America has been buying more from other countries than they have been buying from us. And just as a family or a company cannot go on indefinitely buying more than it sells, neither can a country.

Changing the exchange rates will help us change this picture. It means our exports will be priced more competitively in the international marketplace and should therefore sell better. Our imports, on the other hand, will not grow as fast.

But this step must now be followed by reforms which are more basic.

First, we need a more flexible international monetary system, one that will lead to balance without crisis. The United States set forth fundamental proposals for such a system last September. It is time for other nations to join us in getting action on these proposals.

Secondly, American products must get a fairer shake in a more open world trading system—so that we can extend American markets and expand American jobs. If other countries make it harder for our products to be sold abroad, then our trade imbalance can only grow worse.

Responsibility of the Congress

America is assuredly on the road to a new era of prosperity. The road signs are clear, and we are gathering more momentum with each passing month. But we can easily lose our way unless the Congress is on board, helping to steer the course.

As we face 1973, in fact, we may be sure that the state of our economy in the future will very much depend upon the decisions made this year on Capitol Hill.

Over the course of the next few months, I will urge prompt Congressional action on a variety of economic proposals. Together, these proposals will constitute one of the most important packages of economic initiatives ever considered by any Congress in our history. I hope—as do all of our people—that the Congress will act with both discipline and dispatch.

Among the items included in my 1973 economic package are:

- Extension of the Economic Stabilization Program. Present authority will soon expire, and I have asked the Congress to extend the law for one year to April 30, 1974. I hope this will be done without adding general mandatory standards or prescribing rigid advance decisions—steps that would only hamper sound administration of the program. A highly complex economy simply cannot be regulated effectively for extended periods in that way.

- Tax Program. I shall recommend a tax program that builds further reforms on those we achieved in 1969 and 1971.

- Property Tax Relief. I shall also submit recommendations for alleviating the crushing burdens which property taxes now create for older Americans.

- Tax Credit for Nonpublic Schools. I shall propose legislation which would provide for income tax credit for tuition paid to nonpublic elementary and secondary schools. These institutions are a valuable national resource, relieving the public school system of enrollment pressures, injecting a welcome variety into our educational process, and expanding the options of millions of parents.

- Trade Legislation. Another item high on our agenda will be new trade proposals which I will soon send to the Congress. They would make it easier for us not only to lower our trade barriers when other countries lower theirs but also to raise our barriers when that is necessary to keep things fair.

- Other Reforms. To modernize and make them more equitable and beneficial, I shall also later submit recommendations for improving the performance of our private pension system, our unemployment compensation program, our minimum wage laws and the manner in which we deal with our transportation systems.

- Spending Limits. Finally, but most importantly, I ask the Congress to act this year to impose strict limits on Federal spending.

The cuts I have suggested in this year's budget did not come easily. Thus I can well understand that it may not be easy for the Congress to sustain them, as every special interest group lobbies with its own special Congressional committees for its own special legislation. But the Congress should serve more than the special interest; its first allegiance must always be to the public interest.

We must also recognize that no one in the Congress is now charged with adding all of our Federal expenditures together—and considering their total impact on taxes and prices. It is as if each member of a family went shopping on his own, without knowing how much money was available in the overall family budget or how much other members of the family were spending or charging on various credit accounts.

To overcome these problems, I urge prompt adoption by the Congress of an overall spending ceiling for each fiscal year. This action would allow the Congress to work jointly with me in holding spending to $250 billion in the current fiscal year, $269 billion next year, and $288 billion in fiscal year 1975. Beyond the adoption of an annual ceiling, I also recommend that the Congress consider internal reforms which would establish a regular mechanism for deciding how to maintain the ceiling.

I have no economic recommendation to make to the Congress which is more important to the economic well-being of our people.

I believe that most members of the House and Senate want to hold down spending. Most Congressmen voted for a spending ceiling in principle when the Senate and House approved a ceiling last fall. Unfortunately the two bodies could not get together on a final version. I believe they must get together soon—so that the Congress can proceed this year with a firm sense of budget discipline.

The stakes are high. If we do not restrain spending and if my recommended cuts are reversed, it would take a 15 percent increase in income taxes to pay for the additional expenditures.

The separation of powers between the President and the Congress has become a favorite topic of discussion in recent weeks. We should never, of course, lose our sharp concern for maintaining Constitutional balances.

But we should never overlook the fact we have joint responsibilities as well as separate powers.

There are many areas in which the President and the Congress should and must work together in behalf of all the people—and the level of spending, since it directly affects the pocketbooks of every family in the land, is one of the most critical.

I have fulfilled my pledge that I would not recommend any programs that would require a general tax increase or would create inflationary pressures.

Now it is up to the Congress to match these efforts with a spending ceiling of its own.

Making a Choice

We stand on the threshold of a new era of prolonged and growing prosperity for the United States.

Unlike past booms, this new prosperity will not depend on the stimulus of war.

It will not be eaten away by the blight of inflation.

It will be solid; it will be steady; and it will be sustainable.

If we act responsibly, this new prosperity can be ours for many years to come. If we don't, then, as Franklin Roosevelt once warned, we could be "wrecked on (the) rocks of loose fiscal policy."

The choice is ours. Let us choose responsible prosperity.

State of the Union Message to Congress on Human Resources

March 1, 1973

President Nixon's fourth of six written State of the Union addresses for 1973 focused on human resources. Nixon called for sweeping changes in government social programs, stating that in the 1960s, many of these programs had failed. His own administration, which came into office in 1969, had espoused a "healthy skepticism" about the role of the federal government, he said. Among his goals were having the federal government focus more on providing incentives rather than delivering services, encouraging state and local governments to play more of a role, and maintaining fiscal responsibility.

To the Congress of the United States:

"Information of the State of the Union," which our Constitution directs shall be communicated from time to time to the Congress by the President, must consist above all of information about the well-being of the American people.

As the opening words of the Constitution proclaim, America began with "We the People." The people are the Union, and its condition depends wholly on theirs.

While the Nation's land and resources, its communities, its economy, and its political institutions are also vital concerns to be addressed in my reports to the Congress this year, all of these in the final analysis are no more than means to a greater end. For each of them must ultimately be measured according to a single standard: what will serve the millions of individual Americans for whom all public officials serve as trustees.

Too often in the past that standard has not prevailed. Too often public policy decisions have been founded not on the long-run interests of all the people, but on the short-run interests of special groups of people. Programs once set in motion tend to stay in motion—sometimes long after their useful life has ended. They acquire a constituency of their own, even within the Government, and they cannot easily be reformed or stopped. Means come to be regarded as ends in themselves. And no one suffers more than the people they were designed to serve.

Despite all of the factors which conspire to hinder both the executive and the legislative branches in being as objective and analytical as we should be about the soundness of activities that continue from year to year supposedly in the public interest, we can and must discipline ourselves to take a larger view.

As we consider the subject of human resources in this fourth section of my 1973 State of the Union Message, we must not confine ourselves solely to a discussion of the year past and the year ahead. Nor can we be content to frame the choices we face in strictly governmental and programmatic terms—as though Federal money and programs were the only variables that mattered in meeting human needs.

Fulfilling the American Dream

I am irrevocably committed, as Presidents before me have been and as I know each Member of the Congress is, to fulfilling the American dream for all Americans.

But I also believe deeply that in seeking progress and reform we must neither underestimate our society's present greatness, nor mistake the sources of that greatness. To do so would be to run a serious risk of damaging, with unproven panaceas applied in excessive haste and zeal, the very institutions we seek to improve.

Let us begin then, by recognizing that by almost any measure, life is better for Americans in 1973 than ever before in our history, and better than in any other society of the world in this or any earlier age.

No previous generation of our people has ever enjoyed higher incomes, better health and nutrition, longer life-expectancy, or greater mobility and convenience in their lives than we enjoy today. None before us has had a better chance for fulfillment and advancement in their work, more leisure time and recreational opportunities, more widespread access to culture and the arts, or a higher level of education and awareness of the world around them. None has had greater access to and control over the natural and human forces that shape their lives, or better protection against suffering, inhumanity, injustice, and discrimination. And none has enjoyed greater freedom.

Secondly, let us recognize that the American system which has brought us so far so fast is not simply a system of Government helping people. *Rather it is a system under which Government helps people to help themselves and one another.*

The real miracles in raising millions out of poverty, for example, have been performed by the free-enterprise economy, not by Government anti-poverty programs. The integration of one disadvantaged minority after another into the American mainstream has been accomplished by the inherent responsiveness of our political and social system, not by quotas and coercion. The dramatic gains in health and medical care have come primarily through private medicine, not from federally-operated systems.

Even where the public sector has played a major role, as in education, the great strength of the system has derived from State and local governments' primacy and from the diverse mixture of private and public institutions in the educational process—both factors which have facilitated grass roots influence and popular participation.

We should not tamper lightly, then, with the delicately balanced social, economic, and political system which has been responsible for making this country the best place on earth to live—and which has tremendous potential to rectify whatever shortcomings may still persist.

But we Americans—to our great credit—are a restless and impatient people, a nation of idealists. We dream not simply of alleviating poverty, hunger, discrimination, ignorance, disease, and fear, but of eradicating them altogether—and we would like to do it all today.

During the middle and late 1960's, under the pressure of this impatient idealism, Federal intervention to help meet human needs increased sharply. Provision of services from Federal programs directly to individuals began to be regarded as the rule in human resources policy, rather than the rare exception if had been in the past.

The Government in those years undertook sweeping, sometimes almost utopian, commitments in one area of social concern after another. The State and local governments and the private sector were elbowed aside with little regard for the dislocations that might result. Literally hundreds of new programs were established on the assumption that even the most complex problems could be quickly solved by throwing enough Federal dollars at them.

Well-intentioned as this effort may have been, the results in case after case amounted to dismal failure. It was a classic case of elevating means to the status of ends in themselves. Hard evidence of actual betterment in people's lives was seldom demanded. Ever-larger amounts of funds, new agencies, and increased staff were treated as proof enough of success, simply because the motive was compassionate.

The American people deserve better than this. They deserve compassion that works—not simply compassion that means well. They deserve programs that say yes to human needs by saying no to paternalism, social exploitation and waste.

Protecting and enhancing the greatness of our society is a great goal. It is doubly important, therefore, that we not permit the worthiness of our objective to render us uncritical or careless in the means we select for attaining that objective.

It will increase our greatness as a society, for example, to establish the principle that no American family should be denied good health care because of inability to pay. But it will diminish our greatness if we deprive families of the freedom to make their own health care arrangements without bureaucratic meddling.

It will increase our greatness to ensure that no boy or girl is denied a quality education. But it will diminish our greatness if we force hundreds of thousands of children to ride buses miles away from their neighborhood schools in order to achieve an arbitrary racial balance.

It will increase our greatness to establish an income security system under which no American family will have to suffer for lack of income or break up because welfare regulations encourage it. But it would erode the very foundations of our stability and our prosperity if we ever made it more comfortable or more profitable to live on a welfare check than on a paycheck.

Principles for the 1970's

Consistently since 1969, this Administration has worked to establish a new human resources policy, based on a healthy skepticism about Federal Government omniscience and omnicompetence, and on a strong reaffirmation of the right and the capacity of individuals to chart their own lives and solve their own problems through State and local government and private endeavor. We have achieved a wide variety of significant reforms.

Now the progress made and the experience gained over the past four years, together with the results of careful program reviews which were conducted over this period, have prepared us to seek broader reforms in 1973 than any we have requested before.

In the time since the outlines of these proposals emerged in the new budget, intense controversy and considerable misunderstanding about both their purposes and their effects have understandably arisen among persons of goodwill on all sides.

To provide a more rational, less emotional basis for the national debate which will—and properly should—surround my recommendations, I would invite the Congress to consider four basic principles which I believe should govern our human resources policy in the 1970's:

- Government at all levels should seek to support and nurture, rather than limit, the diversity and freedom of choice which are hallmarks of the American system. The Federal Government in particular must work to guarantee an equal chance at the starting line by removing barriers which might impede an individual's opportunity to realize his or her full potential.

- The Federal Government should concentrate more on providing incentives and opening opportunities, and less on delivering direct services. Such programs of direct assistance to individuals as the Federal Government does conduct must provide evenhanded treatment for all, and must be carefully designed to ensure that the benefits are actually received by those who are intended to receive them.

- Rather than stifling initiative by trying to direct everything from Washington, Federal efforts should encourage State and local governments to make those decisions and supply those services for which their closeness to the people best qualifies them. In addition, the Federal Government should seek means of encouraging the private sector to address social problems, thereby utilizing the market mechanism to marshal resources behind clearly stated national objectives.

- Finally, all Federal policy must adhere to a strict standard of fiscal responsibility. Ballooning deficits which spent our economy into a new inflationary spiral or a recessionary tailspin in the name of social welfare would punish most cruelly the very people whom they seek to help. On the other hand, continued additions to a personal tax burden which has already doubled since 1950 would reduce incentives for excellence and would conflict directly with the goal of allowing each individual to keep as much as possible of what he or she earns to permit maximum personal freedom of choice.

The new post of Counsellor to the President for Human Resources, which I have recently created within the Executive Office of the President, will provide a much needed focal point for our efforts to see that these principles are carried out in all Federal activities aimed at meeting human needs, as well as in the Federal Government's complex relationships with State and local governments in this field. The coordinating function to be performed by this Counsellor should materially increase the unity, coherence, and effectiveness of our policies.

The following sections present a review of the progress we have made over the past four years in bringing each of the various human resources activities into line with these principles, and they outline our agenda for the years ahead.

Health

I am committed to removing financial barriers that would limit access to quality medical care for all American families. To that end, we have nearly doubled Federal outlays for health since the beginning of this Administration. Next year, they will exceed $30 billion.

Nearly 60 percent of these funds will go to finance health care for older Americans, the disabled, and the poor, through Medicare and Medicaid.

But we have taken significant steps to meet other priority needs as well. In the last four years, funding for cancer and heart and lung disease research has more than doubled; it will amount to more than three-quarters of a billion dollars in 1974.

We have supported reform of the health care delivery system and have proposed legislation to assist in the development of health maintenance organizations on a demonstration basis. We have increased funds for programs which help prevent illness, such as those which help carry out our pure food and drug laws and those which promote consumer safety.

We have declared total war on the epidemic problem of drug abuse—and we are winning that war. We have come a long way toward our goal of creating sufficient treatment services so that any addict desiring treatment can obtain it. We are also making substantial investments in research to develop innovative treatment approaches to drug abuse. I will report in greater detail on our anti-drug effort in a later section of this year's State of the Union message.

Strong measures have been taken to ensure that health care costs do not contribute to inflation and price people out of the care they need. The rate of increase in physicians' fees was cut by two-thirds last year alone, and hospital price rises have also been slowed. To build on these gains, controls on the health services industry have been retained and will be strengthened under Phase III of the Economic Stabilization Program.

A major goal of this Administration has been to develop an insurance system which can guarantee adequate financing of health care for every American family. The 92nd Congress failed to act upon my 1971 proposal to accomplish this goal, and now the need for legislation has grown still more pressing. *I shall once again submit to the Congress legislation to help meet the Nation's health insurance needs.*

Federal health policy should seek to safeguard this country's pluralistic health care system and to build on its strengths, minimizing reliance on Government-run arrangements. We must recognize appropriate limits to the Federal role, and we must see that every health care dollar is spent as effectively as possible.

This means discontinuing federally funded health programs which have served their purpose, or which have proved ineffective, or which involve functions more suitably performed by State and local government or the private sector.

The Hill-Burton hospital grants program, for example, can no longer be justified on the basis of the shortage of hospital facilities which prompted its creation in 1946. That shortage has given way to a surplus—so that to continue this program would only add to the Nation's excess of hospital beds and lead to higher charges to patients. It should be terminated.

We are also proposing to phase out the community mental health center demonstration program while providing funding for commitments to existing arrangements extending up to eight years. This program has helped to build and establish some 500 such centers, which have demonstrated new ways to deliver mental health services at the community level.

Regional Medical Programs likewise can now be discontinued. The planning function they have performed can better be conducted by comprehensive State planning efforts. A second function of these programs, the continuing education of physicians who are already licensed, is an inappropriate burden for Federal taxpayers to bear.

Education

1973 must be a year of decisive action to restructure Federal aid programs for education. Our goal is to provide continued Federal financial support for our schools while expanding State and local control over basic educational decisions.

I shall again ask the Congress to establish a new program of Education Revenue Sharing. This program would replace the complex and inefficient tangle of approximately 30 separate programs for elementary and secondary education with a single flexible authority for use in a few broad areas such as compensatory education for the disadvantaged, education for the handicapped, vocational education, needed assistance in federally affected areas, and supporting services.

Education Revenue Sharing would enlarge the opportunities for State and local decision-makers to tailor programs and resources to meet the specific educational needs of their own localities. It would mean less red tape, less paper work, and greater freedom for those at the local level to do what they think is best for their schools—not what someone in Washington tells them is best.

It would help to strengthen the principle of diversity and freedom in education that is as old as America itself, and would give educators a chance to create fresher, more individual approaches to the educational challenges of the Seventies. At the same time, it would affirm and further the national interest in promoting equal educational opportunities for economically disadvantaged children.

If there is any one area of human activity where decisions are best made at the local level by the people who know local conditions and local needs, it is in the field of primary and secondary education. I urge the Congress to join me in making this year, the third in which Education Revenue Sharing has been on the legislative agenda, the year when this much needed reform becomes law.

The time has also come to redefine the Federal role in higher education, by replacing categorical support programs for institutions with substantially increased funds for student assistance. *My budget proposals have already outlined a plan to channel much more of our higher education support through students themselves, including a new grant program which would increase funds provided to $948 million and the number assisted to over 1,500,000 people—almost a five-fold increase over the current academic year.*

These proposals would help to ensure for the first time that no qualified student seeking postsecondary education would be barred from attaining it by a lack of funds—and they would at the same time reinforce the spirit of competition among institutions that has made American higher education strong. I urge their prompt enactment.

As we work to eliminate the unnecessary bureaucratic constraints currently hampering Federal education aid, we will also be devoting more attention to educational research and development through the new National Institute of Education.

Funding for NIE will increase by almost 50 percent in fiscal year 1974, reaching $162 million.

Finally, in order to enhance the diversity provided by our mixed educational system of public and private schools, I will propose to the Congress legislation to provide a tax credit for tuition payments made by parents of children who attend non-public elementary and secondary schools.

Manpower

The Federal manpower program is a vital part of our total effort to conserve and develop our human resources.

Up to the present time, however, the "manpower program" has been not a unified effort, but a collection of separate categorical activities, many of them overlapping. These activities now include such programs as Manpower Development and Training Act Institutional Training programs, on-the-job training, Neighborhood Youth Corps, Public Service Careers, Operation Mainstream, and the Concentrated Employment Program. The net effect of several such programs operating in a single city seldom amounts to a coherent strategy for meeting the needs of people in that community.

While many well-run local programs are more than worth what they cost, many other individual projects are largely ineffective—and their failure wastes money which could be used to bolster the solid accomplishments of the rest.

Manpower programs ought to offer golden "second chances" for the less fortunate to acquire the skills and work habits which will help them become self-supporting, fully productive citizens. But as presently organized and managed, these second chance opportunities too often become just another dead-end exercise in frustration, rather than a genuine entree into a good job.

I believe that the answer to much of this problem lies in our program of Manpower Revenue Sharing—uniting several previously fragmented manpower activities under a single umbrella and then giving most of the responsibility for running this effort to those governments which are closest to the working men and women who need assistance. *In the next 16 months, administrative measures will be taken to institute this needed reform of the manpower system within the present legal framework.*

Manpower Revenue Sharing assistance will be freed from unnecessary Federal constraints, and aimed at developing jobs, equipping unemployed workers with useful work skills, and moving trainees into regular employment.

Welfare

With the failure of the past two Congresses to enact my proposals for fundamental reform of the Nation's public assistance system, that system remains as I described it in a message last year—"a crazy quilt of injustice and contradiction that has developed in bits and pieces over the years."

The major existing program, Aid to Families with Dependent Children (AFDC), is as inequitable, inefficient, and inadequate as ever.

- The administration of this program is unacceptably loose. The latest national data indicate that in round numbers, one of every 20 persons on the AFDC rolls is totally ineligible for welfare; 3 more are paid more benefits than they are entitled to; and another is underpaid. About one-quarter of AFDC recipients, in other words, are receiving improper payments.

- Complex program requirements and administrative red tape at the Federal and State levels have created bureaucracies that are difficult to manage.

- Inconsistent and unclear definitions of need have diluted resources that should be targeted on those who need help most.

- Misguided incentives have discouraged employable persons from work and induced fathers to leave home so that their families can qualify for welfare.

After several years of skyrocketing increases, however, outlays for this program have begun to level off. This results from the strong resurgence of our economy and expansion of the job market, along with some management improvements in the AFDC program and strengthened work requirements which were introduced into the program last year.

Since the legislative outlook seems to preclude passage of an overall structural reform bill in the immediate future, I have directed that vigorous steps be taken to strengthen the management of AFDC through administrative measures and legislative proposals.

Under these reforms, Federal impediments to efficient State administration of the current AFDC system will be removed wherever possible. Changes will be proposed to reduce the complexities of current eligibility and payment processes. Work will continue to be required of all those who can reasonably be considered available for employment, while Federal funds to help welfare recipients acquire needed job skills will increase.

One thing is certain: the welfare mess cannot be permitted to continue. A system which penalizes a person for going to work and rewards a person for going on welfare is totally alien to the American tradition of self-reliance and self-respect. That is why welfare reform has been and will continue to be one of our major goals; and we will work diligently with the Congress in developing ways to achieve it.

Nutrition

During the past four years, Federal outlays for food assistance have increased more than three-fold. Food stamp and food distribution programs for needy families have been extended to virtually every community in the country. More than 15 million persons are now receiving food stamps or distributed foods, more than double the 1969 total. More than 8 million schoolchildren are now being provided with free or reduced-price lunches—up from only 3 million in 1969.

We have made great strides toward banishing hunger and malnutrition from American life—and we shall continue building on that progress until the job is done.

Older Americans

One measure of the Nation's devotion to our older citizens is the fact that programs benefitting them—including Social Security and a wide range of other activities—now account for nearly one-fourth of the entire Federal budget.

Social Security benefits levels have been increased 51 percent in the last four years—the most rapid increase in history. Under new legislation which I initially proposed, benefits have also become inflation-proof, increasing automatically as the cost of living increases.

Over 1½ million older Americans or their dependents can now receive higher Social Security benefits while continuing to work. Nearly 4 million widows and widowers are also starting to receive larger benefits—$1 billion in additional income in the next fiscal year. And millions of older Americans will be helped by the new Supplemental Security Income program which establishes a Federal income floor for the aging, blind, and disabled poor.

Nevertheless, we are confronted with a major item of unfinished business. Approximately two-thirds of the twenty million persons who are 65 and over own their own homes. A disproportionate amount of their fixed income must now be used for property taxes. *I will submit to the Congress recommendations for alleviating the often crushing burdens which property taxes place upon many older Americans.*

I also ask the cooperation of the Congress in passing my 1974 budget request for $200 million to fund the programs of the Administration on Aging—a funding level more than four times that appropriated for AoA programs in fiscal year 1972. Half of this amount will be devoted to nutrition projects for the elderly, with the remainder going to assist States and localities in developing comprehensive service programs for older Americans.

In 1973, we shall continue to carry out the commitment I made in 1971 at the White House Conference on Aging: to help make the last days of our older Americans their best days.

Economic Opportunity

No one who started life in a family at the bottom of the income scale, as I did and as many Members of the Congress did, can ever forget how that condition felt, or ever turn his back on an opportunity to help alleviate it in the lives of others.

We in the Federal Government have such an opportunity to help combat poverty. Our commitment to this fight has grown steadily during the past decade, without regard to which party happened to be in power, from under $8 billion in total Federal anti-poverty expenditures in 1964 to more than $30 billion in my proposed budget for 1974.

And we have moved steadily closer to the goal of a society in which all our citizens, regardless of economic status, will have both the resources and the opportunity to fully control their own destinies.

At the beginning of this period, when Government found itself unprepared to respond to the sharp new national awareness of the plight of the disadvantaged, creation of an institutional structure separate from the regular machinery of Government and specifically charged with helping the poor seemed a wise first step to take. Thus the Office of Economic Opportunity was brought into being in 1964.

A wide range of useful anti-poverty programs has been conceived and put into operation over the years by the Office of Economic Opportunity. Some programs which got their start within OEO have been moved out into the operating departments and agencies of the Government when they matured, and they are thriving there. VISTA, for example, became part of ACTION in 1971, and Head Start was integrated with other activities focused on the first five years of life under HEW's Office of Child Development. OEO's other programs have now developed to a point where they can be similarly integrated.

Accordingly, in keeping with my determination to make every dollar devoted to human resources programs return 100 cents worth of real benefits to the people who most need those benefits, I have decided that most of the anti-poverty activities now conducted by the Office of Economic Opportunity should be delegated or transferred into the Cabinet departments relating to their respective fields of activity. Adhering strictly to statutory procedures, and requesting Congressional approval whenever necessary, I shall take action to effect this change.

This reorganization will increase the efficiency of the various programs by grouping them with other functionally related Federal efforts and by minimizing the overhead costs which in the past have diverted too much money from human needs into staff payrolls and administrative expenses. Funding for the transferred activities will stay level, or in many cases will even increase.

The only major OEO program for which termination of Federal funding is recommended in my budget is Community Action. New funding for Community Action activities in fiscal year 1974 will be at the discretion of local communities.

After more than 7 years of existence, Community Action has had an adequate opportunity to demonstrate its value within the communities it serves, and to build locally based agencies. OEO has taken steps to help Community Action agencies put down local roots through a program of incentives and training, and has incorporated the basic community action concept—participation in programs by the people whom the programs seek to serve—into all Federal anti-poverty activities. Further Federal spending on behalf of this concept, beyond the $2.8 billion which has been spent on it since 1965, no longer seems necessary or desirable.

Legal Services

One other economic opportunity effort deserving special mention is the Legal Services Program. Notwithstanding some abuses, legal services has done much in its seven-year history to breathe new life into the cherished concept of equal justice for all by providing access to quality legal representation for millions of Americans who would otherwise have been denied it for want of funds.

The time has now come to institutionalize legal services as a permanent, responsible, and responsive component of the American system of justice.

I shall soon propose legislation to the Congress to form a legal services corporation so constituted as to permit its attorneys to practice according to the highest professional standards, provided with safeguards against politicization of its activities, and held accountable to the people through appropriate monitoring and evaluation procedures.

Civil Rights

Protecting the civil rights of every American is one of my firmest commitments as President. No citizen should be denied equal justice and equal opportunity in our society because of race, color, sex, religion, or national origin.

This Administration has steadily increased the Federal financial commitment in this field. Outlays for civil rights and equal opportunity in 1974 will pass $3 billion—3½ times what they were when we took office.

We have worked hard—and with good results—to end de jure school segregation, to promote equal job opportunity, to combat housing discrimination, to foster minority business enterprise, to uphold voting rights, to assist minority higher education, to meet minority health problems like sickle cell anemia, and to make progress on many other fronts.

Now that equal opportunity is clearly written into the statute books, the next and in many ways more difficult step involves moving from abstract legal rights to concrete economic opportunities. We must ensure real social mobility—the freedom of all Americans to make their own choices and to go as far and as high as their abilities will take them. Legislation and court decisions play a major part in establishing that freedom. But community attitudes, government programs, and the vigor of the economic system all play large parts as well.

I believe that we have made progress, and we shall continue building on that progress *in the coming year:*

- The Department of Justice will expand its efforts to guarantee equal access to, and equal benefit from, Federal financial assistance programs.
- The Equal Employment Opportunity Commission will receive additional resources to carry out its expanded responsibilities.
- The Civil Service Commission will expand its monitoring of equal employment opportunities within the Federal Government.
- Efforts to assure that Federal contractors provide equal access to job opportunities will be expanded.
- The Small Business Administration will expand its loan program for minority business by nearly one-third.
- The Commission on Civil Rights will receive additional resources to carry out its newly granted responsibilities. Additionally, in the year ahead, we will continue to support ratification of the Equal Rights Amendment to the Constitution so that American women—not a minority group but a majority of the whole population—need never again be denied equal opportunity.

The American Indian

For Indian people the policy of this Administration will continue to be one of advancing their opportunities for self-determination, without termination of the special Federal relationship with recognized Indian tribes.

Just as it is essential to put more decision-making in the hands of State and local governments, I continue to believe that Indian tribal governments should assume greater responsibility for programs of the Bureau of Indian Affairs and the Department of Health, Education, and Welfare which operate on their reservations. *As I first proposed in 1970, I recommend that the Congress enact the necessary legislation to facilitate this take-over of responsibility. Also, I recommend that the 1953 termination resolution be repealed.* Meanwhile the new statutory provisions for Indian tribal governments under General Revenue Sharing will assist responsible tribal governments in allocating extra resources with greater flexibility.

I shall also propose new legislation to foster local Indian self-determination by developing an Interior Department program of bloc grants to Federally recognized tribes as a replacement for a number of existing economic and resource development programs. The primary purpose of these grants would be to provide tribal governments with funds which they could use at their own discretion to promote development of their reservations.

Indian tribal organizations and Indians seeking to enter business need easier access to loan and credit opportunities; I proposed in 1970 and will again propose legislation to accomplish this objective.

Because Indian rights to natural resources need better protection, I am again urging the Congress to create an Indian Trust Counsel Authority to guarantee that protection.

In the two and one-half years that Indians have been waiting for the Congress to enact the major legislation I have proposed, we have moved ahead administratively whenever possible. We have restored 21,000 acres of wrongfully acquired Government land to the Yakima Tribe. We have filed a precedent-setting suit in the Supreme Court to protect Indian water rights in Pyramid Lake. My fiscal year 1974 budget proposes total Federal outlays of $1.45 billion for Indian affairs, an increase of more than 15 percent over 1973.

To accelerate organizational reform, I have directed the Secretary of the Interior to transfer day to day operational activities of the Bureau of Indian Affairs out of Washington to its field offices. *And I am again asking the Congress to create a new Assistant Secretary position within the Interior Department to deal with Indian matters.*

Veterans

With the coming of peace, the Nation's inestimable debt to our veterans and their dependents will continue to command a high priority among the human resource efforts of this Administration.

During the past four years, I have twice signed legislation increasing the allowances for educational assistance to veterans. Nearly 2 million veterans are now in some form of training under the GI Bill for Vietnam-era veterans. Pension payments to veterans or their survivors who need income support have also been raised twice and the test of need has been greatly improved, including a more equitable formula for adjusting the VA pension rate when other sources of income, such as Social Security, are increased. The VA pension program now directly benefits over 2 million individuals.

Compensation payments for service related disabilities have been raised on two occasions, and more than 2 million veterans of all wars now receive this benefit. The service-disabled veteran deserves special concern. In addition to top-priority consideration in medical care, my budget calls for VA outlays to provide disabled Vietnam-era veterans with vocational rehabilitation, housing grants, and specially equipped automobiles to be nearly doubled in 1974 compared to their 1971 level. Disability compensation is also being intensively reviewed to ensure that disabled veterans will receive compensation payments which fully recognize their earnings impairment.

VA guaranteed home loans for veterans have risen by almost two-thirds since we took office. And high-priority job programs have decreased the unemployment rate among Vietnam-era veterans by almost one-third during the past year alone.

Dramatic progress has been made in the veterans medical care program. A high level of construction and modernization of VA medical facilities has been carried on. The total number of medical care personnel staffing VA facilities has increased by one-sixth since 1969. The total number of veterans treated—both in VA facilities and as outpatients—has risen to new highs. Beneficiaries treated as hospital inpatients will go over the million mark in fiscal 1974 for the first time. Outpatient visits will climb to almost 14,000,000—about twice the level of 1969.

Since 1969, there has also been a steady shortening of the average length of stay in VA hospitals, a highly desirable objective from every viewpoint. This means that VA hospitals have fewer patients in bed on an average day, with shorter waiting lists, even though the total number of patients treated has gone up.

Misunderstanding these statistics, some have sought to establish by law a numerical minimum average daily patient census in VA hospitals. But such a fixed daily census would represent a backward step: it would force a sharply increased length-of-stay—an effect that is medically, economically, and socially undesirable. It is far better that our veterans be restored to their families and jobs as rapidly as feasible, consistent with good medical care. A fixed patient census would tie the hands of those seeking to serve veterans' health needs; I urge the Congress not to enact such a requirement.

The Congress is now studying several bills involving the VA pension program and cemetery and burial benefits for veterans. I hope that the Congress will work to see that the veterans pension program is realistically structured and compatible with other major income maintenance programs. On the burial benefits question, I urge that legislative action be deferred until completion of a study currently being conducted by the Administrator of Veterans Affairs to determine the most equitable approach to improving burial and cemetery benefits for veterans. The Administrator's recommendations will be made available to the Congress in the near future.

Consumer Affairs

The self-reliance and resourcefulness of our people when they enter the marketplace as consumers, the generally high standard of ethics and social responsibility upheld by business and industry, and the restrained intervention of government at various levels as a vigorous but not heavy-handed referee of commerce—that combination of factors, in that order, has been largely responsible for confounding predictions that American capitalism would breed its own downfall in the 20th century. We must build on each of these strengths in our efforts to protect the rights of the consumer as well as the vigor of the free enterprise economy in the 1970's.

Early in 1971, after the Congress had failed to act on my "Buyer's Bill of Rights" proposal for a new Office of Consumer Affairs directly under the President, I established such an office by executive order. Under the direction of my Special Assistant for Consumer Affairs, OCA has helped to create a stronger consumer consciousness throughout the executive branch.

This office is now ready to integrate its operations more fully with the line departments of the Government, and has accordingly been transferred into the Department of Health, Education and Welfare—the logical base for an agency concerned with human well-being.

From this new base the Office of Consumer Affairs will continue its policy formation role and educational efforts, and will also take on additional responsibilities, including representing consumer interests in testimony before the Congress and acting as a general ombudsman for the individual consumer.

Voluntary Action

Many thousands of Americans already are volunteering their time to meet human needs in their communities—fighting disease, teaching children to read, working to solve local social problems. But now we must do more to tap the enormous reservoir of energy represented by millions of other potential citizen volunteers.

That is why three years ago I encouraged a number of our leading citizens to create the National Center for Voluntary Action to support private volunteer efforts; that is why two years ago I established the new ACTION agency to strengthen Federal volunteer programs.

We must now continue seeking new avenues of citizen service. As we turn from the concerns of war, may all Americans accept the challenge of peace by volunteering to help meet the needs of their communities—so that we can mobilize a new army of concerned, dedicated, able volunteers across the Nation.

Arts and Humanities

I know that many in the Congress share the concern I have often expressed that some Americans, particularly younger people, lost faith in their country during the 1960's. I believe this faith is now being reborn out of the knowledge that our country is moving toward an era of lasting peace in the world, toward a healthier environment, and toward a new era of progress and equality of opportunity for all our people.

But renewed faith in ourselves also arises from a deeper understanding of who we are, where we have come from, and where we are going—an understanding to which the arts and the humanities can make a great contribution.

Government has a limited but important function in encouraging the arts and the humanities—that of reinforcing local initiatives and helping key institutions to help themselves. With the approach of our Bicentennial, we have a special opportunity to draw on the enrichment and renewal which cultural activity can provide in our national life. With this in mind, my 1974 budget requests further expansion of the funds for the National Foundation on the Arts and the Humanities, to a new high of $168 million. I ask continued full support from the Congress for this funding.

Saying Yes

Carl Sandburg spoke volumes about this country's past and future in three simple words that became the title for one of his greatest poems: "The People, Yes."

America has risen to greatness because again and again when the chips were down, the American people have said yes—yes to the challenge of freedom, yes to the dare of progress, and yes to the hope of peace—even when defending the peace has meant paying the price of war.

America's greatness will endure in the future only if our institutions continually rededicate themselves to saying yes to the people—yes to human needs and aspirations, yes to democracy and the consent of the governed, yes to equal opportunity and unlimited horizons of achievement for every American.

1973 is a year full of opportunity for great advances on this front. After more than a decade of war, we have successfully completed one of the most unselfish missions ever undertaken by one nation in the defense of another. Now the coming of peace permits us to turn our attention more fully to the works of compassion, concern, and social betterment here at home.

The seriousness of my commitment to make the most of this opportunity is demonstrated by the record level of funding for human resource programs proposed in our new budget—$125 billion in all—nearly twice the amount that was being spent on such programs when I took office in 1969.

This is both a generous budget and a reform budget. The reforms it proposes will put muscle behind the generosity it intends. The overall effect of these reforms will be the elimination of programs that are wasteful so that we can concentrate on programs that work. They will make possible the continued growth of Federal efforts to meet human needs—while at the same time helping to prevent a runaway deficit that could lead to higher taxes, higher prices, and higher interest rates for all Americans.

The opportunity is ours, executive and legislative branches together, to lead America to a new standard of fairness, of freedom, and of vitality within our federal system. We can forge a new approach to human services in this country—an approach which will treat people as more than mere statistics—an approach which recognizes that problems like poverty and unemployment, health care and the costs of education are more than cold abstractions in a government file drawer.

We know how tough these problems are, because many of us grew up with them ourselves. But we also know that with the right kind of help and the right kind of spirit they can be overcome.

Let us give all our citizens the help they need. But let us remember that each of us also bears a basic obligation to help himself and to help our fellowman, and that no one else can assume that obligation for us—least of all the Federal Government.

If we shirk our individual responsibility, the American dream will never be more than a dream.

But if the people say yes to this challenge, if government says yes to the people—and if all of us in Washington say no to petty quarrels and partisanship and yes to our public trust—then we can truly bring that dream to life for all Americans in the new day of peace that is dawning.

Richard Nixon, 1973–1974

State of the Union Message to Congress on Community Development

March 8, 1973

Nixon's fifth of six written State of the Union addresses for 1973 focused on community development. The president's agenda included revenue-sharing for community development, creation of a federal department of community development, improved housing and transportation, and more effective preparation for disaster relief.

To the Congress of the United States:

Today, in this fifth report to the Congress on the State of the Union, I want to discuss the quality of life in our cities and towns and set forth new directions for community development in America.

Not long ago we became accustomed to the constant rhetorical drumbeat of the "crisis of our cities." Problems were multiplying so rapidly for our larger urban areas that some observers said our cities were doomed as centers of culture, of commerce, and of constructive change.

Many of these problems still persist, but I believe we have made sufficient progress in recent years that fears of doom are no longer justified.

What is needed today is calm reflection upon the nature of modern community life in the United States, a reassessment of the manner in which we are trying to solve our remaining problems, and a firm resolve to get on with the task.

America's communities are as diverse as our people themselves. They vary tremendously in size from massive cities to medium-sized urban and suburban areas, to small towns and rural communities.

Just as importantly, each of our communities has built up strong individual characteristics over the years, shaped by region, climate, economic influences, ethnic origins and local culture.

Of course, communities do share common needs and concerns. People in every community want adequate housing, transportation, and jobs, a clean environment, good health, education, recreation facilities, security from crime and fear, and other essential services. But local priorities differ; the intensity and order of local needs vary.

Clearly, no single, rigid scheme, imposed by the Federal Government from Washington, is capable of meeting the changing and varied needs of this diverse and dynamic Nation.

There is no "best" way, no magic, universal cure-all, that can be dispensed from hundreds or thousands of miles away.

What is good for New York City is not necessarily good for Chicago, or San Francisco, much less for smaller communities with entirely different economies, traditions and populations.

Too often in the past we have fallen into the trap of letting Washington make the final decisions for St. Louis, Detroit, Miami and our other cities. Sometimes the decisions were right, and programs have succeeded. Too often they were wrong, and we are still paying the price.

The time has come to recognize the errors of past Federal efforts to support community development and to move swiftly to correct them.

The results of past errors form a disturbing catalogue:

- They have distorted local priorities.
- They have spawned a massive glut of red tape.
- They have created an adversary climate between local communities and Washington which has often led to waste, delay and mutual frustration.
- They have contributed to a lack of confidence among our people in the ability of both local and national governments to solve problems and get results.
- They have led to the creation of too many complex and often competing Federal programs.
- Perhaps worst of all, they have undercut the will and the ability of local and State governments to take the initiative to mobilize their own energies and those of their citizens.

The Federal policy that will work best in the last third of this century is not one that tries to force all of our communities into a single restrictive mold. The Federal policy that will work best is one that helps people and their leaders in each community meet their own needs in the way they think best.

It is this policy which binds together the many aspects of our community development programs.

The Better Communities Act

In the near future, I will submit to the Congress the Better Communities Act to provide revenue sharing for community development. Beginning July 1, 1974, this act would provide $2.3 billion a year to communities to be spent as they desire to meet their community development needs. In the interim period before the legislation becomes effective, funds already available to the Department of Housing and Urban Development will be used to maintain and support community development.

The Better Communities Act is intended to replace inflexible and fragmented categorical grant-in-aid programs, and to reduce the excessive Federal control that has been so frustrating to local governments.

Rather than focusing and concentrating resources in a coordinated assault on a set of problems, the categorical system scatters these resources, and diminishes their impact upon the most needy. Excessive Federal influence also limits the variety and diversity of development programs. Local officials should be able to focus their time, their resources and their talents on meeting local needs and producing results, instead of trying to please Washington with an endless torrent of paperwork.

I first proposed such legislation in 1971, and although the Congress failed to enact it, significant support was expressed in both the Senate and the House. Since that time, members of my Administration have been consulting with Congressional leaders, mayors, Governors, other local officials and their representatives. Many constructive suggestions have been received and will be incorporated in my new legislative proposal. As a result, I believe the Better Communities Act will represent our best hope for the future of community development and will deserve rapid approval by the Congress.

Among the most significant features of the Better Communities Act are these:

- Hold-Harmless Provision: The flow of money to cities and urban counties is to be based on a formula reflecting community needs, as determined by objective standards. In the years immediately following enactment, funds would be used to assure that no city receives less money for community development than it has received under the categorical grant programs.

- Assistance for Smaller Communities: Funding is also to be provided for our smaller communities, recognizing the vital importance of small towns and rural communities to the future of the Nation.

- The Role of State Government: State governments have always played an important part in meeting the community development needs of their communities. The Act will recognize this role.

- Local Decision Making: While each of the activities now supported by categorical grants may be continued, it would be up to local leaders to determine how that money will be spent.

- Minimizing Red Tape: Recipients would be required to show the Federal Government only that they are complying with Federal statutes in the way they are spending their revenue sharing money.
- Elimination of Matching: Shared revenues would not have to be matched by local funds.
- Protection for Minorities: Under no circumstances could funds provided under the Better Communities Act be used for purposes that would violate the civil rights of any person.

A Department Of Community Development

One of the most serious deficiencies in the effort of the Federal Government to assist in community development has been the fragmentation and scattering of Federal programs among a variety of departments and agencies. All too often State or local officials seeking help for a particular project must shuttle back and forth from one Federal office to another, wasting precious time and resources in a bureaucratic wild goose chase.

In order to coordinate our community development activities more effectively, I proposed nearly two years ago that we create a Department of Community Development which would pull under one roof various programs now in the Departments of Housing and Urban Development, Transportation, Agriculture, and other agencies.

After extensive hearings on this proposal, the Committee on Government Operations of the House of Representatives reached this conclusion:

"The Department of Community Development will be a constructive center in the Federal Government for assistance to communities, large and small. It will facilitate rational planning, orderly growth, and the effective employment of resources to build viable communities throughout the United States. It will help to strengthen the physical and institutional bases for cooperative action by Federal, State and local governments."

This Administration fully agrees, of course, and will continue to work with the Congress for the prompt creation of a Department of Community Development.

In the interim, I recently appointed a Presidential Counsellor on Community Development who will coordinate community development programs and policies in the executive branch. But only when the Congress approves the basic departmental reorganization proposed by the Administration can our efforts to eliminate waste, confusion and duplication, and to promote community betterment more efficiently, be fully effective.

The Responsive Governments Act

For nearly 20 years, the Federal Government has provided assistance to State and local governments in order to strengthen their planning and management capabilities.

This aid, provided under the Comprehensive Planning Assistance Program, has always been helpful, but the program itself has several major flaws. It has tended, for instance, to stress one aspect of public administration—planning—without adequately recognizing other essential features such as budgeting, management, personnel administration, and information-gathering. Planning has often been irrelevant to the problems and the actual decisions. State and local governments have also found it difficult to coordinate their planning because of the fragmented way in which funds have been sent from Washington.

This Administration proposed new planning and management legislation to the 92nd Congress, but it was not approved. In the meantime, we took what steps we could to improve the existing program. Some progress has been made, but corrective legislation is still needed.

I shall therefore propose that the 93rd Congress enact a new Responsive Governments Act. I shall also propose that we provide $110 million for this act in fiscal year 1974—almost one-fifth of the entire amount that has been spent under the present law in the last two decades.

This Responsive Governments Act would assist State and local governments in meeting several important goals:

- Developing reliable information on their problems and opportunities;
- Developing and analyzing alternative policies and programs;
- Managing the programs;
  - And evaluating the results, so that appropriate adjustments can be made.

The ability to plan and manage is vital to effective government. It will be even more important to State and local governments as they are freed from the restraints of narrow categorical Federal programs and must decide how to spend revenue sharing funds. Thus the Responsive Governments Act is a vitally necessary companion piece to the Better Communities Act.

Housing

This Administration is firmly committed to the goal first set forth for America in the 1949 Housing Act: "a decent home and a suitable living environment for every American family." While we believe that some of our housing programs have failed and should be replaced, we should never waiver in our commitment.

During the past four years, the Federal Government has provided housing assistance to an additional 1.5 million American families of low and moderate income. This represents more housing assistance than the total provided by the Federal Government during the entire 34-year history of our national housing program preceding this Administration.

In addition, a healthy, vigorous, private housing industry has provided 6 million new unsubsidized units of housing for Americans in the last four years. Housing starts for each of the last three years have reached record high levels—levels, in fact, that are more than double the average for the preceding 21 years.

Most importantly, the percentage of Americans living in substandard housing has dropped dramatically from 46 percent in 1940 to 37 percent in 1950 to 18 percent in 1960 to 8 percent in 1970. Americans today are better housed than ever before in our history.

At the same time, however, there has been mounting evidence of basic defects in some of our housing programs. It is now clear that all too frequently the needy have not been the primary beneficiaries of these programs; that the programs have been riddled with inequities; and that the cost for each unit of subsidized housing produced under these programs has been too high. In short, we shall be making far more progress than we have been and we should now move to place our housing policies on a much firmer foundation.

That is why we suspended new activity under Federal subsidized housing programs effective January 5th of this year. I would emphasize, however, that commitments that were made under these programs prior to their suspension will be honored. This will mean that approximately 300,000 units of new subsidized housing will be started in 1973.

In pursuing our goal of decent homes for all Americans, we know that better means are needed—that the old and wasteful programs, programs which have already obligated the taxpayer to payments of between $63 billion and $95 billion during the next 40 years, are not the answer.

One of my highest domestic priorities this year will be the development of new policies that will provide aid to genuinely needy families and eliminate waste.

A major housing study is now underway within the Government, under the direction of my Counsellor for Community Development. Within the next six months, I intend to submit to the Congress my policy recommendations in this field, based upon the results of that study.

Transportation

To thrive, a community must provide for the efficient movement of its people and its products. Yet in recent years, the growing separation of the city from its suburbs and changing employment patterns have made transportation more of a community problem than a community asset. To improve community development we must meet the challenge of transportation planning and provide more flexible means for communities to meet their transportation needs.

Without better transportation, our communities will either stagnate or choke.

Four years ago we initiated programs to renew and redirect our transportation systems. We took action to expand the capacity of our airways, to preserve and improve intercity rail passenger service, to continue the Nation's highway program with greater emphasis on safety, and to bring needed progress to our surface public transportation. The Federal commitment has been substantial:

- The enlarged Airport Development Aid Program established under the Airport-Airways Development Act of 1970 has quadrupled Federal assistance to airports to $295 million per year.

- Under the Rail Passenger Service Act of 1970 we have begun to rejuvenate rail service as part of a balanced transportation system.

- From 1970 through 1974 we will have invested some $23 billion in highways. In 1972 alone we committed $3.3 billion to the Interstate system, which is now 80 percent complete. In that same year, $870 million was designated for primary and secondary roads. Equally important, we have emphasized safety on our highways, both in their design and use.

- We have progressively increased the levels of Federal funding for transportation research, development, and demonstration projects. This support focuses on new transportation technology. It is designed to encourage private industry to join aggressively in the search for better transportation.

- Concurrent with our programs to improve transportation between our cities, we have undertaken programs to develop free flowing corridors for people and commerce within our cities.

- Since 1970, when I proposed and the Congress passed the Urban Mass Transportation Assistance Act, we have committed more than 2 billion Federal dollars to preserve and upgrade public transportation. Nationally, urban public transportation has become a billion-dollar-a-year Federal program.

- Over the past four years, Federal dollars have helped 60 American cities to help those who depend on public systems for transportation to jobs, hospitals, shops and recreational centers. Now we must deal even more aggressively with community development challenges in transportation by building on the strong foundations we have laid.

Nothing can do more to lift the face of our cities, and the spirit of our city dwellers, than truly adequate systems of modern transportation. With the best highway system in the world, and with 75 percent of our people owning and operating automobiles, we have more transportation assets per capita than any other people on earth. Yet the commuter who uses a two ton vehicle to transport only himself to and from work each day is not making the most efficient use of our transportation system and is himself contributing to our transportation and environmental problems.

Good public transportation is essential not only to assure adequate transportation for all citizens, but to forward the common goal of less congested, cleaner and safer communities. As I pointed out a few weeks ago in my message on the environment and natural resources, effective mass transit systems that relieve urban congestion will also reduce pollution and the waste of our limited energy resources.

As we build such systems, we must be aware of the two special challenges in coordinating the needs of the inner city and the suburb and in alleviating potential disruptions which new transportation systems can bring to neighborhood life.

To further these efforts I again continue to urge Congress to permit a portion of the Highway Trust Fund to be used in a more flexible fashion, thus allowing mass transit capital investments where communities so desire.

I recommend that the Congress authorize the expenditure by State and local governments of $3.65 billion over the next three years from the Highway Trust Fund for urban transportation needs, including capital improvements for bus and rapid rail systems. I also recommend continuing the rural highway program at the $1 billion a year level, and providing ample resources to advance the Interstate system as it approaches its 1980 funding completion date. This legislation can meet old needs while at the same time addressing new ones.

Some communities now feel unduly obligated to spend Federal monies on controversial Interstate highway segments in urban areas. I urge the Congress to allow States and localities to transfer such funds to the construction of other Federal-aid highways and mass transit capital improvements. In this way, we can help resolve controversies which have slowed work on a number of Interstate links in urban areas.

It is very important to recognize that this proposal does not represent an arbitrary Federal shift of funds from highways to transit. What it does stress is the right of local governments to choose the best solutions for their urban transportation problems.

This year, in a companion measure to our Federal Highway Bill, I am also proposing that funding for mass transit capital grants be increased by $3 billion, bringing the obligational authority for the mass transit program to $6.1 billion. This provision would maintain a forward looking mass transit program through at least 1977. I am also asking the Congress to amend the Urban Mass Transportation Assistance Act, increasing the Federal share for urban mass transit capital grant assistance programs to 70 percent and thereby achieving parity with Federal aid for urban and rural road building projects.

Rural Development

Community Development is sometimes thought of primarily in terms of urban areas. However, as this Administration has often pointed out—and will continue to emphasize—no element of our national well-being is more important than the health and vitality of our rural communities. Thus, in pursuing a policy of balanced development for our community life, we must always keep the needs of rural America clearly in sight.

Twice in the last two years, I have recommended legislation which would provide new revenues for rural development. Under my latest proposal, loans and guarantees would have been made for projects selected and prepared by the States.

While the 92nd Congress did not enact either of these proposals, it did enact the Rural Development Act of 1972, establishing additional lending authority for rural needs. Like the Administration's proposals, this lending authority provides for insured loans and guaranteed loans which allow maximum participation of the private sector.

Several new programs are proposed to be funded under the Rural Development Act. One is a $200 million loan program to assist communities with a population of less than 50,000 in developing commercial and industrial facilities. A previously existing loan program has been increased by $100 million—to a total of $445 million—and, under the new law, can now be used to construct a wide variety of essential community facilities. In addition, grants and other programs under the act will be funded at a level of $33 million.

This Administration will implement the Rural Development Act in a manner consistent with the revenue sharing concept, allowing major project selections and priority decisions to be made by the State and local governments whenever possible. It is our intent, after fully evaluating the effectiveness of this approach, to seek whatever additional legislation may be needed.

Disaster Assistance

To a community suffering the ravages of a natural disaster, nothing is more important than prompt and effective relief assistance. As our population grows and spreads, each storm, earthquake, drought or freeze affects larger numbers of people.

During the past four years, we have tried to reduce personal injury, deaths, and property damage by emphasizing adequate preventive measures. During the same period, however, I have had to declare III major disasters in 39 States and three Territories. This past year alone set a tragic record for major disaster activity, as I had to declare 48 major disasters—43 caused by storms and floodings. There were a number of especially devastating disaster emergencies in this period: the flooding in Buffalo

Creek, West Virginia; flash flood in Rapid City, South Dakota; and, of course, Tropical Storm Agnes which rampaged through the eastern United States. Agnes alone caused 118 deaths and some $3 billion in property damage.

Until now, disaster relief efforts have involved a number of different agencies and have been coordinated by the Executive Office of the President. The experience of the past few years has demonstrated that:

- We are not doing nearly enough to prepare in advance for disasters.
- States, local governments and private individuals should assume a larger role in preparing for disasters, and in relieving the damage after they have occurred.
- Responsibility for relief is presently too fragmented among too many authorities.
- At the Federal level, disaster relief should be managed by a single agency.

I intend to make 1973 a turning point in the quality of governmental response to natural disasters.

To achieve this goal, I have already proposed Reorganization Plan Number I of 1973, which is now before the Congress. It calls for the delegation of all responsibility for coordinating disaster relief to the Secretary of Housing and Urban Development, who is also my Counsellor for Community Development. This transfer of operations would take place at the beginning of the new fiscal year and would be carried out in such a way that the effective relations which now exist with State disaster officials would in no way be harmed, while a new sense of unity and mobility at the Federal level would be fostered.

If the Congress enacts my proposal for a new Department of Community Development, that new department would be responsible for directing all Federal disaster activities, including those of several other agencies which perform disaster roles.

In addition to the improvements I have proposed in Reorganization Plan Number 1, I will shortly submit a new Disaster Assistance Act to the Congress. This new act is designed to improve the delivery of Federal assistance, to provide a more equitable basis for financing individual property losses, and to forge a more balanced partnership for meeting disasters head-on—a partnership not only among governments at all levels but also between governments and private citizens.

Under these proposals, each level of government would accept responsibility for those things it can do best. While the Federal Government would continue to assist with financing, State and local governments would have far more latitude and responsibility in the use of those funds. They would also be encouraged to assert stronger leadership in efforts to minimize the damage of future disasters.

For homeowners, farmers and businessmen who have suffered disaster losses, the Federal Government would continue to provide direct assistance.

I will also recommend to the Congress an expansion of the national flood insurance program to allow participation by more communities in flood-prone areas and to increase the limits of coverage.

Conclusion

As reflected by the proposals set forth here, I believe that we must strike out on broad, new paths of community development in America.

During the last few years, we have taken genuine, measurable strides toward better communities.

All of this is good; it is not good enough. It is clear that we can and should be accomplishing more in the field of community development. There are too many programs that have been tried and found wanting. There are too many programs that strengthen the bureaucracy in Washington but sap the strength of our State and local governments.

People today want to have a real say in the way their communities are run. They want to feel that, once again, they can play a significant role in shaping the kind of world their children will inherit. And they expect their institutions to respond to their needs and aspirations.

That feeling will never flourish if the Federal Government, however vast its financial resources and however good its intentions, tries to direct the pattern of our lives. That feeling cannot be manufactured in Washington, it must come from within.

But the Federal Government can and should eliminate some of the barriers that have impeded the development of that feeling by returning resources and initiatives to the people and their locally elected leaders. It is in that spirit that I urge the 93rd Congress to give favorable consideration to my proposals for community development.

Richard Nixon, 1973–1974

State of the Union Message to Congress on Law Enforcement and Drug Abuse Prevention
March 14, 1973

Nixon's last of six written State of the Union addresses for 1973 dealt with law enforcement and drug abuse. Nixon touted his administration's record on crime control, stating that it "marked a clear departure" from the past. His recommendations for further action included a revision of federal criminal laws, reinstitution of the death penalty for certain crimes, and tougher law enforcement efforts against heroin traffickers.

To the Congress of the United States:

This sixth message to the Congress on the State of the Union concerns our Federal system of criminal justice. It discusses both the progress we have made in improving that system and the additional steps we must take to consolidate our accomplishments and to further our efforts to achieve a safe, just, and law-abiding society.

In the period from 1960 to 1968 serious crime in the United States increased by 122 percent according to the FBI's Uniform Crime Index. The rate of increase accelerated each year until it reached a peak of 17 percent in 1968.

In 1968 one major public opinion poll showed that Americans considered lawlessness to be the top domestic problem facing the Nation. Another poll showed that four out of five Americans believed that "Law and order has broken down in this country." There was a very real fear that crime and violence were becoming a threat to the stability of our society.

The decade of the 1960s was characterized in many quarters by a growing sense of permissiveness in America—as well intentioned as it was poorly reasoned—in which many people were reluctant to take the steps necessary to control crime. It is no coincidence that within a few years' time, America experienced a crime wave that threatened to become uncontrollable.

This Administration came to office in 1969 with the conviction that the integrity of our free institutions demanded stronger and firmer crime control. I promised that the wave of crime would not be the wave of the future. An all-out attack was mounted against crime in the United States.

- The manpower of Federal enforcement and prosecution agencies was increased.
- New legislation was proposed and passed by the Congress to put teeth into Federal enforcement efforts against organized crime, drug trafficking, and crime in the District of Columbia.
- Federal financial aid to State and local criminal justice systems—a forerunner of revenue sharing—was greatly expanded through Administration budgeting and Congressional appropriations, reaching a total of $1.5 billion in the three fiscal years from 1970 through 1972.

These steps marked a clear departure from the philosophy which had come to dominate Federal crime fighting efforts, and which had brought America to record-breaking levels of lawlessness. Slowly, we began to bring America back. The effort has been long, slow, and difficult. In spite of the difficulties, we have made dramatic progress.

In the last four years the Department of Justice has obtained convictions against more than 2500 organized crime figures, including a number of bosses and underbosses in major cities across the country. The pressure on the underworld is building constantly.

Today, the capital of the United States no longer bears the stigma of also being the Nation's crime capital. As a result of decisive reforms in the criminal justice system the serious crime rate has been cut in half in Washington, D.C. From a peak rate of more than 200 serious crimes per day reached during one month in 1969, the figure has been cut by more than half to 93 per day for the latest month of record in 1973. Felony prosecutions have increased from 2100 to 3800, and the time between arrest and trial for felonies has fallen from ten months to less than two.

Because of the combined efforts of Federal, State, and local agencies, the wave of serious crime in the United States is being brought under control. Latest figures from the FBI's Uniform Crime Index show that serious crime is increasing at the rate of only one percent a year—the lowest recorded rate since 1960. A majority of cities with over 100,000 population have an actual reduction in crime.

These statistics and these indices suggest that our anti-crime program is on the right track. They suggest that we are taking the right measures. They prove that the only way to attack crime in America is the way crime attacks our people—without pity. Our program is based on this philosophy, and it is working.

Now we intend to maintain the momentum we have developed by taking additional steps to further improve law enforcement and to further protect the people of the United States.

Law Enforcement Special Revenue Sharing

Most crime in America does not fall under Federal jurisdiction. Those who serve in the front lines of the battle against crime are the State and local law enforcement authorities. State and local police are supported in turn by many other elements of the criminal justice system, including prosecuting and defending attorneys, judges, and probation and corrections officers. All these elements need assistance and some need dramatic reform, especially the prison systems.

While the Federal Government does not have full jurisdiction in the field of criminal law enforcement, it does have a broad, constitutional responsibility to insure domestic tranquility. I intend to meet that responsibility.

At my direction, the Law Enforcement Assistance Administration (LEAA) has greatly expanded its efforts to aid in the improvement of State and local criminal justice systems. In the last three years of the previous Administration, Federal grants to State and local law enforcement authorities amounted to only $22 million. In the first three years of my Administration, this same assistance totaled more than $1.5 billion—more than 67 times as much. I consider this money to be an investment in justice and safety on our streets, an investment which has been yielding encouraging dividends.

But the job has not been completed. We must now act further to improve the Federal role in the granting of aid for criminal justice. Such improvement can come with the adoption of Special Revenue Sharing for law enforcement.

I believe the transition to Special Revenue Sharing for law enforcement will be a relatively easy one. Since its inception, the LEAA has given block grants which allow State and local authorities somewhat greater discretion than does the old-fashioned categorical grant system. But States and localities still lack both the flexibility and the clear authority they need in spending Federal monies to meet their law enforcement challenges.

Under my proposed legislation, block grants, technical assistance grants, manpower development grants, and aid for correctional institutions would be combined into one $680 million Special Revenue Sharing fund which would be distributed to States and local governments on a formula basis. This money could be used for improving any area of State and local criminal justice systems.

I have repeatedly expressed my conviction that decisions affecting those at State and local levels should be made to the fullest possible extent at State and local levels. This is the guiding principle behind revenue sharing. Experience has demonstrated the validity of this approach and I urge that it now be fully applied to the field of law enforcement and criminal justice.

The Criminal Code Reform Act

The Federal criminal laws of the United States date back to 1790 and are based on statutes then pertinent to effective law enforcement. With the passage of new criminal laws, with the unfolding of new court decisions interpreting those laws, and with the development and growth of our Nation, many of the concepts still reflected in our criminal laws have become inadequate, clumsy, or outmoded.

In 1966, the Congress established the National Commission on Reform of the Federal Criminal Laws to analyze and evaluate the criminal Code. The Commission's final report of January 7, 1971, has been studied and further refined by the Department of Justice, working with the Congress. In some areas this Administration has substantial disagreements with the Commission's recommendations.

But we agree fully with the almost universal recognition that modification of the Code is not merely desirable but absolutely imperative.

Accordingly, I will soon submit to the Congress the Criminal Code Reform Act aimed at a comprehensive revision of existing Federal criminal laws. This act will provide a rational, integrated code of Federal criminal law that is workable and responsive to the demands of a modem Nation.

The act is divided into three parts:

1—general provisions and principles,

2—definitions of Federal offenses, and

3—provisions for sentencing.

Part 1 of the Code establishes general provisions and principles regarding such matters as Federal criminal jurisdiction, culpability, complicity, and legal defenses, and contains a number of significant innovations. Foremost among these is a more effective test for establishing Federal criminal jurisdiction. Those circumstances giving rise to Federal jurisdiction are clearly delineated in the proposed new Code and the extent of jurisdiction is clearly defined.

I am emphatically opposed to encroachment by Federal authorities on State sovereignty, by unnecessarily increasing the areas over which the Federal Government asserts jurisdiction. To the contrary, jurisdiction has been relinquished in those areas where the States have demonstrated no genuine need for assistance in protecting their citizens.

In those instances where jurisdiction is expanded, care has been taken to limit that expansion to areas of compelling Federal interest which are not adequately dealt with under present law. An example of such an instance would be the present law which states that it is a Federal crime to travel in interstate commerce to bribe a witness in a State court proceeding, but it is not a crime to travel in interstate commerce to threaten or intimidate the same witness, though intimidation might even take the form of murdering the witness.

The Federal interest is the same in each case—to assist the State in safeguarding the integrity of its judicial processes. In such a case, an extension of Federal jurisdiction is clearly warranted and is provided for under my proposal.

The rationalization of jurisdictional bases permits greater clarity of drafting, uniformity of interpretation, and the consolidation of numerous statutes presently applying to basically the same conduct.

For example, title 18 of the criminal Code as presently drawn, lists some 70 theft offenses—each written in a different fashion to cover the taking of various kinds of property in different jurisdictional situations. In the proposed new Code, these have been reduced to 5 general sections. Almost 80 forgery, counterfeiting, and related offenses have been replaced by only 3 sections. Over 50 statutes involving perjury and false statements have been reduced to 7 sections. Approximately 70 arson and property destruction offenses have been consolidated into 4 offenses.

Similar changes have been made in the Code's treatment of culpability. Instead of 79 undefined terms or combinations of terms presently found in title 18, the Code uses four clearly defined terms.

Another major innovation reflected in Part One is a codification of general defenses available to a defendant. This change permits clarification of areas in which the law is presently confused and, for the first time, provides uniform Federal standards for defense.

The most significant feature of this chapter is a codification of the "insanity" defense. At present the test is determined by the courts and varies across the country. The standard has become so vague in some instances that it has led to unconscionable abuse by defendants.

My proposed new formulation would provide an insanity defense only if the defendant did not know what he was doing. Under this formulation, which has considerable support in psychiatric and legal circles, the only question considered germane in a murder case, for example, would be whether the defendant knew that he was pulling the trigger of a gun. Questions such as the existence of a mental disease or defect and whether the defendant requires treatment or deserves imprisonment would be reserved for consideration at the time of sentencing.

Part Two of the Code consolidates the definitions of all Federal felonies, as well as certain related Federal offenses of a less serious character. Offenses and, in appropriate instances, specific defenses, are defined in simple, concise terms, and those existing provisions found to be obsolete or unusable have been eliminated—for example, operating a pirate ship on behalf of a "foreign prince," or detaining a United States carrier pigeon. Loopholes in existing law have been closed—for example, statutes concerning the theft of union funds, and new offenses have been created where necessary, as in the case of leaders of organized crime.

We have not indulged in changes merely for the sake of changes. Where existing law has proved satisfactory and where existing statutory language has received favorable interpretation by the courts, the law and the operative language have been retained. In other areas, such as pornography, there has been a thorough revision to reassert the Federal interest in protecting our citizens.

The reforms set forth in Parts One and Two of the Code would be of little practical consequence without a more realistic approach to those problems which arise in the post-conviction phase of dealing with Federal offenses.

For example, the penalty structure prescribed in the present criminal Code is riddled with inconsistencies and inadequacies. Title 18 alone provides 18 different terms of imprisonment and 14 different fines, often with no discernible relationship between the possible term of imprisonment and the possible levying of a fine.

Part Three of the new Code classifies offenses into 8 categories for purposes of assessing and levying imprisonment and fines. It brings the present structure into line with current judgments as to the seriousness of various offenses and with the best opinions of penologists as [to] the efficacy of specific penalties. In some instances, more stringent sanctions are provided. For example, sentences for arson are increased from 5 to 15 years. In other cases penalties are reduced. For example, impersonating a foreign official carries a three year sentence, as opposed to the 10 year term originally prescribed.

To reduce the possibility of unwarranted disparities in sentencing, the Code establishes criteria for the imposition of sentence. At the same time, it provides for parole supervision after all prison sentences, so that even hardened criminals who serve their full prison terms will receive supervision following their release.

There are certain crimes reflecting such a degree of hostility to society that a decent regard for the common welfare requires that a defendant convicted of those crimes be removed from free society. For this reason my proposed new Code provides mandatory minimum prison terms for trafficking in hard narcotics; it provides mandatory minimum prison terms for persons using dangerous weapons in the execution of a crime; and it provides mandatory minimum prison sentences for those convicted as leaders of organized crime.

The magnitude of the proposed revision of the Federal criminal Code will require careful detailed consideration by the Congress. I have no doubt this will be time-consuming. There are, however, two provisions in the Code which I feel require immediate enactment. I have thus directed that provisions relating to the death penalty and to heroin trafficking also be transmitted as separate bills in order that the Congress may act more rapidly on these two measures.

Death Penalty

The sharp reduction in the application of the death penalty was a component of the more permissive attitude toward crime in the last decade.

I do not contend that the death penalty is a panacea that will cure crime. Crime is the product of a variety of different circumstances—sometimes social, sometimes psychological—but it is committed by human beings and at the point of commission it is the product of that individual's motivation. If the incentive not to commit crime is stronger than the incentive to commit it, then logic suggests that crime will be reduced. It is in part the entirely justified feeling of the prospective criminal that he will not suffer for his deed which, in the present circumstances, helps allow those deeds to take place.

Federal crimes are rarely "crimes of passion." Airplane hi-jacking is not done in a blind rage; it has to be carefully planned. The use of incendiary devices and bombs is not a crime of passion, nor is kidnapping; all these must be thought out in advance. At present those who plan these crimes do not have to include in their deliberations the possibility that they will be put to death for their deeds. I believe that in making their plans, they should have to consider the fact that if a death results from their crime, they too may die.

Under those conditions, I am confident that the death penalty can be a valuable deterrent. By making the death penalty available, we will provide Federal enforcement authorities with additional leverage to dissuade those individuals who may commit a Federal crime from taking the lives of others in the course of committing that crime.

Hard experience has taught us that with due regard for the rights of all—including the right to life itself we must return to a greater concern with protecting those who might otherwise be the innocent victims of violent crime than with protecting those who have committed those crimes. The society which fails to recognize this as a reasonable ordering of its priorities must inevitably find itself, in time, at the mercy of criminals.

America was heading in that direction in the last decade, and I believe that we must not risk returning to it again. Accordingly, I am proposing the re-institution of the death penalty for war-related treason, sabotage, and espionage, and for all specifically enumerated crimes under Federal jurisdiction from which death results.

The Department of Justice has examined the constitutionality of the death penalty in the light of the Supreme Court's recent decision in *Furman v. Georgia*. It is the Department's opinion that Furman holds unconstitutional the imposition of the death penalty only insofar as it is applied arbitrarily and capriciously. I believe the best way to accommodate the reservations of the Court is to authorize the automatic imposition of the death penalty where it is warranted.

Under the proposal drafted by the Department of Justice, a hearing would be required after the trial for the purpose of determining the existence or nonexistence of certain rational standards which delineate aggravating factors or mitigating factors.

Among those mitigating factors which would preclude the imposition of a death sentence are the youth of the defendant, his or her mental capacity, or the fact that the crime was committed under duress. Aggravating factors include the creation of a grave risk of danger to the national security, or to the life of another person, or the killing of another person during the commission of one of a circumscribed list of serious offenses, such as treason, kidnapping, or aircraft piracy.

The hearing would be held before the judge who presided at the trial and before either the same jury, or, if circumstances require, a jury specially impaneled. Imposition of the death penalty by the judge would be mandatory if the jury returns a special verdict finding the existence of one or more aggravating factors and the absence of any mitigating factor. The death sentence is prohibited if the jury finds the existence of one or more mitigating factors.

Current statutes containing the death penalty would be amended to eliminate the requirement for jury recommendation, thus limiting the imposition of the death penalty to cases in which the legislative guidelines for its imposition clearly require it, and eliminating arbitrary and capricious application of the death penalty which the Supreme Court has condemned in the Furman case.

Drug Abuse

No single law enforcement problem has occupied more time, effort and money in the past four years than that of drug abuse and drug addiction. We have regarded drugs as "public enemy number one," destroying the most precious resource we have—our young people—and breeding lawlessness, violence and death.

When this Administration assumed Office in 1969, only $82 million was budgeted by the Federal Government for law enforcement, prevention, and rehabilitation in the field of drug abuse.

Today that figure has been increased to $785 million for 1974—nearly 10 times as much. Narcotics production has been disrupted, more traffickers and distributors have been put out of business, and addicts and abusers have been treated and started on the road to rehabilitation.

Since last June, the supply of heroin on the East Coast has been substantially reduced. The scarcity of heroin in our big Eastern cities has driven up the price of an average "fix" from $4.31 to $9.88, encouraging more addicts to seek medical treatment. At the same time the heroin content of that fix has dropped from 6.5 to 3.7 percent.

Meanwhile, through my Cabinet Committee on International Narcotics Control, action plans are underway to help 59 foreign countries develop and carry out their own national control programs. These efforts, linked with those of the Bureau of Customs and the Bureau of Narcotics and Dangerous Drugs, have produced heartening results.

Our worldwide narcotics seizures almost tripled in 1972 over 1971. Seizures by our anti-narcotics allies abroad are at an all-time high.

In January, 1972, the French seized a half-ton of heroin on a shrimp boat headed for this country. Argentine, Brazilian and Venezuelan agents seized 285 pounds of heroin in three raids in 1972, and with twenty arrests crippled the existing French-Latin American connection. The ringleader was extradited to the U.S. by Paraguay and has just begun to serve a 20-year sentence in Federal prison.

Thailand's Special Narcotics Organization recently seized a total of almost eleven tons of opium along the Burmese border, as well as a half-ton of morphine and heroin.

Recently Iran scored the largest opium seizure on record—over 12 tons taken from smugglers along the Afghanistan border.

Turkey, as a result of a courageous decision by the government under Prime Minister Erim in 1971, has prohibited all cultivation of opium within her borders.

These results are all the more gratifying in light of the fact that heroin is wholly a foreign import to the United States. We do not grow opium here; we do not produce heroin here; yet we have the largest addict population in the world. Clearly we will end our problem faster with continued foreign assistance.

Our domestic accomplishments are keeping pace with international efforts and are producing equally encouraging results. Domestic drug seizures, including seizures of marijuana and hashish, almost doubled in 1972 over 1971. Arrests have risen by more than one-third and convictions have doubled.

In January of 1972, a new agency, the Office of Drug Abuse Law Enforcement (DALE), was created within the Department of Justice. Task forces composed of investigators, attorneys, and special prosecuting attorneys have been assigned to more than forty cities with heroin problems. DALE now arrests pushers at the rate of 550 a month and has obtained 750 convictions.

At my direction, the Internal Revenue Service (IRS) established a special unit to make intensive tax investigations of suspected domestic traffickers. To date, IRS has collected $18 million in currency and property, assessed tax penalties of more than $100 million, and obtained 25 convictions. This effort can be particularly effective in reaching the high level traffickers and financiers who never actually touch the heroin, but who profit from the misery of those who do.

The problem of drug abuse in America is not a law enforcement problem alone. Under my Administration, the Federal Government has pursued a balanced, comprehensive approach to ending this problem. Increased law enforcement efforts have been coupled with expanded treatment programs.

The Special Action Office for Drug Abuse Prevention was created to aid in preventing drug abuse before it begins and in rehabilitating those who have fallen victim to it.

In each year of my Administration, more Federal dollars have been spent on treatment, rehabilitation, prevention, and research in the field of drug abuse than has been budgeted for law enforcement in the drug field.

The Special Action Office for Drug Abuse Prevention is currently developing a special program of Treatment Alternatives to Street Crime (TASC) to break the vicious cycle of addiction, crime, arrest, bail, and more crime. Under the TASC program, arrestees who are scientifically identified as heroin-dependent may be assigned by judges to treatment programs as a condition for release on bail, or as a possible alternative to prosecution.

Federally funded treatment programs have increased from sixteen in January, 1969, to a current level of 400. In the last fiscal year, the Special Action Office created more facilities for treating drug addiction than the Federal Government had provided in all the previous fifty years.

Today, federally funded treatment is available for 100,000 addicts a year. We also have sufficient funds available to expand our facilities to treat 250,000 addicts if required.

Nationwide, in the last two years, the rate of new addiction to heroin registered its first decline since 1964. This is a particularly important trend because it is estimated that one addict "infects" six of his peers.

The trend in narcotic-related deaths is also clearly on its way down. My advisers report to me that virtually complete statistics show such fatalities declined approximately 6 percent in 1972 compared to 1971.

In spite of these accomplishments, however, it is still estimated that one-third to one-half of all individuals arrested for street crimes continue to be narcotics abusers and addicts. What this suggests is that in the area of enforcement we are still only holding our own, and we must increase the tools available to do the job.

The work of the Special Action Office for Drug Abuse Prevention has aided in smoothing the large expansion of Federal effort in the area of drug treatment and prevention. Now we must move to improve Federal action in the area of law enforcement.

Drug abuse treatment specialists have continuously emphasized in their discussions with me the need for strong, effective law enforcement to restrict the availability of drugs and to punish the pusher.

One area where I am convinced of the need for immediate action is that of jailing heroin pushers. Under the Bail Reform Act of 1966, a Federal judge is precluded from considering the danger to the community when setting bail for suspects arrested for selling heroin. The effect of this restriction is that many accused pushers are immediately released on bail and are thus given the opportunity to go out and create more misery, generate more violence, and commit more crimes while they are waiting to be tried for these same activities.

In a study of 422 accused violators, the Bureau of Narcotics and Dangerous Drugs found that 71 percent were freed on bail for a period ranging from three months to more than one year between the time of arrest and the time of trial. Nearly 40 percent of the total were free for a period ranging from one-half year to more than one year. As for the major cases, those involving pushers accused of trafficking in large quantities of heroin, it was found that one-fourth were free for over three months to one-half year; one-fourth were free for one-half year to one year; and 16 percent remained free for over one year prior to their trial.

In most cases these individuals had criminal records. One-fifth had been convicted of a previous drug charge and a total of 64 percent had a record of prior felony arrests.

The cost of obtaining such a pre-trial release in most cases was minimal; 19 percent of the total sample were freed on personal recognizance and only 23 percent were required to post bonds of $10,000 or more.

Sentencing practices have also been found to be inadequate in many cases. In a study of 955 narcotics drug violators who were arrested by the Bureau of Narcotics and Dangerous Drugs and convicted in the courts, a total of 27 percent received sentences other than imprisonment. Most of these individuals were placed on probation.

This situation is intolerable. I am therefore calling upon the Congress to promptly enact a new Heroin Trafficking Act.

The first part of my proposed legislation would increase the sentences for heroin and morphine offenses.

For a first offense of trafficking in less than four ounces of a mixture or substance containing heroin or morphine, it provides a mandatory sentence of not less than five years nor more than fifteen years. For a first offense of trafficking in four or more ounces, it provides a mandatory, sentence of not less than ten years or for life.

For those with a prior felony narcotic conviction who are convicted of trafficking in less than four ounces, my proposed legislation provides a mandatory prison term of ten years to life imprisonment. For second offenders who are convicted of trafficking in more than four ounces, I am proposing a mandatory sentence of life imprisonment without parole.

While four ounces of a heroin mixture may seem a very small amount to use as the criterion for major penalties, that amount is actually worth 12–15,000 dollars and would supply about 180 addicts for a day. Anyone selling four or more ounces cannot be considered a small time operator.

For those who are convicted of possessing large amounts of heroin but cannot be convicted of trafficking, I am proposing a series of lesser penalties.

To be sure that judges actually apply these tough sentences, my legislation would provide that the mandatory minimum sentences cannot be suspended, nor probation granted.

The second portion of my proposed legislation would deny pre-trial release to those charged with trafficking in heroin or morphine unless the judicial officer finds that release will not pose a danger to the persons or property of others. It would also prohibit the release of anyone convicted of one of the above felonies who is awaiting sentencing or the results of an appeal.

These are very harsh measures, to be applied within very rigid guidelines and providing only a minimum of sentencing discretion to judges. But circumstances warrant such provisions. All the evidence shows that we are now doing a more effective job in the areas of enforcement and rehabilitation. In spite of this progress, however, we find an intolerably high level of street crime being committed by addicts. Part of the reason, I believe, lies in the court system which takes over after drug pushers have been apprehended. The courts are frequently little more than an escape hatch for those who are responsible for the menace of drugs.

Sometimes it seems that as fast as we bail water out of the boat through law enforcement and rehabilitation, it runs right back in through the holes in our judicial system. I intend to plug those holes. Until then, all the money we spend, all the enforcement we provide, and all the rehabilitation services we offer are not going to solve the drug problem in America.

Finally, I want to emphasize my continued opposition to legalizing the possession, sale or use of marijuana. There is no question about whether marijuana is dangerous, the only question is how dangerous. While the matter is still in dispute, the only responsible governmental approach is to prevent marijuana from being legalized. I intend, as I have said before, to do just that.

Conclusion

This Nation has fought hard and sacrificed greatly to achieve a lasting peace in the world. Peace in the world, however, must be accompanied by peace in our own land. Of what ultimate value is it to end the threat to our national safety in the world if our citizens face a constant threat to their personal safety in our own streets?

The American people are a law-abiding people. They have faith in the law. It is now time for Government to justify that faith by insuring that the law works, that our system of criminal justice works, and that "domestic tranquility" is preserved.

I believe we have gone a long way toward erasing the apprehensions of the last decade. But we must go further if we are to achieve that peace at home which will truly complement peace abroad.

In the coming months I will propose legislation aimed at curbing the manufacture and sale of cheap handguns commonly known as "Saturday night specials," I will propose reforms of the Federal criminal system to provide speedier and more rational criminal trial procedures, and I will continue to press for innovation and improvement in our correctional systems.

The Federal Government cannot do everything. Indeed, it is prohibited from doing everything. But it can do a great deal. The crime legislation I will submit to the Congress can give us the tools we need to do all that we can do. This is sound, responsible legislation. I am confident that the approval of the American people for measures of the sort that I have suggested will be reflected in the actions of the Congress.

Richard Nixon, 1973–1974

Address to Congress on the State of the Union
January 30, 1974

President Richard Nixon delivered his last State of the Union message in January 1974. In his speech before Congress, the president praised his own record over the previous five years, called for major changes, and—perhaps most significantly—addressed the burning issue of the Watergate scandal.

Watergate, a major political scandal that ended with Nixon's resignation less than seven months after his State of the Union speech, began with a break-in on June 17, 1972 at the Democratic National Committee offices in the Watergate complex in Washington. Nixon's reelection campaign and the White House denied any involvement, but subsequent investigations revealed that to be untrue, and by early

1974, the repercussions from this cover-up were threatening to bring down the administration. In February 1974, the House Judiciary Committee started looking into possible impeachment charges.

Nixon waited until the end of his speech to deal with Watergate. He stated that the investigations should come to an end, saying: "One year of Watergate is enough." He pledged to cooperate with the Judiciary Committee, but drew the line at taking any actions that would weaken the presidency. He vowed not to walk away from his job as president, and admitted that 1973 had been a difficult year for him.

Nixon opened the speech with a defense of his administration's policies, stating that since his first inauguration five years earlier, the country had pulled out of Vietnam, had worked to improve the environment, and had clamped down on crime and drug abuse.

He listed ten areas in which he hoped to achieve progress in 1974, including attacking the energy crisis besieging the country—he termed energy "the first priority" for the country—working toward peace in the Middle East, and seeking to curb inflation. In the course of his speech, Nixon mentioned "these final three years of my administration"; he also referred to leaving a legacy of peace from "the eight years of my presidency." Nixon also sent Congress a 22,000-word message detailing his proposals.

Overall, many observers viewed Nixon's State of the Union speech as a sign that he would fight any efforts to impeach him. His backers in Congress hailed his references to his remaining in office, but many Democrats responded negatively to his remarks about the investigation. Nixon's resignation, on August 9, 1974, came only after the House Judiciary Committee voted to recommend articles of impeachment. He was succeeded by his vice president, Gerald Ford. The legacy of Watergate, including mistrust of government, would haunt subsequent presidents.

Mr. Speaker, Mr. President, my colleagues in the Congress, our distinguished guests, my fellow Americans:

We meet here tonight at a time of great challenge and great opportunities for America. We meet at a time when we face great problems at home and abroad that will test the strength of our fiber as a nation. But we also meet at a time when that fiber has been tested, and it has proved strong.

America is a great and good land, and we are a great and good land because we are a strong, free, creative people and because America is the single greatest force for peace anywhere in the world. Today, as always in our history, we can base our confidence in what the American people will achieve in the future on the record of what the American people have achieved in the past.

Tonight, for the first time in 12 years, a President of the United States can report to the Congress on the state of a Union at peace with every nation of the world. Because of this, in the 22,000-word message on the state of the Union that I have just handed to the Speaker of the House and the President of the Senate, I have been able to deal primarily with the problems of peace with what we can do here at home in America for the American people—rather than with the problems of war.

The measures I have outlined in this message set an agenda for truly significant progress for this Nation and the world in 1974. Before we chart where we are going, let us see how far we have come.

It was 5 years ago on the steps of this Capitol that I took the oath of office as your President. In those 5 years, because of the initiatives undertaken by this Administration, the world has changed. America has changed. As a result of those changes, America is safer today, more prosperous today, with greater opportunity for more of its people than ever before in our history.

Five years ago, America was at war in Southeast Asia. We were locked in confrontation with the Soviet Union. We were in hostile isolation from a quarter of the world's people who lived in Mainland China.

Five years ago, our cities were burning and besieged.

Five years ago, our college campuses were a battleground.

Five years ago, crime was increasing at a rate that struck fear across the Nation.

Five years ago, the spiraling rise in drug addiction was threatening human and social tragedy of massive proportion, and there was no program to deal with it.

Five years ago—as young Americans had done for a generation before that—America's youth still lived under the shadow of the military draft.

Five years ago, there was no national program to preserve our environment. Day by day, our air was getting dirtier, our water was getting more foul.

And 5 years ago, American agriculture was practically a depressed industry with 100,000 farm families abandoning the farm every year.

As we look at America today, we find ourselves challenged by new problems. But we also find a record of progress to confound the professional criers of doom and prophets of despair. We met the challenges we faced 5 years ago, and we will be equally confident of meeting those that we face today.

Let us see for a moment how we have met them.

After more than 10 years of military involvement, all of our troops have returned from Southeast Asia, and they have returned with honor. And we can be proud of the fact that our courageous prisoners of war, for whom a dinner was held in Washington tonight, that they came home with their heads high, on their feet and not on their knees.

In our relations with the Soviet Union, we have turned away from a policy of confrontation to one of negotiation. For the first time since World War II, the world's two strongest powers are working together toward peace in the world. With the People's Republic of China after a generation of hostile isolation, we have begun a period of peaceful exchange and expanding trade.

Peace has returned to our cities, to our campuses. The 17-year rise in crime has been stopped. We can confidently say today that we are finally beginning to win the war against crime. Right here in this Nation's Capital—which a few years ago was threatening to become the crime capital of the world—the rate in crime has been cut in half. A massive campaign against drug abuse has been organized. And the rate of new heroin addiction, the most vicious threat of all, is decreasing rather than increasing.

For the first time in a generation, no young Americans are being drafted into the armed services of the United States. And for the first time ever, we have organized a massive national effort to protect the environment. Our air is getting cleaner, our water is getting purer, and our agriculture, which was depressed, is prospering. Farm income is up 70 percent, farm production is setting all-time records, and the billions of dollars the taxpayers were paying in subsidies has been cut to nearly zero.

Overall, Americans are living more abundantly than ever before, today. More than

2½ million new jobs were created in the past year alone. That is the biggest percentage increase in nearly 20 years. People are earning more. What they earn buys more, more than ever before in history. In the past 5 years, the average American's real spendable income—that is, what you really can buy with your income, even after allowing for taxes and inflation—has increased by 16 percent.

Despite this record of achievement, as we turn to the year ahead we hear once again the familiar voice of the perennial prophets of gloom telling us now that because of the need to fight inflation, because of the energy shortage, America may be headed for a recession.

Let me speak to that issue head on. There will be no recession in the United States of America. Primarily due to our energy crisis, our economy is passing through a difficult period. But I pledge to you tonight that the full powers of this Government will be used to keep America's economy producing and to protect the jobs of America's workers.

We are engaged in a long and hard fight against inflation. There have been, and there will be in the future, ups and downs in that fight. But if this Congress cooperates in our efforts to hold down the cost of Government, we shall win our fight to hold down the cost of living for the American people.

As we look back over our history, the years that stand out as the ones of signal achievement are those in which the Administration and the Congress, whether one party or the other, working together, had the wisdom and the foresight to select those particular initiatives for which the Nation was ready and the moment was right—and in which they seized the moment and acted.

Looking at the year 1974 which lies before us, there are 10 key areas in which landmark accomplishments are possible this year in America. If we make these our national agenda, this is what we will achieve in 1974:

We will break the back of the energy crisis; we will lay the foundation for our future capacity to meet America's energy needs from America's own resources.

And we will take another giant stride toward lasting peace in the world—not only by continuing our policy of negotiation rather than confrontation where the great powers are concerned but also by helping toward the achievement of a just and lasting settlement in the Middle East.

We will check the rise in prices without administering the harsh medicine of recession, and we will move the economy into a steady period of growth at a sustainable level.

We will establish a new system that makes high-quality health care available to every American in a dignified manner and at a price he can afford.

We will make our States and localities more responsive to the needs of their own citizens.

We will make a crucial breakthrough toward better transportation in our towns and in our cities across America.

We will reform our system of Federal aid to education, to provide it when it is needed, where it is needed, so that it will do the most for those who need it the most.

We will make an historic beginning on the task of defining and protecting the right of personal privacy for every American.

And we will start on a new road toward reform of a welfare system that bleeds the taxpayer, corrodes the community, and demeans those it is intended to assist.

And together with the other nations of the world, we will establish the economic framework within which Americans will share more fully in an expanding worldwide trade and prosperity in the years ahead, with more open access to both markets and supplies.

In all of the 186 State of the Union messages delivered from this place, in our history this is the first in which the one priority, the first priority, is energy. Let me begin by reporting a new development which I know will be welcome news to every American. As you know, we have committed ourselves to an active role in helping to achieve a just and durable peace in the Middle East, on the basis of full implementation of Security Council Resolutions 242 and 338. The first step in the process is the disengagement of Egyptian and Israeli forces which is now taking place.

Because of this hopeful development, I can announce tonight that I have been assured, through my personal contacts with friendly leaders in the Middle Eastern area, that an urgent meeting will be called in the immediate future to discuss the lifting of the oil embargo.

This is an encouraging sign. However, it should be clearly understood by our friends in the Middle East that the United States will not be coerced on this issue.

Regardless of the outcome of this meeting, the cooperation of the American people in our energy conservation program has already gone a long way towards achieving a goal to which I am deeply dedicated. Let us do everything we can to avoid gasoline rationing in the United States of America.

Last week, I sent to the Congress a comprehensive special message setting forth our energy situation, recommending the legislative measures which are necessary to a program for meeting our needs. If the embargo is lifted, this will ease the crisis, but it will not mean an end to the energy shortage in America. Voluntary conservation will continue to be necessary. And let me take this occasion to pay tribute once again to the splendid spirit of cooperation the American people have shown which has made possible our success in meeting this emergency up to this time.

The new legislation I have requested will also remain necessary. Therefore, I urge again that the energy measures that I have proposed be made the first priority of this session of the Congress. These measures will require the oil companies and other energy producers to provide the public with the necessary information on their supplies. They will prevent the injustice of windfall profits for a few as a result of the sacrifices of the millions of Americans. And they will give us the organization, the incentives, the authorities needed to deal with the short-term emergency and to move toward meeting our long-term needs.

Just as 1970 was the year in which we began a full-scale effort to protect the environment, 1974 must be the year in which we organize a full-scale effort to provide for our energy needs, not only in this decade but through the 21st century.

As we move toward the celebration 2 years from now of the 200th anniversary of this Nation's independence, let us press vigorously on toward the goal I announced last November for Project Independence. Let this be our national goal: At the end of this decade, in the year 1980, the United States will not be dependent on any other country for the energy we need to provide our jobs, to heat our homes, and to keep our transportation moving.

To indicate the size of the Government commitment, to spur energy research and development, we plan to spend $10 billion in Federal funds over the next 5 years.

That is an enormous amount. But during the same 5 years, private enterprise will be investing as much as $200 billion—and in 10 years, $500 billion—to develop the new resources, the new technology, the new capacity America will require for its energy needs in the 1980's. That is just a measure of the magnitude of the project we are undertaking.

But America performs best when called to its biggest tasks. It can truly be said that only in America could a task so tremendous be achieved so quickly, and achieved not by regimentation, but through the effort and ingenuity of a free people, working in a free system.

Turning now to the rest of the agenda for 1974, the time is at hand this year to bring comprehensive, high quality health care within the reach of every American. I shall propose a sweeping new program that will assure comprehensive health insurance protection to millions of Americans who cannot now obtain it or afford it, with vastly improved protection against catastrophic illnesses. This will be a plan that maintains the high standards of quality in America's health care. And it will not require additional taxes.

Now, I recognize that other plans have been put forward that would cost $80 billion or even $100 billion and that would put our whole health care system under the heavy hand of the Federal Government. This is the wrong approach. This has been tried abroad, and it has failed. It is not the way we do things here in America. This kind of plan would threaten the quality of care provided by our whole health care system. The right way is one that builds on the strengths of the present system and one that does not destroy those strengths, one based on partnership, not paternalism. Most important of all, let us keep this as the guiding principle of our health programs. Government has a great role to play, but we must always make sure that our doctors will be working for their patients and not for the Federal Government.

Many of you will recall that in my State of the Union Address 3 years ago, I commented that "Most Americans today are simply fed up with government at all levels," and I recommended a sweeping set of proposals to revitalize State and local governments, to make them more responsive to the people they serve. I can report to you today that as a result of revenue sharing passed by the Congress, and other measures, we have made progress toward that goal. After 40 years of moving power from the States and the communities to Washington, D.C., we have begun moving power back from Washington to the States and communities and, most important, to the people of America.

In this session of the Congress, I believe we are near the breakthrough point on efforts which I have suggested, proposals to let people themselves make their own decisions for their own communities and, in particular, on those to provide broad new flexibility in Federal aid for community development, for economic development, for education. And I look forward to working with the Congress, with members of both parties in resolving whatever remaining differences we have in this legislation so that we can make available nearly $5½ billion to our States and localities to use not for what a Federal bureaucrat may want, but for what their own people in those communities want. The decision should be theirs.

I think all of us recognize that the energy crisis has given new urgency to the need to improve public transportation, not only in our cities but in rural areas as well. The program I have proposed this year will give communities not only more money but also more freedom to balance their own transportation needs. It will mark the strongest Federal commitment ever to the improvement of mass transit as an essential element of the improvement of life in our towns and cities.

One goal on which all Americans agree is that our children should have the very best education this great Nation can provide.

In a special message last week, I recommended a number of important new measures that can make 1974 a year of truly significant advances for our schools and for the children they serve. If the Congress will act on these proposals, more flexible funding will enable each Federal dollar to meet better the particular need of each particular school district. Advance funding will give school authorities a chance to make each year's plans, knowing ahead of time what Federal funds they are going to receive. Special targeting will give special help to the truly disadvantaged among our people. College students faced with rising costs for their education will be able to draw on an expanded program of loans and grants. These advances are a needed investment in America's most precious resource, our next generation. And I urge the Congress to act on this legislation in 1974.

One measure of a truly free society is the vigor with which it protects the liberties of its individual citizens. As technology has advanced in America, it has increasingly encroached on one of those liberties—what I term the right of personal privacy. Modern information systems, data banks, credit records, mailing list abuses, electronic snooping, the collection of personal data for one purpose that may be used for another—all these have left millions of Americans deeply concerned by the privacy they cherish.

And the time has come, therefore, for a major initiative to define the nature and extent of the basic rights of privacy and to erect new safeguards to ensure that those rights are respected.

I shall launch such an effort this year at the highest levels of the Administration, and I look forward again to working with this Congress in establishing a new set of standards that respect the legitimate needs of society, but that also recognize personal privacy as a cardinal principle of American liberty.

Many of those in this Chamber tonight will recall that it was 3 years ago that I termed the Nation's welfare system "a monstrous, consuming outrage—an outrage against the community, against the taxpayer, and particularly against the children that it is supposed to help."

That system is still an outrage. By improving its administration, we have been able to reduce some of the abuses. As a result, last year, for the first time in 18 years, there has been a halt in the growth of the welfare caseload. But as a system, our welfare program still needs reform as urgently today as it did when I first proposed in 1969 that we completely replace it with a different system.

In these final 3 years of my Administration, I urge the Congress to join me in mounting a major new effort to replace the discredited present welfare system with one that works, one that is fair to those who need help or cannot help themselves, fair to the community, and fair to the taxpayer. And let us have as our goal that there will be no Government program which makes it more profitable to go on welfare than to go to work.

I recognize that from the debates that have taken place within the Congress over the past 3 years on this program that we cannot expect enactment overnight of a new reform. But I do propose that the Congress and the Administration together make this the year in which we discuss, debate, and shape such a reform so that it can be enacted as quickly as possible.

America's own prosperity in the years ahead depends on our sharing fully and equitably in an expanding world prosperity. Historic negotiations will take place this year that will enable us to ensure fair treatment in international markets for American workers, American farmers, American investors, and American consumers.

It is vital that the authorities contained in the trade bill I submitted to the Congress be enacted so that the United States can negotiate flexibly and vigorously on behalf of American interests. These negotiations can usher in a new era of international trade that not only increases the prosperity of all nations but also strengthens the peace among all nations.

In the past 5 years, we have made more progress toward a lasting structure of peace in the world than in any comparable time in the Nation's history. We could not have made that progress if we had not maintained the military strength of America. Thomas Jefferson once observed that the price of liberty is eternal vigilance. By the same token, and for the same reason, in today's world the price of peace is a strong defense as far as the United States is concerned.

In the past 5 years, we have steadily reduced the burden of national defense as a share of the budget, bringing it down from 44 percent in 1969 to 29 percent in the current year. We have cut our military manpower over the past 5 years by more than a third, from 3.5 million to 2.2 million.

In the coming year, however, increased expenditures will be needed. They will be needed to assure the continued readiness of our military forces, to preserve present force levels in the face of rising costs, and to give us the military strength we must have if our security is to be maintained and if our initiatives for peace are to succeed.

The question is not whether we can afford to maintain the necessary strength of our defense, the question is whether we can afford not to maintain it, and the answer to that question is no. We must never allow America to become the second strongest nation in the world.

I do not say this with any sense of belligerence, because I recognize the fact that is recognized around the world. America's military strength has always been maintained to keep the peace, never to break it. It has always been used to defend freedom, never to destroy it. The world's peace, as well as our own, depends on our remaining as strong as we need to be as long as we need to be.

In this year 1974, we will be negotiating with the Soviet Union to place further limits on strategic nuclear arms. Together with our allies, we will be negotiating with the nations of the Warsaw Pact on mutual and balanced reduction of forces in Europe. And we will continue our efforts to promote peaceful economic development in Latin America, in Africa, in Asia. We will press for full compliance with the peace accords that brought an end to American fighting in Indochina, including particularly a provision that promised the fullest possible accounting for those Americans who are missing in action.

And having in mind the energy crisis to which I have referred to earlier, we will be working with the other nations of the world toward agreement on means by which oil supplies can be assured at reasonable prices on a stable basis in a fair way to the consuming and producing nations alike.

All of these are steps toward a future in which the world's peace and prosperity, and ours as well as a result, are made more secure.

Throughout the 5 years that I have served as your President, I have had one overriding aim, and that was to establish a new structure of peace in the world that can free future generations of the scourge of war. I can understand that others may have different priorities. This has been and this will remain my first priority and the chief legacy I hope to leave from the 8 years of my Presidency.

This does not mean that we shall not have other priorities, because as we strengthen the peace, we must also continue each year a steady strengthening of our society here at home. Our conscience requires it, our interests require it, and we must insist upon it.

As we create more jobs, as we build a better health care system, as we improve our education, as we develop new sources of energy, as we provide more abundantly for the elderly and the poor, as we strengthen the system of private enterprise that produces our prosperity as we do all of this and even more, we solidify those essential bonds that hold us together as a nation.

Even more importantly, we advance what in the final analysis government in America is all about.

What it is all about is more freedom, more security, a better life for each one of the 211 million people that live in this land.

We cannot afford to neglect progress at home while pursuing peace abroad. But neither can Ave afford to neglect peace abroad while pursuing progress at home. With a stable peace, all is possible, but without peace, nothing is possible.

In the written message that I have just delivered to the Speaker and to the President of the Senate, I commented that one of the continuing challenges facing us in the legislative process is that of the timing and pacing of our initiatives, selecting each year among many worthy projects those that are ripe for action at that time.

What is true in terms of our domestic initiatives is true also in the world. This period we now are in, in the world—and I say this as one who has seen so much of the world, not only in these past 5 years but going back over many years—we are in a period which presents a juncture of historic forces unique in this century. They provide an opportunity we may never have again to create a structure of peace solid enough to last a lifetime and more, not just peace in our time but peace in our children's time as well. It is on the way we respond to this opportunity, more than anything else, that history will judge whether we in America have met our responsibility. And I am confident we will meet that great historic responsibility which is ours today.

It was 27 years ago that John F. Kennedy and I sat in this Chamber, as freshmen Congressmen, hearing our first State of the Union address delivered by Harry Truman. I know from my talks with him, as members of the Labor Committee on which we both served, that neither of us then even dreamed that either one or both might eventually be standing in this place that I now stand in now and that he once stood in, before me. It may well be that one of the freshmen Members of the 93d Congress, one of you out there, will deliver his own State of the Union message 27 years from now, in the year 2001.

Well, whichever one it is, I want you to be able to look back with pride and to say that your first years here were great years and recall that you were here in this 93d Congress when America ended its longest war and began its longest peace.

[At this point, the President paused to acknowledge applause from the audience. He then resumed speaking.]

Mr. Speaker, and Mr. President, and my distinguished colleagues and our guests: I would like to add a personal word with regard to an issue that has been of great concern to all Americans over the past year. I refer, of course, to the investigations of the so-called Watergate affair. As you know, I have provided to the Special Prosecutor voluntarily a great deal of material. I believe that I have provided all the material that he needs to conclude his investigations and to proceed to prosecute the guilty and to clear the innocent.

I believe the time has come to bring that investigation and the other investigations of this matter to an end. One year of Watergate is enough.

And the time has come, my colleagues, for not only the Executive, the President, but the Members of Congress, for all of us to join together in devoting our full energies to these great issues that I have discussed tonight which involve the welfare of all of the American people in so many different ways, as well as the peace of the world.

I recognize that the House Judiciary Committee has a special responsibility in this area, and I want to indicate on this occasion that I will cooperate with the Judiciary Committee in its investigation. I will cooperate so that it can conclude its investigation, make its decision, and I will cooperate in any way that I consider consistent with my responsibilities to the Office of the Presidency of the United States.

There is only one limitation. I will follow the precedent that has been followed by and defended by every President from George Washington to Lyndon B. Johnson of never doing anything that weakens the Office of the President of the United States or impairs the ability of the Presidents of the future to make the great decisions that are so essential to this Nation and the world.

Another point I should like to make very briefly: Like every Member of the House and Senate assembled here tonight, I was elected to the office that I hold. And like every Member of the House and Senate, when I was elected to that office, I knew that I was elected for the purpose of doing a job and doing it as well as I possibly can. And I want you to know that I have no intention whatever of ever walking away from the job that the people elected me to do for the people of the United States.

Now, needless to say, it would be understatement if I were not to admit that the year 1973 was not a very easy year for me personally or for my family. And as I have already indicated, the year 1974 presents very great and serious problems, as very great and serious opportunities are also presented.

But my colleagues, this I believe: With the help of God, who has blessed this land so richly, with the cooperation of the Congress, and with the support of the American people, we can and we will make the year 1974 a year of unprecedented progress toward our goal of building a structure of lasting peace in the world and a new prosperity without war in the United States of America.

Gerald R. Ford

1974–1977

"We must introduce a new balance between the spending on domestic programs and spending on defense—a balance that ensures we will fully meet our obligation to the needy while also protecting our security in a world that is still hostile to freedom."

ADDRESS BEFORE A JOINT SESSION OF CONGRESS REPORTING ON THE
STATE OF THE UNION, JANUARY 19, 1976

Address before a Joint Session of Congress Reporting on the State of the Union

January 15, 1975

Gerald R. Ford was the only president of the United States not to be elected either president or vice president. A longtime House member who was serving as House minority leader, Ford was named Richard Nixon's vice president in 1973 after the resignation of Vice President Spiro Agnew. Ford then became president on August 9, 1974, when Nixon himself resigned rather than face impeachment charges over the Watergate affair.

Ford took office at a time of great disillusionment with the presidency. The Watergate affair, centering on a White House cover-up of a 1972 break-in at Democratic headquarters in Washington, D.C., had resulted in the toppling of a Republican administration that had been in office since 1969. Democrats, who already controlled both the House and Senate, gained a significant number of seats in the post-Watergate midterm congressional elections of 1974.

In addition, the country's economy was suffering. In this State of the Union address, delivered before Congress five months into his presidency, Ford was blunt. He declared that "the state of the union is not good," later adding, "I've got bad news, and I don't expect much, if any, applause."

Ford devoted most of his speech to energy and economic issues. The president stated that creation of new jobs should be a priority and proposed a one-year tax reduction of $16 billion, three-quarters of which would go to individuals and one-quarter to business. He also called for efforts to control federal spending, describing past levels as "self-indulgent." He deemed himself ready to veto new spending programs sought by Congress.

While he acknowledged that the price of petroleum had quadrupled in the past year, he blamed not only the oil-exporting countries but also the United States, stating that the country had not been prepared for an event like the oil embargo that had wreaked havoc in 1973. He called for various energy-related measures, including reduction in oil imports and cuts in consumption.

Democrats agreed with Ford on the need for speedy action on a tax cut and reductions in energy consumption, while disagreeing on an overall approach to getting the economy moving. In the end, the country saw some economic improvement later that year and into 1976, despite continued inflation and high unemployment.

Ford came into office with a reputation for honesty, and he had a good working relationship with Congress. His standing would be tarnished somewhat when he opted to pardon Nixon in September 1974. Ford would seek his own four-year term in 1976 but would lose to Democrat Jimmy Carter.

Mr. Speaker, Mr. Vice President, Members of the 94th Congress, and distinguished guests:

Twenty-six years ago, a freshman Congressman, a young fellow with lots of idealism who was out to change the world, stood before Sam Rayburn in the well of the House and solemnly swore to the same oath that all of you took yesterday—an unforgettable experience, and I congratulate you all.

Two days later, that same freshman stood at the back of this great Chamber—over there someplace—as President Truman, all charged up by his single-handed election victory, reported as the Constitution requires on the state of the Union.

When the bipartisan applause stopped, President Truman said, "I am happy to report to this 81st Congress that the state of the Union is good. Our Nation is better able than ever before to meet the needs of the American people, and to give them their fair chance in the pursuit of happiness. It is foremost among the nations of the world in the search for peace."

Today, that freshman Member from Michigan stands where Mr. Truman stood, and I must say to you that the state of the Union is not good: Millions of Americans are out of work. Recession and inflation are eroding the money of millions more. Prices are too high, and sales are too slow.

This year's Federal deficit will be about $30 billion; next year's probably $45 billion. The national debt will rise to over $500 billion. Our plant capacity and productivity are not increasing fast enough. We depend on others for essential energy.

Some people question their Government's ability to make hard decisions and stick with them; they expect Washington politics as usual.

Yet, what President Truman said on January 5, 1949, is even more true in 1975. We are better able to meet our people's needs. All Americans do have a fairer chance to pursue happiness. Not only are we still the foremost nation in the pursuit of peace but today's prospects of attaining it are infinitely brighter.

There were 59 million Americans employed at the start of 1949; now there are more than 85 million Americans who have jobs. In comparable dollars, the average income of the American family has doubled during the past 26 years.

Now, I want to speak very bluntly. I've got bad news, and I don't expect much, if any, applause. The American people want action, and it will take both the Congress and the President to give them what they want. Progress and solutions can be achieved, and they will be achieved.

My message today is not intended to address all of the complex needs of America. I will send separate messages making specific recommendations for domestic legislation, such as the extension of general revenue sharing and the Voting Rights Act.

The moment has come to move in a new direction. We can do this by fashioning a new partnership between the Congress on the one hand, the White House on the other, and the people we both represent.

Let us mobilize the most powerful and most creative industrial nation that ever existed on this Earth to put all our people to work. The emphasis on our economic efforts must now shift from inflation to jobs.

To bolster business and industry and to create new jobs, I propose a 1-year tax reduction of $16 billion. Three-quarters would go to individuals and one-quarter to promote business investment.

This cash rebate to individuals amounts to 12 percent of 1974 tax payments—a total cut of $12 billion, with a maximum of $1,000 per return.

I call on the Congress to act by April 1. If you do—and I hope you will—the Treasury can send the first check for half of the rebate in May and the second by September.

The other one-fourth of the cut, about $4 billion, will go to business, including farms, to promote expansion and to create more jobs. The 1-year reduction for businesses would be in the form of a liberalized investment tax credit increasing the rate to 12 percent for all businesses.

This tax cut does not include the more fundamental reforms needed in our tax system. But it points us in the right direction—allowing taxpayers rather than the Government to spend their pay.

Cutting taxes now is essential if we are to turn the economy around. A tax cut offers the best hope of creating more jobs. Unfortunately, it will increase the size of the budget deficit. Therefore, it is more important than ever that we take steps to control the growth of Federal expenditures.

Part of our trouble is that we have been self-indulgent. For decades, we have been voting ever-increasing levels of Government benefits, and now the bill has come due. We have been adding so many new programs that the size and the growth of the Federal budget has taken on a life of its own.

One characteristic of these programs is that their cost increases automatically every year because the number of people eligible for most of the benefits increases every year. When these programs are enacted, there is no dollar amount set. No one knows what they will cost. All we know is that whatever they cost last year, they will cost more next year.

It is a question of simple arithmetic. Unless we check the excessive growth of Federal expenditures or impose on ourselves matching increases in taxes, we will continue to run huge inflationary deficits in the Federal budget.

If we project the current built-in momentum of Federal spending through the next 15 years, State, Federal, and local government expenditures could easily comprise half of our gross national product. This compares with less than a third in 1975.

I have just concluded the process of preparing the budget submissions for fiscal year 1976. In that budget, I will propose legislation to restrain the growth of a number of existing programs. I have also concluded that no new spending programs can be initiated this year, except for energy. Further, I will not hesitate to veto any new spending programs adopted by the Congress.

As an additional step toward putting the Federal Government's house in order, I recommend a 5-percent limit on Federal pay increases in 1975. In all Government programs tied to the Consumer Price Index—including social security, civil service and military retirement pay, and food stamps—I also propose a 1-year maximum increase of 5 percent.

None of these recommended ceiling limitations, over which Congress has final authority, are easy to propose, because in most cases they involve anticipated payments to many, many deserving people. Nonetheless, it must be done. I must emphasize that I am not asking to eliminate, to reduce, to freeze these payments. I am merely recommending that we slow down the rate at which these payments increase and these programs grow.

Only a reduction in the growth of spending can keep Federal borrowing down and reduce the damage to the private sector from high interest rates. Only a reduction in spending can make it possible for the Federal Reserve System to avoid an inflationary growth in the money supply and thus restore balance to our economy. A major reduction in the growth of Federal spending can help dispel the uncertainty that so many feel about our economy and put us on the way to curing our economic ills.

If we don't act to slow down the rate of increase in Federal spending, the United States Treasury will be legally obligated to spend more than $360 billion in fiscal year 1976, even if no new programs are enacted. These are not matters of conjecture or prediction, but again, a matter of simple arithmetic. The size of these numbers and their implications for our everyday life and the health of our economic system are shocking.

I submitted to the last Congress a list of budget deferrals and rescissions. There will be more cuts recommended in the budget that I will submit. Even so, the level of outlays for fiscal year 1976 is still much, much too high. Not only is it too high for this year but the decisions we make now will inevitably have a major and growing impact on expenditure levels in future years. I think this is a very fundamental issue that we, the Congress and I, must jointly solve.

Economic disruptions we and others are experiencing stem in part from the fact that the world price of petroleum has quadrupled in the last year. But in all honesty, we cannot put all of the blame on the oil-exporting nations. We, the United States, are not blameless. Our growing dependence upon foreign sources has been adding to our vulnerability for years and years, and we did nothing to prepare ourselves for such an event as the embargo of 1973.

During the 1960's, this country had a surplus capacity of crude oil which we were able to make available to our trading partners whenever there was a disruption of supply. This surplus capacity enabled us to influence both supplies and prices of crude oil throughout the world. Our excess capacity neutralized any effort at establishing an effective cartel, and thus the rest of the world was assured of adequate supplies of oil at reasonable prices.

By 1970, our surplus capacity had vanished, and as a consequence, the latent power of the oil cartel could emerge in full force. Europe and Japan, both heavily dependent on imported oil, now struggle to keep their economies in balance. Even the United States, our country, which is far more self-sufficient than most other industrial countries, has been put under serious pressure.

I am proposing a program which will begin to restore our country's surplus capacity in total energy. In this way, we will be able to assure ourselves reliable and adequate energy and help foster a new world energy stability for other major consuming nations.

But this Nation and, in fact, the world must face the prospect of energy difficulties between now and 1985. This program will impose burdens on all of us with the aim of reducing our consumption of energy and increasing our production. Great attention has been paid to the considerations of fairness, and I can assure you that the burdens will not fall more harshly on those less able to bear them.

I am recommending a plan to make us invulnerable to cutoffs of foreign oil. It will require sacrifices, but it—and this is most important—it will work.

I have set the following national energy goals to assure that our future is as secure and as productive as our past:

First, we must reduce oil imports by 1 million barrels per day by the end of this year and by 2 million barrels per day by the end of 1977.

Second, we must end vulnerability to economic disruption by foreign suppliers by 1985.

Third, we must develop our energy technology and resources so that the United States has the ability to supply a significant share of the energy needs of the free world by the end of this century.

To attain these objectives, we need immediate action to cut imports. Unfortunately, in the short term there are only a limited number of actions which can increase domestic supply. I will press for all of them.

I urge quick action on the necessary legislation to allow commercial production at the Elk Hills, California, Naval Petroleum Reserve. In order that we make greater use of domestic coal resources, I am submitting amendments to the Energy Supply and Environmental Coordination Act which will greatly increase the number of powerplants that can be promptly converted to coal.

Obviously, voluntary conservation continues to be essential, but tougher programs are needed—and needed now. Therefore, I am using Presidential powers to raise the fee on all imported crude oil and petroleum products. The crude oil fee level will be increased $1 per barrel on February 1, by $2 per barrel on March 1, and by $3 per barrel on April 1. I will take actions to reduce undue hardships on any geographical region. The foregoing are interim administrative actions. They will be rescinded when the broader but necessary legislation is enacted.

To that end, I am requesting the Congress to act within 90 days on a more comprehensive energy tax program. It includes: excise taxes and import fees totaling $2 per barrel on product imports and on all crude oil; deregulation of new natural gas and enactment of a natural gas excise tax.

I plan to take Presidential initiative to decontrol the price of domestic crude oil on April 1. I urge the Congress to enact a windfall profits tax by that date to ensure that oil producers do not profit unduly.

The sooner Congress acts, the more effective the oil conservation program will be and the quicker the Federal revenues can be returned to our people.

I am prepared to use Presidential authority to limit imports, as necessary, to guarantee success.

I want you to know that before deciding on my energy conservation program, I considered rationing and higher gasoline taxes as alternatives. In my judgment, neither would achieve the desired results and both would produce unacceptable inequities.

A massive program must be initiated to increase energy supply, to cut demand, and provide new standby emergency programs to achieve the independence we want by 1985. The largest part of increased oil production must come from new frontier areas on the Outer Continental Shelf and from the Naval Petroleum Reserve No. 4 in Alaska. It is the intent of this Administration to move ahead with exploration, leasing, and production on those frontier areas of the Outer Continental Shelf where the environmental risks are acceptable.

Use of our most abundant domestic resource—coal—is severely limited. We must strike a reasonable compromise on environmental concerns with coal. I am submitting Clean Air amendments which will allow greater coal use without sacrificing clean air goals.

I vetoed the strip mining legislation passed by the last Congress. With appropriate changes, I will sign a revised version when it comes to the White House.

I am proposing a number of actions to energize our nuclear power program. I will submit legislation to expedite nuclear leasing and the rapid selection of sites.

In recent months, utilities have cancelled or postponed over 60 percent of planned nuclear expansion and 30 percent of planned additions to non-nuclear capacity. Financing problems for that industry are worsening. I am therefore recommending that the 1-year investment tax credit of 12 percent be extended an additional 2 years to specifically speed the construction of powerplants that do not use natural gas or oil. I am also submitting proposals for selective reform of State utility commission regulations.

To provide the critical stability for our domestic energy production in the face of world price uncertainty, I will request legislation to authorize and require tariffs, import quotas, or price floors to protect our energy prices at levels which will achieve energy independence.

Increasing energy supplies is not enough. We must take additional steps to cut long-term consumption. I therefore propose to the Congress: legislation to make thermal efficiency standards mandatory for all new buildings in the United States; a new tax credit of up to $150 for those homeowners who install insulation equipment; the establishment of an energy conservation program to help low-income families purchase insulation supplies; legislation to modify and defer automotive pollution standards for 5 years, which will enable us to improve automobile gas mileage by 40 percent by 1980.

These proposals and actions, cumulatively, can reduce our dependence on foreign energy supplies from 3 to 5 million barrels per day by 1985. To make the United States invulnerable to foreign disruption, I propose standby emergency legislation and a strategic storage program of 1 billion barrels of oil for domestic needs and 300 million barrels for national defense purposes.

I will ask for the funds needed for energy research and development activities. I have established a goal of 1 million barrels of synthetic fuels and shale oil production per day by 1985 together with an incentive program to achieve it.

I have a very deep belief in America's capabilities. Within the next 10 years, my program envisions: 200 major nuclear powerplants; 250 major new coal mines; 150 major coal-fired powerplants; 30 major new refineries; 20 major new synthetic fuel plants; the drilling of many thousands of new oil wells; the insulation of 18 million homes; and the manufacturing and the sale of millions of new automobiles, trucks, and buses that use much less fuel.

I happen to believe that we can do it. In another crisis—the one in 1942 President Franklin D. Roosevelt said this country would build 60,000 military aircraft. By 1943, production in that program had reached 125,000 aircraft annually. They did it then. We can do it now.

If the Congress and the American people will work with me to attain these targets, they will be achieved and will be surpassed. From adversity, let us seize opportunity. Revenues of some $30 billion from higher energy taxes designed to encourage conservation must be refunded to the American people in a manner which corrects distortions in our tax system wrought by inflation.

People have been pushed into higher tax brackets by inflation, with consequent reduction in their actual spending power. Business taxes are similarly distorted because inflation exaggerates reported profits, resulting in excessive taxes.

Accordingly, I propose that future individual income taxes be reduced by $16.5 billion. This will be done by raising the low-income allowance and reducing tax rates. This continuing tax cut will primarily benefit lower- and middle-income taxpayers.

For example, a typical family of four with a gross income of $5,600 now pays $185 in Federal income taxes. Under this tax cut plan, they would pay nothing. A family of four with a gross income of $12,500 now pays $1,260 in Federal taxes. My proposal reduces that total by $300. Families grossing $20,000 would receive a reduction of $210.

Those with the very lowest incomes, who can least afford higher costs, must also be compensated. I propose a payment of $80 to every person 18 years of age and older in that very limited category.

State and local governments will receive $2 billion in additional revenue sharing to offset their increased energy costs.

To offset inflationary distortions and to generate more economic activity, the corporate tax rate will be reduced from 48 percent to 42 percent.

Now let me turn, if I might, to the international dimension of the present crisis. At no time in our peacetime history has the state of the Nation depended more heavily on the state of the world. And seldom, if ever, has the state of the world depended more heavily on the state of our Nation.

The economic distress is global. We will not solve it at home unless we help to remedy the profound economic dislocation abroad. World trade and monetary structure provides markets, energy, food, and vital raw materials—for all nations. This international system is now in jeopardy.

This Nation can be proud of significant achievements in recent years in solving problems and crises. The Berlin agreement, the SALT agreements, our new relationship with China, the unprecedented efforts in the Middle East are immensely encouraging. But the world is not free from crisis. In a world of 150 nations, where nuclear technology is proliferating and regional conflicts continue, international security cannot be taken for granted.

So, let there be no mistake about it: International cooperation is a vital factor of our lives today. This is not a moment for the American people to turn inward. More than ever before, our own well-being depends on America's determination and America's leadership in the whole wide world.

We are a great Nation—spiritually, politically, militarily, diplomatically, and economically. America's commitment to international security has sustained the safety of allies and friends in many areas—in the Middle East, in Europe, and in Asia. Our turning away would unleash new instabilities, new dangers around the globe, which, in turn, would threaten our own security.

At the end of World War II, we turned a similar challenge into an historic opportunity and, I might add, an historic achievement. An old order was in disarray; political and economic institutions were shattered. In that period, this Nation and its partners built new institutions, new mechanisms of mutual support and cooperation. Today, as then, we face an historic opportunity. If we act imaginatively and boldly, as we acted then, this period will in retrospect be seen as one of the great creative moments of our Nation's history. The whole world is watching to see how we respond.

A resurgent American economy would do more to restore the confidence of the world in its own future than anything else we can do. The program that this

Congress passes can demonstrate to the world that we have started to put our own house in order. If we can show that this Nation is able and willing to help other nations meet the common challenge, it can demonstrate that the United States will fulfill its responsibilities as a leader among nations.

Quite frankly, at stake is the future of industrialized democracies, which have perceived their destiny in common and sustained it in common for 30 years.

The developing nations are also at a turning point. The poorest nations see their hopes of feeding their hungry and developing their societies shattered by the economic crisis. The long-term economic future for the producers of raw materials also depends on cooperative solutions.

Our relations with the Communist countries are a basic factor of the world environment. We must seek to build a long-term basis for coexistence. We will stand by our principles. We will stand by our interests. We will act firmly when challenged. The kind of a world we want depends on a broad policy of creating mutual incentives for restraint and for cooperation.

As we move forward to meet our global challenges and opportunities, we must have the tools to do the job.

Our military forces are strong and ready. This military strength deters aggression against our allies, stabilizes our relations with former adversaries, and protects our homeland. Fully adequate conventional and strategic forces cost many, many billions, but these dollars are sound insurance for our safety and for a more peaceful world.

Military strength alone is not sufficient. Effective diplomacy is also essential in preventing conflict, in building world understanding. The Vladivostok negotiations with the Soviet Union represent a major step in moderating strategic arms competition. My recent discussions with the leaders of the Atlantic community, Japan, and South Korea have contributed to meeting the common challenge.

But we have serious problems before us that require cooperation between the President and the Congress. By the Constitution and tradition, the execution of foreign policy is the responsibility of the President.

In recent years, under the stress of the Vietnam war, legislative restrictions on the President's ability to execute foreign policy and military decisions have proliferated. As a Member of the Congress, I opposed some and I approved others. As President, I welcome the advice and cooperation of the House and the Senate.

But if our foreign policy is to be successful, we cannot rigidly restrict in legislation the ability of the President to act. The conduct of negotiations is ill-suited to such limitations. Legislative restrictions, intended for the best motives and purposes, can have the opposite result, as we have seen most recently in our trade relations with the Soviet Union.

For my part, I pledge this Administration will act in the closest consultation with the Congress as we face delicate situations and troubled times throughout the globe.

When I became President only 5 months ago, I promised the last Congress a policy of communication, conciliation, compromise, and cooperation. I renew that pledge to the new Members of this Congress.

Let me sum it up. America needs a new direction, which I have sought to chart here today—a change of course which will: put the unemployed back to work; increase real income and production; restrain the growth of Federal Government spending; achieve energy independence; and advance the cause of world understanding.

We have the ability. We have the know-how. In partnership with the American people, we will achieve these objectives.

As our 200th anniversary approaches, we owe it to ourselves and to posterity to rebuild our political and economic strength. Let us make America once again and for centuries more to come what it has so long been—a stronghold and a beacon-light of liberty for the whole world.

Thank you.

Gerald R. Ford, 1974–1977

Address before a Joint Session of Congress Reporting on the State of the Union

January 19, 1976

Nineteen seventy-six marked the country's bicentennial, and President Gerald Ford began his 1976 State of the Union message by referring to that anniversary. He spoke of the pride Americans felt in their country, the problems they faced, and his suggestions for change.

The bicentennial year also was a presidential election year, and Ford, who had become president in August 1974 after Richard Nixon's resignation, was seeking his own four-year term in the White House. He would lose narrowly to Democrat Jimmy Carter in November 1976.

In his State of the Union message, Ford called for a "new realism" that included creation of a healthy economy that would curb inflation while adding jobs, set a new balance between government and the individual, and give more responsibility to state and local governments. Opposed to what Republicans thought were the intrusive policies of the New Deal, he stated that the purpose of government was to "create and preserve conditions in which people can translate their ideas into practical reality. In the best of times, much is lost in translation." The president commented that in recent years, the country had become "overconfident" and tried to solve problems with "massive national programs" that often failed to help. "Too often they made things worse," he argued.

The previous year, Ford had declared in his State of the Union message that "the state of the union is not good." This time, he termed it "better" but "still not good enough." He called, as he had before, for slower growth in the rate of federal spending—with defense spending as an exception. He sought tax changes that he said would help create jobs, and he urged Congress to approve additional energy proposals designed to reduce domestic shortages in natural gas, among other goals.

Addressing health and human services, Ford called for catastrophic health insurance for those covered by Medicare but rejected ideas aimed at universal heath care, stating: "We cannot realistically afford federally dictated national health insurance providing full coverage for all 215 million Americans." To strengthen the Social Security trust fund, the president proposed an increase of three-tenths of 1 percent in Social Security taxes. In addition, he asked for a tightening in the rules for welfare eligibility and benefits and called for 500 more federal agents to help fight crime in eleven major cities.

The Central Intelligence Agency had been the subject of a presidential commission's investigation as well as a congressional investigation during Ford's administration. In response, he pledged to reform and strengthen the U.S. intelligence community.

While most of Ford's address focused on domestic issues, he also discussed foreign policy, calling it "sound and strong," and painted a positive picture of the country's relationships with various countries around the world. He criticized Congress for opting to end aid to U.S.-backed forces in the African nation of Angola.

Mr. Speaker, Mr. Vice President, Members of the 94th Congress, and distinguished guests:

As we begin our Bicentennial, America is still one of the youngest nations in recorded history. Long before our forefathers came to these shores, men and women had been struggling on this planet to forge a better life for themselves and their families.

In man's long, upward march from savagery and slavery—throughout the nearly 2,000 years of the Christian calendar, the nearly 6,000 years of Jewish reckoning—there have been many deep, terrifying valleys, but also many bright and towering peaks.

One peak stands highest in the ranges of human history. One example shines forth of a people uniting to produce abundance and to share the good life fairly and with freedom. One union holds out the promise of justice and opportunity for every citizen: That union is the United States of America.

We have not remade paradise on Earth. We know perfection will not be found here. But think for a minute how far we have come in 200 years.

We came from many roots, and we have many branches. Yet all Americans across the eight generations that separate us from the stirring deeds of 1776, those who know no other homeland and those who just found refuge among our shores, say in unison: "I am proud of America, and I am proud to be an American. Life will be a little better here for my children than for me. I believe this not because I am told to believe it, but because life has been better for me than it was for my father and my mother. I know it will be better for my children because my hands, my brains, my voice, and my vote can help make it happen."

It has happened here in America. It has happened to you and to me. Government exists to create and preserve conditions in which people can translate their ideas into practical reality. In the best of times, much is lost in translation. But we try. Sometimes we have tried and failed. Always we have had the best of intentions.

But in the recent past, we sometimes forgot the sound principles that guided us through most of our history. We wanted to accomplish great things and solve age-old problems. And we became overconfident of our abilities. We tried to be a policeman abroad and the indulgent parent here at home.

We thought we could transform the country through massive national programs, but often the programs did not work. Too often they only made things worse. In our rush to accomplish great deeds quickly, we trampled on sound principles of restraint and endangered the rights of individuals. We unbalanced our economic system by the huge and unprecedented growth of Federal expenditures and borrowing. And we were not totally honest with ourselves about how much these programs would cost and how we would pay for them. Finally, we shifted our emphasis from defense to domestic problems while our adversaries continued a massive buildup of arms.

The time has now come for a fundamentally different approach for a new realism that is true to the great principles upon which this Nation was founded.

We must introduce a new balance to our economy—a balance that favors not only sound, active government but also a much more vigorous, healthy economy that can create new jobs and hold down prices.

We must introduce a new balance in the relationship between the individual and the government—a balance that favors greater individual freedom and self-reliance.

We must strike a new balance in our system of federalism—a balance that favors greater responsibility and freedom for the leaders of our State and local governments.

We must introduce a new balance between the spending on domestic programs and spending on defense—a balance that ensures we will fully meet our obligation to the needy while also protecting our security in a world that is still hostile to freedom.

And in all that we do, we must be more honest with the American people, promising them no more than we can deliver and delivering all that we promise.

The genius of America has been its incredible ability to improve the lives of its citizens through a unique combination of governmental and free citizen activity.

History and experience tells us that moral progress cannot come in comfortable and in complacent times, but out of trial and out of confusion. Tom Paine aroused the troubled Americans of 1776 to stand up to the times that try men's souls because the harder the conflict, the more glorious the triumph.

Just a year ago I reported that the state of the Union was not good. Tonight, I report that the state of our Union is better—in many ways a lot better—but still not good enough.

To paraphrase Tom Paine, 1975 was not a year for summer soldiers and sunhine patriots. It was a year of fears and alarms and of dire forecasts—most of which never happened and won't happen.

As you recall, the year 1975 opened with rancor and with bitterness. Political misdeeds of the past had neither been forgotten nor forgiven. The longest, most divisive war in our history was winding toward an unhappy conclusion. Many feared that the end of that foreign war of men and machines meant the beginning of a domestic war of recrimination and reprisal. Friends and adversaries abroad were asking whether America had lost its nerve. Finally, our economy was ravaged by inflation—inflation that was plunging us into the worse recession in four decades. At the same time, Americans became increasingly alienated from big institutions. They were steadily losing confidence, not just in big government but in big business, big labor, and big education, among others. Ours was a troubled land.

And so, 1975 was a year of hard decisions, difficult compromises, and a new realism that taught us something important about America. It brought back a needed measure of common sense, steadfastness, and self-discipline.

Americans did not panic or demand instant but useless cures. In all sectors, people met their difficult problems with the restraint and with responsibility worthy of their great heritage.

Add up the separate pieces of progress in 1975, subtract the setbacks, and the sum total shows that we are not only headed in a new direction, a direction which I proposed 12 months ago, but it turned out to be the right direction.

It is the right direction because it follows the truly revolutionary American concept of 1776, which holds that in a free society the making of public policy and successful problem solving involves much more than government. It involves a full partnership among all branches and all levels of government, private institutions, and individual citizens.

Common sense tells me to stick to that steady course.

Take the state of our economy. Last January, most things were rapidly getting worse. This January, most things are slowly but surely getting better.

The worst recession since World War II turned around in April. The best cost-of-living news of the past year is that double-digit inflation of 12 percent or higher was cut almost in half. The worst—unemployment remains far too high.

Today, nearly 1,700,000 more Americans are working than at the bottom of the recession. At year's end, people were again being hired much faster than they were being laid off.

Yet, let's be honest. Many Americans have not yet felt these changes in their daily lives. They still see prices going up far too fast, and they still know the fear of unemployment.

We are also a growing nation. We need more and more jobs every year. Today's economy has produced over 85 million jobs for Americans, but we need a lot more jobs, especially for the young.

My first objective is to have sound economic growth without inflation.

We all know from recent experience what runaway inflation does to ruin every other worthy purpose. We are slowing it. We must stop it cold.

For many Americans, the way to a healthy, noninflationary economy has become increasingly apparent. The Government must stop spending so much and stop borrowing so much of our money. More money must remain in private hands where it will do the most good. To hold down the cost of living, we must hold down the cost of government.

In the past decade, the Federal budget has been growing at an average rate of over 10 percent a year. The budget I am submitting Wednesday cuts this rate of growth in half. I have kept my promise to submit a budget for the next fiscal year of $395 billion. In fact, it is $394.2 billion.

By holding down the growth of Federal spending, we can afford additional tax cuts and return to the people who pay taxes more decisionmaking power over their own lives.

Last month I signed legislation to extend the 1975 tax reductions for the first 6 months of this year. I now propose that effective July 1, 1976, we give our taxpayers a tax cut of approximately $10 billion more than Congress agreed to in December.

My broader tax reduction would mean that for a family of four making $15,000 a year, there will be $227 more in take-home pay annually. Hardworking Americans caught in the middle can really use that kind of extra cash.

My recommendations for a firm restraint on the growth of Federal spending and for greater tax reduction are simple and straightforward. For every dollar saved in cutting the growth in the Federal budget, we can have an added dollar of Federal tax reduction.

We can achieve a balanced budget by 1979 if we have the courage and the wisdom to continue to reduce the growth of Federal spending.

One test of a healthy economy is a job for every American who wants to work. Government—our kind of government—cannot create that many jobs. But the Federal Government can create conditions and incentives for private business and industry to make more and more jobs.

Five out of six jobs in this country are in private business and in industry. Common sense tells us this is the place to look for more jobs and to find them faster. I mean real, rewarding, permanent jobs.

To achieve this we must offer the American people greater incentives to invest in the future. My tax proposals are a major step in that direction. To supplement these proposals, I ask that Congress enact changes in Federal tax laws that will speed up plant expansion and the purchase of new equipment. My recommendations will concentrate this job-creation tax incentive in areas where the unemployment rate now runs over 7 percent. Legislation to get this started must be approved at the earliest possible date.

Within the strict budget total that I will recommend for the coming year, I will ask for additional housing assistance for 500,000 families. These programs will expand housing opportunities, spur construction, and help to house moderate- and low-income families.

We had a disappointing year in the housing industry in 1975. But with lower interest rates and available mortgage money, we can have a healthy recovery in 1976.

A necessary condition of a healthy economy is freedom from the petty tyranny of massive government regulation. We are wasting literally millions of working hours costing billions of taxpayers' and consumers' dollars because of bureaucratic redtape. The American farmer, who now feeds 215 million Americans, but also millions worldwide, has shown how much more he can produce without the shackles of government control.

Now, we badly need reforms in other key areas in our economy: the airlines, trucking, railroads, and financial institutions. I have submitted concrete plans in each of these areas, not to help this or that industry, but to foster competition and to bring prices down for the consumer.

This administration, in addition, will strictly enforce the Federal antitrust laws for the very same purposes.

Taking a longer look at America's future, there can be neither sustained growth nor more jobs unless we continue to have an assured supply of energy to run our economy. Domestic production of oil and gas is still declining. Our dependence on foreign oil at high prices is still too great, draining jobs and dollars away from our own economy at the rate of $125 per year for every American.

Last month, I signed a compromise national energy bill which enacts a part of my comprehensive energy independence program. This legislation was late, not the complete answer to energy independence, but still a start in the right direction.

I again urge the Congress to move ahead immediately on the remainder of my energy proposals to make America invulnerable to the foreign oil cartel.

My proposals, as all of you know, would reduce domestic natural gas shortages; allow production from Federal petroleum reserves; stimulate effective conservation, including revitalization of our railroads and the expansion of our urban transportation systems; develop more and cleaner energy from our vast coal resources; expedite clean and safe nuclear power production; create a new national energy independence authority to stimulate vital energy investment; and accelerate development of technology to capture energy from the Sun and the Earth for this and future generations.

Also, I ask, for the sake of future generations, that we preserve the family farm and family-owned small business. Both strengthen America and give stability to our economy. I will propose estate tax changes so that family businesses and family farms can be handed down from generation to generation without having to be sold to pay taxes.

I propose tax changes to encourage people to invest in America's future, and their own, through a plan that gives moderate-income families income tax benefits if they make long-term investments in common stock in American companies.

The Federal Government must and will respond to clear-cut national needs—for this and future generations.

Hospital and medical services in America are among the best in the world, but the cost of a serious and extended illness can quickly wipe out a family's lifetime savings. Increasing health costs are of deep concern to all and a powerful force pushing up the cost of living. The burden of catastrophic illness can be borne by very few in our society. We must eliminate this fear from every family.

I propose catastrophic health insurance for everybody covered by Medicare. To finance this added protection, fees for short-term care will go up somewhat, but nobody after reaching age 65 will have to pay more than $500 a year for covered hospital or nursing home care, nor more than $250 for 1 year's doctor bills.

We cannot realistically afford federally dictated national health insurance providing full coverage for all 215 million Americans. The experience of other countries raises questions about the quality as well as the cost of such plans. But I do envision the day when we may use the private health insurance system to offer more middle-income families high quality health services at prices they can afford and shield them also from their catastrophic illnesses.

Using resources now available, I propose improving the Medicare and other Federal health programs to help those who really need protection—older people and the poor. To help States and local governments give better health care to the poor, I propose that we combine 16 existing Federal programs, including Medicaid, into a single $10 billion Federal grant.

Funds would be divided among States under a new formula which provides a larger share of Federal money to those States that have a larger share of low-income families.

I will take further steps to improve the quality of medical and hospital care for those who have served in our Armed Forces.

Now let me speak about social security. Our Federal social security system for people who have worked and contributed to it for all their lives is a vital part of our economic system. Its value is no longer debatable. In my budget for fiscal year 1977, I am recommending that the full cost-of-living increases in the social security benefits be paid during the coming year.

But I am concerned about the integrity of our Social Security Trust Fund that enables people—those retired and those still working who will retire—to count on this source of retirement income. Younger workers watch their deductions rise and wonder if they will be adequately protected in the future. We must meet this challenge head on. Simple arithmetic warns all of us that the Social Security Trust Fund is headed for trouble. Unless we act soon to make sure the fund takes in as much as it pays out, there will be no security for old or for young.

I must, therefore, recommend a three-tenths of 1 percent increase in both employer and employee social security taxes effective January 1, 1977. This will cost each covered employee less than 1 extra dollar a week and will ensure the integrity of the trust fund.

As we rebuild our economy, we have a continuing responsibility to provide a temporary cushion to the unemployed. At my request, the Congress enacted two extensions and two expansions in unemployment insurance which helped those who were jobless during 1975. These programs will continue in 1976.

In my fiscal year 1977 budget, I am also requesting funds to continue proven job training and employment opportunity programs for millions of other Americans.

Compassion and a sense of community—two of America's greatest strengths throughout our history—tell us we must take care of our neighbors who cannot take care of themselves. The host of Federal programs in this field reflect our generosity as a people.

But everyone realizes that when it comes to welfare, government at all levels is not doing the job well. Too many of our welfare programs are inequitable and invite abuse. Too many of our welfare programs have problems from beginning to end. Worse, we are wasting badly needed resources without reaching many of the truly needy.

Complex welfare programs cannot be reformed overnight. Surely we cannot simply dump welfare into the laps of the 50 States, their local taxpayers, or their private charities, and just walk away from it. Nor is it the right time for massive and sweeping changes while we are still recovering from the recession.

Nevertheless, there are still plenty of improvements that we can make. I will ask Congress for Presidential authority to tighten up the rules for eligibility and benefits.

Last year I twice sought long overdue reform of the scandal-riddled food stamp program. This year I say again: Let's give food stamps to those most in need. Let's not give any to those who don't need them.

Protecting the life and property of the citizen at home is the responsibility of all public officials, but is primarily the job of local and State law enforcement authorities.

Americans have always found the very thought of a Federal police force repugnant, and so do I. But there are proper ways in which we can help to insure domestic tranquility as the Constitution charges us.

My recommendations on how to control violent crime were submitted to the Congress last June with strong emphasis on protecting the innocent victims of crime. To keep a convicted criminal from committing more crimes, we must put him in prison so he cannot harm more law-abiding citizens. To be effective, this punishment must be swift and it must be certain.

Too often, criminals are not sent to prison after conviction but are allowed to return to the streets. Some judges are reluctant to send convicted criminals to prison because of inadequate facilities. To alleviate this problem at the Federal level, my new budget proposes the construction of four new Federal facilities.

To speed Federal justice, I propose an increase this year in the United States attorneys prosecuting Federal crimes and the reinforcement of the number of United States marshals. Additional Federal judges are needed, as recommended by me and the Judicial Conference.

Another major threat to every American's person and property is the criminal carrying a handgun. The way to cut down on the criminal use of guns is not to take guns away from the law-abiding citizen, but to impose mandatory sentences for crimes in which a gun is used, make it harder to obtain cheap guns for criminal purposes, and concentrate gun control enforcement in high crime areas.

My budget recommends 500 additional Federal agents in the 11 largest metropolitan high-crime areas to help local authorities stop criminals from selling and using handguns.

The sale of hard drugs is tragically on the increase again. I have directed all agencies of the Federal Government to step up law enforcement efforts against those who deal in drugs. In 1975, I am glad to report, Federal agents seized substantially more heroin coming into our country than in 1974.

As President, I have talked personally with the leaders of Mexico, Colombia, and Turkey to urge greater efforts by their Governments to control effectively the production and shipment of hard drugs.

I recommended months ago that the Congress enact mandatory fixed sentences for persons convicted of Federal crimes involving the sale of hard drugs. Hard drugs, we all know, degrade the spirit as they destroy the body of their users.

It is unrealistic and misleading to hold out the hope that the Federal Government can move into every neighborhood and clean up crime. Under the Constitution, the greatest responsibility for curbing crime lies with State and local authorities. They are the frontline fighters in the war against crime.

There are definite ways in which the Federal Government can help them. I will propose in the new budget that Congress authorize almost $7 billion over the next 5 years to assist State and local governments to protect the safety and property of all their citizens.

As President, I pledge the strict enforcement of Federal laws and—by example, support, and leadership—to help State and local authorities enforce their laws. Together, we must protect the victims of crime and ensure domestic tranquility.

Last year I strongly recommended a 5-year extension of the existing revenue sharing legislation, which thus far has provided $23 1/2 billion to help State and local units of government solve problems at home. This program has been effective with decisionmaking transferred from the Federal Government to locally elected officials. Congress must act this year, or State and local units of government will have to drop programs or raise local taxes.

Including my health care program reforms, I propose to consolidate some 59 separate Federal programs and provide flexible Federal dollar grants to help States, cities, and local agencies in such important areas as education, child nutrition, and social services. This flexible system will do the job better and do it closer to home.

The protection of the lives and property of Americans from foreign enemies is one of my primary responsibilities as President.

In a world of instant communications and intercontinental ballistic missiles, in a world economy that is global and interdependent, our relations with other nations become more, not less, important to the lives of Americans.

America has had a unique role in the world since the day of our independence 200 years ago. And ever since the end of World War II, we have borne—successfully—a heavy responsibility for ensuring a stable world order and hope for human progress.

Today, the state of our foreign policy is sound and strong. We are at peace, and I will do all in my power to keep it that way.

Our military forces are capable and ready. Our military power is without equal, and I intend to keep it that way.

Our principal alliances with the industrial democracies of the Atlantic community and Japan have never been more solid.

A further agreement to limit the strategic arms race may be achieved.

We have an improving relationship with China, the world's most populous nation. The key elements for peace among the nations of the Middle East now exist. Our traditional friendships in Latin America, Africa, and Asia continue.

We have taken the role of leadership in launching a serious and hopeful dialog between the industrial world and the developing world.

We have helped to achieve significant reform of the international monetary system.

We should be proud of what America, what our country, has accomplished in these areas, and I believe the American people are.

The American people have heard too much about how terrible our mistakes, how evil our deeds, and how misguided our purposes. The American people know better.

The truth is we are the world's greatest democracy. We remain the symbol of man's aspiration for liberty and well-being. We are the embodiment of hope for progress.

I say it is time we quit downgrading ourselves as a nation. Of course, it is our responsibility to learn the right lesson from past mistakes. It is our duty to see that they never happen again. But our greater duty is to look to the future. The world's troubles will not go away.

The American people want strong and effective international and defense policies. In our constitutional system, these policies should reflect consultation and accommodation between the President and the Congress. But in the final analysis, as the framers of our Constitution knew from hard experience, the foreign relations of the United States can be conducted effectively only if there is strong central direction that allows flexibility of action. That responsibility clearly rests with the President.

I pledge to the American people policies which seek a secure, just, and peaceful world. I pledge to the Congress to work with you to that end.

We must not face a future in which we can no longer help our friends, such as Angola, even in limited and carefully controlled ways. We must not lose all capacity to respond short of military intervention.

Some hasty actions of the Congress during the past year—most recently in respect to Angola—were, in my view, very shortsighted. Unfortunately, they are still very much on the minds of our allies and our adversaries.

A strong defense posture gives weight to our values and our views in international negotiations. It assures the vigor of our alliances. And it sustains our efforts to promote settlements of international conflicts. Only from a position of strength can we negotiate a balanced agreement to limit the growth of nuclear arms. Only a balanced agreement will serve our interests and minimize the threat of nuclear confrontation.

The defense budget I will submit to the Congress for fiscal year 1977 will show an essential increase over the current year. It provides for real growth in purchasing power over this year's defense budget, which includes the cost of the all-volunteer force.

We are continuing to make economies to enhance the efficiency of our military forces. But the budget I will submit represents the necessity of American strength for the real world in which we live.

As conflict and rivalry persist in the world, our United States intelligence capabilities must be the best in the world.

The crippling of our foreign intelligence services increases the danger of American involvement in direct armed conflict. Our adversaries are encouraged to attempt new adventures while our own ability to monitor events and to influence events short of military action is undermined. Without effective intelligence capability, the United States stands blindfolded and hobbled.

In the near future, I will take actions to reform and strengthen our intelligence community. I ask for your positive cooperation. It is time to go beyond sensationalism and ensure an effective, responsible, and responsive intelligence capability.

Tonight I have spoken about our problems at home and abroad. I have recommended policies that will meet the challenge of our third century. I have no doubt that our Union will endure, better, stronger, and with more individual freedom. We can see forward only dimly—1 year, 5 years, a generation perhaps. Like our forefathers, we know that if we meet the challenges of our own time with a common sense of purpose and conviction, if we remain true to our Constitution and to our ideals, then we can know that the future will be better than the past.

I see America today crossing a threshold, not just because it is our Bicentennial but because we have been tested in adversity. We have taken a new look at what we want to be and what we want our Nation to become.

I see America resurgent, certain once again that life will be better for our children than it is for us, seeking strength that cannot be counted in megatons and riches that cannot be eroded by inflation.

I see these United States of America moving forward as before toward a more perfect Union where the government serves and the people rule.

We will not make this happen simply by making speeches, good or bad, yours or mine, but by hard work and hard decisions made with courage and with common sense.

I have heard many inspiring Presidential speeches, but the words I remember best were spoken by Dwight D. Eisenhower. "America is not good because it is great," the President said. "America is great because it is good."

President Eisenhower was raised in a poor but religious home in the heart of America. His simple words echoed President Lincoln's eloquent testament that "right makes might." And Lincoln in turn evoked the silent image of George Washington kneeling in prayer at Valley Forge.

So, all these magic memories which link eight generations of Americans are summed up in the inscription just above me. How many times have we seen it? "In God We Trust."

Let us engrave it now in each of our hearts as we begin our Bicentennial.

Gerald R. Ford, 1974–1977

Address before a Joint Session of Congress Reporting on the State of the Union

January 12, 1977

Gerald Ford delivered his last State of the Union message as an outgoing president, just eight days before the inauguration of Jimmy Carter.

Ford had become president in August 1974 after Richard Nixon resigned during the Watergate scandal. A longtime House member from Michigan, Ford had served as House minority leader before Nixon named him to replace Spiro Agnew as vice president in 1973. Ford is the only president never to have been elected to either the presidency or the vice presidency.

In 1976 Ford sought his own four-year term as president. He faced, and overcame, a tough challenge in the Republican primary from Ronald Reagan, the conservative former California governor who would win the presidency in 1980. Ford's Democratic opponent in November was former Georgia governor Jimmy Carter. In the end, Carter narrowly defeated Ford, taking 50.1 percent of the popular vote to Ford's 48 percent, and 297 electoral votes to Ford's 240. The Democrats also retained their large majorities in the House and Senate.

The president called the state of the union "good," an upgrade from his 1975 description of "not good" and his 1976 description of "better." He praised the country's tradition of "orderly transitions" of power and said he wanted the new president to have an "easier start than I had."

Ford drew a negative picture of the country's situation upon his accession to the presidency in the wake of Watergate, the Vietnam War, and economic troubles. He proclaimed that Americans' belief in themselves, their leaders, and the future had returned.

In contrast to his previous messages, Ford spent most of this State of the Union message discussing international and defense issues. He highlighted a variety of foreign policy efforts undertaken during his administration, including negotiations with Middle Eastern countries regarding a framework for peace and with the Soviet Union on maintaining a strategic nuclear balance. He also stated that his administration had worked to increase the resources spent on national defense, and he urged a continuation of this trend.

On the domestic front, Ford called jobs the country's "most pressing need," adding that while his administration had created jobs, there were still "too many" unemployed Americans; he termed this "his greatest regret" as he left the White House. He also criticized what he termed unsatisfactory progress toward a goal of energy independence and toward reducing the size and spending of the federal government.

Ford would retire to Palm Springs, California, upon leaving the White House.

Mr. Speaker, Mr. Vice President, Members of the 95th Congress, and distinguished guests:

In accordance with the Constitution, I come before you once again to report on the state of the Union.

This report will be my last—maybe—but for the Union it is only the first of such reports in our third century of independence, the close of which none of us will ever see. We can be confident, however, that 100 years from now a freely elected President will come before a freely elected Congress chosen to renew our great Republic's pledge to the Government of the people, by the people, and for the people.

For my part I pray the third century we are beginning will bring to all Americans, our children and their children's children, a greater measure of individual equality, opportunity, and justice, a greater abundance of spiritual and material blessings, and a higher quality of life, liberty, and the pursuit of happiness.

The state of the Union is a measurement of the many elements of which it is composed—a political union of diverse States, an economic union of varying interests, an intellectual union of common convictions, and a moral union of immutable ideals.

Taken in sum, I can report that the state of the Union is good. There is room for improvement, as always, but today we have a more perfect Union than when my stewardship began.

As a people we discovered that our Bicentennial was much more than a celebration of the past; it became a joyous reaffirmation of all that it means to be Americans, a confirmation before all the world of the vitality and durability of our free institutions. I am proud to have been privileged to preside over the affairs of our Federal Government during these eventful years when we proved, as I said in my first words upon assuming office, that "our Constitution works; our great Republic is a Government of laws and not of men. Here the people rule."

The people have spoken; they have chosen a new President and a new Congress to work their will. I congratulate you—particularly the new Members—as sincerely as I did President-elect Carter. In a few days it will be his duty to outline for you his priorities and legislative recommendations. Tonight I will not infringe on that responsibility, but rather wish him the very best in all that is good for our country.

During the period of my own service in this Capitol and in the White House, I can recall many orderly transitions of governmental responsibility—of problems as well as of position, of burdens as well as of power. The genius of the American system is that we do this so naturally and so normally. There are no soldiers marching in the street except in the Inaugural Parade; no public demonstrations except for some of the dancers at the Inaugural Ball; the opposition party doesn't go underground, but goes on functioning vigorously in the Congress and in the country; and our vigilant press goes right on probing and publishing our faults and our follies, confirming the wisdom of the framers of the first amendment.

Because of the transfer of authority in our form of government affects the state of the Union and of the world, I am happy to report to you that the current transition is proceeding very well. I was determined that it should; I wanted the new President to get off on an easier start than I had.

When I became President on August 9, 1974, our Nation was deeply divided and tormented. In rapid succession the Vice President and the President had resigned in disgrace. We were still struggling with the after-effects of a long, unpopular, and bloody war in Southeast Asia. The economy was unstable and racing toward the worst recession in 40 years. People were losing jobs. The cost of living was soaring. The Congress and the Chief Executive were at loggerheads. The integrity of our constitutional process and other institutions was being questioned. For more than 15 years domestic spending had soared as Federal programs multiplied, and the expense escalated annually. During the same period our national security needs were steadily short-changed. In the grave situation which prevailed in August 1974, our will to maintain our international leadership was in doubt.

I asked for your prayers and went to work.

In January 1975 I reported to the Congress that the state of the Union was not good. I proposed urgent action to improve the economy and to achieve energy independence in 10 years. I reassured America's allies and sought to reduce the danger of confrontation with potential adversaries. I pledged a new direction for America. 1975 was a year of difficult decisions, but Americans responded with realism, common sense, and self-discipline.

By January 1976 we were headed in a new direction, which I hold to be the right direction for a free society. It was guided by the belief that successful problem-solving requires more than Federal action alone, that it involves a full partnership among all branches and all levels of government and public policies which nurture and promote the creative energies of private enterprises, institutions, and individual citizens.

A year ago I reported that the state of the Union was better—in many ways a lot better—but still not good enough. Common sense told me to stick to the steady course we were on, to continue to restrain the inflationary growth of government, to reduce taxes as well as spending, to return local decisions to local officials, to provide for long-range sufficiency in energy and national security needs. I resisted the immense pressures of an election year to open the floodgates of Federal money and the temptation to promise more than I could deliver. I told it as it was to the American people and demonstrated to the world that in our spirited political competition, as in this chamber, Americans can disagree without being disagreeable.

Now, after 30 months as your President, I can say that while we still have a way to go, I am proud of the long way we have come together.

I am proud of the part I have had in rebuilding confidence in the Presidency, confidence in our free system, and confidence in our future. Once again, Americans believe in themselves, in their leaders, and in the promise that tomorrow holds for their children.

I am proud that today America is at peace. None of our sons are fighting and dying in battle anywhere in the world. And the chance for peace among all nations is improved by our determination to honor our vital commitments in defense of peace and freedom.

I am proud that the United States has strong defenses, strong alliances, and a sound and courageous foreign policy.

Our alliances with major partners, the great industrial democracies of Western Europe, Japan, and Canada, have never been more solid. Consultations on mutual security, defense, and East-West relations have grown closer. Collaboration has branched out into new fields such as energy, economic policy, and relations with the Third World. We have used many avenues for cooperation, including summit meetings held among major allied countries. The friendship of the democracies is deeper, warmer, and more effective than at any time in 30 years.

We are maintaining stability in the strategic nuclear balance and pushing back the specter of nuclear war. A decisive step forward was taken in the Vladivostok Accord which I negotiated with General Secretary [Leonid] Brezhnev—joint recognition that an equal ceiling should be placed on the number of strategic weapons on each side. With resolve and wisdom on the part of both nations, a good agreement is well within reach this year.

The framework for peace in the Middle East has been built. Hopes for future progress in the Middle East were stirred by the historic agreements we reached and the trust and confidence that we formed. Thanks to American leadership, the prospects for peace in the Middle East are brighter than they have been in three decades. The Arab states and Israel continue to look to us to lead them from confrontation and war to a new era of accommodation and peace. We have no alternative but to persevere, and I am sure we will. The opportunities for a final settlement are great, and the price of failure is a return to the bloodshed and hatred that for too long have brought tragedy to all of the peoples of this area and repeatedly edged the world to the brink of war.

Our relationship with the People's Republic of China is proving its importance and its durability. We are finding more and more common ground between our two countries on basic questions of international affairs.

In my two trips to Asia as President, we have reaffirmed America's continuing vital interest in the peace and security of Asia and the Pacific Basin, established a new partnership with Japan, confirmed our dedication to the security of Korea, and reinforced our ties with the free nations of Southeast Asia.

An historic dialog has begun between industrial nations and developing nations. Most proposals on the table are the initiatives of the United States, including those on food, energy, technology, trade, investment, and commodities. We are well launched on this process of shaping positive and reliable economic relations between rich nations and poor nations over the long term.

We have made progress in trade negotiations and avoided protectionism during recession. We strengthened the international monetary system. During the past 2 years the free world's most important economic powers have already brought about important changes that serve both developed and developing economies. The momentum already achieved must be nurtured and strengthened, for the prosperity of the rich and poor depends upon it.

In Latin America, our relations have taken on a new maturity and a sense of common enterprise.

In Africa the quest for peace, racial justice, and economic progress is at a crucial point. The United States, in close cooperation with the United Kingdom, is actively engaged in this historic process. Will change come about by warfare and chaos and foreign intervention? Or will it come about by negotiated and fair solutions, ensuring majority rule, minority rights, and economic advance? America is committed to the side of peace and justice and to the principle that Africa should shape its own future, free of outside intervention.

American leadership has helped to stimulate new international efforts to stem the proliferation of nuclear weapons and to shape a comprehensive treaty governing the use of oceans.

I am gratified by these accomplishments. They constitute a record of broad success for America and for the peace and prosperity of all mankind. This administration leaves to its successor a world in better condition than we found. We leave, as well, a solid foundation for progress on a range of issues that are vital to the well-being of America.

What has been achieved in the field of foreign affairs and what can be accomplished by the new administration demonstrate the genius of Americans working together for the common good. It is this, our remarkable ability to work together, that has made us a unique nation. It is Congress, the President, and the people striving for a better world.

I know all patriotic Americans want this Nation's foreign policy to succeed. I urge members of my party in this Congress to give the new President loyal support in this area. I express the hope that this new Congress will reexamine its constitutional role in international affairs.

The exclusive right to declare war, the duty to advise and consent on the part of the Senate, the power of the purse on the part of the House are ample authority for the legislative branch and should be jealously guarded. But because we may have been too careless of these powers in the past does not justify congressional intrusion into, or obstruction of, the proper exercise of Presidential responsibilities now or in the future. There can be only one Commander in Chief. In these times crises cannot be managed and wars cannot be waged by committee, nor can peace be pursued solely by parliamentary debate. To the ears of the world, the President speaks for the Nation. While he is, of course, ultimately accountable to the Congress, the courts, and the people, he and his emissaries must not be handicapped in advance in their relations with foreign governments as has sometimes happened in the past.

At home I am encouraged by the Nation's recovery from the recession and our steady return to sound economic growth. It is now continuing after the recent period of uncertainty, which is part of the price we pay for free elections.

Our most pressing need today and the future is more jobs—productive, permanent jobs created by a thriving economy. We must revise our tax system both to ease the burden of heavy taxation and to encourage the investment necessary for the creation of productive jobs for all Americans who want to work.

Earlier this month I proposed a permanent income tax reduction of $10 billion below current levels, including raising the personal exemption from $750 to $1,000. I also recommended a series of measures to stimulate investment, such as accelerated depreciation for new plants and equipment in areas of high unemployment, a reduction in the corporate tax rate from 48 to 46 percent, and eliminating the present double taxation of dividends. I strongly urge the Congress to pass these measures to help create the productive, permanent jobs in the private economy that are so essential for our future.

All the basic trends are good; we are not on the brink of another recession or economic disaster. If we follow prudent policies that encourage productive investment and discourage destructive inflation, we will come out on top, and I am sure we will.

We have successfully cut inflation by more than half. When I took office, the Consumer Price Index was rising at 12.2 percent a year. During 1976 the rate of inflation was 5 percent.

We have created more jobs—over 4 million more jobs today than in the spring of 1975. Throughout this Nation today we have over 88 million people in useful, productive jobs—more than at any other time in our Nation's history. But there are still too many Americans unemployed. This is the greatest regret that I have as I leave office.

We brought about with the Congress, after much delay, the renewal of the general revenue sharing. We expanded community development and Federal manpower programs. We began a significant urban mass transit program. Federal programs today provide more funds for our States and local governments than ever before—$70 billion for the current fiscal year. Through these programs and others that provide aid directly to individuals, we have kept faith with our tradition of compassionate help for those who need it. As we begin our third century we can be proud of the progress that we have made in meeting human needs for all of our citizens.

We have cut the growth of crime by nearly 90 percent. Two years ago crime was increasing at the rate of 18 percent annually. In the first three quarters of 1976, that growth rate had been cut to 2 percent. But crime, and the fear of crime, remains one of the most serious problems facing our citizens.

We have had some successes, and there have been some disappointments. Bluntly, I must remind you that we have not made satisfactory progress toward achieving energy independence. Energy is absolutely vital to the defense of our country, to the strength of our economy, and to the quality of our lives.

Two years ago I proposed to the Congress the first comprehensive national energy program—a specific and coordinated set of measures that would end our vulnerability to embargo, blockade, or arbitrary price increases and would mobilize U.S. technology and resources to supply a significant share of the free world's energy after 1985. Of the major energy proposals I submitted 2 years ago, only half, belatedly, became law. In 1973 we were dependent upon foreign oil imports for 36 percent of our needs. Today, we are 40-percent dependent, and we'll pay out $34 billion for foreign oil this year. Such vulnerability at present or in the future is intolerable and must be ended.

The answer to where we stand on our national energy effort today reminds me of the old argument about whether the tank is half full or half empty. The pessimist will say we have half failed to achieve our 10-year energy goals; the optimist will say that we have half succeeded. I am always an optimist, but we must make up for lost time.

We have laid a solid foundation for completing the enormous task which confronts us. I have signed into law five major energy bills which contain significant measures for conservation, resource development, stockpiling, and standby authorities. We have moved forward to develop the naval petroleum reserves; to build a 500-million barrel strategic petroleum stockpile; to phase out unnecessary Government allocation and price controls; to develop a lasting relationship with other oil consuming nations; to improve the efficiency of energy use through conservation in automobiles, buildings, and industry; and to expand research on new technology and renewable resources such as wind power, geothermal and solar energy. All these actions, significant as they are for the long term, are only the beginning.

I recently submitted to the Congress my proposals to reorganize the Federal energy structure and the hard choices which remain if we are serious about reducing our dependence upon foreign energy. These include programs to reverse our declining production of natural gas and increase incentives for domestic crude oil production. I proposed to minimize environmental uncertainties affecting coal development, expand nuclear power generation, and create an energy independence authority to provide government financial assistance for vital energy programs where private capital is not available.

We must explore every reasonable prospect for meeting our energy needs when our current domestic reserves of oil and natural gas begin to dwindle in the next decade. I urgently ask Congress and the new administration to move quickly on these issues. This Nation has the resources and the capability to achieve our energy goals if its Government has the will to proceed, and I think we do.

I have been disappointed by inability to complete many of the meaningful organizational reforms which I contemplated for the Federal Government, although a start has been made. For example, the Federal judicial system has long served as a model for other courts. But today it is threatened by a shortage of qualified Federal judges and an explosion of litigation claiming Federal jurisdiction. I commend to the new administration and the Congress the recent report and recommendations of the Department of Justice, undertaken at my request, on "the needs of the Federal Courts." I especially endorse its proposals for a new commission on the judicial appointment process.

While the judicial branch of our Government may require reinforcement, the budgets and payrolls of the other branches remain staggering. I cannot help but observe that while the White House staff and the Executive Office of the President have been reduced and the total number of civilians in the executive branch contained during the 1970's, the legislative branch has increased substantially although the membership of the Congress remains at 535. Congress now costs the taxpayers more than a million dollars per Member; the whole legislative budget has passed the billion dollar mark.

I set out to reduce the growth in the size and spending of the Federal Government, but no President can accomplish this alone. The Congress sidetracked most of my requests for authority to consolidate overlapping programs and agencies, to return more decisionmaking and responsibility to State and local governments through block grants instead of rigid categorical programs, and to eliminate unnecessary red tape and outrageously complex regulations.

We have made some progress in cutting back the expansion of government and its intrusion into individual lives, but believe me, there is much more to be done—and you and I know it. It can only be done by tough and temporarily painful surgery by a Congress as prepared as the President to face up to this very real political problem. Again, I wish my successor, working with a substantial majority of his own party, the best of success in reforming the costly and cumbersome machinery of the Federal Government.

The task of self-government is never finished. The problems are great; the opportunities are greater.

America's first goal is and always will be peace with honor. America must remain first in keeping peace in the world. We can remain first in peace only if we are never second in defense.

In presenting the state of the Union to the Congress and to the American people, I have a special obligation as Commander in Chief to report on our national defense. Our survival as a free and independent people requires, above all, strong military forces that are well equipped and highly trained to perform their assigned mission.

I am particularly gratified to report that over the past 2¹/₂ years, we have been able to reverse the dangerous decline of the previous decade in real resources this country was devoting to national defense. This was an immediate problem I faced in 1974. The evidence was unmistakable that the Soviet Union had been steadily increasing the resources it applied to building its military strength. During this same period the United States real defense spending declined. In my three budgets we not only arrested that dangerous decline, but we have established the positive trend which is essential to our ability to contribute to peace and stability in the world.

The Vietnam war, both materially and psychologically, affected our overall defense posture. The dangerous anti-military sentiment discouraged defense spending and unfairly disparaged the men and women who serve in our Armed Forces.

The challenge that now confronts this country is whether we have the national will and determination to continue this essential defense effort over the long term, as it must be continued. We can no longer afford to oscillate from year to year in so vital a matter; indeed, we have a duty to look beyond the immediate question of budgets and to examine the nature of the problem we will face over the next generation.

I am the first recent President able to address long-term, basic issues without the burden of Vietnam. The war in Indochina consumed enormous resources at the very time that the overwhelming strategic superiority we once enjoyed was disappearing. In past years, as a result of decisions by the United States, our strategic forces leveled off, yet the Soviet Union continued a steady, constant buildup of its own forces, committing a high percentage of its national economic effort to defense.

The United States can never tolerate a shift in strategic balance against us or even a situation where the American people or our allies believe the balance is shifting against us. The United States would risk the most serious political consequences if the world came to believe that our adversaries have a decisive margin of superiority.

To maintain a strategic balance we must look ahead to the 1980's and beyond. The sophistication of modern weapons requires that we make decisions now if we are to ensure our security 10 years from now. Therefore, I have consistently advocated and strongly urged that we pursue three critical strategic programs: the Trident missile launching submarine; the B-1 bomber, with its superior capability to penetrate modern air defenses; and a more advanced intercontinental ballistic missile that will be better able to survive nuclear attack and deliver a devastating retaliatory strike.

In an era where the strategic nuclear forces are in rough equilibrium, the risks of conflict below the nuclear threshold may grow more perilous. A major, long-term objective, therefore, is to maintain capabilities to deal with, and thereby deter, conventional challenges and crises, particularly in Europe.

We cannot rely solely on strategic forces to guarantee our security or to deter all types of aggression. We must have superior naval and marine forces to maintain freedom of the seas, strong multipurpose tactical air forces, and mobile, modern ground forces. Accordingly, I have directed a long-term effort to improve our worldwide capabilities to deal with regional crises.

I have submitted a 5-year naval building program indispensable to the Nation's maritime strategy. Because the security of Europe and the integrity of NATO remain the cornerstone of American defense policy, I have initiated a special, long-term program to ensure the capacity of the Alliance to deter or defeat aggression in Europe.

As I leave office I can report that our national defense is effectively deterring conflict today. Our Armed Forces are capable of carrying out the variety of missions assigned to them. Programs are underway which will assure we can deter war in the years ahead. But I also must warn that it will require a sustained effort over a period of years to maintain these capabilities. We must have the wisdom, the stamina, and the courage to prepare today for the perils of tomorrow, and I believe we will.

As I look to the future—and I assure you I intend to go on doing that for a good many years—I can say with confidence that the state of the Union is good, but we must go on making it better and better.

This gathering symbolizes the constitutional foundation which makes continued progress possible, synchronizing the skills of three independent branches of Government, reserving fundamental sovereignty to the people of this great land. It is only as the temporary representatives and servants of the people that we meet here, we bring no hereditary status or gift of infallibility, and none follows us from this place.

Like President Washington, like the more fortunate of his successors, I look forward to the status of private citizen with gladness and gratitude. To me, being a citizen of the United States of America is the greatest honor and privilege in this world.

From the opportunities which fate and my fellow citizens have given me, as a Member of the House, as Vice President and President of the Senate, and as President of all the people, I have come to understand and place the highest value on the checks and balances which our founders imposed on government through the separation of powers among co-equal legislative, executive, and judicial branches. This often results in difficulty and delay, as I well know, but it also places supreme authority under God, beyond any one person, any one branch, any majority great or small, or any one party. The Constitution is the bedrock of all our freedoms. Guard and cherish it, keep honor and order in your own house, and the Republic will endure.

It is not easy to end these remarks. In this Chamber, along with some of you, I have experienced many, many of the highlights of my life. It was here that I stood 28 years ago with my freshman colleagues, as Speaker Sam Rayburn administered the oath. I see some of you now—Charlie Bennett, Dick Bolling, Carl Perkins, Pete Rodino, Harley Staggers, Tom Steed, Sid Yates, Clem Zablocki—and I remember those who have gone to their rest. It was here we waged many, many a lively battle—won some, lost some, but always remaining friends. It was here, surrounded by such friends, that the distinguished Chief Justice swore me in as Vice President on December 6, 1973. It was here I returned 8 months later as your President to ask not for a honeymoon, but for a good marriage.

I will always treasure those memories and your many, many kindnesses. I thank you for them all.

My fellow Americans, I once asked you for your prayers, and now I give you mine: May God guide this wonderful country, its people, and those they have chosen to lead them. May our third century be illuminated by liberty and blessed with brotherhood, so that we and all who come after us may be the humble servants of thy peace. Amen.

Good night. God bless you.

Jimmy Carter

1977–1981

*"We have no desire to be the world's policeman.
But America does want to be
the world's peacemaker."*

ADDRESS BEFORE A JOINT SESSION OF CONGRESS ON
THE STATE OF THE UNION, JANUARY 25, 1979

Address before a Joint Session of Congress on the State of the Union

January 19, 1978

Jimmy Carter delivered his first State of the Union address before Congress after he had been in office for one year. Carter, a Democratic former governor of Georgia and the first southerner elected president since the Civil War, had defeated incumbent Republican president Gerald Ford in November 1976.

Carter's speech was accompanied by a fifty-page written address that spelled out his proposals in greater detail. In this address, the president stated that the country, being at peace, was at a point where it could focus on "persistent problems and burdens." He called for a partnership between government and the people, stating that government had limits when it came to solving the country's problems—a stance that was similar in theme to what was included in the addresses of Richard Nixon and Gerald Ford and that drew praise from Republicans and some Democrats.

The president termed the economy, particularly energy, the country's main domestic focus. He stated that the country spent more than $120 million a day for foreign oil and that this negatively affected the economy. He urged emphasis on creating a national energy policy, including an increase in production.

Carter described his economic plan as resting on four principles: more job opportunities—he asked Congress for a major increase in funds for public jobs for the young; an expansion led by private business rather than government; efforts to lower the inflation rate; and U.S. contributions to the world economy. He also called for a $25 billion tax cut, which he planned to detail a few days later.

Referring to the newly created Department of Energy, he urged the formation of a Department of Education, a proposal which would come to fruition the next year.

On the foreign policy front, Carter stated his administration's view that human rights were an important part of international relations. He also listed three major goals for U.S. foreign policy: national security, a world at peace, and world economic growth and stability.

In terms of security, Carter mentioned the strategic arms limitation talks (SALT), which were under way with the Soviet Union. The SALT II treaty would be signed the next year, but Carter ended up withdrawing it from Senate consideration in 1980 following the Soviet invasion of Afghanistan.

Carter referred to the Middle East when discussing world peace. One of his foreign policy successes would be the Camp David accords between Israel and Egypt; the two countries would sign a peace treaty in 1979 at the White House. He also urged support for the Panama Canal treaties, which would give Panama control of the canal at the end of the century. Carter believed returning the canal would be a key move toward improving U.S. relations in the developing world; the Senate narrowly approved the return in April 1978.

Mr. President, Mr. Speaker, Members of the 95th Congress, ladies and gentlemen:

Two years ago today we had the first caucus in Iowa, and one year ago tomorrow, I walked from here to the White House to take up the duties of President of the United States. I didn't know it then when I walked, but I've been trying to save energy ever since.

I return tonight to fulfill one of those duties of the Constitution: to give to the Congress—and to the Nation—information on the state of the Union.

Militarily, politically, economically, and in spirit, the state of our Union is sound.

We are a great country, a strong country, a vital and a dynamic country—and so we will remain.

We are a confident people and a hardworking people, a decent and a compassionate people—and so we will remain.

I want to speak to you tonight about where we are and where we must go, about what we have done and what we must do. And I want to pledge to you my best efforts and ask you to pledge yours.

Each generation of Americans has to face circumstances not of its own choosing, but by which its character is measured and its spirit is tested.

There are times of emergency, when a nation and its leaders must bring their energies to bear on a single urgent task. That was the duty Abraham Lincoln faced when our land was torn apart by conflict in the War Between the States. That was the duty faced by Franklin Roosevelt when he led America out of an economic depression and again when he led America to victory in war.

There are other times when there is no single overwhelming crisis, yet profound national interests are at stake.

At such times the risk of inaction can be equally great. It becomes the task of leaders to call forth the vast and restless energies of our people to build for the future.

That is what Harry Truman did in the years after the Second World War, when we helped Europe and Japan rebuild themselves and secured an international order that has protected freedom from aggression.

We live in such times now, and we face such duties.

We've come through a long period of turmoil and doubt, but we've once again found our moral course, and with a new spirit, we are striving to express our best instincts to the rest of the world.

There is all across our land a growing sense of peace and a sense of common purpose. This sense of unity cannot be expressed in programs or in legislation or in dollars. It's an achievement that belongs to every individual American. This unity ties together, and it towers over all our efforts here in Washington, and it serves as an inspiring beacon for all of us who are elected to serve.

This new atmosphere demands a new spirit, a partnership between those of us who lead and those who elect. The foundations of this partnership are truth, the courage to face hard decisions, concern for one another and the common good over special interests, and a basic faith and trust in the wisdom and strength and judgment of the American people.

For the first time in a generation, we are not haunted by a major international crisis or by domestic turmoil, and we now have a rare and a priceless opportunity to address persistent problems and burdens which come to us as a nation—quietly and steadily getting worse over the years.

As President, I've had to ask you, the Members of Congress, and you, the American people, to come to grips with some of the most difficult and hard questions facing our society.

We must make a maximum effort, because if we do not aim for the best, we are very likely to achieve little. I see no benefit to the country if we delay, because the problems will only get worse.

We need patience and good will, but we really need to realize that there is a limit to the role and the function of government. Government cannot solve our problems, it can't set our goals, it cannot define our vision. Government cannot eliminate poverty or provide a bountiful economy or reduce inflation or save our cities or cure illiteracy or provide energy. And government cannot mandate goodness. Only a true partnership between government and the people can ever hope to reach these goals.

Those of us who govern can sometimes inspire, and we can identify needs and marshal resources, but we simply cannot be the managers of everything and everybody.

We here in Washington must move away from crisis management, and we must establish clear goals for the future—immediate and the distant future—which will let us work together and not in conflict. Never again should we neglect a growing crisis like the shortage of energy, where further delay will only lead to more harsh and painful solutions.

Every day we spend more than $120 million for foreign oil. This slows our economic growth, it lowers the value of the dollar overseas, and it aggravates unemployment and inflation here at home.

Now we know what we must do—increase production. We must cut down on waste. And we must use more of those fuels which are plentiful and more permanent. We must be fair to people, and we must not disrupt our Nation's economy and our budget.

Now, that sounds simple. But I recognize the difficulties involved. I know that it is not easy for the Congress to act. But the fact remains that on the energy legislation, we have failed the American people. Almost 5 years after the oil embargo dramatized the problem for us all, we still do not have a national energy program. Not much longer can we tolerate this stalemate. It undermines our national interest both at home and abroad. We must succeed, and I believe we will.

Our main task at home this year, with energy a central element, is the Nation's economy. We must continue the recovery and further cut unemployment and inflation.

Last year was a good one for the United States. We reached all of our major economic goals for 1977. Four million new jobs were created—an all-time record and the number of unemployed dropped by more than a million. Unemployment right now is the lowest it has been since 1974, and not since World War II has such a high percentage of American people been employed.

The rate of inflation went down. There was a good growth in business profits and investments, the source of more jobs for our workers, and a higher standard of living for all our people. After taxes and inflation, there was a healthy increase in workers' wages.

And this year, our country will have the first $2 trillion economy in the history of the world.

Now, we are proud of this progress the first year, but we must do even better in the future.

We still have serious problems on which all of us must work together. Our trade deficit is too large. Inflation is still too high, and too many Americans still do not have a job.

Now, I didn't have any simple answers for all these problems. But we have developed an economic policy that is working, because it's simple, balanced, and fair. It's based on four principles:

First, the economy must keep on expanding to produce new jobs and better income, which our people need. The fruits of growth must be widely shared. More jobs must be made available to those who have been bypassed until now. And the tax system must be made fairer and simpler.

Secondly, private business and not the Government must lead the expansion in the future.

Third, we must lower the rate of inflation and keep it down. Inflation slows down economic growth, and it's the most cruel to the poor and also to the elderly and others who live on fixed incomes.

And fourth, we must contribute to the strength of the world economy.

I will announce detailed proposals for improving our tax system later this week. We can make our tax laws fairer, we can make them simpler and easier to understand, and at the same time, we can—and we will—reduce the tax burden on American citizens by $25 billion.

The tax reforms and the tax reductions go together. Only with the long overdue reforms will the full tax cut be advisable.

Almost $17 billion in income tax cuts will go to individuals. Ninety-six percent of all American taxpayers will see their taxes go down. For a typical family of four, this means an annual saving of more than $250 a year, or a tax reduction of about 20 percent. A further $2 billion cut in excise taxes will give more relief and also contribute directly to lowering the rate of inflation.

And we will also provide strong additional incentives for business investment and growth through substantial cuts in the corporate tax rates and improvement in the investment tax credit.

Now, these tax proposals will increase opportunity everywhere in the Nation. But additional jobs for the disadvantaged deserve special attention.

We've already passed laws to assure equal access to the voting booth and to restaurants and to schools, to housing, and laws to permit access to jobs. But job opportunity—the chance to earn a decent living—is also a basic human right, which we cannot and will not ignore.

A major priority for our Nation is the final elimination of the barriers that restrict the opportunities available to women and also to black people and Hispanics and other minorities. We've come a long way toward that goal. But there is still much to do. What we inherited from the past must not be permitted to shackle us in the future.

I'll be asking you for a substantial increase in funds for public jobs for our young people, and I also am recommending that the Congress continue the public service employment programs at more than twice the level of a year ago. When welfare reform is completed, we will have more than a million additional jobs so that those on welfare who are able to work can work.

However, again, we know that in our free society, private business is still the best source of new jobs. Therefore, I will propose a new program to encourage businesses to hire young and disadvantaged Americans. These young people only need skills and a chance in order to take their place in our economic system. Let's give them the chance they need. A major step in the right direction would be the early passage of a greatly improved Humphrey-Hawkins bill.

My budget for 1979 addresses these national needs, but it is lean and tight. I have cut waste wherever possible.

I am proposing an increase of less than 2 percent after adjusting for inflation—the smallest increase in the Federal budget in 4 years.

Lately, Federal spending has taken a steadily increasing portion of what Americans produce. Our new budget reverses that trend, and later I hope to bring the Government's toll down even further. And with your help, we'll do that.

In time of high employment and a strong economy, deficit spending should not be a feature of our budget. As the economy continues to gain strength and as our unemployment rates continue to fall, revenues will grow. With careful planning, efficient management, and proper restraint on spending, we can move rapidly toward a balanced budget—and we will.

Next year the budget deficit will be only slightly less than this year. But one-third of the deficit is due to the necessary tax cuts that I've proposed. This year the right choice is to reduce the burden on taxpayers and provide more jobs for our people.

The third element in our program is a renewed attack on inflation. We've learned the hard way that high unemployment will not prevent or cure inflation. Government can help us by stimulating private investment and by maintaining a responsible economic policy. Through a new top-level review process, we will do a better job of reducing Government regulation that drives up costs and drives up prices.

But again, Government alone cannot bring down the rate of inflation. When a level of high inflation is expected to continue, then companies raise prices to protect their profit margins against prospective increases in wages and other costs, while workers demand higher wages as protection against expected price increases. It's like an escalation in the arms race, and understandably, no one wants to disarm alone.

Now, no one firm or a group of workers can halt this process. It's an effort that we must all make together. I'm therefore asking government, business, labor, and other groups to join in a voluntary program to moderate inflation by holding wage and price increases in each sector of the economy during 1978 below the average increases of the last 2 years.

I do not believe in wage and price controls. A sincere commitment to voluntary constraint provides a way—perhaps the only way—to fight inflation without Government interference.

As I came into the Capitol tonight, I saw the farmers, my fellow farmers, standing out in the snow. I'm familiar with their problem, and I know from Congress' action that you are too. When I was running Carters Warehouse, we had spread on our own farms 5–10–15 fertilizer for about $40 a ton. The last time I was home, the price was about $100 a ton. The cost of nitrogen has gone up 150 percent, and the price of products that farmers sell has either stayed the same or gone down a little.

Now, this past year in 1977, you, the Congress, and I together passed a new agricultural act. It went into effect October 1. It'll have its first impact on the 1978 crops.

It will help a great deal. It'll add $6½ billion or more to help the farmers with their price supports and target prices.

Last year we had the highest level of exports of farm products in the history of our country—$24 billion. We expect to have more this year. We'll be working together. But I think it's incumbent on us to monitor very carefully the farm situation and continue to work harmoniously with the farmers of our country. What's best for the farmers, the farm families, in the long run is also best for the consumers of our country.

Economic success at home is also the key to success in our international economic policy. An effective energy program, strong investment and productivity, and controlled inflation will improve our trade balance and balance it, and it will help to protect the integrity of the dollar overseas.

By working closely with our friends abroad, we can promote the economic health of the whole world, with fair and balanced agreements lowering the barriers to trade.

Despite the inevitable pressures that build up when the world economy suffers from high unemployment, we must firmly resist the demands for self-defeating protectionism. But free trade must also be fair trade. And I am determined to protect American industry and American workers against foreign trade practices which are unfair or illegal.

In a separate written message to Congress, I've outlined other domestic initiatives, such as welfare reform, consumer protection, basic education skills, urban policy, reform of our labor laws, and national health care later on this year. I will not repeat these tonight. But there are several other points that I would like to make directly to you.

During these past years, Americans have seen our Government grow far from us.

For some citizens, the Government has almost become like a foreign country, so strange and distant that we've often had to deal with it through trained ambassadors who have sometimes become too powerful and too influential—lawyers, accountants, and lobbyists. This cannot go on.

We must have what Abraham Lincoln wanted—a government for the people.

We've made progress toward that kind of government. You've given me the authority I requested to reorganize the Federal bureaucracy. And I am using that authority.

We've already begun a series of reorganization plans which will be completed over a period of 3 years. We have also proposed abolishing almost 500 Federal advisory and other commissions and boards. But I know that the American people are still sick and tired of Federal paperwork and redtape. Bit by bit we are chopping down the thicket of unnecessary Federal regulations by which Government too often interferes in our personal lives and our personal business. We've cut the public's Federal paperwork load by more than 12 percent in less than a year. And we are not through cutting.

We've made a good start on turning the gobbledygook of Federal regulations into plain English that people can understand. But we know that we still have a long way to go.

We've brought together parts of 11 Government agencies to create a new Department of Energy. And now it's time to take another major step by creating a separate Department of Education.

But even the best organized Government will only be as effective as the people who carry out its policies. For this reason, I consider civil service reform to be absolutely vital. Worked out with the civil servants themselves, this reorganization plan will restore the merit principle to a system which has grown into a bureaucratic maze. It will provide greater management flexibility and better rewards for better performance without compromising job security.

Then and only then can we have a government that is efficient, open, and truly worthy of our people's understanding and respect. I have promised that we will have such a government, and I intend to keep that promise.

In our foreign policy, the separation of people from government has been in the past a source of weakness and error. In a democratic system like ours, foreign policy decisions must be able to stand the test of public examination and public debate. If we make a mistake in this administration, it will be on the side of frankness and openness with the American people.

In our modern world, when the deaths of literally millions of people can result from a few terrifying seconds of destruction, the path of national strength and security is identical to the path of peace.

Tonight, I am happy to report that because we are strong, our Nation is at peace with the world.

We are a confident nation. We've restored a moral basis for our foreign policy. The very heart of our identity as a nation is our firm commitment to human rights.

We stand for human rights because we believe that government has as a purpose to promote the well-being of its citizens. This is true in our domestic policy; it's also true in our foreign policy. The world must know that in support of human rights, the United States will stand firm.

We expect no quick or easy results, but there has been significant movement toward greater freedom and humanity in several parts of the world.

Thousands of political prisoners have been freed. The leaders of the world—even our ideological adversaries—now see that their attitude toward fundamental human rights affects their standing in the international community, and it affects their relations with the United States.

To serve the interests of every American, our foreign policy has three major goals.

The first and prime concern is and will remain the security of our country.

Security is based on our national will, and security is based on the strength of our Armed Forces. We have the will, and militarily we are very strong.

Security also comes through the strength of our alliances. We have reconfirmed our commitment to the defense of Europe, and this year we will demonstrate that commitment by further modernizing and strengthening our military capabilities there.

Security can also be enhanced by agreements with potential adversaries which reduce the threat of nuclear disaster while maintaining our own relative strategic capability.

In areas of peaceful competition with the Soviet Union, we will continue to more than hold our own.

At the same time, we are negotiating with quiet confidence, without haste, with careful determination, to ease the tensions between us and to ensure greater stability and security.

The strategic arms limitation talks have been long and difficult. We want a mutual limit on both the quality and the quantity of the giant nuclear arsenals of both nations, and then we want actual reductions in strategic arms as a major step toward the ultimate elimination of nuclear weapons from the face of the Earth.

If these talks result in an agreement this year—and I trust they will—I pledge to you that the agreement will maintain and enhance the stability of the world's strategic balance and the security of the United States.

For 30 years, concerted but unsuccessful efforts have been made to ban the testing of atomic explosives—both military weapons and peaceful nuclear devices.

We are hard at work with Great Britain and the Soviet Union on an agreement which will stop testing and will protect our national security and provide for adequate verification of compliance. We are now making, I believe, good progress toward this comprehensive ban on nuclear explosions.

We are also working vigorously to halt the proliferation of nuclear weapons among the nations of the world which do not now have them and to reduce the deadly global traffic in conventional arms sales. Our stand for peace is suspect if we are also the principal arms merchant of the world. So, we've decided to cut down our arms transfers abroad on a year-by-year basis and to work with other major arms exporters to encourage their similar constraint.

Every American has a stake in our second major goal—a world at peace. In a nuclear age, each of us is threatened when peace is not secured everywhere. We are trying to promote harmony in those parts of the world where major differences exist among other nations and threaten international peace.

In the Middle East, we are contributing our good offices to maintain the momentum of the current negotiations and to keep open the lines of communication among the Middle Eastern leaders. The whole world has a great stake in the success of these efforts. This is a precious opportunity for a historic settlement of a longstanding conflict—an opportunity which may never come again in our lifetime.

Our role has been difficult and sometimes thankless and controversial. But it has been constructive and it has been necessary, and it will continue.

Our third major foreign policy goal is one that touches the life of every American citizen every day—world economic growth and stability.

This requires strong economic performance by the industrialized democracies like ourselves and progress in resolving the global energy crisis. Last fall, with the help of others, we succeeded in our vigorous efforts to maintain the stability of the price of oil. But as many foreign leaders have emphasized to me personally and, I am sure, to you, the greatest future contribution that America can make to the world economy would be an effective energy conservation program here at home. We will not hesitate to take the actions needed to protect the integrity of the American dollar.

We are trying to develop a more just international system. And in this spirit, we are supporting the struggle for human development in Africa, in Asia, and in Latin America.

Finally, the world is watching to see how we act on one of our most important and controversial items of business—approval of the Panama Canal treaties. The treaties now before the Senate are the result of the work of four administrations—two Democratic, two Republican.

They guarantee that the canal will be open always for unrestricted use by the ships of the world. Our ships have the right to go to the head of the line for priority of passage in times of emergency or need. We retain the permanent right to defend the canal with our own military forces, if necessary, to guarantee its openness and its neutrality.

The treaties are to the clear advantage of ourselves, the Panamanians, and the other users of the canal. Ratifying the Panama Canal treaties will demonstrate our good faith to the world, discourage the spread of hostile ideologies in this hemisphere, and directly contribute to the economic well-being and the security of the United States.

I have to say that that's very welcome applause.

There were two moments on my recent journey which, for me, confirmed the final aims of our foreign policy and what it always must be.

One was in a little village in India, where I met a people as passionately attached to their rights and liberties as we are, but whose children have a far smaller chance for good health or food or education or human fulfillment than a child born in this country.

The other moment was in Warsaw, capital of a nation twice devastated by war in this century. There, people have rebuilt the city which war's destruction took from them. But what was new only emphasized clearly what was lost.

What I saw in those two places crystalized for me the purposes of our own Nation's policy: to ensure economic justice, to advance human rights, to resolve conflicts without violence, and to proclaim in our great democracy our constant faith in the liberty and dignity of human beings everywhere.

We Americans have a great deal of work to do together. In the end, how well we do that work will depend on the spirit in which we approach it. We must seek fresh answers, unhindered by the stale prescriptions of the past.

It has been said that our best years are behind us. But I say again that America's best is still ahead. We have emerged from bitter experiences chastened but proud, confident once again, ready to face challenges once again, and united once again.

We come together tonight at a solemn time. Last week the Senate lost a good and honest man—Lee Metcalf of Montana.

And today, the flag of the United States flew at half-mast from this Capitol and from American installations and ships all over the world, in mourning for Senator Hubert Humphrey.

Because he exemplified so well the joy and the zest of living, his death reminds us not so much of our own mortality, but of the possibilities offered to us by life. He always looked to the future with a special American kind of confidence, of hope and enthusiasm. And the best way that we can honor him is by following his example.

Our task—to use the words of Senator Humphrey—is "reconciliation, rebuilding, and rebirth."

Reconciliation of private needs and interests into a higher purpose.

Rebuilding the old dreams of justice and liberty, and country and community.

Rebirth of our faith in the common good.

Each of us here tonight—and all who are listening in your homes—must rededicate ourselves to serving the common good. We are a community, a beloved community, all of us. Our individual fates are linked, our futures intertwined. And if we act in that knowledge and in that spirit, together, as the Bible says, we can move mountains.

Thank you very much.

Address before a Joint Session of Congress on the State of the Union

January 25, 1979

Jimmy Carter delivered his second State of the Union address before Congress in January 1979. He used as his theme the idea of the nation building a "new foundation"—one that would look to long-term solutions for the country's problems. While the "new foundation" idea seemed to echo Woodrow Wilson's "New Freedom," Franklin D. Roosevelt's "New Deal," and John F. Kennedy's "New Frontier," the slogan did not resonate with the public and was dropped.

As he had the previous year, Carter, a Democrat, also submitted a longer, written analysis of his message.

Although it is customary for the president to send his budget message to Congress after his State of the Union, in 1979 Carter sent his budget message first and then used the State of the Union address to illustrate the importance of enacting his fiscal priorities. In the State of the Union, Carter urged Congress to hold "the line on excess federal spending," acknowledging that it would not be easy. The budget, he said, sent a "clear message" that Carter hoped to control inflation, a persistent problem. Both houses of Congress had remained Democratic after the 1978 midterm elections.

Carter also called for a national health plan and restraint in inflation in hospital care. Although he had signed a law in 1978 deregulating the airlines, he proposed additional deregulation in the transportation industry. In addition, he called for reform of the government bureaucracy.

When it came to foreign policy, Carter stated that changes around the world—such as mass communications and literacy—were creating a situation where it was no longer a question of whether one superpower or the other would dominate, but whether cooperation and peace would prevail over anarchy and destruction.

The threat of nuclear weapons loomed over everything, Carter said, and he stated that the United States sought to be "the world's peacemaker." He cited, among other things, his efforts toward Middle East peace; Israel and Egypt would sign a peace treaty later that year at the White House following negotiations brokered by Carter.

Carter chose to devote some time to describing the strategic arms limitation talks then under way with the Soviet Union. The so-called SALT II talks had been ongoing for six years, with almost all the issues resolved, Carter said. He defended the treaty, stating that it was not based on trust but would be verifiable, and that the U.S. nuclear deterrent would remain robust.

In the end, Carter would withdraw the SALT II treaty from Senate consideration in 1980 after Afghanistan was invaded by the Soviets.

Toward the end of his speech, Carter focused on human rights, a theme of his presidency, stating that he wanted the United States to serve as an example to the world on that front.

Mr. President, Mr. Speaker, Members of the 96th Congress, and my fellow citizens:

Tonight I want to examine in a broad sense the state of our American Union—how we are building a new foundation for a peaceful and a prosperous world.

Our children who will be born this year will come of age in the 21st century. What kind of society, what kind of world are we building for them? Will we ourselves be at peace? Will our children enjoy a better quality of life? Will a strong and united America still be a force for freedom and prosperity around the world?

Tonight, there is every sign that the state of our Union is sound.

Our economy offers greater prosperity for more of our people than ever before. Real per capita income and real business profits have risen substantially in the last 2 years. Farm exports are setting an all-time record each year, and farm income last year, net farm income, was up more than 25 percent.

Our liberties are secure. Our military defenses are strong and growing stronger. And more importantly, tonight, America—our beloved country—is at peace.

Our earliest national commitments, modified and reshaped by succeeding generations, have served us well. But the problems that we face today are different from those that confronted earlier generations of Americans. They are more subtle, more complex, and more interrelated. At home, we are recognizing ever more clearly that government alone cannot solve these problems. And abroad, few of them can be solved by the United States alone. But Americans as a united people, working with our allies and friends, have never been afraid to face problems and to solve problems, either here or abroad.

The challenge to us is to build a new and firmer foundation for the future—for a sound economy, for a more effective government, for more political trust, and for a stable peace—so that the America our children inherit will be even stronger and even better than it is today.

We cannot resort to simplistic or extreme solutions which substitute myths for common sense.

In our economy, it is a myth that we must choose endlessly between inflation and recession. Together, we build the foundation for a strong economy, with lower inflation, without contriving either a recession with its high unemployment or unworkable, mandatory government controls.

In our government, it is a myth that we must choose between compassion and competence. Together, we build the foundation for a government that works—and works for people.

In our relations with our potential adversaries, it is a myth that we must choose between confrontation and capitulation. Together, we build the foundation for a stable world of both diversity and peace.

Together, we've already begun to build the foundation for confidence in our economic system. During the last 2 years, in bringing our economy out of the deepest recession since the 1930's, we've created 7,100,000 new jobs. The unemployment rate has gone down 25 percent. And now we must redouble our fight against the persistent inflation that has wracked our country for more than a decade. That's our important domestic issue, and we must do it together.

We know that inflation is a burden for all Americans, but it's a disaster for the poor, the sick, and the old. No American family should be forced to choose among food, warmth, health care, or decent housing because the cost of any of these basic necessities has climbed out of reach.

Three months ago, I outlined to the Nation a balanced anti-inflation program that couples responsible government restraint with responsible wage and price restraint. It's based upon my knowledge that there is a more powerful force than government compulsion—the force created by the cooperative efforts of millions of Americans working toward a common goal.

Business and labor have been increasingly supportive. It's imperative that we in government do our part. We must stop excessive government growth, and we must control government spending habits.

I've sent to this Congress a stringent but a fair budget, one that, since I ran for President in 1976, will have cut the Federal deficit in half. And as a percentage of our gross national product, the deficit will have dropped by almost 75 percent.

This Congress had a good record last year, and I now ask the 96th Congress to continue this partnership in holding the line on excess Federal spending. It will not be easy. But we must be strong, and we must be persistent.

This budget is a clear message that, with the help of you and the American people, I am determined, as President, to bring inflation under control.

The 1980 budget provides enough spending restraint to begin unwinding inflation, but enough support for our country to keep American workers productive and to encourage the investments that provide new jobs. We will continue to mobilize our Nation's resources to reduce our trade deficit substantially this year and to maintain the strength of the American dollar.

We've demonstrated in this restrained budget that we can build on the gains of the past 2 years to provide additional support to educate disadvantaged children, to care for the elderly, to provide nutrition and legal services for the poor, and to strengthen the economic base of our urban communities and, also, our rural areas.

This year, we will take our first steps to develop a national health plan.

We must never accept a permanent group of unemployed Americans, with no hope and no stake in building our society. For those left out of the economy because of discrimination, a lack of skills, or poverty, we must maintain high levels of training, and we must continue to provide jobs.

A responsible budget is not our only weapon to control inflation. We must act now to protect all Americans from health care costs that are rising $1 million per hour, 24 hours a day, doubling every 5 years. We must take control of the largest contributor to that inflation—skyrocketing hospital costs.

There will be no clearer test of the commitment of this Congress to the anti-inflation fight than the legislation that I will submit again this year to hold down inflation in hospital care.

Over the next 5 years, my proposals will save Americans a total of $60 billion, of which $25 billion will be savings to the American taxpayer in the Federal budget itself. The American people have waited long enough. This year we must act on hospital cost containment.

We must also fight inflation by improvements and better enforcement of our antitrust laws and by reducing government obstacles to competition in the private sector.

We must begin to scrutinize the overall effect of regulation in our economy. Through deregulation of the airline industry we've increased profits, cut prices for all Americans, and begun—for one of the few times in the history of our Nation—to actually dismantle a major Federal bureaucracy. This year, we must begin the effort to reform our regulatory processes for the railroad, bus, and the trucking industries.

America has the greatest economic system in the world. Let's reduce government interference and give it a chance to work.

I call on Congress to take other anti-inflation action—to expand our exports to protect American jobs threatened by unfair trade, to conserve energy, to increase production and to speed development of solar power, and to reassess our Nation's technological superiority. American workers who enlist in the fight against inflation deserve not just our gratitude, but they deserve the protection of the real wage insurance proposal that I have already made to the Congress.

To be successful, we must change our attitudes as well as our policies. We cannot afford to live beyond our means. We cannot afford to create programs that we can neither manage nor finance, or to waste our natural resources, and we cannot tolerate mismanagement and fraud. Above all, we must meet the challenges of inflation as a united people.

With the support of the American people, government in recent decades has helped to dismantle racial barriers, has provided assistance for the jobless and the retired, has fed the hungry, has protected the safety, health, and bargaining rights of American workers, and has helped to preserve our natural heritage.

But it's not enough to have created a lot of government programs. Now we must make the good programs more effective and improve or weed out those which are wasteful or unnecessary.

With the support of the Congress, we've begun to reorganize and to get control of the bureaucracy. We are reforming the civil service system, so that we can recognize and reward those who do a good job and correct or remove those who do not.

This year, we must extend major reorganization efforts to education, to economic development, and to the management of our natural resources. We need to enact a sunshine [sunset] law that when government programs have outlived their value, they will automatically be terminated.

There's no such thing as an effective and a noncontroversial reorganization and reform. But we know that honest, effective government is essential to restore public faith in our public action.

None of us can be satisfied when two thirds of the American citizens chose not to vote last year in a national election. Too many Americans feel powerless against the influence of private lobbying groups and the unbelievable flood of private campaign money which threatens our electoral process.

This year, we must regain the public's faith by requiring limited financial funds from public funds for congressional election campaigns. House bill 1 provides for this public financing of campaigns. And I look forward with a great deal of anticipation to signing it at an early date.

A strong economy and an effective government will restore confidence in America. But the path of the future must be charted in peace. We must continue to build a new and a firm foundation for a stable world community.

We are building that new foundation from a position of national strength—the strength of our own defenses, the strength of our friendships with other nations, and of our oldest American ideals.

America's military power is a major force for security and stability in the world. We must maintain our strategic capability and continue the progress of the last 2 years with our NATO Allies, with whom we have increased our readiness, modernized our equipment, and strengthened our defense forces in Europe. I urge you to support the strong defense budget which I have proposed to the Congress.

But our national security in this complicated age requires more than just military might. In less than a lifetime, world population has more than doubled, colonial empires have disappeared, and a hundred new nations have been born. Mass communications, literacy, and migration to the world's cities have all awakened new yearnings for economic justice and human rights among people everywhere.

This demand for justice and human rights is a wave of the future. In such a world, the choice is not which super power will dominate the world. None can and none will. The choice instead is between a world of anarchy and destruction, or a world of cooperation and peace.

In such a world, we seek not to stifle inevitable change, but to influence its course in helpful and constructive ways that enhance our values, our national interests, and the cause of peace.

Towering over this volatile, changing world, like a thundercloud on a summer day, looms the awesome power of nuclear weapons.

We will continue to help shape the forces of change, to anticipate emerging problems of nuclear proliferation and conventional arms sales, and to use our great strength and influence to settle international conflicts in other parts of the world before they erupt and spread.

We have no desire to be the world's policeman. But America does want to be the world's peacemaker.

We are building the foundation for truly global cooperation, not only with Western and industrialized nations but with the developing countries as well. Our ties with Japan and our European allies are stronger than ever, and so are our friendly relations with the people of Latin America, Africa, and the Western Pacific and Asia.

We've won new respect in this hemisphere with the Panama Canal treaties. We've gained new trust with the developing world through our opposition to racism, our commitment to human rights, and our support for majority rule in Africa.

The multilateral trade negotiations are now reaching a successful conclusion, and congressional approval is essential to the economic well-being of our own country and of the world. This will be one of our top priorities in 1979.

We are entering a hopeful era in our relations with one-fourth of the world's people who live in China. The presence of Vice Premier Deng Xiaoping next week will help to inaugurate that new era. And with prompt congressional action on authorizing legislation, we will continue our commitment to a prosperous, peaceful, and secure life for the people of Taiwan.

I'm grateful that in the past year, as in the year before, no American has died in combat anywhere in the world. And in Iran, Nicaragua, Cyprus, Namibia, and Rhodesia, our country is working for peaceful solutions to dangerous conflicts.

In the Middle East, under the most difficult circumstances, we have sought to help ancient enemies lay aside deep-seated differences that have produced four bitter wars in our lifetime.

Our firm commitment to Israel's survival and security is rooted in our deepest convictions and in our knowledge of the strategic importance to our own Nation of a stable Middle East. To promote peace and reconciliation in the region, we must retain the trust and the confidence both of Israel and also of the Arab nations that are sincerely searching for peace.

I am determined, as President, to use the full, beneficial influence of our country so that the precious opportunity for lasting peace between Israel and Egypt will not be lost. The new foundation of international cooperation that we seek excludes no nation. Cooperation with the Soviet Union serves the cause of peace, for in this nuclear age, world peace must include peace between the super powers—and it must mean the control of nuclear arms.

Ten years ago, the United States and the Soviet Union made the historic decision to open the strategic arms limitations talks, or SALT. The purpose of SALT, then as now, is not to gain a unilateral advantage for either nation, but to protect the security of both nations, to reverse the costly and dangerous momentum of the nuclear arms race, to preserve a stable balance of nuclear forces, and to demonstrate to a concerned world that we are determined to help preserve the peace.

The first SALT agreement was concluded in 1972. And since then, during 6 years of negotiation by both Republican and Democratic leaders, nearly all issues of SALT II have been resolved. If the Soviet Union continues to negotiate in good faith, a responsible SALT agreement will be reached.

It's important that the American people understand the nature of the SALT process.

SALT II is not based on sentiment; it's based on self-interest—of the United States and of the Soviet Union. Both nations share a powerful common interest in reducing the threat of a nuclear war. I will sign no agreement which does not enhance our national security.

SALT II does not rely on trust; it will be verifiable. We have very sophisticated, proven means, including our satellites, to determine for ourselves whether or not the Soviet Union is meeting its treaty obligations. I will sign no agreement which cannot be verified.

The American nuclear deterrent will remain strong after SALT II. For example, just one of our relatively invulnerable Poseidon submarines—comprising less than 2 percent of our total nuclear force of submarines, aircraft, and landbased missiles—carries enough warheads to destroy every large- and medium-sized city in the Soviet Union. Our deterrent is overwhelming, and I will sign no agreement unless our deterrent force will remain overwhelming.

A SALT agreement, of course, cannot substitute for wise diplomacy or a strong defense, nor will it end the danger of nuclear war. But it will certainly reduce that danger. It will strengthen our efforts to ban nuclear tests and to stop the spread of atomic weapons to other nations. And it can begin the process of negotiating new agreements which will further limit nuclear arms.

The path of arms control, backed by a strong defense—the path our Nation and every President has walked for 30 years—can lead to a world of law and of international negotiation and consultation in which all peoples might live in peace. In this year 1979, nothing is more important than that the Congress and the people of the United States resolve to continue with me on that path of nuclear arms control and world peace. This is paramount.

I've outlined some of the changes that have transformed the world and which are continuing as we meet here tonight. But we in America need not fear change. The values on which our Nation was founded—individual liberty, self-determination, the potential for human fulfillment in freedom—all of these endure. We find these democratic principles praised, even in books smuggled out of totalitarian nations and on wallposters in lands which we thought were closed to our influence. Our country has regained its special place of leadership in the worldwide struggle for human rights. And that is a commitment that we must keep at home, as well as abroad.

The civil rights revolution freed all Americans, black and white, but its full promise still remains unrealized. I will continue to work with all my strength for equal opportunity for all Americans—and for affirmative action for those who carry the extra burden of past denial of equal opportunity.

We remain committed to improving our labor laws to better protect the rights of American workers. And our Nation must make it clear that the legal rights of women as citizens are guaranteed under the laws of our land by ratifying the equal rights amendment.

As long as I'm President, at home and around the world America's examples and America's influence will be marshaled to advance the cause of human rights.

To establish those values, two centuries ago a bold generation of Americans risked their property, their position, and life itself. We are their heirs, and they are sending us a message across the centuries. The words they made so vivid are now growing faintly indistinct, because they are not heard often enough. They are words like "justice," "equality," "unity," "truth," "sacrifice," "liberty," "faith," and "love."

These words remind us that the duty of our generation of Americans is to renew our Nation's faith—not focused just against foreign threats but against the threats of selfishness, cynicism, and apathy.

The new foundation I've discussed tonight can help us build a nation and a world where every child is nurtured and can look to the future with hope, where the resources now wasted on war can be turned towards meeting human needs, where all people have enough to eat, a decent home, and protection against disease.

It can help us build a nation and a world where all people are free to seek the truth and to add to human understanding, so that all of us may live our lives in peace.

Tonight, I ask you, the Members of the Congress, to join me in building that new foundation—a better foundation—for our beloved country and our world.

Thank you very much.

Jimmy Carter, 1977–1981

Address before a Joint Session of Congress on the State of the Union
January 23, 1980

Jimmy Carter's third State of the Union address was delivered before Congress in the wake of two international crises: the seizing of American embassy personnel in Tehran, Iran, by Iranian militants in November 1979, and the Soviet Union's invasion of Afghanistan the following month.

Departing from his former emphasis on international cooperation, Carter adopted a tough tone in his speech, which focused primarily on international issues. He spoke at a time of national agitation over the hostage crisis; the crisis would continue through the end of Carter's presidency. Those in the House chamber applauded repeatedly during the speech.

The president declared that attempts to control the oil-rich Persian Gulf region by force would be seen as an attack on U.S. vital interests and would be met with all necessary means, including military force; the declaration came to be known as the "Carter Doctrine."

In terms of the hostages, Carter stated that the United States would not "yield to blackmail" and would continue working to gain their release.

He spent considerable time discussing U.S.-Soviet relations, reviewing the Cold War tensions between the two countries since the 1940s; he said that the Soviet invasion of Afghanistan could represent "the most serious threat to the peace since the Second World War." Carter had imposed economic penalties on the Soviet Union in the wake of the invasion, and he stated in his speech that the United States would not send an Olympic team to Moscow in 1980.

The president devoted relatively little time to discussing the strategic arms limitation efforts between the United States and the Soviet Union, which had been a high priority in previous addresses, but he mentioned that attempts to control nuclear weapons would "not be abandoned."

Carter also called for revitalization of the country's Selective Service System, stating that he hoped a military draft would not be necessary but that the country should be prepared. He stressed the need for a "strong defense budget for 1981." Illustrating this, he said that events in Iran and Afghanistan reinforced the point that the United States was too dependent on foreign oil.

The president had sent Congress a longer written message on January 21 that included more details on his proposals. In his speech, he briefly listed some domestic goals, including deficit reduction and job creation.

Carter, a Democrat, sought reelection in 1980, but, battered by the continued Iran hostage crisis as well as economic troubles, would lose in a landslide to Republican Ronald Reagan.

Mr. President, Mr. Speaker, Members of the 96th Congress, fellow citizens:

This last few months has not been an easy time for any of us. As we meet tonight, it has never been more clear that the state of our Union depends on the state of the world. And tonight, as throughout our own generation, freedom and peace in the world depend on the state of our Union.

The 1980's have been born in turmoil, strife, and change. This is a time of challenge to our interests and our values and it's a time that tests our wisdom and our skills.

At this time in Iran, 50 Americans are still held captive, innocent victims of terrorism and anarchy. Also at this moment, massive Soviet troops are attempting to subjugate the fiercely independent and deeply religious people of Afghanistan. These two acts—one of international terrorism and one of military aggression—present a serious challenge to the United States of America and indeed to all the nations of the world. Together, we will meet these threats to peace.

I'm determined that the United States will remain the strongest of all nations, but our power will never be used to initiate a threat to the security of any nation or to the rights of any human being. We seek to be and to remain secure—a nation at peace in a stable world. But to be secure we must face the world as it is.

Three basic developments have helped to shape our challenges: the steady growth and increased projection of Soviet military power beyond its own borders; the overwhelming dependence of the Western democracies on oil supplies from the Middle East; and the press of social and religious and economic and political change in the many nations of the developing world, exemplified by the revolution in Iran.

Each of these factors is important in its own right. Each interacts with the others. All must be faced together, squarely and courageously. We will face these challenges, and we will meet them with the best that is in us. And we will not fail.

In response to the abhorrent act in Iran, our Nation has never been aroused and unified so greatly in peacetime. Our position is clear. The United States will not yield to blackmail.

We continue to pursue these specific goals: first, to protect the present and long-range interests of the United States; secondly, to preserve the lives of the American hostages and to secure, as quickly as possible, their safe release, if possible, to avoid bloodshed which might further endanger the lives of our fellow citizens; to enlist the help of other nations in condemning this act of violence, which is shocking and violates the moral and the legal standards of a civilized world; and also to convince and to persuade the Iranian leaders that the real danger to their nation lies in the north, in the Soviet Union and from the Soviet troops now in Afghanistan, and that the unwarranted Iranian quarrel with the United States hampers their response to this far greater danger to them.

If the American hostages are harmed, a severe price will be paid. We will never rest until every one of the American hostages are released.

But now we face a broader and more fundamental challenge in this region because of the recent military action of the Soviet Union.

Now, as during the last 3½ decades, the relationship between our country, the United States of America, and the Soviet Union is the most critical factor in determining whether the world will live at peace or be engulfed in global conflict.

Since the end of the Second World War, America has led other nations in meeting the challenge of mounting Soviet power. This has not been a simple or a static relationship. Between us there has been cooperation, there has been competition, and at times there has been confrontation.

In the 1940's we took the lead in creating the Atlantic Alliance in response to the Soviet Union's suppression and then consolidation of its East European empire and the resulting threat of the Warsaw Pact to Western Europe.

In the 1950's we helped to contain further Soviet challenges in Korea and in the Middle East, and we rearmed to assure the continuation of that containment.

In the 1960's we met the Soviet challenges in Berlin, and we faced the Cuban missile crisis. And we sought to engage the Soviet Union in the important task of moving beyond the cold war and away from confrontation.

And in the 1970's three American Presidents negotiated with the Soviet leaders in attempts to halt the growth of the nuclear arms race. We sought to establish rules of behavior that would reduce the risks of conflict, and we searched for areas of cooperation that could make our relations reciprocal and productive, not only for the sake of our two nations but for the security and peace of the entire world.

In all these actions, we have maintained two commitments: to be ready to meet any challenge by Soviet military power, and to develop ways to resolve disputes and to keep the peace.

Preventing nuclear war is the foremost responsibility of the two superpowers. That's why we've negotiated the strategic arms limitation treaties—SALT I and SALT II. Especially now, in a time of great tension, observing the mutual constraints imposed by the terms of these treaties will be in the best interest of both countries and will help to preserve world peace. I will consult very closely with the Congress on this matter as we strive to control nuclear weapons. That effort to control nuclear weapons will not be abandoned.

We superpowers also have the responsibility to exercise restraint in the use of our great military force. The integrity and the independence of weaker nations must not be threatened. They must know that in our presence they are secure.

But now the Soviet Union has taken a radical and an aggressive new step. It's using its great military power against a relatively defenseless nation. The implications of the Soviet invasion of Afghanistan could pose the most serious threat to the peace since the Second World War.

The vast majority of nations on Earth have condemned this latest Soviet attempt to extend its colonial domination of others and have demanded the immediate withdrawal of Soviet troops. The Moslem world is especially and justifiably outraged by this aggression against an Islamic people. No action of a world power has ever been so quickly and so overwhelmingly condemned. But verbal condemnation is not enough. The Soviet Union must pay a concrete price for their aggression.

While this invasion continues, we and the other nations of the world cannot conduct business as usual with the Soviet Union. That's why the United States has imposed stiff economic penalties on the Soviet Union. I will not issue any permits for Soviet ships to fish in the coastal waters of the United States. I've cut Soviet access to high-technology equipment and to agricultural products. I've limited other commerce with the Soviet Union, and I've asked our allies and friends to join with us in restraining their own trade with the Soviets and not to replace our own embargoed items. And I have notified the Olympic Committee that with Soviet invading forces in Afghanistan, neither the American people nor I will support sending an Olympic team to Moscow.

The Soviet Union is going to have to answer some basic questions: Will it help promote a more stable international environment in which its own legitimate, peaceful concerns can be pursued? Or will it continue to expand its military power far beyond its genuine security needs, and use that power for colonial conquest? The Soviet Union must realize that its decision to use military force in Afghanistan will be costly to every political and economic relationship it values.

The region which is now threatened by Soviet troops in Afghanistan is of great strategic importance: It contains more than two-thirds of the world's exportable oil. The Soviet effort to dominate Afghanistan has brought Soviet military forces to within 300 miles of the Indian Ocean and close to the Straits of Hormuz, a waterway through which most of the world's oil must flow. The Soviet Union is now attempting to consolidate a strategic position, therefore, that poses a grave threat to the free movement of Middle East oil.

This situation demands careful thought, steady nerves, and resolute action, not only for this year but for many years to come. It demands collective efforts to meet this new threat to security in the Persian Gulf and in Southwest Asia. It demands the participation of all those who rely on oil from the Middle East and who are concerned with global peace and stability. And it demands consultation and close cooperation with countries in the area which might be threatened.

Meeting this challenge will take national will, diplomatic and political wisdom, economic sacrifice, and, of course, military capability. We must call on the best that is in us to preserve the security of this crucial region.

Let our position be absolutely clear: An attempt by any outside force to gain control of the Persian Gulf region will be regarded as an assault on the vital interests of the United States of America, and such an assault will be repelled by any means necessary, including military force.

During the past 3 years, you have joined with me to improve our own security and the prospects for peace, not only in the vital oil-producing area of the Persian Gulf region but around the world. We've increased annually our real commitment for defense, and we will sustain this increase of effort throughout the Five Year Defense Program. It's imperative that Congress approve this strong defense budget for 1981, encompassing a 5-percent real growth in authorizations, without any reduction.

We are also improving our capability to deploy U.S. military forces rapidly to distant areas. We've helped to strengthen NATO and our other alliances, and recently we and other NATO members have decided to develop and to deploy modernized, intermediate-range nuclear forces to meet an unwarranted and increased threat from the nuclear weapons of the Soviet Union.

We are working with our allies to prevent conflict in the Middle East. The peace treaty between Egypt and Israel is a notable achievement which represents a strategic asset for America and which also enhances prospects for regional and world peace. We are now engaged in further negotiations to provide full autonomy for the people of the West Bank and Gaza, to resolve the Palestinian issue in all its aspects, and to preserve the peace and security of Israel. Let no one doubt our commitment to the security of Israel. In a few days we will observe an historic event when Israel makes another major withdrawal from the Sinai and when Ambassadors will be exchanged between Israel and Egypt.

We've also expanded our own sphere of friendship. Our deep commitment to human rights and to meeting human needs has improved our relationship with much of the Third World. Our decision to normalize relations with the People's Republic of China will help to preserve peace and stability in Asia and in the Western Pacific.

We've increased and strengthened our naval presence in the Indian Ocean, and we are now making arrangements for key naval and air facilities to be used by our forces in the region of northeast Africa and the Persian Gulf.

We've reconfirmed our 1959 agreement to help Pakistan preserve its independence and its integrity. The United States will take action consistent with our own laws to assist Pakistan in resisting any outside aggression. And I'm asking the Congress specifically to reaffirm this agreement. I'm also working, along with the leaders of other nations, to provide additional military and economic aid for Pakistan. That request will come to you in just a few days.

In the weeks ahead, we will further strengthen political and military ties with other nations in the region. We believe that there are no irreconcilable differences between us and any Islamic nation. We respect the faith of Islam, and we are ready to cooperate with all Moslem countries.

Finally, we are prepared to work with other countries in the region to share a cooperative security framework that respects differing values and political beliefs, yet which enhances the independence, security, and prosperity of all.

All these efforts combined emphasize our dedication to defend and preserve the vital interests of the region and of the nation which we represent and those of our allies—in Europe and the Pacific, and also in the parts of the world which have such great strategic importance to us, stretching especially through the Middle East and Southwest Asia. With your help, I will pursue these efforts with vigor and with determination. You and I will act as necessary to protect and to preserve our Nation's security.

The men and women of America's Armed Forces are on duty tonight in many parts of the world. I'm proud of the job they are doing, and I know you share that pride. I believe that our volunteer forces are adequate for current defense needs, and I hope that it will not become necessary to impose a draft. However, we must be prepared for that possibility. For this reason, I have determined that the Selective Service System must now be revitalized. I will send legislation and budget proposals to the Congress next month so that we can begin registration and then meet future mobilization needs rapidly if they arise.

We also need clear and quick passage of a new charter to define the legal authority and accountability of our intelligence agencies. We will guarantee that abuses do not recur, but we must tighten our controls on sensitive intelligence information, and we need to remove unwarranted restraints on America's ability to collect intelligence.

The decade ahead will be a time of rapid change, as nations everywhere seek to deal with new problems and age-old tensions. But America need have no fear. We can thrive in a world of change if we remain true to our values and actively engaged in promoting world peace. We will continue to work as we have for peace in the Middle East and southern Africa. We will continue to build our ties with developing nations, respecting and helping to strengthen their national independence which they have struggled so hard to achieve. And we will continue to support the growth of democracy and the protection of human rights.

In repressive regimes, popular frustrations often have no outlet except through violence. But when peoples and their governments can approach their problems together through open, democratic methods, the basis for stability and peace is far more solid and far more enduring. That is why our support for human rights in other countries is in our own national interest as well as part of our own national character.

Peace—a peace that preserves freedom—remains America's first goal. In the coming years, as a mighty nation we will continue to pursue peace. But to be strong abroad we must be strong at home. And in order to be strong, we must continue to face up to the difficult issues that confront us as a nation today.

The crises in Iran and Afghanistan have dramatized a very important lesson: Our excessive dependence on foreign oil is a clear and present danger to our Nation's security. The need has never been more urgent. At long last, we must have a clear, comprehensive energy policy for the United States.

As you well know, I have been working with the Congress in a concentrated and persistent way over the past 3 years to meet this need. We have made progress together.

But Congress must act promptly now to complete final action on this vital energy legislation. Our Nation will then have a major conservation effort, important initiatives to develop solar power, realistic pricing based on the true value of oil, strong incentives for the production of coal and other fossil fuels in the United States, and our Nation's most massive peacetime investment in the development of synthetic fuels.

The American people are making progress in energy conservation. Last year we reduced overall petroleum consumption by 8 percent and gasoline consumption by 5 percent below what it was the year before. Now we must do more.

After consultation with the Governors, we will set gasoline conservation goals for each of the 50 States, and I will make them mandatory if these goals are not met.

I've established an import ceiling for 1980 of 8.2 million barrels a day—well below the level of foreign oil purchases in 1977. I expect our imports to be much lower than this, but the ceiling will be enforced by an oil import fee if necessary. I'm prepared to lower these imports still further if the other oil-consuming countries will join us in a fair and mutual reduction. If we have a serious shortage, I will not hesitate to impose mandatory gasoline rationing immediately.

The single biggest factor in the inflation rate last year, the increase in the inflation rate last year, was from one cause: the skyrocketing prices of OPEC oil. We must take whatever actions are necessary to reduce our dependence on foreign oil—and at the same time reduce inflation.

As individuals and as families, few of us can produce energy by ourselves. But all of us can conserve energy—every one of us, every day of our lives. Tonight I call on you—in fact, all the people of America—to help our Nation. Conserve energy. Eliminate waste. Make 1980 indeed a year of energy conservation.

Of course, we must take other actions to strengthen our Nation's economy.

First, we will continue to reduce the deficit and then to balance the Federal budget.

Second, as we continue to work with business to hold down prices, we'll build also on the historic national accord with organized labor to restrain pay increases in a fair fight against inflation.

Third, we will continue our successful efforts to cut paperwork and to dismantle unnecessary Government regulation.

Fourth, we will continue our progress in providing jobs for America, concentrating on a major new program to provide training and work for our young people, especially minority youth. It has been said that "a mind is a terrible thing to waste." We will give our young people new hope for jobs and a better life in the 1980's.

And fifth, we must use the decade of the 1980's to attack the basic structural weaknesses and problems in our economy through measures to increase productivity, savings, and investment.

With these energy and economic policies, we will make America even stronger at home in this decade—just as our foreign and defense policies will make us stronger and safer throughout the world. We will never abandon our struggle for a just and a decent society here at home. That's the heart of America—and it's the source of our ability to inspire other people to defend their own rights abroad.

Our material resources, great as they are, are limited. Our problems are too complex for simple slogans or for quick solutions. We cannot solve them without effort and sacrifice. Walter Lippmann once reminded us, "You took the good things for granted. Now you must earn them again. For every right that you cherish, you have a duty which you must fulfill. For every good which you wish to preserve, you will have to sacrifice your comfort and your ease. There is nothing for nothing any longer."

Our challenges are formidable. But there's a new spirit of unity and resolve in our country. We move into the 1980's with confidence and hope and a bright vision of the America we want: an America strong and free, an America at peace, an America with equal rights for all citizens—and for women, guaranteed in the United States Constitution—an America with jobs and good health and good education for every citizen, an America with a clean and bountiful life in our cities and on our farms, an America that helps to feed the world, an America secure in filling its own energy needs, an America of justice, tolerance, and compassion. For this vision to come true, we must sacrifice, but this national commitment will be an exciting enterprise that will unify our people.

Together as one people, let us work to build our strength at home, and together as one indivisible union, let us seek peace and security throughout the world.

Together let us make of this time of challenge and danger a decade of national resolve and of brave achievement.

Thank you very much.

Jimmy Carter, 1977–1981

Annual Message to Congress on the State of the Union

January 16, 1981

Jimmy Carter's last State of the Union message was a lengthy, written address dated just days before Carter would leave office. Carter, a Democrat, had lost his bid for reelection the previous November, losing in a landslide to Republican Ronald Reagan.

Carter's popularity had been dragged down by the ongoing problem of a group of American diplomats being held hostage in Iran. Militants had seized the Americans at the U.S. embassy in Tehran in November 1979, and U.S. attempts to free them, most notably a failed April 1980 helicopter raid that killed eight U.S. soldiers, were unsuccessful.

In the Democratic primaries, Carter faced a challenge from Senator Edward Kennedy of Massachusetts; he overcame that only to face Reagan, a conservative, and independent candidate John Anderson, formerly a Republican centrist, in the general election. Although polls had called for a close race, Reagan won 489 electoral votes to Carter's 49, and 51 percent of the popular vote to Carter's 41 percent and Anderson's 7 percent. In addition, Republicans won control of the Senate and picked up some seats in the Democratic-controlled House.

Carter's message of January 16 summed up his four years in office, crediting his administration with a long list of accomplishments ranging from creation of a Department of Energy to breakthroughs in Middle East peace.

Carter wrote that the economy was on its way back from recession, that a national energy plan had been instituted, that dependence on foreign oil was decreasing, and that the United States had been at peace for four years. But he also warned of high inflation, high unemployment, and a difficult world oil market.

The president also referred to the hostages in Iran, calling their captivity "against international law and against every precept of human affairs."

The State of the Union message was overshadowed by developments leading up to the freeing of the hostages; they were freed on January 20, just after Reagan took office. Carter's departure and Reagan's ascent heralded the start of a conservative era in Washington.

Carter returned to his hometown of Plains, Georgia, after leaving office. Among his other activities, he established the Carter Center in Atlanta, which focuses on human rights and other issues. Many observers have given Carter higher marks for his accomplishments after leaving the presidency than they did for his years in the White House. He won the Nobel Peace Prize in 2002 for his efforts in international peacemaking.

To the Congress of the United States:

The State of the Union is sound. Our economy is recovering from a recession. A national energy plan is in place and our dependence on foreign oil is decreasing. We have been at peace for four uninterrupted years.

But, our Nation has serious problems. Inflation and unemployment are unacceptably high. The world oil market is increasingly tight. There are trouble spots throughout the world, and 53 American hostages are being held in Iran against international law and against every precept of human affairs.

However, I firmly believe that, as a result of the progress made in so many domestic and international areas over the past four years, our Nation is stronger, wealthier, more compassionate and freer than it was four years ago. I am proud of that fact. And I believe the Congress should be proud as well, for so much of what has been accomplished over the past four years has been due to the hard work, insights and cooperation of Congress. I applaud the Congress for its efforts and its achievements.

In this State of the Union Message I want to recount the achievements and progress of the last four years and to offer recommendations to the Congress for this year. While my term as President will end before the 97th Congress begins its work in earnest, I hope that my recommendations will serve as a guide for the direction this country should take so we build on the record of the past four years.

Record of Progress

When I took office, our Nation faced a number of serious domestic and international problems:

- no national energy policy existed, and our dependence on foreign oil was rapidly increasing;
- public trust in the integrity and openness of the government was low;
- the Federal government was operating inefficiently in administering essential programs and policies;

- major social problems were being ignored or poorly addressed by the Federal government;
- our defense posture was declining as a result of a defense budget which was continuously shrinking in real terms;
- the strength of the NATO Alliance needed to be bolstered;
- tensions between Israel and Egypt threatened another Middle East war; and
- America's resolve to oppose human rights violations was under serious question.

Over the past 48 months, clear progress has been made in solving the challenges we found in January of 1977:

- almost all of our comprehensive energy programs have been enacted, and the Department of Energy has been established to administer the program;
- confidence in the government's integrity has been restored, and respect for the government's openness and fairness has been renewed;
- the government has been made more effective and efficient: the Civil Service system was completely reformed for the first time this century; 14 reorganization initiatives have been proposed to the Congress, approved, and implemented; two new Cabinet departments have been created to consolidate and streamline the government's handling of energy and education problems; inspectors general have been placed in each Cabinet department to combat fraud, waste and other abuses; the regulatory process has been reformed through creation of the Regulatory Council, implementation of Executive Order 12044 and its requirement for cost-impact analyses, elimination of unnecessary regulation, and passage of the Regulatory Flexibility Act; procedures have been established to assure citizen participation in government; and the airline, trucking, rail and communications industries are being deregulated;
- critical social problems, many long ignored by the Federal government, have been addressed directly; an urban policy was developed and implemented to reverse the decline in our urban areas; the Social Security System was refinanced to put it on a sound financial basis; the Humphrey-Hawkins Full Employment Act was enacted; Federal assistance for education was expanded by more than 75 percent; the minimum wage was increased to levels needed to ease the effects of inflation; affirmative action has been pursued aggressively—more blacks, Hispanics and women have been appointed to senior government positions and to judgeships than at any other time in our history; the ERA ratification deadline was extended to aid the ratification effort; and minority business procurement by the Federal government has more than doubled;
- the Nation's first sectoral policies were put in place, for the auto and steel industries, with my Administration demonstrating the value of cooperation between the government, business and labor;
- reversing previous trends, real defense spending has increased every year since 1977; the real increase in FY [fiscal year] 1980 defense spending is well above 3 percent and I expect FY 1981 defense spending to be even higher; looking ahead,

the defense program I am proposing is premised on a real increase in defense spending over the next five years of 20 percent or more;

• the NATO Alliance has proven its unity in responding to the situations in Eastern Europe and Southwest Asia and in agreeing on the issues to be addressed in the review of the Helsinki Final Act currently underway in Madrid;

• the peace process in the Middle East established at Camp David and by the Peace Treaty between Egypt and Israel is being buttressed on two fronts: steady progress in the normalization of Egyptian-Israeli relations in many fields, and the commitment of both Egypt and Israel, with United States' assistance, to see through to successful conclusion the autonomy negotiations for the West Bank and Gaza;

• the Panama Canal Treaties have been put into effect, which has helped to improve relations with Latin America;

• we have continued this Nation's strong commitment to the pursuit of human rights throughout the world, evenhandedly and objectively; our commitment to a worldwide human rights policy has remained firm; and many other countries have given high priority to it;

• our resolve to oppose aggression, such as the illegal invasion of the Soviet Union into Afghanistan, has been supported by tough action.

I. Ensuring Economic Strength

Economy

During the last decade our Nation has withstood a series of economic shocks unprecedented in peacetime. The most dramatic of these has been the explosive increases of OPEC oil prices. But we have also faced world commodity shortages, natural disasters, agricultural shortages and major challenges to world peace and security. Our ability to deal with these shocks has been impaired because of a decrease in the growth of productivity and the persistence of underlying inflationary forces built up over the past 15 years.

Nevertheless, the economy has proved to be remarkably resilient. Real output has grown at an average rate of 3 percent per year since I took office, and employment has grown by 10 percent. We have added about 8 million productive private sector jobs to the economy. However, unacceptably high inflation—the most difficult economic problem I have faced—persists.

This inflation—which threatens the growth, productivity, and stability of our economy—requires that we restrain the growth of the budget to the maximum extent consistent with national security and human compassion. I have done so in my earlier budgets, and in my FY '82 budget. However, while restraint is essential to any appropriate economic policy, high inflation cannot be attributed solely to government spending. The growth in budget outlays has been more the result of economic factors than the cause of them.

We are now in the early stages of economic recovery following a short recession. Typically, a post-recessionary period has been marked by vigorous economic growth aided by anti-recessionary policy measures such as large tax cuts or big, stimulation spending programs. I have declined to recommend such actions to stimulate economic activity, because the persistent inflationary pressures that beset our economy today dictate a restrained fiscal policy.

Accordingly, I am asking the Congress to postpone until January 1, 1982, the personal tax reductions I had earlier proposed to take effect on January 1 of this year.

However, my 1982 budget proposes significant tax changes to increase the sources of financing for business investment. While emphasizing the need for continued fiscal restraint, this budget takes the first major step in a long-term tax reduction program designed to increase capital formation. The failure of our Nation's capital stock to grow at a rate that keeps pace with its labor force has clearly been one cause of our productivity slowdown. Higher investment rates are also critically needed to meet our Nation's energy needs, and to replace energy-inefficient plants and equipment with new energy-saving physical plants. The level of investment that is called for will not occur in the absence of policies to encourage it.

Therefore, my budget proposes a major liberalization of tax allowances for depreciation, as well as simplified depreciation accounting, increasing the allowable rates by about 40 percent. I am also proposing improvements in the investment tax credit, making it refundable, to meet the investment needs of firms with no current earnings.

These two proposals, along with carefully-phased tax reductions for individuals, will improve both economic efficiency and tax equity. I urge the Congress to enact legislation along the lines and timetable I have proposed.

The 1982 Budget

The FY 1982 budget I have sent to the Congress continues our four-year policy of prudence and restraint. While the budget deficits during my term are higher than I would have liked, their size is determined for the most part by economic conditions. And in spite of these conditions, the relative size of the deficit continues to decline. In 1976, before I took office, the budget deficit equalled 4 percent of gross national product. It had been cut to 2.3 percent in the 1980 fiscal year just ended. My 1982 budget contains a deficit estimated to be less than 1 percent of our gross national product.

The rate of growth in Federal spending has been held to a minimum. Nevertheless, outlays are still rising more rapidly than many had anticipated, the result of many powerful forces in our society.

We face a threat to our security, as events in Afghanistan, the Middle East, and Eastern Europe make clear. We have a steadily aging population and, as a result, the biggest single increase in the Federal budget is the rising cost of retirement programs, particularly social security. We face other important domestic needs: to continue responsibility for the disadvantaged; to provide the capital needed by our cities and our transportation systems; to protect our environment; to revitalize American industry; and to increase the export of American goods and services so essential to the creation of jobs and a trade surplus.

Yet the Federal Government itself may not always be the proper source of such assistance. For example, it must not usurp functions if they can be more appropriately decided upon, managed, and financed by the private sector or by State and local governments. My Administration has always sought to consider the proper focus of responsibility for the most efficient resolution of problems.

We have also recognized the need to simplify the system of grants to State and local governments. I have again proposed several grant consolidations in the 1982 budget, including a new proposal that would consolidate several highway programs.

The pressures for growth in Federal use of national resources are great. My Administration has initiated many new approaches to cope with these pressures. We started a multi-year budget system, and we began a system for controlling Federal credit programs. Yet in spite of increasing needs to limit spending growth, we have consistently adhered to these strong budget principles:

- Our Nation's armed forces must always stand sufficiently strong to deter aggression and to assure our security.
- An effective national energy plan is essential to increase domestic production of oil and gas, to encourage conservation of our scarce energy resources, to stimulate conversion to more abundant fuels, and to reduce our trade deficit.
- The essential human needs for our citizens must be given the highest priority.
- The Federal Government must lead the way in investment in the Nation's technological future.
- The Federal Government has an obligation to nurture and protect our environment—the common resource, birthright, and sustenance of the American people.

My 1982 budget continues to support these principles. It also proposes responsible tax reductions to encourage a more productive economy, and adequate funding of our highest priority programs within an overall policy of constraint.

Fiscal restraint must be continued in the years ahead. Budgets must be tight enough to convince those who set wages and prices that the Federal Government is serious about fighting inflation but not so tight as to choke off all growth.

Careful budget policy should be supplemented by other measures designed to reduce inflation at lower cost in lost output and employment. These other steps include measures to increase investment—such as the tax proposals included in my 1982 budget—and measures to increase competition and productivity in our economy. Voluntary incomes policies can also directly influence wages and prices in the direction of moderation and thereby bring inflation down faster and at lower cost to the economy. Through a tax-based incomes policy (TIP) we could provide tax incentives for firms and workers to moderate their wage and price increases. In the coming years, control of Federal expenditures can make possible periodic tax reductions. The Congress should therefore begin now to evaluate the potentialities of a TIP program so that when the next round of tax reductions is appropriate a TIP program will be seriously considered.

Employment
During the last four years we have given top priority to meeting the needs of workers and providing additional job opportunities to those who seek work. Since the end of 1976:

- almost 9 million new jobs have been added to the nation's economy
- total employment has reached 97 million. More jobs than ever before are held by women, minorities and young people. Employment over the past four years has increased by:
    - —17% for adult women
    - —11% for blacks, and
    - —30% for Hispanics

- employment of black teenagers increased by more than 5%, reversing the decline that occurred in the previous eight years.

Major initiatives launched by this Administration helped bring about these accomplishments and have provided a solid foundation for employment and training policy in the 1980's.

In 1977, as part of the comprehensive economic stimulus program:

- 425,000 public service jobs were created
- A $1 billion youth employment initiative funded 200,000 jobs
- the doubling of the Job Corps to 44,000 slots began and 1 million summer youth jobs were approved—a 25 percent increase.

In 1978:

- the Humphrey-Hawkins Full Employment Act became law
- the $400 million Private Sector Initiatives Program was begun
- a targeted jobs tax credit for disadvantaged youth and others with special employment barriers was enacted
- the Comprehensive Employment and Training Act was reauthorized for four years.

In 1979:

- a $6 billion welfare reform proposal was introduced with funding for 400,000 public service jobs
- welfare reform demonstration projects were launched in communities around the country
- the Vice President initiated a nationwide review of youth unemployment in this country.

In 1980:

- The findings of the Vice President's Task Force revealed the major education and employment deficits that exist for poor and minority youngsters. As a result a $2 billion youth education and jobs initiative was introduced to provide unemployed youth with the basic education and work experience they need to compete in the labor market of the 1980's.
- As part of the economic revitalization program several steps were proposed to aid workers in high unemployment communities:
    —an additional 13 weeks of unemployment benefits for the long term unemployed.
    —$600 million to train the disadvantaged and unemployed for new private sector jobs.

—positive adjustment demonstrations to aid workers in declining industries.

- The important Title VII Private Sector Initiatives Program was reauthorized for an additional two years.

In addition to making significant progress in helping the disadvantaged and unemployed, important gains were realized for all workers:

- an historic national accord with organized labor made it possible for the views of working men and women to be heard as the nation's economic and domestic policies were formulated.
- the Mine Safety and Health Act brought about improved working conditions for the nation's 500,000 miners.
- substantial reforms of the Occupational Safety and Health Administration were accomplished to help reduce unnecessary burdens on business and to focus on major health and safety problems.
- the minimum wage was increased over a four year period from $2.30 to $3.35 an hour.
- the Black Lung Benefit Reform Act was signed into law.
- attempts to weaken the Davis-Bacon Act were defeated.

While substantial gains have been made in the last four years, continued efforts are required to ensure that this progress is continued:

- government must continue to make labor a full partner in the policy decisions that affect the interests of working men and women
- a broad, bipartisan effort to combat youth unemployment must be sustained
- compassionate reform of the nation's welfare system should be continued with employment opportunities provided for those able to work
- workers in declining industries should be provided new skills and help in finding employment

Trade

Over the past year, the U.S. trade picture improved as a result of solid export gains in both manufactured and agricultural products. Agricultural exports reached a new record of over $40 billion, while manufactured exports have grown by 24 percent to a record $144 billion. In these areas the United States recorded significant surpluses of $24 billion and $19 billion respectively. While our oil imports remained a major drain on our foreign exchange earnings, that drain was somewhat moderated by a 19 percent decline in the volume of oil imports.

U.S. trade negotiators made significant progress over the past year in assuring effective implementation of the agreements negotiated during the Tokyo Round of Multilateral Trade Negotiations. Agreements reached with the Japanese government, for example, will assure that the United States will be able to expand its exports to the Japanese market in such key areas as telecommunications equipment, tobacco, and lumber. Efforts by U.S. trade negotiators also helped to persuade a number of key developing countries to accept many of the non-tariff codes negotiated during the Multilateral Trade Negotiations. This will assure that these countries will increasingly assume obligations under the international trading system.

A difficult world economic environment posed a challenge for the management of trade relations. U.S. trade negotiators were called upon to manage serious sectoral problems in such areas as steel, and helped to assure that U.S. chemical exports will have continued access to the European market.

Close consultations with the private sector in the United States have enabled U.S. trade negotiators to pinpoint obstacles to U.S. trade in services, and to build a basis for future negotiations. Services have been an increasingly important source of export earnings for the United States, and the United States must assure continued and increased access to foreign markets.

The trade position of the United States has improved. But vigorous efforts are needed in a number of areas to assure continued market access for U.S. exports, particularly agricultural and high technology products, in which the United States continues to have a strong competitive edge. Continued efforts are also needed to remove many domestic disincentives, which now hamper U.S. export growth. And we must ensure that countries do not manipulate investment, or impose investment performance requirements which distort trade and cost us jobs in this country.

In short, we must continue to seek free—but fair—trade. That is the policy my Administration has pursued from the beginning, even in areas where foreign competition has clearly affected our domestic industry. In the steel industry, for instance, we have put a Trigger Price Mechanism into place to help prevent the dumping of steel. That action has strengthened the domestic steel industry. In the automobile industry, we have worked—without resort to import quotas—to strengthen the industry's ability to modernize and compete effectively.

Small Business

I have often said that there is nothing small about small business in America. These firms account for nearly one-half our gross national product; over half of new technology; and much more than half of the jobs created by industry.

Because this sector of the economy is the very lifeblood of our National economy, we have done much together to improve the competitive climate for smaller firms. These concerted efforts have been an integral part of my program to revitalize the economy.

They include my campaign to shrink substantially the cash and time consuming red tape burden imposed on business. They include my personally-directed policy of ambitiously increasing the Federal contracting dollars going to small firms, especially those owned by women and minorities. And they include my proposals to reinvigorate existing small businesses and assist the creation of new ones through tax reform; financing assistance; market expansion; and support of product innovation.

Many of my initiatives to facilitate the creation and growth of small businesses were made in response to the White House Conference on Small Business, which I convened. My Administration began the implementation of most of the ideas produced last year by that citizen's advisory body; others need to be addressed. I have proposed the reconvening of the Conference next year to review progress; reassess priorities; and set new goals. In the interim I hope that the incoming Administration and the new Congress will work with the committee I have established to keep these business development ideas alive and help implement Conference recommendations.

Minority Business

One of the most successful developments of my Administration has been the growth and strengthening of minority business. This is the first Administration to put the issue on the policy agenda as a matter of major importance. To implement the results of our early efforts in this field I submitted legislation to Congress designed to further the development of minority business.

We have reorganized the Office of Minority Business into the Minority Business Development Administration in the Department of Commerce. MBDA has already proven to be a major factor in assisting minority businesses to achieve equitable competitive positions in the marketplace.

The Federal government's procurement from minority-owned firms has nearly tripled since I took office. Federal deposits in minority-owned banks have more than doubled and minority ownership of radio and television stations has nearly doubled. The SBA administered 8(a) Pilot Program for procurement with the Army proved to be successful and I recently expanded the number of agencies involved to include NASA and the Departments of Energy and Transportation.

I firmly believe the critical path to full freedom and equality for America's minorities rests with the ability of minority communities to participate competitively in the free enterprise system. I believe the government has a fundamental responsibility to assist in the development of minority business and I hope the progress made in the last four years will continue.

II. Creating Energy Security

Since I took office, my highest legislative priorities have involved the reorientation and redirection of U.S. energy activities and for the first time, to establish a coordinated national energy policy. The struggle to achieve that policy has been long and difficult, but the accomplishments of the past four years make clear that our country is finally serious about the problems caused by our overdependence on foreign oil. Our progress should not be lost. We must rely on and encourage multiple forms of energy production—coal, crude oil, natural gas, solar, nuclear, synthetics—and energy conservation. The framework put in place over the last four years will enable us to do this.

National Energy Policy

As a result of actions my Administration and the Congress have taken over the past four years, our country finally has a national energy policy:

- Under my program of phased decontrol, domestic crude oil price controls will end September 30, 1981. As a result exploratory drilling activities have reached an all-time high;

- Prices for new natural gas are being decontrolled under the Natural Gas Policy

Act—and natural gas production is now at an all time high; the supply shortages of several years ago have been eliminated;

- The windfall profits tax on crude oil has been enacted providing $227 billion over ten years for assistance to low-income households, increased mass transit funding, and a massive investment in the production and development of alternative energy sources;

- The Synthetic Fuels Corporation has been established to help private companies build the facilities to produce energy from synthetic fuels;

- Solar energy funding has been quadrupled, solar energy tax credits enacted, and a Solar Energy and Energy Conservation Bank has been established;

- A route has been chosen to bring natural gas from the North Slope of Alaska to the lower 48 states;

- Coal production and consumption incentives have been increased, and coal production is now at its highest level in history;

- A gasoline rationing plan has been approved by Congress for possible use in the event of a severe energy supply shortage or interruption;

- Gasohol production has been dramatically increased, with a program being put in place to produce 500 million gallons of alcohol fuel by the end of this year— an amount that could enable gasohol to meet the demand for 10 percent of all unleaded gasoline;

- New energy conservation incentives have been provided for individuals, businesses and communities and conservation has increased dramatically. The U.S. has reduced oil imports by 25 percent—or 2 million barrels per day—over the past four years.

Increased Development of Domestic Energy Sources
Although it is essential that the Nation reduce its dependence on imported fossil fuels and complete the transition to reliance on domestic renewable sources of energy, it is also important that this transition be accomplished in an orderly, economic, and environmentally sound manner. To this end, the Administration has launched several initiatives.

Leasing of oil and natural gas on federal lands, particularly the outer continental shelf, has been accelerated at the same time as the Administration has reformed leasing procedures through the 1978 amendments to the Outer Continental Shelf Lands Act. In 1979 the Interior Department held six OCS lease sales, the greatest number ever, which resulted in federal receipts of $6.5 billion, another record. The five-year OCS Leasing schedule was completed, requiring 36 sales over the next five years.

Since 1971 no general federal coal lease sales were suspended. Over the past four years the Administration has completely revised the federal coal leasing program to bring it into compliance with the requirements of 1976 Federal Land Planning and Management Act and other statutory provisions. The program is designed to balance the competing interests that affect resource development on public lands and to ensure that adequate supplies of coal will be available to meet national needs. As a result, the first general competitive federal coal lease sale in ten years will be held this month.

In July 1980, I signed into law the Energy Security Act of 1980 which established the Synthetic Fuels Corporation. The Corporation is designed to spur the development of commercial technologies for production of synthetic fuels, such as liquid and gaseous fuels from coal and the production of oil from oil shale. The Act provides the Corporation with an initial $22 billion to accomplish these objectives. The principal purpose of the legislation is to ensure that the nation will have available in the late 1980's the option to undertake commercial development of synthetic fuels if that becomes necessary. The Energy Security Act also provides significant incentives for the development of gasohol and biomass fuels, thereby enhancing the nation's supply of alternative energy sources.

Commitment to a Sustainable Energy Future

The Administration's 1977 National Energy Plan marked an historic departure from the policies of previous Administrations. The plan stressed the importance of both energy production and conservation to achieving our ultimate national goal of relying primarily on secure sources of energy. The National Energy Plan made energy conservation a cornerstone of our national energy policy.

In 1978, I initiated the Administration's Solar Domestic Policy Review. This represented the first step towards widespread introduction of renewable energy sources into the Nation's economy. As a result of the Review, I issued the 1979 Solar Message to Congress, the first such message in the Nation's history. The Message outlined the Administration's solar program and established an ambitious national goal for the year 2000 of obtaining 20 percent of this Nation's energy from solar and renewable sources. The thrust of the federal solar program is to help industry develop solar energy sources by emphasizing basic research and development of solar technologies which are not currently economic, such as photovoltaics, which generate energy directly from the sun. At the same time, through tax incentives, education, and the Solar Energy and Energy Conservation Bank, the solar program seeks to encourage state and local governments, industry, and our citizens to expand their use of solar and renewable resource technologies currently available.

As a result of these policies and programs, the energy efficiency of the American economy has improved markedly and investments in renewable energy sources have grown significantly. It now takes 3 1/2 percent less energy to produce a constant dollar of GNP than it did in January 1977. This increase in efficiency represents a savings of over 1.3 million barrels per day of oil equivalent, about the level of total oil production now occurring in Alaska. Over the same period, Federal support for conservation and solar energy has increased by more than 3000 percent, to $3.3 billion in FY 1981, including the tax credits for solar energy and energy conservation investments—these credits are expected to amount to $1.2 billion in FY 1981 and $1.5 billion in FY 1982.

Commitment to Nuclear Safety and Security

Since January 1977, significant progress has been achieved in resolving three critical problems resulting from the use of nuclear energy: radioactive waste management, nuclear safety and weapons proliferation.

In 1977, the Administration announced its nuclear nonproliferation policy and initiated the International Fuel Cycle Evaluation. In 1978, Congress passed the Nuclear Nonproliferation Act, an historic piece of legislation.

In February 1980, the Administration transmitted its nuclear waste management policy to the Congress. This policy was a major advance over all previous efforts. The principal aspects of that policy are: acknowledging the seriousness of the problem and the numerous technical and institutional issues; adopting a technically and environmentally conservative approach to the first permanent repository; and providing the states with significant involvement in nuclear waste disposal decisions by creating the State Planning Council. While much of the plan can be and is being implemented administratively, some new authorities are needed. The Congress should give early priority to enacting provisions for away-from-reactor storage and the State Planning Council.

The accident at Three Mile Island made the nation acutely aware of the safety risks posed by nuclear power plants. In response, the President established the Kemeny Commission to review the accident and make recommendations. Virtually all of the Commission's substantive recommendations were adopted by the Administration and are now being implemented by the Nuclear Regulatory Commission. The Congress adopted the President's proposed plan for the Nuclear Regulatory Commission and the Nuclear Safety Oversight Committee was established to ensure that the Administration's decisions were implemented.

Nuclear safety will remain a vital concern in the years ahead. We must continue to press ahead for the safe, secure disposal of radioactive wastes, and prevention of nuclear proliferation.

While significant growth in foreign demand for U.S. steam coal is foreseen, congestion must be removed at major U.S. coal exporting ports such as Hampton Roads, Virginia, and Baltimore, Maryland. My Administration has worked through the Interagency Coal Task Force Study to promote cooperation and coordination of resources between shippers, railroads, vessel broker/operators and port operators, and to determine the most appropriate Federal role in expanding and modernizing coal export facilities, including dredging deeper channels at selected ports. As a result of the Task Force's efforts, administrative steps have been taken by the Corps of Engineers to reduce significantly the amount of time required for planning and economic review of port dredging proposals. The Administration has also recommended that the Congress enact legislation to give the President generic authority to recommend appropriations for channel dredging activities. Private industry will, of course, play the major role in developing the United States' coal export facilities, but the government must continue to work to facilitate transportation to foreign markets.

III. Enhancing Basic Human and Social Needs

For too long prior to my Administration, many of our Nation's basic human and social needs were being ignored or handled insensitively by the Federal government. Over the last four years, we have significantly increased funding for many of the vital programs in these areas; developed new programs where needs were unaddressed; targeted Federal support to those individuals and areas most in need of our assistance; and removed barriers that have unnecessarily kept many disadvantaged citizens from obtaining aid for their most basic needs.

Our record has produced clear progress in the effort to solve some of the country's fundamental human and social problems. My Administration and the Congress, working together, have demonstrated that government must and can meet our citizens' basic human and social needs in a responsible and compassionate way.

But there is an unfinished agenda still before the Congress. If we are to meet our obligations to help all Americans realize the dreams of sound health care, decent housing, effective social services, a good education, and a meaningful job, important legislation still must be enacted. National Health Insurance, Welfare Reform, Child Health Assessment Program, are before the Congress and I urge their passage.

Health

National Health Plan. During my Administration, I proposed to Congress a National Health Plan which will enable the country to reach the goal of comprehensive, universal health care coverage. The legislation I submitted lays the foundation for this comprehensive plan and addresses the most serious problems of health financing and delivery. It is realistic and enactable. It does not overpromise or overspend, and, as a result, can be the solution to the thirty years of Congressional battles on national health insurance. My Plan includes the following key features:

- nearly 15 million additional poor would receive fully-subsidized comprehensive coverage;
- pre-natal and delivery services are provided for all pregnant women and coverage is provided for all acute care for infants in their first year of life;
- the elderly and disabled would have a limit of $1,250 placed on annual out-of-pocket medical expenses and would no longer face limits on hospital coverage;
- all full-time employees and their families would receive insurance against at least major medical expenses under mandated employer coverage;
- Medicare and Medicaid would be combined and expanded into an umbrella Federal program, Healthcare, for increased program efficiency, accountability and uniformity; and
- strong cost controls and health system reforms would be implemented, including greater incentives for Health Maintenance Organizations.

I urge the new Congress to compare my Plan with the alternatives—programs which either do too little to improve the health care needs of Americans most in need or programs which would impose substantial financial burdens on the American taxpayers. I hope the Congress will see the need for and the benefits of my Plan and work toward prompt enactment. We cannot afford further delay in this vital area.

Health Care Cost Control. Inflation in health care costs remains unacceptably high. Throughout my Administration, legislation to reduce health care cost inflation was one of my highest priorities, but was not passed by the Congress. Therefore, my FY 1982 budget proposes sharing the responsibility for health care cost control with the private sector, through voluntary hospital cost guidelines and intensified monitoring. In the longer term, the health care reimbursement system must be reformed. We must move away from inflationary cost-based reimbursement and fee-for-service, and toward a system of prospective reimbursement, under which health care providers would operate within predetermined budgets. This reimbursement reform is essential to ultimately control inflation in health care costs, and will be a significant challenge to the new Congress.

Health Promotion and Disease Prevention. During my Administration, the Surgeon General released Healthy People, a landmark report on health promotion and disease prevention. The report signals the growing consensus that the Nation's health strategy must be refocused in the 1980's to emphasize the prevention of disease. Specifically, the report lays out measurable and achievable goals in the reduction of mortality which can be reached by 1990.

I urge the new Congress to endorse the principles of Healthy People, and to adopt the recommendations to achieve its goals. This will necessitate adoption of a broader concept of health care, to include such areas as environmental health, workplace health and safety, commercial product safety, traffic safety, and health education, promotion and information.

Maternal and Child Health. Ensuring a healthy start in life for children remains not only a high priority of my Administration, but also one of the most cost effective forms of health care.

When I took office, immunization levels for preventable childhood diseases had fallen to 70%. As a result of a concerted nationwide effort during my Administration, I am pleased to report that now at least 90% of children under 15, and virtually all school-age children are immunized. In addition, reported cases of measles and mumps are at their lowest levels ever.

Under the National Health Plan I have proposed, there would be no cost-sharing for prenatal and delivery services for all pregnant women and for acute care provided to infants in their first year of life. These preventive services have extremely high returns in terms of improved newborn and long-term child health.

Under the Child Health Assurance Program (CHAP) legislation which I submitted to the Congress, and which passed the House, an additional two million low income children under 18 would become eligible for Medicaid benefits, which would include special health assessments. CHAP would also improve the continuity of care for the nearly 14 million children now eligible for Medicaid. An additional 100,000 low-income pregnant women would become eligible for prenatal care under the proposal. I strongly urge the new Congress to enact CHAP and thereby provide millions of needy children with essential health services. The legislation has had strong bipartisan support, which should continue as the details of the bill are completed.

I also urge the new Congress to provide strong support for two highly successful ongoing programs: the special supplemental food program for women, infants and children (WIC) and Family Planning. The food supplements under WIC have been shown to effectively prevent ill health and thereby reduce later medical costs. The Family Planning program has been effective at reducing unwanted pregnancies among low-income women and adolescents.

Expansion of Services to the Poor and Underserved. During my Administration, health services to the poor and underserved have been dramatically increased. The number of National Health Service Corps (NHSC) assignees providing services in medically underserved communities has grown from 500 in 1977 to nearly 3,000 in 1981. The population served by the NHSC has more than tripled since 1977. The number of Community Health Centers providing services in high priority underserved areas has doubled during my Administration, and will serve an estimated six million people in 1981. I strongly urge the new Congress to support these highly successful programs.

Mental Health. One of the most significant health achievements during my Administration was the recent passage of the Mental Health Systems Act, which grew out of recommendations of my Commission on Mental Health. I join many others in my gratitude to the First Lady for her tireless and effective contribution to the passage of this important legislation.

The Act is designed to inaugurate a new era of Federal and State partnership in the planning and provision of mental health services. In addition, the Act specifically provides for prevention and support services to the chronically mentally ill to prevent unnecessary institutionalization and for the development of community-based mental health services. I urge the new Congress to provide adequate support for the full and timely implementation of this Act.

Health Protection. With my active support, the Congress recently passed "Medigap" legislation, which provides for voluntary certification of health insurance policies supplemental to Medicare, to curb widespread abuses in this area.

In the area of toxic agent control, legislation which I submitted to the Congress recently passed. This will provide for a "super-fund" to cover hazardous waste cleanup costs.

In the area of accidental injury control, we have established automobile safety standards and increased enforcement activities with respect to the 55 MPH speed limit. By the end of the decade these actions are expected to save over 13,000 lives and 100,000 serious injuries each year.

I urge the new Congress to continue strong support for all these activities.

Food and Nutrition. Building on the comprehensive reform of the Food Stamp Program that I proposed and Congress passed in 1977, my Administration and the Congress worked together in 1979 and 1980 to enact several other important changes in the Program. These changes will further simplify administration and reduce fraud and error, will make the program more responsive to the needs of the elderly and disabled, and will increase the cap on allowable program expenditures. The Food Stamp Act will expire at the end of fiscal 1981. It is essential that the new Administration and the Congress continue this program to ensure complete eradication of the debilitating malnutrition witnessed and documented among thousands of children in the 1960's.

Drug Abuse Prevention. At the beginning of my Administration there were over a half million heroin addicts in the United States. Our continued emphasis on reducing the supply of heroin, as well as providing treatment and rehabilitation to its victims, has reduced the heroin addict population, reduced the number of heroin overdose deaths by 80%, and reduced the number of heroin related injuries by 50%. We have also seen and encouraged a national movement of parents and citizens committed to reversing the very serious and disturbing trends of adolescent drug abuse.

Drug abuse in many forms will continue to detract, however, from the quality of life of many Americans. To prevent that, I see four great challenges in the years ahead. First, we must deal aggressively with the supplies of illegal drugs at their source, through joint crop destruction programs with foreign nations and increased law enforcement and border interdiction. Second, we must look to citizens and parents across the country to help educate the increasing numbers of American youth who are experimenting with drugs to the dangers of drug abuse. Education is a key factor in reducing drug abuse. Third, we must focus our efforts on drug and alcohol abuse in the workplace for not only does this abuse contribute to low productivity but it also destroys the satisfaction and sense of purpose all Americans can gain from the work experience. Fourth, we need a change in attitude, from an attitude which condones the casual use of drugs to one that recognizes the appropriate use of drugs for medical purposes and condemns the inappropriate and harmful abuse of drugs. I hope the Congress and the new Administration will take action to meet each of these challenges.

Education

The American people have always recognized that education is one of the soundest investments they can make. The dividends are reflected in every dimension of our national life—from the strength of our economy and national security to the vitality of our music, art, and literature. Among the accomplishments that have given me the most satisfaction over the last four years are the contributions that my Administration has been able to make to the well-being of students and educators throughout the country.

This Administration has collaborated successfully with the Congress on landmark education legislation. Working with the Congressional leadership, my Administration spotlighted the importance of education by creating a new Department of Education. The Department has given education a stronger voice at the Federal level, while at the same time reserving the actual control and operation of education to states, localities, and private institutions. The Department has successfully combined nearly 150 Federal education programs into a cohesive, streamlined organization that is more responsive to the needs of educators and students. The Department has made strides to cut red tape and paperwork and thereby to make the flow of Federal dollars to school districts and institutions of higher education more efficient. It is crucial that the Department be kept intact and strengthened.

Our collaboration with the Congress has resulted in numerous other important legislative accomplishments for education. A little over two years ago, I signed into law on the same day two major bills—one benefiting elementary and secondary education and the other, postsecondary education. The Education Amendments of 1978 embodied nearly all of my Administration's proposals for improvements in the Elementary and Secondary Education Act, including important new programs to improve students' achievement in the basic skills and to aid school districts with exceptionally high concentrations of children from low-income families. The Middle Income Student Assistance Act, legislation jointly sponsored by this Administration and the Congressional leadership, expanded eligibility for need-based Basic Educational Opportunity Grants to approximately one-third of the students enrolled in postsecondary education and made many more students eligible for the first time for other types of grants, work-study, and loans.

Just three and a half months ago, my Administration and the Congress successfully concluded over two years of work on a major reauthorization bill that further expands benefits to postsecondary education. Reflected in the Education Amendments of 1980 are major Administration recommendations for improvements in the Higher Education Act—including proposals for better loan access for students; a new parent loan program; simplified application procedures for student financial aid; a strengthened Federal commitment to developing colleges, particularly the historically Black institutions; a new authorization for equipment and facilities modernization funding for the nation's major research universities; and revitalized international education programs.

Supplementing these legislative accomplishments have been important administrative actions aimed at reducing paperwork and simplifying regulations associated with Federal education programs. We also launched major initiatives to reduce the backlog of defaulted student loans and otherwise to curb fraud, abuse, and waste in education programs.

To insure that the education enterprise is ready to meet the scientific and technological changes of the future, we undertook a major study of the status of science and engineering education throughout the nation. I hope that the findings from this report will serve as a springboard for needed reforms at all levels of education.

I am proud that this Administration has been able to provide the financial means to realize many of our legislative and administrative goals. Compared to the previous administration's last budget, I have requested the largest overall increase in Federal funding for education in our nation's history. My budget requests have been particularly sensitive to the needs of special populations like minorities, women, the educationally and economically disadvantaged, the handicapped, and students with limited English-speaking ability. At the same time, I have requested significant increases for many programs designed to enhance the quality of American education, including programs relating to important areas as diverse as international education, research libraries, museums, and teacher centers.

Last year, I proposed to the Congress a major legislative initiative that would direct $2 billion into education and job training programs designed to alleviate youth unemployment through improved linkages between the schools and the work place. This legislation generated bipartisan support; but unfortunately, action on it was not completed in the final, rushed days of the 96th Congress. I urge the new Congress—as it undertakes broad efforts to strengthen the economy as well as more specific tasks like reauthorizing the Vocational Education Act—to make the needs of our nation's unemployed youth a top priority for action. Only by combining a basic skills education program together with work training and employment incentives can we make substantial progress in eliminating one of the most severe social problems in our nation— youth unemployment, particularly among minorities. I am proud of the progress already made through passage of the Youth Employment and Demonstration Project Act of 1977 and the substantial increase in our investment in youth employment programs. The new legislation would cap these efforts.

Income Security
Social Security. One of the highest priorities of my Administration has been to continue the tradition of effectiveness and efficiency widely associated with the social security program, and to assure present and future beneficiaries that they will receive their benefits as expected. The earned benefits that are paid monthly to retired and disabled American workers and their families provide a significant measure of economic protection to millions of people who might otherwise face retirement or possible disability with fear. I have enacted changes to improve the benefits of many social security beneficiaries during my years as President.

The last four years have presented a special set of concerns over the financial stability of the social security system. Shortly after taking office I proposed and Congress enacted legislation to protect the stability of the old age and survivors trust fund and prevent the imminent exhaustion of the disability insurance trust fund, and to correct a flaw in the benefit formula that was threatening the long run health of the entire social security system. The actions taken by the Congress at my request helped stabilize the system. That legislation was later complemented by the Disability Insurance Amendments of 1980 which further bolstered the disability insurance program, and reduced certain inequities among beneficiaries.

My commitment to the essential retirement and disability protection provided to 35 million people each month has been demonstrated by the fact that without interruption those beneficiaries have continued to receive their social security benefits, including annual cost of living increases. Changing and unpredictable economic circumstances require that we continue to monitor the financial stability of the social security system. To correct anticipated short-term strains on the system, I proposed last year that the three funds be allowed to borrow from one another, and I urge the Congress again this year to adopt such interfund borrowing. To further strengthen the social security system and provide a greater degree of assurance to beneficiaries, given projected future economic uncertainties, additional action should be taken. Among the additional financing options available are borrowing from the general fund, financing half of the hospital insurance fund with general revenues, and increasing the payroll tax rate. The latter option is particularly unpalatable given the significant increase in the tax rate already mandated in law.

This Administration continues to oppose cuts in basic social security benefits and taxing social security benefits. The Administration continues to support annual indexing of social security benefits.

Welfare Reform. In 1979 I proposed a welfare reform package which offers solutions to some of the most urgent problems in our welfare system. This proposal is embodied in two bills—The Work and Training Opportunities Act and The Social Welfare Reform Amendments Act. The House passed the second of these two proposals. Within the framework of our present welfare system, my reform proposals offer achievable means to increase self-sufficiency through work rather than welfare, more adequate assistance to people unable to work, the removal of inequities in coverage under current programs, and fiscal relief needed by States and localities.

Our current welfare system is long overdue for serious reform; the system is wasteful and not fully effective. The legislation I have proposed will help eliminate inequities by establishing a national minimum benefit, and by directly relating benefit levels to the poverty threshold. It will reduce program complexity, which leads to inefficiency and waste, by simplifying and coordinating administration among different programs.

I urge the Congress to take action in this area along the lines I have recommended.

Child Welfare. My Administration has worked closely with the Congress on legislation which is designed to improve greatly the child welfare services and foster care programs and to create a Federal system of adoption assistance. These improvements will be achieved with the recent enactment of H.R. 3434, the Adoption Assistance and Child Welfare Act of 1980. The well-being of children in need of homes and their permanent placement have been a primary concern of my Administration. This legislation will ensure that children are not lost in the foster care system, but instead will be returned to their families where possible or placed in permanent adoptive homes.

Low-Income Energy Assistance. In 1979 I proposed a program to provide an annual total of $1.6 billion to low income households which are hardest hit by rising energy bills. With the cooperation of Congress, we were able to move quickly to provide assistance to eligible households in time to meet their winter heating bills.

In response to the extreme heat conditions affecting many parts of the country during 1980, I directed the Community Services Administration to make available over $27 million to assist low-income individuals, especially the elderly, facing life threatening circumstances due to extreme heat.

Congress amended and reauthorized the low-income energy assistance program for fiscal year 1981, and provided $1.85 billion to meet anticipated increasing need. The need for a program to help low income households with rising energy expenses will not abate in the near future. The low-income energy assistance program should be reauthorized to meet those needs.

Housing

For the past 14 months, high interest rates have had a severe impact on the nation's housing market. Yet the current pressures and uncertainties should not obscure the achievements of the past four years.

Working with the Congress, the regulatory agencies, and the financial community, my Administration has brought about an expanded and steadier flow of funds into home mortgages. Deregulation of the interest rates payable by depository institutions, the evolution of variable and renegotiated rate mortgages, development of high yielding savings certificates, and expansion of the secondary mortgage market have all increased housing's ability to attract capital and have assured that mortgage money would not be cut off when interest rates rose. These actions will diminish the cyclicality of the housing industry. Further, we have secured legislation updating the Federal Government's emergency authority to provide support for the housing industry through the Brooke-Cranston program, and creating a new Section 235 housing stimulus program. These tools will enable the Federal Government to deal quickly and effectively with serious distress in this critical industry.

We have also worked to expand homeownership opportunities for Americans. By using innovative financing mechanisms, such as the graduated payment mortgage, we have increased the access of middle income families to housing credit. By revitalizing the Section 235 program, we have enabled nearly 100,000 moderate income households to purchase new homes. By reducing paperwork and regulation in Federal programs, and by working with State and local governments to ease the regulatory burden, we have helped to hold down housing costs and produce affordable housing.

As a result of these governmentwide efforts, 5^1/$_2$ million more American families bought homes in the past four years than in any equivalent period in history. And more than 7 million homes have begun construction during my Administration, 1 million more than in the previous four years.

We have devoted particular effort to meeting the housing needs of low and moderate income families. In the past four years, more than 1 million subsidized units have been made available for occupancy by lower income Americans and more than 600,000 assisted units have gone into construction. In addition, we have undertaken a series of measures to revitalize and preserve the nation's 2 million units of public and assisted housing.

For Fiscal Year 1982, I am proposing to continue our commitment to lower income housing. I am requesting funds to support 260,000 units of Section 8 and public housing, maintaining these programs at the level provided by Congress in Fiscal 1981.

While we have made progress in the past four years, in the future there are reasons for concern. Home price inflation and high interest rates threaten to put homeownership out of reach for first-time homebuyers. Lower income households, the elderly and those dependent upon rental housing face rising rents, low levels of rental housing construction by historic standards, and the threat of displacement due to conversion to condominiums and other factors. Housing will face strong competition for investment capital from the industrial sector generally and the energy industries, in particular.

To address these issues, I appointed a Presidential Task Force and Advisory Group last October. While this effort will not proceed due to the election result, I hope the incoming Administration will proceed with a similar venture.

The most important action government can take to meet America's housing needs is to restore stability to the economy and bring down the rate of inflation. Inflation has driven up home prices, operating costs and interest rates. Market uncertainty about inflation has contributed to the instability in interest rates, which has been an added burden to homebuilders and homebuyers alike. By making a long-term commitment to provide a framework for greater investment, sustained economic growth, and price stability, my Administration has begun the work of creating a healthy environment for housing.

Transportation

With the passage of the Airline Deregulation Act of 1978, the Motor Carrier Act of 1980, and the Harley O. Staggers Rail Act of 1980, my Administration, working with the Congress, has initiated a new era of reduced regulation of transportation industries. Deregulation will lead to increased productivity and operating efficiencies in the industries involved, and stimulate price and service competition, to the benefit of consumers generally. I urge the new Administration to continue our efforts on behalf of deregulation legislation for the intercity passenger bus industry as well.

In the coming decade, the most significant challenge facing the nation in transportation services will be to improve a deteriorating physical infrastructure of roadways, railroads, waterways and mass transit systems, in order to conserve costly energy supplies while promoting effective transportation services.

Highways. Our vast network of highways, which account for 90 percent of travel and 80 percent by value of freight traffic goods movement, is deteriorating. If current trends continue, a major proportion of the Interstate pavement will have deteriorated by the end of the 1980's.

Arresting the deterioration of the nation's system of highways is a high priority objective for the 1980's. We must reorient the Federal mission from major new construction projects to the stewardship of the existing Interstate Highway System. Interstate gaps should be judged on the connections they make and on their compatibility with community needs.

During this decade, highway investments will be needed to increase productivity, particularly in the elimination of bottlenecks, provide more efficient connections to ports and seek low-cost solutions to traffic demand.

My Administration has therefore recommended redefining completion of the Interstate system, consolidating over 27 categorical assistance programs into nine, and initiating a major repair and rehabilitation program for segments of the Interstate system. This effort should help maintain the condition and performance of the Nation's highways, particularly the Interstate and primary system; provide a realistic means to complete the Interstate system by 1990; ensure better program delivery through consolidation, and assist urban revitalization. In addition, the Congress must address the urgent funding problems of the highway trust fund, and the need to generate greater revenues.

Mass Transit. In the past decade the nation's public transit systems' ridership increased at an annual average of 1.1% each year in the 1970's (6.9% in 1979). Continued increases in the cost of fuel are expected to make transit a growing part of the nation's transportation system.

As a result, my Administration projected a ten year, $43 billion program to increase mass transit capacity by 50 percent, and promote more energy efficient vehicle uses in the next decade. The first part of this proposal was the five year, $24.7 billion Urban Mass Transportation Administration reauthorization legislation I sent to the Congress in March, 1980. I urge the 97th Congress to quickly enact this or similar legislation in 1981.

My Administration was also the first to have proposed and signed into law a nonurban formula grant program to assist rural areas and small communities with public transportation programs to end their dependence on the automobile, promote energy conservation and efficiency, and provide transportation services to impoverished rural communities.

A principal need of the 1980's will be maintaining mobility for all segments of the population in the face of severely increasing transportation costs and uncertainty of fuel supplies. We must improve the flexibility of our transportation system and offer greater choice and diversity in transportation services. While the private automobile will continue to be the principal means of transportation for many Americans, public transportation can become an increasingly attractive alternative. We, therefore, want to explore a variety of paratransit modes, various types of buses, modern rapid transit, regional rail systems and light rail systems.

Highway planning and transit planning must be integrated and related to State, regional, district and neighborhood planning efforts now in place or emerging. Low density development and land use threaten the fiscal capacity of many communities to support needed services and infrastructure.

Elderly and Handicapped Transportation. Transportation policies in the 1980's must pay increasing attention to the needs of the elderly and handicapped. By 1990, the number of people over 65 will have grown from today's 19 million to 27 million. During the same period, the number of handicapped—people who have difficulty using transit as well as autos, including the elderly—is expected to increase from 9 to 11 million, making up 4.5 percent of the population.

We must not retreat from a policy that affords a significant and growing portion of our population accessible public transportation while recognizing that the handicapped are a diverse group and will need flexible, door-to-door service where regular public transportation will not do the job.

Railroads. In addition, the Federal government must reassess the appropriate Federal role of support for passenger and freight rail services such as Amtrak and Conrail. Our goal through federal assistance should be to maintain and enhance adequate rail service, where it is not otherwise available to needy communities. But Federal subsidies must be closely scrutinized to be sure they are a stimulus to, and not a replacement for, private investment and initiative. Federal assistance cannot mean permanent subsidies for unprofitable operations.

Waterways and Rural Transportation. There is a growing need in rural and small communities for improved transportation services. Rail freight service to many communities has declined as railroads abandon unproductive branch lines. At the same time, rural roads are often inadequate to handle large, heavily-loaded trucks. The increased demand for "harvest to harbor" service has also placed an increased burden on rural transportation systems, while bottlenecks along the Mississippi River delay grain shipments to the Gulf of Mexico.

We have made some progress:

- To further develop the nation's waterways, my Administration began construction of a new 1,200 foot lock at the site of Lock and Dam 26 on the Mississippi River. When opened in 1987, the new lock will have a capacity of 86 million tons per year, an 18 percent increase over the present system. The U.S. Army Corps of Engineers has also undertaken studies to assess the feasibility of expanding the Bonneville Locks. Rehabilitation of John Day Lock was begun in 1980 and should be completed in 1982. My Administration also supports the completion of the Upper Mississippi River Master Plan to determine the feasibility of constructing a second lock at Alton, Illinois. These efforts will help alleviate delays in transporting corn, soybeans and other goods along the Mississippi River to the Gulf of Mexico.

- The Department of Transportation's new Small Community and Rural Transportation Policy will target federal assistance for passenger transportation, roads and highways, truck service, and railroad freight service to rural areas. This policy implements and expands upon the earlier White House Initiative, Improving Transportation in Rural America, announced in June, 1979, and the President's Small Community and Rural Development Policy announced in December, 1979. The Congress should seek ways to balance rail branch line abandonment with the service needs of rural and farm communities, provide financial assistance to rail branch line rehabilitation where appropriate, assist shippers to adjust to rail branch line abandonment where it takes place, and help make it possible for trucking firms to serve light density markets with dependable and efficient trucking services.

Maritime Policy. During my Administration I have sought to ensure that the U.S. maritime industry will not have to function at an unfair competitive disadvantage in the international market. As I indicated in my maritime policy statement to the

Congress in July, 1979, the American merchant marine is vital to our Nation's welfare, and Federal actions should promote rather than harm it. In pursuit of this objective, I signed into law the Controlled Carrier Act of 1978, authorizing the Federal Maritime Commission to regulate certain rate cutting practices of some state-controlled carriers, and recently signed a bilateral maritime agreement with the People's Republic of China that will expand the access of American ships to 20 specified Chinese ports, and set aside for American-flag ships a substantial share (at least one-third) of the cargo between our countries. This agreement should officially foster expanded U.S. and Chinese shipping services linking the two countries, and will provide further momentum to the growth of Sino-American trade.

There is also a need to modernize and expand the dry bulk segment of our fleet. Our heavy dependence on foreign carriage of U.S.-bulk cargoes deprives the U.S. economy of seafaring and shipbuilding jobs, adds to the balance-of-payments deficit, deprives the Government of substantial tax revenues, and leaves the United States dependent on foreign-flag shipping for a continued supply of raw materials to support the civil economy and war production in time of war.

I therefore sent to the Congress proposed legislation to strengthen this woefully weak segment of the U.S.-flag fleet by removing certain disincentives to U.S. construction of dry bulkers and their operation under U.S. registry. Enactment of this proposed legislation would establish the basis for accelerating the rebuilding of the U.S.-flag dry bulk fleet toward a level commensurate with the position of the United States as the world's leading bulk trading country.

During the past year the Administration has stated its support for legislation that would provide specific Federal assistance for the installation of fuel-efficient engines in existing American ships, and would strengthen this country's shipbuilding mobilization base. Strengthening the fleet is important, but we must also maintain our shipbuilding base for future ship construction.

Provisions in existing laws calling for substantial or exclusive use of American flag vessels to carry cargoes generated by the Government must be vigorously pursued.

I have therefore supported requirements that 50 percent of oil purchased for the strategic petroleum reserve be transported in U.S.-flag vessels, that the Cargo Preference Act be applied to materials furnished for the U.S. assisted construction of air bases in Israel, and to cargoes transported pursuant to the Chrysler Corporation Loan Guarantee Act. In addition, the Deep Seabed Hard Mineral Resources Act requires that at least one ore carrier per mine site be a U.S.-flag vessel.

Much has been done, and much remains to be done. The FY 1982 budget includes a $107 million authorization for Construction Differential Subsidy ("CDS") funds which, added to the unobligated CDS balance of $100 million from 1980, and the recently enacted $135 million 1981 authorization, will provide an average of $171 million in CDS funds in 1981 and 1982.

Coal Export Policy. While significant growth in foreign demand for U.S. steam coal is foreseen, congestion at major U.S. coal exporting ports such as Hampton Roads, Virginia, and Baltimore, Maryland, could delay and impede exports.

My Administration has worked through the Interagency Coal Task Force Study, which I created, to promote cooperation and coordination of resources between shippers, railroads, vessel broker/operators and port operators, and to determine the most appropriate Federal role in expanding and modernizing coal export facilities, including dredging deeper channels at selected ports.

Some progress has already been made. In addition to action taken by transshippers to reduce the number of coal classifications used whenever possible, by the Norfolk and Western Railroad to upgrade its computer capability to quickly inventory its coal cars in its yards, and by the Chessie Railroad which is reactivating Pier 15 in Newport News and has established a berth near its Curtis Bay Pier in Baltimore to decrease delays in vessel berthing, public activities will include:

- A $26.5 million plan developed by the State of Pennsylvania and Conrail to increase Conrail's coal handling capacity at Philadelphia;
- A proposal by the State of Virginia to construct a steam coal port on the Craney Island Disposal area in Portsmouth harbor;
- Plans by Mobile, Alabama, which operates the only publicly owned coal terminal in the U.S. to enlarge its capacity at McDuffie Island to 10 million tons ground storage and 100 car unit train unloading capability;
- Development at New Orleans of steam coal facilities that are expected to add over 20 million tons of annual capacity by 1983; and
- The Corps of Engineers, working with other interested Federal agencies, will determine which ports should be dredged, to what depth and on what schedule, in order to accommodate larger coal carrying vessels.

Private industry will, of course, play a major role in developing the United States' coal export facilities. The new Administration should continue to work to eliminate transportation bottlenecks that impede our access to foreign markets.

Special Needs

Women. The past four years have been years of rapid advancement for women. Our focus has been two-fold: to provide American women with a full range of opportunities and to make them a part of the mainstream of every aspect of our national life and leadership.

I have appointed a record number of women to judgeships and to top government posts. Fully 22 percent of all my appointees are women, and I nominated 41 of the 46 women who sit on the Federal bench today. For the first time in our history, women occupy policymaking positions at the highest level of every Federal agency and department and have demonstrated their ability to serve our citizens well.

We have strengthened the rights of employed women by consolidating and strengthening enforcement of sex discrimination laws under the EEOC, by expanding employment rights of pregnant women through the Pregnancy Disability Bill, and by increasing federal employment opportunities for women through civil service reform, and flexi-time and part-time employment.

By executive order, I created the first national program to provide women business-owners with technical assistance, grants, loans, and improved access to federal contracts.

We have been sensitive to the needs of women who are homemakers. I established an Office of Families within HHS and sponsored the White House Conference on

Families. We initiated a program targeting CETA funds to help displaced homemakers. The Social Security system was amended to eliminate the widow's penalty and a comprehensive study of discriminatory provisions and possible changes was presented to Congress. Legislation was passed to give divorced spouses of foreign service officers rights to share in pension benefits.

We created an office on domestic violence within HHS to coordinate the 12 agencies that now have domestic violence relief programs, and to distribute information on the problem and the services available to victims.

Despite a stringent budget for FY 1981, the Administration consistently supported the Women's Educational Equity Act and family planning activities, as well as other programs that affect women, such as food stamps, WIC, and social security.

We have been concerned not only about the American woman's opportunities, but ensuring equality for women around the world. In November, 1980, I sent to the Senate the Convention on the Elimination of All Forms of Discrimination Against Women. This United Nations document is the most comprehensive and detailed international agreement which seeks the advancement of women.

On women's issues, I have sought the counsel of men and women in and out of government and from all regions of our country. I established two panels—the President's Advisory Committee for Women and the Interdepartmental Task Force on Women—to advise me on these issues. The mandate for both groups expired on December 31, but they have left behind a comprehensive review of the status of women in our society today. That review provides excellent guidance for the work remaining in our battle against sex discrimination.

Even though we have made progress, much remains on the agenda for women. I remain committed to the Equal Rights Amendment and will continue to work for its passage. It is essential to the goal of bringing America's women fully into the mainstream of American life that the ERA be ratified.

The efforts begun for women in employment, business and education should be continued and strengthened. Money should be available to states to establish programs to help the victims of domestic violence. Congress should pass a national health care plan and a welfare reform program, and these measures should reflect the needs of women.

The talents of women should continue to be used to the fullest inside and outside of government, and efforts should continue to see that they have the widest range of opportunities and options.

Handicapped. I hope that my Administration will be remembered in this area for leading the way toward full civil rights for handicapped Americans. When I took office, no federal agency had yet issued 504 regulations. As I leave office, this first step by every major agency and department in the federal government is almost complete. But it is only a first step. The years ahead will require steadfast dedication by the President to protect and promote these precious rights in the classroom, in the workplace, and in all public facilities so that handicapped individuals may join the American mainstream and contribute to the fullest their resources and talents to our economic and social life.

Just as we supported, in an unprecedented way, the civil rights of disabled persons in schools and in the workplace, other initiatives in health prevention—such as our immunization and nutrition programs for young children and new intense efforts to reverse spinal cord injury must continue so that the incidence of disability continues to decline.

This year is the UN-declared International Year of Disabled Persons. We are organizing activities to celebrate and promote this important commemorative year within the government as well as in cooperation with private sector efforts in this country and around the world. The International Year will give our country the opportunity to recognize the talents and capabilities of our fellow citizens with disabilities. We can also share our rehabilitation and treatment skills with other countries and learn from them as well. I am proud that the United States leads the world in mainstreaming and treating disabled people. However, we have a long way to go before all psychological and physical barriers to disabled people are torn down and they can be full participants in our American way of life. We must pledge our full commitment to this goal during the International Year.

Families. Because of my concern for American families, my Administration convened last year the first White House Conference on Families which involved seven national hearings, over 506 state and local events, three White House Conferences, and the direct participation of more than 125,000 citizens. The Conference reaffirmed the centrality of families in our lives and nation but documented problems American families face as well. We also established the Office of Families within the Department of Health and Human Services to review government policies and programs that affect families.

I expect the departments and agencies within the executive branch of the Federal government as well as Members of Congress, corporate and business leaders, and State and local officials across the country, to study closely the recommendations of the White House Conference and implement them appropriately. As public policy is developed and implemented by the Federal government, cognizance of the work of the Conference should be taken as a pragmatic and essential step.

The Conference has done a good job of establishing an agenda for action to assure that the policies of the Federal government are more sensitive in their impact on families. I hope the Congress will review and seriously consider the Conference's recommendations.

Older Americans. My Administration has taken great strides toward solving the difficult problems faced by older Americans. Early in my term we worked successfully with the Congress to assure adequate revenues for the Social Security Trust Funds. And last year the strength of the Social Security System was strengthened by legislation I proposed to permit borrowing among the separate trust funds. I have also signed into law legislation prohibiting employers from requiring retirement prior to age 70, and removing mandatory retirement for most Federal employees. In addition, my Administration worked very closely with Congress to amend the Older Americans Act in a way that has already improved administration of its housing, social services, food delivery, and employment programs.

This year, I will be submitting to Congress a budget which again demonstrates my commitment to programs for the elderly. It will include, as my previous budgets have, increased funding for nutrition, senior centers and home health care, and will focus added resources on the needs of older Americans.

With the 1981 White House Conference on Aging approaching, I hope the new Administration will make every effort to assure an effective and useful conference. This Conference should enable older Americans to voice their concerns and give us guidance in our continued efforts to ensure the quality of life so richly deserved by our senior citizens.

Refugees. We cannot hope to build a just and humane society at home if we ignore the humanitarian claims of refugees, their lives at stake, who have nowhere else to turn. Our country can be proud that hundreds of thousands of people around the world would risk everything they have—including their own lives—to come to our country.

This Administration initiated and implemented the first comprehensive reform of our refugee and immigration policies in over 25 years. We also established the first refugee coordination office in the Department of State under the leadership of a special ambassador and coordinator for refugee affairs and programs. The new legislation and the coordinator's office will bring common sense and consolidation to our Nation's previously fragmented, inconsistent, and in many ways, outdated, refugee and immigration policies.

With the unexpected arrival of thousands of Cubans and Haitians who sought refuge in our country last year, outside of our regular immigration and refugee admissions process, our country and its government were tested in being compassionate and responsive to a major human emergency. Because we had taken steps to reorganize our refugee programs, we met that test successfully. I am proud that the American people responded to this crisis with their traditional good will and hospitality. Also, we would never have been able to handle this unprecedented emergency without the efforts of the private resettlement agencies who have always been there to help refugees in crises.

Immigrants to this country always contribute more toward making our country stronger than they ever take from the system. I am confident that the newest arrivals to our country will carry on this tradition.

While we must remain committed to aiding and assisting those who come to our shores, at the same time we must uphold our immigration and refugee policies and provide adequate enforcement resources. As a result of our enforcement policy, the illegal flow from Cuba has been halted and an orderly process has been initiated to make certain that our refugee and immigration laws are honored.

This year the Select Commission on Immigration and Refugee Policy will complete its work and forward its advice and recommendations. I hope that the recommendations will be carefully considered by the new Administration and the Congress, for it is clear that we must take additional action to keep our immigration policy responsive to emergencies and ever changing times.

Veterans. This country and its leadership has a continuing and unique obligation to the men and women who served their nation in the armed forces and help maintain or restore peace in the world.

My commitment to veterans—as evidenced by my record—is characterized by a conscientious and consistent emphasis in these general areas:

First, we have worked to honor the Vietnam veteran. During my Administration, and under the leadership of VA Administrator Max Cleland, I was proud to lead our country in an overdue acknowledgement of our Nation's gratitude to the men and women who served their country during the bitter war in Southeast Asia. Their homecoming was deferred and seemed doomed to be ignored. Our country has matured in the last four years and at long last we were able to separate the war from the warrior and honor these veterans. But with our acknowledgement of their service goes an understanding that some Vietnam veterans have unique needs and problems.

My Administration was able to launch a long sought after psychological readjustment and outreach program, unprecedented in its popularity, sensitivity and success. This program must be continued. The Administration has also grappled with the difficult questions posed by some veterans who served in Southeast Asia and were exposed to potentially harmful substances, including the herbicide known as Agent Orange. We have launched scientific inquiries that should answer many veterans' questions about their health and should provide the basis for establishing sound compensation policy. We cannot rest until their concerns are dealt with in a sensitive, expeditious and compassionate fashion.

Second, we have focused the VA health care system in the needs of the service-connected disabled veteran. We initiated and are implementing the first reform of the VA vocational rehabilitation system since its inception in 1943. Also, my Administration was the first to seek a cost-of-living increase for the recipients of VA compensation every year. My last budget also makes such a request. The Administration also launched the Disabled Veterans Outreach Program in the Department of Labor which has successfully placed disabled veterans in jobs. Services provided by the VA health care system will be further targeted to the special needs of disabled veterans during the coming year.

Third, the VA health care system—the largest in the free world—has maintained its independence and high quality during my Administration. We have made the system more efficient and have therefore treated more veterans than ever before by concentrating on out-patient care and through modern management improvements. As the median age of the American veteran population increases, we must concentrate on further changes within the VA system to keep it independent and to serve as a model to the nation and to the world as a center for research, treatment and rehabilitation.

Government Assistance

General Aid to State and Local Governments. Since taking office, I have been strongly committed to strengthening the fiscal and economic condition of our Nation's State and local governments. I have accomplished this goal by encouraging economic development of local communities, and by supporting the General Revenue Sharing and other essential grant-in-aid programs.

Grants-in-Aid to States and Localities. During my Administration, total grants-in-aid to State and local governments have increased by more than 40 percent—from $68 billion in Fiscal Year 1977 to $96 billion in Fiscal Year 1981. This significant increase in aid has allowed States and localities to maintain services that are essential to their citizens without imposing onerous tax burdens. It also has allowed us to establish an unprecedented partnership between the leaders of the Federal government and State and local government elected officials.

General Revenue Sharing. Last year Congress enacted legislation that extends the General Revenue Sharing program for three more years. This program is the cornerstone of our efforts to maintain the fiscal health of our Nation's local government. It will provide $4.6 billion in each of the next three years to cities, counties and towns. This program is essential to the continued ability of our local governments to provide essential police, fire and sanitation services.

This legislation renewing GRS will be the cornerstone of Federal-State-local government relations in the 1980's. This policy will emphasize the need for all levels of government to cooperate in order to meet the needs of the most fiscally strained cities and counties, and also will emphasize the important role that GRS can play in forging this partnership. I am grateful that Congress moved quickly to assure that our Nation's localities can begin the 1980's in sound fiscal condition.

Counter-Cyclical Assistance. Last year, I proposed that Congress enact a $1 billion counter-cyclical fiscal assistance program to protect States and localities from unexpected changes in the national economy. This program unfortunately was not enacted by the [full] Congress. I, therefore, have not included funding for counter-cyclical aid in my Fiscal Year 1982 budget. Nevertheless, I urge Congress to enact a permanent stand-by counter-cyclical program, so that States and cities can be protected during the next economic downturn.

Urban Policy

Three years ago, I proposed the Nation's first comprehensive urban policy. That policy involved more than one hundred improvements in existing Federal programs, four new Executive Orders and nineteen pieces of urban-oriented legislation. With Congress' cooperation, sixteen of these bills have now been signed into law.

Economic Development. One of the principal goals of my domestic policy has been to strengthen the private sector economic base of our Nation's economically troubled urban and rural areas. With Congress' cooperation, we have substantially expanded the Federal government's economic development programs and provided new tax incentives for private investment in urban and rural communities. These programs have helped many communities to attract new private sector jobs and investments and to retain the jobs and investments that already are in place.

When I took office, the Federal government was spending less than $300 million annually on economic development programs, and only $60 million of those funds in our Nation's urban areas. Since that time, we have created the Urban Development Action Grant (UDAG) program and substantially expanded the economic development programs in the Commerce Department. My FY 1982 budget requests more than $1.5 billion for economic development grants, loans and interest subsidies and almost $1.5 billion for loan guarantees. Approximately 60 percent of these funds will be spent in our Nation's urban areas. In addition, we have extended the 10 percent investment credit to include rehabilitation of existing industrial facilities as well as new construction.

I continue to believe that the development of private sector investment and jobs is the key to revitalizing our Nation's economically depressed urban and rural areas. To ensure that the necessary economic development goes forward, the Congress must continue to provide strong support for the UDAG program and the programs for the Economic Development Administration. Those programs provide a foundation for the economic development of our Nation in the 1980's.

Community Development. The partnership among Federal, State and local governments to revitalize our Nation's communities has been a high priority of my Administration. When I took office, I proposed a substantial expansion of the Community Development Block Grant (CDBG) program and the enactment of a new $400 million Urban Development Action Grant (UDAG) program. Both of these programs have provided essential community and economic development assistance to our Nation's cities and counties.

Last year, Congress reauthorized both the CDBG and UDAG programs. The CDBG program was reauthorized for three more years with annual funding increases of $150 million, and the UDAG program was extended for three years at the current funding level of $675 million annually. My 1982 budget requests full funding for both of these programs. These actions should help our Nation's cities and counties to continue the progress they have made in the last three years.

Neighborhoods. During my Administration we have taken numerous positive steps to achieve a full partnership of neighborhood organizations and government at all levels. We have successfully fought against red lining and housing discrimination. We created innovative Self Help funding and technical resource transfer mechanisms. We have created unique methods of access for neighborhood organizations to have a participating role in Federal and State government decision-making. Neighborhood based organizations are the threshold of the American community.

The Federal government will need to develop more innovative and practical ways for neighborhood based organizations to successfully participate in the identification and solution of local and neighborhood concerns. Full partnership will only be achieved with the knowing participation of leaders of government, business, education and unions. Neither state nor Federal solutions imposed from on high will suffice. Neighborhoods are the fabric and soul of this great land. Neighborhoods define the weave that has been used to create a permanent fabric. The Federal government must take every opportunity to provide access and influence to the individuals and organizations affected at the neighborhood level.

Rural Policy

Since the beginning of my Administration, I have been committed to improving the effectiveness with which the Federal government deals with the problems and needs of a rapidly changing rural America. The rapid growth of some rural areas has placed a heavy strain on communities and their resources. There are also persistent problems of poverty and economic stagnation in other parts of rural America. Some rural areas continue to lose population, as they have for the past several decades.

In December, 1979, I announced the Small Community and Rural Development Policy. It was the culmination of several years' work and was designed to address the varying needs of our rural population. In 1980, my Administration worked with the Congress to pass the Rural Development Policy Act of 1980, which when fully implemented will allow us to meet the needs of rural people and their communities more effectively and more efficiently.

As a result of the policy and the accompanying legislation, we have:

- Created the position of Under Secretary of Agriculture for Small Community and Rural Development to provide overall leadership.
- Established a White House Working Group to assist in the implementation of the policy.
- Worked with more than 40 governors to form State rural development councils to work in partnership with the White House Working Group, and the Federal agencies, to better deliver State and Federal programs to rural areas.
- Directed the White House Working Group to annually review existing and proposed policies, programs, and budget levels to determine their adequacy in meeting rural needs and the fulfilling of the policy's objectives and principles.

This effort on the part of my Administration and the Congress has resulted in a landmark policy. For the first time, rural affairs has received the prominence it has always deserved. It is a policy that can truly help alleviate the diverse and differing problems rural America will face in the 1980's.

With the help and dedication of a great many people around the country who are concerned with rural affairs, we have constructed a mechanism for dealing effectively with rural problems. There is now a great opportunity to successfully combine Federal efforts with the efforts of rural community leaders and residents. It is my hope this spirit of cooperation and record of accomplishment will be continued in the coming years.

Consumers

In September, 1979, I signed an Executive Order designed to strengthen and coordinate Federal consumer programs and to establish procedures to improve and facilitate consumer participation in government decision-making. Forty Federal agencies have adopted programs to comply with the requirements of the Order. These programs will improve complaint handling, provide better information to consumers, enhance opportunities for public participation in government proceedings, and assure that the consumer point of view is considered in all programs, policies, and regulations.

While substantial progress has been made in assuring a consumer presence in Federal agencies, work must continue to meet fully the goals of the Executive Order. Close monitoring of agency compliance with the requirements of the Order is necessary. Continued evaluation to assure that the programs are effective and making maximum use of available resources is also essential. As a complement to these initiatives, efforts to provide financial assistance in regulatory proceedings to citizen groups, small businesses, and others whose participation is limited by their economic circumstances must continue to be pursued.

It is essential that consumer representatives in government pay particular attention to the needs and interests of low-income consumers and minorities. The Office of Consumer Affairs' publication, People Power: What Communities Are Doing to Counter Inflation, catalogues some of the ways that government and the private sector can assist the less powerful in our society to help themselves. New ways should be found to help foster this new people's movement which is founded on the principle of self-reliance.

Science and Technology

Science and technology contribute immeasurably to the lives of all Americans. Our high standard of living is largely the product of the technology that surrounds us in the home or factory. Our good health is due in large part to our ever increasing scientific understanding. Our national security is assured by the application of technology. And our environment is protected by the use of science and technology. Indeed, our vision of the future is often largely defined by the bounty that we anticipate science and technology will bring.

The Federal government has a special role to play in science and technology. Although the fruits of scientific achievements surround us, it is often difficult to predict the benefits that will arise from a given scientific venture. And these benefits, even if predictable, do not usually lead to ownership rights. Accordingly, the Government has a special obligation to support science as an investment in our future.

My Administration has sought to reverse a decade-long decline in funding. Despite the need for fiscal restraint, real support of basic research has grown nearly 11% during my term in office. And, my Administration has sought to increase the support of long-term research in the variety of mission agencies. In this way, we can harness the American genius for innovation to meet the economic, energy, health, and security challenges that confront our nation.

- International Relations and National Security. Science and technology are becoming increasingly important elements of our national security and foreign policies. This is especially so in the current age of sophisticated defense systems and of growing dependence among all countries on modern technology for all aspects of their economic strength. For these reasons, scientific and technological considerations have been integral elements of the Administration's decisionmaking on such national security and foreign policy issues as the modernization of our strategic weaponry, arms control, technology transfer, the growing bilateral relationship with China, and our relations with the developing world.

  Four themes have shaped U.S. policy in international scientific and technological cooperation: pursuit of new international initiatives to advance our own research and development objectives; development and strengthening of scientific exchange to bridge politically ideological and cultural divisions between this country and other countries; formulation of programs and institutional relations to help developing countries use science and technology beneficially; and cooperation with other nations to manage technologies with local impact. At my direction, my Science and Technology Adviser has actively pursued international programs in support of these four themes. We have given special attention to scientific and technical relations with China, to new forms of scientific and technical cooperation with Japan, to cooperation with Mexico, other Latin American and Caribbean countries and several states in Black America [Africa], and to the proposed Institute for Scientific and Technological Cooperation.

  In particular our cooperation with developing countries reflects the importance that each of them has placed on the relationship between economic growth and scientific and technological capability. It also reflects their view that the great strength of the U.S. in science and technology makes close relations with the U.S. technical community an especially productive means of enhancing this capability. Scientific and technological assistance is a key linkage between the U.S. and the developing world, a linkage that has been under-utilized in the past and one which we must continue to work to strengthen.

• Space Policy. The Administration has established a framework for a strong and evolving space program for the 1980's.

The Administration's space policy reaffirmed the separation of military space systems and the open civil space program, and at the same time, provided new guidance on technology transfer between the civil and military programs. The civil space program centers on three basic tenets: First, our space policy will reflect a balanced strategy of applications, science, and technology development. Second, activities will be pursued when they can be uniquely or more efficiently accomplished in space. Third, a premature commitment to a high challenge, space-engineering initiative of the complexity of Apollo is inappropriate. As the Shuttle development phases down, however, there will be added flexibility to consider new space applications, space science and new space exploration activities.

• Technology Development. The Shuttle dominates our technology development effort and correctly so. It represents one of the most sophisticated technological challenges ever undertaken, and as a result, has encountered technical problems. Nonetheless, the first manned orbital flight is now scheduled for March, 1981. I have been pleased to support strongly the necessary funds for the Shuttle throughout my Administration.

• Space Applications. Since 1972, the U.S. has conducted experimental civil remote sensing through Landsat satellites, thereby realizing many successful applications. Recognizing this fact, I directed the implementation of an operational civil land satellite remote sensing system, with the operational management responsibility in Commerce's National Oceanic and Atmospheric Administration. In addition, because ocean observations from space can meet common civil and military data requirements, a National Oceanic Satellite System has been proposed as a major FY 1981 new start.

• Space Science Exploration. The goals of this Administration's policy in space science have been to: (1) continue a vigorous program of planetary exploration to understand the origin and evolution of the solar system; (2) utilize the space telescope and free-flying satellites to usher in a new era of astronomy; (3) develop a better understanding of the sun and its interaction with the terrestrial environment; and (4) utilize the Shuttle and Spacelab to conduct basic research that complements earth-based life science investigations.

District of Columbia

Washington, D.C., is home to both the Federal Government and to more than half a million American citizens. I have worked to improve the relationship between the Federal establishment and the Government of the District of Columbia in order to further the goals and spirit of home rule. The City controls more of its own destiny than was the case four years ago. Yet, despite the close cooperation between my Administration and that of Mayor Marion Barry, we have not yet seen the necessary number of states ratify the Constitutional Amendment granting full voting representation in the Congress to the citizens of this city. It is my hope that this inequity will be rectified. The country and the people who inhabit Washington deserve no less.

The Arts

The arts are a precious national resource.

Federal support for the arts has been enhanced during my Administration by expanding government funding and services to arts institutions, individual artists, scholars, and teachers through the National Endowment for the Arts. We have broadened its scope and reach to a more diverse population. We have also reactivated the Federal Council on the Arts and Humanities.

It is my hope that during the coming years the new Administration and the Congress will:

- Continue support of institutions promoting development and understanding of the arts;
- Encourage business participants in a comprehensive effort to achieve a truly mixed economy of support for the arts;
- Explore a variety of mechanisms to nurture the creative talent of our citizens and build audiences for their work;
- Support strong, active National Endowments for the Arts;
- Seek greater recognition for the rich cultural tradition of the nation's minorities;
- Provide grants for the arts in low income neighborhoods.

The Humanities

In recently reauthorizing Federal appropriations for the National Endowment for the Humanities, the Congress has once again reaffirmed that "the encouragement and support of national progress and scholarship in the humanities . . . while primarily a matter for private and local initiative, is also an appropriate matter of concern to the Federal Government" and that "a high civilization must not limit its efforts to science and technology alone but must give full value and support to the other great branches of man's scholarly and cultural activity in order to achieve a better understanding of the past, a better analysis of the present, and a better view of the future."

I believe we are in agreement that the humanities illuminate the values underlying important personal, social, and national questions raised in our society by its multiple links to and increasing dependence on technology, and by the diverse heritage of our many regions and ethnic groups. The humanities cast light on the broad issue of the role in a society of men and women of imagination and energy—those individuals who through their own example define "the spirit of the age," and in so doing move nations. Our Government's support for the humanities, within the framework laid down by the Congress, is a recognition of their essential nourishment of the life of the mind and vital enrichment of our national life.

I will be proposing an increase in funding this year sufficient to enable the Endowment to maintain the same level of support offered our citizens in Fiscal Year 1981.

In the allocation of this funding, special emphasis will be given to:

- Humanities education in the nation's schools, in response to the great needs that have arisen in this area;
- Scholarly research designed to increase our understanding of the cultures, traditions, and historical forces at work in other nations and in our own;
- Drawing attention to the physical disintegration of the raw material of our cultural heritage—books, manuscripts, periodicals, and other documents—and to the development of techniques to prevent the destruction and to preserve those materials; and
- The dissemination of quality programming in the humanities to increasingly large American audiences through the use of radio and television.

The dominant effort in the Endowment's expenditures will be a commitment to strengthen and promulgate scholarly excellence and achievement in work in the humanities in our schools, colleges, universities, libraries, museums and other cultural institutions, as well as in the work of individual scholars or collaborative groups engaged in advanced research in the humanities.

In making its grants the Endowment will increase its emphasis on techniques which stimulate support for the humanities from non-Federal sources, in order to reinforce our tradition of private philanthropy in this field, and to insure and expand the financial viability of our cultural institutions and life.

Insular Areas

I have been firmly committed to self-determination for Puerto Rico, the Virgin Islands, Guam, American Samoa and the Northern Mariana Islands, and have vigorously supported the realization of whatever political status aspirations are democratically chosen by their peoples. This principle was the keystone of the comprehensive territorial policy I sent the Congress last year. I am pleased that most of the legislative elements of that policy were endorsed by the 96th Congress.

The unique cultures, fragile economies, and locations of our Caribbean and Pacific Islands are distinct assets to the United States which require the sensitive application of policy. The United States Government should pursue initiatives begun by my Administration and the Congress to stimulate insular economic development; enhance treatment under Federal programs eliminating current inequities; provide vitally needed special assistance and coordinate and rationalize policies. These measures will result in greater self-sufficiency and balanced growth. In particular, I hope that the new Congress will support funding for fiscal management, comprehensive planning and other technical assistance for the territories, as well as create the commission I have proposed to review the applicability of all Federal laws to the insular areas and make recommendations for appropriate modification.

IV. Removing Governmental Waste and Inefficiency

One of my major commitments has been to restore public faith in our Federal government by cutting out waste and inefficiency. In the past four years, we have made dramatic advances toward this goal, many of them previously considered impossible to achieve. Where government rules and operations were unnecessary, they have been eliminated, as with airline, rail, trucking and financial deregulation. Where government functions are needed, they have been streamlined, through such landmark measures as the Civil Service Reform Act of 1978. I hope that the new administration and the Congress will keep up the momentum we have established for effective and responsible change in this area of crucial public concern.

Civil Service Reform

In March 1978, I submitted the Civil Service Reform Act to Congress. I called it the centerpiece of my efforts to reform and reorganize the government. With bipartisan support from Congress, the bill passed, and I am pleased to say that implementation is running well ahead of the statutory schedule. Throughout the service, we are putting into place the means to assure that reward and retention are based on performance and not simply on length of time on the job. In the first real test of the Reform Act, 98 percent of the eligible top-level managers joined the Senior Executive Service, choosing to relinquish job protections for the challenge and potential reward of this new corps of top executives. Though the Act does not require several of its key elements to be in operation for another year, some Federal agencies already have established merit pay systems for GS 13–15 managers, and most agencies are well on their way to establishing new performance standards for all their employees. All have paid out, or are now in the process of paying out, performance bonuses earned by outstanding members of the Senior Executive Service. Dismissals have increased by 10 percent, and dismissals specifically for inadequate job performance have risen 1500 percent, since the Act was adopted. Finally, we have established a fully independent Merit Systems Protection Board and Special Counsel to protect the rights of whistleblowers and other Federal employees faced with threats to their rights.

In 1981, civil service reform faces critical challenges—all agencies must have fully functioning performance appraisal systems for all employees, and merit pay systems for compensating the government's 130,000 GS 13–15 managers. Performance bonuses for members of the Senior Executive Service will surely receive scrutiny. If this attention is balanced and constructive, it can only enhance the chances for ultimate success of our bipartisan commitment to the revolutionary and crucial pay-for-performance concept.

Regulatory Reform

During the past four years we have made tremendous progress in regulatory reform. We have discarded old economic regulations that prevented competition and raised consumer costs, and we have imposed strong management principles on the regulatory programs the country needs, cutting paperwork and other wasteful burdens. The challenge for the future is to continue the progress in both areas without crippling vital health and safety programs.

Our economic deregulation program has achieved major successes in five areas:

Airlines: The Airline Deregulation Act is generating healthy competition, saving billions in fares, and making the airlines more efficient. The Act provides that in 1985 the CAB [Civil Aeronautics Board] itself will go out of existence.

Trucking: The trucking deregulation bill opens the industry to competition and allows truckers wide latitude on the routes they drive and the goods they haul. The bill also phases out most of the old law's immunity for setting rates. The Congressional Budget Office estimates these reforms will save as much as $8 billion per year and cut as much as half a percentage point from the inflation rate.

Railroads: Overregulation has stifled railroad management initiative, service, and competitive pricing. The new legislation gives the railroads the freedom they need to rebuild a strong, efficient railroad industry.

Financial Institutions: With the help of the Congress, over the past four years we have achieved two major pieces of financial reform legislation—legislation which has provided the basis for the most farreaching changes in the financial services industry since the 1930's. The International Banking Act of 1978 was designed to reduce the advantages that foreign banks operating in the United States possessed in comparison to domestic banks. The Depository Institutions Deregulation and Monetary Control Act, adopted last March, provides for the phased elimination of a variety of anti-competitive barriers to financial institutions and freedom to offer services to and attract the savings of consumers, especially small savers.

Recently, I submitted to the Congress my Administration's recommendations for the phased liberalization of restrictions on geographic expansion by commercial banks. Last year the Administration and financial regulatory agencies proposed legislation to permit the interstate acquisition of failing depository institutions. In view of the difficult outlook for some depository institutions I strongly urge the Congress to take prompt favorable action on the failing bank legislation.

Telecommunications: While Congress did not pass legislation in this area, the Federal Communications Commission has taken dramatic action to open all aspects of communications to competition and to eliminate regulations in the areas where competition made them obsolete. The public is benefitting from an explosion of competition and new services.

While these initiatives represent dramatic progress in economic deregulation, continued work is needed. I urge Congress to act on communications legislation and to consider other proposed deregulation measures, such as legislation on the bus industry. In addition, the regulatory commissions must maintain their commitment to competition as the best regulator of all.

The other part of my reform program covers the regulations that are needed to protect the health, safety, and welfare of our citizens. For these regulations, my Administration has created a management program to cut costs without sacrificing goals. Under my Executive Order 12044, we required agencies to analyze the costs of their major new rules and consider alternative approaches—such as performance standards and voluntary codes—that may make rules less costly and more flexible. We created the Regulatory Analysis Review Group in the White House to analyze the most costly proposed new rules and find ways to improve them. The Regulatory Council was established to provide the first Government-wide listing of upcoming rules and eliminate overlapping and conflicting regulations. Agencies have launched "sunset" programs to weed out outmoded old regulations. We have acted to encourage public participation in regulatory decision-making.

These steps have already saved billions of dollars in regulatory costs and slashed thousands of outmoded regulations. We are moving steadily toward a regulatory system that provides needed protections fairly, predictably, and at minimum cost.

I urge Congress to continue on this steady path and resist the simplistic solutions that have been proposed as alternatives. Proposals like legislative veto and increased judicial review will add another layer to the regulatory process, making it more cumbersome and inefficient. The right approach to reform is to improve the individual statutes—where they need change—and to ensure that the regulatory agencies implement those statutes sensibly.

Paperwork Reduction

The Federal Government imposes a huge paperwork burden on business, local government, and the private sector. Many of these forms are needed for vital government functions, but others are duplicative, overly complex or obsolete.

During my Administration we cut the paperwork burden by 15 percent, and we created procedures to continue this progress. The new Paperwork Reduction Act centralizes, in OMB [Office of Management and Budget], oversight of all agencies' information requirements and strengthens OMB's authority to eliminate needless forms. The "paperwork budget" process, which I established by executive order, applies the discipline of the budget process to the hours of reporting time imposed on the public, forcing agencies to scrutinize all their forms each year. With effective implementation, these steps should allow further, substantial paperwork cuts in the years ahead.

Tightening Standards for Governmental Efficiency and Integrity

To develop a foundation to carry out energy policy, we consolidated scattered energy programs and launched the Synthetic Fuels Corporation; to give education the priority it deserves and at the same time reduce HHS to more manageable size, I gave education a seat at the Cabinet table; to create a stronger system for attacking waste and fraud, I reorganized audit and investigative functions by putting an Inspector General in major agencies. Since I took office, we have submitted 14 reorganization initiatives and had them all approved by Congress.

We have saved hundreds of millions of dollars through the adoption of businesslike cash management principles and set strict standards for personal financial disclosure and conflict of interest avoidance by high Federal officials.

To streamline the structure of the government, we have secured approval of 14 reorganization initiatives, improving the efficiency of the most important sectors of the government, including energy, education, and civil rights enforcement. We have eliminated more than 300 advisory committees as well as other agencies, boards and commissions which were obsolete or ineffective. Independent Inspectors General have been appointed in major agencies to attack fraud and waste. More than a billion dollars of questionable transactions have been identified through their audit activities.

The adoption of business-like cash management and debt collection initiatives will save over $1 billion, by streamlining the processing of receipts, by controlling disbursements more carefully, and by reducing idle cash balances. Finally this Administration has set strict standards for personal financial disclosure and conflict of interest avoidance by high Federal officials, to elevate the level of public trust in the government.

V. Protecting Basic Rights and Liberties

I am extremely proud of the advances we have made in ensuring equality and protecting the basic freedoms of all Americans.

- The Equal Employment Opportunity Commission (EEOC) and the Office of Federal Contract Compliance (OFCCP) have been reorganized and strengthened and a permanent civil rights unit has been established in OMB.
- To avoid fragmented, inconsistent and duplicative enforcement of civil rights laws, three agencies have been given coordinative and standard-setting responsibilities in discrete areas: EEOC for all employment-related activities, HUD for all those relating to housing, and the Department of Justice for all other areas.
- With the enactment of the Right to Financial Privacy Act and a bill limiting police search of newsrooms, we have begun to establish a sound, comprehensive, privacy program.

Ratification of the Equal Rights Amendment must be aggressively pursued. Only one year remains in which to obtain ratification by three additional states.

The Congress must give early attention to a number of important bills which remain. These bills would:

- strengthen the laws against discrimination in housing. Until it is enacted, the 1968 Civil Rights Act's promise of equal access to housing will remain unfulfilled;
- establish a charter for the FBI and the intelligence agencies. The failure to define in law the duties and responsibilities of these agencies has made possible some of the abuses which have occurred in recent years;
- establish privacy safeguards for medical research, bank, insurance, and credit records; and provide special protection for election fund transfer systems.

Equal Rights Amendment

I remain committed as strongly as possible to the ratification of the Equal Rights Amendment.

As a result of our efforts in 1978, the Equal Rights Amendment's deadline for ratification was extended for three years. We have now one year and three States left. We cannot afford any delay in marshalling our resources and efforts to obtain the ratification of those three additional States.

Although the Congress has no official role in the ratification process at this point, you do have the ability to affect public opinion and the support of State Legislators for the Amendment. I urge Members from States which have not yet ratified the Equal Rights Amendment to use their influence to secure ratification. I will continue my own efforts to help ensure ratification of the Equal Rights Amendment.

Martin Luther King, Jr.

Dr. Martin Luther King, Jr. led this Nation's effort to provide all its citizens with civil rights and equal opportunities. His commitment to human rights, peace and non-violence stands as a monument to his humanity and courage. As one of our Nation's most outstanding leaders, it is appropriate that his birthday be commemorated as a national holiday. I hope the Congress will enact legislation this year that will achieve this goal.

Fair Housing

The Fair Housing Act Amendments of 1980 passed the House of Representatives by an overwhelming bipartisan majority only to die in the Senate at the close of the 96th Congress. The leaders of both parties have pledged to make the enactment of fair housing legislation a top priority of the incoming Congress. The need is pressing and a strengthened federal enforcement effort must be the primary method of resolution.

Criminal Code

The Federal criminal laws are often archaic, frequently contradictory and imprecise, and clearly in need of revision and codification. The new Administration should continue the work which has been begun to develop a Federal criminal code which simplifies and clarifies our criminal laws, while maintaining our basic civil liberties and protections.

Privacy

As our public and private institutions collect more and more information and as communications and computer technologies advance, we must act to protect the personal privacy of our citizens.

In the past four years we acted on the report of the Privacy Commission and established a national privacy policy. We worked with Congress to pass legislation restricting wiretaps and law enforcement access to bank records and to reporters' files. We reduced the number of personal files held by the government and restricted the transfer of personal information among Federal agencies. We also worked with the Organization for Economic Cooperation and Development to establish international guidelines to protect the privacy of personal information that is transferred across borders.

VI. Protecting and Developing Our Natural Resources

Two of our Nation's most precious natural resources are our environment and our vast agricultural capacity. From the beginning of my Administration, I have worked with the Congress to enhance and protect, as well as develop our natural resources. In the environmental areas, I have been especially concerned about the importance of balancing the need for resource development with preserving a clean environment, and have taken numerous actions to foster this goal. In the agricultural area, I have taken the steps needed to improve farm incomes and to increase our agricultural production to record levels. That progress must be continued in the 1980's.

Environment

Preserving the quality of our environment has been among the most important objectives of my Administration and of the Congress. As a result of these shared commitments and the dedicated efforts of many members of the Congress and my Administration, we have achieved several historic accomplishments.

Protection of Alaska Lands. Passage of the Alaska National Interest Lands Conservation Act was one of the most important conservation actions of this century. At stake was the fate of millions of acres of beautiful land, outstanding and unique wildlife populations, native cultures, and the opportunity to ensure that future generations of Americans would be able to enjoy the benefits of these nationally significant resources. As a result of the leadership, commitment, and persistence of my Administration and the Congressional leadership, the Alaska Lands Bill was signed into law last December.

The Act adds 97 million acres of new parks and refuges, more than doubling the size of our National Park and National Wildlife Refuge Systems. The bill triples the size of our national wilderness system, increasing its size by 56 million acres. And by adding 25 free-flowing river segments to the Wild and Scenic River System, the bill almost doubles the river mileage in that system. The Alaska Lands Act reaffirms our commitment to the environment and strikes a balance between protecting areas of great beauty and allowing development of Alaska's oil, gas. mineral, and timber resources.

Protection of Natural Resources. In addition to the Alaska Lands Act, over the past four years we have been able to expand significantly the national wilderness and parks systems. In 1978, the Congress passed the historic Omnibus Parks Act, which made 12 additions to the National Park System. The Act also established the first two national trails since the National Trails System Act was passed in 1968. Then, in 1980, as a result of my 1979 Environmental Message, the Federal land management agencies have established almost 300 new National Recreational Trails. With the completion of the RARE II process, which eliminated the uncertainty surrounding the status of millions of acres of land, we called for over 15 million acres of new wilderness in the nation's National Forest, in 1980 the Congress established about 4.5 million acres of wilderness in the lower 48 states. In addition, the Administration recommended legislation to protect Lake Tahoe, and through an Executive Order has already established a mechanism to help ensure the Lake's protection. Finally, in 1980 the Administration established the Channel Islands Marine Sanctuary.

Administration actions over the past four years stressed the importance of providing Federal support only for water resource projects that are economically and environmentally sound. This policy should have a major and lasting influence on the federal government's role in water resource development and management. The Administration's actions to recommend to the Congress only economically and environmentally sound water resource projects for funding resulted not only in our opposing uneconomic projects but also—in 1979—in the first Administration proposal of new project starts in 4 years.

One of the most significant water policy actions of the past four years was the Administration's June 6, 1978 Water Policy Reform Message to the Congress. This Message established a new national water resources policy with the following objectives:

- to give priority emphasis to water conservation;
- to consider environmental requirements and values more fully and along with economic factors in the planning and management of water projects and programs;
- to enhance cooperation between state and federal agencies in water resources planning and management.

In addition, the Executive Office of the President established 11 policy decision criteria to evaluate the proposed federal water projects, the Water Resources Council developed and adopted a new set of Principles and Standards for water projects which is binding on all federal construction agencies, and improved regulations were developed to implement the National Historic Preservation Act and the Fish and Wildlife Coordination Act. As a result, water resource projects must be determined to be economically sound before the Administration will recommend authorization or appropriation. Over the years ahead, this policy will help to reduce wasteful federal spending by targeting federal funds to the highest priority water resource projects.

In the pursuit of this policy, however, we cannot lose sight of the vital role that sound water resource projects play in providing irrigation, power, and flood control. We must also recognize the special needs of particular regions of the country in evaluating the need for additional projects.

Addressing Global Resource and Environmental Problems. The Global 2000 Report to the President, prepared in response to my 1977 Environment Message, is the first of its kind. Never before has our government, or any government, taken such a comprehensive, long-range look at the interrelated global issues of resources, population, and environment.

The Report's conclusions are important. They point to a rapid increase in population and human needs through the year 2000 while at the same time a decline in the earth's capacity to meet those needs—unless nations of the world act decisively to alter current trends.

The United States has contributed actively to a series of UN conferences on the environment, population, and resources, and is preparing for the 1981 Conference on New and Renewable Sources of Energy. Following my 1977 Environmental Message, the Administration development assistance programs have added emphasis to natural resource management and environmental protection. My 1979 Environmental Message called attention to the alarming loss of world forests, particularly in the tropics. An interagency task force on tropical forests has developed a U.S. government program to encourage conservation and wise management of tropical forests. The Administration is encouraging action by other nations and world organizations to the same purpose. The United States is a world leader in wildlife conservation and the assessment of environmental effects of government actions. The January 5, 1979, Executive Order directing U.S. government agencies to consider the effects of their major actions abroad, is another example of this leadership.

Commitment to Control of Pollution and Hazardous Chemicals. Over the past four years, there has been steady progress towards cleaner air and water, sustained by the commitment of Congress and the Administration to these important national objectives. In addition, the Administration has developed several new pollution compliance approaches such as alternative and innovative waste water treatment projects, the "bubble" concept, the "offset" policy, and permit consolidation, all of which are designed to reduce regulatory burdens on the private sector.

One of the most pressing problems to come to light in the past four years has been improper hazardous waste disposal. The Administration has moved on three fronts. First, we proposed the Oil Hazardous Substances and Hazardous Waste Response, Liability and Compensation Act (the "Superfund" bill) to provide comprehensive authority and $1.6 billion in funds to clean up abandoned hazardous waste disposal sites. In November 1980 the Congress passed a Superfund bill which I signed into law.

Second, the administration established a hazardous waste enforcement strike force to ensure that when available, responsible parties are required to clean up sites posing dangers to public health and to the environment. To date, 50 lawsuits have been brought by the strike force.

Third, regulations implementing subtitle C of the Resource Conservation and Recovery Act were issued. The regulations establish comprehensive controls for hazardous waste and, together with vigorous enforcement, will help to ensure that Love Canal will not be repeated.

The Future. For the future, we cannot—and we must not—forget that we are charged with the stewardship of an irreplaceable environment and natural heritage. Our children, and our children's children, are dependent upon our maintaining our commitment to preserving and enhancing the quality of our environment. It is my hope that when our descendants look back on the 1980's they will be able to affirm:

- that we kept our commitment to the restoration of environmental quality;
- that we protected the public health from the continuing dangers of toxic chemicals, from pollution, from hazardous and radioactive waste, and that we made our communities safer, healthier and better places to live;
- that we preserved America's wilderness areas and particularly its last great frontier, Alaska, for the benefit of all Americans in perpetuity;
- that we put this nation on a path to a sustainable energy future, one based increasingly on renewable resources and on energy conservation;
- that we moved to protect America's countryside and coastland from mismanagement and irresponsibility;
- that we redirected the management of the nation's water resources toward water conservation, sound development and environmental protection;
- that we faced squarely such worldwide problems as the destruction of forests, acid rain, carbon dioxide build-up and nuclear proliferation; and
- that we protected the habitat and the existence of our own species on this earth.

Agriculture

The Farm Economy. The farm economy is sound and its future is bright. Agriculture remains a major bulwark of the nation's economy and an even more important factor in the world food system. The demand for America's agricultural abundance, here and abroad, continues to grow. In the near-term, the strength of this demand is expected to press hard against supplies, resulting in continued price strength.

The health and vitality of current-day agriculture represents a significant departure from the situation that existed when I came to office four years ago. In January 1977, the farm economy was in serious trouble. Farm prices and farm income were falling rapidly. Grain prices were at their lowest levels in years and steadily falling. Livestock producers, in their fourth straight year of record losses, were liquidating breeding herds at an unparalleled rate. Dairy farmers were losing money on every hundredweight of milk they produced. Sugar prices were in a nosedive.

Through a combination of improvements in old, established programs and the adoption of new approaches where innovation and change were needed, my Administration turned this situation around. Commodity prices have steadily risen. Farm income turned upward. U.S. farm exports set new records each year, increasing over 80 percent for the four year period. Livestock producers began rebuilding their herds. Dairy farmers began to earn a profit again.

Recent Policy Initiatives. Several major agricultural policy initiatives have been undertaken over the past year. Some are the culmination of policy proposals made earlier in this Administration; others are measures taken to help farmers offset the impact of rapid inflation in production costs. In combination, they represent a significant strengthening of our nation's food and agricultural policy. These initiatives include:

Food Security Reserve: The Congress authorized formation of a 4 million ton food grain reserve for use in international food assistance. This reserve makes it possible for the United States to stand behind its food aid commitment to food deficit nations, even during periods of short supplies and high prices. This corrects a serious fault in our past food assistance policy.

Comprehensive Crop Insurance: The Congress also authorized a significant new crop insurance program during 1980. This measure provides farmers with an important new program tool for sharing the economic risks that are inherent to agriculture. When fully operational, it will replace a hodgepodge of disaster programs that suffered from numerous shortcomings.

Special Loan Rates: Another legislative measure passed late in the 2nd session of the 96th Congress authorizes the Secretary of Agriculture to provide higher loan rates to farmers who enter their grain in the farmer-owned grain reserve. This additional incentive to participate will further strengthen the reserve.

Increased Loan Prices: In July 1980, I administratively raised loan prices for wheat, feedgrains, and soybeans to help offset the effects of a serious cost-price squeeze. At the same time, the release and call prices for the grain reserve were adjusted upward.

Higher Target Prices: The Agricultural Adjustment Act of 1980 raised the target prices for 1980-crop wheat and feed grain crops. This change corrected for shortcomings in the adjustment formula contained in the Food and Agriculture Act of 1977.

Future Agenda. The food and agricultural policies adopted by this Administration over the past four years, including those described above, will provide a firm foundation for future governmental actions in this field. Expiration of the Food and Agriculture Act of 1977 later this year will require early attention by the Congress. With relatively minor changes, most of the authorities contained in the 1977 Act should be extended in their present form. The farmer-owned grain reserve has proven to be a particularly effective means of stabilizing grain markets and should be preserved in essentially its present form.

Beyond this, it will be important for the Congress to keep a close eye on price-cost developments in the farm sector. As noted above, some of the actions I took last year were for the purpose of providing relief from the cost-price squeeze facing farmers. Should these pressures continue, further actions might be required.

My Administration has devoted particular attention to the issues of world hunger, agricultural land use, and the future structure of American agriculture. I encourage the Congress and the next Administration to review the results of these landmark enquiries and, where deemed appropriate, to act on their recommendations.

Following a careful review of the situation, I recently extended the suspension of grain sales to the Soviet Union. I am satisfied that this action has served its purpose effectively and fairly. However, as long as this suspension must remain in effect, it will be important for the next Administration and the Congress to take whatever actions are necessary to ensure that the burden does not fall unfairly on our Nation's farmers. This has been a key feature of my Administration's policy, and it should be maintained.

VII. Foreign Policy

From the time I assumed office four years ago this month, I have stressed the need for this country to assert a leading role in a world undergoing the most extensive and intensive change in human history.

My policies have been directed in particular at three areas of change:

- the steady growth and increased projection abroad of Soviet military power— power that has grown faster than our own over the past two decades.
- the overwhelming dependence of Western nations, which now increasingly includes the United States, on vital oil supplies from the Middle East.
- the pressures of change in many nations of the developing world, in Iran and uncertainty about the future stability of many developing countries.

As a result of those fundamental facts, we face some of the most serious challenges in the history of this nation. The Soviet invasion of Afghanistan is a threat to global peace, to East-West relations, and to regional stability and to the flow of oil. As the unprecedented and overwhelming vote in the General Assembly demonstrated, countries across the world—and particularly the nonaligned—regard the Soviet invasion as a threat to their independence and security. Turmoil within the region adjacent to the Persian Gulf poses risks for the security and prosperity of every oil importing nation and thus for the entire global economy. The continuing holding of American hostages in Iran is both an affront to civilized people everywhere, and a serious impediment to meeting the self-evident threat to widely-shared common interests—including those of Iran.

But as we focus our most urgent efforts on pressing problems, we will continue to pursue the benefits that only change can bring. For it always has been the essence of America that we want to move on—we understand that prosperity, progress and most of all peace cannot be had by standing still. A world of nations striving to preserve their independence, and of peoples aspiring for economic development and political freedom, is not a world hostile to the ideals and interests of the United States. We face powerful adversaries, but we have strong friends and dependable allies. We have common interests with the vast majority of the world's nations and peoples.

There have been encouraging developments in recent years, as well as matters requiring continued vigilance and concern:

- Our alliances with the world's most advanced and democratic states from Western Europe through Japan are stronger than ever.

- We have helped to bring about a dramatic improvement in relations between Egypt and Israel and an historic step towards a comprehensive Arab-Israeli settlement.

- Our relations with China are growing closer, providing a major new dimension in our policy in Asia and the world.

- Across southern Africa from Rhodesia to Namibia we are helping with the peaceful transition to majority rule in a context of respect for minority as well as majority rights.

- We have worked domestically and with our allies to respond to an uncertain energy situation by conservation and diversification of energy supplies based on internationally agreed targets.

- We have unambiguously demonstrated our commitment to defend Western interests in Southwest Asia, and we have significantly increased our ability to do so.

- And over the past four years the U.S. has developed an energy program which is comprehensive and ambitious. New institutions have been established such as the Synthetic Fuels Corporation and Solar Bank. Price decontrol for oil and gas is proceeding. American consumers have risen to the challenge, and we have experienced real improvements in consumption patterns.

The central challenge for us today is to our steadfastness of purpose. We are no longer tempted by isolationism. But we must also learn to deal effectively with the contradictions of the world—the need to cooperate with potential adversaries without euphoria, without undermining our determination to compete with such adversaries and if necessary confront the threats they may pose to our security.

We face a broad range of threats and opportunities. We have and should continue to pursue a broad range of defense, diplomatic and economic capabilities and objectives.

I see six basic goals for America in the world over the 1980's:

- First, we will continue, as we have over the past four years, to build America's military strength and that of our allies and friends. Neither the Soviet Union nor any other nation will have reason to question our will to sustain the strongest and most flexible defense forces.

- Second, we will pursue an active diplomacy in the world, working—together with our friends and allies—to resolve disputes through peaceful means and to make any aggressor pay a heavy price.

- Third, we will strive to resolve pressing international economic problems—particularly energy and inflation—and continue to pursue our still larger objective of global economic growth through expanded trade and development assistance and through the preservation of an open multilateral trading system.

- Fourth, we will continue vigorously to support the process of building democratic institutions and improving human rights protection around the world. We are deeply convinced that the future lies not with dictatorship but democracy.

- Fifth, we remain deeply committed to the process of mutual and verifiable arms control, particularly to the effort to prevent the spread and further development of nuclear weapons. Our decision to defer, but not abandon our efforts to secure ratification of the SALT II Treaty reflects our firm conviction that the United States has a profound national security interest in the constraints on Soviet nuclear forces which only that treaty can provide.

- Sixth, we must continue to look ahead in order to evaluate and respond to resource, environment and population challenges through the end of this century.

One very immediate and pressing objective that is uppermost on our minds and those of the American people is the release of our hostages in Iran.

We have no basic quarrel with the nation, the revolution or the people of Iran. The threat to them comes not from American policy but from Soviet actions in the region. We are prepared to work with the government of Iran to develop a new and mutually beneficial relationship.

But that will not be possible so long as Iran continues to hold Americans hostages, in defiance of the world community and civilized behavior. They must be released unharmed. We have thus far pursued a measured program of peaceful diplomatic and economic steps in an attempt to resolve this issue without resorting to other remedies available to us under international law. This reflects the deep respect of our nation for the rule of law and for the safety of our people being held, and our belief that a great power bears a responsibility to use its strength in a measured and judicious manner. But our patience is not unlimited and our concern for the well-being of our fellow citizens grows each day.

Enhancing National Security—American Military Strength

The maintenance of national security is my first concern, as it has been for every president before me.

We must have both the military power and the political will to deter our adversaries and to support our friends and allies.

We must pay whatever price is required to remain the strongest nation in the world. That price has increased as the military power of our major adversary has grown and its readiness to use that power been made all too evident in Afghanistan. The real increases in defense spending, therefore probably will be higher than previously projected; protecting our security may require a larger share of our national wealth in the future.

The U.S.–Soviet Relationship. We are demonstrating to the Soviet Union across a broad front that it will pay a heavy price for its aggression in terms of our relationship. Throughout the last decades U.S.-Soviet relations have been a mixture of cooperation and competition. The Soviet invasion of Afghanistan and the imposition of a puppet government have highlighted in the starkest terms the darker side of their policies—going well beyond competition and the legitimate pursuit of national interest, and violating all norms of international law and practice.

This attempt to subjugate an independent, non-aligned Islamic people is a callous violation of international law and the United Nations Charter, two fundamentals of international order. Hence, it is also a dangerous threat to world peace. For the first time since the communization of Eastern Europe after World War II, the Soviets have sent combat forces into an area that was not previously under their control, into a non-aligned and sovereign state.

The destruction of the independence of the Afghanistan government and the occupation by the Soviet Union have altered the strategic situation in that part of the world in a very ominous fashion. It has significantly shortened the striking distance to the Indian Ocean and the Persian Gulf for the Soviet Union.

It has also eliminated a buffer between the Soviet Union and Pakistan and presented a new threat to Iran. These two countries are now far more vulnerable to Soviet political intimidation. If that intimidation were to prove effective, the Soviet Union could control an area of vital strategic and economic significance to the survival of Western Europe, the Far East, and ultimately the United States.

It has now been over a year since the Soviet invasion of Afghanistan dealt a major blow to U.S.-Soviet relations and the entire international system. The U.S. response has proven to be serious and far-reaching. It has been increasingly effective, imposing real and sustained costs on the USSR's economy and international image.

Meanwhile, we have encouraged and supported efforts to reach a political settlement in Afghanistan which would lead to a withdrawal of Soviet forces from that country and meet the interests of all concerned. It is Soviet intransigence that has kept those efforts from bearing fruit.

Meanwhile, an overwhelming November resolution of the United Nations General Assembly on Afghanistan has again made clear that the world has not and will not forget Afghanistan. And our response continues to make it clear that Soviet use of force in pursuit of its international objectives is incompatible with the notion of business-as-usual.

Bilateral Communication. U.S.-Soviet relations remain strained by the continued Soviet presence in Afghanistan, by growing Soviet military capabilities, and by the Soviets' apparent willingness to use those capabilities without respect for the most basic norms of international behavior.

But the U.S.-Soviet relationship remains the single most important element in determining whether there will be war or peace. And so, despite serious strains in our relations, we have maintained a dialogue with the Soviet Union over the past year. Through this dialogue, we have ensured against bilateral misunderstandings and miscalculations which might escalate out of control, and have managed to avoid the injection of superpower rivalries into areas of tension like the Iran-Iraq conflict.

Poland. Now, as was the case a year ago, the prospect of Soviet use of force threatens the international order. The Soviet Union has completed preparations for a possible military intervention against Poland. Although the situation in Poland has shown signs of stabilizing recently, Soviet forces remain in a high state of readiness and they could move into Poland on short notice. We continue to believe that the Polish people should be allowed to work out their internal problems themselves, without outside interference, and we have made clear to the Soviet leadership that any intervention in Poland would have severe and prolonged consequences for East-West detente, and U.S.-Soviet relations in particular.

Defense Budget. For many years the Soviets have steadily increased their real defense spending, expanded their strategic forces, strengthened their forces in Europe and Asia, and enhanced their capability for projecting military force around the world directly or through the use of proxies. Afghanistan dramatizes the vastly increased military power of the Soviet Union.

The Soviet Union has built a war machine far beyond any reasonable requirements for their own defense and security. In contrast, our own defense spending declined in real terms every year from 1968 through 1976.

We have reversed this decline in our own effort. Every year since 1976 there has been a real increase in our defense spending—and our lead has encouraged increases by our allies. With the support of the Congress, we must and will make an even greater effort in the years ahead.

The Fiscal Year 1982 budget would increase funding authority for defense to more than $196 billion. This amount, together with a supplemental request for FY 1981 of about $6 billion, will more than meet my Administration's pledge for a sustained growth of 3 percent in real expenditures, and provides for 5 percent in program growth in FY 1982 and beyond.

The trends we mean to correct cannot be remedied overnight; we must be willing to see this program through. To ensure that we do so I am setting a growth rate for defense that we can sustain over the long haul.

The defense program I have proposed for the next five years will require some sacrifice—but sacrifice we can well afford.

The defense program emphasizes four areas:

- It ensures that our strategic nuclear forces will be equivalent to those of the Soviet Union and that deterrence against nuclear war will be maintained;
- It upgrades our forces so that the military balance between NATO and the Warsaw Pact will continue to deter the outbreak of war—conventional or nuclear—in Europe;
- It provides us the ability to come quickly to the aid of friends and allies around the globe;
- And it ensures that our Navy will continue to be the most powerful on the seas.

Strategic Forces. We are strengthening each of the three legs of our strategic forces. The cruise missile production which will begin next year will modernize our strategic air deterrent. B-52 capabilities will also be improved. These steps will maintain and enhance the B-52 fleet by improving its ability to deliver weapons against increasingly heavily defended targets.

We are also modernizing our strategic submarine force. Four more POSEIDON submarines backfitted with new, 4,000 mile *Trident I* missiles began deployments in 1980. Nine *Trident* submarines have been authorized through 1981, and we propose one more each year.

The new *M-X* missile program to enhance our land-based intercontinental ballistic missile force continues to make progress. Technical refinements in the basing design over the last year will result in operational benefits, lower costs, and reduced environmental impact. The *M-X* program continues to be an essential ingredient in our strategic posture—providing survivability, endurance, secure command and control and the capability to threaten targets the Soviets hold dear.

Our new systems will enable U.S. strategic forces to maintain equivalence in the face of the mounting Soviet challenge. We would however need an even greater investment in strategic systems to meet the likely Soviet buildup without SALT.

Strategic Doctrine. This Administration's systematic contributions to the necessary evolution of strategic doctrine began in 1977 when I commissioned a comprehensive net assessment. From that base a number of thorough investigations of specific topics continued. I should emphasize that the need for an evolutionary doctrine is driven not by any change in our basic objective—which remains peace and freedom for all mankind. Rather, the need for change is driven by the inexorable buildup of Soviet military power and the increasing propensity of Soviet leaders to use this power in coercion and outright aggression to impose their will on others.

I have codified our evolving strategic doctrine in a number of interrelated and mutually supporting Presidential Directives. Their overarching theme is to provide a doctrinal basis—and the specific program to implement it—that tells the world that no potential adversary of the United States could ever conclude that the fruits of his aggression would be significant or worth the enormous costs of our retaliation.

The Presidential Directives include:

PD-18: An overview of our strategic objectives

PD-37: Basic space policy

PD-41: Civil Defense

PD-53: Survivability and endurance for telecommunications

PD-57: Mobilization planning

PD-58: Continuity of Government

PD-59: Countervailing Strategy for General War

These policies have been devised to deter, first and foremost, Soviet aggression. As such they confront not only Soviet military forces but also Soviet military doctrine. By definition deterrence requires that we shape Soviet assessments about the risks of war—assessments they will make using their doctrine, not ours.

But at the same time we in no way seek to emulate their doctrine. In particular, nothing in our policy contemplates that nuclear warfare could ever be a deliberate instrument for achieving our own goals of peace and freedom. Moreover, our policies are carefully devised to provide the greatest possible incentives and opportunities for future progress in arms control.

Finally, our doctrinal evolution has been undertaken with appropriate consultation with our NATO Allies and others. We are fully consistent with NATO's strategy of flexible response.

Forces for NATO. We are greatly accelerating our ability to reinforce Western Europe with massive ground and air forces in a crisis. We are undertaking a major modernization program for the Army's weapons and equipment, adding armor, firepower, and tactical mobility.

We are prepositioning more heavy equipment in Europe to help us cope with attacks with little warning, and greatly strengthening our airlift and sealift capabilities.

We are also improving our tactical air forces—buying about 1700 new fighter and attack aircraft over the next five years—and increasing the number of Air Force fighter wings, by over 10 percent.

We are working closely with our European allies to secure the Host Nation Support necessary to enable us to deploy more quickly a greater ratio of combat forces to the European theater at a lower cost to the United States.

Security Assistance. As we move to enhance U.S. defense capabilities, we must not lose sight of the need to assist others in maintaining their own security and independence. Events since World War II, most recently in Southwest Asia, have amply demonstrated that U.S. security cannot exist in a vacuum, and that our own prospects for peace are closely tied to those of our friends. The security assistance programs which I am proposing for the coming fiscal year thus directly promote vital U.S. foreign policy and national security aims—and are integral parts of our efforts to improve and upgrade our own military forces.

More specifically, these programs, which are part of our overall foreign aid request, promote U.S. security in two principal ways. First, they assist friendly and allied nations to develop the capability to defend themselves and maintain their own independence. An example during this past year was the timely support provided Thailand to help bolster that country's defenses against the large numbers of Soviet-backed Vietnamese troops ranged along its eastern frontier. In addition, over the years these programs have been important to the continued independence of other friends and allies such as Israel, Greece, Turkey and Korea. Second, security assistance constitutes an essential element in the broad cooperative relationships we have established with many nations which permit either U.S. bases on their territory or access by U.S. forces to their facilities. These programs have been particularly important with regard to the recently-concluded access agreements with various countries in the Persian Gulf and Indian Ocean regions and have been crucial to the protection of our interests throughout Southwest Asia.

Rapid Deployment Forces. We are systematically enhancing our ability to respond rapidly to non-NATO contingencies wherever required by our commitments or when our vital interests are threatened.

The rapid deployment forces we are assembling will be extraordinarily flexible: They could range in size from a few ships or air squadrons to formations as large as 100,000 men, together with their support. Our forces will be prepared for rapid deployment to any region of strategic significance.

Among the specific initiatives we are taking to help us respond to crises outside of Europe are:

- the development of a new fleet of large cargo aircraft with intercontinental range;
- the design and procurement of a force of Maritime Prepositioning Ships that will carry heavy equipment and supplies for three Marine Corps brigades;
- the procurement of fast sealift ships to move large quantities of men and material quickly from the U.S. to overseas areas of deployment;

- increasing training and exercise activities to ensure that our forces will be well prepared to deploy and operate in distant areas.

In addition, our European allies have agreed on the importance of providing support to U.S. deployments to Southwest Asia.

Naval Forces. Seapower is indispensable to our global position—in peace and also in war. Our shipbuilding program will sustain a 50-ship Navy in the 1990's and we will continue to build the most capable ships afloat.

The program I have proposed will assure the ability of our Navy to operate in high threat areas, to maintain control of the seas and protect vital lines of communication—both military and economic—and to provide the strong maritime component of our rapid deployment forces. This is essential for operations in remote areas of the world, where we cannot predict far in advance the precise location of trouble, or preposition equipment on land.

Military Personnel. No matter how capable or advanced our weapons systems, our military security depends on the abilities, the training and the dedication of the people who serve in our armed forces. I am determined to recruit and to retain under any foreseeable circumstances an ample level of such skilled and experienced military personnel. This Administration has supported for FY 1981 the largest peacetime increase ever in military pay and allowances.

We have enhanced our readiness and combat endurance by improving the Reserve Components. All reservists are assigned to units structured to complement and provide needed depth to our active forces. Some reserve personnel have also now been equipped with new equipment.

Mobilization Planning. We have completed our first phase of mobilization planning—the first such Presidentially-directed effort since World War II. The government-wide exercise of our mobilization plans at the end of 1980 showed, first, that planning pays off and, second, that much more needs to be done.

Our Intelligence Posture. Our national interests are critically dependent on a strong and effective intelligence capability. We will maintain and strengthen the intelligence capabilities needed to assure our national security. Maintenance of and continued improvements in our multi-faceted intelligence effort are essential if we are to cope successfully with the turbulence and uncertainties of today's world.

The intelligence budget I have submitted to the Congress responds to our needs in a responsible way, providing for significant growth over the Fiscal Year 1981 budget. This growth will enable us to develop new technical means of intelligence collection while also assuring that the more traditional methods of intelligence work are also given proper stress. We must continue to integrate both modes of collection in our analyses.

Regional Policies

Every President for over three decades has recognized that America's interests are global and that we must pursue a global foreign policy.

Two world wars have made clear our stake in Western Europe and the North Atlantic area. We are also inextricably linked with the Far East—politically, economically, and militarily. In both of these, the United States has a permanent presence and security commitments which would be automatically triggered. We have become increasingly conscious of our growing interests in a third area—the Middle East and the Persian Gulf area.

We have vital stakes in other major regions of the world as well. We have long recognized that in an era of interdependence, our own security and prosperity depend upon a larger common effort with friends and allies throughout the world.

The Atlantic Alliance. At the outset of this Administration, I emphasized the primacy of our Atlantic relationship in this country's national security agenda. We have made important progress toward making the Atlantic Alliance still more effective in a changing security environment.

In recognition of the threat which the Soviet invasion of Afghanistan posed to Western interests in both Europe and Southwest Asia, NATO foreign and defense ministers have expressed full support for U.S. efforts to develop a capability to respond to a contingency in Southwest Asia and have approved an extensive program to help fill the gap which could be created by the diversion of U.S. forces to that region.

The U.S. has not been alone in seeking to maintain stability in the Southwest Asia area and insure access to the needed resources there. The European nations with the capability to do so are improving their own forces in the region and providing greater economic and political support to the residents of the area. In the face of the potential danger posed by the Iran-Iraq conflict, we have developed coordination among the Western forces in the area of the Persian Gulf in order to be able to safeguard passage in that essential waterway.

Concerning developments in and around Poland, the allies have achieved the highest level of cohesion and unity of purpose in making clear the effects on future East-West relations of a precipitous Soviet act there.

The alliance has continued to build on the progress of the past three years in improving its conventional forces through the Long-Term Defense Program. Though economic conditions throughout Europe today are making its achievement difficult, the yearly real increase of 3 percent in defense spending remains a goal actively sought by the alliance.

The NATO alliance also has moved forward during the past year with the implementation of its historic December 1979 decision to modernize its Theater Nuclear Force capabilities through deployment of improved Pershing ballistic missiles and ground launched cruise missiles in Europe. Our allies continue to cooperate actively with us in this important joint endeavor, whose purpose is to demonstrate convincingly to the Soviet Union the potential costs of a nuclear conflict in Europe. At the same time, we offered convincing evidence of our commitment to arms control in Europe by initiating preliminary consultations with the Soviet Union in Geneva on the subject of negotiated limits on long-range theater nuclear forces. Also, during 1980 we initiated and carried out a withdrawal from our nuclear weapons stockpile in Europe of 1,000 nuclear warheads. This successful drawdown in our nuclear stockpile was a further tangible demonstration of our commitment to the updating of our existing theater nuclear forces in Europe.

In the NATO area, we continued to work closely with other countries in providing resources to help Turkey regain economic health. We regretted that massive political and internal security problems led the Turkish military to take over the government on September 12. The new Turkish authorities are making some progress in resolving those problems, and they have pledged an early return to civilian government. The tradition of the Turkish military gives us cause to take that pledge seriously. We welcomed the reestablishment of Greece's links to the integrated military command structure of the Atlantic Alliance—a move which we had strongly encouraged—as a major step toward strengthening NATO's vital southern flank at a time of international crisis and tension in adjacent areas. Greek reintegration exemplifies the importance which the allies place on cooperating in the common defense and shows that the allies can make the difficult decisions necessary to insure their continued security. We also welcomed the resumption of the intercommunal talks on Cyprus.

The U.S. and the Pacific Nations. The United States is a Pacific nation, as much as it is an Atlantic nation. Our interests in Asia are as important to us as our interests in Europe. Our trade with Asia is as great as our trade with Europe. During the past four years we have regained a strong, dynamic and flexible posture for the United States in this vital region.

Our major alliances with Japan, Australia and New Zealand are now stronger than they ever have been, and together with the nations of western Europe, we have begun to form the basic political structure for dealing with international crises that affect us all. Japan, Australia and New Zealand have given us strong support in developing a strategy for responding to instability in the Persian Gulf.

Normalization of U.S. relations with China has facilitated China's full entry into the international community and encouraged a constructive Chinese role in the Asia-Pacific region. Our relations with China have been rapidly consolidated over the past year through the conclusion of a series of bilateral agreements. We have established a pattern of frequent and frank consultations between our two governments, exemplified by a series of high-level visits and by regular exchanges at the working level, through which we have been able to identify increasingly broad areas of common interest on which we can cooperate.

United States relations with the Association of Southeast Asian Nations (ASEAN) have also expanded dramatically in the past four years. ASEAN is now the focus for U.S. policy in Southeast Asia, and its cohesion and strength are essential to stability in this critical area and beyond.

Soviet-supported Vietnamese aggression in Indochina has posed a major challenge to regional stability. In response, we have reiterated our security commitment to Thailand and have provided emergency security assistance for Thai forces facing a Vietnamese military threat along the Thai-Cambodian border. We have worked closely with ASEAN and the UN to press for withdrawal of Vietnamese forces from Cambodia and to encourage a political settlement in Cambodia which permits that nation to be governed by leaders of its own choice. We still look forward to the day when Cambodia peacefully can begin the process of rebuilding it social, economic and political institutions, after years of devastation and occupation. And, on humanitarian grounds and in support of our friends in the region, we have worked vigorously with international organizations to arrange relief and resettlement for the exodus of Indochinese refugees which threatened to overwhelm these nations.

We have maintained our alliance with Korea and helped assure Korea's security during a difficult period of political transition.

We have amended our military base agreement with the Philippines, ensuring stable access to these bases through 1991. The importance of our Philippine bases to the strategic flexibility of U.S. forces and our access to the Indian Ocean is self-evident.

Finally, we are in the process of concluding a long negotiation establishing Micronesia's status as a freely associated state.

We enter the 1980's with a firm strategic footing in East Asia and the Pacific, based on stable and productive U.S. relations with the majority of countries of the region. We have established a stable level of U.S. involvement in the region, appropriate to our own interests and to the interests of our friends and allies there.

The Middle East and Southwest Asia. The continuing Soviet occupation of Afghanistan and the dislocations caused by the Iraq-Iran war serve as constant reminders of the critical importance for us, and our allies, of a third strategic zone stretching across the Middle East, the Persian Gulf, and much of the Indian subcontinent. This Southwest Asian region has served as a key strategic and commercial link between East and West over the centuries. Today it produces two-thirds of the world's oil exports, providing most of the energy needs of our European allies and Japan. It has experienced almost continuous conflict between nations, internal instabilities in many countries, and regional rivalries, combined with very rapid economic and social change. And now the Soviet Union remains in occupation of one of these nations, ignoring world opinion which has called on it to get out.

We have taken several measures to meet these challenges.

Middle East. In the Middle East, our determination to consolidate what has already been achieved in the peace process—and to buttress that accomplishment with further progress toward a comprehensive peace settlement—must remain a central goal of our foreign policy. Pursuant to their peace treaty, Egypt and Israel have made steady progress in the normalization of their relations in a variety of fields, bringing the benefits of peace directly to their people. The new relationship between Egypt and Israel stands as an example of peaceful cooperation in an increasingly fragmented and turbulent region.

Both President Sadat and Prime Minister Begin remain committed to the current negotiations to provide full autonomy to the inhabitants of the West Bank and Gaza. These negotiations have been complex and difficult, but they have already made significant progress, and it is vital that the two sides, with our assistance, see the process through to a successful conclusion. We also recognize the need to broaden the peace process to include other parties to the conflict and believe that a successful autonomy agreement is an essential first step toward this objective.

We have also taken a number of steps to strengthen our bilateral relations with both Israel and Egypt. We share important strategic interests with both of these countries.

We remain committed to Israel's security and are prepared to take concrete steps to support Israel whenever that security is threatened.

Persian Gulf. The Persian Gulf has been a vital crossroads for trade between Europe and Asia at many key moments in history. It has become essential in recent years for its supply of oil to the United States, our allies, and our friends. We have taken effective measures to control our own consumption of imported fuel, working in cooperation with the other key industrial nations of the world. However, there is little doubt that the healthy growth of our American and world economies will depend for many years on continued safe access to the Persian Gulf's oil production. The denial of these oil supplies would threaten not only our own but world security.

The potent new threat from an advancing Soviet Union, against the background of regional instability of which it can take advantage, requires that we reinforce our ability to defend our regional friends and to protect the flow of oil. We are continuing to build on the strong political, economic, social and humanitarian ties which bind this government and the American people to friendly governments and peoples of the Persian Gulf.

We have also embarked on a course to reinforce the trust and confidence our regional friends have in our ability to come to their assistance rapidly with American military force if needed. We have increased our naval presence in the Indian Ocean. We have created a Rapid Deployment Force which can move quickly to the Gulf—or indeed any other area of the world where outside aggression threatens. We have concluded several agreements with countries which are prepared to let us use their airports and naval facilities in an emergency. We have met requests for reasonable amounts of American weaponry from regional countries which are anxious to defend themselves. And we are discussing with a number of our area friends further ways we can help to improve their security and ours, both for the short and the longer term.

South Asia. We seek a South Asia comprising sovereign and stable states, free of outside interference, which can strengthen their political institutions according to their own national genius and can develop their economies for the betterment of their people.

The Soviet invasion of Afghanistan has posed a new challenge to this region, and particularly to neighboring Pakistan. We are engaged in a continuing dialogue with the Pakistan government concerning its development and security requirements and the economic burden imposed by Afghan refugees who have fled to Pakistan. We are participating with other aid consortium members in debt rescheduling and will continue to cooperate through the UNHCR in providing refugee assistance. We remain committed to Pakistan's territorial integrity and independence.

Developments in the broad South/Southwest Asian region have also lent a new importance to our relations with India, the largest and strongest power in the area. We share India's interest in a more constructive relationship. Indian policies and perceptions at times differ from our own, and we have established a candid dialogue with this sister democracy which seeks to avoid the misunderstandings which have sometimes complicated our ties.

We attach major importance to strong economic assistance programs to the countries in the area, which include a majority of the poor of the non-Communist world. We believe that these programs will help achieve stability in the area, an objective we share with the countries in the region. Great progress has been achieved by these countries in increasing food production; international cooperation in harnessing the great river resources of South Asia would contribute further to this goal and help to increase energy production.

We continue to give high priority to our non-proliferation goals in the area in the context of our broad global and regional priorities. The decision to continue supply of nuclear fuel to the Indian Tarapur reactors was sensitive to this effort.

Africa. The United States has achieved a new level of trust and cooperation with Africa. Our efforts, together with our allies, to achieve peace in southern Africa, our increased efforts to help the poorest countries in Africa to combat poverty, and our expanded efforts to promote trade and investment have led to growing respect for the U.S. and to cooperation in areas of vital interest to the United States.

Africa is a continent of poor nations for the most part. It also contains many of the mineral resources vital for our economy. We have worked with Africa in a spirit of mutual cooperation to help the African nations solve their problems of poverty and to develop stronger ties between our private sector and African economies. Our assistance to Africa has more than doubled in the last four years. Equally important, we set in motion new mechanisms for private investment and trade.

Nigeria is the largest country in Black Africa and the second largest oil supplier to the United States. During this Administration we have greatly expanded and improved our relationship with Nigeria and other West African states whose aspirations for a constitutional democratic order we share and support. This interest was manifested both symbolically and practically by the visit of Vice President Mondale to West Africa in July (1980) and the successful visit to Washington of the President of Nigeria in October.

During Vice President Mondale's visit, a Joint Agricultural Consultative Committee was established, with the U.S. represented entirely by the private sector. This could herald a new role for the American private sector in helping solve the world's serious food shortages. I am pleased to say that our relations with Nigeria are at an all-time high, providing the foundation for an even stronger relationship in the years ahead.

Another tenet of this Administration's approach to African problems has been encouragement and support for regional solutions to Africa's problems. We have supported initiatives by the Organization of African Unity to solve the protracted conflict in the western Sahara, Chad, and the Horn. In Chad, the world is watching with dismay as a country torn by a devastating civil war has become a fertile field for Libya's exploitation, thus demonstrating that threats to peace can come from forces within as well as without Africa.

In southern Africa the United States continues to pursue a policy of encouraging peaceful development toward majority rule. In 1980, Southern Rhodesia became independent as Zimbabwe, a multiracial nation under a system of majority rule. Zimbabwean independence last April was the culmination of a long struggle within the country and diplomatic efforts involving Great Britain, African states neighboring Zimbabwe, and the United States.

The focus of our efforts in pursuit of majority rule in southern Africa has now turned to Namibia. Negotiations are proceeding among concerned parties under the leadership of UN Secretary General Waldheim. This should lead to implementation of the UN plan for self-determination and independence for Namibia during 1981. If these negotiations are successfully concluded, sixty-five years of uncertainty over the status of the territory, including a seven-year-long war, will be ended.

Common efforts to resolve the Zimbabwean and Namibian issues have brought the United States closer both to its Western allies—Great Britain, France, the Federal Republic of Germany, and Canada—and to African states such as Tanzania, Zambia, Mozambique, Angola, and Botswana, with whom relations have at some times in the past been difficult. The success of these common undertakings demonstrates that complex problems with sometimes bitter and bloody histories can be resolved peacefully through negotiation.

In response to our active concern with issues of importance to Africans, African states have cooperated with us on issues of importance to our national interests. African states voted overwhelmingly in favor of the UN Resolution calling for release of the hostages, and for the UN Resolution condemning the Soviet invasion of Afghanistan. Two countries of Africa have signed access agreements with the U.S. allowing us use of naval and air facilities in the Indian Ocean.

Africans have become increasingly vocal on human rights. African leaders have spoken out on the issue of political prisoners, and the OAU is drafting its own Charter on Human Rights. Three countries in Africa—Nigeria, Ghana, and Uganda—have returned to civilian rule during the past year.

U.S. cooperation with Africa on all these matters represents a strong base on which we can build in future years.

Liberia is a country of long-standing ties with the U.S. and the site of considerable U.S. investment and facilities. This past April a coup replaced the government and a period of political and economic uncertainty ensued. The U.S. acted swiftly to meet this situation. We, together with African leaders, urged the release of political prisoners, and many have been released; we provided emergency economic assistance to help avoid economic collapse, and helped to involve the IMF and the banking community to bring about economic stability; and we have worked closely with the new leaders to maintain Liberia's strong ties with the West and to protect America's vital interests.

North Africa. In early 1979, following a Libyan inspired commando attack on a Tunisian provincial city, the U.S. responded promptly to Tunisia's urgent request for assistance, both by airlifting needed military equipment and by making clear our long-standing interest in the security and integrity of this friendly country. The U.S. remains determined to oppose other irresponsible Libyan aspirations. Despairing of a productive dialogue with the Libyan authorities, the U.S. closed down its embassy in Libya and later expelled six Libyan diplomats in Washington in order to deter an intimidation campaign against Libyan citizens in the U.S.

U.S. relations with Algeria have improved, and Algeria has played an indispensable and effective role as intermediary between Iran and the U.S. over the hostage issue.

The strengthening of our arms supply relationship with Morocco has helped to deal with attacks inside its internationally recognized frontiers and to strengthen its confidence in seeking a political settlement of the Western Sahara conflict. While not assuming a mediatory role, the U.S. encouraged all interested parties to turn their energies to a peaceful and sensible compromise resolution of the war in the Sahara and supported efforts by the Organization of African Unity toward that end. As the year drew to a close, the U.S. was encouraged by evolution in the attitudes of all sides, and is hopeful that their differences will be peacefully resolved in the year ahead so that the vast economic potential of North Africa can be developed for the well-being of the people living there.

Latin America and the Caribbean. The principles of our policies in this hemisphere have been clear and constant over the last four years. We support democracy and respect for human rights. We have struggled with many to help free the region of both repression and terrorism. We have respected ideological diversity and opposed outside intervention in purely internal affairs. We will act, though, in response to a request for assistance by a country threatened by external aggression. We support social and economic development within a democratic framework. We support the peaceful settlement of disputes. We strongly encourage regional cooperation and shared responsibilities within the hemisphere to all these ends, and we have eagerly and regularly sought the advice of the leaders of the region on a wide range of issues.

Last November, I spoke to the General Assembly of the Organization of American States of a cause that has been closest to my heart—human rights. It is an issue that has found its time in the hemisphere. The cause is not mine alone, but an historic movement that will endure.

At Riobamba, Ecuador, last September four Andean Pact countries, Costa Rica, and Panama broke new ground by adopting a "Code of Conduct," stating that joint action in defense of human rights does not violate the principles of nonintervention in the internal affairs of states in this hemisphere. The Organization of American States has twice condemned the coup that overturned the democratic process in Bolivia and the widespread abuse of human rights by the regime which seized power. The Inter-American Commission on Human Rights has gained world acclaim for its dispassionate reports. It completed two major country studies this year in addition to its annual report. In a resolution adopted without opposition, the OAS General Assembly in November strongly supported the work of the Commission. The American Convention on Human Rights is in force and an Inter-American Court has been created to judge human rights violations. This convention has been pending before the Senate for two years; I hope the United States this year will join the other nations of the hemisphere in ratifying a convention which embodies principles that are our tradition.

The trend in favor of democracy has continued. During this past year, Peru inaugurated a democratically elected government. Brazil continues its process of liberalization. In Central America, Hondurans voted in record numbers in their first national elections in over eight years. In the Caribbean seven elections have returned governments firmly committed to the democratic traditions of the Commonwealth.

Another major contribution to peace in the hemisphere is Latin America's own Treaty for the Prohibition of Nuclear Weapons. On behalf of the United States, I signed Protocol I of this Treaty in May of 1977 and sent it to the Senate for ratification. I urge that it be acted upon promptly by the Senate in order that it be brought into the widest possible effect in the Latin American region.

Regional cooperation for development is gaining from Central America to the Andes, and throughout the Caribbean. The Caribbean Group for Cooperation in Economic Development, which we established with 29 other nations in 1977, has helped channel $750 million in external support for growth in the Caribbean. The recent meeting of the Chiefs of State of the Eastern Caribbean set a new precedent for cooperation in that region. Mexico and Venezuela jointly and Trinidad and Tobago separately have established oil facilities that will provide substantial assistance to their oil importing neighbors. The peace treaty between El Salvador and Honduras will hopefully stimulate Central America to move forward again toward economic integration. Formation of Caribbean/Central American Action, a private sector organization, has given a major impetus to improving people-to-people bonds and strengthening the role of private enterprise in the development of democratic societies.

The Panama treaties have been in force for over a year. A new partnership has been created with Panama; it is a model for large and small nations. A longstanding issue that divided us from our neighbors has been resolved. The security of the canal has been enhanced. The canal is operating as well as ever, with traffic through it reaching record levels this year. Canal employees, American and Panamanian alike, have remained on the job and have found their living and working conditions virtually unchanged.

In 1980, relations with Mexico continued to improve due in large measure to the effectiveness of the Coordinator for Mexican Affairs and the expanded use of the U.S.-Mexico Consultative Mechanism. By holding periodic meetings of its various working groups, we have been able to prevent mutual concerns from becoming political issues. The Secretary of State visited Mexico City in November, and, along with the Mexican Secretary of Foreign Relations, reviewed the performance of the Consultative Mechanism. The office of the Coordinator has ensured the implementation of my directive to all agencies to accord high priority to Mexican concerns. Trade with Mexico rose by almost 60 percent to nearly $30 billion, making that country our third largest trading partner.

These are all encouraging developments. Other problems remain, however.

The impact of large-scale migration is affecting many countries in the hemisphere. The most serious manifestation was the massive, illegal exodus from Cuba last summer. The Cuban government unilaterally encouraged the disorderly and even deadly migration of 125,000 of its citizens in complete disregard for international law or the immigration laws of its neighbors. Migrations of this nature clearly require concerted action, and we have asked the OAS to explore means of dealing with similar situations which may occur in the future.

We have a long-standing treaty with Colombia on Quita Sueno, Roncador, and Serrano which remains to be ratified by the Senate.

In Central America, the future of Nicaragua is unclear. Recent tensions, the restrictions on the press and political activity, an inordinate Cuban presence in the country and the tragic killing by the security forces of a businessman well known for his democratic orientation, cause us considerable concern. These are not encouraging developments. But those who seek a free society remain in the contest for their nation's destiny. They have asked us to help rebuild their country, and by our assistance, to demonstrate that the democratic nations do not intend to abandon Nicaragua to the Cubans. As long as those who intend to pursue their pluralistic goals play important roles in Nicaragua, it deserves our continuing support.

In El Salvador, we have supported the efforts of the Junta to change the fundamental basis of an inequitable system and to give a stake in a new nation to those millions of people, who for so long, lived without hope or dignity. As the government struggles against those who would restore an old tyranny or impose a new one, the United States will continue to stand behind them.

We have increased our aid to the Caribbean, an area vital to our national security, and we should continue to build close relations based on mutual respect and understanding, and common interests.

As the nations of this hemisphere prepare to move further into the 1980's, I am struck by the depth of underlying commitment that there is to our common principles: non-intervention, peaceful settlement of disputes, cooperation for development, democracy and defense of basic human rights. I leave office satisfied that the political, economic, social and organizational basis for further progress with respect to all these principles have been substantially strengthened in the past four years. I am particularly reassured by the leadership by other nations of the hemisphere in advancing these principles. The success of our common task of improving the circumstances of all peoples and nations in the hemisphere can only be assured by the sharing of responsibility. I look forward to a hemisphere that at the end of this decade has proven itself anew as a leader in the promotion of both national and human dignity.

The International Economy

A growing defense effort and a vigorous foreign policy rest upon a strong economy here in the United States. And the strength of our own economy depends upon our ability to lead and compete in the international marketplace.

Energy. Last year, the war between Iraq and Iran led to the loss of nearly 4 million barrels of oil to world markets, the third major oil market disruption in the past seven years. This crisis has vividly demonstrated once again both the value of lessened dependence on oil imports and the continuing instability of the Persian Gulf area.

Under the leadership of the United States, the 21 members of the International Energy Agency took collective action to ensure that the oil shortfall stemming from the Iran-Iraq war would not be aggravated by competition for scarce spot market supplies. We are also working together to see that those nations most seriously affected by the oil disruption—including our key NATO allies Turkey and Portugal—can get the oil they need. At the most recent IEA Ministerial meeting we joined the other members in pledging to take those policy measures necessary to slice our joint oil imports in the first quarter of 1981 by 2.2 million barrels.

Our international cooperation efforts in the energy field are not limited to crisis management. At the Economic Summit meetings in Tokyo and Venice, the heads of government of the seven major industrial democracies agreed to a series of tough energy conservation and production goals. We are working together with all our allies and friends in this effort.

Construction has begun on a commercial scale coal liquefaction plant in West Virginia co-financed by the United States, Japan and West Germany. An interagency task force has just reported to me on a series of measures we need to take to increase coal production and exports. This report builds on the work of the International Energy Agency's Coal Industry Advisory Board. With the assurances of a reliable United States steam coal supply at reasonable prices, many of the electric power plants to be built in the 1980's and 1990's can be coal-fired rather than oil-burning.

We are working cooperatively with other nations to increase energy security in other areas as well. Joint research and development with our allies is underway in solar energy, nuclear power, industrial conservation and other areas. In addition, we are assisting rapidly industrializing nations to carefully assess their basic energy policy choices, and our development assistance program helps the developing countries to increase indigenous energy production to meet the energy needs of their poorest citizens. We support the proposal for a new World Bank energy affiliate to these same ends, whose fulfillment will contribute to a better global balance between energy supply and demand.

International Monetary Policy. Despite the rapid increase in oil costs, the policy measures we have taken to improve domestic economic performance have had a continued powerful effect on our external accounts and on the strength of the dollar. A strong dollar helps in the fight against inflation.

There has also been considerable forward movement in efforts to improve the functioning of the international monetary system. The stability of the international system of payments and trade is important to the stability and good health of our own economy. We have given strong support to the innovative steps being taken by the International Monetary Fund and World Bank to help promote early adjustment to the difficult international economic problems. Recent agreement to increase quotas by fifty percent will ensure the IMF has sufficient resources to perform its central role in promoting adjustment and financing payments imbalances. The World Bank's new structural adjustment lending program will also make an important contribution to international efforts to help countries achieve a sustainable level of growth and development.

Sugar. In 1980, Congress passed U.S. implementing legislation for the International Sugar Agreement, thus fulfilling a major commitment of this Administration. The agreement is an important element in our international commodity policy with far-reaching implications for our relations with developing countries, particularly sugar producers in Latin America. Producers and consumers alike will benefit from a more stable market for this essential commodity.

Coffee. At year's end, Congress approved implementing legislation permitting the U.S. to carry out fully its commitments under the International Coffee Agreement. Specifically, the legislation enables us to meet our part of an understanding negotiated last fall among members of the Agreement, which defends, by use of export quotas, a price range well below coffee prices of previous years and which commits major coffee producers to eliminate cartel arrangements that manipulated future markets to raise prices. The way is now open to a fully-functioning International Coffee Agreement which can help to stabilize this major world commodity market. The results will be positive for both consumers—who will be less likely to suffer from sharp increases in coffee prices—and producers—who can undertake future investment with assurance of greater protection against disruptive price fluctuations in their exports.

Natural Rubber. In 1980, the International Natural Rubber Agreement entered into force provisionally. U.S. membership in this new body was approved overwhelmingly by the Senate last year. The natural rubber agreement is a model of its kind and should make a substantial contribution to a stable world market in this key industrial commodity. It is thus an excellent example of constructive steps to improve the operation of the world economy in ways which can benefit the developing and industrialized countries alike. In particular, the agreement has improved important U.S. relationships with the major natural rubber-producing countries of Southeast Asia.

Common Fund. The United States joined members of the United Nations Conference on Trade and Development, both developed and developing nations, in concluding Articles of Agreement in 1980 for a Common Fund to help international commodity agreements stabilize the prices of raw materials.

Economic Cooperation with Developing Nations. Our relations with the developing nations are of major importance to the United States. The fabric of our relations with these countries has strong economic and political dimensions. They constitute the most rapidly growing markets for our exports, and are important sources of fuel and raw materials. Their political views are increasingly important, as demonstrated in their overwhelming condemnation of the Soviet invasion of Afghanistan. Our ability to work together with developing nations toward goals we have in common—their political independence, the resolution of regional tensions, and our growing ties of trade for example—require us to maintain the policy of active involvement with the developing world that we have pursued over the past four years.

The actions we have taken in such areas as energy, trade, commodities, and international financial institutions are all important to the welfare of the developing countries. Another important way the United States can directly assist these countries and demonstrate our concern for their future is through our multilateral and bilateral foreign assistance program. The legislation which I will be submitting to you for FY 82 provides the authority and the funds to carry on this activity. Prompt Congressional action on this legislation is essential in order to attack such high priority global problems as food and energy, meet our treaty and base rights agreements, continue our peace efforts in the Middle East, provide economic and development support to countries in need, promote progress on North-South issues, protect Western interests, and counter Soviet influence.

Our proposed FY 1982 bilateral development aid program is directly responsive to the agreement reached at the 1980 Venice Economic Summit that the major industrial nations should increase their aid for food and energy production and for family planning. We understand that other Summit countries plan similar responses. It is also important to honor our international agreements for multilateral assistance by authorizing and appropriating funds for the International Financial Institutions. These multilateral programs enhance the efficiency of U.S. contributions by combining them with those of many other donor countries to promote development; the proposed new World Bank affiliate to increase energy output in developing countries offers particular promise. All these types of aid benefit our long-run economic and political interests.

Progress was made on a number of economic issues in negotiations throughout the UN system. However, in spite of lengthy efforts in the United Nations, agreement has not been reached on how to launch a process of Global Negotiations in which nations might collectively work to solve such important issues as energy, food, protectionism, and population pressures. The United States continues to believe that progress can best be made when nations focus on such specific problems, rather than on procedural and institutional questions. It will continue to work to move the North-South dialogue into a more constructive phase.

Food—The War on Hunger. The War on Hunger must be a continuous urgent priority. Major portions of the world's population continue to be threatened by the specter of hunger and malnutrition. During the past year, some 150 million people in 36 African countries were faced with near disaster as the result of serious drought-induced food shortages. Our government, working in concert with the UN's Food and Agricultural Organization (FAO), helped to respond to that need. But the problems of hunger cannot be solved by short-term measures. We must continue to support those activities, bilateral and multilateral, which aim at improving food production especially in developing countries and assuring global food security. These measures are necessary to the maintenance of a stable and healthy world economy.

I am pleased that negotiation of a new Food Aid Convention, which guarantees a minimum annual level of food assistance, was successfully concluded in March. The establishment of the International Emergency Wheat Reserve will enable the U.S. to meet its commitment under the new Convention to feed hungry people, even in times of short supply.

Of immediate concern is the prospect of millions of Africans threatened by famine because of drought and civil disturbances. The U.S. plea for increased food aid resulted in the organization of an international pledging conference and we are hopeful that widespread starvation will be avoided.

Good progress has been made since the Venice Economic Summit called for increased effort on this front. We and other donor countries have begun to assist poor countries develop long-term strategies to improve their food production. The World Bank will invest up to $4 billion in the next few years in improving the grain storage and food-handling capacity of countries prone to food shortages.

Good progress has been made since the Tokyo Economic Summit called for increased effort on this front. The World Bank is giving this problem top priority, as are some other donor countries. The resources of the consultative Group on International Agricultural Research will be doubled over a five-year period. The work of our own Institute of Scientific and Technological Cooperation will further strengthen the search for relevant new agricultural technologies.

The goal of freeing the world from hunger by the year 2000 should command the full support of all countries.

The Human Dimension of Foreign Policy

Human Rights. The human rights policy of the United States has been an integral part of our overall foreign policy for the past several years. This policy serves the national interest of the United States in several important ways: by encouraging respect by governments for the basic rights of human beings, it promotes peaceful, constructive change, reduces the likelihood of internal pressures for violent change and for the exploitation of these by our adversaries, and thus directly serves our long-term interest in peace and stability; by matching espousal of fundamental American principles of freedom with specific foreign policy actions, we stand out in vivid contrast to our ideological adversaries; by our efforts to expand freedom elsewhere, we render our own freedom, and our own nation, more secure. Countries that respect human rights make stronger allies and better friends.

Rather than attempt to dictate what system of government or institutions other countries should have, the U.S. supports, throughout the world, the internationally recognized human rights which all members of the United Nations have pledged themselves to respect. There is more than one model that can satisfy the continuing human reach for freedom and justice.

1980 has been a year of some disappointments, but has also seen some positive developments in the ongoing struggle for fulfillment of human rights throughout the world. In the year we have seen:

- Free elections were held and democratic governments installed in Peru, Dominica, and Jamaica. Honduras held a free election for installation of a constituent assembly. An interim government was subsequently named pointing toward national presidential elections in 1981. Brazil continues on its course of political liberalization.

- The "Charter of Conduct" signed in Riobamba, Ecuador, by Ecuador, Colombia, Venezuela, Peru, Costa Rica, Panama and Spain, affirms the importance of democracy and human rights for the Andean countries.

- The Organization of American States, in its annual General Assembly, approved a resolution in support of the Inter-American Human Rights Commission's work. The resolution took note of the Commission's annual report, which described the status of human rights in Chile, El Salvador, Paraguay and Uruguay; and the special reports on Argentina and Haiti, which described human rights conditions as investigated during on-site inspections to these countries.

- The awarding of the Nobel Prize for Peace to Adolfo Perez Esquivel of Argentina for his non-violent advocacy of human rights.

- The United States was able to rejoin the International Labor Organization after an absence of two years, as that UN body reformed its procedures to return to its original purpose of strengthening employer-employee-government relations to insure human rights for the working people of the world.

The United States, of course, cannot take credit for all these various developments. But we can take satisfaction in knowing that our policies encourage and perhaps influence them.

Those who see a contradiction between our security and our humanitarian interests forget that the basis for a secure and stable society is the bond of trust between a government and its people. I profoundly believe that the future of our world is not to be found in authoritarianism: that wears the mask of order, or totalitarianism that wears the mask of justice. Instead, let us find our future in the human face of democracy, the human voice of individual liberty, the human hand of economic development.

Humanitarian Aid. The United States has continued to play its traditional role of safehaven for those who flee or are forced to flee their homes because of persecution or war. During 1980, the United States provided resettlement opportunities for 216,000 refugees from countries around the globe. In addition, the United States joined with other nations to provide relief to refugees in country of first asylum in Africa, the Middle East, and Asia.

The great majority of refugee admissions continued to be from Indochina. During 1980, 168,000 Indochinese were resettled in the United States. Although refugee populations persist in camps in Southeast Asia, and refugees continue to flee Vietnam, Laos and Kampuchea, the flow is not as great as in the past. One factor in reducing the flow from Vietnam has been the successful negotiation and commencement of an Orderly Departure Program which permits us to process Vietnamese for resettlement in the United States with direct departure from Ho Chi Minh Ville in an orderly fashion. The first group of 250 departed Vietnam for the United States in December, 1980.

In addition to the refugees admitted last year, the United States accepted for entry into the United States 125,000 Cubans who were expelled by Fidel Castro. Federal and state authorities, as well as private voluntary agencies, responded with unprecedented vigor to coping with the unexpected influx of Cubans.

Major relief efforts to aid refugees in countries of first asylum continued in several areas of the world. In December, 1980, thirty-two nations, meeting in New York City, agreed to contribute $65 million to the continuing famine relief program in Kampuchea. Due in great part to the generosity of the American people and the leadership exercised in the international arena by the United States, we have played the pivotal role in ameliorating massive suffering in Kampuchea.

The United States has taken the lead among a group of donor countries who are providing relief to some two million refugees in the Horn of Africa who have been displaced by fighting in Ethiopia. U.S. assistance, primarily to Somalia, consists of $35 million worth of food and $18 million in cash and kind. Here again, United States efforts can in large part be credited with keeping hundreds of thousands of people alive.

Another major international relief effort has been mounted in Pakistan. The United States is one of 25 countries plus the European Economic Community who have been helping the Government of Pakistan to cope with the problem of feeding and sheltering the more than one million refugees that have been generated by the Soviet invasion of Afghanistan.

In April, 1980, the Congress passed the Refugee Act of 1980 which brought together, for the first time, in one piece of legislation the various threads of U.S. policy towards refugees. The law laid down a new, broader definition of the term refugee, established mechanisms for arriving at a level of refugee admissions through consultation with Congress, and established the Office of the United States Coordinator for Refugees.

It cannot be ignored that the destructive and aggressive policies of the Soviet Union have added immeasurably to the suffering in these three tragic situations.

The Control of Nuclear Weapons

Together with our friends and allies, we are striving to build a world in which peoples with diverse interests can live freely and prosper. But all that humankind has achieved to date, all that we are seeking to accomplish, and human existence itself can be undone in an instant—in the catastrophe of a nuclear war.

Thus one of the central objectives of my Administration has been to control the proliferation of nuclear weapons to those nations which do not have them, and their further development by the existing nuclear powers—notably the Soviet Union and the United States.

Non-Proliferation. My Administration has been committed to stemming the spread of nuclear weapons. Nuclear proliferation would raise the spectre of the use of nuclear explosives in crucial, unstable regions of the world endangering not only our security and that of our Allies, but that of the whole world. Non-proliferation is not and can not be a unilateral U.S. policy, nor should it be an issue of contention between the industrialized and developing states. The international non-proliferation effort requires the support of suppliers as well as importers of nuclear technology and materials.

We have been proceeding on a number of fronts:

- First, we have been seeking to encourage nations to accede to the Non-Proliferation Treaty. The U.S. is also actively encouraging other nations to accept full-scope safeguards on all of their nuclear activities and is asking other nuclear suppliers to adopt a full-scope safeguards requirement as a condition for future supply.

- Second, the International Nuclear Fuel Cycle Evaluation (INFCE), which was completed in 1980, demonstrated that suppliers and recipients can work together on these technically complex and sensitive issues. While differences remain, the INFCE effort provides a broader international basis for national decisions which must balance energy needs with non-proliferation concerns.

- Finally, we are working to encourage regional cooperation and restraint. Protocol I of the Treaty of Tlatelolco which will contribute to the lessening of nuclear dangers for our Latin American neighbors ought now to be ratified by the United States Senate.

Limitations on Strategic Arms. I remain convinced that the SALT II Treaty is in our Nation's security interest and that it would add significantly to the control of nuclear weapons. I strongly support continuation of the SALT process and the negotiation of more far-reaching mutual restraints on nuclear weaponry.

Conclusion

We have new support in the world for our purposes of national independence and individual human dignity. We have a new will at home to do what is required to keep us the strongest nation on earth. We must move together into this decade with the strength which comes from realization of the dangers before us and from the confidence that together we can overcome them.

Ronald Reagan

1981–1989

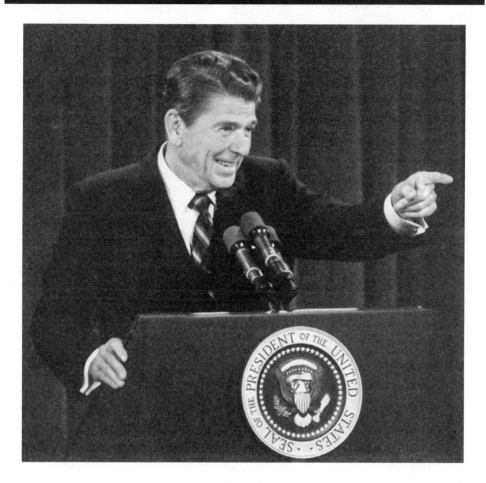

"Every dollar the Federal Government does not take from us, every decision it does not make for us will make our economy stronger, our lives more abundant, our future more free."

ADDRESS BEFORE A JOINT SESSION OF CONGRESS ON THE STATE OF THE UNION, FEBRUARY 6, 1985

Address before a Joint Session of Congress on the State of the Union

January 26, 1982

Ronald Reagan delivered his first State of the Union message in January 1982. Known as the "Great Communicator," the former movie actor and California governor initiated a new twist to the annual message, one that his successors would emulate.

Toward the end of his address, Reagan noted two people present in the audience, whom he referred to as heroes. One was Jeremiah Denton, a former prisoner of war in Vietnam who was serving as a Republican senator from Alabama. The other was Lenny Skutnik, a government worker who two weeks earlier had saved a woman from drowning in the Potomac River after an airplane crash. While Denton, as a senator, would have been present at the speech anyway, Skutnik was specifically invited and thus became the first in a continuing line of people seated in the House gallery and mentioned in presidential State of the Union messages.

Substantively, Reagan's address focused on domestic issues, including the state of the economy and the size of the federal government. A key element of Reagan's ideology was that the government should be smaller.

He also discussed foreign policy, but not in as much detail. He mentioned Cuba and Libya as exporters of terrorism and subversion and stated that the United States would need to negotiate with the Soviet Union on military issues "from a position of strength."

In terms of the economy, Reagan mentioned the ongoing recession, which had begun in late 1981 and would last through 1982. He defended his administration's approach to the economy, mentioning cuts in the rate of increase in government spending as well as the big tax cut Reagan had pushed through in 1981. He blamed the economic problems on the previous decades' policies, stating, "Our current problems are not the product of the recovery program that's only just now getting underway, as some would have you believe; they are the inheritance of decades of tax and tax and spend and spend."

Reagan's most important proposal in the address, called by the press the "New Federalism," called for transferring various federal functions totaling $47 billion to the state and local governments. Under the plan, by 1988 the states would be in control of more than forty grant programs.

Reagan also called for dismantling the departments of energy and education, and he vowed to cut waste and fraud in the Medicare and Medicaid entitlement programs.

Reagan's first year in office was perhaps best known for his having survived an assassination attempt by assailant John Hinckley Jr., on March 31, 1981. The president was rushed into surgery, and doctors removed a bullet that had struck him in the chest.

Mr. Speaker, Mr. President, distinguished Members of the Congress, honored guests, and fellow citizens:

Today marks my first State of the Union address to you, a constitutional duty as old as our Republic itself.

President Washington began this tradition in 1790 after reminding the Nation that the destiny of self-government and the "preservation of the sacred fire of liberty" is "finally staked on the experiment entrusted to the hands of the American people." For our friends in the press, who place a high premium on accuracy, let me say: I did not actually hear George Washington say that. But it is a matter of historic record.

But from this podium, Winston Churchill asked the free world to stand together against the onslaught of aggression. Franklin Delano Roosevelt spoke of a day of infamy and summoned a nation to arms. Douglas MacArthur made an unforgettable farewell to a country he loved and served so well. Dwight Eisenhower reminded us that peace was purchased only at the price of strength. And John F. Kennedy spoke of the burden and glory that is freedom.

When I visited this Chamber last year as a newcomer to Washington, critical of past policies which I believed had failed, I proposed a new spirit of partnership between this Congress and this administration and between Washington and our State and local governments. In forging this new partnership for America, we could achieve the oldest hopes of our Republic—prosperity for our nation, peace for the world, and the blessings of individual liberty for our children and, someday, for all of humanity.

It's my duty to report to you tonight on the progress that we have made in our relations with other nations, on the foundation we've carefully laid for our economic recovery, and finally, on a bold and spirited initiative that I believe can change the face of American government and make it again the servant of the people.

Seldom have the stakes been higher for America. What we do and say here will make all the difference to autoworkers in Detroit, lumberjacks in the Northwest, steelworkers in Steubenville who are in the unemployment lines; to black teenagers in Newark and Chicago; to hard-pressed farmers and small businessmen; and to millions of everyday Americans who harbor the simple wish of a safe and financially secure future for their children. To understand the state of the Union, we must look not only at where we are and where we're going but where we've been. The situation at this time last year was truly ominous.

The last decade has seen a series of recessions. There was a recession in 1970, in 1974, and again in the spring of 1980. Each time, unemployment increased and inflation soon turned up again. We coined the word "stagflation" to describe this.

Government's response to these recessions was to pump up the money supply and increase spending. In the last 6 months of 1980, as an example, the money supply increased at the fastest rate in postwar history—13 percent. Inflation remained in double digits, and government spending increased at an annual rate of 17 percent. Interest rates reached a staggering 21.5 percent. There were 8 million unemployed.

Late in 1981 we sank into the present recession, largely because continued high interest rates hurt the auto industry and construction. And there was a drop in productivity, and the already high unemployment increased.

This time, however, things are different. We have an economic program in place, completely different from the artificial quick fixes of the past. It calls for a reduction of the rate of increase in government spending, and already that rate has been cut nearly in half. But reduced spending the first and smallest phase of a 3-year tax rate reduction designed to stimulate the economy and create jobs. Already interest rates are down to 15³/₄ percent, but they must still go lower. Inflation is down from 12.4 percent to 8.9, and for the month of December it was running at an annualized rate of 5.2 percent. If we had not acted as we did, things would be far worse for all Americans than they are today. Inflation, taxes, and interest rates would all be higher.

A year ago, Americans' faith in their governmental process was steadily declining. Six out of 10 Americans were saying they were pessimistic about their future. A new kind of defeatism was heard. Some said our domestic problems were uncontrollable, that we had to learn to live with this seemingly endless cycle of high inflation and high unemployment.

There were also pessimistic predictions about the relationship between our administration and this Congress. It was said we could never work together. Well, those predictions were wrong. The record is clear, and I believe that history will remember this as an era of American renewal, remember this administration as an administration of change, and remember this Congress as a Congress of destiny.

Together, we not only cut the increase in government spending nearly in half, we brought about the largest tax reductions and the most sweeping changes in our tax structure since the beginning of this century. And because we indexed future taxes to the rate of inflation, we took away government's built-in profit on inflation and its hidden incentive to grow larger at the expense of American workers.

Together, after 50 years of taking power away from the hands of the people in their States and local communities, we have started returning power and resources to them.

Together, we have cut the growth of new Federal regulations nearly in half. In 1981 there were 23,000 fewer pages in the *Federal Register,* which lists new regulations, than there were in 1980. By deregulating oil we've come closer to achieving energy independence and helped bring down the cost of gasoline and heating fuel.

Together, we have created an effective Federal strike force to combat waste and fraud in government. In just 6 months it has saved the taxpayers more than $2 billion, and it's only getting started.

Together we've begun to mobilize the private sector, not to duplicate wasteful and discredited government programs, but to bring thousands of Americans into a volunteer effort to help solve many of America's social problems.

Together we've begun to restore that margin of military safety that ensures peace. Our country's uniform is being worn once again with pride.

Together we have made a New Beginning, but we have only begun.

No one pretends that the way ahead will be easy. In my Inaugural Address last year, I warned that the "ills we suffer have come upon us over several decades. They will not go away in days, weeks, or months, but they will go away . . . because we as Americans have the capacity now, as we've had it in the past, to do whatever needs to be done to preserve this last and greatest bastion of freedom."

The economy will face difficult moments in the months ahead. But the program for economic recovery that is in place will pull the economy out of its slump and put us on the road to prosperity and stable growth by the latter half of this year. And that is why I can report to you tonight that in the near future the state of the Union and the economy will be better—much better—if we summon the strength to continue on the course that we've charted.

And so, the question: If the fundamentals are in place, what now? Well, two things. First, we must understand what's happening at the moment to the economy. Our current problems are not the product of the recovery program that's only just now getting underway, as some would have you believe; they are the inheritance of decades of tax and tax and spend and spend.

Second, because our economic problems are deeply rooted and will not respond to quick political fixes, we must stick to our carefully integrated plan for recovery. That plan is based on four commonsense fundamentals: continued reduction of the growth in Federal spending; preserving the individual and business tax reductions that will stimulate saving and investment; removing unnecessary Federal regulations to spark productivity; and maintaining a healthy dollar and a stable monetary policy, the latter a responsibility of the Federal Reserve System.

The only alternative being offered to this economic program is a return to the policies that gave us a trillion-dollar debt, runaway inflation, runaway interest rates and unemployment. The doubters would have us turn back the clock with tax increases that would offset the personal tax rate reductions already passed by this Congress. Raise present taxes to cut future deficits, they tell us. Well, I don't believe we should buy that argument.

There are too many imponderables for anyone to predict deficits or surpluses several years ahead with any degree of accuracy. The budget in place, when I took office, had been projected as balanced. It turned out to have one of the biggest deficits in history. Another example of the imponderables that can make deficit projections highly questionable—a change of only one percentage point in unemployment can alter a deficit up or down by some $25 billion.

As it now stands, our forecast, which we're required by law to make, will show major deficits starting at less than a hundred billion dollars and declining, but still too high. More important, we're making progress with the three keys to reducing deficits: economic growth, lower interest rates, and spending control. The policies we have in place will reduce the deficit steadily, surely, and in time, completely.

Higher taxes would not mean lower deficits. If they did, how would we explain that tax revenues more than doubled just since 1976; yet in that same 6-year period we ran the largest series of deficits in our history. In 1980 tax revenues increased by $54 billion, and in 1980 we had one of our all-time biggest deficits. Raising taxes won't balance the budget; it will encourage more government spending and less private investment. Raising taxes will slow economic growth, reduce production, and destroy future jobs, making it more difficult for those without jobs to find them and more likely that those who now have jobs could lose them. So, I will not ask you to try to balance the budget on the backs of the American taxpayers.

I will seek no tax increases this year, and I have no intention of retreating from our basic program of tax relief. I promise to bring the American people—to bring their tax rates down and to keep them down, to provide them incentives to rebuild our economy, to save, to invest in America's future. I will stand by my word. Tonight I'm urging the American people: Seize these new opportunities to produce, to save, to invest, and together we'll make this economy a mighty engine of freedom, hope, and prosperity again.

Now, the budget deficit this year will exceed our earlier expectations. The recession did that. It lowered revenues and increased costs. To some extent, we're also victims of our own success. We've brought inflation down faster than we thought we could, and in doing this, we've deprived government of those hidden revenues that occur when inflation pushes people into higher income tax brackets. And the continued high interest rates last year cost the government about $5 billion more than anticipated.

We must cut out more nonessential government spending and rout out more waste, and we will continue our efforts to reduce the number of employees in the Federal work force by 75,000.

The budget plan I submit to you on February 8th will realize major savings by dismantling the Departments of Energy and Education and by eliminating ineffective subsidies for business. We'll continue to redirect our resources to our two highest budget priorities—a strong national defense to keep America free and at peace and a reliable safety net of social programs for those who have contributed and those who are in need.

Contrary to some of the wild charges you may have heard, this administration has not and will not turn its back on America's elderly or America's poor. Under the new budget, funding for social insurance programs will be more than double the amount spent only 6 years ago. But it would be foolish to pretend that these or any programs cannot be made more efficient and economical.

The entitlement programs that make up our safety net for the truly needy have worthy goals and many deserving recipients. We will protect them. But there's only one way to see to it that these programs really help those whom they were designed to help. And that is to bring their spiraling costs under control.

Today we face the absurd situation of a Federal budget with three-quarters of its expenditures routinely referred to as "uncontrollable." And a large part of this goes to entitlement programs.

Committee after committee of this Congress has heard witness after witness describe many of these programs as poorly administered and rife with waste and fraud. Virtually every American who shops in a local supermarket is aware of the daily abuses that take place in the food stamp program, which has grown by 16,000 percent in the last 15 years. Another example is Medicare and Medicaid—programs with worthy goals but whose costs have increased from 11.2 billion to almost 60 billion, more than 5 times as much, in just 10 years.

Waste and fraud are serious problems. Back in 1980 Federal investigators testified before one of your committees that "corruption has permeated virtually every area of the Medicare and Medicaid health care industry." One official said many of the people who are cheating the system were "very confident that nothing was going to happen to them." Well, something is going to happen. Not only the taxpayers are defrauded; the people with real dependency on these programs are deprived of what they need, because available resources are going not to the needy, but to the greedy.

The time has come to control the uncontrollable. In August we made a start. I signed a bill to reduce the growth of these programs by $44 billion over the next 3 years while at the same time preserving essential services for the truly needy. Shortly you will receive from me a message on further reforms we intend to install—some new, but others long recommended by your own congressional committees. I ask you to help make these savings for the American taxpayer.

The savings we propose in entitlement programs will total some $63 billion over 4 Years and will, without affecting social t security, go a long way toward bringing Federal spending under control.

But don't be fooled by those who proclaim that spending cuts will deprive the elderly, the needy, and the helpless. The Federal Government will still subsidize 95 million meals every day. That's one out of seven of all the meals served in America. Head Start, senior nutrition programs, and child welfare programs will not be cut from the levels we proposed last year. More than one-half billion dollars has been proposed for minority business assistance. And research at the National Institute of Health will be increased by over $100 million. While meeting all these needs, we intend to plug unwarranted tax loopholes and strengthen the law which requires all large corporations to pay a minimum tax.

I am confident the economic program we've put into operation will protect the needy while it triggers a recovery that will benefit all Americans. It will stimulate the economy, result in increased savings and provide capital for expansion, mortgages for homebuilding, and jobs for the unemployed.

Now that the essentials of that program are in place, our next major undertaking must be a program—just as bold, just as innovative—to make government again accountable to the people, to make our system of federalism work again.

Our citizens feel they've lost control of even the most basic decisions made about the essential services of government, such as schools, welfare, roads, and even garbage collection. And they're right. A maze of interlocking jurisdictions and levels of government confronts average citizens in trying to solve even the simplest of problems. They don't know where to turn for answers, who to hold accountable, who to praise, who to blame, who to vote for or against. The main reason for this is the overpowering growth of Federal grants-in-aid programs during the past few decades.

In 1960 the Federal Government had 132 categorical grant programs, costing $7 billion. When I took office, there were approximately 500, costing nearly a hundred billion dollars—13 programs for energy, 36 for pollution control, 66 for social services, 90 for education. And here in the Congress, it takes at least 166 committees just to try to keep track of them.

You know and I know that neither the President nor the Congress can properly oversee this jungle of grants-in-aid; indeed, the growth of these grants has led to the distortion in the vital functions of government. As one Democratic Governor put it recently: The National Government should be worrying about "arms control, not potholes."

The growth in these Federal programs has—in the words of one intergovernmental commission—made the Federal Government "more pervasive, more intrusive, more unmanageable, more ineffective and costly, and above all, more unaccountable." Let's solve this problem with a single, bold stroke: the return of some $47 billion in Federal programs to State and local government, together with the means to finance them and a transition period of nearly 10 years to avoid unnecessary disruption.

I will shortly send this Congress a message describing this program. I want to emphasize, however, that its full details will have been worked out only after close consultation with congressional, State, and local officials.

Starting in fiscal 1984, the Federal Government will assume full responsibility for the cost of the rapidly growing Medicaid program to go along with its existing responsibility for Medicare. As part of a financially equal swap, the States will simultaneously take full responsibility for Aid to Families with Dependent Children and food stamps. This will make welfare less costly and more responsive to genuine need, because it'll be designed and administered closer to the grass roots and the people it serves.

In 1984 the Federal Government will apply the full proceeds from certain excise taxes to a grass roots trust fund that will belong in fair shares to the 50 States. The total amount flowing into this fund will be $28 billion a year. Over the next 4 years the States can use this money in either of two ways. If they want to continue receiving Federal grants in such areas as transportation, education, and social services, they can use their trust fund money to pay for the grants. Or to the extent they choose to forgo the Federal grant programs, they can use their trust fund money on their own for those or other purposes. There will be a mandatory pass-through of part of these funds to local governments.

By 1988 the States will be in complete control of over 40 Federal grant programs. The trust fund will start to phase out, eventually to disappear, and the excise taxes will be turned over to the States. They can then preserve, lower, or raise taxes on their own and fund and manage these programs as they see fit.

In a single stroke we will be accomplishing a realignment that will end cumbersome administration and spiraling costs at the Federal level while we ensure these programs will be more responsive to both the people they're meant to help and the people who pay for them.

Hand in hand with this program to strengthen the discretion and flexibility of State and local governments, we're proposing legislation for an experimental effort to improve and develop our depressed urban areas in the 1980's and '90's. This legislation will permit States and localities to apply to the Federal Government for designation as urban enterprise zones. A broad range of special economic incentives in the zones will help attract new business, new jobs, new opportunity to America's inner cities and rural towns. Some will say our mission is to save free enterprise. Well, I say we must free enterprise so that together we can save America.

Some will also say our States and local communities are not up to the challenge of a new and creative partnership. Well, that might have been true 20 years ago before reforms like reapportionment and the Voting Rights Act, the 10-year extension of which I strongly support. It's no longer true today. This administration has faith in State and local governments and the constitutional balance envisioned by the Founding Fathers. We also believe in the integrity, decency, and sound, good sense of grass roots Americans.

Our faith in the American people is reflected in another major endeavor. Our private sector initiatives task force is seeking out successful community models of school, church, business, union, foundation, and civic programs that help community needs. Such groups are almost invariably far more efficient than government in running social programs.

We're not asking them to replace discarded and often discredited government programs dollar for dollar, service for service. We just want to help them perform the good works they choose and help others to profit by their example. Three hundred and eighty-five thousand corporations and private organizations are already working on social programs ranging from drug rehabilitation to job training, and thousands more Americans have written us asking how they can help. The volunteer spirit is still alive and well in America.

Our nation's long journey towards civil rights for all our citizens—once a source of discord, now a source of pride—must continue with no backsliding or slowing down. We must and shall see that those basic laws that guarantee equal rights are preserved and, when necessary, strengthened.

Our concern for equal rights for women is firm and unshakable. We launched a new Task Force on Legal Equity for Women and a Fifty States Project that will examine State laws for discriminatory language. And for the first time in our history, a woman sits on the highest court in the land.

So, too, the problem of crime—one as real and deadly serious as any in America today. It demands that we seek transformation of our legal system, which overly protects the rights of criminals while it leaves society and the innocent victims of crime without justice.

We look forward to the enactment of a responsible clean air act to increase jobs while continuing to improve the quality of our air. We're encouraged by the bipartisan initiative of the House and are hopeful of further progress as the Senate continues its deliberations.

So far, I've concentrated largely, now, on domestic matters. To view the state of the Union in perspective, we must not ignore the rest of the world. There isn't time tonight for a lengthy treatment of social—or foreign policy, I should say, a subject I intend to address in detail in the near future. A few words, however, are in order on the progress we've made over the past year, reestablishing respect for our nation around the globe and some of the challenges and goals that we will approach in the year ahead.

At Ottawa and Cancun, I met with leaders of the major industrial powers and developing nations. Now, some of those I met with were a little surprised that I didn't apologize for America's wealth. Instead, I spoke of the strength of the free marketplace system and how that system could help them realize their aspirations for economic development and political freedom. I believe lasting friendships were made, and the foundation was laid for future cooperation.

In the vital region of the Caribbean Basin, we're developing a program of aid, trade, and investment incentives to promote self-sustaining growth and a better, more secure life for our neighbors to the south. Toward those who would export terrorism and subversion in the Caribbean and elsewhere, especially Cuba and Libya, we will act with firmness.

Our foreign policy is a policy of strength, fairness, and balance. By restoring America's military credibility, by pursuing peace at the negotiating table wherever both sides are willing to sit down in good faith, and by regaining the respect of America's allies and adversaries alike, we have strengthened our country's position as a force for peace and progress in the world.

When action is called for, we're taking it. Our sanctions against the military dictatorship that has attempted to crush human rights in Poland—and against the Soviet regime behind that military dictatorship—clearly demonstrated to the world that America will not conduct "business as usual" with the forces of oppression. If the events in Poland continue to deteriorate, further measures will follow.

Now, let me also note that private American groups have taken the lead in making January 30th a day of solidarity with the people of Poland. So, too, the European Parliament has called for March 21st to be an international day of support for Afghanistan. Well, I urge all peace-loving peoples to join together on those days, to raise their voices, to speak and pray for freedom.

Meanwhile, we're working for reduction of arms and military activities, as I announced in my address to the Nation last November 18th. We have proposed to the Soviet Union a far-reaching agenda for mutual reduction of military forces and have already initiated negotiations with them in Geneva on intermediate-range nuclear forces. In those talks it is essential that we negotiate from a position of strength. There must be a real incentive for the Soviets to take these talks seriously. This requires that we rebuild our defenses.

In the last decade, while we sought the moderation of Soviet power through a process of restraint and accommodation, the Soviets engaged in an unrelenting buildup of their military forces. The protection of our national security has required that we undertake a substantial program to enhance our military forces.

We have not neglected to strengthen our traditional alliances in Europe and Asia, or to develop key relationships with our partners in the Middle East and other countries. Building a more peaceful world requires a sound strategy and the national resolve to back it up. When radical forces threaten our friends, when economic misfortune creates conditions of instability, when strategically vital parts of the world fall under the shadow of Soviet power, our response can make the difference between peaceful change or disorder and violence. That's why we've laid such stress not only on our own defense but on our vital foreign assistance program. Your recent passage of the Foreign Assistance Act sent a signal to the world that America will not shrink from making the investments necessary for both peace and security. Our foreign policy must be rooted in realism, not naiveté or self-delusion.

A recognition of what the Soviet empire is about is the starting point. Winston Churchill, in negotiating with the Soviets, observed that they respect only strength and resolve in their dealings with other nations. That's why we've moved to reconstruct our national defenses. We intend to keep the peace. We will also keep our freedom.

We have made pledges of a new frankness in our public statements and worldwide broadcasts. In the face of a climate of falsehood and misinformation, we've promised the world a season of truth—the truth of our great civilized ideas: individual liberty, representative government, the rule of law under God. We've never needed walls or minefields or barbed wire to keep our people in. Nor do we declare martial law to keep our people from voting for the kind of government they want.

Yes, we have our problems; yes, we're in a time of recession. And it's true, there's no quick fix, as I said, to instantly end the tragic pain of unemployment. But we will end it. The process has already begun, and we'll see its effect as the year goes on.

We speak with pride and admiration of that little band of Americans who overcame insuperable odds to set this nation on course 200 years ago. But our glory didn't end with them. Americans ever since have emulated their deeds.

We don't have to turn to our history books for heroes. They're all around us. One who sits among you here tonight epitomized that heroism at the end of the longest imprisonment ever inflicted on men of our Armed Forces. Who will ever forget that night when we waited for television to bring us the scene of that first plane landing at Clark Field in the Philippines, bringing our POW's home? The plane door opened and Jeremiah Denton came slowly down the ramp. He caught sight of our flag, saluted it, said, "God bless America," and then thanked us for bringing him home.

Just 2 weeks ago, in the midst of a terrible tragedy on the Potomac, we saw again the spirit of American heroism at its finest—the heroism of dedicated rescue workers saving crash victims from icy waters. And we saw the heroism of one of our young government employees, Lenny Skutnik, who, when he saw a woman lose her grip on the helicopter line, dived into the water and dragged her to safety.

And then there are countless, quiet, everyday heroes of American who sacrifice long and hard so their children will know a better life than they've known; church and civic volunteers who help to feed, clothe, nurse, and teach the needy; millions who've made our nation and our nation's destiny so very special—unsung heroes who may not have realized their own dreams themselves but then who reinvest those dreams in their children. Don't let anyone tell you that America's best days are behind her, that the American spirit has been vanquished. We've seen it triumph too often in our lives to stop believing in it now.

A hundred and twenty years ago, the greatest of all our Presidents delivered his second State of the Union message in this Chamber. "We cannot escape history," Abraham Lincoln warned. "We of this Congress and this administration will be remembered in spite of ourselves." The "trial through which we pass will light us down, in honor or dishonor, to the last generation."

Well, that President and that Congress did not fail the American people. Together they weathered the storm and preserved the Union. Let it be said of us that we, too, did not fail; that we, too, worked together to bring America through difficult times. Let us so conduct ourselves that two centuries from now, another Congress and another President, meeting in this Chamber as we are meeting, will speak of us with pride, saying that we met the test and preserved for them in their day the sacred flame of liberty—this last, best hope of man on Earth.

God bless you, and thank you.

Ronald Reagan, 1981–1985

Address before a Joint Session of Congress on the State of the Union
January 25, 1983

Ronald Reagan's second State of the Union address focused primarily on domestic issues, particularly the economy and the budget.

The president described the economy as "troubled" and said that, while the country "had a long way to go," it was "on the mend." The country had been in recession since late 1981 and would start to recover in early 1983.

As one example of his optimism, Reagan praised the bipartisan Commission on Social Security, which recently had unveiled a plan to reform the entitlement program. The president urged Congress to enact the commission's plan, which he said asked everyone for sacrifices but did not unfairly burden anyone. Congress passed amendments to the Social Security program that year, based on the commission's work.

Overall, Reagan recommended that Congress focus on long-term, bipartisan solutions to the country's problems. He stated that the challenges inherited by his administration had been worse than expected. To counter this, he called for a decrease in the growth of federal spending, which would become a key theme for his administration. He maintained that the deficits at that time were caused not by defense spending or by tax cuts, as some critics had charged, but by domestic spending.

Among his proposals was a four-part plan to reduce deficits and increase economic growth. He suggested a federal spending freeze, specific methods to control domestic programs such as food stamps, $55 billion in defense cuts over five years, and a "standby tax" that would start in fiscal 1986 under certain conditions.

Reagan also vowed to resist any efforts to reverse the tax reforms already enacted during his presidency.

In addition, he mentioned "a comprehensive federalism program" he planned to submit that would send some government functions back to the states—a scaled-back version of the plan featured in his 1982 State of the Union message.

On the foreign policy front, Reagan vowed to continue negotiations with the Soviet Union on verifiable arms reductions, carry on the Middle East peace process, and push for passage of the entire Caribbean Basin Initiative, which aimed to foster economic development for Caribbean nations.

Reagan, a Republican, was still working with a Republican-controlled Senate and a Democratic-controlled House; the midterm elections the previous November had not changed party control in either chamber.

Mr. Speaker, Mr. President, distinguished Members of the Congress, honored guests, and fellow citizens:

This solemn occasion marks the 196th time that a President of the United States has reported on the State of the Union since George Washington first did so in 1790. That's a lot of reports, but there's no shortage of new things to say about the State of the Union. The very key to our success has been our ability, foremost among nations, to preserve our lasting values by making change work for us rather than against us.

I would like to talk with you this evening about what we can do together—not as Republicans and Democrats, but as Americans—to make tomorrow's America happy and prosperous at home, strong and respected abroad, and at peace in the world.

As we gather here tonight, the state of our Union is strong, but our economy is troubled. For too many of our fellow citizens—farmers, steel and auto workers, lumbermen, black teenagers, working mothers—this is a painful period. We must all do everything in our power to bring their ordeal to an end. It has fallen to us, in our time, to undo damage that was a long time in the making, and to begin the hard but necessary task of building a better future for ourselves and our children.

We have a long way to go, but thanks to the courage, patience, and strength of our people, America is on the mend.

But let me give you just one important reason why I believe this—it involves many members of this body.

Just 10 days ago, after months of debate and deadlock, the bipartisan Commission on Social Security accomplished the seemingly impossible. Social security, as some of us had warned for so long, faced disaster. I, myself, have been talking about this problem for almost 30 years. As 1983 began, the system stood on the brink of bankruptcy, a double victim of our economic ills. First, a decade of rampant inflation drained its reserves as we tried to protect beneficiaries from the spiraling cost of living. Then the recession and the sudden end of inflation withered the expanding wage base and increasing revenues the system needs to support the 36 million Americans who depend on it.

When the Speaker of the House, the Senate majority leader, and I performed the bipartisan—or formed the bipartisan Commission on Social Security, pundits and experts predicted that party divisions and conflicting interests would prevent the Commission from agreeing on a plan to save social security. Well, sometimes, even here in Washington, the cynics are wrong. Through compromise and cooperation, the members of the Commission overcame their differences and achieved a fair, workable plan. They proved that, when it comes to the national welfare, Americans can still pull together for the common good.

Tonight, I'm especially pleased to join with the Speaker and the Senate majority leader in urging the Congress to enact this plan by Easter.

There are elements in it, of course, that none of us prefers, but taken together it performs a package that all of us can support. It asks for some sacrifice by all—the self-employed, beneficiaries, workers, government employees, and the better-off among the retired—but it imposes an undue burden on none. And, in supporting it, we keep an important pledge to the American people: The integrity of the social security system will be preserved, and no one's payments will be reduced.

The Commission's plan will do the job; indeed, it must do the job. We owe it to today's older Americans and today's younger workers. So, before we go any further, I ask you to join with me in saluting the members of the Commission who are here tonight and Senate Majority Leader Howard Baker and Speaker Tip O'Neill for a job well done. I hope and pray the bipartisan spirit that guided you in this endeavor will inspire all of us as we face the challenges of the year ahead.

Nearly half a century ago, in this Chamber, another American President, Franklin Delano Roosevelt, in his second State of the Union message, urged America to look to the future, to meet the challenge of change and the need for leadership that looks forward, not backward.

"Throughout the world," he said, "change is the order of the day. In every nation economic problems long in the making have brought crises of many kinds for which the masters of old practice and theory were unprepared." He also reminded us that "the future lies with those wise political leaders who realize that the great public is interested more in Government than in politics."

So, let us, in these next 2 years—men and women of both parties, every political shade—concentrate on the long-range, bipartisan responsibilities of government, not the short-range or short-term temptations of partisan politics.

The problems we inherited were far worse than most inside and out of government had expected; the recession was deeper than most inside and out of government had predicted. Curing those problems has taken more time and a higher toll than any of us wanted. Unemployment is far too high. Projected Federal spending—if government refuses to tighten its own belt—will also be far too high and could weaken and shorten the economic recovery now underway.

This recovery will bring with it a revival of economic confidence and spending for consumer items and capital goods—the stimulus we need to restart our stalled economic engines. The American people have already stepped up their rate of saving, assuring that the funds needed to modernize our factories and improve our technology will once again flow to business and industry.

The inflationary expectations that led to a 21½ percent interest prime rate and soaring mortgage rates 2 years ago are now reduced by almost half. Leaders have started to realize that double-digit inflation is no longer a way of life. I misspoke there. I should have said "lenders."

So, interest rates have tumbled, paving the way for recovery in vital industries like housing and autos.

The early evidence of that recovery has started coming in. Housing starts for the fourth quarter of 1982 were up 45 percent from a year ago, and housing permits, a sure indicator of future growth, were up a whopping 60 percent.

We're witnessing an upsurge of productivity and impressive evidence that American industry will once again become competitive in markets at home and abroad, ensuring more jobs and better incomes for the Nation's work force. But our confidence must also be tempered by realism and patience. Quick fixes and artificial stimulants repeatedly applied over decades are what brought us the inflationary disorders that we've now paid such a heavy price to cure.

The permanent recovery in employment, production, and investment we seek won't come in a sharp, short spurt. It'll build carefully and steadily in the months and years ahead. In the meantime, the challenge of government is to identify the things that we can do now to ease the massive economic transition for the American people.

The Federal budget is both a symptom and a cause of our economic problems. Unless we reduce the dangerous growth rate in government spending, we could face the prospect of sluggish economic growth into the indefinite future. Failure to cope with this problem now could mean as much as a trillion dollars more in national debt in the next 4 years alone. That would average $4,300 in additional debt for every man, woman, child, and baby in our nation.

To assure a sustained recovery, we must continue getting runaway spending under control to bring those deficits down. If we don't, the recovery will be too short, unemployment will remain too high, and we will leave an unconscionable burden of national debt for our children. That we must not do.

Let's be clear about where the deficit problem comes from. Contrary to the drumbeat we've been hearing for the last few months, the deficits we face are not rooted in defense spending. Taken as a percentage of the gross national product, our defense spending happens to be only about four-fifths of what it was in 1970. Nor is the deficit, as some would have it, rooted in tax cuts. Even with our tax cuts, taxes as a fraction of gross national product remain about the same as they were in 1970. The fact is, our deficits come from the uncontrolled growth of the budget for domestic spending.

During the 1970's, the share of our national income devoted to this domestic spending increased by more than 60 percent, from 10 cents out of every dollar produced by the American people to 16 cents. In spite of all our economies and efficiencies, and without adding any new programs, basic, necessary domestic spending provided for in this year's budget will grow to almost a trillion dollars over the next 5 years.

The deficit problem is a clear and present danger to the basic health of our Republic. We need a plan to overcome this danger—a plan based on these principles. It must be bipartisan. Conquering the deficits and putting the Government's house in order will require the best effort of all of us. It must be fair. Just as all will share in the benefits that will come from recovery, all would share fairly in the burden of transition. It must be prudent. The strength of our national defense must be restored so that we can pursue prosperity and peace and freedom while maintaining our commitment to the truly needy. And finally, it must be realistic. We can't rely on hope alone.

With these guiding principles in mind, let me outline a four-part plan to increase economic growth and reduce deficits.

First, in my budget message, I will recommend a Federal spending freeze. I know this is strong medicine, but so far, we have only cut the rate of increase in Federal spending. The Government has continued to spend more money each year, though not as much more as it did in the past. Taken as a whole, the budget I'm proposing for the fiscal year will increase no more than the rate of inflation. In other words, the Federal Government will hold the line on real spending. Now, that's far less than many American families have had to do in these difficult times.

I will request that the proposed 6-month freeze in cost-of-living adjustments recommended by the bipartisan Social Security Commission be applied to other government-related retirement programs. I will, also, propose a 1-year freeze on a broad range of domestic spending programs, and for Federal civilian and military pay and pension programs. And let me say right here, I'm sorry, with regard to the military, in asking that of them, because for so many years they have been so far behind and so low in reward for what the men and women in uniform are doing. But I'm sure they will understand that this must be across the board and fair.

Second, I will ask the Congress to adopt specific measures to control the growth of the so-called uncontrollable spending programs. These are the automatic spending programs, such as food stamps, that cannot be simply frozen and that have grown by over 400 percent since 1970. They are the largest single cause of the built-in or structural deficit problem. Our standard here will be fairness, ensuring that the taxpayers' hard-earned dollars go only to the truly needy; that none of them are turned away, but that fraud and waste are stamped out. And I'm sorry to say, there's a lot of it out there. In the food stamp program alone, last year, we identified almost 1.1 billion in over-payments. The taxpayers aren't the only victims of this kind of abuse. The truly needy suffer as funds intended for them are taken not by the needy, but by the greedy. For everyone's sake, we must put an end to such waste and corruption.

Third, I will adjust our program to restore America's defenses by proposing $55 billion in defense savings over the next 5 years. These are savings recommended to me by the Secretary of Defense, who has assured me they can be safely achieved and will not diminish our ability to negotiate arms reductions or endanger America's security. We will not gamble with our national survival.

And fourth, because we must ensure reduction and eventual elimination of deficits over the next several years, I will propose a standby tax, limited to no more than 1 percent of the gross national product, to start in fiscal 1986. It would last no more than 3 years, and it would start only if the Congress has first approved our spending freeze and budget control program. And there are several other conditions also that must be met, all of them in order for this program to be triggered.

Now, you could say that this is an insurance policy for the future, a remedy that will be at hand if needed but only resorted to if absolutely necessary. In the meantime, we'll continue to study ways to simplify the tax code and make it more fair for all Americans. This is a goal that every American who's ever struggled with a tax form can understand.

At the same time, however, I will oppose any efforts to undo the basic tax reforms that we've already enacted, including the 10-percent tax break coming to taxpayers this July and the tax indexing which will protect all Americans from inflationary bracket creep in the years ahead.

Now, I realize that this four-part plan is easier to describe than it will be to enact. But the looming deficits that hang over us and over America's future must be reduced. The path I've outlined is fair, balanced, and realistic. If enacted, it will ensure a steady decline in deficits, aiming toward a balanced budget by the end of the decade. It's the only path that will lead to a strong, sustained recovery. Let us follow that path together.

No domestic challenge is more crucial than providing stable, permanent jobs for all Americans who want to work. The recovery program will provide jobs for most, but others will need special help and training for new skills. Shortly, I will submit to the Congress the Employment Act of 1983, designed to get at the special problems of the long-term unemployed, as well as young people trying to enter the job market. I'll propose extending unemployment benefits, including special incentives to employers who hire the long-term unemployed, providing programs for displaced workers, and helping federally funded and State-administered unemployment insurance programs provide workers with training and relocation assistance. Finally, our proposal will include new incentives for summer youth employment to help young people get a start in the job market.

We must offer both short-term help and long-term hope for our unemployed. I hope we can work together on this. I hope we can work together as we did last year in enacting the landmark Job Training Partnership Act. Regulatory reform legislation, a responsible clean air act, and passage of enterprise zone legislation will also create new incentives for jobs and opportunity.

One of out of every five jobs in our country depends on trade. So, I will propose a broader strategy in the field of international trade—one that increases the openness of our trading system and is fairer to America's farmers and workers in the world marketplace. We must have adequate export financing to sell American products overseas. I will ask for new negotiating authority to remove barriers and to get more of our products into foreign markets. We must strengthen the organization of our trade agencies and make changes in our domestic laws and international trade policy to promote free trade and the increased flow of American goods, services, and investments.

Our trade position can also be improved by making our port system more efficient. Better, more active harbors translate into stable jobs in our coalfields, railroads, trucking industry, and ports. After 2 years of debate, it's time for us to get together and enact a port modernization bill.

Education, training, and retraining are fundamental to our success as are research and development and productivity. Labor, management, and government at all levels can and must participate in improving these tools of growth. Tax policy, regulatory practices, and government programs all need constant reevaluation in terms of our competitiveness. Every American has a role and a stake in international trade.

We Americans are still the technological leaders in most fields. We must keep that edge, and to do so we need to begin renewing the basics—starting with our educational system. While we grew complacent, others have acted. Japan, with a population only about half the size of ours, graduates from its universities more engineers than we do. If a child doesn't receive adequate math and science teaching by the age of 16, he or she has lost the chance to be a scientist or an engineer. We must join together— parents, teachers, grass roots groups, organized labor, and the business community— to revitalize American education by setting a standard of excellence.

In 1983 we seek four major education goals: a quality education initiative to encourage a substantial upgrading of math and science instruction through block grants to the States; establishment of education savings accounts that will give middle and lower-income families an incentive to save for their children's college education and, at the same time, encourage a real increase in savings for economic growth; passage of tuition tax credits for parents who want to send their children to private or religiously affiliated schools; a constitutional amendment to permit voluntary school prayer. God should never have been expelled from America's classrooms in the first place.

Our commitment to fairness means that we must assure legal and economic equity for women, and eliminate, once and for all, all traces of unjust discrimination against women from the United States Code. We will not tolerate wage discrimination based on sex, and we intend to strengthen enforcement of child support laws to ensure that single parents, most of whom are women, do not suffer unfair financial hardship. We will also take action to remedy inequities in pensions. These initiatives will be joined by others to continue our efforts to promote equity for women.

Also in the area of fairness and equity, we will ask for extension of the Civil Rights Commission, which is due to expire this year. The Commission is an important part of the ongoing struggle for justice in America, and we strongly support its reauthorization. Effective enforcement of our nation's fair housing laws is also essential to ensuring equal opportunity. In the year ahead, we'll work to strengthen enforcement of fair housing laws for all Americans.

The time has also come for major reform of our criminal justice statutes and acceleration of the drive against organized crime and drug trafficking. It's high time that we make our cities safe again. This administration hereby declares an all-out war on big-time organized crime and the drug racketeers who are poisoning our young people. We will also implement recommendations of our Task Force on Victims of Crime, which will report to me this week.

American agriculture, the envy of the world, has become the victim of its own successes. With one farmer now producing enough food to feed himself and 77 other people, America is confronted with record surplus crops and commodity prices below the cost of production. We must strive, through innovations like the payment-in-kind crop swap approach and an aggressive export policy, to restore health and vitality to rural America. Meanwhile, I have instructed the Department of Agriculture to work individually with farmers with debt problems to help them through these tough times.

Over the past year, our Task Force on Private Sector Initiatives has successfully forged a working partnership involving leaders of business, labor, education, and government to address the training needs of American workers. Thanks to the Task Force, private sector initiatives are now underway in all 50 States of the Union, and thousands of working people have been helped in making the shift from dead-end jobs and low-demand skills to the growth areas of high technology and the service economy. Additionally, a major effort will be focused on encouraging the expansion of private community child care. The new advisory council on private sector initiatives will carry on and extend this vital work of encouraging private initiative in 1983.

In the coming year, we will also act to improve the quality of life for Americans by curbing the skyrocketing cost of health care that is becoming an unbearable financial burden for so many. And we will submit legislation to provide catastrophic illness insurance coverage for older Americans.

I will also shortly submit a comprehensive federalism proposal that will continue our efforts to restore to States and local governments their roles as dynamic laboratories of change in a creative society.

During the next several weeks, I will send to the Congress a series of detailed proposals on these and other topics and look forward to working with you on the development of these initiatives.

So far, now, I've concentrated mainly on the problems posed by the future. But in almost every home and workplace in America, we're already witnessing reason for great hope—the first flowering of the manmade miracles of high technology, a field pioneered and still led by our country.

To many of us now, computers, silicon chips, data processing, cybernetics, and all the other innovations of the dawning high technology age are as mystifying as the workings of the combustion engine must have been when that first Model T rattled down Main Street, U.S.A. But as surely as America's pioneer spirit made us the industrial giant of the 20th century, the same pioneer spirit today is opening up on another vast front of opportunity, the frontier of high technology.

In conquering the frontier we cannot write off our traditional industries, but we must develop the skills and industries that will make us a pioneer of tomorrow. This administration is committed to keeping America the technological leader of the world now and into the 21st century.

But let us turn briefly to the international arena. America's leadership in the world came to us because of our own strength and because of the values which guide us as a society: free elections, a free press, freedom of religious choice, free trade unions, and above all, freedom for the individual and rejection of the arbitrary power of the state. These values are the bedrock of our strength. They unite us in a stewardship of peace and freedom with our allies and friends in NATO, in Asia, in Latin America, and elsewhere. They are also the values which in the recent past some among us had begun to doubt and view with a cynical eye.

Fortunately, we and our allies have rediscovered the strength of our common democratic values, and we're applying them as a cornerstone of a comprehensive strategy for peace with freedom. In London last year, I announced the commitment of the United States to developing the infrastructure of democracy throughout the world. We intend to pursue this democratic initiative vigorously. The future belongs not to governments and ideologies which oppress their peoples, but to democratic systems of self-government which encourage individual initiative and guarantee personal freedom.

But our strategy for peace with freedom must also be based on strength—economic strength and military strength. A strong American economy is essential to the well-being and security of our friends and allies. The restoration of a strong, healthy American economy has been and remains one of the central pillars of our foreign policy. The progress I've been able to report to you tonight will, I know, be as warmly welcomed by the rest of the world as it is by the American people.

We must also recognize that our own economic well-being is inextricably linked to the world economy. We export over 20 percent of our industrial production, and 40 percent of our farmland produces for export. We will continue to work closely with the industrialized democracies of Europe and Japan and with the International Monetary Fund to ensure it has adequate resources to help bring the world economy back to strong, noninflationary growth.

As the leader of the West and as a country that has become great and rich because of economic freedom, America must be an unrelenting advocate of free trade. As some nations are tempted to turn to protectionism, our strategy cannot be to follow them, but to lead the way toward freer trade. To this end, in May of this year America will host an economic summit meeting in Williamsburg, Virginia.

As we begin our third year, we have put in place a defense program that redeems the neglect of the past decade. We have developed a realistic military strategy to deter threats to peace and to protect freedom if deterrence fails. Our Armed Forces are finally properly paid; after years of neglect are well trained and becoming better equipped and supplied. And the American uniform is once again worn with pride. Most of the major systems needed for modernizing our defenses are already underway, and we will be addressing one key system, the MX missile, in consultation with the Congress in a few months.

America's foreign policy is once again based on bipartisanship, on realism, strength, full partnership, in consultation with our allies, and constructive negotiation with potential adversaries. From the Middle East to southern Africa to Geneva, American diplomats are taking the initiative to make peace and lower arms levels. We should be proud of our role as peacemakers.

In the Middle East last year, the United States played the major role in ending the tragic fighting in Lebanon and negotiated the withdrawal of the PLO from Beirut.

Last September, I outlined principles to carry on the peace process begun so promisingly at Camp David. All the people of the Middle East should know that in the year ahead we will not flag in our efforts to build on that foundation to bring them the blessings of peace.

In Central America and the Caribbean Basin, we are likewise engaged in a partnership for peace, prosperity, and democracy. Final passage of the remaining portions of our Caribbean Basin Initiative, which passed the House last year, is one of this administration's top legislative priorities for 1983.

The security and economic assistance policies of this administration in Latin America and elsewhere are based on realism and represent a critical investment in the future of the human race. This undertaking is a joint responsibility of the executive and legislative branches, and I'm counting on the cooperation and statesmanship of the Congress to help us meet this essential foreign policy goal.

At the heart of our strategy for peace is our relationship with the Soviet Union. The past year saw a change in Soviet leadership. We're prepared for a positive change in Soviet-American relations. But the Soviet Union must show by deeds as well as words a sincere commitment to respect the rights and sovereignty of the family of nations. Responsible members of the world community do not threaten or invade their neighbors. And they restrain their allies from aggression.

For our part, we're vigorously pursuing arms reduction negotiations with the Soviet Union. Supported by our allies, we've put forward draft agreements proposing significant weapon reductions to equal and verifiable lower levels. We insist on an equal balance of forces. And given the overwhelming evidence of Soviet violations of international treaties concerning chemical and biological weapons, we also insist that any agreement we sign can and will be verifiable.

In the case of intermediate-range nuclear forces, we have proposed the complete elimination of the entire class of land-based missiles. We're also prepared to carefully explore serious Soviet proposals. At the same time, let me emphasize that allied stead-fastness remains a key to achieving arms reductions.

With firmness and dedication, we'll continue to negotiate. Deep down, the Soviets must know it's in their interest as well as ours to prevent a wasteful arms race. And once they recognize our unshakable resolve to maintain adequate deterrence, they will have every reason to join us in the search for greater security and major arms reductions. When that moment comes—and I'm confident that it will—we will have taken an important step toward a more peaceful future for all the world's people.

A very wise man, Bernard Baruch, once said that America has never forgotten the nobler things that brought her into being and that light her path. Our country is a special place, because we Americans have always been sustained, through good times and bad, by a noble vision—a vision not only of what the world around us is today but what we as a free people can make it be tomorrow.

We're realists; we solve our problems instead of ignoring them, no matter how loud the chorus of despair around us. But we're also idealists, for it was an ideal that brought our ancestors to these shores from every corner of the world.

Right now we need both realism and idealism. Millions of our neighbors are without work. It is up to us to see they aren't without hope. This is a task for all of us. And may I say, Americans have rallied to this cause, proving once again that we are the most generous people on Earth.

We who are in government must take the lead in restoring the economy. And here all that time, I thought you were reading the paper.

The single thing—the single thing that can start the wheels of industry turning again is further reduction of interest rates. Just another 1 or 2 points can mean tens of thousands of jobs.

Right now, with inflation as low as it is, 3.9 percent, there is room for interest rates to come down. Only fear prevents their reduction. A lender, as we know, must charge an interest rate that recovers the depreciated value of the dollars loaned. And that depreciation is, of course, the amount of inflation. Today, interest rates are based on fear—fear that government will resort to measures, as it has in the past, that will send inflation zooming again.

We who serve here in this Capital must erase that fear by making it absolutely clear that we will not stop fighting inflation; that, together, we will do only those things that will lead to lasting economic growth.

Yes, the problems confronting us are large and forbidding. And, certainly, no one can or should minimize the plight of millions of our friends and neighbors who are living in the bleak emptiness of unemployment. But we must and can give them good reason to be hopeful.

Back over the years, citizens like ourselves have gathered within these walls when our nation was threatened; sometimes when its very existence was at stake. Always with courage and common sense, they met the crises of their time and lived to see a stronger, better, and more prosperous country. The present situation is no worse and, in fact, is not as bad as some of those they faced. Time and again, they proved that there is nothing we Americans cannot achieve as free men and women.

Yes, we still have problems—plenty of them. But it's just plain wrong—unjust to our country and unjust to our people—to let those problems stand in the way of the most important truth of all: America is on the mend.

We owe it to the unfortunate to be aware of their plight and to help them in every way we can. No one can quarrel with that. We must and do have compassion for all the victims of this economic crisis. But the big story about America today is the way that millions of confident, caring people—those extraordinary "ordinary" Americans who never make the headlines and will never be interviewed—are laying the foundation, not just for recovery from our present problems but for a better tomorrow for all our people.

From coast to coast, on the job and in classrooms and laboratories, at new construction sites and in churches and community groups, neighbors are helping neighbors. And they've already begun the building, the research, the work, and the giving that will make our country great again.

I believe this, because I believe in them—in the strength of their hearts and minds, in the commitment that each one of them brings to their daily lives, be they high or humble. The challenge for us in government is to be worthy of them—to make government a help, not a hindrance to our people in the challenging but promising days ahead.

If we do that, if we care what our children and our children's children will say of us, if we want them one day to be thankful for what we did here in these temples of freedom, we will work together to make America better for our having been here— not just in this year or this decade but in the next century and beyond.

Thank you, and God bless you.

Ronald Reagan, 1981–1985

Address before a Joint Session of Congress on the State of the Union

January 25, 1984

Ronald Reagan's third State of the Union message, delivered at the start of a presidential election year, seemed designed to rally supporters by highlighting accomplishments of the president's past three years in office.

Reagan delivered his speech before Congress amidst extra-tight security in the wake of a terrorist bombing in the Capitol in November 1983. He began by listing various difficulties the country faced as he took office; he mentioned lack of confidence, inflation, a "web" of government rules and regulations, and a loss of respect around the world.

During his administration, he said, taxes had been cut and inflation reduced, leading to entrepreneurial initiative. He mentioned two people in particular as examples of this trend, calling them "heroes for the eighties": Barbara Proctor, who "rose from a ghetto" and built a successful Chicago advertising agency, and Carlos Perez, a Cuban immigrant who created a Florida importing business.

The president cited several goals; the first was economic growth. He reiterated a familiar theme of his presidency: limiting the size of government. He rejected the idea of cuts in defense spending and pledged to bring budget deficits down over the next five years. Deficits, however, would remain high throughout his presidency. He also called for tax simplification.

Another goal Reagan put forth was to build within a decade a permanently manned space station, which would involve other countries as well. Eventually, a joint U.S.-Soviet international space station would become operational in 1998.

Reagan also called for increased funding for the Environmental Protection Agency; his administration had come under criticism for cutting its budget.

He also mentioned issues tailored toward conservative voters, such as support for school prayer and opposition to abortion.

On the international front, Reagan called for "a lasting and meaningful peace." He directed some remarks to the Soviet people, stating that "a nuclear war cannot be won and must never be fought."

In a manner similar to that of his 1982 State of the Union address, Reagan mentioned several more "heroes" toward the end of his address: Sergeant Stephen Trujillo, a medic who had fought in the U.S. invasion of Grenada in 1983; Father Bruce Ritter, whose Covenant House shelters helped children in New York and Houston; and Dr. Charles Carson, who was paralyzed in a plane crash and worked on computer-controlled walking techniques. Trujillo was mentioned as an example of U.S. forces fighting for freedom; the other two were mentioned as examples of American unsung heroes.

In November 1984, Reagan, a Republican, would win a landslide victory over his Democratic opponent, former vice president Walter Mondale, taking forty-nine of fifty states and earning another four years in the White House.

Mr. Speaker, Mr. President, distinguished Members of the Congress, honored guests, and fellow citizens:

Once again, in keeping with time-honored tradition, I have come to report to you on the state of the Union, and I'm pleased to report that America is much improved, and there's good reason to believe that improvement will continue through the days to come.

You and I have had some honest and open differences in the year past. But they didn't keep us from joining hands in bipartisan cooperation to stop a long decline that had drained this nation's spirit and eroded its health. There is renewed energy and optimism throughout the land. America is back, standing tall, looking to the eighties with courage, confidence, and hope.

The problems we're overcoming are not the heritage of one person, party, or even one generation. It's just the tendency of government to grow, for practices and programs to become the nearest thing to eternal life we'll ever see on this Earth. And there's always that well-intentioned chorus of voices saying, "With a little more power and a little more money, we could do so much for the people." For a time we forgot the American dream isn't one of making government bigger; it's keeping faith with the mighty spirit of free people under God.

As we came to the decade of the eighties, we faced the worst crisis in our postwar history. In the seventies were years of rising problems and falling confidence. There was a feeling government had grown beyond the consent of the governed. Families felt helpless in the face of mounting inflation and the indignity of taxes that reduced reward for hard work, thrift, and risktaking. All this was overlaid by an ever-growing web of rules and regulations.

On the international scene, we had an uncomfortable feeling that we'd lost the respect of friend and foe. Some questioned whether we had the will to defend peace and freedom. But America is too great for small dreams. There was a hunger in the land for a spiritual revival; if you will, a crusade for renewal. The American people said: Let us look to the future with confidence, both at home and abroad. Let us give freedom a chance.

Americans were ready to make a new beginning, and together we have done it. We're confronting our problems one by one. Hope is alive tonight for millions of young families and senior citizens set free from unfair tax increases and crushing inflation. Inflation has been beaten down from 12.4 to 3.2 percent, and that's a great victory for all the people. The prime rate has been cut almost in half, and we must work together to bring it down even more.

Together, we passed the first across-the-board tax reduction for everyone since the Kennedy tax cuts. Next year, tax rates will be indexed so inflation can't push people into higher brackets when they get cost-of-living pay raises. Government must never again use inflation to profit at the people's expense.

Today a working family earning $25,000 has $1,100 more in purchasing power than if tax and inflation rates were still at the 1980 levels. Real after-tax income increased 5 percent last year. And economic deregulation of key industries like transportation has offered more chances—or choices, I should say, to consumers and new changes—or chances for entrepreneurs and protecting safety. Tonight, we can report and be proud of one of the best recoveries in decades. Send away the handwringers and the doubting Thomases. Hope is reborn for couples dreaming of owning homes and for risktakers with vision to create tomorrow's opportunities.

The spirit of enterprise is sparked by the sunrise industries of high-tech and by small business people with big ideas—people like Barbara Proctor, who rose from a ghetto to build a multimillion-dollar advertising agency in Chicago; Carlos Perez, a Cuban refugee, who turned $27 and a dream into a successful importing business in Coral Gables, Florida.

People like these are heroes for the eighties. They helped 4 million Americans find jobs in 1983. More people are drawing paychecks tonight than ever before. And Congress helps—or progress helps everyone—well, Congress does too—everyone. In 1983 women filled 73 percent of all the new jobs in managerial, professional, and technical fields.

But we know that many of our fellow countrymen are still out of work, wondering what will come of their hopes and dreams. Can we love America and not reach out to tell them: You are not forgotten; we will not rest until each of you can reach as high as your God-given talents will take you.

The heart of America is strong; it's good and true. The cynics were wrong; America never was a sick society. We're seeing rededication to bedrock values of faith, family, work, neighborhood, peace, and freedom—values that help bring us together as one people, from the youngest child to the most senior citizen.

The Congress deserves America's thanks for helping us restore pride and credibility to our military. And I hope that you're as proud as I am of the young men and women in uniform who have volunteered to man the ramparts in defense of freedom and whose dedication, valor, and skill increases so much our chance of living in a world at peace.

People everywhere hunger for peace and a better life. The tide of the future is a freedom tide, and our struggle for democracy cannot and will not be denied. This nation champions peace that enshrines liberty, democratic rights, and dignity for every individual. America's new strength, confidence, and purpose are carrying hope and opportunity far from our shores. A world economic recovery is underway. It began here.

We've journeyed far, but we have much farther to go. Franklin Roosevelt told us 50 years ago this month: "Civilization can not go back; civilization must not stand still. We have undertaken new methods. It is our task to perfect, to improve, to alter when necessary, but in all cases to go forward."

It's time to move forward again, time for America to take freedom's next step. Let us unite tonight behind four great goals to keep America free, secure, and at peace in the eighties together.

We can ensure steady economic growth. We can develop America's next frontier. We can strengthen our traditional values. And we can build a meaningful peace to protect our loved ones and this shining star of faith that has guided millions from tyranny to the safe harbor of freedom, progress, and hope.

Doing these things will open wider the gates of opportunity, provide greater security for all, with no barriers of bigotry or discrimination.

The key to a dynamic decade is vigorous economic growth, our first great goal. We might well begin with common sense in Federal budgeting: government spending no more than government takes in.

We must bring Federal deficits down. But how we do that makes all the difference.

We can begin by limiting the size and scope of government. Under the leadership of Vice President Bush, we have reduced the growth of Federal regulations by more than 25 percent and cut well over 300 million hours of government-required paperwork each year. This will save the public more than $150 billion over the next 10 years.

The Grace commission has given us some 2,500 recommendations for reducing wasteful spending, and they're being examined throughout the administration. Federal spending growth has been cut from 17.4 percent in 1980 to less than half of that today, and we have already achieved over $300 billion in budget savings for the period of 1982 to '86. But that's only a little more than half of what we sought. Government is still spending too large a percentage of the total economy.

Now, some insist that any further budget savings must be obtained by reducing the portion spent on defense. This ignores the fact that national defense is solely the responsibility of the Federal Government; indeed, it is its prime responsibility. And yet defense spending is less than a third of the total budget. During the years of President Kennedy and of the years before that, defense was almost half the total budget. And then came several years in which our military capability was allowed to deteriorate to a very dangerous degree. We are just now restoring, through the essential modernization of our conventional and strategic forces, our capability to meet our present and future security needs. We dare not shirk our responsibility to keep America free, secure, and at peace.

The last decade saw domestic spending surge literally out of control. But the basis for such spending had been laid in previous years. A pattern of overspending has been in place for half a century. As the national debt grew, we were told not to worry, that we owed it to ourselves.

Now we know that deficits are a cause for worry. But there's a difference of opinion as to whether taxes should be increased, spending cut, or some of both. Fear is expressed that government borrowing to fund the deficit could inhibit the economic recovery by taking capital needed for business and industrial expansion. Well, I think that debate is missing an important point. Whether government borrows or increases taxes, it will be taking the same amount of money from the private sector, and, either way, that's too much. Simple fairness dictates that government must not raise taxes on families struggling to pay their bills. The root of the problem is that government's share is more than we can afford if we're to have a sound economy.

We must bring down the deficits to ensure continued economic growth. In the budget that I will submit on February 1st, I will recommend measures that will reduce the deficit over the next 5 years. Many of these will be unfinished business from last year's budget.

Some could be enacted quickly if we could join in a serious effort to address this problem. I spoke today with Speaker of the House [Tip] O'Neill, Senate Majority Leader [Howard] Baker, Senate Minority Leader [Robert] Byrd, and House Minority Leader [Robert] Michel. I asked them if they would designate congressional representatives to meet with representatives of the administration to try to reach prompt agreement on a bipartisan deficit reduction plan. I know it would take a long, hard struggle to agree on a full-scale plan. So, what I have proposed is that we first see if we can agree on a down payment.

Now, I believe there is basis for such an agreement, one that could reduce the deficits by about a hundred billion dollars over the next 3 years. We could focus on some of the less contentious spending cuts that are still pending before the Congress. These could be combined with measures to close certain tax loopholes, measures that the Treasury Department has previously said to be worthy of support. In addition, we could examine the possibility of achieving further outlay savings based on the work of the Grace commission.

If the congressional leadership is willing, my representatives will be prepared to meet with theirs at the earliest possible time. I would hope the leadership might agree on an expedited timetable in which to develop and enact that down payment.

But a down payment alone is not enough to break us out of the deficit problem. It could help us start on the right path. Yet, we must do more. So, I propose that we begin exploring how together we can make structural reforms to curb the built-in growth of spending.

I also propose improvements in the budgeting process. Some 43 of our 50 States grant their Governors the right to veto individual items in appropriation bills without having to veto the entire bill. California is one of those 43 States. As Governor, I found this line-item veto was a powerful tool against wasteful or extravagant spending. It works in 43 States. Let's put it to work in Washington for all the people.

It would be most effective if done by constitutional amendment. The majority of Americans approve of such an amendment, just as they and I approve of an amendment mandating a balanced Federal budget. Many States also have this protection in their constitutions.

To talk of meeting the present situation by increasing taxes is a Band-Aid solution which does nothing to cure an illness that's been coming on for half a century—to say nothing of the fact that it poses a real threat to economic recovery. Let's remember that a substantial amount of income tax is presently owed and not paid by people in the underground economy. It would be immoral to make those who are paying taxes pay more to compensate for those who aren't paying their share.

There's a better way. Let us go forward with an historic reform for fairness, simplicity, and incentives for growth. I am asking Secretary Don Regan for a plan for action to simplify the entire tax code, so all taxpayers, big and small, are treated more fairly. And I believe such a plan could result in that underground economy being brought into the sunlight of honest tax compliance. And it could make the tax base broader, so personal tax rates could come down, not go up. I've asked that specific recommendations, consistent with those objectives, be presented to me by December 1984.

Our second great goal is to build on America's pioneer spirit—I said something funny? I said America's next frontier—and that's to develop that frontier. A sparkling economy spurs initiatives, sunrise industries, and makes older ones more competitive.

Nowhere is this more important than our next frontier: space. Nowhere do we so effectively demonstrate our technological leadership and ability to make life better on Earth. The Space Age is barely a quarter of a century old. But already we've pushed civilization forward with our advances in science and technology. Opportunities and jobs will multiply as we cross new thresholds of knowledge and reach deeper into the unknown.

Our progress in space—taking giant steps for all mankind—is a tribute to American teamwork and excellence. Our finest minds in government, industry, and academia have all pulled together. And we can be proud to say: We are first; we are the best; and we are so because we're free.

America has always been greatest when we dared to be great. We can reach for greatness again. We can follow our dreams to distant stars, living and working in space for peaceful, economic, and scientific gain. Tonight, I am directing NASA to develop a permanently manned space station and to do it within a decade.

A space station will permit quantum leaps in our research in science, communications, in metals, and in lifesaving medicines which could be manufactured only in space. We want our friends to help us meet these challenges and share in their benefits. NASA will invite other countries to participate so we can strengthen peace, build prosperity, and expand freedom for all who share our goals.

Just as the oceans opened up a new world for clipper ships and Yankee traders, space holds enormous potential for commerce today. The market for space transportation could surpass our capacity to develop it. Companies interested in putting payloads into space must have ready access to private sector launch services. The Department of Transportation will help an expendable launch services industry to get off the ground. We'll soon implement a number of executive initiatives, develop proposals to ease regulatory constraints, and, with NASA's help, promote private sector investment in space.

And as we develop the frontier of space, let us remember our responsibility to preserve our older resources here on Earth. Preservation of our environment is not a liberal or conservative challenge, it's common sense.

Though this is a time of budget constraints, I have requested for EPA one of the largest percentage budget increases of any agency. We will begin the long, necessary effort to clean up a productive recreational area and a special national resource—the Chesapeake Bay.

To reduce the threat posed by abandoned hazardous waste dumps, EPA will spend $410 million. And I will request a supplemental increase of 50 million. And because the Superfund law expires in 1985, I've asked Bill Ruckelshaus to develop a proposal for its extension so there'll be additional time to complete this important task.

On the question of acid rain, which concerns people in many areas of the United States and Canada, I'm proposing a research program that doubles our current funding. And we'll take additional action to restore our lakes and develop new technology to reduce pollution that causes acid rain.

We have greatly improved the conditions of our natural resources. We'll ask the Congress for $157 million beginning in 1985 to acquire new park and conservation lands. The Department of the Interior will encourage careful, selective exploration and production on our vital resources in an Exclusive Economic Zone within the 200-mile limit off our coasts—but with strict adherence to environmental laws and with fuller State and public participation.

But our most precious resources, our greatest hope for the future, are the minds and hearts of our people, especially our children. We can help them build tomorrow by strengthening our community of shared values. This must be our third great goal. For us, faith, work, family, neighborhood, freedom, and peace are not just words; they're expressions of what America means, definitions of what makes us a good and loving people.

Families stand at the center of our society. And every family has a personal stake in promoting excellence in education. Excellence does not begin in Washington. A 600-percent increase in Federal spending on education between 1960 and 1980 was accompanied by a steady decline in Scholastic Aptitude Test scores. Excellence must begin in our homes and neighborhood schools, where it's the responsibility of every parent and teacher and the right of every child.

Our children come first, and that's why I established a bipartisan National Commission on Excellence in Education, to help us chart a commonsense course for better education. And already, communities are implementing the Commission's recommendations. Schools are reporting progress in math and reading skills. But we must do more to restore discipline to schools; and we must encourage the teaching of new basics, reward teachers of merit, enforce tougher standards, and put our parents back in charge.

I will continue to press for tuition tax credits to expand opportunities for families and to soften the double payment for those paying public school taxes and private school tuition. Our proposal would target assistance to low- and middle-income families. Just as more incentives are needed within our schools, greater competition is needed among our schools. Without standards and competition, there can be no champions, no records broken, no excellence in education or any other walk of life.

And while I'm on this subject, each day your Members observe a 200-year-old tradition meant to signify America is one nation under God. I must ask: If you can begin your day with a member of the clergy standing right here leading you in prayer, then why can't freedom to acknowledge God be enjoyed again by children in every schoolroom across this land?

America was founded by people who believed that God was their rock of safety. He is ours. I recognize we must be cautious in claiming that God is on our side, but I think it's all right to keep asking if we're on His side.

During our first 3 years, we have joined bipartisan efforts to restore protection of the law to unborn children. Now, I know this issue is very controversial. But unless and until it can be proven that an unborn child is not a living human being, can we justify assuming without proof that it isn't? No one has yet offered such proof; indeed, all the evidence is to the contrary. We should rise above bitterness and reproach, and if Americans could come together in a spirit of understanding and helping, then we could find positive solutions to the tragedy of abortion.

Economic recovery, better education, rededication to values, all show the spirit of renewal gaining the upper hand. And all will improve family life in the eighties. But families need more. They need assurance that they and their loved ones can walk the streets of America without being afraid. Parents need to know their children will not be victims of child pornography and abduction. This year we will intensify our drive against these and other horrible crimes like sexual abuse and family violence.

Already our efforts to crack down on career criminals, organized crime, drug push-ers, and to enforce tougher sentences and paroles are having effect. In 1982 the crime rate dropped by 4.3 percent, the biggest decline since 1972. Protecting victims is just as important as safeguarding the rights of defendants.

Opportunities for all Americans will increase if we move forward in fair housing and work to ensure women's rights, provide for equitable treatment in pension bene-fits and Individual Retirement Accounts, facilitate child care, and enforce delinquent parent support payments.

It's not just the home but the workplace and community that sustain our values and shape our future. So, I ask your help in assisting more communities to break the bondage of dependency. Help us to free enterprise by permitting debate and voting "yes" on our proposal for enterprise zones in America. This has been before you for 2 years. Its passage can help high-unemployment areas by creating jobs and restoring neighborhoods.

A society bursting with opportunities, reaching for its future with confidence, sus-tained by faith, fair play, and a conviction that good and courageous people will flour-ish when they're free—these are the secrets of a strong and prosperous America at peace with itself and the world.

A lasting and meaningful peace is our fourth great goal. It is our highest aspiration. And our record is clear: Americans resort to force only when we must. We have never been aggressors. We have always struggled to defend freedom and democracy.

We have no territorial ambitions. We occupy no countries. We build no walls to lock people in. Americans build the future. And our vision of a better life for farm-ers, merchants, and working people, from the Americas to Asia, begins with a simple premise: The future is best decided by ballots, not bullets.

Governments which rest upon the consent of the governed do not wage war on their neighbors. Only when people are given a personal stake in deciding their own destiny, benefiting from their own risks, do they create societies that are prosperous, progressive, and free. Tonight, it is democracies that offer hope by feeding the hun-gry, prolonging life, and eliminating drudgery.

When it comes to keeping America strong, free, and at peace, there should be no Republicans or Democrats, just patriotic Americans. We can decide the tough issues not by who is right, but by what is right.

Together, we can continue to advance our agenda for peace. We can establish a more stable basis for peaceful relations with the Soviet Union; strengthen allied relations across the board; achieve real and equitable reductions in the levels of nuclear arms; reinforce our peacemaking efforts in the Middle East, Central America, and southern Africa; or assist developing countries, particularly our neighbors in the Western Hemi-sphere; and assist in the development of democratic institutions throughout the world.

The wisdom of our bipartisan cooperation was seen in the work of the Scowcroft commission, which strengthened our ability to deter war and protect peace. In that same spirit, I urge you to move forward with the Henry Jackson plan to implement the recommendations of the Bipartisan Commission on Central America.

Your joint resolution on the multinational peacekeeping force in Lebanon is also serving the cause of peace. We are making progress in Lebanon. For nearly 10 years, the Lebanese have lived from tragedy to tragedy with no hope for their future. Now the multinational peacekeeping force and our marines are helping them break their cycle of despair. There is hope for a free, independent, and sovereign Lebanon. We must have the courage to give peace a chance. And we must not be driven from our objectives for peace in Lebanon by state-sponsored terrorism. We have seen this ugly specter in Beirut, Kuwait, and Rangoon. It demands international attention. I will forward shortly legislative proposals to help combat terrorism. And I will be seeking support from our allies for concerted action.

Our NATO alliance is strong. 1983 was a banner year for political courage. And we have strengthened our partnerships and our friendships in the Far East. We're committed to dialog, deterrence, and promoting prosperity. We'll work with our trading partners for a new round of negotiations in support of freer world trade, greater competition, and more open markets.

A rebirth of bipartisan cooperation, of economic growth, and military deterrence, and a growing spirit of unity among our people at home and our allies abroad underline a fundamental and far-reaching change: The United States is safer, stronger, and more secure in 1984 than before. We can now move with confidence to seize the opportunities for peace, and we will.

Tonight, I want to speak to the people of the Soviet Union, to tell them it's true that our governments have had serious differences, but our sons and daughters have never fought each other in war. And if we Americans have our way, they never will.

People of the Soviet Union, there is only one sane policy, for your country and mine, to preserve our civilization in this modern age: A nuclear war cannot be won and must never be fought. The only value in our two nations possessing nuclear weapons is to make sure they will never be used. But then would it not be better to do away with them entirely?

People of the Soviet, President Dwight Eisenhower, who fought by your side in World War II, said the essential struggle "is not merely man against man or nation against nation. It is man against war." Americans are people of peace. If your government wants peace, there will be peace. We can come together in faith and friendship to build a safer and far better world for our children and our children's children. And the whole world will rejoice. That is my message to you.

Some days when life seems hard and we reach out for values to sustain us or a friend to help us, we find a person who reminds us what it means to be Americans.

Sergeant Stephen Trujillo, a medic in the 2d Ranger Battalion, 75th Infantry, was in the first helicopter to land at the compound held by Cuban forces in Grenada. He saw three other helicopters crash. Despite the imminent explosion of the burning aircraft, he never hesitated. He ran across 25 yards of open terrain through enemy fire to rescue wounded soldiers. He directed two other medics, administered first aid, and returned again and again to the crash site to carry his wounded friends to safety.

Sergeant Trujillo, you and your fellow service men and women not only saved innocent lives; you set a nation free. You inspire us as a force for freedom, not for despotism; and, yes, for peace, not conquest. God bless you.

And then there are unsung heroes: single parents, couples, church and civic volunteers. Their hearts carry without complaint the pains of family and community problems. They soothe our sorrow, heal our wounds, calm our fears, and share our joy.

A person like Father Ritter is always there. His Covenant House programs in New York and Houston provide shelter and help to thousands of frightened and abused children each year. The same is true of Dr. Charles Carson. Paralyzed in a plane crash, he still believed nothing is impossible. Today in Minnesota, he works 80 hours a week without pay, helping pioneer the field of computer-controlled walking. He has given hope to 500,000 paralyzed Americans that some day they may walk again.

How can we not believe in the greatness of America? How can we not do what is right and needed to preserve this last best hope of man on Earth? After all our struggles to restore America, to revive confidence in our country, hope for our future, after all our hard-won victories earned through the patience and courage of every citizen, we cannot, must not, and will not turn back. We will finish our job. How could we do less? We're Americans.

Carl Sandburg said, "I see America not in the setting sun of a black night of despair. . . . I see America in the crimson light of a rising sun fresh from the burning, creative hand of God. . . . I see great days ahead for men and women of will and vision."

I've never felt more strongly that America's best days and democracy's best days lie ahead. We're a powerful force for good. With faith and courage, we can perform great deeds and take freedom's next step. And we will. We will carry on the tradition of a good and worthy people who have brought light where there was darkness, warmth where there was cold, medicine where there was disease, food where there was hunger, and peace where there was only bloodshed.

Let us be sure that those who come after will say of us in our time, that in our time we did everything that could be done. We finished the race; we kept them free; we kept the faith.

Thank you very much. God bless you, and God bless America.

Ronald Reagan, 1985–1989

Address before a Joint Session of Congress on the State of the Union

February 6, 1985

Ronald Reagan delivered his fourth State of the Union address before Congress in February 1985. The president had been sworn in for a second term the month before, having scored a landslide victory the previous November over his Democratic opponent, former vice president Walter Mondale.

Reagan, with his trademark conservative philosophy and optimistic outlook, won 49 states, with Mondale taking only his home state of Minnesota plus the District of Columbia. Reagan took 525 electoral votes to Mondale's 13, and 58.8 percent of the popular vote to Mondale's 40.6 percent. Republicans held the Senate while Democrats maintained control of the House.

In his State of the Union speech, the president stated that the country had become stronger in the four years of his first term; he cited sustained economic growth, lower inflation, and an increase in employment. Reagan added, however, that more needed to be done. He called for a "second American Revolution of hope and opportunity," citing freedom as a key ingredient for such change.

One key proposal in his speech involved tax reform, which he said would reduce barriers to growth. Although the president had called for tax reform in his previous State of the Union addresses, in this speech Reagan offered a few specifics of his revised plan, including that the top rate would be capped at 35 percent, that people living at or near the poverty line would be exempt from federal income taxes, and that corporate rate reductions would be proposed. Congress went on to pass major tax reform legislation in 1986.

Reagan faced large budget deficits during his presidency, and in this speech he stated that economic growth was the best method of reducing the deficit. He called for 1986 spending to remain at 1985 levels, while maintaining a social safety net for the elderly and poor and continuing efforts to "restore military strength." He also called for reductions or eliminations in "costly government subsidies," such as those allocated to Amtrak.

While discussing defense policy, Reagan pushed for his controversial Strategic Defense Initiative missile-defense plan, saying, "Let's get started." He also urged support for Nicaraguan "freedom fighters" battling the country's communist government.

At the end of the speech, after talking about "great plans and great dreams," Reagan introduced two American women who he felt exemplified this theme: Jean Nguyen, who fled Vietnam in 1975 and ten years later was about to graduate from West Point, and Clara "Mother" Hale, who cared for children whose mothers were heroin addicts.

M r. Speaker, Mr. President, distinguished Members of the Congress, honored guests, and fellow citizens:

I come before you to report on the state of our Union, and I'm pleased to report that after 4 years of united effort, the American people have brought forth a nation renewed, stronger, freer, and more secure than before.

Four years ago we began to change, forever I hope, our assumptions about government and its place in our lives. Out of that change has come great and robust growth—in our confidence, our economy, and our role in the world.

Tonight America is stronger because of the values that we hold dear. We believe faith and freedom must be our guiding stars, for they show us truth, they make us brave, give us hope, and leave us wiser than we were. Our progress began not in Washington, DC, but in the hearts of our families, communities, workplaces, and voluntary groups which, together, are unleashing the invincible spirit of one great nation under God.

Four years ago we said we would invigorate our economy by giving people greater freedom and incentives to take risks and letting them keep more of what they earned. We did what we promised, and a great industrial giant is reborn.

Tonight we can take pride in 25 straight months of economic growth, the strongest in 34 years; a 3-year inflation average of 3.9 percent, the lowest in 17 years; and 7.3 million new jobs in 2 years, with more of our citizens working than ever before.

New freedom in our lives has planted the rich seeds for future success:

For an America of wisdom that honors the family, knowing that as the family goes, so goes our civilization;

For an America of vision that sees tomorrow's dreams in the learning and hard work we do today;

For an America of courage whose service men and women, even as we meet, proudly stand watch on the frontiers of freedom;

For an America of compassion that opens its heart to those who cry out for help.

We have begun well. But it's only a beginning. We're not here to congratulate ourselves on what we have done but to challenge ourselves to finish what has not yet been done.

We're here to speak for millions in our inner cities who long for real jobs, safe neighborhoods, and schools that truly teach. We're here to speak for the American farmer, the entrepreneur, and every worker in industries fighting to modernize and compete. And, yes, we're here to stand, and proudly so, for all who struggle to break free from totalitarianism, for all who know in their hearts that freedom is the one true path to peace and human happiness.

Proverbs tell us, without a vision the people perish. When asked what great principle holds our Union together, Abraham Lincoln said: "Something in the Declaration giving liberty, not alone to the people of this country, but hope to the world for all future time."

We honor the giants of our history not by going back but forward to the dreams their vision foresaw. My fellow citizens, this nation is poised for greatness. The time has come to proceed toward a great new challenge—a second American Revolution of hope and opportunity; a revolution carrying us to new heights of progress by pushing back frontiers of knowledge and space; a revolution of spirit that taps the soul of America, enabling us to summon greater strength than we've ever known; and a revolution that carries beyond our shores the golden promise of human freedom in a world of peace.

Let us begin by challenging our conventional wisdom. There are no constraints on the human mind, no walls around the human spirit, no barriers to our progress except those we ourselves erect. Already, pushing down tax rates has freed our economy to vault forward to record growth.

In Europe, they're calling it "the American Miracle." Day by day, we're shattering accepted notions of what is possible. When I was growing up, we failed to see how a new thing called radio would transform our marketplace. Well, today, many have not yet seen how advances in technology are transforming our lives.

In the late 1950's workers at the AT&T semiconductor plant in Pennsylvania produced five transistors a day for $7.50 apiece. They now produce over a million for less than a penny apiece.

New laser techniques could revolutionize heart bypass surgery, cut diagnosis time for viruses linked to cancer from weeks to minutes, reduce hospital costs dramatically, and hold out new promise for saving human lives.

Our automobile industry has overhauled assembly lines, increased worker productivity, and is competitive once again.

We stand on the threshold of a great ability to produce more, do more, be more. Our economy is not getting older and weaker; it's getting younger and stronger. It doesn't need rest and supervision; it needs new challenge, greater freedom. And that word "freedom" is the key to the second American revolution that we need to bring about.

Let us move together with an historic reform of tax simplification for fairness and growth. Last year I asked Treasury Secretary—then—[Donald] Regan to develop a plan to simplify the tax code, so all taxpayers would be treated more fairly and personal tax rates could come further down.

We have cut tax rates by almost 25 percent, yet the tax system remains unfair and limits our potential for growth. Exclusions and exemptions cause similar incomes to be taxed at different levels. Low-income families face steep tax barriers that make hard lives even harder. The Treasury Department has produced an excellent reform plan, whose principles will guide the final proposal that we will ask you to enact.

One thing that tax reform will not be is a tax increase in disguise. We will not jeopardize the mortgage interest deduction that families need. We will reduce personal tax rates as low as possible by removing many tax preferences. We will propose a top rate of no more than 35 percent, and possibly lower. And we will propose reducing corporate rates, while maintaining incentives for capital formation.

To encourage opportunity and jobs rather than dependency and welfare, we will propose that individuals living at or near the poverty line be totally exempt from Federal income tax. To restore fairness to families, we will propose increasing significantly the personal exemption.

And tonight, I am instructing Treasury Secretary James Baker—I have to get used to saying that—to begin working with congressional authors and committees for bipartisan legislation conforming to these principles. We will call upon the American people for support and upon every man and woman in this Chamber. Together, we can pass, this year, a tax bill for fairness, simplicity, and growth, making this economy the engine of our dreams and America the investment capital of the world. So let us begin.

Tax simplification will be a giant step toward unleashing the tremendous pent-up power of our economy. But a second American revolution must carry the promise of opportunity for all. It is time to liberate the spirit of enterprise in the most distressed areas of our country.

This government will meet its responsibility to help those in need. But policies that increase dependency, break up families, and destroy self-respect are not progressive; they're reactionary. Despite our strides in civil rights, blacks, Hispanics, and all minorities will not have full and equal power until they have full economic power.

We have repeatedly sought passage of enterprise zones to help those in the abandoned corners of our land find jobs, learn skills, and build better lives. This legislation is supported by a majority of you.

Mr. Speaker, I know we agree that there must be no forgotten Americans. Let us place new dreams in a million hearts and create a new generation of entrepreneurs by passing enterprise zones this year. And, Tip, you could make that a birthday present.

Nor must we lose the chance to pass our youth employment opportunity wage proposal. We can help teenagers, who have the highest unemployment rate, find summer jobs, so they can know the pride of work and have confidence in their futures.

We'll continue to support the Job Training Partnership Act, which has a nearly two-thirds job placement rate. Credits in education and health care vouchers will help working families shop for services that they need.

Our administration is already encouraging certain low-income public housing residents to own and manage their own dwellings. It's time that all public housing residents have that opportunity of ownership.

The Federal Government can help create a new atmosphere of freedom. But States and localities, many of which enjoy surpluses from the recovery, must not permit their tax and regulatory policies to stand as barriers to growth.

Let us resolve that we will stop spreading dependency and start spreading opportunity; that we will stop spreading bondage and start spreading freedom.

There are some who say that growth initiatives must await final action on deficit reductions. Well, the best way to reduce deficits is through economic growth. More businesses will be started, more investments made, more jobs created, and more people will be on payrolls paying taxes. The best way to reduce government spending is to reduce the need for spending by increasing prosperity. Each added percentage point per year of real GNP growth will lead to cumulative reduction in deficits of nearly $200 billion over 5 years.

To move steadily toward a balanced budget, we must also lighten government's claim on our total economy. We will not do this by raising taxes. We must make sure that our economy grows faster than the growth in spending by the Federal Government. In our fiscal year 1986 budget, overall government program spending will be frozen at the current level. It must not be one dime higher than fiscal year 1985, and three points are key.

First, the social safety net for the elderly, the needy, the disabled, and unemployed will be left intact. Growth of our major health care programs, Medicare and Medicaid, will be slowed, but protections for the elderly and needy will be preserved.

Second, we must not relax our efforts to restore military strength just as we near our goal of a fully equipped, trained, and ready professional corps. National security is government's first responsibility; so in past years defense spending took about half the Federal budget. Today it takes less than a third. We've already reduced our planned defense expenditures by nearly a hundred billion dollars over the past 4 years and reduced projected spending again this year.

You know, we only have a military-industrial complex until a time of danger, and then it becomes the arsenal of democracy. Spending for defense is investing in things that are priceless—peace and freedom.

Third, we must reduce or eliminate costly government subsidies. For example, deregulation of the airline industry has led to cheaper airfares, but on Amtrak taxpayers pay about $35 per passenger every time an Amtrak train leaves the station. It's time we ended this huge Federal subsidy.

Our farm program costs have quadrupled in recent years. Yet I know from visiting farmers, many in great financial distress, that we need an orderly transition to a market-oriented farm economy. We can help farmers best not by expanding Federal payments but by making fundamental reforms, keeping interest rates heading down, and knocking down foreign trade barriers to American farm exports.

We're moving ahead with Grace commission reforms to eliminate waste and improve government's management practices. In the long run, we must protect the taxpayers from government. And I ask again that you pass, as 32 States have now called for, an amendment mandating the Federal Government spend no more than it takes in. And I ask for the authority, used responsibly by 43 Governors, to veto individual items in appropriation bills. Senator Mattingly has introduced a bill permitting a 2-year trial run of the line-item veto. I hope you'll pass and send that legislation to my desk.

Nearly 50 years of government living beyond its means has brought us to a time of reckoning. Ours is but a moment in history. But one moment of courage, idealism, and bipartisan unity can change American history forever.

Sound monetary policy is key to long-running economic strength and stability. We will continue to cooperate with the Federal Reserve Board, seeking a steady policy that ensures price stability without keeping interest rates artificially high or needlessly holding down growth.

Reducing unneeded red tape and regulations, and deregulating the energy, transportation, and financial industries have unleashed new competition, giving consumers more choices, better services, and lower prices. In just one set of grant programs we have reduced 905 pages of regulations to 31. We seek to fully deregulate natural gas to bring on new supplies and bring us closer to energy independence. Consistent with safety standards, we will continue removing restraints on the bus and railroad industries, we will soon end up legislation—or send up legislation, I should say—to return Conrail to the private sector where it belongs, and we will support further deregulation of the trucking industry.

Every dollar the Federal Government does not take from us, every decision it does not make for us will make our economy stronger, our lives more abundant, our future more free.

Our second American revolution will push on to new possibilities not only on Earth but in the next frontier of space. Despite budget restraints, we will seek record funding for research and development.

We've seen the success of the space shuttle. Now we're going to develop a permanently manned space station and new opportunities for free enterprise, because in the next decade Americans and our friends around the world will be living and working together in space.

In the zero gravity of space, we could manufacture in 30 days lifesaving medicines it would take 30 years to make on Earth. We can make crystals of exceptional purity to produce super computers, creating jobs, technologies, and medical breakthroughs beyond anything we ever dreamed possible.

As we do all this, we'll continue to protect our natural resources. We will seek reauthorization and expanded funding for the Superfund program to continue cleaning up hazardous waste sites which threaten human health and the environment.

Now, there's another great heritage to speak of this evening. Of all the changes that have swept America the past 4 years, none brings greater promise than our rediscovery of the values of faith, freedom, family, work, and neighborhood.

We see signs of renewal in increased attendance in places of worship; renewed optimism and faith in our future; love of country rediscovered by our young, who are leading the way. We've rediscovered that work is good in and of itself, that it ennobles us to create and contribute no matter how seemingly humble our jobs. We've seen a powerful new current from an old and honorable tradition—American generosity.

From thousands answering Peace Corps appeals to help boost food production in Africa, to millions volunteering time, corporations adopting schools, and communities pulling together to help the neediest among us at home, we have re-found our values. Private sector initiatives are crucial to our future.

I thank the Congress for passing equal access legislation giving religious groups the same right to use classrooms after school that other groups enjoy. But no citizen need tremble, nor the world shudder, if a child stands in a classroom and breathes a prayer. We ask you again, give children back a right they had for a century and a half or more in this country.

The question of abortion grips our nation. Abortion is either the taking of a human life or it isn't. And if it is—and medical technology is increasingly showing it is—it must be stopped. It is a terrible irony that while some turn to abortion, so many others who cannot become parents cry out for children to adopt. We have room for these children. We can fill the cradles of those who want a child to love. And tonight I ask you in the Congress to move this year on legislation to protect the unborn.

In the area of education, we're returning to excellence, and again, the heroes are our people, not government. We're stressing basics of discipline, rigorous testing, and homework, while helping children become computer-smart as well. For 20 years scholastic aptitude test scores of our high school students went down, but now they have gone up 2 of the last 3 years. We must go forward in our commitment to the new basics, giving parents greater authority and making sure good teachers are rewarded for hard work and achievement through merit pay.

Of all the changes in the past 20 years, none has more threatened our sense of national well-being than the explosion of violent crime. One does not have to be attacked to be a victim. The woman who must run to her car after shopping at night is a victim. The couple draping their door with locks and chains are victims; as is the tired, decent cleaning woman who can't ride a subway home without being afraid.

We do not seek to violate the rights of defendants. But shouldn't we feel more compassion for the victims of crime than for those who commit crime? For the first time in 20 years, the crime index has fallen 2 years in a row. We've convicted over 7,400 drug offenders and put them, as well as leaders of organized crime, behind bars in record numbers.

But we must do more. I urge the House to follow the Senate and enact proposals permitting use of all reliable evidence that police officers acquire in good faith. These proposals would also reform the habeas corpus laws and allow, in keeping with the will of the overwhelming majority of Americans, the use of the death penalty where necessary.

There can be no economic revival in ghettos when the most violent among us are allowed to roam free. It's time we restored domestic tranquility. And we mean to do just that.

Just as we're positioned as never before to secure justice in our economy, we're poised as never before to create a safer, freer, more peaceful world. Our alliances are stronger than ever. Our economy is stronger than ever. We have resumed our historic role as a leader of the free world. And all of these together are a great force for peace.

Since 1981 we've been committed to seeking fair and verifiable arms agreements that would lower the risk of war and reduce the size of nuclear arsenals. Now our determination to maintain a strong defense has influenced the Soviet Union to return to the bargaining table. Our negotiators must be able to go to that table with the united support of the American people. All of us have no greater dream than to see the day when nuclear weapons are banned from this Earth forever.

Each Member of the Congress has a role to play in modernizing our defenses, thus supporting our chances for a meaningful arms agreement. Your vote this spring on the Peacekeeper missile will be a critical test of our resolve to maintain the strength we need and move toward mutual and verifiable arms reductions.

For the past 20 years we've believed that no war will be launched as long as each side knows it can retaliate with a deadly counterstrike. Well, I believe there's a better way of eliminating the threat of nuclear war. It is a Strategic Defense Initiative aimed ultimately at finding a non-nuclear defense against ballistic missiles. It's the most hopeful possibility of the nuclear age. But it's not very well understood.

Some say it will bring war to the heavens, but its purpose is to deter war in the heavens and on Earth. Now, some say the research would be expensive. Perhaps, but it could save millions of lives, indeed humanity itself. And some say if we build such a system, the Soviets will build a defense system of their own. Well, they already have strategic defenses that surpass ours; a civil defense system, where we have almost none; and a research program covering roughly the same areas of technology that we're now exploring. And finally some say the research will take a long time. Well, the answer to that is: Let's get started.

Harry Truman once said that, ultimately, our security and the world's hopes for peace and human progress "lie not in measures of defense or in the control of weapons, but in the growth and expansion of freedom and self-government."

And tonight, we declare anew to our fellow citizens of the world: Freedom is not the sole prerogative of a chosen few; it is the universal right of all God's children. Look to where peace and prosperity flourish today. It is in homes that freedom built. Victories against poverty are greatest and peace most secure where people live by laws that ensure free press, free speech, and freedom to worship, vote, and create wealth.

Our mission is to nourish and defend freedom and democracy, and to communicate these ideals everywhere we can. America's economic success is freedom's success; it can be repeated a hundred times in a hundred different nations. Many countries in east Asia and the Pacific have few resources other than the enterprise of their own people. But through low tax rates and free markets they've soared ahead of centralized economies. And now China is opening up its economy to meet its needs.

We need a stronger and simpler approach to the process of making and implementing trade policy, and we'll be studying potential changes in that process in the next few weeks. We've seen the benefits of free trade and lived through the disasters of protectionism. Tonight I ask all our trading partners, developed and developing alike, to join us in a new round of trade negotiations to expand trade and competition and strengthen the global economy—and to begin it in this next year.

There are more than 3 billion human beings living in Third World countries with an average per capita income of $650 a year. Many are victims of dictatorships that impoverished them with taxation and corruption. Let us ask our allies to join us in a practical program of trade and assistance that fosters economic development through personal incentives to help these people climb from poverty on their own.

We cannot play innocents abroad in a world that's not innocent; nor can we be passive when freedom is under siege. Without resources, diplomacy cannot succeed. Our security assistance programs help friendly governments defend themselves and give them confidence to work for peace. And I hope that you in the Congress will understand that, dollar for dollar, security assistance contributes as much to global security as our own defense budget.

We must stand by all our democratic allies. And we must not break faith with those who are risking their lives—on every continent, from Afghanistan to Nicaragua—to defy Soviet-supported aggression and secure rights which have been ours from birth.

The Sandinista dictatorship of Nicaragua, with full Cuban-Soviet bloc support, not only persecutes its people, the church, and denies a free press, but arms and provides bases for Communist terrorists attacking neighboring states. Support for freedom fighters is self-defense and totally consistent with the OAS [Organization of American States] and U.N. Charters. It is essential that the Congress continue all facets of our assistance to Central America. I want to work with you to support the democratic forces whose struggle is tied to our own security.

And tonight, I've spoken of great plans and great dreams. They're dreams we can make come true. Two hundred years of American history should have taught us that nothing is impossible.

Ten years ago a young girl left Vietnam with her family, part of the exodus that followed the fall of Saigon. They came to the United States with no possessions and not knowing a word of English. Ten years ago—the young girl studied hard, learned English, and finished high school in the top of her class. And this May, May 22d to be exact, is a big date on her calendar. Just 10 years from the time she left Vietnam, she will graduate from the United States Military Academy at West Point. I thought you might like to meet an American hero named Jean Nguyen.

Now, there's someone else here tonight, born 79 years ago. She lives in the inner city, where she cares for infants born of mothers who are heroin addicts. The children, born in withdrawal, are sometimes even dropped on her doorstep. She helps them with love. Go to her house some night, and maybe you'll see her silhouette against the window as she walks the floor talking softly, soothing a child in her arms— Mother Hale of Harlem, and she, too, is an American hero.

Jean, Mother Hale, your lives tell us that the oldest American saying is new again: Anything is possible in America if we have the faith, the will, and the heart. History is asking us once again to be a force for good in the world. Let us begin in unity, with justice, and love.

Thank you, and God bless you.

Ronald Reagan, 1985–1989

Address before a Joint Session of Congress on the State of the Union
February 4, 1986

Ronald Reagan delivered his fifth State of the Union address after delaying his visit to the Capitol by one week due to the tragic explosion of the space shuttle *Challenger* on January 28, the original scheduled date for the address. At the start of his speech, Reagan paid tribute to the seven crew members who had died.

The president's message was shorter than usual and consisted of many of the same themes he had discussed in previous State of the Union messages. He voiced his usual optimism, stating that "America is on the move," and cited continued economic growth, creation of new jobs, lower inflation, and $74 billion in voluntary giving the previous year.

But, he said, more needed to be done. "We cannot stop at the foothills when Everest beckons," he declared. Although the Reagan presidency was known for large budget deficits, he reiterated his calls for deficit reduction, as he had done in previous State of the Union addresses. In December 1985 Reagan had signed the Gramm-Rudman-Hollings law, which provided for automatic spending cuts unless certain deficit targets were met. But in order to further reduce government spending, Reagan also pleaded with Congress to approve line-item veto power, which would allow the president to veto specific provisions in a bill. Finally, he urged passage of tax reform, and later that year Congress heeded his suggestion.

When it came to foreign policy, Reagan spoke of his hope that his summit meetings with new Soviet leader Mikhail Gorbachev would lead to a better relationship between the two countries. The leaders had met for the first time the previous November, and they would hold a series of meetings over Reagan's last few years in office that did, in fact, improve relations between the two longtime adversaries. In this speech, Reagan also asked for a continued commitment to defense spending.

Reagan maintained his State of the Union tradition of introducing guests invited to sit in the House gallery. This time he mentioned Richard Cavoli, a young man who had designed an exhibit that had gone on the space shuttle; twelve-year-old Tyrone Ford, a gospel prodigy; thirteen-year-old Shelby Butler, a safety patrol who saved another student's life; and thirteen-year-old Trevor Ferrell, who helped the homeless in Philadelphia. He cited them as examples of the American dream.

Reagan, who was almost seventy when he first took the oath of office, was the oldest president to be inaugurated. Although vigorous, he did have some health issues; in July 1985 he had undergone surgery for colon cancer.

Mr. Speaker, Mr. President, distinguished Members of the Congress, honored guests, and fellow citizens:

Thank you for allowing me to delay my address until this evening. We paused together to mourn and honor the valor of our seven *Challenger* heroes. And I hope that we are now ready to do what they would want us to do: Go forward, America, and reach for the stars. We will never forget those brave seven, but we shall go forward.

Mr. Speaker, before I begin my prepared remarks, may I point out that tonight marks the 10th and last State of the Union Message that you've presided over. And on behalf of the American people, I want to salute you for your service to Congress and country. Here's to you!

I have come to review with you the progress of our nation, to speak of unfinished work, and to set our sights on the future. I am pleased to report the state of our Union is stronger than a year ago and growing stronger each day. Tonight we look out on a rising America, firm of heart, united in spirit, powerful in pride and patriotism. America is on the move! But it wasn't long ago that we looked out on a different land: locked factory gates, long gasoline lines, intolerable prices, and interest rates turning the greatest country on Earth into a land of broken dreams. Government growing beyond our consent had become a lumbering giant, slamming shut the gates of opportunity, threatening to crush the very roots of our freedom. What brought America back? The American people brought us back with quiet courage and common sense, with undying faith that in this nation under God the future will be ours; for the future belongs to the free.

Tonight the American people deserve our thanks for 37 straight months of economic growth, for sunrise firms and modernized industries creating 9 million new jobs in 3 years, interest rates cut in half, inflation falling over from 12 percent in 1980 to under 4 today, and a mighty river of good works—a record $74 billion in voluntary giving just last year alone. And despite the pressures of our modern world, family and community remain the moral core of our society, guardians of our values and hopes for the future. Family and community are the costars of this great American comeback. They are why we say tonight: Private values must be at the heart of public policies.

What is true for families in America is true for America in the family of free nations. History is no captive of some inevitable force. History is made by men and women of vision and courage. Tonight freedom is on the march. The United States is the economic miracle, the model to which the world once again turns. We stand for an idea whose time is now: Only by lifting the weights from the shoulders of all can people truly prosper and can peace among all nations be secure. Teddy Roosevelt said that a nation that does great work lives forever. We have done well, but we cannot stop at the foothills when Everest beckons. It's time for America to be all that we can be.

We speak tonight of an agenda for the future, an agenda for a safer, more secure world. And we speak about the necessity for actions to steel us for the challenges of growth, trade, and security in the next decade and the year 2000. And we will do it—not by breaking faith with bedrock principles but by breaking free from failed policies. Let us begin where storm clouds loom darkest—right here in Washington, D.C. This week I will send you our detailed proposals; tonight let us speak of our responsibility to redefine government's role: not to control, not to demand or command, not to contain us, but to help in times of need and, above all, to create a ladder of opportunity to full employment so that all Americans can climb toward economic power and justice on their own.

But we cannot win the race to the future shackled to a system that can't even pass a Federal budget. We cannot win that race held back by horse-and-buggy programs that waste tax dollars and squander human potential. We cannot win that race if we're swamped in a sea of red ink. Now, Mr. Speaker, you know, I know, and the American people know the Federal budget system is broken. It doesn't work. Before we leave this city, let's you and I work together to fix it, and then we can finally give the American people a balanced budget.

Members of Congress, passage of Gramm-Rudman-Hollings gives us an historic opportunity to achieve what has eluded our national leadership for decades: forcing the Federal Government to live within its means. Your schedule now requires that the budget resolution be passed by April 15th, the very day America's families have to foot the bill for the budgets that you produce. How often we read of a husband and wife both working, struggling from paycheck to paycheck to raise a family, meet a mortgage, pay their taxes and bills. And yet some in Congress say taxes must be raised. Well, I'm sorry; they're asking the wrong people to tighten their belts. It's time we reduce the Federal budget and left the family budget alone. We do not face large deficits because American families are undertaxed; we face those deficits because the Federal Government overspends.

The detailed budget that we will submit will meet the Gramm-Rudman-Hollings target for deficit reductions, meet our commitment to ensure a strong national defense, meet our commitment to protect Social Security and the truly less fortunate, and, yes, meet our commitment to not raise taxes. How should we accomplish this? Well, not by taking from those in need. As families take care of their own, government must provide shelter and nourishment for those who cannot provide for themselves. But we must revise or replace programs enacted in the name of compassion that degrade the moral worth of work, encourage family breakups, and drive entire communities into a bleak and heartless dependency. Gramm-Rudman-Hollings can mark a dramatic improvement. But experience shows that simply setting deficit targets does not assure they'll be met. We must proceed with Grace commission reforms against waste.

And tonight I ask you to give me what 43 Governors have: Give me a line-item veto this year. Give me the authority to veto waste, and I'll take the responsibility, I'll make the cuts, I'll take the heat. This authority would not give me any monopoly power, but simply prevent spending measures from sneaking through that could not pass on their own merit. And you can sustain or override my veto; that's the way the system should work. Once we've made the hard choices, we should lock in our gains with a balanced budget amendment to the Constitution.

I mentioned that we will meet our commitment to national defense. We must meet it. Defense is not just another budget expense. Keeping America strong, free, and at peace is solely the responsibility of the Federal Government; it is government's prime responsibility. We have devoted 5 years trying to narrow a dangerous gap born of illusion and neglect, and we've made important gains. Yet the threat from Soviet forces, conventional and strategic, from the Soviet drive for domination, from the increase in espionage and state terror remains great. This is reality. Closing our eyes will not make reality disappear. We pledged together to hold real growth in defense spending to the bare minimum. My budget honors that pledge, and I'm now asking you, the Congress, to keep its end of the bargain. The Soviets must know that if America reduces her defenses, it will be because of a reduced threat, not a reduced resolve.

Keeping America strong is as vital to the national security as controlling Federal spending is to our economic security. But, as I have said before, the most powerful force we can enlist against the Federal deficit is an ever-expanding American economy, unfettered and free. The magic of opportunity—unreserved, unfailing, unrestrained— isn't this the calling that unites us? I believe our tax rate cuts for the people have done more to spur a spirit of risk-taking and help America's economy break free than any program since John Kennedy's tax cut almost a quarter century ago.

Now history calls us to press on, to complete efforts for an historic tax reform providing new opportunity for all and ensuring that all pay their fair share, but no more. We've come this far. Will you join me now, and we'll walk this last mile together? You know my views on this. We cannot and we will not accept tax reform that is a tax increase in disguise. True reform must be an engine of productivity and growth, and that means a top personal rate no higher than 35 percent. True reform must be truly fair, and that means raising personal exemptions to $2,000. True reform means a tax system that at long last is pro-family, pro-jobs, pro-future, and pro-America.

As we knock down the barriers to growth, we must redouble our efforts for freer and fairer trade. We have already taken actions to counter unfair trading practices and to pry open closed foreign markets. We will continue to do so. We will also oppose legislation touted as providing protection that in reality pits one American worker against another, one industry against another, one community against another, and that raises prices for us all. If the United States can trade with other nations on a level playing field, we can out produce, out compete, and outsell anybody, anywhere in the world.

The constant expansion of our economy and exports requires a sound and stable dollar at home and reliable exchange rates around the world. We must never again permit wild currency swings to cripple our farmers and other exporters. Farmers, in particular, have suffered from past unwise government policies. They must not be abandoned with problems they did not create and cannot control. We've begun coordinating economic and monetary policy among our major trading partners. But there's more to do, and tonight I am directing Treasury Secretary Jim Baker to determine if the nations of the world should convene to discuss the role and relationship of our currencies.

Confident in our future and secure in our values, Americans are striving forward to embrace the future. We see it not only in our recovery but in 3 straight years of falling crime rates, as families and communities band together to fight pornography, drugs, and lawlessness and to give back to their children the safe and, yes, innocent childhood they deserve. We see it in the renaissance in education, the rising SAT scores for 3 years—last year's increase, the greatest since 1963. It wasn't government and Washington lobbies that turned education around; it was the American people who, in reaching for excellence, knew to reach back to basics. We must continue the advance by supporting discipline in our schools, vouchers that give parents freedom of choice; and we must give back to our children their lost right to acknowledge God in their classrooms.

We are a nation of idealists, yet today there is a wound in our national conscience. America will never be whole as long as the right to life granted by our Creator is denied to the unborn. For the rest of my time, I shall do what I can to see that this wound is one day healed.

As we work to make the American dream real for all, we must also look to the condition of America's families. Struggling parents today worry how they will provide their children the advantages that their parents gave them. In the welfare culture, the breakdown of the family, the most basic support system, has reached crisis proportions—female and child poverty, child abandonment, horrible crimes, and deteriorating schools. After hundreds of billions of dollars in poverty programs, the plight of the poor grows more painful. But the waste in dollars and cents pales before the most tragic loss: the sinful waste of human spirit and potential. We can ignore this terrible truth no longer. As Franklin Roosevelt warned 51 years ago, standing before this Chamber, he said, "Welfare is a narcotic, a subtle destroyer of the human spirit." And we must now escape the spider's web of dependency.

Tonight I am charging the White House Domestic Council to present me by December 1, 1986, an evaluation of programs and a strategy for immediate action to meet the financial, educational, social, and safety concerns of poor families. I'm talking about real and lasting emancipation, because the success of welfare should be judged by how many of its recipients become independent of welfare. Further, after seeing how devastating illness can destroy the financial security of the family, I am directing the Secretary of Health and Human Services, Dr. Otis Bowen, to report to me by year end with recommendations on how the private sector and government can work together to address the problems of affordable insurance for those whose life savings would otherwise be threatened when catastrophic illness strikes.

And tonight I want to speak directly to America's younger generation, because you hold the destiny of our nation in your hands. With all the temptations young people face, it sometimes seems the allure of the permissive society requires superhuman feats of self-control. But the call of the future is too strong, the challenge too great to get lost in the blind alleyways of dissolution, drugs, and despair. Never has there been a more exciting time to be alive, a time of rousing wonder and heroic achievement. As they said in the film "Back to the Future," "Where we're going, we don't need roads."

Well, today physicists peering into the infinitely small realms of subatomic particles find reaffirmations of religious faith. Astronomers build a space telescope that can see to the edge of the universe and possibly back to the moment of creation. So, yes, this nation remains fully committed to America's space program. We're going forward with our shuttle flights. We're going forward to build our space station. And we are going forward with research on a new Orient Express that could, by the end of the next decade, take off from Dulles Airport, accelerate up to 25 times the speed of sound, attaining low Earth orbit or flying to Tokyo within 2 hours. And the same technology transforming our lives can solve the greatest problem of the 20th century. A security shield can one day render nuclear weapons obsolete and free mankind from the prison of nuclear terror. America met one historic challenge and went to the Moon. Now America must meet another: to make our strategic defense real for all the citizens of planet Earth.

Let us speak of our deepest longing for the future: to leave our children a land that is free and just and a world at peace. It is my hope that our fireside summit in Geneva and Mr. Gorbachev's upcoming visit to America can lead to a more stable relationship. Surely no people on Earth hate war or love peace more than we Americans. But we cannot stroll into the future with childlike faith. Our differences with a system that openly proclaims and practices an alleged right to command people's lives and to export its ideology by force are deep and abiding. Logic and history compel us to accept that our relationship be guided by realism—rock-hard, clear-eyed, steady, and sure. Our negotiators in Geneva have proposed a radical cut in offensive forces by each side with no cheating. They have made clear that Soviet compliance with the letter and spirit of agreements is essential. If the Soviet Government wants an agreement that truly reduces nuclear arms, there will be such an agreement.

But arms control is no substitute for peace. We know that peace follows in freedom's path and conflicts erupt when the will of the people is denied. So, we must prepare for peace not only by reducing weapons but by bolstering prosperity, liberty, and democracy however and wherever we can. We advance the promise of opportunity every time we speak out on behalf of lower tax rates, freer markets, sound currencies around the world. We strengthen the family of freedom every time we work with allies and come to the aid of friends under siege. And we can enlarge the family of free nations if we will defend the unalienable rights of all God's children to follow their dreams.

To those imprisoned in regimes held captive, to those beaten for daring to fight for freedom and democracy—for their right to worship, to speak, to live, and to prosper in the family of free nations—we say to you tonight: You are not alone, freedom fighters. America will support with moral and material assistance your right not just to fight and die for freedom but to fight and win freedom—to win freedom in Afghanistan, in Angola, in Cambodia, and in Nicaragua. This is a great moral challenge for the entire free world.

Surely no issue is more important for peace in our own hemisphere, for the security of our frontiers, for the protection of our vital interests, than to achieve democracy in Nicaragua and to protect Nicaragua's democratic neighbors. This year I will be asking Congress for the means to do what must be done for that great and good cause. As Scoop Jackson, the inspiration for our Bipartisan Commission on Central America, once said, "In matters of national security, the best politics is no politics."

What we accomplish this year, in each challenge we face, will set our course for the balance of the decade, indeed, for the remainder of the century. After all we've done so far, let no one say that this nation cannot reach the destiny of our dreams. America believes, America is ready, America can win the race to the future—and we shall. The American dream is a song of hope that rings through night winter air; vivid, tender music that warms our hearts when the least among us aspire to the greatest things: to venture a daring enterprise; to unearth new beauty in music, literature, and art; to discover a new universe inside a tiny silicon chip or a single human cell.

We see the dream coming true in the spirit of discovery of Richard Cavoli. All his life he's been enthralled by the mysteries of medicine. And, Richard, we know that the experiment that you began in high school was launched and lost last week, yet your dream lives. And as long as it's real, work of noble note will yet be done, work that could reduce the harmful effects of x-rays on patients and enable astronomers to view the golden gateways of the farthest stars.

We see the dream glow in the towering talent of a 12-year-old, Tyrone Ford. A child prodigy of gospel music, he has surmounted personal adversity to become an accomplished pianist and singer. He also directs the choirs of three churches and has performed at the Kennedy Center. With God as your composer, Tyrone, your music will be the music of angels.

We see the dream being saved by the courage of the 13-year-old Shelby Butler, honor student and member of her school's safety patrol. Seeing another girl freeze in terror before an out-of-control school bus, she risked her life and pulled her to safety. With bravery like yours, Shelby, America need never fear for our future.

And we see the dream born again in the joyful compassion of a 13 year old, Trevor Ferrell. Two years ago, age 11, watching men and women bedding down in abandoned doorways—on television he was watching—Trevor left his suburban Philadelphia home to bring blankets and food to the helpless and homeless. And now 250 people help him fulfill his nightly vigil. Trevor, yours is the living spirit of brotherly love.

Would you four stand up for a moment? Thank you, thank you. You are heroes of our hearts. We look at you and know it's true: In this land of dreams fulfilled, where greater dreams may be imagined, nothing is impossible, no victory is beyond our reach, no glory will ever be too great.

So, now it's up to us, all of us, to prepare America for that day when our work will pale before the greatness of America's champions in the 21st century. The world's hopes rest with America's future; America's hopes rest with us. So, let us go forward to create our world of tomorrow in faith, in unity, and in love.

God bless you, and God bless America.

Address before a Joint Session of Congress on the State of the Union

January 27, 1987

Ronald Reagan's sixth State of the Union message came at a time when the Iran-contra affair, which had come to light in late 1986, was looming over his presidency. It involved Reagan administration officials secretly selling weapons to Iran and unlawfully sending some of the profits to aid contra rebels in Nicaragua. While it was never clear whether Reagan knew about the diversion, his approval rating dipped for a period, and his presidency was tarnished by the scandal.

Reagan did not devote much attention in his speech to the affair, but he did briefly note it early in the address. He stated that he had "one major regret" in having taken "a risk with regard to our action in Iran." Administration officials had hoped, through dealing with the revolutionary Iranian regime, to ameliorate relations with that country and help win freedom for American hostages held by pro-Iranian kidnappers in Lebanon.

Reagan defended the goals of the Iranian overture as "worthy," although he said that "serious mistakes were made" and that the effort had failed. He pledged to "get to the bottom" of the matter. He did not explicitly discuss any arms sales to Iran or the diversion of funds to the contras.

In the section of the address devoted to foreign policy, Reagan spent some time talking about what he saw as the threat to freedom posed by Nicaragua's communist government. "There must be no Soviet beachhead in Central America," he declared.

He also defended the administration's controversial Strategic Defense Initiative (SDI), an antimissile defense program. He commented that a summit the previous October with the Soviet Union had failed over the issue of SDI, and he pledged that the program would continue.

On the domestic side, Reagan urged support for various initiatives that were also themes in some of his previous State of the Union messages: a constitutional amendment to balance the budget, school prayer, and welfare reform.

He criticized the entire budgeting process, calling it "a sorry spectacle," and he again asked for line-item veto powers.

Reagan was now working with a Democratic-controlled House and Senate; Democrats had taken control of the Senate in the 1986 midterm elections, while maintaining their hold on the House. The seventy-five-year-old president had recently experienced another health challenge, having undergone prostate surgery on January 5.

Nineteen eighty-seven was the two hundredth anniversary of the Constitution, and Reagan spent the last section of his speech discussing the "we the people" concept and how it had defined the country. He mentioned his own mother, Nelle Reagan, whom he remembered as helping the hungry, as an example of the American spirit.

A Gallup poll taken two days after this speech of people who had watched or listened to his message found that 22.35 percent of respondents thought it made them feel more confident in him as a leader, 28.67 percent felt less confident, 48.11 percent said it had no effect, and 0.87 percent did not know.

Mr. Speaker, Mr. President, distinguished Members of Congress, honored guests, and fellow citizens:

May I congratulate all of you who are Members of this historic 100th Congress of the United States of America. In this 200th anniversary year of our Constitution, you and I stand on the shoulders of giants—men whose words and deeds put wind in the sails of freedom. However, we must always remember that our Constitution is to be celebrated not for being old, but for being young—young with the same energy, spirit, and promise that filled each eventful day in Philadelphia's statehouse. We will be guided tonight by their acts, and we will be guided forever by their words.

Now, forgive me, but I can't resist sharing a story from those historic days. Philadelphia was bursting with civic pride in the spring of 1787, and its newspapers began embellishing the arrival of the Convention delegates with elaborate social classifications. Governors of States were called Excellency. Justices and Chancellors had reserved for them honorable with a capital "H." For Congressmen, it was honorable with a small "h." And all others were referred to as "the following respectable characters." Well, for this 100th Congress, I invoke special executive powers to declare that each of you must never be titled less than honorable with a capital "H." Incidentally, I'm delighted you are celebrating the 100th birthday of the Congress. It's always a pleasure to congratulate someone with more birthdays than I've had.

Now, there's a new face at this place of honor tonight. And please join me in warm congratulations to the Speaker of the House, Jim Wright. Mr. Speaker, you might recall a similar situation in your very first session of Congress 32 years ago. Then, as now, the speakership had changed hands and another great son of Texas, Sam Rayburn—"Mr. Sam"—sat in your chair. I cannot find better words than those used by President Eisenhower that evening. He said, "We shall have much to do together; I am sure that we will get it done and that we shall do it in harmony and good will." Tonight I renew that pledge. To you, Mr. Speaker, and to Senate Majority Leader Robert Byrd, who brings 34 years of distinguished service to the Congress, may I say: Though there are changes in the Congress, America's interests remain the same. And I am confident that, along with Republican leaders Bob Michel and Bob Dole, this Congress can make history.

Six years ago I was here to ask the Congress to join me in America's new beginning. Well, the results are something of which we can all be proud. Our inflation rate is now the lowest in a quarter of a century. The prime interest rate has fallen from the 21½ percent the month before we took office to 7½ percent today. And those rates have triggered the most housing starts in 8 years. The unemployment rate—still too high—is the lowest in nearly 7 years, and our people have created nearly 13 million new jobs. Over 61 percent of everyone over the age of 16, male and female, is employed—the highest percentage on record. Let's roll up our sleeves and go to work and put America's economic engine at full throttle. We can also be heartened by our progress across the world. Most important, America is at peace tonight, and freedom is on the march. And we've done much these past years to restore our defenses, our alliances, and our leadership in the world. Our sons and daughters in the services once again wear their uniforms with pride.

But though we've made much progress, I have one major regret: I took a risk with regard to our action in Iran. It did not work, and for that I assume full responsibility. The goals were worthy. I do not believe it was wrong to try to establish contacts with a country of strategic importance or to try to save lives. And certainly it was not wrong to try to secure freedom for our citizens held in barbaric captivity. But we did not achieve what we wished, and serious mistakes were made in trying to do so. We will get to the bottom of this, and I will take whatever action is called for. But in debating the past, we must not deny ourselves the successes of the future. Let it never be said of this generation of Americans that we became so obsessed with failure that we refused to take risks that could further the cause of peace and freedom in the world. Much is at stake here, and the Nation and the world are watching to see if we go forward together in the national interest or if we let partisanship weaken us. And let there be no mistake about American policy: We will not sit idly by if our interests or our friends in the Middle East are threatened, nor will we yield to terrorist blackmail.

And now, ladies and gentlemen of the Congress, why don't we get to work? I am pleased to report that because of our efforts to rebuild the strength of America, the world is a safer place. Earlier this month I submitted a budget to defend America and maintain our momentum to make up for neglect in the last decade. Well, I ask you to vote out a defense and foreign affairs budget that says yes to protecting our country. While the world is safer, it is not safe.

Since 1970 the Soviets have invested $500 billion more on their military forces than we have. Even today, though nearly 1 in 3 Soviet families is without running hot water and the average family spends 2 hours a day shopping for the basic necessities of life, their government still found the resources to transfer $75 billion in weapons to client states in the past 5 years—clients like Syria, Vietnam, Cuba, Libya, Angola, Ethiopia, Afghanistan, and Nicaragua. With 120,000 Soviet combat and military personnel and 15,000 military advisers in Asia, Africa, and Latin America, can anyone still doubt their single-minded determination to expand their power? Despite this, the Congress cut my request for critical U.S. security assistance to free nations by 21 percent this year, and cut defense requests by $85 billion in the last 3 years.

These assistance programs serve our national interests as well as mutual interests. And when the programs are devastated, American interests are harmed. My friends, it's my duty as President to say to you again tonight that there is no surer way to lose freedom than to lose our resolve. Today the brave people of Afghanistan are showing that resolve. The Soviet Union says it wants a peaceful settlement in Afghanistan, yet it continues a brutal war and props up a regime whose days are clearly numbered. We are ready to support a political solution that guarantees the rapid withdrawal of all Soviet troops and genuine self-determination for the Afghan people.

In Central America, too, the cause of freedom is being tested. And our resolve is being tested there as well. Here, especially, the world is watching to see how this nation responds. Today over 90 percent of the people of Latin America live in democracy. Democracy is on the march in Central and South America. Communist Nicaragua is the odd man out—suppressing the church, the press, and democratic dissent and promoting subversion in the region. We support diplomatic efforts, but these efforts can never succeed if the Sandinistas win their war against the Nicaraguan people.

Our commitment to a Western Hemisphere safe from aggression did not occur by spontaneous generation on the day that we took office. It began with the Monroe Doctrine in 1823 and continues our historic bipartisan American policy. Franklin Roosevelt said we "are determined to do everything possible to maintain peace on this hemisphere." President Truman was very blunt: "International communism seeks to crush and undermine and destroy the independence of the Americas. We cannot let that happen here." And John F. Kennedy made clear that "Communist domination in this hemisphere can never be negotiated." Some in this Congress may choose to depart from this historic commitment, but I will not.

This year we celebrate the second century of our Constitution. The Sandinistas just signed theirs 2 weeks ago, and then suspended it. We won't know how my words tonight will be reported there for one simple reason: There is no free press in Nicaragua. Nicaraguan freedom fighters have never asked us to wage their battle, but I will fight any effort to shut off their lifeblood and consign them to death, defeat, or a life without freedom. There must be no Soviet beachhead in Central America.

You know, we Americans have always preferred dialog to conflict, and so, we always remain open to more constructive relations with the Soviet Union. But more responsible Soviet conduct around the world is a key element of the U.S.-Soviet agenda. Progress is also required on the other items of our agenda as well—real respect for human rights and more open contacts between our societies and, of course, arms reduction.

In Iceland, last October, we had one moment of opportunity that the Soviets dashed because they sought to cripple our Strategic Defense Initiative, SDI. I wouldn't let them do it then; I won't let them do it now or in the future. This is the most positive and promising defense program we have undertaken. It's the path, for both sides, to a safer future—a system that defends human life instead of threatening it. SDI will go forward. The United States has made serious, fair, and far-reaching proposals to the Soviet Union, and this is a moment of rare opportunity for arms reduction. But I will need, and American negotiators in Geneva will need, Congress' support. Enacting the Soviet negotiating position into American law would not be the way to win a good agreement. So, I must tell you in this Congress I will veto any effort that undercuts our national security and our negotiating leverage.

Now, today, we also find ourselves engaged in expanding peaceful commerce across the world. We will work to expand our opportunities in international markets through the Uruguay round of trade negotiations and to complete an historic free trade arrangement between the world's two largest trading partners, Canada and the United States. Our basic trade policy remains the same: We remain opposed as ever to protectionism, because America's growth and future depend on trade. But we would insist on trade that is fair and free. We are always willing to be trade partners but never trade patsies.

Now, from foreign borders let us return to our own, because America in the world is only as strong as America at home. This 100th Congress has high responsibilities. I begin with a gentle reminder that many of these are simply the incomplete obligations of the past. The American people deserve to be impatient, because we do not yet have the public house in order. We've had great success in restoring our economic integrity, and we've rescued our nation from the worst economic mess since the Depression. But there's more to do. For starters, the Federal deficit is outrageous. For years I've asked that we stop pushing onto our children the excesses of our government.

And what the Congress finally needs to do is pass a constitutional amendment that mandates a balanced budget and forces government to live within its means. States, cities, and the families of America balance their budgets. Why can't we?

Next, the budget process is a sorry spectacle. The missing of deadlines and the nightmare of monstrous continuing resolutions packing hundreds of billions of dollars of spending into one bill must be stopped. We ask the Congress once again: Give us the same tool that 43 Governors have a line-item veto so we can carve out the boondoggles and pork, those items that would never survive on their own. I will send the Congress broad recommendations on the budget, but first I'd like to see yours. Let's go to work and get this done together.

But now let's talk about this year's budget. Even though I have submitted it within the Gramm-Rudman-Hollings deficit reduction target, I have seen suggestions that we might postpone that timetable. Well, I think the American people are tired of hearing the same old excuses. Together we made a commitment to balance the budget. Now let's keep it. As for those suggestions that the answer is higher taxes, the American people have repeatedly rejected that shop-worn advice. They know that we don't have deficits because people are taxed too little. We have deficits because big government spends too much.

Now, next month I'll place two additional reforms before the Congress. We've created a welfare monster that is a shocking indictment of our sense of priorities. Our national welfare system consists of some 59 major programs and over 6,000 pages of Federal laws and regulations on which more than $132 billion was spent in 1985. I will propose a new national welfare strategy, a program of welfare reform through State-sponsored, community-based demonstration projects. This is the time to reform this outmoded social dinosaur and finally break the poverty trap. Now, we will never abandon those who, through no fault of their own, must have our help. But let us work to see how many can be freed from the dependency of welfare and made self-supporting, which the great majority of welfare recipients want more than anything else. Next, let us remove a financial specter facing our older Americans: the fear of an illness so expensive that it can result in having to make an intolerable choice between bankruptcy and death. I will submit legislation shortly to help free the elderly from the fear of catastrophic illness.

Now let's turn to the future. It's widely said that America is losing her competitive edge. Well, that won't happen if we act now. How well prepared are we to enter the 21st century? In my lifetime, America set the standard for the world. It is now time to determine that we should enter the next century having achieved a level of excellence unsurpassed in history. We will achieve this, first, by guaranteeing that government does everything possible to promote America's ability to compete. Second, we must act as individuals in a quest for excellence that will not be measured by new proposals or billions in new funding. Rather, it involves an expenditure of American spirit and just plain American grit. The Congress will soon receive my comprehensive proposals to enhance our competitiveness, including new science and technology centers and strong new funding for basic research. The bill will include legal and regulatory reforms and weapons to fight unfair trade practices. Competitiveness also means giving our farmers a shot at participating fairly and fully in a changing world market.

Preparing for the future must begin, as always, with our children. We need to set for them new and more rigorous goals. We must demand more of ourselves and our children by raising literacy levels dramatically by the year 2000. Our children should master the basic concepts of math and science, and let's insist that students not leave high school until they have studied and understood the basic documents of our national heritage. There's one more thing we can't let up on: Let's redouble our personal efforts to provide for every child a safe and drug-free learning environment. If our crusade against drugs succeeds with our children, we will defeat that scourge all over the country.

Finally, let's stop suppressing the spiritual core of our national being. Our nation could not have been conceived without divine help. Why is it that we can build a nation with our prayers, but we can't use a schoolroom for voluntary prayer? The 100th Congress of the United States should be remembered as the one that ended the expulsion of God from America's classrooms.

The quest for excellence into the 21st century begins in the schoolroom but must go next to the workplace. More than 20 million new jobs will be created before the new century unfolds, and by then, our economy should be able to provide a job for everyone who wants to work. We must also enable our workers to adapt to the rapidly changing nature of the workplace. And I will propose substantial, new Federal commitments keyed to retraining and job mobility.

Over the next few weeks, I'll be sending the Congress a complete series of these special messages—on budget reform, welfare reform, competitiveness, including education, trade, worker training and assistance, agriculture, and other subjects. The Congress can give us these tools, but to make these tools work, it really comes down to just being our best. And that is the core of American greatness. The responsibility of freedom presses us towards higher knowledge and, I believe, moral and spiritual greatness. Through lower taxes and smaller government, government has its ways of freeing people's spirits. But only we, each of us, can let the spirit soar against our own individual standards. Excellence is what makes freedom ring. And isn't that what we do best?

We're entering our third century now, but it's wrong to judge our nation by its years. The calendar can't measure America because we were meant to be an endless experiment in freedom—with no limit to our reaches, no boundaries to what we can do, no end point to our hopes. The United States Constitution is the impassioned and inspired vehicle by which we travel through history. It grew out of the most fundamental inspiration of our existence: that we are here to serve Him by living free—that living free releases in us the noblest of impulses and the best of our abilities; that we would use these gifts for good and generous purposes and would secure them not just for ourselves and for our children but for all mankind.

Over the years—I won't count if you don't—nothing has been so heartwarming to me as speaking to America's young, and the little ones especially, so fresh-faced and so eager to know. Well, from time to time I've been with them—they will ask about our Constitution. And I hope you Members of Congress will not deem this a breach of protocol if you'll permit me to share these thoughts again with the young people who might be listening or watching this evening. I've read the constitutions of a number of countries, including the Soviet Union's. Now, some people are surprised to hear that they have a constitution, and it even supposedly grants a number of freedoms to its people. Many countries have written into their constitution provisions for freedom of speech and freedom of assembly. Well, if this is true, why is the Constitution of the United States so exceptional?

Well, the difference is so small that it almost escapes you, but it's so great it tells you the whole story in just three words: We the people. In those other constitutions, the Government tells the people of those countries what they're allowed to do. In our Constitution, we the people tell the Government what it can do, and it can do only those things listed in that document and no others. Virtually every other revolution in history has just exchanged one set of rulers for another set of rulers. Our revolution is the first to say the people are the masters and government is their servant. And you young people out there, don't ever forget that. Someday you could be in this room, but wherever you are, America is depending on you to reach your highest and be your best—because here in America, we the people are in charge.

Just three words: We the people—those are the kids on Christmas Day looking out from a frozen sentry post on the 38th parallel in Korea or aboard an aircraft carrier in the Mediterranean. A million miles from home, but doing their duty.

We the people—those are the warmhearted whose numbers we can't begin to count, who'll begin the day with a little prayer for hostages they will never know and MIA families they will never meet. Why? Because that's the way we are, this unique breed we call Americans.

We the people—they're farmers on tough times, but who never stop feeding a hungry world. They're the volunteers at the hospital choking back their tears for the hundredth time, caring for a baby struggling for life because of a mother who used drugs. And you'll forgive me a special memory—it's a million mothers like Nelle Reagan who never knew a stranger or turned a hungry person away from her kitchen door.

We the people—they refute last week's television commentary downgrading our optimism and our idealism. They are the entrepreneurs, the builders, the pioneers, and a lot of regular folks—the true heroes of our land who make up the most uncommon nation of doers in history. You know they're Americans because their spirit is as big as the universe and their hearts are bigger than their spirits.

We the people—starting the third century of a dream and standing up to some cynic who's trying to tell us we're not going to get any better. Are we at the end? Well, I can't tell it any better than the real thing—a story recorded by James Madison from the final moments of the Constitutional Convention, September 17th, 1787. As the last few members signed the document, Benjamin Franklin—the oldest delegate at 81 years and in frail health—looked over toward the chair where George Washington daily presided. At the back of the chair was painted the picture of a Sun on the horizon. And turning to those sitting next to him, Franklin observed that artists found it difficult in their painting to distinguish between a rising and a setting Sun.

Well, I know if we were there, we could see those delegates sitting around Franklin—leaning in to listen more closely to him. And then Dr. Franklin began to share his deepest hopes and fears about the outcome of their efforts, and this is what he said: "I have often looked at that picture behind the President without being able to tell whether it was a rising or setting Sun: But now at length I have the happiness to know that it is a rising and not a setting Sun." Well, you can bet it's rising because, my fellow citizens, America isn't finished. Her best days have just begun.

Thank you, God bless you, and God bless America.

Address before a Joint Session of Congress on the State of the Union

January 25, 1988

Ronald Reagan's last State of the Union address was delivered before Congress in January 1988. Reagan was approaching the end of his second term and thus could not run again. But he vowed throughout the speech that he would continue to push hard on his agenda during his last year in office, declaring that "it's all out—right to the finish line."

He made a plea for bipartisanship despite the fact that 1988 was an election year, and he touted his administration's record during its seven years in office. On the domestic front, he cited "the longest peacetime expansion in history"; on the international side, he stated that a "revolution" had been undertaken with an increase in American strength and democratic efforts under way "from Central America to East Asia."

One of the first issues he discussed was the importance of eliminating federal deficits—a constant refrain throughout his administration even though the Reagan years saw the largest deficits in the nation's history. He summed up the problem: "The federal government is too big, and it spends too much money."

He also criticized the budget process, which he described as "broken down." He painted a picture of lawmakers missing deadlines and passing huge "behemoths" that they did not have time to study before having to cast their votes; he even brought copies of the hefty bills to the podium as visual aids.

Speaking on foreign policy, one of the issues Reagan mentioned—although he did not devote much attention to it—was the U.S.-Soviet treaty on banning intermediate-range nuclear forces, which he and Soviet leader Mikhail Gorbachev had signed the previous year. He urged the Senate to ratify the treaty.

The president pointed out First Lady Nancy Reagan in the audience when he mentioned efforts to combat drugs, and he praised her work on the issue. Nancy Reagan had focused on urging people to "just say no" to drugs.

Reagan's tone was upbeat; he did not mention the Iran-contra scandal that had tarnished his presidency. In addition, the president had seen two of his Supreme Court nominations fail.

Despite the fallout caused by the Iran-contra affair, the economy continued to be good, and Reagan would ultimately overcome the scandal. His presidency, which lasted eight years, would transform the political discourse, turning it in a rightward direction that would continue after he left office and would help his vice president, George Bush, win the 1988 presidential election.

Reagan returned to California, where he died in 2004 at age ninety-three, many years after being diagnosed with Alzheimer's disease.

Mr. Speaker, Mr. President, and distinguished Members of the House and Senate:

When we first met here 7 years ago—many of us for the first time—it was with the hope of beginning something new for America. We meet here tonight in this historic Chamber to continue that work. If anyone expects just a proud recitation of the accomplishments of my administration, I say let's leave that to history; we're not finished yet. So, my message to you tonight is put on your work shoes; we're still on the job.

History records the power of the ideas that brought us here those 7 years ago—ideas like the individual's right to reach as far and as high as his or her talents will permit; the free market as an engine of economic progress. And as an ancient Chinese philosopher, Lao-tzu, said: "Govern a great nation as you would cook a small fish; do not overdo it." Well, these ideas were part of a larger notion, a vision, if you will, of America herself—an America not only rich in opportunity for the individual but an America, too, of strong families and vibrant neighborhoods; an America whose divergent but harmonizing communities were a reflection of a deeper community of values: the value of work, of family, of religion, and of the love of freedom that God places in each of us and whose defense He has entrusted in a special way to this nation.

All of this was made possible by an idea I spoke of when Mr. Gorbachev was here—the belief that the most exciting revolution ever known to humankind began with three simple words: "We the People," the revolutionary notion that the people grant government its rights, and not the other way around. And there's one lesson that has come home powerfully to me, which I would offer to you now. Just as those who created this Republic pledged to each other their lives, their fortunes, and their sacred honor, so, too, America's leaders today must pledge to each other that we will keep foremost in our hearts and minds not what is best for ourselves or for our party but what is best for America.

In the spirit of Jefferson, let us affirm that in this Chamber tonight there are no Republicans, no Democrats—just Americans. Yes, we will have our differences, but let us always remember what unites us far outweighs whatever divides us. Those who sent us here to serve them—the millions of Americans watching and listening tonight—expect this of us. Let's prove to them and to ourselves that democracy works even in an election year. We've done this before. And as we have worked together to bring down spending, tax rates, and inflation, employment has climbed to record heights; America has created more jobs and better, higher paying jobs; family income has risen for 4 straight years, and America's poor climbed out of poverty at the fastest rate in more than 10 years.

Our record is not just the longest peacetime expansion in history but an economic and social revolution of hope based on work, incentives, growth, and opportunity; a revolution of compassion that led to private sector initiatives and a 77-percent increase in charitable giving; a revolution that at a critical moment in world history reclaimed and restored the American dream.

In international relations, too, there's only one description for what, together, we have achieved: a complete turnabout, a revolution. Seven years ago, America was weak, and freedom everywhere was under siege. Today America is strong, and democracy is everywhere on the move. From Central America to East Asia, ideas like free markets and democratic reforms and human rights are taking hold. We've replaced "Blame America" with "Look up to America." We've rebuilt our defenses. And of all our accomplishments, none can give us more satisfaction than knowing that our young people are again proud to wear our country's uniform.

And in a few moments, I'm going to talk about three developments—arms reduction, the Strategic Defense Initiative, and the global democratic revolution—that, when taken together, offer a chance none of us would have dared imagine 7 years ago, a chance to rid the world of the two great nightmares of the postwar era. I speak of the startling hope of giving our children a future free of both totalitarianism and nuclear terror.

Tonight, then, we're strong, prosperous, at peace, and we are free. This is the state of our Union. And if we will work together this year, I believe we can give a future President and a future Congress the chance to make that prosperity, that peace, that freedom not just the state of our Union but the state of our world.

Toward this end, we have four basic objectives tonight. First, steps we can take this year to keep our economy strong and growing, to give our children a future of low inflation and full employment. Second, let's check our progress in attacking social problems, where important gains have been made, but which still need critical attention. I mean schools that work, economic independence for the poor, restoring respect for family life and family values. Our third objective tonight is global: continuing the exciting economic and democratic revolutions we've seen around the world. Fourth and finally, our nation has remained at peace for nearly a decade and a half, as we move toward our goals of world prosperity and world freedom. We must protect that peace and deter war by making sure the next President inherits what you and I have a moral obligation to give that President: a national security that is unassailable and a national defense that takes full advantage of new technology and is fully funded.

This is a full agenda. It's meant to be. You see, my thinking on the next year is quite simple: Let's make this the best of 8. And that means it's all out—right to the finish line. I don't buy the idea that this is the last year of anything, because we're not talking here tonight about registering temporary gains but ways of making permanent our successes. And that's why our focus is the values, the principles, and ideas that made America great. Let's be clear on this point. We're for limited government, because we understand, as the Founding Fathers did, that it is the best way of ensuring personal liberty and empowering the individual so that every American of every race and region shares fully in the flowering of American prosperity and freedom.

One other thing we Americans like—the future—like the sound of it, the idea of it, the hope of it. Where others fear trade and economic growth, we see opportunities for creating new wealth and undreamed-of opportunities for millions in our own land and beyond. Where others seek to throw up barriers, we seek to bring them down. Where others take counsel of their fears, we follow our hopes. Yes, we Americans like the future and like making the most of it. Let's do that now.

And let's begin by discussing how to maintain economic growth by controlling and eventually eliminating the problem of Federal deficits. We have had a balanced budget only eight times in the last 57 years. For the first time in 14 years, the Federal Government spent less in real terms last year than the year before. We took $73 billion off last year's deficit compared to the year before. The deficit itself has moved from

6.3 percent of the gross national product to only 3.4 percent. And perhaps the most important sign of progress has been the change in our view of deficits. You know, a few of us can remember when, not too many years ago, those who created the deficits said they would make us prosperous and not to worry about the debt, because we owe it to ourselves. Well, at last there is agreement that we can't spend ourselves rich.

Our recent budget agreement, designed to reduce Federal deficits by $76 billion over the next 2 years, builds on this consensus. But this agreement must be adhered to without slipping into the errors of the past: more broken promises and more unchecked spending. As I indicated in my first State of the Union, what ails us can be simply put: The Federal Government is too big, and it spends too much money. I can assure you, the bipartisan leadership of Congress, of my help in fighting off any attempt to bust our budget agreement. And this includes the swift and certain use of the veto power.

Now, it's also time for some plain talk about the most immediate obstacle to controlling Federal deficits. The simple but frustrating problem of making expenses match revenues—something American families do and the Federal Government can't—has caused crisis after crisis in this city.

Mr. Speaker, Mr. President, I will say to you tonight what I have said before and will continue to say: The budget process has broken down; it needs a drastic overhaul. With each ensuing year, the spectacle before the American people is the same as it was this Christmas: budget deadlines delayed or missed completely, monstrous continuing resolutions that pack hundreds of billions of dollars worth of spending into one bill, and a Federal Government on the brink of default.

I know I'm echoing what you here in the Congress have said, because you suffered so directly. But let's recall that in 7 years, of 91 appropriations bills scheduled to arrive on my desk by a certain date, only 10 made it on time. Last year, of the 13 appropriations bills due by October 1st, none of them made it. Instead, we had four continuing resolutions lasting 41 days, then 36 days, and 2 days, and 3 days, respectively.

And then, along came these behemoths. This is the conference report—1,053 pages, report weighing 14 pounds. Then this—a reconciliation bill 6 months late that was 1,186 pages long, weighing 15 pounds. And the long-term continuing resolution—this one was 2 months late, and it's 1,057 pages long, weighing 14 pounds. That was a total of 43 pounds of paper and ink. You had 3 hours—yes, 3 hours—to consider each, and it took 300 people at my Office of Management and Budget just to read the bill so the Government wouldn't shut down. Congress shouldn't send another one of these. No, and if you do, I will not sign it.

Let's change all this. Instead of a Presidential budget that gets discarded and a congressional budget resolution that is not enforced, why not a simple partnership, a joint agreement that sets out the spending priorities within the available revenues? And let's remember our deadline is October 1st, not Christmas. Let's get the people's work done in time to avoid a footrace with Santa Claus. And, yes, this year—to coin a phrase—a new beginning: 13 individual bills, on time and fully reviewed by Congress.

I'm also certain you join me in saying: Let's help ensure our future of prosperity by giving the President a tool that, though I will not get to use it, is one I know future Presidents of either party must have. Give the President the same authority that 43 Governors use in their States: the right to reach into massive appropriation bills, pare away the waste, and enforce budget discipline. Let's approve the line-item veto.

And let's take a partial step in this direction. Most of you in this Chamber didn't know what was in this catchall bill and report. Over the past few weeks, we've all learned what was tucked away behind a little comma here and there. For example, there's millions for items such as cranberry research, blueberry research, the study of crawfish, and the commercialization of wildflowers. And that's not to mention the five or so million that—so that people from developing nations could come here to watch Congress at work. I won't even touch that. So, tonight I offer you this challenge. In 30 days I will send back to you those items as rescissions, which if I had the authority to line them out I would do so.

Now, review this multibillion-dollar package that will not undercut our bipartisan budget agreement. As a matter of fact, if adopted, it will improve our deficit reduction goals. And what an example we can set, that we're serious about getting our financial accounts in order. By acting and approving this plan, you have the opportunity to override a congressional process that is out of control.

There is another vital reform. Yes, Gramm-Rudman-Hollings has been profoundly helpful, but let us take its goal of a balanced budget and make it permanent. Let us do now what so many States do to hold down spending and what 32 State legislatures have asked us to do. Let us heed the wishes of an overwhelming plurality of Americans and pass a constitutional amendment that mandates a balanced budget and forces the Federal Government to live within its means. Reform of the budget process—including the line-item veto and balanced budget amendment—will, together with real restraint on government spending, prevent the Federal budget from ever again ravaging the family budget.

Let's ensure that the Federal Government never again legislates against the family and the home. Last September I signed an Executive order on the family requiring that every department and agency review its activities in light of seven standards designed to promote and not harm the family. But let us make certain that the family is always at the center of the public policy process not just in this administration but in all future administrations. It's time for Congress to consider, at the beginning, a statement of the impact that legislation will have on the basic unit of American society, the family.

And speaking of the family, let's turn to a matter on the mind of every American parent tonight: education. We all know the sorry story of the sixties and seventies—soaring spending, plummeting test scores—and that hopeful trend of the eighties, when we replaced an obsession with dollars with a commitment to quality, and test scores started back up. There's a lesson here that we all should write on the blackboard a hundred times: In a child's education, money can never take the place of basics like discipline, hard work, and, yes, homework.

As a nation we do, of course, spend heavily on education—more than we spend on defense. Yet across our country, Governors like New Jersey's Tom Kean are giving classroom demonstrations that how we spend is as important as how much we spend. Opening up the teaching profession to all qualified candidates, merit pay—so that good teachers get A's as well as apples—and stronger curriculum, as Secretary Bennett has proposed for high schools—these imaginative reforms are making common sense the most popular new kid in America's schools. How can we help? Well, we can talk about and push for these reforms. But the most important thing we can do is to reaffirm that control of our schools belongs to the States, local communities and, most of all, to the parents and teachers.

My friends, some years ago, the Federal Government declared war on poverty, and poverty won. Today the Federal Government has 59 major welfare programs and spends more than $100 billion a year on them. What has all this money done? Well, too often it has only made poverty harder to escape. Federal welfare programs have created a massive social problem. With the best of intentions, government created a poverty trap that wreaks havoc on the very support system the poor need most to lift themselves out of poverty: the family. Dependency has become the one enduring heirloom, passed from one generation to the next, of too many fragmented families.

It is time—this may be the most radical thing I've said in 7 years in this office—it's time for Washington to show a little humility. There are a thousand sparks of genius in 50 States and a thousand communities around the Nation. It is time to nurture them and see which ones can catch fire and become guiding lights. States have begun to show us the way. They've demonstrated that successful welfare programs can be built around more effective child support enforcement practices and innovative programs requiring welfare recipients to work or prepare for work. Let us give the States more flexibility and encourage more reforms. Let's start making our welfare system the first rung on America's ladder of opportunity, a boost up from dependency, not a graveyard but a birthplace of hope.

And now let me turn to three other matters vital to family values and the quality of family life. The first is an untold American success story. Recently, we released our annual survey of what graduating high school seniors have to say about drugs. Cocaine use is declining, and marijuana use was the lowest since surveying began. We can be proud that our students are just saying no to drugs. But let us remember what this menace requires: commitment from every part of America and every single American, a commitment to a drug free America. The war against drugs is a war of individual battles, a crusade with many heroes, including America's young people and also someone very special to me. She has helped so many of our young people to say no to drugs. Nancy, much credit belongs to you, and I want to express to you your husband's pride and your country's thanks. Surprised you, didn't I?

Well, now we come to a family issue that we must have the courage to confront. Tonight, I call America—a good nation, a moral people—to charitable but realistic consideration of the terrible cost of abortion on demand. To those who say this violates a woman's right to control of her own body: Can they deny that now medical evidence confirms the unborn child is a living human being entitled to life, liberty, and the pursuit of happiness? Let us unite as a nation and protect the unborn with legislation that would stop all Federal funding for abortion and with a human life amendment making, of course, an exception where the unborn child threatens the life of the mother. Our Judeo-Christian tradition recognizes the right of taking a life in self-defense. But with that one exception, let us look to those others in our land who cry out for children to adopt. I pledge to you tonight I will work to remove barriers to adoption and extend full sharing in family life to millions of Americans so that children who need homes can be welcomed to families who want them and love them.

And let me add here: So many of our greatest statesmen have reminded us that spiritual values alone are essential to our nation's health and vigor. The Congress opens its proceedings each day, as does the Supreme Court, with an acknowledgment of the Supreme Being. Yet we are denied the right to set aside in our schools a moment each day for those who wish to pray. I believe Congress should pass our school prayer amendment.

Now, to make sure there is a full nine member Supreme Court to interpret the law, to protect the rights of all Americans, I urge the Senate to move quickly and decisively in confirming Judge Anthony Kennedy to the highest Court in the land and to also confirm 27 nominees now waiting to fill vacancies in the Federal judiciary.

Here then are our domestic priorities. Yet if the Congress and the administration work together, even greater opportunities lie ahead to expand a growing world economy, to continue to reduce the threat of nuclear arms, and to extend the frontiers of freedom and the growth of democratic institutions.

Our policies consistently received the strongest support of the late Congressman Dan Daniel of Virginia. I'm sure all of you join me in expressing heartfelt condolences on his passing.

One of the greatest contributions the United States can make to the world is to promote freedom as the key to economic growth. A creative, competitive America is the answer to a changing world, not trade wars that would close doors, create greater barriers, and destroy millions of jobs. We should always remember: Protectionism is destructionism. America's jobs, America's growth, America's future depend on trade—trade that is free, open, and fair.

This year, we have it within our power to take a major step toward a growing global economy and an expanding cycle of prosperity that reaches to all the free nations of this Earth. I'm speaking of the historic free trade agreement negotiated between our country and Canada. And I can also tell you that we're determined to expand this concept, south as well as north. Next month I will be traveling to Mexico, where trade matters will be of foremost concern. And over the next several months, our Congress and the Canadian Parliament can make the start of such a North American accord a reality. Our goal must be a day when the free flow of trade, from the tip of Tierra del Fuego to the Arctic Circle, unites the people of the Western Hemisphere in a bond of mutually beneficial exchange, when all borders become what the U.S.-Canadian border so long has been: a meeting place rather than a dividing line.

This movement we see in so many places toward economic freedom is indivisible from the worldwide movement toward political freedom and against totalitarian rule. This global democratic revolution has removed the specter, so frightening a decade ago, of democracy doomed to permanent minority status in the world. In South and Central America, only a third of the people enjoyed democratic rule in 1976. Today over 90 percent of Latin Americans live in nations committed to democratic principles. And the resurgence of democracy is owed to these courageous people on almost every continent who have struggled to take control of their own destiny.

In Nicaragua the struggle has extra meaning, because that nation is so near our own borders. The recent revelations of a former high-level Sandinista major, Roger Miranda, show us that, even as they talk peace, the Communist Sandinista government of Nicaragua has established plans for a large 600,000-man army. Yet even as these plans are made, the Sandinista regime knows the tide is turning, and the cause of Nicaraguan freedom is riding at its crest. Because of the freedom fighters, who are resisting Communist rule, the Sandinistas have been forced to extend some democratic rights, negotiate with church authorities, and release a few political prisoners.

The focus is on the Sandinistas, their promises and their actions. There is a consensus among the four Central American democratic Presidents that the Sandinistas have not complied with the plan to bring peace and democracy to all of Central

America. The Sandinistas again have promised reforms. Their challenge is to take irreversible steps toward democracy. On Wednesday my request to sustain the freedom fighters will be submitted, which reflects our mutual desire for peace, freedom, and democracy in Nicaragua. I ask Congress to pass this request. Let us be for the people of Nicaragua what Lafayette, Pulaski, and Von Steuben were for our forefathers and the cause of American independence.

So, too, in Afghanistan, the freedom fighters are the key to peace. We support the Mujahidin. There can be no settlement unless all Soviet troops are removed and the Afghan people are allowed genuine self-determination. I have made my views on this matter known to Mr. Gorbachev. But not just Nicaragua or Afghanistan—yes, everywhere we see a swelling freedom tide across the world: freedom fighters rising up in Cambodia and Angola, fighting and dying for the same democratic liberties we hold sacred. Their cause is our cause: freedom.

Yet even as we work to expand world freedom, we must build a safer peace and reduce the danger of nuclear war. But let's have no illusions. Three years of steady decline in the value of our annual defense investment have increased the risk of our most basic security interests, jeopardizing earlier hard-won goals. We must face squarely the implications of this negative trend and make adequate, stable defense spending a top goal both this year and in the future.

This same concern applies to economic and security assistance programs as well. But the resolve of America and its NATO allies has opened the way for unprecedented achievement in arms reduction. Our recently signed INF treaty is historic, because it reduces nuclear arms and establishes the most stringent verification regime in arms control history, including several forms of short-notice, on-site inspection. I submitted the treaty today, and I urge the Senate to give its advice and consent to ratification of this landmark agreement. Thank you very much.

In addition to the INF [Intermediate Range Nuclear Forces] treaty, we're within reach of an even more significant START [Strategic Arms Reduction Treaty] agreement that will reduce U.S. and Soviet long-range missile—or strategic arsenals by half. But let me be clear. Our approach is not to seek agreement for agreement's sake but to settle only for agreements that truly enhance our national security and that of our allies. We will never put our security at risk—or that of our allies—just to reach an agreement with the Soviets. No agreement is better than a bad agreement.

As I mentioned earlier, our efforts are to give future generations what we never had—a future free of nuclear terror. Reduction of strategic offensive arms is one step, SDI another. Our funding request for our Strategic Defense Initiative is less than 2 percent of the total defense budget. SDI funding is money wisely appropriated and money well spent. SDI has the same purpose and supports the same goals of arms reduction. It reduces the risk of war and the threat of nuclear weapons to all mankind. Strategic defenses that threaten no one could offer the world a safer, more stable basis for deterrence. We must also remember that SDI is our insurance policy against a nuclear accident, a Chernobyl of the sky, or an accidental launch or some madman who might come along.

We've seen such changes in the world in 7 years. As totalitarianism struggles to avoid being overwhelmed by the forces of economic advance and the aspiration for human freedom, it is the free nations that are resilient and resurgent. As the global democratic revolution has put totalitarianism on the defensive, we have left behind the days of retreat. America is again a vigorous leader of the free world, a nation that acts decisively and firmly in the furtherance of her principles and vital interests. No legacy would make me more proud than leaving in place a bipartisan consensus for the cause of world freedom, a consensus that prevents a paralysis of American power from ever occurring again.

But my thoughts tonight go beyond this, and I hope you'll let me end this evening with a personal reflection. You know, the world could never be quite the same again after Jacob Shallus, a trustworthy and dependable clerk of the Pennsylvania General Assembly, took his pen and engrossed those words about representative government in the preamble of our Constitution. And in a quiet but final way, the course of human events was forever altered when, on a ridge overlooking the Emmitsburg Pike in an obscure Pennsylvania town called Gettysburg, Lincoln spoke of our duty to government of and by the people and never letting it perish from the Earth.

At the start of this decade, I suggested that we live in equally momentous times, that it is up to us now to decide whether our form of government would endure and whether history still had a place of greatness for a quiet, pleasant, greening land called America. Not everything has been made perfect in 7 years, nor will it be made perfect in seven times 70 years, but before us, this year and beyond, are great prospects for the cause of peace and world freedom.

It means, too, that the young Americans I spoke of 7 years ago, as well as those who might be coming along the Virginia or Maryland shores this night and seeing for the first time the lights of this Capital City—the lights that cast their glow on our great halls of government and the monuments to the memory of our great men—it means those young Americans will find a city of hope in a land that is free.

We can be proud that for them and for us, as those lights along the Potomac are still seen this night signaling as they have for nearly two centuries and as we pray God they always will, that another generation of Americans has protected and passed on lovingly this place called America, this shining city on a hill, this government of, by, and for the people.

Thank you, and God bless you.

George H.W. Bush

1989–1993

*"Much good can come from the prudent use
of power. And much good can come of this:
A world once divided into two armed camps
now recognizes one sole and preeminent power,
the United States of America."*

ADDRESS BEFORE A JOINT SESSION OF CONGRESS ON THE
STATE OF THE UNION, JANUARY 28, 1992

Address before a Joint Session of Congress on Administration Goals

February 9, 1989

George Bush delivered a speech to the nation in February 1989 that was not an official State of the Union message. The president had taken the oath of office the previous month, and the address sought to lay out his budget priorities.

Bush had served as Ronald Reagan's vice president for eight years, from 1981 to 1989, before ascending to the presidency—the first sitting vice president to do so since Martin Van Buren in 1836. Bush had also served as a member of the House, an ambassador, chairman of the Republican National Committee, and director of the Central Intelligence Agency. He defeated Democrat Michael Dukakis, the governor of Massachusetts, in a campaign remembered for negative campaigning.

Bush was aided by the peace and prosperity that had characterized much of Reagan's presidency. But the negativity of the 1988 contest contributed to a low voter turnout—just over 50 percent of eligible voters turned out. Bush won 426 electoral votes to Dukakis's 111 and took 54 percent of the popular vote to Dukakis's 46 percent.

The new president was following a giant. The popular Reagan had reshaped the political dialogue, moving it to the conservative right and ushering in a new era in domestic and international priorities.

In this February 9 address, Bush picked up on a theme his predecessor also had discussed: the need to tackle the federal budget deficit. Bush pledged to work with Congress to meet targets set out in federal law and produce a budget in a timely fashion. The bipartisan congressional leadership would negotiate with the White House to produce an agreement, which Bush, who called it a first step, signed on April 14. Congress was controlled by Democrats; both the Senate and House had remained Democratic in the 1988 elections.

In his February 9 speech, Bush also called for two-year, rather than annual, budgets; for line-item veto power; and for a constitutional balanced budget amendment.

On other domestic issues, he called for additional spending on education, antidrug, and environmental programs. He mentioned a mother in Pennsylvania who had written to him about her son who was addicted to cocaine; she had urged him to curb the supply of the drug. "The scourge of drugs must be stopped," he declared.

Bush termed international peace a key priority, stating that "we meet at a time of extraordinary hope." Changes were under way in the Soviet Union and Eastern Europe; Bush expressed cautious optimism about these developments while also vowing to continue pursuing the Strategic Defense Initiative antimissile defense program.

Mr. Speaker, Mr. President, and distinguished Members of the House and Senate, honored guests, and fellow citizens:

Less than 3 weeks ago, I joined you on the West Front of this very building and, looking over the monuments to our proud past, offered you my hand in filling the next page of American history with a story of extended prosperity and continued peace. And tonight I'm back to offer you my plans as well. The hand remains extended; the sleeves are rolled up; America is waiting; and now we must produce. Together, we can build a better America.

It is comforting to return to this historic Chamber. Here, 22 years ago, I first raised my hand to be sworn into public life. So, tonight I feel as if I'm returning home to friends. And I intend, in the months and years to come, to give you what friends deserve: frankness, respect, and my best judgment about ways to improve America's future. In return, I ask for an honest commitment to our common mission of progress. If we seize the opportunities on the road before us, there'll be praise enough for all. The people didn't send us here to bicker, and it's time to govern.

And many Presidents have come to this Chamber in times of great crisis: war and depression, loss of national spirit. And 8 years ago, I sat in that very chair as President Reagan spoke of punishing inflation and devastatingly high interest rates and people out of work—American confidence on the wane. And our challenge is different. We're fortunate—a much changed landscape lies before us tonight. So, I don't propose to reverse direction. We're headed the right way, but we cannot rest. We're a people whose energy and drive have fueled our rise to greatness. And we're a forward-looking nation—generous, yes, but ambitious, not for ourselves but for the world. Complacency is not in our character—not before, not now, not ever.

And so, tonight we must take a strong America and make it even better. We must address some very real problems. We must establish some very clear priorities. And we must make a very substantial cut in the Federal budget deficit. Some people find that agenda impossible, but I'm presenting to you tonight a realistic plan for tackling it. My plan has four broad features: attention to urgent priorities, investment in the future, an attack on the deficit, and no new taxes. This budget represents my best judgment of how we can address our priorities. There are many areas in which we would all like to spend more than I propose; I understand that. But we cannot until we get our fiscal house in order.

Next year alone, thanks to economic growth, without any change in the law, the Federal Government will take in over $80 billion more than it does this year. That's right—over $80 billion in new revenues, with no increases in taxes. And our job is to allocate those new resources wisely. We can afford to increase spending by a modest amount, but enough to invest in key priorities and still cut the deficit by almost 40 percent in 1 year. And that will allow us to meet the targets set forth in the Gramm-Rudman-Hollings law. But to do that, we must recognize that growth above inflation in Federal programs is not preordained, that not all spending initiatives were designed to be immortal.

I make this pledge tonight: My team and I are ready to work with the Congress, to form a special leadership group, to negotiate in good faith, to work day and night—if that's what it takes—to meet the budget targets and to produce a budget on time.

We cannot settle for business as usual. Government by continuing resolution, or government by crisis, will not do. And I ask the Congress tonight to approve several measures which will make budgeting more sensible. We could save time and improve efficiency by enacting 2-year budgets. Forty-three Governors have the line-item veto. Presidents should have it, too. And at the very least, when a President proposes to rescind Federal spending, the Congress should be required to vote on that proposal instead of killing it by inaction. And I ask the Congress to honor the public's wishes by passing a constitutional amendment to require a balanced budget. Such an amendment, once phased in, will discipline both the Congress and the executive branch.

Several principles describe the kind of America I hope to build with your help in the years ahead. We will not have the luxury of taking the easy, spendthrift approach to solving problems because higher spending and higher taxes put economic growth at risk. Economic growth provides jobs and hope. Economic growth enables us to pay for social programs. Economic growth enhances the security of the Nation, and low tax rates create economic growth.

I believe in giving Americans greater freedom and greater choice. And I will work for choice for American families, whether in the housing in which they live, the schools to which they send their children, or the child care they select for their young. You see, I believe that we have an obligation to those in need, but that government should not be the provider of first resort for things that the private sector can produce better. I believe in a society that is free from discrimination and bigotry of any kind. And I will work to knock down the barriers left by past discrimination and to build a more tolerant society that will stop such barriers from ever being built again.

I believe that family and faith represent the moral compass of the Nation. And I'll work to make them strong, for as Benjamin Franklin said: "If a sparrow cannot fall to the ground without His notice, can a great nation rise without His aid?" And I believe in giving people the power to make their own lives better through growth and opportunity. And together, let's put power in the hands of people.

Three weeks ago, we celebrated the bicentennial inaugural, the 200th anniversary of the first Presidency. And if you look back, one thing is so striking about the way the Founding Fathers looked at America. They didn't talk about themselves. They talked about posterity. They talked about the future. And we, too, must think in terms bigger than ourselves. We must take actions today that will ensure a better tomorrow. We must extend American leadership in technology, increase long-term investment, improve our educational system, and boost productivity. These are the keys to building a better future, and here are some of my recommendations:

I propose almost $2.2 billion for the National Science Foundation to promote basic research and keep us on track to double its budget by 1993.

I propose to make permanent the tax credit for research and development.

I've asked Vice President [Dan] Quayle to chair a new Task Force on Competitiveness.

And I request funding for NASA and a strong space program, an increase of almost $2.4 billion over the current fiscal year. We must have a manned space station; a vigorous, safe space shuttle program; and more commercial development in space. The space program should always go "full throttle up." And that's not just our ambition; it's our destiny.

I propose that we cut the maximum tax rate on capital gains to increase long-term investment. History on this is clear—this will increase revenues, help savings, and create new jobs. We won't be competitive if we leave whole sectors of America behind. This is the year we should finally enact urban enterprise zones and bring hope to the inner cities.

But the most important competitiveness program of all is one which improves education in America. When some of our students actually have trouble locating America on a map of the world, it is time for us to map a new approach to education. We must reward excellence and cut through bureaucracy. We must help schools that need help the most. We must give choice to parents, students, teachers, and principals; and we must hold all concerned accountable. In education, we cannot tolerate mediocrity. I want to cut that dropout rate and make America a more literate nation, because what it really comes down to is this: The longer our graduation lines are today, the shorter our unemployment lines will be tomorrow.

So, tonight I'm proposing the following initiatives: the beginning of a $500 million program to reward America's best schools, merit schools; the creation of special Presidential awards for the best teachers in every State, because excellence should be rewarded; the establishment of a new program of National Science Scholars, one each year for every Member of the House and Senate, to give this generation of students a special incentive to excel in science and mathematics; the expanded use of magnet schools, which give families and students greater choice; and a new program to encourage alternative certification, which will let talented people from all fields teach in our classrooms. I've said I'd like to be the "Education President." And tonight, I'd ask you to join me by becoming the "Education Congress."

Just last week, as I settled into this new office, I received a letter from a mother in Pennsylvania who had been struck by my message in the Inaugural Address. "Not 12 hours before," she wrote, "my husband and I received word that our son was addicted to cocaine. He had the world at his feet. Bright, gifted, personable—he could have done anything with his life. And now he has chosen cocaine." "And please," she wrote, "find a way to curb the supply of cocaine. Get tough with the pushers. Our son needs your help."

My friends, that voice crying out for help could be the voice of your own neighbor, your own friend, your own son. Over 23 million Americans used illegal drugs last year, at a staggering cost to our nation's well-being. Let this be recorded as the time when America rose up and said no to drugs. The scourge of drugs must be stopped. And I am asking tonight for an increase of almost a billion dollars in budget outlays to escalate the war against drugs. The war must be waged on all fronts. Our new drug czar, Bill Bennett, and I will be shoulder to shoulder in the executive branch leading the charge.

Some money will be used to expand treatment to the poor and to young mothers. This will offer the helping hand to the many innocent victims of drugs, like the thousands of babies born addicted or with AIDS because of the mother's addiction. Some will be used to cut the waiting time for treatment. Some money will be devoted to those urban schools where the emergency is now the worst. And much of it will be used to protect our borders, with help from the Coast Guard and the Customs Service, the Departments of State and Justice, and, yes, the U.S. military.

I mean to get tough on the drug criminals. And let me be clear: This President will back up those who put their lives on the line every single day—our local police officers. My budget asks for beefed-up prosecution, for a new attack on organized crime, and for enforcement of tough sentences—and for the worst kingpins, that means the death penalty. I also want to make sure that when a drug dealer is convicted there's a cell waiting for him. And he should not go free because prisons are too full. And so, let the word go out: If you're caught and convicted, you will do time.

But for all we do in law enforcement, in interdiction and treatment, we will never win this war on drugs unless we stop the demand for drugs. So, some of this increase will be used to educate the young about the dangers of drugs. We must involve the parents. We must involve the teachers. We must involve the communities. And, my friends, we must involve ourselves, each and every one of us in this concern.

One problem related to drug use demands our urgent attention and our continuing compassion, and that is the terrible tragedy of AIDS. I'm asking for $1.6 billion for education to prevent the disease and for research to find a cure.

If we're to protect our future, we need a new attitude about the environment. We must protect the air we breathe. I will send to you shortly legislation for a new, more effective Clean Air Act. It will include a plan to reduce by date certain the emissions which cause acid rain, because the time for study alone has passed, and the time for action is now. We must make use of clean coal. My budget contains full funding, on schedule, for the clean coal technology agreement that we've made with Canada. We've made that agreement with Canada, and we intend to honor that agreement. We must not neglect our parks. So, I'm asking to fund new acquisitions under the Land and Water Conservation Fund. We must protect our oceans. And I support new penalties against those who would dump medical waste and other trash into our oceans. The age of the needle on the beaches must end.

And in some cases, the gulfs and oceans off our shores hold the promise of oil and gas reserves which can make our nation more secure and less dependent on foreign oil. And when those with the most promise can be tapped safely, as with much of the Alaska National Wildlife Refuge, we should proceed. But we must use caution; we must respect the environment. And so, tonight I'm calling for the indefinite postponement of three lease sales which have raised troubling questions, two off the coast of California and one which could threaten the Everglades in Florida. Action on these three lease sales will await the conclusion of a special task force set up to measure the potential for environmental damage.

I'm directing the Attorney General and the Administrator of the Environmental Protection Agency to use every tool at their disposal to speed and toughen the enforcement of our laws against toxic-waste dumpers. I want faster cleanups and tougher enforcement of penalties against polluters.

In addition to caring for our future, we must care for those around us. A decent society shows compassion for the young, the elderly, the vulnerable, and the poor. Our first obligation is to the most vulnerable—infants, poor mothers, children living in poverty—and my proposed budget recognizes this. I ask for full funding of Medicaid, an increase of over $3 billion, and an expansion of the program to include coverage of pregnant women who are near the poverty line. I believe we should help working families cope with the burden of child care. Our help should be aimed at those who need it most: low-income families with young children. I support a new child care tax credit that will aim our efforts at exactly those families, without discriminating against mothers who choose to stay at home.

Now, I know there are competing proposals. But remember this: The overwhelming majority of all preschool child care is now provided by relatives and neighbors and churches and community groups. Families who choose these options should remain eligible for help. Parents should have choice. And for those children who are unwanted or abused or whose parents are deceased, we should encourage adoption. I propose to reenact the tax deduction for adoption expenses and to double it to $3,000. Let's make it easier for these kids to have parents who love them.

We have a moral contract with our senior citizens. And in this budget, Social Security is fully funded, including a full cost-of-living adjustment. We must honor our contract.

We must care about those in the shadow of life, and I, like many Americans, am deeply troubled by the plight of the homeless. The causes of homelessness are many; the history is long. But the moral imperative to act is clear. Thanks to the deep well of generosity in this great land, many organizations already contribute, but we in government cannot stand on the sidelines. In my budget, I ask for greater support for emergency food and shelter, for health services and measures to prevent substance abuse, and for clinics for the mentally ill. And I propose a new initiative involving the full range of government agencies. We must confront this national shame.

There's another issue that I've decided to mention here tonight. I've long believed that the people of Puerto Rico should have the right to determine their own political future. Personally, I strongly favor statehood. But I urge the Congress to take the necessary steps to allow the people to decide in a referendum.

Certain problems, the result of decades of unwise practices, threaten the health and security of our people. Left unattended, they will only get worse. But we can act now to put them behind us.

Earlier this week, I announced my support for a plan to restore the financial and moral integrity of our savings system. I ask Congress to enact our reform proposals within 45 days. We must not let this situation fester. We owe it to the savers in this country to solve this problem. Certainly, the savings of Americans must remain secure. Let me be clear: Insured depositors will continue to be fully protected, but any plan to refinance the system must be accompanied by major reform. Our proposals will prevent such a crisis from recurring. The best answer is to make sure that a mess like this will never happen again. The majority of thrifts in communities across the Nation have been honest. They've played a major role in helping families achieve the dream of home ownership. But make no mistake, those who are corrupt, those who break the law, must be kicked out of the business; and they should go to jail.

We face a massive task in cleaning up the waste left from decades of environmental neglect at America's nuclear weapons plants. Clearly, we must modernize these plants and operate them safely. That's not at issue; our national security depends on it. But beyond that, we must clean up the old mess that's been left behind. And I propose in this budget to more than double our current effort to do so. This will allow us to identify the exact nature of the various problems so we can clean them up, and clean them up we will.

We've been fortunate during these past 8 years. America is a stronger nation than it was in 1980. Morale in our Armed Forces has been restored; our resolve has been shown. Our readiness has been improved, and we are at peace. There can no longer be any doubt that peace has been made more secure through strength. And when America is stronger, the world is safer.

Most people don't realize that after the successful restoration of our strength, the Pentagon budget has actually been reduced in real terms for each of the last 4 years. We cannot tolerate continued real reduction in defense. In light of the compelling need to reduce the deficit, however, I support a 1-year freeze in the military budget, something I proposed last fall in my flexible freeze plan. And this freeze will apply for only 1 year, and after that, increases above inflation will be required. I will not sacrifice American preparedness, and I will not compromise American strength.

I should be clear on the conditions attached to my recommendation for the coming year: The savings must be allocated to those priorities for investing in our future that I've spoken about tonight. This defense freeze must be a part of a comprehensive budget agreement which meets the targets spelled out in Gramm-Rudman-Hollings law without raising taxes and which incorporates reforms in the budget process.

I've directed the National Security Council to review our national security and defense policies and report back to me within 90 days to ensure that our capabilities and resources meet our commitments and strategies. I'm also charging the Department of Defense with the task of developing a plan to improve the defense procurement process and management of the Pentagon, one which will fully implement the Packard commission report. Many of these changes can only be made with the participation of the Congress, and so, I ask for your help. We need fewer regulations. We need less bureaucracy. We need multiyear procurement and 2-year budgeting. And frankly— and don't take this wrong—we need less congressional micromanagement of our nation's military policy. I detect a slight division on that question, but nevertheless.

Securing a more peaceful world is perhaps the most important priority I'd like to address tonight. You know, we meet at a time of extraordinary hope. Never before in this century have our values of freedom, democracy, and economic opportunity been such a powerful and intellectual force around the globe. Never before has our leadership been so crucial, because while America has its eyes on the future, the world has its eyes on America.

And it's a time of great change in the world, and especially in the Soviet Union. Prudence and common sense dictate that we try to understand the full meaning of the change going on there, review our policies, and then proceed with caution. But I've personally assured General Secretary [Mikhail] Gorbachev that at the conclusion of such a review we will be ready to move forward. We will not miss any opportunity to work for peace. The fundamental facts remain that the Soviets retain a very powerful military machine in the service of objectives which are still too often in conflict with ours. So, let us take the new openness seriously, but let's also be realistic. And let's always be strong.

There are some pressing issues we must address. I will vigorously pursue the Strategic Defense Initiative. The spread, and even use, of sophisticated weaponry threatens global security as never before. Chemical weapons must be banned from the face of the Earth, never to be used again. And look, this won't be easy. Verification—extraordinarily difficult, but civilization and human decency demand that we try. And the spread of nuclear weapons must be stopped. And I'll work to strengthen the hand of the International Atomic Energy Agency. Our diplomacy must work every day against the proliferation of nuclear weapons.

And around the globe, we must continue to be freedom's best friend. And we must stand firm for self-determination and democracy in Central America, including in Nicaragua. It is my strongly held conviction that when people are given the chance they inevitably will choose a free press, freedom of worship, and certifiably free and fair elections.

We must strengthen the alliance of the industrial democracies, as solid a force for peace as the world has ever known. And this is an alliance forged by the power of our ideals, not the pettiness of our differences. So, let's lift our sights to rise above fighting about beef hormones, to building a better future, to move from protectionism to progress.

I've asked the Secretary of State to visit Europe next week and to consult with our allies on the wide range of challenges and opportunities we face together, including East-West relations. And I look forward to meeting with our NATO partners in the near future.

And I, too, shall begin a trip shortly to the far reaches of the Pacific Basin, where the winds of democracy are creating new hope and the power of free markets is unleashing a new force. When I served as our representative in China 14 or 15 years ago, few would have predicted the scope of the changes we've witnessed since then. But in preparing for this trip, I was struck by something I came across from a Chinese writer. He was speaking of his country, decades ago, but his words speak to each of us in America tonight. "Today," he said, "we're afraid of the simple words like 'goodness' and 'mercy' and 'kindness.'" My friends, if we're to succeed as a nation, we must rediscover those words.

In just 3 days, we mark the birthday of Abraham Lincoln, the man who saved our Union and gave new meaning to the word "opportunity." Lincoln once said: "I hold that while man exists, it is his duty to improve not only his own condition but to assist in ameliorating that of mankind." It is this broader mission to which I call all Americans, because the definition of a successful life must include serving others.

And to the young people of America, who sometimes feel left out, I ask you tonight to give us the benefit of your talent and energy through a new program called YES, for Youth Entering Service to America.

To those men and women in business, remember the ultimate end of your work: to make a better product, to create better lives. I ask you to plan for the longer term and avoid that temptation of quick and easy paper profits.

To the brave men and women who wear the uniform of the United States of America, thank you. Your calling is a high one: to be the defenders of freedom and the guarantors of liberty. And I want you to know that this nation is grateful for your service.

To the farmers of America, we appreciate the bounty you provide. We will work with you to open foreign markets to American agricultural products.

And to the parents of America, I ask you to get involved in your child's schooling. Check on the homework, go to the school, meet the teachers, care about what is happening there. It's not only your child's future on the line, it's America's.

To kids in our cities, don't give up hope. Say no to drugs; stay in school. And, yes, "Keep hope alive."

To those 37 million Americans with some form of disability, you belong in the economic mainstream. We need your talents in America's work force. Disabled Americans must become full partners in America's opportunity society.

To the families of America watching tonight in your living rooms, hold fast to your dreams because ultimately America's future rests in your hands.

And to my friends in this Chamber, I ask your cooperation to keep America growing while cutting the deficit. That's only fair to those who now have no vote: the generations to come. Let them look back and say that we had the foresight to understand that a time of peace and prosperity is not the time to rest but a time to press forward, a time to invest in the future.

And let all Americans remember that no problem of human making is too great to be overcome by human ingenuity, human energy, and the untiring hope of the human spirit. I believe this. I would not have asked to be your President if I didn't. And tomorrow the debate on the plan I've put forward begins, and I ask the Congress to come forward with your own proposals. Let's not question each other's motives. Let's debate, let's negotiate; but let us solve the problem.

Recalling anniversaries may not be my specialty in speeches but tonight is one of some note. On February 9th, 1941, just 48 years ago tonight, Sir Winston Churchill took to the airwaves during Britain's hour of peril. He'd received from President Roosevelt a hand-carried letter quoting Longfellow's famous poem: "Sail on, O Ship of State! Sail on, O Union, strong and great! Humanity with all its fears, With all the hopes of future years, Is hanging breathless on thy fate!" And Churchill responded on this night by radio broadcast to a nation at war, but he directed his words to Franklin Roosevelt. "We shall not fail or falter," he said. "We shall not weaken or tire. Give us the tools, and we will finish the job."

Tonight, almost half a century later, our peril may be less immediate, but the need for perseverance and clear-sighted fortitude is just as great. Now, as then, there are those who say it can't be done. There are voices who say that America's best days have passed, that we're bound by constraints, threatened by problems, surrounded by troubles which limit our ability to hope. Well, tonight I remain full of hope. We Americans have only begun on our mission of goodness and greatness. And to those timid souls, I repeat the plea: "Give us the tools, and we will do the job."

Thank you. God bless you, and God bless America.

George H. W. Bush, 1989–1993

Address before a Joint Session of Congress on the State of the Union

January 31, 1990

George Bush delivered his first official State of the Union address before Congress in January 1990. It had been a momentous year on the international front, with the Soviet empire crumbling, the Berlin Wall falling, and Eastern European countries forming new democratic governments. In addition, the United States had sent troops to topple the Panamanian regime of strongman Manuel Noriega in late 1989. Bush began his speech by discussing foreign policy, declaring that the previous year had ushered in the start of "a new era in the world's affairs." He stated that U.S. forces in Panama would all be home by the end of February.

On the European front, he cited the fall of the Berlin Wall and new democratic governments in Poland and Czechoslovakia, stating that these events served to "validate" American policy goals and devotion to freedom. "America stands at the center of a widening circle of freedom," the president declared.

He moved on to domestic issues, focusing on education in particular. He had met with governors at an education summit the previous year, and he discussed various goals—including increasing the rate of high school graduation to no less than 90 percent.

While much of his address was not especially partisan, one line, in which he pledged to balance the budget by 1993 with no new taxes, resulted in a standing ovation from his fellow Republicans while Democrats remained in their seats. Another phrase that drew a partisan reaction was when the president reiterated his support for a capital gains tax cut.

Bush returned to international issues toward the end of the speech. He read from a letter written by Private First Class James Markwell, who had written before his death in the Panama invasion that he joined the army to protect freedom. Bush discussed Markwell's letter in the context of Americans living up to their ideals.

In the wake of the changes in Europe, Bush called for a reduction in U.S. and Soviet forces in the region to 195,000 on each side.

He concluded by discussing the birth of his twelfth grandchild and spoke on how children around the world share similar dreams. He asked grandparents to tell grandchildren about sacrifices made for freedom and parents to teach children about liberty.

Bush came into office with a strong background in foreign affairs, having served as ambassador to the United Nations and as chief diplomat in China, as well as head of the Central Intelligence Agency. International relations would dominate his presidency, with the leadup later that year to the 1991 Persian Gulf War.

Mr. President, Mr. Speaker, Members of the United States Congress:

I return as a former President of the Senate and a former Member of this great House. And now, as President, it is my privilege to report to you on the state of the Union.

Tonight I come not to speak about the state of the Government, not to detail every new initiative we plan for the coming year nor to describe every line in the budget. I'm here to speak to you and to the American people about the state of the Union, about our world—the changes we've seen, the challenges we face—and what that means for America.

There are singular moments in history, dates that divide all that goes before from all that comes after. And many of us in this Chamber have lived much of our lives in a world whose fundamental features were defined in 1945; and the events of that year decreed the shape of nations, the pace of progress, freedom or oppression for millions of people around the world.

Nineteen forty-five provided the common frame of reference, the compass points of the postwar era we've relied upon to understand ourselves. And that was our world, until now. The events of the year just ended, the Revolution of '89, have been a chain reaction, changes so striking that it marks the beginning of a new era in the world's affairs.

Think back—think back just 12 short months ago to the world we knew as 1989 began.

One year—one year ago, the people of Panama lived in fear, under the thumb of a dictator. Today democracy is restored; Panama is free. Operation Just Cause has achieved its objective. The number of military personnel in Panama is now very close to what it was before the operation began. And tonight I am announcing that well before the end of February, the additional numbers of American troops, the brave men and women of our Armed Forces who made this mission a success, will be back home.

A year ago in Poland, Lech Walesa declared that he was ready to open a dialog with the Communist rulers of that country; and today, with the future of a free Poland in their own hands, members of Solidarity lead the Polish Government.

A year ago, freedom's playwright, Vaclav Havel, languished as a prisoner in Prague. And today it's Vaclav Havel, President of Czechoslovakia.

And 1 year ago, Erich Hoenecker of East Germany claimed history as his guide, and he predicted the Berlin Wall would last another hundred years. And today, less than 1 year later, it's the Wall that's history.

Remarkable events—events that fulfill the long-held hopes of the American people; events that validate the longstanding goals of American policy, a policy based on a single, shining principle: the cause of freedom.

America, not just the nation but an idea, alive in the minds of people everywhere. As this new world takes shape, America stands at the center of a widening circle of freedom—today, tomorrow, and into the next century. Our nation is the enduring dream of every immigrant who ever set foot on these shores, and the millions still struggling to be free. This nation, this idea called America, was and always will be a new world—our new world.

At a workers' rally, in a place called Branik on the outskirts of Prague, the idea called America is alive. A worker, dressed in grimy overalls, rises to speak at the factory gates. He begins his speech to his fellow citizens with these words, words of a distant revolution: "We hold these truths to be self-evident, that all men are created equal, that they are endowed by their Creator with certain unalienable Rights, and that among these are Life, Liberty and the pursuit of Happiness."

It's no secret that here at home freedom's door opened long ago. The cornerstones of this free society have already been set in place: democracy, competition, opportunity, private investment, stewardship, and of course leadership. And our challenge today is to take this democratic system of ours, a system second to none, and make it better: a better America, where there's a job for everyone who wants one; where women working outside the home can be confident their children are in safe and loving care and where government works to expand child-care alternatives for parents; where we reconcile the needs of a clean environment and a strong economy; where "Made in the USA" is recognized around the world as the symbol of quality and progress; where every one of us enjoys the same opportunities to live, to work, and to contribute to society and where, for the first time, the American mainstream includes all of our disabled citizens; where everyone has a roof over his head and where the homeless get the help they need to live in dignity; where our schools challenge and support our kids and our teachers and where all of them make the grade; where every street, every city, every school, and every child is drug-free; and finally, where no American is forgotten—our hearts go out to our hostages who are ceaselessly on our minds and in our efforts.

That's part of the future we want to see, the future we can make for ourselves, but dreams alone won't get us there. We need to extend our horizon, commit to the long view. And our mission for the future starts today.

In the tough competitive markets around the world, America faces the great challenges and great opportunities. And we know that we can succeed in the global economic arena of the nineties, but to meet that challenge, we must make some fundamental changes—some crucial investment in ourselves.

Yes, we are going to invest in America. This administration is determined to encourage the creation of capital, capital of all kinds: physical capital—everything from our farms and factories to our workshops and production lines, all that is needed to produce and deliver quality goods and quality services; intellectual capital—the source of ideas that spark tomorrow's products; and of course our human capital—the talented work force that we'll need to compete in the global market.

Let me tell you, if we ignore human capital, if we lose the spirit of American ingenuity, the spirit that is the hallmark of the American worker, that would be bad. The American worker is the most productive worker in the world.

We need to save more. We need to expand the pool of capital for new investments that need more jobs and more growth. And that's the idea behind a new initiative I call the Family Savings Plan, which I will send to Congress tomorrow.

We need to cut the tax on capital gains, encourage risktakers, especially those in our small businesses, to take those steps that translate into economic reward, jobs, and a better life for all of us.

We'll do what it takes to invest in America's future. The budget commitment is there. The money is there. It's there for research and development, R&D—a record high. It's there for our housing initiative—HOPE [Home Ownership Participation for Everyone]—to help everyone from first-time homebuyers to the homeless. The money's there to keep our kids drug-free—70 percent more than when I took office in 1989. It's there for space exploration. And it's there for education—another record high.

And one more thing: Last fall at the education summit, the Governors and I agreed to look for ways to help make sure that our kids are ready to learn the very first day they walk into the classroom. And I've made good on that commitment by proposing a record increase in funds—an extra half-a-billion dollars—for something near and dear to all of us: Head Start.

Education is the one investment that means more for our future because it means the most for our children. Real improvement in our schools is not simply a matter of spending more: It's a matter of asking more—expecting more—of our schools, our teachers, of our kids, of our parents, and ourselves. And that's why tonight I am announcing America's education goals, goals developed with enormous cooperation from the Nation's Governors. And if I might, I'd like to say I'm very pleased that Governor [Booth] Gardner and Governor [Bill] Clinton, Governor [Terry] Branstad, Governor [Carroll] Campbell, all of whom were very key in these discussions, these deliberations, are with us here tonight.

By the year 2000, every child must start school ready to learn.

The United States must increase the high school graduation rate to no less than 90 percent.

And we are going to make sure our schools' diplomas mean something. In critical subjects—at the 4th, 8th, and 12th grades—we must assess our students' performance.

By the year 2000, U.S. students must be first in the world in math and science achievement.

Every American adult must be a skilled, literate worker and citizen.

Every school must offer the kind of disciplined environment that makes it possible for our kids to learn. And every school in America must be drug-free.

Ambitious aims? Of course. Easy to do? Far from it. But the future's at stake. The Nation will not accept anything less than excellence in education.

These investments will keep America competitive. And I know this about the American people: We welcome competition. We'll match our ingenuity, our energy, our experience and technology, our spirit and enterprise against anyone. But let the competition be free, but let it also be fair. America is ready.

Since we really mean it and since we're serious about being ready to meet that challenge, we're getting our own house in order. We have made real progress. Seven years ago, the Federal deficit was 6 percent of our gross national product—6 percent. In the new budget I sent up 2 days ago, the deficit is down to 1 percent of gross national product.

That budget brings Federal spending under control. It meets the Gramm-Rudman target. It brings that deficit down further and balances the budget by 1993 with no new taxes. And let me tell you, there's still more than enough Federal spending. For most of us, $1.2 trillion is still a lot of money.

And once the budget is balanced, we can operate the way every family must when it has bills to pay. We won't leave it to our children and our grandchildren. Once it's balanced, we will start paying off the national debt.

And there's something more we owe the generations of the future: stewardship, the safekeeping of America's precious environmental inheritance. It's just one sign of how serious we are. We will elevate the Environmental Protection Agency to Cabinet rank—not more bureaucracy, not more red tape, but the certainty that here at home, and especially in our dealings with other nations, environmental issues have the status they deserve.

This year's budget provides over $2 billion in new spending to protect our environment, with over $1 billion for global change research, and a new initiative I call America the Beautiful to expand our national parks and wildlife preserves that improve recreational facilities on public lands, and something else, something that will help keep this country clean from our forestland to the inner cities and keep America beautiful for generations to come: the money to plant a billion trees a year.

And tonight let me say again to all the Members of the Congress: The American people did not send us here to bicker. There is work to do, and they sent us here to get it done. And once again, in the spirit of cooperation, I offer my hand to all of you. Let's work together to do the will of the people: clean air, child care, the Educational Excellence Act, crime, and drugs. It's time to act. The farm bill, transportation policy, product-liability reform, enterprise zones—it's time to act together.

And there's one thing I hope we will be able to agree on. It's about our commitments. I'm talking about Social Security. To every American out there on Social Security, to every American supporting that system today, and to everyone counting on it when they retire, we made a promise to you, and we are going to keep it.

We rescued the system in 1983, and it's sound again—bipartisan arrangement. Our budget fully funds today's benefits, and it assures that future benefits will be funded as well. The last thing we need to do is mess around with Social Security.

There's one more problem we need to address. We must give careful consideration to the recommendations of the health-care studies underway now. That's why tonight

I'm asking Dr. Sullivan, Lou Sullivan, Secretary of Health and Human Services, to lead a Domestic Policy Council review of recommendations on the quality, accessibility, and cost of our nation's health-care system. I am committed to bring the staggering costs of health care under control.

The state of the Government does indeed depend on many of us in this very chamber. But the state of the Union depends on all Americans. We must maintain the democratic decency that makes a nation out of millions of individuals. I've been appalled at the recent mail bombings across this country. Every one of us must confront and condemn racism, anti-Semitism, bigotry, and hate, not next week, not tomorrow, but right now—every single one of us.

The state of the Union depends on whether we help our neighbor—claim the problems of our community as our own. We've got to step forward when there's trouble, lend a hand, be what I call a point of light to a stranger in need. We've got to take the time after a busy day to sit down and read with our kids, help them with their homework, pass along the values we learned as children. That's how we sustain the state of the Union. Every effort is important. It all adds up. It's doing the things that give democracy meaning. It all adds up to who we are and who we will be.

Let me say that so long as we remember the American idea, so long as we live up to the American ideal, the state of the Union will remain sound and strong.

And to those who worry that we've lost our way—well, I want you to listen to parts of a letter written by Private First Class James Markwell, a 20-year-old Army medic of the 1st Battalion, 75th Rangers. It's dated December 18th, the night before our armed forces went into action in Panama. It's a letter servicemen write and hope will never be sent. And sadly, Private Markwell's mother did receive this letter. She passed it along to me out there in Cincinnati.

And here is some of what he wrote: "I've never been afraid of death, but I know he is waiting at the corner. I've been trained to kill and to save, and so has everyone else. I am frightened what lays beyond the fog, and yet do not mourn for me. Revel in the life that I have died to give you. But most of all, don't forget the Army was my choice. Something that I wanted to do. Remember I joined the Army to serve my country and ensure that you are free to do what you want and live your lives freely."

Let me add that Private Markwell was among the first to see battle in Panama, and one of the first to fall. But he knew what he believed in. He carried the idea we call America in his heart.

I began tonight speaking about the changes we've seen this past year. There is a new world of challenges and opportunities before us, and there's a need for leadership that only America can provide. Nearly 40 years ago, in his last address to the Congress, President Harry Truman predicted such a time would come. He said: "As our world grows stronger, more united, more attractive to men on both sides of the Iron Curtain, then inevitably there will come a time of change within the Communist world." Today, that change is taking place.

For more than 40 years, America and its allies held communism in check and ensured that democracy would continue to exist. And today, with communism crumbling, our aim must be to ensure democracy's advance, to take the lead in forging peace and freedom's best hope: a great and growing commonwealth of free nations. And to the Congress and to all Americans, I say it is time to acclaim a new consensus at home and abroad, a common vision of the peaceful world we want to see.

Here in our own hemisphere, it is time for all the peoples of the Americas, North and South, to live in freedom. In the Far East and Africa, it's time for the full flowering of free governments and free markets that have served as the engine of progress. It's time to offer our hand to the emerging democracies of Eastern Europe so that continent—for too long a continent divided—can see a future whole and free. It's time to build on our new relationship with the Soviet Union, to endorse and encourage a peaceful process of internal change toward democracy and economic opportunity.

We are in a period of great transition, great hope, and yet great uncertainty. We recognize that the Soviet military threat in Europe is diminishing, but we see little change in Soviet strategic modernization. Therefore, we must sustain our own strategic offense modernization and the Strategic Defense Initiative.

But the time is right to move forward on a conventional arms control agreement to move us to more appropriate levels of military forces in Europe, a coherent defense program that ensures the U.S. will continue to be a catalyst for peaceful change in Europe. And I've consulted with leaders of NATO. In fact, I spoke by phone with President Gorbachev just today.

I agree with our European allies that an American military presence in Europe is essential and that it should not be tied solely to the Soviet military presence in Eastern Europe. But our troop levels can still be lower. And so, tonight I am announcing a major new step for a further reduction in U.S. and Soviet manpower in Central and Eastern Europe to 195,000 on each side. This level reflects the advice of our senior military advisers. It's designed to protect American and European interests and sustain NATO's defense strategy. A swift conclusion to our arms control talks—conventional, chemical, and strategic—must now be our goal. And that time has come.

Still, we must recognize an unfortunate fact: In many regions of the world tonight, the reality is conflict, not peace. Enduring animosities and opposing interests remain. And thus, the cause of peace must be served by an America strong enough and sure enough to defend our interests and our ideals. It's this American idea that for the past four decades helped inspire this Revolution of '89.

Here at home and in the world, there's history in the making, history to be made. Six months ago, early in this season of change, I stood at the gates of the Gdansk shipyard in Poland at the monument to the fallen workers of Solidarity. It's a monument of simple majesty. Three tall crosses rise up from the stones, and atop each cross, an anchor—an ancient symbol of hope.

The anchor in our world today is freedom, holding us steady in times of change, a symbol of hope to all the world. And freedom is at the very heart of the idea that is America. Giving life to that idea depends on every one of us. Our anchor has always been faith and family.

In the last few days of this past momentous year, our family was blessed once more, celebrating the joy of life when a little boy became our 12th grandchild. When I held the little guy for the first time, the troubles at home and abroad seemed manageable and totally in perspective.

Now, I know you're probably thinking, well, that's just a grandfather talking. Well, maybe you're right. But I've met a lot of children this past year across this country, as all of you have, everywhere from the Far East to Eastern Europe. And all kids are unique, and yet all kids are alike—the budding young environmentalists I met this month who joined me in exploring the Florida Everglades; the little leaguers I played catch with in Poland, ready to go from Warsaw to the World Series; and even the kids who are ill or alone—and God bless those boarder babies, born addicted to drugs and AIDS and coping with problems no child should have to face. But you know, when it comes to hope and the future, every kid is the same—full of dreams, ready to take on the world—all special, because they are the very future of freedom. And to them belongs this new world I've been speaking about.

And so, tonight I'm going to ask something of every one of you. Now, let me start with my generation, with the grandparents out there. You are our living link to the past. Tell your grandchildren the story of struggles waged at home and abroad, of sacrifices freely made for freedom's sake. And tell them your own story as well, because every American has a story to tell.

And, parents, your children look to you for direction and guidance. Tell them of faith and family. Tell them we are one nation under God. Teach them that of all the many gifts they can receive liberty is their most precious legacy, and of all the gifts they can give the greatest is helping others.

And to the children and young people out there tonight: With you rests our hope, all that America will mean in the years and decades ahead. Fix your vision on a new century—your century, on dreams we cannot see, on the destiny that is yours and yours alone.

And finally, let all Americans—all of us together here in this Chamber, the symbolic center of democracy—affirm our allegiance to this idea we call America. And let us remember that the state of the Union depends on each and every one of us.

God bless all of you, and may God bless this great nation, the United States of America.

George H. W. Bush, 1989–1993

Address before a Joint Session of Congress on the State of the Union

January 29, 1991

Operation Desert Storm, a military effort in the Persian Gulf to remove Iraqi forces from neighboring Kuwait, was launched in mid-January 1991. It formed the backdrop of George Bush's second State of the Union address before Congress. The Capitol was under tight security, with bomb-sniffing dogs on duty and adjacent streets blocked off.

On August 2, 1990, Iraq had invaded Kuwait; the United States saw this as a dangerous precedent as well as a threat to oil reserves in the region. Having been invited to send troops to Saudi Arabia, the Bush administration organized a coalition of European and Arab states in support. After diplomatic efforts failed, the coalition forces began bombing Iraq on January 17, 1991—twelve days before the State of the Union address.

At the time of the speech, it was not clear whether Operation Desert Storm would succeed. In the end, Bush ordered a cease-fire on February 28, after Iraq had been driven from Kuwait. The six-week military operation was considered a success, with most Americans rallying behind the president. Iraqi leader Saddam Hussein remained in power, however; his regime would not be toppled until U.S. troops again went to war in Iraq in 2003, under the presidency of Bush's son, George W. Bush.

In this January 29 speech, Bush sought to gain support for the operation, declaring that "we lead the world in facing down a threat to decency and humanity." He praised the troops serving in the Gulf and spoke of ensuring the "stability and security" of the region. He acknowledged the presence in the audience of Brenda Schwarzkopf and Alma Powell, wives of two of the nation's top military leaders— General Norman Schwarzkopf, commander of the coalition forces in the Gulf War, and General Colin Powell, chairman of the Joint Chiefs of Staff.

Turning to issues outside the Persian Gulf region, Bush discussed the end of the Cold War between the United States and the Soviet Union, calling it "a victory for all humanity." He credited America's leadership as being "instrumental" in the crumbling of the Soviet empire and pledged to work toward U.S.-Soviet cooperation.

On the domestic side, Bush's political fortunes were deteriorating. The country had been in a recession since the previous summer, and the president read from a letter written by Kathy Blackwell of Massachusetts, who said that "people out here are hurting badly." Bush vowed to move forward with the economy, mentioning both short- and long-term fixes, including control of federal spending, lower interest rates, and competition in world markets.

The president referred to the "controversial" budget agreement of the previous fall, which included a tax raise for those with high-incomes; this conflicted with Bush's 1988 campaign pledge of no new taxes and angered voters.

A Gallup poll taken between January 30 and February 2, 1991, found that 80.9 percent of viewers and listeners thought Bush did a good job of explaining why the U.S. military was in the Persian Gulf. Only 16.26 percent disagreed; 2.84 percent did not know or refused to answer.

M r. President and Mr. Speaker and Members of the United States Congress:

I come to this House of the people to speak to you and all Americans, certain that we stand at a defining hour. Halfway around the world, we are engaged in a great struggle in the skies and on the seas and sands. We know why we're there: We are Americans, part of something larger than ourselves. For two centuries, we've done the hard work of freedom. And tonight, we lead the world in facing down a threat to decency and humanity.

What is at stake is more than one small country; it is a big idea: a new world order, where diverse nations are drawn together in common cause to achieve the universal aspirations of mankind—peace and security, freedom, and the rule of law. Such is a world worthy of our struggle and worthy of our children's future.

The community of nations has resolutely gathered to condemn and repel lawless aggression. Saddam Hussein's unprovoked invasion—his ruthless, systematic rape of a peaceful neighbor—violated everything the community of nations holds dear. The world has said this aggression would not stand, and it will not stand. Together, we have resisted the trap of appeasement, cynicism, and isolation that gives temptation to tyrants. The world has answered Saddam's invasion with 12 United Nations resolutions, starting with a demand for Iraq's immediate and unconditional withdrawal, and backed up by forces from 28 countries of 6 continents. With few exceptions, the world now stands as one.

The end of the cold war has been a victory for all humanity. A year and a half ago, in Germany, I said that our goal was a Europe whole and free. Tonight, Germany is united. Europe has become whole and free, and America's leadership was instrumental in making it possible.

Our relationship to the Soviet Union is important, not only to us but to the world. That relationship has helped to shape these and other historic changes. But like many other nations, we have been deeply concerned by the violence in the Baltics, and we have communicated that concern to the Soviet leadership. The principle that has guided us is simple: Our objective is to help the Baltic peoples achieve their aspirations, not to punish the Soviet Union. In our recent discussions with the Soviet leadership we have been given representations which, if fulfilled, would result in the withdrawal of some Soviet forces, a reopening of dialog with the Republics, and a move away from violence.

We will watch carefully as the situation develops. And we will maintain our contact with the Soviet leadership to encourage continued commitment to democratization and reform. If it is possible, I want to continue to build a lasting basis for U.S.-Soviet cooperation—for a more peaceful future for all mankind.

The triumph of democratic ideas in Eastern Europe and Latin America and the continuing struggle for freedom elsewhere all around the world all confirm the wisdom of our nation's founders. Tonight, we work to achieve another victory, a victory over tyranny and savage aggression.

We in this Union enter the last decade of the 20th century thankful for our blessings, steadfast in our purpose, aware of our difficulties, and responsive to our duties at home and around the world. For two centuries, America has served the world as an inspiring example of freedom and democracy. For generations, America has led the struggle to preserve and extend the blessings of liberty. And today, in a rapidly changing world, American leadership is indispensable. Americans know that leadership brings burdens and sacrifices. But we also know why the hopes of humanity turn to us. We are Americans; we have a unique responsibility to do the hard work of freedom. And when we do, freedom works.

The conviction and courage we see in the Persian Gulf today is simply the American character in action. The indomitable spirit that is contributing to this victory for world peace and justice is the same spirit that gives us the power and the potential to meet our toughest challenges at home. We are resolute and resourceful. If we can selflessly confront the evil for the sake of good in a land so far away, then surely we can make this land all that it should be. If anyone tells you that America's best days are behind her, they're looking the wrong way.

Tonight I come before this House and the American people with an appeal for renewal. This is not merely a call for new government initiatives; it is a call for new initiatives in government, in our communities, and from every American to prepare for the next American century.

America has always led by example. So, who among us will set the example? Which of our citizens will lead us in this next American century? Everyone who steps forward today—to get one addict off drugs, to convince one troubled teenager not to give up on life, to comfort one AIDS patient, to help one hungry child.

We have within our reach the promise of a renewed America. We can find meaning and reward by serving some higher purpose than ourselves, a shining purpose, the illumination of a Thousand Points of Light. And it is expressed by all who know the irresistible force of a child's hand, of a friend who stands by you and stays there, a volunteer's generous gesture, an idea that is simply right.

The problems before us may be different, but the key to solving them remains the same. It is the individual—the individual who steps forward. And the state of our Union is the union of each of us, one to the other—the sum of our friendships, marriages, families, and communities.

We all have something to give. So, if you know how to read, find someone who can't. If you've got a hammer, find a nail. If you're not hungry, not lonely, not in trouble, seek out someone who is. Join the community of conscience. Do the hard work of freedom. And that will define the state of our Union.

Since the birth of our nation, "We the People" has been the source of our strength. What government can do alone is limited, but the potential of the American people knows no limits.

We are a nation of rock-solid realism and clear-eyed idealism. We are Americans. We are the Nation that believes in the future. We are the Nation that can shape the future. And we've begun to do just that, by strengthening the power and choice of individuals and families.

Together, these last 2 years, we've put dollars for child care directly in the hands of parents instead of bureaucracies; unshackled the potential of Americans with disabilities; applied the creativity of the marketplace in the service of the environment, for clean air; and made home ownership possible for more Americans.

The strength of a democracy is not in bureaucracy. It is in the people and their communities. In everything we do, let us unleash the potential of our most precious resource—our citizens, our citizens themselves. We must return to families, communities, counties, cities, States, and institutions of every kind the power to chart their own destiny and the freedom and opportunity provided by strong economic growth. And that's what America is all about.

I know that tonight, in some regions of our country, people are in genuine economic distress. And I hear them. Earlier this month, Kathy Blackwell, of Massachusetts, wrote me about what can happen when the economy slows down, saying, "My heart is aching, and I think that you should know your people out here are hurting badly."

I understand, and I'm not unrealistic about the future. But there are reasons to be optimistic about our economy. First, we don't have to fight double-digit inflation. Second, most industries won't have to make big cuts in production because they don't have big inventories piled up. And third, our exports are running solid and strong. In fact, American businesses are exporting at a record rate.

So, let's put these times in perspective. Together, since 1981, we've created almost 20 million jobs, cut inflation in half, and cut interest rates in half. And yes, the largest peacetime economic expansion in history has been temporarily interrupted. But our economy is still over twice as large as our closest competitor.

We will get this recession behind us and return to growth soon. We will get on our way to a new record of expansion and achieve the competitive strength that will carry us into the next American century. We should focus our efforts today on encouraging economic growth, investing in the future, and giving power and opportunity to the individual.

We must begin with control of Federal spending. That's why I'm submitting a budget that holds the growth in spending to less than the rate of inflation. And that's why, amid all the sound and fury of last year's budget debate, we put into law new, enforceable spending caps, so that future spending debates will mean a battle of ideas, not a bidding war.

Though controversial, the budget agreement finally put the Federal Government on a pay-as-you-go plan and cut the growth of debt by nearly $500 billion. And that frees funds for saving and job-creating investment.

Now, let's do more. My budget again includes tax-free family savings accounts; penalty-free withdrawals from IRA's for first-time home buyers; and to increase jobs and growth, a reduced tax for long-term capital gains.

I know there are differences among us about the impact and the effects of a capital gains incentive. So tonight, I'm asking the congressional leaders and the Federal Reserve to cooperate with us in a study, led by Chairman Alan Greenspan, to sort out our technical differences so that we can avoid a return to unproductive partisan bickering.

But just as our efforts will bring economic growth now and in the future, they must also be matched by long-term investments for the next American century. That requires a forward-looking plan of action, and that's exactly what we will be sending to the Congress. We've prepared a detailed series of proposals that include: a budget that promotes investment in America's future—in children, education, infrastructure, space, and high technology; legislation to achieve excellence in education, building on the partnership forged with the 50 Governors at the education summit, enabling parents to choose their children's schools and helping to make America number one in math and science; a blueprint for a new national highway system, a critical investment in our transportation infrastructure; a research and development agenda that includes record levels of Federal investment, and a permanent tax credit to strengthen private R&D and to create jobs; a comprehensive national energy strategy that calls for energy conservation and efficiency, increased development, and greater use of alternative fuels; a banking reform plan to bring America's financial system into the 21st century so that our banks remain safe and secure and can continue to make job-creating loans for our factories, our businesses, and home buyers.

You know, I do think there has been too much pessimism. Sound banks should be making sound loans now, and interest rates should be lower, now.

In addition to these proposals, we must recognize that our economic strength depends on being competitive in world markets. We must continue to expand American exports. A successful Uruguay round of world trade negotiations will create more real jobs and more real growth for all nations. You and I know that if the playing field is level, America's workers and farmers can out-work, out-produce anyone, anytime, anywhere.

And with a Mexican free trade agreement and our Enterprise for the Americas Initiative, we can help our partners strengthen their economies and move toward a free trade zone throughout this entire hemisphere.

The budget also includes a plan of action right here at home to put more power and opportunity in the hands of the individual. And that means new incentives to create jobs in our inner cities by encouraging investment through enterprise zones. It also means tenant control and ownership of public housing. Freedom and the power to choose should not be the privilege of wealth. They are the birthright of every American.

Civil rights are also crucial to protecting equal opportunity. Every one of us has a responsibility to speak out against racism, bigotry, and hate. We will continue our vigorous enforcement of existing statutes, and I will once again press the Congress to strengthen the laws against employment discrimination without resorting to the use of unfair preferences.

We're determined to protect another fundamental civil right: freedom from crime and the fear that stalks our cities. The Attorney General will soon convene a crime summit of our nation's law enforcement officials. And to help us support them, we need tough crime control legislation, and we need it now.

And as we fight crime, we will fully implement our national strategy for combating drug abuse. Recent data show that we are making progress, but much remains to be done. We will not rest until the day of the dealer is over, forever.

Good health care is every American's right and every American's responsibility. And so, we are proposing an aggressive program of new prevention initiatives—for infants, for children, for adults, and for the elderly—to promote a healthier America and to help keep costs from spiraling.

It's time to give people more choice in government by reviving the ideal of the citizen politician who comes not to stay but to serve. And one of the reasons that there is so much support across this country for term limitations is that the American people are increasingly concerned about big-money influence in politics. So, we must look beyond the next election to the next generation. And the time has come to put the national interest above the special interest and to totally eliminate political action committees. And that would truly put more competition in elections and more power in the hands of individuals.

And where power cannot be put directly in the hands of the individual, it should be moved closer to the people, away from Washington. The Federal Government too often treats government programs as if they are of Washington, by Washington, and for Washington. Once established, Federal programs seem to become immortal. It's time for a more dynamic program life cycle. Some programs should increase. Some should decrease. Some should be terminated. And some should be consolidated and turned over to the States.

My budget includes a list of programs for potential turnover totaling more than $20 billion. Working with Congress and the Governors, I propose we select at least $15 billion in such programs and turn them over to the States in a single consolidated grant, fully funded, for flexible management by the States.

The value, the value of this turnover approach is straightforward. It allows the Federal Government to reduce overhead. It allows States to manage more flexibly and more efficiently. It moves power and decisionmaking closer to the people. And it reinforces a theme of this administration: appreciation and encouragement of the innovative powers of States as laboratories.

This nation was founded by leaders who understood that power belongs in the hands of people. And they planned for the future. And so must we, here and all around the world.

As Americans, we know that there are times when we must step forward and accept our responsibility to lead the world away from the dark chaos of dictators, toward the brighter promise of a better day. Almost 50 years ago we began a long struggle against aggressive totalitarianism. Now we face another defining hour for America and the world.

There is no one more devoted, more committed to the hard work of freedom than every soldier and sailor, every marine, airman, and coastguardsman, every man and woman now serving in the Persian Gulf. Oh, how they deserve and what a fitting tribute to them.

You see—what a wonderful, fitting tribute to them. Each of them has volunteered, volunteered to provide for this nation's defense, and now they bravely struggle to earn for America, for the world, and for future generations a just and lasting peace. Our commitment to them must be equal to their commitment to their country. They are truly America's finest.

The war in the Gulf is not a war we wanted. We worked hard to avoid war. For more than 5 months we—along with the Arab League, the European Community, the United Nations—tried every diplomatic avenue. U.N. Secretary-General [Javier] Perez de Cuellar; Presidents [Mikhail] Gorbachev, [François] Mitterrand, [Turgut] Ozal, [Hosni] Mubarak, and [Chadli] Bendjedid; Kings Fahd [Bin Abdul Aziz] and Hassan [II]; Prime Ministers [John] Major and [Giulio] Andreotti—just to name a few—all worked for a solution. But time and again, Saddam Hussein flatly rejected the path of diplomacy and peace.

The world well knows how this conflict began and when: It began on August 2d, when Saddam invaded and sacked a small, defenseless neighbor. And I am certain of how it will end. So that peace can prevail, we will prevail. Thank you.

Tonight I am pleased to report that we are on course. Iraq's capacity to sustain war is being destroyed. Our investment, our training, our planning—all are paying off. Time will not be Saddam's salvation.

Our purpose in the Persian Gulf remains constant: to drive Iraq out of Kuwait, to restore Kuwait's legitimate government, and to ensure the stability and security of this critical region.

Let me make clear what I mean by the region's stability and security. We do not seek the destruction of Iraq, its culture, or its people. Rather, we seek an Iraq that uses its great resources not to destroy, not to serve the ambitions of a tyrant, but to build a better life for itself and its neighbors. We seek a Persian Gulf where conflict is no longer the rule, where the strong are neither tempted nor able to intimidate the weak.

Most Americans know instinctively why we are in the Gulf. They know we had to stop Saddam now, not later. They know that this brutal dictator will do anything, will use any weapon, will commit any outrage, no matter how many innocents suffer.

They know we must make sure that control of the world's oil resources does not fall into his hands, only to finance further aggression. They know that we need to build a new, enduring peace, based not on arms races and confrontation but on shared principles and the rule of law.

And we all realize that our responsibility to be the catalyst for peace in the region does not end with the successful conclusion of this war.

Democracy brings the undeniable value of thoughtful dissent, and we've heard some dissenting voices here at home—some, a handful, reckless; most responsible. But the fact that all voices have the right to speak out is one of the reasons we've been united in purpose and principle for 200 years.

Our progress in this great struggle is the result of years of vigilance and a steadfast commitment to a strong defense. Now, with remarkable technological advances like the Patriot missile, we can defend against ballistic missile attacks aimed at innocent civilians.

Looking forward, I have directed that the SDI program be refocused on providing protection from limited ballistic missile strikes, whatever their source. Let us pursue an SDI program that can deal with any future threat to the United States, to our forces overseas, and to our friends and allies.

The quality of American technology, thanks to the American worker, has enabled us to successfully deal with difficult military conditions and help minimize precious loss of life. We have given our men and women the very best. And they deserve it.

We all have a special place in our hearts for the families of our men and women serving in the Gulf. They are represented here tonight by Mrs. Norman Schwarzkopf. We are all very grateful to General Schwarzkopf and to all those serving with him. And I might also recognize one who came with Mrs. Schwarzkopf: Alma Powell, the wife of the distinguished Chairman of the Joint Chiefs. And to the families, let me say our forces in the Gulf will not stay there one day longer than is necessary to complete their mission.

The courage and success of the RAF pilots, of the Kuwaiti, Saudi, French, the Canadians, the Italians, the pilots of Qatar and Bahrain—all are proof that for the first time since World War II, the international community is united. The leadership of the United Nations, once only a hoped-for ideal, is now confirming its founders' vision.

I am heartened that we are not being asked to bear alone the financial burdens of this struggle. Last year, our friends and allies provided the bulk of the economic costs of Desert Shield. And now, having received commitments of over $40 billion for the first 3 months of 1991, I am confident they will do no less as we move through Desert Storm.

But the world has to wonder what the dictator of Iraq is thinking. If he thinks that by targeting innocent civilians in Israel and Saudi Arabia, that he will gain advantage, he is dead wrong. If he thinks that he will advance his cause through tragic and despicable environmental terrorism, he is dead wrong. And if he thinks that by abusing the coalition prisoners of war he will benefit, he is dead wrong.

We will succeed in the Gulf. And when we do, the world community will have sent an enduring warning to any dictator or despot, present or future, who contemplates outlaw aggression.

The world can, therefore, seize this opportunity to fulfill the long-held promise of a new world order, where brutality will go unrewarded and aggression will meet collective resistance.

Yes, the United States bears a major share of leadership in this effort. Among the nations of the world, only the United States of America has both the moral standing and the means to back it up. We're the only nation on this Earth that could assemble the forces of peace. This is the burden of leadership and the strength that has made America the beacon of freedom in a searching world.

This nation has never found glory in war. Our people have never wanted to abandon the blessings of home and work for distant lands and deadly conflict. If we fight in anger, it is only because we have to fight at all. And all of us yearn for a world where we will never have to fight again.

Each of us will measure within ourselves the value of this great struggle. Any cost in lives—any cost—is beyond our power to measure. But the cost of closing our eyes to aggression is beyond mankind's power to imagine. This we do know: Our cause is just; our cause is moral; our cause is right.

Let future generations understand the burden and the blessings of freedom. Let them say we stood where duty required us to stand. Let them know that, together, we affirmed America and the world as a community of conscience.

The winds of change are with us now. The forces of freedom are together, united. We move toward the next century more confident than ever that we have the will at home and abroad to do what must be done—the hard work of freedom.

May God bless the United States of America. Thank you very, very much.

George H. W. Bush, 1989–1993

Address before a Joint Session of Congress on the State of the Union
January 28, 1992

George Bush's third and last State of the Union message was delivered before Congress at the start of an election year, and Bush, a Republican, was seeking another four-year term in office.

The president's address focused primarily on the faltering economy. He set out some short-term measures, including a ninety-day moratorium on new federal regulations that he said could hurt growth, as well as a change in the federal tax-withholding tables that would let Americans withhold less from their paychecks. In addition, he urged Congress to pass a capital gains tax reduction, a goal he had sought before but had yet to achieve.

Bush noted that it was an election year, but said that he was putting the country before politics when it came to his plan for the economy. Some observers, though, saw this speech as the start of his presidential campaign. He laid out a series of long-term economic plans, including working to open world markets, improving American education, encouraging research and development, and fighting crime and drugs.

He began his speech with a look at the international scene, which was a more pleasing prospect given the end of the Soviet Union as well as the American success in the Persian Gulf War. He declared that "communism died this year," and that "America won the cold war." He spoke of major cuts in the U.S. nuclear force, including elimination of or reductions in various types of missiles. He commented that, with the decades-long conflict over, "we can look homeward even more" to deal with domestic problems. On the issue of the Gulf War, Bush quoted from a telegram written by Joanne Speicher, whose husband had been the first pilot killed in the Gulf, stating that the war had been the right thing to do.

Bush's popularity had taken a major dive the previous year, falling below 50 percent at the time of this address. At the end of the war, he had near record-breaking ratings of about 90 percent. But they plummeted as the war receded from people's minds and the sour economy continued.

A Gallup poll taken on January 28 found that the speech made 38 percent of respondents more likely to vote to reelect Bush and 8 percent less likely; 50 percent said the speech made no difference to their voting plans, and 3 percent did not know or refused to answer.

The president faced Democrat Bill Clinton and independent billionaire Ross Perot in the November elections, in which an anti-incumbent mood prevailed. Clinton won the three-way race, taking 43 percent of the popular vote to Bush's 38 percent and Perot's 19. Clinton took 370 electoral votes; Bush won 168. Both houses of Congress remained Democratic, giving Democrats control of both ends of Pennsylvania Avenue.

Bush later had the satisfaction of seeing his son George W. Bush win two terms as president, in 2000 and 2004. They became the second father-son presidential duo, after John Adams and John Quincy Adams.

Mr. Speaker and Mr. President, distinguished Members of Congress, honored guests, and fellow citizens:

Thank you very much for that warm reception. You know, with the big buildup this address has had, I wanted to make sure it would be a big hit, but I couldn't convince Barbara to deliver it for me.

I see the Speaker and the Vice President are laughing. They saw what I did in Japan, and they're just happy they're sitting behind me.

I mean to speak tonight of big things, of big changes and the promises they hold, and of some big problems and how, together, we can solve them and move our country forward as the undisputed leader of the age.

We gather tonight at a dramatic and deeply promising time in our history and in the history of man on Earth. For in the past 12 months, the world has known changes of almost Biblical proportions. And even now, months after the failed coup that doomed a failed system, I'm not sure we've absorbed the full impact, the full import of what happened. But communism died this year.

Even as President, with the most fascinating possible vantage point, there were times when I was so busy managing progress and helping to lead change that I didn't always show the joy that was in my heart. But the biggest thing that has happened in the world in my life, in our lives, is this: By the grace of God, America won the cold war.

I mean to speak this evening of the changes that can take place in our country, now that we can stop making the sacrifices we had to make when we had an avowed enemy that was a superpower. Now we can look homeward even more and move to set right what needs to be set right.

I will speak of those things. But let me tell you something I've been thinking these past few months. It's a kind of rollcall of honor. For the cold war didn't end; it was won. And I think of those who won it, in places like Korea and Vietnam. And some of them didn't come back. Back then they were heroes, but this year they were victors.

The long rollcall, all the G.I. Joes and Janes, all the ones who fought faithfully for freedom, who hit the ground and sucked the dust and knew their share of horror.

This may seem frivolous, and I don't mean it so, but it's moving to me how the world saw them. The world saw not only their special valor but their special style: their rambunctious, optimistic bravery, their do-or-die unity unhampered by class or race or region. What a group we've put forth, for generations now, from the ones who wrote "Kilroy was here" on the walls of the German stalags to those who left signs in the Iraqi desert that said, "I saw Elvis." What a group of kids we've sent out into the world.

And there's another to be singled out, though it may seem inelegant, and I mean a mass of people called the American taxpayer. No one ever thinks to thank the people who pay a country's bill or an alliance's bill. But for half a century now, the American people have shouldered the burden and paid taxes that were higher than they would have been to support a defense that was bigger than it would have been if imperial communism had never existed. But it did; doesn't anymore. And here's a fact I wouldn't mind the world acknowledging: The American taxpayer bore the brunt of the burden and deserves a hunk of the glory.

So now, for the first time in 35 years, our strategic bombers stand down. No longer are they on 'round-the-clock alert. Tomorrow our children will go to school and study history and how plants grow. And they won't have, as my children did, air raid drills in which they crawl under their desks and cover their heads in case of nuclear war. My grandchildren don't have to do that and won't have the bad dreams children had once, in decades past. There are still threats. But the long, drawn-out dread is over.

A year ago tonight, I spoke to you at a moment of high peril. American forces had just unleashed Operation Desert Storm. And after 40 days in the desert skies and 4 days on the ground, the men and women of America's Armed Forces and our allies accomplished the goals that I declared and that you endorsed: We liberated Kuwait. Soon after, the Arab world and Israel sat down to talk seriously and comprehensively about peace, an historic first. And soon after that, at Christmas, the last American hostages came home. Our policies were vindicated.

Much good can come from the prudent use of power. And much good can come of this: A world once divided into two armed camps now recognizes one sole and preeminent power, the United States of America. And they regard this with no dread. For the world trusts us with power, and the world is right. They trust us to be fair and restrained. They trust us to be on the side of decency. They trust us to do what's right.

I use those words advisedly. A few days after the war began, I received a telegram from Joanne Speicher, the wife of the first pilot killed in the Gulf, Lieutenant Commander Scott Speicher. Even in her grief, she wanted me to know that some day when her children were old enough, she would tell them "that their father went away to war because it was the right thing to do." And she said it all: It was the right thing to do.

And we did it together. There were honest differences right here in this Chamber. But when the war began, you put partisanship aside, and we supported our troops. This is still a time for pride, but this is no time to boast. For problems face us, and we must stand together once again and solve them and not let our country down.

Two years ago, I began planning cuts in military spending that reflected the changes of the new era. But now, this year, with imperial communism gone, that process can be accelerated. Tonight I can tell you of dramatic changes in our strategic nuclear force. These are actions we are taking on our own because they are the right thing to do. After completing 20 planes for which we have begun procurement, we will shut down further production of the B-2 bombers. We will cancel the small ICBM [intercontinental ballistic missile] program. We will cease production of new warheads for our sea-based ballistic missiles. We will stop all new production of the Peacekeeper missile. And we will not purchase any more advanced cruise missiles.

This weekend I will meet at Camp David with Boris Yeltsin of the Russian Federation. I've informed President Yeltsin that if the Commonwealth, the former Soviet Union, will eliminate all land-based multiple-warhead ballistic missiles, I will do the following: We will eliminate all Peacekeeper missiles. We will reduce the number of warheads on Minuteman missiles to one and reduce the number of warheads on our sea-based missiles by about one-third. And we will convert a substantial portion of our strategic bombers to primarily conventional use. President Yeltsin's early response has been very positive, and I expect our talks at Camp David to be fruitful.

I want you to know that for half a century, American Presidents have longed to make such decisions and say such words. But even in the midst of celebration, we must keep caution as a friend. For the world is still a dangerous place. Only the dead have seen the end of conflict. And though yesterday's challenges are behind us, tomorrow's are being born.

The Secretary of Defense recommended these cuts after consultation with the Joint Chiefs of Staff. And I make them with confidence. But do not misunderstand me. The reductions I have approved will save us an additional $50 billion over the next 5 years. By 1997, we will have cut defense by 30 percent since I took office. These cuts are deep, and you must know my resolve: This deep, and no deeper. To do less would be insensible to progress, but to do more would be ignorant of history. We must not go back to the days of "the hollow army." We cannot repeat the mistakes made twice in this century when armistice was followed by recklessness and defense was purged as if the world were permanently safe.

I remind you this evening that I have asked for your support in funding a program to protect our country from limited nuclear missile attack. We must have this protection because too many people in too many countries have access to nuclear arms. And I urge you again to pass the Strategic Defense Initiative, SDI.

There are those who say that now we can turn away from the world, that we have no special role, no special place. But we are the United States of America, the leader of the West that has become the leader of the world. And as long as I am President, I will continue to lead in support of freedom everywhere, not out of arrogance, not out of altruism, but for the safety and security of our children. This is a fact: Strength in the pursuit of peace is no vice; isolationism in the pursuit of security is no virtue.

And now to our troubles at home. They're not all economic; the primary problem is our economy. There are some good signs. Inflation, that thief, is down. And interest rates are down. But unemployment is too high, some industries are in trouble, and growth is not what it should be. Let me tell you right from the start and right from the heart, I know we're in hard times. But I know something else: This will not stand.

In this Chamber, in this Chamber we can bring the same courage and sense of common purpose to the economy that we brought to Desert Storm. And we can defeat hard times together. I believe you'll help. One reason is that you're patriots, and you want the best for your country. And I believe that in your hearts you want to put partisanship aside and get the job done because it's the right thing to do.

The power of America rests in a stirring but simple idea, that people will do great things if only you set them free. Well, we're going to set the economy free. For if this age of miracles and wonders has taught us anything, it's that if we can change the world we can change America. We must encourage investment. We must make it easier for people to invest money and create new products, new industries, and new jobs. We must clear away the obstacles to growth: high taxes, high regulation, red tape, and yes, wasteful Government spending.

None of this will happen with a snap of the fingers, but it will happen. And the test of a plan isn't whether it's called new or dazzling. The American people aren't impressed by gimmicks; they're smarter on this score than all of us in this room. The only test of a plan is: Is it sound, and will it work?

We must have a short-term plan to address our immediate needs and heat up the economy. And then we need a longer term plan to keep combustion going and to guarantee our place in the world economy. There are certain things that a President can do without Congress, and I'm going to do them.

I have, this evening, asked major Cabinet departments and Federal agencies to institute a 90-day moratorium on any new Federal regulations that could hinder growth. In those 90 days, major departments and agencies will carry out a top-to-bottom review of all regulations, old and new, to stop the ones that will hurt growth and speed up those that will help growth.

Further, for the untold number of hard-working, responsible American workers and business men and women who've been forced to go without needed bank loans, the banking credit crunch must end. I won't neglect my responsibility for sound regulations that serve the public good, but regulatory overkill must be stopped. And I've instructed our Government regulators to stop it.

I have directed Cabinet departments and Federal agencies to speed up pro-growth expenditures as quickly as possible. This should put an extra $10 billion into the economy in the next 6 months. And our new transportation bill provides more than $150 billion for construction and maintenance projects that are vital to our growth and well-being. And that means jobs building roads, jobs building bridges, and jobs building railways.

And I have, this evening, directed the Secretary of the Treasury to change the Federal tax withholding tables. With this change, millions of Americans from whom the Government withholds more than necessary can now choose to have the Government withhold less from their paychecks. Something tells me a number of taxpayers may take us up on this one. This initiative could return about $25 billion back into our economy over the next 12 months, money people can use to help pay for clothing, college, or to get a new car. Finally, working with the Federal Reserve, we will continue to support monetary policy that keeps both interest rates and inflation down.

Now, these are the things I can do. And now, Members of Congress, let me tell you what you can do for your country. You must pass the other elements of my plan to meet our economic needs. Everyone knows that investment spurs recovery. I am proposing this evening a change in the alternative minimum tax and the creation of a new 15-percent investment tax allowance. This will encourage businesses to accelerate investment and bring people back to work.

Real estate has led our economy out of almost all the tough times we've ever had. Once building starts, carpenters and plumbers work; people buy homes and take out mortgages. My plan would modify the passive loss rule for active real estate developers. And it would make it easier for pension plans to purchase real estate. For those Americans who dream of buying a first home but who can't quite afford it, my plan would allow first-time homebuyers to withdraw savings from IRA's without penalty and provide a $5,000 tax credit for the first purchase of that home.

And finally, my immediate plan calls on Congress to give crucial help to people who own a home, to everyone who has a business or a farm or a single investment. This time, at this hour, I cannot take no for an answer. You must cut the capital gains tax on the people of our country. Never has an issue been more demagogued by its opponents. But the demagogs are wrong. They are wrong, and they know it. Sixty percent of the people who benefit from lower capital gains have incomes under $50,000. A cut in the capital gains tax increases jobs and helps just about everyone in our country. And so, I'm asking you to cut the capital gains tax to a maximum of 15.4 percent.

I'll tell you, those of you who say, "Oh, no, someone who's comfortable may benefit from that," you kind of remind me of the old definition of the Puritan who couldn't sleep at night, worrying that somehow, someone somewhere was out having a good time. The opponents of this measure and those who have authored various so-called soak-the-rich bills that are floating around this Chamber should be reminded of something: When they aim at the big guy, they usually hit the little guy. And maybe it's time that stopped.

This, then, is my short-term plan. Your part, Members of Congress, requires enactment of these commonsense proposals that will have a strong effect on the economy without breaking the budget agreement and without raising tax rates.

While my plan is being passed and kicking in, we've got to care for those in trouble today. I have provided for up to $4.4 billion in my budget to extend Federal unemployment benefits. And I ask for congressional action right away. And I thank the committee. Well, at last.

Let's be frank. Let's be frank. Let me level with you. I know and you know that my plan is unveiled in a political season. I know and you know that everything I propose will be viewed by some in merely partisan terms. But I ask you to know what is in my heart. And my aim is to increase our Nation's good. I'm doing what I think is right, and I am proposing what I know will help.

I pride myself that I'm a prudent man, and I believe that patience is a virtue. But I understand that politics is, for some, a game and that sometimes the game is to stop all progress and then decry the lack of improvement. But let me tell you: Far more important than my political future and far more important than yours is the well-being of our country. Members of this Chamber are practical people, and I know you won't resent some practical advice. When people put their party's fortunes, whatever the party, whatever side of this aisle, before the public good, they court defeat not only for their country but for themselves. And they will certainly deserve it.

I submit my plan tomorrow, and I'm asking you to pass it by March 20th. And I ask the American people to let you know they want this action by March 20th. From the day after that, if it must be, the battle is joined. And you know, when principle is at stake I relish a good, fair fight.

I said my plan has two parts, and it does. And it's the second part that is the heart of the matter. For it's not enough to get an immediate burst. We need long-term improvement in our economic position. We all know that the key to our economic future is to ensure that America continues as an economic leader of the world. We have that in our power. Here, then, is my long-term plan to guarantee our future.

First, trade: We will work to break down the walls that stop world trade. We will work to open markets everywhere. And in our major trade negotiations, I will continue pushing to eliminate tariffs and subsidies that damage America's farmers and workers. And we'll get more good American jobs within our own hemisphere through the North American free trade agreement and through the Enterprise for the Americas Initiative.

But changes are here, and more are coming. The workplace of the future will demand more highly skilled workers than ever, more people who are computer-literate, highly educated. We must be the world's leader in education. And we must revolutionize America's schools. My America 2000 strategy will help us reach that goal. My plan will give parents more choice, give teachers more flexibility, and help communities create new American schools. Thirty States across the Nation have established America 2000 programs. Hundreds of cities and towns have joined in. Now Congress must join this great movement: Pass my proposals for new American schools.

That was my second long-term proposal, and here's my third: We must make commonsense investments that will help us compete, long-term, in the marketplace. We must encourage research and development. My plan is to make the R&D tax credit permanent and to provide record levels of support, over $76 billion this year alone, for people who will explore the promise of emerging technologies.

Fourth, we must do something about crime and drugs. It is time for a major, renewed investment in fighting violent street crime. It saps our strength and hurts our faith in our society and in our future together. Surely a tired woman on her way to work at 6 in the morning on a subway deserves the right to get there safely. And surely it's true that everyone who changes his or her life because of crime, from those afraid to go out at night to those afraid to walk in the parks they pay for, surely these people have been denied a basic civil right. It is time to restore it. Congress, pass my comprehensive crime bill. It is tough on criminals and supportive of police, and it has been languishing in these hallowed halls for years now. Pass it. Help your country.

Fifth, I ask you tonight to fund our HOPE housing proposal and to pass my enterprise zone legislation which will get businesses into the inner city. We must empower the poor with the pride that comes from owning a home, getting a job, becoming a part of things. My plan would encourage real estate construction by extending tax incentives for mortgage revenue bonds and low-income housing. And I ask tonight for record expenditures for the program that helps children born into want move into excellence, Head Start.

Step six, we must reform our health care system. For this, too, bears on whether or not we can compete in the world. American health costs have been exploding. This year America will spend over $800 billion on health, and that is expected to grow to 1.6 trillion by the end of the decade. We simply cannot afford this. The cost of health care shows up not only in your family budget but in the price of everything we buy and everything we sell. When health coverage for a fellow on an assembly line costs thousands of dollars, the cost goes into the products he makes, and you pay the bill.

We must make a choice. Now, some pretend we can have it both ways. They call it "play or pay," but that expensive approach is unstable. It will mean higher taxes, fewer jobs, and eventually a system under complete Government control.

Really, there are only two options. And we can move toward a nationalized system, a system which will restrict patient choice in picking a doctor and force the Government to ration services arbitrarily. And what we'll get is patients in long lines, indifferent service, and a huge new tax burden. Or we can reform our own private health care system, which still gives us, for all its flaws, the best quality health care in the world.

Well, let's build on our strengths. My plan provides insurance security for all Americans while preserving and increasing the idea of choice. We make basic health insurance affordable for all low-income people not now covered, and we do it by providing a health insurance tax credit of up to $3,750 for each low-income family. And the middle class gets help, too. And by reforming the health insurance market, my plan assures that Americans will have access to basic health insurance even if they change jobs or develop serious health problems. We must bring costs under control, preserve quality, preserve choice, and reduce the people's nagging daily worry about health insurance. My plan, the details of which I'll announce very shortly, does just that.

Seventh, we must get the Federal deficit under control. We now have, in law, enforceable spending caps and a requirement that we pay for the programs we create. There are those in Congress who would ease that discipline now. But I cannot let them do it, and I won't.

My plan would freeze all domestic discretionary budget authority, which means no more next year than this year. I will not tamper with Social Security, but I would put real caps on the growth of uncontrolled spending. And I would also freeze Federal domestic Government employment. And with the help of Congress, my plan will get rid of 246 programs that don't deserve Federal funding. Some of them have noble titles, but none of them is indispensable. We can get rid of each and every one of them.

You know, it's time we rediscovered a home truth the American people have never forgotten: This Government is too big and spends too much. And I call upon Congress to adopt a measure that will help put an end to the annual ritual of filling the budget with pork barrel appropriations. Every year, the press has a field day making fun of outrageous examples: a Lawrence Welk museum, research grants for Belgian endive. We all know how these things get into the budget, and maybe you need someone to help you say no. I know how to say it, and I know what I need to make it stick. Give me the same thing 43 Governors have, the line-item veto, and let me help you control spending.

We must put an end to unfinanced Federal Government mandates. These are the requirements Congress puts on our cities, counties, and States without supplying the money. If Congress passes a mandate, it should be forced to pay for it and balance the cost with savings elsewhere. After all, a mandate just increases someone else's burden, and that means higher taxes at the State and local level.

Step eight, Congress should enact the bold reform proposals that are still awaiting congressional action: bank reform, civil justice reform, tort reform, and my national energy strategy.

And finally, we must strengthen the family because it is the family that has the greatest bearing on our future. When Barbara holds an AIDS baby in her arms and reads to children, she's saying to every person in this country: Family matters.

And I am announcing tonight a new Commission on America's Urban Families. I've asked Missouri's Governor John Ashcroft to be Chairman, former Dallas Mayor

Annette Strauss to be Co-chair. You know, I had mayors, the leading mayors from the League of Cities, in the other day at the White House, and they told me something striking. They said that every one of them, Republican or Democrat, agreed on one thing, that the major cause of the problems of the cities is the dissolution of the family. They asked for this Commission, and they were right to ask because it's time to determine what we can do to keep families together, strong and sound.

There's one thing we can do right away: Ease the burden of rearing a child. I ask you tonight to raise the personal exemption by $500 per child for every family. For a family with four kids, that's an increase of $2,000. This is a good start in the right direction, and it's what we can afford.

It's time to allow families to deduct the interest they pay on student loans. I am asking you to do just that. And I'm asking you to allow people to use money from their IRA's to pay medical and education expenses, all without penalties.

And I'm asking for more. Ask American parents what they dislike about how things are going in our country, and chances are good that pretty soon they'll get to welfare. Americans are the most generous people on Earth. But we have to go back to the insight of Franklin Roosevelt who, when he spoke of what became the welfare program, warned that it must not become "a narcotic" and a "subtle destroyer" of the spirit. Welfare was never meant to be a lifestyle. It was never meant to be a habit. It was never supposed to be passed from generation to generation like a legacy. It's time to replace the assumptions of the welfare state and help reform the welfare system.

States throughout the country are beginning to operate with new assumptions that when able-bodied people receive Government assistance, they have responsibilities to the taxpayer: A responsibility to seek work, education, or job training; a responsibility to get their lives in order; a responsibility to hold their families together and refrain from having children out of wedlock; and a responsibility to obey the law. We are going to help this movement. Often, State reform requires waiving certain Federal regulations. I will act to make that process easier and quicker for every State that asks for our help.

I want to add, as we make these changes, we work together to improve this system, that our intention is not scapegoating or finger-pointing. If you read the papers and watch TV, you know there's been a rise these days in a certain kind of ugliness: racist comments, anti-Semitism, an increased sense of division. Really, this is not us. This is not who we are. And this is not acceptable.

And so, you have my plan for America. And I'm asking for big things, but I believe in my heart you'll do what's right.

You know, it's kind of an American tradition to show a certain skepticism toward our democratic institutions. I myself have sometimes thought the aging process could be delayed if it had to make its way through Congress. You will deliberate, and you will discuss, and that is fine. But, my friends, the people cannot wait. They need help now.

There's a mood among us. People are worried. There's been talk of decline. Someone even said our workers are lazy and uninspired. And I thought: Really? You go tell Neil Armstrong standing on the moon. Tell the men and women who put him there. Tell the American farmer who feeds his country and the world. Tell the men and women of Desert Storm.

Moods come and go, but greatness endures. Ours does. And maybe for a moment it's good to remember what, in the dailiness of our lives, we forget: We are still and ever the freest nation on Earth, the kindest nation on Earth, the strongest nation on Earth. And we have always risen to the occasion. And we are going to lift this Nation out of hard times inch by inch and day by day, and those who would stop us had better step aside. Because I look at hard times, and I make this vow: This will not stand.

And so, we move on together, a rising nation, the once and future miracle that is still, this night, the hope of the world. Thank you. God bless you, and God bless our beloved country. Thank you very, very much.

William J. Clinton

1993–2001

*"We have moved past the sterile debate
between those who say government is the enemy
and those who say government is the answer.
My fellow Americans, we have found
a third way."*

ADDRESS BEFORE A JOINT SESSION OF CONGRESS ON THE
STATE OF THE UNION, JANUARY 27, 1998

Address before a Joint Session of Congress on Administration Goals

February 17, 1993

William J. "Bill" Clinton delivered an address to Congress in February 1993 that outlined his economic plans, particularly when it came to deficit reduction. While not officially a State of the Union message, the speech served the same function that year as it was framed by the media as a "state of the union address."

Clinton, a Democrat, had been sworn in almost a month earlier, after winning a three-way presidential contest the previous November against incumbent Republican president George Bush and independent billionaire Ross Perot. With the country in an economic slump, Bush was not able to win a second term; Clinton took a plurality of 43 percent of the vote to Bush's 38 percent and Perot's 19 percent. Clinton won 370 electoral votes to Bush's 168.

In this speech the new president called for a "new direction." He mentioned a series of problems facing the country, including unemployment, deficits, increasing health care costs, and children in poverty.

Among the specifics Clinton offered in his deficit-reduction package was an income tax increase that he said would affect the wealthiest 1.2 percent of Americans. He also called for a raise in the corporate tax rate for businesses with taxable incomes over $10 million.

The plan also sought a "broad-based" energy tax. The president stated that a family earning less than $30,000 would not be affected by any of these changes due to other proposals, such as a raise in the earned-income tax credit. The plan included a one-year freeze in federal government salaries and 150 specific budget cuts.

The president also listed a series of other items on his domestic agenda. One of them, the Family and Medical Leave Act, which gave time off to people with a new child or a family emergency, had already been passed by Congress. He also mentioned completion of a North American Free Trade Agreement (NAFTA), health care reform, welfare reform, and the Brady handgun control bill, among other goals.

Later that year, the Democratic-controlled Congress, without Republican support, would narrowly pass a huge five-year bill known as the Omnibus Budget Reconciliation Act, which incorporated a great deal of Clinton's budget plan; the president would sign it less than six months after his speech. Clinton also would see successes with the passage of the Brady bill and approval of NAFTA.

Clinton, a gifted politician, would become a controversial leader over his eight years in office, surviving impeachment as well as six years of a Republican-controlled Congress. The economy recovered well during his years in office, leading to budget surpluses in the later years of his presidency.

Mr. President, Mr. Speaker, Members of the House and the Senate, distinguished Americans here as visitors in this Chamber, as am I. It is nice to have a fresh excuse for giving a long speech.

When Presidents speak to Congress and the Nation from this podium, typically they comment on the full range in challenges and opportunities that face the United States. But this is not an ordinary time, and for all the many tasks that require our attention, I believe tonight one calls on us to focus, to unite, and to act. And that is our economy. For more than anything else, our task tonight as Americans is to make our economy thrive again.

Let me begin by saying that it has been too long, at least three decades, since a President has come and challenged Americans to join him on a great national journey, not merely to consume the bounty of today but to invest for a much greater one tomorrow.

Like individuals, nations must ultimately decide how they wish to conduct themselves, how they wish to be thought of by those with whom they live, and later, how they wish to be judged by history. Like every individual man and woman, nations must decide whether they are prepared to rise to the occasions history presents them.

We have always been a people of youthful energy and daring spirit. And at this historic moment, as communism has fallen, as freedom is spreading around the world, as a global economy is taking shape before our eyes, Americans have called for change. And now it is up to those of us in this room to deliver for them.

Our Nation needs a new direction. Tonight I present to you a comprehensive plan to set our Nation on that new course. I believe we will find our new direction in the basic old values that brought us here over the last two centuries: a commitment to opportunity, to individual responsibility, to community, to work, to family, and to faith. We must now break the habits of both political parties and say there can be no more something for nothing and admit frankly that we are all in this together.

The conditions which brought us as a nation to this point are well-known: two decades of low productivity, growth, and stagnant wages; persistent unemployment and underemployment; years of huge Government deficits and declining investment in our future; exploding health care costs and lack of coverage for millions of Americans; legions of poor children; education and job training opportunities inadequate to the demands of this tough, global economy. For too long we have drifted without a strong sense of purpose or responsibility or community.

And our political system so often has seemed paralyzed by special interest groups, by partisan bickering, and by the sheer complexity of our problems. I believe we can do better because we remain the greatest nation on Earth, the world's strongest economy, the world's only military superpower. If we have the vision, the will, and the heart to make the changes we must, we can still enter the 21st century with possibilities our parents could not even have imagined and enter it having secured the American dream for ourselves and for future generations.

I well remember 12 years ago President Reagan stood at this very podium and told you and the American people that if our national debt were stacked in thousand-dollar bills, the stack would reach 67 miles into space. Well, today that stack would reach 267 miles. I tell you this not to assign blame for this problem. There is plenty of blame to go around in both branches of the Government and both parties. The time has come for the blame to end. I did not seek this office to place blame. I come here tonight to accept responsibility, and I want you to accept responsibility with me. And if we do right by this country, I do not care who gets the credit for it.

The plan I offer you has four fundamental components. First, it shifts our emphasis in public and private spending from consumption to investment, initially by jump-starting the economy in the short term and investing in our people, their jobs, and their incomes over the long run. Second, it changes the rhetoric of the past into the actions of the present by honoring work and families in every part of our public decision-making. Third, it substantially reduces the Federal deficit honestly and credibly by using in the beginning the most conservative estimates of Government revenues, not, as the executive branch has done so often in the past, using the most optimistic ones. And finally, it seeks to earn the trust of the American people by paying for these plans first with cuts in Government waste and efficiency; second, with cuts, not gimmicks, in Government spending; and by fairness, for a change, in the way additional burdens are borne.

Tonight I want to talk with you about what Government can do because I believe Government must do more. But let me say first that the real engine of economic growth in this country is the private sector, and second, that each of us must be an engine of growth and change. The truth is that as Government creates more opportunity in this new and different time, we must also demand more responsibility in turn.

Our immediate priority must be to create jobs, create jobs now. Some people say, "Well, we're in a recovery, and we don't have to do that." Well, we all hope we're in a recovery, but we're sure not creating new jobs. And there's no recovery worth its salt that doesn't put the American people back to work.

To create jobs and guarantee a strong recovery, I call on Congress to enact an immediate package of jobs investments of over $30 billion to put people to work now, to create a half a million jobs: jobs to rebuild our highways and airports, to renovate housing, to bring new life to rural communities, and spread hope and opportunity among our Nation's youth. Especially I want to emphasize, after the events of last year in Los Angeles and the countless stories of despair in our cities and in our poor rural communities, this proposal will create almost 700,000 new summer jobs for displaced, unemployed young people alone this summer. And tonight I invite America's business leaders to join us in this effort so that together we can provide over one million summer jobs in cities and poor rural areas for our young people.

Second, our plan looks beyond today's business cycle because our aspirations extend into the next century. The heart of this plan deals with the long term. It is an investment program designed to increase public and private investment in areas critical to our economic future. And it has a deficit reduction program that will increase the savings available for the private sector to invest, will lower interest rates, will decrease the percentage of the Federal budget claimed by interest payments, and decrease the risk of financial market disruptions that could adversely affect our economy.

Over the long run, all this will bring us a higher rate of economic growth, improved productivity, more high-quality jobs, and an improved economic competitive position in the world. In order to accomplish both increased investment and deficit reduction, something no American Government has ever been called upon to do at the same time before, spending must be cut and taxes must be raised.

The spending cuts I recommend were carefully thought through in a way to minimize any adverse economic impact, to capture the peace dividend for investment purposes, and to switch the balance in the budget from consumption to more investment. The tax increases and the spending cuts were both designed to assure that the cost of this historic program to face and deal with our problems will be borne by those who could readily afford it the most. Our plan is designed, furthermore, and perhaps in some ways most importantly, to improve the health of American business through lower interest rates, more incentives to invest, and better trained workers.

Because small business has created such a high percentage of all the new jobs in our Nation over the last 10 or 15 years, our plan includes the boldest targeted incentives for small business in history. We propose a permanent investment tax credit for the smallest firms in this country, with revenues of under $5 million. That's about 90 percent of the firms in America, employing about 40 percent of the work force but creating a big majority of the net new jobs for more than a decade. And we propose new rewards for entrepreneurs who take new risks. We propose to give small business access to all the new technologies of our time. And we propose to attack this credit crunch which has denied small business the credit they need to flourish and prosper.

With a new network of community development banks and $1 billion to make the dream of enterprise zones real, we propose to bring new hope and new jobs to storefronts and factories from south Boston to south Texas to south central Los Angeles. This plan invests in our roads, our bridges, our transit systems, in high-speed railways and high-tech information systems. And it provides the most ambitious environmental cleanup in partnership with State and local government of our time, to put people to work and to preserve the environment for our future.

Standing as we are on the edge of a new century, we know that economic growth depends as never before on opening up new markets overseas and expanding the volume of world trade. And so, we will insist on fair trade rules in international markets as a part of a national economic strategy to expand trade, including the successful completion of the latest round of world trade talks and the successful completion of a North American Free Trade Agreement with appropriate safeguards for our workers and for the environment.

At the same time—and I say this to you in both parties and across America tonight, all the people who are listening—it is not enough to pass a budget or even to have a trade agreement. This world is changing so fast that we must have aggressive, targeted attempts to create the high-wage jobs of the future. That's what all our competitors are doing. We must give special attention to those critical industries that are going to explode in the 21st century but that are in trouble in America today, like aerospace. We must provide special assistance to areas and to workers displaced by cuts in the defense budget and by other unavoidable economic dislocations.

And again I will say we must do this together. I pledge to you that I will do my best to see that business and labor and Government work together for a change.

But all of our efforts to strengthen the economy will fail—let me say this again; I feel so strongly about this—all of our efforts to strengthen the economy will fail unless we also take this year, not next year, not 5 years from now but this year, bold steps to reform our health care system.

In 1992, we spent 14 percent of our income on health care, more than 30 percent more than any other country in the world, and yet we were the only advanced nation that did not provide a basic package of health care benefits to all of its citizens. Unless we change the present pattern, 50 percent of the growth in the deficit between now and the year 2000 will be in health care costs. By the year 2000 almost 20 percent of our income will be in health care. Our families will never be secure, our businesses will never be strong, and our Government will never again be fully solvent until we tackle the health care crisis. We must do it this year.

The combination of the rising cost of care and the lack of care and the fear of losing care are endangering the security and the very lives of millions of our people. And they are weakening our economy every day. Reducing health care costs can liberate literally hundreds of billions of dollars for new investment in growth and jobs. Bringing health costs in line with inflation would do more for the private sector in this country than any tax cut we could give and any spending program we could promote. Reforming health care over the long run is critically essential to reducing not only our deficit but to expanding investment in America.

Later this spring, after the First Lady and the many good people who are helping her all across the country complete their work, I will deliver to Congress a comprehensive plan for health care reform that finally will bring costs under control and provide security to all of our families, so that no one will be denied the coverage they need but so that our economic future will not be compromised either. We'll have to root out fraud and overcharges and make sure that paperwork no longer chokes your doctor. We'll have to maintain the highest American standards and the right to choose in a system that is the world's finest for all those who can access it. But first we must make choices. We must choose to give the American people the quality they demand and deserve with a system that will not bankrupt the country or further drive more Americans into agony.

Let me further say that I want to work with all of you on this. I realize this is a complicated issue. But we must address it. And I believe if there is any chance that Republicans and Democrats who disagree on taxes and spending or anything else could agree on one thing, surely we can all look at these numbers and go home and tell our people the truth. We cannot continue these spending patterns in public or private dollars for health care for less and less and less every year. We can do better. And I will work to do better.

Perhaps the most fundamental change the new direction I propose offers is its focus on the future and its investment which I seek in our children. Each day we delay really making a commitment to our children carries a dear cost. Half of the 2-year-olds in this country today don't receive the immunizations they need against deadly diseases. Our plan will provide them for every eligible child. And we know now that we will save $10 later for every $1 we spend by eliminating preventable childhood diseases. That's a good investment no matter how you measure it.

I recommend that the women, infants, and children's nutrition program be expanded so that every expectant mother who needs the help gets it. We all know that Head Start, a program that prepares children for school, is a success story. We all know that it saves money. But today it just reaches barely over one-third of all the eligible children. Under this plan, every eligible child will be able to get a head start. This is not just the right thing to do; it is the smart thing to do. For every dollar we invest today, we'll save $3 tomorrow. We have to start thinking about tomorrow. I've heard that somewhere before.

We have to ask more in our schools of our students, our teachers, our principals, our parents. Yes, we must give them the resources they need to meet high standards, but we must also use the authority and the influence and the funding of the Education Department to promote strategies that really work in learning. Money alone is not enough. We have to do what really works to increase learning in our schools.

We have to recognize that all of our high school graduates need some further education in order to be competitive in this global economy. So we have to establish a partnership between businesses and education and the Government for apprenticeship programs in every State in this country to give our people the skills they need. Life-long learning must benefit not just young high school graduates but workers, too, throughout their career. The average 18-year-old today will change jobs seven times in a lifetime. We have done a lot in this country on worker training in the last few years, but the system is too fractured. We must develop a unified, simplified, sensible, streamlined worker-training program so that workers receive the training they need regardless of why they lost their jobs or whether they simply need to learn something new to keep them. We have got to do better on this.

And finally, I propose a program that got a great response from the American people all across this country last year: a program of national service to make college loans available to all Americans and to challenge them at the same time to give something back to their country as teachers or police officers or community service workers; to give them the option to pay the loans back, but at tax time so they can't beat the bill, but to encourage them instead to pay it back by making their country stronger and making their country better and giving us the benefit of their knowledge.

A generation ago when President Kennedy proposed and the United States Congress embraced the Peace Corps, it defined the character of a whole generation of Americans committed to serving people around the world. In this national service program, we will provide more than twice as many slots for people before they go to college to be in national service than ever served in the Peace Corps. This program could do for this generation of Members of Congress what the land grant college act did and what the GI bill did for former Congressmen. In the future, historians who got their education through the national service loan will look back on you and thank you for giving America a new lease on life, if you meet this challenge.

If we believe in jobs and we believe in learning, we must believe in rewarding work. If we believe in restoring the values that make America special, we must believe that there is dignity in all work, and there must be dignity for all workers. To those who care for our sick, who tend our children, who do our most difficult and tiring jobs, the new direction I propose will make this solemn, simple commitment: By expanding the refundable earned-income tax credit, we will make history. We will reward the work of millions of working poor Americans by realizing the principle that if you work 40 hours a week and you've got a child in the house, you will no longer be in poverty.

Later this year, we will offer a plan to end welfare as we know it. I have worked on this issue for the better part of a decade. And I know from personal conversations with many people that no one, no one wants to change the welfare system as badly as those who are trapped in it. I want to offer the people on welfare the education, the training, the child care, the health care they need to get back on their feet, but say after 2 years they must get back to work, too, in private business if possible, in public service if necessary. We have to end welfare as a way of life and make it a path to independence and dignity.

Our next great goal should be to strengthen our families. I compliment the Congress for passing the Family and Medical Leave Act as a good first step, but it is time to do more. This plan will give this country the toughest child support enforcement system it has ever had. It is time to demand that people take responsibility for the children they bring in this world.

And I ask you to help to protect our families against the violent crime which terrorizes our people and which tears our communities apart. We must pass a tough crime bill. I support not only the bill which didn't quite make it to the President's desk last year but also an initiative to put 100,000 more police officers on the street, to provide boot camps for first-time nonviolent offenders for more space for the hardened criminals in jail. And I support an initiative to do what we can to keep guns out of the hands of criminals. Let me say this. I will make you this bargain: If you will pass the Brady bill, I'll sure sign it.

Let me say now, we should move to the harder parts.

I think it is clear to every American, including every Member of Congress of both parties, that the confidence of the people who pay our bills in our institutions in Washington is not high. We must restore it. We must begin again to make Government work for ordinary taxpayers, not simply for organized interest groups. And that beginning must start with real political reform. I am asking the United States Congress to pass a real campaign finance reform bill this year. I ask you to increase the participation of the American people by passing the motor voter bill promptly. I ask you to deal with the undue influence of special interests by passing a bill to end the tax deduction for lobbying and to act quickly to require all the people who lobby you to register as lobbyists by passing the lobbying registration bill.

Believe me, they were cheering that last section at home. I believe lobby reform and campaign finance reform are a sure path to increased popularity for Republicans and Democrats alike because it says to the voters back home, "This is your House. This is your Senate. We're your hired hands, and every penny we draw is your money."

Next, to revolutionize Government we have to ensure that we live within our means, and that should start at the top and with the White House. In the last few days I have announced a cut in the White House staff of 25 percent, saving approximately $10 million. I have ordered administrative cuts in budgets of agencies and departments. I have cut the Federal bureaucracy, or will over the next 4 years, by approximately 100,000 positions, for a combined savings of $9 billion. It is time for Government to demonstrate, in the condition we're in, that we can be as frugal as any household in America.

And that's why I also want to congratulate the Congress. I noticed the announcement of the leadership today that Congress is taking similar steps to cut its costs. I think that is important. I think it will send a very clear signal to the American people.

But if we really want to cut spending, we're going to have to do more, and some of it will be difficult. Tonight I call for an across-the-board freeze in Federal Government salaries for one year. And thereafter, during this 4-year period, I recommend that salaries rise at one point lower than the cost of living allowance normally involved in Federal pay increases.

Next, I recommend that we make 150 specific budget cuts, as you know, and that all those who say we should cut more be as specific as I have been.

Finally, let me say to my friends on both sides of the aisle, it is not enough simply to cut Government; we have to rethink the whole way it works. When I became President I was amazed at just the way the White House worked, in ways that added lots of money to what taxpayers had to pay, outmoded ways that didn't take maximum advantage of technology and didn't do things that any business would have done years ago to save taxpayers' money.

So I want to bring a new spirit of innovation into every Government Department. I want to push education reform, as I said, not just to spend more money but to really improve learning. Some things work, and some things don't. We ought to be subsidizing the things that work and discouraging the things that don't. I'd like to use that Superfund to clean up pollution for a change and not just pay lawyers.

In the aftermath of all the difficulties with the savings and loans, we must use Federal bank regulators to protect the security and safety of our financial institutions, but they should not be used to continue the credit crunch and to stop people from making sensible loans.

I'd like for us to not only have welfare reform but to reexamine the whole focus of all of our programs that help people, to shift them from entitlement programs to empowerment programs. In the end we want people not to need us anymore. I think that's important.

But in the end we have to get back to the deficit. For years there's been a lot of talk about it but very few credible efforts to deal with it. And now I understand why, having dealt with the real numbers for 4 weeks. But I believe this plan does; it tackles the budget deficit seriously and over the long term. It puts in place one of the biggest deficit reductions and one of the biggest changes in Federal priorities, from consumption to investment, in the history of this country at the same time over the next 4 years.

Let me say to all the people watching us tonight who will ask me these questions beginning tomorrow as I go around the country and who've asked it in the past: We're not cutting the deficit just because experts say it's the thing to do or because it has some intrinsic merit. We have to cut the deficit because the more we spend paying off the debt, the less tax dollars we have to invest in jobs and education and the future of this country. And the more money we take out of the pool of available savings, the harder it is for people in the private sector to borrow money at affordable interest rates for a college loan for their children, for a home mortgage, or to start a new business.

That's why we've got to reduce the debt, because it is crowding out other activities that we ought to be engaged in and that the American people ought to be engaged in. We cut the deficit so that our children will be able to buy a home, so that our companies can invest in the future and in retraining their workers, so that our Government can make the kinds of investments we need to be a stronger and smarter and safer nation.

If we don't act now, you and I might not even recognize this Government 10 years from now. If we just stay with the same trends of the last 4 years, by the end of the decade the deficit will be $635 billion a year, almost 80 percent of our gross domestic product. And paying interest on that debt will be the costliest Government program of all. We'll still be the world's largest debtor. And when Members of Congress come here, they'll be devoting over 20 cents on the dollar to interest payments, more than half of the budget to health care and to other entitlements. And you'll come here and deliberate and argue over 6 or 7 cents on the dollar, no matter what America's problems are. We will not be able to have the independence we need to chart the future that we must. And we'll be terribly dependent on foreign funds for a large portion of our investment.

This budget plan, by contrast, will by 1997 cut $140 billion in that year alone from the deficit, a real spending cut, a real revenue increase, a real deficit reduction, using the independent numbers of the Congressional Budget Office. Well, you can laugh, my fellow Republicans, but I'll point out that the Congressional Budget Office was normally more conservative in what was going to happen and closer to right than previous Presidents have been.

I did this so that we could argue about priorities with the same set of numbers. I did this so that no one could say I was estimating my way out of this difficulty. I did this because if we can agree together on the most prudent revenues we're likely to get if the recovery stays and we do right things economically, then it will turn out better for the American people than we say. In the last 12 years, because there were differences over the revenue estimates, you and I know that both parties were given greater elbow room for irresponsibility. This is tightening the rein on the Democrats as well as the Republicans. Let's at least argue about the same set of numbers so the American people will think we're shooting straight with them.

As I said earlier, my recommendation makes more than 150 difficult reductions to cut the Federal spending by a total of $246 billion. We are eliminating programs that are no longer needed, such as nuclear power research and development. We're slashing subsidies and canceling wasteful projects. But many of these programs were justified in their time, and a lot of them are difficult for me to recommend reductions in, some really tough ones for me personally. I recommend that we reduce interest subsidies to the Rural Electric Administration. That's a difficult thing for me to recommend. But I think that I cannot exempt the things that exist in my State or in my experience, if I ask you to deal with things that are difficult for you to deal with. We're going to have to have no sacred cows except the fundamental abiding interest of the American people.

I have to say that we all know our Government has been just great at building programs. The time has come to show the American people that we can limit them too; that we can not only start things, that we can actually stop things.

About the defense budget, I raise a hope and a caution. As we restructure our military forces to meet the new threats of the post-cold-war world, it is true that we can responsibly reduce our defense budget. And we may all doubt what that range of reductions is, but let me say that as long as I am President, I will do everything I can to make sure that the men and women who serve under the American flag will remain the best trained, the best prepared, the best equipped fighting force in the world. And every one of you should make that solemn pledge. We still have responsibilities around the world. We are the world's only superpower. This is still a dangerous and uncertain time, and we owe it to the people in uniform to make sure that we adequately provide for the national defense and for their interests and needs. Backed by an effective national defense and a stronger economy, our Nation will be prepared to lead a world challenged as it is everywhere by ethnic conflict, by the proliferation of weapons of mass destruction, by the global democratic revolution, and by challenges to the health of our global environment.

I know this economic plan is ambitious, but I honestly believe it is necessary for the continued greatness of the United States. And I think it is paid for fairly, first by cutting Government, then by asking the most of those who benefited the most in the past, and by asking more Americans to contribute today so that all of us can prosper tomorrow.

For the wealthiest, those earning more than $180,000 per year, I ask you all who are listening tonight to support a raise in the top rate for Federal income taxes from 31 to 36 percent. We recommend a 10 percent surtax on incomes over $250,000 a year, and we recommend closing some loopholes that let some people get away without paying any tax at all.

For businesses with taxable incomes in excess of $10 million, we recommend a raise in the corporate tax rate, also to 36 percent, as well as a cut in the deduction for business entertainment expenses. Our plan seeks to attack tax subsidies that actually reward companies more for shutting their operations down here and moving them overseas than for staying here and reinvesting in America. I say that as someone who believes that American companies should be free to invest around the world and as a former Governor who actively sought investment of foreign companies in my State. But the Tax Code should not express a preference to American companies for moving somewhere else, and it does in particular cases today.

We will seek to ensure that, through effective tax enforcement, foreign corporations who do make money in America simply pay the same taxes that American companies make on the same income.

To middle class Americans who have paid a great deal for the last 12 years and from whom I ask a contribution tonight, I will say again as I did on Monday night: You're not going alone any more, you're certainly not going first, and you're not going to pay more for less as you have too often in the past. I want to emphasize the facts about this plan: 98.8 percent of America's families will have no increase in their income tax rates, only 1.2 percent at the top.

Let me be clear: There will also be no new cuts in benefits for Medicare. As we move toward the 4th year, with the explosion in health care costs, as I said, projected to account for 50 percent of the growth of the deficit between now and the year 2000, there must be planned cuts in payments to providers, to doctors, to hospitals, to labs, as a way of controlling health care costs. But I see these only as a stopgap until we can reform the entire health care system. If you'll help me do that, we can be fair to the providers and to the consumers of health care. Let me repeat this, because I know it matters to a lot of you on both sides of the aisle. This plan does not make a recommendation for new cuts in Medicare benefits for any beneficiary.

Secondly, the only change we are making in Social Security is one that has already been publicized. The plan does ask older Americans with higher incomes, who do not rely solely on Social Security to get by, to contribute more. This plan will not affect the 80 percent of Social Security recipients who do not pay taxes on Social Security now. Those who do not pay tax on Social Security now will not be affected by this plan.

Our plan does include a broad-based tax on energy, and I want to tell you why I selected this and why I think it's a good idea. I recommend that we adopt a Btu tax on the heat content of energy as the best way to provide us with revenue to lower the deficit because it also combats pollution, promotes energy efficiency, promotes the independence, economically, of this country as well as helping to reduce the debt, and because it does not discriminate against any area. Unlike a carbon tax, that's not too hard on the coal States; unlike a gas tax, that's not too tough on people who drive a long way to work; unlike an ad valorem tax, it doesn't increase just when the price of an energy source goes up. And it is environmentally responsible. It will help us in the future as well as in the present with the deficit.

Taken together, these measures will cost an American family with an income of about $40,000 a year less than $17 a month. It will cost American families with incomes under $30,000 nothing because of other programs we propose, principally those raising the earned-income tax credit.

Because of our publicly stated determination to reduce the deficit, if we do these things, we will see the continuation of what's happened just since the election. Just since the election, since the Secretary of the Treasury, the Director of the Office of Management and Budget, and others who have begun to speak out publicly in favor of a tough deficit reduction plan, interest rates have continued to fall long-term. That means that for the middle class who will pay something more each month, if they had any credit needs or demands, their increased energy costs will be more than offset by lower interest costs for mortgages, consumer loans, credit cards. This can be a wise investment for them and their country now.

I would also point out what the American people already know, and that is, because we're a big, vast country where we drive long distances, we have maintained far lower burdens on energy than any other advanced country. We will still have far lower burdens on energy than any other advanced country. And these will be spread fairly, with real attempts to make sure that no cost is imposed on families with incomes under $30,000 and that the costs are very modest until you get into the higher income groups where the income taxes trigger in.

Now, I ask all of you to consider this: Whatever you think of the tax program, whatever you think of the spending cuts, consider the cost of not changing. Remember the numbers that you all know. If we just keep on doing what we're doing, by the end of the decade we'll have a $650-billion-a-year deficit. If we just keep on doing what we're doing, by the end of the decade 20 percent of our national income will go to health care every year, twice as much as any other country on the face of the globe. If we just keep on doing what we're doing, over 20 cents on the dollar will have to go to service the debt.

Unless we have the courage now to start building our future and stop borrowing from it, we're condemning ourselves to years of stagnation interrupted by occasional recessions, to slow growth in jobs, to no more growth in income, to more debt, to more disappointment. Worse, unless we change, unless we increase investment and reduce the debt to raise productivity so that we can generate both jobs and incomes, we will be condemning our children and our children's children to a lesser life than we enjoyed. Once Americans looked forward to doubling their living standards every 25 years. At present productivity rates, it will take 100 years to double living standards, until our grandchildren's grandchildren are born. I say that is too long to wait.

Tonight the American people know we have to change. But they're also likely to ask me tomorrow and all of you for the weeks and months ahead whether we have the fortitude to make the changes happen in the right way. They know that as soon as I leave this Chamber and you go home, various interest groups will be out in force lobbying against this or that piece of this plan, and that the forces of conventional wisdom will offer a thousand reasons why we well ought to do this but we just can't do it.

Our people will be watching and wondering, not to see whether you disagree with me on a particular issue but just to see whether this is going to be business as usual or a real new day, whether we're all going to conduct ourselves as if we know we're working for them. We must scale the walls of the people's skepticisms, not with our words but with our deeds. After so many years of gridlock and indecision, after so many hopeful beginnings and so few promising results, the American people are going to be harsh in their judgments of all of us if we fail to seize this moment.

This economic plan can't please everybody. If the package is picked apart, there will be something that will anger each of us, won't please anybody. But if it is taken as a whole, it will help all of us. So I ask you all to begin by resisting the temptation to focus only on a particular spending cut you don't like or some particular investment that wasn't made. And nobody likes the tax increases, but let's just face facts. For 20 years, through administrations of both parties, incomes have stalled and debt has exploded and productivity has not grown as it should. We cannot deny the reality of our condition. We have got to play the hand we were dealt and play it as best we can.

My fellow Americans, the test of this plan cannot be "what is in it for me." It has got to be "what is in it for us." If we work hard and if we work together, if we rededicate ourselves to creating jobs, to rewarding work, to strengthening our families, to reinventing our Government, we can lift our country's fortunes again.

Tonight I ask everyone in this Chamber and every American to look simply into your heart, to spark your own hopes, to fire your own imagination. There is so much good, so much possibility, so much excitement in this country now that if we act boldly and honestly, as leaders should, our legacy will be one of prosperity and progress. This must be America's new direction. Let us summon the courage to seize it.

Thank you. God bless America.

William J. Clinton, 1993–1997

Address before a Joint Session of Congress on the State of the Union
January 25, 1994

Bill Clinton's first official State of the Union message was delivered before Congress when Clinton had been in office for a year. His first year in the White House had seen a series of successes, including passage of the Brady handgun control law, the Family and Medical Leave Act, and a budget reconciliation law. He had run into problems on some other fronts, including the "don't ask, don't tell" compromise on homosexuals in the military.

The speech's central focus was Clinton's desire to reform the country's health care system. The first lady, Hillary Rodham Clinton, headed a commission charged with developing such a plan. In the speech, Clinton noted that the first lady had received almost a million letters from people across the country. He read from one written by Richard Anderson, who had lost his job and his health insurance, after which his wife, Judy, suffered a cerebral aneurysm. The medical costs associated with her treatment forced the couple into bankruptcy. Clinton used them as an example of what he saw as the importance of reforming the system.

He criticized America's private health care system, particularly the insurance companies and their lobbyists, and called for guaranteed private insurance. In a dramatic moment, he held his pen in the air and threatened to veto any measure that did not guarantee private insurance to every American—the same type of insurance members of Congress had, he noted.

In the end, health care reform would be a dismal failure for the Clintons; their controversial plan would be withdrawn later that year before a final vote was taken in either the House or the Senate.

Another focus of the speech was crime, a top concern for many Americans. Clinton pushed the crime bill then pending before Congress, stating, "I care a lot about this issue." He ran through a list of priorities in the crime bill, including a "three strikes and you're out" provision, an extra 100,000 police officers in communities around the country, a gun control measure focusing on assault weapons, and additional money for drug treatment. Clinton introduced an audience member, New York police detective Kevin Jett, to symbolize the importance of funding for additional police officers. Congress approved a sweeping crime bill later that year.

The president also touched on foreign affairs, particularly the new post-Cold War situation in the former Soviet Union; he called for continued U.S. support for democratic and market reforms in that area. In addition, Clinton praised the U.S. troops that were involved in Bosnia and Somalia, and he pledged to build on the historic Israeli-Palestinian breakthrough of the previous year.

A Gallup poll taken January 28–30 found that 11 percent of respondents rated the speech as outstanding, 29 percent as above average, 40 percent as average, 3 percent as below average, and 3 percent as poor. Another 14 percent did not know or refused to answer.

Thank you very much. Mr. Speaker, Mr. President, Members of the 103d Congress, my fellow Americans:

I'm not at all sure what speech is in the TelePrompter tonight but I hope we can talk about the state of the Union.

I ask you to begin by recalling the memory of the giant who presided over this Chamber with such force and grace. Tip O'Neill liked to call himself "a man of the House." And he surely was that. But even more, he was a man of the people, a bricklayer's son who helped to build the great American middle class. Tip O'Neill never forgot who he was, where he came from, or who sent him here. Tonight he's smiling down on us for the first time from the Lord's gallery. But in his honor, may we, too, always remember who we are, where we come from, and who sent us here. If we do that we will return over and over again to the principle that if we simply give ordinary people equal opportunity, quality education, and a fair shot at the American dream, they will do extraordinary things.

We gather tonight in a world of changes so profound and rapid that all nations are tested. Our American heritage has always been to master such change, to use it to expand opportunity at home and our leadership abroad. But for too long and in too many ways, that heritage was abandoned, and our country drifted.

For 30 years, family life in America has been breaking down. For 20 years, the wages of working people have been stagnant or declining. For the 12 years of trickle-down economics, we built a false prosperity on a hollow base as our national debt quadrupled. From 1989 to 1992, we experienced the slowest growth in a half century. For too many families, even when both parents were working, the American dream has been slipping away.

In 1992, the American people demanded that we change. A year ago I asked all of you to join me in accepting responsibility for the future of our country. Well, we did. We replaced drift and deadlock with renewal and reform. And I want to thank every one of you here who heard the American people, who broke gridlock, who gave them the most successful teamwork between a President and a Congress in 30 years.

This Congress produced a budget that cut the deficit by half a trillion dollars, cut spending, and raised income taxes on only the wealthiest Americans. This Congress produced tax relief for millions of low-income workers to reward work over welfare. It produced NAFTA. It produced the Brady bill, now the Brady law. And thank you, Jim Brady, for being here, and God bless you, sir.

This Congress produced tax cuts to reduce the taxes of 9 out of 10 small businesses who use the money to invest more and create more jobs. It produced more research and treatment for AIDS, more childhood immunizations, more support for women's health research, more affordable college loans for the middle class, a new national service program for those who want to give something back to their country and their communities for higher education, a dramatic increase in high-tech investments to move us from a defense to a domestic high-tech economy. This Congress produced a new law, the motor voter bill, to help millions of people register to vote. It produced family and medical leave. All passed. All signed into law with not one single veto. These accomplishments were all commitments I made when I sought this office. And in fairness, they all had to be passed by you in this Congress. But I am persuaded that the real credit belongs to the people who sent us here, who pay our salaries, who hold our feet to the fire.

But what we do here is really beginning to change lives. Let me just give you one example. I will never forget what the family and medical leave law meant to just one father I met early one Sunday morning in the White House. It was unusual to see a family there touring early Sunday morning, but he had his wife and his three children there, one of them in a wheelchair. I came up, and after we had our picture taken and had a little visit, I was walking off and that man grabbed me by the arm and he said, "Mr. President, let me tell you something. My little girl here is desperately ill. She's probably not going to make it. But because of the family leave law, I was able to take time off to spend with her, the most important time I ever spent in my life, without losing my job and hurting the rest of my family. It means more to me than I will ever be able to say. Don't you people up here ever think what you do doesn't make a difference. It does."

Though we are making a difference, our work has just begun. Many Americans still haven't felt the impact of what we've done. The recovery still hasn't touched every community or created enough jobs. Incomes are still stagnant. There's still too much violence and not enough hope in too many places. Abroad, the young democracies we are strongly supporting still face very difficult times and look to us for leadership. And so tonight, let us resolve to continue the journey of renewal, to create more and better jobs, to guarantee health security for all, to reward work over welfare, to promote democracy abroad, and to begin to reclaim our streets from violent crime and drugs and gangs, to renew our own American community.

Last year we began to put our house in order by tackling the budget deficit that was driving us toward bankruptcy. We cut $255 billion in spending, including entitlements, and over 340 separate budget items. We froze domestic spending and used honest budget numbers.

Led by the Vice President, we launched a campaign to reinvent Government. We cut staff, cut perks, even trimmed the fleet of Federal limousines. After years of leaders whose rhetoric attacked bureaucracy but whose action expanded it, we will actually reduce it by 252,000 people over the next 5 years. By the time we have finished, the Federal bureaucracy will be at its lowest point in 30 years.

Because the deficit was so large and because they benefited from tax cuts in the 1980's, we did ask the wealthiest Americans to pay more to reduce the deficit. So on April the 15th, the American people will discover the truth about what we did last year on taxes. Only the top 1, yes, listen, the top 1.2 percent of Americans, as I said all along, will pay higher income tax rates. Let me repeat: Only the wealthiest 1.2 percent of Americans will face higher income tax rates, and no one else will. And that is the truth.

Of course, there were, as there always are in politics, naysayers who said this plan wouldn't work. But they were wrong. When I became President, the experts predicted that next year's deficit would be $300 billion. But because we acted, those same people now say the deficit is going to be under $180 billion, 40 percent lower than was previously predicted.

Our economic program has helped to produce the lowest core inflation rate and the lowest interest rates in 20 years. And because those interest rates are down, business investment and equipment is growing at 7 times the rate of the previous 4 years. Auto sales are way up. Home sales are at a record high. Millions of Americans have refinanced their homes, and our economy has produced 1.6 million private sector jobs in 1993, more than were created in the previous 4 years combined.

The people who supported this economic plan should be proud of its early results. Proud. But everyone in this Chamber should know and acknowledge that there is more to do.

Next month I will send you one of the toughest budgets ever presented to Congress. It will cut spending in more than 300 programs, eliminate 100 domestic programs, and reform the ways in which governments buy goods and services. This year we must again make the hard choices to live within the hard spending ceilings we have set. We must do it. We have proved we can bring the deficit down without choking off recovery, without punishing seniors or the middle class, and without putting our national security at risk. If you will stick with this plan, we will post 3 consecutive years of declining deficits for the first time since Harry Truman lived in the White House. And once again, the buck stops here.

Our economic plan also bolsters our strength and our credibility around the world. Once we reduced the deficit and put the steel back into our competitive edge, the world echoed with the sound of falling trade barriers. In one year, with NAFTA, with GATT, with our efforts in Asia and the National Export Strategy, we did more to open world markets to American products than at any time in the last two generations. That means more jobs and rising living standards for the American people, low deficits, low inflation, low interest rates, low trade barriers, and high investments. These are the building blocks of our recovery. But if we want to take full advantage of the opportunities before us in the global economy, you all know we must do more.

As we reduce defense spending, I ask Congress to invest more in the technologies of tomorrow. Defense conversion will keep us strong militarily and create jobs for our people here at home. As we protect our environment, we must invest in the environmental technologies of the future which will create jobs. This year we will fight for a revitalized Clean Water Act and a Safe Drinking Water Act and a reformed Superfund program. And the Vice President is right, we must also work with the private sector to connect every classroom, every clinic, every library, every hospital in America into a national information super highway by the year 2000.

Think of it, instant access to information will increase productivity, will help to educate our children. It will provide better medical care. It will create jobs. And I call on the Congress to pass legislation to establish that information super highway this year.

As we expand opportunity and create jobs, no one can be left out. We must continue to enforce fair lending and fair housing and all civil rights laws, because America will never be complete in its renewal until everyone shares in its bounty.

But we all know, too, we can do all these things, put our economic house in order, expand world trade, target the jobs of the future, guarantee equal opportunity, but if we're honest, we'll all admit that this strategy still cannot work unless we also give our people the education, training, and skills they need to seize the opportunities of tomorrow.

We must set tough, world-class academic and occupational standards for all our children and give our teachers and students the tools they need to meet them. Our Goals 2000 proposal will empower individual school districts to experiment with ideas like chartering their schools to be run by private corporations or having more public school choice, to do whatever they wish to do as long as we measure every school by one high standard: Are our children learning what they need to know to compete and win in the global economy? Goals 2000 links world-class standards to grassroots reforms. And I hope Congress will pass it without delay.

Our school to work initiative will for the first time link school to the world of work, providing at least one year of apprenticeship beyond high school. After all, most of the people we're counting on to build our economic future won't graduate from college. It's time to stop ignoring them and start empowering them.

We must literally transform our outdated unemployment system into a new reemployment system. The old unemployment system just sort of kept you going while you waited for your old job to come back. We've got to have a new system to move people into new and better jobs, because most of those old jobs just don't come back. And we know that the only way to have real job security in the future, to get a good job with a growing income, is to have real skills and the ability to learn new ones. So we've got to streamline today's patchwork of training programs and make them a source of new skills for our people who lose their jobs. Reemployment, not unemployment, must become the centerpiece of our economic renewal. I urge you to pass it in this session of Congress.

And just as we must transform our unemployment system, so must we also revolutionize our welfare system. It doesn't work. It defies our values as a Nation. If we value work, we can't justify a system that makes welfare more attractive than work if people are worried about losing their health care. If we value responsibility, we can't ignore the $34 billion in child support absent parents ought to be paying to millions of parents who are taking care of their children. If we value strong families, we can't perpetuate a system that actually penalizes those who stay together. Can you believe that a child who has a child gets more money from the Government for leaving home than for staying home with a parent or a grandparent? That's not just bad policy, it's wrong. And we ought to change it.

I worked on this problem for years before I became President, with other Governors and with Members of Congress of both parties and with the previous administration of another party. I worked on it with people who were on welfare, lots of them. And I want to say something to everybody here who cares about this issue. The people who most want to change this system are the people who are dependent on it. They want to get off welfare. They want to go back to work. They want to do right by their kids.

I once had a hearing when I was a Governor, and I brought in people on welfare from all over America who had found their way to work. The woman from my State who testified was asked this question: What's the best thing about being off welfare and in a job? And without blinking an eye, she looked at 40 Governors, and she said, "When my boy goes to school and they say what does you mother do for a living, he can give an answer." These people want a better system, and we ought to give it to them.

Last year we began this. We gave the States more power to innovate because we know that a lot of great ideas come from outside Washington, and many States are already using it. Then this Congress took a dramatic step. Instead of taxing people with modest incomes into poverty, we helped them to work their way out of poverty by dramatically increasing the earned-income tax credit. It will lift 15 million working families out of poverty, rewarding work over welfare, making it possible for people to be successful workers and successful parents. Now that's real welfare reform.

But there is more to be done. This spring I will send you a comprehensive welfare reform bill that builds on the Family Support Act of 1988 and restores the basic values of work and responsibility. We'll say to teenagers, "If you have a child out of wedlock, we will no longer give you a check to set up a separate household. We want families to stay together;" say to absent parents who aren't paying their child support, "If you're not providing for your children, we'll garnish your wages, suspend your license, track you across State lines, and if necessary, make some of you work off what you owe." People who bring children into this world cannot and must not walk away from them. But to all those who depend on welfare, we should offer ultimately a simple compact. We'll provide the support, the job training, the child care you need for up to 2 years. But after that, anyone who can work, must, in the private sector wherever possible, in community service, if necessary. That's the only way we'll ever make welfare what it ought to be, a second chance, not a way of life.

I know it will be difficult to tackle welfare reform in 1994 at the same time we tackle health care. But let me point out, I think it is inevitable and imperative. It is estimated that one million people are on welfare today because it's the only way they can get health care coverage for their children. Those who choose to leave welfare for jobs without health benefits, and many entry-level jobs don't have health benefits, find themselves in the incredible position of paying taxes that help to pay for health care coverage for those who made the other choice to stay on welfare. No wonder people leave work and go back to welfare to get health care coverage. We've got to solve the health care problem to have real welfare reform.

So this year, we will make history by reforming the health care system. And I would say to you, all of you, my fellow public servants, this is another issue where the people are way ahead of the politicians. That may not be popular with either party, but it happens to be the truth.

You know, the First Lady has received now almost a million letters from people all across America and from all walks of life. I'd like to share just one of them with you. Richard Anderson of Reno, Nevada, lost his job and with it, his health insurance. Two weeks later his wife, Judy, suffered a cerebral aneurysm. He rushed her to the hospital, where she stayed in intensive care for 21 days. The Andersons' bills were over $120,000. Although Judy recovered and Richard went back to work at $8 an hour, the bills were too much for them, and they were literally forced into bankruptcy. "Mrs. Clinton," he wrote to Hillary, "no one in the United States of America should have to lose everything they've worked for all their lives because they were unfortunate enough to become ill." It was to help the Richard and Judy Andersons of America that the First Lady and so many others have worked so hard and so long on this health care reform issue. We owe them our thanks and our action.

I know there are people here who say there's no health care crisis. Tell it to Richard and Judy Anderson. Tell it to the 58 million Americans who have no coverage at all for some time each year. Tell it to the 81 million Americans with those preexisting conditions. Those folks are paying more, or they can't get insurance at all. Or they can't ever change their jobs because they or someone in their family has one of those preexisting conditions. Tell it to the small businesses burdened by the skyrocketing cost of insurance. Most small businesses cover their employees, and they pay on average 35 percent more in premiums than big businesses or Government. Or tell it to the 76 percent of insured Americans, three out of four whose policies have lifetime limits. And that means they can find themselves without any coverage at all just when they need it the most. So if any of you believe there's no crisis, you tell it to those people, because I can't.

There are some people who literally do not understand the impact of this problem on people's lives. And all you have to do is go out and listen to them. Just go talk to them anywhere in any congressional district in this country. They're Republicans and Democrats and independents; it doesn't have a lick to do with party. They think we don't get it. And it's time we show them that we do get it.

From the day we began, our health care initiative has been designed to strengthen what is good about our health care system: the world's best health care professionals, cutting-edge research and wonderful research institutions, Medicare for older Americans. None of this, none of it should be put at risk.

But we're paying more and more money for less and less care. Every year fewer and fewer Americans even get to choose their doctors. Every year doctors and nurses spend more time on paperwork and less time with patients because of the absolute bureaucratic nightmare the present system has become. This system is riddled with inefficiency, with abuse, with fraud, and everybody knows it. In today's health care system, insurance companies call the shots. They pick whom they cover and how they cover them. They can cut off your benefits when you need your coverage the most. They are in charge.

What does it mean? It means every night millions of well-insured Americans go to bed just an illness, an accident, or a pink slip away from having no coverage or financial ruin. It means every morning millions of Americans go to work without any health insurance at all, something the workers in no other advanced country in the world do. It means that every year, more and more hard-working people are told to pick a new doctor because their boss has had to pick a new plan. And countless others turn down better jobs because they know if they take the better job, they will lose their health insurance. If we just let the health care system continue to drift, our country will have people with less care, fewer choices, and higher bills.

Now, our approach protects the quality of care and people's choices. It builds on what works today in the private sector, to expand employer-based coverage, to guarantee private insurance for every American. And I might say, employer-based private insurance for every American was proposed 20 years ago by President Richard Nixon to the United States Congress. It was a good idea then, and it's a better idea today.

Why do we want guaranteed private insurance? Because right now 9 out of 10 people who have insurance get it through their employers. And that should continue. And if your employer is providing good benefits at reasonable prices, that should continue, too. That ought to make the Congress and the President feel better.

Our goal is health insurance everybody can depend on: comprehensive benefits that cover preventive care and prescription drugs; health premiums that don't just explode when you get sick or you get older; the power, no matter how small your business is, to choose dependable insurance at the same competitive rates governments and big business get today; one simple form for people who are sick; and most of all, the freedom to choose a plan and the right to choose your own doctor.

Our approach protects older Americans. Every plan before the Congress proposes to slow the growth of Medicare. The difference is this: We believe those savings should be used to improve health care for senior citizens. Medicare must be protected, and it should cover prescription drugs, and we should take the first steps in covering long-term care. To those who would cut Medicare without protecting seniors, I say the solution to today's squeeze on middle-class working people's health care is not to put the squeeze on middle-class retired people's health care. We can do better than that.

When it's all said and done, it's pretty simple to me. Insurance ought to mean what it used to mean: You pay a fair price for security, and when you get sick, health care's always there, no matter what.

Along with the guarantee of health security, we all have to admit, too, there must be more responsibility on the part of all of us in how we use this system. People have to take their kids to get immunized. We should all take advantage of preventive care. We must all work together to stop the violence that explodes our emergency rooms. We have to practice better health habits, and we can't abuse the system. And those who don't have insurance under our approach will get coverage, but they'll have to pay something for it, too. The minority of businesses that provide no insurance at all and in so doing shift the cost of the care of their employees to others, should contribute something. People who smoke should pay more for a pack of cigarettes.

Everybody can contribute something if we want to solve the health care crisis. There can't be any more something for nothing. It will not be easy but it can be done.

Now, in the coming months I hope very much to work with both Democrats and Republicans to reform a health care system by using the market to bring down costs and to achieve lasting health security. But if you look at history we see that for 60 years this country has tried to reform health care. President Roosevelt tried. President Truman tried. President Nixon tried. President Carter tried. Every time the special interests were powerful enough to defeat them. But not this time.

I know that facing up to these interests will require courage. It will raise critical questions about the way we finance our campaigns and how lobbyists yield their influence. The work of change, frankly, will never get any easier until we limit the influence of well-financed interests who profit from this current system. So I also must now call on you to finish the job both Houses began last year by passing tough and meaningful campaign finance reform and lobby reform legislation this year.

You know, my fellow Americans, this is really a test for all of us. The American people provide those of us in Government service with terrific health care benefits at reasonable costs. We have health care that's always there. I think we need to give every hard-working, tax-paying American the same health care security they have already given to us.

I want to make this very clear. I am open, as I have said repeatedly, to the best ideas of concerned Members of both parties. I have no special brief for any specific approach, even in our own bill, except this: If you send me legislation that does not guarantee every American private health insurance that can never be taken away, you will force me to take this pen, veto the legislation, and we'll come right back here and start all over again.

But I don't think that's going to happen. I think we're ready to act now. I believe that you're ready to act now. And if you're ready to guarantee every American the same health care that you have, health care that can never be taken away, now, not next year or the year after, now is the time to stand with the people who sent us here. Now.

As we take these steps together to renew our strength at home, we cannot turn away from our obligation to renew our leadership abroad. This is a promising moment. Because of the agreements we have reached this year, last year, Russia's strategic nuclear missiles soon will no longer be pointed at the United States, nor will we point ours at them. Instead of building weapons in space, Russian scientists will help us to build the international space station.

Of course, there are still dangers in the world: rampant arms proliferation, bitter regional conflicts, ethnic and nationalist tensions in many new democracies, severe environmental degradation the world over, and fanatics who seek to cripple the world's cities with terror. As the world's greatest power, we must, therefore, maintain our defenses and our responsibilities.

This year, we secured indictments against terrorists and sanctions against those who harbor them. We worked to promote environmentally sustainable economic growth. We achieved agreements with Ukraine, with Belarus, with Kazahkstan to eliminate completely their nuclear arsenal. We are working to achieve a Korean Peninsula free of nuclear weapons. We will seek early ratification of a treaty to ban chemical weapons worldwide. And earlier today, we joined with over 30 nations to begin negotiations on a comprehensive ban to stop all nuclear testing.

But nothing, nothing is more important to our security than our Nation's Armed Forces. We honor their contributions, including those who are carrying out the longest humanitarian air lift in history in Bosnia, those who will complete their mission in Somalia this year and their brave comrades who gave their lives there. Our forces are the finest military our Nation has ever had. And I have pledged that as long as I am President, they will remain the best equipped, the best trained, and the best prepared fighting force on the face of the Earth.

Last year I proposed a defense plan that maintains our post-cold-war security at a lower cost. This year many people urged me to cut our defense spending further to pay for other Government programs. I said, no. The budget I send to Congress draws the line against further defense cuts. It protects the readiness and quality of our forces. Ultimately, the best strategy is to do that. We must not cut defense further. I hope the Congress, without regard to party, will support that position.

Ultimately, the best strategy to ensure our security and to build a durable peace is to support the advance of democracy elsewhere. Democracies don't attack each other, they make better trading partners and partners in diplomacy. That is why we have supported, you and I, the democratic reformers in Russia and in the other states of the former Soviet bloc. I applaud the bipartisan support this Congress provided last year for our initiatives to help Russia, Ukraine, and the other states through their epic transformations.

Our support of reform must combine patience for the enormity of the task and vigilance for our fundamental interest and values. We will continue to urge Russia and the other states to press ahead with economic reforms. And we will seek to cooperate with Russia to solve regional problems, while insisting that if Russian troops operate in neighboring states, they do so only when those states agree to their presence and in strict accord with international standards.

But we must also remember as these nations chart their own futures—and they must chart their own futures—how much more secure and more prosperous our own people will be if democratic and market reforms succeed all across the former Communist bloc. Our policy has been to support that move, and that has been the policy of the Congress. We should continue it.

That is why I went to Europe earlier this month, to work with our European partners, to help to integrate all the former Communist countries into a Europe that has a possibility of becoming unified for the first time in its entire history, its entire history, based on the simple commitments of all nations in Europe to democracy, to free markets, and to respect for existing borders.

With our allies we have created a Partnership For Peace that invites states from the former Soviet bloc and other non-NATO members to work with NATO in military cooperation. When I met with Central Europe's leaders, including Lech Walesa and Václav Havel, men who put their lives on the line for freedom, I told them that the security of their region is important to our country's security.

This year we must also do more to support democratic renewal and human rights and sustainable development all around the world. We will ask Congress to ratify the new GATT [General Agreement on Tariffs and Trade] accord. We will continue standing by South Africa as it works its way through its bold and hopeful and difficult transition to democracy. We will convene a summit of the Western Hemisphere's democratic leaders from Canada to the tip of South America. And we will continue to press for the restoration of true democracy in Haiti. And as we build a more constructive relationship with China, we must continue to insist on clear signs of improvement in that nation's human rights record.

We will also work for new progress toward the Middle East peace. Last year the world watched Yitzhak Rabin and Yasser Arafat at the White House when they had their historic handshake of reconciliation. But there is a long, hard road ahead. And on that road I am determined that I and our administration will do all we can to achieve a comprehensive and lasting peace for all the peoples of the region.

Now, there are some in our country who argue that with the cold war, America should turn its back on the rest of the world. Many around the world were afraid we would do just that. But I took this office on a pledge that had no partisan tinge, to keep our Nation secure by remaining engaged in the rest of the world. And this year, because of our work together, enacting NAFTA, keeping our military strong and prepared, supporting democracy abroad, we have reaffirmed America's leadership, America's engagement. And as a result, the American people are more secure than they were before.

But while Americans are more secure from threats abroad, I think we all know that in many ways we are less secure from threats here at home. Every day the national peace is shattered by crime. In Petaluma, California, an innocent slumber party gives way to agonizing tragedy for the family of Polly Klaas. An ordinary train ride on Long Island ends in a hail of 9-millimeter rounds. A tourist in Florida is nearly burned alive by bigots simply because he is black. Right here in our Nation's Capital, a brave young man named Jason White, a policeman, the son and grandson of policemen, is ruthlessly gunned down. Violent crime and the fear it provokes are crippling our society, limiting personal freedom, and fraying the ties that bind us.

The crime bill before Congress gives you a chance to do something about it, a chance to be tough and smart. What does that mean? Let me begin by saying I care a lot about this issue. Many years ago, when I started out in public life, I was the attorney general of my State. I served as a Governor for a dozen years. I know what it's like to sign laws increasing penalties, to build more prison cells, to carry out the death penalty. I understand this issue. And it is not a simple thing.

First, we must recognize that most violent crimes are committed by a small percentage of criminals who too often break the laws even when they are on parole. Now those who commit crimes should be punished. And those who commit repeated, violent crimes should be told, "When you commit a third violent crime, you will be put away, and put away for good. Three strikes, and you are out."

Second, we must take serious steps to reduce violence and prevent crime, beginning with more police officers and more community policing. We know right now that police who work the streets, know the folks, have the respect of the neighborhood kids, focus on high crime areas, we know that they are more likely to prevent crime as well as catch criminals. Look at the experience of Houston, where the crime rate dropped 17 percent in one year when that approach was taken.

Here tonight is one of those community policemen, a brave, young detective, Kevin Jett, whose beat is eight square blocks in one of the toughest neighborhoods in New York. Every day he restores some sanity and safety and a sense of values and connections to the people whose lives he protects. I'd like to ask him to stand up and be recognized tonight. Thank you, sir.

You will be given a chance to give the children of this country, the law-abiding working people of this country—and don't forget, in the toughest neighborhoods in this country, in the highest crime neighborhoods in this country, the vast majority of people get up every day and obey the law, pay their taxes, do their best to raise their kids. They deserve people like Kevin Jett. And you're going to be given a chance to give the American people another 100,000 of them, well trained. And I urge you to do it.

You have before you crime legislation which also establishes a police corps to encourage young people to get an education and pay it off by serving as police officers; which encourages retiring military personnel to move into police forces, an inordinate resource for our country; one which has a safe schools provision which will give our young people the chance to walk to school in safety and to be in school in safety instead of dodging bullets. These are important things.

The third thing we have to do is to build on the Brady bill, the Brady law, to take further steps to keep guns out of the hands of criminals. I want to say something about this issue. Hunters must always be free to hunt. Law-abiding adults should always be free to own guns and protect their homes. I respect that part of our culture; I grew up in it. But I want to ask the sportsmen and others who lawfully own guns to join us in this campaign to reduce gun violence. I say to you, I know you didn't create this problem, but we need your help to solve it. There is no sporting purpose on Earth that should stop the United States Congress from banishing assault weapons that outgun police and cut down children.

Fourth, we must remember that drugs are a factor in an enormous percentage of crimes. Recent studies indicate, sadly, that drug use is on the rise again among our young people. The crime bill contains—all the crime bills contain—more money for drug treatment for criminal addicts and boot camps for youthful offenders that include incentives to get off drugs and to stay off drugs. Our administration's budget, with all its cuts, contains a large increase in funding for drug treatment and drug education. You must pass them both. We need them desperately.

My fellow Americans, the problem of violence is an American problem. It has no partisan or philosophical element. Therefore, I urge you to find ways as quickly as possible to set aside partisan differences and pass a strong, smart, tough crime bill. But further, I urge you to consider this: As you demand tougher penalties for those who choose violence, let us also remember how we came to this sad point. In our toughest neighborhoods, on our meanest streets, in our poorest rural areas, we have seen a stunning and simultaneous breakdown of community, family, and work, the heart and soul of civilized society. This has created a vast vacuum which has been filled by violence and drugs and gangs. So I ask you to remember that even as we say "no" to crime, we must give people, especially our young people, something to say "yes" to.

Many of our initiatives, from job training to welfare reform to health care to national service, will help to rebuild distressed communities, to strengthen families, to provide work. But more needs to be done. That's what our community empowerment agenda is all about, challenging businesses to provide more investment through empowerment zones, ensuring banks will make loans in the same communities their deposits come from, passing legislation to unleash the power of capital through community development banks to create jobs, opportunity, and hope where they're needed most.

I think you know that to really solve this problem, we'll all have to put our heads together, leave our ideological armor aside, and find some new ideas to do even more. And let's be honest, we all know something else too: Our problems go way beyond the reach of Government. They're rooted in the loss of values, in the disappearance of work, and the breakdown of our families and our communities.

My fellow Americans, we can cut the deficit, create jobs, promote democracy around the world, pass welfare reform and health care, pass the toughest crime bill in history, but still leave too many of our people behind. The American people have got to want to change from within if we're going to bring back work and family and community. We cannot renew our country when within a decade more than half of the children will be born into families where there has been no marriage. We cannot renew this country when 13-year-old boys get semi-automatic weapons to shoot 9-year-olds for kicks. We can't renew our country when children are having children, and the fathers walk away as if the kids don't amount to anything. We can't renew the country when our businesses eagerly look for new investments and new customers abroad but ignore those people right here at home who would give anything to have their jobs and would gladly buy their products if they had the money to do it. We can't renew our country unless more of us, I mean, all of us—are willing to join the churches and the other good citizens, people like all the ministers I've worked with over the years or the priests and the nuns I met at Our Lady of Help in east Los Angeles or my good friend Tony Campollo in Philadelphia, unless we're willing to work with people like that, people who are saving kids, adopting schools, making streets safer. All of us can do that. We can't renew our country until we realize that governments don't raise children, parents do.

Parents who know their children's teachers and turn off the television and help with the homework and teach their kids right from wrong, those kinds of parents can make all the difference. I know, I had one. I'm telling you, we have got to stop pointing our fingers at these kids who have no future and reach our hands out to them. Our country needs it, we need it, and they deserve it.

So I say to you tonight, let's give our children a future. Let us take away their guns and give them books. Let us overcome their despair and replace it with hope. Let us, by our example, teach them to obey the law, respect our neighbors, and cherish our values. Let us weave these sturdy threads into a new American community that can once more stand strong against the forces of despair and evil because everybody has a chance to walk into a better tomorrow.

Oh, there will be naysayers who fear that we won't be equal to the challenges of this time. But they misread our history, our heritage. Even today's headlines, all those things tell us we can and we will overcome any challenge.

When the Earth shook and fires raged in California, when I saw the Mississippi deluge the farmlands of the Midwest in a 500-year flood, when the century's bitterest cold swept from North Dakota to Newport News, it seemed as though the world itself was coming apart at the seams. But the American people, they just came together. They rose to the occasion, neighbor helping neighbor, strangers risking life and limb to save total strangers, showing the better angels of our nature.

Let us not reserve the better angels only for natural disasters, leaving our deepest and most profound problems to petty political fighting. Let us instead be true to our spirit, facing facts, coming together, bringing hope, and moving forward.

Tonight, my fellow Americans, we are summoned to answer a question as old as the Republic itself: What is the state of our Union? It is growing stronger, but it must be stronger still. With your help, and God's help, it will be.

Thank you, and God bless America.

William J. Clinton, 1993–1997

Address before a Joint Session of Congress on the State of the Union

January 24, 1995

Bill Clinton delivered his second State of the Union address in an environment of divided government. The Republicans, united behind their "Contract with America" platform, swept their way into power in both the House and Senate in the 1994 midterm elections, which were viewed as a widespread desire for change.

Clinton, a Democrat, took note of this upheaval at the start of his speech, saying that "the American people certainly voted for change in 1992 [his own election] and 1994." He mentioned Harry Truman and Ronald Reagan, two previous presidents who had worked with Congresses controlled by the opposition party. Clinton acknowledged having made mistakes and having "learned again the importance of humility in all human endeavor." He also commented that the country was stronger than it had been when he took office two years earlier.

Throughout his speech, Clinton referred to a "new social compact" he wanted to start, which he termed the "New Covenant." He called for a bipartisan effort to achieve this new beginning and stated that the test for any action should be, "Is it good for the American people?"

Clinton's speech, which was mostly centrist in tone, ran eighty-two minutes—the longest State of the Union ever delivered orally. One issue he addressed was health care reform, which had been on the top of his agenda a year earlier. But it ended up being a failure for the Clinton administration in 1994, and this time around the president opted to discuss incremental reform rather than the sweeping plan he had not achieved the previous year.

The president reiterated his desire for welfare reform, which he had sought since arriving in the White House. In this context, he mentioned Lynn Woolsey, a Democratic representative from California who had been on welfare earlier in her life.

Congress had passed a crime bill in 1994 that included the Brady handgun-control bill as well as a ban on nineteen assault weapons. Clinton made a point of mentioning that several members of Congress had lost their seats in November because they had voted for that legislation. He stated that he would oppose any attempt by the new Congress to repeal the law.

At the end of the speech, Clinton emphasized the idea of citizenship in the context of building the New Covenant. He lauded the audience members sitting with First Lady Hillary Clinton as examples of what the country should be doing: Cindy Perry, who was teaching in the new AmeriCorps program; Stephen Bishop, the Kansas City police chief who was active in community policing; Corporal Gregory

Depestre, a Haitian-American who was involved in the U.S. effort in Haiti; the Reverends John and Diana Cherry, who founded a large church in Maryland focused on keeping families together; and Jack Lucas, who saved the lives of two companions during his World War II service and won the Congressional Medal of Honor.

Mr. President, Mr. Speaker, Members of the 104th Congress, my fellow Americans:

Again we are here in the sanctuary of democracy, and once again our democracy has spoken. So let me begin by congratulating all of you here in the 104th Congress and congratulating you, Mr. Speaker.

If we agree on nothing else tonight, we must agree that the American people certainly voted for change in 1992 and in 1994. And as I look out at you, I know how some of you must have felt in 1992.

I must say that in both years we didn't hear America singing, we heard America shouting. And now all of us, Republicans and Democrats alike, must say, "We hear you. We will work together to earn the jobs you have given us. For we are the keepers of a sacred trust, and we must be faithful to it in this new and very demanding era."

Over 200 years ago, our Founders changed the entire course of human history by joining together to create a new country based on a single powerful idea: "We hold these truths to be self-evident, that all men are created equal, . . . endowed by their Creator with certain unalienable Rights, and among these are Life, Liberty and the pursuit of Happiness."

It has fallen to every generation since then to preserve that idea, the American idea, and to deepen and expand its meaning in new and different times: to Lincoln and to his Congress to preserve the Union and to end slavery; to Theodore Roosevelt and Woodrow Wilson to restrain the abuses and excesses of the industrial revolution and to assert our leadership in the world; to Franklin Roosevelt to fight the failure and pain of the Great Depression and to win our country's great struggle against fascism; and to all our Presidents since to fight the cold war. Especially, I recall two who struggled to fight that cold war in partnership with Congresses where the majority was of a different party: to Harry Truman, who summoned us to unparalleled prosperity at home and who built the architecture of the cold war; and to Ronald Reagan, whom we wish well tonight and who exhorted us to carry on until the twilight struggle against communism was won.

In another time of change and challenge, I had the honor to be the first President to be elected in the post-cold-war era, an era marked by the global economy, the information revolution, unparalleled change and opportunity and insecurity for the American people. I came to this hallowed Chamber 2 years ago on a mission, to restore the American dream for all our people and to make sure that we move into the 21st century still the strongest force for freedom and democracy in the entire world. I was determined then to tackle the tough problems too long ignored. In this effort I am frank to say that I have made my mistakes, and I have learned again the importance of humility in all human endeavor. But I am also proud to say tonight that our country is stronger than it was 2 years ago. Thank you.

Record numbers of Americans are succeeding in the new global economy. We are at peace, and we are a force for peace and freedom throughout the world. We have almost 6 million new jobs since I became President, and we have the lowest combined rate of unemployment and inflation in 25 years. Our businesses are more productive. And here we have worked to bring the deficit down, to expand trade, to put more police on our streets, to give our citizens more of the tools they need to get an education and to rebuild their own communities.

But the rising tide is not lifting all boats. While our Nation is enjoying peace and prosperity, too many of our people are still working harder and harder, for less and less. While our businesses are restructuring and growing more productive and competitive, too many of our people still can't be sure of having a job next year or even next month. And far more than our material riches are threatened, things far more precious to us, our children, our families, our values.

Our civil life is suffering in America today. Citizens are working together less and shouting at each other more. The common bonds of community which have been the great strength of our country from its very beginning are badly frayed. What are we to do about it?

More than 60 years ago, at the dawn of another new era, President Roosevelt told our Nation, "New conditions impose new requirements on Government and those who conduct Government." And from that simple proposition, he shaped the New Deal, which helped to restore our Nation to prosperity and define the relationship between our people and their Government for half a century.

That approach worked in its time. But we today, we face a very different time and very different conditions. We are moving from an industrial age built on gears and sweat to an information age demanding skills and learning and flexibility. Our Government, once a champion of national purpose, is now seen by many as simply a captive of narrow interests, putting more burdens on our citizens rather than equipping them to get ahead. The values that used to hold us all together seem to be coming apart.

So tonight we must forge a new social compact to meet the challenges of this time. As we enter a new era, we need a new set of understandings, not just with Government but, even more important, with one another as Americans.

That's what I want to talk with you about tonight. I call it the New Covenant. But it's grounded in a very, very old idea, that all Americans have not just a right but a solemn responsibility to rise as far as their God-given talents and determination can take them and to give something back to their communities and their country in return. Opportunity and responsibility: They go hand in hand. We can't have one without the other. And our national community can't hold together without both.

Our New Covenant is a new set of understandings for how we can equip our people to meet the challenges of a new economy, how we can change the way our Government works to fit a different time, and, above all, how we can repair the damaged bonds in our society and come together behind our common purpose. We must have dramatic change in our economy, our Government, and ourselves.

My fellow Americans, without regard to party, let us rise to the occasion. Let us put aside partisanship and pettiness and pride. As we embark on this new course, let us put our country first, remembering that regardless of party label, we are all Americans. And let the final test of everything we do be a simple one: Is it good for the American people?

Let me begin by saying that we cannot ask Americans to be better citizens if we are not better servants. You made a good start by passing that law which applies to

Congress all the laws you put on the private sector, and I was proud to sign it yesterday. But we have a lot more to do before people really trust the way things work around here. Three times as many lobbyists are in the streets and corridors of Washington as were here 20 years ago. The American people look at their Capital, and they see a city where the well-connected and the well-protected can work the system, but the interests of ordinary citizens are often left out.

As the new Congress opened its doors, lobbyists were still doing business as usual; the gifts, the trips, all the things that people are concerned about haven't stopped. Twice this month you missed opportunities to stop these practices. I know there were other considerations in those votes, but I want to use something that I've heard my Republican friends say from time to time, "There doesn't have to be a law for everything." So tonight I ask you to just stop taking the lobbyists' perks. Just stop. We don't have to wait for legislation to pass to send a strong signal to the American people that things are really changing. But I also hope you will send me the strongest possible lobby reform bill, and I'll sign that, too.

We should require lobbyists to tell the people for whom they work what they're spending, what they want. We should also curb the role of big money in elections by capping the cost of campaigns and limiting the influence of PAC's. And as I have said for 3 years, we should work to open the airwaves so that they can be an instrument of democracy, not a weapon of destruction, by giving free TV time to candidates for public office.

When the last Congress killed political reform last year, it was reported in the press that the lobbyists actually stood in the Halls of this sacred building and cheered. This year, let's give the folks at home something to cheer about.

More important, I think we all agree that we have to change the way the Government works. Let's make it smaller, less costly, and smarter; leaner, not meaner.

I just told the Speaker the equal time doctrine is alive and well.

The New Covenant approach to governing is as different from the old bureaucratic way as the computer is from the manual typewriter. The old way of governing around here protected organized interests. We should look out for the interests of ordinary people. The old way divided us by interest, constituency, or class. The New Covenant way should unite us behind a common vision of what's best for our country. The old way dispensed services through large, top-down, inflexible bureaucracies. The New Covenant way should shift these resources and decision-making from bureaucrats to citizens, injecting choice and competition and individual responsibility into national policy. The old way of governing around here actually seemed to reward failure. The New Covenant way should have built-in incentives to reward success. The old way was centralized here in Washington. The New Covenant way must take hold in the communities all across America. And we should help them to do that.

Our job here is to expand opportunity, not bureaucracy, to empower people to make the most of their own lives, and to enhance our security here at home and abroad. We must not ask Government to do what we should do for ourselves. We should rely on Government as a partner to help us to do more for ourselves and for each other.

I hope very much that as we debate these specific and exciting matters, we can go beyond the sterile discussion between the illusion that there is somehow a program for every problem, on the one hand, and the other illusion that the Government is a source of every problem we have. Our job is to get rid of yesterday's Government so that our own people can meet today's and tomorrow's needs. And we ought to do it together.

You know, for years before I became President, I heard others say they would cut Government and how bad it was, but not much happened. We actually did it. We cut over a quarter of a trillion dollars in spending, more than 300 domestic programs, more than 100,000 positions from the Federal bureaucracy in the last 2 years alone. Based on decisions already made, we will have cut a total of more than a quarter of a million positions from the Federal Government, making it the smallest it has been since John Kennedy was President, by the time I come here again next year.

Under the leadership of Vice President [Al] Gore, our initiatives have already saved taxpayers $63 billion. The age of the $500 hammer and the ashtray you can break on "David Letterman" is gone. Deadwood programs, like mohair subsidies, are gone. We've streamlined the Agriculture Department by reducing it by more than 1,200 offices. We've slashed the small business loan form from an inch thick to a single page. We've thrown away the Government's 10,000-page personnel manual.

And the Government is working better in important ways: FEMA, the Federal Emergency Management Agency, has gone from being a disaster to helping people in disasters. You can ask the farmers in the Middle West who fought the flood there or the people in California who have dealt with floods and earthquakes and fires, and they'll tell you that. Government workers, working hand in hand with private business, rebuilt southern California's fractured freeways in record time and under budget. And because the Federal Government moved fast, all but one of the 5,600 schools damaged in the earthquake are back in business.

Now, there are a lot of other things that I could talk about. I want to just mention one because it will be discussed here in the next few weeks. University administrators all over the country have told me that they are saving weeks and weeks of bureaucratic time now because of our direct college loan program, which makes college loans cheaper and more affordable with better repayment terms for students, costs the Government less, and cuts out paperwork and bureaucracy for the Government and for the universities. We shouldn't cap that program. We should give every college in America the opportunity to be a part of it.

Previous Government programs gathered dust. The reinventing Government report is getting results. And we're not through. There's going to be a second round of reinventing Government. We propose to cut $130 billion in spending by shrinking departments, extending our freeze on domestic spending, cutting 60 public housing programs down to 3, getting rid of over 100 programs we do not need, like the Interstate Commerce Commission and the Helium Reserve Program. And we're working on getting rid of unnecessary regulations and making them more sensible. The programs and regulations that have outlived their usefulness should go. We have to cut yesterday's Government to help solve tomorrow's problems.

And we need to get Government closer to the people it's meant to serve. We need to help move programs down to the point where States and communities and private citizens in the private sector can do a better job. If they can do it, we ought to let them do it. We should get out of the way and let them do what they can do better. Taking power away from Federal bureaucracies and giving it back to communities and individuals is something everyone should be able to be for.

It's time for Congress to stop passing on to the States the cost of decisions we make here in Washington. I know there are still serious differences over the details of the unfunded mandates legislation, but I want to work with you to make sure we pass a reasonable bill which will protect the national interests and give justified relief where we need to give it.

For years, Congress concealed in the budget scores of pet spending projects. Last year was no different. There was a $1 million to study stress in plants and $12 million for a tick removal program that didn't work. It's hard to remove ticks. Those of us who have had them know. But I'll tell you something, if you'll give me line-item veto, I'll remove some of that unnecessary spending.

But I think we should all remember, and almost all of us would agree, that Government still has important responsibilities. Our young people—we should think of this when we cut—our young people hold our future in their hands. We still owe a debt to our veterans. And our senior citizens have made us what we are. Now, my budget cuts a lot. But it protects education, veterans, Social Security, and Medicare, and I hope you will do the same thing. You should, and I hope you will.

And when we give more flexibility to the States, let us remember that there are certain fundamental national needs that should be addressed in every State, North and South, East and West: Immunization against childhood disease, school lunches in all our schools, Head Start, medical care and nutrition for pregnant women and infants—medical care and nutrition for pregnant women and infants, all these things, all these things are in the national interest.

I applaud your desire to get rid of costly and unnecessary regulations. But when we deregulate, let's remember what national action in the national interest has given us: safer food for our families, safer toys for our children, safer nursing homes for our parents, safer cars and highways, and safer workplaces, cleaner air, and cleaner water. Do we need common sense and fairness in our regulations? You bet we do. But we can have common sense and still provide for safe drinking water. We can have fairness and still clean up toxic dumps, and we ought to do it.

Should we cut the deficit more? Well, of course we should. Of course we should. But we can bring it down in a way that still protects our economic recovery and does not unduly punish people who should not be punished but instead should be helped.

I know many of you in this Chamber support the balanced budget amendment. I certainly want to balance the budget. Our administration has done more to bring the budget down and to save money than any in a very, very long time. If you believe passing this amendment is the right thing to do, then you have to be straight with the American people. They have a right to know what you're going to cut, what taxes you're going to raise, and how it's going to affect them. We should be doing things in the open around here. For example, everybody ought to know if this proposal is going to endanger Social Security. I would oppose that, and I think most Americans would.

Nothing has done more to undermine our sense of common responsibility than our failed welfare system. This is one of the problems we have to face here in Washington in our New Covenant. It rewards welfare over work. It undermines family values. It lets millions of parents get away without paying their child support. It keeps a minority but a significant minority of the people on welfare trapped on it for a very long time.

I've worked on this problem for a long time, nearly 15 years now. As a Governor, I had the honor of working with the Reagan administration to write the last welfare reform bill back in 1988. In the last 2 years, we made a good start at continuing the work of welfare reform. Our administration gave two dozen States the right to slash through Federal rules and regulations to reform their own welfare systems and to try to promote work and responsibility over welfare and dependency.

Last year I introduced the most sweeping welfare reform plan ever presented by an administration. We have to make welfare what it was meant to be, a second chance, not a way of life. We have to help those on welfare move to work as quickly as possible, to provide child care and teach them skills, if that's what they need, for up to 2 years. And after that, there ought to be a simple, hard rule: Anyone who can work must go to work. If a parent isn't paying child support, they should be forced to pay. We should suspend drivers' license, track them across State lines, make them work off what they owe. That is what we should do. Governments do not raise children, people do. And the parents must take responsibility for the children they bring into this world.

I want to work with you, with all of you, to pass welfare reform. But our goal must be to liberate people and lift them up from dependence to independence, from welfare to work, from mere childbearing to responsible parenting. Our goal should not be to punish them because they happen to be poor.

We should, we should require work and mutual responsibility. But we shouldn't cut people off just because they're poor, they're young, or even because they're unmarried. We should promote responsibility by requiring young mothers to live at home with their parents or in other supervised settings, by requiring them to finish school. But we shouldn't put them and their children out on the street. And I know all the arguments, pro and con, and I have read and thought about this for a long time. I still don't think we can in good conscience punish poor children for the mistakes of their parents.

My fellow Americans, every single survey shows that all the American people care about this without regard to party or race or region. So let this be the year we end welfare as we know it. But also let this be the year that we are all able to stop using this issue to divide America. No one is more eager to end welfare—I may be the only President who has actually had the opportunity to sit in a welfare office, who's actually spent hours and hours talking to people on welfare. And I am telling you, the people who are trapped on it know it doesn't work; they also want to get off. So we can promote, together, education and work and good parenting. I have no problem with punishing bad behavior or the refusal to be a worker or a student or a responsible parent. I just don't want to punish poverty and past mistakes. All of us have made our mistakes, and none of us can change our yesterdays. But every one of us can change our tomorrows. And America's best example of that may be Lynn Woolsey, who worked her way off welfare to become a Congresswoman from the State of California.

I know the Members of this Congress are concerned about crime, as are all the citizens of our country. And I remind you that last year we passed a very tough crime bill: longer sentences, "three strikes and you're out," almost 60 new capital punishment offenses, more prisons, more prevention, 100,000 more police. And we paid for it all by reducing the size of the Federal bureaucracy and giving the money back to local communities to lower the crime rate.

There may be other things we can do to be tougher on crime, to be smarter with crime, to help to lower that rate first. Well, if there are, let's talk about them, and let's do them. But let's not go back on the things that we did last year that we know work, that we know work because the local law enforcement officers tell us that we did the right thing, because local community leaders who have worked for years and years to lower the crime rate tell us that they work. Let's look at the experience of our cities and our rural areas where the crime rate has gone down and ask the people who did it how they did it. And if what we did last year supports the decline in the crime rate—and I am convinced that it does—let us not go back on it. Let's stick with it, implement it. We've got 4 more hard years of work to do to do that.

I don't want to destroy the good atmosphere in the room or in the country tonight, but I have to mention one issue that divided this body greatly last year. The last Congress also passed the Brady bill and, in the crime bill, the ban on 19 assault weapons. I don't think it's a secret to anybody in this room that several Members of the last Congress who voted for that aren't here tonight because they voted for it. And I know, therefore, that some of you who are here because they voted for it are under enormous pressure to repeal it. I just have to tell you how I feel about it.

The Members of Congress who voted for that bill and I would never do anything to infringe on the right to keep and bear arms to hunt and to engage in other appropriate sporting activities. I've done it since I was a boy, and I'm going to keep right on doing it until I can't do it anymore. But a lot of people laid down their seats in Congress so that police officers and kids wouldn't have to lay down their lives under a hail of assault weapon attack, and I will not let that be repealed. I will not let it be repealed.

I'd like to talk about a couple of other issues we have to deal with. I want us to cut more spending, but I hope we won't cut Government programs that help to prepare us for the new economy, promote responsibility, and are organized from the grassroots up, not by Federal bureaucracy. The very best example of this is the national service corps, AmeriCorps. It passed with strong bipartisan support. And now there are 20,000 Americans, more than ever served in one year in the Peace Corps, working all over this country, helping people person-to-person in local grassroots volunteer groups, solving problems, and in the process earning some money for their education. This is citizenship at its best. It's good for the AmeriCorps members, but it's good for the rest of us, too. It's the essence of the New Covenant, and we shouldn't stop it.

All Americans, not only in the States most heavily affected but in every place in this country, are rightly disturbed by the large numbers of illegal aliens entering our country. The jobs they hold might otherwise be held by citizens or legal immigrants. The public service they use impose burdens on our taxpayers. That's why our administration has moved aggressively to secure our borders more by hiring a record number of new border guards, by deporting twice as many criminal aliens as ever before, by cracking down on illegal hiring, by barring welfare benefits to illegal aliens. In the budget I will present to you, we will try to do more to speed the deportation of illegal aliens who are arrested for crimes, to better identify illegal aliens in the workplace as recommended by the commission headed by former Congresswoman Barbara Jordan. We are a nation of immigrants. But we are also a nation of laws. It is wrong and ultimately self-defeating for a nation of immigrants to permit the kind of abuse of our immigration laws we have seen in recent years, and we must do more to stop it.

The most important job of our Government in this new era is to empower the American people to succeed in the global economy. America has always been a land of opportunity, a land where, if you work hard, you can get ahead. We've become a great middle class country. Middle class values sustain us. We must expand that middle class and shrink the underclass, even as we do everything we can to support the millions of Americans who are already successful in the new economy.

America is once again the world's strongest economic power: almost 6 million new jobs in the last 2 years, exports booming, inflation down. High-wage jobs are coming back. A record number of American entrepreneurs are living the American dream. If we want it to stay that way, those who work and lift our Nation must have more of its benefits.

Today, too many of those people are being left out. They're working harder for less. They have less security, less income, less certainty that they can even afford a vacation, much less college for their kids or retirement for themselves. We cannot let this continue. If we don't act, our economy will probably keep doing what it's been doing since about 1978, when the income growth began to go to those at the very top of our economic scale and the people in the vast middle got very little growth, and people who worked like crazy but were on the bottom then fell even further and further behind in the years afterward, no matter how hard they worked.

We've got to have a Government that can be a real partner in making this new economy work for all of our people, a Government that helps each and every one of us to get an education and to have the opportunity to renew our skills. That's why we worked so hard to increase educational opportunities in the last 2 years, from Head Start to public schools, to apprenticeships for young people who don't go to college, to making college loans more available and more affordable. That's the first thing we have to do. We've got to do something to empower people to improve their skills.

The second thing we ought to do is to help people raise their incomes immediately by lowering their taxes. We took the first step in 1993 with a working family tax cut for 15 million families with incomes under $27,000, a tax cut that this year will average about $1,000 a family. And we also gave tax reductions to most small and new businesses. Before we could do more than that, we first had to bring down the deficit we inherited, and we had to get economic growth up. Now we've done both. And now we can cut taxes in a more comprehensive way. But tax cuts should reinforce and promote our first obligation: to empower our citizens through education and training to make the most of their own lives. The spotlight should shine on those who make the right choices for themselves, their families, and their communities.

I have proposed the middle class bill of rights, which should properly be called the bill of rights and responsibilities because its provisions only benefit those who are working to educate and raise their children and to educate themselves. It will, therefore, give needed tax relief and raise incomes in both the short run and the long run in a way that benefits all of us.

There are four provisions. First, a tax deduction for all education and training after high school. If you think about it, we permit businesses to deduct their investment, we permit individuals to deduct interest on their home mortgages, but today an education is even more important to the economic well-being of our whole country than even those things are. We should do everything we can to encourage it. And I hope you will support it. Second, we ought to cut taxes $500 for families with children under 13. Third, we ought to foster more savings and personal responsibility by permitting people to establish an individual retirement account and withdraw from it tax free for the cost of education, health care, first-time homebuying, or the care of a parent. And fourth, we should pass a GI bill for America's workers. We propose to collapse nearly 70 Federal programs and not give the money to the States but give the money directly to the American people, offer vouchers to them so that they, if they're laid off or if they're working for a very low wage, can get a voucher worth $2,600 a year for up to 2 years to go to their local community colleges or wherever else they want to get the skills they need to improve their lives. Let's empower people in this way, move it from the Government directly to the workers of America.

Now, any one of us can call for a tax cut, but I won't accept one that explodes the deficit or puts our recovery at risk. We ought to pay for our tax cuts fully and honestly.

Just 2 years ago, it was an open question whether we would find the strength to cut the deficit. Thanks to the courage of the people who were here then, many of whom didn't return, we did cut the deficit. We began to do what others said would not be done. We cut the deficit by over $600 billion, about $10,000 for every family in this country. It's coming down 3 years in a row for the first time since Mr. Truman was President, and I don't think anybody in America wants us to let it explode again.

In the budget I will send you, the middle class bill of rights is fully paid for by budget cuts in bureaucracy, cuts in programs, cuts in special interest subsidies. And the spending cuts will more than double the tax cuts. My budget pays for the middle class bill of rights without any cuts in Medicare. And I will oppose any attempts to pay for tax cuts with Medicare cuts. That's not the right thing to do.

I know that a lot of you have your own ideas about tax relief, and some of them I find quite interesting. I really want to work with all of you. My test for our proposals will be: Will it create jobs and raise incomes; will it strengthen our families and support our children; is it paid for; will it build the middle class and shrink the underclass? If it does, I'll support it. But if it doesn't, I won't.

The goal of building the middle class and shrinking the underclass is also why I believe that you should raise the minimum wage. It rewards work. Two and a half million Americans, two and a half million Americans, often women with children, are working out there today for $4.25 an hour. In terms of real buying power, by next year that minimum wage will be at a 40-year low. That's not my idea of how the new economy ought to work.

Now, I've studied the arguments and the evidence for and against a minimum wage increase. I believe the weight of the evidence is that a modest increase does not cost jobs and may even lure people back into the job market. But the most important thing is, you can't make a living on $4.25 an hour, especially if you have children, even with the working families tax cut we passed last year. In the past, the minimum wage has been a bipartisan issue, and I think it should be again. So I want to challenge you to have honest hearings on this, to get together, to find a way to make the minimum wage a living wage.

Members of Congress have been here less than a month, but by the end of the week, 28 days into the new year, every Member of Congress will have earned as much in congressional salary as a minimum wage worker makes all year long.

Everybody else here, including the President, has something else that too many Americans do without, and that's health care. Now, last year we almost came to blows over health care, but we didn't do anything. And the cold, hard fact is that, since last year, since I was here, another 1.1 million Americans in working families have lost their health care. And the cold, hard fact is that many millions more, most of them farmers and small business people and self-employed people, have seen their premiums skyrocket, their copays and deductibles go up. There's a whole bunch of people in this country that in the statistics have health insurance but really what they've got is a piece of paper that says they won't lose their home if they get sick.

Now, I still believe our country has got to move toward providing health security for every American family. But I know that last year, as the evidence indicates, we bit off more than we could chew. So I'm asking you that we work together. Let's do it step by step. Let's do whatever we have to do to get something done. Let's at least pass meaningful insurance reform so that no American risks losing coverage for facing skyrocketing prices, that nobody loses their coverage because they face high prices or unavailable insurance when they change jobs or lose a job or a family member gets sick.

I want to work together with all of you who have an interest in this, with the Democrats who worked on it last time, with the Republican leaders like Senator Dole, who has a longtime commitment to health care reform and made some constructive proposals in this area last year. We ought to make sure that self-employed people in small businesses can buy insurance at more affordable rates through voluntary purchasing pools. We ought to help families provide long-term care for a sick parent or a disabled child. We can work to help workers who lose their jobs at least keep their health insurance coverage for a year while they look for work. And we can find a way—it may take some time, but we can find a way—to make sure that our children have health care.

You know, I think everybody in this room, without regard to party, can be proud of the fact that our country was rated as having the world's most productive economy for the first time in nearly a decade. But we can't be proud of the fact that we're the only wealthy country in the world that has a smaller percentage of the work force and their children with health insurance today than we did 10 years ago, the last time we were the most productive economy in the world. So let's work together on this. It is too important for politics as usual.

Much of what the American people are thinking about tonight is what we've already talked about. A lot of people think that the security concerns of America today are entirely internal to our borders. They relate to the security of our jobs and our homes and our incomes and our children, our streets, our health, and protecting those borders. Now that the cold war has passed, it's tempting to believe that all the security issues, with the possible exception of trade, reside here at home. But it's not so. Our security still depends upon our continued world leadership for peace and freedom and democracy. We still can't be strong at home unless we're strong abroad.

The financial crisis in Mexico is a case in point. I know it's not popular to say it tonight, but we have to act, not for the Mexican people but for the sake of the millions of Americans whose livelihoods are tied to Mexico's well-being. If we want to secure American jobs, preserve American exports, safeguard America's borders, then we must pass the stabilization program and help to put Mexico back on track.

Now let me repeat: It's not a loan; it's not foreign aid; it's not a bailout. We will be given a guarantee like cosigning a note, with good collateral that will cover our risks. This legislation is the right thing for America. That's why the bipartisan leadership has supported it. And I hope you in Congress will pass it quickly. It is in our interest, and we can explain it to the American people because we're going to do it in the right way.

You know, tonight, this is the first State of the Union Address ever delivered since the beginning of the cold war when not a single Russian missile is pointed at the children of America. And along with the Russians, we're on our way to destroying the missiles and the bombers that carry 9,000 nuclear warheads. We've come so far so fast in this post-cold-war world that it's easy to take the decline of the nuclear threat for granted. But it's still there, and we aren't finished yet.

This year I'll ask the Senate to approve START II to eliminate weapons that carry 5,000 more warheads. The United States will lead the charge to extend indefinitely the Nuclear Non-Proliferation Treaty, to enact a comprehensive nuclear test ban, and to eliminate chemical weapons. To stop and roll back North Korea's potentially deadly nuclear program, we'll continue to implement the agreement we have reached with that nation. It's smart. It's tough. It's a deal based on continuing inspection with safeguards for our allies and ourselves.

This year I'll submit to Congress comprehensive legislation to strengthen our hand in combating terrorists, whether they strike at home or abroad. As the cowards who bombed the World Trade Center found out, this country will hunt down terrorists and bring them to justice.

Just this week, another horrendous terrorist act in Israel killed 19 and injured scores more. On behalf of the American people and all of you, I send our deepest sympathy to the families of the victims. I know that in the face of such evil, it is hard for the people in the Middle East to go forward. But the terrorists represent the past, not the future. We must and we will pursue a comprehensive peace between Israel and all her neighbors in the Middle East.

Accordingly, last night I signed an Executive order that will block the assets in the United States of terrorist organizations that threaten to disrupt the peace process. It prohibits financial transactions with these groups. And tonight I call on all our allies and peace-loving nations throughout the world to join us with renewed fervor in a global effort to combat terrorism. We cannot permit the future to be marred by terror and fear and paralysis.

From the day I took the oath of office, I pledged that our Nation would maintain the best equipped, best trained, and best prepared military on Earth. We have, and they are. They have managed the dramatic downsizing of our forces after the cold war with remarkable skill and spirit. But to make sure our military is ready for action and to provide the pay and the quality of life the military and their families deserve, I'm asking the Congress to add $25 billion in defense spending over the next 6 years.

I have visited many bases at home and around the world since I became President. Tonight I repeat that request with renewed conviction. We ask a very great deal of our Armed Forces. Now that they are smaller in number, we ask more of them. They go out more often to more different places and stay longer. They are called to service in many, many ways. And we must give them and their families what the times demand and what they have earned.

Just think about what our troops have done in the last year, showing America at its best, helping to save hundreds of thousands of people in Rwanda, moving with lightning speed to head off another threat to Kuwait, giving freedom and democracy back to the people of Haiti. We have proudly supported peace and prosperity and freedom from South Africa to Northern Ireland, from Central and Eastern Europe to Asia, from Latin America to the Middle East. All these endeavors are good in those places, but they make our future more confident and more secure.

Well, my fellow Americans, that's my agenda for America's future: expanding opportunity, not bureaucracy; enhancing security at home and abroad; empowering our people to make the most of their own lives. It's ambitious and achievable, but it's not enough. We even need more than new ideas for changing the world or equipping Americans to compete in the new economy, more than a Government that's smaller, smarter, and wiser, more than all of the changes we can make in Government and in the private sector from the outside in.

Our fortunes and our posterity also depend upon our ability to answer some questions from within, from the values and voices that speak to our hearts as well as our heads; voices that tell us we have to do more to accept responsibility for ourselves and our families, for our communities, and yes, for our fellow citizens. We see our families and our communities all over this country coming apart, and we feel the common ground shifting from under us. The PTA, the town hall meeting, the ball park, it's hard for a lot of overworked parents to find the time and space for those things that strengthen the bonds of trust and cooperation. Too many of our children don't even have parents and grandparents who can give them those experiences that they need to build their own character and their sense of identity.

We all know what while we here in this Chamber can make a difference on those things, that the real differences will be made by our fellow citizens, where they work and where they live and that it will be made almost without regard to party. When I used to go to the softball park in Little Rock to watch my daughter's league, and people would come up to me, fathers and mothers, and talk to me, I can honestly say I had no idea whether 90 percent of them were Republicans or Democrats. When I visited the relief centers after the floods in California, northern California, last week, a woman came up to me and did something that very few of you would do. She hugged me and said, "Mr. President, I'm a Republican, but I'm glad you're here."

Now, why? We can't wait for disasters to act the way we used to act every day, because as we move into this next century, everybody matters. We don't have a person to waste. And a lot of people are losing a lot of chances to do better. That means that we need a New Covenant for everybody.

For our corporate and business leaders, we're going to work here to keep bringing the deficit down, to expand markets, to support their success in every possible way. But they have an obligation when they're doing well to keep jobs in our communities and give their workers a fair share of the prosperity they generate.

For people in the entertainment industry in this country, we applaud your creativity and your worldwide success, and we support your freedom of expression. But you do have a responsibility to assess the impact of your work and to understand the damage that comes from the incessant, repetitive, mindless violence and irresponsible conduct that permeates our media all the time.

We've got to ask our community leaders and all kinds of organizations to help us stop our most serious social problem, the epidemic of teen pregnancies and births where there is no marriage. I have sent to Congress a plan to target schools all over this country with anti-pregnancy programs that work. But Government can only do so much. Tonight I call on parents and leaders all across this country to join together in a national campaign against teen pregnancy to make a difference. We can do this, and we must.

And I would like to say a special word to our religious leaders. You know, I'm proud of the fact the United States has more houses of worship per capita than any country in the world. These people who lead our houses of worship can ignite their congregations to carry their faith into action, can reach out to all of our children, to all of the people in distress, to those who have been savaged by the breakdown of all we hold dear. Because so much of what must be done must come from the inside out and our religious leaders and their congregations can make all the difference, they have a role in the New Covenant as well.

There must be more responsibility for all of our citizens. You know, it takes a lot of people to help all the kids in trouble stay off the streets and in school. It takes a lot of people to build the Habitat for Humanity houses that the Speaker celebrates on his lapel pin. It takes a lot of people to provide the people power for all of the civic organizations in this country that made our communities mean so much to most of us when we were kids. It takes every parent to teach the children the difference between right and wrong and to encourage them to learn and grow and to say no to the wrong things but also to believe that they can be whatever they want to be.

I know it's hard when you're working harder for less, when you're under great stress to do these things. A lot of our people don't have the time or the emotional stress, they think, to do the work of citizenship.

Most of us in politics haven't helped very much. For years, we've mostly treated citizens like they were consumers or spectators, sort of political couch potatoes who were supposed to watch the TV ads either promise them something for nothing or play on their fears and frustrations. And more and more of our citizens now get most of their information in very negative and aggressive ways that are hardly conducive to honest and open conversations. But the truth is, we have got to stop seeing each other as enemies just because we have different views.

If you go back to the beginning of this country, the great strength of America, as de Tocqueville pointed out when he came here a long time ago, has always been our ability to associate with people who were different from ourselves and to work together to find common ground. And in this day, everybody has a responsibility to do more of that. We simply cannot want for a tornado, a fire, or a flood to behave like Americans ought to behave in dealing with one another.

I want to finish up here by pointing out some folks that are up with the First Lady that represent what I'm trying to talk about—citizens. I have no idea what their party affiliation is or who they voted for in the last election. But they represent what we ought to be doing.

Cindy Perry teaches second graders to read in AmeriCorps in rural Kentucky. She gains when she gives. She's a mother of four. She says that her service inspired her to get her high school equivalency last year. She was married when she was a teenager—stand up, Cindy. She was married when she was a teenager. She had four children. But she had time to serve other people, to get her high school equivalency, and she's going to use her AmeriCorps money to go back to college.

Chief Stephen Bishop is the police chief of Kansas City. He's been a national leader—stand up, Steve. He's been a national leader in using more police in community policing, and he's worked with AmeriCorps to do it. And the crime rate in Kansas City has gone down as a result of what he did.

Corporal Gregory Depestre went to Haiti as part of his adopted country's force to help secure democracy in his native land. And I might add, we must be the only country in the world that could have gone to Haiti and taken Haitian-Americans there who could speak the language and talk to the people. And he was one of them, and we're proud of him.

The next two folks I've had the honor of meeting and getting to know a little bit, the Reverend John and the Reverend Diana Cherry of the AME Zion Church in Temple Hills, Maryland. I'd like to ask them to stand. I want to tell you about them. In the early eighties, they left Government service and formed a church in a small living room in a small house, in the early eighties. Today that church has 17,000 members. It is one of the three or four biggest churches in the entire United States. It grows by 200 a month. They do it together. And the special focus of their ministry is keeping families together.

Two things they did make a big impression on me. I visited their church once, and I learned they were building a new sanctuary closer to the Washington, DC, line in a higher crime, higher drug rate area because they thought it was part of their ministry to change the lives of the people who needed them. The second thing I want to say is that once Reverend Cherry was at a meeting at the White House with some other religious leaders, and he left early to go back to this church to minister to 150 couples that he had brought back to his church from all over America to convince them to come back together, to save their marriages, and to raise their kids. This is the kind of work that citizens are doing in America. We need more of it, and it ought to be lifted up and supported.

The last person I want to introduce is Jack Lucas from Hattiesburg, Mississippi. Jack, would you stand up? Fifty years ago, in the sands of Iwo Jima, Jack Lucas taught and learned the lessons of citizenship. On February 20th, 1945, he and three of his buddies encountered the enemy and two grenades at their feet. Jack Lucas threw himself on both of them. In that moment, he saved the lives of his companions, and miraculously in the next instant, a medic saved his life. He gained a foothold for freedom, and at the age of 17, just a year older than his grandson who is up there with him today—and his son, who is a West Point graduate and a veteran—at 17, Jack Lucas became the youngest Marine in history and the youngest soldier in this century to win the Congressional Medal of Honor. All these years later, yesterday, here's what he said about that day: "It didn't matter where you were from or who you were, you relied on one another. You did it for your country."

We all gain when we give, and we reap what we sow. That's at the heart of this New Covenant. Responsibility, opportunity, and citizenship, more than stale chapters in some remote civic book, they're still the virtue by which we can fulfill ourselves and reach our God-given potential and be like them and also to fulfill the eternal promise of this country, the enduring dream from that first and most sacred covenant. I believe every person in this country still believes that we are created equal and given by our Creator the right to life, liberty and the pursuit of happiness. This is a very, very great country. And our best days are still to come.

Thank you, and God bless you all.

William J. Clinton, 1993–1997

Address before a Joint Session of Congress on the State of the Union

January 23, 1996

Democratic president Bill Clinton delivered his third State of the Union address before Congress at the start of a presidential election year, and the night would provide something of a preview of the upcoming November. After Clinton's address aired, Senate Majority Leader Bob Dole of Kansas, who would become the Republican nominee that year, delivered the GOP response. Clinton, successfully steering a centrist course, would defeat Dole in November, winning 49.2 percent of the popular vote to Dole's 40.7 percent and Reform Party candidate Ross Perot's 8.4 percent.

The Republican-controlled Congress, which had swept to power in the 1994 midterm elections, had come out on the short end of a battle with Clinton over the budget in late 1995 that resulted in two government shutdowns. Clinton had vetoed Republican balanced-budget legislation, calling its cuts in some domestic programs too harsh; the public seemed to agree with the president's position.

In this State of the Union address, Clinton declared that the "era of big government is over." The line came to symbolize the centrist rhetoric, or "triangulation," that the president would use to win a second term.

He discussed a variety of challenges facing the country, including the budget, which he said should be balanced in a fair manner. In 1997 Clinton and the Congress would reach agreement on balancing the budget in five years. The strong economy, however, resulted in a surplus only one year later.

Other priorities on Clinton's election-year agenda included strengthening families, reforming the welfare system, improving the country's education, a "G.I. Bill" for American workers, a crackdown on crime, a focus on the environment, and an effort to keep America strong in the world. Welfare-reform legislation would pass later that year.

The president gave special mention and praise to First Lady Hillary Clinton, who was in the midst of dealing with troubles relating to investigations of the failed Arkansas land deal known as Whitewater.

He also noted the presence in the audience of Richard Dean, a federal government worker who had saved three women in the 1995 terrorist attack in Oklahoma City. Clinton commented on the dedication of federal workers and challenged Congress to "never, ever" shut down the federal government again.

Clinton also recognized audience members Lucius Wright, a teacher in Mississippi who worked on antigang efforts, and Jennifer Rodgers, an Oklahoma City police sergeant. He commented that they symbolized the need for Americans to work together.

Thank you very much. Mr. Speaker, Mr. Vice President, Members of the 104th Congress, distinguished guests, my fellow Americans all across our land:

Let me begin tonight by saying to our men and women in uniform around the world, and especially those helping peace take root in Bosnia and to their families, I thank you. America is very, very proud of you.

My duty tonight is to report on the state of the Union, not the state of our Government but of our American community, and to set forth our responsibilities, in the words of our Founders, to form a more perfect Union.

The state of the Union is strong. Our economy is the healthiest it has been in three decades. We have the lowest combined rates of unemployment and inflation in 27 years. We have completed—created nearly 8 million new jobs, over a million of them in basic industries like construction and automobiles. America is selling more cars than Japan for the first time since the 1970's. And for 3 years in a row, we have had a record number of new businesses started in our country.

Our leadership in the world is also strong, bringing hope for new peace. And perhaps most important, we are gaining ground in restoring our fundamental values. The crime rate, the welfare and food stamp rolls, the poverty rate, and the teen pregnancy rate are all down. And as they go down, prospects for America's future go up.

We live in an age of possibility. A hundred years ago we moved from farm to factory. Now we move to an age of technology, information, and global competition. These changes have opened vast new opportunities for our people, but they have also presented them with stiff challenges. While more Americans are living better, too many of our fellow citizens are working harder just to keep up, and they are rightly concerned about the security of their families.

We must answer here three fundamental questions: First, how do we make the American dream of opportunity for all a reality for all Americans who are willing to work for it? Second, how do we preserve our old and enduring values as we move into the future? And third, how do we meet these challenges together, as one America?

We know big Government does not have all the answers. We know there's not a program for every problem. We know, and we have worked to give the American people a smaller, less bureaucratic Government in Washington. And we have to give the American people one that lives within its means. The era of big Government is over. But we cannot go back to the time when our citizens were left to fend for themselves.

Instead, we must go forward as one America, one nation working together to meet the challenges we face together. Self-reliance and teamwork are not opposing virtues; we must have both. I believe our new, smaller Government must work in an old-fashioned American way, together with all of our citizens through State and local governments, in the workplace, in religious, charitable, and civic associations. Our goal must be to enable all our people to make the most of their own lives, with stronger families, more educational opportunity, economic security, safer streets, a cleaner environment in a safer world.

To improve the state of our Union, we must ask more of ourselves, we must expect more of each other, and we must face our challenges together.

Here, in this place, our responsibility begins with balancing the budget in a way that is fair to all Americans. There is now broad bipartisan agreement that permanent deficit spending must come to an end.

I compliment the Republican leadership and the membership for the energy and determination you have brought to this task of balancing the budget. And I thank the Democrats for passing the largest deficit reduction plan in history in 1993, which has already cut the deficit nearly in half in 3 years.

Since 1993, we have all begun to see the benefits of deficit reduction. Lower interest rates have made it easier for businesses to borrow and to invest and to create new jobs. Lower interest rates have brought down the cost of home mortgages, car payments, and credit card rates to ordinary citizens. Now, it is time to finish the job and balance the budget.

Though differences remain among us which are significant, the combined total of the proposed savings that are common to both plans is more than enough, using the numbers from your Congressional Budget Office to balance the budget in 7 years and to provide a modest tax cut.

These cuts are real. They will require sacrifice from everyone. But these cuts do not undermine our fundamental obligations to our parents, our children, and our future, by endangering Medicare or Medicaid or education or the environment or by raising taxes on working families.

I have said before, and let me say again, many good ideas have come out of our negotiations. I have learned a lot about the way both Republicans and Democrats view the debate before us. I have learned a lot about the good ideas that each side has that we could all embrace.

We ought to resolve our remaining differences. I am willing to work to resolve them. I am ready to meet tomorrow. But I ask you to consider that we should at least enact these savings that both plans have in common and give the American people their balanced budget, a tax cut, lower interest rates, and a brighter future. We should do that now and make permanent deficits yesterday's legacy.

Now it is time for us to look also to the challenges of today and tomorrow, beyond the burdens of yesterday. The challenges are significant. But our Nation was built on challenges. America was built on challenges, not promises. And when we work together to meet them, we never fail. That is the key to a more perfect Union. Our individual dreams must be realized by our common efforts.

Tonight I want to speak to you about the challenges we all face as a people. Our first challenge is to cherish our children and strengthen America's families. Family is the foundation of American life. If we have stronger families, we will have a stronger America.

Before I go on, I'd like to take just a moment to thank my own family, and to thank the person who has taught me more than anyone else over 25 years about the importance of families and children, a wonderful wife, a magnificent mother, and a great First Lady. Thank you, Hillary.

All strong families begin with taking more responsibility for our children. I've heard Mrs. Gore say that it's hard to be a parent today, but it's even harder to be a child. So all of us, not just as parents but all of us in our other roles—our media, our schools, our teachers, our communities, our churches and synagogues, our businesses, our governments—all of us have a responsibility to help our children to make it and to make the most of their lives and their God-given capacities.

To the media, I say you should create movies and CD's and television shows you'd want your own children and grandchildren to enjoy.

I call on Congress to pass the requirement for a V-chip in TV sets so that parents can screen out programs they believe are inappropriate for their children. When parents control what their young children see, that is not censorship; that is enabling parents to assume more personal responsibility for their children's upbringing. And I urge them to do it. The V-chip requirement is part of the important telecommunications bill now pending in this Congress. It has bipartisan support, and I urge you to pass it now.

To make the V-chip work, I challenge the broadcast industry to do what movies have done, to identify your program in ways that help parents to protect their children. And I invite the leaders of major media corporations in the entertainment industry to come to the White House next month to work with us in a positive way on concrete ways to improve what our children see on television. I am ready to work with you.

I say to those who make and market cigarettes, every year a million children take up smoking, even though it's against the law. Three hundred thousand of them will have their lives shortened as a result. Our administration has taken steps to stop the massive marketing campaigns that appeal to our children. We are simply saying: Market your products to adults, if you wish, but draw the line on children.

I say to those who are on welfare, and especially to those who have been trapped on welfare for a long time: For too long our welfare system has undermined the values of family and work, instead of supporting them. The Congress and I are near agreement on sweeping welfare reform. We agree on time limits, tough work requirements, and the toughest possible child support enforcement. But I believe we must also provide child care so that mothers who are required to go to work can do so without worrying about what is happening to their children.

I challenge this Congress to send me a bipartisan welfare reform bill that will really move people from welfare to work and do the right thing by our children. I will sign it immediately.

Let us be candid about this difficult problem. Passing a law, even the best possible law, is only a first step. The next step is to make it work. I challenge people on welfare to make the most of this opportunity for independence. I challenge American businesses to give people on welfare the chance to move into the work force. I applaud the work of religious groups and others who care for the poor. More than anyone else in our society, they know the true difficulty of the task before us, and they are in a position to help.

Every one of us should join them. That is the only way we can make real welfare reform a reality in the lives of the American people.

To strengthen the family we must do everything we can to keep the teen pregnancy rate going down. I am gratified, as I'm sure all Americans are, that it has dropped for 2 years in a row. But we all know it is still far too high.

Tonight I am pleased to announce that a group of prominent Americans is responding to that challenge by forming an organization that will support grassroots community efforts all across our country in a national campaign against teen pregnancy. And I challenge all of us and every American to join their efforts.

I call on American men and women in families to give greater respect to one another. We must end the deadly scourge of domestic violence in our country. And I challenge America's families to work harder to stay together. For families who stay together not only do better economically, their children do better as well.

In particular, I challenge the fathers of this country to love and care for their children. If your family has separated, you must pay your child support. We're doing more than ever to make sure you do, and we're going to do more. But let's all admit something about that, too: A check will not substitute for a parent's love and guidance. And only you—only you can make the decision to help raise your children. No matter who you are, how low or high your station in life, it is the most basic human duty of every American to do that job to the best of his or her ability.

Our second challenge is to provide Americans with the educational opportunities we'll all need for this new century. In our schools, every classroom in America must be connected to the information superhighway, with computers and good software and well-trained teachers. We are working with the telecommunications industry, educators, and parents to connect 20 percent of California's classrooms by this spring, and every classroom and every library in the entire United States by the year 2000. I ask Congress to support this education technology initiative so that we can make sure this national partnership succeeds.

Every diploma ought to mean something. I challenge every community, every school, and every State to adopt national standards of excellence, to measure whether schools are meeting those standards, to cut bureaucratic redtape so that schools and teachers have more flexibility for grassroots reform, and to hold them accountable for results. That's what our Goals 2000 initiative is all about. I challenge every State to give all parents the right to choose which public school their children will attend, and to let teachers form new schools with a charter they can keep only if they do a good job.

I challenge all our schools to teach character education, to teach good values and good citizenship. And if it means that teenagers will stop killing each other over designer jackets, then our public schools should be able to require their students to wear school uniforms.

I challenge our parents to become their children's first teachers. Turn off the TV. See that the homework is done. And visit your children's classroom. No program, no teacher, no one else can do that for you.

My fellow Americans, higher education is more important today than ever before. We've created a new student loan program that's made it easier to borrow and repay those loans, and we have dramatically cut the student loan default rate. That's something we should all be proud of because it was unconscionably high just a few years ago.

Through AmeriCorps, our national service program, this year 25,000 young people will earn college money by serving their local communities to improve the lives of their friends and neighbors.

These initiatives are right for America, and we should keep them going. And we should also work hard to open the doors of college even wider. I challenge Congress to expand work-study and help one million young Americans work their way through college by the year 2000, to provide a $1,000 merit scholarship for the top 5 percent of graduates in every high school in the United States, to expand Pell Grant scholarships for deserving and needy students, and to make up to $10,000 a year of college tuition tax deductible. It's a good idea for America.

Our third challenge is to help every American who is willing to work for it, achieve economic security in this new age. People who work hard still need support to get ahead in the new economy. They need education and training for a lifetime. They need more support for families raising children. They need retirement security. They need access to health care. More and more Americans are finding that the education of their childhood simply doesn't last a lifetime.

So I challenge Congress to consolidate 70 overlapping, antiquated job-training programs into a simple voucher worth $2,600 for unemployed or underemployed workers to use as they please for community college tuition or other training. This is a "GI bill" for America's workers we should all be able to agree on.

More and more Americans are working hard without a raise. Congress sets the minimum wage. Within a year, the minimum wage will fall to a 40-year low in purchasing power. Four dollars and 25 cents an hour is no longer a living wage, but millions of Americans and their children are trying to live on it. I challenge you to raise their minimum wage.

In 1993, Congress cut the taxes of 15 million hard-pressed working families to make sure that no parents who work full-time would have to raise their children in poverty and to encourage people to move from welfare to work. This expanded earned-income tax credit is now worth about $1,800 a year to a family of four living on $20,000. The budget bill I vetoed would have reversed this achievement and raised taxes on nearly 8 million of these people. We should not do that. We should not do that.

I also agree that the people who are helped under this initiative are not all those in our country who are working hard to do a good job raising their children and at work. I agree that we need a tax credit for working families with children. That's one of the things most of us in this Chamber, I hope, can agree on. I know it is strongly supported by the Republican majority. And it should be part of any final budget agreement.

I want to challenge every business that can possibly afford it to provide pensions for your employees. And I challenge Congress to pass a proposal recommended by the White House Conference on Small Business that would make it easier for small businesses and farmers to establish their own pension plans. That is something we should all agree on.

We should also protect existing pension plans. Two years ago, with bipartisan support that was almost unanimous on both sides of the aisle, we moved to protect the pensions of 8 million working people and to stabilize the pensions of 32 million more. Congress should not now let companies endanger those workers' pension funds.

I know the proposal to liberalize the ability of employers to take money out of pension funds for other purposes would raise money for the Treasury. But I believe it is false economy. I vetoed that proposal last year, and I would have to do so again.

Finally, if our working families are going to succeed in the new economy, they must be able to buy health insurance policies that they do not lose when they change jobs or when someone in their family gets sick. Over the past 2 years, over one million Americans in working families have lost their health insurance. We have to do more to make health care available to every American. And Congress should start by passing the bipartisan bill sponsored by Senator Kennedy and Senator Kassebaum that would require insurance companies to stop dropping people when they switch jobs and stop denying coverage for preexisting conditions. Let's all do that.

And even as we enact savings in these programs, we must have a common commitment to preserve the basic protections of Medicare and Medicaid, not just to the poor but to people in working families, including children, people with disabilities, people with AIDS, senior citizens in nursing homes.

In the past 3 years, we've saved $15 billion just by fighting health care fraud and abuse. We have all agreed to save much more. We have all agreed to stabilize the Medicare Trust Fund. But we must not abandon our fundamental obligations to the people who need Medicare and Medicaid. America cannot become stronger if they become weaker.

The "GI bill" for workers, tax relief for education and child rearing, pension availability and protection, access to health care, preservation of Medicare and Medicaid, these things, along with the Family and Medical Leave Act passed in 1993, these things will help responsible, hard-working American families to make the most of their own lives.

But employers and employees must do their part, as well, as they are doing in so many of our finest companies, working together, putting the long-term prosperity ahead of the short-term gain. As workers increase their hours and their productivity, employers should make sure they get the skills they need and share the benefits of the good years, as well as the burdens of the bad ones. When companies and workers work as a team they do better, and so does America.

Our fourth great challenge is to take our streets back from crime and gangs and drugs. At last we have begun to find a way to reduce crime, forming community partnerships with local police forces to catch criminals and prevent crime. This strategy, called community policing, is clearly working. Violent crime is coming down all across America. In New York City murders are down 25 percent, in St. Louis, 18 percent, in Seattle, 32 percent. But we still have a long way to go before our streets are safe and our people are free from fear.

The crime bill of 1994 is critical to the success of community policing. It provides funds for 100,000 new police in communities of all sizes. We're already a third of the way there. And I challenge the Congress to finish the job. Let us stick with a strategy that's working and keep the crime rate coming down.

Community policing also requires bonds of trust between citizens and police. I ask all Americans to respect and support our law enforcement officers. And to our police, I say, our children need you as role models and heroes. Don't let them down.

The Brady bill has already stopped 44,000 people with criminal records from buying guns. The assault weapons ban is keeping 19 kinds of assault weapons out of the hands of violent gangs. I challenge the Congress to keep those laws on the books.

Our next step in the fight against crime is to take on gangs the way we once took on the mob. I'm directing the FBI and other investigative agencies to target gangs that involve juveniles and violent crime, and to seek authority to prosecute as adults teenagers who maim and kill like adults.

And I challenge local housing authorities and tenant associations: Criminal gang members and drug dealers are destroying the lives of decent tenants. From now on, the rule for residents who commit crime and pedal drugs should be one strike and you're out.

I challenge every State to match Federal policy to assure that serious violent criminals serve at least 85 percent of their sentence.

More police and punishment are important, but they're not enough. We have got to keep more of our young people out of trouble, with prevention strategies not dictated by Washington but developed in communities. I challenge all of our communities, all of our adults, to give our children futures to say yes to. And I challenge Congress not to abandon the crime bill's support of these grassroots prevention efforts.

Finally, to reduce crime and violence we have to reduce the drug problem. The challenge begins in our homes, with parents talking to their children openly and firmly. It embraces our churches and synagogues, our youth groups and our schools.

I challenge Congress not to cut our support for drug-free schools. People like the D.A.R.E. officers are making a real impression on grade schoolchildren that will give them the strength to say no when the time comes.

Meanwhile, we continue our efforts to cut the flow of drugs into America. For the last 2 years, one man in particular has been on the front lines of that effort. Tonight I am nominating him, a hero of the Persian Gulf War and the Commander in Chief of the United States Military Southern Command, General Barry McCaffrey, as America's new drug czar.

General McCaffrey has earned three Purple Hearts and two Silver Stars fighting for this country. Tonight I ask that he lead our Nation's battle against drugs at home and abroad. To succeed, he needs a force far larger than he has ever commanded before. He needs all of us. Every one of us has a role to play on this team.

Thank you, General McCaffrey, for agreeing to serve your country one more time.

Our fifth challenge: to leave our environment safe and clean for the next generation. Because of a generation of bipartisan effort we do have cleaner water and air, lead levels in children's blood has been cut by 70 percent, toxic emissions from factories cut in half. Lake Erie was dead, and now it's a thriving resource. But 10 million children under 12 still live within 4 miles of a toxic waste dump. A third of us breathe air that endangers our health. And in too many communities the water is not safe to drink. We still have much to do.

Yet Congress has voted to cut environmental enforcement by 25 percent. That means more toxic chemicals in our water, more smog in our air, more pesticides in our food. Lobbyists for polluters have been allowed to write their own loopholes into bills to weaken laws that protect the health and safety of our children. Some say that the taxpayer should pick up the tab for toxic waste and let polluters who can afford to fix it off the hook. I challenge Congress to reexamine those policies and to reverse them.

This issue has not been a partisan issue. The most significant environmental gains in the last 30 years were made under a Democratic Congress and President Richard Nixon. We can work together. We have to believe some basic things. Do you believe we can expand the economy without hurting the environment? I do. Do you believe we can create more jobs over the long run by cleaning the environment up? I know we can. That should be our commitment.

We must challenge businesses and communities to take more initiative in protecting the environment, and we have to make it easier for them to do it. To businesses this administration is saying: If you can find a cheaper, more efficient way than Government regulations require to meet tough pollution standards, do it, as long as you do it right. To communities we say: We must strengthen community right-to-know laws requiring polluters to disclose their emissions, but you have to use the information to work with business to cut pollution. People do have a right to know that their air and their water are safe.

Our sixth challenge is to maintain America's leadership in the fight for freedom and peace throughout the world. Because of American leadership, more people than ever before live free and at peace. And Americans have known 50 years of prosperity and security.

We owe thanks especially to our veterans of World War II. I would like to say to Senator Bob Dole and to all others in this Chamber who fought in World War II, and to all others on both sides of the aisle who have fought bravely in all our conflicts since: I salute your service and so do the American people.

All over the world, even after the cold war, people still look to us and trust us to help them seek the blessings of peace and freedom. But as the cold war fades into memory, voices of isolation say America should retreat from its responsibilities. I say they are wrong.

The threats we face today as Americans respect no Nation's borders. Think of them: terrorism, the spread of weapons of mass destruction, organized crime, drug trafficking, ethnic and religious hatred, aggression by rogue states, environmental degradation. If we fail to address these threats today, we will suffer the consequences in all our tomorrows.

Of course, we can't be everywhere. Of course, we can't do everything. But where our interests and our values are at stake, and where we can make a difference, America must lead. We must not be isolationist. We must not be the world's policeman. But we can and should be the world's very best peacemaker.

By keeping our military strong, by using diplomacy where we can and force where we must, by working with others to share the risk and the cost of our efforts, America is making a difference for people here and around the world. For the first time since the dawn of the nuclear age—for the first time since the dawn of the nuclear age—there is not a single Russian missile pointed at America's children.

North Korea has now frozen its dangerous nuclear weapons program. In Haiti, the dictators are gone, democracy has a new day, the flow of desperate refugees to our shores has subsided. Through tougher trade deals for America, over 80 of them, we have opened markets abroad, and now exports are at an all-time high, growing faster than imports and creating good American jobs.

We stood with those taking risks for peace: in Northern Ireland, where Catholic and Protestant children now tell their parents, violence must never return; in the Middle East, where Arabs and Jews who once seemed destined to fight forever now share knowledge and resources and even dreams.

And we stood up for peace in Bosnia. Remember the skeletal prisoners, the mass graves, the campaign to rape and torture, the endless lines of refugees, the threat of a spreading war. All these threats, all these horrors have now begun to give way to the promise of peace. Now our troops and a strong NATO, together with our new partners from central Europe and elsewhere, are helping that peace to take hold.

As all of you know, I was just there with a bipartisan congressional group, and I was so proud not only of what our troops were doing but of the pride they evidenced in what they were doing. They knew what America's mission in this world is, and they were proud to be carrying it out.

Through these efforts, we have enhanced the security of the American people, but make no mistake about it: Important challenges remain.

The START II treaty with Russia will cut our nuclear stockpiles by another 25 percent. I urge the Senate to ratify it now. We must end the race to create new nuclear weapons by signing a truly comprehensive nuclear test ban treaty this year.

As we remember what happened in the Japanese subway, we can outlaw poison gas forever if the Senate ratifies the Chemical Weapons Convention this year. We can intensify the fight against terrorists and organized criminals at home and abroad if Congress passes the antiterrorism legislation I proposed after the Oklahoma City bombing, now. We can help more people move from hatred to hope all across the world in our own interest if Congress gives us the means to remain the world's leader for peace.

My fellow Americans, the six challenges I have just discussed are for all of us. Our seventh challenge is really America's challenge to those of us in this hallowed Hall tonight: to reinvent our Government and make our democracy work for them.

Last year this Congress applied to itself the laws it applies to everyone else. This Congress banned gifts and meals from lobbyists. This Congress forced lobbyists to disclose who pays them and what legislation they are trying to pass or kill. This Congress did that, and I applaud you for it.

Now I challenge Congress to go further, to curb special interest influence in politics by passing the first truly bipartisan campaign finance reform bill in a generation. You, Republicans and Democrats alike, can show the American people that we can limit spending and we can open the airwaves to all candidates.

I also appeal to Congress to pass the line-item veto you promised the American people.

Our administration is working hard to give the American people a Government that works better and costs less. Thanks to the work of Vice President Gore, we are eliminating 16,000 pages of unnecessary rules and regulations, shifting more decision-making out of Washington, back to States and local communities.

As we move into the era of balanced budgets and smaller Government, we must work in new ways to enable people to make the most of their own lives. We are helping America's communities, not with more bureaucracy but with more opportunities. Through our successful empowerment zones and community development banks, we're helping people to find jobs, to start businesses. And with tax incentives for companies that clean up abandoned industrial property, we can bring jobs back to places that desperately, desperately need them.

But there are some areas that the Federal Government should not leave and should address and address strongly. One of these areas is the problem of illegal immigration. After years of neglect, this administration has taken a strong stand to stiffen the protection of our borders. We are increasing border controls by 50 percent. We are increasing inspections to prevent the hiring of illegal immigrants. And tonight, I announce I will sign an Executive order to deny Federal contracts to businesses that hire illegal immigrants.

Let me be very clear about this: We are still a nation of immigrants; we should be proud of it. We should honor every legal immigrant here, working hard to be a good citizen, working hard to become a new citizen. But we are also a nation of laws.

I want to say a special word now to those who work for our Federal Government. Today the Federal work force is 200,000 employees smaller than it was the day I took office as President. Our Federal Government today is the smallest it has been in 30 years, and it's getting smaller every day. Most of our fellow Americans probably don't know that. And there's a good reason—a good reason: The remaining Federal work force is composed of hard-working Americans who are now working harder and working smarter than ever before to make sure the quality of our services does not decline.

I'd like to give you one example. His name is Richard Dean. He's a 49-year-old

Vietnam veteran who's worked for the Social Security Administration for 22 years now. Last year he was hard at work in the Federal Building in Oklahoma City when the blast killed 169 people and brought the rubble down all around him. He reentered that building four times. He saved the lives of three women. He's here with us this evening, and I want to recognize Richard and applaud both his public service and his extraordinary personal heroism. But Richard Dean's story doesn't end there. This last November, he was forced out of his office when the Government shut down. And the second time the Government shut down he continued helping Social Security recipients, but he was working without pay.

On behalf of Richard Dean and his family, and all the other people who are out there working every day doing a good job for the American people, I challenge all of you in this Chamber: Let's never, ever shut the Federal Government down again.

On behalf of all Americans, especially those who need their Social Security payments at the beginning of March, I also challenge the Congress to preserve the full faith and credit of the United States, to honor the obligations of this great Nation as we have for 220 years, to rise above partisanship and pass a straightforward extension of the debt limit and show people America keeps its word.

I know that this evening I have asked a lot of Congress and even more from America. But I am confident: When Americans work together in their homes, their schools, their churches, their synagogues, their civic groups, their workplace, they can meet any challenge.

I say again, the era of big Government is over. But we can't go back to the era of fending for yourself. We have to go forward to the era of working together as a community, as a team, as one America, with all of us reaching across these lines that divide us— the division, the discrimination, the rancor—we have to reach across it to find common ground. We have got to work together if we want America to work.

I want you to meet two more people tonight who do just that. Lucius Wright is a teacher in the Jackson, Mississippi, public school system. A Vietnam veteran, he has created groups to help inner-city children turn away from gangs and build futures they can believe in. Sergeant Jennifer Rodgers is a police officer in Oklahoma City. Like Richard Dean, she helped to pull her fellow citizens out of the rubble and deal with that awful tragedy. She reminds us that in their response to that atrocity the people of Oklahoma City lifted all of us with their basic sense of decency and community.

Lucius Wright and Jennifer Rodgers are special Americans. And I have the honor to announce tonight that they are the very first of several thousand Americans who will be chosen to carry the Olympic torch on its long journey from Los Angeles to the centennial of the modern Olympics in Atlanta this summer, not because they are star athletes but because they are star citizens, community heroes meeting America's challenges. They are our real champions.

Please stand up.

Now each of us must hold high the torch of citizenship in our own lives. None of us can finish the race alone. We can only achieve our destiny together, one hand, one generation, one American connecting to another.

There have always been things we could do together, dreams we could make real which we could never have done on our own. We Americans have forged our identity, our very Union, from the very point of view that we can accommodate every point on the planet, every different opinion. But we must be bound together by a faith more powerful than any doctrine that divides us, by our belief in progress, our love of liberty, and our relentless search for common ground.

America has always sought and always risen to every challenge. Who would say that having come so far together, we will not go forward from here? Who would say that this age of possibility is not for all Americans?

Our country is and always has been a great and good nation. But the best is yet to come if we all do our parts.

Thank you. God bless you, and God bless the United States of America. Thank you.

William J. Clinton, 1997–2001

Address before a Joint Session of Congress on the State of the Union

February 4, 1997

Bill Clinton delivered his fourth State of the Union address in February 1997. He had been sworn in for a second term as president the previous month, after having won the November 1996 presidential election. Clinton, a Democrat, had easily defeated Republican Bob Dole, a longtime senator from Kansas, as well as Ross Perot, a billionaire who was running as the Reform Party candidate.

Clinton, who ran as a centrist, took 49.2 percent of the popular vote to Dole's 40.7 percent and Perot's 8.4 percent. The president won 379 electoral votes to Dole's 159. The Republicans, who had taken both houses of Congress in a landslide in the 1994 midterm elections, retained that control in the 1996 contests.

Education was the top issue in Clinton's speech. He declared it his "number one priority for the next four years." He cited several goals: every eight-year-old in the country should be able to read, every twelve-year-old should be able to log onto the Internet, every eighteen-year-old should be able to attend college, and every adult should have the chance to learn for an entire lifetime. Among the solutions he proposed were national education standards, certification for "master teachers," an effort to increase literacy, a focus on early learning, and character education.

The president introduced three people sitting in the audience: Illinois eighth-graders Kristen Tanner and Chris Getsler, who were among a group of students who tied for first place in the world on a science test and placed second in math, and their teacher, Sue Winski. He said they proved that "when we aim high and challenge our students, they will be the best in the world."

He also introduced Kristen Zarfos, a doctor from Connecticut who had served as the inspiration for proposed legislation that would allow a woman to stay in the hospital for forty-eight hours after a mastectomy; Clinton urged Congress to support that legislation.

Clinton listed some "unfinished business" that he wanted to accomplish. One item was to achieve a balanced budget, an issue that resulted in an agreement with the GOP Congress in 1997. Ironically, due to a strong economy, the budget quickly went into surplus the following year. He also called for campaign finance reform and a continuation of the previous year's welfare reform.

At the end of his speech, Clinton recognized in the House gallery Governor Gary Locke of Washington state, the first Chinese-American governor; he also welcomed the mother and sister of recently deceased Representative Frank Tejeda of Texas.

Clinton's speech competed for national attention with the jury verdict in O.J. Simpson's civil trial, which was to be announced that night.

Mr. Speaker, Mr. Vice President, Members of the 105th Congress, distinguished guests, and my fellow Americans.

I think I should start by saying, thanks for inviting me back. I come before you tonight with a challenge as great as any in our peacetime history and a plan of action to meet that challenge, to prepare our people for the bold new world of the 21st century.

We have much to be thankful for. With 4 years of growth, we have won back the basic strength of our economy. With crime and welfare rolls declining, we are winning back our optimism, the enduring faith that we can master any difficulty. With the cold war receding and global commerce at record levels, we are helping to win an unrivaled peace and prosperity all across the world.

My fellow Americans, the state of our Union is strong. But now we must rise to the decisive moment, to make a nation and a world better than any we have ever known. The new promise of the global economy, the information age, unimagined new work, life-enhancing technology, all these are ours to seize. That is our honor and our challenge. We must be shapers of events, not observers. For if we do not act, the moment will pass, and we will lose the best possibilities of our future.

We face no imminent threat, but we do have an enemy. The enemy of our time is inaction. So tonight I issue a call to action: action by this Congress, action by our States, by our people, to prepare America for the 21st century; action to keep our economy and our democracy strong and working for all our people; action to strengthen education and harness the forces of technology and science; action to build stronger families and stronger communities and a safer environment; action to keep America the world's strongest force for peace, freedom, and prosperity; and above all, action to build a more perfect Union here at home.

The spirit we bring to our work will make all the difference. We must be committed to the pursuit of opportunity for all Americans, responsibility from all Americans, in a community of all Americans. And we must be committed to a new kind of Government, not to solve all our problems for us but to give our people, all our people, the tools they need to make the most of their own lives.

And we must work together. The people of this Nation elected us all. They want us to be partners, not partisans. They put us all right here in the same boat, they gave us all oars, and they told us to row. Now, here is the direction I believe we should take.

First, we must move quickly to complete the unfinished business of our country, to balance the budget, renew our democracy, and finish the job of welfare reform.

Over the last 4 years, we have brought new economic growth by investing in our people, expanding our exports, cutting our deficits, creating over 11 million new jobs, a 4-year record. Now we must keep our economy the strongest in the world. We here tonight have an historic opportunity. Let this Congress be the Congress that finally balances the budget. Thank you.

In 2 days, I will propose a detailed plan to balance the budget by 2002. This plan will balance the budget and invest in our people while protecting Medicare, Medicaid, education, and the environment. It will balance the budget and build on the Vice President's efforts to make our Government work better, even as it costs less. It will balance the budget and provide middle class tax relief to pay for education and health care, to help to raise a child, to buy and sell a home.

Balancing the budget requires only your vote and my signature. It does not require us to rewrite our Constitution. I believe it is both unnecessary and unwise to adopt a balanced budget amendment that could cripple our country in time of economic crisis and force unwanted results, such as judges halting Social Security checks or increasing taxes. Let us at least agree, we should not pass any measure—no measure should be passed that threatens Social Security. Whatever your view on that, we all must concede: We don't need a constitutional amendment; we need action.

Whatever our differences, we should balance the budget now. And then, for the long-term health of our society, we must agree to a bipartisan process to preserve Social Security and reform Medicare for the long run, so that these fundamental programs will be as strong for our children as they are for our parents.

And let me say something that's not in my script tonight. I know this is not going to be easy. But I really believe one of the reasons the American people gave me a second term was to take the tough decisions in the next 4 years that will carry our country through the next 50 years. I know it is easier for me than for you to say or do. But another reason I was elected is to support all of you, without regard to party, to give you what is necessary to join in these decisions. We owe it to our country and to our future.

Our second piece of unfinished business requires us to commit ourselves tonight, before the eyes of America, to finally enacting bipartisan campaign finance reform. Now, Senators McCain and Feingold, Representatives Shays and Meehan, have reached across party lines here to craft tough and fair reform. Their proposal would curb spending, reduce the role of special interests, create a level playing field between challengers and incumbents, and ban contributions from non-citizens, all corporate sources, and the other large soft money contributions that both parties receive.

You know and I know that this can be delayed. And you know and I know the delay will mean the death of reform. So let's set our own deadline. Let's work together to write bipartisan campaign finance reform into law and pass McCain-Feingold by the day we celebrate the birth of our democracy, July the Fourth.

There is a third piece of unfinished business. Over the last 4 years, we moved a record 2.25 million people off the welfare rolls. Then last year, Congress enacted landmark welfare reform legislation, demanding that all able-bodied recipients assume the responsibility of moving from welfare to work. Now each and every one of us has to fulfill our responsibility, indeed, our moral obligation, to make sure that people who now must work, can work.

Now we must act to meet a new goal: 2 million more people off the welfare rolls by the year 2000. Here is my plan: Tax credits and other incentives for businesses that hire people off welfare; incentives for job placement firms and States to create more jobs for welfare recipients; training, transportation, and child care to help people go to work.

Now I challenge every State: Turn those welfare checks into private sector pay-checks. I challenge every religious congregation, every community nonprofit, every business to hire someone off welfare. And I'd like to say especially to every employer in our country who ever criticized the old welfare system, you can't blame that old system anymore. We have torn it down. Now do your part. Give someone on welfare the chance to go to work.

Tonight I am pleased to announce that five major corporations, Sprint, Monsanto, UPS, Burger King, and United Airlines, will be the first to join in a new national effort to marshal America's businesses, large and small, to create jobs so that people can move from welfare to work.

We passed welfare reform. All of you know I believe we were right to do it. But no one can walk out of this Chamber with a clear conscience unless you are prepared to finish the job.

And we must join together to do something else, too, something both Republican and Democratic Governors have asked us to do, to restore basic health and disability benefits when misfortune strikes immigrants who came to this country legally, who work hard, pay taxes, and obey the law. To do otherwise is simply unworthy of a great nation of immigrants.

Now, looking ahead, the greatest step of all, the high threshold of the future we must now cross, and my number one priority for the next 4 years is to ensure that all Americans have the best education in the world.

Let's work together to meet these three goals: Every 8-year-old must be able to read; every 12-year-old must be able to log on to the Internet; every 18-year-old must be able to go to college; and every adult American must be able to keep on learning for a lifetime.

My balanced budget makes an unprecedented commitment to these goals, $51 billion next year. But far more than money is required. I have a plan, a call to action for American education, based on these 10 principles:

First, a national crusade for education standards, not Federal Government standards but national standards, representing what all our students must know to succeed in the knowledge economy of the 21st century. Every State and school must shape the curriculum to reflect these standards and train teachers to lift students up to them. To help schools meet the standards and measure their progress, we will lead an effort over the next 2 years to develop national tests of student achievement in reading and math. Tonight I issue a challenge to the Nation: Every State should adopt high national standards, and by 1999, every State should test every fourth grader in reading and every eighth grader in math to make sure these standards are met.

Raising standards will not be easy, and some of our children will not be able to meet them at first. The point is not to put our children down but to lift them up. Good tests will show us who needs help, what changes in teaching to make, and which schools need to improve. They can help us end social promotions, for no child should move from grade school to junior high or junior high to high school until he or she is ready.

Last month, our Secretary of Education Dick Riley and I visited Northern Illinois, where eighth grade students from 20 school districts, in a project aptly called First in the World, took the Third International Math and Science Study. That's a test that reflects the world-class standards our children must meet for the new era. And those students in Illinois tied for first in the world in science and came in second in math. Two of them, Kristen Tanner and Chris Getsler, are here tonight, along with their teacher Sue Winski. They're up there with the First Lady. And they prove that when we aim high and challenge our students, they will be the best in the world. Let's give them a hand. Stand up, please.

Second, to have the best schools, we must have the best teachers. Most of us in this Chamber would not be here tonight without the help of those teachers. I know that I wouldn't be here. For years, many of our educators, led by North Carolina's Governor Jim Hunt and the National Board for Professional Teaching Standards, have worked very hard to establish nationally accepted credentials for excellence in teaching. Just 500 of these teachers have been certified since 1995. My budget will enable 100,000 more to seek national certification as master teachers. We should reward and recognize our best teachers. And as we reward them, we should quickly and fairly remove those few who don't measure up, and we should challenge more of our finest young people to consider teaching as a career.

Third, we must do more to help all our children read. Forty percent—40 percent—of our 8-year-olds cannot read on their own. That's why we have just launched the America Reads initiative, to build a citizen army of one million volunteer tutors to make sure every child can read independently by the end of the third grade. We will use thousands of AmeriCorps volunteers to mobilize this citizen army. We want at least 100,000 college students to help. And tonight I am pleased that 60 college presidents have answered my call, pledging that thousands of their work-study students will serve for one year as reading tutors. This is also a challenge to every teacher and every principal. You must use these tutors to help students read. And it is especially a challenge to our parents. You must read with your children every night.

This leads to the fourth principle: Learning begins in the first days of life. Scientists are now discovering how young children develop emotionally and intellectually from their very first days and how important it is for parents to begin immediately talking, singing, even reading to their infants. The First Lady has spent years writing about this issue, studying it. And she and I are going to convene a White House conference on early learning and the brain this spring, to explore how parents and educators can best use these startling new findings.

We already know we should start teaching children before they start school. That's why this balanced budget expands Head Start to one million children by 2002. And that is why the Vice President and Mrs. Gore will host their annual family conference this June on what we can do to make sure that parents are an active part of their children's learning all the way through school.

They've done a great deal to highlight the importance of family in our life, and now they're turning their attention to getting more parents involved in their children's learning all the way through school. And I thank you, Mr. Vice President, and I thank you especially, Tipper, for what you do.

Fifth, every State should give parents the power to choose the right public school for their children. Their right to choose will foster competition and innovation that can make public schools better. We should also make it possible for more parents and teachers to start charter schools, schools that set and meet the highest standards and exist only as long as they do. Our plan will help America to create 3,000 of these charter schools by the next century, nearly 7 times as there are in the country today, so that parents will have even more choices in sending their children to the best schools.

Sixth, character education must be taught in our schools. We must teach our children to be good citizens. And we must continue to promote order and discipline, supporting communities that introduce school uniforms, impose curfews, enforce truancy laws, remove disruptive students from the classroom, and have zero tolerance for guns and drugs in school.

Seventh, we cannot expect our children to raise themselves up in schools that are literally falling down. With the student population at an all-time high and record numbers of school buildings falling into disrepair, this has now become a serious national concern. Therefore, my budget includes a new initiative, $5 billion to help communities finance $20 billion in school construction over the next 4 years.

Eighth, we must make the 13th and 14th years of education, at least 2 years of college, just as universal in America by the 21st century as a high school education is today, and we must open the doors of college to all Americans. To do that, I propose America's HOPE scholarship, based on Georgia's pioneering program: 2 years of a $1,500 tax credit for college tuition, enough to pay for the typical community college. I also propose a tax deduction of up to $10,000 a year for all tuition after high school, an expanded IRA you can withdraw from tax free for education, and the largest increase in Pell grant scholarships in 20 years. Now, this plan will give most families the ability to pay no taxes on money they save for college tuition. I ask you to pass it and give every American who works hard the chance to go to college.

Ninth, in the 21st century, we must expand the frontiers of learning across a lifetime. All our people, of whatever age, must have the chance to learn new skills. Most Americans live near a community college. The roads that take them there can be paths to a better future. My "GI bill" for America's workers will transform the confusing tangle of Federal training programs into a simple skill grant to go directly into eligible workers' hands. For too long, this bill has been sitting on that desk there without action. I ask you to pass it now. Let's give more of our workers the ability to learn and to earn for a lifetime.

Tenth, we must bring the power of the information age into all our schools. Last year, I challenged America to connect every classroom and library to the Internet by the year 2000, so that, for the first time in our history, children in the most isolated rural towns, the most comfortable suburbs, the poorest inner-city schools, will have the same access to the same universe of knowledge.

That is my plan, a call to action for American education. Some may say that it is unusual for a President to pay this kind of attention to education. Some may say it is simply because the President and his wonderful wife have been obsessed with this subject for more years than they can recall. That is not what is driving these proposals.

We must understand the significance of this endeavor: One of the greatest sources of our strength throughout the cold war was a bipartisan foreign policy; because our future was at stake, politics stopped at the water's edge. Now I ask you and I ask all our Nation's Governors; I ask parents, teachers, and citizens all across America for a new nonpartisan commitment to education because education is a critical national security issue for our future, and politics must stop at the schoolhouse door.

To prepare America for the 21st century, we must harness the powerful forces of science and technology to benefit all Americans. This is the first State of the Union carried live in video over the Internet. But we've only begun to spread the benefits of a technology revolution that should become the modern birthright of every citizen.

Our effort to connect every classroom is just the beginning. Now we should connect every hospital to the Internet, so that doctors can instantly share data about their patients with the best specialists in the field. And I challenge the private sector tonight to start by connecting every children's hospital as soon as possible, so that a child in bed can stay in touch with school, family, and friends. A sick child need no longer be a child alone.

We must build the second generation of the Internet so that our leading universities and national laboratories can communicate in speeds 1,000 times faster than today, to develop new medical treatments, new sources of energy, new ways of working together.

But we cannot stop there. As the Internet becomes our new town square, a computer in every home, a teacher of all subjects, a connection to all cultures, this will no longer be a dream but a necessity. And over the next decade, that must be our goal.

We must continue to explore the heavens, pressing on with the Mars probes and the international space station, both of which will have practical applications for our everyday living.

We must speed the remarkable advances in medical science. The human genome project is now decoding the genetic mysteries of life. American scientists have discovered genes linked to breast cancer and ovarian cancer and medication that stops a stroke in progress and begins to reverse its effects and treatments that dramatically lengthen the lives of people with HIV and AIDS.

Since I took office, funding for AIDS research at the National Institutes of Health [NIH] has increased dramatically to $1.5 billion. With new resources, NIH will now become the most powerful discovery engine for an AIDS vaccine, working with other scientists to finally end the threat of AIDS. Remember that every year—every year we move up the discovery of an AIDS vaccine will save millions of lives around the world. We must reinforce our commitment to medical science.

To prepare America for the 21st century, we must build stronger families. Over the past 4 years, the family and medical leave law has helped millions of Americans to take time off to be with their families. With new pressures on people in the way they work and live, I believe we must expand family leave so that workers can take time off for teacher conferences and a child's medical checkup. We should pass flex-time, so workers can choose to be paid for overtime in income or trade it in for time off to be with their families.

We must continue, step by step, to give more families access to affordable, quality health care. Forty million Americans still lack health insurance. Ten million children still lack health insurance; 80 percent of them have working parents who pay taxes. That is wrong. My balanced budget will extend health coverage to up to 5 million of those children. Since nearly half of all children who lose their insurance do so because their parents lose or change a job, my budget will also ensure that people who temporarily lose their jobs can still afford to keep their health insurance. No child should be without a doctor just because a parent is without a job.

My Medicare plan modernizes Medicare, increases the life of the Trust Fund to 10 years, provides support for respite care for the many families with loved ones afflicted with Alzheimer's, and for the first time, it would fully pay for annual mammograms.

Just as we ended drive-through deliveries of babies last year, we must now end the dangerous and demeaning practice of forcing women home from the hospital only hours after a mastectomy. I ask your support for bipartisan legislation to guarantee that a woman can stay in the hospital for 48 hours after a mastectomy. With us tonight is Dr. Kristen Zarfos, a Connecticut surgeon whose outrage at this practice spurred a national movement and inspired this legislation. I'd like her to stand so we can thank her for her efforts. Dr. Zarfos, thank you.

In the last 4 years, we have increased child support collections by 50 percent. Now we should go further and do better by making it a felony for any parent to cross a State line in an attempt to flee from this, his or her most sacred obligation.

Finally, we must also protect our children by standing firm in our determination to ban the advertising and marketing of cigarettes that endanger their lives.

To prepare America for the 21st century, we must build stronger communities. We should start with safe streets. Serious crime has dropped 5 years in a row. The key has been community policing. We must finish the job of putting 100,000 community police on the streets of the United States. We should pass the victims' rights amendment to the Constitution. And I ask you to mount a full-scale assault on juvenile crime, with legislation that declares war on gangs, with new prosecutors and tougher penalties; extends the Brady bill so violent teen criminals will not be able to buy handguns; requires child safety locks on handguns to prevent unauthorized use; and helps to keep our schools open after hours, on weekends, and in the summer, so our young people will have someplace to go and something to say yes to.

This balanced budget includes the largest anti-drug effort ever, to stop drugs at their source, punish those who push them, and teach our young people that drugs are wrong, drugs are illegal, and drugs will kill them. I hope you will support it.

Our growing economy has helped to revive poor urban and rural neighborhoods. But we must do more to empower them to create the conditions in which all families can flourish and to create jobs through investment by business and loans by banks. We should double the number of empowerment zones. They've already brought so much hope to communities like Detroit, where the unemployment rate has been cut in half in 4 years. We should restore contaminated urban land and buildings to productive use. We should expand the network of community development banks. And together we must pledge tonight that we will use this empowerment approach, including private-sector tax incentives, to renew our Capital City, so that Washington is a great place to work and live and once again the proud face America shows the world.

We must protect our environment in every community. In the last 4 years, we cleaned up 250 toxic waste sites, as many as in the previous 12. Now we should clean up 500 more, so that our children grow up next to parks, not poison. I urge you to pass my proposal to make big polluters live by a simple rule: If you pollute our environment, you should pay to clean it up.

In the last 4 years, we strengthened our Nation's safe food and clean drinking water laws; we protected some of America's rarest, most beautiful land in Utah's Red Rocks region, created three new national parks in the California desert, and began to restore the Florida Everglades. Now we must be as vigilant with our rivers as we are with our lands. Tonight, I announce that this year I will designate 10 American Heritage Rivers, to help communities alongside them revitalize their waterfronts and clean up pollution in the rivers, proving once again that we can grow the economy as we protect the environment.

We must also protect our global environment, working to ban the worst toxic chemicals and to reduce the greenhouse gases that challenge our health even as they change our climate.

Now, we all know that in all of our communities, some of our children simply don't have what they need to grow and learn in their own homes or schools or neighborhoods. And that means the rest of us must do more, for they are our children, too. That's why President Bush, General Colin Powell, former Housing Secretary Henry Cisneros will join the Vice President and me to lead the President's summit of service in Philadelphia in April.

Our national service program, AmeriCorps, has already helped 70,000 young people to work their way through college as they serve America. Now we intend to mobilize millions of Americans to serve in thousands of ways. Citizen service is an American responsibility which all Americans should embrace, and I ask your support for that endeavor.

I'd like to make just one last point about our national community. Our economy is measured in numbers and statistics, and it's very important. But the enduring worth of our Nation lies in our shared values and our soaring spirit. So instead of cutting back on our modest efforts to support the arts and humanities, I believe we should stand by them and challenge our artists, musicians, and writers, challenge our museums, libraries, and theaters. We should challenge all Americans in the arts and humanities to join with our fellow citizens to make the year 2000 a national celebration of the American spirit in every community, a celebration of our common culture in the century that has passed and in the new one to come in the new millennium, so that we can remain in the world's beacon not only of liberty but of creativity, long after the fireworks have faded.

To prepare America for the 21st century, we must master the forces of change in the world and keep American leadership strong and sure for an uncharted time.

Fifty years ago, a farsighted America led in creating the institutions that secured victory in the cold war and built a growing world economy. As a result, today more people than ever embrace our ideals and share our interests. Already we have dismantled many of the blocs and barriers that divided our parents' world. For the first time, more people live under democracy than dictatorship, including every nation in our own hemisphere but one, and its day, too, will come.

Now, we stand at another moment of change and choice and another time to be farsighted, to bring America 50 more years of security and prosperity. In this endeavor, our first task is to help to build, for the very first time, an undivided, democratic Europe. When Europe is stable, prosperous, and at peace, America is more secure. To that end, we must expand NATO by 1999, so that countries that were once our adversaries can become our allies. At the special NATO summit this summer, that is what we will begin to do. We must strengthen NATO's Partnership For Peace with non-member allies. And we must build a stable partnership between NATO and a democratic Russia. An expanded NATO is good for America; and a Europe in which all democracies define their future not in terms of what they can do to each other but in terms of what they can do together for the good of all—that kind of Europe is good for America.

Second, America must look to the East no less than to the West. Our security demands it. Americans fought three wars in Asia in this century. Our prosperity requires it. More than 2 million American jobs depend upon trade with Asia.

There, too, we are helping to shape an Asia-Pacific community of cooperation, not conflict. Let our progress there not mask the peril that remains. Together with South Korea, we must advance peace talks with North Korea and bridge the cold war's last divide. And I call on Congress to fund our share of the agreement under which North Korea must continue to freeze and then dismantle its nuclear weapons program.

We must pursue a deeper dialog with China for the sake of our interests and our ideals. An isolated China is not good for America; a China playing its proper role in the world is. I will go to China, and I have invited China's President to come here, not because we agree on everything but because engaging China is the best way to work on our common challenges like ending nuclear testing and to deal frankly with our fundamental differences like human rights.

The American people must prosper in the global economy. We've worked hard to tear down trade barriers abroad so that we can create good jobs at home. I am proud to say that today America is once again the most competitive nation and the number one exporter in the world.

Now we must act to expand our exports, especially to Asia and Latin America, two of the fastest growing regions on Earth, or be left behind as these emerging economies forge new ties with other nations. That is why we need the authority now to conclude new trade agreements that open markets to our goods and services even as we preserve our values.

We need not shrink from the challenge of the global economy. After all, we have the best workers and the best products. In a truly open market, we can out-compete anyone, anywhere on Earth.

But this is about more than economics. By expanding trade, we can advance the cause of freedom and democracy around the world. There is no better example of this truth than Latin America where democracy and open markets are on the march together. That is why I will visit there in the spring to reinforce our important tie.

We should all be proud that America led the effort to rescue our neighbor Mexico from its economic crises. And we should all be proud that last month Mexico repaid the United States, 3 full years ahead of schedule, with half a billion dollar profit to us.

America must continue to be an unrelenting force for peace from the Middle East to Haiti, from Northern Ireland to Africa. Taking reasonable risks for peace keeps us from being drawn into far more costly conflicts later.

With American leadership, the killing has stopped in Bosnia. Now the habits of peace must take hold. The new NATO force will allow reconstruction and reconciliation to accelerate. Tonight I ask Congress to continue its strong support of our troops. They are doing a remarkable job there for America, and America must do right by them.

Fifth, we must move strongly against new threats to our security. In the past 4 years, we agreed to ban—we led the way to a worldwide agreement to ban nuclear testing. With Russia, we dramatically cut nuclear arsenals, and we stopped targeting each others' citizens. We are acting to prevent nuclear materials from falling into the wrong hands and to rid the world of landmines. We are working with other nations with renewed intensity to fight drug traffickers and to stop terrorists before they act and hold them fully accountable if they do.

Now we must rise to a new test of leadership, ratifying the Chemical Weapons Convention. Make no mistake about it, it will make our troops safer from chemical attack;

it will help us to fight terrorism. We have no more important obligations, especially in the wake of what we now know about the Gulf war. This treaty has been bipartisan from the beginning, supported by Republican and Democratic administrations and Republican and Democratic Members of Congress and already approved by 68 nations.

But if we do not act by April 29th, when this convention goes into force with or without us, we will lose the chance to have Americans leading and enforcing this effort. Together we must make the Chemical Weapons Convention law, so that at last we can begin to outlaw poison gas from the Earth.

Finally, we must have the tools to meet all these challenges. We must maintain a strong and ready military. We must increase funding for weapons modernization by the year 2000, and we must take good care of our men and women in uniform. They are the world's finest.

We must also renew our commitment to America's diplomacy and pay our debts and dues to international financial institutions like the World Bank and to a reforming United Nations. Every dollar we devote to preventing conflicts, to promoting democracy, to stopping the spread of disease and starvation, brings a sure return in security and savings. Yet international-affairs spending today is just one percent of the Federal budget, a small fraction of what America invested in diplomacy to choose leadership over escapism at the start of the cold war. If America is to continue to lead the world, we here who lead America simply must find the will to pay our way.

A farsighted America moved the world to a better place over these last 50 years. And so it can be for another 50 years. But a shortsighted America will soon find its words falling on deaf ears all around the world.

Almost exactly 50 years ago, in the first winter of the cold war, President Truman stood before a Republican Congress and called upon our country to meet its responsibilities of leadership. This was his warning; he said, "If we falter, we may endanger the peace of the world, and we shall surely endanger the welfare of this Nation." That Congress, led by Republicans like Senator Arthur Vandenberg, answered President Truman's call. Together, they made the commitments that strengthened our country for 50 years. Now let us do the same. Let us do what it takes to remain the indispensable nation, to keep America strong, secure, and prosperous for another 50 years.

In the end, more than anything else, our world leadership grows out of the power of our example here at home, out of our ability to remain strong as one America.

All over the world, people are being torn asunder by racial, ethnic, and religious conflicts that fuel fanaticism and terror. We are the world's most diverse democracy, and the world looks to us to show that it is possible to live and advance together across those kinds of differences.

America has always been a nation of immigrants. From the start, a steady stream of people in search of freedom and opportunity have left their own lands to make this land their home. We started as an experiment in democracy fueled by Europeans. We have grown into an experiment in democratic diversity fueled by openness and promise.

My fellow Americans, we must never, ever believe that our diversity is a weakness. It is our greatest strength. Americans speak every language, know every country. People on every continent can look to us and see the reflection of their own great potential, and they always will, as long as we strive to give all of our citizens, whatever their background, an opportunity to achieve their own greatness.

We're not there yet. We still see evidence of abiding bigotry and intolerance in ugly words and awful violence, in burned churches and bombed buildings. We must fight against this, in our country and in our hearts.

Just a few days before my second Inauguration, one of our country's best known pastors, Reverend Robert Schuller, suggested that I read Isaiah 58:12. Here's what it says: "Thou shalt raise up the foundations of many generations, and thou shalt be called the repairer of the breach, the restorer of paths to dwell in." I placed my hand on that verse when I took the oath of office, on behalf of all Americans, for no matter what our differences in our faiths, our backgrounds, our politics, we must all be repairers of the breach.

I want to say a word about two other Americans who show us how. Congressman Frank Tejeda was buried yesterday, a proud American whose family came from Mexico. He was only 51 years old. He was awarded the Silver Star, the Bronze Star, and the Purple Heart fighting for his country in Vietnam. And he went on to serve Texas and America fighting for our future here in this Chamber. We are grateful for his service and honored that his mother, Lillie Tejeda, and his sister, Mary Alice, have come from Texas to be with us here tonight. And we welcome you.

Gary Locke, the newly elected Governor of Washington State, is the first Chinese-American Governor in the history of our country. He's the proud son of two of the millions of Asian-American immigrants who have strengthened America with their hard work, family values, and good citizenship. He represents the future we can all achieve. Thank you, Governor, for being here. Please stand up.

Reverend Schuller, Congressman Tejeda, Governor Locke, along with Kristen Tanner and Chris Getsler, Sue Winski and Dr. Kristen Zarfos, they're all Americans from different roots whose lives reflect the best of what we can become when we are one America. We may not share a common past, but we surely do share a common future. Building one America is our most important mission, the foundation for many generations of every other strength we must build for this new century. Money cannot buy it. Power cannot compel it. Technology cannot create it. It can only come from the human spirit.

America is far more than a place. It is an idea, the most powerful idea in the history of nations. And all of us in this Chamber, we are now the bearers of that idea, leading a great people into a new world. A child born tonight will have almost no memory of the 20th century. Everything that child will know about America will be because of what we do now to build a new century.

We don't have a moment to waste. Tomorrow there will be just over 1,000 days until the year 2000; 1,000 days to prepare our people; 1,000 days to work together; 1,000 days to build a bridge to a land of new promise. My fellow Americans, we have work to do. Let us seize those days and the century.

Thank you, God bless you, and God bless America.

Address before a Joint Session of Congress on the State of the Union

January 27, 1998

Bill Clinton's fifth State of the Union message was an unusual one. The president had faced reports for the previous week that he had an affair with a former White House intern, Monica Lewinsky, and had asked her to lie about it. There was speculation that Clinton might be impeached—which he later was—or forced to resign. But the president, a natural politician and communicator, delivered a seventy-two-minute speech that made no mention of the burgeoning controversy. Instead, he touted the country's strong economy and proposed a variety of new programs. "These are good times for America," he declared. The speech was interrupted repeatedly by Democrats who stood and applauded; even Republicans seemed to welcome some of Clinton's remarks.

Clinton stated that there were only 700 days remaining in the twentieth century, and that the progress already made should continue. He described a "third way" of looking at government, between those who viewed it as the enemy and those who saw it as the answer.

He praised the balanced budget agreement reached the previous year and projected future surpluses. He stated that the solvency of Social Security should be the priority under a budget surplus.

Among the initiatives Clinton proposed were raising the minimum wage and reducing class sizes in the early grades. He also called for a crackdown on abusive child labor and requested that an effort be made to help more families pay for child care. He reflected on his own childhood, when his widowed mother was able to leave young Bill with her parents while she obtained her education.

Clinton praised the reforms that had been under way in the welfare system and recognized audience member Elaine Kinslow of Indianapolis, a former welfare recipient who now held a good job and had moved her family to a better neighborhood.

Among the international issues mentioned, the president urged continued support for U.S. troops in Bosnia. He recognized another audience member, Army Sergeant Michael Tolbert, who had been stationed in Bosnia and, with his unit, stopped insurgents from taking over a democratic radio station.

Clinton also singled out John Glenn, a senator from Ohio and former astronaut who was about to return to space for one last mission.

Although Clinton did not mention the Lewinsky scandal, it would lead to his impeachment by the House of Representatives, voting mostly along party lines, that December. He would become the second president, after Andrew Johnson, to be impeached. The Senate, however, acquitted Clinton of the two counts against him.

A Gallup poll taken the day after the speech found that 61 percent of respondents said the policies Clinton described represented the correct approach; only 14 percent said they represented the wrong approach. Another 25 percent did not know or refused to answer.

Mr. Speaker, Mr. Vice President, Members of the 105th Congress, distinguished guests, my fellow Americans:

Since the last time we met in this Chamber, America has lost two patriots and fine public servants. Though they sat on opposite sides of the aisle, Representatives Walter Capps and Sonny Bono shared a deep love for this House and an unshakable commitment to improving the lives of all our people. In the past few weeks they've both been eulogized. Tonight I think we should begin by sending a message to their families and their friends that we celebrate their lives and give thanks for their service to our Nation.

For 209 years it has been the President's duty to report to you on the state of the Union. Because of the hard work and high purpose of the American people, these are good times for America. We have more than 14 million new jobs, the lowest unemployment in 24 years, the lowest core inflation in 30 years; incomes are rising; and we have the highest homeownership in history. Crime has dropped for a record 5 years in a row, and the welfare rolls are at their lowest levels in 27 years. Our leadership in the world is unrivaled. Ladies and gentlemen, the state of our Union is strong.

But with barely 700 days left in the 20th century, this is not a time to rest. It is a time to build, to build the America within reach, an America where everybody has a chance to get ahead with hard work; where every citizen can live in a safe community; where families are strong, schools are good, and all our young people can go on to college; an America where scientists find cures for diseases, from diabetes to Alzheimer's to AIDS; an America where every child can stretch a hand across a keyboard and reach every book ever written, every painting ever painted, every symphony ever composed; where government provides opportunity and citizens honor the responsibility to give something back to their communities; an America which leads the world to new heights of peace and prosperity. This is the America we have begun to build; this is the America we can leave to our children if we join together to finish the work at hand. Let us strengthen our Nation for the 21st century.

Rarely have Americans lived through so much change in so many ways in so short a time. Quietly, but with gathering force, the ground has shifted beneath our feet as we have moved into an information age, a global economy, a truly new world. For 5 years now, we have met the challenge of these changes, as Americans have at every turning point in our history, by renewing the very idea of America: widening the circle of opportunity, deepening the meaning of our freedom, forging a more perfect Union.

We shaped a new kind of Government for the information age. I thank the Vice President for his leadership and the Congress for its support in building a Government that is leaner, more flexible, a catalyst for new ideas, and most of all, a Government that gives the American people the tools they need to make the most of their own lives.

We have moved past the sterile debate between those who say government is the enemy and those who say government is the answer. My fellow Americans, we have found a third way. We have the smallest Government in 35 years, but a more progressive one. We have a smaller Government, but a stronger Nation. We are moving steadily toward an even stronger America in the 21st century: an economy that offers opportunity, a society rooted in responsibility, and a nation that lives as a community.

First, Americans in this Chamber and across our Nation have pursued a new strategy for prosperity: fiscal discipline to cut interest rates and spur growth; investments in education and skills, in science and technology and transportation, to prepare our people for the new economy; new markets for American products and American workers.

When I took office, the deficit for 1998 was projected to be $357 billion and heading higher. This year, our deficit is projected to be $10 billion and heading lower. For three decades, six Presidents have come before you to warn of the damage deficits pose to our Nation. Tonight I come before you to announce that the Federal deficit, once so incomprehensibly large that it had 11 zeros, will be, simply, zero. I will submit to Congress for 1999 the first balanced budget in 30 years. And if we hold fast to fiscal discipline, we may balance the budget this year—4 years ahead of schedule.

You can all be proud of that, because turning a sea of red ink into black is no miracle. It is the product of hard work by the American people and of two visionary actions in Congress: the courageous vote in 1993 that led to a cut in the deficit of 90 percent, and the truly historic bipartisan balanced budget agreement passed by this Congress. Here's the really good news: If we maintain our resolve, we will produce balanced budgets as far as the eye can see.

We must not go back to unwise spending or untargeted tax cuts that risk reopening the deficit. Last year, together, we enacted targeted tax cuts so that the typical middle class family will now have the lowest tax rates in 20 years. My plan to balance the budget next year includes both new investments and new tax cuts targeted to the needs of working families, for education, for child care, for the environment.

But whether the issue is tax cuts or spending, I ask all of you to meet this test: Approve only those priorities that can actually be accomplished without adding a dime to the deficit.

Now, if we balance the budget for next year, it is projected that we'll then have a sizable surplus in the years that immediately follow. What should we do with this projected surplus? I have a simple four-word answer: Save Social Security first. Thank you.

Tonight I propose that we reserve 100 percent of the surplus—that's every penny of any surplus—until we have taken all the necessary measures to strengthen the Social Security system for the 21st century. Let us say to all Americans watching tonight— whether you're 70 or 50, or whether you just started paying into the system—Social Security will be there when you need it. Let us make this commitment: Social Security first. Let's do that together.

I also want to say that all the American people who are watching us tonight should be invited to join in this discussion, in facing these issues squarely and forming a true consensus on how we should proceed. We'll start by conducting nonpartisan forums in every region of the country, and I hope that lawmakers of both parties will participate. We'll hold a White House conference on Social Security in December. And one year from now I will convene the leaders of Congress to craft historic, bipartisan legislation to achieve a landmark for our generation: a Social Security system that is strong in the 21st century. Thank you.

In an economy that honors opportunity, all Americans must be able to reap the rewards of prosperity. Because these times are good, we can afford to take one simple, sensible step to help millions of workers struggling to provide for their families: We should raise the minimum wage.

The information age is, first and foremost, an education age, in which education must start at birth and continue throughout a lifetime. Last year, from this podium, I said that education has to be our highest priority. I laid out a 10-point plan to move us forward and urged all of us to let politics stop at the schoolhouse door. Since then, this Congress—across party lines—and the American people have responded, in the most important year for education in a generation, expanding public school choice, opening the way to 3,000 new charter schools, working to connect every classroom in the country to the information superhighway, committing to expand Head Start to a million children, launching America Reads, sending literally thousands of college students into our elementary schools to make sure all our 8-year-olds can read.

Last year I proposed and you passed 220,000 new Pell grant scholarships for deserving students. Student loans, already less expensive and easier to repay—now you get to deduct the interest. Families all over America now can put their savings into new tax-free education IRA's. And this year, for the first 2 years of college, families will get a $1,500 tax credit—a HOPE scholarship that will cover the cost of most community college tuition. And for junior and senior year, graduate school, and job training, there is a lifetime learning credit. You did that, and you should be very proud of it.

And because of these actions, I have something to say to every family listening to us tonight: Your children can go on to college. If you know a child from a poor family, tell her not to give up; she can go on to college. If you know a young couple struggling with bills, worried they won't be able to send their children to college, tell them not to give up; their children can go on to college. If you know somebody who's caught in a dead-end job and afraid he can't afford the classes necessary to get better jobs for the rest of his life, tell him not to give up; he can go on to college. Because of the things that have been done, we can make college as universal in the 21st century as high school is today. And my friends, that will change the face and future of America.

We have opened wide the doors of the world's best system of higher education. Now we must make our public elementary and secondary schools the world's best as well by raising standards, raising expectations, and raising accountability. Thanks to the actions of this Congress last year, we will soon have, for the very first time, a voluntary national test based on national standards in fourth grade reading and eighth grade math. Parents have a right to know whether their children are mastering the basics. And every parent already knows the key: good teachers and small classes.

Tonight I propose the first ever national effort to reduce class size in the early grades. Thank you. My balanced budget will help to hire 100,000 new teachers who've passed a State competency test. Now, with these teachers—listen—with these teachers, we will actually be able to reduce class size in the first, second, and third grades to an average of 18 students a class, all across America.

If I've got the math right, more teachers teaching smaller classes requires more classrooms. So I also propose a school construction tax cut to help communities modernize or build 5,000 schools.

We must also demand greater accountability. When we promote a child from grade to grade who hasn't mastered the work, we don't do that child any favors. It is time to end social promotion in America's schools. Last year, in Chicago, they made that decision—not to hold our children back but to lift them up. Chicago stopped social promotion and started mandatory summer school to help students who are behind to catch up. I propose to help other communities follow Chicago's lead. Let's say to them:

Stop promoting children who don't learn, and we will give you the tools to make sure they do.

I also ask this Congress to support our efforts to enlist colleges and universities to reach out to disadvantaged children, starting in the sixth grade, so that they can get the guidance and hope they need so they can know that they, too, will be able to go on to college.

As we enter the 21st century, the global economy requires us to seek opportunity not just at home but in all the markets of the world. We must shape this global economy, not shrink from it. In the last 5 years, we have led the way in opening new markets, with 240 trade agreements that remove foreign barriers to products bearing the proud stamp "Made in the USA." Today, record high exports account for fully one-third of our economic growth. I want to keep them going, because that's the way to keep America growing and to advance a safer, more stable world.

All of you know, whatever your views are, that I think this is a great opportunity for America. I know there is opposition to more comprehensive trade agreements. I have listened carefully, and I believe that the opposition is rooted in two fears: first, that our trading partners will have lower environmental and labor standards which will give them an unfair advantage in our market and do their own people no favors, even if there's more business; and, second, that if we have more trade, more of our workers will lose their jobs and have to start over. I think we should seek to advance worker and environmental standards around the world. I have made it abundantly clear that it should be a part of our trade agenda. But we cannot influence other countries' decisions if we send them a message that we're backing away from trade with them.

This year I will send legislation to Congress, and ask other nations to join us, to fight the most intolerable labor practice of all: abusive child labor. We should also offer help and hope to those Americans temporarily left behind by the global marketplace or by the march of technology, which may have nothing to do with trade. That's why we have more than doubled funding for training dislocated workers since 1993. And if my new budget is adopted, we will triple funding. That's why we must do more, and more quickly, to help workers who lose their jobs for whatever reason.

You know, we help communities in a special way when their military base closes; we ought to help them in the same way if their factory closes. Again, I ask the Congress to continue its bipartisan work to consolidate the tangle of training programs we have today into one single "GI bill" for workers, a simple skills grant so people can, on their own, move quickly to new jobs, to higher incomes, and brighter futures.

We all know, in every way in life, change is not always easy, but we have to decide whether we're going to try to hold it back and hide from it or reap its benefits. And remember the big picture here: While we've been entering into hundreds of new trade agreements, we've been creating millions of new jobs.

So this year we will forge new partnerships with Latin America, Asia, and Europe. And we should pass the new "African Trade Act"; it has bipartisan support. I will also renew my request for the fast-track negotiating authority necessary to open more new markets, create more new jobs, which every President has had for two decades.

You know, whether we like it or not, in ways that are mostly positive, the world's economies are more and more interconnected and interdependent. Today, an economic crisis anywhere can affect economies everywhere. Recent months have brought serious financial problems to Thailand, Indonesia, South Korea, and beyond.

Now, why should Americans be concerned about this? First, these countries are our customers. If they sink into recession, they won't be able to buy the goods we'd like to sell them. Second, they're also our competitors. So if their currencies lose their value and go down, then the price of their goods will drop, flooding our market and others with much cheaper goods, which makes it a lot tougher for our people to compete. And finally, they are our strategic partners. Their stability bolsters our security.

The American economy remains sound and strong, and I want to keep it that way. But because the turmoil in Asia will have an impact on all the world's economies, including ours, making that negative impact as small as possible is the right thing to do for America and the right thing to do for a safer world.

Our policy is clear: No nation can recover if it does not reform itself. But when nations are willing to undertake serious economic reform, we should help them do it. So I call on Congress to renew America's commitment to the International Monetary Fund. And I think we should say to all the people we're trying to represent here that preparing for a far-off storm that may reach our shores is far wiser than ignoring the thunder till the clouds are just overhead.

A strong nation rests on the rock of responsibility. A society rooted in responsibility must first promote the value of work, not welfare. We can be proud that after decades of finger-pointing and failure, together we ended the old welfare system. And we're now replacing welfare checks with paychecks.

Last year, after a record 4-year decline in welfare rolls, I challenged our Nation to move 2 million more Americans off welfare by the year 2000. I'm pleased to report we have also met that goal, 2 full years ahead of schedule.

This is a grand achievement, the sum of many acts of individual courage, persistence, and hope. For 13 years, Elaine Kinslow of Indianapolis, Indiana, was on and off welfare. Today, she's a dispatcher with a van company. She's saved enough money to move her family into a good neighborhood, and she's helping other welfare recipients go to work. Elaine Kinslow and all those like her are the real heroes of the welfare revolution. There are millions like her all across America. And I'm happy she could join the First Lady tonight. Elaine, we're very proud of you. Please stand up.

We still have a lot more to do, all of us, to make welfare reform a success—providing child care, helping families move closer to available jobs, challenging more companies to join our welfare-to-work partnership, increasing child support collections from deadbeat parents who have a duty to support their own children. I also want to thank Congress for restoring some of the benefits to immigrants who are here legally and working hard, and I hope you will finish that job this year.

We have to make it possible for all hard-working families to meet their most important responsibilities. Two years ago we helped guarantee that Americans can keep their health insurance when they change jobs. Last year we extended health care to up to 5 million children. This year, I challenge Congress to take the next historic steps.

A hundred and sixty million of our fellow citizens are in managed care plans. These plans save money, and they can improve care. But medical decisions ought to be made by medical doctors, not insurance company accountants. I urge this Congress to reach across the aisle and write into law a consumer bill of rights that says this: You have the right to know all your medical options, not just the cheapest. You have the right to choose the doctor you want for the care you need. You have the right to emergency room care, wherever and whenever you need it. You have the right to keep your medical records confidential. Traditional care or managed care, every American deserves quality care.

Millions of Americans between the ages of 55 and 65 have lost their health insurance. Some are retired; some are laid off; some lose their coverage when their spouses retire. After a lifetime of work, they are left with nowhere to turn. So I ask the Congress, let these hard-working Americans buy into the Medicare system. It won't add a dime to the deficit, but the peace of mind it will provide will be priceless.

Next, we must help parents protect their children from the gravest health threat that they face: an epidemic of teen smoking, spread by multimillion-dollar marketing campaigns. I challenge Congress: Let's pass bipartisan, comprehensive legislation that will improve public health, protect our tobacco farmers, and change the way tobacco companies do business forever. Let's do what it takes to bring teen smoking down. Let's raise the price of cigarettes by up to a dollar and a half a pack over the next 10 years, with penalties on the tobacco industry if it keeps marketing to our children. Tomorrow, like every day, 3,000 children will start smoking, and 1,000 will die early as a result. Let this Congress be remembered as the Congress that saved their lives.

In the new economy, most parents work harder than ever. They face a constant struggle to balance their obligations to be good workers and their even more important obligations to be good parents. The Family and Medical Leave Act was the very first bill I was privileged to sign into law as President in 1993. Since then, about 15 million people have taken advantage of it, and I've met a lot of them all across this country. I ask you to extend that law to cover 10 million more workers and to give parents time off when they have to go see their children's teachers or take them to the doctor.

Child care is the next frontier we must face to enable people to succeed at home and at work. Last year I co-hosted the very first White House Conference on Child Care with one of our foremost experts, America's First Lady. From all corners of America, we heard the same message, without regard to region or income or political affiliation: We've got to raise the quality of child care. We've got to make it safer. We've got to make it more affordable.

So here's my plan: Help families to pay for child care for a million more children; scholarships and background checks for child care workers, and a new emphasis on early learning; tax credits for businesses that provide child care for their employees; and a larger child care tax credit for working families. Now, if you pass my plan, what this means is that a family of four with an income of $35,000 and high child care costs will no longer pay a single penny of Federal income tax.

I think this is such a big issue with me because of my own personal experience. I have often wondered how my mother, when she was a young widow, would have been able to go away to school and get an education and come back and support me if my grandparents hadn't been able to take care of me. She and I were really very lucky. How many other families have never had that same opportunity? The truth is, we don't know the answer to that question. But we do know what the answer should be: Not a single American family should ever have to choose between the job they need and the child they love.

A society rooted in responsibility must provide safe streets, safe schools, and safe neighborhoods. We pursued a strategy of more police, tougher punishment, smarter prevention, with crimefighting partnerships with local law enforcement and citizen groups, where the rubber hits the road. I can report to you tonight that it's working. Violent crime is down; robbery is down; assault is down; burglary is down—for 5 years in a row, all across America. We need to finish the job of putting 100,000 more police on our streets.

Again, I ask Congress to pass a juvenile crime bill that provides more prosecutors and probation officers, to crack down on gangs and guns and drugs, and bar violent juveniles from buying guns for life. And I ask you to dramatically expand our support for after-school programs. I think every American should know that most juvenile crime is committed between the hours of 3 in the afternoon and 8 at night. We can keep so many of our children out of trouble in the first place if we give them someplace to go other than the streets, and we ought to do it.

Drug use is on the decline. I thank General McCaffrey for his leadership, and I thank this Congress for passing the largest anti-drug budget in history. Now I ask you to join me in a groundbreaking effort to hire 1,000 new Border Patrol agents and to deploy the most sophisticated available new technologies to help close the door on drugs at our borders.

Police, prosecutors, and prevention programs, as good as they are, they can't work if our court system doesn't work. Today there are large number of vacancies in the Federal courts. Here is what the Chief Justice of the United States wrote: "Judicial vacancies cannot remain at such high levels indefinitely without eroding the quality of justice." I simply ask the United States Senate to heed this plea and vote on the highly qualified judicial nominees before you, up or down.

We must exercise responsibility not just at home but around the world. On the eve of a new century, we have the power and the duty to build a new era of peace and security. But make no mistake about it, today's possibilities are not tomorrow's guarantees. America must stand against the poisoned appeals of extreme nationalism. We must combat an unholy axis of new threats from terrorists, international criminals, and drug traffickers. These 21st century predators feed on technology and the free flow of information and ideas and people. And they will be all the more lethal if weapons of mass destruction fall into their hands.

To meet these challenges, we are helping to write international rules of the road for the 21st century, protecting those who join the family of nations and isolating those who do not. Within days, I will ask the Senate for its advice and consent to make Hungary, Poland, and the Czech Republic the newest members of NATO. For 50 years, NATO contained communism and kept America and Europe secure. Now these three formerly Communist countries have said yes to democracy. I ask the Senate to say yes to them, our new allies. By taking in new members and working closely with new partners, including Russia and Ukraine, NATO can help to assure that Europe is a stronghold for peace in the 21st century.

Next, I will ask Congress to continue its support of our troops and their mission in Bosnia. This Christmas, Hillary and I traveled to Sarajevo with Senator [Bob] and Mrs. [Elizabeth] Dole and a bipartisan congressional delegation. We saw children playing in the streets, where 2 years ago they were hiding from snipers and shells. The shops are filled with food; the cafes were alive with conversation. The progress there is unmistakable, but it is not yet irreversible. To take firm root, Bosnia's fragile peace still needs the support of American and allied troops when the current NATO mission ends in June. I think Senator Dole actually said it best. He said, "This is like being ahead in the 4th quarter of a football game. Now is not the time to walk off the field and forfeit the victory."

I wish all of you could have seen our troops in Tuzla. They're very proud of what they're doing in Bosnia, and we're all very proud of them. One of those—thank you—one of those brave soldiers is sitting with the First Lady tonight: Army Sergeant Michael Tolbert. His father was a decorated Vietnam vet. After college in Colorado, he joined the Army. Last year he led an infantry unit that stopped a mob of extremists from taking over a radio station that is a voice of democracy and tolerance in Bosnia. Thank you very much, Sergeant, for what you represent. Please stand up.

In Bosnia and around the world, our men and women in uniform always do their mission well. Our mission must be to keep them well-trained and ready, to improve their quality of life, and to provide the 21st century weapons they need to defeat any enemy.

I ask Congress to join me in pursuing an ambitious agenda to reduce the serious threat of weapons of mass destruction. This year, four decades after it was first proposed by President Eisenhower, a comprehensive nuclear test ban is within reach. By ending nuclear testing, we can help to prevent the development of new and more dangerous weapons and make it more difficult for non-nuclear states to build them. I'm pleased to announce that four former Chairmen of the Joint Chiefs of Staff—Generals John Shalikashvili, Colin Powell, and David Jones and Admiral William Crowe—have endorsed this treaty. And I ask the Senate to approve it this year. Thank you.

Together, we must confront the new hazards of chemical and biological weapons and the outlaw states, terrorists, and organized criminals seeking to acquire them. Saddam Hussein has spent the better part of this decade and much of his nation's wealth not on providing for the Iraqi people but on developing nuclear, chemical, and biological weapons and the missiles to deliver them. The United Nations weapons inspectors have done a truly remarkable job finding and destroying more of Iraq's arsenal than was destroyed during the entire Gulf war. Now Saddam Hussein wants to stop them from completing their mission.

I know I speak for everyone in this chamber, Republicans and Democrats, when I say to Saddam Hussein, "You cannot defy the will of the world," and when I say to him, "You have used weapons of mass destruction before. We are determined to deny you the capacity to use them again."

Last year the Senate ratified the Chemical Weapons Convention to protect our soldiers and citizens from poison gas. Now we must act to prevent the use of disease as a weapon of war and terror. The Biological Weapons Convention has been in effect for 23 years now. The rules are good, but the enforcement is weak. We must strengthen it with a new international inspection system to detect and deter cheating.

In the months ahead, I will pursue our security strategy with old allies in Asia and Europe and new partners from Africa to India and Pakistan, from South America to China. And from Belfast to Korea to the Middle East, America will continue to stand with those who stand for peace.

Finally, it's long past time to make good on our debt to the United Nations. Thank you. More and more, we are working with other nations to achieve common goals. If we want America to lead, we've got to set a good example. As we see so clearly in Bosnia, allies who share our goals can also share our burdens. In this new era, our freedom and independence are actually enriched, not weakened, by our increasing interdependence with other nations. But we have to do our part.

Our Founders set America on a permanent course toward a more perfect Union. To all of you I say, it is a journey we can only make together, living as one community. First, we have to continue to reform our Government, the instrument of our national community. Everyone knows elections have become too expensive, fueling a fundraising arms race. This year, by March 6th, at long last the Senate will actually vote on bipartisan campaign finance reform proposed by Senators [John] McCain and [Russell] Feingold. Let's be clear: A vote against McCain-Feingold is a vote for soft money and for the status quo. I ask you to strengthen our democracy and pass campaign finance reform this year.

At least equally important, we have to address the real reason for the explosion in campaign costs: the high cost of media advertising.

To the folks watching at home, those were the groans of pain in the audience. I will formally request that the Federal Communications Commission act to provide free or reduced-cost television time for candidates who observe spending limits voluntarily. The airwaves are a public trust, and broadcasters also have to help us in this effort to strengthen our democracy.

Under the leadership of Vice President Gore, we've reduced the Federal payroll by 300,000 workers, cut 16,000 pages of regulation, eliminated hundreds of programs, and improved the operations of virtually every Government agency. But we can do more. Like every taxpayer, I'm outraged by the reports of abuses by the IRS. We need some changes there: new citizen advocacy panels, a stronger taxpayer advocate, phone lines open 24 hours a day, relief for innocent taxpayers. Last year, by an overwhelming bipartisan margin, the House of Representatives passed sweeping IRS reforms. This bill must not now languish in the Senate. Tonight I ask the Senate: Follow the House; pass the bipartisan package as your first order of business.

I hope to goodness before I finish I can think of something to say "follow the Senate" on, so I'll be out of trouble.

A nation that lives as a community must value all its communities. For the past 5 years, we have worked to bring the spark of private enterprise to inner city and poor rural areas, with community development banks, more commercial loans in the poor neighborhoods, cleanup of polluted sites for development. Under the continued leadership of the Vice President, we propose to triple the number of empowerment zones to give business incentives to invest in those areas. We should—thank you—we should also give poor families more help to move into homes of their own, and we should use tax cuts to spur the construction of more low-income housing.

Last year, this Congress took strong action to help the District of Columbia. Let us renew our resolve to make our Capital City a great city for all who live and visit here. Our cities are the vibrant hubs of great metropolitan areas. They are still the gateways for new immigrants, from every continent, who come here to work for their own American dreams. Let's keep our cities going strong into the 21st century; they're a very important part of our future.

Our communities are only as healthy as the air our children breathe, the water they drink, the Earth they will inherit. Last year we put in place the toughest-ever controls on smog and soot. We moved to protect Yellowstone, the Everglades, Lake Tahoe. We expanded every community's right to know about the toxins that threaten their children. Just yesterday, our food safety plan took effect, using new science to protect consumers from dangers like E. coli and salmonella.

Tonight I ask you to join me in launching a new clean water initiative, a far-reaching effort to clean our rivers, our lakes, and our coastal waters for our children. Thank you.

Our overriding environmental challenge tonight is the worldwide problem of climate change, global warming, the gathering crisis that requires worldwide action. The vast majority of scientists have concluded unequivocally that if we don't reduce the emission of greenhouse gases, at some point in the next century, we'll disrupt our climate and put our children and grandchildren at risk. This past December, America led the world to reach a historic agreement committing our Nation to reduce greenhouse gas emissions through market forces, new technologies, energy efficiency. We have it in our power to act right here, right now. I propose $6 billion in tax cuts and research and development to encourage innovation, renewable energy, fuel-efficient cars, energy-efficient homes.

Every time we have acted to heal our environment, pessimists have told us it would hurt the economy. Well, today our economy is the strongest in a generation, and our environment is the cleanest in a generation. We have always found a way to clean the environment and grow the economy at the same time. And when it comes to global warming, we'll do it again.

Finally, community means living by the defining American value, the ideal heard 'round the world that we are all created equal. Throughout our history, we haven't always honored that ideal and we've never fully lived up to it. Often it's easier to believe that our differences matter more than what we have in common. It may be easier, but it's wrong.

What we have to do in our day and generation to make sure that America becomes truly one nation—what do we have to do? We're becoming more and more and more diverse. Do you believe we can become one nation? The answer cannot be to dwell on our differences but to build on our shared values. We all cherish family and faith, freedom and responsibility. We all want our children to grow up in a world where their talents are matched by their opportunities.

I've launched this national initiative on race to help us recognize our common interests and to bridge the opportunity gaps that are keeping us from becoming one America. Let us begin by recognizing what we still must overcome. Discrimination against any American is un-American. We must vigorously enforce the laws that make it illegal. I ask your help to end the backlog at the Equal Employment Opportunity Commission. Sixty thousand of our fellow citizens are waiting in line for justice, and we should act now to end their wait.

We also should recognize that the greatest progress we can make toward building one America lies in the progress we make for all Americans, without regard to race. When we open the doors of college to all Americans, when we rid all our streets of crime, when there are jobs available to people from all our neighborhoods, when we make sure all parents have the child care they need, we're helping to build one nation.

We, in this Chamber and in this Government, must do all we can to address the continuing American challenge to build one America. But we'll only move forward if all our fellow citizens, including every one of you at home watching tonight, is also committed to this cause. We must work together, learn together, live together, serve together. On the forge of common enterprise, Americans of all backgrounds can hammer out a common identity. We see it today in the United States military, in the Peace Corps, in AmeriCorps. Wherever people of all races and backgrounds come together in a shared endeavor and get a fair chance, we do just fine. With shared values and meaningful opportunities and honest communication and citizen service, we can unite a diverse people in freedom and mutual respect. We are many; we must be one.

In that spirit, let us lift our eyes to the new millennium. How will we mark that passage? It just happens once every 1,000 years. This year Hillary and I launched the White House Millennium Program to promote America's creativity and innovation, and to preserve our heritage and culture into the 21st century. Our culture lives in every community, and every community has places of historic value that tell our stories as Americans. We should protect them. I am proposing a public-private partnership to advance our arts and humanities and to celebrate the millennium by saving American's treasures, great and small.

And while we honor the past, let us imagine the future. Now, think about this: The entire store of human knowledge now doubles every 5 years. In the 1980's, scientists identified the gene causing cystic fibrosis; it took 9 years. Last year scientists located the gene that causes Parkinson's Disease—in only 9 days. Within a decade, "gene chips" will offer a roadmap for prevention of illnesses throughout a lifetime. Soon we'll be able to carry all the phone calls on Mother's Day on a single strand of fiber the width of a human hair. A child born in 1998 may well live to see the 22d century.

Tonight, as part of our gift to the millennium, I propose a 21st century research fund for path-breaking scientific inquiry, the largest funding increase in history for the National Institutes of Health, the National Science Foundation, the National Cancer Institute. We have already discovered genes for breast cancer and diabetes. I ask you to support this initiative so ours will be the generation that finally wins the war against cancer and begins a revolution in our fight against all deadly diseases.

As important as all this scientific progress is, we must continue to see that science serves humanity, not the other way around. We must prevent the misuse of genetic tests to discriminate against any American. And we must ratify the ethical consensus of the scientific and religious communities and ban the cloning of human beings.

We should enable all the world's people to explore the far reaches of cyberspace. Think of this: The first time I made a State of the Union speech to you, only a handful of physicists used the World Wide Web—literally, just a handful of people. Now, in schools, in libraries, homes, and businesses, millions and millions of Americans surf the Net every day. We must give parents the tools they need to help protect their children from inappropriate material on the Internet, but we also must make sure that we protect the exploding global commercial potential of the Internet. We can do the kinds of things that we need to do and still protect our kids.

For one thing, I ask Congress to step up support for building the next-generation Internet. It's getting kind of clogged, you know, and the next-generation Internet will operate at speeds up to 1,000 times faster than today.

Even as we explore this inner space in the new millennium, we're going to open new frontiers in outer space. Throughout all history, humankind has had only one place to call home, our planet, Earth. Beginning this year, 1998, men and women from 16 countries will build a foothold in the heavens, the international space station.

With its vast expanses, scientists and engineers will actually set sail on an uncharted sea of limitless mystery and unlimited potential.

And this October, a true American hero, a veteran pilot of 149 combat missions and one 5-hour space flight that changed the world, will return to the heavens. Godspeed, John Glenn. John, you will carry with you America's hopes. And on your uniform, once again, you will carry America's flag, marking the unbroken connection between the deeds of America's past and the daring of America's future.

Nearly 200 years ago, a tattered flag, its broad stripes and bright stars still gleaming through the smoke of a fierce battle, moved Francis Scott Key to scribble a few words on the back of an envelope, the words that became our national anthem. Today, that Star-Spangled Banner, along with the Declaration of Independence, the Constitution, and the Bill of Rights, are on display just a short walk from here. They are America's treasures, and we must also save them for the ages.

I ask all Americans to support our project to restore all our treasures so that the generations of the 21st century can see for themselves the images and the words that are the old and continuing glory of America; an America that has continued to rise through every age, against every challenge, a people of great works and greater possibilities, who have always, always found the wisdom and strength to come together as one nation—to widen the circle of opportunity, to deepen the meaning of our freedom, to form that more perfect Union. Let that be our gift to the 21st century.

God bless you, and God bless the United States.

William J. Clinton, 1997–2001

Address before a Joint Session of Congress on the State of the Union
January 19, 1999

Bill Clinton delivered his sixth State of the Union message before Congress in January 1999. The previous month, the House of Representatives had voted to impeach him on charges related to his affair with former White House intern Monica Lewinsky, and the Senate was considering whether to find him guilty on both counts of impeachment.

Clinton delivered a lengthy, seventy-seven-minute speech that did not directly mention anything relating to the impeachment scandal; instead, he focused on the progress the country had made during his presidency and proposed new initiatives. It was reminiscent of his 1998 State of the Union message, which had taken place a week after reports about his affair with Lewinsky had first surfaced.

In the end, the Senate on February 12 voted Clinton not guilty on the two impeachment counts, an outcome that had been expected as Clinton's popularity remained strong during the impeachment process.

Clinton began this speech by introducing Lyn Gibson and Wenling Chestnut, whose husbands, Capitol Hill police officers, had been killed the previous year in a shooting incident in the Capitol.

He then reported that the country had the first balanced budget in three decades, that the violent crime rate was the lowest in a quarter-century, and that the environment was the cleanest in a quarter-century.

The president repeated a proposal he had focused on the previous year: that future budget surpluses should be used to save the Social Security program from going bankrupt. Other goals, he said, would be to save the Medicare program, to initiate a new pension plan for retirement security, and to start a tax credit of $1,000 for the aged, sick and disabled, and their families.

He also listed a series of goals on the education front, including additional funding for summer and after-school programs, improvements in failing schools, and performance exams for new teachers.

Clinton mentioned some audience members, including Air Force Captain Jeff Taliaferro, who had participated in Operation Desert Fox over Iraq; baseball player Sammy Sosa, who Clinton described as a hero in both the Dominican Republic and the United States; Suzann Wilson, who spoke out for gun control after her daughter died in a school shooting in Arkansas; and civil rights figure Rosa Parks. He also praised First Lady Hillary Clinton, saying, "I honor her."

An NBC News poll taken after the speech showed Clinton's popularity at a record 76 percent.

Mr. Speaker, Mr. Vice President, Members of Congress, honored guests, my fellow Americans:

Tonight, I have the honor of reporting to you on the State of the Union.

Let me begin by saluting the new Speaker of the House [Dennis Hastert], and thanking him, especially tonight, for extending an invitation to two guests sitting in the gallery with Mrs. Hastert: Lyn Gibson and Wenling Chestnut are the widows of the two brave Capitol Hill police officers who gave their lives to defend freedom's house.

Mr. Speaker, at your swearing-in, you asked us all to work together in a spirit of civility and bipartisanship. Mr. Speaker, let's do exactly that.

Tonight, I stand before you to report that America has created the longest peacetime economic expansion in our history with nearly 18 million new jobs, wages rising at more than twice the rate of inflation, the highest homeownership in history, the smallest welfare rolls in 30 years, and the lowest peacetime unemployment since 1957.

For the first time in three decades, the budget is balanced. From a deficit of $290 billion in 1992, we had a surplus of $70 billion last year. And now we are on course for budget surpluses for the next 25 years.

Thanks to the pioneering leadership of all of you, we have the lowest violent crime rate in a quarter century and the cleanest environment in a quarter century. America is a strong force for peace from Northern Ireland to Bosnia to the Middle East.

Thanks to the leadership of Vice President Gore, we have a Government for the information age. Once again, a Government that is a progressive instrument of the common good, rooted in our oldest values of opportunity, responsibility, and community; devoted to fiscal responsibility; determined to give our people the tools they need to make the most of their own lives in the 21st century; a 21st century Government for 21st century America.

My fellow Americans, I stand before you tonight to report that the state of our Union is strong.

Now, America is working again. The promise of our future is limitless. But we cannot realize that promise if we allow the hum of our prosperity to lull us into complacency. How we fare as a nation far into the 21st century depends upon what we do as a nation today. So with our budget surplus growing, our economy expanding, our confidence rising, now is the moment for this generation to meet our historic responsibility to the 21st century.

Our fiscal discipline gives us an unsurpassed opportunity to address a remarkable new challenge, the aging of America. With the number of elderly Americans set to double by 2030, the baby boom will become a senior boom. So first, and above all, we must save Social Security for the 21st century.

Early in this century, being old meant being poor. When President Roosevelt created Social Security, thousands wrote to thank him for eliminating what one woman called "the stark terror of penniless, helpless old age." Even today, without Social Security, half our Nation's elderly would be forced into poverty.

Today, Social Security is strong. But by 2013, payroll taxes will no longer be sufficient to cover monthly payments. By 2032, the Trust Fund will be exhausted and Social Security will be unable to pay the full benefits older Americans have been promised.

The best way to keep Social Security a rock-solid guarantee is not to make drastic cuts in benefits, not to raise payroll tax rates, not to drain resources from Social Security in the name of saving it. Instead, I propose that we make the historic decision to invest the surplus to save Social Security.

Specifically, I propose that we commit 60 percent of the budget surplus for the next 15 years to Social Security, investing a small portion in the private sector, just as any private or State Government pension would do. This will earn a higher return and keep Social Security sound for 55 years.

But we must aim higher. We should put Social Security on a sound footing for the next 75 years. We should reduce poverty among elderly women, who are nearly twice as likely to be poor as our other seniors. And we should eliminate the limits on what seniors on Social Security can earn.

Now, these changes will require difficult but fully achievable choices over and above the dedication of the surplus. They must be made on a bipartisan basis. They should be made this year. So let me say to you tonight, I reach out my hand to all of you in both Houses, in both parties, and ask that we join together in saying to the American people: We will save Social Security now.

Now, last year we wisely reserved all of the surplus until we knew what it would take to save Social Security. Again, I say, we shouldn't spend any of it, not any of it, until after Social Security is truly saved. First things first.

Second, once we have saved Social Security, we must fulfill our obligation to save and improve Medicare. Already, we have extended the life of the Medicare Trust Fund by 10 years, but we should extend it for at least another decade. Tonight, I propose that we use one out of every $6 in the surplus for the next 15 years to guarantee the soundness of Medicare until the year 2020.

But again, we should aim higher. We must be willing to work in a bipartisan way and look at new ideas, including the upcoming report of the bipartisan Medicare Commission. If we work together, we can secure Medicare for the next two decades and cover the greatest growing need of seniors, affordable prescription drugs.

Third, we must help all Americans, from their first day on the job to save, to invest, to create wealth. From its beginning, Americans have supplemented Social Security with private pensions and savings. Yet, today, millions of people retire with little to live on other than Social Security. Americans living longer than ever simply must save more than ever.

Therefore, in addition to saving Social Security and Medicare, I propose a new pension initiative for retirement security in the 21st century. I propose that we use a little over 11 percent of the surplus to establish universal savings accounts—USA accounts—to give all Americans the means to save. With these new accounts Americans can invest as they choose and receive funds to match a portion of their savings, with extra help for those least able to save. USA accounts will help all Americans to share in our Nation's wealth and to enjoy a more secure retirement. I ask you to support them.

Fourth, we must invest in long-term care. I propose a tax credit of $1,000 for the aged, ailing or disabled, and the families who care for them. Long-term care will become a bigger and bigger challenge with the aging of America, and we must do more to help our families deal with it.

I was born in 1946, the first year of the baby boom. I can tell you that one of the greatest concerns of our generation is our absolute determination not to let our growing old place an intolerable burden on our children and their ability to raise our grandchildren. Our economic success and our fiscal discipline now give us an opportunity to lift that burden from their shoulders, and we should take it.

Saving Social Security, Medicare, creating USA accounts: This is the right way to use the surplus. If we do so—if we do so—we will still have resources to meet critical needs in education and defense. And I want to point out that this proposal is fiscally sound. Listen to this: If we set aside 60 percent of the surplus for Social Security and 16 percent for Medicare, over the next 15 years, that saving will achieve the lowest level of publicly held debt since right before World War I, in 1917.

So with these four measures—saving Social Security, strengthening Medicare, establishing the USA accounts, supporting long-term care—we can begin to meet our generation's historic responsibility to establish true security for 21st century seniors.

Now, there are more children from more diverse backgrounds in our public schools than at any time in our history. Their education must provide the knowledge and nurture the creativity that will allow our entire Nation to thrive in the new economy.

Today we can say something we couldn't say 6 years ago: With tax credits and more affordable student loans, with more work-study grants and more Pell grants, with education IRA's and the new HOPE scholarship tax cut that more than 5 million Americans will receive this year, we have finally opened the doors of college to all Americans.

With our support, nearly every State has set higher academic standards for public schools, and a voluntary national test is being developed to measure the progress of our students. With over $1 billion in discounts available this year, we are well on our way to our goal of connecting every classroom and library to the Internet.

Last fall, you passed our proposal to start hiring 100,000 new teachers to reduce class size in the early grades. Now I ask you to finish the job.

You know, our children are doing better. SAT scores are up; math scores have risen in nearly all grades. But there's a problem. While our fourth graders outperform their peers in other countries in math and science, our eighth graders are around average, and our twelfth graders rank near the bottom. We must do better. Now, each year the National Government invests more than $15 billion in our public schools. I believe we must change the way we invest that money, to support what works and to stop supporting what does not work.

First, later this year, I will send to Congress a plan that, for the first time, holds States and school districts accountable for progress and rewards them for results. My "Education Accountability Act" will require every school district receiving Federal help to take the following five steps.

First, all schools must end social promotion. No child should graduate from high school with a diploma he or she can't read. We do our children no favors when we allow them to pass from grade to grade without mastering the material. But we can't just hold students back because the system fails them. So my balanced budget triples the funding for summer school and after-school programs, to keep a million children learning.

Now, if you doubt this will work, just look at Chicago, which ended social promotion and made summer school mandatory for those who don't master the basics. Math and reading scores are up 3 years running with some of the biggest gains in some of the poorest neighborhoods. It will work, and we should do it.

Second, all States and school districts must turn around their worst-performing schools or shut them down. That's the policy established in North Carolina by Governor Jim Hunt. North Carolina made the biggest gains in test scores in the Nation last year. Our budget includes $200 million to help States turn around their own failing schools.

Third, all States and school districts must be held responsible for the quality of their teachers. The great majority of our teachers do a fine job. But in too many schools, teachers don't have college majors—or even minors—in the subjects they teach. New teachers should be required to pass performance exams, and all teachers should know the subjects they're teaching. This year's balanced budget contains resources to help them reach higher standards.

And to attract talented young teachers to the toughest assignments, I recommend a sixfold increase in our program for college scholarships for students who commit to teach in the inner cities and isolated rural areas and in Indian communities. Let us bring excellence in every part of America.

Fourth, we must empower parents with more information and more choices. In too many communities, it's easier to get information on the quality of the local restaurants than on the quality of the local schools. Every school district should issue report cards on every school. And parents should be given more choices in selecting their public school.

When I became President, there was just one independent public charter school in all America. With our support, on a bipartisan basis, today there are 1,100. My budget assures that early in the next century, there will be 3,000.

Fifth, to assure that our classrooms are truly places of learning and to respond to what teachers have been asking us to do for years, we should say that all States and school districts must both adopt and implement sensible discipline policies.

Now, let's do one more thing for our children. Today, too many schools are so old they're falling apart, or so over-crowded students are learning in trailers. Last fall, Congress missed the opportunity to change that. This year, with 53 million children in our schools, Congress must not miss that opportunity again. I ask you to help our communities build or modernize 5,000 schools.

If we do these things—end social promotion; turn around failing schools; build modern ones; support qualified teachers; promote innovation, competition and discipline—then we will begin to meet our generation's historic responsibility to create 21st century schools.

Now, we also have to do more to support the millions of parents who give their all every day at home and at work. The most basic tool of all is a decent income. So let's raise the minimum wage by a dollar an hour over the next 2 years. And let's make sure that women and men get equal pay for equal work by strengthening enforcement of equal pay laws.

That was encouraging, you know. There was more balance on the seesaw. I like that. Let's give them a hand. That's great.

Working parents also need quality child care. So again this year, I ask Congress to support our plan for tax credits and subsidies for working families, for improved safety and quality, for expanded after-school programs. And our plan also includes a new tax credit for stay-at-home parents, too. They need support, as well.

Parents should never have to worry about choosing between their children and their work. Now, the Family and Medical Leave Act, the very first bill I signed into law, has now, since 1993, helped millions and millions of Americans to care for a newborn baby or an ailing relative without risking their jobs. I think it's time, with all the evidence that it has been so little burdensome to employers, to extend family leave to 10 million more Americans working for smaller companies. And I hope you will support it.

Finally on the matter of work, parents should never have to face discrimination in the workplace. So I want to ask Congress to prohibit companies from refusing to hire or promote workers simply because they have children. That is not right.

America's families deserve the world's best medical care. Thanks to bipartisan Federal support for medical research, we are now on the verge of new treatments to prevent or delay diseases from Parkinson's to Alzheimer's, to arthritis to cancer. But as we continue our advances in medical science, we can't let our medical system lag behind. Managed care has literally transformed medicine in America, driving down costs but threatening to drive down quality as well.

I think we ought to say to every American: You should have the right to know all your medical options, not just the cheapest. If you need a specialist, you should have a right to see one. You have a right to the nearest emergency care if you're in an accident. These are things that we ought to say. And I think we ought to say: You should have a right to keep your doctor during a period of treatment, whether it's a pregnancy or a chemotherapy treatment, or anything else. I believe this.

Now, I've ordered these rights to be extended to the 85 million Americans served by Medicare, Medicaid, and other Federal health programs. But only Congress can pass a Patients' Bill of Rights for all Americans. Now, last year, Congress missed that opportunity, and we must not miss that opportunity again. For the sake of our families, I ask us to join together across party lines and pass a strong, enforceable Patients' Bill of Rights.

As more of our medical records are stored electronically, the threats to all our privacy increase. Because Congress has given me the authority to act if it does not do so by August, one way or another, we can all say to the American people, "We will protect the privacy of medical records, and we will do it this year."

Now 2 years ago, the Congress extended health coverage to up to 5 million children. Now we should go beyond that. We should make it easier for small businesses to offer health insurance. We should give people between the ages of 55 and 65 who lose their health insurance the chance to buy into Medicare. And we should continue to ensure access to family planning.

No one should have to choose between keeping health care and taking a job. And therefore, I especially ask you tonight to join hands to pass the landmark bipartisan legislation, proposed by Senators [Ted] Kennedy and [James] Jeffords, [William] Roth, and [Daniel] Moynihan to allow people with disabilities to keep their health insurance when they go to work.

We need to enable our public hospitals, our community, our university health centers to provide basic, affordable care for all the millions of working families who don't have any insurance. They do a lot of that today, but much more can be done. And my balanced budget makes a good down payment toward that goal. I hope you will think about them and support that provision.

Let me say we must step up our efforts to treat and prevent mental illness. No American should ever be afraid—ever—to address this disease. This year, we will host a White House Conference on Mental Health. With sensitivity, commitment, and passion, Tipper Gore is leading our efforts here, and I'd like to thank her for what she's done. Thank you. Thank you.

As everyone knows, our children are targets of a massive media campaign to hook them on cigarettes. Now, I ask this Congress to resist the tobacco lobby, to reaffirm the FDA's authority to protect our children from tobacco, and to hold tobacco companies accountable while protecting tobacco farmers.

Smoking has cost taxpayers hundreds of billions of dollars under Medicare and other programs. You know, the States have been right about this: Taxpayers shouldn't pay for the cost of lung cancer, emphysema, and other smoking-related illnesses; the tobacco companies should. So tonight I announce that the Justice Department is preparing a litigation plan to take the tobacco companies to court and, with the funds we recover, to strengthen Medicare.

Now, if we act in these areas—minimum wage, family leave, child care, health care, the safety of our children—then we will begin to meet our generation's historic responsibilities to strengthen our families for the 21st century.

Today, America is the most dynamic, competitive, job-creating economy in history. But we can do even better in building a 21st century economy that embraces all Americans.

Today's income gap is largely a skills gap. Last year, the Congress passed a law enabling workers to get a skills grant to choose the training they need. And I applaud all of you here who were part of that. This year, I recommend a 5-year commitment to the new system so that we can provide, over the next 5 years, appropriate training opportunities for all Americans who lose their jobs and expand rapid response teams to help all towns which have been really hurt when businesses close. I hope you will support this.

Also, I ask your support for a dramatic increase in Federal support for adult literacy, to mount a national campaign aimed at helping the millions and millions of working people who still read at less than a fifth grade level. We need to do this.

Here's some good news: In the past 6 years, we have cut the welfare rolls nearly in half. You can all be proud of that. Two years ago, from this podium, I asked five companies to lead a national effort to hire people off welfare. Tonight, our Welfare to Work Partnership includes 10,000 companies who have hired hundreds of thousands of people. And our balanced budget will help another 200,000 people move to the dignity and pride of work. I hope you will support it.

We must do more to bring the spark of private enterprise to every corner of America, to build a bridge from Wall Street to Appalachia to the Mississippi Delta to our Native American communities, with more support for community development banks, for empowerment zones, for 100,000 more vouchers for affordable housing. And I ask Congress to support our bold new plan to help businesses raise up to $15 billion in private sector capital to bring jobs and opportunities to our inner cities and rural areas with tax credits, loan guarantees, including the new "American Private Investment Company," modeled on the Overseas Private Investment Company.

For years and years and years, we've had this OPIC, this Overseas Private Investment Corporation, because we knew we had untapped markets overseas. But our greatest untapped markets are not overseas; they are right here at home. And we should go after them.

We must work hard to help bring prosperity back to the family farm. As this Congress knows very well, dropping prices and the loss of foreign markets have devastated too many family farms. Last year, the Congress provided substantial assistance to help stave off a disaster in American agriculture. And I am ready to work with lawmakers of both parties to create a farm safety net that will include crop insurance reform and farm income assistance. I ask you to join with me and do this. This should not be a political issue. Everyone knows what an economic problem is going on out there in rural America today, and we need an appropriate means to address it.

We must strengthen our lead in technology. It was Government investment that led to the creation of the Internet. I propose a 28-percent increase in long-term computing research. We also must be ready for the 21st century from its very first moment, by solving the so-called Y2K computer problem.

We had one Member of Congress stand up and applaud. And we may have about that ratio out there applauding at home, in front of their television sets. But remember, this is a big, big problem. And we've been working hard on it. Already, we've made sure that the Social Security checks will come on time. But I want all the folks at home listening to this to know that we need every State and local government, every business, large and small, to work with us to make sure that this Y2K computer bug will be remembered as the last headache of the 20th century, not the first crisis of the 21st.

For our own prosperity, we must support economic growth abroad. You know, until recently, a third of our economic growth came from exports. But over the past year and a half, financial turmoil overseas has put that growth at risk. Today, much of the world is in recession, with Asia hit especially hard. This is the most serious financial crisis in half a century. To meet it, the United States and other nations have reduced interest rates and strengthened the International Monetary Fund. And while the turmoil is not over, we have worked very hard with other nations to contain it.

At the same time, we have to continue to work on the long-term project, building a global financial system for the 21st century that promotes prosperity and tames the cycle of boom and bust that has engulfed so much of Asia. This June I will meet with other world leaders to advance this historic purpose, and I ask all of you to support our endeavors.

I also ask you to support creating a freer and fairer trading system for 21st century America. I'd like to say something really serious to everyone in this Chamber in both parties. I think trade has divided us, and divided Americans outside this Chamber, for too long. Somehow we have to find a common ground on which business and workers and environmentalists and farmers and Government can stand together. I believe these are the things we ought to all agree on. So let me try.

First, we ought to tear down barriers, open markets, and expand trade. But at the same time, we must ensure that ordinary citizens in all countries actually benefit from trade, a trade that promotes the dignity of work and the rights of workers and protects the environment. We must insist that international trade organizations be more open to public scrutiny, instead of mysterious, secret things subject to wild criticism.

When you come right down to it, now that the world economy is becoming more and more integrated, we have to do in the world what we spent the better part of this century doing here at home. We have got to put a human face on the global economy.

We must enforce our trade laws when imports unlawfully flood our Nation. I have already informed the Government of Japan that if that nation's sudden surge of steel imports into our country is not reversed, America will respond.

We must help all manufacturers hit hard by the present crisis with loan guarantees and other incentives to increase American exports by nearly $2 billion. I'd like to believe we can achieve a new consensus on trade, based on these principles. And I ask the Congress again to join me in this common approach and to give the President the trade authority long used and now overdue and necessary to advance our prosperity in the 21st century.

Tonight I issue a call to the nations of the world to join the United States in a new round of global trade negotiations to expand exports of services, manufactures, and farm products. Tonight I say we will work with the International Labor Organization on a new initiative to raise labor standards around the world. And this year, we will lead the international community to conclude a treaty to ban abusive child labor everywhere in the world.

If we do these things—invest in our people, our communities, our technology, and lead in the global economy—then we will begin to meet our historic responsibility to build a 21st century prosperity for America.

You know, no nation in history has had the opportunity and the responsibility we now have to shape a world that is more peaceful, more secure, more free. All Americans can be proud that our leadership helped to bring peace in Northern Ireland. All Americans can be proud that our leadership has put Bosnia on the path to peace. And with our NATO allies, we are pressing the Serbian Government to stop its brutal repression in Kosovo, to bring those responsible to justice, and to give the people of Kosovo the self-government they deserve.

All Americans can be proud that our leadership renewed hope for lasting peace in the Middle East. Some of you were with me last December as we watched the Palestinian National Council completely renounce its call for the destruction of Israel. Now I ask Congress to provide resources so that all parties can implement the Wye agreement to protect Israel's security, to stimulate the Palestinian economy, to support our friends in Jordan. We must not—we dare not—let them down. I hope you will help.

As we work for peace, we must also meet threats to our Nation's security, including increased dangers from outlaw nations and terrorism. We will defend our security wherever we are threatened, as we did this summer when we struck at Usama bin Ladin's network of terror. The bombing of our Embassies in Kenya and Tanzania reminds us again of the risks faced every day by those who represent America to the world. So let's give them the support they need, the safest possible workplaces, and the resources they must have so America can continue to lead.

We must work to keep terrorists from disrupting computer networks. We must work to prepare local communities for biological and chemical emergencies, to support research into vaccines and treatments.

We must increase our efforts to restrain the spread of nuclear weapons and missiles, from Korea to India and Pakistan. We must expand our work with Russia, Ukraine, and other former Soviet nations to safeguard nuclear materials and technology so they never fall into the wrong hands. Our balanced budget will increase funding for these critical efforts by almost two-thirds over the next 5 years.

With Russia, we must continue to reduce our nuclear arsenals. The START II treaty and the framework we have already agreed to for START III could cut them by 80 percent from their cold war height.

It's been 2 years since I signed the Comprehensive Test Ban Treaty. If we don't do the right thing, other nations won't either. I ask the Senate to take this vital step: Approve the treaty now, to make it harder for other nations to develop nuclear arms, and to make sure we can end nuclear testing forever.

For nearly a decade, Iraq has defied its obligations to destroy its weapons of terror and the missiles to deliver them. America will continue to contain Saddam, and we will work for the day when Iraq has a Government worthy of its people.

Now, last month, in our action over Iraq, our troops were superb. Their mission was so flawlessly executed that we risk taking for granted the bravery and the skill it required. Captain Jeff Taliaferro, a 10-year veteran of the Air Force, flew a B-1B bomber over Iraq as we attacked Saddam's war machine. He's here with us tonight. I'd like to ask you to honor him and all the 33,000 men and women of Operation Desert Fox.

Captain Taliaferro.

It is time to reverse the decline in defense spending that began in 1985. Since April, together we have added nearly $6 billion to maintain our military readiness. My balanced budget calls for a sustained increase over the next 6 years for readiness, for modernization, and for pay and benefits for our troops and their families.

We are the heirs of a legacy of bravery represented in every community in America by millions of our veterans. America's defenders today still stand ready at a moment's notice to go where comforts are few and dangers are many, to do what needs to be done as no one else can. They always come through for America. We must come through for them.

The new century demands new partnerships for peace and security. The United Nations plays a crucial role, with allies sharing burdens America might otherwise bear alone. America needs a strong and effective U.N. I want to work with this new Congress to pay our dues and our debts.

We must continue to support security and stability in Europe and Asia, expanding NATO and defining its new missions, maintaining our alliance with Japan, with Korea, with our other Asian allies, and engaging China.

In China, last year, I said to the leaders and the people what I'd like to say again tonight: Stability can no longer be bought at the expense of liberty. But I'd also like to say again to the American people: It's important not to isolate China. The more we bring China into the world, the more the world will bring change and freedom to China.

Last spring, with some of you, I traveled to Africa, where I saw democracy and reform rising but still held back by violence and disease. We must fortify African democracy and peace by launching Radio Democracy for Africa, supporting the transition to democracy now beginning to take place in Nigeria, and passing the "African Trade and Development Act."

We must continue to deepen our ties to the Americas and the Caribbean, our common work to educate children, fight drugs, strengthen democracy and increase trade. In this hemisphere, every government but one is freely chosen by its people. We are determined that Cuba, too, will know the blessings of liberty.

The American people have opened their hearts and their arms to our Central American and Caribbean neighbors who have been so devastated by the recent hurricanes. Working with Congress, I am committed to help them rebuild. When the First Lady and Tipper Gore visited the region, they saw thousands of our troops and thousands of American volunteers. In the Dominican Republic, Hillary helped to rededicate a hospital that had been rebuilt by Dominicans and Americans, working side-by-side. With her was someone else who has been very important to the relief efforts.

You know, sports records are made and, sooner or later, they're broken. But making other people's lives better, and showing our children the true meaning of brotherhood—that lasts forever. So, for far more than baseball, Sammy Sosa, you're a hero in two countries tonight. Thank you.

So I say to all of you, if we do these things—if we pursue peace, fight terrorism, increase our strength, renew our alliances—we will begin to meet our generation's historic responsibility to build a stronger 21st century America in a freer, more peaceful world.

As the world has changed, so have our own communities. We must make them safer, more livable, and more united. This year, we will reach our goal of 100,000 community police officers ahead of schedule and under budget. The Brady bill has stopped a quarter million felons, fugitives, and stalkers from buying handguns. And now, the murder rate is the lowest in 30 years and the crime rate has dropped for 6 straight years.

Tonight I propose a 21st century crime bill to deploy the latest technologies and tactics to make our communities even safer. Our balanced budget will help put up to 50,000 more police on the street in the areas hardest hit by crime and then to equip them with new tools, from crime-mapping computers to digital mug shots.

We must break the deadly cycle of drugs and crime. Our budget expands support for drug testing and treatment, saying to prisoners: If you stay on drugs, you have to stay behind bars; and to those on parole: If you want to keep your freedom, you must stay free of drugs.

I ask Congress to restore the 5-day waiting period for buying a handgun and extend the Brady bill to prevent juveniles who commit violent crimes from buying a gun.

We must do more to keep our schools the safest places in our communities. Last year, every American was horrified and heartbroken by the tragic killings in Jonesboro,

Paducah, Pearl, Edinboro, Springfield. We were deeply moved by the courageous parents now working to keep guns out of the hands of children and to make other efforts so that other parents don't have to live through their loss.

After she lost her daughter, Suzann Wilson of Jonesboro, Arkansas, came here to the White House with a powerful plea. She said, "Please, please, for the sake of your children, lock up your guns. Don't let what happened in Jonesboro happen in your town." It's a message she is passionately advocating every day. Suzann is here with us tonight, with the First Lady. I'd like to thank her for her courage and her commitment. Thank you.

In memory of all the children who lost their lives to school violence, I ask you to strengthen the Safe and Drug-Free School Act, to pass legislation to require child trigger locks, to do everything possible to keep our children safe.

A century ago, President Theodore Roosevelt defined our "great, central task" as "leaving this land even a better land for our descendants than it is for us." Today, we're restoring the Florida Everglades, saving Yellowstone, preserving the red rock canyons of Utah, protecting California's redwoods and our precious coasts. But our most fateful new challenge is the threat of global warming; 1998 was the warmest year ever recorded. Last year's heat waves, floods, and storms are but a hint of what future generations may endure if we do not act now.

Tonight I propose a new clean air fund to help communities reduce greenhouse and other pollution, and tax incentives and investments to spur clean energy technology. And I want to work with Members of Congress in both parties to reward companies that take early, voluntary action to reduce greenhouse gases.

All our communities face a preservation challenge, as they grow and green space shrinks. Seven thousand acres of farmland and open space are lost every day. In response, I propose two major initiatives: First, a $1-billion livability agenda to help communities save open space, ease traffic congestion, and grow in ways that enhance every citizen's quality of life; and second, a $1-billion lands legacy initiative to preserve places of natural beauty all across America from the most remote wilderness to the nearest city park.

These are truly landmark initiatives, which could not have been developed without the visionary leadership of the Vice President, and I want to thank him very much for his commitment here.

Now, to get the most out of your community, you have to give something back. That's why we created AmeriCorps, our national service program that gives today's generation a chance to serve their communities and earn money for college.

So far, in just 4 years, 100,000 young Americans have built low-income homes with Habitat for Humanity, helped to tutor children with churches, worked with FEMA to ease the burden of natural disasters, and performed countless other acts of service that have made America better. I ask Congress to give more young Americans the chance to follow their lead and serve America in AmeriCorps.

Now, we must work to renew our national community as well for the 21st century. Last year the House passed the bipartisan campaign finance reform legislation sponsored by Representatives [Christopher] Shays and [Martin] Meehan and Senators [John] McCain and [Russell] Feingold. But a partisan minority in the Senate blocked reform. So I'd like to say to the House: Pass it again, quickly. And I'd like to say to the Senate: I hope you will say yes to a stronger American democracy in the year 2000.

Since 1997, our initiative on race has sought to bridge the divides between and among our people. In its report last fall, the initiative's advisory board found that Americans really do want to bring our people together across racial lines.

We know it's been a long journey. For some, it goes back to before the beginning of our Republic; for others, back since the Civil War; for others, throughout the 20th century. But for most of us alive today, in a very real sense, this journey began 43 years ago, when a woman named Rosa Parks sat down on a bus in Alabama and wouldn't get up. She's sitting down with the First Lady tonight, and she may get up or not, as she chooses. We thank her. Thank you, Rosa.

We know that our continuing racial problems are aggravated, as the Presidential initiative said, by opportunity gaps. The initiative I've outlined tonight will help to close them. But we know that the discrimination gap has not been fully closed either. Discrimination or violence because of race or religion, ancestry or gender, disability or sexual orientation, is wrong, and it ought to be illegal. Therefore, I ask Congress to make the "Employment Non-Discrimination Act" and the "Hate Crimes Prevention Act" the law of the land.

Now, since every person in America counts, every American ought to be counted. We need a census that uses modern scientific methods to do that.

Our new immigrants must be part of our One America. After all, they're revitalizing our cities; they're energizing our culture; they're building up our economy. We have a responsibility to make them welcome here, and they have a responsibility to enter the mainstream of American life. That means learning English and learning about our democratic system of government. There are now long waiting lines of immigrants that are trying to do just that. Therefore, our budget significantly expands our efforts to help them meet their responsibility. I hope you will support it.

Whether our ancestors came here on the Mayflower, on slave ships, whether they came to Ellis Island or LAX in Los Angeles, whether they came yesterday or walked this land a thousand years ago, our great challenge for the 21st century is to find a way to be one America. We can meet all the other challenges if we can go forward as one America.

You know, barely more than 300 days from now, we will cross that bridge into the new millennium. This is a moment, as the First Lady has said, "to honor the past and imagine the future."

I'd like to take just a minute to honor her. For leading our Millennium Project, for all she's done for our children, for all she has done in her historic role to serve our Nation and our best ideals at home and abroad, I honor her.

Last year, I called on Congress and every citizen to mark the millennium by saving America's treasures. Hillary has traveled all across the country to inspire recognition and support for saving places like Thomas Edison's invention factory or Harriet Tubman's home. Now we have to preserve our treasures in every community. And tonight, before I close, I want to invite every town, every city, every community to become a nationally recognized "millennium community," by launching projects that save our history, promote our arts and humanities, prepare our children for the 21st century.

Already, the response has been remarkable. And I want to say a special word of thanks to our private sector partners and to Members in Congress of both parties for their support. Just one example: Because of you, the Star-Spangled Banner will be preserved for the ages. In ways large and small, as we look to the millennium we are keeping alive what George Washington called "the sacred fire of liberty."

Six years ago, I came to office in a time of doubt for America, with our economy troubled, our deficit high, our people divided. Some even wondered whether our best days were behind us. But across this country, in a thousand neighborhoods, I have seen, even amidst the pain and uncertainty of recession, the real heart and character of America. I knew then that we Americans could renew this country.

Tonight, as I deliver the last State of the Union Address of the 20th century, no one anywhere in the world can doubt the enduring resolve and boundless capacity of the American people to work toward that "more perfect Union" of our Founders' dream.

We're now at the end of a century when generation after generation of Americans answered the call to greatness, overcoming depression, lifting up the disposed, bringing down barriers to racial prejudice, building the largest middle class in history, winning two World Wars and the long twilight struggle of the cold war. We must all be profoundly grateful for the magnificent achievement of our forebears in this century. Yet, perhaps, in the daily press of events, in the clash of controversy, we don't see our own time for what it truly is, a new dawn for America.

A hundred years from tonight, another American President will stand in this place and report on the state of the Union. He—or she—he or she will look back on a 21st century shaped in so many ways by the decisions we make here and now. So let it be said of us then that we were thinking not only of our time but of their time, that we reached as high as our ideals, that we put aside our divisions and found a new hour of healing and hopefulness, that we joined together to serve and strengthen the land we love.

My fellow Americans, this is our moment. Let us lift our eyes as one Nation, and from the mountaintop of this American Century, look ahead to the next one, asking God's blessing on our endeavors and on our beloved country.

Thank you, and good evening.

William J. Clinton, 1997–2001

Address before a Joint Session of Congress on the State of the Union

January 27, 2000

Bill Clinton's last State of the Union address was the longest ever spoken; at ninety minutes, it broke the previous record, held by Clinton's eighty-one-minute 1995 address.

Clinton was by this point a lame-duck president with less than one year left in his second term. He had survived being impeached by the House of Representatives in December 1998 when the Senate acquitted him in February 1999. At this point, he was looking toward the 2000 presidential election, where his vice president, Al Gore, was the likely Democratic nominee. Gore eventually would lose to Republican George W. Bush after a protracted dispute following the closely fought 2000 presidential election.

In this speech Clinton declared that the state of the union was "the strongest it has ever been." He made some comparisons between 1992, when he was elected, and the current situation, stating that the government had turned budget deficits into surpluses and reformed the welfare system, among other accomplishments. He recognized his first Treasury secretary, former senator Lloyd Bentsen, who was in the audience.

He also urged additional efforts to improve the country's education, health care, and child care, as well as efforts to crack down on deadbeat dads and help those fathers who sought to assist their children. He introduced audience member Carlos Rosas of St. Paul, Minnesota, who "wanted to do right by his son, and he got the help to do it."

Clinton offered thanks to his wife, Hillary, for her work on children and families. Mrs. Clinton would be elected as a Democratic senator from New York that year, marking the first time in U.S. history that a first lady had won elected office.

In his last two State of the Union addresses, Clinton had made a point of calling for the budget surpluses to be used to strengthen Social Security; he did not repeat that call this time, choosing to mention Social Security only briefly.

On the issue of crime, the president called for 50,000 more police officers to be added to the 100,000 new positions that had already been funded during his presidency, and he urged passage of additional gun control measures. He introduced audience member Tom Mauser, who was fighting for gun safety laws in the wake of the death of his son, Daniel, in the 1999 Columbine school shooting tragedy.

Clinton also singled out others in the audience: Captain John Cherrey, who had saved the life of another pilot during action in Serbia; Defense Secretary William Cohen and his wife, Janet; and baseball legend Hank Aaron, whom Clinton discussed as an example of racial healing.

Clinton's legacy would be mixed. His skills as a politician, combined with the strong economy during much of his presidency, enabled him to withstand the impeachment scandal and other controversies. But he was a polarizing figure as president and would continue to be so, as his wife was touted as a possible 2008 White House contender.

Mr. Speaker, Mr. Vice President, Members of Congress, honored guests, my fellow Americans:

We are fortunate to be alive at this moment in history. Never before has our Nation enjoyed, at once, so much prosperity and social progress with so little internal crisis and so few external threats. Never before have we had such a blessed opportunity and, therefore, such a profound obligation to build the more perfect Union of our Founders' dreams.

We begin the new century with over 20 million new jobs; the fastest economic growth in more than 30 years; the lowest unemployment rates in 30 years; the lowest poverty rates in 20 years; the lowest African-American and Hispanic unemployment rates on record; the first back-to-back surpluses in 42 years; and next month, America will achieve the longest period of economic growth in our entire history. We have built a new economy.

And our economic revolution has been matched by a revival of the American spirit: crime down by 20 percent, to its lowest level in 25 years; teen births down 7 years in a row; adoptions up by 30 percent; welfare rolls cut in half, to their lowest levels in 30 years.

My fellow Americans, the state of our Union is the strongest it has ever been.

As always, the real credit belongs to the American people. My gratitude also goes to those of you in this Chamber who have worked with us to put progress over partisanship.

Eight years ago, it was not so clear to most Americans there would be much to celebrate in the year 2000. Then our Nation was gripped by economic distress, social decline, political gridlock. The title of a best-selling book asked: "America: What Went Wrong?"

In the best traditions of our Nation, Americans determined to set things right. We restored the vital center, replacing outmoded ideologies with a new vision anchored in basic, enduring values: opportunity for all, responsibility from all, a community of all Americans. We reinvented Government, transforming it into a catalyst for new ideas that stress both opportunity and responsibility and give our people the tools they need to solve their own problems.

With the smallest Federal work force in 40 years, we turned record deficits into record surpluses and doubled our investment in education. We cut crime with 100,000 community police and the Brady law, which has kept guns out of the hands of half a million criminals.

We ended welfare as we knew it, requiring work while protecting health care and nutrition for children and investing more in child care, transportation, and housing to help their parents go to work. We've helped parents to succeed at home and at work with family leave, which 20 million Americans have now used to care for a new-born child or a sick loved one. We've engaged 150,000 young Americans in citizen service through AmeriCorps, while helping them earn money for college.

In 1992, we just had a roadmap. Today, we have results.

Even more important, America again has the confidence to dream big dreams. But we must not let this confidence drift into complacency. For we, all of us, will be judged by the dreams and deeds we pass on to our children. And on that score, we will be held to a high standard, indeed, because our chance to do good is so great.

My fellow Americans, we have crossed the bridge we built to the 21st century. Now, we must shape a 21st century American revolution of opportunity, responsibility, and community. We must be now, as we were in the beginning, a new nation.

At the dawn of the last century, Theodore Roosevelt said, "The one characteristic more essential than any other is foresight . . . it should be the growing Nation with a future that takes the long look ahead." So tonight let us take our long look ahead and set great goals for our Nation.

To 21st century America, let us pledge these things: Every child will begin school ready to learn and graduate ready to succeed. Every family will be able to succeed at home and at work, and no child will be raised in poverty. We will meet the challenge of the aging of America. We will assure quality, affordable health care, at last, for all Americans. We will make America the safest big country on Earth. We will pay off our national debt for the first time since 1835. We will bring prosperity to every American community. We will reverse the course of climate change and leave a safer, cleaner planet. America will lead the world toward shared peace and prosperity and the far frontiers of science and technology. And we will become at last what our Founders pledged us to be so long ago—one Nation, under God, indivisible, with liberty and justice for all.

These are great goals, worthy of a great nation. We will not reach them all this year, not even in this decade. But we will reach them. Let us remember that the first American Revolution was not won with a single shot; the continent was not settled in a single year. The lesson of our history and the lesson of the last 7 years is that great goals are reached step by step, always building on our progress, always gaining ground.

Of course, you can't gain ground if you're standing still. And for too long this Congress has been standing still on some of our most pressing national priorities. So let's begin tonight with them.

Again, I ask you to pass a real Patients' Bill of Rights. I ask you to pass common-sense gun safety legislation. I ask you to pass campaign finance reform. I ask you to vote up or down on judicial nominations and other important appointees. And again, I ask you—I implore you to raise the minimum wage.

Now, 2 years ago—let me try to balance the seesaw here—2 years ago, as we reached across party lines to reach our first balanced budget, I asked that we meet our responsibility to the next generation by maintaining our fiscal discipline. Because we refused to stray from that path, we are doing something that would have seemed unimaginable 7 years ago. We are actually paying down the national debt. Now, if we stay on this path, we can pay down the debt entirely in just 13 years now and make America debt-free for the first time since Andrew Jackson was President in 1835.

In 1993 we began to put our fiscal house in order with the Deficit Reduction Act, which you'll all remember won passages in both Houses by just a single vote. Your former colleague, my first Secretary of the Treasury, led that effort and sparked our long boom. He's here with us tonight. Lloyd Bentsen, you have served America well, and we thank you.

Beyond paying off the debt, we must ensure that the benefits of debt reduction go to preserving two of the most important guarantees we make to every American, Social Security and Medicare. Tonight I ask you to work with me to make a bipartisan downpayment on Social Security reform by crediting the interest savings from debt reduction to the Social Security Trust

Fund so that it will be strong and sound for the next 50 years.

But this is just the start of our journey. We must also take the right steps toward reaching our great goals. First and foremost, we need a 21st century revolution in education, guided by our faith that every single child can learn. Because education is more important than ever, more than ever the key to our children's future, we must make sure all our children have that key. That means quality preschool and after-school, the best trained teachers in the classroom, and college opportunities for all our children.

For 7 years now, we've worked hard to improve our schools, with opportunity and responsibility, investing more but demanding more in turn. Reading, math, college entrance scores are up. Some of the most impressive gains are in schools in very poor neighborhoods.

But all successful schools have followed the same proven formula: higher standards, more accountability, and extra help so children who need it can get it to reach those standards. I have sent Congress a reform plan based on that formula. It holds States and school districts accountable for progress and rewards them for results. Each year, our National Government invests more than $15 billion in our schools. It is time to support what works and stop supporting what doesn't.

Now, as we demand more from our schools, we should also invest more in our schools. Let's double our investment to help States and districts turn around their worst performing schools or shut them down. Let's double our investments in after-school and summer school programs, which boost achievement and keep people off the streets and out of trouble. If we do this, we can give every single child in every failing school in America—everyone—the chance to meet high standards.

Since 1993, we've nearly doubled our investment in Head Start and improved its quality. Tonight I ask you for another $1 billion for Head Start, the largest increase in the history of the program.

We know that children learn best in smaller classes with good teachers. For 2 years in a row, Congress has supported my plan to hire 100,000 new qualified teachers to lower class size in the early grades. I thank you for that, and I ask you to make it 3 in a row. And to make sure all teachers know the subjects they teach, tonight I propose a new teacher quality initiative, to recruit more talented people into the classroom, reward good teachers for staying there, and give all teachers the training they need.

We know charter schools provide real public school choice. When I became President, there was just one independent public charter school in all America. Today, thanks to you, there are 1,700. I ask you now to help us meet our goal of 3,000 charter schools by next year.

We know we must connect all our classrooms to the Internet, and we're getting there. In 1994, only 3 percent of our classrooms were connected. Today, with the help of the Vice President's E-rate program, more than half of them are, and 90 percent of our schools have at least one Internet connection. But we cannot finish the job when a third of all our schools are in serious disrepair. Many of them have walls and wires so old, they're too old for the Internet. So tonight I propose to help 5,000 schools a year make immediate and urgent repairs and, again, to help build or modernize 6,000 more, to get students out of trailers and into high-tech classrooms.

I ask all of you to help me double our bipartisan GEAR UP program, which provides mentors for disadvantaged young people. If we double it, we can provide mentors for 1.4 million of them. Let's also offer these kids from disadvantaged backgrounds the same chance to take the same college test-prep courses wealthier students use to boost their test scores.

To make the American dream achievable for all, we must make college affordable for all. For 7 years, on a bipartisan basis, we have taken action toward that goal: larger Pell grants, more affordable student loans, education IRA's, and our HOPE scholarships, which have already benefited 5 million young people.

Now, 67 percent of high school graduates are going on to college. That's up 10 percent since 1993. Yet millions of families still strain to pay college tuition. They need help. So I propose a landmark $30 billion college opportunity tax cut, a middle class tax deduction for up to $10,000 in college tuition costs. The previous actions of this Congress have already made 2 years of college affordable for all. It's time make 4 years of college affordable for all. If we take all these steps, we'll move a long way toward making sure every child starts school ready to learn and graduates ready to succeed.

We also need a 21st century revolution to reward work and strengthen families by giving every parent the tools to succeed at work and at the most important work of all, raising children. That means making sure every family has health care and the support to care for aging parents, the tools to bring their children up right, and that no child grows up in poverty.

From my first days as President, we've worked to give families better access to better health care. In 1997, we passed the Children's Health Insurance Program—CHIP—so that workers who don't have coverage through their employers at least can get it for their children. So far, we've enrolled 2 million children. We're well on our way to our goal of 5 million.

But there are still more than 40 million of our fellow Americans without health insurance, more than there were in 1993. Tonight I propose that we follow Vice President Gore's suggestion to make low income parents eligible for the insurance that covers their children. Together with our children's initiative—think of this—together with our children's initiative, this action would enable us to cover nearly a quarter of all the uninsured people in America.

Again, I want to ask you to let people between the ages of 55 and 65, the fastest growing group of uninsured, buy into Medicare. And this year I propose to give them a tax credit to make that choice an affordable one. I hope you will support that, as well.

When the baby boomers retire, Medicare will be faced with caring for twice as many of our citizens; yet, it is far from ready to do so. My generation must not ask our children's generation to shoulder our burden. We simply must act now to strengthen and modernize Medicare.

My budget includes a comprehensive plan to reform Medicare, to make it more efficient and more competitive. And it dedicates nearly $400 billion of our budget surplus to keep Medicare solvent past 2025. And at long last, it also provides funds to give every senior a voluntary choice of affordable coverage for prescription drugs.

Lifesaving drugs are an indispensable part of modern medicine. No one creating a Medicare program today would even think of excluding coverage for prescription drugs. Yet more than three in five of our seniors now lack dependable drug coverage which can lengthen and enrich their lives. Millions of older Americans, who need prescription drugs the most, pay the highest prices for them. In good conscience, we cannot let another year pass without extending to all our seniors this lifeline of affordable prescription drugs.

Record numbers of Americans are providing for aging or ailing loved ones at home. It's a loving but a difficult and often very expensive choice. Last year, I proposed a $1,000 tax credit for long-term care. Frankly, it wasn't enough. This year, let's triple it to $3,000. But this year, let's pass it.

We also have to make needed investments to expand access to mental health care. I want to take a moment to thank the person who led our first White House Conference on Mental Health last year and who for 7 years has led all our efforts to break down the barriers to decent treatment of people with mental illness. Thank you, Tipper Gore.

Taken together, these proposals would mark the largest investment in health care in the 35 years since Medicare was created—the largest investment in 35 years. That would be a big step toward assuring quality health care for all Americans, young and old. And I ask you to embrace them and pass them.

We must also make investments that reward work and support families. Nothing does that better than the earned-income tax credit, the EITC. The "E" in the EITC is about earning, working, taking responsibility, and being rewarded for it. In my very first address to you, I asked Congress to greatly expand this credit, and you did. As a result, in 1998 alone, the EITC helped more than 4.3 million Americans work their way out of poverty toward the middle class. That's double the number in 1993.

Tonight I propose another major expansion of the EITC: to reduce the marriage penalty, to make sure it rewards marriage as it rewards work, and also to expand the tax credit for families that have more than two children. It punishes people with more than two children today. Our proposal would allow families with three or more children to get up to $1,100 more in tax relief. These are working families; their children should not be in poverty.

We also can't reward work and family unless men and women get equal pay for equal work. Today the female unemployment rate is the lowest it has been in 46 years. Yet, women still only earn about 75 cents for every dollar men earn. We must do better, by providing the resources to enforce present equal pay laws, training more women for high-paying, high-tech jobs, and passing the "Paycheck Fairness Act."

Many working parents spend up to a quarter—a quarter—of their income on child care. Last year, we helped parents provide child care for about 2 million children. My child care initiative before you now, along with funds already secured in welfare reform, would make child care better, safer, and more affordable for another 400,000 children. I ask you to pass that. They need it out there.

For hard-pressed middle income families, we should also expand the child care tax credit. And I believe strongly we should take the next big step and make that tax credit refundable for low income families. For people making under $30,000 a year, that could mean up to $2,400 for child care costs. You know, we all say we're pro-work and pro-family. Passing this proposal would prove it.

Ten of millions of Americans live from paycheck to paycheck. As hard as they work, they still don't have the opportunity to save. Too few can make use of IRA's and 401k plans. We should do more to help all working families save and accumulate wealth. That's the idea behind the Individual Development Accounts, the IDA's. I ask you to take that idea to a new level, with new retirement savings accounts that enable every low and moderate income family in America to save for retirement, a first home, a medical emergency, or a college education. I propose to match their contributions, however small, dollar for dollar, every year they save. And I propose to give a major new tax credit to any small business that will provide a meaningful pension to its workers. Those people ought to have retirement as well as the rest of us.

Nearly one in three American children grows up without a father. These children are 5 times more likely to live in poverty than children with both parents at home. Clearly, demanding and supporting responsible fatherhood is critical to lifting all our children out of poverty. We've doubled child support collections since 1992. And I'm proposing to you tough new measures to hold still more fathers responsible.

But we should recognize that a lot of fathers want to do right by their children but need help to do it. Carlos Rosas of St. Paul, Minnesota, wanted to do right by his son, and he got the help to do it. Now he's got a good job, and he supports his little boy. My budget will help 40,000 more fathers make the same choices Carlos Rosas did. I thank him for being here tonight. Stand up, Carlos. Thank you.

If there is any single issue on which we should be able to reach across party lines, it is in our common commitment to reward work and strengthen families. Just remember what we did last year. We came together to help people with disabilities keep their health insurance when they go to work. And I thank you for that. Thanks to overwhelming bipartisan support from this Congress, we have improved foster care. We've helped those young people who leave it when they turn 18, and we have dramatically increased the number of foster care children going into adoptive homes. I thank all of you for all of that.

Of course, I am forever grateful to the person who has led our efforts from the beginning and who's worked so tirelessly for children and families for 30 years now, my wife, Hillary, and I thank her.

If we take the steps just discussed, we can go a long, long way toward empowering parents to succeed at home and at work and ensuring that no child is raised in poverty. We can make these vital investments in health care, education, support for working families, and still offer tax cuts to help pay for college, for retirement, to care for aging parents, to reduce the marriage penalty. We can do these things without forsaking the path of fiscal discipline that got us to this point here tonight. Indeed, we must make these investments and these tax cuts in the context of a balanced budget that strengthens and extends the life of Social Security and Medicare and pays down the national debt.

Crime in America has dropped for the past 7 years—that's the longest decline on record— thanks to a national consensus we helped to forge on community police, sensible gun safety laws, and effective prevention. But nobody, nobody here, nobody in America believes we're safe enough. So again, I ask you to set a higher goal. Let's make this country the safest big country in the world.

Last fall, Congress supported my plan to hire, in addition to the 100,000 community police we've already funded, 50,000 more, concentrated in high-crime neighborhoods. I ask your continued support for that.

Soon after the Columbine tragedy, Congress considered commonsense gun legislation, to require Brady background checks at the gun shows, child safety locks for new handguns, and a ban on the importation of large capacity ammunition clips. With courage and a tie-breaking vote by the Vice President—the Senate faced down the gun lobby, stood up for the American people, and passed this legislation. But the House failed to follow suit.

Now, we have all seen what happens when guns fall into the wrong hands. Daniel Mauser was only 15 years old when he was gunned down at Columbine. He was an amazing kid, a straight-A student, a good skier. Like all parents who lose their children, his father, Tom, has borne unimaginable grief. Somehow he has found the strength to honor his son by transforming his grief into action. Earlier this month, he took a leave of absence from his job to fight for tougher gun safety laws. I pray that his courage and wisdom will at long last move this Congress to make commonsense gun legislation the very next order of business. Tom Mauser, stand up. We thank you for being here tonight. Tom. Thank you, Tom.

We must strengthen our gun laws and enforce those already on the books better. Federal gun crime prosecutions are up 16 percent since I took office. But we must do more. I propose to hire more Federal and local gun prosecutors and more ATF agents to crack down on illegal gun traffickers and bad-apple dealers. And we must give them the enforcement tools that they need, tools to trace every gun and every bullet used in every gun crime in the United States. I ask you to help us do that.

Every State in this country already requires hunters and automobile drivers to have a license. I think they ought to do the same thing for handgun purchases. Now, specifically, I propose a plan to ensure that all new handgun buyers must first have a photo license from their State showing they passed the Brady background check and a gun safety course, before they get the gun. I hope you'll help me pass that in this Congress.

Listen to this. The accidental gun death rate of children under 15 in the United States is 9 times higher than in the other 25 industrialized countries combined. Technologies now exist that could lead to guns that can only be fired by the adults who own them. I ask Congress to fund research into smart gun technology to save these children's lives. I ask responsible leaders in the gun industry to work with us on smart guns and other steps to keep guns out of the wrong hands, to keep our children safe.

You know, every parent I know worries about the impact of violence in the media on their children. I want to begin by thanking the entertainment industry for accepting my challenge to put voluntary ratings on TV programs and video and Internet games. But frankly, the ratings are too numerous, diverse, and confusing to be really useful to parents. So tonight I ask the industry to accept the First Lady's challenge to develop a single voluntary rating system for all children's entertainment that is easier for parents to understand and enforce.

The steps I outline will take us well on our way to making America the safest big country in the world.

Now, to keep our historic economic expansion going, the subject of a lot of discussion in this community and others, I believe we need a 21st century revolution to open new markets, start new businesses, hire new workers right here in America, in our inner cities, poor rural areas, and Native American reservations.

Our Nation's prosperity hasn't yet reached these places. Over the last 6 months, I've traveled to a lot of them, joined by many of you and many far-sighted business people, to shine a spotlight on the enormous potential in communities from Appalachia to the Mississippi Delta, from Watts to the Pine Ridge Reservation. Everywhere I go, I meet talented people eager for opportunity and able to work. Tonight I ask you, let's put them to work. For business, it's the smart thing to do. For America, it's the right thing to do. And let me ask you something: If we don't do this now, when in the wide world will we ever get around to it?

So I ask Congress to give businesses the same incentives to invest in America's new markets they now have to invest in markets overseas. Tonight I propose a large new markets tax credit and other incentives to spur $22 billion in private-sector capital to create new businesses and new investments in our inner cities and rural areas. Because empowerment zones have been creating these opportunities for 5 years now, I also ask you to increase incentives to invest in them and to create more of them.

And let me say to all of you again what I have tried to say at every turn: This is not a Democratic or a Republican issue. Giving people a chance to live their dreams is an American issue.

Mr. Speaker, it was a powerful moment last November when you joined Reverend Jesse Jackson and me in your home State of Illinois and committed to working toward our common goal by combining the best ideas from both sides of the aisle. I want to thank you again and to tell you, Mr. Speaker, I look forward to working with you. This is a worthy joint endeavor. Thank you.

I also ask you to make special efforts to address the areas of our Nation with the highest rates of poverty, our Native American reservations and the Mississippi Delta. My budget includes a $110 million initiative to promote economic development in the Delta and a billion dollars to increase economic opportunity, health care, education, and law enforcement for our Native American communities. We should begin this new century by honoring our historic responsibility to empower the first Americans. And I want to thank tonight the leaders and the members from both parties who've expressed to me an interest in working with us on these efforts. They are profoundly important.

There's another part of our American community in trouble tonight, our family farmers. When I signed the farm bill in 1996, I said there was great danger it would work well in good times but not in bad. Well, droughts, floods, and historically low prices have made these times very bad for the farmers. We must work together to strengthen the farm safety net, invest in land conservation, and create some new markets for them by expanding our programs for bio-based fuels and products. Please, they need help. Let's do it together.

Opportunity for all requires something else today, having access to a computer and knowing how to use it. That means we must close the digital divide between those who've got the tools and those who don't. Connecting classrooms and libraries to the Internet is crucial, but it's just a start. My budget ensures that all new teachers are trained to teach 21st century skills, and it creates technology centers in 1,000 communities to serve adults. This spring, I'll invite high-tech leaders to join me on another new markets tour, to close the digital divide and open opportunity for our people. I want to thank the high-tech companies that already are doing so much in this area. I hope the new tax incentives I have proposed will get all the rest of them to join us. This is a national crusade. We have got to do this and do it quickly.

Now, again I say to you, these are steps, but step by step, we can go a long way toward our goal of bringing opportunity to every community.

To realize the full possibilities of this economy, we must reach beyond our own borders to shape the revolution that is tearing down barriers and building new networks among nations and individuals and economies and cultures: globalization. It's the central reality of our time.

Of course, change this profound is both liberating and threatening to people. But there's no turning back. And our open, creative society stands to benefit more than any other if we understand and act on the realities of interdependence. We have to be at the center of every vital global network, as a good neighbor and a good partner. We have to recognize that we cannot build our future without helping others to build theirs.

The first thing we have got to do is to forge a new consensus on trade. Now, those of us who believe passionately in the power of open trade, we have to ensure that it lifts both our living standards and our values, never tolerating abusive child labor or a race to the bottom in the environment and worker protection. But others must recognize that open markets and rule-based trade are the best engines we know of for raising living standards, reducing global poverty and environmental destruction, and assuring the free flow of ideas.

I believe, as strongly tonight as I did the first day I got here, the only direction forward for America on trade—the only direction for America on trade is to keep going forward. I ask you to help me forge that consensus. We have to make developing economies our partners in prosperity. That's why I would like to ask you again to finalize our groundbreaking African and Caribbean Basin trade initiatives.

But globalization is about more than economics. Our purpose must be to bring together the world around freedom and democracy and peace and to oppose those who would tear it apart. Here are the fundamental challenges I believe America must meet to shape the 21st century world.

First, we must continue to encourage our former adversaries, Russia and China, to emerge as stable, prosperous, democratic nations. Both are being held back today from reaching their full potential: Russia by the legacy of communism, an economy in turmoil, a cruel and self-defeating war in Chechnya; China by the illusion that it can buy stability at the expense of freedom.

But think how much has changed in the past decade: 5,000 former Soviet nuclear weapons taken out of commission; Russian soldiers actually serving with ours in the Balkans; Russian people electing their leaders for the first time in 1,000 years; and in China, an economy more open to the world than ever before.

Of course, no one, not a single person in this Chamber tonight can know for sure what direction these great nations will take. But we do know for sure that we can choose what we do. And we should do everything in our power to increase the chance that they will choose wisely, to be constructive members of our global community.

That's why we should support those Russians who are struggling for a democratic, prosperous future; continue to reduce both our nuclear arsenals; and help Russia to safeguard weapons and materials that remain.

And that's why I believe Congress should support the agreement we negotiated to bring China into the WTO [World Trade Organization], by passing permanent normal trade relations with China as soon as possible this year. I think you ought to do it for two reasons: First of all, our markets are already open to China; this agreement will open China's markets to us. And second, it will plainly advance the cause of peace in Asia and promote the cause of change in China. No, we don't know where it's going. All we can do is decide what we're going to do. But when all is said and done, we need to know we did everything we possibly could to maximize the chance that China will choose the right future.

A second challenge we've got is to protect our own security from conflicts that pose the risk of wider war and threaten our common humanity. We can't prevent every conflict or stop every outrage. But where our interests are at stake and we can make a difference, we should be, and we must be, peacemakers.

We should be proud of our role in bringing the Middle East closer to a lasting peace, building peace in Northern Ireland, working for peace in East Timor and Africa, promoting reconciliation between Greece and Turkey and in Cyprus, working to defuse these crises between India and Pakistan, in defending human rights and religious freedom. And we should be proud of the men and women of our Armed Forces and those of our allies who stopped the ethnic cleansing in Kosovo, enabling a million people to return to their homes.

When Slobodan Milosevic unleashed his terror on Kosovo, Captain John Cherry was one of the brave airmen who turned the tide. And when another American plane was shot down over Serbia, he flew into the teeth of enemy air defenses to bring his fellow pilot home. Thanks to our Armed Forces' skill and bravery, we prevailed in Kosovo without losing a single American in combat. I want to introduce Captain Cherrey to you. We honor Captain Cherrey, and we promise you, Captain, we'll finish the job you began. Stand up so we can see you.

A third challenge we have is to keep this inexorable march of technology from giving terrorists and potentially hostile nations the means to undermine our defenses. Keep in mind, the same technological advances that have shrunk cell phones to fit in the palms of our hands can also make weapons of terror easier to conceal and easier to use.

We must meet this threat by making effective agreements to restrain nuclear and missile programs in North Korea, curbing the flow of lethal technology to Iran, preventing Iraq from threatening its neighbors, increasing our preparedness against chemical and biological attack, protecting our vital computer systems from hackers and criminals, and developing a system to defend against new missile threats, while working to preserve our ABM missile treaty with Russia. We must do all these things.

I predict to you, when most of us are long gone but some time in the next 10 to 20 years, the major security threat this country will face will come from the enemies of the nation-state, the narcotraffickers and the terrorists and the organized criminals who will be organized together, working together, with increasing access to ever more sophisticated chemical and biological weapons. And I want to thank the Pentagon and others for doing what they're doing right now to try to help protect us and plan for that, so that our defenses will be strong. I ask for your support to ensure they can succeed.

I also want to ask you for a constructive bipartisan dialog this year to work to build a consensus which I hope will eventually lead to the ratification of the Comprehensive Nuclear-Test-Ban Treaty.

I hope we can also have a constructive effort to meet the challenge that is presented to our planet by the huge gulf between rich and poor. We cannot accept a world in which part of humanity lives on the cutting edge of a new economy and the rest live on the bare edge of survival. I think we have to do our part to change that with expanded trade, expanded aid, and the expansion of freedom.

This is interesting: From Nigeria to Indonesia, more people got the right to choose their leaders in 1999 than in 1989, when the Berlin Wall fell. We've got to stand by these democracies, including and especially tonight Colombia, which is fighting narcotraffickers, for its own people's lives and our children's lives. I have proposed a strong 2-year package to help Colombia win this fight. I want to thank the leaders in both parties in both Houses for listening to me and the President of Colombia about it. We have got to pass this. I want to ask your help. A lot is riding on it. And it's so important for the long-term stability of our country and for what happens in Latin America.

I also want you to know I'm going to send you new legislation to go after what these drug barons value the most, their money. And I hope you'll pass that as well.

In a world where over a billion people live on less than a dollar a day, we also have got to do our part in the global endeavor to reduce the debts of the poorest countries, so they can invest in education, health care, and economic growth. That's what the Pope and other religious leaders have urged us to do. And last year, Congress made a downpayment on America's share. I ask you to continue that. I thank you for what you did and ask you to stay the course.

I also want to say that America must help more nations to break the bonds of disease. Last year in Africa, 10 times as many people died from AIDS as were killed in wars—10 times. The budget I give you invests $150 million more in the fight against this and other infectious killers. And today I propose a tax credit to speed the development of vaccines for diseases like malaria, TB, and AIDS. I ask the private sector and our partners around the world to join us in embracing this cause. We can save millions of lives together, and we ought to do it.

I also want to mention our final challenge, which, as always, is the most important. I ask you to pass a national security budget that keeps our military the best trained and best equipped in the world, with heightened readiness and 21st century weapons, which raises salaries for our service men and women, which protects our veterans, which fully funds the diplomacy that keeps our soldiers out of war, which makes good on our commitment to our U.N. dues and arrears. I ask you to pass this budget.

I also want to say something, if I might, very personal tonight. The American people watching us at home, with the help of all the commentators, can tell, from who stands and who sits and who claps and who doesn't, that there's still modest differences of opinion in this room. But I want to thank you for something, every one of you. I want to thank you for the extraordinary support you have given, Republicans and Democrats alike, to our men and women in uniform. I thank you for that.

I also want to thank, especially, two people. First, I want to thank our Secretary of Defense, Bill Cohen, for symbolizing our bipartisan commitment to national security. Thank you, sir. Even more, I want to thank his wife, Janet, who, more than any other American citizen, has tirelessly traveled this world to show the support we all feel for our troops. Thank you, Janet Cohen. I appreciate that. Thank you.

These are the challenges we have to meet so that we can lead the world toward peace and freedom in an era of globalization.

I want to tell you that I am very grateful for many things as President. But one of the things I'm grateful for is the opportunity that the Vice President and I have had to finally put to rest the bogus idea that you cannot grow the economy and protect the environment at the same time.

As our economy has grown, we've rid more than 500 neighborhoods of toxic waste, ensured cleaner air and water for millions of people. In the past 3 months alone, we've helped preserve 40 million acres of roadless lands in the national forests, created three new national monuments.

But as our communities grow, our commitment to conservation must continue to grow.

Tonight I propose creating a permanent conservation fund, to restore wildlife, protect coastlines, save natural treasures, from the California redwoods to the Florida Everglades. This lands legacy endowment would represent by far the most enduring investment in land preservation ever proposed in this House. I hope we can get together with all the people with different ideas and do this. This is a gift we should give to our children and our grandchildren for all time, across party lines. We can make an agreement to do this.

Last year the Vice President launched a new effort to make communities more liberal—livable—liberal, I know. Wait a minute, I've got a punchline now. That's this year's agenda; last year was livable, right? That's what Senator [Trent] Lott is going to say in the commentary afterwards—to make our communities more livable. This is big business. This is a big issue. What does that mean? You ask anybody that lives in an unlivable community, and they'll tell you. They want their kids to grow up next to parks, not parking lots; the parents don't have to spend all their time stalled in traffic when they could be home with their children.

Tonight I ask you to support new funding for the following things, to make American communities more liberal—livable. I've done pretty well with this speech, but I can't say that.

One, I want you to help us to do three things. We need more funding for advanced transit systems. We need more funding for saving open spaces in places of heavy development. And we need more funding—this ought to have bipartisan appeal—we need more funding for helping major cities around the Great Lakes protect their waterways and enhance their quality of life. We need these things, and I want you to help us.

The greatest environmental challenge of the new century is global warming. The scientists tell us the 1990's were the hottest decade of the entire millennium. If we fail to reduce the emission of greenhouse gases, deadly heat waves and droughts will become more frequent, coastal areas will flood, and economies will be disrupted. That is going to happen, unless we act.

Many people in the United States, some people in this Chamber, and lots of folks around the world still believe you cannot cut greenhouse gas emissions without slowing economic growth. In the industrial age, that may well have been true. But in this digital economy, it is not true anymore. New technologies make it possible to cut harmful emissions and provide even more growth.

For example, just last week, automakers unveiled cars that get 70 to 80 miles a gallon, the fruits of a unique research partnership between Government and industry. And before you know it, efficient production of bio-fuels will give us the equivalent of hundreds of miles from a gallon of gasoline.

To speed innovation in these kind of technologies, I think we should give a major tax incentive to business for the production of clean energy and to families for buying energy-saving homes and appliances and the next generation of super efficient cars when they hit the showroom floor. I also ask the auto industry to use the available technologies to make all new cars more fuel-efficient right away.

And I ask this Congress to do something else. Please help us make more of our clean energy technology available to the developing world. That will create cleaner growth abroad and a lot more new jobs here in the United States of America.

In the new century, innovations in science and technology will be key not only to the health of the environment but to miraculous improvements in the quality of our lives and advances in the economy. Later this year, researchers will complete the first draft of the entire human genome, the very blueprint of life. It is important for all our fellow Americans to recognize that Federal tax dollars have funded much of this research and that this and other wise investments in science are leading to a revolution in our ability to detect, treat, and prevent disease.

For example, researchers have identified genes that cause Parkinson's, diabetes, and certain kinds of cancer. They are designing precision therapies that will block the harmful effect of these genes for good. Researchers already are using this new technique to target and destroy cells that cause breast cancer. Soon, we may be able to use it to prevent the onset of Alzheimer's. Scientists are also working on an artificial retina to help many blind people to see and—listen to this—microchips that would actually directly stimulate damaged spinal cords in a way that could allow people now paralyzed to stand up and walk.

These kinds of innovations are also propelling our remarkable prosperity. Information technology only includes 8 percent of our employment but now accounts for a third of our economic growth along with jobs that pay, by the way, about 80 percent above the private sector average. Again, we ought to keep in mind, Government-funded research brought supercomputers, the Internet, and communications satellites into being. Soon researchers will bring us devices that can translate foreign languages as fast as you can talk, materials 10 times stronger than steel at a fraction of the weight, and— this is unbelievable to me—molecular computers the size of a teardrop with the power of today's fastest supercomputers.

To accelerate the march of discovery across all these disciplines in science and technology, I ask you to support my recommendation of an unprecedented $3 billion in the 21st century research fund, the largest increase in civilian research in a generation. We owe it to our future.

Now, these new breakthroughs have to be used in ways that reflect our values. First and foremost, we have to safeguard our citizens' privacy. Last year we proposed to protect every citizen's medical record. This year we will finalize those rules. We've also taken the first steps to protect the privacy of bank and credit card records and other financial statements. Soon I will send legislation to you to finish that job. We must also act to prevent any genetic discrimination whatever by employers or insurers. I hope you will support that.

These steps will allow us to lead toward the far frontiers of science and technology. They will enhance our health, the environment, the economy in ways we can't even imagine today. But we all know that at a time when science, technology, and the forces of globalization are bringing so many changes into all our lives, it's more important than ever that we strengthen the bonds that root us in our local communities and in our national community.

No tie binds different people together like citizen service. There's a new spirit of service in America, a movement we've tried to support with AmeriCorps, expanded Peace Corps, unprecedented new partnerships with businesses, foundations, community groups; partnerships, for example, like the one that enlisted 12,000 companies which have now moved 650,000 of our fellow citizens from welfare to work; partnerships to battle drug abuse, AIDS, teach young people to read, save America's treasures, strengthen the arts, fight teen pregnancy, prevent violence among young people, promote racial healing. The American people are working together.

But we should do more to help Americans help each other. First, we should help faith-based organizations to do more to fight poverty and drug abuse and help people get back on the right track, with initiatives like Second Chance Homes that do so much to help unwed teen mothers. Second, we should support Americans who tithe and contribute to charities but don't earn enough to claim a tax deduction for it. Tonight I propose new tax incentives that would allow low and middle income citizens who don't itemize to get that deduction. It's nothing but fair, and it will get more people to give.

We should do more to help new immigrants to fully participate in our community. That's why I recommend spending more to teach them civics and English. And since everybody in our community counts, we've got to make sure everyone is counted in this year's census.

Within 10 years—just 10 years—there will be no majority race in our largest State of California. In a little more than 50 years, there will be no majority race in America. In a more interconnected world, this diversity can be our greatest strength. Just look around this Chamber. Look around. We have Members in this Congress from virtually every racial, ethnic, and religious background. And I think you would agree that America is stronger because of it.

You also have to agree that all those differences you just clapped for all too often spark hatred and division even here at home. Just in the last couple of years, we've seen a man dragged to death in Texas just because he was black. We saw a young man murdered in Wyoming just because he was gay. Last year we saw the shootings of African-Americans, Asian-Americans, and Jewish children just because of who they were. This is not the American way, and we must draw the line.

I ask you to draw that line by passing without delay the "Hate Crimes Prevention Act" and the "Employment Non-Discrimination Act." And I ask you to reauthorize the Violence Against Women Act.

Finally tonight, I propose the largest ever investment in our civil rights laws for enforcement, because no American should be subjected to discrimination in finding a home, getting a job, going to school, or securing a loan. Protections in law should be protections in fact.

Last February, because I thought this was so important, I created the White House Office of One America to promote racial reconciliation. That's what one of my personal heroes, Hank Aaron, has done all his life. From his days as our all-time home run king to his recent acts of healing, he has always brought people together. We should follow his example, and we're honored to have him with us tonight. Stand up, Hank Aaron.

I just want to say one more thing about this, and I want every one of you to think about this the next time you get mad at one of your colleagues on the other side of the aisle. This fall, at the White House, Hillary had one of her millennium dinners, and we had this very distinguished scientist there, who is an expert in this whole work in the human genome. And he said that we are all, regardless of race, genetically 99.9 percent the same.

Now, you may find that uncomfortable when you look around here. But it is worth remembering. We can laugh about this, but you think about it. Modern science has confirmed what ancient faiths have always taught: the most important fact of life is our common humanity. Therefore, we should do more than just tolerate our diversity; we should honor it and celebrate it.

My fellow Americans, every time I prepare for the State of the Union, I approach it with hope and expectation and excitement for our Nation. But tonight is very special, because we stand on the mountaintop of a new millennium. Behind us we can look back and see the great expanse of American achievement, and before us we can see even greater, grander frontiers of possibility. We should, all of us, be filled with gratitude and humility for our present progress and prosperity. We should be filled with awe and joy at what lies over the horizon. And we should be filled with absolute determination to make the most of it.

You know, when the Framers finished crafting our Constitution in Philadelphia, Benjamin Franklin stood in Independence Hall, and he reflected on the carving of the Sun that was on the back of a chair he saw. The Sun was low on the horizon. So he said this—he said, "I've often wondered whether that Sun was rising or setting. Today," Franklin said, "I have the happiness to know it's a rising Sun." Today, because each succeeding generation of Americans has kept the fire of freedom burning brightly, lighting those frontiers of possibility, we all still bask in the glow and the warmth of Mr. Franklin's rising Sun.

After 224 years, the American revolution continues. We remain a new nation. And as long as our dreams outweigh our memories, America will be forever young. That is our destiny. And this is our moment.

Thank you, God bless you, and God bless America.

George W. Bush

2001–2006

*"I will not wait on events
while dangers gather. I will not stand by
as peril draws closer and closer.
The United States of America will not permit
the world's most dangerous regimes to threaten us
with the world's most destructive weapons."*

ADDRESS BEFORE A JOINT SESSION OF CONGRESS ON THE
STATE OF THE UNION, JANUARY 29, 2002

Address before a Joint Session of Congress on Administration Goals

February 27, 2001

Just over one month into his presidency, George W. Bush addressed the nation and both houses of Congress in what was not strictly a State of the Union message. Unlike his inaugural address a month earlier, in which Bush had focused mostly on overarching themes, this speech featured a long list of priorities, many of which Bush had highlighted in his campaign.

Bush came into office facing a divided country, in the wake of the disputed 2000 election that took thirty-six days to resolve. While his supporters hailed the Republican's victory over his opponent, Democrat Al Gore, many Gore supporters remained bitter, convinced that their candidate should have prevailed.

Nevertheless, Bush confidently took office, preparing to push for his conservative agenda. Tax cuts were his top priority, and they took star billing in this address; other priorities included education reform—a more popular bipartisan issue—and increased military spending. While Bush, unlike his predecessor, Bill Clinton, was not considered much of an orator, the new president won praise from many observers of the speech for his humor and his man-of-the-people persona.

Bush began his speech by joking about the closeness of the election. "It's a great privilege to be here to outline a new budget and a new approach for governing our great country. I thank you for your invitation to speak here tonight. I know Congress had to formally invite me, and it could have been a close vote. So, Mr. Vice President, I appreciate you being here to break the tie."

His vice president was Dick Cheney, who had headed Bush's transition team and had been defense secretary under Bush's father, President George H. W. Bush. While both the House and Senate had remained in Republican hands after the 2000 election, the Senate was divided 50–50, so Cheney's presence as president of the Senate (a vice-presidential responsibility) made the difference for the GOP. Democrats took control just months later when Senator James Jeffords of Vermont left the Republican Party to become an independent and caucus with the Democrats.

Another of Bush's priorities advocated allowing certain social service programs run by religious organizations to apply for federal funds. Bush noted the presence in the audience of Philadelphia mayor John Street, a Democrat who, Bush said, had "encouraged faith-based and community organizations to make a significant difference in Philadelphia." Bush also introduced Pennsylvania taxpayers Steven and Josefina Ramos, who he said would save $2,000 under the president's tax-cut plan. While many Republicans hailed the idea of a large tax cut, Democrats and some GOP centrists argued that more of the tax relief should go to lower- and middle-income taxpayers than to the wealthy.

Bush spent only a small portion of his address on international issues, a balance that would shift dramatically after the terrorist attacks on the United States the following September 11.

$\mathbf{M}$r. Speaker, Mr. Vice President, Members of Congress:

It's a great privilege to be here to outline a new budget and a new approach for governing our great country. I thank you for your invitation to speak here tonight. I know Congress had to formally invite me, and it could have been a close vote. So, Mr. Vice President, I appreciate you being here to break the tie.

I want to thank so many of you who have accepted my invitation to come to the White House to discuss important issues. We're off to a good start. I will continue to meet with you and ask for your input. You have been kind and candid, and I thank you for making a new President feel welcome.

The last time I visited the Capitol, I came to take an oath on the steps of this building. I pledged to honor our Constitution and laws, and I asked you to join me in setting a tone of civility and respect in Washington. I hope America is noticing the difference, because we're making progress.

Together, we are changing the tone in the Nation's Capital. And this spirit of respect and cooperation is vital, because, in the end, we will be judged not only by what we say or how we say it, we will be judged by what we're able to accomplish.

America today is a nation with great challenges but greater resources. An artist using statistics as a brush could paint two very different pictures of our country. One would have warning signs: increasing layoffs, rising energy prices, too many failing schools, persistent poverty, the stubborn vestiges of racism. Another picture would be full of blessings: a balanced budget, big surpluses, a military that is second to none, a country at peace with its neighbors, technology that is revolutionizing the world, and our greatest strength, concerned citizens who care for our country and care for each other.

Neither picture is complete in and of itself. And tonight I challenge and invite Congress to work with me to use the resources of one picture to repaint the other; to direct the advantages of our time to solve the problems of our people. Some of these resources will come from Government—some but not all.

Year after year in Washington, budget debates seem to come down to an old, tired argument: on one side, those who want more Government, regardless of the cost; on the other, those who want less Government, regardless of the need. We should leave those arguments to the last century and chart a different course.

Government has a role, and an important role. Yet, too much Government crowds out initiative and hard work, private charity and the private economy. Our new governing vision says Government should be active but limited, engaged but not overbearing. And my budget is based on that philosophy.

It is reasonable, and it is responsible. It meets our obligations and funds our growing needs. We increase spending next year for Social Security and Medicare, and other entitlement programs, by $81 billion. We've increased spending for discretionary programs by a very responsible 4 percent, above the rate of inflation. My plan pays down an unprecedented amount of our national debt. And then, when money is still left over, my plan returns it to the people who earned it in the first place.

A budget's impact is counted in dollars but measured in lives. Excellent schools, quality health care, a secure retirement, a cleaner environment, a stronger defense: These are all important needs, and we fund them. The highest percentage increase in our budget should go to our children's education. Education is not my top priority—

education is my top priority, and by supporting this budget, you'll make it yours, as well.

Reading is the foundation of all learning. So during the next 5 years, we triple spending, adding $5 billion to help every child in America learn to read. Values are important, so we've tripled funding for character education to teach our children not only reading and writing but right from wrong. We've increased funding to train and recruit teachers, because we know a good education starts with a good teacher. And I have a wonderful partner in this effort. I like teachers so much, I married one. Laura has begun a new effort to recruit Americans to the profession that will shape our future—teaching. She will travel across America to promote sound teaching practices and early reading skills in our schools and in programs such as Head Start.

When it comes to our schools, dollars alone do not always make the difference. Funding is important, and so is reform. So we must tie funding to higher standards and accountability for results.

I believe in local control of schools. We should not, and we will not, run public schools from Washington, D.C. Yet when the Federal Government spends tax dollars, we must insist on results. Children should be tested on basic reading and math skills every year between grades three and eight. Measuring is the only way to know whether all our children are learning. And I want to know, because I refuse to leave any child behind in America.

Critics of testing contend it distracts from learning. They talk about teaching to the test. But let's put that logic to the test. If you test a child on basic math and reading skills and you're teaching to the test, you're teaching math and reading. And that's the whole idea. As standards rise, local schools will need more flexibility to meet them, so we must streamline the dozens of Federal education programs into five and let States spend money in those categories as they see fit.

Schools will be given a reasonable chance to improve and the support to do so. Yet if they don't, if they continue to fail, we must give parents and students different options: a better public school, a private school, tutoring, or a charter school. In the end, every child in a bad situation must be given a better choice because, when it comes to our children, failure is simply not an option.

Another priority in my budget is to keep the vital promises of Medicare and Social Security, and together we will do so. To meet the health care needs of all America's seniors, we double the Medicare budget over the next 10 years. My budget dedicates $238 billion to Medicare next year alone, enough to fund all current programs and to begin a new prescription drug benefit for low income seniors. No senior in America should have to choose between buying food and buying prescriptions.

To make sure the retirement savings of America's seniors are not diverted into any other program, my budget protects all $2.6 trillion of the Social Security surplus for Social Security and for Social Security alone.

My budget puts a priority on access to health care, without telling Americans what doctor they have to see or what coverage they must choose. Many working Americans do not have health care coverage, so we will help them buy their own insurance with refundable tax credits. And to provide quality care in low income neighborhoods, over the next 5 years we will double the number of people served at community health care centers. And we will address the concerns of those who have health coverage, yet worry their insurance company doesn't care and won't pay.

Together this Congress and this President will find common ground to make sure doctors make medical decisions, and patients get the health care they deserve with a Patients' Bill of Rights.

When it comes to their health, people want to get the medical care they need, not be forced to go to court because they didn't get it. We will ensure access to the courts for those with legitimate claims. But first, let's put in place a strong, independent review so we promote quality health care, not frivolous lawsuits.

My budget also increases funding for medical research, which gives hope to many who struggle with serious disease. Our prayers tonight are with one of your own who is engaged in his own fight against cancer, a fine Representative, and a good man, Congressman Joe Moakley. I can think of no more appropriate tribute to Joe than to have the Congress finish the job of doubling the budget for the National Institutes of Health.

My New Freedom Initiative for Americans with disabilities funds new technologies, expands opportunities to work, and makes our society more welcoming. For the more than 50 million Americans with disabilities, we must continue to break down barriers to equality.

The budget I propose to you also supports the people who keep our country strong and free, the men and women who serve in the United States military. I'm requesting $5.7 billion in increased military pay and benefits and health care and housing. Our men and women in uniform give America their best, and we owe them our support.

America's veterans honored their commitment to our country through their military service. I will honor our commitment to them with a billion-dollar increase to ensure better access to quality care and faster decisions on benefit claims.

My budget will improve our environment by accelerating the cleanup of toxic brownfields. And I propose we make a major investment in conservation by fully funding the Land and Water Conservation Fund. Our national parks have a special place in our country's life. Our parks are places of great natural beauty and history. As good stewards, we must leave them better than we found them. So I propose providing $4.9 billion over 5 years for the upkeep of these national treasures.

And my budget adopts a hopeful new approach to help the poor and the disadvantaged. We must encourage and support the work of charities and faith-based and community groups that offer help and love, one person at a time. These groups are working in every neighborhood in America to fight homelessness and addiction and domestic violence, to provide a hot meal or a mentor or a safe haven for our children. Government should welcome these groups to apply for funds, not discriminate against them.

Government cannot be replaced by charities or volunteers. Government should not fund religious activities. But our Nation should support the good works of these good people who are helping their neighbors in need. So I propose allowing all taxpayers, whether they itemize or not, to deduct their charitable contributions. Estimates show this could encourage as much as $14 billion a year in new charitable giving, money that will save and change lives.

Our budget provides more than $700 million over the next 10 years for a Federal compassion capital fund, with a focused and noble mission, to provide a mentor to the more than one million children with a parent in prison and to support other local efforts to fight illiteracy, teen pregnancy, drug addiction, and other difficult problems.

With us tonight is the mayor of Philadelphia. Please help me welcome Mayor John Street. Mayor Street has encouraged faith-based and community organizations to make a significant difference in Philadelphia. He's invited me to his city this summer to see compassionate action. I'm personally aware of just how effective the mayor is. Mayor Street's a Democrat. Let the record show, I lost his city—big time. But some things are bigger than politics. So I look forward to coming to your city, to see your faith-based programs in action.

As Government promotes compassion, it also must promote justice. Too many of our citizens have cause to doubt our Nation's justice, when the law points a finger of suspicion at groups instead of individuals. All our citizens are created equal and must be treated equally.

Earlier today I asked John Ashcroft, the Attorney General, to develop specific recommendations to end racial profiling. It's wrong, and we will end it in America. In so doing, we will not hinder the work of our Nation's brave police officers. They protect us every day, often at great risk. But by stopping the abuses of a few, we will add to the public confidence our police officers earn and deserve.

My budget has funded a responsible increase in our ongoing operations. It has funded our Nation's important priorities. It has protected Social Security and Medicare. And our surpluses are big enough that there is still money left over.

Many of you have talked about the need to pay down our national debt. I listened, and I agree. We owe it to our children and grandchildren to act now, and I hope you will join me to pay down $2 trillion in debt during the next 10 years. At the end of those 10 years, we will have paid down all the debt that is available to retire. That is more debt, repaid more quickly than has ever been repaid by any nation at any time in history.

We should also prepare for the unexpected, for the uncertainties of the future. We should approach our Nation's budget as any prudent family would, with a contingency fund for emergencies or additional spending needs. For example, after a strategic review, we may need to increase defense spending; we may need to increase spending for our farmers or additional money to reform Medicare. And so, my budget sets aside almost a trillion dollars over 10 years for additional needs. That is one trillion additional reasons you can feel comfortable supporting this budget.

We have increased our budget at a responsible 4 percent. We have funded our priorities. We paid down all the available debt. We have prepared for contingencies. And we still have money left over.

Yogi Berra once said, "When you come to a fork in the road, take it." Now, we come to a fork in the road; we have two choices. Even though we have already met our needs, we could spend the money on more and bigger Government. That's the road our Nation has traveled in recent years.

Last year Government spending shot up 8 percent. That's far more than our economy grew, far more than personal income grew, and far more than the rate of inflation. If you continue on that road, you will spend the surplus and have to dip into Social Security to pay other bills. Unrestrained Government spending is a dangerous road to deficits, so we must take a different path.

The other choice is to let the American people spend their own money to meet their own needs. I hope you will join me in standing firmly on the side of the people. You see, the growing surplus exists because taxes are too high and Government is charging more than it needs. The people of America have been overcharged, and on their behalf, I am here asking for a refund.

Some say my tax plan is too big. Others say it's too small. I respectfully disagree. This plan is just right. I didn't throw darts at a board to come up with a number for tax relief. I didn't take a poll or develop an arbitrary formula that might sound good. I looked at problems in the Tax Code and calculated the cost to fix them.

A tax rate of 15 percent is too high for those who earn low wages, so we must lower the rate to 10 percent. No one should pay more than a third of the money they earn in Federal income taxes, so we lowered the top rate to 33 percent.

This reform will be welcome relief for America's small businesses, which often pay taxes at the highest rate. And help for small business means jobs for Americans. We simplified the Tax Code by reducing the number of tax rates from the current five rates to four lower ones, 10 percent, 15, 25, and 33 percent. In my plan, no one is targeted in or targeted out. Everyone who pays income taxes will get relief.

Our Government should not tax and, thereby, discourage marriage, so we reduced the marriage penalty. I want to help families rear and support their children, so we doubled the child credit to $1,000 per child. It's not fair to tax the same earnings twice— once when you earn them, and again when you die—so we must repeal the death tax.

These changes add up to significant help. A typical family with two children will save $1,600 a year on their Federal income taxes. Now, $1,600 may not sound like a lot to some, but it means a lot to many families: $1,600 buys gas for two cars for an entire year; it pays tuition for a year at a community college; it pays the average family grocery bill for 3 months. That's real money.

With us tonight representing many American families are Steven and Josefina Ramos. They are from Pennsylvania, but they could be from any one of your districts. Steven is the network administrator for a school district. Josefina is a Spanish teacher at a charter school. And they have a 2-year-old daughter.

Steven and Josefina tell me they pay almost $8,000 a year in Federal income taxes. My plan will save them more than $2,000. Let me tell you what Steven says: "Two thousand dollars a year means a lot to my family. If we had this money, it would help us reach our goal of paying off our personal debt in 2 years' time." After that, Steven and Josefina want to start saving for Lianna's college education.

My attitude is, Government should never stand in the way of families achieving their dreams. And as we debate this issue, always remember, the surplus is not the Government's money; the surplus is the people's money.

For lower income families, my tax plan restores basic fairness. Right now, complicated tax rules punish hard work. A waitress supporting two children on $25,000 a year can lose nearly half of every additional dollar she earns above the $25,000. Her overtime, her hardest hours, are taxed at nearly 50 percent. This sends a terrible message: "You'll never get ahead."

But America's message must be different. We must honor hard work, never punish it. With tax relief, overtime will no longer be over-taxed-time for the waitress. People with the smallest incomes will get the highest percentage of reductions. And millions of additional American families will be removed from the income tax rolls entirely.

Tax relief is right, and tax relief is urgent. The long economic expansion that began almost 10 years ago is faltering. Lower interest rates will eventually help, but we cannot assume they will do the job all by themselves.

Forty years ago, and then 20 years ago, two Presidents, one Democrat, one Republican, John F. Kennedy and Ronald Reagan, advocated tax cuts to, in President Kennedy's words, "get this country moving again." They knew then what we must do now. To create economic growth and opportunity, we must put money back into the hands of the people who buy goods and create jobs.

We must act quickly. The Chairman of the Federal Reserve has testified before Congress that tax cuts often come too late to stimulate economic recovery. So I want to work with you to give our economy an important jump-start by making tax relief retroactive.

We must act now because it is the right thing to do. We must also act now because we have other things to do. We must show courage to confront and resolve tough challenges, to restructure our Nation's defenses, to meet our growing need for energy, and to reform Medicare and Social Security.

America has a window of opportunity to extend and secure our present peace by promoting a distinctly American internationalism. We will work with our allies and friends to be a force for good and a champion of freedom. We will work for free markets, free trade, and freedom from oppression. Nations making progress toward freedom will find America is their friend. We will promote our values. We will promote the peace, and we need a strong military to keep the peace.

But our military was shaped to confront the challenges of the past. So I've asked the Secretary of Defense to review America's Armed Forces and prepare to transform them to meet emerging threats. My budget makes a downpayment on the research and development that will be required. Yet, in our broader transformation effort, we must put strategy first, then spending. Our defense vision will drive our defense budget, not the other way around.

Our Nation also needs a clear strategy to confront the threats of the 21st century, threats that are more widespread and less certain. They range from terrorists who threaten with bombs to tyrants in rogue nations intent upon developing weapons of mass destruction. To protect our own people, our allies, and friends, we must develop and we must deploy effective missile defenses.

And as we transform our military, we can discard cold war relics and reduce our own nuclear forces to reflect today's needs. A strong America is the world's best hope for peace and freedom.

Yet the cause of freedom rests on more than our ability to defend ourselves and our allies. Freedom is exported every day, as we ship goods and products that improve the lives of millions of people. Free trade brings greater political and personal freedom. Each of the previous five Presidents has had the ability to negotiate far-reaching trade agreements. Tonight I ask you to give me the strong hand of Presidential trade promotion authority and to do so quickly.

As we meet tonight, many citizens are struggling with the high cost of energy. We have a serious energy problem that demands a national energy policy. The West is confronting a major energy shortage that has resulted in high prices and uncertainty. I've asked Federal agencies to work with California officials to help speed construction of new energy sources, and I have directed Vice President Cheney, Commerce Secretary [Donald] Evans, Energy Secretary [Spencer] Abraham, and other senior members in my administration to develop a national energy policy.

Our energy demand outstrips our supply. We can produce more energy at home while protecting our environment, and we must. We can produce more electricity to meet demand, and we must. We can promote alternative energy sources and conservation, and we must. America must become more energy independent, and we will.

Perhaps the biggest test of our foresight and courage will be reforming Medicare and Social Security. Medicare's finances are strained, and its coverage is outdated. Ninety-nine percent of employer-provided health plans offer some form of prescription drug coverage. Medicare does not. The framework for reform has been developed by Senators Frist and Breaux and Congressman Thomas, and now is the time to act.

Medicare must be modernized, and we must make sure that every senior on Medicare can choose a health care plan that offers prescription drugs.

Seven years from now, the baby boom generation will begin to claim Social Security benefits. Every one in this Chamber knows that Social Security is not prepared to fully fund their retirement. And we only have a couple of years to get prepared. Without reform, this country will one day awaken to a stark choice: Either a drastic rise in payroll taxes or a radical cut in retirement benefits. There is a better way.

This spring I will form a Presidential commission to reform Social Security. The commission will make its recommendations by next fall. Reform should be based on these principles: It must preserve the benefits of all current retirees and those nearing retirement; it must return Social Security to sound financial footing; and it must offer personal savings accounts to younger workers who want them.

Social Security now offers workers a return of less than 2 percent on the money they pay into the system. To save the system, we must increase that by allowing younger workers to make safe, sound investments that yield a higher rate of return. Ownership, access to wealth, and independence should not be the privilege of the few. They are the hope of every American, and we must make them the foundation of Social Security.

By confronting the tough challenge of reform, by being responsible with our budget, we can earn the trust of the American people. And we can add to that trust by enacting fair and balanced election and campaign reforms.

The agenda I have set before you tonight is worthy of a great nation. America is a nation at peace but not a nation at rest. Much has been given to us, and much is expected. Let us agree to bridge old divides. But let us also agree that our good will must be dedicated to great goals. Bipartisanship is more than minding our manners; it is doing our duty.

No one can speak in this Capitol and not be awed by its history. At so many turning points, debates in these chambers have reflected the collected or divided conscience of our country. And when we walk through Statuary Hall and see those men and women of marble, we're reminded of their courage and achievement.

Yet America's purpose is never found only in statues or history. America's purpose always stands before us. Our generation must show courage in a time of blessing, as our Nation has always shown in times of crisis. And our courage, issue by issue, can gather to greatness and serve our country. This is the privilege and responsibility we share. And if we work together, we can prove that public service is noble.

We all came here for a reason. We all have things we want to accomplish and promises to keep. *Juntos podemos*—together we can.

We can make Americans proud of their Government. Together we can share in the credit of making our country more prosperous and generous and just and earn from our conscience and from our fellow citizens the highest possible praise: Well done, good and faithful servants.

Thank you all. Good night, and God bless.

Address before a Joint Session of Congress on the State of the Union

January 29, 2002

George W. Bush's 2002 State of the Union address came just four and a half months after the shock of the September 11, 2001, terrorist attacks on the United States, and much of the speech focused on national security and the war on terror. Bush's popularity, which had risen dramatically after September 11, was still high, and the country—so divided after the 2000 presidential election—was relatively united behind the commander in chief.

In the wake of the terrorist attacks, the United States and allied countries had launched a military action in Afghanistan that succeeded in ousting the country's Taliban regime, which had supported al Qaeda—the group behind the September 11 attacks—and its leader, Osama bin Laden. In addition, Bush had created a White House Office of Homeland Security, led by former Pennsylvania governor Tom Ridge.

In his remarks, Bush recognized Afghan leader Hamid Karzai and Afghanistan's new minister of women's affairs, Sima Samar, who were guests of First Lady Laura Bush. He also singled out Shannon Spann, whose husband had been killed in Afghanistan, and Hermis Moutardier and Christina Jones, two flight attendants who had helped foil an attempted terrorist attack on a passenger plane a month earlier. "Our first priority must always be the security of our nation, and that will be reflected in the budget I send to Congress," Bush said, later adding, "It costs a lot to fight this war. We have spent more than a billion dollars a month—over $30 million a day—and we must be prepared for future operations."

Perhaps the most controversial part of the president's speech involved his description of three countries—Iran, Iraq, and North Korea—as an "axis of evil." While some observers welcomed Bush's remarks, others found it unwise to group the three countries, each with its own problems, into one villainous mass.

In his 2001 address to Congress, Bush had focused primarily on domestic matters, including his proposal for a massive tax cut and his push for education reform. After some changes initiated by Senate moderates, Congress in May 2001 had approved a $1.35 trillion, ten-year tax cut plan. Congress also passed education reforms, with more bipartisan support than the tax cut.

"And I was so proud of our work, I even had nice things to say about my friend, Ted Kennedy," Bush quipped in his 2002 State of the Union about the famously liberal Democratic senator from Massachusetts, with whom he had worked on the bipartisan education reform package. In addition, the president noted the economic downturn the country faced as of early 2002.

Thank you very much. Mr. Speaker, Vice President Cheney, Members of Congress, distinguished guests, fellow citizens:

As we gather tonight, our Nation is at war; our economy is in recession; and the civilized world faces unprecedented dangers. Yet, the state of our Union has never been stronger.

We last met in an hour of shock and suffering. In 4 short months, our Nation has comforted the victims, begun to rebuild New York and the Pentagon, rallied a great coalition, captured, arrested, and rid the world of thousands of terrorists, destroyed Afghanistan's terrorist training camps, saved a people from starvation, and freed a country from brutal oppression.

The American flag flies again over our Embassy in Kabul. Terrorists who once occupied Afghanistan now occupy cells at Guantanamo Bay. And terrorist leaders who urged followers to sacrifice their lives are running for their own.

America and Afghanistan are now allies against terror. We'll be partners in rebuilding that country. And this evening we welcomed the distinguished interim leader of a liberated Afghanistan, Chairman Hamid Karzai.

The last time we met in this Chamber, the mothers and daughters of Afghanistan were captives in their own homes, forbidden from working or going to school. Today women are free and are part of Afghanistan's new Government. And we welcome the new Minister of Women's Affairs, Dr. Sima Samar.

Our progress is a tribute to the spirit of the Afghan people, to the resolve of our coalition, and to the might of the United States military. When I called our troops into action, I did so with complete confidence in their courage and skill. And tonight, thanks to them, we are winning the war on terror. The men and women of our Armed Forces have delivered a message now clear to every enemy of the United States: Even 7,000 miles away, across oceans and continents, on mountaintops and in caves, you will not escape the justice of this Nation.

For many Americans, these 4 months have brought sorrow and pain that will never completely go away. Every day a retired firefighter returns to Ground Zero to feel closer to his two sons who died there. At a memorial in New York, a little boy left his football with a note for his lost father: "Dear Daddy, please take this to heaven. I don't want to play football until I can play with you again some day."

Last month, at the grave of her husband, Michael, a CIA officer and Marine who died in Mazur-e-Sharif, Shannon Spann said these words of farewell, "Semper Fi, my love." Shannon is with us tonight. Shannon, I assure you and all who have lost a loved one that our cause is just, and our country will never forget the debt we owe Michael and all who gave their lives for freedom.

Our cause is just, and it continues. Our discoveries in Afghanistan confirmed our worst fears and showed us the true scope of the task ahead. We have seen the depth of our enemies' hatred in videos where they laugh about the loss of innocent life. And the depth of their hatred is equaled by the madness of the destruction they design. We have found diagrams of American nuclear powerplants and public water facilities, detailed instructions for making chemical weapons, surveillance maps of American cities, and thorough descriptions of landmarks in America and throughout the world.

What we have found in Afghanistan confirms that, far from ending there, our war against terror is only beginning. Most of the 19 men who hijacked planes on

September the 11th were trained in Afghanistan's camps, and so were tens of thousands of others. Thousands of dangerous killers, schooled in the methods of murder, often supported by outlaw regimes, are now spread throughout the world like ticking timebombs, set to go off without warning.

Thanks to the work of our law enforcement officials and coalition partners, hundreds of terrorists have been arrested. Yet, tens of thousands of trained terrorists are still at large. These enemies view the entire world as a battlefield, and we must pursue them wherever they are. So long as training camps operate, so long as nations harbor terrorists, freedom is at risk. And America and our allies must not and will not allow it.

Our Nation will continue to be steadfast and patient and persistent in the pursuit of two great objectives. First, we will shut down terrorist camps, disrupt terrorist plans, and bring terrorists to justice. And second, we must prevent the terrorists and regimes who seek chemical, biological, or nuclear weapons from threatening the United States and the world.

Our military has put the terror training camps of Afghanistan out of business, yet camps still exist in at least a dozen countries. A terrorist underworld, including groups like Hamas, Hezbollah, Islamic Jihad, Jaish-i-Mohammed, operates in remote jungles and deserts and hides in the centers of large cities.

While the most visible military action is in Afghanistan, America is acting elsewhere. We now have troops in the Philippines, helping to train that country's armed forces to go after terrorist cells that have executed an American and still hold hostages. Our soldiers, working with the Bosnian Government, seized terrorists who were plotting to bomb our Embassy. Our Navy is patrolling the coast of Africa to block the shipment of weapons and the establishment of terrorist camps in Somalia.

My hope is that all nations will heed our call and eliminate the terrorist parasites who threaten their countries and our own. Many nations are acting forcefully. Pakistan is now cracking down on terror, and I admire the strong leadership of President Musharraf. But some governments will be timid in the face of terror. And make no mistake about it: If they do not act, America will.

Our second goal is to prevent regimes that sponsor terror from threatening America or our friends and allies with weapons of mass destruction. Some of these regimes have been pretty quiet since September the 11th, but we know their true nature.

North Korea is a regime arming with missiles and weapons of mass destruction, while starving its citizens.

Iran aggressively pursues these weapons and exports terror, while an unelected few repress the Iranian people's hope for freedom.

Iraq continues to flaunt its hostility toward America and to support terror. The Iraqi regime has plotted to develop anthrax and nerve gas and nuclear weapons for over a decade. This is a regime that has already used poison gas to murder thousands of its own citizens, leaving the bodies of mothers huddled over their dead children. This is a regime that agreed to international inspections, then kicked out the inspectors. This is a regime that has something to hide from the civilized world.

States like these and their terrorist allies constitute an axis of evil, arming to threaten the peace of the world. By seeking weapons of mass destruction, these regimes pose a grave and growing danger. They could provide these arms to terrorists, giving them the means to match their hatred. They could attack our allies or attempt to blackmail the United States. In any of these cases, the price of indifference would be catastrophic.

We will work closely with our coalition to deny terrorists and their state sponsors the materials, technology, and expertise to make and deliver weapons of mass destruction. We will develop and deploy effective missile defenses to protect America and our allies from sudden attack. And all nations should know: America will do what is necessary to ensure our Nation's security.

We'll be deliberate; yet, time is not on our side. I will not wait on events while dangers gather. I will not stand by as peril draws closer and closer. The United States of America will not permit the world's most dangerous regimes to threaten us with the world's most destructive weapons.

Our war on terror is well begun, but it is only begun. This campaign may not be finished on our watch; yet, it must be and it will be waged on our watch. We can't stop short. If we stop now, leaving terror camps intact and terrorist states unchecked, our sense of security would be false and temporary. History has called America and our allies to action, and it is both our responsibility and our privilege to fight freedom's fight.

Our first priority must always be the security of our Nation, and that will be reflected in the budget I send to Congress. My budget supports three great goals for America: We will win this war; we will protect our homeland; and we will revive our economy.

September the 11th brought out the best in America and the best in this Congress. And I join the American people in applauding your unity and resolve. Now Americans deserve to have this same spirit directed toward addressing problems here at home. I'm a proud member of my party. Yet as we act to win the war, protect our people, and create jobs in America, we must act, first and foremost, not as Republicans, not as Democrats but as Americans.

It costs a lot to fight this war. We have spent more than a billion dollars a month, over $30 million a day, and we must be prepared for future operations. Afghanistan proved that expensive precision weapons defeat the enemy and spare innocent lives, and we need more of them. We need to replace aging aircraft and make our military more agile to put our troops anywhere in the world quickly and safely. Our men and women in uniform deserve the best weapons, the best equipment, the best training, and they also deserve another pay raise.

My budget includes the largest increase in defense spending in two decades, because while the price of freedom and security is high, it is never too high. Whatever it costs to defend our country, we will pay.

The next priority of my budget is to do everything possible to protect our citizens and strengthen our Nation against the ongoing threat of another attack. Time and distance from the events of September the 11th will not make us safer unless we act on its lessons. America is no longer protected by vast oceans. We are protected from attack only by vigorous action abroad and increased vigilance at home.

My budget nearly doubles funding for a sustained strategy of homeland security, focused on four key areas: bioterrorism, emergency response, airport and border security, and improved intelligence. We will develop vaccines to fight anthrax and other deadly diseases. We'll increase funding to help States and communities train and equip our heroic police and firefighters. We will improve intelligence collection and sharing, expand patrols at our borders, strengthen the security of air travel, and use technology to track the arrivals and departures of visitors to the United States.

Homeland security will make America not only stronger but, in many ways, better. Knowledge gained from bioterrorism research will improve public health. Stronger police and fire departments will mean safer neighborhoods. Stricter border enforcement will help combat illegal drugs. And as government works to better secure our homeland, America will continue to depend on the eyes and ears of alert citizens.

A few days before Christmas, an airline flight attendant spotted a passenger lighting a match. The crew and passengers quickly subdued the man, who had been trained by Al Qaida and was armed with explosives. The people on that plane were alert and, as a result, likely saved nearly 200 lives. And tonight we welcome and thank flight attendants Hermis Moutardier and Christina Jones.

Once we have funded our national security and our homeland security, the final great priority of my budget is economic security for the American people. To achieve these great national objectives—to win the war, protect the homeland, and revitalize our economy—our budget will run a deficit that will be small and short term, so long as Congress restrains spending and acts in a fiscally responsible manner. We have clear priorities, and we must act at home with the same purpose and resolve we have shown overseas. We'll prevail in the war, and we will defeat this recession.

Americans who have lost their jobs need our help, and I support extending unemployment benefits and direct assistance for health care coverage. Yet, American workers want more than unemployment checks; they want a steady paycheck. When America works, America prospers, so my economic security plan can be summed up in one word: jobs.

Good jobs begin with good schools, and here we've made a fine start. Republicans and Democrats worked together to achieve historic education reform so that no child is left behind. I was proud to work with members of both parties: Chairman John Boehner and Congressman George Miller; Senator Judd Gregg. And I was so proud of our work, I even had nice things to say about my friend Ted Kennedy. I know the folks at the Crawford coffee shop couldn't believe I'd say such a thing, but our work on this bill shows what is possible if we set aside posturing and focus on results.

There is more to do. We need to prepare our children to read and succeed in school with improved Head Start and early childhood development programs. We must upgrade our teacher colleges and teacher training and launch a major recruiting drive with a great goal for America, a quality teacher in every classroom.

Good jobs also depend on reliable and affordable energy. This Congress must act to encourage conservation, promote technology, build infrastructure, and it must act to increase energy production at home so America is less dependent on foreign oil.

Good jobs depend on expanded trade. Selling into new markets creates new jobs, so I ask Congress to finally approve trade promotion authority.

On these two key issues, trade and energy, the House of Representatives has acted to create jobs, and I urge the Senate to pass this legislation.

Good jobs depend on sound tax policy. Last year, some in this Hall thought my tax relief plan was too small; some thought it was too big. But when the checks arrived in the mail, most Americans thought tax relief was just about right. Congress listened to the people and responded by reducing tax rates, doubling the child credit, and ending the death tax. For the sake of long-term growth and to help Americans plan for the future, let's make these tax cuts permanent.

The way out of this recession, the way to create jobs, is to grow the economy by encouraging investment in factories and equipment and by speeding up tax relief so people have more money to spend. For the sake of American workers, let's pass a stimulus package.

Good jobs must be the aim of welfare reform. As we reauthorize these important reforms, we must always remember the goal is to reduce dependency on government and offer every American the dignity of a job.

Americans know economic security can vanish in an instant without health security. I ask Congress to join me this year to enact a patients' bill of rights, to give uninsured workers credits to help buy health coverage, to approve an historic increase in the spending for veterans' health, and to give seniors a sound and modern Medicare system that includes coverage for prescription drugs.

A good job should lead to security in retirement. I ask Congress to enact new safeguards for 401K and pension plans. Employees who have worked hard and saved all their lives should not have to risk losing everything if their company fails. Through stricter accounting standards and tougher disclosure requirements, corporate America must be made more accountable to employees and shareholders and held to the highest standards of conduct.

Retirement security also depends upon keeping the commitments of Social Security, and we will. We must make Social Security financially stable and allow personal retirement accounts for younger workers who choose them.

Members, you and I will work together in the months ahead on other issues: productive farm policy; a cleaner environment; broader homeownership, especially among minorities; and ways to encourage the good work of charities and faith-based groups. I ask you to join me on these important domestic issues in the same spirit of cooperation we've applied to our war against terrorism.

During these last few months, I've been humbled and privileged to see the true character of this country in a time of testing. Our enemies believed America was weak and materialistic, that we would splinter in fear and selfishness. They were as wrong as they are evil.

The American people have responded magnificently, with courage and compassion, strength and resolve. As I have met the heroes, hugged the families, and looked into the tired faces of rescuers, I have stood in awe of the American people.

And I hope you will join me—I hope you will join me in expressing thanks to one American for the strength and calm and comfort she brings to our Nation in crisis, our First Lady, Laura Bush.

None of us would ever wish the evil that was done on September the 11th. Yet, after America was attacked, it was as if our entire country looked into a mirror and saw our better selves. We were reminded that we are citizens with obligations to each other, to our country, and to history. We began to think less of the goods we can accumulate and more about the good we can do.

For too long our culture has said, "If it feels good, do it." Now America is embracing a new ethic and a new creed, "Let's roll." In the sacrifice of soldiers, the fierce brotherhood of firefighters, and the bravery and generosity of ordinary citizens, we have glimpsed what a new culture of responsibility could look like. We want to be a nation that serves goals larger than self. We've been offered a unique opportunity, and we must not let this moment pass.

My call tonight is for every American to commit at least 2 years, 4,000 hours over the rest of your lifetime, to the service of your neighbors and your Nation. Many are already serving, and I thank you. If you aren't sure how to help, I've got a good place to start. To sustain and extend the best that has emerged in America, I invite you to join the new USA Freedom Corps. The Freedom Corps will focus on three areas of need: responding in case of crisis at home; rebuilding our communities; and extending American compassion throughout the world.

One purpose of the USA Freedom Corps will be homeland security. America needs retired doctors and nurses who can be mobilized in major emergencies, volunteers to help police and fire departments, transportation and utility workers well-trained in spotting danger.

Our country also needs citizens working to rebuild our communities. We need mentors to love children, especially children whose parents are in prison. And we need more talented teachers in troubled schools. USA Freedom Corps will expand and improve the good efforts of AmeriCorps and Senior Corps to recruit more than 200,000 new volunteers.

And America needs citizens to extend the compassion of our country to every part of the world. So we will renew the promise of the Peace Corps, double its volunteers over the next 5 years, and ask it to join a new effort to encourage development and education and opportunity in the Islamic world.

This time of adversity offers a unique moment of opportunity, a moment we must seize to change our culture. Through the gathering momentum of millions of acts of service and decency and kindness, I know we can overcome evil with greater good.

And we have a great opportunity during this time of war to lead the world toward the values that will bring lasting peace. All fathers and mothers, in all societies, want their children to be educated and live free from poverty and violence. No people on Earth yearn to be oppressed or aspire to servitude or eagerly await the midnight knock of the secret police. If anyone doubts this, let them look to Afghanistan, where the Islamic "street" greeted the fall of tyranny with song and celebration. Let the skeptics look to Islam's own rich history, with its centuries of learning and tolerance and progress. America will lead by defending liberty and justice because they are right and true and unchanging for all people everywhere.

No nation owns these aspirations, and no nation is exempt from them. We have no intention of imposing our culture. But America will always stand firm for the non-negotiable demands of human dignity: the rule of law; limits on the power of the state; respect for women; private property; free speech; equal justice; and religious tolerance.

America will take the side of brave men and women who advocate these values around the world, including the Islamic world, because we have a greater objective than eliminating threats and containing resentment. We seek a just and peaceful world beyond the war on terror.

In this moment of opportunity, a common danger is erasing old rivalries. America is working with Russia and China and India, in ways we have never before, to achieve peace and prosperity. In every region, free markets and free trade and free societies are proving their power to lift lives. Together with friends and allies from Europe to Asia and Africa to Latin America, we will demonstrate that the forces of terror cannot stop the momentum of freedom.

The last time I spoke here, I expressed the hope that life would return to normal. In some ways, it has. In others, it never will. Those of us who have lived through these challenging times have been changed by them. We've come to know truths that we will never question: Evil is real, and it must be opposed. Beyond all differences of race or creed, we are one country, mourning together and facing danger together. Deep in the American character, there is honor, and it is stronger than cynicism. And many have discovered again that even in tragedy—especially in tragedy—God is near.

In a single instant, we realized that this will be a decisive decade in the history of liberty, that we've been called to a unique role in human events. Rarely has the world faced a choice more clear or consequential.

Our enemies send other people's children on missions of suicide and murder. They embrace tyranny and death as a cause and a creed. We stand for a different choice, made long ago on the day of our founding. We affirm it again today. We choose freedom and the dignity of every life.

Steadfast in our purpose, we now press on. We have known freedom's price. We have shown freedom's power. And in this great conflict, my fellow Americans, we will see freedom's victory.

Thank you all. May God bless.

George W. Bush, 2001–2005

Address before a Joint Session of Congress on the State of the Union

January 28, 2003

President George W. Bush's 2003 State of the Union address was delivered to a nation poised on the brink of war with Iraq, and the primary focus of the speech was aimed at rallying the nation for support of military action. In his remarks, the president linked Iraq to the terrorists of al Qaeda, who had attacked the United States on September 11, 2001, and spoke forcefully of the need to take action against its leader, Saddam Hussein.

"A brutal dictator, with a history of reckless aggression . . . with ties to terrorism . . . with great potential wealth . . . will not be permitted to dominate a vital region and threaten the United States," Bush said.

In his speech the president did not dwell only on Iraq and national security. He also sought a massive ten-year, $726 billion tax cut, focusing in part on reducing taxes on stock dividends; proposed that a prescription-drug benefit be added to the Medicare health care system; and called for billions of dollars to combat AIDS in Africa and the Caribbean.

Bush was riding fairly high in January 2003. He had campaigned hard for Republican candidates in the November 2002 congressional elections, and, counter to the trend in most midterm contests, the president's party scored historic gains—increasing its margin in the House of Representatives and winning back control of the Senate. However, some doubts about the administration's handling of the economy and Iraq were creeping into the polls.

The president had been making his case for war with Iraq for months, highlighting the country's apparent possession of weapons of mass destruction. He had dubbed Iraq, along with Iran and North Korea, part of the "axis of evil" in his 2002

State of the Union message and had delivered major speeches in the fall of 2002 calling for action against Iraq. Congress had authorized the use of force against Saddam Hussein's country that fall, and by January the world was waiting to see when—not whether—war would break out. The action against Iraq began on March 20, less than two months after this State of the Union address.

While the "axis of evil" phrase had proved controversial in 2002, another presidential sentence roiled the waters in 2003: "The British Government has learned that Saddam Hussein recently sought significant quantities of uranium from Africa." The administration later admitted that the information was not correct, but that did not end the brouhaha, which spiraled into CIA-related controversies that dogged the Bush White House for years.

Mr. Speaker, Vice President Cheney, Members of Congress, distinguished citizens and fellow citizens:

Every year, by law and by custom, we meet here to consider the state of the Union. This year, we gather in this Chamber deeply aware of decisive days that lie ahead.

You and I serve our country in a time of great consequence. During this session of Congress, we have the duty to reform domestic programs vital to our country. We have the opportunity to save millions of lives abroad from a terrible disease. We will work for a prosperity that is broadly shared, and we will answer every danger and every enemy that threatens the American people.

In all these days of promise and days of reckoning, we can be confident. In a whirlwind of change and hope and peril, our faith is sure; our resolve is firm; and our Union is strong.

This country has many challenges. We will not deny, we will not ignore, we will not pass along our problems to other Congresses, to other Presidents, and other generations. We will confront them with focus and clarity and courage.

During the last 2 years, we have seen what can be accomplished when we work together. To lift the standards of our public schools, we achieved historic education reform, which must now be carried out in every school and in every classroom so that every child in America can read and learn and succeed in life. To protect our country, we reorganized our Government and created the Department of Homeland Security, which is mobilizing against the threats of a new era. To bring our economy out of recession, we delivered the largest tax relief in a generation. To insist on integrity in American business, we passed tough reforms, and we are holding corporate criminals to account.

Some might call this a good record. I call it a good start. Tonight I ask the House and the Senate to join me in the next bold steps to serve our fellow citizens.

Our first goal is clear: We must have an economy that grows fast enough to employ every man and woman who seeks a job. After recession, terrorist attacks, corporate scandals, and stock market declines, our economy is recovering. Yet, it's not growing fast enough or strongly enough. With unemployment rising, our Nation needs more small businesses to open, more companies to invest and expand, more employers to put up the sign that says, "Help Wanted."

Jobs are created when the economy grows. The economy grows when Americans have more money to spend and invest, and the best and fairest way to make sure Americans have that money is not to tax it away in the first place.

I am proposing that all the income-tax reductions set for 2004 and 2006 be made permanent and effective this year. And under my plan, as soon as I've signed the bill, this extra money will start showing up in workers' paychecks. Instead of gradually reducing the marriage penalty, we should do it now. Instead of slowly raising the child credit to $1,000, we should send the checks to American families now.

The tax relief is for everyone who pays income taxes, and it will help our economy immediately: 92 million Americans will keep, this year, an average of almost $1,100 more of their own money; a family of 4 with an income of $40,000 would see their Federal income taxes fall from $1,178 to $45 per year; our plan will improve the bottom line for more than 23 million small businesses.

You, the Congress, have already passed all these reductions and promised them for future years. If this tax relief is good for Americans 3, or 5, or 7 years from now, it is even better for Americans today.

We should also strengthen the economy by treating investors equally in our tax laws. It's fair to tax a company's profits. It is not fair to again tax the shareholder on the same profits. To boost investor confidence and to help the nearly 10 million seniors who receive dividend income, I ask you to end the unfair double taxation of dividends.

Lower taxes and greater investment will help this economy expand. More jobs mean more taxpayers and higher revenues to our Government. The best way to address the deficit and move toward a balanced budget is to encourage economic growth and to show some spending discipline in Washington, DC.

We must work together to fund only our most important priorities. I will send you a budget that increases discretionary spending by 4 percent next year, about as much as the average family's income is expected to grow. And that is a good benchmark for us. Federal spending should not rise any faster than the paychecks of American families.

A growing economy and a focus on essential priorities will be crucial to the future of Social Security. As we continue to work together to keep Social Security sound and reliable, we must offer younger workers a chance to invest in retirement accounts that they will control and they will own.

Our second goal is high quality, affordable health for all Americans. The American system of medicine is a model of skill and innovation, with a pace of discovery that is adding good years to our lives. Yet for many people, medical care costs too much, and many have no health coverage at all. These problems will not be solved with a nationalized health care system that dictates coverage and rations care.

Instead, we must work toward a system in which all Americans have a good insurance policy, choose their own doctors, and seniors and low-income Americans receive the help they need. Instead of bureaucrats and trial lawyers and HMOs, we must put doctors and nurses and patients back in charge of American medicine.

Health care reform must begin with Medicare. Medicare is the binding commitment of a caring society. We must renew that commitment by giving seniors access to preventive medicine and new drugs that are transforming health care in America.

Seniors happy with the current Medicare system should be able to keep their coverage just the way it is. And just like you, the Members of Congress, and your staffs and other Federal employees, all seniors should have the choice of a health care plan that provides prescription drugs.

My budget will commit an additional $400 billion over the next decade to reform and strengthen Medicare. Leaders of both political parties have talked for years about strengthening Medicare. I urge the Members of this new Congress to act this year.

To improve our health care system, we must address one of the prime causes of higher cost, the constant threat that physicians and hospitals will be unfairly sued. Because of excessive litigation, everybody pays more for health care, and many parts of America are losing fine doctors. No one has ever been healed by a frivolous lawsuit. I urge the Congress to pass medical liability reform.

Our third goal is to promote energy independence for our country, while dramatically improving the environment. I have sent you a comprehensive energy plan to promote energy efficiency and conservation, to develop cleaner technology, and to produce more energy at home. I have sent you Clear Skies legislation that mandates a 70-percent cut in air pollution from powerplants over the next 15 years. I have sent you a Healthy Forests Initiative, to help prevent the catastrophic fires that devastate communities, kill wildlife, and burn away millions of acres of treasured forests.

I urge you to pass these measures, for the good of both our environment and our economy. Even more, I ask you to take a crucial step and protect our environment in ways that generations before us could not have imagined.

In this century, the greatest environmental progress will come about not through endless lawsuits or command-and-control regulations but through technology and innovation. Tonight I'm proposing $1.2 billion in research funding so that America can lead the world in developing clean, hydrogen-powered automobiles.

A simple chemical reaction between hydrogen and oxygen generates energy, which can be used to power a car, producing only water, not exhaust fumes. With a new national commitment, our scientists and engineers will overcome obstacles to taking these cars from laboratory to showroom, so that the first car driven by a child born today could be powered by hydrogen and pollution-free. Join me in this important innovation to make our air significantly cleaner and our country much less dependent on foreign sources of energy.

Our fourth goal is to apply the compassion of America to the deepest problems of America. For so many in our country, the homeless and the fatherless, the addicted, the need is great. Yet there's power, wonder-working power, in the goodness and idealism and faith of the American people.

Americans are doing the work of compassion every day, visiting prisoners, providing shelter for battered women, bringing companionship to lonely seniors. These good works deserve our praise. They deserve our personal support, and when appropriate, they deserve the assistance of the Federal Government.

I urge you to pass both my Faith-Based Initiative and the Citizen Service Act, to encourage acts of compassion that can transform America, one heart and one soul at a time.

Last year, I called on my fellow citizens to participate in the USA Freedom Corps, which is enlisting tens of thousands of new volunteers across America. Tonight I ask Congress and the American people to focus the spirit of service and the resources of Government on the needs of some of our most vulnerable citizens, boys and girls trying to grow up without guidance and attention and children who have to go through a prison gate to be hugged by their mom or dad. I propose a $450 million initiative to bring mentors to more than a million disadvantaged junior high students and children of prisoners. Government will support the training and recruiting of mentors. Yet it is the men and women of America who will fill the need. One mentor, one person can change a life forever, and I urge you to be that one person.

Another cause of hopelessness is addiction to drugs. Addiction crowds out friendship, ambition, moral conviction and reduces all the richness of life to a single destructive desire. As a government, we are fighting illegal drugs by cutting off supplies and reducing demand through anti-drug education programs. Yet for those already addicted, the fight against drugs is a fight for their own lives. Too many Americans in search of treatment cannot get it. So tonight I propose a new $600 million program to help an additional 300,000 Americans receive treatment over the next 3 years.

Our Nation is blessed with recovery programs that do amazing work. One of them is found at the Healing Place Church in Baton Rouge, Louisiana. A man in the program said, "God does miracles in people's lives, and you never think it could be you." Tonight let us bring to all Americans who struggle with drug addiction this message of hope: The miracle of recovery is possible, and it could be you.

By caring for children who need mentors and for addicted men and women who need treatment, we are building a more welcoming society, a culture that values every life. And in this work, we must not overlook the weakest among us. I ask you to protect infants at the very hour of their birth and end the practice of partial-birth abortion. And because no human life should be started or ended as the object of an experiment, I ask you to set a high standard for humanity and pass a law against all human cloning.

The qualities of courage and compassion that we strive for in America also determine our conduct abroad. The American flag stands for more than our power and our interests. Our Founders dedicated this country to the cause of human dignity, the rights of every person, and the possibilities of every life. This conviction leads us into the world to help the afflicted and defend the peace and confound the designs of evil men.

In Afghanistan, we helped to liberate an oppressed people. And we will continue helping them secure their country, rebuild their society, and educate all their children, boys and girls. In the Middle East, we will continue to seek peace between a secure Israel and a democratic Palestine. Across the Earth, America is feeding the hungry. More than 60 percent of international food aid comes as a gift from the people of the United States. As our Nation moves troops and builds alliances to make our world safer, we must also remember our calling as a blessed country is to make the world better.

Today, on the continent of Africa, nearly 30 million people have the AIDS virus, including 3 million children under the age 15. There are whole countries in Africa where more than one-third of the adult population carries the infection. More than 4 million require immediate drug treatment. Yet across that continent, only 50,000 AIDS victims—only 50,000—are receiving the medicine they need.

Because the AIDS diagnosis is considered a death sentence, many do not seek treatment. Almost all who do are turned away. A doctor in rural South Africa describes his frustration. He says, "We have no medicines. Many hospitals tell people, 'You've got AIDS. We can't help you. Go home and die.' " In an age of miraculous medicines, no person should have to hear those words.

AIDS can be prevented. Antiretroviral drugs can extend life for many years. And the cost of those drugs has dropped from $12,000 a year to under $300 a year, which places a tremendous possibility within our grasp. Ladies and gentlemen, seldom has history offered a greater opportunity to do so much for so many.

We have confronted and will continue to confront HIV/AIDS in our own country. And to meet a severe and urgent crisis abroad, tonight I propose the Emergency Plan for AIDS Relief, a work of mercy beyond all current international efforts to help the people of Africa. This comprehensive plan will prevent 7 million new AIDS infections, treat at least 2 million people with life-extending drugs, and provide humane care for millions of people suffering from AIDS and for children orphaned by AIDS. I ask the Congress to commit $15 billion over the next 5 years, including nearly $10 billion in new money, to turn the tide against AIDS in the most afflicted nations of Africa and the Caribbean.

This Nation can lead the world in sparing innocent people from a plague of nature. And this Nation is leading the world in confronting and defeating the manmade evil of international terrorism.

There are days when our fellow citizens do not hear news about the war on terror. There's never a day when I do not learn of another threat or receive reports of operations in progress or give an order in this global war against a scattered network of killers. The war goes on, and we are winning.

To date, we've arrested or otherwise dealt with many key commanders of Al Qaida. They include a man who directed logistics and funding for the September the 11th attacks, the chief of Al Qaida operations in the Persian Gulf who planned the bombings of our embassies in east Africa and the U.S.S. Cole, an Al Qaida operations chief from Southeast Asia, a former director of Al Qaida's training camps in Afghanistan, a key Al Qaida operative in Europe, a major Al Qaida leader in Yemen. All told, more than 3,000 suspected terrorists have been arrested in many countries. Many others have met a different fate. Let's put it this way: They are no longer a problem to the United States and our friends and allies.

We are working closely with other nations to prevent further attacks. America and coalition countries have uncovered and stopped terrorist conspiracies targeting the Embassy in Yemen, the American Embassy in Singapore, a Saudi military base, ships in the Straits of Hormuz and the Straits of Gibraltar. We've broken Al Qaida cells in Hamburg, Milan, Madrid, London, Paris, as well as Buffalo, New York.

We have the terrorists on the run. We're keeping them on the run. One by one, the terrorists are learning the meaning of American justice.

As we fight this war, we will remember where it began: Here, in our own country. This Government is taking unprecedented measures to protect our people and defend our homeland. We've intensified security at the borders and ports of entry, posted more than 50,000 newly trained Federal screeners in airports, begun inoculating troops and first-responders against smallpox, and are deploying the Nation's first early warning network of sensors to detect biological attack. And this year, for the first time, we are beginning to field a defense to protect this Nation against ballistic missiles.

I thank the Congress for supporting these measures. I ask you tonight to add to our future security with a major research and production effort to guard our people against bioterrorism, called Project BioShield. The budget I send you will propose almost $6 billion to quickly make available effective vaccines and treatments against agents like anthrax, botulinum toxin, Ebola, and plague. We must assume that our enemies would use these diseases as weapons, and we must act before the dangers are upon us.

Since September the 11th, our intelligence and law enforcement agencies have worked more closely than ever to track and disrupt the terrorists. The FBI is improving its ability to analyze intelligence and is transforming itself to meet new threats. Tonight I am instructing the leaders of the FBI, the CIA, the Homeland Security, and the Department of Defense to develop a Terrorist Threat Integration Center, to merge and analyze all threat information in a single location. Our Government must have the very best information possible, and we will use it to make sure the right people are in the right places to protect all our citizens.

Our war against terror is a contest of will in which perseverance is power. In the ruins of two towers, at the western wall of the Pentagon, on a field in Pennsylvania, this Nation made a pledge, and we renew that pledge tonight: Whatever the duration of this struggle and whatever the difficulties, we will not permit the triumph of violence in the affairs of men; free people will set the course of history.

Today, the gravest danger in the war on terror, the gravest danger facing America and the world, is outlaw regimes that seek and possess nuclear, chemical, and biological weapons. These regimes could use such weapons for blackmail, terror, and mass murder. They could also give or sell those weapons to terrorist allies, who would use them without the least hesitation.

This threat is new. America's duty is familiar. Throughout the 20th century, small groups of men seized control of great nations, built armies and arsenals, and set out to dominate the weak and intimidate the world. In each case, their ambitions of cruelty and murder had no limit. In each case, the ambitions of Hitlerism, militarism, and communism were defeated by the will of free peoples, by the strength of great alliances, and by the might of the United States of America.

Now, in this century, the ideology of power and domination has appeared again and seeks to gain the ultimate weapons of terror. Once again, this Nation and all our friends are all that stand between a world at peace and a world of chaos and constant alarm. Once again, we are called to defend the safety of our people and the hopes of all mankind. And we accept this responsibility.

America is making a broad and determined effort to confront these dangers. We have called on the United Nations to fulfill its charter and stand by its demand that Iraq disarm. We're strongly supporting the International Atomic Energy Agency in its mission to track and control nuclear materials around the world. We're working with other governments to secure nuclear materials in the former Soviet Union and to strengthen global treaties banning the production and shipment of missile technologies and weapons of mass destruction.

In all these efforts, however, America's purpose is more than to follow a process; it is to achieve a result, the end of terrible threats to the civilized world. All free nations have a stake in preventing sudden and catastrophic attacks. And we're asking them to join us, and many are doing so. Yet the course of this Nation does not depend on the decisions of others. Whatever action is required, whenever action is necessary, I will defend the freedom and security of the American people.

Different threats require different strategies. In Iran, we continue to see a Government that represses its people, pursues weapons of mass destruction, and supports terror. We also see Iranian citizens risking intimidation and death as they speak out for liberty and human rights and democracy. Iranians, like all people, have a right to choose their own Government and determine their own destiny, and the United States supports their aspirations to live in freedom.

On the Korean Peninsula, an oppressive regime rules a people living in fear and starvation. Throughout the 1990s, the United States relied on a negotiated framework to keep North Korea from gaining nuclear weapons. We now know that that regime was deceiving the world and developing those weapons all along. And today the North Korean regime is using its nuclear program to incite fear and seek concessions. America and the world will not be blackmailed.

America is working with the countries of the region, South Korea, Japan, China, and Russia, to find a peaceful solution and to show the North Korean Government that nuclear weapons will bring only isolation, economic stagnation, and continued hardship. The North Korean regime will find respect in the world and revival for its people only when it turns away from its nuclear ambitions.

Our Nation and the world must learn the lessons of the Korean Peninsula and not allow an even greater threat to rise up in Iraq. A brutal dictator, with a history of reckless aggression, with ties to terrorism, with great potential wealth, will not be permitted to dominate a vital region and threaten the United States.

Twelve years ago, Saddam Hussein faced the prospect of being the last casualty in a war he had started and lost. To spare himself, he agreed to disarm of all weapons of mass destruction. For the next 12 years, he systematically violated that agreement. He pursued chemical, biological, and nuclear weapons, even while inspectors were in his country. Nothing to date has restrained him from his pursuit of these weapons, not economic sanctions, not isolation from the civilized world, not even cruise missile strikes on his military facilities.

Almost 3 months ago, the United Nations Security Council gave Saddam Hussein his final chance to disarm. He has shown instead utter contempt for the United Nations and for the opinion of the world. The 108 U.N. inspectors were sent to conduct—were not sent to conduct a scavenger hunt for hidden materials across a country the size of California. The job of the inspectors is to verify that Iraq's regime is disarming. It is up to Iraq to show exactly where it is hiding its banned weapons, lay those weapons out for the world to see, and destroy them as directed. Nothing like this has happened.

The United Nations concluded in 1999 that Saddam Hussein had biological weapons sufficient to produce over 25,000 liters of anthrax, enough doses to kill several million people. He hasn't accounted for that material. He's given no evidence that he has destroyed it. The United Nations concluded that Saddam Hussein had materials sufficient to produce more than 38,000 liters of botulinum toxin, enough to subject millions of people to death by respiratory failure. He hasn't accounted for that material. He's given no evidence that he has destroyed it. Our intelligence officials estimate that Saddam Hussein had the materials to produce as much as 500 tons of sarin, mustard, and VX nerve agent. In such quantities, these chemical agents could also kill untold thousands. He's not accounted for these materials. He has given no evidence that he has destroyed them. U.S. intelligence indicates that Saddam Hussein had upwards of 30,000 munitions capable of delivering chemical agents. Inspectors recently turned up 16 of them, despite Iraq's recent declaration denying their existence. Saddam Hussein has not accounted for the remaining 29,984 of these prohibited munitions. He's given no evidence that he has destroyed them.

From three Iraqi defectors we know that Iraq, in the late 1990s, had several mobile biological weapons labs. These are designed to produce germ warfare agents and can be moved from place to a place to evade inspectors. Saddam Hussein has not disclosed these facilities. He's given no evidence that he has destroyed them.

The International Atomic Energy Agency confirmed in the 1990s that Saddam Hussein had an advanced nuclear weapons development program, had a design for a nuclear weapon, and was working on five different methods of enriching uranium for a bomb. The British Government has learned that Saddam Hussein recently sought significant quantities of uranium from Africa. Our intelligence sources tell us that he has attempted to purchase high-strength aluminum tubes suitable for nuclear weapons production. Saddam Hussein has not credibly explained these activities. He clearly has much to hide.

The dictator of Iraq is not disarming. To the contrary, he is deceiving. From intelligence sources we know, for instance, that thousands of Iraqi security personnel are at work hiding documents and materials from the U.N. inspectors, sanitizing inspection sites, and monitoring the inspectors themselves. Iraqi officials accompany the inspectors in order to intimidate witnesses.

Iraq is blocking U-2 surveillance flights requested by the United Nations. Iraqi intelligence officers are posing as the scientists inspectors are supposed to interview. Real scientists have been coached by Iraqi officials on what to say. Intelligence sources indicate that Saddam Hussein has ordered that scientists who cooperate with U.N. inspectors in disarming Iraq will be killed, along with their families.

Year after year, Saddam Hussein has gone to elaborate lengths, spent enormous sums, taken great risks to build and keep weapons of mass destruction. But why? The only possible explanation, the only possible use he could have for those weapons, is to dominate, intimidate, or attack.

With nuclear arms or a full arsenal of chemical and biological weapons, Saddam Hussein could resume his ambitions of conquest in the Middle East and create deadly havoc in that region. And this Congress and the American people must recognize another threat. Evidence from intelligence sources, secret communications, and statements by people now in custody reveal that Saddam Hussein aids and protects terrorists, including members of Al Qaida. Secretly and without fingerprints, he could provide one of his hidden weapons to terrorists or help them develop their own.

Before September the 11th, many in the world believed that Saddam Hussein could be contained. But chemical agents, lethal viruses, and shadowy terrorist networks are not easily contained. Imagine those 19 hijackers with other weapons and other plans, this time armed by Saddam Hussein. It would take one vial, one canister, one crate slipped into this country to bring a day of horror like none we have ever known. We will do everything in our power to make sure that that day never comes.

Some have said we must not act until the threat is imminent. Since when have terrorists and tyrants announced their intentions, politely putting us on notice before they strike? If this threat is permitted to fully and suddenly emerge, all actions, all words, and all recriminations would come too late. Trusting in the sanity and restraint of Saddam Hussein is not a strategy, and it is not an option.

The dictator who is assembling the world's most dangerous weapons has already used them on whole villages, leaving thousands of his own citizens dead, blind, or disfigured. Iraqi refugees tell us how forced confessions are obtained, by torturing children while their parents are made to watch. International human rights groups have cataloged other methods used in the torture chambers of Iraq: electric shock, burning with hot irons, dripping acid on the skin, mutilation with electric drills, cutting out tongues, and rape. If this is not evil, then evil has no meaning.

And tonight I have a message for the brave and oppressed people of Iraq: Your enemy is not surrounding your country; your enemy is ruling your country. And the day he and his regime are removed from power will be the day of your liberation.

The world has waited 12 years for Iraq to disarm. America will not accept a serious and mounting threat to our country and our friends and our allies. The United States will ask the U.N. Security Council to convene on February the 5th to consider the facts of Iraq's ongoing defiance of the world. Secretary of State Powell will present information and intelligence about Iraqi's legal—Iraq's illegal weapons programs, its attempt to hide those weapons from inspectors, and its links to terrorist groups.

We will consult. But let there be no misunderstanding: If Saddam Hussein does not fully disarm, for the safety of our people and for the peace of the world, we will lead a coalition to disarm him.

Tonight I have a message for the men and women who will keep the peace, members of the American Armed Forces: Many of you are assembling in or near the Middle East, and some crucial hours may lay ahead. In those hours, the success of our cause will depend on you. Your training has prepared you. Your honor will guide you. You believe in America, and America believes in you.

Sending Americans into battle is the most profound decision a President can make. The technologies of war have changed; the risks and suffering of war have not. For the brave Americans who bear the risk, no victory is free from sorrow. This Nation fights reluctantly, because we know the cost and we dread the days of mourning that always come.

We seek peace. We strive for peace. And sometimes peace must be defended. A future lived at the mercy of terrible threats is no peace at all. If war is forced upon us, we will fight in a just cause and by just means, sparing, in every way we can, the innocent. And if war is forced upon us, we will fight with the full force and might of the United States military, and we will prevail.

And as we and our coalition partners are doing in Afghanistan, we will bring to the Iraqi people food and medicines and supplies and freedom.

Many challenges, abroad and at home, have arrived in a single season. In 2 years, America has gone from a sense of invulnerability to an awareness of peril, from bitter division in small matters to calm unity in great causes. And we go forward with confidence, because this call of history has come to the right country.

Americans are a resolute people who have risen to every test of our time. Adversity has revealed the character of our country, to the world and to ourselves. America is a strong nation and honorable in the use of our strength. We exercise power without conquest, and we sacrifice for the liberty of strangers.

Americans are a free people, who know that freedom is the right of every person and the future of every nation. The liberty we prize is not America's gift to the world, it is God's gift to humanity.

We Americans have faith in ourselves, but not in ourselves alone. We do not know—we do not claim to know all the ways of providence, yet we can trust in them, placing our confidence in the loving God behind all of life and all of history.

May He guide us now. And may God continue to bless the United States of America.

George W. Bush, 2001–2005

Address before a Joint Session of Congress on the State of the Union

January 20, 2004

By January 2004 George W. Bush was looking ahead to the November elections, where he ultimately would win a second term in the White House. His State of the Union address, delivered the day after Democrat John Kerry, Bush's eventual opponent, scored a win in the critical Iowa caucus, was a preview of the themes Bush would highlight in his campaign.

"We have faced serious challenges together—and now we face a choice," the president said. "We can go forward with confidence and resolve—or we can turn back to the dangerous illusion that terrorists are not plotting and outlaw regimes are no threat to us. We can press on with economic growth, and reforms in education and Medicare—or we can turn back to the old policies and old divisions. We have not come all this way—through tragedy, and trial, and war—only to falter and leave our work unfinished."

As had been the case since the September 11, 2001, terrorist attacks against the United States, much of the president's address dealt with national security and the war against terrorism. In his remarks, the president described a successful prosecution of the war against terrorism and the fighting in Iraq, stating that many terrorist leaders had been captured or killed. He also mentioned the capture of former Iraqi leader Saddam Hussein, whose regime had been overthrown in the U.S.-led military action of 2003. Bush also detailed political progress in Afghanistan, whose Taliban government had been overthrown by U.S.-led forces in the wake of the September 11 attacks.

Bush did not refer to the apparent failure to find weapons of mass destruction in Iraq, the supposed presence of which he had used as one of the key reasons for embarking on the war. In his remarks, Bush spoke of investigators finding "weapons of mass destruction-related program activities and significant amounts of equipment that Iraq concealed from the United Nations," and he defended the decision to go to war as a necessary step toward a better world.

The president did not neglect domestic matters in this speech. He focused on various initiatives implemented during his presidency, including massive tax cuts, an education-reform law known as No Child Left Behind, and the addition of a prescription drug benefit to Medicare. He called for the tax cuts to be made permanent, stating that "Congress has some unfinished business on the issue of taxes." Priming his upcoming reelection campaign, Bush touched on issues of interest to conservatives, including gay marriage. Although he later endorsed a constitutional marriage amendment, he chose to use less direct wording in his speech, saying that if "judges insist on forcing their arbitrary will upon the people, the only alternative left to the people would be the constitutional process."

M r. Speaker, Vice President Cheney, Members of Congress, distinguished guests, and fellow citizens:

America this evening is a Nation called to great responsibilities. And we are rising to meet them.

As we gather tonight, hundreds of thousands of American servicemen and women are deployed across the world in the war on terror. By bringing hope to the oppressed, and delivering justice to the violent, they are making America more secure.

Each day, law enforcement personnel and intelligence officers are tracking terrorist threats; analysts are examining airline passenger lists; the men and women of our new Homeland Security Department are patrolling our coasts and borders. And their vigilance is protecting America.

Americans are proving once again to be the hardest working people in the world. The American economy is growing stronger. The tax relief you passed is working.

Tonight, Members of Congress can take pride in great works of compassion and reform that skeptics had thought impossible. You are raising the standards of our public schools; and you are giving our senior citizens prescription drug coverage under Medicare.

We have faced serious challenges together—and now we face a choice. We can go forward with confidence and resolve—or we can turn back to the dangerous illusion that terrorists are not plotting and outlaw regimes are no threat to us. We can press on with economic growth, and reforms in education and Medicare—or we can turn back to the old policies and old divisions.

We have not come all this way—through tragedy, and trial, and war—only to falter and leave our work unfinished. Americans are rising to the tasks of history, and they expect the same of us. In their efforts, their enterprise, and their character, the American people are showing that the state of our Union is confident and strong.

Our greatest responsibility is the active defense of the American people. Twenty-eight months have passed since September 11th, 2001—over two years without an attack on American soil—and it is tempting to believe that the danger is behind us. That hope is understandable, comforting—and false. The killing has continued in Bali, Jakarta, Casablanca, Riyadh, Mombassa, Jerusalem, Istanbul, and Baghdad. The terrorists continue to plot against America and the civilized world. And by our will and courage, this danger will be defeated.

Inside the United States, where the war began, we must continue to give homeland security and law enforcement personnel every tool they need to defend us. And one of those essential tools is the PATRIOT Act, which allows Federal law enforcement to better share information, to track terrorists, to disrupt their cells, and to seize their assets. For years, we have used similar provisions to catch embezzlers and drug traffickers. If these methods are good for hunting criminals, they are even more important for hunting terrorists. Key provisions of the PATRIOT [Providing Appropriate Tools Required to Intercept and Obstruct Terrorism] Act are set to expire next year. The terrorist threat will not expire on that schedule. Our law enforcement needs this vital legislation to protect our citizens—you need to renew the PATRIOT Act.

America is on the offensive against the terrorists who started this war. Last March, Khalid Shaikh Mohammed, a mastermind of September 11th, awoke to find himself in the custody of U.S. and Pakistani authorities. Last August 11th brought the capture of the terrorist Hambali, who was a key player in the attack in Indonesia that killed over 200 people. We are tracking al-Qaida around the world—and nearly two-thirds of their known leaders have now been captured or killed. Thousands of very skilled and determined military personnel are on a manhunt, going after the remaining killers who hide in cities and caves—and, one by one, we will bring the terrorists to justice.

As part of the offensive against terror, we are also confronting the regimes that harbor and support terrorists, and could supply them with nuclear, chemical, or biological weapons. The United States and our allies are determined: We refuse to live in the shadow of this ultimate danger.

The first to see our determination were the Taliban, who made Afghanistan the primary training base of al-Qaida killers. As of this month, that country has a new constitution, guaranteeing free elections and full participation by women. Businesses are opening, health care centers are being established, and the boys and girls of Afghanistan are back in school. With help from the new Afghan Army, our coalition is leading aggressive raids against surviving members of the Taliban and al-Qaida. The men and women of Afghanistan are building a nation that is free, and proud, and fighting terror—and America is honored to be their friend.

Since we last met in this chamber, combat forces of the United States, Great Britain, Australia, Poland, and other countries enforced the demands of the United Nations, ended the rule of Saddam Hussein—and the people of Iraq are free. Having broken the Baathist regime, we face a remnant of violent Saddam supporters. Men who ran away from our troops in battle are now dispersed and attack from the shadows.

These killers, joined by foreign terrorists, are a serious, continuing danger. Yet we are making progress against them. The once all-powerful ruler of Iraq was found in a hole, and now sits in a prison cell. Of the top 55 officials of the former regime, we have captured or killed 45. Our forces are on the offensive, leading over 1,600 patrols a day, and conducting an average of 180 raids every week. We are dealing with these thugs in Iraq, just as surely as we dealt with Saddam Hussein's evil regime.

The work of building a new Iraq is hard, and it is right. And America has always been willing to do what it takes for what is right. Last January, Iraq's only law was the whim of one brutal man. Today our coalition is working with the Iraqi Governing Council to draft a basic law, with a bill of rights. We are working with Iraqis and the United Nations to prepare for a transition to full Iraqi sovereignty by the end of June. As democracy takes hold in Iraq, the enemies of freedom will do all in their power to spread violence and fear. They are trying to shake the will of our country and our friends—but the United States of America will never be intimidated by thugs and assassins. The killers will fail, and the Iraqi people will live in freedom.

Month by month, Iraqis are assuming more responsibility for their own security and their own future. And tonight we are honored to welcome one of Iraq's most respected leaders: the current President of the Iraqi Governing Council, Adnan Pachachi. Sir, America stands with you and the Iraqi people as you build a free and peaceful nation.

Because of American leadership and resolve, the world is changing for the better. Last month, the leader of Libya voluntarily pledged to disclose and dismantle all of his regime's weapons of mass destruction programs, including a uranium enrichment project for nuclear weapons. Colonel [Muammar al] Qadhafi correctly judged that his country would be better off, and far more secure, without weapons of mass murder.

Nine months of intense negotiations involving the United States and Great Britain succeeded with Libya, while 12 years of diplomacy with Iraq did not. And one reason is clear: For diplomacy to be effective, words must be credible—and no one can now doubt the word of America.

Different threats require different strategies. Along with nations in the region, we are insisting that North Korea eliminate its nuclear program. America and the international community are demanding that Iran meet its commitments and not develop nuclear weapons. America is committed to keeping the world's most dangerous weapons out of the hands of the world's most dangerous regimes.

When I came to this rostrum on September 20th, 2001, I brought the police shield of a fallen officer, my reminder of lives that ended, and a task that does not end. I gave to you and to all Americans my complete commitment to securing our country and defeating our enemies. And this pledge, given by one, has been kept by many. You in the Congress have provided the resources for our defense, and cast the difficult votes of war and peace. Our closest allies have been unwavering. America's intelligence personnel and diplomats have been skilled and tireless.

And the men and women of the American military—they have taken the hardest duty. We have seen their skill and courage in armored charges, and midnight raids, and lonely hours on faithful watch. We have seen the joy when they return, and felt the sorrow when one is lost. I have had the honor of meeting our servicemen and women at many posts, from the deck of a carrier in the Pacific, to a mess hall in Baghdad. Many of our troops are listening tonight. And I want you and your families to know: America is proud of you. And my Administration, and this Congress, will give you the resources you need to fight and win the war on terror.

I know that some people question if America is really in a war at all. They view terrorism more as a crime—a problem to be solved mainly with law enforcement and indictments. After the World Trade Center was first attacked in 1993, some of the guilty were indicted, tried, convicted, and sent to prison. But the matter was not settled. The terrorists were still training and plotting in other nations, and drawing up more ambitious plans. After the chaos and carnage of September 11th, it is not enough to serve our enemies with legal papers. The terrorists and their supporters declared war on the United States—and war is what they got.

Some in this chamber, and in our country, did not support the liberation of Iraq. Objections to war often come from principled motives. But let us be candid about the consequences of leaving Saddam Hussein in power. We are seeking all the facts—already the Kay Report identified dozens of weapons of mass destruction-related program activities and significant amounts of equipment that Iraq concealed from the United Nations. Had we failed to act, the dictator's weapons of mass destruction programs would continue to this day. Had we failed to act, Security Council resolutions on Iraq would have been revealed as empty threats, weakening the United Nations and encouraging defiance by dictators around the world. Iraq's torture chambers would still be filled with victims—terrified and innocent. The killing fields of Iraq—where hundreds of thousands of men, women, and children vanished into the sands—would still be known only to the killers. For all who love freedom and peace, the world without Saddam Hussein's regime is a better and safer place.

Some critics have said our duties in Iraq must be internationalized. This particular criticism is hard to explain to our partners in Britain, Australia, Japan, South Korea, the Philippines, Thailand, Italy, Spain, Poland, Denmark, Hungary, Bulgaria, Ukraine, Romania, the Netherlands, Norway, El Salvador, and the 17 other countries that have committed troops to Iraq. As we debate at home, we must never ignore the vital contributions of our international partners, or dismiss their sacrifices. From the beginning, America has sought international support for operations in Afghanistan and Iraq, and we have gained much support. There is a difference, however, between leading a coalition of many nations, and submitting to the objections of a few. America will never seek a permission slip to defend the security of our people.

We also hear doubts that democracy is a realistic goal for the greater Middle East, where freedom is rare. Yet it is mistaken, and condescending, to assume that whole cultures and great religions are incompatible with liberty and self-government. I believe that God has planted in every heart the desire to live in freedom. And even when that desire is crushed by tyranny for decades, it will rise again.

As long as the Middle East remains a place of tyranny, despair, and anger, it will continue to produce men and movements that threaten the safety of America and our friends. So America is pursuing a forward strategy of freedom in the greater Middle East. We will challenge the enemies of reform, confront the allies of terror, and expect a higher standard from our friends. To cut through the barriers of hateful propaganda, the Voice of America and other broadcast services are expanding their programming in Arabic and Persian—and soon, a new television service will begin providing reliable news and information across the region. I will send you a proposal to double the budget of the National Endowment for Democracy, and to focus its new work on the development of free elections, free markets, free press, and free labor unions in the Middle East. And above all, we will finish the historic work of democracy in Afghanistan and Iraq, so those nations can light the way for others, and help transform a troubled part of the world.

America is a Nation with a mission—and that mission comes from our most basic beliefs. We have no desire to dominate, no ambitions of empire. Our aim is a democratic peace—a peace founded upon the dignity and rights of every man and woman. America acts in this cause with friends and allies at our side, yet we understand our special calling: This great Republic will lead the cause of freedom.

In these last three years, adversity has also revealed the fundamental strengths of the American economy. We have come through recession, and terrorist attack, and corporate scandals, and the uncertainties of war. And because you acted to stimulate our economy with tax relief, this economy is strong, and growing stronger.

You have doubled the child tax credit from 500 to a thousand dollars, reduced the marriage penalty, begun to phase out the death tax, reduced taxes on capital gains and stock dividends, cut taxes on small businesses, and you have lowered taxes for every American who pays income taxes.

Americans took those dollars and put them to work, driving this economy forward. The pace of economic growth in the third quarter of 2003 was the fastest in nearly 20 years. New home construction: the highest in almost 20 years. Home ownership rates: the highest ever. Manufacturing activity is increasing. Inflation is low. Interest rates are low. Exports are growing. Productivity is high. And jobs are on the rise.

These numbers confirm that the American people are using their money far better than government would have—and you were right to return it.

America's growing economy is also a changing economy. As technology transforms the way almost every job is done, America becomes more productive, and workers need new skills. Much of our job growth will be found in high-skilled fields like health care and biotechnology. So we must respond by helping more Americans gain the skills to find good jobs in our new economy.

All skills begin with the basics of reading and math, which are supposed to be learned in the early grades of our schools. Yet for too long, for too many children, those skills were never mastered. By passing the No Child Left Behind Act, you have made the expectation of literacy the law of our country. We are providing more funding for our schools—a 36 percent increase since 2001. We are requiring higher standards. We are regularly testing every child on the fundamentals. We are reporting results to parents, and making sure they have better options when schools are not performing. We are making progress toward excellence for every child.

But the status quo always has defenders. Some want to undermine the No Child Left Behind Act by weakening standards and accountability. Yet the results we require are really a matter of common sense: We expect third graders to read and do math at third grade level—and that is not asking too much. Testing is the only way to identify and help students who are falling behind.

This Nation will not go back to the days of simply shuffling children along from grade to grade without them learning the basics. I refuse to give up on any child— and the No Child Left Behind Act is opening the door of opportunity to all of America's children.

At the same time, we must ensure that older students and adults can gain the skills they need to find work now. Many of the fastest-growing occupations require strong math and science preparation, and training beyond the high school level. So tonight I propose a series of measures called Jobs for the 21st Century. This program will provide extra help to middle- and high school students who fall behind in reading and math, expand Advanced Placement programs in low-income schools, and invite math and science professionals from the private sector to teach part-time in our high schools. I propose larger Pell Grants for students who prepare for college with demanding courses in high school. I propose increasing our support for America's fine community colleges, so they can train workers for the industries that are creating the most new jobs. By all these actions, we will help more and more Americans to join in the growing prosperity of our country.

Job training is important, and so is job creation. We must continue to pursue an aggressive, pro-growth economic agenda.

Congress has some unfinished business on the issue of taxes. The tax reductions you passed are set to expire. Unless you act, the unfair tax on marriage will go back up. Unless you act, millions of families will be charged 300 dollars more in Federal taxes for every child. Unless you act, small businesses will pay higher taxes. Unless you act, the death tax will eventually come back to life. Unless you act, Americans face a tax increase. What the Congress has given, the Congress should not take away: For the sake of job growth, the tax cuts you passed should be permanent.

Our agenda for jobs and growth must help small business owners and employees with relief from needless Federal regulation, and protect them from junk and frivolous lawsuits. Consumers and businesses need reliable supplies of energy to make our economy run—so I urge you to pass legislation to modernize our electricity system, promote conservation, and make America less dependent on foreign sources of energy. My Administration is promoting free and fair trade, to open up new markets for America's entrepreneurs, and manufacturers, and farmers, and to create jobs for America's workers. Younger workers should have the opportunity to build a nest egg by saving part of their Social Security taxes in a personal retirement account. We should make the Social Security system a source of ownership for the American people.

And we should limit the burden of government on this economy by acting as good stewards of taxpayer dollars. In two weeks, I will send you a budget that funds the war, protects the homeland, and meets important domestic needs, while limiting the growth in discretionary spending to less than four percent. This will require that Congress focus on priorities, cut wasteful spending, and be wise with the people's money. By doing so, we can cut the deficit in half over the next five years.

Tonight I also ask you to reform our immigration laws, so they reflect our values and benefit our economy. I propose a new temporary worker program to match willing foreign workers with willing employers, when no Americans can be found to fill the job. This reform will be good for our economy—because employers will find needed workers in an honest and orderly system. A temporary worker program will help protect our homeland—allowing border patrol and law enforcement to focus on true threats to our national security. I oppose amnesty, because it would encourage further illegal immigration, and unfairly reward those who break our laws. My temporary worker program will preserve the citizenship path for those who respect the law, while bringing millions of hardworking men and women out from the shadows of American life.

Our Nation's health care system, like our economy, is also in a time of change. Amazing medical technologies are improving and saving lives. This dramatic progress has brought its own challenge, in the rising costs of medical care and health insurance. Members of Congress, we must work together to help control those costs and extend the benefits of modern medicine throughout our country.

Meeting these goals requires bipartisan effort—and two months ago, you showed the way. By strengthening Medicare and adding a prescription drug benefit, you kept a basic commitment to our seniors: You are giving them the modern medicine they deserve.

Starting this year, under the law you passed, seniors can choose to receive a drug discount card, saving them 10 to 25 percent off the retail price of most prescription drugs—and millions of low-income seniors can get an additional 600 dollars to buy medicine. Beginning next year, seniors will have new coverage for preventive screenings against diabetes and heart disease, and seniors just entering Medicare can receive wellness exams.

In January of 2006, seniors can get prescription drug coverage under Medicare. For a monthly premium of about 35 dollars, most seniors who do not have that coverage today can expect to see their drug bills cut roughly in half. Under this reform, senior citizens will be able to keep their Medicare just as it is, or they can choose a Medicare plan that fits them best—just as you, as Members of Congress, can choose an insurance plan that meets your needs. And starting this year, millions of Americans will be able to save money tax-free for their medical expenses, in a health savings account.

I signed this measure proudly, and any attempt to limit the choices of our seniors, or to take away their prescription drug coverage under Medicare, will meet my veto.

On the critical issue of health care, our goal is to ensure that Americans can choose and afford private health care coverage that best fits their individual needs. To make insurance more affordable, Congress must act to address rapidly rising health care costs. Small businesses should be able to band together and negotiate for lower insurance rates, so they can cover more workers with health insurance—I urge you to pass Association Health Plans. I ask you to give lower-income Americans a refundable tax credit that would allow millions to buy their own basic health insurance. By computerizing health records, we can avoid dangerous medical mistakes, reduce costs, and improve care. To protect the doctor-patient relationship, and keep good doctors doing good work, we must eliminate wasteful and frivolous medical lawsuits. And tonight I propose that individuals who buy catastrophic health care coverage, as part of our new health savings accounts, be allowed to deduct 100 percent of the premiums from their taxes.

A government-run health care system is the wrong prescription. By keeping costs under control, expanding access, and helping more Americans afford coverage, we will preserve the system of private medicine that makes America's health care the best in the world.

We are living in a time of great change—in our world, in our economy, and in science and medicine. Yet some things endure—courage and compassion, reverence and integrity, respect for differences of faith and race. The values we try to live by never change. And they are instilled in us by fundamental institutions, such as families, and schools, and religious congregations. These institutions—the unseen pillars of civilization—must remain strong in America, and we will defend them.

We must stand with our families to help them raise healthy, responsible children. And when it comes to helping children make right choices, there is work for all of us to do.

One of the worst decisions our children can make is to gamble their lives and futures on drugs. Our government is helping parents confront this problem, with aggressive education, treatment, and law enforcement. Drug use in high school has declined by 11 percent over the past two years. Four hundred thousand fewer young people are using illegal drugs than in the year 2001. In my budget, I have proposed new funding to continue our aggressive, community-based strategy to reduce demand for illegal drugs. Drug testing in our schools has proven to be an effective part of this effort. So tonight I propose an additional 23 million dollars for schools that want to use drug testing as a tool to save children's lives. The aim here is not to punish children, but to send them this message: We love you, and we don't want to lose you.

To help children make right choices, they need good examples. Athletics play such an important role in our society, but, unfortunately, some in professional sports are not setting much of an example. The use of performance-enhancing drugs like steroids in baseball, football, and other sports is dangerous, and it sends the wrong message—that there are shortcuts to accomplishment, and that performance is more important than character. So tonight I call on team owners, union representatives, coaches, and players to take the lead, to send the right signal, to get tough, and to get rid of steroids now.

To encourage right choices, we must be willing to confront the dangers young people face—even when they are difficult to talk about. Each year, about three million teenagers contract sexually transmitted diseases that can harm them, or kill them, or prevent them from ever becoming parents. In my budget, I propose a grassroots campaign to help inform families about these medical risks. We will double Federal funding for abstinence programs, so schools can teach this fact of life: Abstinence for young people is the only certain way to avoid sexually transmitted diseases. Decisions children make now can affect their health and character for the rest of their lives. All of us—parents, schools, government—must work together to counter the negative influence of the culture, and to send the right messages to our children.

A strong America must also value the institution of marriage. I believe we should respect individuals as we take a principled stand for one of the most fundamental, enduring institutions of our civilization. Congress has already taken a stand on this issue by passing the Defense of Marriage Act, signed in 1996 by President Clinton. That statute protects marriage under Federal law as the union of a man and a woman, and declares that one state may not redefine marriage for other states. Activist judges, however, have begun redefining marriage by court order, without regard for the will of the people and their elected representatives. On an issue of such great consequence, the people's voice must be heard. If judges insist on forcing their arbitrary will upon the people, the only alternative left to the people would be the constitutional process. Our Nation must defend the sanctity of marriage.

The outcome of this debate is important—and so is the way we conduct it. The same moral tradition that defines marriage also teaches that each individual has dignity and value in God's sight.

It is also important to strengthen our communities by unleashing the compassion of America's religious institutions. Religious charities of every creed are doing some of the most vital work in our country—mentoring children, feeding the hungry, taking the hand of the lonely. Yet government has often denied social service grants and contracts to these groups, just because they have a cross or Star of David or crescent on the wall. By Executive Order, I have opened billions of dollars in grant money to competition that includes faith-based charities. Tonight I ask you to codify this into law, so people of faith can know that the law will never discriminate against them again.

In the past, we have worked together to bring mentors to the children of prisoners, and provide treatment for the addicted, and help for the homeless. Tonight I ask you to consider another group of Americans in need of help. This year, some 600,000 inmates will be released from prison back into society. We know from long experience that if they can't find work, or a home, or help, they are much more likely to commit more crimes and return to prison. So tonight, I propose a four-year, 300 million dollar Prisoner Re-Entry Initiative to expand job training and placement services, to provide transitional housing, and to help newly released prisoners get mentoring, including from faith-based groups. America is the land of the second chance—and when the gates of the prison open, the path ahead should lead to a better life.

For all Americans, the last three years have brought tests we did not ask for, and achievements shared by all. By our actions, we have shown what kind of Nation we are. In grief, we found the grace to go on. In challenge, we rediscovered the courage and daring of a free people. In victory, we have shown the noble aims and good heart of America. And having come this far, we sense that we live in a time set apart.

I have been a witness to the character of the American people, who have shown calm in times of danger, compassion for one another, and toughness for the long haul. All of us have been partners in a great enterprise. And even some of the youngest understand that we are living in historic times. Last month a girl in Lincoln, Rhode Island, sent me a letter. It began, "Dear George W. Bush." "If there is anything you know, I Ashley Pearson age 10 can do to help anyone, please send me a letter and tell me what I can do to save our country." She added this P.S.: "If you can send a letter to the troops . . . please put, 'Ashley Pearson believes in you.'" Tonight, Ashley, your message to our troops has just been conveyed. And yes, you have some duties yourself. Study hard in school, listen to your mom and dad, help someone in need, and when you and your friends see a man or woman in uniform, say "thank you." And while you do your part, all of us here in this great chamber will do our best to keep you and the rest of America safe and free.

My fellow citizens, we now move forward, with confidence and faith. Our Nation is strong and steadfast. The cause we serve is right, because it is the cause of all mankind. The momentum of freedom in our world is unmistakable—and it is not carried forward by our power alone. We can trust in that greater power Who guides the unfolding of the years. And in all that is to come, we can know that His purposes are just and true.

May God bless the United States of America. Thank you.

George W. Bush, 2005–2006

Address before a Joint Session of Congress on the State of the Union

February 2, 2005

George W. Bush's 2005 State of the Union address came on the heels of his second inauguration as president on January 20. After being reelected the previous November, Bush had declared, "I earned capital in the campaign, political capital, and now I intend to spend it." Indeed, the president put forth a lengthy agenda in his State of the Union speech, which focused on both international and domestic priorities.

The item that received the most attention was a new White House plan to revamp the country's Social Security system. In this address, Bush called for "voluntary personal retirement accounts" for workers under age fifty-five, stating that, without changes, the entitlement program would go bankrupt by the year 2042. "For younger workers, the Social Security system has serious problems that will grow worse with time," Bush said. "Social Security was created decades ago, for a very different era."

Bush pledged to "work with members of Congress to find the most effective combination of reforms" and to "listen to anyone who has a good idea to offer." While he campaigned hard for changes in Social Security, Congress was less enthusiastic, and the idea of reforming the program stalled.

Continuing on domestic themes, Bush spoke in favor of a constitutional marriage amendment, a popular subject among conservatives. He also pushed to reform the tax code and revamp the country's immigration system, among other issues.

As had been the case since the terrorist attacks of September 11, 2001, Bush devoted a great deal of his State of the Union speech to foreign policy matters. He touched on some of the same themes about the importance of spreading freedom throughout the world that he had stressed in his second inaugural address.

The ongoing and increasingly unpopular war in Iraq, where U.S. troops continued to battle insurgent forces, was a key focus of this State of the Union address. Bush recognized Janet and Bill Norwood, whose son Byron, a Marine, had died in Iraq. He also noted the presence of Safia Taleb al-Suhail, an Iraqi human rights advocate. The two women embraced, in what seemed to be a gesture of thanks from the Iraqi for the sacrifice of the Norwoods' son. Bush also spoke of the recent National Assembly elections in Iraq, pledging that the United States would not abandon its commitment to the Iraqis. "While our military strategy is adapting to circumstances, our commitment remains firm and unchanging," Bush said.

 M r. Speaker, Vice President Cheney, Members of Congress, fellow citizens:

As a new Congress gathers, all of us in the elected branches of government share a great privilege: we have been placed in office by the votes of the people we serve. And tonight that is a privilege we share with newly elected leaders of Afghanistan, the Palestinian territories, Ukraine, and a free and sovereign Iraq.

Two weeks ago, I stood on the steps of this Capitol and renewed the commitment of our Nation to the guiding ideal of liberty for all. This evening I will set forth policies to advance that ideal at home and around the world.

Tonight, with a healthy, growing economy, with more Americans going back to work, with our Nation an active force for good in the world—the state of our union is confident and strong. Our generation has been blessed—by the expansion of opportunity, by advances in medicine, and by the security purchased by our parents' sacrifice. Now, as we see a little gray in the mirror—or a lot of gray—and we watch our children moving into adulthood, we ask the question: What will be the state of their union?

Members of Congress, the choices we make together will answer that question. Over the next several months, on issue after issue, let us do what Americans have always done, and build a better world for our children and grandchildren.

First, we must be good stewards of this economy, and renew the great institutions on which millions of our fellow citizens rely.

America's economy is the fastest growing of any major industrialized nation. In the past four years, we have provided tax relief to every person who pays income taxes, overcome a recession, opened up new markets abroad, prosecuted corporate criminals, raised homeownership to the highest level in history, and in the last year alone, the United States has added 2.3 million new jobs. When action was needed, the Congress delivered—and the Nation is grateful.

Now we must add to these achievements. By making our economy more flexible, more innovative, and more competitive, we will keep America the economic leader of the world.

America's prosperity requires restraining the spending appetite of the federal government. I welcome the bipartisan enthusiasm for spending discipline. So next week I will send you a budget that holds the growth of discretionary spending below inflation, makes tax relief permanent, and stays on track to cut the deficit in half by 2009. My budget substantially reduces or eliminates more than 150 government programs that are not getting results, or duplicate current efforts, or do not fulfill essential priorities. The principle here is clear: a taxpayer dollar must be spent wisely, or not at all.

To make our economy stronger and more dynamic, we must prepare a rising generation to fill the jobs of the 21st century. Under the No Child Left Behind Act, standards are higher, test scores are on the rise, and we are closing the achievement gap for minority students. Now we must demand better results from our high schools, so every high school diploma is a ticket to success. We will help an additional 200,000 workers to get training for a better career, by reforming our job training system and strengthening America's community colleges. And we will make it easier for Americans to afford a college education, by increasing the size of Pell Grants.

To make our economy stronger and more competitive, America must reward, not punish, the efforts and dreams of entrepreneurs. Small business is the path of advancement, especially for women and minorities, so we must free small businesses from needless regulation and protect honest job-creators from junk lawsuits. Justice is distorted, and our economy is held back, by irresponsible class actions and frivolous asbestos claims—and I urge Congress to pass legal reforms this year.

To make our economy stronger and more productive, we must make health care more affordable, and give families greater access to good coverage, and more control over their health decisions. I ask Congress to move forward on a comprehensive health care agenda—with tax credits to help low-income workers buy insurance, a community health center in every poor county, improved information technology to prevent medical errors and needless costs, association health plans for small businesses and their employees, expanded health savings accounts, and medical liability reform that will reduce health care costs, and make sure patients have the doctors and care they need.

To keep our economy growing, we also need reliable supplies of affordable, environmentally responsible energy. Nearly four years ago, I submitted a comprehensive energy strategy that encourages conservation, alternative sources, a modernized electricity grid, and more production here at home, including safe, clean nuclear energy. My Clear Skies legislation will cut power plant pollution and improve the health of our citizens. And my budget provides strong funding for leading-edge technology—from hydrogen-fueled cars, to clean coal, to renewable sources such as ethanol. Four years of debate is enough—I urge Congress to pass legislation that makes America more secure and less dependent on foreign energy.

All these proposals are essential to expand this economy and add new jobs—but they are just the beginning of our duty. To build the prosperity of future generations, we must update institutions that were created to meet the needs of an earlier time. Year after year, Americans are burdened by an archaic, incoherent federal tax code. I have appointed a bipartisan panel to examine the tax code from top to bottom. And when their recommendations are delivered, you and I will work together to give this Nation a tax code that is pro-growth, easy to understand, and fair to all.

America's immigration system is also outdated—unsuited to the needs of our economy and to the values of our country. We should not be content with laws that punish hardworking people who want only to provide for their families, and deny businesses willing workers, and invite chaos at our border. It is time for an immigration policy that permits temporary guest workers to fill jobs Americans will not take, that rejects amnesty, that tells us who is entering and leaving our country, and that closes the border to drug dealers and terrorists.

One of America's most important institutions—a symbol of the trust between generations—is also in need of wise and effective reform. Social Security was a great moral success of the 20th Century, and we must honor its great purposes in this new century. The system, however, on its current path, is headed toward bankruptcy. And so we must join together to strengthen and save Social Security.

Today, more than 45 million Americans receive Social Security benefits, and millions more are nearing retirement—and for them the system is strong and fiscally sound. I have a message for every American who is 55 or older: Do not let anyone mislead you. For you, the Social Security system will not change in any way.

For younger workers, the Social Security system has serious problems that will grow worse with time. Social Security was created decades ago, for a very different era. In those days people didn't live as long, benefits were much lower than they are today, and a half century ago, about 16 workers paid into the system for each person drawing benefits. Our society has changed in ways the founders of Social Security could not have foreseen. In today's world, people are living longer and therefore drawing benefits longer—and those benefits are scheduled to rise dramatically over the next few decades. And instead of 16 workers paying in for every beneficiary, right now it's only about three workers—and over the next few decades, that number will fall to just two workers per beneficiary. With each passing year, fewer workers are paying ever-higher benefits to an ever-larger number of retirees.

So here is the result: Thirteen years from now, in 2018, Social Security will be paying out more than it takes in. And every year afterward will bring a new shortfall, bigger than the year before. For example, in the year 2027, the government will somehow have to come up with an extra 200 billion dollars to keep the system afloat—and by 2033, the annual shortfall would be more than 300 billion dollars. By the year 2042, the entire system would be exhausted and bankrupt. If steps are not taken to avert that outcome, the only solutions would be drastically higher taxes, massive new borrowing, or sudden and severe cuts in Social Security benefits or other government programs.

I recognize that 2018 and 2042 may seem like a long way off. But those dates are not so distant, as any parent will tell you. If you have a five-year-old, you're already concerned about how you'll pay for college tuition 13 years down the road. If you've got children in their 20s, as some of us do, the idea of Social Security collapsing before they retire does not seem like a small matter. And it should not be a small matter to the United States Congress.

You and I share a responsibility. We must pass reforms that solve the financial problems of Social Security once and for all.

Fixing Social Security permanently will require an open, candid review of the options. Some have suggested limiting benefits for wealthy retirees. Former Congressman Tim Penny has raised the possibility of indexing benefits to prices rather than wages. During the 1990s, my predecessor, President Clinton, spoke of increasing the retirement age. Former Senator John Breaux suggested discouraging early collection of Social Security benefits. The late Senator Daniel Patrick Moynihan recommended changing the way benefits are calculated.

All these ideas are on the table. I know that none of these reforms would be easy. But we have to move ahead with courage and honesty, because our children's retirement security is more important than partisan politics. I will work with members of Congress to find the most effective combination of reforms. I will listen to anyone who has a good idea to offer. We must, however, be guided by some basic principles.

We must make Social Security permanently sound, not leave that task for another day. We must not jeopardize our economic strength by increasing payroll taxes. We must ensure that lower income Americans get the help they need to have dignity and peace of mind in their retirement. We must guarantee that there is no change for those now retired or nearing retirement. And we must take care that any changes in the system are gradual, so younger workers have years to prepare and plan for their future.

As we fix Social Security, we also have the responsibility to make the system a better deal for younger workers. And the best way to reach that goal is through voluntary personal retirement accounts. Here is how the idea works. Right now, a set portion of the money you earn is taken out of your paycheck to pay for the Social Security benefits of today's retirees. If you are a younger worker, I believe you should be able to set aside part of that money in your own retirement account, so you can build a nest egg for your own future.

Here is why personal accounts are a better deal. Your money will grow, over time, at a greater rate than anything the current system can deliver—and your account will provide money for retirement over and above the check you will receive from Social Security. In addition, you'll be able to pass along the money that accumulates in your personal account, if you wish, to your children or grandchildren. And best of all, the money in the account is yours, and the government can never take it away.

The goal here is greater security in retirement, so we will set careful guidelines for personal accounts. We will make sure the money can only go into a conservative mix of bonds and stock funds. We will make sure that your earnings are not eaten up by hidden Wall Street fees. We will make sure there are good options to protect your investments from sudden market swings on the eve of your retirement. We will make sure a personal account can't be emptied out all at once, but rather paid out over time, as an addition to traditional Social Security benefits. And we will make sure this plan is fiscally responsible, by starting personal retirement accounts gradually, and raising the yearly limits on contributions over time, eventually permitting all workers to set aside four percentage points of their payroll taxes in their accounts.

Personal retirement accounts should be familiar to federal employees, because you already have something similar, called the Thrift Savings Plan, which lets workers deposit a portion of their paychecks into any of five different broadly based investment funds. It is time to extend the same security, and choice, and ownership to young Americans.

Our second great responsibility to our children and grandchildren is to honor and to pass along the values that sustain a free society. So many of my generation, after a long journey, have come home to family and faith, and are determined to bring up responsible, moral children. Government is not the source of these values, but government should never undermine them.

Because marriage is a sacred institution and the foundation of society, it should not be re-defined by activist judges. For the good of families, children, and society, I support a constitutional amendment to protect the institution of marriage.

Because a society is measured by how it treats the weak and vulnerable, we must strive to build a culture of life. Medical research can help us reach that goal, by developing treatments and cures that save lives and help people overcome disabilities—and I thank Congress for doubling the funding of the National Institutes of Health. To build a culture of life, we must also ensure that scientific advances always serve human dignity, not take advantage of some lives for the benefit of others. We should all be able to agree on some clear standards. I will work with Congress to ensure that human embryos are not created for experimentation or grown for body parts, and that human life is never bought and sold as a commodity. America will continue to lead the world in medical research that is ambitious, aggressive, and always ethical.

Because courts must always deliver impartial justice, judges have a duty to faithfully interpret the law, not legislate from the bench. As President, I have a constitutional responsibility to nominate men and women who understand the role of courts in our democracy, and are well qualified to serve on the bench—and I have done so. The Constitution also gives the Senate a responsibility: Every judicial nominee deserves an up-or-down vote.

Because one of the deepest values of our country is compassion, we must never turn away from any citizen who feels isolated from the opportunities of America. Our government will continue to support faith-based and community groups that bring hope to harsh places. Now we need to focus on giving young people, especially young men in our cities, better options than apathy, or gangs, or jail. Tonight I propose a three-year initiative to help organizations keep young people out of gangs, and show young men an ideal of manhood that respects women and rejects violence. Taking on gang life will be one part of a broader outreach to at-risk youth, which involves parents and pastors, coaches and community leaders, in programs ranging from literacy to sports. And I am proud that the leader of this nationwide effort will be our First Lady, Laura Bush.

Because HIV/AIDS brings suffering and fear into so many lives, I ask you to reauthorize the Ryan White Act to encourage prevention, and provide care and treatment to the victims of that disease. And as we update this important law, we must focus our efforts on fellow citizens with the highest rates of new cases, African-American men and women.

Because one of the main sources of our national unity is our belief in equal justice, we need to make sure Americans of all races and backgrounds have confidence in the system that provides justice. In America we must make doubly sure no person is held to account for a crime he or she did not commit—so we are dramatically expanding the use of DNA evidence to prevent wrongful conviction. Soon I will send to Congress a proposal to fund special training for defense counsel in capital cases, because people on trial for their lives must have competent lawyers by their side.

Our third responsibility to future generations is to leave them an America that is safe from danger, and protected by peace. We will pass along to our children all the freedoms we enjoy—and chief among them is freedom from fear.

In the three and a half years since September 11th, 2001, we have taken unprecedented actions to protect Americans. We have created a new department of government to defend our homeland, focused the FBI on preventing terrorism, begun to reform our intelligence agencies, broken up terror cells across the country, expanded research on defenses against biological and chemical attack, improved border security, and trained more than a half million first responders. Police and firefighters, air marshals, researchers, and so many others are working every day to make our homeland safer, and we thank them all.

Our Nation, working with allies and friends, has also confronted the enemy abroad, with measures that are determined, successful, and continuing. The al-Qaida terror network that attacked our country still has leaders—but many of its top commanders have been removed. There are still governments that sponsor and harbor terrorists—but their number has declined. There are still regimes seeking weapons of mass destruction—but no longer without attention and without consequence. Our country is still the target of terrorists who want to kill many, and intimidate us all—and we will stay on the offensive against them, until the fight is won.

Pursuing our enemies is a vital commitment of the war on terror—and I thank the Congress for providing our servicemen and women with the resources they have needed. During this time of war, we must continue to support our military and give them the tools for victory.

Other nations around the globe have stood with us. In Afghanistan, an international force is helping provide security. In Iraq, 28 countries have troops on the ground, the United Nations and the European Union provided technical assistance for elections, and NATO is leading a mission to help train Iraqi officers. We are cooperating with 60 governments in the Proliferation Security Initiative, to detect and stop the transit of dangerous materials. We are working closely with governments in Asia to convince North Korea to abandon its nuclear ambitions. Pakistan, Saudi Arabia, and nine other countries have captured or detained al-Qaida terrorists. In the next four years, my Administration will continue to build the coalitions that will defeat the dangers of our time.

In the long term, the peace we seek will only be achieved by eliminating the conditions that feed radicalism and ideologies of murder. If whole regions of the world remain in despair and grow in hatred, they will be the recruiting grounds for terror, and that terror will stalk America and other free nations for decades. The only force powerful enough to stop the rise of tyranny and terror, and replace hatred with hope, is the force of human freedom. Our enemies know this, and that is why the terrorist Zarqawi recently declared war on what he called the "evil principle" of democracy. And we have declared our own intention: America will stand with the allies of freedom to support democratic movements in the Middle East and beyond, with the ultimate goal of ending tyranny in our world.

The United States has no right, no desire, and no intention to impose our form of government on anyone else. That is one of the main differences between us and our enemies. They seek to impose and expand an empire of oppression, in which a tiny group of brutal, self-appointed rulers control every aspect of every life. Our aim is to build and preserve a community of free and independent nations, with governments that answer to their citizens, and reflect their own cultures. And because democracies respect their own people and their neighbors, the advance of freedom will lead to peace. That advance has great momentum in our time—shown by women voting in Afghanistan, and Palestinians choosing a new direction, and the people of Ukraine asserting their democratic rights and electing a president. We are witnessing landmark events in the history of liberty. And in the coming years, we will add to that story.

The beginnings of reform and democracy in the Palestinian territories are showing the power of freedom to break old patterns of violence and failure. Tomorrow morning, Secretary of State [Condoleezza] Rice departs on a trip that will take her to Israel and the West Bank for meetings with Prime Minister Sharon and President Abbas. She will discuss with them how we and our friends can help the Palestinian people end terror and build the institutions of a peaceful, independent democratic state. To promote this democracy, I will ask Congress for 350 million dollars to support Palestinian political, economic, and security reforms. The goal of two democratic states, Israel and Palestine, living side by side in peace is within reach—and America will help them achieve that goal.

To promote peace and stability in the broader Middle East, the United States will work with our friends in the region to fight the common threat of terror, while we encourage a higher standard of freedom. Hopeful reform is already taking hold in an arc from Morocco to Jordan to Bahrain. The government of Saudi Arabia can demonstrate its leadership in the region by expanding the role of its people in determining their future. And the great and proud nation of Egypt, which showed the way toward peace in the Middle East, can now show the way toward democracy in the Middle East.

To promote peace in the broader Middle East, we must confront regimes that continue to harbor terrorists and pursue weapons of mass murder. Syria still allows its territory, and parts of Lebanon, to be used by terrorists who seek to destroy every chance of peace in the region. You have passed, and we are applying, the Syrian Accountability Act—and we expect the Syrian government to end all support for terror and open the door to freedom. Today, Iran remains the world's primary state sponsor of terror—pursuing nuclear weapons while depriving its people of the freedom they seek and deserve. We are working with European allies to make clear to the Iranian regime that it must give up its uranium enrichment program and any plutonium re-processing, and end its support for terror. And to the Iranian people, I say tonight: As you stand for your own liberty, America stands with you.

Our generational commitment to the advance of freedom, especially in the Middle East, is now being tested and honored in Iraq. That country is a vital front in the war on terror, which is why the terrorists have chosen to make a stand there. Our men and women in uniform are fighting terrorists in Iraq, so we do not have to face them here at home. And the victory of freedom in Iraq will strengthen a new ally in the war on terror, inspire democratic reformers from Damascus to Tehran, bring more hope and progress to a troubled region, and thereby lift a terrible threat from the lives of our children and grandchildren.

We will succeed because the Iraqi people value their own liberty—as they showed the world last Sunday. Across Iraq, often at great risk, millions of citizens went to the polls and elected 275 men and women to represent them in a new Transitional National Assembly. A young woman in Baghdad told of waking to the sound of mortar fire on election day, and wondering if it might be too dangerous to vote. She said, "hearing those explosions, it occurred to me—the insurgents are weak, they are afraid of democracy, they are losing. . . . So I got my husband, and I got my parents, and we all came out and voted together." Americans recognize that spirit of liberty, because we share it. In any nation, casting your vote is an act of civic responsibility; for millions of Iraqis, it was also an act of personal courage, and they have earned the respect of us all.

One of Iraq's leading democracy and human rights advocates is Safia Taleb al-Suhail. She says of her country, "we were occupied for 35 years by Saddam Hussein. That was the real occupation. . . . Thank you to the American people who paid the cost . . . but most of all to the soldiers." Eleven years ago, Safia's father was assassinated by Saddam's intelligence service. Three days ago in Baghdad, Safia was finally able to vote for the leaders of her country—and we are honored that she is with us tonight.

The terrorists and insurgents are violently opposed to democracy, and will continue to attack it. Yet the terrorists' most powerful myth is being destroyed. The whole world is seeing that the car bombers and assassins are not only fighting coalition forces, they are trying to destroy the hopes of Iraqis, expressed in free elections. And the whole world now knows that a small group of extremists will not overturn the will of the Iraqi people.

We will succeed in Iraq because Iraqis are determined to fight for their own freedom, and to write their own history. As Prime Minister Allawi said in his speech to Congress last September, "Ordinary Iraqis are anxious . . . to shoulder all the security burdens of our country as quickly as possible." This is the natural desire of an independent nation, and it also is the stated mission of our coalition in Iraq. The new political situation in Iraq opens a new phase of our work in that country. At the recommendation of our commanders on the ground, and in consultation with the Iraqi government, we will increasingly focus our efforts on helping prepare more capable Iraqi security forces—forces with skilled officers, and an effective command structure. As those forces become more self-reliant and take on greater security responsibilities, America and its coalition partners will increasingly be in a supporting role. In the end, Iraqis must be able to defend their own country—and we will help that proud, new nation secure its liberty.

Recently an Iraqi interpreter said to a reporter, "Tell America not to abandon us." He and all Iraqis can be certain: While our military strategy is adapting to circumstances, our commitment remains firm and unchanging. We are standing for the freedom of our Iraqi friends, and freedom in Iraq will make America safer for generations to come. We will not set an artificial timetable for leaving Iraq, because that would embolden the terrorists and make them believe they can wait us out. We are in Iraq to achieve a result: A country that is democratic, representative of all its people, at peace with its neighbors, and able to defend itself. And when that result is achieved, our men and women serving in Iraq will return home with the honor they have earned.

Right now, Americans in uniform are serving at posts across the world, often taking great risks on my orders. We have given them training and equipment; and they have given us an example of idealism and character that makes every American proud. The volunteers of our military are unrelenting in battle, unwavering in loyalty, unmatched in honor and decency, and every day they are making our nation more secure. Some of our servicemen and women have survived terrible injuries, and this grateful country will do everything we can to help them recover. And we have said farewell to some very good men and women, who died for our freedom, and whose memory this nation will honor forever.

One name we honor is Marine Corps Sergeant Byron Norwood of Pflugerville, Texas, who was killed during the assault on Fallujah. His mom, Janet, sent me a letter and told me how much Byron loved being a Marine, and how proud he was to be on the front line against terror. She wrote, "When Byron was home the last time, I said that I wanted to protect him like I had since he was born. He just hugged me and said: 'You've done your job, mom. Now it's my turn to protect you.'" Ladies and gentlemen, with grateful hearts, we honor freedom's defenders, and our military families, represented here this evening by Sergeant Norwood's mom and dad, Janet and Bill Norwood.

In these four years, Americans have seen the unfolding of large events. We have known times of sorrow, and hours of uncertainty, and days of victory. In all this history, even when we have disagreed, we have seen threads of purpose that unite us. The attack on freedom in our world has reaffirmed our confidence in freedom's power to change the world. We are all part of a great venture: To extend the promise of freedom in our country, to renew the values that sustain our liberty, and to spread the peace that freedom brings.

As Franklin Roosevelt once reminded Americans, "each age is a dream that is dying, or one that is coming to birth." And we live in the country where the biggest dreams are born. The abolition of slavery was only a dream—until it was fulfilled. The liberation of Europe from fascism was only a dream—until it was achieved. The fall of imperial communism was only a dream—until, one day, it was accomplished. Our generation has dreams of its own, and we also go forward with confidence. The road of Providence is uneven and unpredictable—yet we know where it leads: It leads to freedom.

Thank you, and may God bless America.

George W. Bush, 2005–2006

Address before a Joint Session of Congress on the State of the Union

January 31, 2006

George W. Bush's popularity had been on the wane for months as he delivered his 2006 State of the Union address. The ongoing war in Iraq, with its increasing casualty list, was one reason. Another was what many perceived as a bungled response by the administration to Hurricane Katrina, which had devastated the city of New Orleans along with other areas along the Gulf Coast in August 2005. Additionally, the White House had been touched by scandal when a key adviser to Vice President Dick Cheney was indicted by a federal grand jury.

It was a somewhat beleaguered president who came to the podium in the House of Representatives chamber on January 31 to give his speech, with congressional midterm elections just about nine months away. The president defended his Iraq policy, answering critics who were calling for a definitive date to bring U.S. troops home. "A sudden withdrawal of our forces from Iraq would abandon our Iraqi allies to death and prison, would put men like [Osama] bin Laden and [Abu Musab al-] Zarqawi in charge of a strategic country, and show that a pledge from America means little," Bush said, referring to top leaders of al Qaeda. "Members of Congress, however we feel about the decisions and debates of the past, our nation has only one option: We must keep our word, defeat our enemies, and stand behind the American military in this vital mission."

Bush introduced the family of Dan Clay, a Marine who had died in Iraq, and read from a letter Clay had written them. He also introduced the country's two new

Supreme Court justices: Chief Justice John Roberts Jr. and Associate Justice Samuel Alito Jr., both strong conservatives whose ascension to the high court marked a political win for the president.

In addition, Bush offered a defense of what had become a controversial administration program involving the interception, without warrants, of communications between people in the United States and people in other countries with possible links to terrorism.

In an interesting sideshow to the main event, two women's Iraq-related T-shirts caused a commotion the night of the president's speech. One, famed antiwar protestor Cindy Sheehan, whose son had been killed in Iraq, was arrested by Capitol police in the House gallery for wearing a T-shirt with an antiwar slogan. The other, Beverly Young, the wife of a Republican representative from Florida, was told to leave on account of her T-shirt, which bore a message of support for U.S. troops.

Thank you all. Mr. Speaker, Vice President [Dick] Cheney, Members of Congress, members of the Supreme Court and diplomatic corps, distinguished guests, and fellow citizens:

Today our Nation lost a beloved, graceful, courageous woman who called America to its founding ideals and carried on a noble dream. Tonight we are comforted by the hope of a glad reunion with the husband who was taken so long ago, and we are grateful for the good life of Coretta Scott King.

Every time I'm invited to this rostrum, I'm humbled by the privilege and mindful of the history we've seen together. We have gathered under this Capitol dome in moments of national mourning and national achievement. We have served America through one of the most consequential periods of our history, and it has been my honor to serve with you.

In a system of two parties, two chambers, and two elected branches, there will always be differences and debate. But even tough debates can be conducted in a civil tone, and our differences cannot be allowed to harden into anger. To confront the great issues before us, we must act in a spirit of goodwill and respect for one another—and I will do my part. Tonight the state of our Union is strong, and together we will make it stronger.

In this decisive year, you and I will make choices that determine both the future and the character of our country. We will choose to act confidently in pursuing the enemies of freedom, or retreat from our duties in the hope of an easier life. We will choose to build our prosperity by leading the world economy, or shut ourselves off from trade and opportunity. In a complex and challenging time, the road of isolationism and protectionism may seem broad and inviting, yet it ends in danger and decline. The only way to protect our people, the only way to secure the peace, the only way to control our destiny is by our leadership. So the United States of America will continue to lead.

Abroad, our Nation is committed to an historic, long-term goal: We seek the end of tyranny in our world. Some dismiss that goal as misguided idealism. In reality, the future security of America depends on it. On September the 11th, 2001, we found that problems originating in a failed and oppressive state 7,000 miles away could bring murder and destruction to our country. Dictatorships shelter terrorists, and feed resentment and radicalism, and seek weapons of mass destruction. Democracies replace resentment with hope, respect the rights of their citizens and their neighbors, and join the fight against terror. Every step toward freedom in the world makes our country safer, so we will act boldly in freedom's cause.

Far from being a hopeless dream, the advance of freedom is the great story of our time. In 1945, there were about two dozen lonely democracies in the world. Today, there are 122. And we're writing a new chapter in the story of self-government—with women lining up to vote in Afghanistan, and millions of Iraqis marking their liberty with purple ink, and men and women from Lebanon to Egypt debating the rights of individuals and the necessity of freedom. At the start of 2006, more than half the people of our world live in democratic nations. And we do not forget the other half— in places like Syria and Burma, Zimbabwe, North Korea, and Iran—because the demands of justice and the peace of this world require their freedom as well.

No one can deny the success of freedom, but some men rage and fight against it. And one of the main sources of reaction and opposition is radical Islam—the perversion by a few of a noble faith into an ideology of terror and death. Terrorists like bin Laden are serious about mass murder, and all of us must take their declared intentions seriously. They seek to impose a heartless system of totalitarian control throughout the Middle East and arm themselves with weapons of mass murder.

Their aim is to seize power in Iraq and use it as a safe haven to launch attacks against America and the world. Lacking the military strength to challenge us directly, the terrorists have chosen the weapon of fear. When they murder children at a school in Beslan or blow up commuters in London or behead a bound captive, the terrorists hope these horrors will break our will, allowing the violent to inherit the Earth. But they have miscalculated: We love our freedom, and we will fight to keep it.

In a time of testing, we cannot find security by abandoning our commitments and retreating within our borders. If we were to leave these vicious attackers alone, they would not leave us alone. They would simply move the battlefield to our own shores. There is no peace in retreat, and there is no honor in retreat. By allowing radical Islam to work its will, by leaving an assaulted world to fend for itself, we would signal to all that we no longer believe in our own ideals or even in our own courage. But our enemies and our friends can be certain: The United States will not retreat from the world, and we will never surrender to evil.

America rejects the false comfort of isolationism. We are the nation that saved liberty in Europe and liberated death camps and helped raise up democracies and faced down an evil empire. Once again, we accept the call of history to deliver the oppressed and move this world toward peace. We remain on the offensive against terror networks. We have killed or captured many of their leaders—and for the others, their day will come.

We remain on the offensive in Afghanistan, where a fine President and a National Assembly are fighting terror while building the institutions of a new democracy. We're on the offensive in Iraq with a clear plan for victory.

First, we're helping Iraqis build an inclusive government, so that old resentments will be eased and the insurgency will be marginalized. Second, we're continuing reconstruction efforts and helping the Iraqi Government to fight corruption and build a modern economy, so all Iraqis can experience the benefits of freedom. And third, we're striking terrorist targets while we train Iraqi forces that are increasingly capable of defeating the enemy. Iraqis are showing their courage every day, and we are proud to be their allies in the cause of freedom.

Our work in Iraq is difficult because our enemy is brutal. But that brutality has not stopped the dramatic progress of a new democracy. In less than 3 years, the nation has gone from dictatorship to liberation, to sovereignty, to a Constitution, to national elections. At the same time, our coalition has been relentless in shutting off terrorist infiltration, clearing out insurgent strongholds, and turning over territory to Iraqi security forces. I am confident in our plan for victory; I am confident in the will of the Iraqi people; I am confident in the skill and spirit of our military. Fellow citizens, we are in this fight to win, and we are winning.

The road of victory is the road that will take our troops home. As we make progress on the ground and Iraqi forces increasingly take the lead, we should be able to further decrease our troop levels. But those decisions will be made by our military commanders, not by politicians in Washington, DC.

Our coalition has learned from our experience in Iraq. We've adjusted our military tactics and changed our approach to reconstruction. Along the way, we have benefited from responsible criticism and counsel offered by Members of Congress of both parties. In the coming year, I will continue to reach out and seek your good advice. Yet there is a difference between responsible criticism that aims for success and defeatism that refuses to acknowledge anything but failure. Hindsight alone is not wisdom, and second-guessing is not a strategy.

With so much in the balance, those of us in public office have a duty to speak with candor. A sudden withdrawal of our forces from Iraq would abandon our Iraqi allies to death and prison, would put men like bin Laden and Zarqawi in charge of a strategic country, and show that a pledge from America means little. Members of Congress, however we feel about the decisions and debates of the past, our Nation has only one option: We must keep our word, defeat our enemies, and stand behind the American military in this vital mission.

Our men and women in uniform are making sacrifices and showing a sense of duty stronger than all fear. They know what it's like to fight house to house in a maze of streets, to wear heavy gear in the desert heat, to see a comrade killed by a roadside bomb. And those who know the costs also know the stakes. Marine Staff Sergeant Dan Clay was killed last month fighting in Fallujah. He left behind a letter to his family, but his words could just as well be addressed to every American. Here is what Dan wrote: "I know what honor is—it has been an honor to protect and serve all of you. I faced death with the secure knowledge that you would not have to. Never falter. Don't hesitate to honor and support those of us who have the honor of protecting that which is worth protecting."

Staff Sergeant Dan Clay's wife, Lisa, and his mom and dad, Sara Jo and Bud, are with us this evening. Welcome.

Our Nation is grateful to the fallen, who live in the memory of our country. We're grateful to all who volunteer to wear our Nation's uniform. And as we honor our brave troops, let us never forget the sacrifices of America's military families.

Our offensive against terror involves more than military action. Ultimately, the only way to defeat the terrorists is to defeat their dark vision of hatred and fear by offering the hopeful alternative of political freedom and peaceful change. So the United States of America supports democratic reform across the broader Middle East. Elections are vital, but they are only the beginning. Raising up a democracy requires the rule of law and protection of minorities and strong, accountable institutions that last longer than a single vote.

The great people of Egypt have voted in a multiparty Presidential election, and now their Government should open paths of peaceful opposition that will reduce the appeal of radicalism. The Palestinian people have voted in elections, and now the leaders of Hamas must recognize Israel, disarm, reject terrorism, and work for lasting peace. Saudi Arabia has taken the first steps of reform; now it can offer its people a better future by pressing forward with those efforts. Democracies in the Middle East will not look like our own because they will reflect the traditions of their own citizens. Yet liberty is the future of every nation in the Middle East because liberty is the right and hope of all humanity.

The same is true of Iran, a nation now held hostage by a small clerical elite that is isolating and repressing its people. The regime in that country sponsors terrorists in the Palestinian territories and in Lebanon, and that must come to an end. The Iranian Government is defying the world with its nuclear ambitions, and the nations of the world must not permit the Iranian regime to gain nuclear weapons. America will continue to rally the world to confront these threats.

Tonight let me speak directly to the citizens of Iran: America respects you, and we respect your country. We respect your right to choose your own future and win your own freedom. And our Nation hopes one day to be the closest of friends with a free and democratic Iran.

To overcome dangers in our world, we must also take the offensive by encouraging economic progress and fighting disease and spreading hope in hopeless lands. Isolationism would not only tie our hands in fighting enemies, it would keep us from helping our friends in desperate need. We show compassion abroad because Americans believe in the God-given dignity and worth of a villager with HIV/AIDS or an infant with malaria or a refugee fleeing genocide or a young girl sold into slavery. We also show compassion abroad because regions overwhelmed by poverty, corruption, and despair are sources of terrorism and organized crime and human trafficking and the drug trade.

In recent years, you and I have taken unprecedented action to fight AIDS and malaria, expand the education of girls, and reward developing nations that are moving forward with economic and political reform. For people everywhere, the United States is a partner for a better life. Shortchanging these efforts would increase the suffering and chaos of our world, undercut our long-term security, and dull the conscience of our country. I urge Members of Congress to serve the interests of America by showing the compassion of America.

Our country must also remain on the offensive against terrorism here at home. The enemy has not lost the desire or capability to attack us. Fortunately, this Nation has superb professionals in law enforcement, intelligence, the military, and homeland security. These men and women are dedicating their lives, protecting us all, and they deserve our support and our thanks. They also deserve the same tools they already use to fight drug trafficking and organized crime, so I ask you to reauthorize the PATRIOT Act.

It is said that prior to the attacks of September the 11th, our Government failed to connect the dots of the conspiracy. We now know that two of the hijackers in the United States placed telephone calls to Al Qaida operatives overseas. But we did not know about their plans until it was too late. So to prevent another attack—based on authority given to me by the Constitution and by statute—I have authorized a terrorist surveillance program to aggressively pursue the international communications of suspected Al Qaida operatives and affiliates to and from America. Previous Presidents have used the same constitutional authority I have, and Federal courts have approved the use of that authority. Appropriate Members of Congress have been kept informed. The terrorist surveillance program has helped prevent terrorist attacks. It remains essential to the security of America. If there are people inside our country who are talking with Al Qaida, we want to know about it, because we will not sit back and wait to be hit again.

In all these areas—from the disruption of terror networks, to victory in Iraq, to the spread of freedom and hope in troubled regions—we need the support of our friends and allies. To draw that support, we must always be clear in our principles and willing to act. The only alternative to American leadership is a dramatically more dangerous and anxious world. Yet we also choose to lead because it is a privilege to serve the values that gave us birth. American leaders—from Roosevelt to Truman to Kennedy to Reagan—rejected isolation and retreat, because they knew that America is always more secure when freedom is on the march.

Our own generation is in a long war against a determined enemy, a war that will be fought by Presidents of both parties, who will need steady bipartisan support from the Congress. And tonight I ask for yours. Together, let us protect our country, support the men and women who defend us, and lead this world toward freedom.

Here at home, America also has a great opportunity: We will build the prosperity of our country by strengthening our economic leadership in the world.

Our economy is healthy and vigorous and growing faster than other major industrialized nations. In the last 2½ years, America has created 4.6 million new jobs—more than Japan and the European Union combined. Even in the face of higher energy prices and natural disasters, the American people have turned in an economic performance that is the envy of the world.

The American economy is preeminent, but we cannot afford to be complacent. In a dynamic world economy, we are seeing new competitors like China and India, and this creates uncertainty, which makes it easier to feed people's fears. So we're seeing some old temptations return. Protectionists want to escape competition, pretending that we can keep our high standard of living while walling off our economy. Others say that the government needs to take a larger role in directing the economy, centralizing more power in Washington and increasing taxes. We hear claims that immigrants are somehow bad for the economy—even though this economy could not function without them. All these are forms of economic retreat, and they lead in the same direction, toward a stagnant and second-rate economy.

Tonight I will set out a better path: An agenda for a nation that competes with confidence; an agenda that will raise standards of living and generate new jobs. Americans should not fear our economic future because we intend to shape it.

Keeping America competitive begins with keeping our economy growing. And our economy grows when Americans have more of their own money to spend, save, and invest. In the last 5 years, the tax relief you passed has left $880 billion in the hands of American workers, investors, small businesses, and families. And they have used it to help produce more than 4 years of uninterrupted economic growth. Yet the tax relief is set to expire in the next few years. If we do nothing, American families will face a massive tax increase they do not expect and will not welcome. Because America needs more than a temporary expansion, we need more than temporary tax relief. I urge the Congress to act responsibly and make the tax cuts permanent.

Keeping America competitive requires us to be good stewards of tax dollars. Every year of my Presidency, we've reduced the growth of non-security discretionary spending, and last year you passed bills that cut this spending. This year my budget will cut it again, and reduce or eliminate more than 140 programs that are performing poorly or not fulfilling essential priorities. By passing these reforms, we will save the American taxpayer another $14 billion next year and stay on track to cut the deficit in half by 2009.

I am pleased that Members of Congress are working on earmark reform, because the Federal budget has too many special interest projects. And we can tackle this problem together, if you pass the line-item veto.

We must also confront the larger challenge of mandatory spending, or entitlements. This year, the first of about 78 million baby boomers turn 60, including two of my Dad's favorite people—me and President Clinton. This milestone is more than a personal crisis it is a national challenge. The retirement of the baby boom generation will put unprecedented strains on the Federal Government. By 2030, spending for Social Security, Medicare, and Medicaid alone will be almost 60 percent of the entire Federal budget. And that will present future Congresses with impossible choices—staggering tax increases, immense deficits, or deep cuts in every category of spending. Congress did not act last year on my proposal to save Social Security, yet the rising cost of entitlements is a problem that is not going away. And every year we fail to act, the situation gets worse.

So tonight I ask you to join me in creating a commission to examine the full impact of baby boom retirements on Social Security, Medicare, and Medicaid. This commission should include Members of Congress of both parties, and offer bipartisan solutions. We need to put aside partisan politics and work together and get this problem solved.

Keeping America competitive requires us to open more markets for all that Americans make and grow. One out of every five factory jobs in America is related to global trade, and we want people everywhere to buy American. With open markets and a level playing field, no one can outproduce or outcompete the American worker.

Keeping America competitive requires an immigration system that upholds our laws, reflects our values, and serves the interests of our economy. Our Nation needs orderly and secure borders. To meet this goal, we must have stronger immigration enforcement and border protection. And we must have a rational, humane guest worker program that rejects amnesty, allows temporary jobs for people who seek them legally, and reduces smuggling and crime at the border.

Keeping America competitive requires affordable health care. Our Government has a responsibility to provide health care for the poor and the elderly, and we are meeting that responsibility. For all Americans, we must confront the rising cost of care, strengthen the doctor-patient relationship, and help people afford the insurance coverage they need.

We will make wider use of electronic records and other health information technology, to help control costs and reduce dangerous medical errors. We will strengthen health savings accounts, making sure individuals and small-business employees can buy insurance with the same advantages that people working for big businesses now get. We will do more to make this coverage portable, so workers can switch jobs without having to worry about losing their health insurance. And because lawsuits are driving many good doctors out of practice, leaving women in nearly 1,500 American counties without a single ob-gyn, I ask the Congress to pass medical liability reform this year.

Keeping America competitive requires affordable energy. And here we have a serious problem: America is addicted to oil, which is often imported from unstable parts of the world. The best way to break this addiction is through technology. Since 2001, we have spent nearly $10 billion to develop cleaner, cheaper, and more reliable alternative energy sources. And we are on the threshold of incredible advances.

So tonight I announce the Advanced Energy Initiative—a 22-percent increase in clean-energy research—at the Department of Energy, to push for breakthroughs in two vital areas. To change how we power our homes and offices, we will invest more in zero-emission coal-fired plants, revolutionary solar and wind technologies, and clean, safe nuclear energy.

We must also change how we power our automobiles. We will increase our research in better batteries for hybrid and electric cars and in pollution-free cars that run on hydrogen. We'll also fund additional research in cutting-edge methods of producing ethanol, not just from corn but from wood chips and stalks or switch grass. Our goal is to make this new kind of ethanol practical and competitive within 6 years.

Breakthroughs on this and other new technologies will help us reach another great goal: To replace more than 75 percent of our oil imports from the Middle East by 2025. By applying the talent and technology of America, this country can dramatically improve our environment, move beyond a petroleum-based economy, and make our dependence on Middle Eastern oil a thing of the past.

And to keep America competitive, one commitment is necessary above all: We must continue to lead the world in human talent and creativity. Our greatest advantage in the world has always been our educated, hard-working, ambitious people. And we're going to keep that edge. Tonight I announce an American Competitiveness Initiative, to encourage innovation throughout our economy and to give our Nation's children a firm grounding in math and science.

First, I propose to double the Federal commitment to the most critical basic research programs in the physical sciences over the next 10 years. This funding will support the work of America's most creative minds as they explore promising areas such as nanotechnology, supercomputing, and alternative energy sources.

Second, I propose to make permanent the research and development tax credit to encourage bolder private-sector initiatives in technology. With more research in both the public and private sectors, we will improve our quality of life and ensure that America will lead the world in opportunity and innovation for decades to come.

Third, we need to encourage children to take more math and science, and to make sure those courses are rigorous enough to compete with other nations. We've made a good start in the early grades with the No Child Left Behind Act, which is raising standards and lifting test scores across our country. Tonight I propose to train 70,000 high school teachers to lead advanced-placement courses in math and science, bring 30,000 math and science professionals to teach in classrooms, and give early help to students who struggle with math, so they have a better chance at good, high-wage jobs.

If we ensure that America's children succeed in life, they will ensure that America succeeds in the world.

Preparing our Nation to compete in the world is a goal that all of us can share. I urge you to support the American Competitiveness Initiative, and together we will show the world what the American people can achieve.

America is a great force for freedom and prosperity. Yet our greatness is not measured in power or luxuries but by who we are and how we treat one another. So we strive to be a compassionate, decent, hopeful society.

In recent years, America has become a more hopeful nation. Violent crime rates have fallen to their lowest levels since the 1970s. Welfare cases have dropped by more than half over the past decade. Drug use among youth is down 19 percent since 2001. There are fewer abortions in America than at any point in the last three decades, and the number of children born to teenage mothers has been falling for a dozen years in a row.

These gains are evidence of a quiet transformation, a revolution of conscience, in which a rising generation is finding that a life of personal responsibility is a life of fulfillment. Government has played a role. Wise policies, such as welfare reform and drug education and support for abstinence and adoption have made a difference in the character of our country. And everyone here tonight, Democrat and Republican, has a right to be proud of this record.

Yet many Americans, especially parents, still have deep concerns about the direction of our culture and the health of our most basic institutions. They're concerned about unethical conduct by public officials and discouraged by activist courts that try to redefine marriage. They worry about children in our society who need direction and love, and about fellow citizens still displaced by natural disaster, and about suffering caused by treatable diseases.

As we look at these challenges, we must never give in to the belief that America is in decline or that our culture is doomed to unravel. The American people know better than that. We have proven the pessimists wrong before, and we will do it again.

A hopeful society depends on courts that deliver equal justice under the law. The Supreme Court now has two superb new members on its bench, Chief Justice John Roberts and Justice Sam Alito. I thank the Senate for confirming both of them. I will continue to nominate men and women who understand that judges must be servants of the law and not legislate from the bench.

Today marks the official retirement of a very special American. For 24 years of faithful service to our Nation, the United States is grateful to Justice Sandra Day O'Connor.

A hopeful society has institutions of science and medicine that do not cut ethical corners and that recognize the matchless value of every life. Tonight I ask you to pass legislation to prohibit the most egregious abuses of medical research: Human cloning in all its forms; creating or implanting embryos for experiments; creating human-animal hybrids; and buying, selling, or patenting human embryos. Human life is a gift from our Creator, and that gift should never be discarded, devalued, or put up for sale.

A hopeful society expects elected officials to uphold the public trust. Honorable people in both parties are working on reforms to strengthen the ethical standards of Washington. I support your efforts. Each of us has made a pledge to be worthy of public responsibility, and that is a pledge we must never forget, never dismiss, and never betray.

As we renew the promise of our institutions, let us also show the character of America in our compassion and care for one another.

A hopeful society gives special attention to children who lack direction and love. Through the Helping America's Youth Initiative, we are encouraging caring adults to get involved in the life of a child. And this good work is being led by our First Lady, Laura Bush. This year we will add resources to encourage young people to stay in school, so more of America's youth can raise their sights and achieve their dreams.

A hopeful society comes to the aid of fellow citizens in times of suffering and emergency, and stays at it until they're back on their feet. So far the Federal Government has committed $85 billion to the people of the gulf coast and New Orleans. We're removing debris and repairing highways and rebuilding stronger levees. We're providing business loans and housing assistance. Yet as we meet these immediate needs, we must also address deeper challenges that existed before the storm arrived.

In New Orleans and in other places, many of our fellow citizens have felt excluded from the promise of our country. The answer is not only temporary relief but schools that teach every child and job skills that bring upward mobility and more opportunities to own a home and start a business. As we recover from a disaster, let us also work for the day when all Americans are protected by justice, equal in hope, and rich in opportunity.

A hopeful society acts boldly to fight diseases like HIV/AIDS, which can be prevented and treated and defeated. More than a million Americans live with HIV, and half of all AIDS cases occur among African Americans. I ask Congress to reform and reauthorize the Ryan White Act and provide new funding to States, so we end the waiting lists for AIDS medicines in America. We will also lead a nationwide effort, working closely with African American churches and faith-based groups, to deliver rapid HIV tests to millions, end the stigma of AIDS, and come closer to the day when there are no new infections in America.

Fellow citizens, we've been called to leadership in a period of consequence. We've entered a great ideological conflict we did nothing to invite. We see great changes in science and commerce that will influence all our lives. Sometimes it can seem that history is turning in a wide arc toward an unknown shore. Yet the destination of history is determined by human action, and every great movement of history comes to a point of choosing.

Lincoln could have accepted peace at the cost of disunity and continued slavery. Martin Luther King could have stopped at Birmingham or at Selma and achieved only half a victory over segregation. The United States could have accepted the permanent division of Europe and been complicit in the oppression of others. Today, having come far in our own historical journey, we must decide: Will we turn back or finish well?

Before history is written down in books, it is written in courage. Like Americans before us, we will show that courage, and we will finish well. We will lead freedom's advance. We will compete and excel in the global economy. We will renew the defining moral commitments of this land. And so we move forward—optimistic about our country, faithful to its cause, and confident of the victories to come.

May God bless America.

Appendix

Woodrow Wilson's Address to a Joint Session of Congress on Tariff Reform

April 8, 1913

Woodrow Wilson's address to Congress on tariff reform should be viewed as the precursor to the modern State of the Union speech. Although this address was not one of Wilson's annual messages, his appearance at a joint session of Congress on April 8, 1913, along with an address on the banking system in June and on Mexican affairs in August, were instrumental in shattering the precedent set by Thomas Jefferson in 1801 that presidents should send written communications to Congress. According to Jefferson, a personal appearance by the president before a gathered Congress should be avoided, as it reckoned back to the "Speech from the Throne," where the British monarch reads a prepared speech to the assembled parliament. So, for 112 years no president formally addressed Congress in person.

Wilson's decision to ask Congress for an invitation to speak on tariff reform was not without controversy, as even some of his fellow Democrats serving in the Senate expressed reservations with the idea. Central to their concerns was the notion that Wilson, newly inaugurated, was attempting to shift the focus of public and media attention at the federal level from the Congress to the presidency—a tectonic change that created the potential for political demagoguery. Wilson, however, was not interested in fundamentally altering the necessary balance of power institutionalized by the Constitution. Instead, his object was to continue the transformation of the presidency started incrementally after the Civil War, then accelerating markedly under Theodore Roosevelt, from a sterile impersonal institution to what Wilson considered the office's rightful place as a dynamic actor in the American political stage. Rather than increase the president's constitutional powers, Wilson sought to enhance the chief executive's power to bargain within the legislative process.

Wilson, a reform-minded Democrat, had won the presidency in a three-way contest in 1912 that also featured incumbent Republican president William Howard Taft and former Republican president Theodore Roosevelt, who was running as a Progressive. Wilson was inaugurated as president on March 4, 1913.

Tariff reform was high on Wilson's "New Freedom" agenda, and in this April 8, 1913, speech he stated that he had brought Congress into "extraordinary session" in order to focus lawmakers' attention on the need to change the tariff laws. The Underwood Tariff Act, which resulted in tariffs' dropping to pre-Civil War levels, was approved during Wilson's first year as president.

M
r. Speaker, Mr. President, Gentlemen of the Congress:

I am very glad indeed to have this opportunity to address the two Houses directly and to verify for myself the impression that the President of the United States is a person, not a mere department of the Government hailing Congress from some isolated island of jealous power, sending messages, not speaking naturally and with his own voice—that he is a human being trying to cooperate with other human beings in a common service. After this pleasant experience I shall feel quite normal in all our dealings with one another.

I have called the Congress together in extraordinary session because a duty was laid upon the party now in power at the recent elections which it ought to perform promptly, in order that the burden carried by the people under existing law may be lightened as soon as possible and in order, also, that the business interests of the country may not be kept too long in suspense as to what the fiscal changes are to be to which they will be required to adjust themselves. It is clear to the whole country that the tariff duties must be altered. They must be changed to meet the radical alteration in the conditions of our economic life which the country has witnessed within the last generation. While the whole face and method of our industrial and commercial life were being changed beyond recognition the tariff schedules have remained what they were before the change began, or have moved in the direction they were given when no large circumstance of our industrial development was what it is to-day. Our task is to square them with the actual facts. The sooner that is done the sooner we shall escape from suffering from the facts and the sooner our men of business will be free to thrive by the law of nature (the nature of free business) instead of by the law of legislation and artificial arrangement.

We have seen tariff legislation wander very far afield in our day—very far indeed from the field in which our prosperity might have had a normal growth and stimulation. No one who looks the facts squarely in the face or knows anything that lies beneath the surface of action can fail to perceive the principles upon which recent tariff legislation has been based. We long ago passed beyond the modest notion of "protecting" the industries of the country and moved boldly forward to the idea that they were entitled to the direct patronage of the Government. For a long time—a time so long that the men now active in public policy hardly remember the conditions that preceded it—we have sought in our tariff schedules to give each group of manufacturers or producers what they themselves thought that they needed in order to maintain a practically exclusive market as against the rest of the world. Consciously or unconsciously, we have built up a set of privileges and exemptions from competition behind which it was easy by any, even the crudest, forms of combination to organize monopoly; until at last nothing is normal, nothing is obliged to stand the tests of efficiency and economy, in our world of big business, but everything thrives by concerted arrangement. Only new principles of action will save us from a final hard crystallization of monopoly and a complete loss of the influences that quicken enterprise and keep independent energy alive.

It is plain what those principles must be. We must abolish everything that bears even the semblance of privilege or of any kind of artificial advantage, and put our business men and producers under the stimulation of a constant necessity to be efficient, economical, and enterprising, masters of competitive supremacy, better workers and merchants than any in the world. Aside from the duties laid upon articles which we do not, and probably cannot, produce, therefore, and the duties laid upon luxuries and merely for the sake of the revenues they yield, the object of the tariff duties henceforth laid must be effective competition, the whetting of American wits by contest with the wits of the rest of the world.

It would be unwise to move toward this end headlong, with reckless haste, or with strokes that cut at the very roots of what has grown up amongst us by long process and at our own invitation. It does not alter a thing to upset it and break it and deprive it of a chance to change. It destroys it. We must make changes in our fiscal laws, in our fiscal system, whose object is development, a more free and wholesome development, not revolution or upset or confusion. We must build up trade, especially foreign trade. We need the outlet and the enlarged field of energy more than we ever did before. We must build up industry as well, and must adopt freedom in the place of artificial stimulation only so far as it will build, not pull down. In dealing with the tariff the method by which this may be done will be a matter of judgment, exercised item by item. To some not accustomed to the excitements and responsibilities of greater freedom our methods may in some respects and at some points seem heroic, but remedies may be heroic and yet be remedies. It is our business to make sure that they are genuine remedies. Our object is clear. If our motive is above just challenge and only an occasional error of judgment is chargeable against us, we shall be fortunate.

We are called upon to render the country a great service in more matters than one. Our responsibility should be met and our methods should be thorough, as thorough as moderate and well considered, based upon the facts as they are, and not worked out as if we were beginners. We are to deal with the facts of our own day, with the facts of no other, and to make laws which square with those facts. It is best, indeed it is necessary, to begin with the tariff. I will urge nothing upon you now at the opening of your session which can obscure that first object or divert our energies from that clearly defined duty. At a later time I may take the liberty of calling your attention to reforms which should press close upon the heels of the tariff changes, if not accompany them, of which the chief is the reform of our banking and currency laws; but just now I refrain. For the present, I put these matters on one side and think only of this one thing—of the changes in our fiscal system which may best serve to open once more the free channels of prosperity to a great people whom we would serve to the utmost and throughout both rank and file.

I thank you for your courtesy.

Franklin D. Roosevelt's Inaugural Address

March 4, 1933

Franklin D. Roosevelt's first inaugural address, delivered to a Depression-weary nation, became one of the most famous American political speeches. His phrase—"the only thing we have to fear is fear itself"—resonated strongly with the public.

Roosevelt scored a landslide victory in November 1932 over incumbent Republican president Herbert Hoover. Plagued by the ongoing Great Depression, which he approached in a cautious manner, Hoover had become deeply unpopular. In the election, Roosevelt, whose outgoing, debonair personality contrasted sharply with that of the more withdrawn Hoover, won 57.4 percent of the popular vote and 472 of 531 electoral votes.

In this address, Roosevelt urged quick action to combat the nation's economic woes, which included a banking crisis that was paralyzing the country. He lashed out at "money changers," stating that they had "fled from their high seats in the temple of our civilization." He added: "This nation asks for action, and action now."

The new president, a distant cousin of former president Theodore Roosevelt, opted to treat the difficult economic situation as if it were a war and he a wartime president. He announced that he would present Congress, in special session, with "detailed measures" to act upon, and asked for "broad Executive power." While he did not spell out many specifics in this address, FDR definitely followed through. The "First Hundred Days" of his administration are viewed as the most productive period of legislation ever at the start of a presidential term.

Just five days after Roosevelt's inauguration, Congress—now also controlled by Democrats—passed his Emergency Banking bill, which was designed to address the banking crisis. During those first hundred days, other major pieces of legislation were passed, including the Agricultural Adjustment Act, which set out a national agricultural plan, the National Industrial Recovery Act, and the Tennessee Valley Authority Act.

This inaugural address marked the start of the New Deal and the Roosevelt era in American politics—and a presidency unlike any other. His time in the White House would last through the Depression of the 1930s, as well as the first half of the 1940s—which was dominated by the horrors of World War II—and would encompass a sea-change in the power of the presidency. Ultimately, Roosevelt would win four terms as president and would die just after the start of the fourth, in 1945.

I am certain that my fellow Americans expect that on my induction into the Presidency I will address them with a candor and a decision which the present situation of our Nation impels. This is preeminently the time to speak the truth, the whole truth, frankly and boldly. Nor need we shrink from honestly facing conditions in our country today. This great Nation will endure as it has endured, will revive and will prosper. So, first of all, let me assert my firm belief that the only thing we have to fear is fear itself—nameless, unreasoning, unjustified terror which paralyzes needed efforts to convert retreat into advance. In every dark hour of our national life a leadership of frankness and vigor has met with that understanding and support of the people themselves which is essential to victory. I am convinced that you will again give that support to leadership in these critical days.

In such a spirit on my part and on yours we face our common difficulties. They concern, thank God, only material things. Values have shrunken to fantastic levels; taxes have risen; our ability to pay has fallen; government of all kinds is faced by serious curtailment of income; the means of exchange are frozen in the currents of trade; the withered leaves of industrial enterprise lie on every side; farmers find no markets for their produce; the savings of many years in thousands of families are gone.

More important, a host of unemployed citizens face the grim problem of existence, and an equally great number toil with little return. Only a foolish optimist can deny the dark realities of the moment.

Yet our distress comes from no failure of substance. We are stricken by no plague of locusts. Compared with the perils which our forefathers conquered because they believed and were not afraid, we have still much to be thankful for. Nature still offers her bounty and human efforts have multiplied it. Plenty is at our doorstep, but a generous use of it languishes in the very sight of the supply. Primarily this is because rulers of the exchange of mankind's goods have failed through their own stubbornness and their own incompetence, have admitted their failure, and have abdicated. Practices of the unscrupulous money changers stand indicted in the court of public opinion, rejected by the hearts and minds of men.

True they have tried, but their efforts have been cast in the pattern of an outworn tradition. Faced by failure of credit they have proposed only the lending of more money. Stripped of the lure of profit by which to induce our people to follow their false leadership, they have resorted to exhortations, pleading tearfully for restored confidence. They know only the rules of a generation of self-seekers. They have no vision, and when there is no vision the people perish.

The money changers have fled from their high seats in the temple of our civilization. We may now restore that temple to the ancient truths. The measure of the restoration lies in the extent to which we apply social values more noble than mere monetary profit.

Happiness lies not in the mere possession of money; it lies in the joy of achievement, in the thrill of creative effort. The joy and moral stimulation of work no longer must be forgotten in the mad chase of evanescent profits. These dark days will be worth all they cost us if they teach us that our true destiny is not to be ministered unto but to minister to ourselves and to our fellow men.

Recognition of the falsity of material wealth as the standard of success goes hand in hand with the abandonment of the false belief that public office and high political position are to be valued only by the standards of pride of place and personal profit; and there must be an end to a conduct in banking and in business which too often has given to a sacred trust the likeness of callous and selfish wrongdoing. Small wonder that confidence languishes, for it thrives only on honesty, on honor, on the sacredness of obligations, on faithful protection, on unselfish performance; without them it cannot live. Restoration calls, however, not for changes in ethics alone. This Nation asks for action, and action now.

Our greatest primary task is to put people to work. This is no unsolvable problem if we face it wisely and courageously. It can be accomplished in part by direct recruiting by the Government itself, treating the task as we would treat the emergency of a war, but at the same time, through this employment, accomplishing greatly needed projects to stimulate and reorganize the use of our natural resources.

Hand in hand with this we must frankly recognize the overbalance of population in our industrial centers and, by engaging on a national scale in a redistribution, endeavor to provide a better use of the land for those best fitted for the land. The task can be helped by definite efforts to raise the values of agricultural products and with this the power to purchase the output of our cities. It can be helped by preventing realistically the tragedy of the growing loss through foreclosure of our small homes and our farms. It can be helped by insistence that the Federal, State, and local governments act forthwith on the demand that their cost be drastically reduced. It can be helped by the unifying of relief activities which today are often scattered, uneconomical, and unequal. It can be helped by national planning for and supervision of all forms of transportation and of communications and other utilities which have a definitely public character. There are many ways in which it can be helped, but it can never be helped merely by talking about it. We must act and act quickly.

Finally, in our progress toward a resumption of work we require two safeguards against a return of the evils of the old order: there must be a strict supervision of all banking and credits and investments, so that there will be an end to speculation with other people's money; and there must be provision for an adequate but sound currency.

These are the lines of attack. I shall presently urge upon a new Congress, in special session, detailed measures for their fulfillment, and I shall seek the immediate assistance of the several States.

Through this program of action we address ourselves to putting our own national house in order and making income balance outgo. Our international trade relations, though vastly important, are in point of time and necessity secondary to the establishment of a sound national economy. I favor as a practical policy the putting of first things first. I shall spare no effort to restore world trade by international economic readjustment, but the emergency at home cannot wait on that accomplishment.

The basic thought that guides these specific means of national recovery is not narrowly nationalistic. It is the insistence, as a first considerations, upon the interdependence of the various elements in and parts of the United States—a recognition of the old and permanently important manifestation of the American spirit of the pioneer. It is the way to recovery. It is the immediate way. It is the strongest assurance that the recovery will endure.

In the field of world policy I would dedicate this Nation to the policy of the good neighbor—the neighbor who resolutely respects himself and, because he does so, respects the rights of others—the neighbor who respects his obligations and respects the sanctity of his agreements in and with a world of neighbors.

If I read the temper of our people correctly, we now realize as we have never realized before our interdependence on each other; that we cannot merely take but we must give as well; that if we are to go forward, we must move as a trained and loyal army willing to sacrifice for the good of a common discipline, because without such discipline no progress is made, no leadership becomes effective. We are, I know, ready and willing to submit our lives and property to such discipline, because it makes possible a leadership which aims at a larger good. This I propose to offer, pledging that the larger purposes will bind upon us all as a sacred obligation with a unity of duty hitherto evoked only in time of armed strife.

With this pledge taken, I assume unhesitatingly the leadership of this great army of our people dedicated to a disciplined attack upon our common problems.

Action in this image and to this end is feasible under the form of government which we have inherited from our ancestors. Our Constitution is so simple and practical that it is possible always to meet extraordinary needs by changes in emphasis and arrangement without loss of essential form. That is why our constitutional system has proved itself the most superbly enduring political mechanism the modern world has produced. It has met every stress of vast expansion of territory, of foreign wars, of bitter internal strife, of world relations.

It is to be hoped that the normal balance of Executive and legislative authority may be wholly adequate to meet the unprecedented task before us. But it may be that an unprecedented demand and need for undelayed action may call for temporary departure from that normal balance of public procedure.

I am prepared under my constitutional duty to recommend the measures that a stricken Nation in the midst of a stricken world may require. These measures, or such other measures as the Congress may build out of its experience and wisdom, I shall seek, within my constitutional authority, to bring to speedy adoption.

But in the event that the Congress shall fail to take one of these two courses, and in the event that the national emergency is still critical, I shall not evade the clear course of duty that will then confront me. I shall ask the Congress for the one remaining instrument to meet the crisis—broad Executive power to wage a war against the emergency, as great as the power that would be given to me if we were in fact invaded by a foreign foe.

For the trust reposed in me I will return the courage and the devotion that befit the time. I can do no less.

We face the arduous days that lie before us in the warm courage of national unity; with the clear consciousness of seeking old and precious moral values; with the clean satisfaction that comes from the stern performance of duty by old and young alike. We aim at the assurance of a rounded and permanent national life.

We do not distrust the future of essential democracy. The people of the United States have not failed. In their need they have registered a mandate that they want direct, vigorous action. They have asked for discipline and direction under leadership. They have made me the present instrument of their wishes. In the spirit of the gift I take it.

In this dedication of a Nation we humbly ask the blessing of God. May He protect each and every one of us. May He guide me in the days to come.

Ronald Reagan's Inaugural Address
January 20, 1981

Ronald Reagan's inauguration was historic not only because of the political realignment it represented, but also because the Americans held hostage in Iran since November 1979 were released immediately after he took the oath of office.

Reagan, a conservative Republican who had served as governor of California and been a movie actor, defeated Democratic incumbent Jimmy Carter in the November 1980 presidential election. Reagan scored a landslide victory, taking 489 electoral votes to Carter's 49; he won 51 percent of the popular vote to Carter's 41 percent and independent candidate John Anderson's 7 percent. The Republicans also took control of the Senate and cut into the Democrats' majority in the House.

Reagan's presidency marked the start of a conservative era in government. The new president favored lower taxes and a shrunken role for the federal government, as well as a tough foreign policy toward the Soviet Union and its communist allies. Reagan became a towering force in U.S. and international politics, and his inaugural address showed the stark contrast between his ideals and the activist role of the federal government started under Franklin Roosevelt's New Deal, which Reagan sought to reverse.

In his twenty-minute inaugural address, Reagan made his views of government clear, stating that the country was in the midst of an economic crisis that had been in the making for decades. "In this present crisis, government is not the solution to our problem; government is the problem," he declared. He spoke of reversing the growth of government and of curbing its influence—although he said he did not want to "do away" with it. He said he wanted to restore the "balance" between the different levels of government, reminding the nation that "the Federal Government did not create the States; the States created the Federal Government."

To personify his philosophy that the common man was the engine of American greatness and resolve, Reagan spoke of heroes, saying that such people were around if you knew where to look for them: factory workers, entrepreneurs, and patriots. He quoted from a diary kept by Martin Treptow, a soldier killed in World War I; the young man had pledged to do his utmost during his service in the war.

Meanwhile, the two planes bearing the American hostages, who had been held by Iranian militants, remained on the runway in Tehran until Reagan had become president, at which point they took off. Carter had hoped to deliver the news of their release; negotiations that led to their freedom had concluded that morning.

Reagan's inaugural marked the first time a president took the oath on the West Front of the Capitol. At nearly seventy, Reagan became the country's oldest president to be inaugurated. His vice president was George H.W. Bush, who would himself become president after Reagan's eight years in office.

Senator Hatfield, Mr. Chief Justice, Mr. President, Vice President Bush, Vice President Mondale, Senator Baker, Speaker O'Neill, Reverend Moomaw, and my fellow citizens:

To a few of us here today this is a solemn and most momentous occasion, and yet in the history of our nation it is a commonplace occurrence. The orderly transfer of authority as called for in the Constitution routinely takes place, as it has for almost two centuries, and few of us stop to think how unique we really are. In the eyes of many in the world, this every 4-year ceremony we accept as normal is nothing less than a miracle.

Mr. President, I want our fellow citizens to know how much you did to carry on this tradition. By your gracious cooperation in the transition process, you have shown a watching world that we are a united people pledged to maintaining a political system which guarantees individual liberty to a greater degree than any other, and I thank you and your people for all your help in maintaining the continuity which is the bulwark of our Republic.

The business of our nation goes forward. These United States are confronted with an economic affliction of great proportions. We suffer from the longest and one of the worst sustained inflations in our national history. It distorts our economic decisions, penalizes thrift, and crushes the struggling young and the fixed-income elderly alike. It threatens to shatter the lives of millions of our people.

Idle industries have cast workers into unemployment, human misery, and personal indignity. Those who do work are denied a fair return for their labor by a tax system which penalizes successful achievement and keeps us from maintaining full productivity.

But great as our tax burden is, it has not kept pace with public spending. For decades we have piled deficit upon deficit, mortgaging our future and our children's future for the temporary convenience of the present. To continue this long trend is to guarantee tremendous social, cultural, political, and economic upheavals.

You and I, as individuals, can, by borrowing, live beyond our means, but for only a limited period of time. Why, then, should we think that collectively, as a nation, we're not bound by that same limitation? We must act today in order to preserve tomorrow. And let there be no misunderstanding: We are going to begin to act, beginning today.

The economic ills we suffer have come upon us over several decades. They will not go away in days, weeks, or months, but they will go away. They will go away because we as Americans have the capacity now, as we've had in the past, to do whatever needs to be done to preserve this last and greatest bastion of freedom.

In this present crisis, government is not the solution to our problem; government is the problem. From time to time we've been tempted to believe that society has become too complex to be managed by self-rule, that government by an elite group is superior to government for, by, and of the people. Well, if no one among us is capable of governing himself, then who among us has the capacity to govern someone else? All of us together, in and out of government, must bear the burden. The solutions we seek must be equitable, with no one group singled out to pay a higher price.

We hear much of special interest groups. Well, our concern must be for a special interest group that has been too long neglected. It knows no sectional boundaries or ethnic and racial divisions, and it crosses political party lines. It is made up of men and women who raise our food, patrol our streets, man our mines and factories, teach our children, keep our homes, and heal us when we're sick—professionals, industrialists, shopkeepers, clerks, tabbies, and truck drivers. They are, in short, "We the people," this breed called Americans.

Well, this administration's objective will be a healthy, vigorous, growing economy that provides equal opportunities for all Americans, with no barriers born of bigotry or discrimination. Putting America back to work means putting all Americans back to work. Ending inflation means freeing all Americans from the terror of runaway living costs. All must share in the productive work of this "new beginning," and all must share in the bounty of a revived economy. With the idealism and fair play which are the core of our system and our strength, we can have a strong and prosperous America, at peace with itself and the world.

So, as we begin, let us take inventory. We are a nation that has a government—not the other way around. And this makes us special among the nations of the Earth. Our government has no power except that granted it by the people. It is time to check and reverse the growth of government, which shows signs of having grown beyond the consent of the governed.

It is my intention to curb the size and influence of the Federal establishment and to demand recognition of the distinction between the powers granted to the Federal Government and those reserved to the States or to the people. All of us need to be reminded that the Federal Government did not create the States; the States created the Federal Government.

Now, so there will be no misunderstanding, it's not my intention to do away with government. It is rather to make it work-work with us, not over us; to stand by our side, not ride on our back. Government can and must provide opportunity, not smother it; foster productivity, not stifle it.

If we look to the answer as to why for so many years we achieved so much, prospered as no other people on Earth, it was because here in this land we unleashed the energy and individual genius of man to a greater extent than has ever been done before. Freedom and the dignity of the individual have been more available and assured here than in any other place on Earth. The price for this freedom at times has been high, but we have never been unwilling to pay that price.

It is no coincidence that our present troubles parallel and are proportionate to the intervention and intrusion in our lives that result from unnecessary and excessive growth of government. It is time for us to realize that we're too great a nation to limit ourselves to small dreams. We're not, as some would have us believe, doomed to an inevitable decline. I do not believe in a fate that will fall on us no matter what we do. I do believe in a fate that will fall on us if we do nothing. So, with all the creative energy at our command, let us begin an era of national renewal. Let us renew our determination, our courage, and our strength. And let us renew our faith and our hope.

We have every right to dream heroic dreams. Those who say that we're in a time when there are not heroes, they just don't know where to look. You can see heroes every day going in and out of factory gates. Others, a handful in number, produce enough food to feed all of us and then the world beyond. You meet heroes across a counter, and they're on both sides of that counter. There are entrepreneurs with faith in themselves and faith in an idea who create new jobs, new wealth and opportunity. They're individuals and families whose taxes support the government and whose voluntary gifts support church, charity, culture, art, and education. Their patriotism is quiet, but deep. Their values sustain our national life.

Now, I have used the words "they" and "their" in speaking of these heroes. I could say "you" and "your," because I'm addressing the heroes of whom I speak—you, the citizens of this blessed land. Your dreams, your hopes, your goals are going to be the dreams, the hopes, and the goals of this administration, so help me God.

We shall reflect the compassion that is so much a part of your makeup. How can we love our country and not love our countrymen; and loving them, reach out a hand when they fall, heal them when they're sick, and provide opportunity to make them self-sufficient so they will be equal in fact and not just in theory?

Can we solve the problems confronting us? Well, the answer is an unequivocal and emphatic "yes." To paraphrase Winston Churchill, I did not take the oath I've just taken with the intention of presiding over the dissolution of the world's strongest economy.

In the days ahead I will propose removing the roadblocks that have slowed our economy and reduced productivity. Steps will be taken aimed at restoring the balance between the various levels of government. Progress may be slow, measured in inches and feet, not miles, but we will progress. It is time to reawaken this industrial giant, to get government back within its means, and to lighten our punitive tax burden. And these will be our first priorities, and on these principles there will be no compromise.

On the eve of our struggle for independence a man who might have been one of the greatest among the Founding Fathers, Dr. Joseph Warren, president of the Massachusetts Congress, said to his fellow Americans, "Our country is in danger, but not to be despaired of. . . . On you depend the fortunes of America. You are to decide the important questions upon which rests the happiness and the liberty of millions yet unborn. Act worthy of yourselves."

Well, I believe we, the Americans of today, are ready to act worthy of ourselves, ready to do what must be done to ensure happiness and liberty for ourselves, our children, and our children's children. And as we renew ourselves here in our own land, we will be seen as having greater strength throughout the world. We will again be the exemplar of freedom and a beacon of hope for those who do not now have freedom.

To those neighbors and allies who share our freedom, we will strengthen our historic ties and assure them of our support and firm commitment. We will match loyalty with loyalty. We will strive for mutually beneficial relations. We will not use our friendship to impose on their sovereignty, for our own sovereignty is not for sale.

As for the enemies of freedom, those who are potential adversaries, they will be reminded that peace is the highest aspiration of the American people. We will negotiate for it, sacrifice for it; we will not surrender for it, now or ever.

Our forbearance should never be misunderstood. Our reluctance for conflict should not be misjudged as a failure of will. When action is required to preserve our national security, we will act. We will maintain sufficient strength to prevail if need be, knowing that if we do so we have the best chance of never having to use that strength.

Above all, we must realize that no arsenal or no weapon in the arsenals of the world is so formidable as the will and moral courage of free men and women. It is a weapon our adversaries in today's world do not have. It is a weapon that we as Americans do have. Let that be understood by those who practice terrorism and prey upon their neighbors.

I'm told that tens of thousands of prayer meetings are being held on this day, and for that I'm deeply grateful. We are a nation under God, and I believe God intended for us to be free. It would be fitting and good, I think, if on each Inaugural Day in future years it should be declared a day of prayer.

This is the first time in our history that this ceremony has been held, as you've been told, on this West Front of the Capitol. Standing here, one faces a magnificent vista, opening up on this city's special beauty and history. At the end of this open mall are those shrines to the giants on whose shoulders we stand.

Directly in front of me, the monument to a monumental man, George Washington, father of our country. A man of humility who came to greatness reluctantly. He led America out of revolutionary victory into infant nationhood. Off to one side, the stately memorial to Thomas Jefferson. The Declaration of Independence flames with his eloquence. And then, beyond the Reflecting Pool, the dignified columns of the Lincoln Memorial. Whoever would understand in his heart the meaning of America will find it in the life of Abraham Lincoln.

Beyond those monuments to heroism is the Potomac River, and on the far shore the sloping hills of Arlington National Cemetery, with its row upon row of simple white markers bearing crosses or Stars of David. They add up to only a tiny fraction of the price that has been paid for our freedom.

Each one of those markers is a monument to the kind of hero I spoke of earlier. Their lives ended in places called Belleau Wood, The Argonne, Omaha Beach, Salerno, and halfway around the world on Guadalcanal, Tarawa, Pork Chop Hill, the Chosin Reservoir, and in a hundred rice paddies and jungles of a place called Vietnam.

Under one such marker lies a young man, Martin Treptow, who left his job in a small town barbershop in 1917 to go to France with the famed Rainbow Division. There, on the western front, he was killed trying to carry a message between battalions under heavy artillery fire.

We're told that on his body was found a diary. On the flyleaf under the heading, "My Pledge," he had written these words: "America must win this war. Therefore I will work, I will save, I will sacrifice, I will endure, I will fight cheerfully and do my utmost, as if the issue of the whole struggle depended on me alone."

The crisis we are facing today does not require of us the kind of sacrifice that Martin Treptow and so many thousands of others were called upon to make. It does require, however, our best effort and our willingness to believe in ourselves and to believe in our capacity to perform great deeds, to believe that together with God's help we can and will resolve the problems which now confront us.

And after all, why shouldn't we believe that? We are Americans.

God bless you, and thank you.

Opposition Responses to
State of the Union Speeches, 1966–2006

Beginning in 1966, television networks have provided free airtime for the party out of the White House to respond to the State of the Union speech. The following list gives the names of all those who have given opposition responses.

A recurring practice has been for the response to be given by those in congressional leadership positions—typically Senate majority and minority leaders, Speakers of the House, and House minority leaders. As a measure of respect for outgoing presidents, opposition responses have not been given to speeches delivered by presidents in their last year in office. The last three presidents—George H.W. Bush, Bill Clinton, and George W. Bush—have delivered speeches before joint sessions of Congress following their first inaugurals. While these have not technically been considered State of the Union addresses, they have functioned in much the same way and the opposition party has chosen to deliver a response in two of the three instances, declining only in George W. Bush's 2001 address.

President and Date of Address	Oppostition Party	Response
Lyndon B. Johnson:		
January 12, 1966	Republican	Sen. Everett Dirksen (Ill.) and Rep. Gerald Ford (Mich.)
January 10, 1967	Republican	Sen. Everett Dirksen (Ill.) and Rep. Gerald Ford (Mich.)
January 17, 1968	Republican	Rep. William Steiger (Wis.), Sen. Thomas Kuchel (Calif.), Rep. Gerald Ford (Mich.), Sen. Charles Percy (Ill.), Rep. Richard Poff (Va.), Rep. George Bush (Texas), Rep. Robert Mathias (Calif.), Sen. Howard Baker (Tenn.), Sen. Hugh Scott (Pa.), Sen. John Tower (Texas), Rep. Charlotte Reid (Ill.), Sen. Peter Dominick (Colo.), Rep. Albert Quie (Minn.), Rep. Melvin Laird (Wis.), Sen. Robert P. Griffin (Mich.), and Sen. George Murphy (Calif.).
January 14, 1969	Republican	No response
Richard M. Nixon:		
January 22, 1970	Democrat	Sen. William Proxmire (Wis.), Rep. Donald Fraser (Minn.), Sen. Mike Mansfield (Mont.), Sen. Henry "Scoop" Jackson (Wash.), Sen. Edmund Muskie (Maine), Rep. Patsy Mink (Hawaii), and Rep. John McCormack (Mass.).
January 22, 1971	Democrat	Sen. Mike Mansfield (Mont.)
January 20, 1972	Democrat	Sens. William Proxmire (Wis.), Frank Church (Idaho), Thomas Eagleton (Mo.), Lloyd Bentsen (Texas); Reps. Leonor Sullivan (Mo.), John Melcher (Mont.), John Brademas (Ind.), Martha Griffiths (Mich.), Ralph Metcalfe (Ill.), Carl Albert (Okla.), and Hale Boggs (La.).
February 2, 1973	Democrat	No response
January 30, 1974	Democrat	Sen. Mike Mansfield (Mont.)

President and Date of Address	Opposition Party	Response
Gerald R. Ford:		
January 15, 1975	Democrat	Sen. Hubert Humphrey (Minn.) and Rep. Carl Albert (Okla.)
January 19, 1976	Democrat	Sen. Edmund Muskie (Maine)
January 12, 1977		No response
Jimmy Carter:		
January 19, 1978	Republican	Sen. Howard Baker Jr. (Tenn.) and Rep. John Rhodes (Ariz.)
January 25, 1979	Republican	Sen. Howard Baker Jr. (Tenn.) and Rep. John Rhodes (Ariz.)
January 19, 1980	Republican	Sen. Ted Stevens (Ark.) and Rep. John Rhodes (Ariz.)
January 19, 1981		No response
Ronald Reagan:		
January 26, 1982	Democrat	Sen. Donald Riegle (Mich.), Sen. James Sasser (Tenn.), Rep. Albert Gore Jr. (Tenn.), Sen. Robert Byrd (W.Va.), Sen. Edward Kennedy (Mass.), Rep. Thomas P. O'Neill (Mass.), Sen. Gary Hart (Colo.), Sen. Paul Sarbanes (Md.), Sen. J. Bennett Johnston (La.), and Sen. Alan Cranston (Calif.).
January 25, 1983	Democrat	Sens. Robert Byrd (W.Va.), Paul Tsongas (Mass.), Bill Bradley (N.J.), Joe Biden (Dele.); Reps. Tom Daschle (S.D.), Barbara Kennelly (Conn.), Thomas P. O'Neill (Mass.), George Miller (Calif.), Les AuCoin (Ore.), Paul Simon (Ill.), Timothy Wirth (Colo.), and W.G. "Bill" Hefner (N.C.).
January 25, 1984	Democrat	Sens. Joe Biden (Dele.), David Boren (Okla.), Carl M. Levin (Mich.), Max S. Baucus (Mont.), Robert Byrd (W.Va.), Clairborne Pell (R.I.), Walter Huddleston (Ky.); Reps. Dante B. Fascell (Fla.), Tom Harkin (Iowa), William Gray (Pa.), Thomas P. O'Neill (Mass.), and Barbara Boxer (Calif.).
February 6, 1985	Democrat	Govs. Bill Clinton (Ark.), Bob Graham (Fla.); Rep. Thomas P. O'Neill (Mass.).
February 4, 1986	Democrat	Sen. George Mitchell (Maine), Lt. Gov. Harriett Woods (Mo.), Gov. Charles Robb (Va.), Reps. Thomas Daschle (S.D.) and William Gray (Pa.)
January 27, 1987	Democrat	Sen. Robert Byrd (W.Va.) and Rep. Jim Wright (Texas)
January 25, 1988	Democrat	Sen. Robert Byrd (W.Va.) and Rep. Jim Wright (Texas)
George H.W. Bush:		
February 9, 1989	Democrat	Rep. Jim Wright (Texas) and Sen. Lloyd Bentsen (Texas)
January 31, 1990	Democrat	Rep. Tom Foley (Wash.)
January 29, 1991	Democrat	Sen. George Mitchell (Maine)
January 28, 1992	Democrat	Rep. Tom Foley (Wash.)

President and Date of Address	Opposition Party	Response
William J. Clinton:		
February 17, 1993	Republican	Rep. Bob Michel (R-Ill.)
January 25, 1994	Republican	Sen. Robert Dole (Kan.)
January 24, 1995	Republican	Gov. Christine Todd Whitman (N.J.)
January 23, 1996	Republican	Sen. Robert Dole (Kan.)
February 4, 1997	Republican	Rep. J.C. Watts (Okla.)
January 27, 1998	Republican	Sen. Trent Lott (Miss.)
January 19, 1999	Republican	Reps. Jennifer Dunn (Wash.) and Steven Largent (Okla.)
January 27, 2000	Republican	Sens. Susan Collins (Maine) and William Frist (Tenn.)
George W. Bush:		
February 27, 2001		No response
January 29, 2002	Democrat	Rep. Richard Gephardt (Mo.)
January 28, 2003	Democrat	Gov. Gary Lock (Wash.)
January 20, 2004	Democrat	Sen. Tom Daschle (S.D.) and Rep. Nancy Pelosi (Calif.)
February 2, 2005	Democrat	Rep. Nancy Pelosi (Calif.) and Sen. Harry Reid (NV)
January 31, 2006	Democrat	Gov. Timothy Kaine (Va.)

State of the Union
Gallery Visitors, 1982–2006

Presidents starting with Ronald Reagan in 1982 have frequently invited guests to sit in the House gallery during the State of the Union address, often next to the First Lady. The following is a list of all gallery visitors to State of the Union addresses and a brief description of each guest.

President and Date of Address	Visitor	Additional Details
Ronald Reagan:		
January 26, 1982	Lenny Skutnik	Federal government employee who rescued a passenger from the Potomac River after the crash of Air Florida Flight 90 on January 13, 1982, in Washington, D.C.
January 25, 1983	None	
January 25, 1984	Sgt. Stephen Trujillo	U.S. Army sergeant who participated in the U.S. invasion of Grenada
February 6, 1985	Jean Nguyen	Vietnamese immigrant and West Point cadet
	Clara Hale	Harlem, N.Y., woman who cared for infants born to heroin-addicted mothers
February 4, 1986	Richard Cavoli	Private citizen who designed a science experiment in high school that was lost during the explosion of the space shuttle Challenger
	Tyrone Ford	Twelve-year old gospel music prodigy from Washington, D.C.
	Shelby Butler	Thirteen-year old school safety patrol
	Trevor Ferrell	Thirteen-year old advocate for the homeless from Philadelphia
January 27, 1987	None	
January 25, 1988	Nancy Reagan	First Lady, in recognition of her antidrug efforts
George H.W. Bush:		
February 9, 1989	None	
January 31, 1990	Booth Gardner	Former governor (D-Wash.), who worked with the president in setting national education goals
	Bill Clinton	Governor (D-Ark.), who worked with the president in setting national education goals
	Terry Branstad	Governor (R-Iowa), who worked with the president in setting national education goals
	Carroll Campbell	Governor (R-S.C.), who worked with the president in setting national education goals
January 29, 1991	Brenda Schwarzkopf	Wife of Gen. Norman Schwarzkopf, representing the families of soldiers serving in the Persian Gulf
	Alma Powell	Wife of Colin Powell, chairman of the Joint Chiefs of Staff, representing the families of soldiers serving in the Persian Gulf
January 28, 1992	None	

President and Date of Address	Visitor	Additional Details
William J. Clinton:		
February 17, 1993	None	
January 25, 1994	Jim Brady	Former press secretary wounded in the 1981 assassination attempt on President Reagan
	Kevin Jett	New York City police officer
January 24, 1995	Cindy Perry	Kentucky teacher in the AmeriCorps Program
	Stephen Bishop	Police chief, Kansas City, Mo., active in community policing
	Cpl. Gregory Depestre	Haitian native and American citizen who participated in U.S. intervention in Haiti
	Rev. John Cherry	Cofounder of the AME Zion Church in Temple Hills, Md.
	Rev. Diana Cherry	Cofounder of the AME Zion Church in Temple Hills, Md.
	Jack Lucas	Congressional Medal of Honor recipient from Hattiesburg, Miss.
January 23, 1996	Gen. Barry McCaffrey	Nominee to become director of the Office of National Drug Control Policy
	Richard Dean	Social Security Administration employee who rescued three coworkers from the Alfred P. Murrah Federal Building following the Oklahoma City bombing on April 19, 1995
	Lucius Wright	Teacher and anti-gang activist from Jackson, Mississippi
	Sgt. Jennifer Rodgers	Sergeant, Oklahoma City Police Department, and one of the first responders to the scene of the bombing of the Alfred P. Murrah Federal Building on April 19, 1995
February 4, 1997	Kristen Tanner	Illinois student who garnered award in the Third International Math and Science Study
	Chris Getsler	Illinois student who garnered award in the Third International Math and Science Study
	Sue Winski	Illinois teacher of students Kristen Tanner and Chris Getsler
	Dr. Kristen Zarfos	Connecticut surgeon
	Lillie Tejeda	Mother of Rep. Frank Tejeda, D-Texas, who was buried the day before the address
	Mary Alice [Tejeda]	Sister of Rep. Frank Tejeda, D-Texas, who was buried the day before the address
	Gary Locke	Governor (D-Wash.), who was the first Chinese-American state governor
January 27, 1998	Elaine Kinslow	Private citizen from Indianapolis, Ind., who exemplified the president's goals of reducing the number of Americans dependent on welfare
	Sgt. Michael Tolbert	U.S. Army sergeant who participated in U.S. operations in Bosnia

President and Date of Address	Visitor	Additional Details
January 19, 1999	Lyn Gibson	Widow of Capitol police officer killed during a shooting rampage at the U.S. Capitol
	Wenling Chestnut	Widow of Capitol police officer killed during a shooting rampage at the U.S. Capitol
	Tipper Gore	Wife of Vice President Al Gore and mental illness reform activist
	Captain Jeff Taliaferro	U.S. Air Force pilot who flew a B-1B bomber over Iraq in Operation Desert Fox
	Sammy Sosa	Professional baseball player
	Suzann Wilson	Gun-control advocate from Jonesboro, Ark.
	Rosa Parks	Civil rights pioneer
January 27, 2000	Lloyd Bentsen	Former U.S. senator from Texas and Clinton's first Treasury secretary
	Carlos Rosas	Private citizen from St. Paul, Minn., cited as a potential beneficiary of the president's proposed plan to help fathers support their children
	Tom Mauser	Father of Daniel Mauser, who was killed during a deadly shooting at Columbine High School in Colorado
	Capt. John Cherrey	U.S. Air Force pilot who rescued another American pilot shot down over Bosnia
	Janet Cohen	Wife of Defense Secretary William Cohen who worked to show public support for service personnel
	Hank Aaron	Former professional baseball player
George W. Bush:		
February 27, 2001	John Street	Mayor of Philadelphia, who promoted faith-based initiatives
	Steven Ramos	Private citizen from Pennsylvania cited as a potential beneficiary of the president's proposed tax cut plan
	Josefina Ramos	Private citizen from Pennsylvania cited as a potential beneficiary of the president's proposed tax cut plan
January 29, 2002	Hamid Karzai	Interim leader of Afghanistan, later elected president in 2004
	Dr. Sima Samar	Minister of women's affairs in Afghanistan
	Shannon Spann	Widow of CIA officer Michael Spann, who was killed in Afghanistan
	Hermis Moutardier	Flight attendant who helped thwart attempted shoe bomb attack on flight from Paris to Miami
	Christina Jones	Flight attendant who helped thwart attempted shoe bomb attack on flight from Paris to Miami
January 28, 2003	None	
January 20, 2004	Adnan Pachachi	President of the Iraqi Governing Council
February 2, 2005	Janet Norwood	Mother of Marine Corps Sgt. Byron Norwood, who was killed in Fallujah, Iraq
	Bill Norwood	Father of Marine Corps Sgt. Byron Norwood, who was killed in Fallujah, Iraq
	Safia Taleb al-Suhail	Iraqi democracy and human rights activist whose father was killed by Saddam Hussein

President and Date of Address	Visitor	Additional Details
January 31, 2006	Lisa Clay	Widow of Marine Corps Staff Sgt. Dan Clay, who was killed in Fallujah, Iraq
	Sara Jo Clay	Mother of Marine Corps Staff Sgt. Dan Clay, who was killed in Fallujah, Iraq
	Bud Clay	Father of Marine Corps Staff Sgt. Dan Clay, who was killed in Fallujah, Iraq

President's Annual Messages to Congress, 1790–1913

The first twelve annual messages to Congress, as they were then known, were delivered by George Washington and John Adams to a joint session of the House and Senate. Beginning with Thomas Jefferson, the practice of delivering the address in person was abandoned, not to be resumed until Woodrow Wilson revived it in 1913.

George Washington (1789–1793)
First annual message, January 8, 1790
Second annual message, December 8, 1790
Third annual message, October 25, 1791
Fourth annual message, November 6, 1792
Fifth annual message, December 3, 1793
Sixth annual message, November 19, 1794
Seventh annual message, December 8, 1795
Eighth annual message, December 7, 1796

John Adams (1797–1801)
First annual message, November 22, 1797
Second annual message, December 8, 1798
Third annual message, December 3, 1799
Fourth annual message, November 11, 1800

Thomas Jefferson (1801–1809)
First annual message, December 8, 1801
Second annual message, December 15, 1802
Third annual message, October 17, 1803
Fourth annual message, November 8, 1804
Fifth annual message, December 3, 1805
Sixth annual message, December 2, 1806
Seventh annual message, October 27, 1807
Eighth annual message, November 8, 1808

James Madison (1809–1817)
First annual message, November 29, 1809
Second annual message, December 5, 1810
Third annual message, November 5, 1811
Fourth annual message, November 4, 1812
Fifth annual message, December 7, 1813
Sixth annual message, September 20, 1814
Seventh annual message, December 5, 1815
Eighth annual message, December 3, 1816

James Monroe (1817–1825)
First annual message, December 12, 1817
Second annual message, November 16, 1818
Third annual message, December 7, 1819
Fourth annual message, November 14, 1820
Fifth annual message, December 3, 1821
Sixth annual message, December 3, 1822
Seventh annual message, December 2, 1823
Eighth annual message, December 7, 1824

John Quincy Adams (1825–1829)
First annual message, December 6, 1825
Second annual message, December 5, 1826
Third annual message, December 4, 1827
Fourth annual message, December 2, 1828

Andrew Jackson (1829–1837)
First annual message, December 8, 1829
Second annual message, December 6, 1830
Third annual message, December 6, 1831
Fourth annual message, December 4, 1832
Fifth annual message, December 3, 1833
Sixth annual message, December 1st, 1834
Seventh annual message, December 7, 1835
Eighth annual message, December 5, 1836

Martin Van Buren (1837–1841)
First annual message, December 5, 1837
Second annual message, December 3, 1838
Third annual message, December 2, 1839
Fourth annual message, December 5, 1840

William Henry Harrison (1841)
No messages. Harrison died on April 4, 1841—exactly one month after his inauguration.

John Tyler (1841–1845)
First annual message, December 7, 1841
Second annual message, December 6, 1842
Third annual message, December 0, 1843
Fourth annual message, December 3, 1844

James K. Polk (1845–1849)
First annual message, December 2, 1845
Second annual message, December 8, 1846
Third annual message, December 7, 1847
Fourth annual message, December 5, 1848

Zachary Taylor (1849–1850)
annual message, December 4, 1849

Millard Fillmore (1850–1853)
First annual message, December 2, 1850
Second annual message, December 2, 1851
Third annual message, December 6, 1852

Franklin Pierce (1853–1857)
First annual message, December 5, 1853
Second annual message, December 4, 1854
Third annual message, December 31st, 1855
Fourth annual message, December 2, 1856

James Buchanan (1857–1861)
First annual message, December 8, 1857
Second annual message, December 6, 1858
Third annual message, December 19, 1859
Fourth annual message, December 3, 1860

Abraham Lincoln (1861–1865)
First annual message, December 3, 1861
Second annual message, December 1st, 1862
Third annual message, December 8, 1863
Fourth annual message, December 6, 1864

Andrew Johnson (1865–1869)
First annual message, December 4, 1865
Second annual message, December 3, 1866
Third annual message, December 3, 1867
Fourth annual message, December 9, 1868

Ulysses S. Grant (1869–1877)
First annual message, December 6, 1869
Second annual message, December 5, 1870
Third annual message, December 4, 1871
Fourth annual message, December 2, 1872
Fifth annual message, December 1st, 1873
Sixth annual message, December 7, 1874
Seventh annual message, December 7, 1875
Eighth annual message, December 5, 1876

Rutherford B. Hayes (1877–1881)
First annual message, December 3, 1877
Second annual message, December 2, 1878
Third annual message, December 1st, 1879
Fourth annual message, December 6, 1880

James A. Garfield (1881)
No messages. Garfield died from an assassin's bullet on September 19, 1881.

Chester A. Arthur (1881–1885)
First annual message, December 6, 1881
Second annual message, December 4, 1882
Third annual message, December 4, 1883
Fourth annual message, December 1st, 1884

Grover Cleveland (1885–1889)
First annual message (first term),
   December 8, 1885
Second annual message (first term),
   December 6, 1886
Third annual message (first term),
   December 6, 1887
Fourth annual message (first term),
   December 3, 1888

Benjamin Harrison (1889–1893)
First annual message, December 3, 1889
Second annual message, December 1st, 1890
Third annual message, December 9, 1891
Fourth annual message, December 6, 1892

Grover Cleveland (1893–1897)
First annual message (second term),
   December 4, 1893
Second annual message (second term),
   December 3, 1894
Third annual message (second term),
   December 2, 1895
Fourth annual message (second term),
   December 7, 1896

William McKinley (1897–1901)
First annual message, December 6, 1897
Second annual message, December 5, 1898
Third annual message, December 5, 1899
Fourth annual message, December 3, 1900

Theodore Roosevelt (1901–1909)
First annual message, December 3, 1901
Second annual message, December 2, 1902
Third annual message, December 7, 1903
Fourth annual message, December 6, 1904
Fifth annual message, December 5, 1905
Sixth annual message, December 3, 1906
Seventh annual message, December 3, 1907
Eighth annual message, December 8, 1908

William Howard Taft (1909–1913)
First annual message, December 7, 1909
Second annual message, December 6, 1910
Third annual message, December 5, 1911
Fourth annual message, December 3, 1912

Captions and Credits

Page 4: "President Wilson Delivers His Message to Congress in Person," cartoon by Clifford Berryman, 1913. Courtesy of the U.S. Senate Collection.

Page 13: Woodrow Wilson delivers his second inaugural address, 1917, Washington, D.C. Courtesy of the Library of Congress.

Page 75: Warren G. Harding is presented with a chair made from the first American battleship, *The Revenge,* by a committee of newspaper editors on the White House lawn, July 13, 1921. Courtesy of the Library of Congress.

Page 97: Calvin Coolidge standing on the south lawn of the White House, February 26, 1925. Courtesy of the Library of Congress.

Page 197: Herbert Hoover seated on sofa, 1929. Courtesy of the Library of Congress.

Page 251: Franklin D. Roosevelt in Casablanca, January 18, 1943. Courtesy of the Franklin D. Roosevelt Presidential Library.

Page 345: Harry S. Truman seated at desk, April 19, 1945. Courtesy of the Library of Congress.

Page 451: Dwight D. Eisenhower addresses a joint session of Congress, 1953. Courtesy of the Granger Collection, New York.

Page 563: John F. Kennedy addresses the U.N. General Assembly, September 20, 1963. Courtesy of the Granger Collection, New York.

Page 599: Lyndon B. Johnson delivers remarks in the Capitol Rotunda on the signing of the Voting Rights Act, August 6, 1965. Courtesy of the LBJ Library, photo by Yoichi R. Okamoto.

Page 661: Richard Nixon delivers a speech, October 31, 1970. Courtesy of the National Archives and Records Administration.

Page 751: Gerald R. Ford in the Oval Office, March 25, 1975. Courtesy of the Gerald R. Ford Presidential Library.

Page 779: Jimmy Carter announces the results of the Camp David Accords to Congress, September 18, 1978. Courtesy of the Library of Congress.

Page 871: Ronald Reagan at a press conference, June 16, 1981. Courtesy of the Ronald Reagan Library.

Page 931: George H. Bush addresses a joint session of Congress, March 6, 1991, following the end of the war with Iraq. Courtesy of the George Bush Presidential Library.

Page 965: Bill Clinton delivers his sixth State of the Union Address, January 19, 1999. Courtesy of the AP/Wide World Photos/Ron Edmonds.

Page 1071: George W. Bush delivers a speech at a Pentagon ceremony, November 24, 2003, before signing the Defense Authorization bill for fiscal year 2004. Photo courtesy of U.S. Army/Spc. Bill Putnam.

Index